Using Special Edition

Using Microsoft® Excel 97

Bestseller Edition

Bruce Hallberg,
Sherry Kinkoph, Bill Ray, et al.

QUE®

Special Edition Using Microsoft® Excel 97, Bestseller Edition

Library of Congress Catalog No.: 97-68763

ISBN: 0-7897-1399-3

99 98 97 6 5 4 3 2 1

Interpretation of the printing code: the rightmost double-digit number is the year of the book's printing; the rightmost single-digit number, the number of the book's printing. For example, a printing code of 97-1 shows that the first printing of the book occurred in 1997.

Screen reproductions in this book were created using Collage Plus from Inner Media, Inc., Hollis, NH.

Contents at a Glance

Table of Contents

III Creating Charts and Graphics

VI Networking and Integration with Excel

Credits

PRESIDENT
Roland Elgey

SENIOR VICE PRESIDENT/PUBLISHING
Don Fowley

PUBLISHER
Joseph B. Wikert

GENERAL MANAGER
Joe Muldoon

MANAGER OF PUBLISHING OPERATIONS
Linda H. Buehler

PUBLISHING DIRECTOR
Karen Reinisch

EDITORIAL SERVICES DIRECTOR
Carla Hall

MANAGING EDITOR
Thomas F. Hayes

ACQUISITIONS MANAGER
Cheryl D. Willoughby

ACQUISITIONS EDITOR
Lisa Swayne

PRODUCT DIRECTOR
Melanie Palaisa

PRODUCTION EDITOR
Audra McFarland

EDITORS
Kristin Ivanetich
Theresa Mathias
Judy Ohm
San Dee Phillips
Sarah Rudy
Leah Williams

COORDINATOR OF EDITORIAL SERVICES
Maureen A. McDaniel

WEBMASTER
Thomas H. Bennett

PRODUCT MARKETING MANAGER
Kourtnaye Sturgeon

ASSISTANT PRODUCT MARKETING MANAGER
Gretchen Schlesinger

TECHNICAL EDITORS
Rick Brown
Curtis Knight
Marty Wyatt

SOFTWARE SPECIALIST
David Garratt

ACQUISITIONS COORDINATOR
Travis Bartlett

SOFTWARE RELATIONS COORDINATOR
Susan D. Gallagher

EDITORIAL ASSISTANT
Jennifer L. Chisholm

BOOK DESIGNERS
Ruth Harvey
Kim Scott

COVER DESIGNER
Sandra Schroeder

PRODUCTION TEAM
Kay Hoskin
Darlena Murray
Timothy S. Neville I
Lisa Stumpf

INDEXERS
Craig Small
Chris Wilcox

Composed in *Century Old Style* and *ITC Franklin Gothic* by Que Corporation.

About the Authors

Bruce Hallberg has been a computer professional for the past 14 years, and presently is Director of Corporate Services for a public biotechnology company in California. He has authored or co-authored many other computer books, including the *OS/2 Certification Handbook*, *Byte's OS/2 Programmer's Cookbook*, and *Inside OS/2 Warp*. He particularly enjoys making complex computer topics understandable for beginning and intermediate computer users.

Forrest Houlette is a computer writer, trainer, and consultant who lives in Muncie, Indiana. He is president of Write Environment, Inc., a consulting firm that specializes in Visual Basic software development, custom documentation, training, and software for both education and business. Forrest holds a Ph.D. in Linguistics and Rhetoric from the University of Louisville. He began working with computers when he took a course in FORTRAN in 1979. Since then, he has programmed in BASIC, the Digital Authoring Language, C, C++, WordBasic, and Visual Basic. During his career as a university professor, he taught linguistics and focused on using artificial intelligence techniques to improve software for writing. He has written computer-based education programs for the teaching of writing, one of which—Write Environment—won the Zenith Masters of Innovation competition. Forrest now focuses on writing about computers and creating custom software. He teaches courses on Windows 95, Windows NT, Office 97, and Visual Basic for Learning Tree International. He has authored or co-authored books for IDG, New Riders Publishing, Que, and Sybex. He is also a Microsoft Certified Product Specialist.

Sherry Kinkoph has authored more than 25 computer books for Macmillan Publishing over the past five years, including books for both adults and children. Her recent publications include *The Complete Idiot's Guide to Microsoft Office for Windows 95*, *Easy Word 97*, *Office 97 Small Business Edition 6 in 1*, *The 10 Minute Guide to Lotus Organizer 97*, and *The Big Basics Book of Microsoft Office 97*. Sherry started exploring computers back in college and claims that many a term paper was whipped out using a trusty 128K Macintosh. Today, Sherry's still churning out words, but now they're in the form of books, and instead of using a Mac, she has moved on to a trusty PC. A native of the Midwest, Sherry currently resides in Fishers, IN, and continues in her quest to help users of all levels master the ever-changing computer technologies. You can e-mail Sherry at **skinkoph@inetdirect.net**.

Diane Koers owns and operates All Business Service, a software training and consulting company formed in 1988 that services the central Indiana area. Her area of expertise has long been in the word processing, spreadsheet, and graphics areas of computing, as well as in providing training and support for several popular accounting packages. Diane's authoring experience includes developing and writing software training manuals for her clients' use.

Joyce J. Nielsen is an independent computer consultant, specializing in writing and developing books based on microcomputer software applications. Prior to her work as a consultant, Joyce was a Senior Product Development Specialist for Que Corporation. She is the author or co-author of more than 20 computer books, including Que's *Special Edition Using 1-2-3 97 for Windows 95*, *Microsoft Office 97 Quick Reference*, and *Word for Windows 95 Visual Quick Reference*. Nielsen also worked as a Research Analyst for a shopping mall developer, where she developed and documented computer applications used nationwide. She received a Bachelor of Science degree in Quantitative Business Analysis from Indiana University. You may contact her via CompuServe at **76507,2712** or via the Internet at **jnielsen@iquest.net**.

Gail Perry is a CPA and a graduate of Indiana University, where she studied journalism, computer science, and music. In her spare time, she took accounting classes at Illinois State University and passed the CPA exam. Gail is a tax humor columnist for the ***Indianapolis Star*** and is the author of several computer and tax-related books, including ***The Complete Idiot's Guide to Doing Your Income Taxes,*** and ***Using Quicken 5 for Windows.*** In addition to writing, Gail teaches computer classes (including Excel) at the Indiana CPA society.

Bill Ray is a Microsoft Certified Solution Developer and a Product Specialist. He is the Training Manager Advanced Training Group for the Center for Professional Computer Education (CPCE, Inc.), of Shelton, CT, a Microsoft Authorized Technical Education Center and Microsoft Solution Provider Partner. His previous position as Senior Consultant for CPCE involved the design and implementation of customized solutions using Microsoft Office applications in the corporate marketplace. Bill is also a codeveloper of CPCE's Word for Windows Productivity Pack, which is a customizable set of macros and templates for improved office productivity. Bill holds an M.A in Music Education from Teachers College, Columbia University, and an M.S. in Computer Science from Union College. Bill can be reached via Compuserve at **71101,3402** or the Internet at **wgray@cpce.com**.

Robert E. Simanski, ABC, is the President of Your Publications Pro!, a publications and Web site management firm in Herndon, Virginia. An Accredited Business Communicator, he is an award-winning publications editor and director with more than 30 years of experience in the field. Bob has been working with personal computers since 1986 and is an active member of the Capital PC User Group, Inc., where he has served on the Member Help Line since 1990.

We'd Like to Hear from You!

QUE Corporation has a long-standing reputation for high-quality books and products. To ensure your continued satisfaction, we also understand the importance of customer service and support.

Tech Support

If you need assistance with the information in this book or with a CD/disk accompanying the book, please access Macmillan Computer Publishing's online Knowledge Base at **http://www.superlibrary.com/general/support**. If you do not find the answer to your questions on our Web site, you may contact Macmillan Technical Support by phone at **317/581-3833** or via e-mail at **support@mcp.com**.

Also be sure to visit QUE's Web resource center for all the latest information, enhancements, errata, downloads, and more. It's located at **http://www.quecorp.com/**.

Orders, Catalogs, and Customer Service

To order other QUE or Macmillan Computer Publishing books, catalogs, or products, please contact our Customer Service Department at **800/428-5331** or fax us at **800/835-3202** (International Fax: 317/228-4400). Or visit our online bookstore at **http://www.mcp.com/**.

Comments and Suggestions

We want you to let us know what you like or dislike most about this book or other QUE products. Your comments will help us to continue publishing the best books available on computer topics in today's market.

Melanie Palaisa
Product Director
QUE Corporation
201 West 103rd Street, 4B
Indianapolis, Indiana 46290 USA
Fax: 317/581-4663 E-mail: **mpalaisa@que.mcp.com**

Please be sure to include the book's title and author, as well as your name and phone or fax number. We will carefully review your comments and share them with the author. Please note that due to the high volume of mail we receive, we may not be able to reply to every message.

Thank you for choosing QUE!

Introduction

Welcome to *Special Edition Using Microsoft Excel 97, Bestseller Edition*!

This book is the most comprehensive and useful reference available for Excel 97, which is part of Microsoft's Office 97 suite of productivity applications. A team of the best Excel authors available explains to you how to make the fullest use of Excel 97, how to take advantage of its extensive features, and how to put it to work immediately. Through the use of explanations, demonstrations, examples, and a variety of files found on the accompanying CD-ROM, *Special Edition Using Microsoft Excel 97, Bestseller Edition* is one-stop shopping for getting the most out of Excel 97.

This book is designed for people who are already familiar with Excel. However, if you're brand-new to Excel, don't worry—Chapter 1 contains Excel basics and is designed to get you up to speed quickly and easily. ■

New Excel 97 Features

Excel 97 is a substantial upgrade from Excel 95. Many features requested by users through Microsoft's wish line (1-800-226-WISH) have been incorporated into Excel, along with some features that support Microsoft's strategy of focusing on the Internet. The following sections summarize the most valuable new features in Excel 97. If you're upgrading to Excel 97 from Excel 95, reading the following sections will help you quickly master these new capabilities.

Increased Capacity

Spreadsheet programs only give you a certain number of rows and columns within which to work. Although you can extend these limits by linking worksheets together in creative ways, there are times when you simply need to be able to store more information in a worksheet. With computers gaining more and more memory, there's no real hardware limitation that keeps you from having just about as many rows of information as you need.

Earlier versions of Excel limited you to 16,384 rows of data. This is quite a lot by anyone's standard, but Excel 97 increases the limit to 65,535 rows. You can also store up to 32,767 characters within a single Excel cell, whereas earlier versions of Excel limited you to 255 characters in a cell.

Another limit that's increased in Excel 97 is the number of data points that can be included in a chart. Excel 97 ups the number of data points from 4,000 to 32,000.

Multiple Level Undo

One thing has been frustrating Excel users for quite a while now: the single-level Undo command. Although Word has had the capability to reverse multiple actions for quite some time, until now Excel only let you undo the most recent action you took when working in your worksheets. If you made a mistake and then performed another action, you could not go back and undo the earlier mistake. Excel 97 now includes this invaluable feature, called ***multiple-level undo***, so you can undo your most recent 16 actions. If you make a mistake and then perform another action, you can still go back and reverse your changes.

Formula AutoCorrect

Microsoft usability testing indicated that people frequently make common mistakes when entering formulas. For example, a user might leave off a closing parenthesis, or type two operators—like two plus signs—together by mistake. In previous versions of Excel, you just got an error message if you made such a typo, and you had to fix it manually. In Excel 97, however, the 15 most common formula entry mistakes are corrected automatically for you. And, if Excel 97 isn't sure how to correct an error, it will pop up a dialog box offering to make the correction for you and suggesting a corrected version.

Shared Workbooks

Many people rely on Excel to enhance their ability to work within a team. For example, most accounting departments couldn't get along without Excel. Any time you have a team of people constantly using Excel, it's natural to want to share files and collaborate on projects. In Excel 95, a feature called *shared lists* was introduced, which let several people edit data in worksheets simultaneously. Excel 97 includes improvements to this feature—now called shared workbooks—that make it even easier to let multiple people work on a single workbook at the same time. Changes made to each person's copy are now automatically consolidated together, and each person's view and print settings are now maintained for them.

Natural Language Formulas

Consider the sample worksheet shown in Figure I.1. In particular, notice that the formula shown for cell C21 in the formula bar is **=C14+C19**. How quickly can you check to see if the correct cells are being used in that formula? Not very!

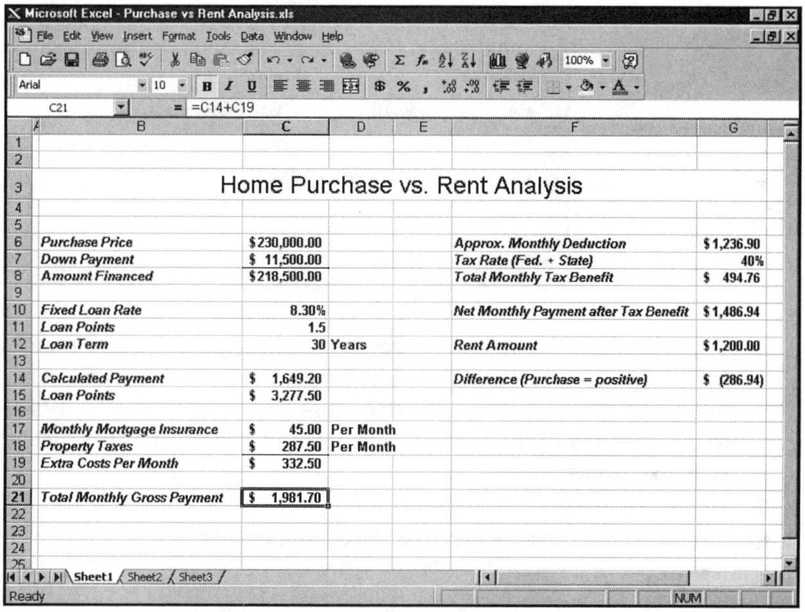

FIG. I.1
How easy is it to check that the right cells are being referenced?

Excel now recognizes something called *natural language formulas*. Using the labels associated with cells, you can enter formulas using plain English. For example, look at the formula bar in Figure I.2.

It was possible to enter formulas using these types of references in previous versions of Excel, but only after assigning names to the various cells manually. Excel 97 now simply understands what you mean! And, if you still want to manually assign cell names, you can do that, too.

Data Validation

It's very important that the information you and others enter in a shared workbook be correct. One way to assure that information isn't entered in error is to develop some method that checks the contents of specific cells in such a way that any obviously-wrong entries are immediately pointed out for the person entering the data.

FIG. I.2
Using natural language formulas makes your worksheets much more readable, and therefore more accurate.

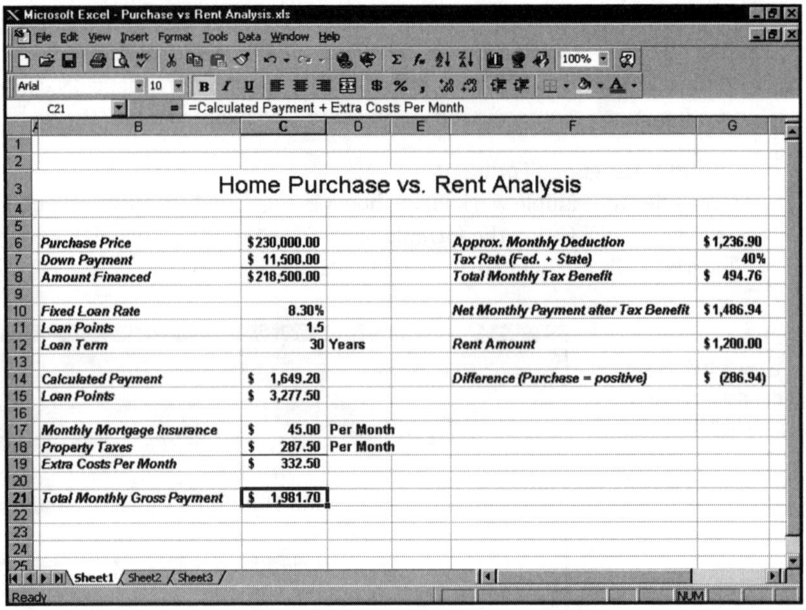

Excel 97 makes this validation process much easier with a new Data Validation dialog box that lets you set up rules for cell entries. For each cell you can specify a message that reminds the user what data is required. An error message is displayed if the data entered doesn't conform to the rules you define. For example, Figure I.3 shows the Data Validation dialog box with a sample Input Message defined.

FIG. I.3
One of the features of the Data Validation dialog box is that you can define messages that tell the user what information is required.

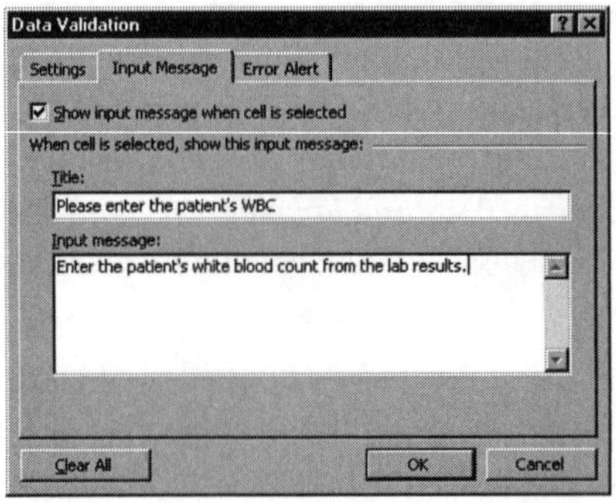

Track Changes

For quite some time Word has had the capability to track changes made by various people editing a document. Each change was highlighted and the person's name was attached to the change so others could quickly and easily see what was new in the document. You now have similar capabilities with Excel 97. The new Track Changes command makes it much easier to have multiple people revising a document together, without losing track of who makes which change.

NOTE Learn about Track Changes in Chapter 23, "Collaborating with Excel."

AutoCorrect and Spell Checking

Another feature added to Excel 97 that has been available in Word for a while is AutoCorrect. When you enter data into cells, Excel 97 now automatically corrects common spelling errors instantly. Excel 97 also now includes the capability to spell-check your worksheets, which makes turning out professional-quality work easier than ever.

Collapse/Expand Dialog Boxes

If you've used Excel 95, you probably appreciated the capability to directly select cells from within dialog boxes fields. Click a field in the dialog box, then click a cell or range of cells in your worksheet and the cell reference is automatically entered into the dialog box. However, in many cases the dialog box was still in your way as you tried to select cells! In Excel 97, any dialog box that lets you perform direct selection now includes a Collapse/Expand button at the end of the field, as shown in Figure I.4.

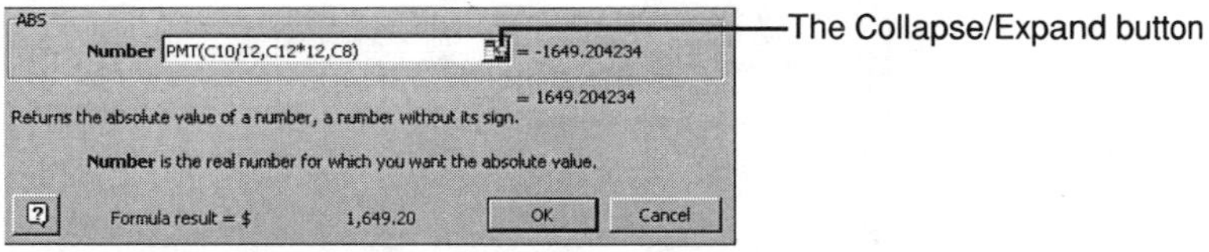

FIG. I.4 Click the Collapse/Expand button to shrink the dialog box out of your way, then click it again to restore it once you've selected the cells.

Range Finder

Making Excel 97 even easier to use than before was a major design goal for Microsoft. One of the neat new features that makes it easier to see what you're doing is called Range Finder. When you edit a formula in a cell, the parts of the formula that reference other cells are highlighted with different colors, and the same colors are used to highlight the actual cells that are being referenced. This makes it much easier to see if your formulas are correct, as shown in Figure I.5.

CellTips

When you attach notes to cells, you used to have to activate a dialog box to see what the note said. Now, with Excel 97, you can review annotations in cells much faster than before! In Figure I.6, you can see how this new reviewing feature, called *CellTips,* appears on-screen. You just place your mouse pointer over a cell with a comment for a moment, and the CellTip appears.

AutoCalculate

If you've used Excel before, you've probably had situations where you needed a quick sum of a series of numbers, or perhaps a quick count of how many numbers there are in a range. In the past, you would have to enter a formula into an empty cell in order to get the quick answer you wanted, such as **=COUNT(B2:B255)**. Now, with AutoCalculate, you can get quick answers much faster. In Figure I.7, you see AutoCalculate in action. Simply select a range of cells, and the sum appears in the status bar. You can also right-click the box with the sum to choose from other popular quick calculations.

FIG. I.5
Range Finder lets you easily see what cells are being referenced by a formula.

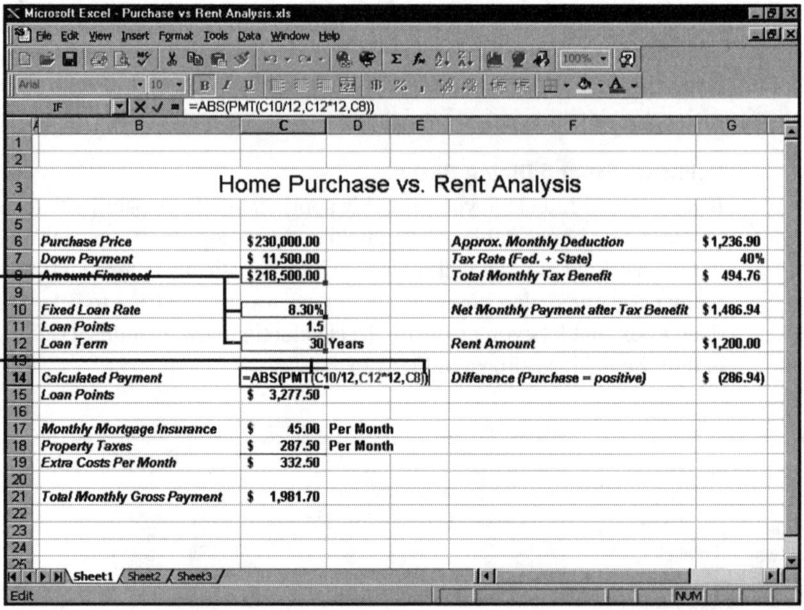

The colors used to highlight the cell references...

...are the same ones used to highlight the cells being referenced

FIG. I.6
CellTips make it faster to review worksheet comments.

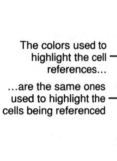

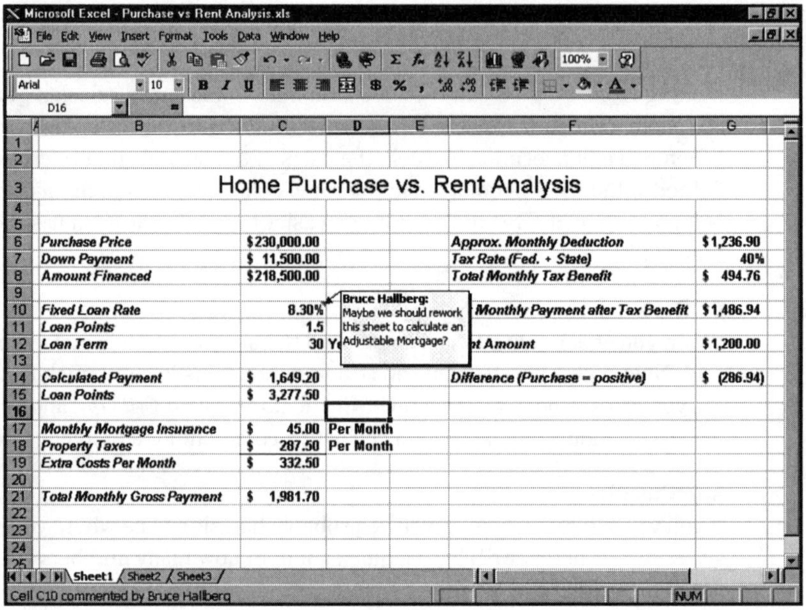

FIG. I.7
AutoCalculate gives you quick answers to your questions!

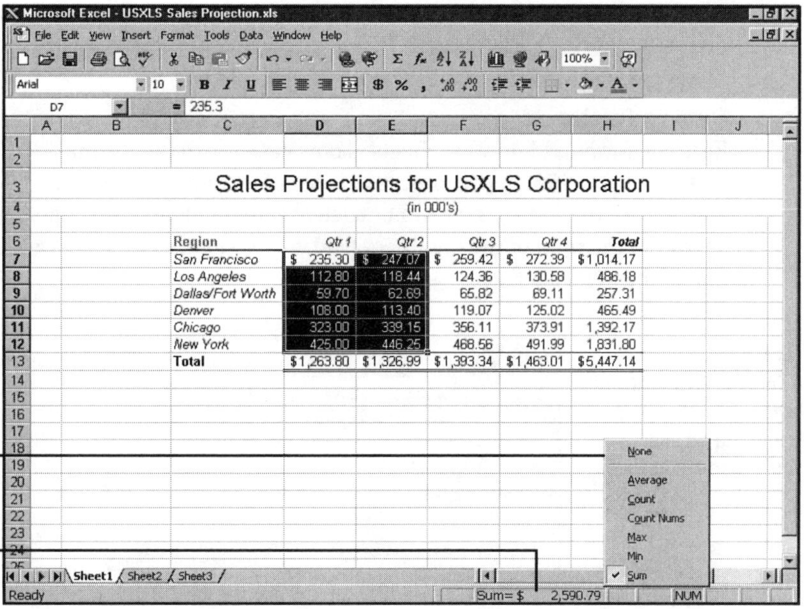

Popular AutoCalculate choices shown when you right-click on the AutoCalculate box

The AutoCalculate sum

Improved Page Break Management

Handling page breaks in Excel has long been a sore subject with users. Before Excel 97, you really had to do backflips to get your worksheet page breaks to occur exactly where you wanted them. With Excel 97, however, you can now preview exactly where the page breaks will occur, and you can easily drag and drop them to get just the effect you need.

NOTE You can learn how to use Excel's new page break features in Chapter 5, "Printing Worksheets."

Conditional Formatting

Another new improvement to Excel 97 surrounds conditional formatting, where you can set rules that determine how a cell is formatted. You can, for example, set rules that say that if one cell is less than some number in another cell, that it will be displayed with a particular format. And you can actually do much more than this. Figure I.8 shows the new Conditional Formatting dialog box, with a simple conditional formatting rule applied.

FIG. I.8
Conditional formatting lets you format your worksheet cells based on their results.

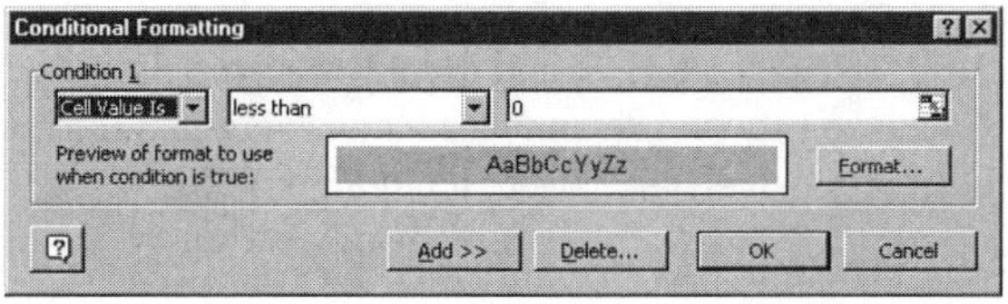

NOTE Chapter 4, "Formatting Your Worksheets," shows you how to use conditional formatting.

Formula Palette

Entering formulas into worksheets is now easier with the Formula Palette, an easy-to-use tool that walks you through the process of using functions. In Figure I.9, you can see the Formula Palette with the PMT function. For each argument of the PMT function, you can see a quick answer to the right of the argument field, and you get a quick answer displayed near the bottom of the Formula Palette.

FIG. I.9
The Formula Palette is an easier way of entering and editing formulas and functions.

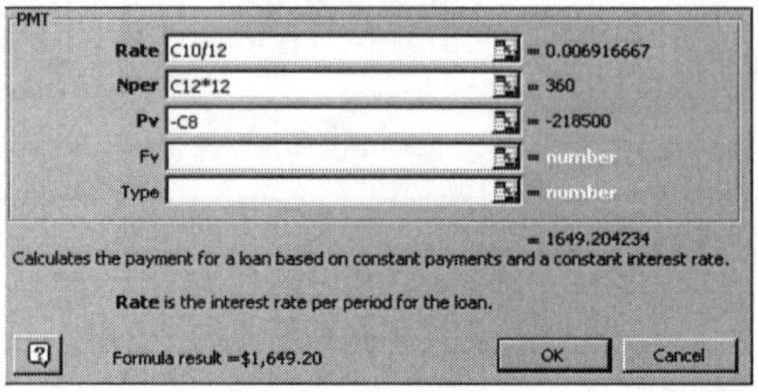

NOTE Learn the ins and outs of using the Formula Palette in Chapter 6, "Using Excel Functions."

Improved Database Queries

In corporate environments, people often use Excel to query databases and return the results to a worksheet, after which they perform their analyses or reports on the data with Excel. Excel 97 improves this important function in a variety of ways. First, a new Query Wizard makes creating basic queries easier than using the full-fledged Microsoft Query tool (which is still available if you need it). Second, queries now take up less memory on the system (running out of memory during queries used to be a big problem). Third, queries can run in the background, so you can continue to work with your worksheet as you wait for the query data to be returned.

NOTE Learn about the Query Wizard in Chapter 16, "Retrieving Data with the Query Wizard." Learn about the more advanced Microsoft Query in Chapter 17, "Advanced Queries Using Microsoft Query."

Better PivotTables

PivotTables were introduced in Excel 95 and quickly became one of people's favorite features. They let you easily analyze lists of data and extract answers in different ways. Excel 97's PivotTables have been extensively improved, including the following:

- *Persistent Formatting* lets you format PivotTables, and retains their formatting when you refresh their data or rearrange them.

- *Automatic Sorting* keeps your data sorted as you want it, even after refreshing the PivotTable data.
- *Reduced Memory Requirements* let PivotTables do more work before exhausting your computer's memory resources.
- *Smart Page Fields* let you only retrieve the data from an external database related to a particular page field. Choosing a different page field then retrieves the new data. This lets PivotTables remain useful with very large external databases.
- *A Special PivotTable Selection feature* lets you choose parts of the PivotTable for formatting or for use in other formulas.

These are only a few of the new features and improvements made to PivotTables. As you'll learn in Chapter 20, "Analyzing Data: PivotTables!," PivotTables are better than ever in Excel 97.

NOTE PivotTables are covered extensively in Chapter 20, "Analyzing Data: PivotTables!"

Improved Charts

If one area of Excel really didn't need much improvement, it was Excel's charting functions. Just the same, Microsoft managed to both increase Excel's charting capabilities ***and*** make them easier to use at the same time (quite an accomplishment!). Look for these new features in Excel 97's charting features:

- *An improved Chart Wizard* makes choosing just the options you want in your charts quick and easy.
- *New chart types* are available in Excel 97. Look for Pie of Pie, Bar of Pie, Bubble, and new 3-D charts in Chapter 12, "A Field Guide to Excel Chart Types."
- *You can have up to 32,000 data points* in 2-D charts now!
- *Data Tables in charts* let you easily add a table that shows the tabular data on which the chart is based on the chart itself. Before, you had to embed a chart on a worksheet and create the data table below the chart manually.
- *Time Scale Axes* in charts automatically display a date axis in chronological order, even if the underlying worksheet range isn't ordered that way. Time Scale Axes also let you easily change the base unit of time shown, so you can quickly switch between showing days, weeks, months, and so forth.
- *Chart Tips* let you easily see which data series corresponds to which range on the underlying worksheet.

These are just the most notable improvements to Excel 97's charting features, but as you can see they're extensive and increase the power of this important Excel tool.

NOTE Learn about all of Excel's charting features—both new and old—in Part III, "Creating Charts and Graphics."

Office Assistant

A new help tool in all of the Office 97 applications is the Office Assistant, shown in Figure I.10. This tool is an animated assistant that "watches over your shoulder" as you use Excel and lets you enter questions using plain English and get help and advice on using Excel. You can choose from a variety of Office Assistant characters, each one providing a different personality and level of animation. You should definitely try the Office Assistant, and even if you don't like to leave it on your screen all the time, you'll find that you can call it up anytime and get quick answers to your Excel questions.

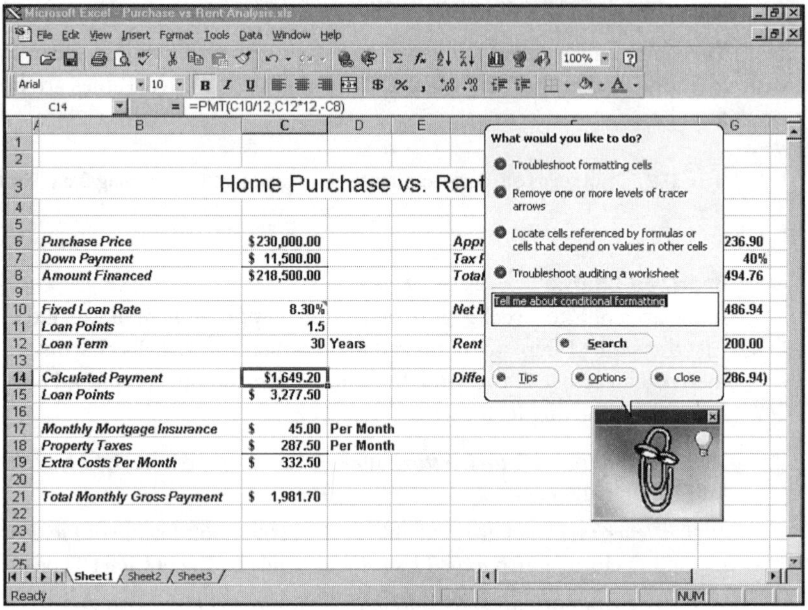

FIG. I.10
The Office Assistant is a powerful new help tool in the Office 97 suite of applications.

How This Book Is Organized

Special Edition Using Microsoft Excel 97, Bestseller Edition is organized into sections to make it easier for you to find the information you need. Each section deals with a different area of Excel.

Part I: Using Excel Worksheets

The first part in the book deals with working with worksheets, the fundamental tool in Excel. Chapter 1 begins with basic information for people new to Excel, and then the section (and the book) assumes you have some experience with Excel. In this section, you learn about how to get further help for Excel, how to manage Excel workbooks, worksheets, and windows, how to enter and edit data in worksheets, how to format worksheets, and how to print worksheets.

Part II: Advanced Excel Worksheet Features

The second part extends your knowledge of Excel worksheets. Here, you learn about using Excel's powerful built-in functions, its array of add-ins that extend Excel's utility, how to customize Excel to your preferences, and about a number of sample worksheet solutions that can solve a variety of problems or can just serve as a starting point for you to develop your own solutions with Excel.

Part III: Creating Charts and Graphics

You're not done with your worksheets until you communicate their results to someone. You can make communicating important data or ideas much easier through the use of Excel charts. Part III covers everything there is to know about creating charts. You learn about creating charts, about advanced chart features, and about all the different chart types built-into Excel. You also learn about using Excel's built-in drawing tools to annotate charts and worksheets.

Part IV: Creating and Using Excel Databases

Excel is often used as an analysis tool, but it's also a rudimentary data management tool. In Part IV you learn how to build databases using Excel 97. You also learn about accessing and querying data from other sources, such as Access, corporate databases, and the Internet.

Part V: Analyzing Your Data

Since Excel is most-used as an analysis tool, you would expect it to have strong features that make analyzing data easier and faster. In this section you learn how to outline worksheets, work with multiple scenarios, audit and validate worksheets, use Excel's Solver, use Excel's PivotTables, and how to make the best use of the Analysis ToolPak.

Part VI: Networking and Integration with Excel

"No program is an island," to paraphrase a famous quotation, and Excel 97 includes features that make it easier to work with other people using Excel, interoperate with other programs, and work seamlessly with the Internet. In this part, you learn how to do all of these things with Excel.

Part VII: Programming Excel

One of the best parts of Excel is its programmability. You can use Excel's built-in programming language, Visual Basic for Applications (VBA), to make Excel do many things. You can create programs that range from automating routine chores in Excel, to building sophisticated applications in Excel. Part VII shows you what you need to know to get up to speed and gain some mastery of VBA in Excel.

Conventions Used in This Book

Que has over a decade of experience writing and developing the most successful computer books available. With that experience, we've learned what special features help readers the most. Look for these special features throughout the book to enhance your learning experience.

Chapter Roadmaps

As a sidebar on the first page of each chapter there is a list of topics to be covered in the chapter. This list serves as a roadmap to the chapter so you can tell at a glance what is covered. It also provides a useful outline of the key topics you'll be reading about.

Notes

Notes present interesting or useful information that isn't necessarily essential to the discussion. This secondary track of information enhances your understanding of Windows, but you can safely skip notes and not be in danger of missing crucial information. Notes look like this:

NOTE Ctrl+Esc is a shortcut key combination used to access the Start menu. Throughout this book, when you see a key+key combination, that signifies a shortcut to accessing an application or opening a menu.

Tips

Tips present short advice on quick or often overlooked procedures. These include shortcuts that save you time. A tip looks like this:

TIP Nearly every item in Windows 95 contains a property sheet you can customize. Right-click an item and choose Properties to see its property sheet.

Cautions

Cautions serve to warn you about potential problems that a procedure may cause, unexpected results, and mistakes to avoid.

CAUTION

If you have a similar printer that could use the same drivers, do not remove the software. Deleting the associated software might remove that driver from use by other printers.

Common Problems and Solutions

No matter how carefully you follow the steps in the book, you eventually come across something that just doesn't work the way you think it should. These troubleshooting sections anticipate common errors or hidden pitfalls and present solutions. Each chapter ends with a list of common problems.

Cross References

Throughout the book, you see references to other sections and pages in the book, like the one that follows this paragraph. These cross references point you to related topics and discussions in other parts of the book.

▶ **See** "Starting and Exiting Excel," **p. 18**

In addition to these special features, there are several conventions used in this book to make it easier to read and understand. These conventions include the following.

Underlined Hot Keys, or Mnemonics

Hot keys in this book appear underlined, like they appear on-screen. In Windows, many menus, commands, buttons, and other options have these hot keys. To use a hot-key shortcut, press Alt and the key for the underlined character. For instance, to choose the Properties button, press Alt and then R.

Shortcut Key Combinations

In this book, shortcut key combinations are joined with plus signs (+). For example, Ctrl+V means hold down the Ctrl key, while you press the V key.

Menu Commands

Instructions for choosing menu commands have this form:

> Choose File, New.

This example means open the File menu and select New, which in this case opens a new file.

Instructions involving the new Windows 95 Start menu are an exception. When you are to choose something through this menu, the form is

> Open the Start menu and choose Programs, Accessories, WordPad.

In this case, you open the WordPad word processing accessory. Notice that in the Start menu you simply drag the mouse pointer and point at the option or command you want to choose (even through a whole series of submenus); you don't need to click anything.

This book also has the following typeface enhancements to indicate special text, as indicated in the following table.

Typeface	Description
Italic	Italics are used to indicate terms and variables in commands or addresses.
Boldface	Bold is used to indicate text you type, and Internet addresses and other locators in the online world.
`Computer type`	This command is used for on-screen messages and commands (such as DOS copy or UNIX commands).
MYFILE.DOC	File names and directories are set in all caps to distinguish them from regular text, as in MYFILE.DOC.

PART I

Using Excel Worksheets

CHAPTER 1

Excel: Quick Start!

by Sherry Kinkoph

By far the most popular spreadsheet program around today, Microsoft Excel is a perfect tool for juggling numbers and formulas, organizing and manipulating data, and producing polished, professional worksheets and reports. With Excel, you can create worksheets, for example, to total sales for your company or to track your personal expenses. You can use Excel to set up a budget or to create an invoice. You can also use Excel as a simple database program and to create charts.

If you're new to Excel, or want to gain a solid understanding of the basic features of the application, then this chapter is just for you. ■

Starting and exiting Excel

Find out how to quickly start and exit the program and create an Excel shortcut icon.

Navigating and working with worksheets

Discover how to move around a typical Excel worksheet, add and delete worksheets, and name worksheet tabs, and view multiple workbook windows.

Using Excel's toolbars

Excel has 13 toolbars you can use to help you quickly access commonly used commands. Learn how to change and customize the toolbars to suit your needs.

Using Excel's help features

Explore Excel's help options for assisting you with the program, including the new Excel 97 Office Assistant tool and Web page help.

Building a sample workbook and worksheet

Create a sample workbook that includes formulas, functions, and formatting.

Building a sample chart

Turn the sample worksheet data you create into a graphical chart using the Chart Wizard tool.

Starting and Exiting Excel

Before plunging into the Excel program, you should first familiarize yourself with the various methods for starting and exiting the program:

- For a straightforward startup, click the Start button on the Windows 95 taskbar, select Programs, Microsoft Excel. The Excel window opens onto your screen.
- If you're looking for a faster startup, add an Excel shortcut icon to your Windows 95 desktop. Right-click a blank area of the desktop and select New, Shortcut. In the Create Shortcut box that appears (see Figure 1.1), type in the path to the Excel program, or use the Browse button to locate the Excel executable file.

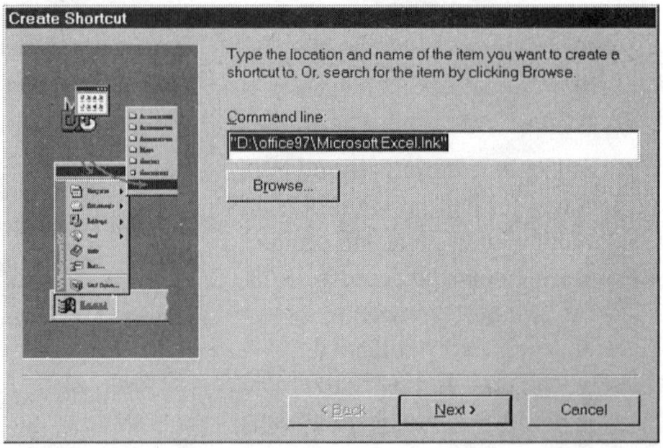

FIG. 1.1
Use the Create Shortcut dialog boxes to insert an Excel shortcut icon on your desktop.

Click the Next button to continue to the next dialog box where you can type in a name for the shortcut icon or use the default name, Microsoft Excel. Click the Finish button and the icon is added to your desktop To start Excel, double-click the shortcut icon.

NOTE If a shortcut icon isn't fast enough for you, you can choose to start Excel automatically whenever you start your computer. Simply place a copy of the Excel shortcut icon into the Startup folder (if you don't have an Excel shortcut icon, you can create one as instructed in the previous paragraphs). Open Windows Explorer and open the contents of the WINDOWS folder. Open the START MENU folder, then open the PROGRAM folder. Now hold the Ctrl key and drag the Excel shortcut icon from your desktop into the STARTUP folder (make sure the Explorer window is resized so you can see the Excel shortcut icon on the desktop).

- You can also start Excel when you click Excel files in the Explorer window or the My Computer window. Locate the Excel file you want to open, then double-click to open Excel.

To exit Excel at any time, use any of the following methods:

- Open the File menu and select Exit.
- Click the Close (X) button located at the far right end of the Excel title bar.

- Press Alt+F4 on the keyboard.
- Double-click the Control-menu icon (located in the upper-left corner of the Excel window).

If you haven't saved your work before exiting, you'll be prompted to do so.

▶ **See** "Opening and Closing Workbook Files," **p. 68**

▶ **See** "Saving Workbooks," **p. 62**

Excel Screen Elements

When you start Excel, you see a blank worksheet on-screen, as shown in Figure 1.2. In Excel, each individual spreadsheet is called a *worksheet*. The worksheet is a grid of rows and columns that intersect to form little boxes, called *cells*. Within each worksheet page in Excel, you can enter data, perform calculations, organize information, and more.

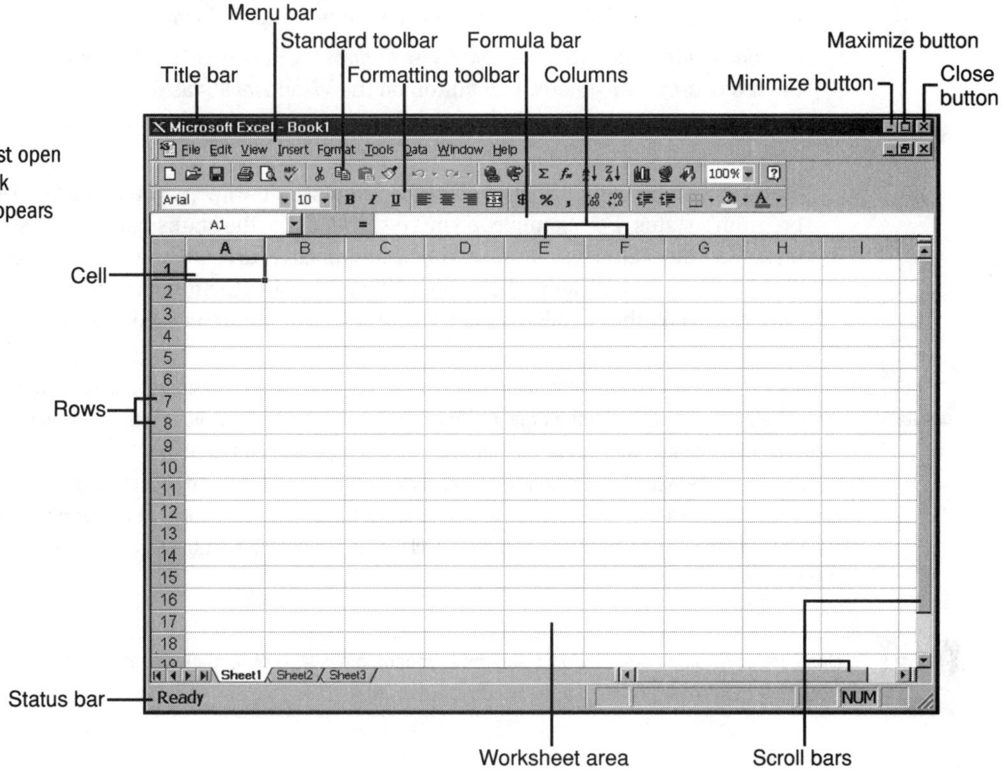

FIG. 1.2
When you first open Excel, a blank worksheet appears on-screen.

The Excel window displays the basic program elements found in other Windows programs, including a title bar, menu bar, toolbars, status bar, and scroll bars, plus buttons for controlling the window's appearance.

Title bar The bar at the top of the Excel program window that displays the name of the file you're currently working on.

Menu bar Click any menu name to display a menu list of Excel commands. Some commands, when selected, will display additional menus (submenus) or dialog boxes. Click a menu command to activate it.

Standard toolbar Excel's toolbars contain shortcut buttons for activating commonly used commands. The Standard toolbar has a variety of buttons for controlling the file and manipulating the data. Click a toolbar button to activate the command.

Formatting toolbar Contains buttons for controlling your worksheet's appearance.

Formula bar Use this area of the window to enter Excel formulas and functions into your worksheet, or edit cell contents. At the far left end of the formula bar is the name box, which displays the address of the currently selected cell or range.

Scroll bars Both the vertical and horizontal scroll bars allow you to view different portions of the overall worksheet. Use the horizontal scroll bar to move your view left or right; use the vertical scroll bar to move your view up or down.

Minimize, Maximize/Restore, and Close buttons Click the Minimize button to minimize the Excel program window to a button on the Windows 95 taskbar. The Maximize/Restore button enlarges the window to full screen or restores the window to its original size. Use the Close button to close the Excel program.

Status bar The bar at the bottom of the Excel window keeps you posted on the program's status. For example, if you're saving a file, the status bar will say so. In some instances, the status bar prompts you or identifies a current command you've activated. The bar also has indicators that tell you if you're using the numeric keypad (NUM), or have turned on the Scroll Lock key (SCRL), or using Extend mode (EXT).

TIP The worksheet window also has control buttons you can use to minimize, maximize, and close the worksheet without closing the entire Excel program window. For example, a click on the worksheet window's Minimize button will reduce the worksheet to a button located just above the horizontal scroll bar. To distinguish between the program window's control buttons and the worksheet window's control buttons, just remember that the program window's control buttons always appear at the far right end of the title bar and the worksheet window's buttons will vary in their placement based on the display of the worksheet window itself.

TIP To close the active workbook window using the keyboard, press Ctrl+W. To minimize the window, press Ctrl+F9, and to maximize or restore the window, press Ctrl+F10.

Navigating and Working with Worksheets

Each Excel worksheet is comprised of 256 columns and 65,536 rows. Sometimes, you can get lost in the vast forest of worksheet cells, so one of the first things you need to learn is how to read cell names, called *addresses*. Excel worksheets are laid out like grids, and each cell in the grid has a name or *reference* based on which row and column it's in.

Excel labels columns with alphabet letters, and rows with numbers. Cell names always reference the column letter first, and then the row number. For example, the cell in the top left corner in a worksheet is A1. If you become confused about which cell you're in, look at the reference area at the far left end of the formula bar, called the Name box (if you've worked with other spreadsheet programs, you may know this box as the *Reference* box). This is kind of like a "you-are-here" marker; it will always show you which cell you're in. Figure 1.5 points out the Name box.

Navigating with the Mouse and Keyboard

You can move around an Excel worksheet using the mouse or the keyboard. As you move your mouse pointer around on-screen, you'll notice it changes shape, ranging from a plus symbol to a pointer arrow. Also, depending on the action you're performing, the pointer may take on other shapes as well.

- To move from cell to cell, simply click the cell to which you want to move. The cell you click becomes highlighted, or selected. (A dark line, called a *selector*, always surrounds a selected cell.) When you select a cell, it is active and ready to accept any numbers or text you type.
- You can also select more than one cell at a time. To do this, click the first cell you want to select, hold down the left mouse button, and drag over the other cells you want to select. This highlights all the cells you drag over. Let go of the mouse button and they're selected.
- Use the scroll bars to move around different portions of a worksheet. Click the up or down scroll arrow on the vertical scroll bar to move your view of the worksheet up or down. Click the right or left scroll arrow to move your view to the right or left. You can also drag the scroll box, shown in Figure 1.3, to move the worksheet view. When you drag the scroll box, the row number or column heading is displayed to help you know where you are in a worksheet. A single click on the scroll bar itself, directly above the scroll box, will move the screen up one page. A click below the scroll box will move one page down.

TIP If the active (selected) cell isn't visible in the current worksheet view, press Ctrl+Backspace and the window scrolls to display the active cell.

97

TIP If you're using Microsoft's IntelliMouse, you can scroll around worksheets using the center wheel button. To pan a worksheet, hold down the wheel button and drag.

You can also use the keyboard to move around in Excel. Table 1.1 is a helpful chart of key combinations you can use to navigate a worksheet.

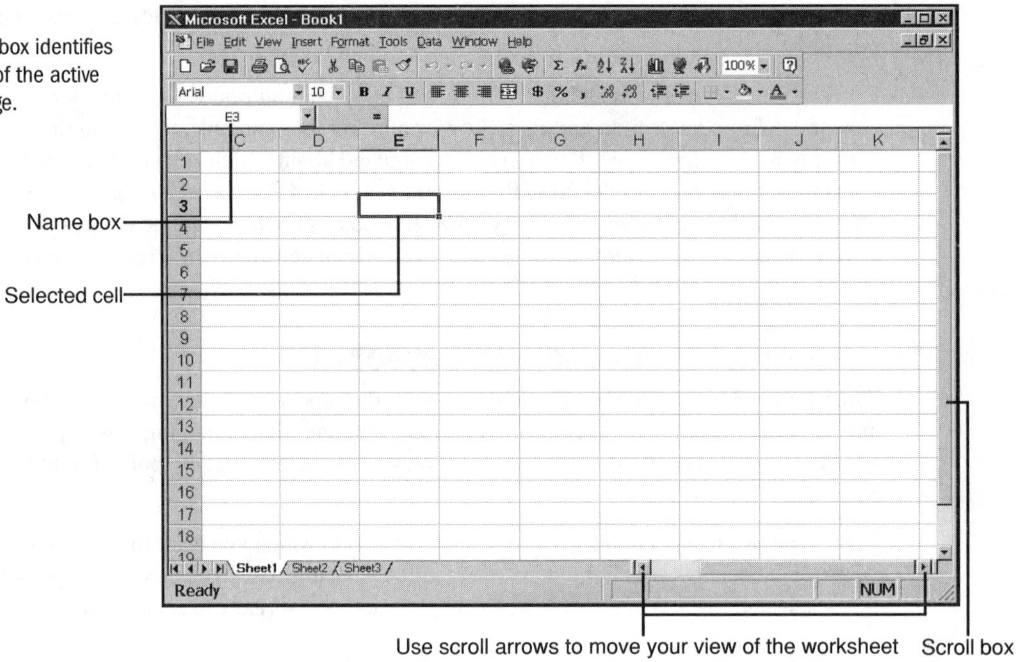

FIG. 1.3
The Name box identifies the name of the active cell or range.

Table 1.1 Navigation Keys

Press	To Move
Enter	One cell down or to the next cell in the sequence
Shift+Tab	One cell to the left
Shift+Enter	One cell up
→	Right one cell
←	Left one cell
↓	Down one cell
↑	Up one cell
Ctrl+→	To right edge of current region
Ctrl+←	To left edge of current region
Ctrl+↓	To bottom edge of current region
Ctrl+↑	To top edge of current region
Home	To first cell in the row
Ctrl+Home	To first cell in the worksheet
Ctrl+End	To lower-right cell in the worksheet

Press	To Move
PgDn	Down one screen
PgUp	Up one screen
Alt+PgDn	Right one screen
Alt+PgUp	Left one screen
Ctrl+PgDn	To next sheet
Ctrl+PgUp	To previous sheet
F5 or Ctrl+G	Into the Go To dialog box

NOTE You can move to a specific cell in the worksheet by selecting the Go To command from the Edit menu. In the Reference text box that appears, type the name of the cell to which you want to move, and click OK or press Enter. You can also move to a specific cell by typing the cell name in the Name box on the Formula bar, then press Enter.

Understanding Worksheets

The grid of columns and rows that you see on-screen is a *worksheet*. In addition to the first sheet you see, you have two more sheets available—but you can always add more if you need them. By default, Excel starts you out with three worksheets, and stores all the worksheets together in one file, called a *workbook*.

To select a specific sheet to work with, you click the sheet tab (labeled as Sheet1, Sheet2 and Sheet3) to make it active in the worksheet window. If you've added additional worksheets (see the information later in this section to learn how), things get a little crowded when trying to read the tabs. If you want to select a worksheet that is not on-screen, you can use the worksheet scroll arrow buttons at the far left end of the horizontal scroll bar to scroll through the sheet names until the one you want appears. Then click the sheet you want. Table 1.2 shows each worksheet scroll arrow's action.

Table 1.2 Worksheet Scroll Arrows

Click This Button	To
	Scroll to the first sheet in the workbook.
	Scroll to the previous sheet.

continues

Table 1.2 Continued

Click This Button	To
	Scroll to the next sheet.
	Scroll to the last sheet in the workbook.

Naming Worksheets By default, Excel's worksheets are named Sheet1, Sheet2, and so on. You can rename your worksheets at any time to better describe the data they contain. Although you can use up to 31 characters in a sheet name, it's a good idea to keep the name short so the tab doesn't take up too much room. To rename a worksheet:

1. Right-click the sheet tab of the sheet you want to rename.
2. A shortcut menu pops up on-screen (see Figure 1.4). Select the Rename command.

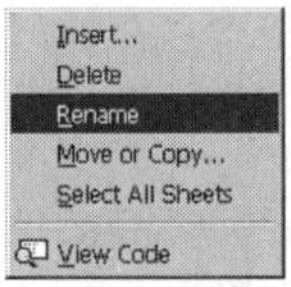

FIG. 1.4
Use the pop-up menu to rename your worksheet.

3. The sheet's tab name is highlighted. Type a new name (up to 31 characters) and press Enter.
4. Excel displays the new name on the worksheet tab.

TIP A quick way to rename a sheet is to double-click the tab and then type a new name. Press Enter when finished.

Adding and Deleting Worksheets You can also add and delete worksheets from your workbook file. Remember that Excel will delete not only the sheet but all the data on that sheet. Be sure that you don't delete sheets that contain information you need. When Excel deletes a worksheet, it's permanently gone.

You can easily add more worksheets to your workbook:

1. Click the worksheet tab *before* which you want to insert a new sheet.
2. Open the Insert menu and select Worksheet.
3. Excel inserts a new sheet and gives it a default name.

TIP To quickly insert a new worksheet using the keyboard, press Shift+F11.

You can also use the shortcut menu to add new sheets. Right-click over the sheet tab name and choose Insert from the shortcut menu. In the Insert dialog box that appears, select the Worksheet icon from the General tab and click OK. The sheet is now added to your workbook.

TIP To add a worksheet after the last sheet in your workbook, just insert a new sheet anywhere and drag its tab to the end of the tab display.

To delete a worksheet from your workbook:

1. Select the sheet you want to delete.
2. Open the Edit menu and select the Delete Sheet command. (You can also right-click the sheet, choose Delete from the shortcut menu.)
3. You are prompted to confirm the deletion. Click OK. Excel deletes the worksheet and all its data. Excel does not automatically renumber existing sheet names.

TIP You can adjust the order of the worksheet tabs by simply selecting a tab name and dragging it into a new location among the other tabs. You can copy your worksheets, too—press and hold the Ctrl key while dragging the tab name to a new location.

Viewing Multiple Workbooks

Although Excel opens a blank workbook window when you first start the program, you're not limited to using that workbook, you can open another workbook you may have saved, or you can open a second workbook window. You can also display more than one window on-screen at a time. Multiple-opened workbook windows make it easier to move items from one workbook and place them in another (see Figure 1.5). However, there's a downside to multiple windows, as the more you open, the more cluttered your desktop becomes.

TIP The active window's title bar is always a solid color so you know which one you're currently using.

One way you can keep things tidy is with the Window menu. It has several commands for controlling the appearance of workbook windows:

- To switch from one open workbook window to another, display the Window menu and select the workbook name you want to open from the bottom of the Window menu list. The name of each opened workbook appears at the bottom of the Windows menu. (You can also cycle through each workbook by pressing Ctrl+F6.)
- If you're working with a particularly large worksheet, you may want to view different portions of the sheet at the same time. Select Window, New Window. This opens a new window of the same worksheet (see the worksheet name in the title bar change accordingly). You can now view another portion of the sheet, then switch back to the original view in the active window.

FIG. 1.5
You can view more than one workbook window at a time.

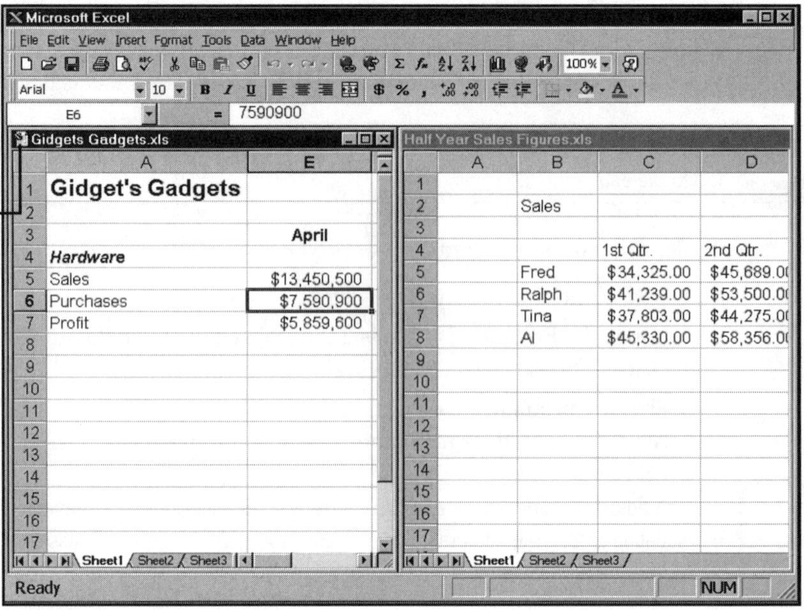

The active worksheet's title bar appears highlighted

- Select Window, Arrange to open the Arrange dialog box. Here you can select options for viewing multiple windows on-screen at the same time. (To return a workbook window to full size, select the window's Maximize button.)
- Select Window, Hide to hide the active workbook window. Although hidden, the file remains open. Select Window, Unhide to display it again.
- Select Window, Split to split the active window into panes (select Window, Remove Split to rid your screen of the split panes). Select Window, Freeze Panes to freeze the top and left panes to keep column or row titles in view at all times while you're scrolling across the worksheet.

TIP To switch to another open workbook using the keyboard, press Ctrl+F6. To switch to the previous workbook, press Ctrl+Shift+F6.

97 **TIP** Another way to move from one Excel file to another is with hyperlinks. Hyperlinks are linked words or images you can click to jump you to another file, worksheet, or Web page. To learn more about using hyperlinks in Excel, see Chapter 24, "Integrating Excel with Other Office Applications," on page 581.

▶ **See** "Opening and Closing Workbook Files," **p. 68**
▶ **See** "Saving Workbooks," **p. 62**

Using Excel Toolbars

Excel's toolbars are full of shortcuts to commonly-used commands. For example, if you want to save your file, click the Save button on the Standard toolbar. This is much faster than opening the File menu and then selecting the Save command. Along with buttons, Excel's toolbars may also display drop-down lists and palettes. In some instances, a click on a toolbar button will open a dialog box offering you more choices pertaining to the command.

NOTE If you're ever in doubt about what task a button performs, move your mouse pointer over the button, and the button's name appears. This is a ScreenTip. This won't work if the ScreenTip feature is turned off. By default, it's on when you first use Excel. If it is off, select View, Toolbars, Customize to open the Customize dialog box. Click the Options tab, then select the Show ScreenTips on toolbars check box. This turns the ScreenTips feature on again. ■

Table 1.3 explains each of the buttons on Excel's Standard toolbar.

Table 1.3 Standard Toolbar Buttons

Button	Function
	Opens a new workbook file
	Displays the Open dialog box
	Saves the file
	Prints the current worksheet
	Previews the worksheet
	Opens the spell check tool
	Cuts selected data to the Windows Clipboard
	Copies selected data to the Clipboard
	Pastes data from the Clipboard
	Copies formatting from one area to another

continues

Table 1.3 Continued

Button	Function
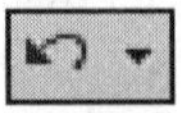	Undoes your last action
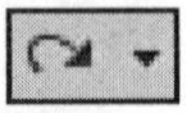	Reverses the Undo command
	Inserts hyperlinks into your worksheet
	Displays the Web toolbar
	Activates the AutoSum function for summing numbers
	Activates the Paste Function command
	Sorts data in ascending order
	Sorts data in descending order
	Opens the Chart Wizard for building charts and graphs
	Creates a map based on selected data
	Displays the Drawing toolbar
	Lets you zoom your worksheet view in and out
	Opens Excel's Office Assistant help feature

▶ **See** "Using Excel Functions," **p. 189**

▶ **See** "Creating Charts," **p. 285**

▶ **See** "Drawing with Excel," **p. 361**

Table 1.4 describes each of the tools available on the Formatting toolbar.

Table 1.4 Formatting Toolbar Buttons

Button	Function
	Displays a drop-down list of font styles
	Displays a drop-down list of font sizes
	Bolds selected data
	Italicizes selected data
	Underlines selected data
	Aligns data to the left in a cell
	Centers data in a cell
	Aligns data to the right in a cell
	Combines adjacent cells to create a single cell
	Assigns Currency Style format to numbers
	Assigns Percent Style format to numbers
	Assigns Decimal Style format to numbers
	Inscreases decimal points
	Decreases decimal points
	Increases the indent
	Decreases the indent
	Add borders to selected cells

continues

Table 1.4 Continued

Button	Function
	Changes the fill color of cells
	Changes font color

▶ **See** "Formatting Your Worksheets," **p. 129**

Selecting, Moving, and Customizing Toolbars

As you work with the Excel, you can change toolbars to access the icon buttons that meet your current needs. To change which toolbars are displayed on-screen, move your mouse pointer over any toolbar and right-click. This displays a shortcut menu listing available toolbars, with a check mark next to each one that currently appears. To change toolbars, click the one you want from the list, and the new toolbar is displayed. You can also change toolbars by selecting View, Toolbars, and then select a toolbar from the submenu. For additional toolbars you may want displayed, select View, Toolbars, Customize and select which toolbars you want in the Toolbars tab.

Microsoft has tried to come up with every possible toolbar combination you could want, but they've also made it easy for you to tailor the toolbars to fit your needs. You can edit the toolbars with the Customize dialog box.

1. Select View, Toolbars, Customize. This opens the Customize dialog box, shown in Figure 1.6. (You can also access the box by selecting Tools, Customize.)
2. From the Commands tab, use the Categories list box to display different buttons in the Commands list box.

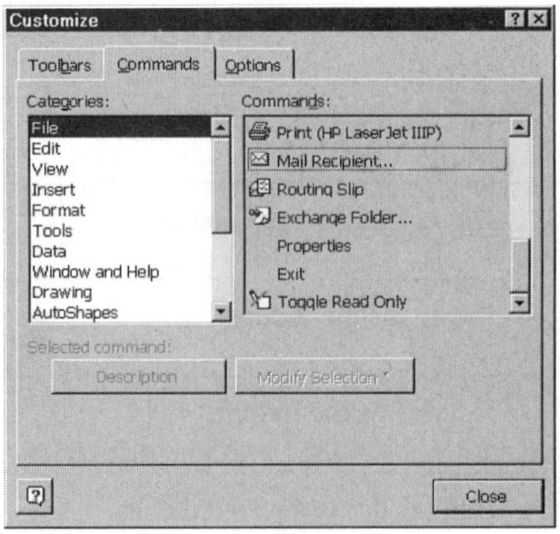

FIG. 1.6
The Customize dialog box.

3. To select a button to place on the toolbar, click the button in the Commands list box and drag it up to the toolbar to the location where you want the button added. Release the mouse button and the button is inserted onto the toolbar.
4. To remove a button from the toolbar, simply drag it off the toolbar.
5. To add a button to a toolbar that's not currently on-screen, click the Toolbars tab and highlight the toolbar you want to see, then return to the Commands tab and add or remove buttons from the toolbar.
6. When finished customizing your toolbars, click the Close button to exit the Customize dialog box.

Excel keeps track of the toolbars you have open when you exit the program. The next time you start Excel, the same toolbars will appear on-screen.

Excel's toolbars are very versatile, you can move them around on-screen and reshape their appearance. By default, toolbars appear docked at the top of the Excel window. To turn a toolbar into a floating toolbar, locate a divider or blank area on the toolbar, then drag the toolbar to a new location on-screen (see Figure 1.7).

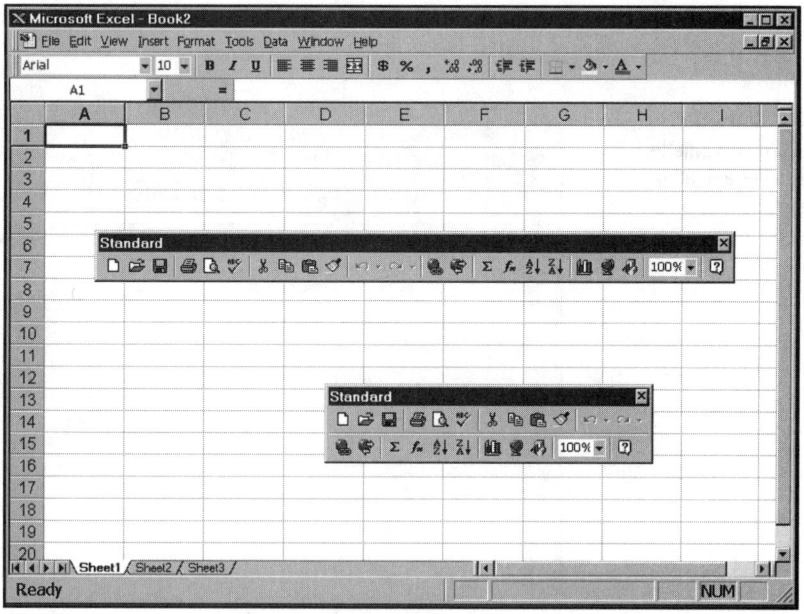

FIG. 1.7 You can make the Standard toolbar a floating toolbar and then resize it.

To move a floating toolbar, drag its title bar to a new location on-screen. To reshape the floating toolbar, drag the edge of the toolbar (refer to Figure 1.7). To dock the toolbar in its original location, double-click the toolbar's title bar.

NOTE If a toolbar's icons appear too small for you to read, you can enlarge them. Select View, Toolbars, Customize to open the Customize dialog box. Click the Options tab, then select the Large icons check box. Click Close to exit the dialog box.

Working with Tear Off Palettes

As you begin using the Excel toolbars, you'll notice some contain drop-down lists or palettes that offer you more selections to make. You can tear off these palettes and display them as a floating palette.

Use these steps to tear off a palette:

1. Click the drop-down arrow to the right of the toolbar button. For example, to tear off the Borders palette, click the tiny arrow next to the Borders button on the Formatting toolbar (see Figure 1.8).

FIG. 1.8
Display drop-down palettes by clicking the button's arrow.

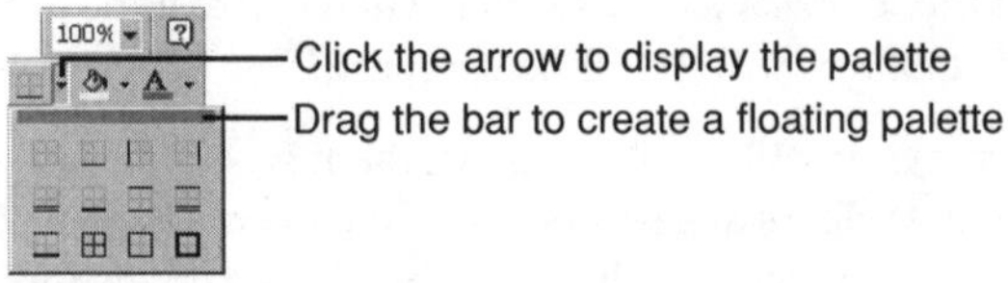

2. Click the title bar at the top of the palette and drag it to a new location on-screen.
3. Release the mouse button and the palette becomes a floating palette you can reposition and use as needed (see Figure 1.9).

FIG. 1.9
The Borders palette becomes a floating palette.

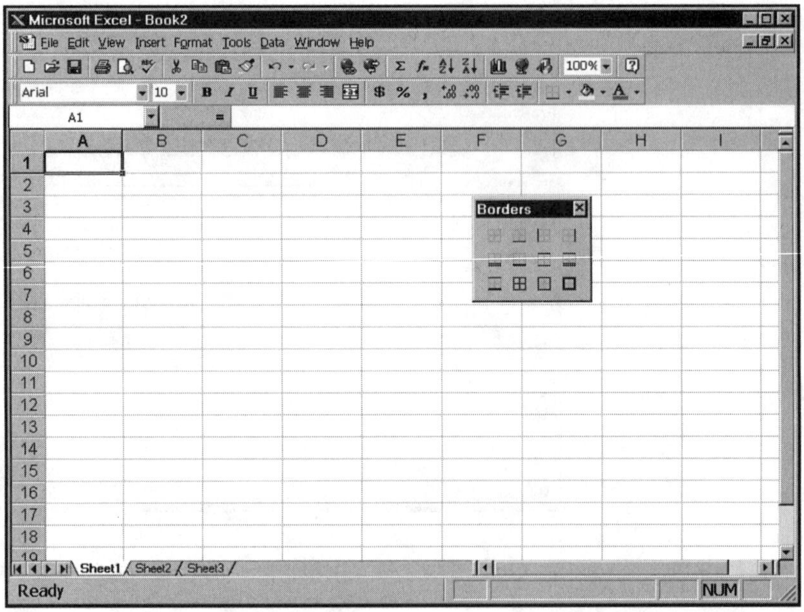

You won't be able to reshape the floating palette, but you can easily move it around on-screen by dragging it's title bar. To close the palette, click its Close button in the top-right corner.

Using Excel's Help Features

With all of Excel's many features and on-screen elements, it's not always easy to remember which item does what or what procedure to follow to accomplish a particular task. Excel 97 offers an extensive help system you can tap into anytime you want to learn more about a task or feature. Many of the help tools are located on Excel's Help menu, including links to help pages on the Web. There's also a new animated help feature, called the Office Assistant, that provides an interactive way of finding help. The more you utilize Excel's many help features, the more you'll learn how to use the program itself.

Using and Customizing the Office Assistant

97

The Office Assistant is a new animated help feature that readily assists you with any questions or tasks you may have while using Excel 97. You can access the Office Assistant by opening the Help menu and selecting Microsoft Excel Help, pressing F1 on the keyboard, or you can click the Office Assistant button on the Standard toolbar (the button with a question mark icon). Once you've accessed Office Assistant, a message balloon appears and you can type in a question, conduct a search, or view tips about the particular feature you're using. You can even customize the appearance of the animated feature and make changes to the options associated with the feature.

TIP The Office Assistant may appear the very first time you use Excel or attempt a new task. If you want help with the task or wish to proceed without the Office Assistant on-screen, select the appropriate option in the Office Assistant message balloon.

When the Office Assistant is displayed on-screen, as shown in Figure 1.10, you're prompted to enter a question. Simply type in your question and click the Search button or press Enter. Don't worry about capitalization or punctuation. In fact, you don't have to type in a complete question. You can type in a single word, such as "bold," or "formatting" and Office Assistant will attempt to find related topics.

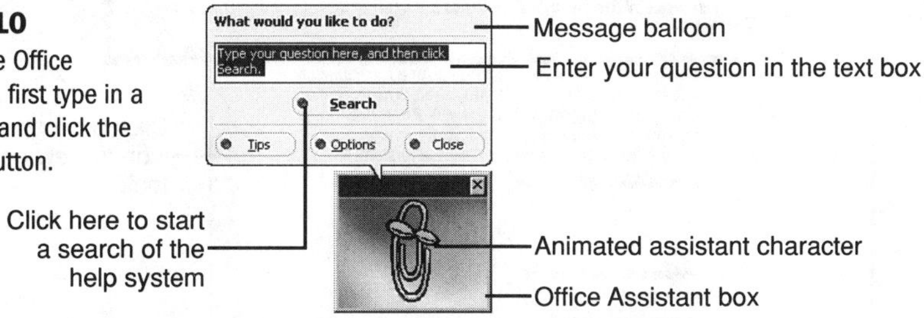

FIG. 1.10
To use the Office Assistant, first type in a question and click the Search button.

As soon as you start the search, Office Assistant looks through it's help database and responds with a list of possible topics, as shown in Figure 1.11. The contents of the Office Assistant box may vary slightly, depending on the action you're performing. However, much of the contents will remind you of options and buttons found in ordinary Windows dialog boxes. The message balloon includes command buttons, a text box for entering questions, and option buttons that open additional help boxes or topics lists.

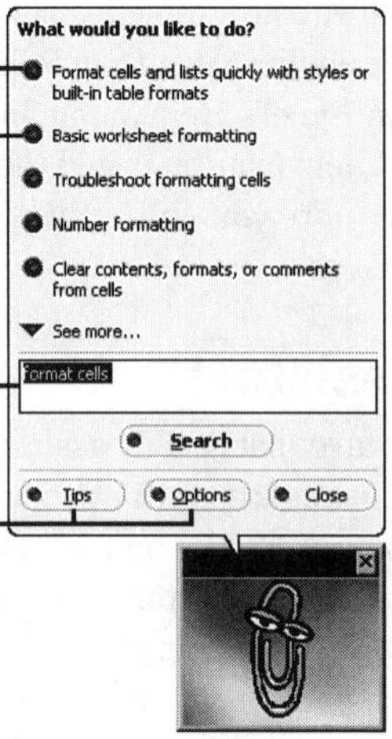

FIG. 1.11
Office Assistant responds with a list of possible topics you can explore to find more information.

To select a topic, click the option button in front of the topic. This opens a Help window, which displays information about the topic you selected (see Figure 1.12).

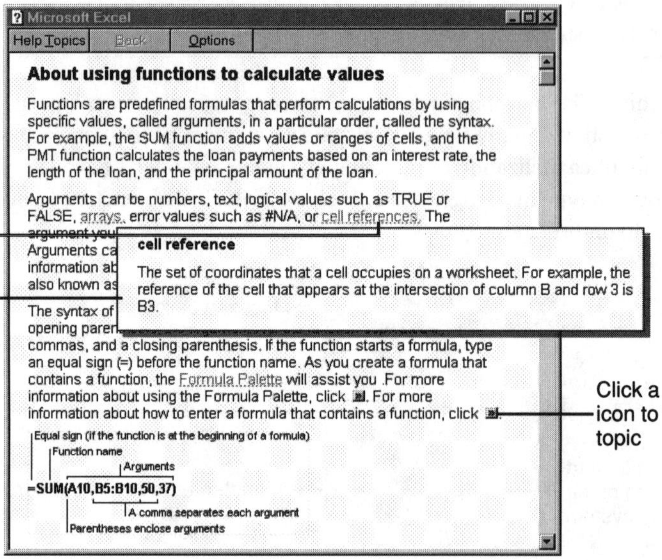

FIG. 1.12
Use the Excel Help window to look up specific help topics.

Within a Help window are several options you can pursue:

- Click on dotted underlined text to view a definition of the term.
- Double arrows display related help topics.

- Some Help windows may display more text than others; use the scroll bar to view the text.
- Click icons to view more information about the topic.
- Click Show Me buttons to see an animated demo of how a feature works.
- Use the command buttons at the top of the Help window to activate other Help features.
- To close the Help window, click on the window's Close (X) button. The message balloon is redisplayed.

TIP To see additional topics in the Office Assistant message balloon, click the See More button (downward-pointing arrow) in the Message Balloon. If the Office Assistant fails to display any topics related to your question, you can type in a new question and perform another search.

In addition to using Office Assistant to search for help topics, you can also use the Tips button (shown in Figure 1.11) to display a tip box (see Figure 1.13). When the tip box opens on-screen, use the Back and Next buttons to view different tips.

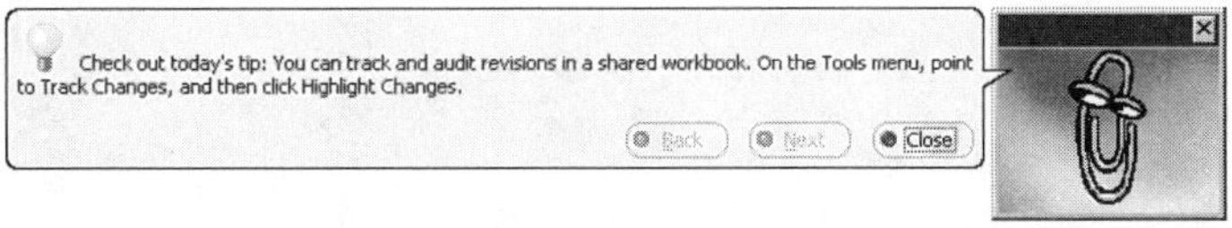

FIG. 1.13
The Tips box displays a tip of the day.

To exit the Tip screen, click the Close button. The Office Assistant box is displayed. To reopen the message balloon again, click anywhere on the Office Assistant box, or press F1.

If you're in the midst of performing a new Excel task, you may want to keep Office Assistant opened and ready to assist you. If the box is in your way, you can easily move it around on-screen by dragging its title bar. However, if you no longer anticipate needing the feature, you can close it entirely. Right-click the box and select Hide Assistant from the pop-up menu, or click on the Close (X) button.

TIP The Office Assistant may pop up on-screen from time to time to help you with common tasks. If you leave Office Assistant opened on-screen when you exit Excel, it will automatically appear on-screen again when you reopen Excel.

While the Office Assistant can be a very useful tool as is, you can also customize it to suit your needs or fancy. For example, by default, Office Assistant uses the animated character Clippit, but you can choose from several others. You can also customize the types of tips displayed, capabilities associated with Office Assistant, such as sounds and positioning, and the keyboard shortcuts associated with Office Assistant. Use the steps below to customize Office Assistant:

1. To open the Office Assistant, click the Office Assistant button on the toolbar, press F1 on the keyboard, or open the Help menu and select Microsoft Excel Help.
2. Click the Office Assistant's Option button.

3. The Office Assistant dialog box appears with the Options tab displayed, as shown in Figure 1.14. From here you can turn options on or off pertaining to the Office Assistant feature. Click an option to turn it on or off (a check mark indicates the option is on, no check mark means the option is off). The Options tab displays three categories of check boxes:

   Assistant Capabilities Use these options to control Office Assistant's appearance, associated sounds, and alerts.

   Show Tips About These options control the types of tips displayed in the Tips box.

   Other Tip Options More options for controlling the Tips box.

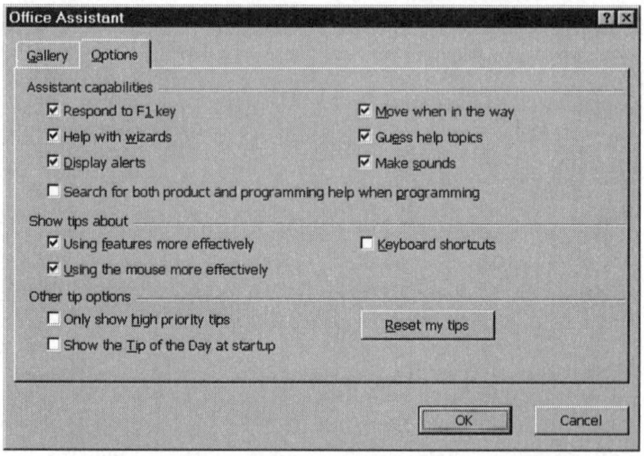

FIG. 1.14
The Office Assistant dialog box lets you customize the Office Assistant help feature.

4. To change the animated character that appears each time you access Office Assistant, click the Gallery tab (see Figure 1.15).

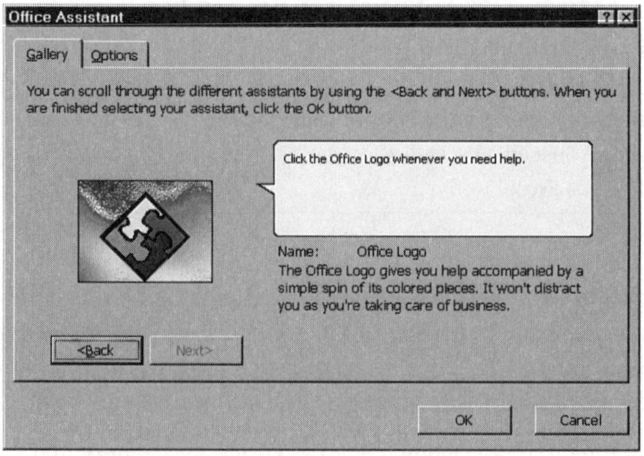

FIG. 1.15
Customize the animated assistant using the Gallery tab.

5. Click the Next and Back buttons to scroll through a gallery of different animated characters and icons and read their descriptions. (It may be necessary to load the Excel 97 CD-ROM to view other characters.)
6. To select a particular character, simply click the OK button. This closes the dialog box.

Using Excel's Help System

Another way to find help is through the Help Topics dialog box. Open the Help menu and select Contents and Index. The Help Topics dialog box appears, as shown in Figure 1.16.

FIG. 1.16
The Help Topics dialog box displaying the Contents tab.

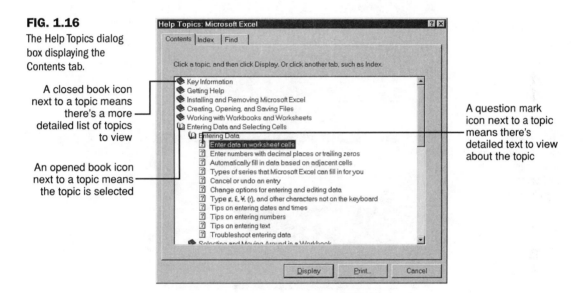

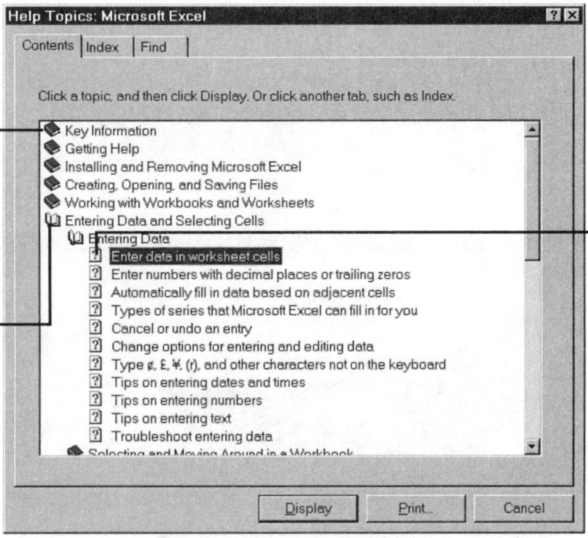

The Help Topics dialog box has three tabs you can use to access help:

- *Contents* Use this tab to view available help topics, much like the table of contents in a book. To choose a topic, double-click its name or icon. In many instances, this reveals a sublist of more topics. Keep double-clicking to find the exact topic you want to view information about.
- *Index* Use this tab to look up specific terms in the Excel help system. Type in the word you're looking for, and the bottom portion of the tab scrolls to the appropriate alphabetical listing (see Figure 1.17). To view help on the term displayed in the index list, double-click the term to open a Help window.
- *Find* The options in this tab (see Figure 1.18) allow you to search the entire Excel help database. Type in the word or words you're looking for, use matching words to narrow your search, and a list of topics appears. Double-click the topic to open a Help window (see Figure 1.19).

To close the Help Topics dialog box, click its Close (X) button or click Cancel.

FIG. 1.17
Use the Index tab to look up Help terms.

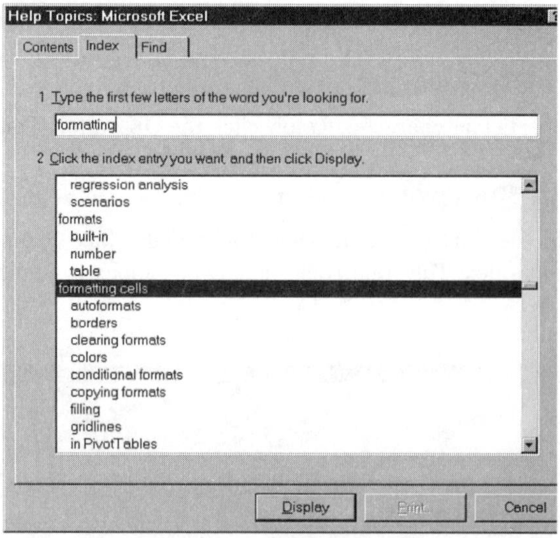

FIG. 1.18
Use the Find tab to search through Excel's Help database for specific information.

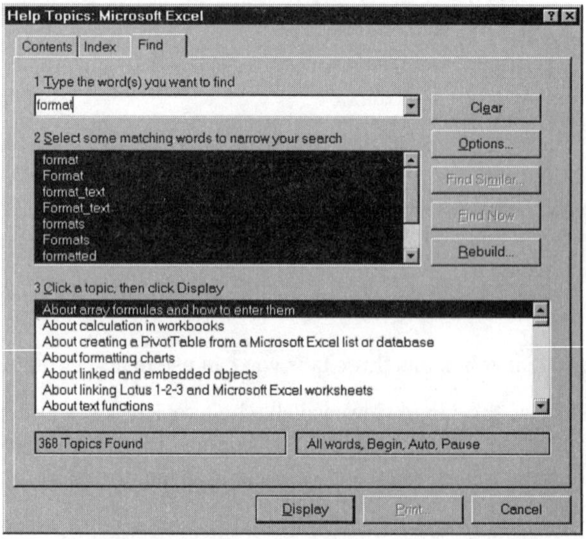

TIP Another help feature to use are ScreenTips. By default, Excel's ScreenTips feature is turned on. To find out what a particular toolbar button does, hover your mouse pointer over the button for a moment. A ScreenTip box appears identifying the button. (If your ScreenTips are turned off, select View, Toolbars, Customize to open the Customize dialog box. Click the Options tab, then select the Show ScreenTips on toolbars check box.)

Working with the Help Window The Help window displays information about a topic, as shown in Figure 1.19. Depending on the topic, the content will vary. Some topics include icons and buttons you can click to view tutorials or additional help boxes. Other topics display step-by-step instructions to perform a task, lists of related topics, or term definitions.

FIG. 1.19
The Help window.

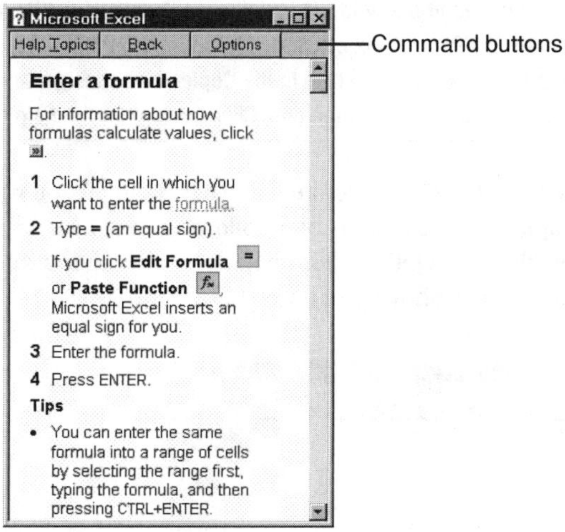

In addition, the Help window has command buttons you can use to navigate the topics you display:

- *Help Topics* Click this command button to open the Help Topics dialog box (see Figure 1.16)
- *Back* Use this button to return to the last help topic you displayed.
- *Options* Click this button to open a menu of options for printing, copying, and annotating the help topics.

Table 1.5 explains the options available when you select the Options button.

Table 1.5 Help Window Options

Menu Command	Function
Annotate Help	You can add notes to a topic with this feature.
Copy Windows	Copy a help topic to Clipboard, then place it in another file using the Paste command.
Print Topic	Prints the current topic.
Font	Changes the size of the font displayed in the Help window.
Keep Help on Top	Keeps the Help window displayed on top even if you switch to another application window.
Use System Colors	Switches the Help window colors to the colors defined in the Windows 95 Control Panel.

TIP Right-click anywhere on the help page window to display the Options menu.

TIP To print the topic currently displayed in the Help window, choose Options, Print Topic, or right-click and select Print Topic. This displays the Print dialog box. If necessary, in the Printer area, use the Name drop-down list to select the printer you want to use. In the Copies area, designate how many copies you want to print, if you plan on printing more than one. Click OK to print the help topic.

Using the Annotate Feature The Annotate feature is handy if you want to add your own comments to a help topic, such as a note about following the steps or how you might use the feature. To add a note, click the Options button in the Help window and select Annotate. This opens the Annotate dialog box, shown in Figure 1.20.

FIG. 1.20
The Annotate dialog box.

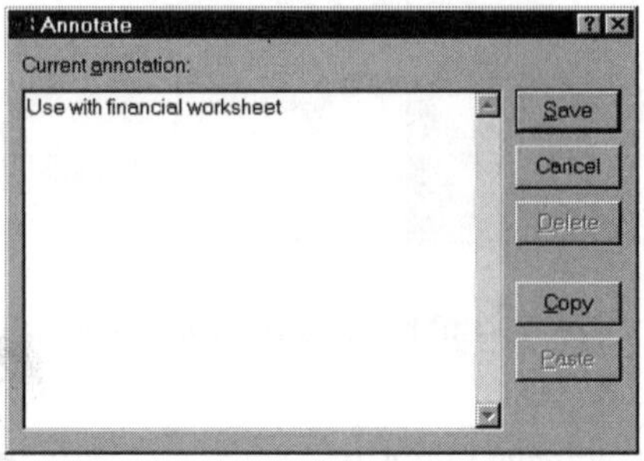

In the Current Annotation text box, type your comments. When finished, click the Save button. The note now appears on the Help topics page as a paper clip icon in the upper left corner. To view the note, simply click the paper clip icon. This opens the Annotate dialog box again with the note.

To remove a note, click the Options button and choose Annotate, then click the Delete button.

TIP To exit the Help window at any time, click the window's Close (X) button.

Using the What's This? Feature

To get help on a particular on-screen element or command, open the Help menu and select What's This, or press Shift+F1 on the keyboard. Your mouse pointer changes to the shape of a question mark. Click the on-screen item or command for which you want help and a description box appears detailing that item and how it's used (see Figure 1.21).

To close the description box, press Esc or click anywhere inside or outside the box.

Some dialog boxes include What's This icons located in the upper-right corner, next to the Close button. To learn more about a particular element or option within the dialog box, select the What's This icon, then click the element you want to learn more about. A description box appears explaining how the element is used.

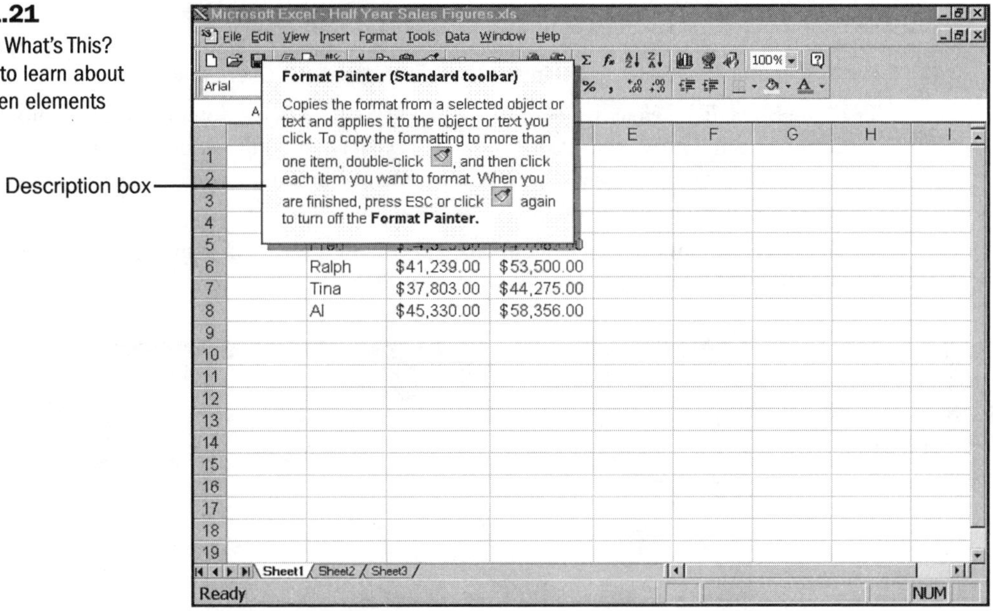

FIG. 1.21
Use the What's This? feature to learn about on-screen elements

> **TIP** You can also right-click to display the What's This command in some Excel dialog boxes. Select the command, then point and click to the dialog box element you need help with.

Using Lotus 1-2-3 Help

If you're switching from Lotus 1-2-3 to Microsoft Excel, you'll find plenty of assistance to help you with the transition of learning a new spreadsheet program. Be aware that there are some differences between the two programs, for example Excel calculates certain formulas and functions differently than 1-2-3. For a complete list of differences, open the Help menu and select Lotus 1-2-3 Help to display the Help for Lotus 1-2-3 Users dialog box (see Figure 1.22).

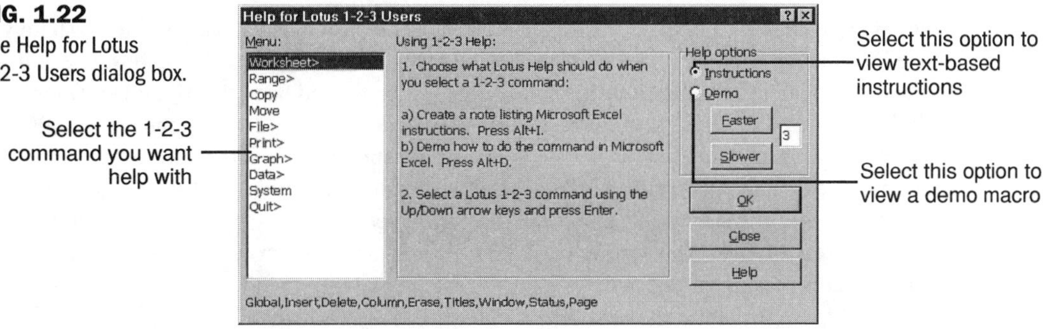

FIG. 1.22
The Help for Lotus 1-2-3 Users dialog box.

To learn more about Lotus 1-2-3 Help, click the Help button in the dialog box. This opens a Help window with related topics, such as the differences between the two programs, equivalent spreadsheet terminology, and tips for converting 1-2-3 worksheets into Excel worksheets.

To see step-by-step instructions of how to perform a 1-2-3 task in Excel:

1. Click the Instructions option in the Help for Lotus 1-2-3 Users dialog box.
2. In the Menu list, select the 1-2-3 command and click OK, or double-click the command. Commands followed by a greater sign (>) reveal submenus, which contain additional command choices. Double click on the submenu commands until you reach the command instructions you want.
3. The Excel window displays a help box, shown in Figure 1.23, listing the instructions you need to follow to carry out the command in Excel.

FIG. 1.23
Lotus 1-2-3 Help appears as a text box in the Excel window.

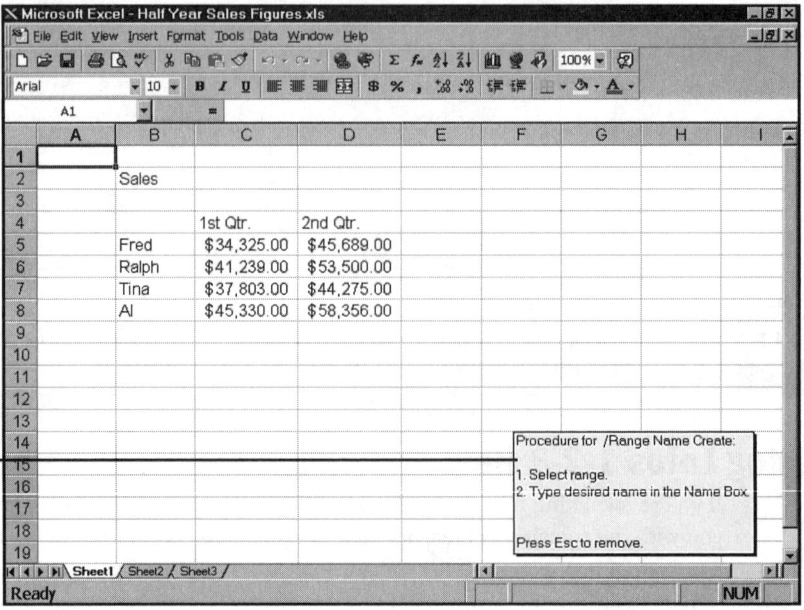

Lotus 1-2-3 Help

You can keep the help box on-screen as long as you need it. To close the box, press Esc.

In addition to text-based help, Lotus 1-2-3 Help also features demos you can play to learn how to use Excel to perform 1-2-3 tasks. From the Help for Lotus 1-2-3 Users dialog box, select the Demo option under Help options, then select the 1-2-3 command from the Menu list. Double-click the command to reveal the submenu list. After selecting the 1-2-3 command, click OK. The next box that appears on-screen lets you enter the spreadsheet data to use in the demonstration. For example, if you choose Range, Name, Create from the Menu list and click OK, a box similar to the one shown in Figure 1.24 appears. Type in or select any spreadsheet data you want help with, then click OK. Lotus 1-2-3 Help starts a prerecorded demo macro that shows you how to perform the task.

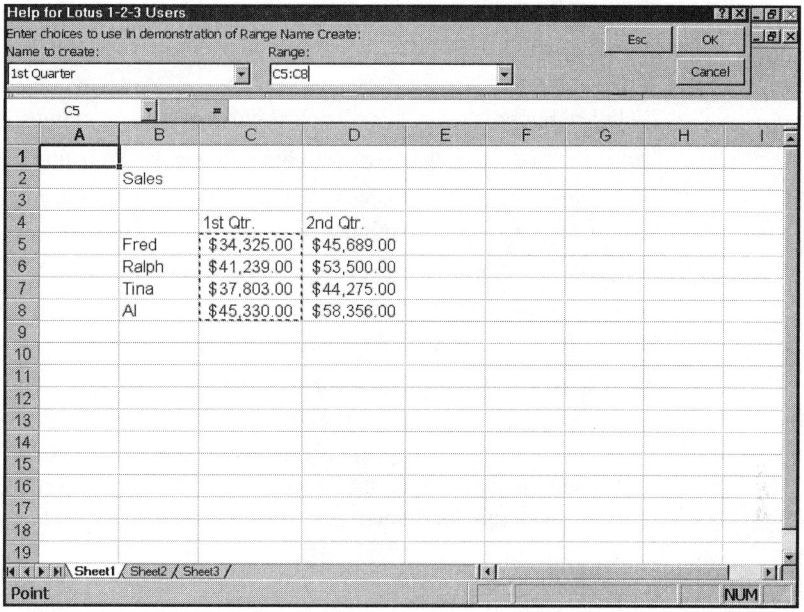

FIG. 1.24
Enter the spreadsheet data you want to see used in the demonstration.

TIP In the Help for Lotus 1-2-3 Users dialog box, the Faster and Slower buttons let you determine how quickly the demo plays. To slow things down, click the Slower button and replay the demo.

Finding Excel Help on the Web

With Excel 97, you can now log onto the Internet without leaving the Excel window. From the Help menu, select Microsoft on the Web, and then choose an option from a submenu of information, which includes:

NOTE You can access Microsoft's Help Web pages only if your computer system is set up to connect to the Internet automatically when you select a Microsoft on the Web command and if you have a Web browser program (such as Microsoft's Internet Explorer) installed. For more information, see Chapter 26, "Working with Web Pages."

- *Free Stuff* Opens the Excel Free Stuff Web page with links to free program enhancements you can download and use with Excel. Visit this page often for new enhancements you might find useful.
- *Product News* Opens the Microsoft Excel Home Page with news about Excel and other Microsoft products.
- *Frequently Asked Questions* Opens a Web page you can use to look through FAQs (frequently asked questions) and answers about Microsoft products.
- *Online Support* Opens the Technical Support Home Page where you can find help with your Excel problems.

- *Microsoft Office Home Page* Opens Microsoft's Office Home Page where you can browse other Office 97 product links and news.
- *Send Feedback...* Opens a page where you can send e-mail messages to Microsoft's Technical Support people, feedback about products, or suggestions.
- *Best of the Web* Opens a page with links to popular Web sites.
- *Search the Web...* Opens a page with a Web search engine you can use to search the Web for topics and information.
- *Web Tutorial* View a demo on how to use the Web.
- *Microsoft Home Page* Opens Microsoft's Home Page where you can browse other Microsoft product links and news.

Depending on the type of help you need, the Web page you open will display different information. For example, if you need to look up information about a problem you're experiencing with Excel, open the Online Support page. If you want to learn more about an Excel program enhancement, open the Free Stuff page. If you need to ask a question of the Microsoft Technical Support group, open the Send Feedback page and send an e-mail question to technical support.

When you've finished working on the Web, exit the browser window and close your Internet account.

Building a Sample Workbook and Worksheet

There are four basic aspects to creating a worksheet: entering data, applying formulas, utilizing functions, and formatting the data to look its best. There are special techniques for accomplishing each of these worksheet tasks. In this section, you'll find instructions for constructing a worksheet in the quickest way possible. For more detailed information on entering data, formulas, and formatting, see Chapters 2, 3, and 4.

Basic Data Entry

To begin entering data into a worksheet, click inside a cell and start typing. It's usually a good idea to plan out where you want data placed in a worksheet. To help you create your first sample workbook and worksheet, let's build a sheet that records 1st quarter sales for a fictional company called "Hales Hardware," a hardware supplier. Let's say there are four sales people. The sheet will record the name of each sales person, one name per row. There are three months in one sales quarter, so the worksheet will include January, February, and March in three columns. The data will look something like this:

January	**February**	**March**
Ralph		
Ed		
Jane		
Andy		

Each name and month should have its own cell in the worksheet. The months are heading titles for three columns. The names are row titles for four rows. Be sure to leave room at the top of the worksheet to add a worksheet title or other headings later. Follow these steps to set up the sample worksheet:

1. Click inside cell C4 and type in *January*.
2. Press Tab or click inside cell D4 and type *February*. Notice that pressing the Tab key takes you to the next adjacent cell to the right.
3. Press Tab or click inside cell E4 and type *March*.
4. Click inside cell B5 and type in the first salesperson's name, *Ralph*.
5. Press Enter or click inside cell B6 and type *Ed*. Notice pressing Enter takes you to the next adjacent cell below.
6. Press Enter or click inside cell B7 and type *Jane*.
7. Press Enter or click inside cell B8 and type *Andy*. The worksheet should now resemble Figure 1.25.

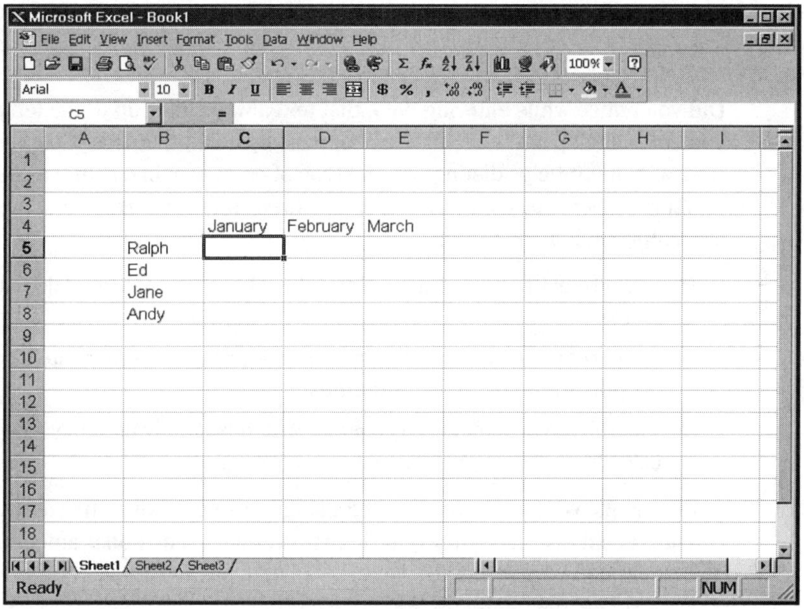

FIG. 1.25
Type in the row headings for each salesperson.

8. Now you're ready to start entering sales numbers for each salesperson. Click inside cell C5 and proceed to enter sales figures for Ralph. Click inside cell C6 and proceed to enter dollar amounts for Ed. Use the figures shown in Figure 1.26. The figures should represent dollar amounts, but don't worry about adding dollar signs yet. (Remember to press Tab to move to each cell in Ralph's row.)
9. Continue entering the dollar amounts for each salesperson, as shown in Figure 1.26. After inserting your data, you're ready to try out formulas and add formatting.

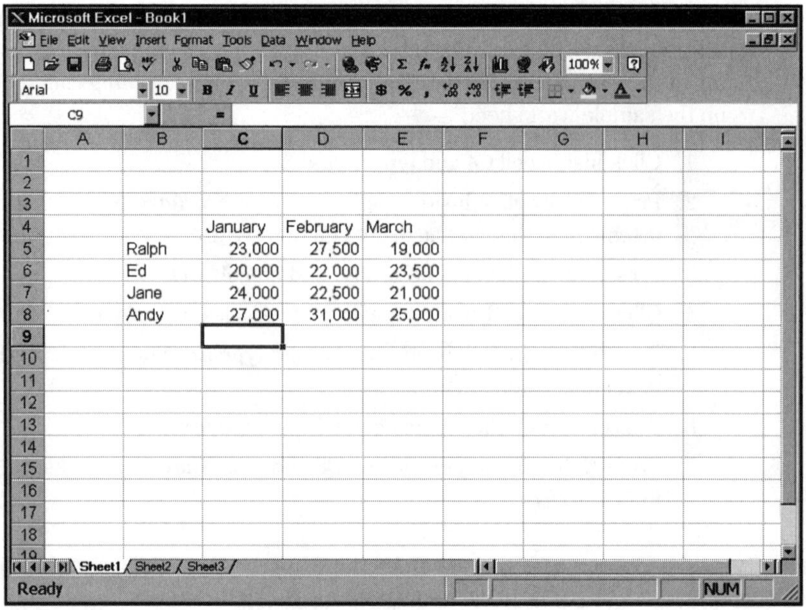

FIG. 1.26
When you finish entering data, your worksheet will look similar to this.

Did you notice while entering data, that text always lines up to the left of a cell and numbers you enter line up to the right? This happens by default, unless you change the cell's alignment. Data alignment helps distinguish the type of entry you insert into a cell. A worksheet can contain three basic types of entries: *labels, values*, and *formulas*. (There are also *functions*, which are simply built-in formulas.)

- Excel refers to text data as a *label*; Excel cannot perform calculations on entries that are labels.
- Excel refers to numerical data as a *value*; Excel can calculate value entries. Values include numbers, dates, and times
- The third type of data is a *formula*, which is simply an entry that tells Excel to perform calculations on the values in a cell or group of cells.

In the sample worksheet you created using the steps above, the column and row heading are considered labels, since they're strictly text entries. The dollar amounts entered for each salesperson are considered values.

▶ **See** "Basic Data Entry," **p. 44**

▶ **See** "Inserting Formulas," **p. 47**

Using the Formula Bar to Enter Data

When you start typing data into a selected cell, the data immediately appears in that cell and also in the Formula Bar above the worksheet window, as shown in Figure 1.27. You can use the Formula Bar buttons to help you enter data. When you finish typing in data, press Enter or click the Enter button (the button with a check mark) on the Formula Bar. You can also click in the next cell in which you want to enter data. If you change your mind about the entry, click the Cancel button.

FIG. 1.27
You can also enter data using the Formula bar.

Formula bar

An entry appears in the formula bar as well as inside the selected cell

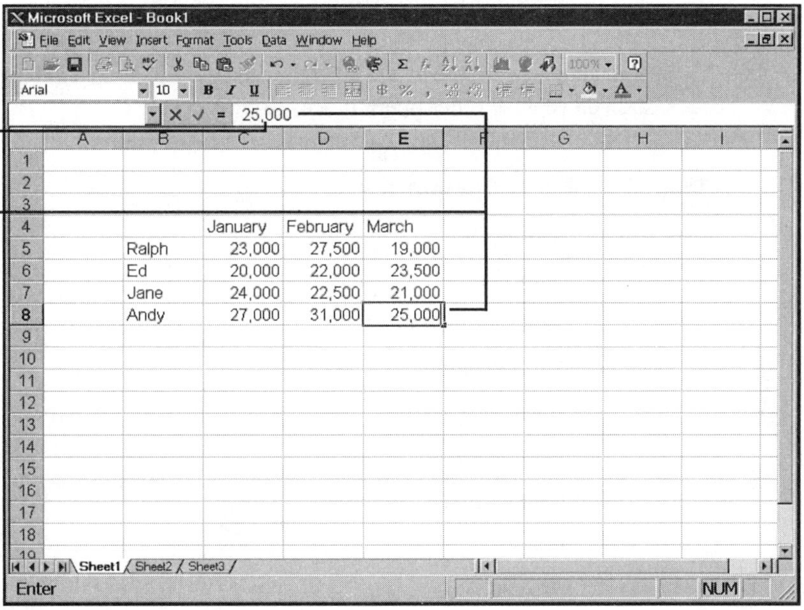

Three new buttons appear in the Formula Bar as you enter data (see Table 1.6):

Table 1.6 Formula Bar Buttons

Button	Name	Description
	Cancel button	Click it to cancel your entry.
	Enter button	Click it to confirm your entry.
	Edit Formula button	Opens the Formula Palette to help you build a worksheet formula.

▶ **See** "Entering and Editing Data," **p. 85**

Inserting Formulas

In a spreadsheet program like Excel, you can use formulas to figure totals and perform all kinds of other calculations for you. *Formulas* are simply mathematical operations you can perform on the entries in your worksheet: addition, subtraction, multiplication, and division.

A formula consists of these key elements: the equal sign (=), the values or cell references you want to calculate, and the operators (mathematical operations such as addition and multiplication). All formulas start with an equal sign. Take a look at this simple formula:

=A1+A2

This formula takes the value in cell A1 and adds it to A2. You can include more than two references, and you can use other operators, as listed in Table 1.7.

Table 1.7 Excel Operators

Operator	Description
+	Addition
-	Subtraction or negation
*	Multiplication
/	Division
%	Percentage
^	Exponentiation
=	Equal
<	Less than
<=	Less than or equal to
>	Greater than
>=	Greater than or equal to
<>	Not

To get an idea of how formulas work, practice using a formula in the sample worksheet you created. Perhaps you want to total all the amounts for Ralph in cell F5. Follow these steps to create a formula:

1. Click inside cell F5.
2. Type an equal sign (=). This tells Excel you're about to enter a formula. Notice the equal sign appears in both the cell and the Formula bar.
3. Type C5+D5+E5 and press Enter. The result of the formula appears in cell F5, as shown in Figure 1.28. Select cell F5 again and you'll see the formula you entered up in the Formula bar and the result of the formula in the cell.

To add the dollar amounts for Ed, the formula would be =C6+D6+E6.

Another thing to keep in mind when creating Excel formulas is *operator precedence*. In any given formula, Excel performs the series of operations from left to right in the following order:

1st All operations in parentheses

2nd Exponential equations or operations

3rd Multiplication and division

4th Addition and subtraction

FIG. 1.28
Formulas appear in the Formula bar, results in the cells.

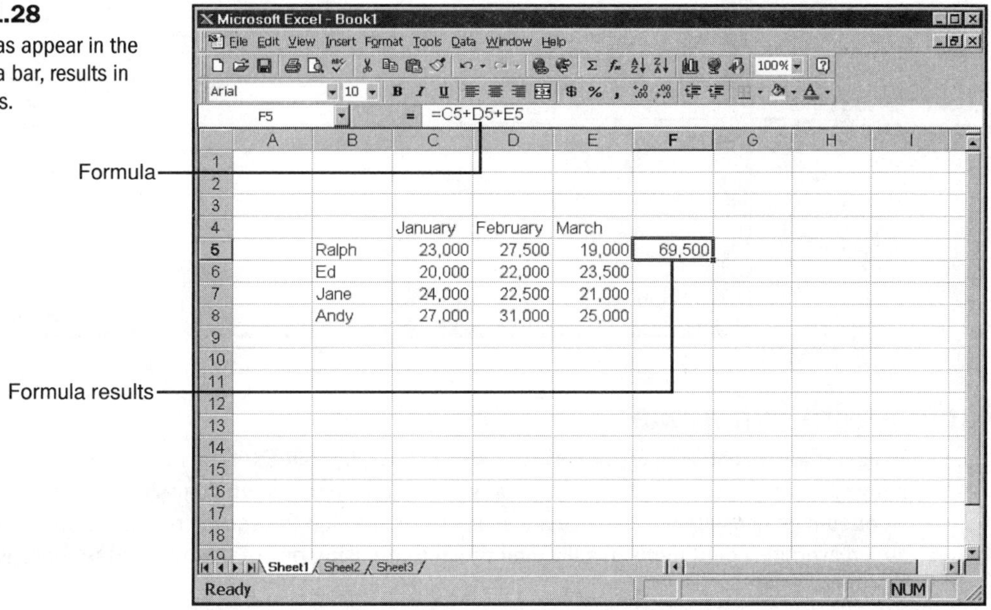

The order of operations determines the result of your formula. For example, if you want to determine the average values in cells C5, C6, C7, and C8, and you enter the formula =C5+C6+C7+C8/4, you'll probably get the wrong answer. Why? Because Excel will divide the value in C8 by 4, then add that result to C5+C6+C7. That's because division takes precedence over addition—the rule of operator precedence. One way around this problem is to group your values in parentheses. In the previous example, =C5+C6+C7+C8/4, enclose the values in parentheses to instruct Excel to do the addition first, then divide the result by 4. The formula looks like this now, ==(C5+C6+C7+C8)/4. Take a look at Figure 1.29 to see the formula in action.

TIP If you get an error message after typing in a formula, check and make sure you didn't designate a blank cell, divide by zero or a blank cell, delete a cell being used in the formula, or use a range name when a single cell address is expected.

NOTE In some formulas, you may want to perform two calculations. To make sure you get the results you want, use parentheses to surround the part of the formula you want to calculate first–the rule of operator precedence. Compare these two formulas: (10*3)+5=35 and 10*(3+5)=80. See how the results differ greatly?

FIG. 1.29
Use operator precedence to tell Excel which parts of the formula to calculate first.

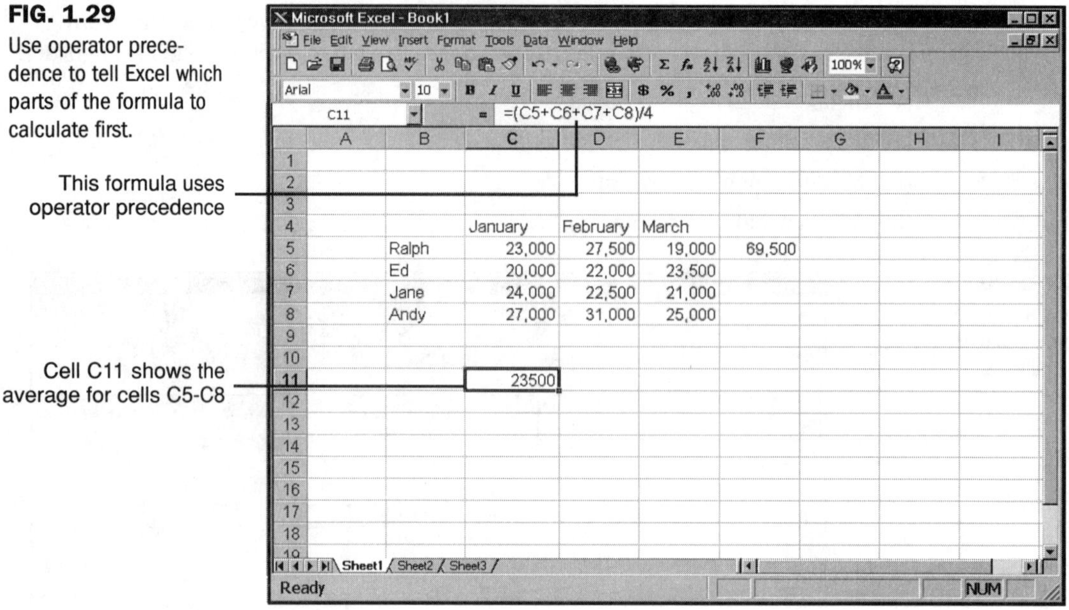

Working with Functions

An easier way of entering formulas is to use *functions*, built-in Excel formulas. Excel provides many calculation functions for you so that you don't have to get out your slide rule and old trigonometry books. You can calculate a loan payment, find the square root of a number, calculate an average, count items in a list, and much more using one of the hundred or more Excel functions.

Quite simply, functions are a shorthand way for entering complex formulas. For example, the AVERAGE function condenses a longer formula into a shorthand version. Rather than have this formula

=(A1+A2+A3+A4+A5)/5

You can use this function

=AVERAGE(A1:A5)

TIP Instead of typing entire strings of cell addresses to include in a formula, you can use a cell range.

Like a formula, the function starts with an equal (=) sign. The next part is the function name: usually a short, abbreviated word that indicates what the function does. After the function name, you see a set of parentheses, and inside the parentheses, you see the arguments—the values used in the calculation. Arguments can be a single value, a single cell reference, a series of cell references or values, or a range. Different functions require different arguments. Some arguments are mandatory; some are optional.

Chapter 6 covers functions in details, but to practice using a simple function, total all the dollar amounts for each column using the AutoSum feature. When selected, the AutoSum feature attempts to sum up the data in adjacent cells. If you prefer to sum up the values in other cells, you'll need to enter the cell references in the formula.

Follow these steps to use the SUM function in the sample worksheet:

1. Click inside cell C9 to total the sales amounts for the month of January.
2. Click the AutoSum button on the Standard toolbar (see Figure 1.30). This automatically enters the SUM function and selects the adjacent cells on which to perform the function.

FIG. 1.30
Use operator precedence to tell Excel which parts of the formula to calculate first.

The SUM function appears in the Formula bar

Selected cells

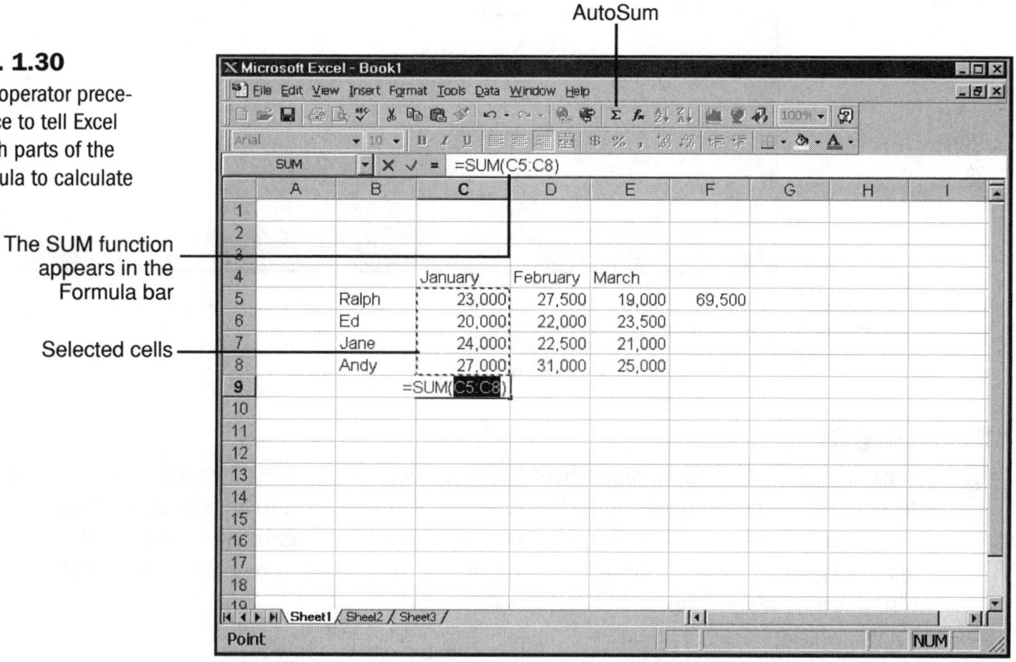

3. Press Enter to sum the selected cells. Select cell C9 again (see Figure 1.31). The cell contains the results of summing up the values in column C. The Formula bar shows the SUM function and its formula.

Continue using the SUM function to total the sales for February and March in the sample worksheet.

N O T E Another way to enter functions is with the Paste Function button on the Standard toolbar. For the function to work properly, you must enter the parts in the correct order and format. You can type the function and hope you remember the right order for the arguments, or you can have Excel build the function for you using the Paste Function button. Learn more about this feature in Chapter 6, "Using Excel Functions," page 189. ▪

FIG. 1.31
Use operator precedence to tell Excel which parts of the formula to calculate first.

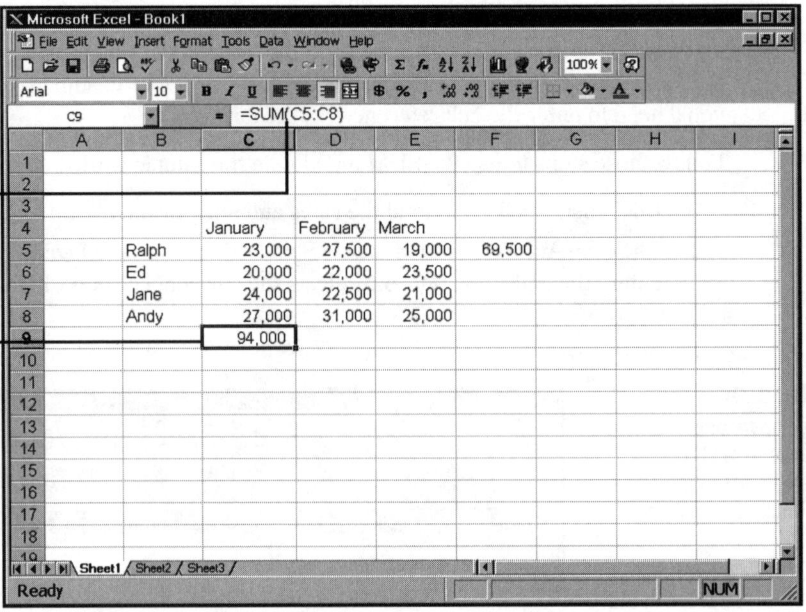

The SUM function and its formula

The total for January sales

▶ **See** "Entering Formulas," **p. 107**

▶ **See** "Using Excel Functions," **p. 189**

Fast Formatting

After entering data into your worksheet, you may want to add some formatting. Formatting effects the appearance of your data. For example, you may want to bold column headings or change number format. Or perhaps you want to change the alignment of data inside a cell, or add a background color or border. The fastest way to format worksheet data is with the buttons on the Formatting toolbar.

In the sample worksheet you created, follow these steps to apply formatting:

1. To change the column headings (January, February, March) to bold, first select the cells, as shown in Figure 1.32. Click the first cell, then drag over the adjacent cells.
2. Click the Bold button on the Formatting toolbar. The column headings now appear bold.
3. To change the number formatting for the sales figures in the sample worksheet, first select the cells you want to apply the formatting to.
4. To add dollar signs to the numbers, click the Currency Style button on the Formatting toolbar.

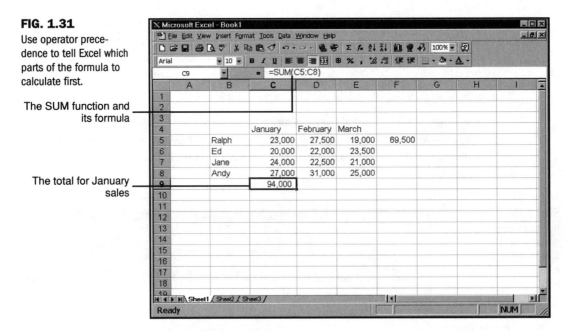

▶ **See** "Formatting Your Worksheets," **p. 129**

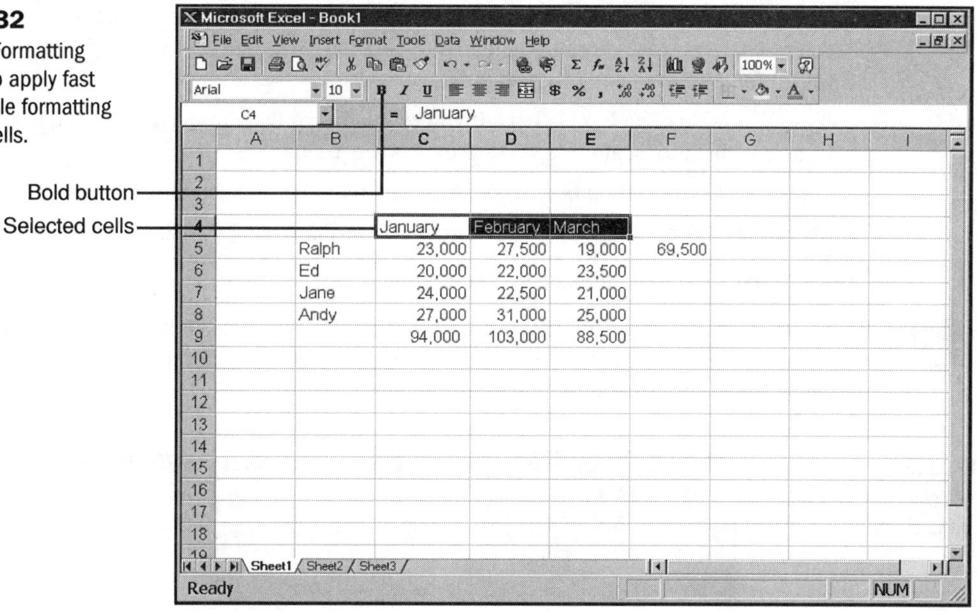

FIG. 1.32
Use the Formatting toolbar to apply fast and simple formatting to your cells.

Building a Sample Chart

Excel makes charting easy and relatively painless. The ChartWizard tool can walk you through each step in the process of turning worksheet data into a professional looking chart or graph. A chart takes your data and represents it visually. You can think of a chart as a snapshot picture of your data. With this picture, you or your intended audience can more easily see the relationship among the data. For example, if you chart sales by division, you can see, at a glance, which division leads in sales. If you create a pie chart of household spending, you can easily see which area has the biggest slice of the pie. You not only can visually see the relationship, but you can see patterns and trends, and you can quickly summarize data in a chart.

You can choose to add a chart on the worksheet or as a separate sheet in the workbook. If you create a chart on the same sheet as your data, Excel prints it side-by-side with your worksheet data. If you create a chart on a separate worksheet, you can print it separately. Both types of charts link to the worksheet data that they represent, so when you change the data, Excel automatically updates the chart.

Excel also offers you great flexibility when it comes to types of charts (there are a total of 14 standard chart types you can apply). After you select the data to chart, Excel will prompt you to select the type of chart you want to create. What's the difference among the chart types? Each has a specific purpose; you can select the chart type that best conveys your message. Excel provides 14 chart types to choose from, and each chart has several subtypes, or styles, which gives you even more flexibility.

As you're working with charts, you may come across charting terms that you're unfamiliar with. Here's a list of explanations for the various chart terms you'll encounter:

Data Series A collection of related data that you want to plot on a chart. For example, if you're charting your monthly household spending, the data series would include the values (amounts) of your spending categories.

Axis One side of an Excel chart. If you're building a two-dimensional chart, the horizontal axis is the X-axis, and the vertical axis is the Y-axis.

Legend An information box inside the chart that defines the chart elements.

Chart Title A name for the chart, usually describing what the chart illustrates.

To create a chart based on the data you entered in the sample worksheet, follow these steps:

1. Select the cells containing the data that you want to chart, as shown in Figure 1.33. (Keep in mind that the type of data you select effects how your chart appears.) Click the Chart Wizard button on the Standard toolbar.

FIG. 1.33
First select the data you want to chart.

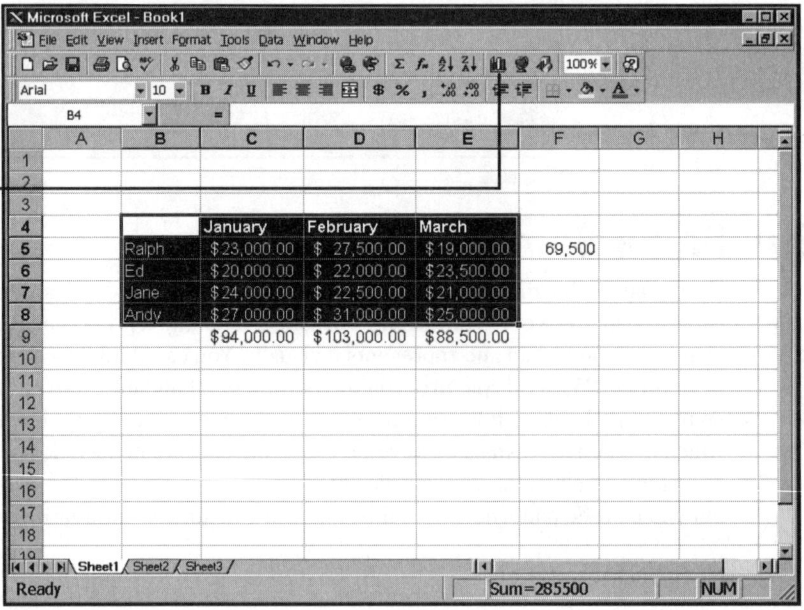

2. The Chart Wizard - Step 1 of 4 box appears, as shown in Figure 1.34. Click the Standard Types tab to bring it to the front of the dialog box, if necessary.

TIP The first time you use Excel's Chart Wizard, the Office Assistant help feature will pop up and offer to help you. Click the Office Assistant's Close (X) button to close the feature.

3. In the Chart Type list box, select the chart type you want to use. For our sample, select the Column chart type.

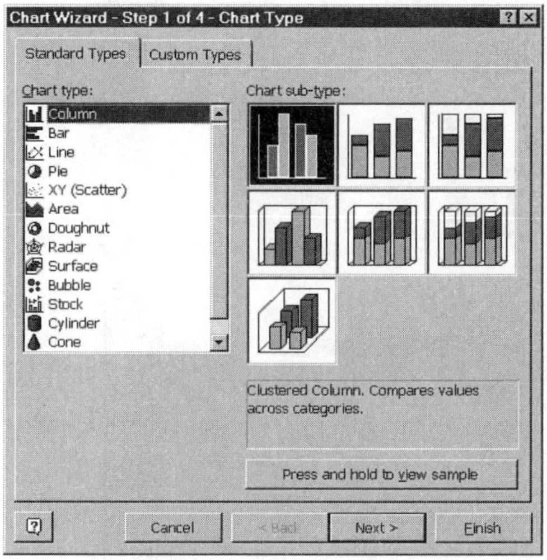

FIG. 1.34
In the first Chart Wizard box, select the chart type you want to use.

4. The Chart Sub-Type area displays several renditions of the chart type you selected. Click the sub-type you want to use. For our sample, select the 3-D column sub-type (second row, far left).
5. To preview how the chart style looks, point to the Press and hold to view sample button. Press and hold the button with the mouse pointer and you see a sample of the chart type using the worksheet data you specified. Release the button when finished viewing.
6. Click the Next button to continue.

TIP If your chart correctly graphs the worksheet data you selected and appears okay when you preview it, you can click the Finish button and Excel creates the chart for you. If you want to add more details, such as a chart legend, continue using the Chart Wizard dialog boxes to help you.

7. The Step 2 of 4 box appears, as shown in Figure 1.35. In step 1, you selected the worksheet data, but this box lets you verify the information. In the Data Range tab, make sure the correct data range is specified. If it's not, click on the Collapse Dialog Box button (at the far right end of the Data Range text box) and drag over the correct data in your worksheet.
8. Under Series In, select the Rows or Columns option to tell Excel how you want the data charted. The preview area at the top of the box will help you tell which option to select. For example, if you click Rows and the sample picture doesn't look like a chart, then click Columns instead. For the sample worksheet, the Columns option should be selected.
9. Click the Next button to continue.

TIP If you change your mind while working through the ChartWizard, click the Back button to go back a step. Also, if you don't like the chart type that you selected, you can change it by using Chart Wizard's Back button to revisit the step where you choose a chart type.

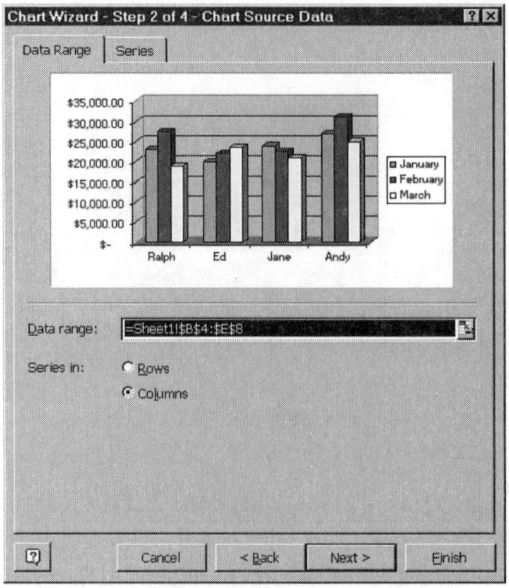

FIG. 1.35 In the second Chart Wizard box, verify the data range or series you want to use.

10. The Step 3 of 4 box appears, as shown in Figure 1.36. Use the various tabs in this box to give your chart a title, name the X- and Y-axes, turn on gridlines, include a legend, and type in data labels. Depending on the chart type you've selected, fill in the appropriate preferences. For the sample chart you're creating, type **1st Quarter Sales** in the Chart Title text box (see Figure 1.36).

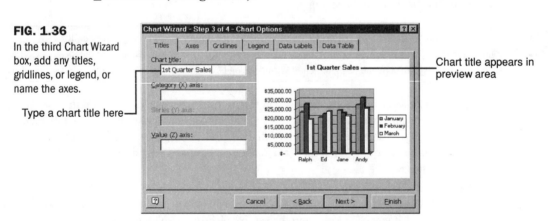

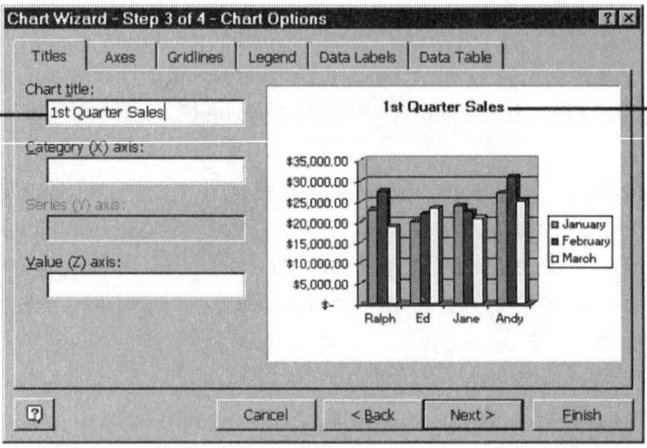

Chart title appears in preview area

Type a chart title here

FIG. 1.36 In the third Chart Wizard box, add any titles, gridlines, or legend, or name the axes.

11. Click the Next button to continue. The Step 4 of 4 box appears, shown in Figure 1.37. In this box, you can tell Excel whether you want to insert the chart onto the current worksheet, or place the chart onto a new worksheet. For our sample chart, select the As Object In option and place the chart in Sheet 1 of our workbook.
12. Click the Finish button and Excel creates the chart.

FIG. 1.37
In the fourth Chart Wizard box, designate a chart location.

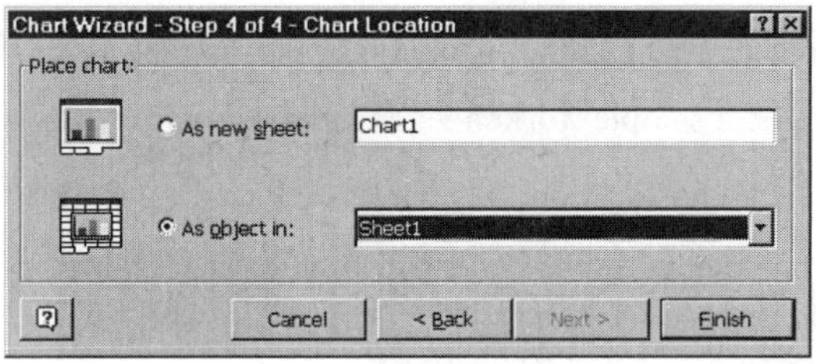

13. Depending on the choices you made with Chart Wizard, the new chart is placed on the current worksheet or in a new worksheet. If you followed step 11, the chart now appears (rather small) on the sample worksheet along with a floating Chart toolbar.

14. To resize the chart, make sure the chart is selected, then drag one of the object handles (small black boxes surrounding the selected chart). To move the chart, point to the chart and drag it to a new location on the worksheet. Figure 1.38 shows an example of how the chart may appear on the worksheet.

FIG. 1.38
Excel inserts a chart onto your worksheet.

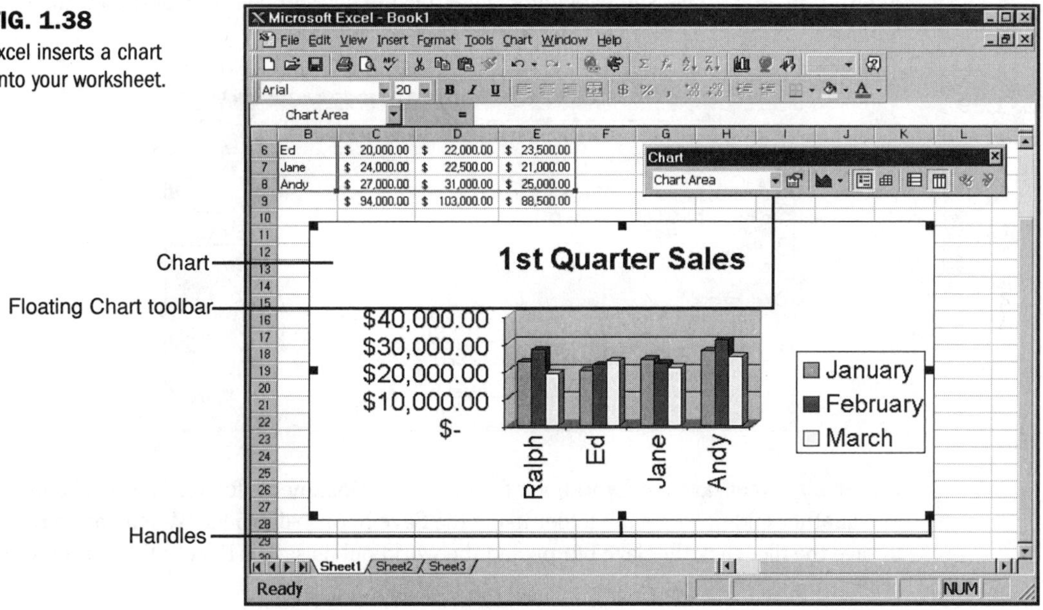

TIP Excel may place the new chart on top of existing data in your worksheet. To move the chart, click it, then drag it to a new location on the worksheet.

▶ **See** "Creating Charts," **p. 285**

▶ **See** "Advanced Chart Topics," **p. 311**

▶ **See** "A Field Guide to Excel Chart Types," **p. 337**

Printing and Saving Your Sample Worksheet

Now that you've created a sample worksheet and chart, you're ready to print and save the workbook.

NOTE When you print the sample, only the worksheet containing data will be printed. Sheet2 and Sheet3 of the workbook are empty.

- Before printing, you may want to preview how the worksheet will appear. Click the Preview button on the Standard toolbar. This opens up the worksheet in the Preview window. From this window, you can zoom in and out for a closer look. (Click the Close button to return to the worksheet window.)
- For a quick print, click the Print button on the Standard toolbar. This immediately sends the workbook file to the default printer.
- To save the sample worksheet and workbook, click the Save button on the Standard toolbar. If this is the first time saving the file, the Save As dialog box appears, as shown in Figure 1.39. In the File Name text box, enter a name for your sample workbook, such as *Sample1*.

FIG. 1.39
The Save As dialog box.

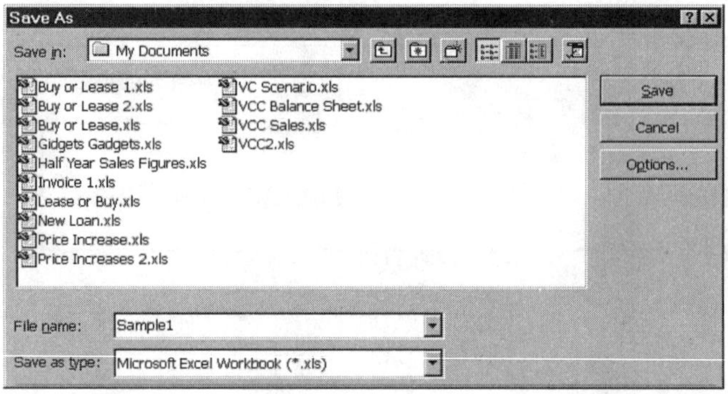

- By default, Excel saves the workbook file in the My Documents folder. To save the file into another folder, locate the folder using the Save In drop-down list. When you're ready to save the file, click the Save button and the workbook is saved. Excel's title bar now reflects the new file name, as shown in Figure 1.40.

▶ **See** "Starting and Exiting Excel," **p. 18**

▶ **See** "Saving Workbooks," **p. 62**

▶ **See** "Printing Worksheets," **p. 165**

FIG. 1.40
The workbook file is saved.

New file name

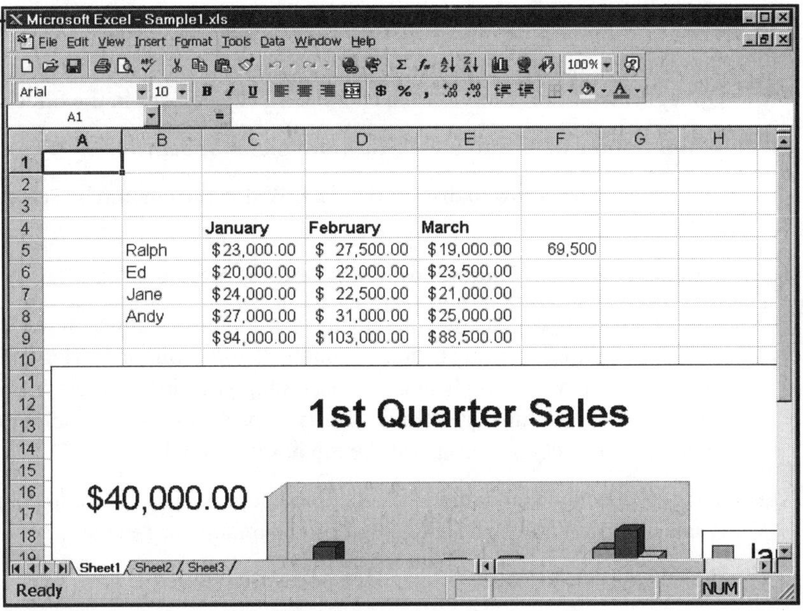

Common Problems and Solutions

If you're new to Excel, you may encounter some common beginner-related problems, as explained in this section. The following problems and solutions may help alleviate some of your frustrations encountered while learning how to use the program.

My Excel program window doesn't fill the display screen on my monitor.

Click the program window's Maximize button. To minimize the program window to a button on the Windows 95 taskbar, click the Minimize button. To open the program window again, click its button on the taskbar.

My toolbars look different from those pictured in this book.

If someone has used the Excel program before you, they may have made modifications to the toolbars. To restore the original toolbars, see "Customizing Toolbars and Menus," on page 248.

My toolbar buttons are too small to see.

You can select to display larger toolbar buttons in the Customize dialog box. Choose View, Toolbars, Customize, then display the Options tab and select the Large icons check box.

There are no worksheet tabs on my worksheets.

The sheet names option is turned off. To turn it on again and display tab names, choose Tools, Options, then select the View tab and place a check mark in the Sheet Tabs check box

When I enter data into a cell, number signs appear.

Your cell is too narrow to display the data. Widen the column by selecting Format, Column, Autofit Selection.

97 **When I select the Undo command, nothing happens.**

The Undo command can only undo your last action. You must choose it immediately after an action in order to undo the action. If you don't and continue working in the worksheet, a click the Undo button will simply undo the last thing you did. However, you can click the Undo button's arrow and display a list of your last few actions and make selections from the list to undo. The last action is always at the top of the Undo list.

To redo an action you undid, click the Redo button. Like the Undo command, the Redo arrow displays a list of previous actions that can be undone or redone.

When I type a formula, it appears as text in the cell.

All formulas must be preceded by an equal sign. Add an equal sign to the beginning of the entry.

From Here...

In this chapter, you learned the fundamentals for using Excel and building worksheets fast. The next two chapters will show you how to manager workbook files and provide more details about data entry.

- Chapter 2, "Managing Workbooks, Windows, and Sheets," shows you how to work with Excel's workbooks, including password-protecting your files, and working with windows and panes.
- Chapter 3, "Entering and Editing Data," explains the various ways of entering data types into your worksheets and how to edit your worksheet data.

CHAPTER 2

Managing Workbooks, Windows, and Sheets

by Sherry Kinkoph

The steps to managing files are identical for most programs. In this chapter, you'll learn how to save workbook files, save them as other file formats, and search for workbooks and worksheet data. You'll also learn how to protect your data by assigning passwords to workbook files and hiding sensitive data.

Sometimes half the battle of learning to use a new program is wrestling with the program window itself and learning how to view your data. This chapter also covers how to work with worksheet windows and panes, and to view different portions of your worksheet data. ■

Saving workbooks

Learn how to save your work using different file formats, rename files, and set up an automatic save.

Opening and closing workbook files

Find out how to open existing workbooks, new workbooks, and close workbook files.

Protecting yourself from macro viruses

Learn how to deal with Excel macro viruses.

Password-protecting files

Steps for protecting your workbooks from unauthorized users and create read-only files.

Searching for files

Learn how to use Excel's search tools to locate workbook files throughout your computer system.

Navigating shortcuts

Tips and tricks for navigating the Excel window, such as using shortcut menus, the Go To command, and splitting a worksheet window into panes to view different portions of your data.

Saving Workbooks

When it comes to saving files, you have several options to consider:

- You can save a new file to a folder on your hard disk drive or save the file to a floppy disk.
- You can save previously saved files, and even give them new names and put them in different folders.
- You can save files of different types to use with other programs.

When you save a file, the application automatically saves the document to the My Document folder. If you want to put the document in a different location or folder, you can use the Save In drop-down list in the Save As dialog box to change drives or folders.

NOTE Although file extensions aren't displayed in Windows 95 by default, all Excel files include the extention .xls. A file extension provides a unique way of identifying which program you created the file in and what type of file it was. You don't need to see a file extension to identify an Excel file, instead you can identify an Excel file by the Excel icon next to the file name. (You can still view extensions in Windows 95, however. While in Explorer, open the View menu, select Options, click the View tab, and deselect the Hide MS-DOS File Extensions check box.)

Also, when you save a file, Excel saves it in Microsoft Excel 97 format. If your coworkers use an earlier version of Excel, you can save your workbook in an appropriate file format they can work with. If your company widely uses Excel 5.0 or Excel 95, but some use Excel 97, you can choose to save Excel 97 workbooks in a dual file format (Microsoft Excel 97 and 5.0/95) that all users can handle. Keep in mind that saving a file in dual format increases the size of the file.

If you share Excel worksheets with users who have different programs, you might want to save an Excel file as another file type. For example, if a coworker uses Lotus 1-2-3 for Windows, you can save your Excel workbook as a 1-2-3 file that your coworker can use. Your coworker won't be able to use the file you've created unless it's converted to a usable format. Thankfully, most programs today let you convert a file's format. You can easily save your Excel workbooks as other file types using the Save As dialog box. Table 2.1 lists the various file formats you can use.

CAUTION

While any of the Microsoft Excel 97 workbook file formats preserve your worksheet data, including charts and macros, the other file formats may not preserve such data. For example, any formatting you apply in Excel 97 may be lost if you save the file in another format, such as dBase or an earlier version of Excel.

97

NOTE If your colleagues use various versions of Excel, you may want to change the default format. For example, if only a few people use Excel 97 and everyone else uses Excel 5 or Excel 95, save your worksheets as Microsoft Excel 97 and 5.0/95 file types. To do so, choose Tools, Options and select the Transition tab. Choose the format you want to save your files as, then choose OK.

Table 2.1 Excel File Formats

Format	File Extension
Microsoft Excel 97 Workbook	.xls
Microsoft Excel 5.0/95 Workbook	.xls
Microsoft Excel 97 and 5.0/95 Workbook	.xls
Microsoft Excel 4.0 Workbook	.xlw
Microsoft Excel 4.0 Worksheet	.xls
Microsoft Excel 3.0 Worksheet	.xls
Microsoft Excel 2.1 Worksheet	.xls
Lotus WK4 (1-2-3)	.wk4
Lotus WK3 (1-2-3)	.wk3
Lotus WK1, FMT (1-2-3)	.wk1
Lotus WK1, ALL (1-2-3)	.wk1
Lotus WK1 (1-2-3)	.wk1
Lotus WKS (1-2-3)	.wks
Quattro Pro WQ1 (Quattro Pro/DOS)	.wq1
dBase DBF 4 (dBase IV)	.dbf
dBase DBF 3 (dBase III)	.dbf
dBase DBF 2 (dBase II)	.dbf
Template	.xlt
Formatted Text (Space delimited)	.prn
Text (Tab delimited)	.txt
CSV (Comma delimited)	.csv
Text (Macintosh)	.txt
Text (OS/2 or MS-DOS)	.txt
CSV (Macintosh)	.csv
CSV (OS/2 or MS-DOS)	.csv
DIF (Data Interchange Format)	.dif
SYLK (Symbolic Link)	.slk
Microsoft Excel Add-In	.xla

TIP If you work in Microsoft Multiplan, Excel 97 doesn't include file format converters for Multiplan. Instead, use the SYLK file format to save workbook files for use in Multiplan.

Saving a File the First Time

To save a file for the first time:

1. In your new, unsaved workbook, choose File, Save. (You also can click the Save button on the Standard toolbar.)

TIP If you've previously saved the file, clicking the Save button on the toolbar will not open the Save As dialog box. Instead, it saves the file under the existing name. If you want to rename the file, choose File, Save As.

2. The Save As dialog box appears, as shown in Figure 2.1. Type a name for your workbook in the File Name text box. You can type up to 255 characters.

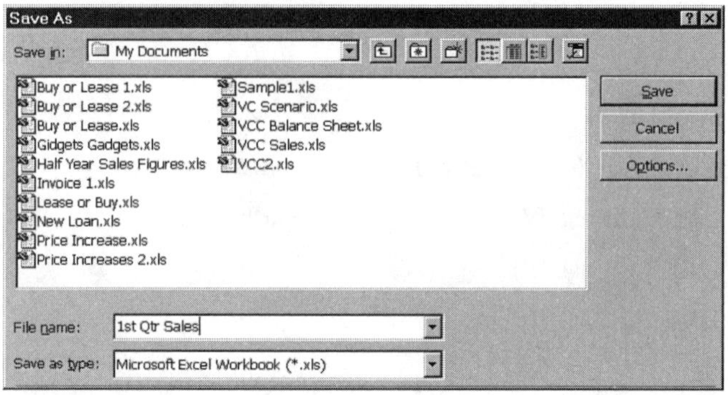

FIG. 2.1 Use the Save As dialog box to assign a unique name to the workbook file.

3. To save the workbook to another drive, click the Save In drop-down arrow and select the drive you want from the list that appears. (If you are saving to a floppy drive, be sure to insert the disk into the floppy drive.)
4. To save the workbook to another folder, click the folder name in the list box; then choose the Open button, or double-click the folder name to open it. If the folder doesn't appear in the list box, you can use the Save In drop-down list to look for the folder.

NOTE You might have to back up through the folder/directory tree to get to the folder you want. You can do so by clicking the Up One Level toolbar button in the dialog box. For example, if you are in the SALES subfolder of EXCEL and want to move to the INVENTORY folder (another subfolder you may have created in EXCEL), you have to back up to EXCEL and then change to INVENTORY.

5. To save the file in a different format, click the down arrow to the right of the Save as Type text box and select the file format you want to use.

6. Once you give the file a name and decide which folder to save it in, choose Save.
7. The workbook is saved and you see the new file name in Excel's title bar.

TIP To save a previously saved file you're working on, simply click the Save button on the Standard toolbar. If you want to rename the file or save it to a different location, choose File, Save As, and then type in a new file name and/or location for the workbook.

It's a good idea to get in the habit of saving every 10 or 15 minutes so that your computer updates the disk version with the changes you make. After you've saved the first time, you simply select File, Save to save again, or click the Save button on the toolbar. You won't be prompted to give the file a name; it will be saved under the existing name.

TIP With some DOS and Windows 3.1 programs, the longer file names you create in Windows 95 may be truncated to eight characters. When this happens, a tilde (~) is added to the name to indicate the name has been shortened and appears as EXPENS~1.XLS.

NOTE You can create a new folder to save your workbook file in from within the Save As dialog box. Click the Create New Folder button in the Save As toolbar. This opens the New Folder dialog box. Enter a folder name (up to 255 characters, including spaces) and choose OK. You can now select the new folder to save to.

Saving an Existing File Under a New Name

Use the File, Save As command to save an existing file under a new name. For example, if you've created a file called INVENTORY1 and you want to base a new workbook on the data in INVENTORY1, you can use the Save As command to create a new file based on the old file. The original file remains the same.

To save an existing file under a new name, choose File, Save As. In the Save As dialog box, give the file a new name. If you want to save the new file in a different folder or drive do so now. When finished, choose Save and the new copy of the file is saved under the new name. The original file is closed and left unchanged.

Setting Up an Automatic Save

Instead of having to remember to save your workbook every few minutes, why not have Excel save it for you? The AutoSave add-in lets you save Excel periodically, in the amount of time you specify. To use this feature, choose Tools, AutoSave. The AutoSave dialog box appears (see Figure 2.2).

Make sure the Automatic Save Every check box is selected and use the Minutes box to designate the save frequency, such as 10 minutes. Use the Save Options to choose to save all open workbooks, or only the active workbook. To display a prompt before saving, select the Prompt Before Saving check box. If you decide the prompts are annoying, deselect the option. Choose

OK to exit the box. Now Excel will automatically save the file you're working on every few minutes.

FIG. 2.2
Use the AutoSave dialog box to set up an automatic file save.

If the AutoSave command does not appear in your Tools menu, you'll have to load the add-in. Choose Tools, Add-Ins and select AutoSave in the Add-ins Available list. Choose OK to exit. If AutoSave still isn't added to the menu, you'll need to run Excel's Setup program and install the add-in.

Once you have AutoSave running, you can turn the option off whenever necessary. Simply open the Tools menu and deselect the AutoSave command, and clear the Automatic Save Every check box.

See "Using Excel Add-Ins," **p. 213**

Creating Backup Files

Another useful save option you might apply is backup files. Turn on Excel's backup option to create a backup copy of your workbook every time you save the file. That way, in case the original file is damaged or lost, you can always open the backup copy. Backup copies are saved in the same folder as the original file. Since the backup file is created after the original has been saved, you must save a file more than once to create a backup copy. If you do need to locate a backup file, the backup is stored under the name "Backup of *filename*."

To turn the backup option on for the current file:

1. Choose File, Save As to open the Save As dialog box.
2. Choose the Options button. The Save Options dialog box appears, as shown in Figure 2.3.

FIG. 2.3
To create a backup file, use the backup option in the Save Options dialog box.

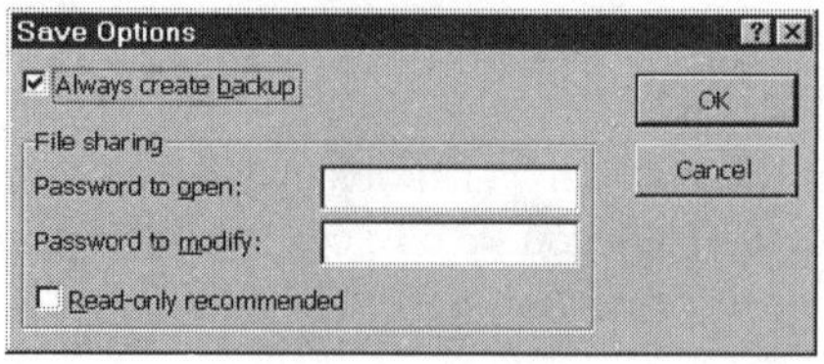

3. Select the Always Create Backup check box.
4. Choose OK to exit; then choose Save to save the file, or choose Cancel to close the Save As dialog box.

Using the Save Workspace Command

If you're the type of user that likes having several workbooks open on-screen to work between them, you may want to use the Save Workspace command. With this command, you can save all the workbooks you have open, plus their present location on the screen. This saves you time in reopening each file and arranging it on-screen to your liking. To use this command:

1. First, open and arrange the workbooks you want to work with.
2. Choose File, Save Workspace. The Save Workspace dialog box appears (see Figure 2.4).

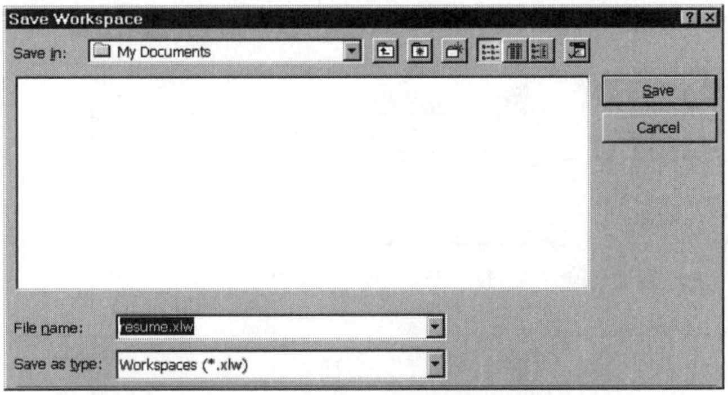

FIG. 2.4
Use the Save Workspace dialog box to save all the opened workbook files as a single group.

3. You can enter a new file name for the group in the File Name text box, or use the default name. You also can choose another folder or drive to save to.
4. When finished, choose Save.

The next time you want to open the files, open the workspace file the same as you open a workbook file. To save data in the individual workbooks within a workspace file, you must save each workbook using the File, Save command.

Saving Workbook Summary Information

Use the Properties dialog box to include summary information with the workbook file you save. Summary information, such as notes about the file contents, file author, or file title may be useful when you need to find the file later. Once you've added summary information to the file, you can make changes to it at any time.

To include summary information with your file, use these steps:

1. Choose File, Properties. The Properties dialog box appears (see Figure 2.5).
2. Fill in the fields as desired. You can type up to 255 characters in each field, but to keep things simple, less text is better.
3. Choose OK to exit the dialog box.

To view the summary information, choose File, Properties. To set up Excel to display the Properties dialog box every time you save a file, choose Tools, Options, and display the General tab. Select the Prompt for Workbook Properties option, then click OK. Each time you save a workbook file, the Properties dialog box appears for you to enter summary information. To disregard the dialog box, choose OK.

FIG. 2.5
The Properties dialog box allows you to assign summary information to a file.

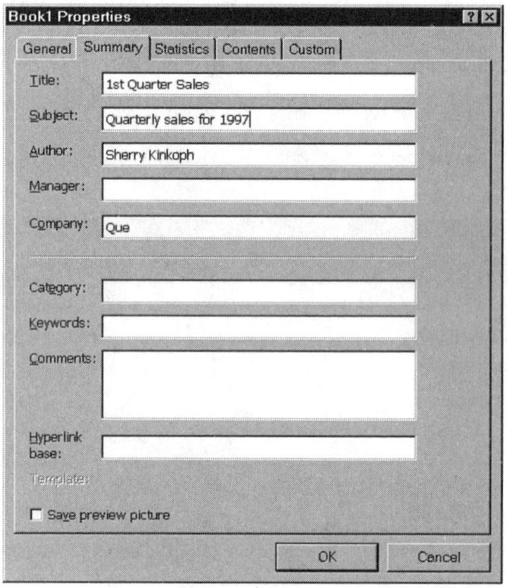

Opening and Closing Workbook Files

Opening a file is fairly straightforward: Choose File, Open (or press Ctrl+O), then double-click the file name in the Open dialog box. You can also use the Open button on the toolbar to display the Open dialog box.

The key is getting the Open dialog box to display the workbook name you want to open. You'll find that the Open dialog box, shown in Figure 2.6, looks very similar to the Save As dialog box (covered in the previous section). Files and folders appear in the list box, and you can change the display at any time. If the file you want is in the current drive or folder, you'll see it listed. If it's not, you can switch to the appropriate drive or folder using the Look In drop-down list or by clicking open any of the folders listed in the list box.

TIP If you like shortcuts, another way to open a file is to open the File menu and notice files listed at the bottom of the menu. The last four files you worked on appear listed. To open one of these files, click the file name.

The Open dialog box also has options for opening workbooks in another file format. For example, you can open Lotus 1-2-3 or Quattro Pro worksheet files. To display other file types in the Open dialog box, use the Files of Type drop-down list and select the file format you want. Table 2.2 lists the file types read by Excel.

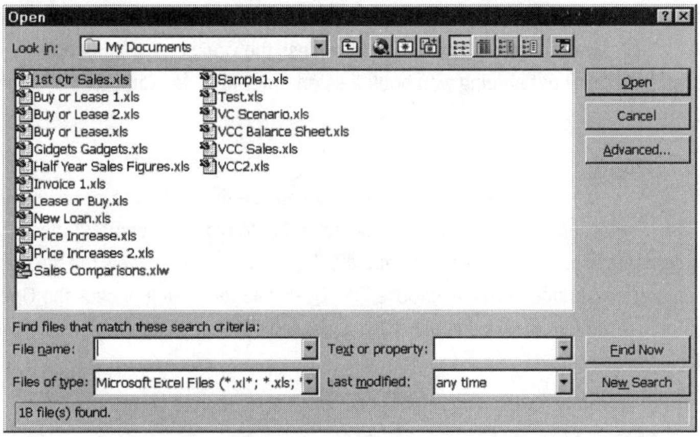

FIG. 2.6
Use the Open dialog box to open previously saved files.

Table 2.2 File Formats You Can Open in Excel

File Format	Extension
Excel workbook	.xls
Excel chart	.xlc
Excel macro sheet	.xlm
Lotus 1-2-3 worksheets	.wk*
Quattro Pro/DOS	.wq1
Microsoft Works	.wks
dBase files	.db*
Comma-separated values	.csv
Text files (tab separated values)	.txt
Backup files	.back
HTML Documents	.html, .htm

When you find the file you want to open in the Open dialog box and select it, choose the Open button to display the file in the Excel program window, or simply double-click the file name in the list box.

TIP To open more than one file at a time, hold down the Ctrl key as you highlight the file names in the list box. If the files are adjacent, hold down the Shift key while selecting files.

NOTE If you're using Excel on a network and sharing files, you won't be able to open a file that's currently in use by someone else unless the workbook sharing option is turned on. For more information about sharing workbook files on a network, see Chapter 23 "Collaborating with Excel."

NOTE If you have Quick View installed, you can use the feature to preview a workbook before selecting it. Right-click over a selected file to display a shortcut menu. Choose Quick View and a separate window opens with the file displayed. You can then view the file and decide if you want to open it or not. To open the file, choose File, Open File for Editing or click the Open File for Editing button on the toolbar. (If you don't see Quick View on the menu, you must install the feature from Windows 95 setup.)

Opening a New Workbook

When you start Excel, a new workbook is waiting for you to start working in. You can begin entering the figures and data for the worksheet. If you want to create another new workbook at any time, you can do so using the New button in the Standard toolbar. A click on this button immediately opens a new workbook on-screen.

Another way to start a new file is to use the New dialog box. To access this box, choose File, New, or press Ctrl+N. In the dialog box that appears, you'll see tabs that list sample workbooks and templates you can use to help you build your file. A *template* is simply a premade design and structure for a file. Depending on the templates you have installed, the New dialog box may show different icons. By default, Excel bases workbooks on the Workbook template, a basic, blank workbook with three worksheets. However, you can select from other templates, such as an invoice or purchase order. You also can create new templates or customize an existing one. Here's how:

1. Choose File, New.
2. The New dialog box appears on-screen (see Figure 2.7). Click the two tabs to see sample workbooks you can use to base your file on.
3. Select the template you want to use (if you haven't already). Look in the Preview area to see what the worksheet sample looks like (if applicable). Choose the OK button. You see a new workbook on-screen.

NOTE You also can open Excel workbooks from other sources. For example, you can open an Excel file from within Windows Explorer or My Computer by double-clicking the file name. If you use Microsoft's Outlook personal information manager, you can even open Excel files using the Other group on the Outlook bar.

▶ **See** "Spreadsheet Solutions Overview," **p. 264**

FIG. 2.7
Use the New dialog box to open specific types of Excel files, such as templates.

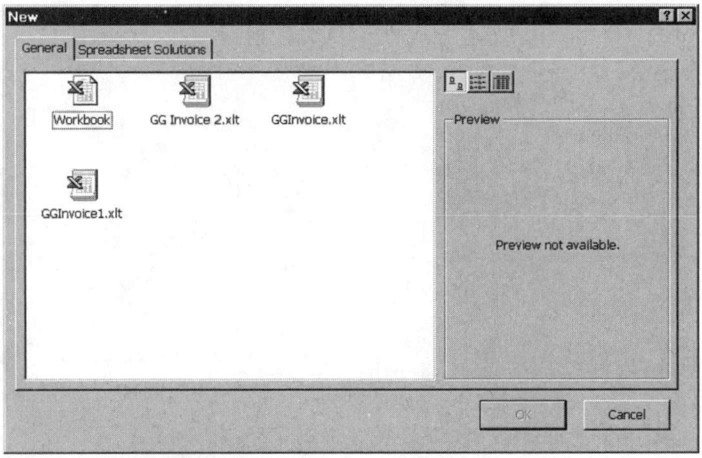

Opening Workbooks Automatically

If you find yourself working with the same workbook over and over again, you may find it useful to set up Excel to open this workbook automatically every time you start the program. You can place the workbook file in Excel's startup folder (XLSTART). Excel opens all workbooks, macros, or charts found in this folder. Or you can set up an alternate startup folder to hold files you want opened automatically. For example, create an alternate startup folder in Windows Explorer and give it a unique name. (If you already have an existing working folder you use, such as SALES or INVENTORY, you can use it instead of creating a new folder.) To create the startup folder, follow these steps:

1. From the Excel program window, choose Tools, Options. This displays the Options dialog box.
2. Select the General tab, as shown in Figure 2.8. In the Alternate Startup File Location text box, type the path to the alternate startup folder containing the file or files you want to open automatically.
3. Choose OK.

Make sure you save the file you want opened in the alternate startup folder you specified. The next time you start Excel, the file you saved in the alternate folder will open.

Closing Workbooks

You can have a lot of workbooks open at once, but doing so ties up your computer's memory and may slow down the performance of your computer. Instead, you should close a workbook when you finish working on it. After you close all Excel files, you see only two menu names on the Excel menu bar: File and Help. Using the File menu, you can choose to create a new workbook or open an existing workbook.

There are several different ways you can close a file. You can choose to close the entire application, which also closes the file, or you can choose to close only the opened workbook.

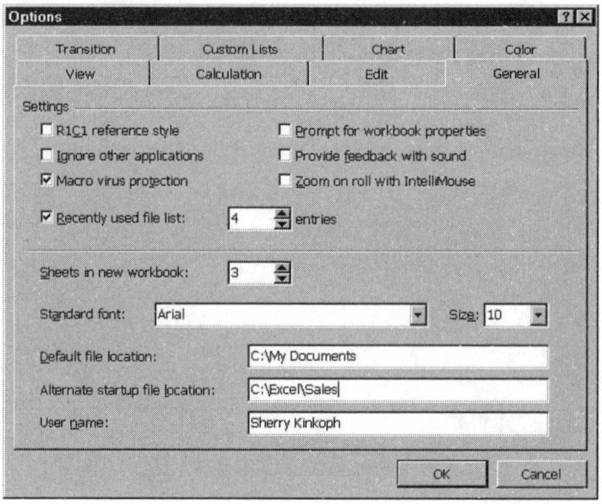

FIG. 2.8
The Options dialog box has options for setting an automatic startup.

If you're closing the entire program, you can use any of these methods:

- Click Excel's Close (X) button in the upper-right corner.
- Choose File, Exit.
- Double-click Excel's Control-menu icon located in the upper-left corner.
- Press Alt+F4 on the keyboard.

If you're only closing the open file, you don't have to close the entire program. You can use one of these methods:

- Click the workbook window's Close button.
- Double-click the workbook window's Control-menu icon.
- Choose File, Close.

If you haven't saved your work before closing the workbook, Excel will prompt you to do so before exiting. A dialog box pops up on your screen with three choices: Yes, No, and Cancel. If you don't want to save your work, click No to close the file. If you want to save your work, click the Yes button. The Save As dialog box appears (if you haven't named the file yet), and you can give the file a name. If you change your mind about exiting, click the Cancel button and you'll return to your workbook window.

Protecting Yourself from Macro Viruses

Excel users today have an additional concern to lookout for—macro viruses. Macro viruses are a new kind of virus embedded in Microsoft Excel and Word macros. (*Macro's* are simply prerecorded commands that simplify a computer task.) Many of Excel's templates use macros, and if you're sharing files (via disk or e-mail), all it takes is one infected macro to infect your system. A virus can be activated by running an infected macro, and any workbooks you save with the infected macro from that point onward can be infected, too. Although Excel can't scan your workbook files for macro viruses, it can help you watch for them. When you attempt to open a workbook that contains macros, Excel displays a warning box, as shown in Figure 2.9.

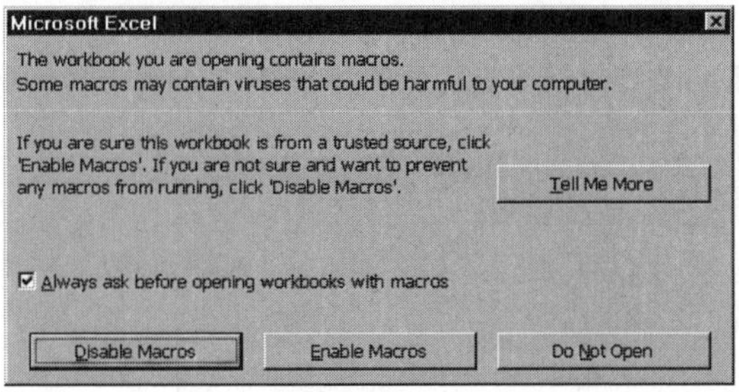

FIG. 2.9
The Macro warning box brings your attention to possible macro usage and the danger of macro viruses.

When you see this warning box, you have several options to pursue:

- If you're unsure about the source of the file, select the Disable Macros button. This lets you open the file but you won't be able to run any macros. This also means some of the workbook's features may not work.
- If you trust the source of the file, and need to use the macros contained within the workbook, choose the Enable Macros button. Before you make this choice, however, it's a good idea to check the file with a virus protection program.
- Choose the Do Not Open button if you want to stop and check the file for viruses before proceeding any further.

Excel's macro warning feature is turned on by default. If you already check files for viruses, you may want to turn the feature off. To do so, choose Tools, Options and select the General tab. Deselect the Macro Virus Protection check box. Choose OK to exit the dialog box. The warning box will not appear again.

Password-Protecting Files

If your workbooks contain sensitive data, you might want to protect the files from unauthorized use through the use of passwords. To assign a password to a workbook file, first open the file, then follow these steps:

1. Display the Save As dialog box by choosing File, Save As.
2. Choose the Options button to open the Save Options dialog box (see Figure 2.10).

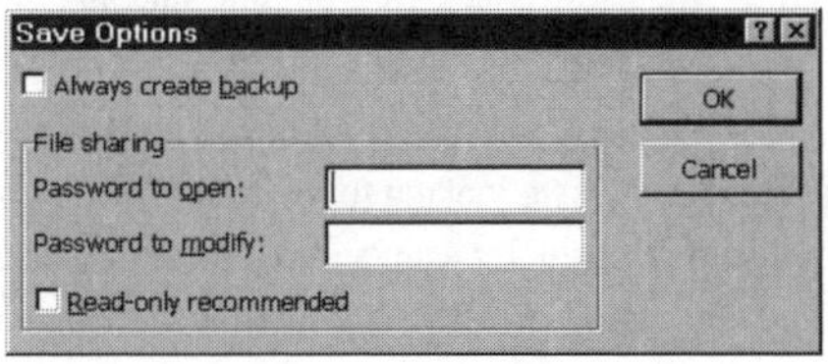

FIG. 2.10
The Save Options dialog box lets you add password protection to a file.

3. To assign a password to the file, type a password in the Password to Open text box. You can use up to 15 characters in a password, including text, numbers, spaces, and symbols. You also can use upper- and lowercase letters, but remember that passwords are case-sensitive, which means you must use the exact same upper- and lowercase letters to open the file.
4. Press Enter and the Confirm Password box appears, as shown in Figure 2.11.

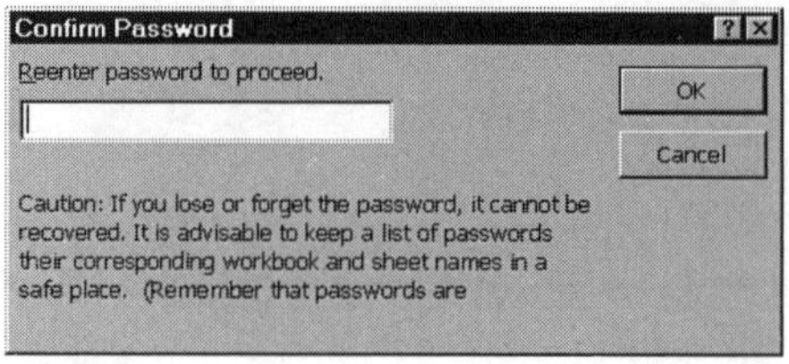

FIG. 2.11
Confirm your password by typing it in again.

5. Enter the password exactly the same as before, and choose OK.
6. Choose OK again to exit the dialog box and the password is assigned to the file.

The next time you want to open the file, Excel displays the Password dialog box. In the Password text box, enter the password you assigned, exactly as you previously typed it, then choose OK or press Enter. You cannot open the file without the password. If you lose or forget the password, you won't be able to open the file.

After you open a password-protected file, you can make changes and save the file as you normally would. You can share your password with others, but this means they, too, can access the file and make changes to the data.

Creating a Read-Only File

If you prefer another user to only view a workbook file and not save any changes they might make to the data, you can turn on the read-only option. You can use this option without password-protecting the file. Simply select the Read-Only Recommended check box in the Save Options dialog box (refer to Figure 2.10). When the read-only option is assigned, the person viewing the file can open the file (if it's not password-protected), and read its contents. When you attempt to open a read-only file a warning box appears. Click Yes to open the file as a read-only file. When the file opens, the title bar shows the file name with the words "Read-Only" in parentheses.

CAUTION

Keep in mind that the read-only option does not protect your data. It only recommends other users read the file contents and not make changes. Any changes they do make can be saved as a new file, but the original file and its data remain intact. If a user chooses No in the read-only warning box, the file still opens and changes can be made to the original data. If you're looking for better protection than this, use Explorer to assign read-only status. Locate the file in the Explorer window, right-click and select Properties from the shortcut menu. Select the Read-Only option and click OK. Now the file will only open in read-only status.

After opening a read-only file, you can make changes to the file contents. But if you try to save the changes, the warning box shown in Figure 2.12 appears.

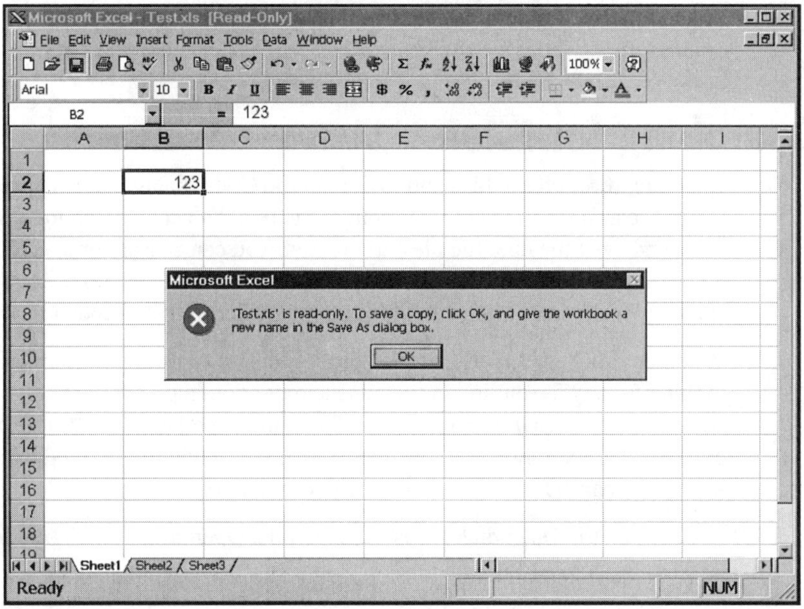

FIG. 2.12
A warning box is displayed when you attempt to save changes to a read-only file.

As noted in the warning box, the user can choose to save the file with their changes under another file name. Choose OK and the Save As dialog box appears and you can save the same file under a new name.

Assigning Modification Status

If you decide to let someone else view a sensitive workbook file, plus allow them to make changes, you can add a special password that only lets certain people (who know the appropriate password) modify the file. Follow these steps to assign this type of password:

1. Display the Save As dialog box by choosing File, Save As.
2. Choose the Options button to open the Save Options dialog box (refer to Figure 2.10).
3. In the Password To Modify text box, type a password.
4. Press Enter and the Confirm Password dialog box appears.
5. Type in the password exactly the same as before, and choose OK.
6. Choose OK again to exit the dialog box and the password is assigned to the file.

Now if someone attempts to open the file, the Password dialog box shown in Figure 2.13 appears. The user can type in the Password and press Enter to open the file. If a user doesn't know the password, he can still open the file by clicking the Read-Only button. This opens the file, but the user can't save any changes he makes to the data. He can only save his changes as a new file.

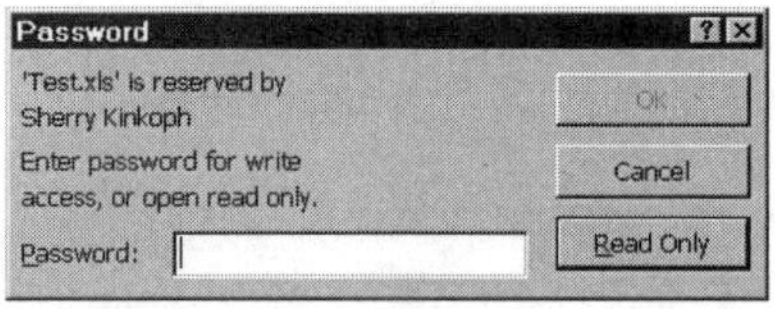

FIG. 2.13
This Password box lets users who have write access open the file.

Searching for Files

If looking through the files and folders in the Open dialog box isn't producing the file you want, try the search features at the bottom of the box. You can search for a file by name, author, file type, and even the date the file was created. You can search for specific text or numbers found within worksheets. You can even use the data you entered into the Properties dialog box (see "Saving Workbook Summary Information" earlier in this chapter) in your search.

When entering search criteria, use the * and ? symbols as wild cards. For example, if you're looking for any file ending in the .xls file extention, type ***.xls**. Or, if you're looking for all files with the text BUDGET as part of the file name, type **BUDGET***. Use the ? symbol to represent any one character. For example, type **SALES??** to find files named SALES01, SALES02, and so on. To search for a file by name or partial name:

1. Open the Open dialog box (choose File, Open or press Ctrl+O on the keyboard).
2. In the File Name text box, enter the name or partial name of the file you're looking for.
3. To search a specific drive and folder, select the drive from the Look In drop-down list and display the folder in the list box.
4. Click the Find Now button. Excel searches the selected folder. The results of the search appear in the list box and the bottom of the dialog box lists the number of matching files found (see Figure 2.14).

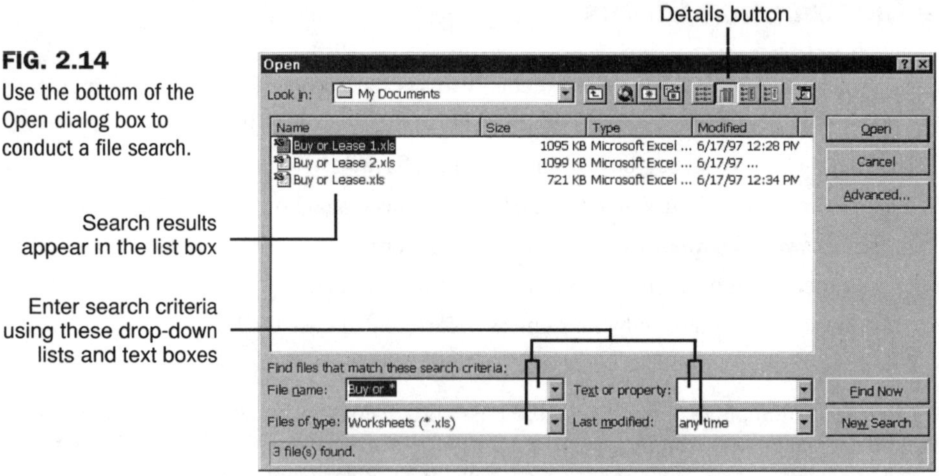

FIG. 2.14
Use the bottom of the Open dialog box to conduct a file search.

To see details about the files displayed in the list box, click the Details button in the Open toolbar. To preview the contents of any of the files found by Excel's search, select the file from the list box and click the Preview button in the Open toolbar. If Excel didn't display the results you were looking for, clear the search results from the list box by clicking the New Search button and try entering new search criteria.

Aside from searching for file names, you also can enter other search criteria:

- *Files of Type.* To search for a specific file type, select a type from this drop-down list. Leave the File Name text box blank to list all files of a certain type.
- *Text or Property.* If you've saved summary information for your files using the Properties dialog box (see "Saving Workbook Summary Information" earlier in this chapter), you can enter text from the summary information fields in the Text or Property box to search for. If you're looking for a particular word or phrase in a worksheet, you also can enter the data in the Text or Property box.
- *Last Modified.* Use this drop-down list to search for files based on the date you last changed the file. Select from specific time intervals: Yesterday, Today, Last Week, Last Month, This Month, or Any Time. Any Time is the default setting.

97

NOTE If you're using Excel as part of the Microsoft Office 97 suite, you can use the new Find Fast search feature. Find Fast creates an index of Office 97 files from which you can perform quick searches of an entire drive.

Using Advanced Search Options

A click on the Advanced button in the Open dialog box will reveal more search criteria options you can use. Figure 2.15 shows the Advanced Find dialog box. From this dialog box, you can define more search criteria, for example, you can choose to search for an exact match of upper- and lowercase letters or search for specific properties, such as the last printed file.

FIG. 2.15
The Advanced Find dialog box has more search criteria options you can apply.

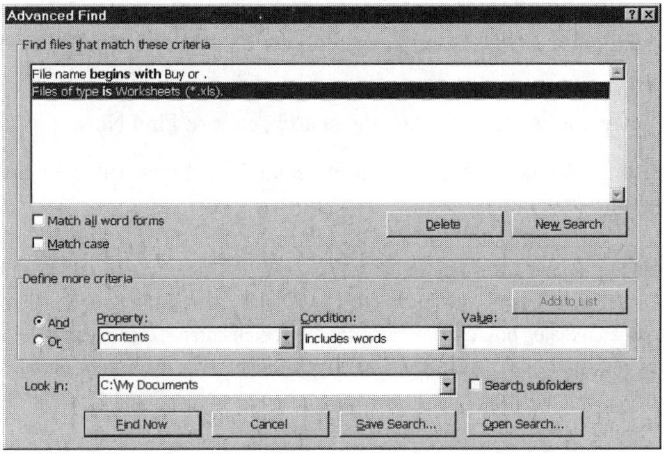

When entering search criteria, you can use partial words, wild cards (* and ?), and upper- and lowercase letters. Table 2.3 lists the rules that can help you with entering search criteria.

Table 2.3 Search Rules

To Search for	Type
A phrase	" " ("quarterly sales")
A single character	? (SALE?)
String of characters	* (budget*)
One word or another word	, (Inventory, Sales)
One word and another word	& (Inventory & Sales)
Files not containing	~ (Inventory~Sales)

To use the Advanced Find options, follow these steps:

1. In the Open dialog box, choose the Advanced button.
2. To select a folder or drive to search, use the Look In drop-down list, or enter the path of the folder you want to search. To search any subfolders included in the folder you select, select the Search Subfolders check box.
3. Type any search criteria you want to include in the Find Files That Match These Criteria list box.
4. To match upper- and lowercase letters exactly, make sure the Match Case check box is selected. To match word variations, select the Match All Word Forms check box.
5. Under the Define More Criteria options, use the Property drop-down list to select a property to search for. The list has 34 properties to choose from, ranging from Last author to Title to Number of paragraphs.
6. Use the Condition drop-down list to designate how you want to make the match. The conditions listed will vary based on your selection in the Property list.
7. Enter a value for the property and condition in the Value text box.
8. When you're ready to start the search, choose Find Now.

If the search results don't meet your expectations, choose the New Search button and try entering new criteria.

TIP If you plan to use the same search criteria again, save the criteria so you won't have to retype and reselect the search options. After conducting the search, choose the Save Search button. This opens the Save Search dialog box. Enter a name for the search criteria, then choose OK. You return to the Advanced Find dialog box. To use the search criteria right away, choose the Find Now button. To use the criteria at a later time, display the Open dialog box, click on the Commands and Settings button in the

Open dialog box toolbar, then select the Saved Searches command and highlight the name of the search from the list that appears.

Navigating Shortcuts

Excel offers many ways to save yourself time as you move around a worksheet:

- One way to save time when using a mouse is to utilize Excel's many shortcut menus. You can right-click to display a shortcut menu. Like the toolbars, shortcut menus display commonly-used commands that relate to the item you're currently working on. For example, if you right-click a selected cell, a menu appears displaying commands related the the item you clicked.
- Excel's Go To command can speedily locate the cell you want to view. For example, if you're currently viewing the bottom of a long worksheet and need to view the contents of cell D13, press F5 and type D13 in the Reference text box, then press Enter. Excel immediately takes you to cell D13 and selects the cell.

Another way to use Go To is to use the Edit, Go To command:

1. Choose Edit, Go To (or press Ctrl+G) to open the Go To dialog box, as shown in Figure 2.16.

FIG. 2.16
Use the Go To box to locate any cell in your worksheet.

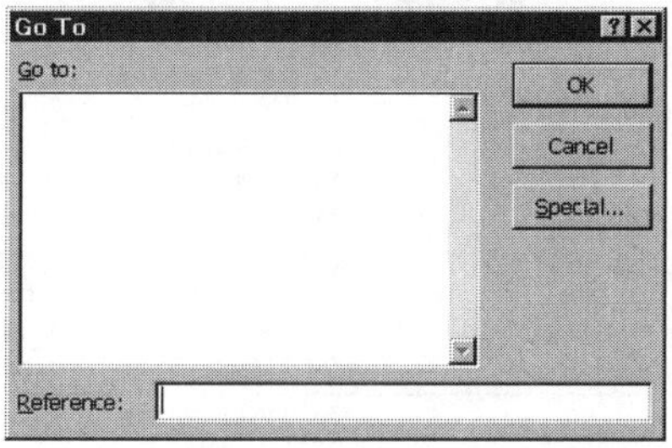

2. In the Reference text box, enter the cell address or range you want to go to.
3. Choose OK or press Enter. Excel moves to the cell you requested and highlights it.

The Go To dialog box keeps track of the last four locations you entered. To revisit a cell, open the Go To dialog box and double-click the cell reference listed in the Go To list box.

Split a Worksheet into Panes

To help speed up navigation between open workbooks, consider viewing multiple workbooks at the same time. You can set up your Excel window to view several portions of the same file. For example, if you're working with an exceptionally long worksheet, you might find yourself scrolling endlessly from one end to another, up and down, and side to side. Instead of scrolling around, you can divide the window into two or four parts. Each part of the window, called a *pane*, lets you view portions of your worksheet.

Perhaps you have a large database you're working with. Each record in the database has a column heading describing its field and each row is a record containing information for each field. If you scroll down a bit in the window, you lose sight of the column headings. To refer to them again, you must scroll back up to the top. But if you split the window into panes, the top portion can remain focused on the column headings, and you can scroll down the database in the second pane without losing track of which column contains which data.

To divide a workbook window into panes, follow these steps:

1. Display the window you want to split into panes.
2. Select a cell directly below and to the right of where you want to split the window. Depending on which cell you select, the window can be divided horizontally, vertically, or both. To split the window horizontally, place the active cell in column A below where you want the split to occur. To split the window vertically, place the active cell in the first row in the column to the right of where you want the split to occur.
3. Choose Window, Split. The worksheet is split into two (see Figure 2.17).

FIG. 2.17
This figure shows an example of a split worksheet.

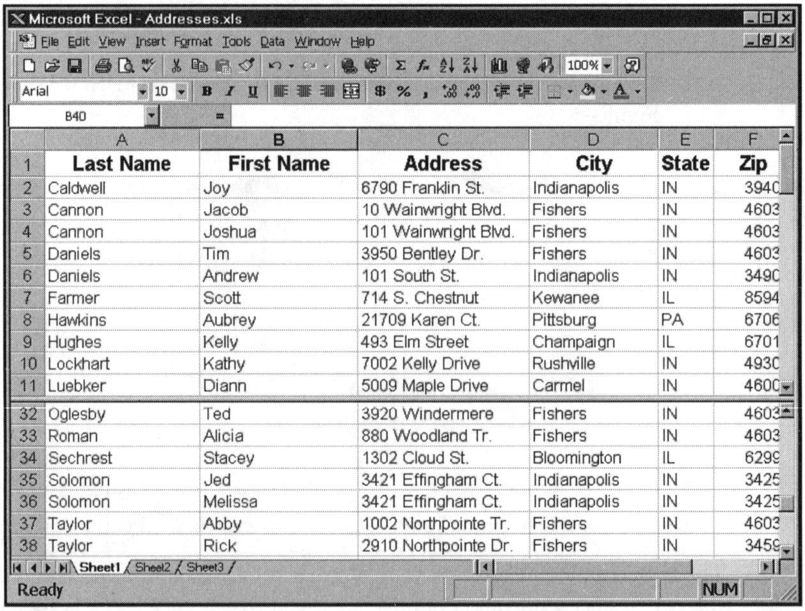

Another way to split a window into panes is to use the split boxes on the scroll bars, as pointed out in Figure 2.18. The boxes are very tiny, and rather hard to see. To use a split box, hover your mouse pointer over the box, hold down the mouse button and drag the split box across the screen. A split bar (which looks like a gray divider line) moves with the mouse. Release the mouse button where you want the split to occur. The window is divided into panes. Figure 2.19 shows a vertical split.

FIG. 2.18
Use the split boxes to create panes using the mouse.

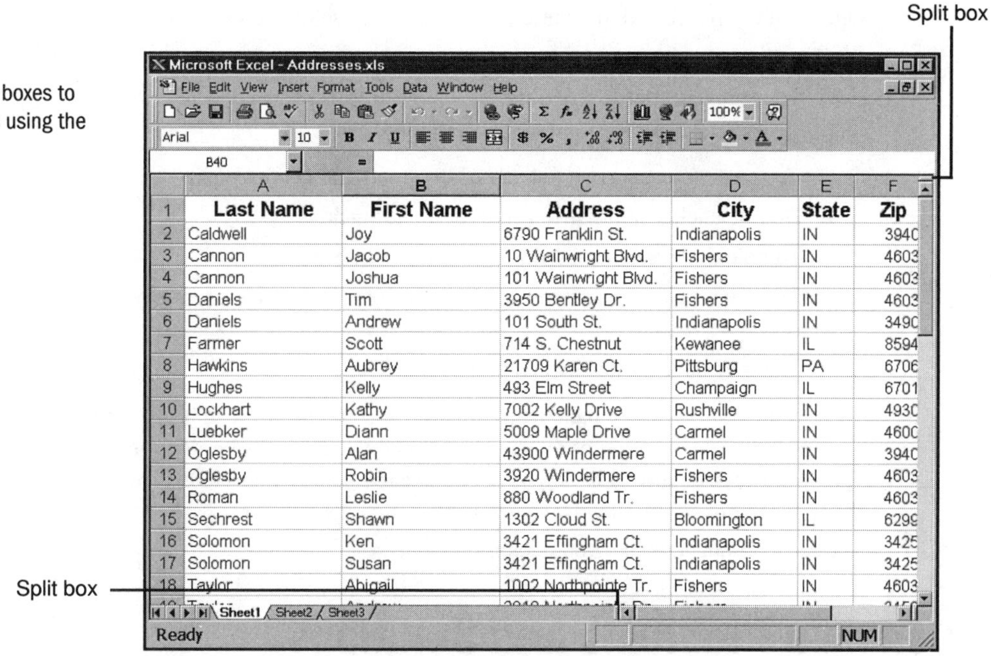

FIG. 2.19
In this figure you see an example of a vertical split.

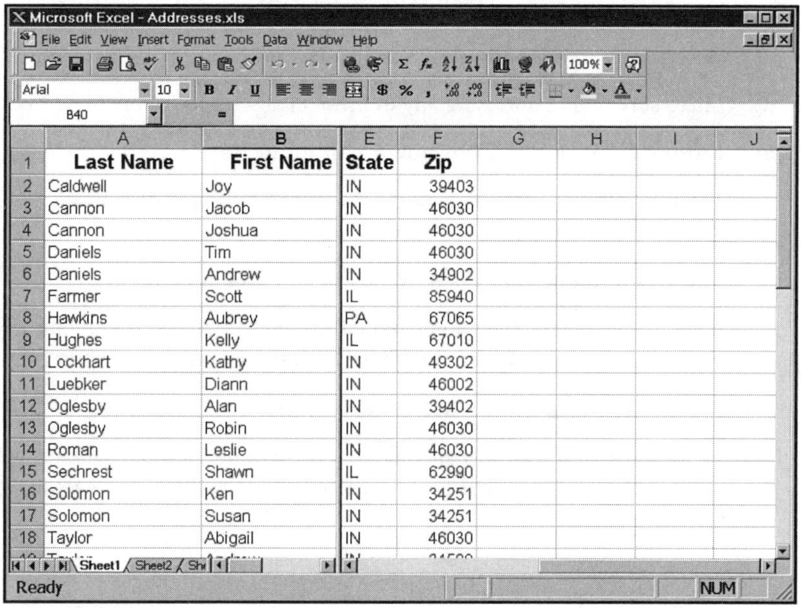

Part I
Ch 2

Once you've split the window into panes, you can use the scroll bars to scroll your view in each pane.

- To remove a split at any time, choose Window, Remove Split.
- To resize a pane, just drag the split bar on-screen.
- To create four panes, use both a horizontal and vertical split.
- Double-click a split bar to remove a split quickly.
- To quickly create a split, double-click a split box.
- To move around the panes quickly, press F6. This moves you clockwise from pane to pane.
- To move counter-clockwise, press Shift+F6

To prevent your view of a pane from moving, you can freeze it so it stays put on-screen. When you freeze panes, the split bar becomes a thin line across the screen. To freeze panes, choose Window, Freeze Panes. The top or left pane can no longer scroll. It's frozen in place. To remove the freeze, choose Window Unfreeze Panes.

▶ **See** "Viewing Multiple Workbooks" **p. 25**

Common Problems and Solutions

File management can become a headache when things go wrong. Listed below are a few common problems users typically face and the solutions that can be applied.

When I try to save my file, Excel tells me I'm not using a valid file name.

Make sure you're not using any of these characters to name files: ? \ < > | / * ' ; ;.

I know I saved a file, but now I can't find it.

Try conducting a search using the Advanced button in the Open dialog box. Follow the steps in the section "Hunting Down Excel Files" in this chapter.

The Open dialog box does not show my files listed.

If you made any modifications to the file type, you may not immediately see the file listed until you select the format from the Files of Type drop-down list in the Open dialog box.

I forgot the password I assigned to a file.

Sadly, there's no way to reopen the file without the original password. Always remember to write down the passwords you've created and keep them in a safe place.

From Here...

In this chapter, you learned the fundamentals for using Excel and building worksheets fast. The next two chapters will show you how to manage workbook files and provide more details about data entry.

- Chapter 3, "Entering and Editing Data," explains the various ways of entering data types into your worksheets and how to edit your worksheet data.
- Chapter 4, "Formatting Your Worksheets," shows you how to turn ordinary worksheet data into a professional-looking presentation of information using formatting commands that change fonts, sizes, alignment, and more.

CHAPTER 3

Entering and Editing Data

by Sherry Kinkoph

Before you can start manipulating data and performing calculations in your Excel workbook, you must first enter any data you plan to use. Although entering data is a fairly straightforward task (you select a cell and start typing), there are a few ground rules to be aware of, such as knowing the differences between text, values, and formulas. This chapter covers the unique ways in which each data type is entered. You'll also learn how to move data around in a worksheet, group cells into ranges, and use special Excel techniques, such as AutoFill, for speedier data entry.

Also covered in this chapter are the basics for building and using Excel formulas. Formulas are where the real action is in any spreadsheet program, and Excel 97 makes constructing formulas easier than ever. Formulas range from simple calculations to complex statistical or scientific problems, all of which Excel handles with ease. Formulas are the key to analyzing and manipulating data; without them you might as well be using a word processing program. ■

Entering information

Learn the differences between text entries, values, and formulas and learn how to enter these data types into your Excel worksheets.

Working with ranges

Learn how to work with ranges in a worksheet and assign range names to use in formulas.

Speeding up data entry

Find out all the shortcuts for making data entry easy. Use Excel's AutoFill feature to automatically create fill series in your worksheets, and let AutoComplete help you enter repetitive data.

Working with formulas

Learn how to construct a formula using operators, cell references, and range names. Create array formulas and 3-D references. Learn the difference between absolute and relative cell references.

Rearranging worksheet data

Familiarize yourself with the various methods used to move data around in a worksheet, to edit entries, and to add columns and rows.

Entering Text and Values

A worksheet can contain three basic types of entries: *text*, *values*, and *formulas*. (There are also *functions*, which are simply built-in formulas—you'll learn more about those in Chapter 6, "Using Excel Functions.") You can type up to 255 characters in a cell, text or numbers. Depending on the purpose of the data, the characters you type will fall into one of these categories:

- *Text.* Excel refers to text data as *text* (sometime known as labels); Excel cannot perform calculations on entries that are strictly text. For example, if you type the word *February* into a cell, you won't be able to perform a mathematical function or calculation with it—it's just a word.
- *Values.* Excel refers to numerical data as a *value*; Excel can calculate value entries. Values include numbers, dates, and times. For example, if you type the number 1,024, you can do something with it, such as multiply or add.
- *Formulas.* The third type of data is a *formula*, which is simply an entry that tells Excel to perform calculations on the values in a cell or group of cells. You'll learn more about entering formulas later in the chapter.

  ▶ **See** "Working with Formulas," **p. 103**

Say you've created a budget worksheet. In this type of worksheet, you might include a worksheet title, column labels for each month, and row labels for each expense category. All of these entries would be text. Within the columns for each month, you might enter the expenses for that category. These entries would be numbers (values). For each month, you might want to calculate the total expenses. This entry would be a formula. Figure 3.1 shows a sample budget worksheet under construction.

As shown in Figure 3.1, Excel displays different data types in different positions in your worksheet cells. A text entry always lines up to the left side of the cell it's in. However, you can change the alignment. If the text entry is too long, it will spill over to the cells next to it, unless those cells contain data. If those cells contain data, the displayed entry will be truncated; the actual entry is still intact, you just can't see it in its entirety. You need to widen the column to see the whole entry. One way to do so is to choose Format, Column, AutoFit Selection.

▶ **See** "Changing Cell Appearance," **p. 158**

Numbers always line up to the right of the cell. By default, numbers appear in the General number format (no specific number format). You can change how the numbers appear: change the alignment, use a number format (such as currency), make entries bold, and more. If you enter a number and see something strange, such as ####, it means the number is too big to fit in the cell. To fix this problem, you can change the number format or widen the column. Choose Format, Column, AutoFit Selection.

▶ **See** "Mastering Number Formats," **p. 148**

FIG. 3.1
An Excel worksheet can contain labels, values, and formulas.

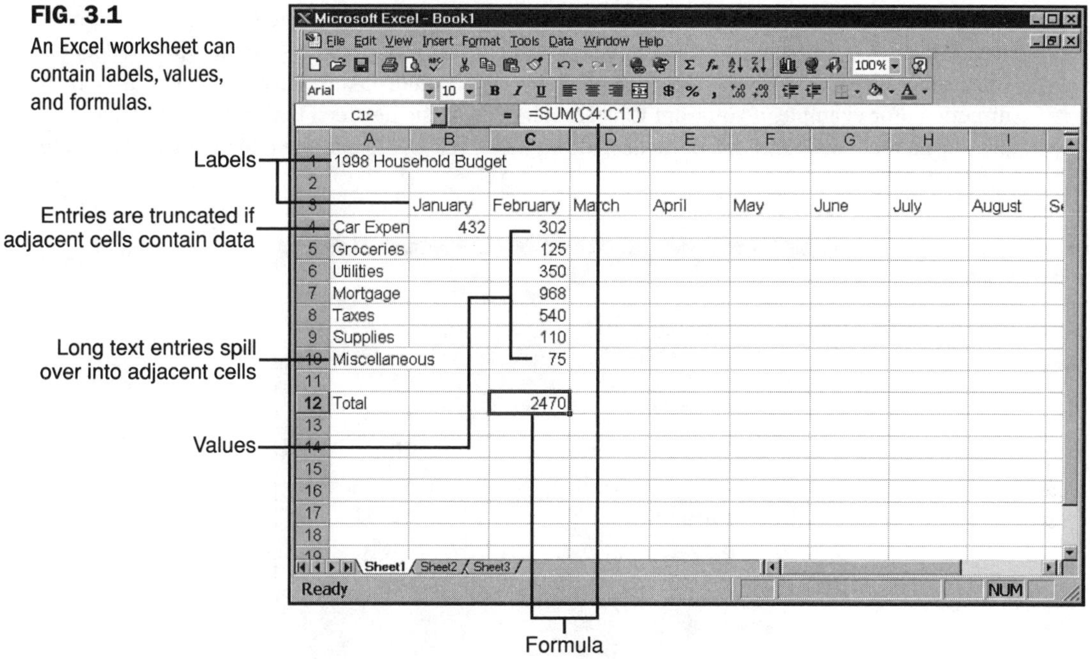

To start entering data into a worksheet, select a cell and begin typing. The data you type appears in the cell, as well as in the Formula Bar. Depending on the method you prefer to use, you can insert entries directly into cells, you can use the Formula Bar, or you can use a combination of the two. To enter data into the Formula Bar, click inside the text box and start typing. Figure 3.2 identifies each of the Formula Bar buttons as they appear to the left of the text box.

FIG. 3.2
You can enter data directly into the Formula Bar.

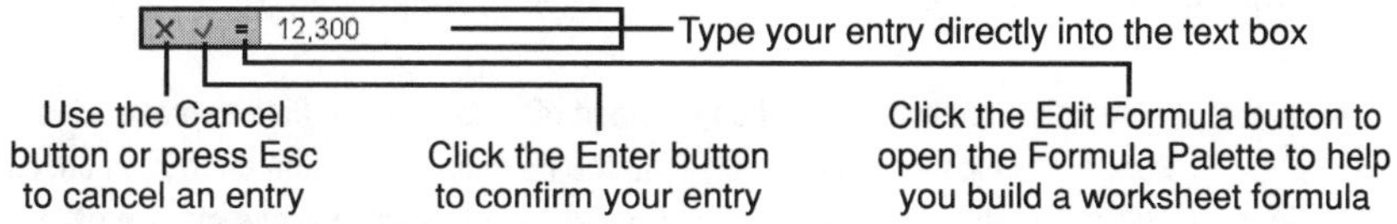

After typing an entry, press Enter on the keyboard, or click the Enter button in the Formula Bar (the check mark icon), or click in the cell you want to type in next. Use any of the navigation keys to move to the next cell you want to enter data in. For example, press Tab to move horizontally across the worksheet from cell to cell.

For most users, pressing Enter after creating an entry is a habit. By default, when you press Enter, Excel moves the cursor to the next cell directly below the active cell. This is fine if that's the next cell you want to use, but if it's not, you might find it a little frustrating when you want to continue entering data without having to figure out which cell you're in. You can easily change the direction the Enter key takes by changing the settings in the Options dialog box (see Figure 3.3). Choose Tools, Options, and click the Edit tab. Make sure the Move Selection After Enter check box is selected; then click the Direction drop-down arrow and choose a new direction. For example, if you want Excel to take you to the next cell to the right when you press Enter, choose Right from the drop-down list. Click OK to exit the dialog box and activate the new settings.

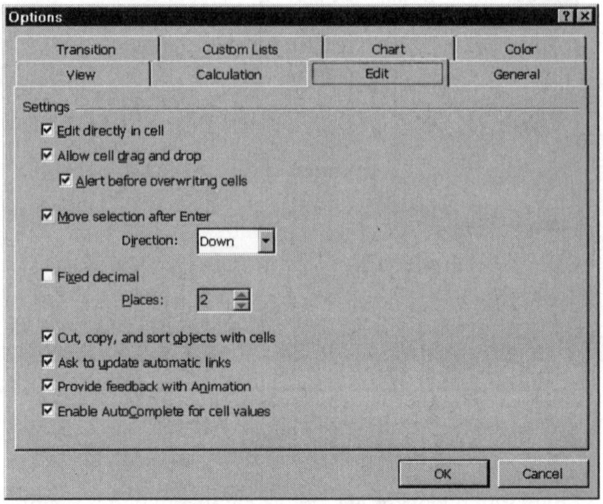

FIG. 3.3
Use the Options dialog box to change the Enter key's direction.

To make any edits to an entry, double-click inside the cell, and move the cursor to the place you want to edit. You also can click inside the text box in the Formula Bar and make edits from there. You can edit your worksheet entries just like you edit data in many other programs. You can select data and type over it to add new data, insert data in the midst of existing data, and delete data. Use the Backspace and Delete keys to remove characters and make corrections.

NOTE If the Edit Directly in Cell option is turned off, you won't be able to make edits directly in a worksheet cell; you can edit only from the Formula Bar. To turn the option on, choose Tools, Options, and click the Edit tab. Check the Edit Directly in Cell check box and choose OK to exit the dialog box. You can now double-click inside a cell and make changes.

To undo any mistakes, click the Undo button immediately after performing the action you want to undo, or choose Edit, Undo. If you change your mind, you can redo the action by clicking the Redo button or selecting Edit, Redo.

Unlike previous versions of Excel, you can choose to undo or redo multiple actions. Next to the Undo and Redo buttons on the toolbar are drop-down arrows you can click to display a list of your recent actions. Your most recent action appears at the top of the list. Select an action from the list by clicking it, and Excel undoes or redoes that action, as well as all the actions listed above it. For example, if you select the third action from the top of the list, Excel will also undo the first and second actions.

TIP Another way to delete cell contents is to select the cell and choose Edit, Clear. From the submenu that appears, select the command that describes what you want removed from the cell. Choose All to clear everything in the cell, choose Formats to clear all formatting applied to the cell, choose Contents to remove the data but leave the formatting, or choose Comments to clear any cell comments attached to the cell.

When entering numbers (values), you need to know the difference between *valid numbers* and *invalid numbers*:

- Valid numbers include the numeric characters 0-9 and any of these special characters: . + – ( ) , $ %
- Invalid numbers are any characters not mentioned as valid numbers. (So the letter Z, for example, would not be considered a valid number because it's a letter.)

Special characters are considered valid numbers because they are used to create mathematical problems, equations, formulas, and so on. When you enter numeric values, you can include commas, decimal points, dollar signs, percentage signs, and parentheses.

To enter a fraction, type the integer, a space, then the fraction, such as 2¾. If you leave out the space, Excel assumes the value is a text entry. If you want to enter only the fractional part, such as ¾, you must type a zero, a space, and then the fraction (0¾); otherwise, Excel assumes the value is a date (4-Mar).

NOTE What if you want your numbers to be treated like text? Say you want to use numbers for a ZIP code instead of a value. To do this, precede your entry with a single quotation mark (') as in '90255. The single quotation mark is an alignment prefix that tells Excel to treat the following characters as text and left-align them in the cell. To quickly format values as text, select the cell or range, choose Format, Cells, and then choose Text from the Category list.

Other types of values you can include in a worksheet are dates and times. Excel keeps track of dates by assigning each date a serial number, starting with the first day in the century. No matter how the date appears in the cell, Excel thinks of the date as this serial number. With this tracking method, you can use a date in a calculation.

Excel keeps track of times by storing them as a fractional part of 24 hours (military time). For example, 8:20 p.m. is 20:20. Again, this tracking method enables you to create calculations with times.

To enter the date, use one of the following formats:

4/4/98

4-Apr-98

4-Apr (assumes current year)

Apr-4 (assumes current year)

Apr-98

To enter a time, type the time using one of these formats:

9:45 PM

9:45:55 PM

21:45

21:45:55

TIP To enter the current date in a cell, press Ctrl+;. To enter the current time, press Ctrl+Shift+:.

▶ **See** "Working with Formulas," **p. 103**

▶ **See** "Excel Shortcuts," **p. 891**

Using Ranges

One way you can organize and work with Excel data is to use ranges. A ***range*** is a rectangular group of related cells (or even a single cell) that you can connect in a column, a row, a combination of columns and rows, or even an entire worksheet.

You can use ranges for a variety of worksheet tasks. You can select a range and use it to format a group of cells with one simple step. You can also use a range to print only a selected group of cells. Ranges are particularly handy when you use them with formulas. Instead of referring to each cell reference that you want to include in a formula, you can specify a range of cells. Cell ranges also can be given distinct names to help you identify their contents.

To select a range with the mouse, follow these steps:

1. Click the first cell in the range.
2. Hold down the mouse button and drag across the cells you want to include.
3. The range appears highlighted on-screen (see Figure 3.4). When you have selected the range you want, release the mouse button. Now you're ready to name the range.

To use the keyboard to select a range, follow these steps:

1. Move to the first cell of the range you want to create.
2. Hold down the Shift key and use any of the arrow or movement keys to highlight the range.

To deselect a range you've selected, click outside the selected range or press any arrow key.

TIP To select multiple ranges in a worksheet, hold down the Ctrl key and continue selecting ranges. If you're using the keyboard, press Shift+F8, press Shift, and then select another range. To keep adding more ranges, press Shift+F8 between selections.

Excel indicates a range with a range reference (name), which refers to its specific anchor points: the upper-left corner and the lower-right corner. A range with more than one cell uses a colon to separate the anchor points. For example, range A1:B3 would include cells A1, A2, A3, B1, B2, and B3.

FIG. 3.4
You can group worksheet cells into ranges.

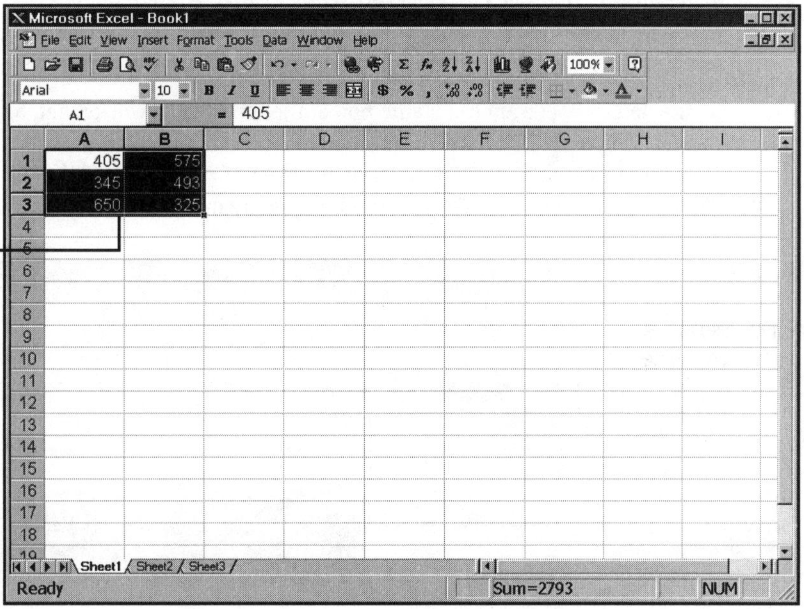

NOTE When you select a range of cells containing data, Excel's AutoCalculate feature kicks in and displays a summary of the selected ranges in the status bar. Notice in Figure 3.4, the status bar shows the sum of cells in range A1:B3. You also can display the average or total count of a selected range by right-clicking the status bar and selecting Average or Count from the shortcut menu that appears.

When selecting ranges, you can use some shortcuts. Table 3.1 describes the mouse and keyboard shortcuts for selecting ranges.

Table 3.1 Range Shortcuts

To Select	Mouse Shortcut	Keyboard Shortcut
A column	Click the column letter	Press Ctrl+Spacebar
A row	Click the row number	Press Shift+Spacebar
The entire worksheet	Click the Select All button (the blank spot above the row numbers and to the left of the column letters)	Press Ctrl+Shift+Spacebar

Naming Ranges

Excel's default range names don't readily identify a range's contents. To clarify your data, you can give a specific range name to a single cell or a large group of cells. It's much easier to refer to your data by a name than with a meaningless cell address. For example, a range named *Sales_Totals* is a lot easier to decipher than a range named *B2:F1;* the formula =INCOME–EXPENSE is easier to understand than =B8:B24–C8:C24. Giving cells recognizable names will make your formulas more logical and easier to manage.

Range names appear in the Name box at the top of your worksheet, to the left of the Formula Bar (see Figure 3.5). When you have at least one defined range name in a worksheet, you can click the Name box drop-down list to see a list of ranges and make your selection from the list. You can also use the Go To command to quickly move to and select a named range.

FIG. 3.5
The Name box drop-down list displays assigned range names.

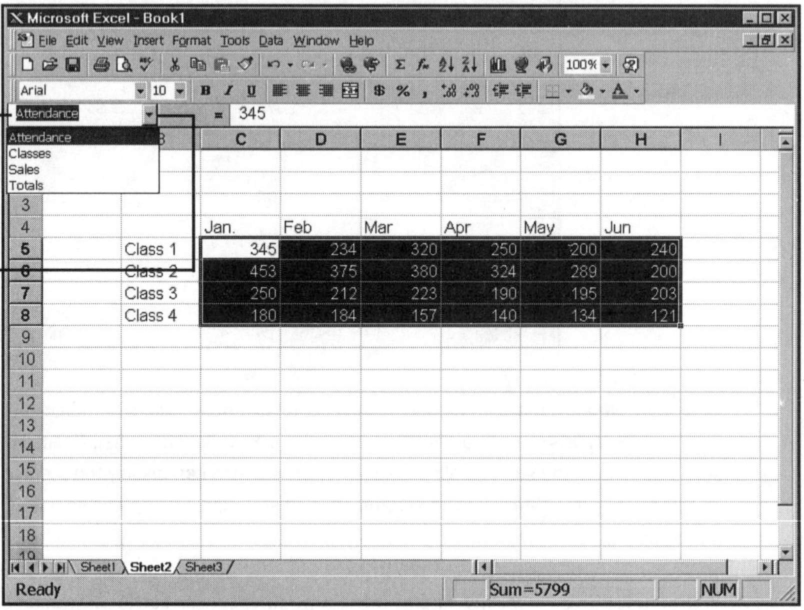

There are a few rules to follow when it comes to naming ranges:

- Range names must start with a letter or an underscore. After that, you can use any character except the hyphen or the space.
- You can use upper- or lowercase letters with range names.
- Don't use spaces—use the underscore instead (_) or a period (.). Spaces aren't allowed in range names.

- You can type up to 255 characters, but it's best to keep range names short. This makes them easier to see when you insert them into formulas.
- Try to avoid making range names look like cell addresses. The whole purpose of being able to name a range is to get away from the confusion of cell addresses.

To further illustrate, here's a comparison of invalid and valid range names:

Invalid Names	**Valid Names**
Sales Totals	Sales_Totals
Year-End Totals	Year_End_Totals
1998	YR1998

To name a range, use these steps:

1. Select the cell or range you want to name and choose Insert, Name, Define. The Define Name dialog box appears (see Figure 3.6).
2. Type the range name you want to use in the Names in Workbook text box. Notice Excel proposes a range name for you based on the text name found in the row or column of the selected range, and replaces any spaces with underscores. If you prefer another name, type over the proposed name.

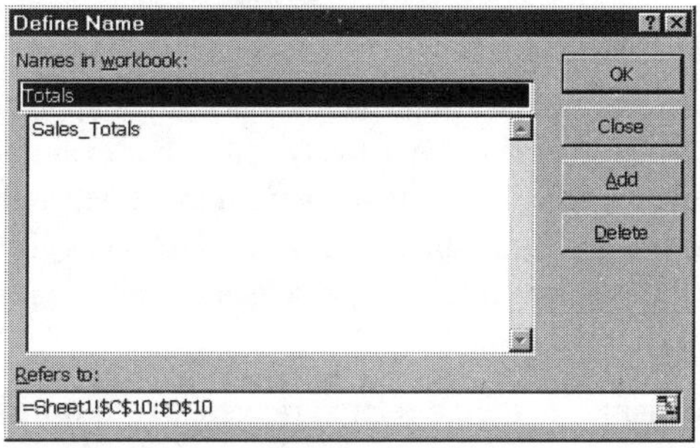

FIG. 3.6
Use the Define Name dialog box to create a range name.

3. The Refers To box shows the cell reference(s) for the range. If the references are incorrect, click the Collapse Dialog button at the far right end of the Refers To box (this reduces the dialog box) and select the correct cells for the range. To reopen the full dialog box, click the button again. (If necessary, you can drag the dialog box out of the way by its title bar to select cells in the worksheet.)
4. Choose OK to exit the box. You have named the range, and the reference name appears in the Name box to the left of the Formula Bar, as shown in Figure 3.7.

Another way to assign a range name is to type the name directly into the Name box. Select the cells you want included in the range; then, click inside the box and type a name. Press Enter when finished. The name is added to the list as well as assigned to the selected cells.

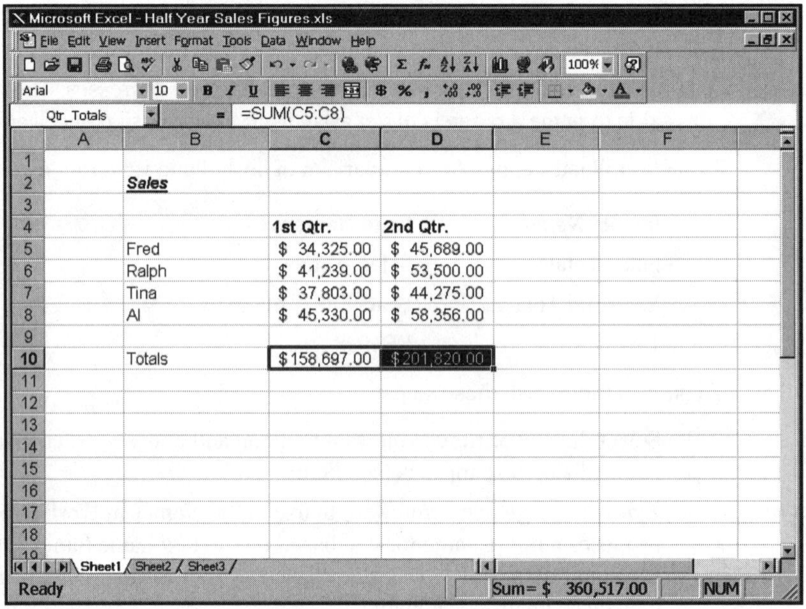

FIG. 3.7
The range name now appears in the Name box.

Working with Multilevel Ranges

The range names you create using the Define Name dialog box apply to all the sheets in the current workbook, not just the sheet you're actively using. For example, perhaps you've created a range on Sheet1 called Sales_Totals. If you switch to Sheet2 and display the Name drop-down list, the range name Sales_Totals appears. If you select Sales_Totals from the list, Sheet1 becomes active again with the Sales_Totals range selected. For this reason, you cannot use the same range name in another worksheet.

You can create sheet-level names to define related ranges across worksheets. For example, perhaps you have a worksheet for each quarter's sales, and all four worksheets need a range named Sales_Totals. When naming such ranges, you must precede the range name with the name of the sheet followed by an exclamation mark, for example, *Sheet2!Sales_Totals*. If you want to refer to a sheet-level range name from another sheet, be sure to include the entire sheet name.

Editing Range Names

After you've created a range name, you can edit it at any time, or delete it completely. Open the Define Name dialog box (select Insert, Name, Define) and select the range name you want to change. Type a new range name in the Names in Workbook text box. Use the Refers To box to change cell references. To delete a name, just choose the Delete button.

NOTE If you create a range name after using the cell references in a formula, you will need to update the formula with the new range name. To apply a range name to an existing formula, choose Insert, Name, Apply. In the Apply Names dialog box, select the range name you want. If you want to replace absolute and relative references, select the Ignore Relative/Absolute check box. Click OK to exit the dialog box and apply the range name.

Speeding Up Data Entry

To make it as quick as possible to create a worksheet, Excel provides some automated features for entering data. For example, if you find yourself entering repetitive data or a data series, such as days of the month or week, you can use Excel's fill features to automatically finish entering the information for you. Another example is Excel's AutoCorrect feature, which automatically corrects your typing mistakes as you type.

Using AutoCorrect

To keep your entries accurate, Excel's AutoCorrect feature is turned on by default. AutoCorrect recognizes commonly misspelled words and automatically corrects them as you type. For example, if you type "adn," AutoCorrect automatically changes the spelling to "and" as soon as you press the spacebar or the Enter key. If there are certain words you constantly type incorrectly, you can add them to the AutoCorrect list.

You also can use AutoCorrect to expand abbreviations you repeatedly type. Instead of typing the complete word each time, simply type the abbreviation and AutoCorrect expands the entry for you. To add your own typographical or abbreviation entries to AutoCorrect, follow these steps:

1. Choose Tools, AutoCorrect. The AutoCorrect dialog box appears (see Figure 3.8).

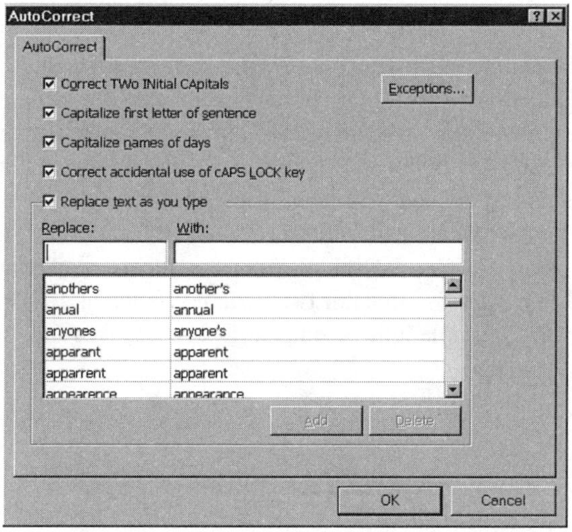

FIG. 3.8
The two-column list of entries shows the incorrect text on the left and the correct spelling on the right.

2. Type the entry you want to add in the Replace text box.
3. In the With text box, type the correct spelling or the unabbreviated text.
4. Choose the Add button and the entry is added to AutoCorrect's list.
5. Click OK to exit the dialog box.

Notice at the top of the AutoCorrect dialog box there are additional options you can turn on or off:

- *Correct Two Initial Capitals.* If you have a tendency to hold down the Shift key while capitalizing a word, sometimes you end up capitalizing more than the first letter. With this option on, AutoCorrect makes sure only the first letter is capitalized.
- *Capitalize First Letter of Sentence.* To make sure every sentence starts with a capital letter, turn this option on.
- *Capitalize Names of Days.* If you prefer the days of the week entries to be capitalized, select this option.
- *Correct Accidental Use of Caps Lock Key.* If you've accidentally left the Caps Lock key on, this option corrects your entries.
- *Replace Text As You Type.* To turn off the AutoCorrect feature, make sure this check box is not selected.

To delete an entry from the AutoCorrect list, open the AutoCorrect dialog box, scroll through the list of entries and select the word or phrase you want to delete, and then choose the Delete button.

TIP You can easily add AutoCorrect entries when you spell check your worksheet. Select the AutoCorrect button from the Spelling dialog box and add a new entry.

▶ **See** "Spell Check Your Worksheet," **p. 183**

Using AutoFill

One of the handiest shortcuts for data entry is the *AutoFill* feature. AutoFill lets you quickly enter a series of data into your worksheet cells or duplicate the same data as many times as necessary. A data series is any series of related information, such as days of the week, number sequences, months, and so on. For example, you can use the AutoFill feature to fill a series of months (such as January, February, March), a series of dates (such as Monday, Tuesday, Wednesday), or a series of formulas. You simply enter the first value, and then let Excel fill in the rest. If you're using a series of dates, all you have to type is one date to start the series. If you're using numbers, you need to enter two variables (such as 1, 2 or 5, 10 and so on) to start the fill series in order to establish the sequence. Table 3.2 gives some examples of fill series and their results.

Table 3.2 Fill Series Examples

If You Type...	AutoFill Inserts the Sequence...
Qtr 1	Qtr 2, Qtr 3, Qtr 4
Sales 1	Sales 2, Sales 3, Sales 4
Mon	Tue, Wed, Thur
Jan	Feb, Mar, Apr
1, 2	3, 4, 5, 6
5, 10	15, 20, 25, 30
1997	1998, 1999, 2000

The easiest method of creating a data series is to use the fill handle of the cell border. If you need to create a different kind of series or assign additional series options, use the Fill command on the Edit menu. These two methods are explained in the following sections.

Using the Fill Handle When you select a cell or range of cells, the lower-right corner of the selected cell(s) outline shows a tiny square known as the *fill handle* (see Figure 3.9). Use the handle to drag a fill series across adjacent cells. You can create the following types of series using the fill handle:

- If you simply want to copy the same entry into other cells, type the entry once, select the cell, and then drag the fill handle with the mouse to fill adjacent cells with the same data.
- If you want to enter a month (Jan., Feb., Mar.) or week day (Mon., Tue., Wed.) series, type the first entry, and then drag the fill handle to fill adjacent cells with the complete series. Excel's AutoFill feature completes the series in the correct order.
- If you want to use a number series, you must remember to type the first two entries in order to tell Excel how to present the series. For example, if you type 5 and 10 into the first two cells, select the cells, and drag the fill handle to complete the series, Excel enters 15, 20, and so on in the adjacent cells.

To fill cells using the fill handle and the mouse, follow these steps:

1. Type the first entry in the first cell. (If you want to use a number series, remember to enter the first two values in adjacent cells.) Then select the cell or cells that contain the entry.
2. Position the mouse pointer over the fill handle in the lower-right corner of the cell (see Figure 3.9). The pointer should look like a small crosshair.
3. Drag across the range you want to fill. An outline appears as you drag, and a ScreenTip displays the value of the cell the pointer is currently over.
4. Release the mouse button, and Excel fills in the series (see Figure 3.10).

FIG. 3.9
To start a fill, enter the first item in the active cell.

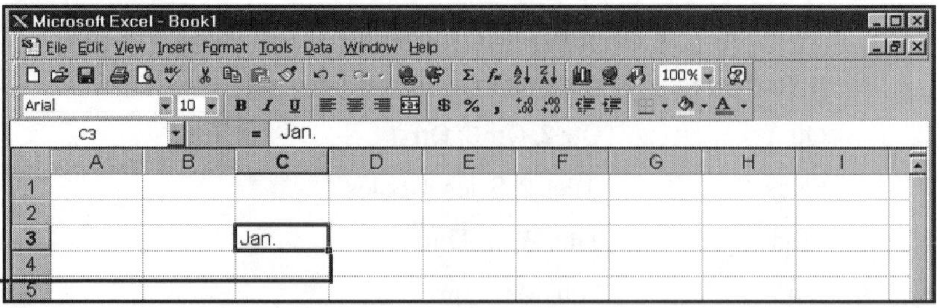

FIG. 3.10
Drag the fill handle over the cells you want to fill, and AutoFill automatically fills in the data.

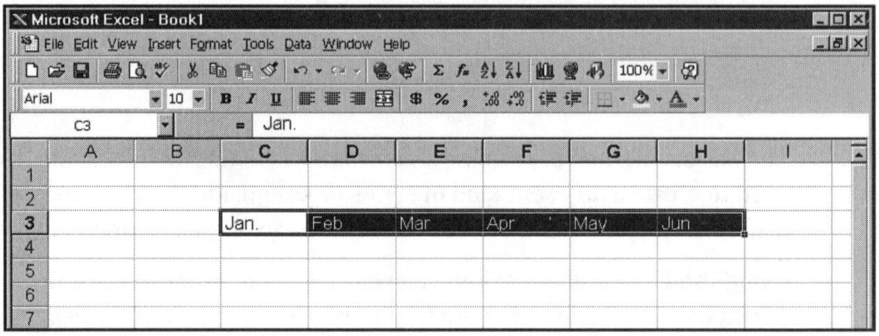

Using the Fill Command Another way to create a fill series is with the Fill command. If you want to use the same data in neighboring cells (if you're copying a category heading, for example), select the cell containing the entry, and then drag over the cells you want to fill. You can drag up, down, left, or right. Next, choose Edit, Fill and choose the direction you want to go (up, down, left, or right). Excel fills the cells with a copy of the original data.

You can specify a specific start and stop value for a data series using the Series dialog box. To use this dialog box to create a data fill, follow these steps:

1. Select the first cell of the fill series and enter the starting data.
2. Select the range of cells you want to fill.
3. Choose Edit, Fill, Series to open the Series dialog box (see Figure 3.11).

FIG. 3.11
You can specify a specific start and stop value with the Series dialog box.

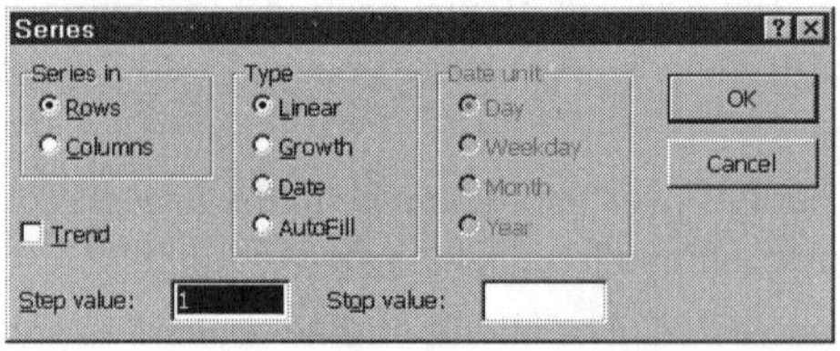

4. From the Series In options, select how you want the series filled: by Rows or Columns.
5. From the Type options, select the type of series you want to create:

   Linear Adds the Step Value you define in step 6 to the series start value you established in step 1.

   Growth Multiplies the Step Value you define in step 6 to the series start value you established in step 1.

   Date Enables the Date Unit options for establishing a series of dates.

   AutoFill Excel creates automatic data series for you based on your start entry in step 1 (such as Qtr 1, Qtr 2, Qtr 3 or Part 1, Part 2, Part 3, and so on). Skip to step 8 to finish using the Series dialog box.
6. If you chose the Linear, Growth, or Date series type, use the Step Value box to enter the amount by which the series changes from cell to cell. In the Stop Value box, enter the last value you want filled in the series (use this option only if you think you've highlighted too many cells for the series in step 1).
7. If you chose the Date series type, select a date unit to apply under the Date Unit options.
8. Click OK to exit the dialog box. Excel fills in the data series and type you specified.

Using AutoComplete

Many spreadsheet users spend a lot of time entering repetitive data, such as entering the same text labels over and over again. You can use Excel's AutoComplete feature to avoid such tedious procedures. To use the AutoComplete feature, follow these steps:

1. Type the labels in the first cells of the column.
2. When you're ready to enter a duplicate label in another cell, right-click the empty cell.
3. Choose Pick from the shortcut menu that appears. A list of previously typed words appears beneath your cell (see Figure 3.12).
4. Choose the word you want from the list, and Excel automatically inserts it in the cell.

You might notice the AutoComplete feature kicking in while you enter text. If you repeat the first few letters of a previous entry, AutoComplete guesses that you're typing repeat information and finishes your word for you. If it's not the correct word, however, just keep typing and ignore AutoComplete.

Adding Comments

You can add comment notes to any cell in your worksheet to help you identify data or to explain the contents. Any comments you add do not affect the data nor do they appear when you print them. Anytime you pass the pointer over a cell with comments, a comment box pops up. Cells containing comment notes are identified by tiny red triangles that appear in the upper-right corner of the cell, as shown in Figure 3.13.

FIG. 3.12
Use AutoComplete to help with repetitious entries.

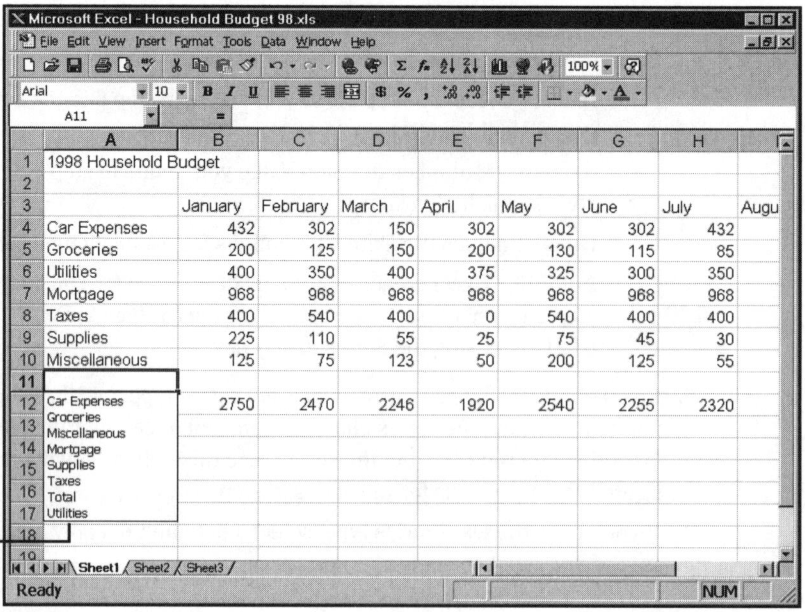

Previously typed words appear in a list

FIG. 3.13
To see a cell comment, pass the pointer over the cell.

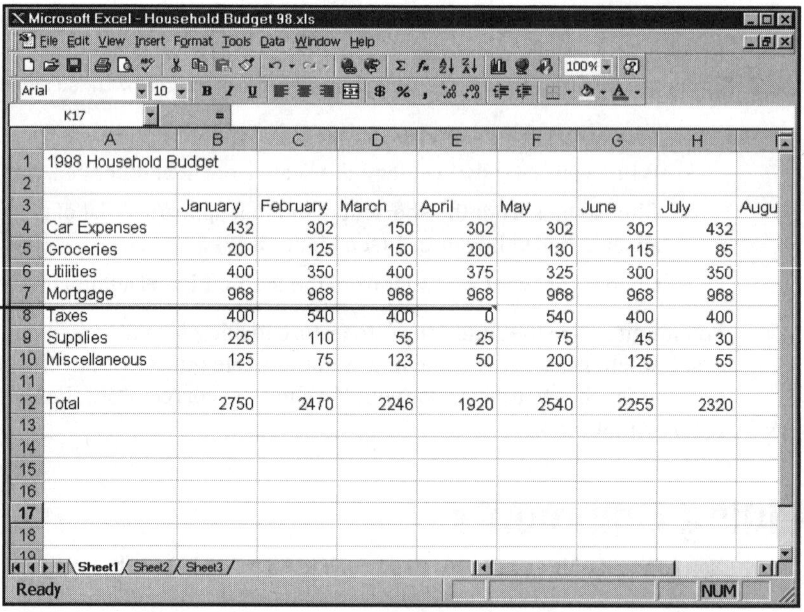

Comment symbol

To add a comment note to your own worksheet, first select the cell you want to add a comment to, and then choose Insert, Comment (or right-click and select Insert Comment from the shortcut menu). Type your comment, as shown in Figure 3.14, and click anywhere outside the box. A red triangle appears in the upper-right corner of the cell, indicating it has a comment attached. To display the comment, pass the pointer over the cell.

TIP If the comment note stays put on-screen, you may have trouble seeing cells underneath the comment box. You can use the shortcut menu to hide the comment box so that it appears only when you pass the pointer over the cell. To hide the box, right-click the cell containing the comment and choose Hide Comment. If you prefer to see the comment all the time, right-click and select Show Comment.

FIG. 3.14
Use comment notes to explain or identify cell contents.

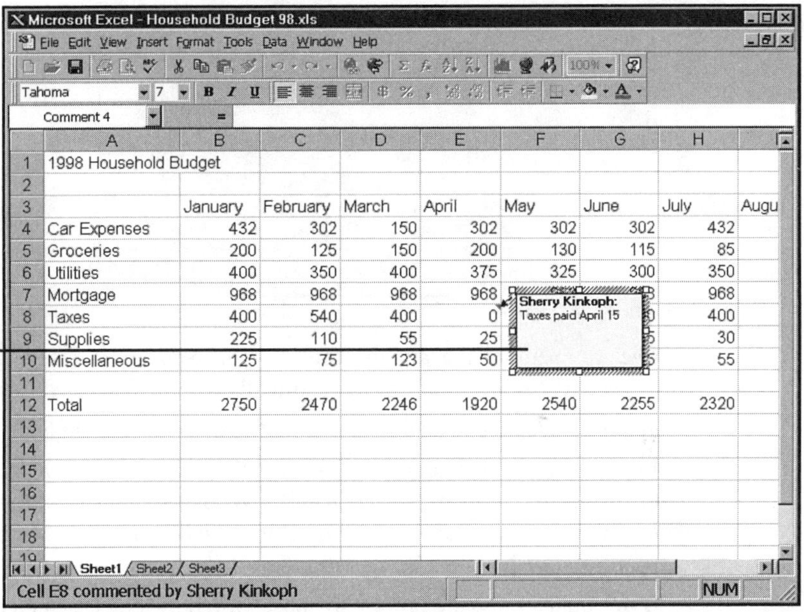

To edit a cell comment note, choose Insert, Edit Comment (or right-click and select Edit Comment from the shortcut menu). This reopens the comment box, and you can make changes to the text. To delete a comment note, right-click the note and select Delete Comment from the shortcut menu.

Using the Validate Data Feature to Reduce Errors

In some worksheets, you might want certain columns or rows to contain specific kinds of data entries, particularly if another user will be adding information to the worksheet you create. You can set up criteria using Excel's Validate Data feature. This feature lets you establish input for a cell or range of cells, and if the data entered doesn't match the criteria you set up, an error message or prompt appears.

For example, let's say you create an inventory worksheet with criteria assigned to the type of data entered into the inventory columns. If another user attempts to update the worksheet and enters data that doesn't match the criteria you establish, a warning or prompt box appears.

Follow these steps to set up the Validate Data feature:

1. Select the cell or range of cells you want to assign criteria to.
2. Choose Data, Validation. The Data Validation dialog box appears (see Figure 3.15).

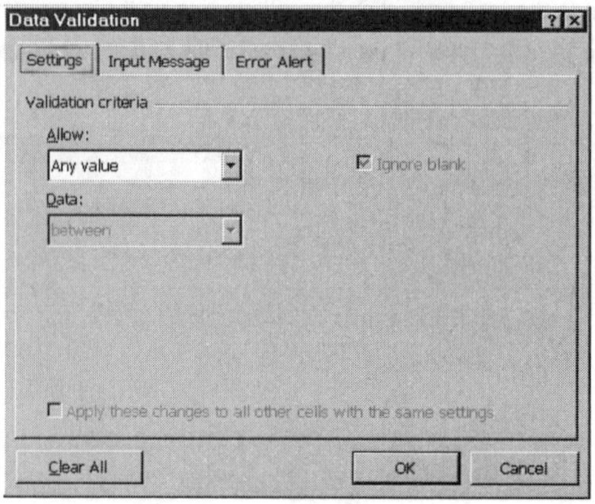

FIG. 3.15
Use the Settings tab in the Data Validation dialog box to define validation settings.

3. Click the Settings tab, and use the Allow drop-down list to select the type of data. If you select a type other than Any Value, the dialog box displays different settings.
4. If applicable, choose an operator from the Data drop-down list.
5. Depending on the data type you select in step 3, there may be additional settings for you to designate. For example, if you select Whole Number from the Allow list box and an operator from the Data list, you must use the Maximum or Minimum box to enter the appropriate values for the operator.
6. If you want a message prompt to appear when the cell is selected, click the Input Message tab and make sure the Show Input Message When Cell Is Selected check box is selected (see Figure 3.16).
7. Enter a title and text for the message.
8. If you want an error box to appear when an incorrect value is entered, click the Error Alert tab and make sure the Show Error Alert After Invalid Data Is Entered check box is selected (see Figure 3.17).
9. Choose a style for the message box, and enter a title and text.
10. Click OK to exit the Data Validation dialog box.

Depending on the options you selected, the next time a user attempts to enter incorrect data in the cell or range, a message or prompt may appear similar to the one shown in Figure 3.18. The Validate Data feature is a handy tool for designing your own error messages to alert you or other users to a worksheet element or problem.

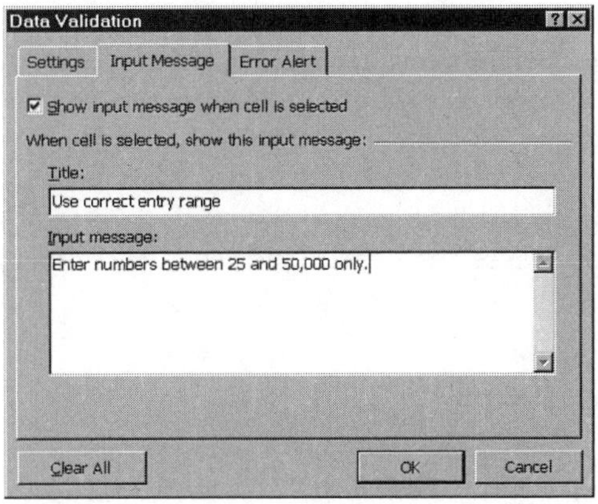

FIG. 3.16
Use the Input Message tab to insert an input message for the Validate Data feature.

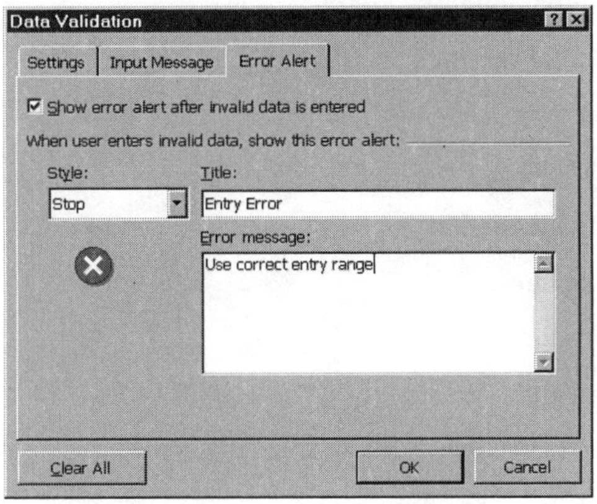

FIG. 3.17
Use the Error Alert tab to create your own error message prompt.

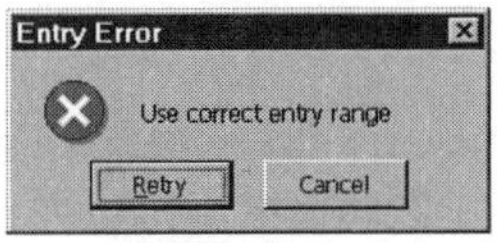

FIG. 3.18
Customize your own error message boxes with the Data Validation feature.

Working with Formulas

In such a spreadsheet program as Excel, formulas are used to figure totals and to perform many other kinds of calculations for you. *Formulas* are simply mathematical operations you can perform on the entries in your worksheet: addition, subtraction, multiplication, and division.

The real thrill of using a worksheet is seeing how quickly you can create a formula by pointing to the values, or arguments, you want to use and adding the appropriate operators. You don't have to worry that the calculation is incorrect; Excel won't make a mistake. Also, you can change any of the values included in the formula, and Excel will update the formula automatically.

A formula consists of these key elements: the equal sign (=), the values or cell references you want to calculate, and the operators (mathematical operations, such as addition and multiplication). All formulas start with an equal sign. Take a look at this simple formula:

=A1+A2

This formula takes the value in cell A1 and adds it to the value in cell A2. With Excel formulas, you can include more than two cell references, and you can use other operators, as listed in Table 3.3.

Table 3.3 Formula Operators

Operator	Description
+	Addition
–	Subtraction or negation
*	Multiplication
/	Division
%	Percentage
^	Exponentiation
=	Equal to
<	Less than
<=	Less than or equal to
>	Greater than
>=	Greater than or equal to
<>	Not equal to

Without an equal sign, Excel doesn't recognize the data as a formula, but only as a regular cell entry. For example, if you enter the formula A1*A2 without the equal sign, Excel simply places the data A1*A2 into the cell. No calculations are performed. The only way to make Excel multiply the contents of the two references is to add the equal sign to the beginning of the formula, as in (=A1*A2).

TIP If you're a former Lotus 1-2-3 user, you might be used to entering formulas with the plus (+) sign rather than the equal (=) sign. Lucky for you, Excel will treat cell entries started with a plus sign as formulas and automatically add an equal sign to the start of the formula for you.

When creating Excel formulas, *operator precedence* dictates the order in which the calculations are performed. In any given formula, Excel performs the series of operations from left to right in the following order:

1st All operations in parenthesis

2nd Exponential equations or operations

3rd Multiplication and division

4th Addition and subtraction

The order of operations determines the result of your formula. For example, if you want to determine the average values in cells A1, B1, and C1, and you enter the formula =A1+B1+C1/3, you'll probably get the wrong answer. Why? Because Excel will divide the value in C1 by 3 and then add that result to A1+B1.

One way around this problem is to group your values in parentheses. Group into parentheses any references and operators you want calculated first in the formula. In the previous example, =A1+B1+C1/3, enclose the values in cells A1, B1, and C1 in parentheses to instruct Excel to do the addition first, then divide the result by 3. The formula looks like this now, =(A1+B1+C1)/3.

If you include terms (such as Sheet1 or another file name) in a formula, be sure to separate them with parentheses or operators.

Table 3.4 lists the exact order in which Excel evaluates operators, starting with the first operator Excel evaluates and ending with the last. Regardless of the placement of these operators in a formula, Excel always evaluates them based on this order.

Table 3.4 Operator Precedence Order

Operator	Type
:	Range
space	Intersect
,	Union
–	Negation
%	Percentage
^	Exponentiation
* and /	Multiplication and division
+ and –	Addition and subtraction
&	Text joining
=, <, and <= >, >=, and <>	Comparisons

Using Reference Operators in Formulas

You can use Excel's reference operators to control how a formula groups cells and ranges to perform calculations. Reference operators allow you to combine named ranges and absolute and relative cell references (you'll learn more about absolute and relative references later in this chapter). Not only do reference operators let you join cells and treat them as a whole, they also let you refer to a common area where ranges intersect.

For example, perhaps your formula needs to refer to the range C3:C20 and to cell D12. To instruct Excel to evaluate all of the data contained in these references, use a reference operator, in this case a comma (,). The formula would look like this: =SUM(C3:C20,D12).

In another example, perhaps you need to perform a calculation on the intersecting cells in two different ranges. Using the intersect operator, which is simply a space, your formula might look like this: =SUM(C3:C20 C5:E15). The space operator tells Excel to evaluate the common cells where the two ranges intersect. (If there are no common cells, you'll see the result #NULL!.)

Table 3.5 explains each of the reference operators and how they are used.

Table 3.5 Reference Operators

Operator	Example	Description
:	=SUM(C3:D12)	Range operator: Evaluates the reference as a single reference, including all the cells in the range from both corners in the reference.
,	=SUM(C3:C20,D12)	Union operator: Evaluates the two references as a single reference.
space	=SUM(C3:C20 C10:D15)	Intersect operator: Evaluates the cells common to both references.
space	=SUM(Totals Sales)	Intersect operator: Evaluates the intersecting cell(s) of the column labeled Totals and the row labeled Sales.

Using Comparative Operators

In addition to arithmetic and reference operators, you can use comparative operators in your Excel formulas. This type of operator lets you compare values and evaluate results. For example, suppose you have an inventory worksheet in which you want to easily see the levels of in-stock product at a glance. You can insert a formula that shows you if the stock is above or below acceptable levels. Perhaps you want cell D30 to show you if the contents of row 12 fall above or below a certain level. To do so, you might enter a formula like this: =SUM(B12:H12)<D29. If the value is less than the level established in cell D29, Excel displays a TRUE result. If the value is greater than the contents of D29, the result is FALSE.

Table 3.6 lists each of the comparative operators used in Excel.

Operator	Type
=	Equal to
<	Less than
<=	Less than or equal to
>	Greater than
>=	Greater than or equal to
<>	Not equal to

Table 3.6 Comparative Operators

NOTE Use text operators (&) to join text (concatenation) contained in quotation marks or in referenced cells. For example, the formula ="Total"&D5 will return the text label Total followed by the value of cell D5 (such as Total 28).

Entering Formulas

As with any other cell entry (such as text or numbers), you can enter a formula directly into a cell or use the Formula Bar. To enter a formula, follow these steps:

1. Select the cell that will contain the formula and type an equal (=) sign. That tells Excel you are about to enter a formula (see Figure 3.19).

FIG. 3.19
Notice the equal sign appears in both the cell and the Formula Bar.

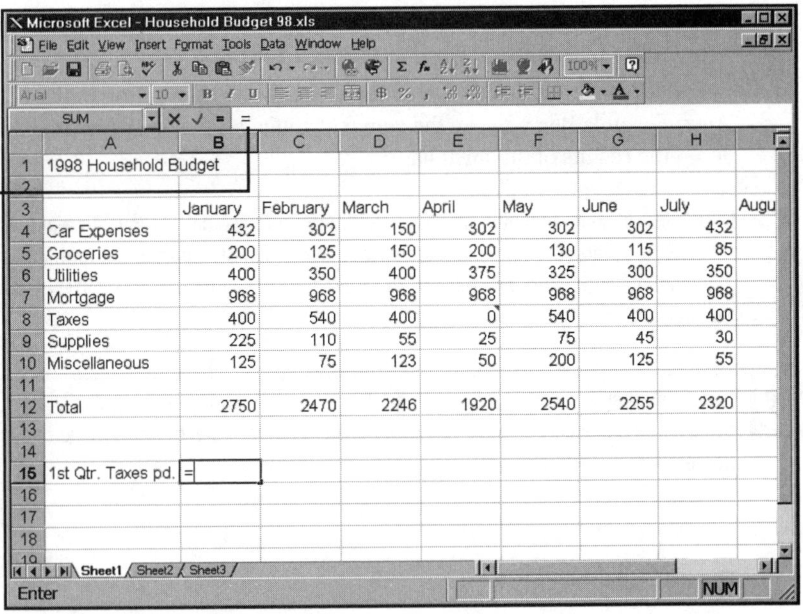

2. Select the first cell or range you want to include in the formula. (You also can directly type the cell reference.) The cell reference appears in the active cell and in the Formula Bar, as shown in Figure 3.20.

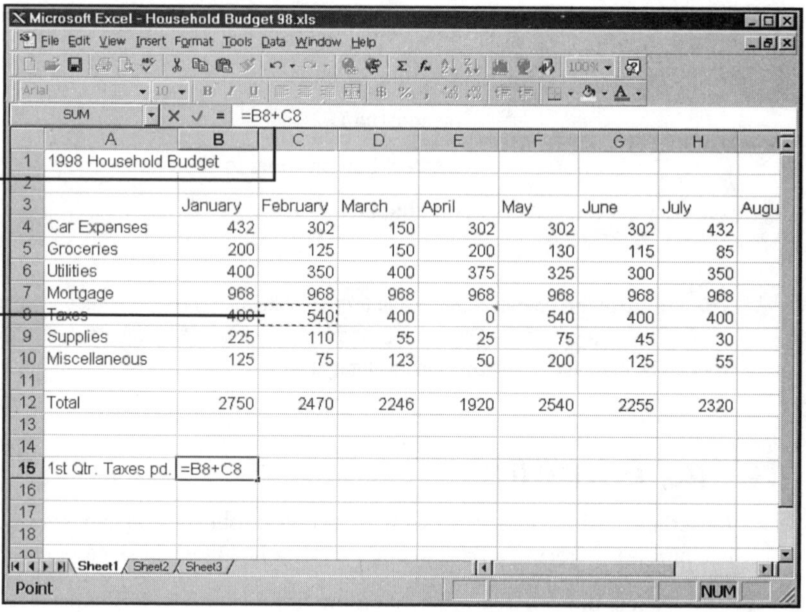

FIG. 3.20

Begin selecting the cells you want to use in the formula, and then enter the operators.

Use operators to build your formula

Each time you select a cell in the worksheet, it's added to the formula

	A	B	C	D	E	F	G	H	
1	1998 Household Budget								
2									
3		January	February	March	April	May	June	July	Augu
4	Car Expenses	432	302	150	302	302	302	432	
5	Groceries	200	125	150	200	130	115	85	
6	Utilities	400	350	400	375	325	300	350	
7	Mortgage	968	968	968	968	968	968	968	
8	Taxes	400	540	400	0	540	400	400	
9	Supplies	225	110	55	25	75	45	30	
10	Miscellaneous	125	75	123	50	200	125	55	
11									
12	Total	2750	2470	2246	1920	2540	2255	2320	
13									
14									
15	1st Qtr. Taxes pd.	=B8+C8							
16									
17									
18									

SUM × ✓ = =B8+C8

Microsoft Excel - Household Budget 98.xls

File Edit View Insert Format Tools Data Window Help

Sheet1 / Sheet2 / Sheet3 /

Point · NUM

3. Type an operator, such as the + sign.

4. Click the next cell you want included in the formula. Continue typing operators and selecting cells until you complete the formula.

5. When you complete the formula, click the Enter button in the Formula Bar. In the Formula Bar, you see the actual formula, as shown in Figure 3.21. The cell displays the results of the formula.

> **N O T E** In some formulas, you may want to perform two calculations. To make sure you get the results you want, use parentheses to surround the part of the formula you want calculated first—the rule of operator precedence. Compare these two formulas: (10*3)+5=35 and 10*(3+5)=80. See how the results differ greatly? ▪

T I P If you get an error message after typing a formula, make sure you didn't designate a blank cell, divide by zero or a blank cell, delete a cell being used in the formula, or use a range name when a single cell address was expected.

FIG. 3.21
The formula appears in the Formula Bar, the results appear in the cell.

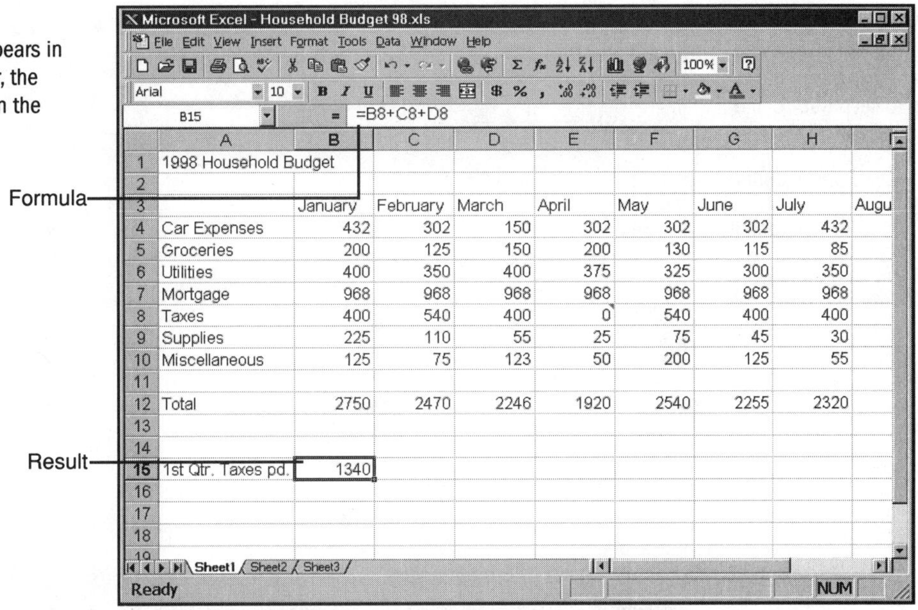

Another way of entering formulas is to use the Formula palette. Select the cell to contain the formula, then click the Edit Formula button in the Formula Bar. This opens the Formula palette, as shown in Figure 3.22. An equal sign is automatically inserted for you. Begin entering the cells you want to use in the formula and the operators necessary to perform the calculations; click the cell you want to include, and select an operator. Notice the Formula palette keeps track of the formula results. After completing the formula, click OK. The formula now appears in the Formula Bar and the results in the worksheet cell.

TIP To cancel a formula, click the Cancel button before pressing Enter. You also can press Esc. Formulas aren't assigned to a cell until you press Enter or click the Enter button in the Formula Bar.

One of the easiest ways to place cell references in your formula is to simply click the appropriate cell in the worksheet. For example, if you're building a formula that adds cells C3 and C4, instead of typing the cell addresses into the formula, click the cells in the worksheet, inserting an operator where necessary. Start by typing an equal sign, and then click cell C3, type a plus sign (+), and click cell C4. Press Enter to see the formula results.

TIP If the cell you want to use doesn't appear in your current view of the worksheet, use the navigation keys, such as the scroll bars or the Go To command to locate the cell you want to select for the formula.

FIG. 3.22
Use the Formula palette to assemble formulas and to keep track of the results.

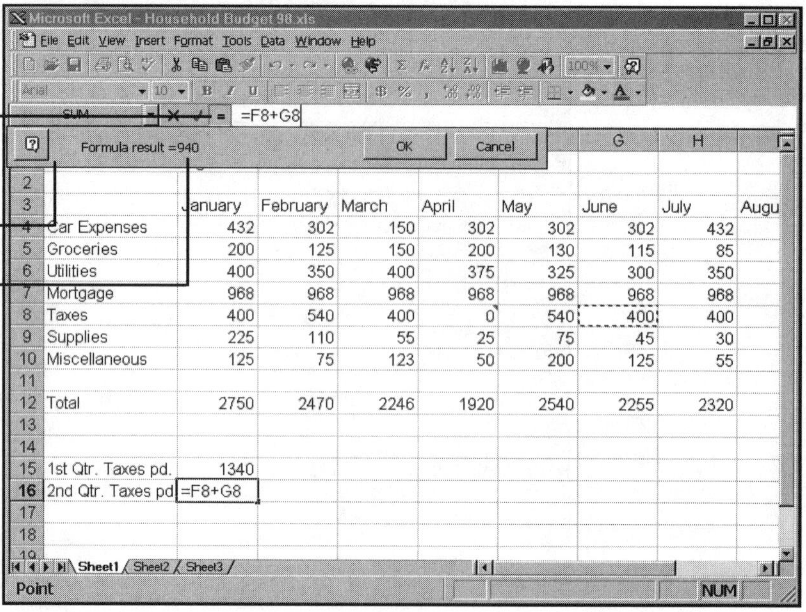

After you've entered a formula and pressed Enter or clicked the Enter button, the results are calculated and displayed in the cell. You can edit the formula at any time. Select the cell containing the formula, click in the Formula Bar, and make the necessary changes. You can use the mouse to select new cells or ranges to include. Press Enter or click the Enter button and Excel calculates the new results.

97

When editing formulas, cell references become color-coded. Each cell reference appears in a different color and the matching cell in the worksheet takes on the same color. This is a new feature in Excel 97 and it helps you readily identify the cells you're working with.

▶ **See** "Auditing and Validating Worksheets," **p. 455**

Using Absolute and Relative Cell Addresses

To make it easy to copy and move formulas, Excel uses a concept that is known as *relative addressing*. Excel doesn't think of the cells you include in the formula as a set location. Instead, Excel thinks of the cells as a relative location. For example, say you've filled the first three cells in column A with the following data:

A1 50

A2 100

A3 =A1+A2

When you create the formula in cell A3, Excel doesn't think "Go to A1." Instead, it identifies the first cell in the formula as two above the current one. Basically, Excel thinks this: "Go up two cells, get this value, go up one cell, get this value, and add the two." Therefore, if you move or copy the formula, the same set of instructions work. If you copied this formula to cell B3, you'd get =B1+B2. This type of referencing saves you from having to create the same formula over and over again. You can just copy it. The formula is relative to its location in the worksheet.

In some formulas, however, you might want to refer to a specific cell; that is, you don't want the formula to adjust to its location. For example, suppose you have several columns of pricing information that refer to one discount rate in cell A1. When you create this formula, you always want to refer to cell A1; you don't want the references to adjust. In this case, you use a different type of cell reference: an ***absolute reference***. An absolute reference stays put, it doesn't change just because the formula might move to another cell.

With this type of reference, you can tell Excel to adjust the column but keep the row reference the same, or adjust the row but keep the column reference the same, or both. To change a reference from relative to absolute, type a **$** sign before the part you want to make absolute. Here are some examples:

$A1	Refers always to column A, row will vary
A$1	Refers always to row 1, column will vary
$A$1	Refers always to cell A1

Follow these steps to enter an absolute reference:

1. Select the cell that will contain the formula and type an equal (=) sign.
2. Click the cell reference you want to include in the formula as an absolute reference.
3. Press F4. Excel enters dollar signs before the column letter and row number of the cell reference. (You also can type in a dollar sign in front of the cell reference.) Figure 3.23 shows an example.
4. Continue building the formula until it is complete, pressing F4 every time you want to make a cell reference absolute. When finished, click the Enter button in the Formula Bar (or press Enter on the keyboard) and Excel creates the formula.

In some instances, you might want to use a mixed reference in a formula. For example, you might want the row reference to stay fixed and the column to be relative. Mixed references can contain both absolute and relative cell addresses. For example, $C6 keeps the column from changing, but the row is relative. If the address is written C$6, the column is relative, but the row is absolute.

You can enter mixed references the same way you enter absolute references. Use the F4 key to cycle through adding dollar signs to the reference. For example, if you enter the reference C6, pressing F4 will cycle through $C$6, C$6, $C6, and C6.

FIG. 3.23
When you press F4 while building a formula, Excel cycles through absolute and relative cell addressing.

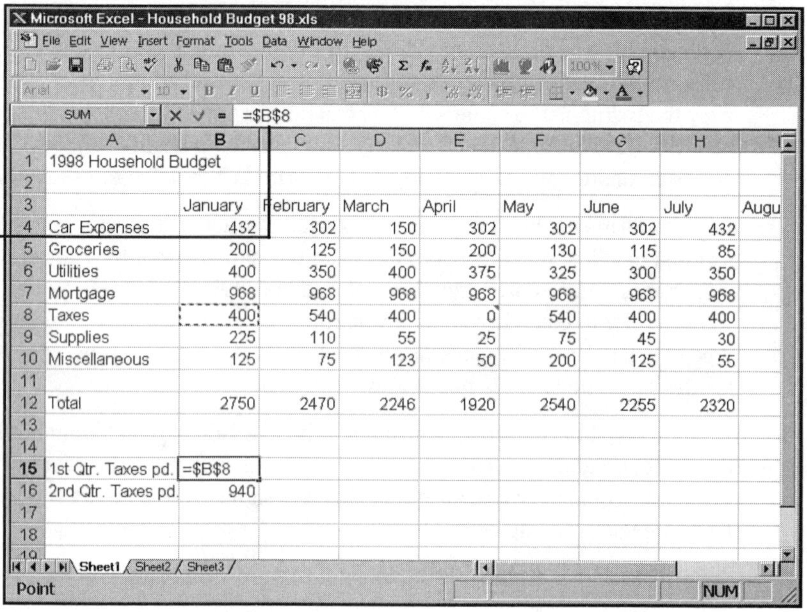

Referencing Formulas from Other Worksheets and Workbooks

In addition to using absolute and relative cell addressing in your formulas, you can also reference cells or ranges from other worksheets and other workbook files. To refer to cells in other sheets, use the sheet name as part of the address. For example, to refer to cell C10 on Sheet4, enter the address Sheet4!C10 in your formula. Anytime you reference a sheet name, you must include an exclamation mark. If you've given the sheet a specific name, such as SALES, use the specific name and an exclamation mark (SALES!C10). If the sheet name includes spaces, such as SALES TOTALS, you must surround the name with single quotation marks ('SALES TOTALS'!C10).

Another way to enter a cell address from another sheet is to use the mouse. When you get to the point in the formula where you need to enter a cell reference from another sheet, click the sheet's tab and select the cell or range you want to use. Excel inserts the complete reference, including the sheet name, into the Formula Bar.

Use 3-D references to designate a cell range that includes two or more sheets in the workbook. When entering 3-D references, use a colon to indicate the range of worksheets. For example, if you're creating a formula that uses data from the same range in four different worksheets, the 3-D reference might look something like this:

```
Sheet1:Sheet4!$D$5:$G$12
```

You can type 3-D references or select them with the mouse. When you get to a point in the formula where you need to enter a 3-D reference, click the first worksheet tab containing the cell or range you want to reference, hold down the Shift key, and select the last worksheet tab containing the data you want to use; then select the cell or range you want to reference.

NOTE Several of Excel's functions also can use 3-D references: AVERAGE, COUNT, COUNTA, MAX, MIN, PRODUCT, STDEV, STDEVP, SUM, VAR, VARP.

If you're using Microsoft Multiplan, you might be used to entering the R1C1 style of referencing cells. This style identifies a cell by its row number, then its column number. If you prefer this style of cell referencing, you can set up Excel to use the same style. Choose Tools, Options, and click the General tab. Select the R1C1 Reference Style check box.

Using Name References in Formulas

If you've assigned names to the ranges in your worksheet, you can easily use a range name to speed up formula building. If you know the range name, you can type it into the formula. But if you don't, you easily can paste the name into the formula using the Paste Name dialog box. To paste a name into a formula:

1. When you come to a place in the formula where you want to insert a name, activate the worksheet or workbook containing the name.
2. Choose Insert, Name, Paste. The Paste Name dialog box appears (see Figure 3.24).

FIG. 3.24 Use range names from the Paste Name dialog box to paste into formulas.

3. Select the range name you want to use from the Paste Name list box.
4. Click OK to exit the dialog box.
5. Return to the current worksheet and continue building the formula.

If you have not named any ranges in the active worksheet, you won't be able to select the Paste command in step 2.

▶ **See** "Naming Ranges," **p. 92**

Turning Formulas into Values

For most formulas you calculate, you only need the results—not the formula itself. Excel lets you convert a formula to its actual value. When you convert a formula, it's essentially frozen and you no longer see the formula in the Formula Bar, only the results.

To convert a single formula into a value, follow these steps:

1. Select the cell containing the formula.
2. Double-click the cell or press F2.
3. Press F9 and Excel replaces the formula with the value.
4. Press Enter when you finish.

To convert a range of formulas into values, follow these steps:

1. Select the range that contains the formulas you want to change to values.
2. Choose Edit, Copy.
3. Choose Edit, Paste Special. The Paste Special dialog box appears.
4. Under the Paste options, select Values.
5. Choose OK. Excel turns the formulas into values.

NOTE To help you keep your formulas organized and understandable, you might want to assign names, much like you do with ranges. But unlike range names, a formula name isn't assigned to any particular worksheet; you can use it with any workbook. To assign a name to a formula, choose Insert, Name, Define. The Define Name dialog box appears. Just as you would to name a range, type a name in the Names in Workbook box. Unlike you would when naming a range, however, enter the actual formula in the Refers To box. Click OK. If you reference a cell in your formula, remember to use absolute references. You can enter the formula just like you do using the Formula Bar.

Using Functions in Formulas

If you're looking for a speedier way to enter formulas, Excel's functions are the way to go. ***Functions*** are built-in Excel formulas. Excel provides many calculation functions for you. For example, you can calculate a loan payment, find the square root of a number, calculate an average, count items in a list, and do much more using the hundred or more Excel functions. Although you'll learn more about using functions in formulas extensively in Chapter 6, "Using Excel Functions," you need to know what they are and how they're used with formulas.

▶ **See** "Excel Function Reference," **p. 875**

Functions are simply a shorthand way for entering complex formulas. For example, the AVERAGE function condenses a longer formula into a shorthand version. Rather than have this formula:

=(A1+A2+A3+A4+A5)/5

You can use this function:

=AVERAGE(A1:A5)

Like a formula, the function starts with an equal (=) sign. The next part is the function name, usually a short, abbreviated word that indicates what the function does. After the function name, you see a set of parentheses and the arguments; like a formula, the function starts with an equal (=) sign. The next part is the function name, usually a short, abbreviated word that indicates what the function does. After the function name, you see a set of parentheses and the arguments. If a function uses more than one argument, commas are used to separate the arguments.

The more you work with functions, you'll notice they can save considerable room in the Formula Bar and cut down on the amount of typographical errors you might make when manually entering formulas. Excel even includes a button on the Standard toolbar for the most commonly used function, SUM (summarizes the specified arguments).

Excel has more than two hundred functions you can use. They're grouped by type:

Database

Date and Time

Financial

Information

Logical

Lookup and Reference

Mathematical and Trigonometric

Statistical

Text

This wide variety of functions allows you to create formulas and complex calculations for business, engineering, and scientific applications. For a complete reference of Excel's functions, see Appendix B, "Excel Function Reference."

To enter a function, select the cell and type an equal sign (=), the function name, and the arguments you want to use. Press Enter to calculate the function. Excel will display the results of the function formula in the selected cell or range. For example, the function SUM used in a formula will add all the values in the arguments. One of the easiest ways to enter a function is with Excel's Paste Function feature. It guides you through the process of using a function. To use the feature, choose Insert, Function or click the Paste Function button.

Edit functions in the same way you edit formulas. Select the cell containing the function and make your changes to the arguments.

▶ **See** "Using Excel Functions," **p. 189**

▶ **See** "Excel Function Reference," **p. 875**

Using Array Formulas

Array formulas are used to perform large calculations and return them as a single result or multiple results. Arrays are simply rectangular ranges of values or formulas that are treated as a group. What makes arrays useful is that they can perform powerful calculations in a small space. Instead of entering repetitive formulas throughout the worksheet, you can save memory by entering a single array formula that spans a range of cells, yet produces multiple results for every cell where you want a result to appear.

For example, an inventory worksheet might include a column of values listing prices and another column of values listing quantities. You might want to create an array formula that totals price and quantity values for each item in the inventory list. Instead of copying such a formula for each row and producing a single result, you can use an array formula that performs such a calculation for every item in the list. Take a look at Figure 3.25.

FIG. 3.25
Use array formulas to repeat the same formula for a range of cells.

Array formulas are identified by curly brackets

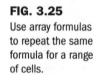

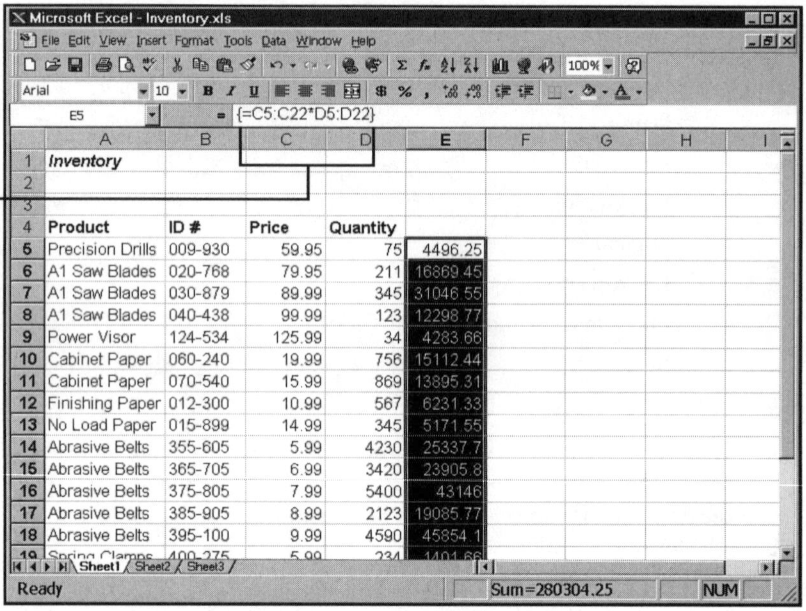

Notice the array formula entered in range E5:E22 produces results for each item in column E.

Array formulas are created like any other formula: You select the cells you want to include and build the formula. The only difference is that you identify the formula as an array by pressing Shift+Ctrl+Enter. Array formulas are enclosed in curly braces ({}), as shown in Figure 3.25.

To enter an array formula, use these steps:

1. Select the range or cell to contain the array formula.
2. Enter the formula and specify all references and operators to use in the formula, then press Shift+Ctrl+Enter.
3. Excel performs the calculations and displays the results.

You'll notice that each cell in the array range contains the same formula in braces. Because the array formula and the range you specified is treated as a single entry, despite the fact that its results may appear in multiple cells, you cannot insert new cells or rows within the array range. You cannot edit or delete any cell within an array range without first selecting the entire array. To edit an array formula or function, move the mouse pointer within the array range and press F2. Make your edits to the formula or function and press Shift+Ctrl+Enter to recalculate and display the results.

Working with Formula Errors

When you enter an incorrect value, reference, function, or operator in a formula, Excel displays an error value in the cell. Error values always begin with a pound sign (#). To help you figure out what's causing an error, choose Tools, Auditing, Trace Error. In many cases, a simple oversight, such as typing over part of the formula or using an invalid cell reference, is all that's causing the error. You'll learn more about finding error sources in Chapter 19, "Auditing and Validating Worksheets." In the meantime, Table 3.7 lists the various types of formula errors and possible solutions.

Table 3.7 Formula Errors

Error Message	Problem and Solution
#DIV/0!	The formula is attempting to divide by zero. Make sure you have not referenced any blank cells or ranges, or deleted a value needed in the formula.
#N/A	A cell has a #N/A entry, or the array is the wrong size, or you've left out a function argument. Recheck the formula, function, and cell references.
#NAME?	Excel doesn't recognize the name. Make sure you used the correct name and defined it properly. You might be referencing a nonexistent name.
#NULL!	The formula references two areas that are not intersecting. Double-check the cell or range references.

continues

Table 3.7 Continued

Error Message	Problem and Solution
#NUM!	The formula is having a problem with the number entered. Make sure you haven't deleted cells used in the formula, or recheck the function arguments you entered.
#REF!	The formula is having a problem with the cell or range reference. Recheck the references.
#VALUE!	The formula is having a problem with the value not being the type expected in the argument or intersect operation. Recheck all values used in the formula.

As you would to find any other computer error, re-examine the Excel formula and check for missing items, such as a parenthesis, a reference, or an operator. Typos are the biggest cause of formula errors, along with referencing the wrong cell or range. Always recheck your work to verify it's accuracy.

▶ **See** "Auditing and Validating Worksheets," **p. 455**

Rearranging Worksheet Data

When you create a new worksheet, it's always beneficial to spend some time planning the layout. What is the purpose of the worksheet? Think about what information you need to enter and what information you need to calculate. Spend some time considering the best way to set up and enter the data. Of course, if you've already entered your data, you can easily rearrange it afterwards to suit your needs. Excel has plenty of commands, such as Cut, Copy, and Paste, that you can use to move data around.

Using Cut, Copy, and Paste

Excel provides some shortcuts for entering the data, for example, the Copy command. Say your budgeted amounts for your categories are the same from month to month. Rather than type them over and over again, you can copy the values. (You also can fill data as a shortcut for entering information. See the "Speeding Up Data Entry" section earlier in this chapter.)

If you don't get things in the right spot, you can move them. You might want to move something over to make room for something else, for example. (You also can insert new rows and columns, as covered later in this section.)

To copy or move information, use the Cut, Copy, and Paste commands. These commands work the same from application to application, and they all use the Windows 95 Clipboard. When you cut or copy something, it is placed on the Clipboard. You can then use the Paste command to paste the item into the same file, into another file, or even into another application.

TIP Like to use keyboard shortcuts? Press Ctrl+C for Copy, Ctrl+X for Cut, or Ctrl+V for Paste.

Note that when you move or copy values, the values are pasted identically. Formulas are handled differently, though. What happens to the formula when your move or copy depends on the type of reference? Excel adjusts all relative references. All absolute references stay the same.

To move data in a worksheet, follow these steps:

1. Select the cell or range you want to move, and click the Cut button (or choose Edit, Cut).
2. A message at the bottom of the screen prompts you to select a destination. Select the cell at the upper-left corner of where you want the pasted cells. Keep in mind that Excel will overwrite any cells in the destination area.

3. Click the Paste button (or choose Edit, Paste). Excel moves the selected cell or range.

TIP If you don't want to paste the cut cells on top of existing cells, use the Insert, Cut Cells command. This command moves existing cells aside to make room for the cells you're moving into a new location.

Follow these steps to copy data from one cell or range to another:

1. Select the cell or range you want to copy, and click the Copy button (or choose Edit, Copy).
2. The status bar prompts you to select a destination. Select the cell at the upper-left corner of where you want the pasted cells.

3. Choose Edit, Paste or click the Paste button. Excel copies the selected cell or range.

TIP If you don't want to paste the copied cells on top of existing cells, use the Insert, Copied Cells command. This command moves existing cells aside to make room for the cells you're copying into the new location.

Use the Drag-and-Drop Technique

If you want to move or copy a selected range, you can drag and drop it. To use this method, you have to get the mouse pointer in just the right spot. You then have to drag the range to the new location.

TIP The drag-and-drop technique is best suited for moving items in the visible work area. If you need to move data to a far location in the worksheet (a location that's not readily visible on-screen), it's better to use the Cut, Copy, and Paste method.

Use these steps to drag and drop data:

1. Select the cell or range you want to move or copy.
2. Move the mouse pointer over the selection's border. The mouse pointer should change to an arrow, as shown in Figure 3.26.

FIG. 3.26
To start a drag and drop, select the cell or range and click the border.

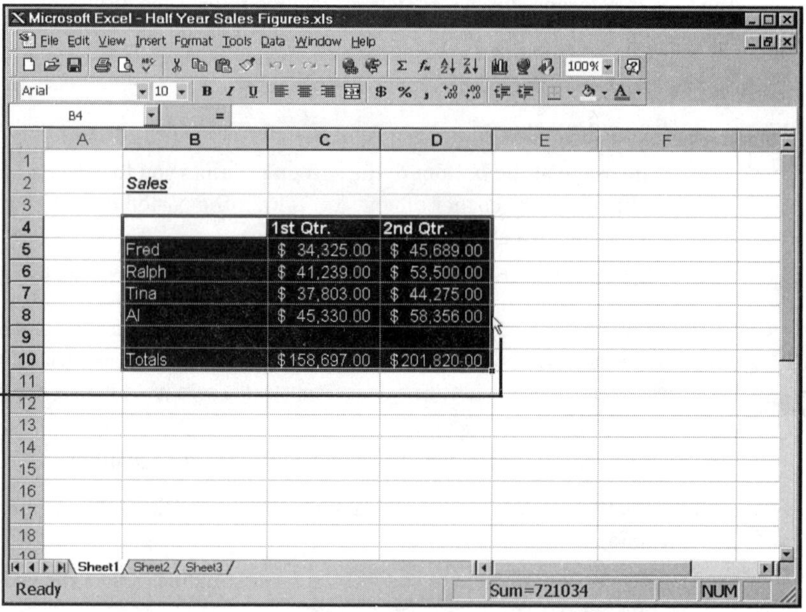

The mouse pointer becomes an arrow

3. To copy the range, hold down the Ctrl key. To move a range, you don't need to press any keys; just use the mouse button.
4. Drag the border. As you drag, you see an outline of the selected data. When the data is in the spot you want, release the mouse button. The data is moved or copied (see Figure 3.27).

NOTE To copy the contents and formatting of cells from one worksheet to another, first click the tab for the worksheet containing the cells you want to copy. Next, hold down the Ctrl key and click the worksheet tab you want to copy to. Select the cells you want to copy. Choose Edit, Fill, Across Worksheets. The Fill Across Worksheets dialog box appears. Select All (to copy cell contents and formatting), Contents (to copy contents only), or Formats (to copy formatting only). Click OK and Excel copies the data.

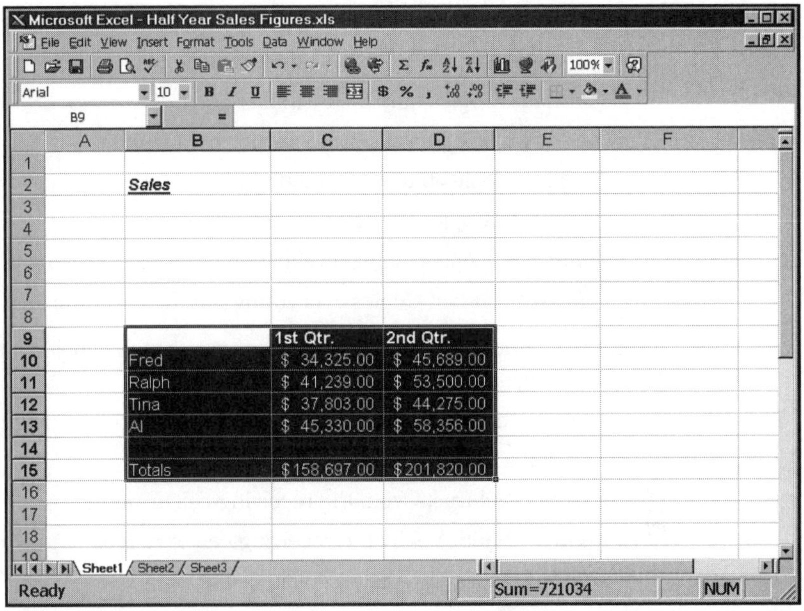

FIG. 3.27
Drag the data to a new location and release the mouse button.

Using the Paste Special Command

Although the Paste command copies entire cell contents from one place to another, you might only want to copy certain cell attributes. For example, you might want to copy only the formula or just the values. If this is the case, you can use Excel's Paste Special command. The Paste Special command combines cell attributes with another cell or range. To use the Paste Special command, follow these steps:

1. Select the cell or range you want to copy.

2. Choose Edit, Copy or click the Copy button.
3. Select the cell or range where you want to copy to.
4. Choose Edit, Paste Special. The Paste Special dialog box appears (see Figure 3.28).

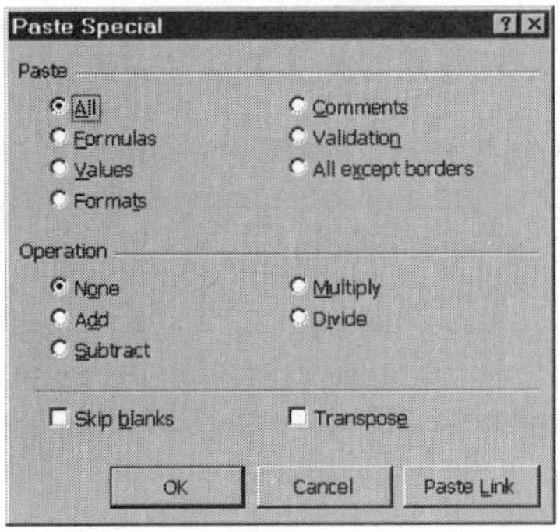

FIG. 3.28
Use the Paste Special dialog box to copy cell contents.

5. Under the Paste options, choose the attributes you want to copy to the new cell or range:

    All. Copies the cell contents and it's attributes.

    Formulas. Copies only the formulas.

    Values. Copies the values and any formula results.

    Formats. Copies the cell formatting.

    Comments. Copies the cell's comment notes.

    Validation. Copies the data validation criteria.

    All Except Border. Copies everything but the border formatting.

6. Under the Operation options, choose how you want the copied attributes combined with the cell or range you're copying to:

    None. Completely replaces the contents in the cell or range you're copying to.

    Add. Adds to the receiving cell or range.

    Subtract. Subtracts from the receiving cell or range.

    Multiply. Multiplies by the receiving cell or range.

    Divide. Divides into the receiving cell or range.

7. If you don't want to paste any blank cells on top of existing cells, select the Skip Blanks check box.
8. To change columns to rows or rows to columns, select the Transpose check box.
9. Click OK, and Excel transfers the attributes you selected.

NOTE If you're linking data from another application into an Excel cell or range, use the Paste Link button in the Paste Special dialog box. Learn more about linking and embedding data in Chapter 24, "Integrating Excel with Other Office Applications."

Find and Replace Data

If you have a worksheet that fits on one screen, you can quickly spot an entry. In a bigger worksheet, though, you may have to scroll and look, and then scroll and look some more to find an entry. Suppose that you keep track of customer orders in a worksheet that contains hundreds of rows. Finding a customer by scanning would be difficult. Instead, you can use Excel's Find command to quickly move to the customer you want.

The companion to the Find command is Replace. With this command, you can find and then replace a value. For example, if you changed a product name from Widget to Wadget, you could search and replace to make the changes automatically.

If Excel can't find a match, you see a message saying so. You can try the command again and double-check your spelling. Also, make sure you're searching the right type of item. You can tell Excel to look in formulas, values, or notes. Be sure to choose the correct option.

To find data in a worksheet, follow these steps:

1. Choose Edit, Find. The Find dialog box appears (see Figure 3.29).
2. In the Find What text box, type the information you want to find.

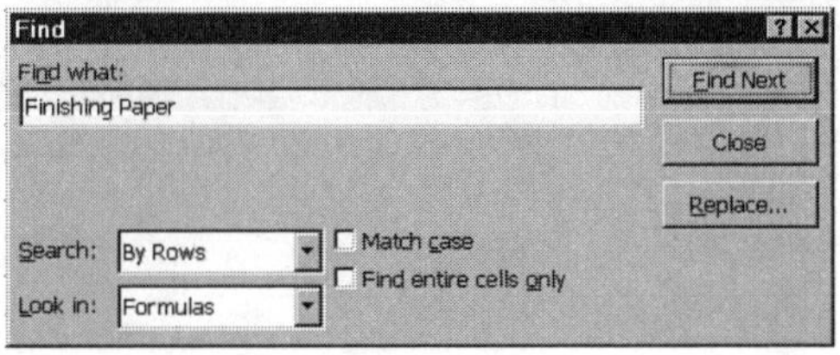

FIG. 3.29
Enter the data you want to search for in the Find dialog box.

3. Select how to search by displaying the Search drop-down list and choosing By Rows or By Columns. These options determine the direction you want the search to proceed. To search across rows, use the By Rows option. To search down columns, use the By Columns option.
4. Select where to look by displaying the Look in drop-down list and choosing one of the following: Formulas, Values, or Notes.
5. (Optional) If you want Excel to match the case as you've typed it, check the Match case check box. If you want to find only entire entries (not partial entries), check the Find Entire Cells Only check box.
6. After you enter the text to find and select any search options, click the Find Next button to find the first matching entry.
7. Excel moves to and highlights the first matching entry, as shown in Figure 3.30. Continue clicking Find Next until you find the entry you want; then click the Close button to close the dialog box.

Follow these steps to replace data in a worksheet:

1. Choose Edit, Replace. The Replace dialog box appears (see Figure 3.31).
2. In the Find What text box, type the information you want to find.
3. In the Replace With text box, type the entry you want to use as the replacement.
4. Select how to search by displaying the Search drop-down list and choosing By Rows or By Columns.
5. If you want Excel to match the case as you've typed it, select the Match Case check box. If you want to find only entire entries (not partial entries), select the Find Entire Cells Only check box.
6. After you make your selections, click the Find Next button to find the first matching entry.

FIG. 3.30
When Excel finds the entry, its cell is selected in the worksheet.

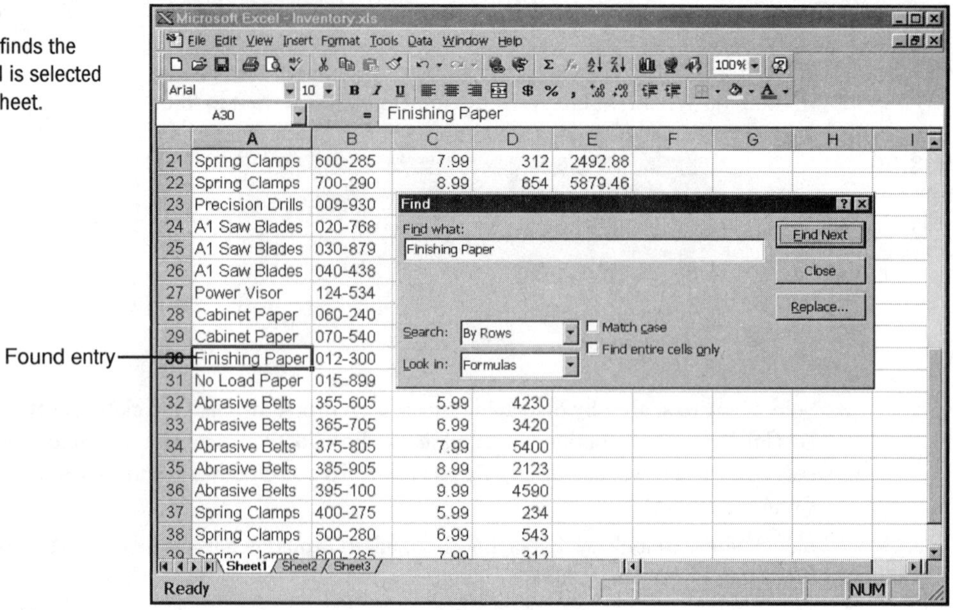

FIG. 3.31
Enter the data you're looking for and the data you want to replace it with in the Replace dialog box.

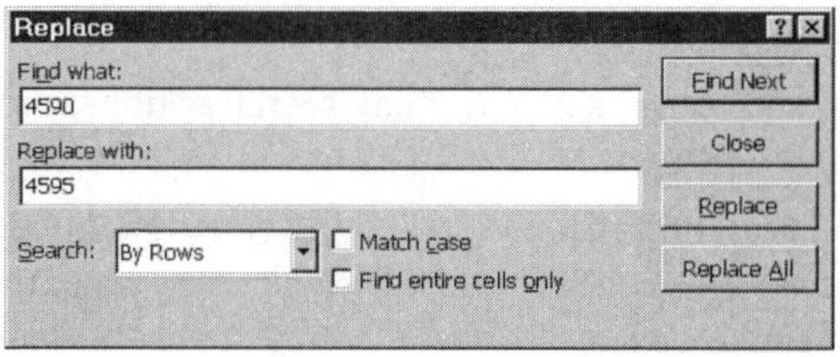

7. Excel moves to the first match; the Replace dialog box remains open (see Figure 3.32). Do one of the following:
   - Choose Replace to replace this occurrence and move to the next.
   - Choose Find Next to skip this occurrence and move to the next.
   - Choose Replace All to replace all occurrences.
8. When all the replacements you want are made, click the Close button to close the dialog box.

FIG. 3.32
When Excel finds the entry, its cell is selected on the worksheet.

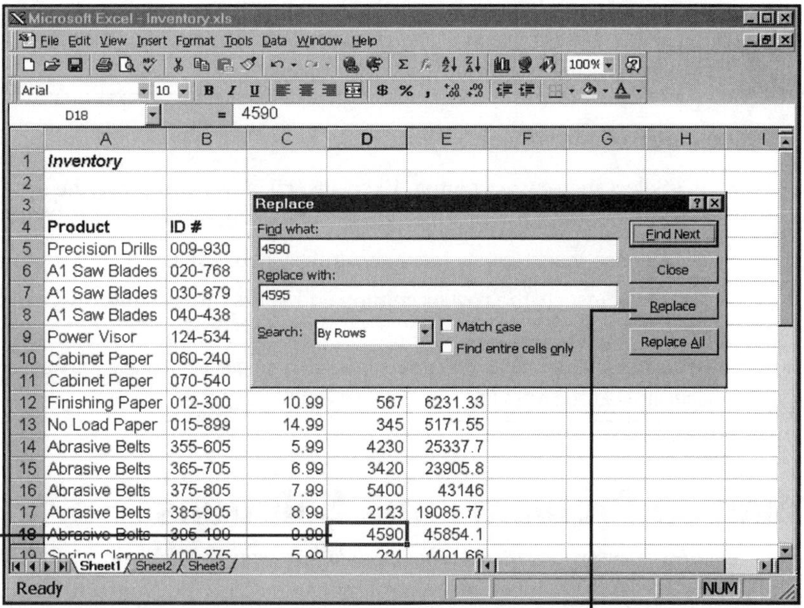
Found entry
Click here to replace the entry with the data you specified

Insert and Delete Rows and Columns

In Excel, you can easily insert and delete rows or columns as needed. When you delete a row or column, you not only remove the row or column from the worksheet, you also remove all the data in that row. Be sure that's what you intend. If you make a mistake, immediately undo the deletion.

If you forget to include something in the worksheet, you can easily add a new row or column, and Excel will move existing rows down or columns over to make room. You can easily rearrange your worksheet to include all the data you need.

One thing to remember when you insert a row or column is that the new row or column does not include any formatting (styles, font sizes, and so on) you might have applied to the existing rows or columns. You need to format the new row or column. (You can learn more about formatting in Excel in the next chapter.)

To delete a row or column, follow these steps:

1. Select the column(s) or row(s) you want to delete.
2. Choose Edit, Delete.
3. Excel deletes the column(s) or row(s) and shifts the remaining cells over.

TIP To delete only the cell contents in a row or column, choose Edit, Clear. This leaves the original row or column intact, but deletes the contents of the cell(s).

To insert a row or column, follow these steps:

1. Select the row or column. Excel inserts new rows above the selected row. Excel inserts new columns to the left of the selected column.
2. Choose Insert, Rows to insert a row. Choose Insert, Columns to insert a column.
3. Excel inserts the row or column and shifts the existing cells over.

TIP For a quick insert, select the row or column below or to the left of where you want the new row or column inserted and press Ctrl++.

Common Problems and Solutions

As you're entering various types of data into your worksheets, problems will inevitably arise. Here are some of the errors you might encounter with your own data entry tasks and possible solutions you can apply.

When I enter data into a cell, number signs appear.

Your cell is too narrow to display the data. Widen the column by choosing Format, Column, Autofit Selection.

When I enter a value, Excel adds decimals.

The fixed decimal options is on. To switch it off, choose Tools, Options, and click the Edit tab. Deselect the Fixed Decimal check box, and then click OK to exit.

When I enter a date, Excel turns it into a number.

Make sure you're entering the date in a format Excel accepts (such as 6/25/98 or 6 Jun 98). See the section "Entering Text and Values."

When I try to undo an action with the Edit, Undo command, nothing happens.

You must use the command immediately after performing the action. If you wait, you might inadvertently perform other actions. If you remember how many tasks you've performed since the original action, use the Undo button's drop-down list to select the action and undo the task.

When I delete a cell's contents, the entire cell is deleted.

To delete only the contents of a cell, use the Edit, Clear command not Edit, Delete.

When I delete a row, my formulas show errors.

Make sure you didn't delete a cell reference used by the formula. If you did, an error such as #REF appears in the formula cells. To make sure you don't inadvertently delete cell references, select the row or column you want to delete, choose Edit, Go To, and select the Special option. Next, select the Dependents Direct Only option and click OK. If Excel displays the `No cells found` message, you can delete the row or column without effecting your formula(s).

When I choose Edit, Fill, Series, the entire range is filled with the same text.

Excel's Fill feature might not be able to recognize the fill pattern you're trying to establish. Make sure you're using an acceptable fill series. See the section "Using AutoFill" for more details.

When I press Enter after building a formula, Excel displays an alert box saying an error exists.

Re-examine the formula, did you remember to use the correct operators and cell references? To find the most common formula errors, press F1 and consult Excel's Office Assistant.

When I enter a name in a formula, the #NAME? error is displayed.

Make sure you typed the correct name and that the name has been defined correctly. Also make sure the name hasn't been accidentally deleted. Do not enclose the name in quotation marks.

I want to use a range I labeled with the Insert, Name, Label command in a formula, but when I add new cells to the range, the formula doesn't change to reflect the new data.

Range labels are not updated automatically. To update the formula results, select the formula cell and press F2, and press Enter.

From Here...

In this chapter, you learned the various ways to enter data types, including formulas. The next two chapters help you with worksheet formatting and printing out your data.

- Chapter 4, "Formatting Your Worksheets," explains the various methods used to format data and change the appearance of your worksheets.
- Chapter 5, "Printing Worksheets," leads you through the steps for printing and previewing worksheet pages and adding additional page layout features.

CHAPTER 4

Formatting Your Worksheets

by Sherry Kinkoph

Once you enter data and formulas into a worksheet, you will probably want to spend some time enhancing the appearance of the data to make sure that the worksheet is easy to read and understand.

Take a moment to examine how the worksheet looks on the page. Do the headings align over the columns of data or do you need to make adjustments? Does the data fit on the page or do you need to adjust the margins? Do you need to clarify numbers or subtotals or emphasize the contents of a cell or range? This chapter covers all of the formatting options you can use with Excel. Use this information to make your worksheets look polished and professional. ■

Basic worksheet formatting

Learn how to use basic formatting commands; change fonts and sizes, style (bold, italics, and underline), and alignment.

Formatting tips and tricks

Speed up your formatting tasks using Excel's special formatting tools, such as AutoFormat and the Format Painter.

Mastering number formats

Learn to add formatting, such as currency or comma styles, to your numbers to define their meaning. Also, find out how to create custom number formats and use Excel's preset number styles.

Changing cell appearance

Add borders, patterns, color, and shading to your worksheet cells to give your data a polished, professional look.

Changing rows and columns

Tips and tricks for altering the size of rows and columns, hiding confidential data, and merging cells.

Using Excel's Basic Formatting Tools

There are a few universal formatting styles that are commonly used when polishing a worksheet's appearance, or any other document for that matter. Users want to be able to change the font and font size, alignment, and styles of data (bold, italics, and underline). Most of these formatting styles are available in all the Office 97 programs (including Excel), as well as other Windows-based applications. The successful employment of these particular formatting options can make the difference between data that makes an impact on the intended audience, or data that is lost in a sea of information.

Figure 4.1 shows examples of basic formatting applied to a worksheet. To organize and clearly identify column labels, try underlining the text. To keep your worksheets looking professional, center the titles across columns. Fonts, alignment, and styles play an important part in the look and feel of your data.

FIG. 4.1
Use Excel's formatting tools to create a professional looking worksheet.

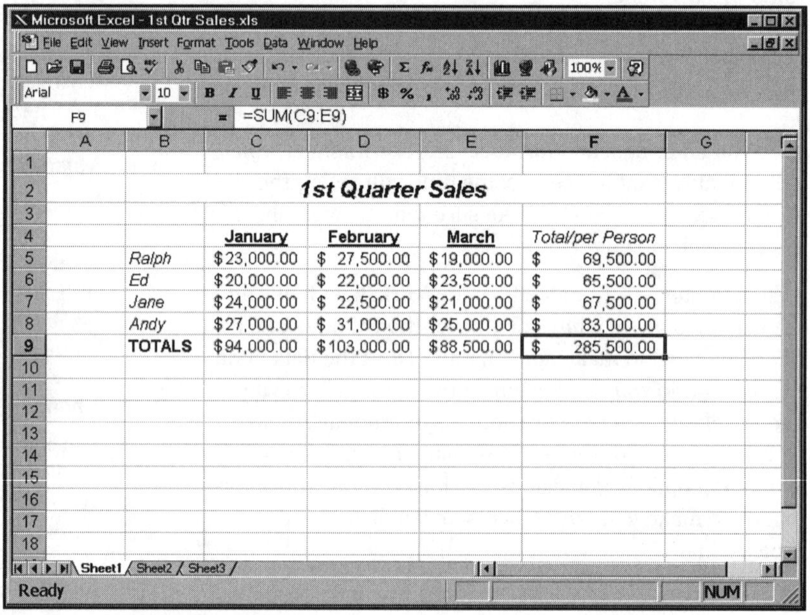

Of course, these same elements can be misused to create a look of visual chaos or a busy worksheet that overwhelms the eyes (see Figure 4.2). Don't overapply Excel's formatting styles or you'll detract from the emphasis of your data.

Using the Formatting Toolbar

For quick formatting, look no further than Excel's Formatting toolbar. On it you'll find quick access to commands that change fonts, sizes, boldness, and more. Many of the toolbar commands toggle on or off. The Formatting toolbar has buttons for changing alignment, number formats, adding shading or borders to cells, and other formatting options. If the Formatting toolbar is not displayed, choose View, Toolbars, Formatting. You also can right-click over a blank area in the Standard toolbar (or any other toolbar displayed) and select Formatting from the shortcut menu that appears.

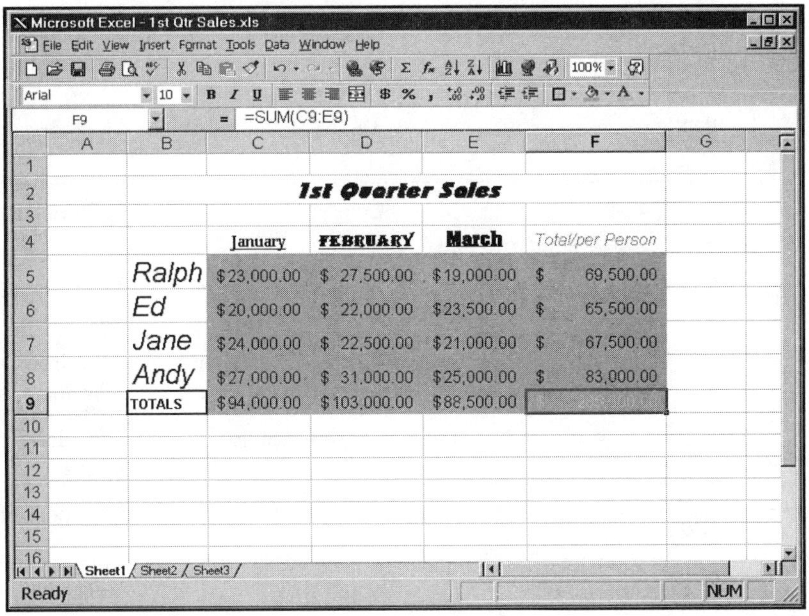

FIG. 4.2
Don't get too carried away with the formatting tools or you'll end up with an unappealing worksheet that detracts from the information you're trying to present.

TIP You can't see a preview of formatting selections you make using the toolbar buttons. If you prefer to preview your choices before applying them to your data, use the Format Cells dialog box instead. See the section "Using the Format Cells Dialog Box" to learn more.

Table 4.1 lists each of the default buttons found on the Formatting toolbar and gives a description of what each button does.

Table 4.1 Formatting Toolbar Buttons

Button	Name	Description
Arial ▾	Font	Displays a list of fonts to choose from
10 ▾	Font Size	Displays a list of font sizes
B	Bold	Bolds data

continues

Table 4.1 Continued

Button	Name	Description
	Italics	Italicized data
	Underline	Underlines data
	Align left	Aligns data to the left inside a cell
	Center	Centers data in a cell
	Align right	Aligns data to the right inside a cell
	Merge and Center	Combines two or more adjacent cells and centers data within
	Currency Style	Adds dollar signs and decimals to values
	Percent Style	Adds percent signs to values
	Comma Style	Adds commas to values
	Increase Decimal	Increases decimal points by one
	Decrease Decimal	Decreases decimal points by one
	Decrease Indent	Decreases indent by one level
	Increase Indent	Increases indent by one level
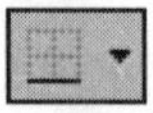	Borders	Displays a palette of border styles to choose from
	Fill Color	Displays a palette of fill colors to use as cell backgrounds
	Font Color	Displays a palette of colors to change font color

If you make a change using the formatting buttons and realize immediately that you don't like it, you can undo it with the Undo command. Click the Undo button on the Standard toolbar, or select Edit, Undo.

▶ **See** "Using Excel Toolbars," **p. 27**

Using the Format Cells Dialog Box

You can also control formatting through the Format Cells dialog box, shown in Figure 4.3. Unlike the Formatting toolbar buttons, the Format Cells dialog box allows you to preview your formatting selections before applying them to worksheet data. Select Format, Cells to open the dialog box. You can easily change many of the formatting features for your data by clicking the appropriate tabs in this dialog box and selecting from the available options. If you're looking for more formatting options, the Format Cells dialog box is the route to take. The tabs in this dialog box offer a greater variety of options, many of which are not found on the Formatting toolbar.

FIG. 4.3
The Format Cells dialog box offers you a wider variety of formatting controls.

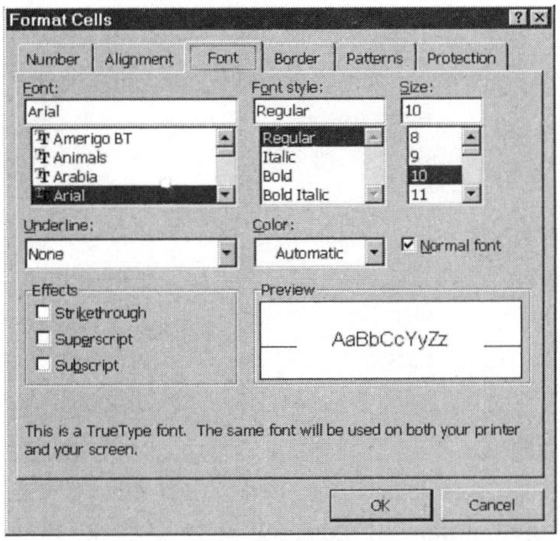

For example, you can use the Font tab to select subscript or superscript characters. In addition, the Font tab's Font Style options let you choose from Regular (plain), Italic, Bold, and Bold Italic.

In the Preview area of the dialog box, you can see a sample of what your selections will look like. Every time you change an option, the Preview area reflects the change.

NOTE Got a color printer? You can easily add color to the data you enter in Excel. Just select the data you want to color, and then click the Font Color drop-down button on the Formatting toolbar or open the Format menu, select Cells, click the Font tab, and choose a color from the Color drop-down list.

Making Entries Bold, Italic, and Underline

Your worksheet is going to be a mix of information, numbers, and text. Usually, each set of numbers has a row and column heading that identifies what the data means. To make it easy to spot these headings, you may want to add emphasis; you can make them **bold**, *italic*, or underline, or apply all three styles. You may also want to use these font styles to call attention to other data in the worksheet (see Figure 4.4). For example, you may want to boldface the totals so that they are easy to see on the page, or you may want to italicize the worksheet title.

FIG. 4.4
Use Excel's basic formatting tools to make an entry bold, italicized, or underlined.

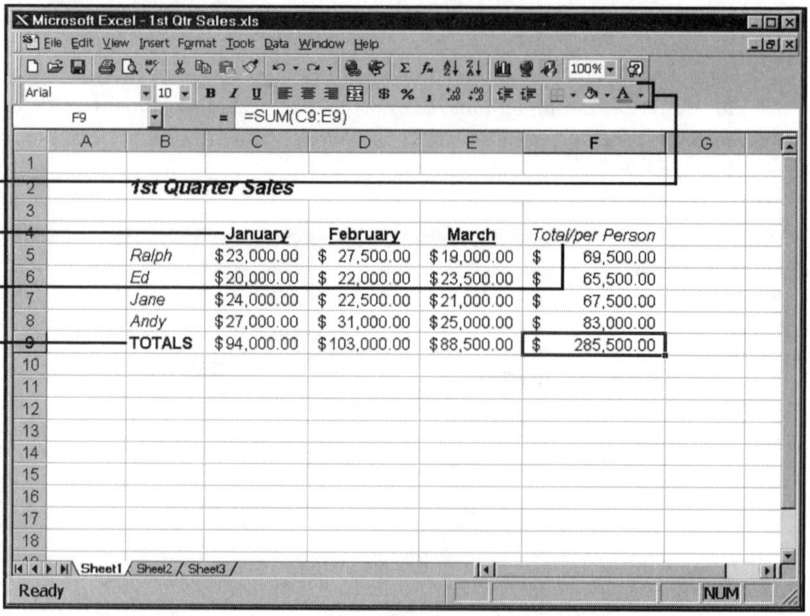

B *I* U

Excel's Formatting toolbar holds many of the same buttons as the Formatting toolbars in other Microsoft programs, such as Word and PowerPoint. Because the Bold, Italic, and Underline styles are so commonly used, just about every Windows program has these commands available as toolbar buttons. To apply bold, italic, or underline using the toolbar buttons, select the data and click the appropriate button.

TIP If you like to use the keyboard, you should learn these shortcuts: Ctrl+B applies bold, Ctrl+I applies italics, and Ctrl+U applies underline. You can use these same shortcuts to toggle the formatting off again.

TIP Notice that some of the buttons on the Formatting toolbar toggle on and off. You can turn off Bold, Italic, or Underline by selecting the affected cell or range and clicking the appropriate button again.

To make an entry bold, italic, or underlined using the Format Cells dialog box, follow these steps:

1. Select the cell or range you want to format.
2. Select Format, Cells, or right-click and choose Format Cells from the shortcut menu. The Format Cells dialog box is displayed (see Figure 4.3).
3. Click the Font tab, if necessary, to bring it to the front. In the Font Style area, select the style you want for the selected cells: Regular, Italic, Bold, or Bold Italic.
4. Choose an underline style for the selected text by using the Underline drop-down list.
5. You can see how your formatting options look in the Preview area of the dialog box. When you're satisfied with what you see, click OK to exit the dialog box and apply your selections.

TIP The Underline button on the Formatting toolbar applies only one line style to selected data. To apply a different line style (such as a double underline), use the Underline drop-down list in the Format Cells dialog box.

Changing Fonts and Sizes

When you create a new worksheet and enter data, Excel uses the default font and font size (Arial 10-point type). With this formatting, all the data has the same emphasis and looks the same. If you find this font is too small or if you prefer a different font, you can make a change.

With Excel, you can change the font for the entire worksheet or for only a selected cell or range. Perhaps you have a single word or character in a cell that needs formatting, or maybe you want to use a larger point size for the entire worksheet. The fastest way to change the font and size is by using the Font and Font Size drop-down lists on the Formatting toolbar. However, with this method, you can't preview the font or size before applying it, and you can make only one change at a time. If you want to change font, size, and style all at once, use the Format Cells dialog box.

NOTE Font sizes are measured in points; 72 points equal one inch in height.

Changing Font and Size with the Formatting Toolbar

To use the Formatting toolbar to change a font style and size, follow these steps:

1. Select the cell or range you want to change (you can also select the entire worksheet or just a single character).
2. Next, click the down arrow next to the Font list (see Figure 4.5) to display a drop-down list of font choices. Select the font you want. Excel makes the font change to the cell or range you selected.

FIG. 4.5
Use the Font drop-down list to change fonts quickly from the toolbar.

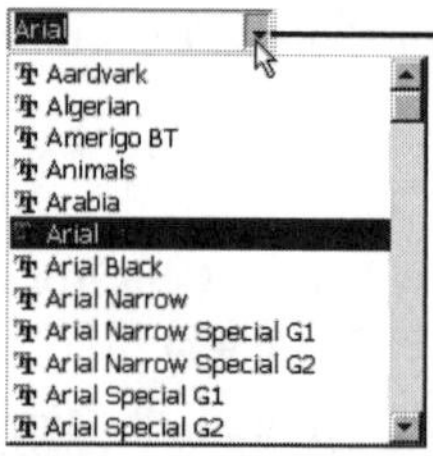

Click here to display a list of fonts

3. To change the size of the font, click the drop-down arrow next to the Font Size list (see Figure 4.6). Excel displays a list of font sizes. Click the size you want.

FIG. 4.6
Use the Font Size drop-down list to change sizes. Note that the list starts with the smallest size and ends with the largest.

Click here to display a list of sizes

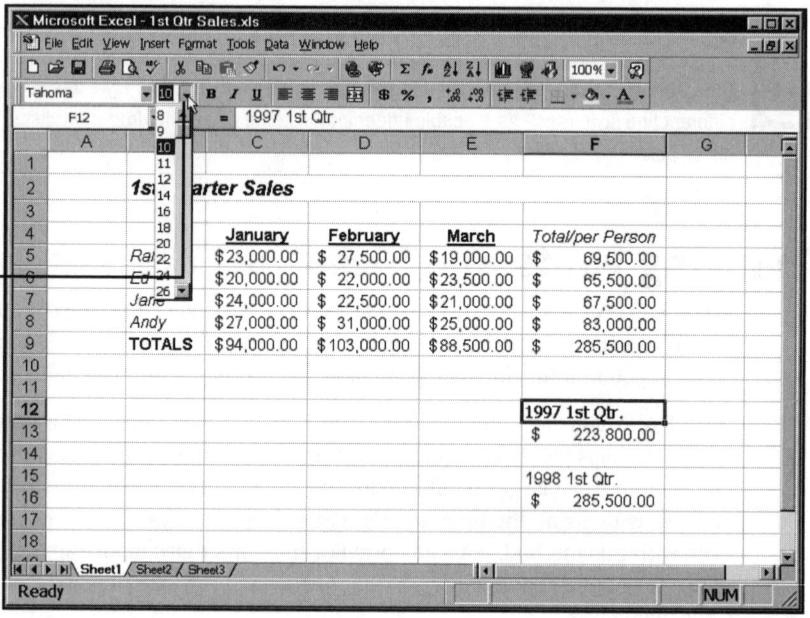

4. Excel formats the cell or range with the new size. If necessary, Excel also adjusts the row height but not the column width.

TIP You can type a font size directly into the Font Size box on the Formatting toolbar. Click inside the box and type a new size.

If you choose a font or size that makes your data wider than the existing column, you can resize the column. One way is to move the mouse pointer to the column border you want to resize until it becomes a two-sided arrow pointer. Then drag the border to a new size.

▶ **See** "Formatting Columns and Rows," **p. 158**

If after changing a font or size you realize immediately that you don't like it, you can undo it with the Undo command. Click the Undo button on the Standard toolbar, or select Edit, Undo.

If you didn't undo the command immediately but you decide you want to later, you can clear formatting by selecting the cell or range and choosing the Edit, Clear, Formats command. Excel clears all the applied formatting.

Changing Font and Size with the Format Cells Dialog Box

If you'd rather preview how a font or size looks before actually applying the changes to your worksheet data, use the Format Cells dialog box. To change the font or size using this dialog box, follow these steps:

1. Select the cell or range you want to change, and then choose Format, Cells.
2. The Format Cells dialog box appears. If necessary, click the Font tab of the Format Cells dialog box to bring it to the front.
3. In the Font list, click the font you want.
4. Click the size you want in the Size list.
5. If you want to use a different type of underline, display the Underline drop-down list and click the underline style you want.
6. To add color to your data, select the Color drop-down box and choose a color from the list.
7. If you want any special effects, check the check box for any of these special effects: Strikethrough, Superscript, or Subscript.
8. Look in the Preview area to see what the selected formatting will look like (see Figure 4.7). When you finish making changes, click OK. Excel formats the selected range with the options you selected.

FIG. 4.7
Look in the Preview area to see a sample of the font choices you selected. If you don't like the looks of your choices, change them.

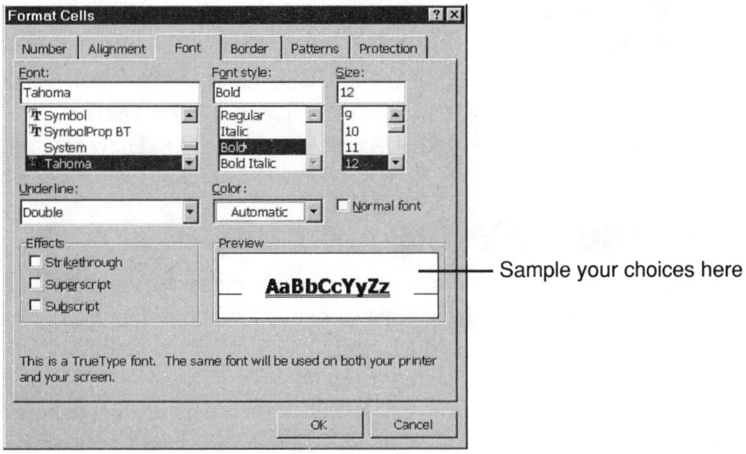

TIP To quickly access the Format Cells dialog box, right-click over the selected cell(s) and choose Format Cells.

Changing the Default Font

If you don't like the default font for new worksheets, you can change the font each time you create a new worksheet, or you can change the default. When you change the default, Excel will use the new font for all new worksheets, which will save you time.

1. Choose Tools, Options. Excel opens the Options dialog box.
2. Click the General tab, as shown in Figure 4.8. To change the font used, click the drop-down arrow next to the Standard Font drop-down list. Then click the font you want.

FIG. 4.8
Use the Options dialog box to change the default font used in your Excel worksheets. The new font you assign will take effect the next time you open Excel.

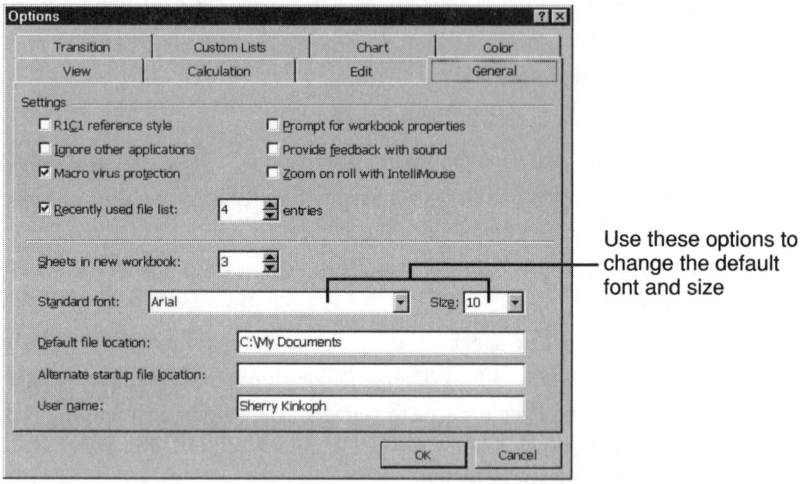

3. To change the font size, click the Size drop-down arrow. Then click the new size you want.
4. Click OK twice. You'll see the following message: `For your changes to the standard font to take effect, you must quit and then restart Microsoft Excel.` Exit the program and reopen Excel. All new worksheets will now use the font you selected.

Aligning and Rotating Cell Entries

By default, Excel automatically aligns data as soon as you enter it into a cell, depending on what type of data it is. Excel aligns text on the left and numbers on the right. In addition, text and numbers are initially set flush with the bottom of the cell. After you make the entries, you may need to make some adjustments to these default alignments. You can align cell entries on the left, center, or right, or you can justify cell contents to align at both the left and right sides of the cell. Excel's alignment commands also include options for wrapping text within a cell, centering entries across a selected group of cells, or rotating entries. Figure 4.9 shows a few examples of alignment options applied to a worksheet.

FIG. 4.9
Use Excel's alignment commands to change the way data is positioned in a cell.

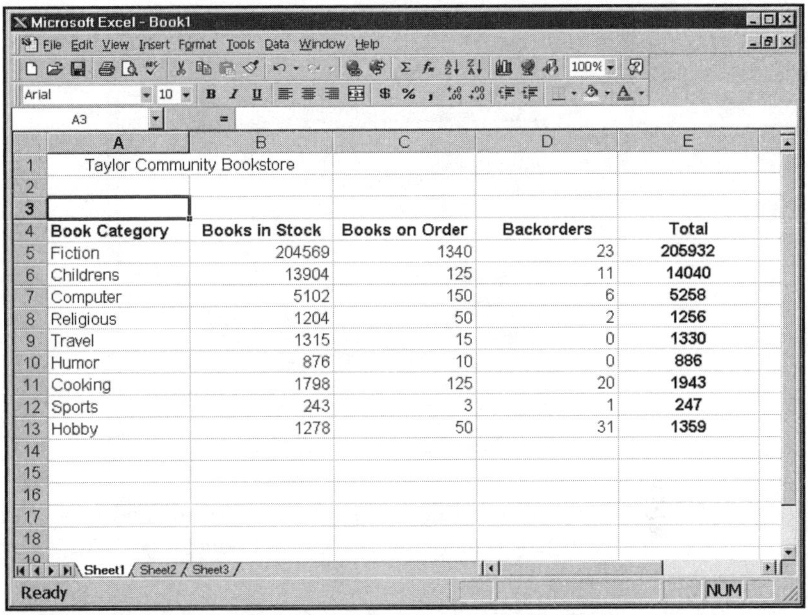

The easiest way to make any simple alignment changes is to use the alignment toolbar buttons. The Formatting toolbar contains three alignment buttons you can choose from: Left, Center, and Right. To change entry alignment using the toolbar, select the cell or range you want to change and click the desired alignment button on the toolbar.

Changing Alignment with the Format Cells Dialog Box

You can also use the Format Cells dialog box to designate alignment. In addition to left, center, and right alignment options, the Alignment tab offers additional options you can apply. Take a look at this list to help you decipher your choices:

- *Horizontal* options enable you to specify a left/right alignment in the cell(s). With the Center across selection option, you can center a title or other text inside a range of cells.
- *Vertical* options enable you to specify how you want the data aligned in relation to the top and bottom of the cell(s).
- *Orientation* options let you flip the text sideways or print it from top to bottom (as opposed to left to right).
- The *Text Control* check boxes allow you to wrap long lines of text within a cell (normally, Excel displays all text in a cell on one line), shrink text to fit inside a cell, and merge cells.

To change alignment using the Format Cells dialog box, follow these steps:

1. Select the cell or range you want to change; then choose Format, Cells.
2. This opens the Format Cells dialog box. Click the Alignment tab to bring it to the front (see Figure 4.10).

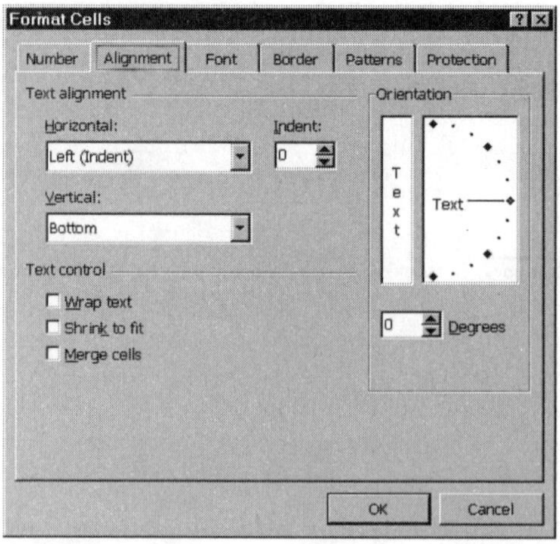

FIG. 4.10
The Alignment tab in the Format Cells dialog box lets you change horizontal and vertical alignment.

3. To change horizontal alignment, choose an option under the Horizontal drop-down list. Choices include General (default), Left, Center, Right, Fill, Justify, and Center Across Selection.
4. To change vertical alignment, select an option from the Vertical drop-down list. Choices include Top, Center, Bottom, or Justify.
5. To wrap text onto other lines inside your cell, select the Wrap Text check box. Use this option if you have a lengthy text entry and want the cell to contain multiple text lines.
6. If you're having trouble fitting text in a cell, you may want to use the Shrink to Fit option. It automatically shrinks the size of the text to fit into the cell.
7. Use the Merge Cells option to combine two or more cells into one.
8. Click OK to exit the box and implement your alignment changes.

TIP You can repeat an alignment format command in another cell. Just use the Repeat Format Cells command from the Edit menu.

Centering a Heading

One of the most common alignment tasks you'll want to perform in a worksheet is centering a title or heading across a range of cells. For that reason, the creator's of Excel have placed a Merge and Center button on the Formatting toolbar. Use these steps to center a heading:

1. Select the cell that contains the heading and the range that you want to center across (see Figure 4.11). If you just select the cell with the entry, this feature won't work properly.

FIG. 4.11
To center a heading in your worksheet, first select the range you want to center across.

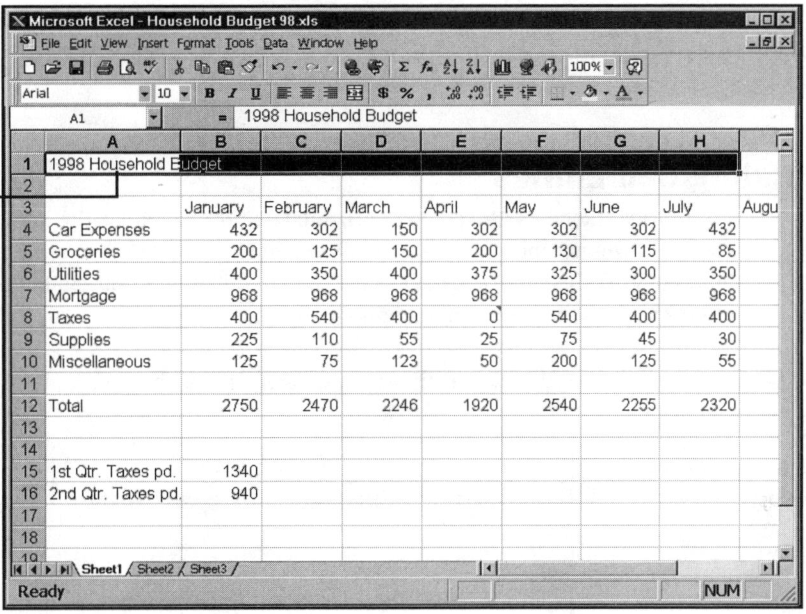

2. Then click the Merge and Center button.
3. Excel centers the headings across the selected columns, as shown in Figure 4.12.

FIG. 4.12
With a click of the Merge and Center button, Excel centers the heading across the range.

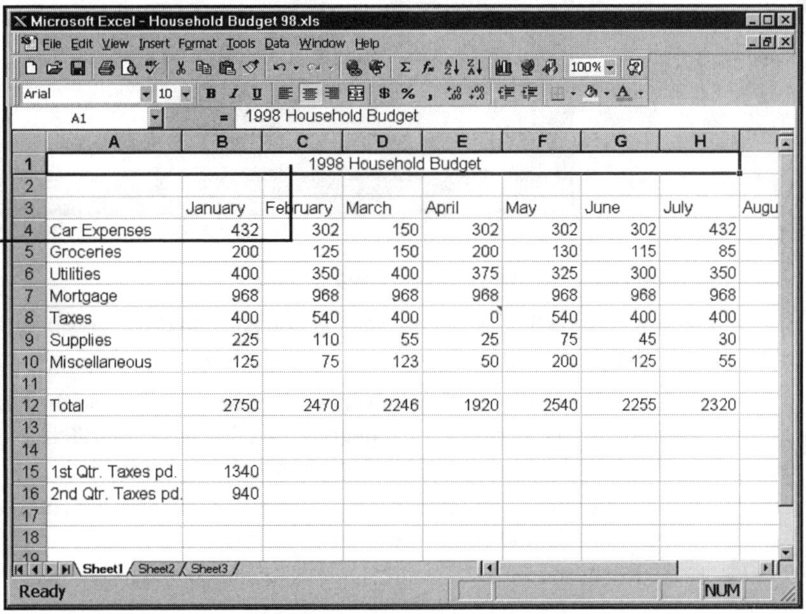

NOTE Even though a centered title looks as if it is in a different cell, it is still in the same cell that you originally entered it in. If you try to edit the cell and it looks blank, try selecting the first cell in the row.

Rotating Cell Entries

For most worksheets, the default horizontal text orientation is the norm. However, to help clarify drawings, tables, or charts you insert into your worksheets, you can apply vertical orientation to worksheet entries. Excel's orientation option lets you rotate text or numbers to create effects such as those shown in Figure 4.13.

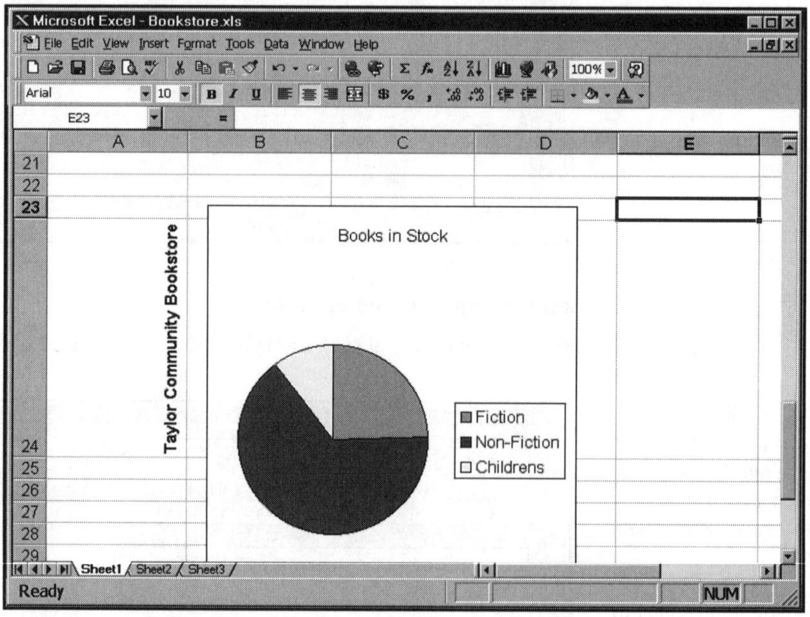

FIG. 4.13 Use rotated text to help label drawings and charts in your Excel worksheets.

To apply rotation effects, use these steps:

1. Select the cell or range you want to change, and then choose Format, Cells.
2. The Format Cells dialog box appears. Click the Alignment tab to bring it to the front.
3. Under the Orientation options, drag or click the pointer in the Orientation gauge up or down to specify a rotation in degrees (see Figure 4.14). Alternatively, you can specify degrees of rotation with the Degrees spin box.
4. To set a stacked orientation, where letters or numbers are stacked to be read from top to bottom, click the box to the left of the gauge.
5. Click OK to exit the box and implement your rotation settings.

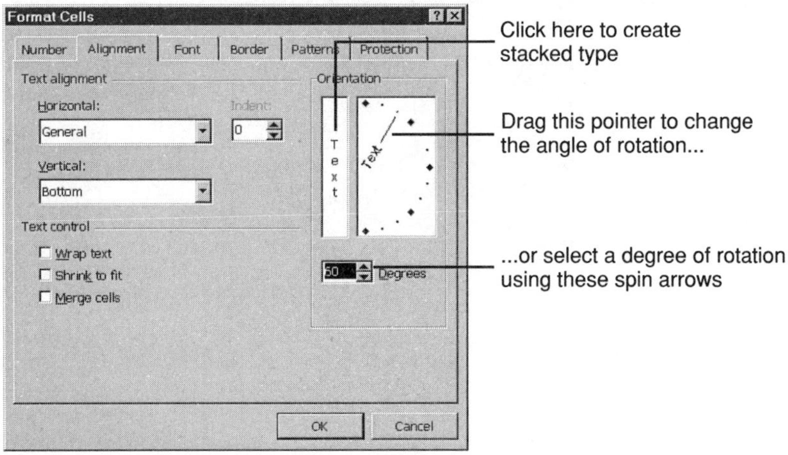

FIG. 4.14
Drag or click the pointer in the Orientation gauge to change the rotation setting.

Using AutoFormat

If you don't know how to format your spreadsheet, let Excel's AutoFormat feature give you some professional help. Excel provides 16 different autoformats to choose from. Figures 4.15 and 4.16 show just two.

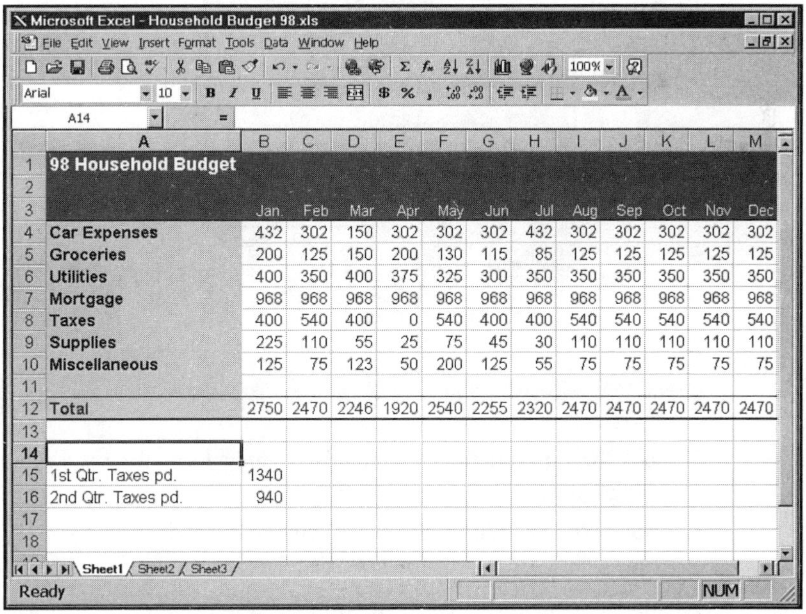

FIG. 4.15
This example shows the Classic 2 AutoFormat style.

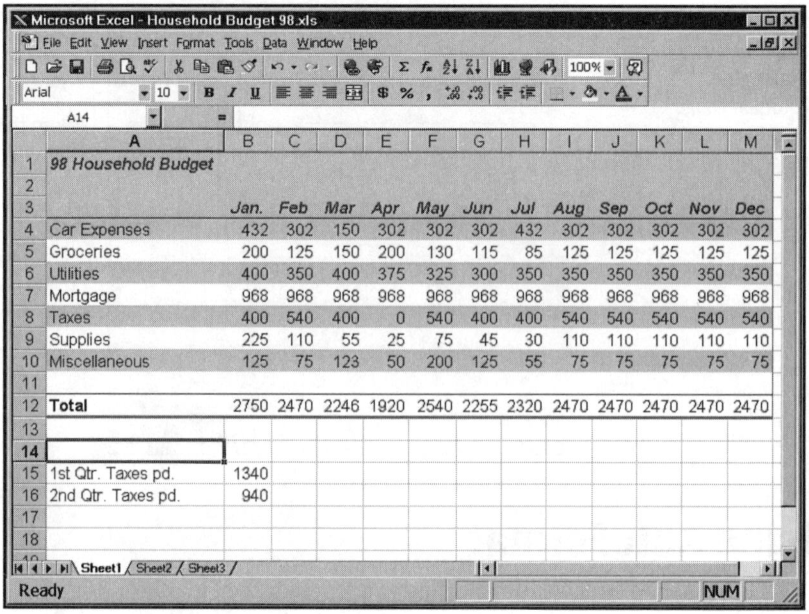

FIG. 4.16
This example shows the List 1 AutoFormat style applied.

To use AutoFormat, follow these steps:

1. Select the data you want to format.
2. Choose Format, AutoFormat. The AutoFormat dialog box appears, as shown in Figure 4.17. Notice the many formatting styles you can try.

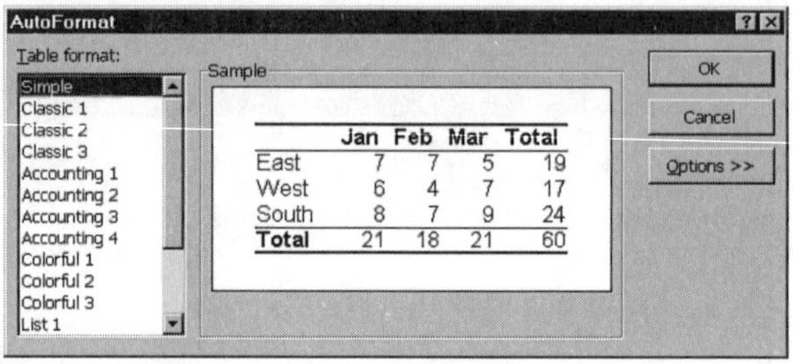

FIG. 4.17
The AutoFormat dialog box has 16 formats you can use.

3. Look through the Table Format list to find a formatting style you want to use, then select a style from the list.
4. Look at the Sample area to see if you like the style. When you're satisfied with your choice, click OK to exit the box. Excel formats your data accordingly.

If you don't like the format you've chosen, click the Undo button or select Edit, Undo immediately. If you make any edits to the data in a formatted table, the new data will reflect the formatting you've chosen. To remove the formatting completely, choose Format, AutoFormat, and select None from the Table Format list.

> **TIP** Keyboard devotees can press Ctrl+Z to quickly undo an action.

If you like certain parts of a preset format, you can choose to apply the formatting only to certain portions of your data or cells. Click the Options button in the AutoFormat dialog box to display a group of options (see Figure 4.18). For example, if you want to apply only the font or pattern of a particular format, you can select check boxes for those particular options and deselect the rest. When you click OK, only the formatting options you selected are applied.

FIG. 4.18
When you want to apply only certain parts of an AutoFormat style, click the Options button and choose the options you want to apply.

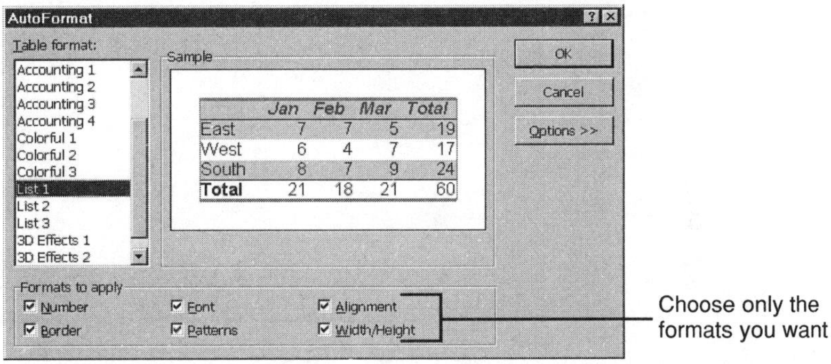

Copying Formatting with the Format Painter Tool

Once you get a range formatted the way you want it, you may like the look so much that you want to use it on other cells or ranges in the worksheet. Instead of going through all the same formatting steps again, you can copy the formatting with the Format Painter button on the Standard toolbar.

1. Select the cell or cells that contain the formatting you want to copy.

2. Then click the Format Painter button on the toolbar. The mouse pointer displays a little paintbrush next to the cross, as shown in Figure 4.19.
3. Select the cells that you want to format with the same options. When you release the mouse button, Excel applies the formatting to the selected range.

Applying Conditional Formatting

With conditional formatting, you can instruct Excel to change the formatting for a cell automatically if the cell's value changes, based on the criteria you establish for change. For example, if the value of a cell in your inventory spreadsheet falls below zero, you can instruct Excel to flag the cell with a heavy red line and shading, and boldfacing the text. The formatting change will alert you to the cell and its contents. This is helpful when you're trying to keep an eye out for changing values. Conditional formatting can help you with error checking your entries and performing exception reporting for analysis. In order for Excel to apply the formatting, however, it must first meet the criteria you establish.

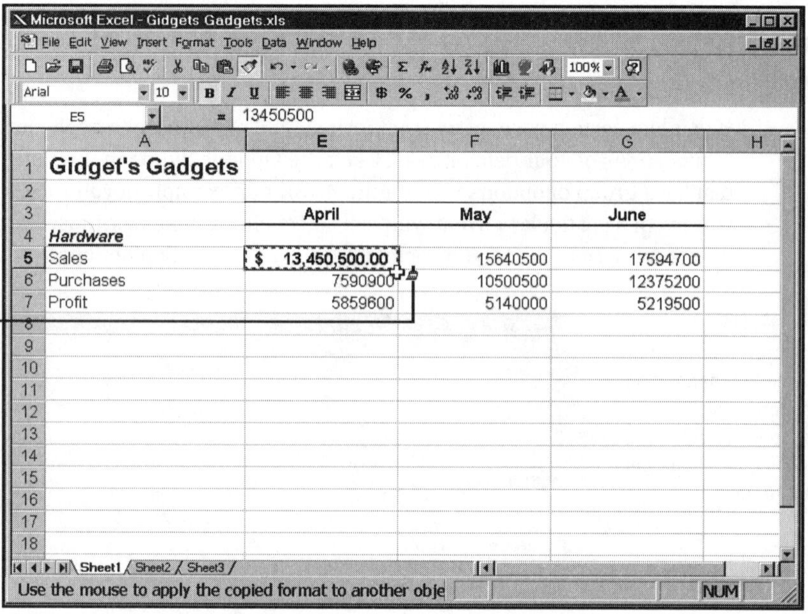

FIG. 4.19
Use the Format Painter tool to copy formatting from one cell or range to another.

To assign conditional formatting, use these steps:

1. Select the cell(s) containing the value or formula you want to format with conditional formatting.
2. Choose Format, Conditional Formatting. The Conditional Formatting dialog box appears, as shown in Figure 4.20.

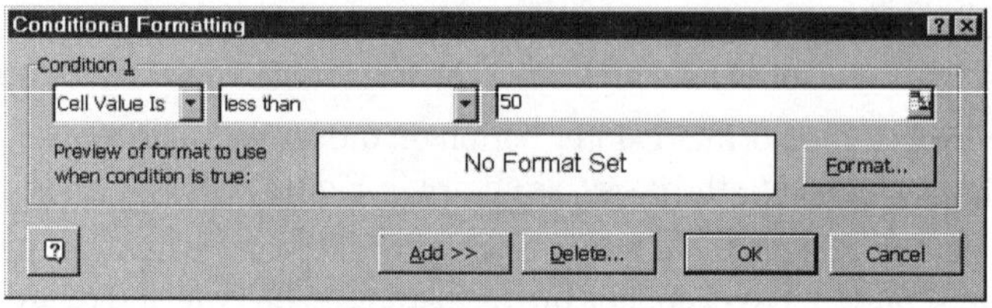

FIG. 4.20
Use the Conditional Formatting dialog box to specify conditional criteria.

3. Click the drop-down list at the far left end of the box and choose the Cell Value Is option. In most cases, that's the option you want to use—if the cell's formula produces a value, for example. However, if the cell contains a formula whose result is True or False, choose the Formula Is option.
4. Use the next drop-down list to designate an argument to activate the conditional format in the cell. Click the drop-down arrow to display the list of arguments. For example, to red flag the cell if the value falls below a particular number, select the Less Than option. Depending on the argument you select from the list, the remaining text boxes will vary.

5. In the remaining text boxes, finish entering the data to complete the condition for formatting the cell. In the example shown in Figure 4.20, to have Excel flag the cell if the value falls below (less than) 50, you would type 50 in the next text box.
6. To specify formatting for the cell, click the Format button.
7. The Format Cells dialog box appears (see Figure 4.21). Use the Font, Border, and Patterns tabs to change the formatting, such as cell shading or color. For example, if you want to format the cell with a color or pattern background, click the Patterns tab.

FIG. 4.21
Use the abbreviated Format Cells dialog box to format the conditional flag.

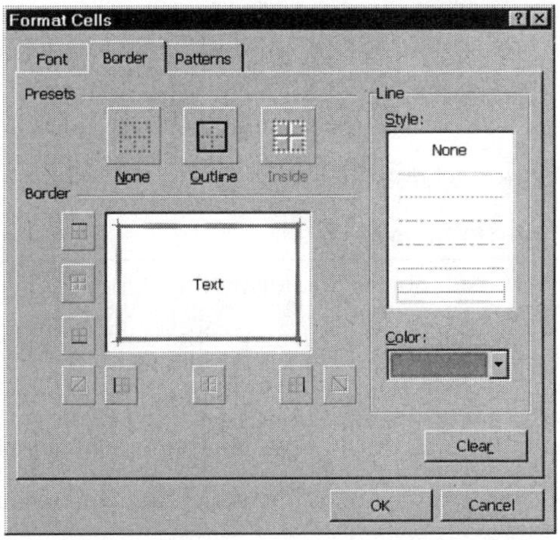

Part I Ch 4

NOTE When you use the Format Cells dialog box by clicking the Format button in the Conditional Formatting dialog box, only three formatting tabs appear (Font, Border, and Patterns); the regular Format Cells dialog box (Format, Cells) offers six tabs of formatting options.

8. To choose a background color from the Patterns tab, simply click a color in the palette. To choose a pattern, click the Pattern drop-down list and select a background pattern.
9. Use the Font tab to change the formatting of the font, such as to make it bold or another color.
10. Use the Border tab to set a line around the cell to draw attention to it, and then select a color if necessary.
11. When you finish assigning formatting, click OK. You're returned to the Conditional Formatting dialog box, where you can see a preview of the formatting you selected. Click OK to exit the dialog box.
12. Anytime the cell value meets the requirements for conditional formatting, Excel applies the formatting options you selected.

TIP To delete a conditional format, reopen the Conditional Formatting dialog box and click the Delete button. Then select the conditions you want to delete and click OK. Click OK again to exit the Conditional Formatting dialog box.

Mastering Number Formats

When you enter a number in Excel, it's entered as a plain number—25, for example. But that number can mean different things. For example, does 25 mean $25, .25, or 25%? The way you format a number changes its meaning. In your worksheet, you need to apply the appropriate number format so that the meaning of the numbers is clear.

The formatting of a number is called a *style*. By default, Excel assigns the General style to number entries, which has no specified formatting. There are ten other number styles you can apply to convey the meaning of values in a cell or range. You can also create your own number format to apply (see "Creating Custom Number Formats," later in this chapter). Table 4.2 lists each of the number styles you can use.

Table 4.2 Number Format Styles

Style	Description
General	Default, no specific formatting applied
Number	General number display with two default decimal places
Currency	Use to display monetary values
Accounting	Lines up currency symbols and decimal points in a column
Date	Displays date and time serial numbers as date values
Time	Displays date and time serial numbers as time values
Percentage	Multiplies cell value by 100 and displays percent sign
Fraction	Displays value as specified fraction
Scientific	Uses scientific or exponential notation
Text	Treats values as text
Special	Works with list and database values
Custom	Enables you to create your own custom format

Changing Number Formats with the Toolbar

The three most common number formats are available as toolbar buttons on the Formatting toolbar (Currency, Comma, and Percent).To quickly format an entry with one of those number styles, select the cell or range you want to change and do one of the following:

To use currency style, click the Currency Style button (or press Shift+Ctrl+$).

To use percent style, click the Percent Style button (or press Shift+Ctrl+%).

To use comma style, click the Comma Style button (or press Shift+Ctrl+!).

Excel applies the style. (Remember that if you don't like the outcome, you can use the Undo feature immediately after the action to remove the formatting.)

If necessary, change the number of decimals that appear by clicking the Increase Decimal or Decrease Decimal buttons on the toolbar (to the right of the Number format buttons).

NOTE If you see number signs (######) in a cell or range after formatting, you know the number with the new formatting is too wide to appear within the current column width. To resize a column, select the column and choose Format, Column, AutoFit Selection.

Changing Number Formats with the Format Cells Dialog Box

To assign a number format other than General (which is the default format), use the Format Cells dialog box. The Number tab, shown in Figure 4.22, lists each number style available and lets you view a sample of the style. With some of the styles, you can specify the number of decimal places displayed or how negative numbers appear.

To use the Format Cells dialog box to assign number formatting, follow these steps:

1. Select the cell or range you want to change.
2. Choose Format, Cells. Click the Number tab to bring it to the front.
3. In the Category list, click the category you want (see Figure 4.22).

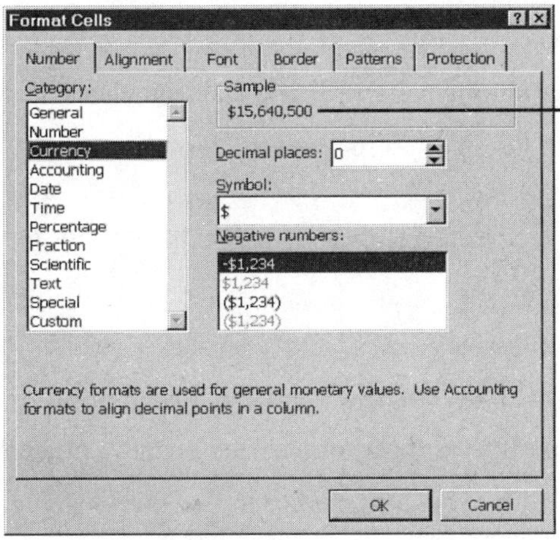

FIG. 4.22
Choose a number category, and additional options pertaining to that category appear.

4. Excel displays the styles and options for this category. If you select a format that requires you to specify additional options, make your selections. For example, if you choose the Currency category, you can designate the number of decimal points to be displayed, which dollar sign symbol to use, and how you want negative numbers displayed.
5. You can preview what the selected number style will look like in the Sample area of the Number tab. When you're satisfied with your choice, click OK to exit the box. Excel makes the number format change.

TIP Another way to display the Format Cells dialog box is to right-click over the selected cell or range and choose Format Cells from the shortcut menu.

Creating Custom Number Formats

If none of the predefined formats fits your needs, you can create your own custom format. For example, you may need a special numeric format for international currency or financial and scientific data. Elect a format that's close to what you want and then edit its code to match the custom format you want to create.

In order to create your own custom code, you will need to know a little about the symbols that define number formats. You can include up to four parts in a numeric format code: a positive number format, a negative number format, a format for zeroes, and a format for text. The parts are separated by semicolons. Take a look at this sample code:

```
$#,##0_);($#,##0)
```

Within each part, a code represents digits, or placeholders. Table 4.3 explains the most common digits used in a style.

Table 4.3 Numeric Formatting Codes

Code	Description
#	Placeholder for digits. If the digit is an insignificant zero, it does not appear.
0	Placeholder for digits. Zeroes appear. (For example, 9.5 in the format #.00 would display as 9.50.)
?	Placeholder for digits. Uses a space for insignificant zeroes.
.	Decimal point.
,	Thousands separator.
%	Percent sign. Excel multiplies entry by 100.
;	Separates positive number format from negative number format.
_	Skips the width of the next character. Use this to align positive numbers and negative numbers displayed in parentheses.

Code	Description
/	Use as a separator for fractions.
"text"	Use quotation marks to insert text you specify.
[color]	Use to format entry as a color you specify.
@	A placeholder where user-input text will appear.

In the sample code *$#,##0_);($#,##0)* the symbols _) following the positive number format inserts a space to the right of the last digit that's the same width as the right parenthesis. The reason for this code is to ensure that negative numbers, which are enclosed in parentheses, are aligned evenly with positive numbers. You can use the underscore code (_) to skip the width of any character following the underscore code.

To format data with color, use brackets and type the color name. For example, in our sample code *$#,##0_);($#,##0)*, you can add color codes at the beginning of each part to format the data in color. The color codes may look something like this:

```
[GREEN]$#,##0_);[RED]($#,##0)
```

According to the code above, the positive format data will appear in green and the negative format data will appear in red.

Remember dates and times can be treated as values, too, and you can customize how they appear in your worksheets. When you enter a format such as 5-15-98, Excel automatically knows it's a date and displays the entry in a date format, but it stores the entry as a serial number. If you enter 10:45, Excel displays the entry as a time format, but it stores the entry as a serial number. To create a custom date or time format, you need to know which date and time format codes to use. Table 4.4 lists the codes you can use.

Table 4.4 Date and Time Formatting Codes

Code	Description
m	Month as a number (1, 2, 3, and so on)
mm	Month as a number with leading zero (01, 02, and so on)
mmm	Month as three-letter abbreviation (Jan, Feb, Mar)
mmmm	Month as full name (January, February, March)
d	Day of month as a number (1, 13, 31)
dd	Day of month as a number with leading zero (01, 02, and so on)
ddd	Day of week with three-letter abbreviation (Mon, Tue, Wed)
dddd	Day of week as full name (Monday, Tuesday, Wednesday)
yy	Year as two digit number (97 for 1997, 98 for 1998)

continues

Table 4.4 Continued

Code	Description
yyyy	Year as full number (1998, 1999, 2000)
h	Hour as a number (1 for 1:00, and so on)
hh	Hour as a number with leading zero (01, 02, 03)
m	Minute as number (1, 10, 23)
mm	Minute as number with leading zero (01, 02, 03)
s	Seconds as number (1,12,45)
ss	Seconds as number with leading zero (01, 02, 03)
AM/PM	Indicates AM or PM time
A/P	Indicates AM or PM time

NOTE When entering time formats, Excel interprets any m character entered after an h character as minutes.

To create a custom number, date, or time format, follow these steps:

1. Select the cells or range you want to format.
2. Choose Format, Cells to display the Format Cells dialog box, then click the Number tab.
3. In the Category list box, select Custom.
4. If a format exists that closely matches the format you want to create, select it from the Type list.
5. The code is displayed in the Type text box. Make your edits to modify the format (see Figure 4.23).
6. Click OK, and Excel applies the custom format to the selected cells and adds it to the list of custom formats in the Format Cells dialog box.

To apply a custom format to other cells or ranges, select the cell or range, and then open the Format Cells dialog box. Click the Number tab and choose Custom in the Category list. The format code you defined will be listed with this category in the Type list box. Click it and click OK.

To remove a custom format, select it from the Type list box and click the Delete button.

Formatting with the Styles Dialog Box

To help speed up number formatting, try using Excel's Style dialog box. It contains a list of predefined number formats you can choose from, as explained in Table 4.5.

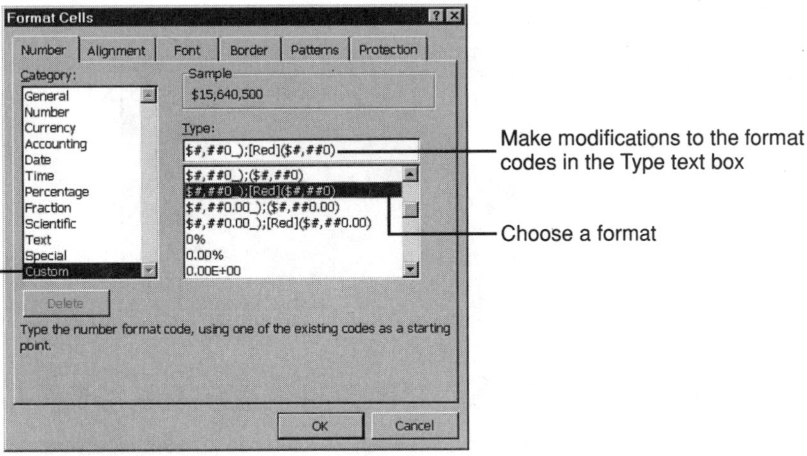

FIG. 4.23
Use the Custom format to create your own number format.

Table 4.5 Number Styles

Style	Description	Example
Comma	Adds commas to numbers with four or more digits and two decimal points.	5000 becomes 5,000.00
Comma (0)	Same as Comma style, but rounds decimals.	5000.75 becomes $5,001
Currency	Adds number signs to numbers, commas, and two decimal points.	5000 becomes $5,000
Currency (0)	Same as Currency style, but rounds decimals.	5000.75 becomes $5,001
Hyperlink	Formats text to Arial, 10-point type, blue, underline.	5000 becomes 5000
Normal	Applies default formatting.	5000 becomes 5000
Percent	Multiples by 100 and adds a percentage sign.	50 becomes 50%.

To assign a style, select the cell or range you want to format and choose Format, Style. This opens the Style dialog box, shown in Figure 4.24. From the Style Name drop-down list, select the style you want to use. Then click OK.

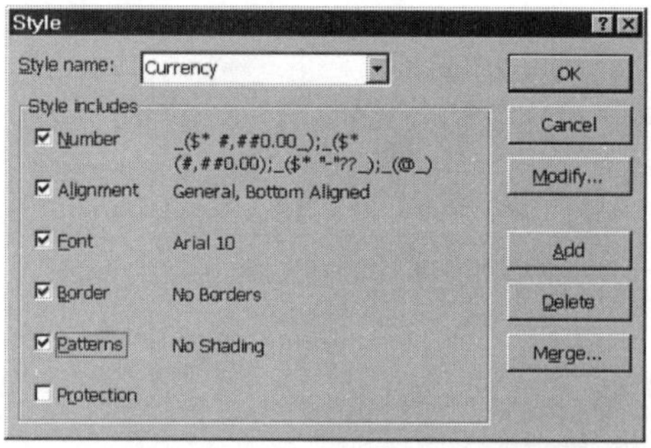

FIG. 4.24
You can assign Excel's preset styles using the Style dialog box.

Formatting with Borders, Patterns, and Colors

Use Excel's border, pattern, shading, and color features to apply formatting techniques that effect overall worksheet appearance. These features can help add emphasis to important data or add polish to a report. There are a variety of combinations you can create with borders, patterns, and colors to format cells, ranges, column headings, and more. For example, you can combine a border with a shaded background, or you can use a pattern background with color text. Remember to keep your combinations simple; too many formatting effects can make your data illegible.

Although many of these formatting features look their best when printed from a color printer, you can still benefit from the effects when printing in black and white. Take advantage of Excel's preview feature to see how formatting appears before you actually commit the worksheet to paper.

▶ **See** "Preview a Worksheet," **p. 166**

Adding Borders to Cells and Ranges

You can add a complete border to any cell or range, or you can add partial borders to one or more sides of a cell. You also can select from several line styles. For example, you can add a double-underline to your totals, or you can draw a thick outline around your headings to make them stand out.

To quickly add a border using the toolbar buttons, follow these steps:

1. Select the cell or range to which you want to add a border.

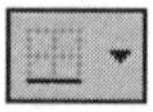

2. Click the Border drop-down arrow. Excel displays a palette of border styles, as shown in Figure 4.25.

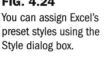

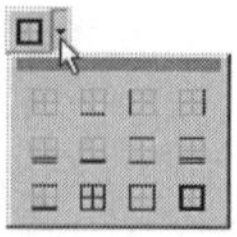

FIG. 4.25
Click the Border button's drop-down arrow to display a palette of border styles.

3. Click the style that represents the side(s) you want to border and the line style you want to use. Excel applies the border to the selected cells.

TIP If you use the toolbar button to apply a border, Excel remembers the last border style you used and applies it again. You can select a range and click the button to apply the same border to another selection.

TIP The Borders palette is one of Excel's tear-off palettes you can reposition on-screen as a floating palette.

▶ **See** "Working with Tear Off Palettes," **p. 32**

After you add a border, you can easily delete it at any time. To remove a border, select the cell or range again, click the Borders button and click the None option on the Borders palette. Excel removes the border. Remember that a cell or range can have a border on the left or right, the top or bottom, or on all four sides. If you can't find the border to turn off, try selecting the cell next to, above, or below the cell you *think* has the border.

For more border options, use the Format Cells dialog box. With the options in the Borders tab, you can customize the border you apply.

1. Select the cell or range you want to change.
2. Choose Format, Cells to display the Format Cells dialog box, and then select the Border tab to bring it to the front of the dialog box, as shown in Figure 4.26.

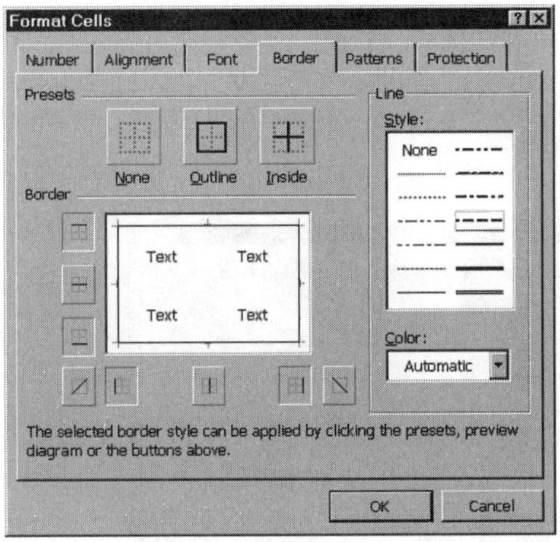

FIG. 4.26
The Border tab in the Format Cells dialog box lets you control which sides of the cell have borders.

3. In the Presets area, click the border style you want: None, Outline (all sides), Inside (inside lines only).
4. In the Line area, select a line style to use.
5. If you want to add color to the border, click the Color drop-down list and choose a color.

6. To customize which sides of the border are included, in the Border area click, the individual buttons representing the sides you want. Then preview how the border will look.
7. Click OK to exit the dialog box, and Excel applies the border.

Adding Patterns, Color, and Shading

You can add a pattern to a cell, or you can change the color of either the cell background or the cell contents. Keep in mind that data that appears in color will print in color only if you have a color printer.

If you don't have a color printer, you'll still be able to see a difference in background and pattern; however, it will print out as shades of gray. Use caution when assigning backgrounds and colors to your spreadsheet data. You still want the data to be readable, and if you choose too dark a color or too busy a pattern, the data may become illegible.

It's important to note that colors and backgrounds can greatly enhance the presentation of your data. You'll even find colors and backgrounds recommended by Excel's AutoFormat feature, which you learned about earlier in this chapter.

Adding Background Pattern and Color

To add a background pattern or color to your data, use Excel's Format Cells dialog box. You'll find plenty of pattern options to choose from, and when you combine them with colors, there's even more variety. Just remember that some patterns may affect the legibility of your cell contents.

1. Select the cell or range you want to change.
2. Choose Format, Cells to display the Format Cells dialog box, and then click the Pattern tab (see Figure 4.27).

FIG. 4.27
Use the Pattern tab to specify patterns for your cell or range backgrounds.

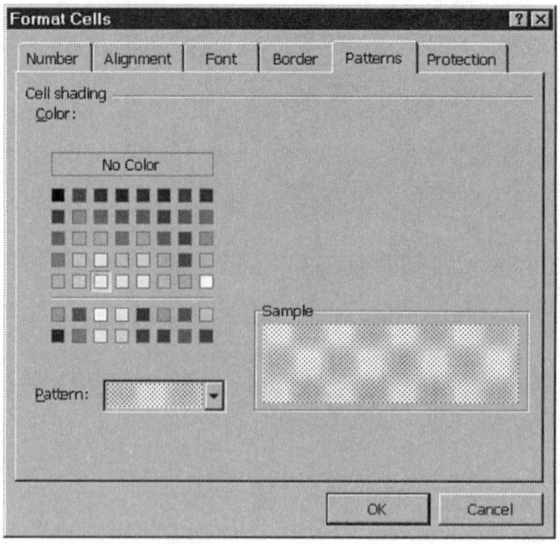

3. Click the Pattern drop-down arrow and select a pattern. The Sample area shows a preview of the selected pattern.
4. To add color to the selected pattern, choose a color from the Color palette.
5. Click OK, and Excel applies the pattern to the selected cells.

Changing Background Color with the Toolbar

A fast way to add a background color to your worksheet cells is to use the Fill Color button on the Formatting toolbar. The Fill Color button displays a palette of colors you can use, plus it's one of Excel's tear-off palettes that you can reposition anywhere on-screen.

1. Select the cell or range you want to change.

2. Click the Fill Color drop-down arrow.
3. Click a color in the palette, and Excel applies the background color.

You can also change background color shading using the Format Cells dialog box and the Patterns tab, as explained in the previous steps.

Changing the Text Color

In addition to changing the cell background, you can change the color of cell contents. Ideally, colors work best with color printers, but you can still use colors to alter the appearance of your data even without a color printer. The colors you select will appear as varying shades of gray.

The fastest way to change the color of your cell's contents is to use the Font Color button on the Formatting toolbar. Like the Pattern and Fill Color buttons, the Font Color button displays a tear-off palette you can reposition around the screen.

1. Select the cell or range you want to change.

2. Click the Font Color drop-down arrow. You see a palette of colors, as shown in Figure 4.28.
3. Click the color you want to use, and Excel changes the text color in the cell or cells.

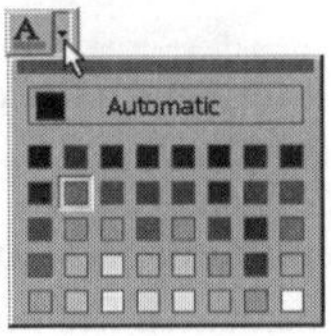

FIG. 4.28
Use the Font Color palette to change your data's color.

You can also change text or number color using the Format Cells dialog box. Select the Font tab and use the Color drop-down list to choose a different text color.

▶ **See** "Working with Tear Off Palettes," **p. 32**

Formatting Columns and Rows

Another way of formatting your worksheet is to manipulate the appearance of columns and rows. You can easily change the size of columns and rows and insert new columns and rows as needed. You can also choose to hide data you want to keep confidential by hiding columns and rows, or you can merge the data from several cells into one. Making an adjustment to a column or row can greatly improve the appearance of your data.

For example, in a new worksheet, all the columns are the same size. As you enter data, you'll find that this size isn't going to work for all your entries. You may have an entry that is too big. When you enter a long entry, several things can happen. If it's text that is too long, Excel truncates the entry. If it's a number that is too long, Excel displays number signs (#####) in the cell. In these instances, you can widen the column to make more room for your data.

In some cases, you may have a really short column that contains as few as two or three characters. In this case, you can narrow the column to avoid wasting the space.

When resizing columns and rows, keep the following tips and shortcuts in mind:

- You can change the width of several columns or rows at once by selecting the ones you want to change. Then drag one border to change them all. To select non-adjacent columns, hold down the Ctrl key while selecting columns.
- To have Excel adjust the column width to fit the largest entry in that column, double-click the right column border next to the column letter.
- Want Excel to fit your data into the column for you? Select the cell or column, choose Format, Column, AutoFit Selection. Excel fits the column to the longest entry.
- If you change the column width and then want to return to the default width, choose Format, Column, Standard Width, and click OK.

NOTE To insert a new column or row, select the row or column next to where you want the new row or column inserted. Then choose Insert, Rows or Insert, Columns.

Changing Column Width

You can adjust column width with the mouse or the Column Width dialog box. Follow these steps to manually adjust the column width with the mouse pointer:

1. Point to the right column heading border. The pointer changes to a thick line with arrows on either side of it (see Figure 4.29). This indicates the pointer is in the right place.
2. Hold down the mouse button and drag to a new width (expressed in points). As you drag, you see an outline of the column border. A measurement of the width appears as a ScreenTip near the pointer.
3. When the column reaches the width you want, release the mouse button. Excel adjusts the width.

FIG. 4.29
To adjust the column width or row height, drag the appropriate border.

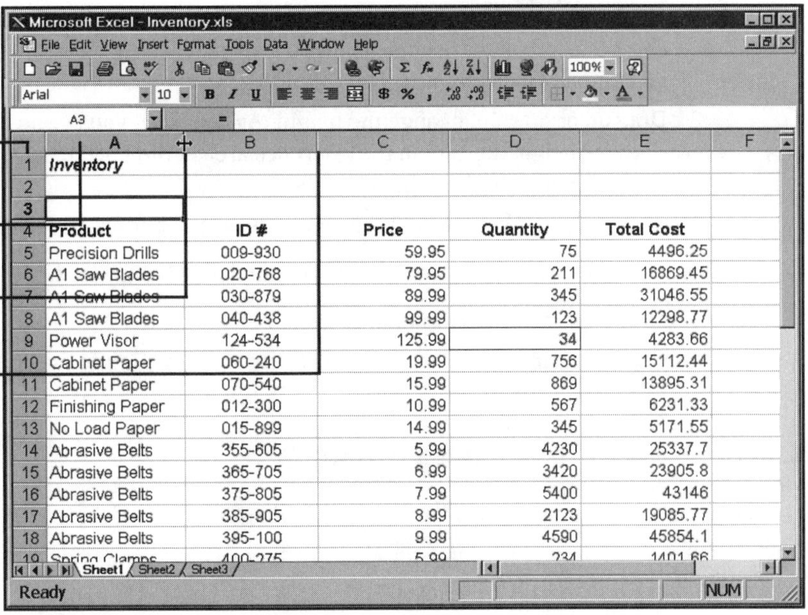

To specify an exact width, use the Column Width dialog box as explained here:

1. Select the column(s) you want to change.
2. Choose Format, Column, Width. This opens the Column Width dialog box, shown in Figure 4.30.

FIG. 4.30
The Column Width dialog box lets you specify an exact column width measurement.

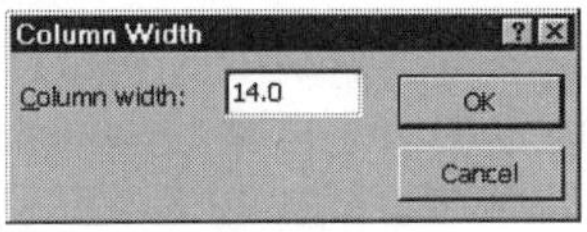

3. Type a width in the Column Width box.
4. Click OK, and Excel adjusts the column to the measurement you specified.

To let Excel automatically adjust the column width to fit the widest cell contents, use the AutoFit Selection command. Choose Format, Column, AutoFit Selection.

Changing Row Height

You can adjust row height with the mouse pointer on-screen, or you can use the Row Height dialog box. Follow these steps to manually adjust the row height with the mouse pointer:

1. Point to the border below the row number that you want to change. The pointer will change to a thick horizontal line with arrows on either side of it. This indicates the pointer is in the right place.
2. Drag up or down to change the height. As you drag, you see an outline of the row border. The row height appears in the reference area of the Formula Bar, as well as in a ScreenTip next to the pointer.
3. Stop dragging the mouse. When you release the button, Excel adjusts the row height.

To specify an exact height, use the Row Height dialog box instead.

1. Select the row(s) you want to change.
2. Choose Format, Row, Height. This opens the Row Height dialog box, shown in Figure 4.31.

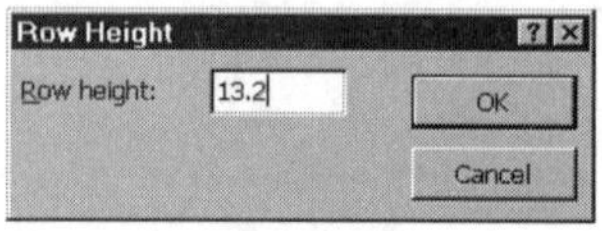

FIG. 4.31
The Row Height dialog box lets you specify an exact row height measurement.

3. Type a height in the Row Height box.
4. Click OK, and the Excel adjusts the row to the measurement you specified.

To let Excel automatically adjust the row height to fit the tallest cell contents, use the AutoFit command. Choose Format, Row, AutoFit.

Hiding Columns and Rows

If you plan to share your worksheets with other users, you may want to hide confidential information from view. You can also hide columns and rows before printing your workbook so that the confidential data doesn't appear on the printout. There are a couple of ways to hide a column or row.

To quickly hide a column, drag the right border past the left. To quickly hide a row, drag the bottom border up past the top. To unhide the data, move the pointer so it touches the column or row border, and then drag the border to the right or down to display the column or row again.

Another way to hide a column or row is with the Hide command. Use these steps:

1. Select the column(s) or row(s) you want to hide.
2. To hide a column, choose Format, Column, Hide. To hide a row, choose Format, Row, Hide. Excel hides the column or row you specified.

To unhide your data, choose Format, Column, Unhide or Format, Row, Unhide.

Merging Cells in Columns or Rows

You can use the Alignment tab in the Format Cells dialog box to merge cells in your worksheets. To merge cells, follow these steps:

1. Select the cells or range you want to merge.
2. Choose Format, Cells to display the Format Cells dialog box, and then click the Alignment tab (see Figure 4.32).

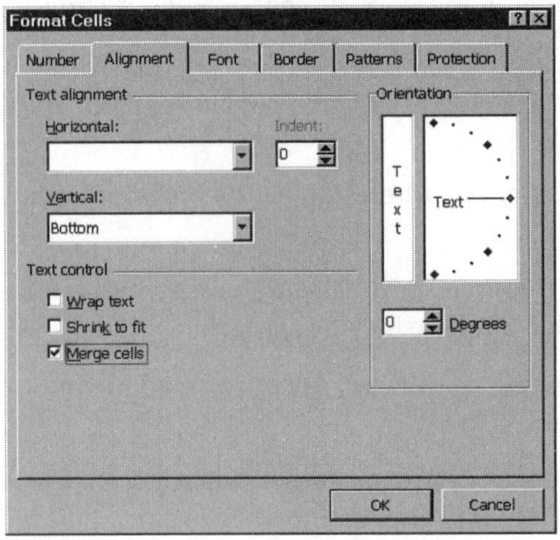

FIG. 4.32
Open the Format Cells dialog box to the Alignment tab and choose the Merge Cells command.

3. Select the Merge Cells check box.
4. Click OK, and Excel merges the selected cells into one.

In addition to merging cells, you can also join the contents of two cells—a process that's called *concatenation*. For example, you may want the text "Amount Owed" in cell E70 joined with the dollar amount in G74. Instead of typing the text, you can concatenate it with the concatenation operator (&). The entry may look something like this:

=E70&TEXT(E12,"$#,##0")

The end result in the cell you select would look something like this:

Amount Owed $5,250

▶ **See** "Creating Custom Number Formats," **p. 156**

Common Problems and Solutions

When you start changing the way your data appears, formatting problems may arise. This list outlines some of the formatting glitches you might run into and possible solutions you can try.

After I add formatting to a cell, number signs appear.

Your cell is too narrow to display the data. Widen the column by selecting Format, Column, AutoFit Selection.

When I apply an AutoFormat the titles suddenly make the column widths too wide.

Try centering the titles across cells instead. See the instructions under "Center a Heading," earlier in this chapter.

When I select AutoFormat, a message appears saying it cannot detect a table around the active cell.

You've selected a single cell instead of a range. AutoFormat won't work unless you select more than one cell.

I centered text across cells, but when I select the cell containing the title, it doesn't appear.

You're probably selecting the wrong cell. If the title is centered across a range, you may need to click the cell to the far left of where the title appears.

I tried to center a title using the Center Across Selection command, but it won't center.

Perhaps one of the cells you're centering across has data or even a space character. Select the cell and press Delete, and then try to center the title again.

I've rotated the text in a cell, and now it isn't completely visible.

You need to adjust the row's height. Select Format, Row, AutoFit, or choose the Height command and specify a larger row height.

I tried to create a custom number format for international currency by modifying the settings in my Control Panel, but now all the currency formats have changed.

To create a custom number format for international currency in Excel, you don't need to change the settings in the Windows Control Panel. Instead, select the Custom category from the Number tab in the Format Cells dialog box (as explained in the section "Creating a Custom Number Format," earlier in this chapter) and enter the code for the currency symbol you want to use.

I'm having trouble seeing the borders I've added to my cells.

It's easier to view border formatting if you turn off Excel's worksheet gridlines. To do so, choose Tools, Options, and then deselect the Gridlines check box.

I changed the color format for a cell, and now I can't see the entry.

You may have selected a background color that's the same as the cell entry color. Try another color for the background, or change the color of the cell entry text.

I can't seem to unhide a column.

If you're having trouble unhiding a column by dragging its border, select that column and the columns on either side, and then choose Format, Column, Standard Width. Click OK. Then you should be able to resize the column as needed.

From Here...

In this chapter, you learned how to apply Excel's formatting tools to improve the appearance of your worksheet data. The next two chapters focus on printing your worksheets and learning more about Excel functions.

- Chapter 5, "Printing Worksheets," shows you how to use Excel's many print features and add additional page layout elements to better organize and present your data.
- Chapter 6, "Using Excel Functions," explains Excel's functions in detail, showing you how to construct function arguments, use the Function Palette, and troubleshoot function errors.

CHAPTER 5

Printing Worksheets

by Sherry Kinkoph

All roads inevitably lead to printing; it's the easiest way to share your data. While printing an Excel worksheet only takes a simple click, there are quite a few additional printing options available and formatting features you can use to improve the appearance of your worksheet pages.

In this chapter, you'll learn how to preview your worksheet pages before committing them to paper. Find out if your data is legible and if you've used the appropriate fonts and sizes. Learn to change page margins, paper size, and printer setup options. Add headers and footers to your worksheets to identify page contents, and use Excel's page break features to control how your data prints out.

Printing and previewing worksheets

Learn how to print and preview a worksheet, print selected ranges, and change the default printer.

Setting up worksheet pages with Page Setup

Use Excel's Page Setup dialog box to control how your pages are layed out, paper size and orientation, margins, scaling, and more.

Creating headers and footers

Give your printouts headers and footers to easily identify worksheet contents and keep your pages organized.

Mastering Excel's page break features

Discover how to use the new Page Break Preview command to view and manipulate page breaks on-screen, plus insert manual page breaks to adjust how your worksheet pages print.

Preview a Worksheet

When you are working in a worksheet, you see only a small part of the sheet in the Excel window. You can't tell how the whole page looks or how the fonts and sizes will appear on the printed page. In Excel's preview mode, you see a full-page view of the file. You can examine how each worksheet page looks before ever committing a single piece of data to paper.

To open Excel's Preview window, click the Print Preview button on the Standard toolbar, or choose File, Print Preview. The Preview window appears, as shown in Figure 5.1. You can click any of the toolbar buttons on the Preview toolbar to adjust your preview of the worksheet. Table 5.1 explains each of the Preview buttons and their function.

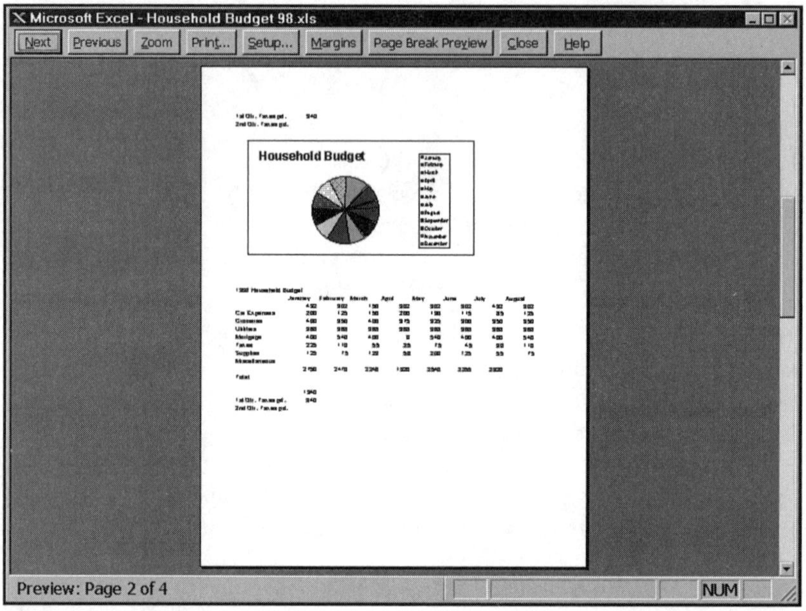

FIG. 5.1
Excel's Print Preview window lets you see what your entire worksheet looks like before printing.

Table 5.1 Print Preview Buttons

Button	Function
	Displays the next page. If your worksheet uses more than one page, you can click this button to view other pages.
	Displays the previous page. Click this button to go back and view the previous page (if your worksheet uses multiple pages).
	Makes the preview screen larger. Click the button again to return to the original size. You can do the same thing by clicking the mouse on the worksheet. (The pointer should look like a magnifying glass when you point to the worksheet.)

Button	Function
Print...	Prints the worksheet.
Setup...	Displays the Page Setup dialog box where you can make changes to the layout of the page.
Margins	Displays on-screen margin indicators. You can then drag the margin indicators (see Figure 5.2) to change the margins. The margin markers look like black squares; column markers look like black Ts.
Page Break Preview	Lets you designate page breaks within your worksheets.
Close	Closes the preview window.
Help	Displays help information about preview.

NOTE If you're looking for more control of the zoom, use the Zoom command in the Excel window. You can quickly zoom a worksheet using the Zoom button on the toolbar, or if you want to customize your zoom percentage, use the View menu and select the Zoom command. When you select the Zoom command, you choose the zoom percentage you want. To return to the regular view, select the Zoom command and set the zoom to 100%.

FIG. 5.2
Use the column markers to change column widths and margin markers to adjust the page margins.

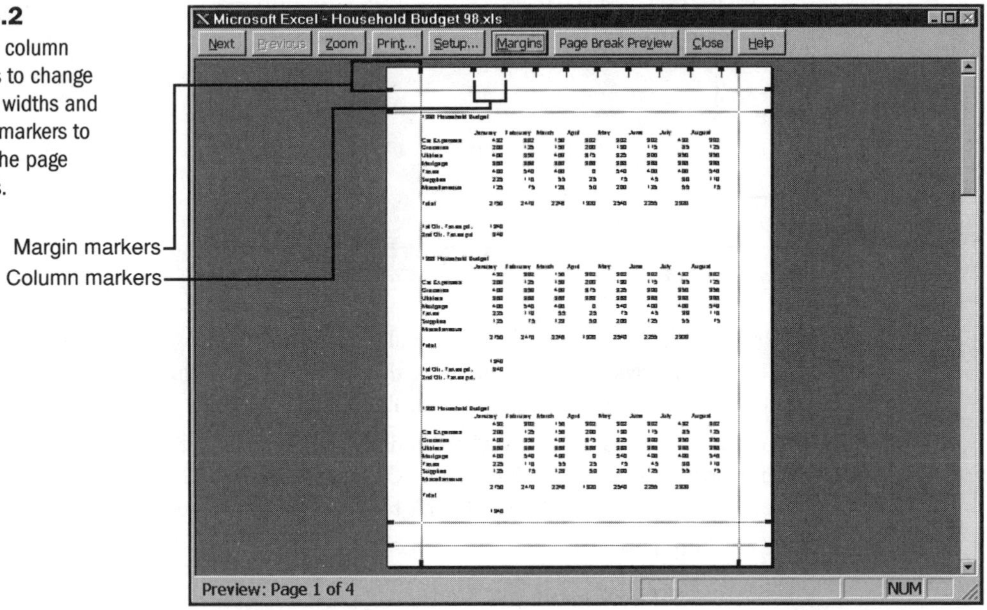

▶ **See** "Changing Margins," **p. 171**
▶ **See** "Mastering Excel's Page Break Features," **p. 180**

Printing Files

All your hard work pays off when you can print your final worksheet. You may want to print a copy to review and mark up editing changes, or you may print a copy to distribute to others.

To print an entire file, you can simply click the Print button. This instructs Excel to immediately start printing one copy of the entire file. To print only certain pages or selected text in a file, to print multiple copies, or to control how the file is printed, you'll need to use the Print dialog box.

Follow these steps to print from the Print dialog box:

1. Choose File, Print to open the Print dialog box. (If you want to print only the contents of a single cell or range, first select the cell or range before opening the Print dialog box.)
2. Under the Print Range options, select which pages to print. To print the entire file, select All. To print a particular page or range of pages, select Page(s) and use the From and To boxes to identify the pages to print. You can type in the page numbers or use the spin arrows to set the exact page numbers (see Figure 5.3).

FIG. 5.3
Use the Print dialog box to set your print options.

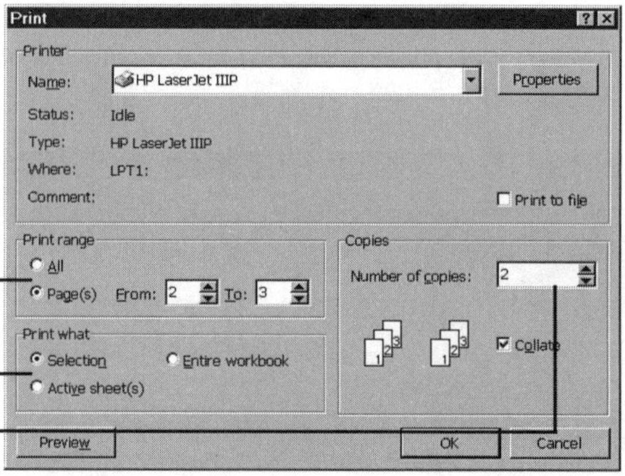

3. If you're printing just one copy of the file, make sure the Number of Copies box under the Copies options says 1. If you want more than one copy, type the number of copies you want or use the spin arrows to set a number.
4. To print certain portions of your worksheet data, use the Print What options. Choose Selection to print the selected cell or range. Choose Active Sheet(s) to print only the active worksheet. Choose Entire Workbook to print each worksheet in the file.
5. Click the OK button to print.

If you haven't previewed the file yet, select the Preview button to display the file in Excel's Preview window. To exit the window, click Close.

Click the Properties button in the Print dialog box to open the Properties dialog box shown in Figure 5.4. Here you'll find options for changing paper size, orientation, and paper source (which you can use to change which printer paper tray is used). If you select any of the options in the Properties dialog box, those selections are used for every application, not just Excel. For example, if you change the paper size, the new size becomes the default for every program. If you only want to change the paper size used for the current file, use Excel's Page Setup dialog box instead. (You learn how to use the Page Setup dialog box in the following section.)

▶ **See** "Report Manager," **p. 228**

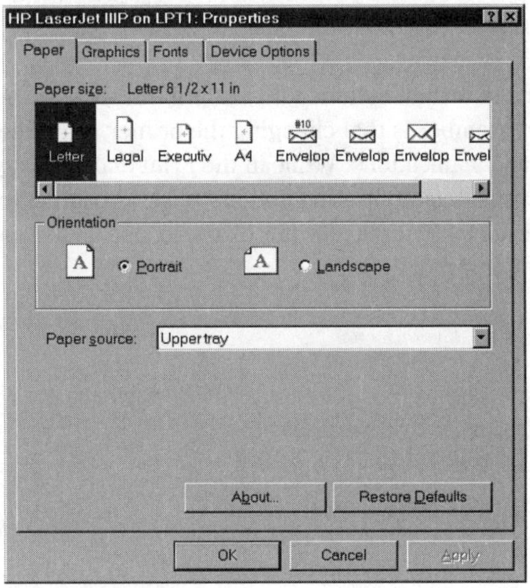

FIG. 5.4
Use the Properties dialog box to change the default paper size and the orientation settings.

Changing the Default Printer

Microsoft Office 97 applications, including Excel, always print to the default printer. In some situations, you may have more than one printer available, and you can select which printer is the default. For example, if you work in an office and are hooked up to a network, you may be able to select which network printer you want to use. If you work at home, you may have a printer and a computer fax machine. Your computer treats the fax machine like a printer; to fax something, you select the fax as a printer source and to print a worksheet, you select the printer.

You can control which printer you use in the Print dialog box (see Figure 5.5). In this dialog box, you'll find controls for determining which printer to use, as well as other printing options.

FIG. 5.5
Use the Print dialog box to designate which printer to use.

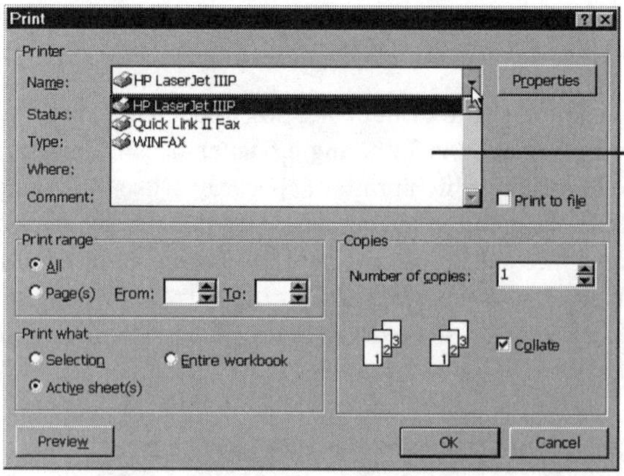

You also can change certain default options for your printer, such as the page size and orientation. What you want to remember is that changing the printer setup this way changes the options for all documents and applications. While in the Print dialog box, you can choose the Properties button to change default printing options, such as page orientation. If you want to change the page orientation for just one file (for example, use landscape for a worksheet), use the Page Setup command instead.

CAUTION

Remember that once you change the default, all Microsoft Office applications will use this default printer—even if you didn't change the printer in that application.

To select a printer, follow these steps:

1. Choose File, Print to open the Print dialog box (refer to Figure 5.5).
2. Under the Printer options, select a printer name from the Name drop-down list.
3. Click OK to print to the printer you selected. To close the dialog box without printing, choose Cancel.

The next time you go to print, the printer you selected in step 2 will be the default printer.

Setting Up Worksheet Pages with Page Setup

Excel's Page Setup dialog box has four tabs, each with a set of options that affect page layout. Use these options to fine tune your worksheet before printing. For example, you may want to change the page margins, paper size and orientation, or add titles that repeat on every page.

- The Page tab has options for controlling paper size, print quality, and page orientation for the current worksheet.
- The Margins tab lets you specify top, bottom, left, and right margins.

- The Header/Footer tab lets you create headers and footers to print on each worksheet page.
- The Sheet tab has options for printing titles, changing print order, and other sheet-related options.

In this section and the following section, you'll learn how to apply these page layout options to your own worksheets.

Changing Margins

By default, Excel uses a one-inch top and bottom margin and a .75-inch left and right margin. Headers and footers have a .5-inch margin (learn more about adding headers and footers in the next section). All margins are measured in inch-increments, from the edge of the paper inward. For your worksheet, you may want to use bigger or smaller margins. Often you can keep your data from spilling over to a second page by simply adjusting the margins. Some printers are incapable of printing to the edge of the paper, so you may need to set the margins accordingly.

You can change any of the margins using the Margins tab in the Page Setup dialog box. If you prefer to see the effects of the changes as you make them, you can modify the margins in Print Preview, covered earlier in this chapter.

Follow these steps to change margins:

1. Choose File, Page Setup. This opens the Page Setup dialog box.
2. Click the Margins tab to bring it to the front of the dialog box, as shown in Figure 5.6. In the middle of the Margins tab is a sample page surrounded by spin boxes for controlling top, left, right, and bottom margins (as well as headers and footers).

FIG. 5.6
Select the Margins tab in the Page Setup dialog box and modify margin settings you want to apply to the current worksheet file.

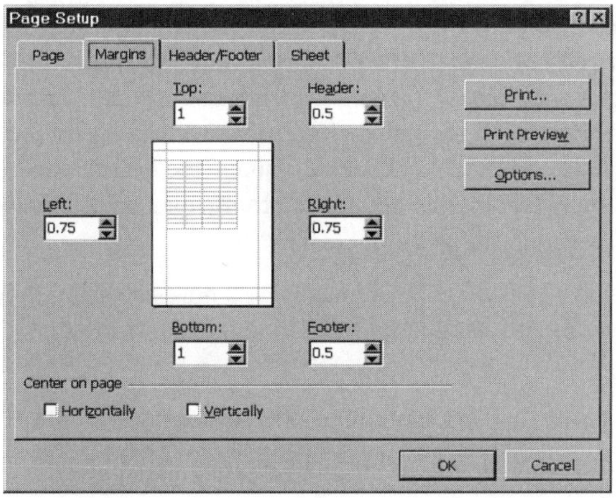

3. To change a margin, click in the appropriate spin box you want to change and then delete and retype the entry, or use the arrows to edit the existing entry. For example, to adjust the top margin, type a new setting in the Top text box or use the arrow buttons to change the setting.

4. If you want to change the header or footer margin, click in the Header or Footer spin box and then delete and retype the entry, or edit the existing entry using the up/down arrows.
5. At the bottom of the Margins tab are options for centering the worksheet on the printed page. Use the Horizontally option to center the worksheet horizontally; use the Vertically option to center the worksheet vertically on the page.
6. Check the sample area, then click OK to exit the dialog box. Excel makes the changes.
7. (Optional) You can print your worksheet with the new margins by clicking the Print button in the Page Setup dialog box. This opens the Print dialog box. Click OK to continue printing.

In the worksheet, you won't notice the changes, but if you click the Print Preview button on the Standard toolbar, you can preview the worksheet to see the changes. To preview the settings before clicking OK and exiting the Page Setup dialog box, select the Print Preview button. This opens the file in the Preview window and shows you how the margin changes effect your worksheet. To close the window again and return to the Page Setup dialog box, click Close.

NOTE If you can't get your printout to look right on the page, try centering it. Select the Horizontally check box in the Page Setup dialog box to center the page horizontally (across). Select the Vertically check box to center the page vertically (up and down). You can use both methods on a single page.

Changing Paper Size or Orientation

Depending on the placement of your data, your worksheet may be wider than tall or taller than wide. Use the paper orientation options to print the data to its best advantage. The Portrait option lets you print down the longest edge of the paper. If you're using a standard 8½ × 11 paper size, the Portrait option prints across the 8" width and down the 11½" length. The Landscape option lets you print across the widest length of the paper; across the 11½" width and down the 8" length. Both of these options let you take advantage of the long and short lengths of an 8½ × 11 paper size (letter size), which is usually the default paper size most people use. However, you can apply these same options to other paper sizes handled by your printer, too, such as legal size paper.

You can easily change the paper size or customize a new size using the options found in the Page tab of the Page Setup dialog box. Depending on your printer type, the choice of paper sizes may vary.

To change the paper size and orientation, use these steps:

1. Choose File, Page Setup to open the Page Setup dialog box.
2. Click the Page tab to bring it to the front of the dialog box, as shown in Figure 5.7.
3. Under Orientation, select the paper orientation option you wish to use: Portrait or Landscape.

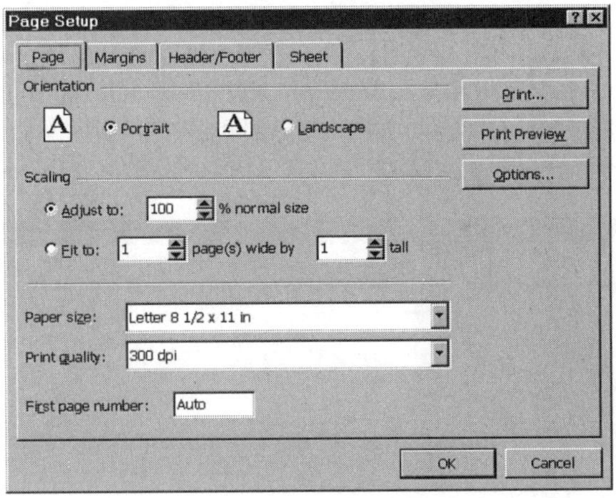

FIG. 5.7
Change paper size and orientation for the current file by selecting from the options in the Page tab of the Page Setup dialog box.

4. To change the paper size, use the Paper Size drop-down arrow to display a list of sizes to choose from.
5. Click OK to exit.

Instead of closing the dialog box, you can print the file immediately using the new settings you assigned. Click the Print button to open the Print dialog box; then click OK to begin printing. To preview the new settings, click the Print Preview button in the Page Setup dialog box. This file opens in Excel's Preview window (click Close to exit).

TIP If you select the Options button from any of the four Page Setup tabs, the Properties dialog box (refer to Figure 5.4) appears. Any changes you make in the Properties dialog box become the default settings for every application.

CAUTION

To change the default paper size and orientation, use the Print dialog box instead of the Page Setup dialog box. The Page Setup dialog box lets you set controls for the current workbook. Use the Print dialog box to set default printing options for Excel and other programs.

Scaling Data to Fit on a Page

If you're having trouble fitting all of your data onto one page, you can fudge a few things to help with the layout. Adjusting margins can help you make more use of a page, and adjusting column widths and row heights can save some space too. Other tricks include decreasing the font size or trying a more condensed font style. If none of these options help, try using the scaling options found on the Page tab in the Page Setup dialog box (refer to Figure 5.7).

To fit more of a worksheet onto the page, use the Adjust to or Fit to options. To scale the worksheet to a percentage of its full size, enter a size in the Adjust To text box or use the spin arrows to enter a new setting. Any number you enter less than 100 will reduce the page to that percentage. For example, if you enter 50 in the Adjust To box, the page is reduced by 50%. Figure 5.8 shows an example of a three-page worksheet scaled to 50% to fit onto one page.

FIG. 5.8
Use Excel's scaling options to fit data from multiple pages onto a single page.

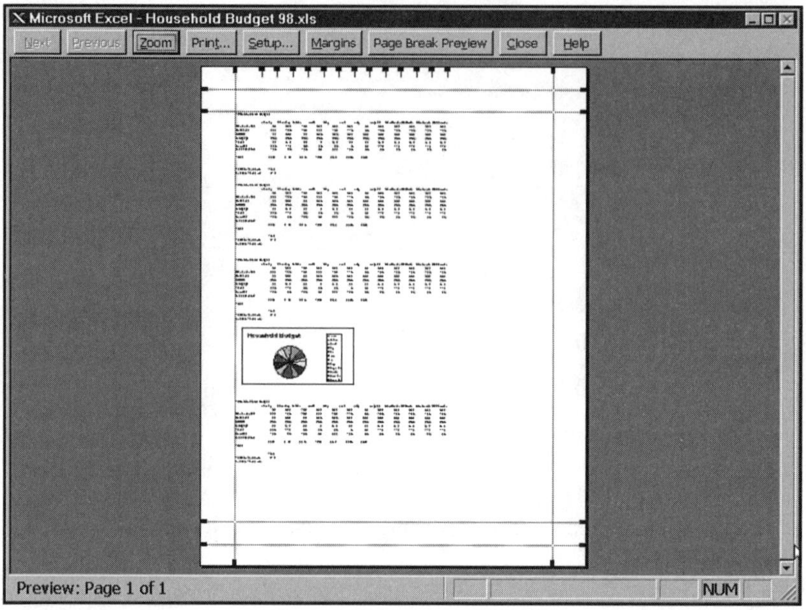

To instruct Excel to fit the worksheet onto a specified number of pages, use the Fit To option on the Page tab (refer to Figure 5.7). In the first text box, choose how many pages to fit to. This number will represent the number of page widths. In the second text box, enter the number of pages tall to fit the document to. For example, to fit a two-page worksheet onto one page, each text box should specify the value 1. To fit a four-page worksheet onto two pages, the values in each box will be 2.

CAUTION

If your printer doesn't support scalable fonts or TrueType fonts, you won't be able to use Page Setup's scaling options. Be sure to check your printer documentation to find out what fonts are supported.

Setting Up Repeating Titles

To help keep your printouts organized, add titles to print on every page. You can repeat row or column titles on each page using the Sheet tab in the Page Setup dialog box. To set up repeating titles, follow these steps:

1. Choose File, Page Setup to open the Page Setup dialog box.
2. Click the Sheet tab to bring it to the front of the dialog box, as shown in Figure 5.9.

FIG. 5.9
To set repeating titles, use the Sheet tab in the Page Setup dialog box.

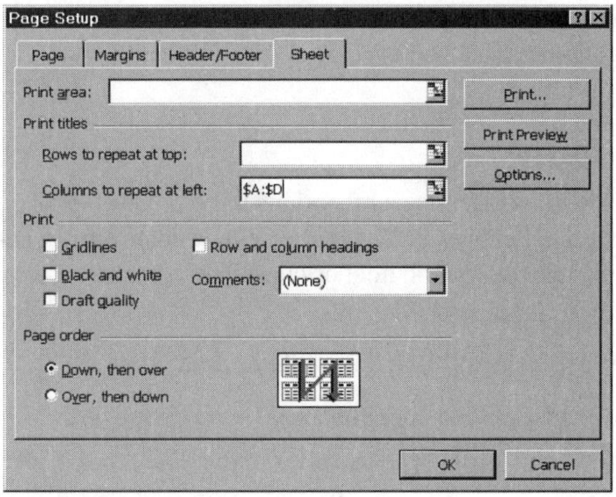

3. To set repeating row titles, click inside the Rows to Repeat at Top text box. To set column titles, click inside the Columns to Repeat at Left text box.
4. On the worksheet, select the row or column titles to use (they must be adjacent). If the Page Setup dialog box is in the way, click the Collapse Dialog button at the end of the row or column text box, then select the titles in the worksheet. To return to the Page Setup dialog box, click the Expand Dialog button. (If you know the range you want to print, you can enter its cell references into the appropriate text box, too.)
5. Click OK to exit.

When you print the worksheet, the titles will print out on each page. To remove the titles, re-open the Page Setup dialog box to the Sheet tab and clear the appropriate text box.

TIP To control which page starts printing page numbers, enter a page number in the First Page Number text box on the Page tab of the Page Setup dialog box.

Printing Gridlines

By default, Excel's gridlines do not print out along with the data. In most instances, you wouldn't want the gridlines to appear on your printouts. However, if you're working with an exceptionally long database or list of values, you may want gridlines printed on the pages to help with the legibility of the data.

To setup your pages to print with gridlines, use these steps:

1. Choose File, Page Setup to open the Page Setup dialog box.
2. Click the Sheet tab to bring it to the front of the dialog box (refer to Figure 5.9).

3. Under the Print options, select the Gridlines check box.
4. Click OK to exit.

TIP To turn off the gridlines while working on your Excel worksheets, select Tools, Options, display the View tab, and deselect the Gridlines check box.

Changing Print Quality

The Page Setup dialog box offers several options to help you control print quality and the time it takes to printout a file. If, for example, you're using a color printer and want to avoid the time it takes to print out a full-color worksheet or chart, you can choose to print only in black and white or draft mode.

Follow these steps to change to black and white or draft quality:

1. Choose File, Page Setup to open the Page Setup dialog box.
2. Click the Sheet tab to bring it to the front of the dialog box (refer to Figure 5.9).
3. Under the Print options, select the Black and White or Draft Quality check box.
4. Click OK to exit.

TIP If you need any cell comment notes printed out, use the Sheet tab to specify whether to print the comments where they fall in the worksheet or print them at the end of the printout. Use the Comments drop-down list to make your selection.

To avoid some of the time spent printing high-quality graphics and fancy fonts, switch to a lower print quality. Depending on your printer, you may have options for printing in draft quality, others may let you specify how many dots-per-inch, or dpi, are printed on a page. Naturally, the higher the dpi, the longer it takes to print the file out. The previous steps showed you how to set the file for draft quality; these steps show you how to change the Print Quality setting.

1. Choose File, Page Setup to open the Page Setup dialog box.
2. Click the Page tab to bring it to the front of the dialog box.
3. Display the Print Quality drop-down list and choose a dpi setting.
4. Click OK to exit.

Defining a Print Area

Unless you tell Excel differently, your entire worksheet is printed when you choose the Print command. You can select a specific range to print and use the Selection option in the Print dialog box to print it out. But if you find yourself printing the same range over and over, you may want to define the print area so you don't have to keep selecting the same printing options repeatedly. When you define a range as a print area, only the print area prints out when you go to print the worksheet.

To define a print area, use these steps:

1. Choose File, Page Setup to open the Page Setup dialog box.
2. Click the Sheet tab to bring it to the front of the dialog box.
3. Click in the Print Area text box.
4. Select the range of cells you want to define as the print area. If you know the range references, you can type them into the text box. If not, click the Collapse Dialog button at the far right end of the Print Area text box and use the mouse pointer to select the cells in the worksheet. Click the Expand Dialog button to reopen the Page Setup dialog box.
5. Click OK to exit.

TIP Another way to define a print area is with the File menu. Select the range you want to use, choose File, Print Area, Set Print Area.

After defining the print area, you'll notice it's marked with dashed lines on the worksheet, as shown in Figure 5.10. The range is now named *Print_Area*, and it is listed in the Name drop-down box. Excel's gridlines make it rather hard to see the dashed lines. To turn off the gridlines, choose Tools, Options, display the General tab, and deselect the Gridlines check box.

FIG. 5.10
A defined print range appears surrounded with dashed lines in the worksheet.

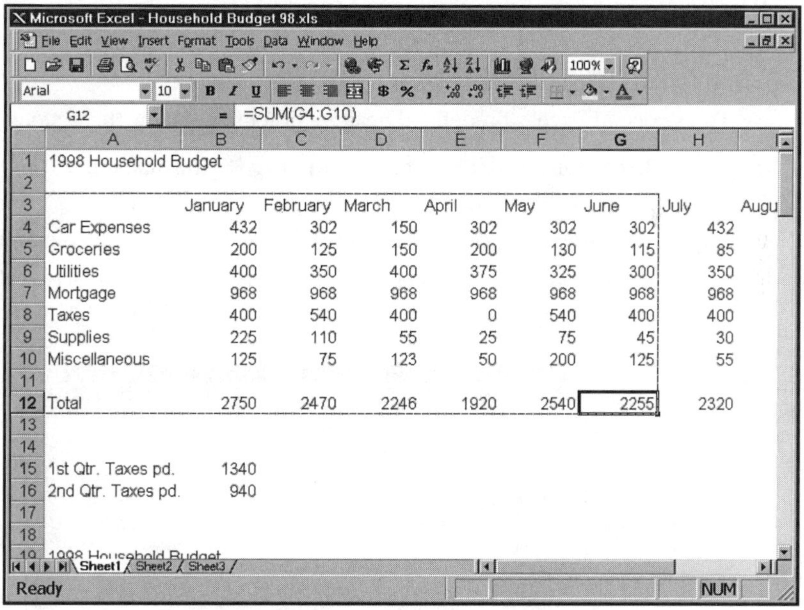

To remove a defined print area and return to printing out the entire worksheet, reopen the Page Setup dialog box and clear the Print Area text box, or choose File, Print Area, Clear Print Area.

You can also select multiple print areas. In steps 3 and 4 of the previous procedure, select each range you want to include in the print area, separating each reference with a comma (,) in the Print Area text box. For example, an entry may look like this: C3:D10, E4:G12.

TIP To change the order in which your pages print, left to right or up and down, use the Page Order options in the Sheet tab (see Figure 5.11).

Adding Headers and Footers

If you print a worksheet, you may wonder why the sheet name and page number appear at the top and bottom of the worksheet. These are the default header and footer that print on all worksheets unless you change them. You may want to use different information such as the date, the worksheet title, or your name; or you may not want to use any headers or footers. You can select to use another predefined header or footer, turn off the header or footer, or create a custom header or footer.

Before you go to the trouble of creating a custom header or footer, check some of the ones Excel has set up for you. Excel provides many combinations of the key data you are likely to want to include: your name, page number, sheet name, company name, workbook name, and date.

Use a Predefined Header or Footer

To use one of Excel's predefined headers or footers, follow these steps:

1. Choose File, Page Setup to open the Page Setup dialog box. (You can also choose View, Header and Footer.)
2. Click the Header/Footer tab to bring it to the front of the dialog box, if necessary.
3. To use a predefined header, click the Header drop-down arrow. You see a list of predefined headers, as shown in Figure 5.11. Click the one you want.

FIG. 5.11
Choose a predefined header from the Header drop-down list.

An example of the selected header appears here

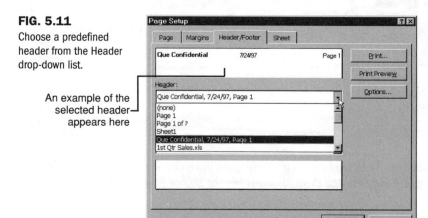

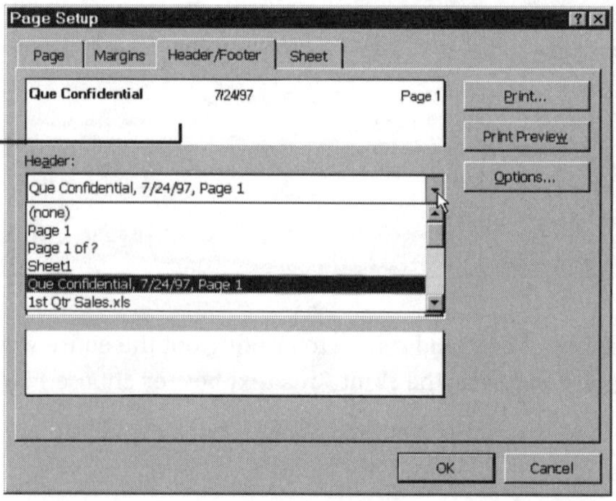

4. Excel displays a preview of the header in the dialog box. If you only want to add a header, skip to step 6.
5. If you want to change the footer, click the Footer drop-down arrow. Then click a predefined footer. Excel displays a preview of the footer in the dialog box.
6. Click OK to exit the dialog box.

In the worksheet, the headers and footers aren't displayed. To see them, click the Print Preview button or choose File, Print Preview. (You can also choose the Print Preview button in the Page Setup dialog box and view your headers or footers.) Excel displays a preview of the worksheet with the headers and footers you selected. (Click the Close button on the Preview toolbar to exit Print Preview.)

TIP Headers are printed 1/2-inch from the top of the page, and footers are printed 1/2-inch from the bottom. You can change these margins in the Margins tab in the Page Setup dialog box.

▶ **See** "Changing Margins," **p. 171**

To remove a header or footer, reopen the Page Setup dialog box and the Header/Footer tab and select (none) from the Header or Footer drop-down list, then click OK to exit.

Create a Custom Header or Footer

If none of the predefined headers or footers is what you need, you can create your own. Excel provides some buttons that enable you to quickly insert the special information, such as the page number, current date or time, as explained in Table 5.2.

Table 5.2 Header and Footer Toolbar Buttons

Button	Description
	Changes the font (opens the Font dialog box)
	Inserts page number
	Inserts number of pages (for instance, you can print Page 1 of 12 using this button and the preceding button)
	Inserts the date
	Inserts the time
	Inserts the file name
	Inserts the worksheet name

To create your own custom header or footer, use these steps:

1. Choose File, Page Setup to open the Page Setup dialog box. (You can also choose View, Header and Footer.)
2. Click the Header/Footer tab to bring it to the front of the dialog box.
3. To create a custom header or footer, click the Custom Header or Custom Footer button.
4. You see the Header or Footer dialog box (see Figure 5.12), which has three sections: Left, Center, and Right (these represent parts of the header, not the alignment of text). Move to the section in which you want to enter text. Enter the text and codes (see Table 5.2) you want to use. (To insert a code, click the appropriate button in the dialog box.)

FIG. 5.12
Create your own custom header or footer using the special buttons.

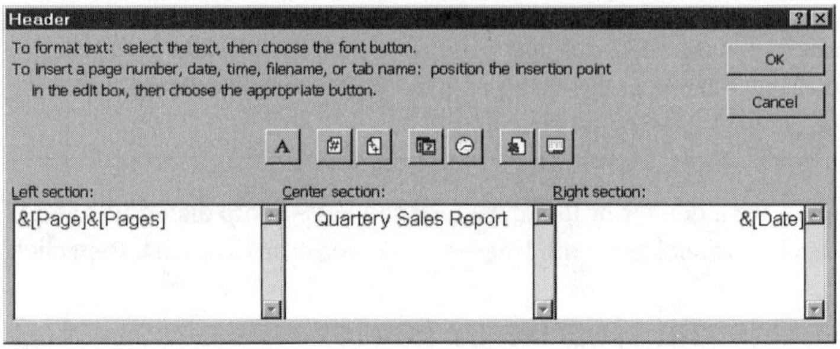

5. When you complete the header or footer, click the OK button.
6. You're returned to the Page Setup dialog box, which shows your custom headers and footers. Click OK to exit the dialog box.

TIP Keyboard shortcut users can enter header or footer text into the section text boxes using the Alt key plus the section letter. Alt+L (left), Alt+C (center), or Alt+R (right). Use the tab key to select the header or footer buttons.

To view your custom header or footer, click the Print Preview button. Excel displays the worksheet with the custom header or footer. To exit the Print Preview feature, click the Close button on the Preview toolbar.

Once you create a custom header or footer, it's added to the predefined header and footer lists.

Mastering Excel's Page Break Features

When you print a worksheet, Excel breaks up the pages based on the margins you have selected, the column width, the scaling options, and other page setup selections. Excel also automatically inserts page breaks when you define a print area. Page breaks appear as dashed lines on the worksheet. They aren't always easy to see, unless you're in Preview mode or if you have Excel's gridlines turned off (to do so, choose Tools, Options, display the General tab, and deselect the Gridlines check box).

With Excel, you can insert two types of page breaks: vertical and horizontal. A vertical page break will break the print range at the current column. A horizontal page break will break the print range at the current row.

You can check where the page breaks will occur by previewing the worksheet and viewing each page or by printing the worksheet.

Setting a Manual Page Break

In some cases, you won't like where Excel inserted a page break, or you may want to force page breaks. For example, if you had a worksheet with sales for each division, you could print each division on a separate page. In both cases, you can insert a hard page break.

To insert a vertical page break, use these steps:

1. Click the column heading to the right of where you want the vertical page break to appear.
2. Choose Insert, Page Break, and Excel inserts the page break. On-screen you see a dotted line indicating the page break (see Figure 5.13).

To insert a horizontal page break, use these steps:

1. Click the row heading to the right of where you want the horizontal page break to appear.
2. Choose Insert, Page Break, and Excel inserts the horizontal page break, as shown in Figure 5.13.

FIG. 5.13
Here you see an example of both vertical and horizontal page breaks.

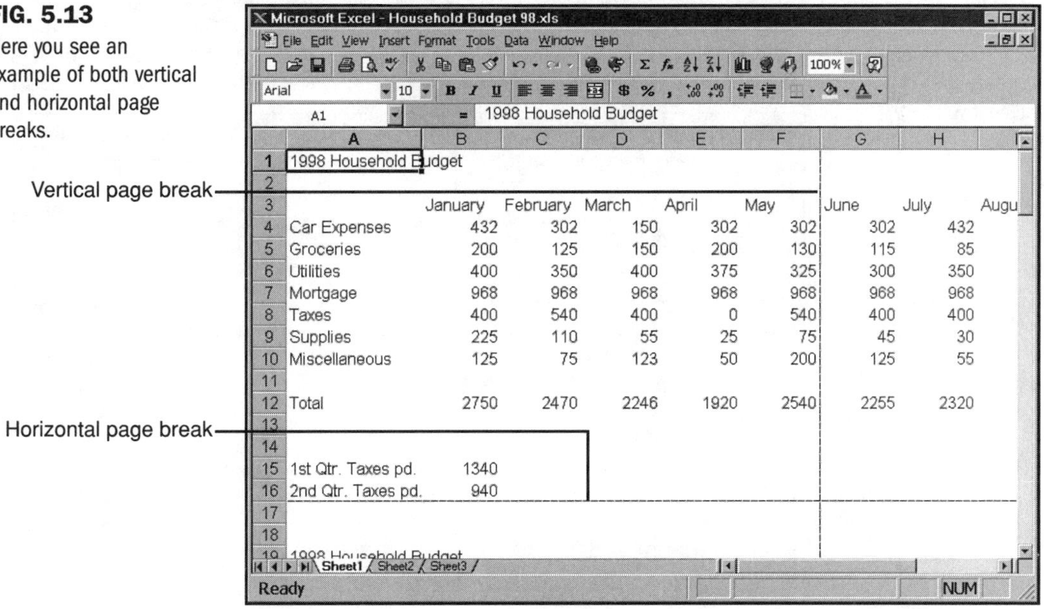

Manual page breaks (those you insert yourself) appear with longer dashed lines than automatic page breaks (those Excel inserts automatically when it reaches the bottom or the edge of a page).

To edit a page break, hover the mouse pointer over the page break line until it becomes a two-headed arrow icon. Drag the page break line to a new location and release the mouse button.

To remove a page break, select the cell immediately below or to the right of the page break. Then choose Insert, Remove Page Break command. (You can't remove automatic page breaks.)

Using the New Page Break Preview Mode

The Page Break Preview command is new to Excel 97. It lets you view where your page breaks fall and make adjustments from the Preview window. To use the feature, choose View, Page Break Preview. You can also click the Print Preview button on the Standard toolbar and then click the Page Break Preview button. A Welcome to Page Break Preview dialog box appears. Click OK to continue. If you don't want to see the welcome dialog box again, select the Do Not Show This Dialog Again check box.

In Page Break Preview mode, page breaks appear as thick blue lines, as shown in Figure 5.14. Page numbers appear as shaded background numerals. To change the position of any page break, hover your mouse pointer over the line until it changes to a double-sided arrow, then drag the break to a new location on the worksheet. You can change the positions of both hard page breaks and automatic page breaks.

FIG. 5.14
Use Excel's new Page Break Preview mode to adjust page breaks throughout your worksheet.

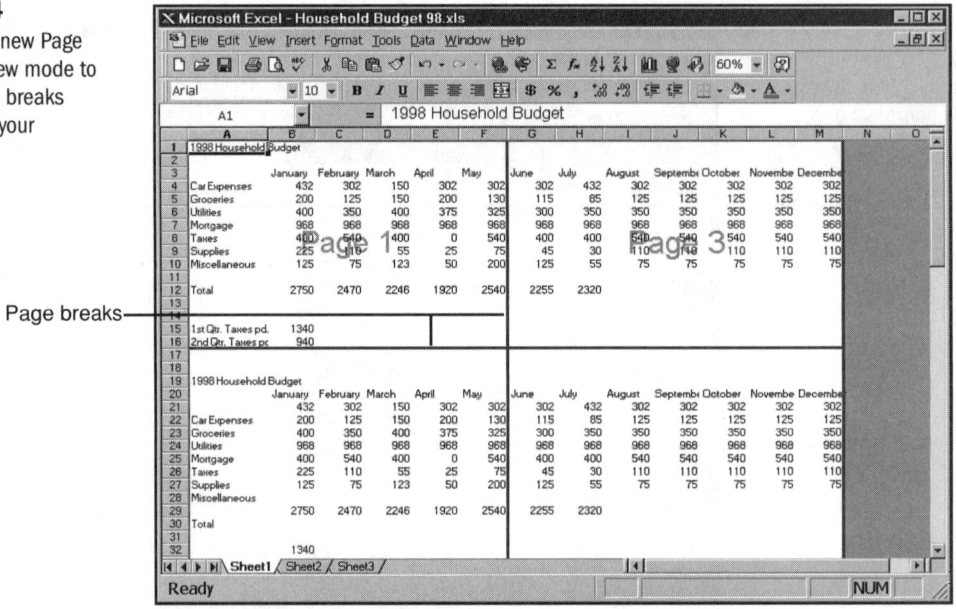

When you adjust an automatic page break, the contents of the page above the break is reduced and the contents below are scaled up to fit more onto a page. To remove a manual page break, select a cell directly below or to the right of the break and choose Insert, Remove Page Break. To remove all of the manual page breaks, select the entire worksheet and choose Insert, Reset All Page Breaks. To exit Page Break Preview mode, choose View, Normal.

Spell Check Your Worksheet

Use Excel's built-in spell check feature to check the accuracy of your worksheet's entries before printing. You can check a single word, a chart, or the entire worksheet (including text found in charts, headers and footers, and cell comment notes). Excel's spell check feature compares words in your worksheet against the Windows dictionary by default. However, you can choose to have it checked against a custom dictionary you compile with terms common to your type of business or clients.

To spell check an Excel worksheet, use these steps:

1. To check the entire worksheet, click inside any cell. To limit the spell check to a range, chart, or single word, select the item to check.

TIP To spell check every worksheet in a workbook, right-click over the sheet tab and choose Select All Sheets before activating the spell check command.

2. Click the Spelling button on the Standard toolbar, or choose Tools, Spelling. The spell check begins.

TIP Keyboard shortcut users can press F7 to start a spell check.

3. If Excel cannot find a word in the Windows dictionary or the custom dictionary, it displays the Spelling dialog box, and it highlights the word in the worksheet (see Figure 5.15). If Excel does not find any misspelled words, no dialog box appears.
4. The word in question appears in the upper-left corner of the Spelling dialog box. If the Always Suggest check box is selected, the Spelling dialog box provides alternative spellings in the Suggestions list box, and the closest match appears in the Change To box.
5. To use the word in the Change To box, click the Change button. To use another word from the Suggestions list box, select the word and then click the Change button. You can also choose from these other options:

   Ignore. Ignores the word and continues the spell check.

   Ignore All. Ignores all occurrences of the word throughout the file.

   Change All. Changes all occurrences of the word throughout the file.

Add. Adds the word to the custom dictionary.

Suggest. Suggests alternative words from the dictionary.

AutoCorrect. Adds the misspelled word to the AutoCorrect list.

▶ **See** "Using AutoCorrect," **p. 95**

FIG. 5.15
The Spelling dialog box appears only if Excel cannot find a word in the standard or custom dictionary.

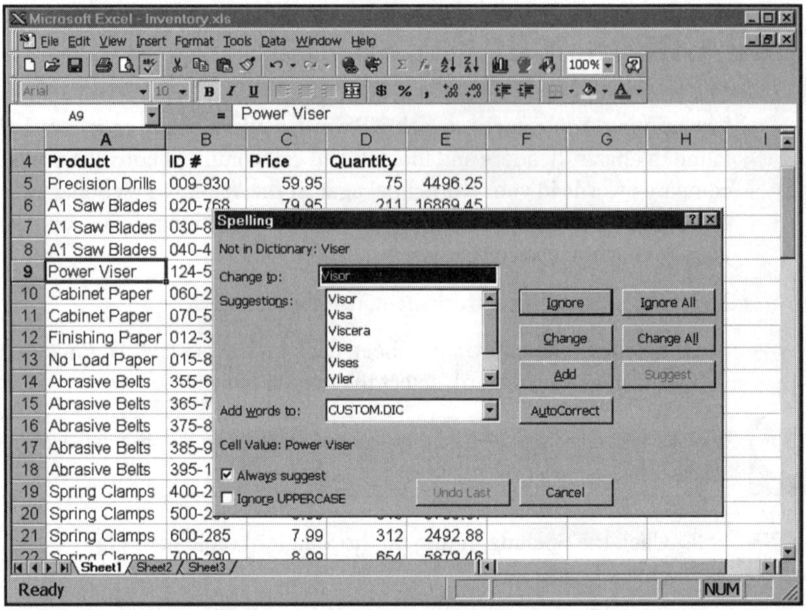

6. Depending on where you started the spell check, a message box may appear asking if you want to continue checking from the beginning of the worksheet. Choose Yes to keep checking.
7. When the spell check is complete, a message box alerts you. Choose OK.

Creating a Custom Dictionary

You can create your own custom dictionary that lists words you use frequently with your business. For example, you may want to include correct spellings of clients' names, industry terms, abbreviations, and words associated with products and services. Excel will compare the worksheet data against words in both the standard Windows dictionary and the custom dictionary.

By default, all words you choose to add using the Add command in the Spelling dialog box (see previous steps) are placed in the CUSTOM.DIC dictionary. If you prefer to build your own dictionary, you can do so through the Spelling dialog box. Here's how:

1. Choose Tools, Spelling to open the Spelling dialog box (refer to Figure 5.15).
2. In the Add Words To text box, type in a name for the custom dictionary.
3. Click the Add button, and the new dictionary is added.

When you're performing a spell check, be sure to specify the custom dictionary name in the Add Words To drop-down list. To add words to the dictionary, start the spell check and use the Add button to add terms to the custom dictionary.

Common Problems and Solutions

The problems you may encounter with printing Excel worksheets will vary greatly based on the type of printer you use. This list outlines a few of the problems you may run into and possible solutions you can try.

The data won't fit on the page when I print.

Try using the Fit to option in the Page tab of the Page Setup dialog box, as explained in "Scaling Data to Fit on a Page." You can also adjust the margins, decrease font size, or try another page orientation.

When I select multiple print areas, only one prints.

Use commas to separate print ranges in the Print area text box. If you don't, Excel won't recognize the multiple ranges and treats the references as a single area.

When I add a custom header, it overflows into my data when I print.

Change the spacing between the header and the data; choose File, Page Setup, and click the Margin tab. Edit the header margin setting. To increase space between the header and the data, decrease the margin setting (from .5 to .25, for example). Use this same technique for adding space between the data and the footer.

How do I set left and right margins for my headers and footers?

You cannot adjust the left and right margins for headers and footers; they always use a .75 setting even if your page margins are set differently.

When I try to remove a page break, the Remove Page Break command is unavailable on the Insert menu.

You first have to select the cell containing the page break before using the Remove Page Break command.

I selected Insert, Remove Page Break, but Excel removed only some of the breaks.

Some of the page breaks are automatically added by Excel and cannot be removed without clearing the defined print area. To do so, choose File, Print Area, Clear Print Area.

From Here...

In this chapter, you learned how to utilize Excel's many print features. The next two chapters focus on more advanced worksheet concepts.

- Chapter 6, "Using Excel Functions," shows you how to work with Excel's functions, building powerful arguments and dealing with function errors.
- Chapter 7, "Using Excel Add-Ins," shows you how to work with Report Manager, Conditional Sum Wizard, Template Wizard, and other useful add-in utilities.

PART II

Advanced Excel Worksheet Features

CHAPTER 6

Using Excel Functions

by Bruce Hallberg

A large part of Excel's power to tackle just about any job lies in its extensive list of *functions*. A function takes information you provide and returns some sort of answer. Functions can be thought of as predefined formulas. Different functions need different types of information to do their work. For example, a function like SUM requires a list of numbers to add together. A function like PV, which computes the present value of a stream of payments, requires information about the payment amount, interest rate, length of the term, and so on.

Using functions in Excel is relatively easy, especially with such tools as the Formula Palette that walk you through creating functions in your worksheets. In this chapter, you'll learn about how functions work, how to use functions, and what types of functions exist. See Appendix B, "Excel Function Reference," for a detailed list of all Excel 97 functions. ■

Learning how functions work

Excel has many built-in functions, each designed to perform specific types of calculations. You'll learn about function syntax, function arguments, and result types and how to create nested functions as arguments.

Using the Paste function and Formula Palette

Building functions from scratch requires that you remember all the required and optional arguments and the syntax for each function. Excel automates function building to reduce time and errors.

An overview of the most commonly used Excel functions

This chapter discusses some of the more commonly used Excel functions in some detail. For a comprehensive list of Excel functions, see Appendix B.

How Do Functions Work?

Although they all do different things, functions follow certain simple rules. When a function is the only thing in a cell on a worksheet, it starts with an equals sign, like any formula; then, the name of the function is entered. Finally, the *arguments* to the function—the information you give the function so it can come up with its answer—are contained within a set of parentheses. For example, consider the following function:

```
=SUM(12,25,34)
```

If you move to any cell in a worksheet, type this function exactly as it appears, and press Enter after entering the final parenthesis, the answer 71 will immediately appear in the cell. If you select the cell with the answer 71 showing, you will see the function in the formula bar (see Figure 6.1).

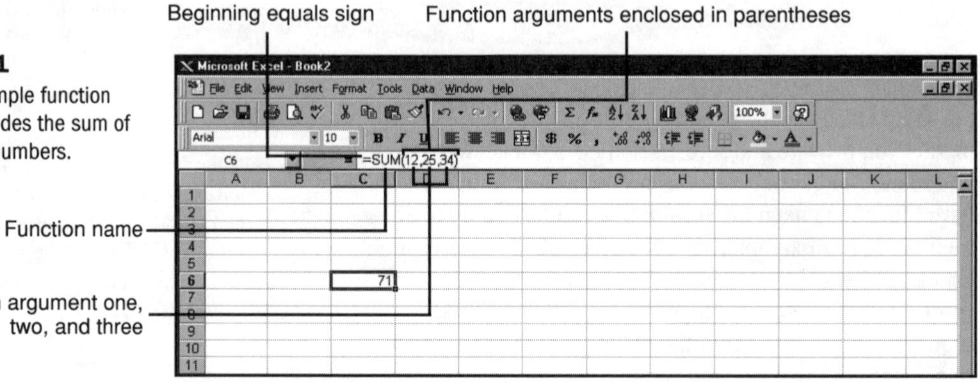

FIG. 6.1
A very simple function that provides the sum of a set of numbers.

Understanding Function Arguments

The simplest functions do not require any arguments. For example, the function =NOW( ) returns the current date and time and requires no arguments. (However, notice that it still includes the required opening and closing parentheses.)

Other functions require only one argument. For example, =INT(23.456) will return the integer portion of a number, or 23 in this case.

Most functions require more than one argument; some can take up to 30 arguments. A good example of this is the SUM function, which can take up to 30 arguments. When you use multiple arguments with a function, each argument is separated from the next by a comma. So, for example, =SUM(12,24) contains two arguments, 12 and 24. Just as valid would be =SUM(12,24,36,45), which contains four arguments.

Examining an Example Function Although some functions, such as SUM, can take a variable number of arguments, most functions have a fixed number of arguments. Many functions also have arguments that are optional. For example, consider the PMT function that computes a payment given certain information. PMT uses the following arguments:

- *Rate.* The first argument is the interest rate of the borrowed money, expressed as a percentage rate per payment period.
- *NPer.* This argument specifies the number of payment periods for the transaction. A three-year loan with monthly payments has 36 periods.
- *PV.* The Present Value defines the amount of money borrowed or loaned at the beginning of the transaction. Generally, use a negative value if you're borrowing money and a positive value if you're loaning money. Whether you use a positive or negative present value doesn't change the numerical result of the calculation, it just affects whether the answer is displayed as a positive or negative payment.
- *FV.* The Future Value defines the amount of value remaining at the end of the loan. This might be used for a loan with a balloon payment at the end of its term, or a lease with a purchase option (also called a *residual*). The FV argument is optional. If you do not provide it, Excel will assume the FV is zero.
- *Type.* The Type argument, also optional, defines whether payments on the loan are made at the beginning of each payment period or at the end of each payment period. (In financial terms, payments made at the beginning of each period are said to be *in advance* and payments made at the end of a payment period are said to be *in arrears*.) The Type argument is given in two possible ways: blank or 0 means the payments are at the end of each payment period; a 1 means the payments are at the beginning of each period.

So, given this function description, here are three valid examples of the PMT function in action:

```
=PMT(0.01,60,-12000)
=PMT(0.18/12,36,-10000,1500,1)
=PMT(B5,B6,B7,,1)
```

In the first example, a five-year loan with monthly payments (60 payment periods) is calculated with an interest rate of 12 percent per year. (Twelve percent equals .12 expressed as a decimal, and then divided by 12 months to arrive at the monthly rate of 0.01.) The beginning loan balance is $12,000 and, in this case, you're borrowing the money so this is expressed as a negative value. There is no future value, and payments are assumed to be at the end of each period (in arrears) because no FV or Type arguments are specified. The answer for this is $266.93, which is the amount of each monthly payment on the loan.

In the second example, an equipment lease is calculated (note that this isn't an automobile lease, which is considerably more complex to calculate). The first argument does the calculation *within the argument* to arrive at the interest rate per period. This is an 18 percent interest rate, divided by 12 to arrive at the monthly rate (you could also simply type .015 for that argument). There are 36 lease payments, and the initial value of the lease is $10,000. The lease has a future value of $1,500 (in other words, a purchase option at the end of the lease), and lease payments are always calculated as being paid in advance of each payment period so a type argument of 1 is given. If you enter this function yourself, the monthly lease payment is $324.92.

In the third example, cells are referenced for most of the arguments. You can see, however, that no future value is defined, but the payments are assumed to be in advance because of the final argument in the function. This illustrates an important point: to skip an optional argument but then define one further to the right, you enter a comma just as if there was a value to the missing optional argument. Without that extra comma, Excel would assume you were specifying a future value of 1, instead of a type of 1.

Function Arguments and Result Types Most functions accept numbers as arguments and return numbers as results. This isn't always the case, however. Functions also can accept other types of arguments, and they can return other types of answers. Here is a list of valid function arguments and result types:

- *Number.* Any integer or decimal number.
- *Time and Date.* Dates and times expressed using any valid date and time entry format.
- *Text.* Text comprised of any characters, surrounded with quotation marks.
- *Logical values.* Examples include TRUE/FALSE, YES/NO, 1/0, and calculated logic like 1+1=2.
- *Arrays.* Array formulas operate on multiple cells.
- *Error Values.* Virtually any function can return an error value, but some functions also accept error values as arguments. For instance, the ISERROR function returns a logical TRUE or FALSE depending on whether its argument is an error value.
- *Named Constants.* A named constant can be used in place of any argument type, provided that the named constant contains the argument type the function expects.
- *Cell References.* Most arguments can reference the results of other cells (or groups of cells) in place of using actual values in the functions.
- *Functions.* You can use a function in place of any argument, provided the function returns the type of data expected by the surrounding function. See the section titled "Using Nested Functions As Arguments," later in this chapter, for more information.

It's critical that you provide the right types of arguments to a function. For example, if a function is expecting a text argument, entering a number without surrounding quote marks would produce an error. Many people experience errors when working with functions as a direct result of not observing this rule. It's a good idea to use the Formula Palette (covered later in this chapter) when building functions because it tests each argument as it is entered and indicates whether the argument is the correct type.

Function arguments can be—and usually are—made up of references to cells. At the most basic level, you just reference cells in place of the argument values.

Suppose you have four values in cells C3 through C6 and want to create a sum in cell C7. You could enter the function **=SUM(C3,C4,C5,C6)** to do just that. However, you also can use a *cell range* as an argument. When you use a cell range as a function argument, you define the first and last cell in the range, and separate them with a colon. So, in this example, the function **=SUM(C3:C6)** would provide the exact same answer as if you had used a list of cell references.

A cell range isn't limited to a single row or column. You also can define a block of cells. For example, if you have a 3–3 series of values in the cells from C3 to E5 that you want to sum together, you can use the function arguments **C3:E5** to define the range. A cell range reference always starts at the upper-left corner of the range, and ends at the lower-right corner of the range. You can enter a cell range reference from the lower-right to the upper-left or from lower-left to upper-right, but Excel always transforms such references so that they are stored and displayed as upper-left to lower-right.

How Excel Automatically Transforms Some Values In the preceding section, you read about how functions take different types of arguments and return different types of values and that these always need to be in agreement. There are certain cases, however, in which Excel automatically transforms arguments for you, changing information you provide into the information it expects. These are the automatic transformations Excel makes:

- **Numbers represented as text used in numerical formulas** are automatically treated as numbers. For instance, the function =SUM("12", "34") will return the number 46. Note that including a non-numeric character in either argument would cause Excel to return the #VALUE error instead.
- **Dates represented as text used in numerical formulas** are automatically treated as dates. The function =MONTH("12/5/97") will return the month number 12, even though technically the argument is a simple text string. Excel recognizes that a date was intended and makes the conversion automatically.
- **Numbers and logical values used in text formulas** are automatically treated as text. The function =CONCATENATE(12,False) will return 12FALSE.

NOTE If you use a date in a formula where Excel expects text, Excel will automatically convert the date into its serial number and then treat the *resulting serial number* as text. For example, if you enter the function =CONCATENATE("Date",5/12/98), the answer you get is Date0.00425170068027211 because the date is converted to its serial number and then the serial number is treated as text. If you want to force Excel to accept the date as you actually entered it, you would have to put the date in quotation marks.

Using Nested Functions as Arguments You aren't limited to using just one function in any given cell. Functions can be as complex as you want them to be, and can contain formulas and other functions as their arguments. For example, consider this function:

```
=SUM(C5:E10,AVERAGE(F10:F20))
```

Here, one of the arguments to the SUM function is another function called AVERAGE. In this particular case, the result will be the sum of cells C5 through E10, plus whatever the average is of cells F10 through F20.

You can have up to seven levels of nested functions. So, for example, using the simple SUM function, this is a valid example that contains seven levels of nested SUM functions:

```
=SUM(SUM(SUM(SUM(SUM(SUM(SUM(SUM(14,15),16),17),18),19),20),21),22)
```

If you exceed this limit, Excel will report an error and will not accept the function.

> **CAUTION**
>
> Using nested functions several levels deep can make it much harder to troubleshoot your formulas when you get error messages. If you have trouble with nested functions, try breaking down each function into a separate cell and then using cell references in the outside function. Doing so helps you see what each function is returning and, therefore, what it is providing to the higher-level functions.

When nesting functions, keep careful track of what types of arguments are required by each function, and what each nested function returns. These must be in agreement. For example, consider this nested function:

```
=SUM(12,34,45,LEFT(ABC,1))
```

In this example, an error code (#NAME?) is returned, because the LEFT function is returning text (the letter "A"), which the SUM function can't work with. This doesn't mean that there can't be certain kinds of mixing of functions. Now consider this example:

```
=SUM(12,34,45,LEN("This is some text"))
```

This example is perfectly valid, because the LEN function returns the length of the text given as its argument. In this particular case, the LEN function is returning the answer 17, which is merely treated by the SUM function as another numerical argument in the list.

Using the Paste Function and the Formula Palette

If you use a function frequently, you'll find that it's often easiest to simply type the function yourself. There are two problems with using this approach that might confuse you until you fully understand all the Excel functions. First, you would have to memorize all of the different functions available in Excel, their arguments, return values, and so on. Second, it becomes difficult to see how each argument is working within the function.

Using two integrated tools in Excel makes using functions much easier than otherwise. The Paste Function dialog box coupled with the Formula Palette walk you through selecting and completing any of Excel's functions.

Using the Paste Function Dialog Box

To choose a function to use in a given situation, start with the Paste Function dialog box. You access it in one of two ways:

- Choose Insert, Function.
- Click the Paste Function button on the Standard toolbar.

Figure 6.2 shows the Paste Function dialog box.

FIG. 6.2
The Paste Function dialog box lets you choose any of Excel's functions to work with.

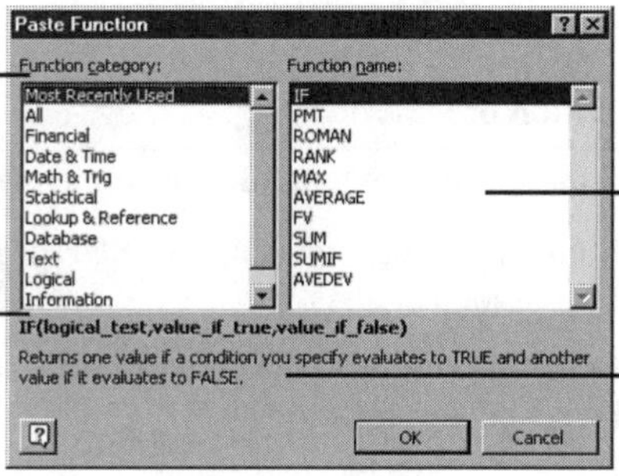

The following two sections describe how to choose functions from the Paste Function dialog box. After that, you'll learn how to build the selected function with the Formula Palette (which appears after you choose a function in the Paste Function dialog box).

Categories Excel's functions are divided into categories. The first thing you do in the Paste Function dialog box is choose a category of functions. Each function category contains functions that solve different kinds of problems in Excel. Table 6.1 details the different categories of functions available in Excel 97 and displayed in the Paste Function dialog box.

Table 6.1 Function Categories in Excel 97

Category Name	Description of Functions
Most Recently Used	The 10 most recently used functions. (Much of the time, this category makes selecting the function you want quick and easy because you'll tend to use a few functions much more often than others.)
All	All Excel functions are displayed if you choose the All category. If you know a function's name but not its category, you can find it in the All category listing.
Financial	Functions related to financial problems, such as computing the present value of a stream of payments, calculating interest rates, internal rates of return, and others.
Date & Time	Functions that perform conversions or calculations based on dates or times.
Math & Trig	Mathematical and trigonometric functions.
Statistical	Functions relating to statistical analysis of data, such as regression analyses, distributions, and so on.
Lookup & Reference	Functions that can find information within a range you define using rules you define.
Database	Functions relating to data management.

continues

Table 6.1 Continued

Category Name	Description of Functions
Text	Functions that act on text information in certain ways.
Logical	Functions that return, typically, a TRUE or FALSE answer based on different logical tests.
Information	Functions that return information for different aspects of an Excel workbook.
User Defined	Functions added to Excel either through the addition of an Excel Add-in, an open workbook that contains programmed functions, or developed by you using Visual Basic for Applications.

Function Names Once you choose a function category in the Paste Function dialog box, a list of the functions within that category display in the Function Name list. You generally can tell what a function does from its name, but you also can click each function to see a brief description of what the function does and its arguments, as illustrated in Figure 6.3.

FIG. 6.3
Click any function you're interested in to read a brief description of the function in the dialog box.

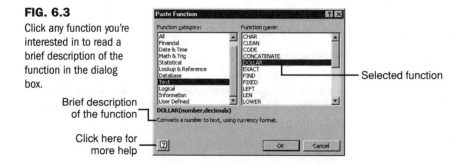

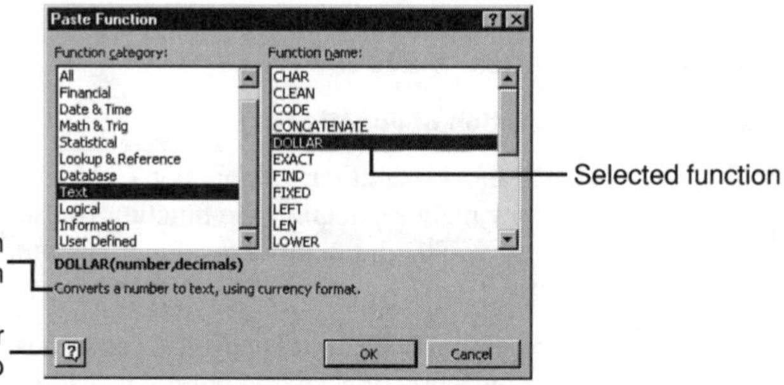

To get more information about a function that you're considering using, click the Office Assistant button on the Paste Function dialog box. Once you activate the Office Assistant this way, click Help With This Feature, and then click Help on Selected Function in the Office Assistant bubble. This activates the Excel 97 help system with the selected function detailed, as shown in Figure 6.4.

Once you've selected the function you want to use, click the OK button, and the Formula Palette appears.

Using the Formula Palette

97

The Formula Palette is entirely new in Excel 97. It provides an easy-to-use way to complete functions without having to laboriously look up all the details of the function in question. You will see the Formula Palette after you select a function in the Paste Function dialog box. The Formula Palette helps you build the function you select. Figure 6.5 shows the Formula Palette.

FIG. 6.4
Accessing detailed function help in Excel 97.

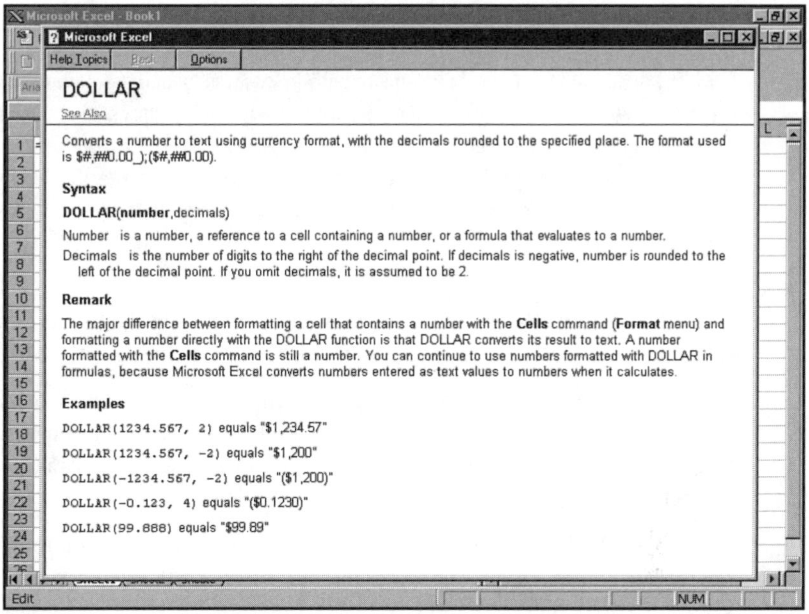

FIG. 6.5
Use the Formula Palette to quickly and accurately complete functions.

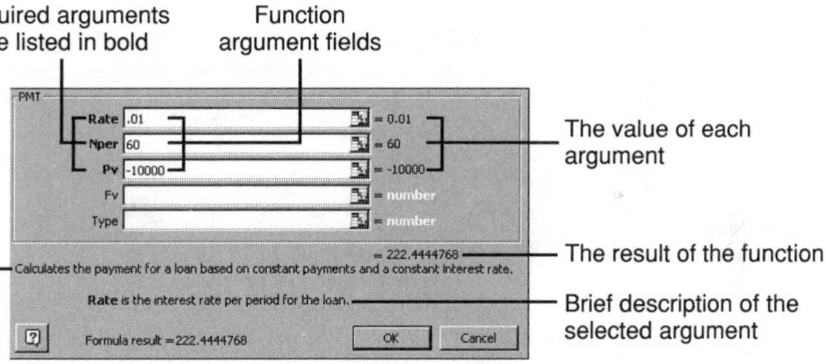

The Formula Palette can be invoked in several different ways:

- When you select a function from the Paste Function dialog box and click OK, you are taken to the Formula Palette with that function selected.

- If you select a cell with an existing function and click the Paste Function button on the Standard toolbar, the Formula Palette appears ready to edit the function.

- When you click the equals sign button on the formula bar, the Formula Palette appears. Type the name of the function you want to work with in the formula bar (which is also active) and the Formula Palette helps you with that function as soon as you type the opening parenthesis.

Part II
Ch 6

CAUTION

When you activate the Formula Palette for an existing formula, and that formula uses named cell references, the Formula Palette may misconstrue part of the cell name references as a function name. For example, say you had a cell that contained the formula **=Calculated Payment + Extra Costs Per Month**. If you select that cell and click the Paste Function button to activate the Formula Palette, the Formula Palette will try to edit the MONTH function. Pressing the Esc key will restore the formula to its original form, and you'll need to edit the formula manually.

Once the Formula Palette is active, your cursor will be in the first argument's field. Type the information for each argument and use the Tab key to move to the next argument's field.

Direct-Selection in the Formula Palette You can also directly select cells that you want to reference in your arguments. In the Formula Palette, place your cursor in the field in which you want the cell reference. Then click in the worksheet to select a cell or range of cells. The cell reference appears in the Formula Palette's field.

Sometimes the Formula Palette is in the way of the cells you want to select. If this happens, use the Collapse/Expand buttons to temporarily move it out of your way. For example, examine Figure 6.6. In this example, you want to choose the PV argument (Present Value) from a cell on the worksheet that is obscured by the Formula Palette.

FIG. 6.6
Sometimes you want to select a cell that the Formula Palette obscures.

Collapse/Expand buttons

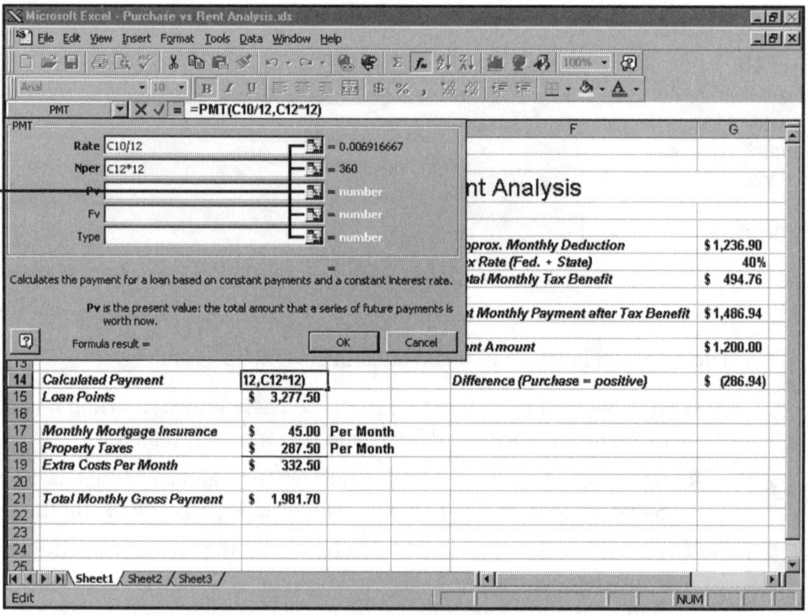

Once you click the appropriate Collapse/Expand button (like the one at the end of the PV field), the Formula Palette temporarily shrinks out of your way, as shown in Figure 6.7.

After choosing the cell or cells you need, click the Collapse/Expand button again to restore the Formula Palette and continue.

FIG. 6.7
With the Formula Palette collapsed, you can direct-select cell C8.

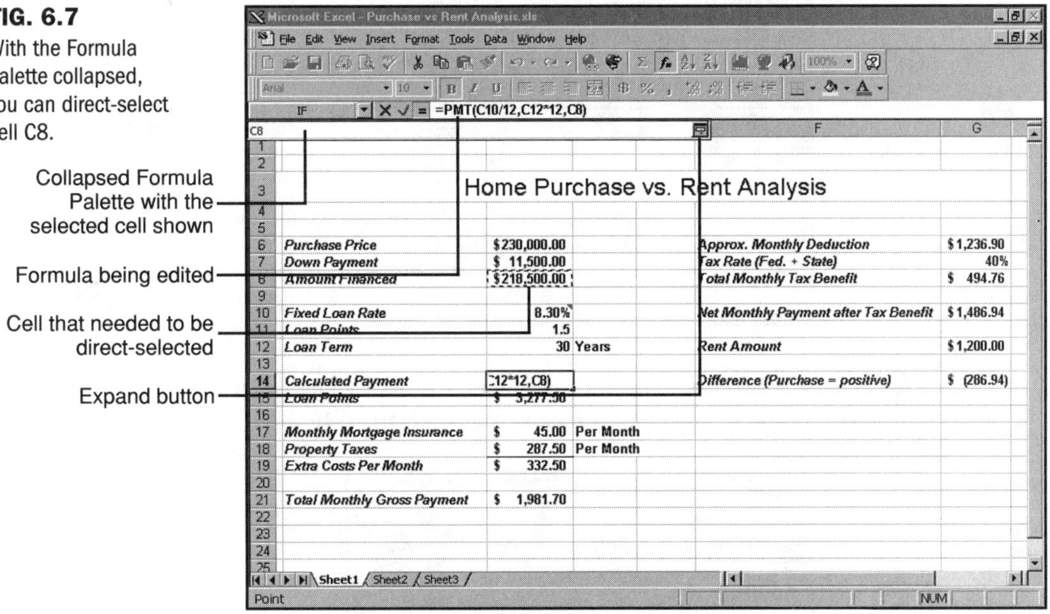

Nesting Functions with the Formula Palette Just as you can nest functions when you type them into an Excel formula, you can do the same thing from within the Formula Palette. To see how this works, you'll learn how to make an Excel "Coin Flipper" that yields a heads or tails result randomly. To do this, you use a combination of the IF and RAND functions. Follow these steps to learn how this works:

1. Click the Paste Function button and choose the IF function from the Logical category. You then see the Formula Palette with the IF function, as shown in Figure 6.8.

   The first argument of the IF function is Logical_test. This argument specifies the test that will be either true or false and that determines what the IF function returns. It is in the Logical_test argument that the RAND function will be nested.

2. Click the down arrow indicated in Figure 6.9 to open the list of recently used functions.

3. Choose a function from the list, or click the More Functions… choice to choose a function from the Paste Function dialog box. For example, if RAND is not on the recently used function list, you have to choose More Functions and then select it from the Paste Function dialog box.

FIG. 6.8
The Formula Palette with the IF function.

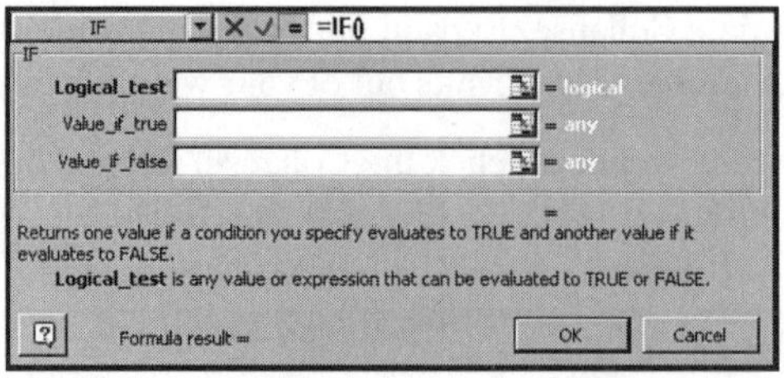

FIG. 6.9
Choosing a function to nest within another using the Formula Palette.

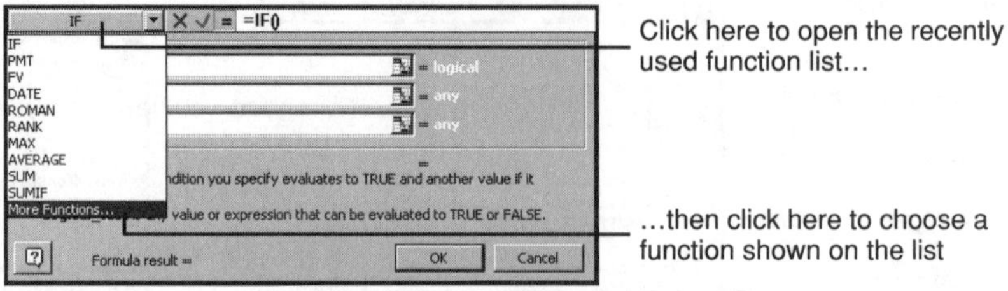

4. From the Paste Function dialog box, choose the RAND function from the Math & Trig category. Click OK, and your screen looks like Figure 6.10.

FIG. 6.10
After you choose a nested function, the Formula Palette changes to show you the new function.

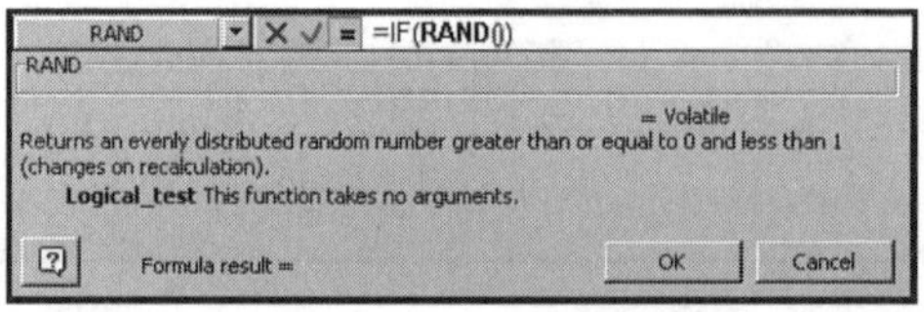

5. As you can see in Figure 6.10, the Formula Palette now shows the RAND function, which takes no arguments. To complete the IF function, you must return to Formula Palette for IF. In the Formula bar, click the function you want to edit in the Formula Palette (IF in this example). The Formula Palette returns to that function, as shown in Figure 6.11.

FIG. 6.11
After nesting a function, click the previous function to return to that level with the Formula Palette.

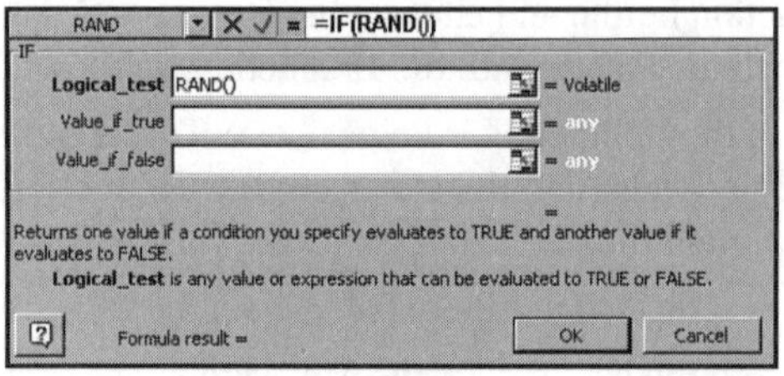

6. Complete the Logical_test argument so that it reads **RAND()>.5**.
7. Set the Value_if_true argument to **"Heads"** (include the quotation marks to force Excel to treat this as a text entry).
8. Set the Value_if_false argument to **"Tails"** (again, include the quotation marks).

Figure 6.12 shows the complete formula.

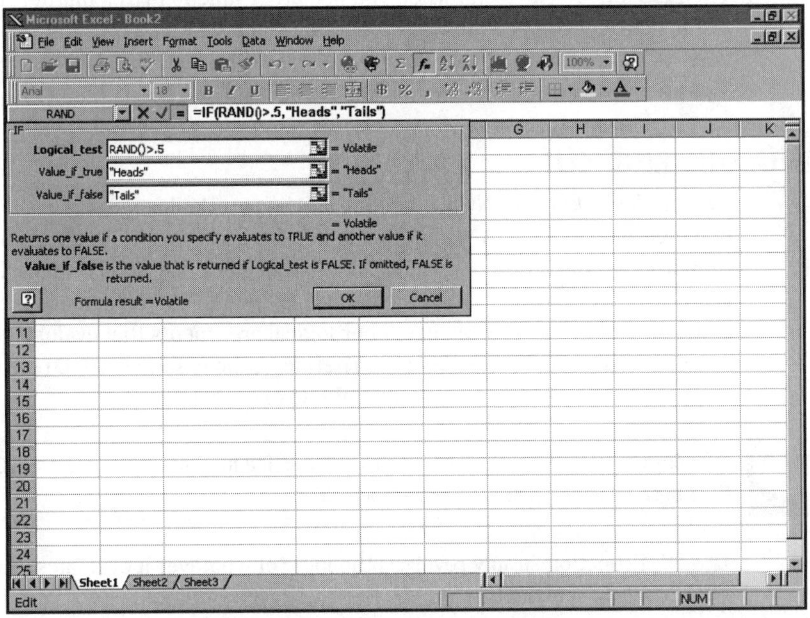

FIG. 6.12
The completed "Coin Flipper" formula demonstrates how to build nested functions using the Formula Palette.

After saving the formula, the worksheet cell that contains this formula will show either "Heads" or "Tails." Moreover, every time the worksheet is recalculated (you can press F9 to force it to recalculate at any time), a new, random value is chosen by the RAND function and "Heads" or "Tails" is displayed accordingly by the IF function.

Most Useful Excel Functions

The old adage generally holds true: 20% of the whole generally accounts for 80% of the results. It's true in your use of Excel functions, too. You'll find that about 20% of the available Excel functions will satisfy most of your needs. In this section, you learn about the most-used (and most broadly useful) Excel functions. When your needs go beyond these functions, refer to Appendix A of this book to explore other available Excel functions. You can then use the Paste Function dialog box and the Formula Palette to tap the power of the other Excel functions.

ABS

The ABS function returns the absolute number of a single argument number. If the argument is a negative number, a positive number is returned, and if the argument is a positive number, a positive number is returned. The syntax is as follows:

=ABS(***number***)

The ABS function is useful when you use other functions that might return a negative number. For instance, if you use the PMT function to calculate a payment on a loan, and you use all positive values for PMT, a negative number is returned. To avoid this, you can use ABS to force a positive result.

AND, OR, and NOT

Use the AND, OR, and NOT functions to perform Boolean algebra in which you can test certain logical conditions. AND and OR take up to 30 logical (TRUE/FALSE) arguments and return TRUE or FALSE depending on those arguments. AND returns TRUE if ***all*** arguments are TRUE; OR returns TRUE if ***any*** argument is TRUE. You can use the arguments 1 for TRUE and 0 for FALSE, or you can use other logical arguments that evaluate to TRUE or FALSE (like 2+2=17, which of course is FALSE). Therefore, the result of =AND(TRUE,0,2+2=4) is FALSE because one of the arguments—the middle one—is FALSE.

TIP *Any* non-zero value (not just a 1) evaluates as TRUE. The function =AND(-1,3,4,2223) evaluates to TRUE because all the arguments represent TRUE.

The NOT function simply reverses the logic of whatever it evaluates. For instance, =NOT(2+2=4) returns FALSE.

You can use these functions in combination with other functions to test values in a worksheet. For instance, you can test to see if salespeople met their quotas and other requirements for a bonus.

AVERAGE

The AVERAGE function returns the average of a set of numbers. The syntax is as follows:

=AVERAGE(***number1, number2, …***)

You can use up to 30 arguments for AVERAGE, and each argument can reference a range of cells, a named range, or an array.

The AVERAGE function ignores cells that are empty or that contain text or logical values. You can use dates with AVERAGE.

CONCATENATE

Use CONCATENATE to join text strings together. Its syntax is as follows:

=CONCATENATE(***string1, string2, …***)

If, for example, cell A1 contains "Fred" and cell B1 contains "Flintstone" the function =CONCATENATE(A1,B1) will return FredFlintstone. To insert the space between the first and last name, you would use the function =CONCATENATE(A1," ",B1).

TIP You can also concatenate text strings with the & operator. Typing **=A1&" "&B1** is the same as using the function =CONCATENATE(A1," ",B1).

COUNT, COUNTBLANK, AND COUNTIF

Use these COUNT functions to find out how many values exist in a range, how many blanks exist, or how many values that meet a certain criteria exist.

The COUNT function returns the number of numbers within its list of arguments. You can use up to 30 numbers or cell references with COUNT. The COUNT function counts numbers, dates, and text strings that represent numbers. Error values, empty cells, logical values, and text are not counted. The syntax for COUNT is as follows:

=COUNT(*number1, number2, ...*)

The COUNTBLANK function counts the number of blank cells within a range of cells. Cells containing "" (an empty text string) are counted. The syntax is as follows:

=COUNTBLANK(*range*)

Use the COUNTIF function to count how many values in a range of cells match criteria you specify. The COUNTIF function's syntax is:

=COUNTIF(*range, criteria*)

COUNTIF is most useful for counting how many values are greater than or less than a set value. For instance, =COUNTIF(A1:B213,">45") will return the number of cells within the range that contain values greater than 45. Note that the criteria argument is surrounded with quotation marks. You can also use static text criteria, such as =COUNTIF(A1:B213,"Jones"), which will count all of the cells that contain Jones.

DATEVALUE

DATEVALUE takes a text-based date and converts it to an Excel serial-number date. DATEVALUE is very useful when you're working with imported data such as dates that were imported into Excel as text. Here is the syntax for DATEVALUE:

=DATEVALUE(*date_text*)

NOTE If the cell that contains the DATEVALUE function is not formatted to display dates, the Excel serial number will appear instead of the date it represents.

IF

One of the more useful functions, IF performs a logical test that you specify, and then returns one of two values depending on whether the logical test is true or false. The IF function's syntax is as follows:

=IF(*logical_test,value_if_true,value_if_false*)

The logical_test is any test that can be evaluated as being true or false. Value_if_true and value_if_false are optional; if they are not supplied, IF returns either TRUE or FALSE depending on the result of logical_test.

Use the IF function to include intelligent labels in your worksheets. For instance, if cell C10 contains actual dollars spent and cell D10 contains the budgeted dollars, the formula =IF(C10>D10,"Overspent","Underspent") can make it easy to quickly see how the values compare.

The IF function, like all functions, can be nested. Nested IF functions can provide more complex logic in formulas. For example, suppose you want to compare actual spending and budgeted spending and then create three different results based on the comparison. If the spending is more than 10% over the budget, you want a cell to indicate "Overspent"; if the spending is more than 10% under budget, you want the cell to indicate "Underspent"; and if the spending is equal to the budget plus or minus 10%, you want to indicate "At budget." The following formula will do this (given that cell C10 contains the actual amount and D10 contains the budgeted amount):

=IF(D10>(C10*1.1),"Underspent",IF(C10>(D10*1.1),"Overspent","At budget))

Value_if_true and value_if_false can contain formulas. For instance, if Actuals and Budget are named ranges, the function =IF(A1="Actuals",SUM(Actuals),SUM(Budget)) lets you build formulas that can take different actions based on the contents of a cell.

IS Functions

There are nine IS functions that test whether the contents of a cell contain a certain type of value or result:

- ISBLANK returns TRUE if a cell is blank.
- ISERR returns TRUE if a cell contains an error result other than #N/A.
- ISERROR returns TRUE if a cell contains any error result.
- ISLOGICAL returns TRUE if a cell contains TRUE or FALSE as a logical value.
- ISNA returns TRUE if a cell contains the #N/A error result.
- ISNONTEXT returns TRUE if a cell contains something other than text.
- ISNUMBER returns TRUE if a cell contains a number.
- ISREF returns TRUE if a cell contains a cell reference.
- ISTEXT returns TRUE if a cell contains text.

The most common use of the IS functions is combined with the IF function. For instance, you can use IF and ISERR to remove error results from worksheets. Consider the case where a formula may display a #DIV/0! error before you enter the data for the worksheet. You don't want to display the #DIV/0! error. The following formula will eliminate it:

=IF(ISERROR(A1/B1),"",A1/B1)

In this example, the IF function first tests to find out if A1/B1 results in an error. If so, a blank result ("") is returned. If not, the A1/B1 formula is carried out, and its result appears normally.

LEFT, RIGHT, and MID

When working with data imported from some other source, you often have to manipulate text values and extract substrings from the full string. The LEFT, RIGHT, and MID functions do this work for you. For the following examples, assume that cell A1 contains the string "Microsoft Corporation."

The LEFT function returns a specified number of characters starting from the left of the string. The syntax is:

=LEFT(*string,number_of_chars*)

The formula =LEFT(A1,5) returns the string "Micro."

The RIGHT function returns a specified number of characters starting from the right of the string. The syntax is:

=RIGHT(*string,number_of_chars*)

The formula =RIGHT(A1,11) returns the string "Corporation."

The MID function returns a specified number of characters starting from a specified part of a string. The syntax is:

=MID(*string,start_char_from_left,number_of_chars*)

The formula =MID(A1,6,4) returns the string "soft." Notice that the *start_char_from_left* argument specifies the actual starting character, and not the one before it.

The following rules apply to LEFT, RIGHT, and MID:

- If *number_of_chars* is greater than the length of the source string, all of the string is returned.
- If you omit *number_of_chars*, it is assumed to be 1.
- *Number_of_chars* must be greater than 0.
- For MID, *start_char_from_left* must be greater than 0.
- For MID, if *start_char_from_left* is greater than the length of the text, a null text string is returned.

MAX AND MIN

Use MAX and MIN to return the largest or smallest number in a range. The syntax is:

=MAX(*range1, range2, ...*)

=MIN(*range1, range2, ...*)

You can specify up to 30 range arguments for MAX and MIN. Non-number entries within the tested ranges are ignored.

PERMUT and COMBIN

Useful for certain probability calculations, PERMUT and COMBIN calculate the number of possible permutations of a set of items. COMBIN is useful when you want to know how many combinations exist, exclusive of their ordering. The formula =COMBIN(52,5) will tell you how many possible Five Card Stud poker hands are possible. You use COMBIN because Ace, King, Queen, Jack, Ten are the same, no matter what order you get them in. You can also use COMBIN to calculate the odds of lottery or Keno games. For instance, to pick 8 numbers from a field of 80, the formula =COMBIN(80,8) yields 28,987,537,150. The odds, therefore, of choosing the right 8 numbers from a field of 80 is approximately 1:29 million. Again, the order in which the numbers appear is unimportant.

PERMUT is useful when you want to see how many possible *orders* exist within a set. For instance, if you have three letters (A, B, and C), how many possible ways are there to represent them? You can have ABC, ACB, BAC, BCA, CAB, and CBA. Therefore, the result of =PERMUT(3,3) is 6.

The syntax for both functions is:

=COMBIN(*number, number_chosen*)

=PERMUT(*number, number_chosen*)

TIP When you want to calculate the number of combinations possible when there is no fixed set from which to draw, you just multiply the probabilities together. For instance, if you want to see how many different ways there are to represent the letters A, B, and C (AAA, ABA, and CCC are all valid examples), you would use the formula =3*3*3, which results in 27. If you wanted to see how many possible 5-letter combinations are possible using the 26 alphabetic characters of English (A to Z), you would use =26*26*26*26*26.

When there is a fixed set, you can duplicate the results of the PERMUT function by multiplying the probabilities together but reducing each argument by one. For instance, if you had 26 Scrabble™ letter blocks for A to Z and wanted to see how many four letter combinations you could possibly form, you could use the formula =26*25*24*23. Each argument is reduced by one, because you have one fewer possibility available as you fill in the previous choices.

PI

One of the simplest functions to use, PI returns the value of PI to 15 digits of accuracy. The syntax for PI is:

=PI()

PMT

The PMT function calculates the payment required to pay back a loan in a specified period of time. It can also be used to calculate how much money must be deposited, or paid, on a regular basis to achieve an investment goal. The syntax for PMT is as follows:

=PMT(*interest_rate, number_of_periods, present_value, future_value, type*)

The details of the PMT function are discussed earlier in this chapter in the section titled "Examining an Example Function."

ROUND

The ROUND function rounds a number to a number of digits that you specify. Its syntax is:

=ROUND(*number,number_of_digits*)

The *number_of_digits* specifies where the number should be rounded. A *number_of_digits* less than 0 rounds the portion of a number to the left of the decimal place, while a *number_of_digits* greater than zero rounds the number to the right of the decimal place. A *number_of_digits* equal to zero rounds the number to the nearest integer. For example, =ROUND(123.456,1) returns 123.5, while =ROUND(123.456,-1) returns 120.

SUBTOTAL

The SUBTOTAL function provides a subtotal within a range. Successive SUBTOTALs ignore previous SUBTOTALs. Moreover, SUBTOTAL ignores any hidden rows, so only visible cells are included. The syntax for SUBTOTAL is:

=SUBTOTAL(*sub_function, range1, range2, ...*)

The SUBTOTAL function performs different functions depending on the setting of *sub_function*. You can choose from the following sub_function settings:

Sub_function	Action
1	AVERAGE
2	COUNT
3	COUNTA
4	MAX

continues

continued

Sub_function	Action
5	MIN
6	PRODUCT
7	STDEV
8	STDEVP
9	SUM
10	VAR
11	VARP

SUM & SUMIF

The SUM function sums a series of numbers. It translates any text numbers into their numerical equivalent automatically. The logical value TRUE is translated into a 1. The syntax for SUM is as follows:

=SUM(*number1, number2, ...*)

In some cases you want to sum only certain values within a range. When that's true, use SUMIF. The syntax for SUMIF is:

=SUMIF(*test_range, logical_criteria, range_to_sum*)

The *test_range* argument specifies the range to be tested against the *logical_criteria*. Cells that meet the criteria are summed if *range_to_sum* is omitted.

You can use *range_to_sum* to sum cells that correspond to the *test_range*. For example, you can test cells A1:A10 against the *logical_criteria*, and then sum the corresponding cells in the range B1:B10 if their matching cell (in *test_range*) meets the *logical_criteria*.

TODAY and NOW

The TODAY and NOW functions return the computer's current date and time. TODAY returns only the current date; NOW returns the current date and time. Both are updated each time you recalculate the worksheet. The syntax for both is:

=TODAY()

=NOW()

Common Problems and Solutions

Troubleshooting problems with functions can often be aggravating. Excel provides error messages when something is amiss with a function, but often the error codes aren't quite specific enough to quickly identify and fix the problem. In the following sections, you learn about common function problems and their solutions.

Common Function Troubleshooting

There are some common problems that occur with functions that you should watch out for. If a function isn't working at all, or isn't working as you expect, check the following:

- Are the parentheses correctly balanced and paired? In complex formulas within functions that contain multiple levels of parentheses, make sure that each one is where you want it and that none are missing. Remember, also, that parentheses control the order of evaluation in formulas.

TIP Excel colors the parentheses in a formula as you edit, using matching colors to represent matching parentheses.

- Are you using the right type of data for each function argument? For example, if you use a number where a function is expecting text, you're likely to get an error.
- Is the data on which a function is operating what it is expecting to work with? Similar to the previous point, make sure the source data you are referencing in a function matches what the function expects.
- Are you missing any arguments in the function? Check the detailed information about the function, particularly the examples given, to look for problems.
- Trying to nest more than seven levels will cause an error. You can nest functions to only seven levels in Excel.
- If you are referring to another worksheet or workbook in an external reference, make sure any names that contain spaces are set off with quotation marks.
- Some functions will not work properly if you enter numbers using some sort of format code, like the percent symbol. Functions almost always require just plain numbers for their number arguments.

The #NULL Error

You see a #NULL error when you use a range operator or cell reference incorrectly. This error usually occurs when you forget to use a comma to separate two distinct ranges in a function or formula.

The #REF! Error

The #REF! error means that a cell reference is invalid. This can come from several common causes. Often, this error comes up when a cell or range of cells on which other cells rely is deleted (or overwritten). You should check all of the cells referenced by the function to ensure that they all contain valid data for the function in question.

The #DIV/0! Error

You see the #DIV/0! error when you try to divide a number by zero. If this happens, make sure that all of the cells being referenced in a division operation contain non-zero numeric values.

The #VALUE! Error

The #VALUE! error is seen when an incorrect data type is used as an argument for a function or formula. For example, **=25/"Hello"** will yield a #VALUE! error.

> **TIP** Some functions explicitly ignore text within their ranges, such as SUM. Also, if you need to perform math operations on a set of data that contains scattered text, consider deriving a new range of data using the IF and ISNUMBER functions to build a new range without any of the text values.

You also see the #VALUE! error when you incorrectly enter an array formula by pressing Enter. Array formulas need to be entered using Ctrl+Shift+Enter.

The #N/A Error

You see the #N/A error when a required value is not available. It often occurs in the various lookup functions (HLOOKUP, LOOKUP, MATCH, and VLOOKUP).

You can use the #N/A error to your advantage. For example, if you are building a worksheet that already contains calculations on a range of data that is incomplete, you can enter #N/A manually into cells that do not yet contain data, but that will. Then, formulas and functions that refer to that data will return #N/A instead of trying to calculate results based on erroneous data. In this way, the #N/A entry and value becomes a sort of placeholder during the process of building a worksheet.

The #NUM! Error

The #NUM! error occurs in two cases: when an argument that requires a numeric value instead receives some other sort of value, and when a number exceeds Excel's maximum. The largest and smallest numbers that can be represented in Excel are $-1*10^{307}$ and $1*10^{307}$.

The #NAME? Error

You see a #NAME? error when you refer to a name in a formula that doesn't exist. Check these sources of trouble when you encounter this error:

- Use the Insert, Name, Define command to see if the name you want to refer to is assigned. If not, assign the name to the cell or range.
- Make sure all names you reference are typed correctly.
- You can see this error when you mistype a function name. Check the spelling of any functions used in this formula.

> **TIP** When you type a function name using lowercase letters, Excel converts the lowercase letters to uppercase automatically. For instance, if you type =now() and press Enter, Excel changes the formula to =NOW(). You can use this to your advantage by getting in the habit of typing function names using lowercase letters; if you've mistyped a function name, the fact that it's still displayed with lowercase letters tells you instantly that it's mistyped.

- Text in a formula that is not enclosed in parentheses can also cause this error. Even when a function is expecting text, it's always a good idea to surround text with parentheses.

From Here...

In this chapter, you learned how to enter and use Excel functions. You learned about the Paste Function dialog box and how to use the Formula Palette to build your functions. You also learned about a number of common Excel functions. Continue your exploration of Excel with the following:

- Chapter 3, "Entering and Editing Data," discusses how formulas are entered and used with Excel.
- Chapter 19, "Auditing and Validating Worksheets," shows you how to trace the precedent and dependent cells in a formula, which can help you troubleshoot functions in your worksheets.
- Appendix B, "Excel Function Reference," lists all of the functions available in Excel and tells you what tasks they perform.

CHAPTER 7

Using Excel Add-Ins

by Bruce Hallberg

In any program, each added feature consumes some memory and makes the program larger than otherwise. If you don't want a particular feature, why have it loaded into memory every time you use the application? That's the concept behind Excel 97's various add-ins. You can select which of the add-ins are installed along with Excel, and then which of them are active at any given time. You can have all of them installed and activated, or just the few that you commonly work with. In this chapter, you'll learn how to select Excel's Add-Ins during installation, as well as how to activate and deactivate them. Since most add-ins cause Excel to take more time to start, and consume some of your computer's memory when Excel is running, controlling whether or not they are active gives you some control over the amount of computer resources Excel consumes.

You also learn how to use many of the add-ins in this chapter. Other add-ins such as the Web Form Wizard or the Analysis Toolpak are covered in chapters related to those topics. ■

Installing and activating add-ins

Excel 97 comes with a number of add-in utilities that extend its power.

Using the Conditional Sum Wizard

You can use the Conditional Sum Wizard to calculate sums in a list based on criteria you specify.

Using the File Conversion Wizard

If you're upgrading to Excel 97 from another spreadsheet program or an earlier version of Excel, use the File Conversion Wizard to convert a group of files into Excel 97's workbook format.

Using the Lookup Wizard

Lookup functions can be difficult to master. The Lookup Wizard makes them easy!

Using AutoSave

Everyone who has used a computer has experienced losing their work because of some problem. Judicious use of the AutoSave Add-in protects you from these losses.

Using the Report Manager

The Report Manager lets you define complex reports that then enable you to print reports with a single action.

Installing Add-Ins

Whether you install Excel as part of Microsoft Office or as a stand-alone product, you can choose which of the various Excel 97 Add-Ins are installed.

When you perform a Typical installation of Microsoft Office 97, the following Excel Add-Ins are automatically installed:

- Analysis Toolpak
- Analysis Toolpak - VBA
- AutoSave
- Conditional Sum Wizard
- Lookup Wizard
- Microsoft Bookshelf Integration
- MS Query Add-In for Excel 5 Compatibility
- ODBC Add-In
- Template Utilities
- Update Add-In Links

As part of a Typical installation of Office 97, you may choose to install the Web Authoring components of Office. If you choose that option, the following two add-ins are also installed for Excel:

- Internet Assistant Wizard
- Web Form Wizard

There are some additional add-ins available to you that aren't installed in the Typical Office 97 installation. To access these other add-ins, you can either perform a Custom installation of Office 97 and then choose the appropriate options, or you can rerun the Office setup utility and then use the Add/Remove button to add the remaining add-ins. The other add-ins available to you are:

- AccessLinks
- File Conversion Wizard
- Report Manager
- Solver
- Template Wizard with Data Tracking

If you have an add-in to install that did not come with your version of Office 97 or Excel 97, you can add it using the Add-Ins dialog box with these steps:

1. Select Tools, Add-Ins and the Add-Ins dialog box appears (see Figure 7.1).
2. Click the Browse button to activate the Browse dialog box.

FIG. 7.1
The Add-Ins dialog box lets you install, activate, and deactivate Excel's Add-Ins.

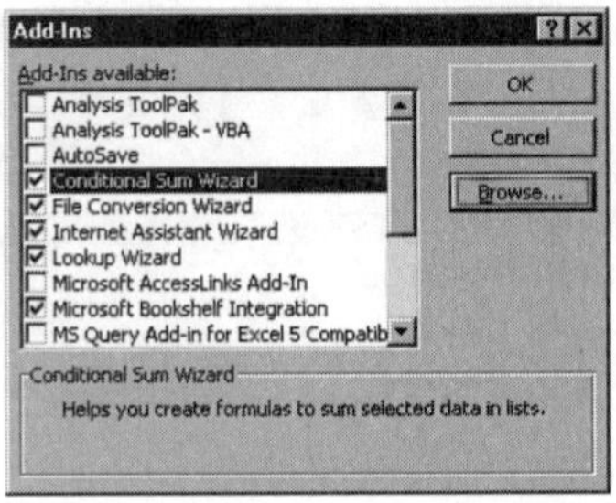

3. In the Browse dialog box locate the add-in file you want to use. Add-ins normally use either an .XLA or .XLL file extension.
4. Click OK.

The add-in you selected will appear in the Add-Ins dialog box and can be activated and deactivated the same as any other add-in.

Activating and Deactivating Add-Ins

Once you have the add-ins you want installed, you then need to choose which ones are active at any given time. Any activated add-ins are automatically loaded into memory when you start Excel, or when you activate them by selecting Tools, Add-Ins (refer to Figure 7.1).

To activate any of the listed add-ins, simply click its respective check box. When you close the Add-Ins dialog box, your changes are implemented instantly. Depending on which add-ins you activate, changes are made in Excel's menus, function list, or available VBA commands so that the features of the chosen add-ins are available to you.

If you need to free up some of your computer's memory while using Excel, you can deactivate any of the active add-ins. Simply deselect the check box beside the name of the add-in in the Add-Ins dialog box and click OK.

Using the Conditional Sum Wizard

If you work with lists of data, you often need to sum values in the list, but only using values that meet certain criteria. For instance, consider the example worksheet shown in Figure 7.2.

In this example, you see a list of invoices for March listed by invoice number. Suppose you now want to calculate the total sales for a particular salesperson? There are many ways to do this, including:

- Copy the worksheet to another sheet; then delete all of the rows except the ones for the salesperson for which you want to total the sales. Then do a simple SUM formula against the resulting list.
- Write a formula in which you manually choose each invoice amount cell for the salesperson for which you want to see total sales. For instance, to see total sales for Frank, you would use the formula **=F4+F9+F10+F15**.

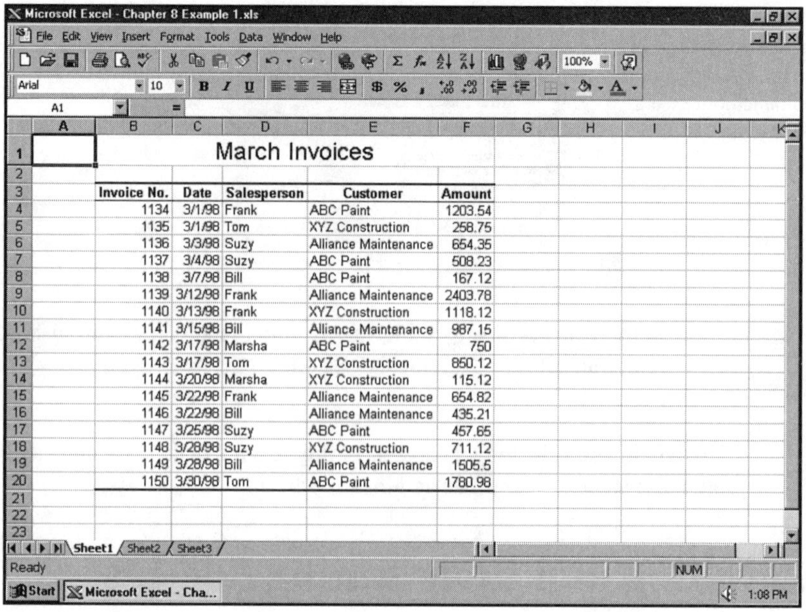

	Invoice No.	Date	Salesperson	Customer	Amount
	1134	3/1/98	Frank	ABC Paint	1203.54
	1135	3/1/98	Tom	XYZ Construction	258.75
	1136	3/3/98	Suzy	Alliance Maintenance	654.35
	1137	3/4/98	Suzy	ABC Paint	508.23
	1138	3/7/98	Bill	ABC Paint	167.12
	1139	3/12/98	Frank	Alliance Maintenance	2403.78
	1140	3/13/98	Frank	XYZ Construction	1118.12
	1141	3/15/98	Bill	Alliance Maintenance	987.15
	1142	3/17/98	Marsha	ABC Paint	750
	1143	3/17/98	Tom	XYZ Construction	850.12
	1144	3/20/98	Marsha	XYZ Construction	115.12
	1145	3/22/98	Frank	Alliance Maintenance	654.82
	1146	3/22/98	Bill	Alliance Maintenance	435.21
	1147	3/25/98	Suzy	ABC Paint	457.65
	1148	3/28/98	Suzy	XYZ Construction	711.12
	1149	3/28/98	Bill	Alliance Maintenance	1505.5
	1150	3/30/98	Tom	ABC Paint	1780.98

FIG. 7.2
A list of invoices in a worksheet. How can you calculate the total sales for any salesperson? How about for a particular customer? What about a range of dates?

- Sort the list by salesperson, and then perform a SUM against the range that includes that salesperson's invoices.
- Write a complex array formula.

While all of these solutions would work, each one has different problems. In some cases, they involve multiple steps that might consume too much time, especially if you need to do this for different salespeople or see totals in different ways. Some of the examples are impractical if you are working with a large list. In the last preceding example, the array formula required is complex to develop and validate if you don't commonly use array formulas.

The Conditional Sum Wizard is designed for jobs just like this one. Using it, you can create sums for lists of data, but only using values that meet criteria that you set. The Conditional Sum Wizard works by building an array formula that calculates the conditional sum using your criteria, but hides from you the complexity of building such a formula. As you will see, you can develop complex criteria for these conditional sum formulas. To use the Conditional Sum Wizard, follow these steps:

1. Select Tools, Wizard, Conditional Sum. The Conditional Sum Wizard dialog box appears, as shown in Figure 7.3.
2. Select the range from which the conditional sum will be derived. You can use the Collapse/Restore button to move the Conditional Sum Wizard dialog box out of your way as you select the range. Click Next after you select the range.

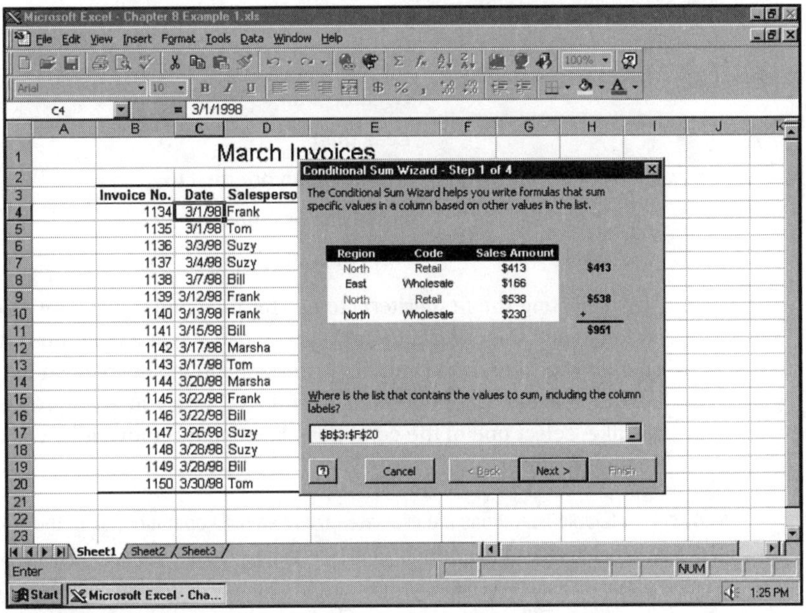

FIG. 7.3
Step 1 of the Conditional Sum Wizard lets you define the worksheet range to use as the source.

TIP If your active cell is within a contiguous list of data when you first activate the Conditional Sum Wizard, the range in step 2 is automatically selected for you. You can just double-check the range and then click Next to proceed.

3. Select the criteria to use for the conditional sum in the next dialog box that appears, shown in Figure 7.4.

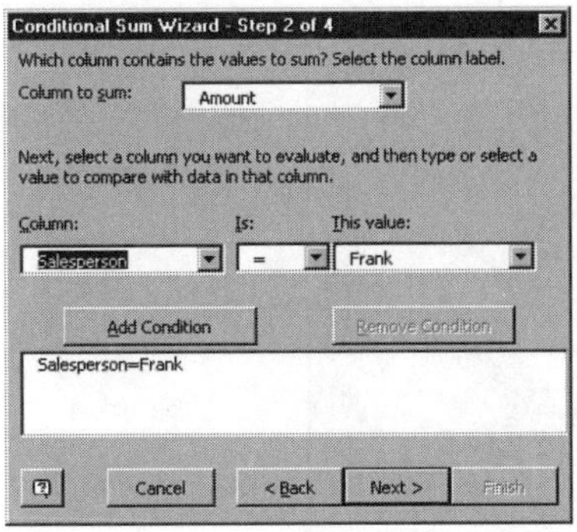

FIG. 7.4
You can define multiple conditions using Step 2 of the Conditional Sum Wizard.

4. First choose the Column to Sum. Then use the Column, Is, and This Value drop-down lists to choose the column you want to evaluate, the operator you want to use, and the possible value (respectively). In the Is drop-down list, you can choose to use the following operators:

Operator	Description
=	Equals
>	Greater than
<	Less than
>=	Greater than or equal to
<=	Less than or equal to
<>	Not equal to

5. After selecting the first criteria to use for the conditional sum, click the Add Condition button to add the criteria to the list (you can see one condition defined in Figure 7.4). Then, if you want, build another criteria using the drop-down list boxes and click Add Condition again. Continue until all of the criteria you need are defined. If you make a mistake, select one of the conditions listed and remove it by clicking the Remove Condition button.

NOTE Multiple conditions are evaluated using an AND operation; all of the conditions must be true in order for any record in the list to be included in the conditional sum. So, for example, if you defined two criteria in this example, one where **Salesperson=Frank** and the other where **Salesperson=Bill**, you would have a result of 0, because no record meets *both* conditions. You can, however, set two criteria where the first is **Salesperson=Frank** and **Customer=ABC Paint**, and only invoices where Frank was the salesperson for ABC Paint would be included in the conditional sum.

6. After defining your criteria, click Next to proceed. You see Step 3 of the Conditional Sum Wizard, as shown in Figure 7.5, in which you choose to only insert the result, or the result and the conditions. For this example, both the result and conditional value is selected. Click Next after you choose one of the options.

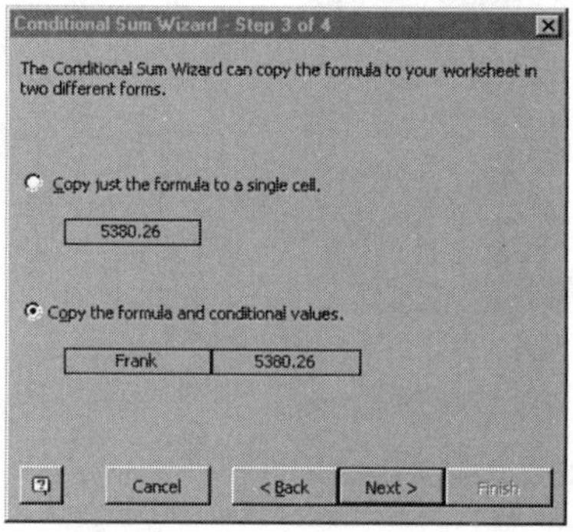

FIG. 7.5
Step 3 of the Conditional Sum Wizard lets you choose whether to include just the result or the result and the conditional values.

7. In Step 4 (and if necessary, additional steps) of the Conditional Sum Wizard, you choose which cell or cells will contain the conditions and result of the conditional sum (see Figure 7.6). Type the cell that you want to contain the condition or result, or click it; then click Next or Finish, as appropriate.

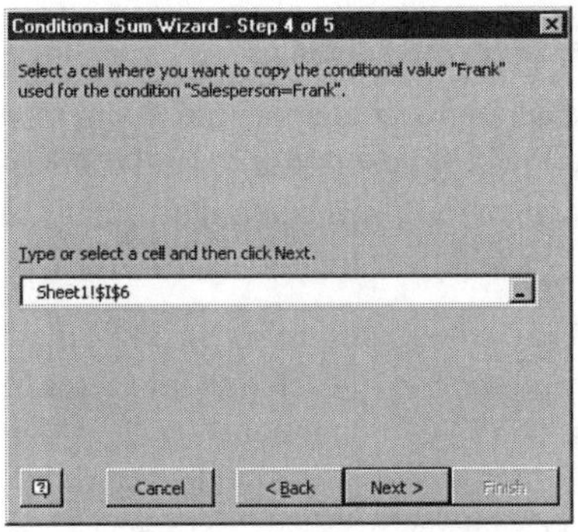

FIG. 7.6
In Step 4 of the Conditional Sum Wizard, you choose which cell contains the result.

Figure 7.7 shows you the result of this example. Notice that the result cell now contains the array formula:

```
{=SUM(IF($D$4:$D$20=H6,$F$4:$F$20,0))}
```

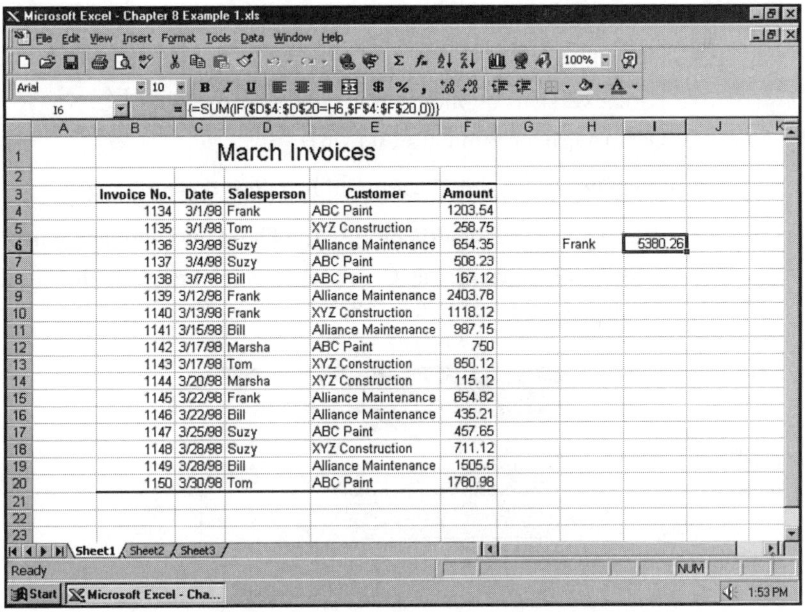

Invoice No.	Date	Salesperson	Customer	Amount
1134	3/1/98	Frank	ABC Paint	1203.54
1135	3/1/98	Tom	XYZ Construction	258.75
1136	3/3/98	Suzy	Alliance Maintenance	654.35
1137	3/4/98	Suzy	ABC Paint	508.23
1138	3/7/98	Bill	ABC Paint	167.12
1139	3/12/98	Frank	Alliance Maintenance	2403.78
1140	3/13/98	Frank	XYZ Construction	1118.12
1141	3/15/98	Bill	Alliance Maintenance	987.15
1142	3/17/98	Marsha	ABC Paint	750
1143	3/17/98	Tom	XYZ Construction	850.12
1144	3/20/98	Marsha	XYZ Construction	115.12
1145	3/22/98	Frank	Alliance Maintenance	654.82
1146	3/22/98	Bill	Alliance Maintenance	435.21
1147	3/25/98	Suzy	ABC Paint	457.65
1148	3/28/98	Suzy	XYZ Construction	711.12
1149	3/28/98	Bill	Alliance Maintenance	1505.5
1150	3/30/98	Tom	ABC Paint	1780.98

FIG. 7.7
The result of the Conditional Sum Wizard shows you the array formula it created.

Examining the array formulas generated by the Conditional Sum Wizard is a good way to learn more about array formulas. In this example, you see that the IF formula evaluates cells D4 through D20, examining each one to see if it meets the criteria set in cell H6 ("Frank"). If TRUE, the appropriate cell in the range F4:F20 is returned, and if FALSE, 0 is returned. The IF function in this array formula returns its multiple values to the SUM formula, which then simply sums them.

Using the File Conversion Wizard

You undoubtedly know that Excel can open spreadsheet files from many different spreadsheets, such as Lotus 1-2-3, Quattro Pro, Microsoft Works, and other types of files that contain similar types of data. Once open, you can then save such files into Excel's native .XLS format using the Save As command.

If you want to convert a large number of files from a non-Excel format into Excel workbooks, you can laboriously open each one and then save each one into Excel's native workbook format. However, an easier way exists. The File Conversion Wizard is designed expressly for this purpose and takes the drudgery out of converting many files. With it, you can convert multiple files in a single folder into Excel's .XLS format from any of these source types:

- Lotus 1-2-3 (.wk?)
- Quattro Pro for DOS (.wq1)
- Microsoft Works 2.0 (.wks)
- dBASE (.dbf)
- SYLK (.slk)
- DIF (.dif)
- Earlier versions of Microsoft Excel (.xls; .xlc; .xlm)
- Quattro Pro for Windows 1.0 (.wb1)

To use the File Conversion Wizard Add-In, follow these steps:

1. Start with a blank workbook (use the File, New command if necessary).
2. Select Tools, Wizard, File Conversion, which brings up the File Conversion Wizard dialog box shown in Figure 7.8.

FIG. 7.8
Use the File Conversion Wizard to convert multiple files into Excel XLS format.

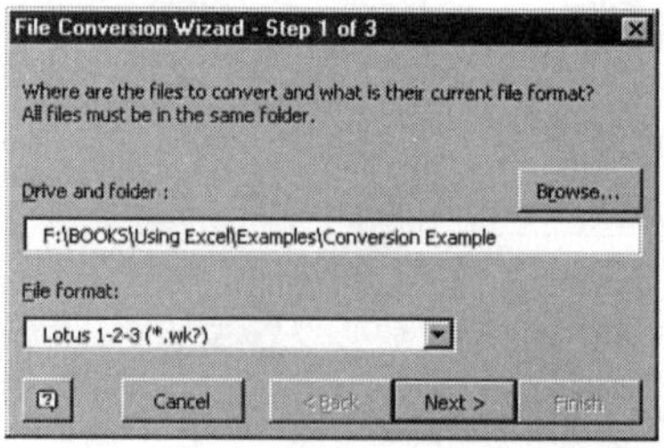

3. In the Drive and Folder field, indicate the folder that contains the source files. If necessary, use the Browse button to locate the folder.
4. Choose the file format from which you want to convert the files with the File Format drop-down list. Click Next to proceed.
5. In this dialog box, all candidate files with the extension you specified in step 4 appear (see Figure 7.9). Select each one you want to convert (click the check box next to each), or click the Select All button to convert all of them. Click Next to proceed.

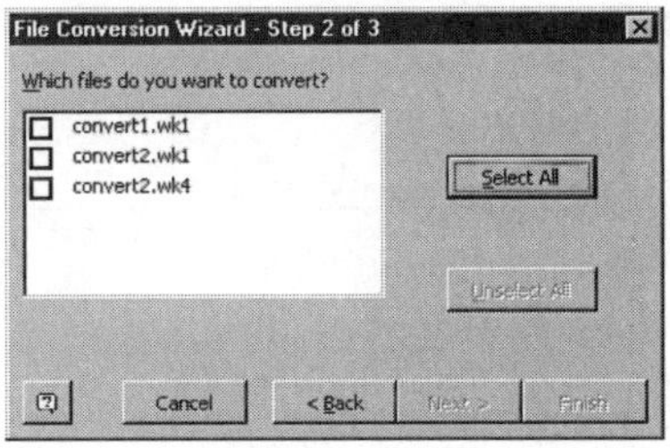

FIG. 7.9
Choose which files you want to convert.

6. The final step of the File Conversion Wizard appears (see Figure 7.10), in which you choose the folder that will contain the converted files. By default, the source folder is chosen. You can use the Browse button to select a new folder, or the New Folder button to create one. Click Finish.

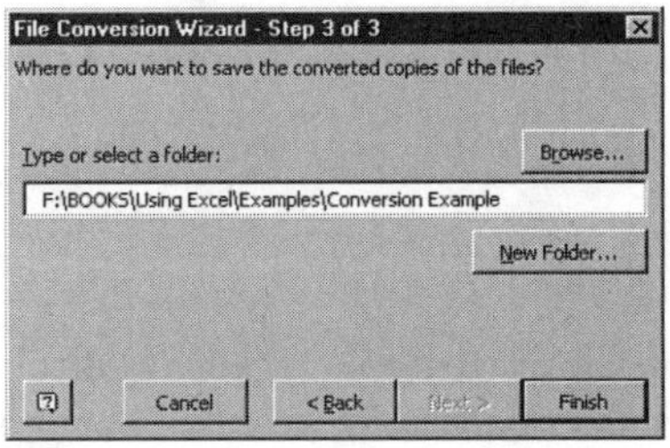

FIG. 7.10
In the final step of the File Conversion Wizard you choose the destination folder for the converted files.

The wizard then opens each of the files to be converted and saves them into Excel XLS format without any further intervention from you. At the end of this process (which may take quite a while for many large files), a summary sheet is generated for you in a new workbook. This summary sheet shows you the results of the File Conversion Wizard. An example summary sheet is shown in Figure 7.11; you can see that all files successfully converted, although one had to be renamed during the conversion to avoid a file name conflict.

The File Conversion Wizard operates on only a single folder at a time and cannot be changed to include subfolders. Because of this, you may want to use Windows Explorer to move all of the files you want to convert into a single folder before you begin the conversion process. In addition, if you are converting multiple files, the File Conversion Wizard may need a long time to complete all of the conversions. If you are converting hundreds of files, for example, it may be a good idea to start the wizard before you leave the office and let it run until it finishes.

Using the Lookup Wizard

When you build worksheets, particularly worksheets that are replacing forms, you often want to look up information in a table and use the matching information in the worksheet or template you're building. You can do this using a variety of functions, but you can more easily do it using the Lookup Wizard.

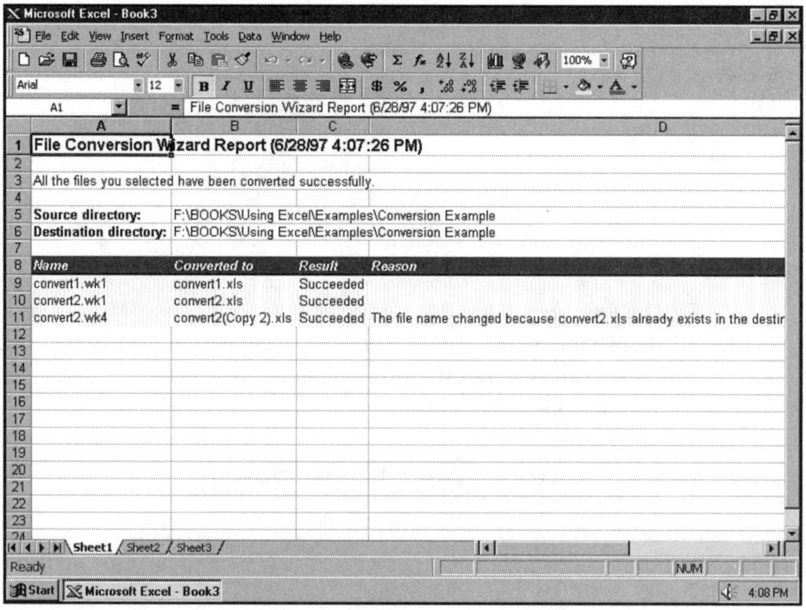

FIG. 7.11
A summary worksheet appears after the File Conversion Wizard runs showing you the results of its work.

For example, consider this situation: you are designing a sales quotation workbook that your salespeople can use to generate customer quotations. You don't want them to make mistakes when looking up product prices, and you want to maintain a worksheet with the correct values. The salesperson would only have to enter in the appropriate product code, and Excel would automatically fill in the product description and price. And if you want to change the quote prices, you can do so simply by changing the Excel list from which the quote form finds the prices. Figure 7.12 shows the quotation form before the lookup formulas are added with the Lookup Wizard. Figure 7.13 shows the list of products that will be linked to the quotation form using the Lookup Wizard.

Notice there are two columns in the sales quotation that need lookup formulas: the Description and Price Each columns. Both columns will be filled in automatically once the salesperson using the form provides a part number. To use the Lookup Wizard:

1. Select Tools, Wizard, Lookup. This starts the Lookup Wizard, shown in Figure 7.14.
2. Select the range of cells that contain the list you want to use. Include the row and column labels for the list. In this case, the range **'Quote Prices'!$A$3:$C$9** is selected. Click Next to proceed.
3. Select the row and column intersections that will be used. In our example, the lookup for the Description field is being created; therefore, the Description column label is selected, along with the 1125 part number, as shown in Figure 7.15. After selecting the appropriate row and column label, click Next to continue.

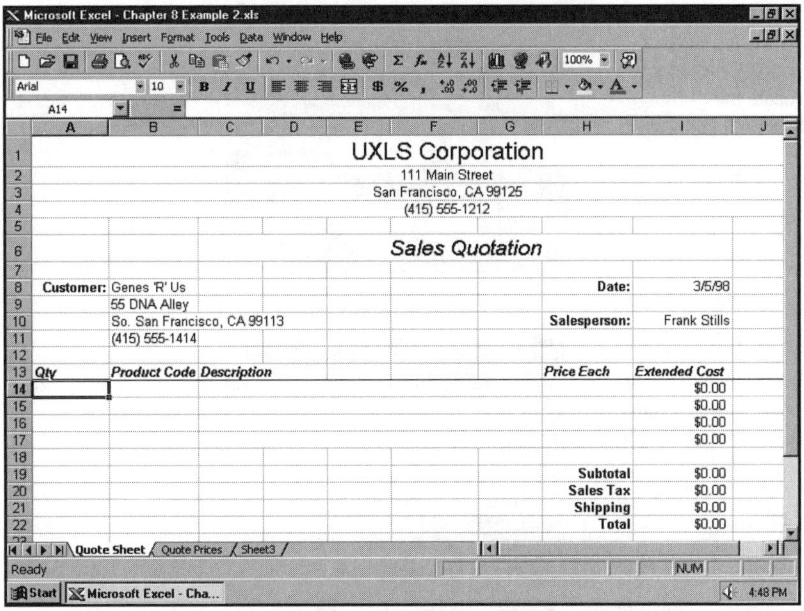

FIG. 7.12
A sample quotation form provides the canvas to learn about the Lookup Wizard.

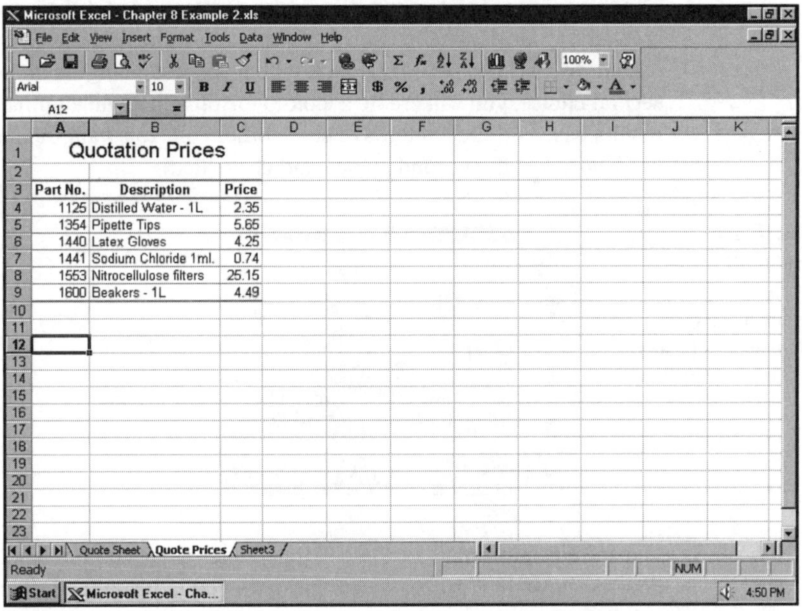

FIG. 7.13
This example list contains products that your salespeople quote to customers. Here the list is used to provide data for the quote form.

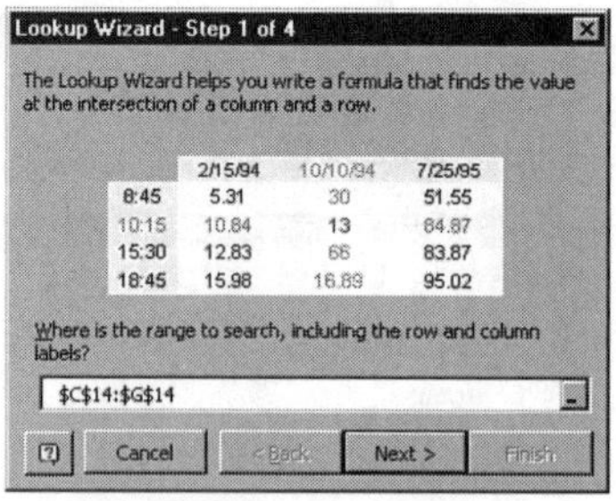

FIG. 7.14
The first step of the Lookup Wizard asks you to locate the list in which it will find values.

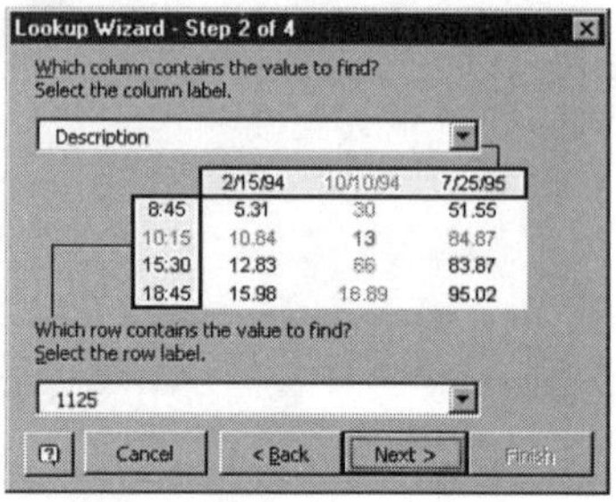

FIG. 7.15
The second step of the Lookup Wizard requires that you choose the row and column that contains the data you want found.

4. The third step of the Lookup Wizard (see Figure 7.16) defines what information will be created in your destination sheet. If you choose the first option, where only the result is pasted, you will create a static lookup that will not change. If instead you choose the second choice, you will create a lookup formula that will automatically return different results based on the contents of some other cell. You want the form to change as it is used, so select the second choice and click Next.

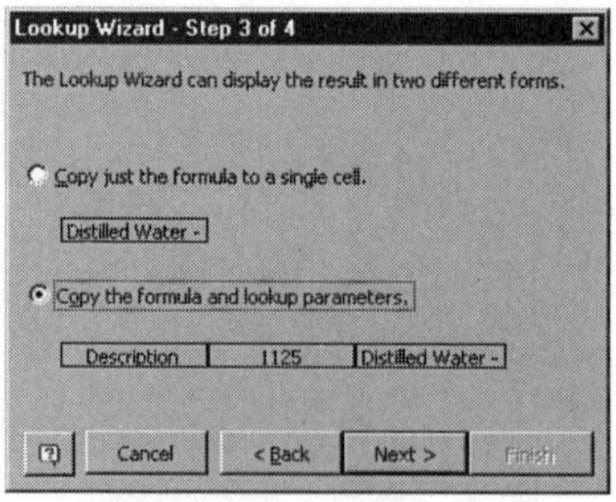

FIG. 7.16
Use Step 3 of the Lookup Wizard to determine how the information is pasted into the worksheet.

5. You are now prompted for the cell that contains the column label for the lookup information, as shown in Figure 7.17. In this case, you indicate the Description column label in cell C13. The column label you indicate must match exactly the column label in the source data in order for the lookup to function correctly. Click Next.

FIG. 7.17
After the third step is complete, you are prompted by successive dialog boxes for the location of the information used by and returned by the lookup formula.

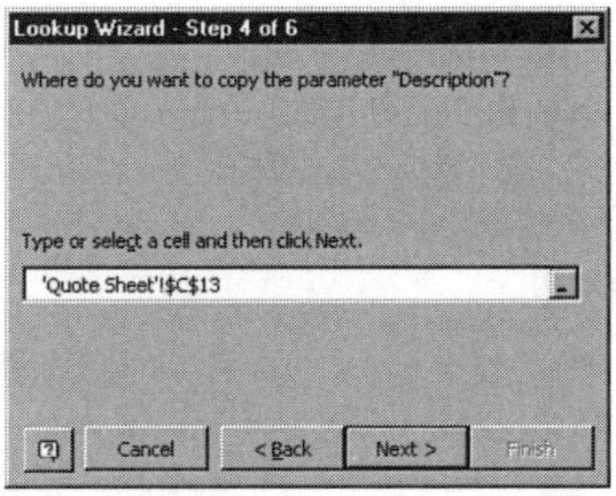

6. Complete the successive dialog boxes as requested, which work the same way as the Step 4 dialog box. Step 5 requests the cell of the parameter—Product Code—used to find the information (which, in this case, will be cell B14). Step 6 requests the cell for the result of the lookup (cell C14). After completing these dialog boxes, click Finish to return to your worksheet.

The result of the Lookup Wizard is shown in Figure 7.18. The first cell containing the lookup formula is selected, and the formula generated by the lookup formula is shown in the formula bar. At this point, you can enter any product code found in the list on the Quote Prices worksheet, and the matching description will appear automatically in the Description column.

FIG. 7.18
The result of the Lookup Wizard.

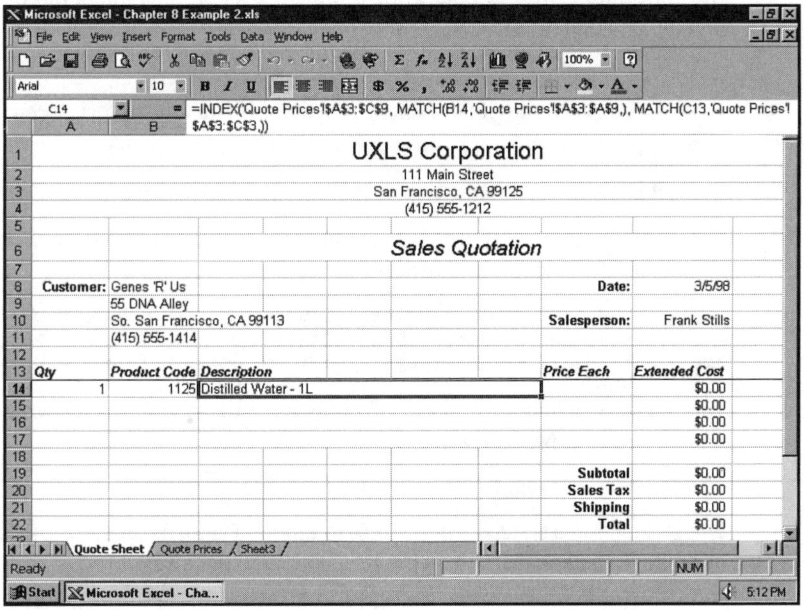

You now complete the same series of steps for the Price Each column, substituting that column in the quote price list in Step 3 of the wizard.

Copying and Refining Lookup Formulas

Once you have both the description and price cell lookup formulas defined, you naturally want to copy those formulas down into the remaining rows of the quote form. However, in this particular application, there exists a problem with doing so. Consider the Description lookup formula generated by the Lookup Wizard:

```
=INDEX('Quote Prices'!$A$3:$C$9, MATCH(B14,'Quote Prices'!$A$3:$A$9,),
MATCH(C13,'Quote Prices'!$A$3:$C$3,))
```

In the second MATCH function, cell **C13** refers to the Description heading. If you copy this formula down, the copied formula will refer to the preceding line for the column portion of the match, instead of the word "Description." To fix this, change the cell reference **C13**, in this example, to the absolute reference **$C$13** before copying the formula down. The other relative reference, **B14**, refers to the part number, and you want that cell reference to adjust for the remaining lines so that the lookup formula works for that line and not the first line only.

The preceding solves the first problem of how to copy the lookup formula down into the remaining lines, but there exists another problem that becomes apparent once you do this. Any lines in the sales quotation that don't have a part number return the #N/A error in place of lookup data. You don't want #N/A to appear in the form, because it looks unprofessional. Instead, if a line of the sales quotation isn't used, you simply want the lookup cells to be blank.

You can address this second problem by using a combination of the IF and ISERROR functions. (In fact, it's best to solve this problem before copying the lookup formulas down). Conceptually, you want Excel to do the following to solve the problem:

1. First, determine if the lookup function is returning an error code.
2. If it is returning an error code, it should display no data.
3. If it is not returning an error code, it should display the result of the lookup.

In order to implement this solution, you can wrap the lookup formula in the IF and ISERROR functions. The solution is shown here:

```
=IF(ISERROR(INDEX('Quote Prices'!$A$3:$C$9, MATCH(B17,'Quote Prices'!$A$3:$A$9,),
MATCH($C$13,'Quote Prices'!$A$3:$C$3,))),"",INDEX('Quote Prices'!$A$3:$C$9,
MATCH(B17,'Quote Prices'!$A$3:$A$9,), MATCH($C$13,'Quote Prices'!$A$3:$C$3,)))
```

This is clearly a long formula! To simplify it a little so you can see what's happening, here is the same formula in pseudo-code:

```
=IF(ISERROR(lookup_function), If_true_display_null, If_false_do_lookup_function)
```

The IF function's test asks if the lookup function returns an error by using the ISERROR function. Then, the value if true in the IF function returns a null (two quotes is equivalent to null) and if false—in other words, there is no error result from the lookup function—the lookup function is actually performed and its result displayed.

Figure 7.19 shows the completed sales quote form with these two solutions implemented.

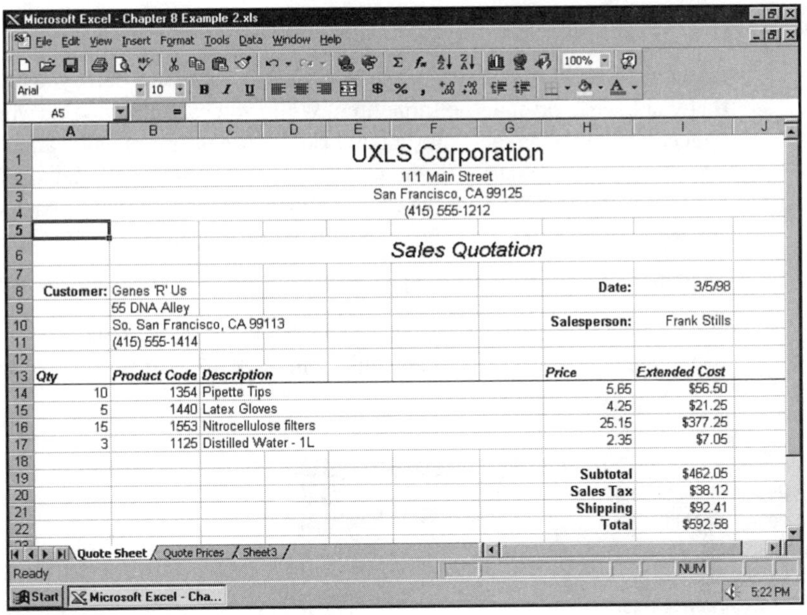

FIG. 7.19
The completed sales quote form using the Lookup Wizard results.

AutoSave

You can help protect yourself from disasters such as losing data by using Excel's AutoSave Add-In, which periodically saves your open workbooks for you automatically.

AutoSave is not turned on by default. You must first enable it by using the Tools, AutoSave command, which displays the AutoSave dialog box shown in Figure 7.20.

FIG. 7.20
Protect yourself with the AutoSave Add-in!

Using the AutoSave dialog box is easy. Simply make sure that the Automatic Save Every field is set with the number of minutes you want (and that its check box is selected). Then choose whether you want to Save Active Workbook Only or Save All Open Workbooks every time an automatic save is performed. You can also select or deselect the Prompt Before Saving check box depending on whether you want to be made aware of each save or simply want it to be performed without your intervention.

When AutoSave runs, it saves your work on a periodic basis, the same as if you use the File, Save command. If you experience a crash while using AutoSave, you can simply re-open the file you were last working with. All of your work up to the most recent AutoSave action should be present.

Report Manager

If you use Excel to prepare worksheet-based reports for others, you often have multiple reports that you have to print at the same time. While you can often do this with Excel's Print function (selecting just the sheets you want to print before printing), you cannot easily incorporate custom views or scenarios in such printouts. This is where the Report Manager comes in handy. The Report Manager lets you define different report sets, each of which can reference any worksheets you want combined with selected scenarios or views.

To define a new report, follow these steps:

1. Select View, Report Manager to access the Report Manager. You then see the Report Manager's main dialog box shown in Figure 7.21 (the example workbook has one report already defined).

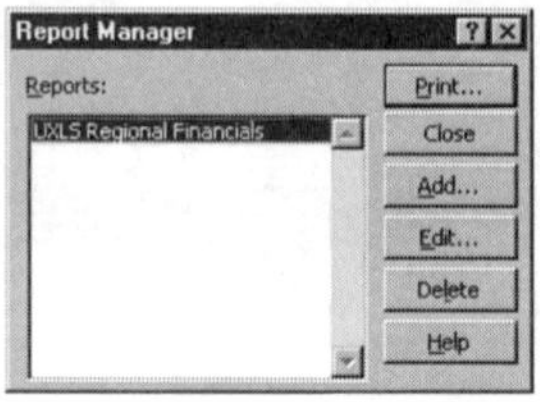

FIG. 7.21 The Report Manager lets you define different report settings, which you can manipulate to print sets of worksheets, scenarios, and custom views.

2. Click Add. The Add Report dialog box shown in Figure 7.22 appears.

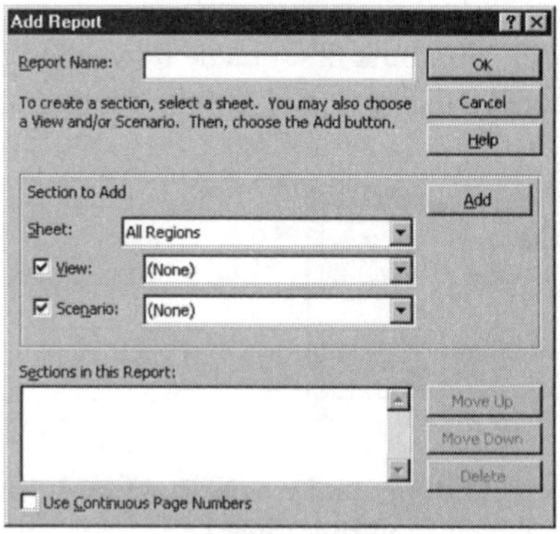

FIG. 7.22 Define what sections you want to include in your report in the Add Report dialog box.

3. In the Add Report dialog box, first assign the report a name in the Report Name field. This is the name that appears in the main Report Manager dialog box and with which you identify the report settings.
4. You can then select a specific Sheet, View, and Scenario. After choosing the combination of worksheet, custom view, and scenario, click the Add button, which adds that report page to the Sections in This Report list.

5. Keep selecting report pages in this manner until all the pages you want are listed. Then use the Move Up and Move Down buttons to order the reports in the way you want (or use the Delete button to remove one from the list). If you want all of the pages in the report to use sequential page numbers, select the Use Continuous Page Numbers check box. Click OK when you are finished.

After you've created a report using the Report Manager, you may want to edit the report by adding or deleting pages, or rearranging the order of the pages. Access the Report Manager dialog box, select the report you want to change, and click the Edit button. In the Edit Report dialog box (which is similar to the Add Report dialog box discussed previously), make the desired changes, and then click OK.

When you are ready to print a report, simply access the Report Manager dialog box, select the report in the Reports list, and click the Print button.

Common Problems and Solutions

Excel Add-Ins solve problems that can't be easily solved within the core set of Excel features. Developed by Microsoft (as well as third parties) and licensed by Microsoft, the add-ins that come with Excel offer powerful solutions to thorny problems.

There are generally few problems that you might experience with add-ins, but there are some common tips that can help you out in different situations. The following sections discuss these tips for working with add-ins.

Other Conditional Formulas

You've seen how useful the Conditional Sum Wizard is in this chapter. How about a Conditional Average Wizard or a Conditional Median Wizard? While no such wizards are included in Excel, you can use a simple trick to achieve the same result. Follow these steps:

1. Use the Conditional Sum Wizard normally to generate a conditional sum.
2. Edit the resulting array formula with the F2 key.
3. Change the SUM formula name to some other that operates on a range, such as AVERAGE or MEDIAN.
4. Press Ctrl+Shift+Enter to save the modified array formula (you must save array formulas with this key combination or they don't work).

Removing Add-Ins

There's no easy way to permanently remove individual Excel Add-Ins, but you can follow this procedure to do so:

1. Exit Excel, if it is open, then use Explorer to open the folder Office97\Office\Library. This is the folder in which Excel's Add-Ins are stored.

2. Locate the add-in you want to remove. You can tell which file name corresponds to which add-in by its name. For instance, the AutoSave Add-In is named AUTOSAVE.XLA. Remove the .XLA file in the Library folder to remove it from Excel. (You may want to simply move it to another folder if you just want to make it unavailable).
3. Start Excel. You will see an error message informing you that the add-in file needed isn't found. Acknowledge the error and continue starting Excel.
4. Select Tools, Add-Ins to access the Add-Ins dialog box. In the Add-In list, click the name of the add-in you removed in step 2.
5. You will see an error message informing you that the add-in is not found and offering to remove it from the list of add-ins. Click Yes to do so.
6. Exit and restart Excel.

You can reinstall add-ins in the same way. Simply place them back into the Library folder and start Excel. When you access the Add-Ins dialog box, they should reappear automatically and can then be activated.

If you want to remove an add-in from the Add-Ins dialog box without moving or removing the underlying add-in's .XLA file, you can directly edit the Registry to remove its reference. Open REGEDIT and navigate to the following key:

```
HKEY_CURRENT_USER\Software\Microsoft\Office\ 7.0\Excel\Init Commands
```

After selecting that key in the Registry Editor, you can locate the appropriate add-in entry, select it, and press the Del key to remove it.

CAUTION

Always take extreme care when editing the Windows Registry. Inadvertent mistakes in editing the Registry can make your system unusable.

Additional Add-Ins

Microsoft occasionally makes new or updated add-ins available for you to download. Point your Web browser to **http://www.microsoft.com/excel** to see what's new for Excel 97. At the time of this writing, the following add-ins were available for download:

- Power Utility Pak 97, a collection of tools available for a free trial period.
- Updated Internet Assistant Add-In that improves this tool when creating Web pages with Excel.
- Updated add-ins that extend the power of Microsoft Map in Excel.

There are also other tools available on Microsoft's Excel Web site, such as example workbooks, white papers, tips, and troubleshooting information in the Knowledge Base. If you're a frequent user of Excel, visit this Web page often to check for new items.

From Here...

In this chapter you learned about installing Excel Add-Ins, activating and deactivating them, and about using some of the add-ins not discussed in other chapters of the book. From here, consider the following chapters:

- Chapter 8, "Customizing Excel," shows you how to set Excel options to change the way Excel works.
- Chapter 9, "Excel Solution Templates," shows you how to install and use all of the included example solution templates that come with Excel. While designed to demonstrate Excel features, many of the solution templates offer useful tools applicable to a number of different needs.
- Chapter 21, "Mastering Excel's Solver," discusses using the Solver, another add-in included with Excel.
- Chapter 22, "Mastering the Analysis ToolPak," shows you how to use the Analysis ToolPak add-in.

CHAPTER 8

Customizing Excel

by Bruce Hallberg

You can customize Excel in a number of ways. You can, for example, choose to display formulas in cells instead of the results of the formulas. You also can hide (and unhide) an entire workbook, worksheets within a workbook, and row and column headings. In addition, Excel enables you to customize on-screen menus and toolbars.

In Excel, you can adjust how you view data in your workbooks. You can display a worksheet in full-screen view, for example, so that more of the worksheet data is visible at one time. You also can more easily compare data in separate worksheets by displaying the worksheets in separate windows. ■

Changing Excel's options

In this section, you learn about Excel's myriad options to change the way it works to suit your needs.

Customizing menus and toolbars

You can change Excel's menus and toolbars or create your own, to make your use of Excel more convenient and productive.

Customizing additional settings

In addition to customizing settings within Excel, you also can change some Windows settings to make Excel easier to use. For example, you'll learn how to open a workbook along with Excel, either from the Windows Start menu or the desktop.

Changing Excel's Options

One of Excel's hallmarks is its flexibility. In this section, you learn about all of Excel's options, each of which changes some aspect of how Excel works. Select Tools, Options from the menu to display the Options dialog box.

View Options

The View tab on the Options dialog box, shown in Figure 8.1, lets you control what elements of Excel appear on the screen. Table 8.1 details the options available on the View tab.

FIG. 8.1
Use the View tab to control what appears on Excel's display.

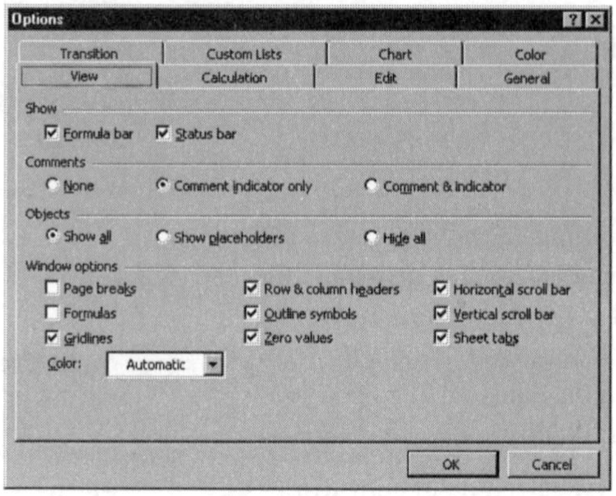

Table 8.1 View Settings in the Options Dialog Box

Option	Function
Show Section	
Formula Bar	Hides or displays Excel's formula bar.
Status Bar	Hides or displays Excel's status bar.
Comments Section	
None	Hides all cell comments and indicators.
Comment Indicator Only	Displays only cell comment indicators.
Comment & Indicator	Displays both cell comments and their indicators.
Objects Section	
Show All	Displays all embedded objects, such as buttons, graphic images, drawings, and text boxes.
Show Placeholders	Displays a rectangle in place of embedded images and charts.
Hide All	Hides all embedded objects.

Option	Function
Window Options Section	
Page Breaks	Displays automatic page breaks.
Formulas	Displays formulas in cells instead of their results.
Gridlines	Displays the gridlines that border cells.
Color	Sets the color of the gridlines.
Row & Column Headers	Displays the row and column labels.
Outline Symbols	Displays the symbols you see when you outline a portion of a worksheet.
Zero Values	Displays zeros. Deselecting this causes nothing to display with cells that contain a zero or zero result.
Horizontal Scroll Bar	Displays the horizontal scroll bar.
Vertical Scroll Bar	Displays the vertical scroll bar.
Sheet Tabs	Displays sheet tabs.

Most of the View option defaults are acceptable for almost all uses. An example when you will change the default settings is when you set up Excel for a user that will only use it to fill out online forms or for other limited uses, and who therefore doesn't need many of Excel's screen elements displayed. Or, perhaps, you may find that you prefer to hide some of the elements that are otherwise displayed in order to make more room to display your data, or simply because you don't ever use some particular option.

TIP On slower computers, you can sometimes dramatically improve the speed at which Excel scrolls through a worksheet by choosing the Show Placeholders option in the Objects section of the View tab. Then, when you're doing final formatting and want to see all the detail associated with any embedded graphic images, you can reactivate their display.

Calculation Options

When developing workbooks, controlling how Excel calculates and recalculates the workbook values is important. You do this on the Calculation tab in the Options dialog box, shown in Figure 8.2. Table 8.2 details the settings on the Calculation tab.

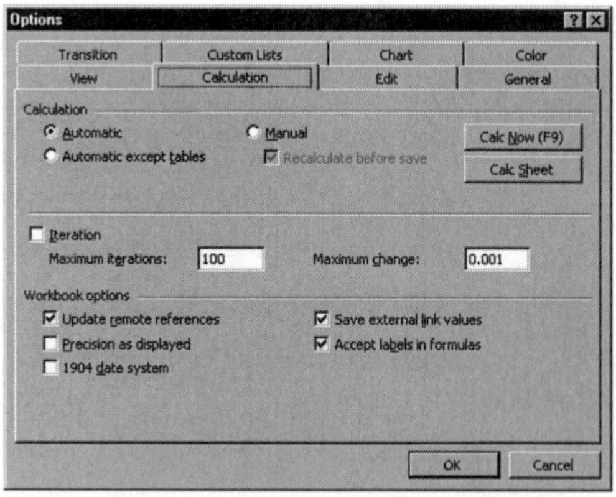

FIG. 8.2
The Calculation tab of the Options dialog box lets you control how Excel calculates workbooks.

Table 8.2 Calculation Settings in the Options Dialog Box

Option	Function
Calculation Section	
Automatic	Excel automatically recalculates all dependent formulas when you change a value, a name, or a formula.
Automatic Except Tables	All formulas recalculate when values, names, or formulas are changed, except those found in data tables. When this option is selected, you must press F9 to recalculate formulas within tables.
Manual	Turns off all automatic recalculation, so that recalculation only occurs when you click the Calc Now button or press F9.
Recalculate Before Save	Only available if the Manual option is chosen; Excel recalculates workbooks before they are saved.
Calc Now	Excel immediately recalculates. You can also press F9 while working with the workbook to achieve the same result.
Calc Sheet	Excel recalculates only the current worksheet.
Iteration Section	
Iteration	You can limit the number of iterations Excel will perform for circular references. With a complex worksheet, limiting the number of iterations Excel performs can dramatically improve your calculation time, although it may decrease the accuracy of any results (depending on the exact formulas involved).

Option	Function
Maximum Iterations	Only active when the Iteration check box is selected, this field specifies the maximum number of iterations Excel will perform for circular references or goal seek operations. The default value, used when Iteration is not checked, is 100 iterations. The maximum number of iterations allowed is 32,767.
Maximum Change	Excel can also limit iterations based on the largest change achieved on any given iteration. The default, 0.001, is used. You can increase or decrease this maximum change setting using this field.
Workbook Options Section	
Update Remote References	When this is selected (it's the default), recalculation automatically updates any cell or formula references to other workbooks or applications.
Precision As Displayed	When this is selected, the full precision stored by Excel is identical to the displayed precision. When this is not selected (it's the default), Excel stores full precision, or 15 digits.
1904 Date System	Changes Excel to use the 1904 date system.
Save External Link Values	If you are linking a workbook to a different (and large) workbook, it can take a lot of time to update the references to that other workbook. Selecting this check box (the default) causes the values from that linked workbook to be stored so that the other workbook doesn't have to be loaded every time its references are recalculated.
Accept Labels in Formulas	Allows you to use label names in formulas. When this is not selected, you must use row and column labels.

When you build a large worksheet, you find that making small changes takes increasing amounts of time to recalculate as the worksheet grows. This becomes a particular problem when you're still developing the workbook or when you make frequent changes but don't need to constantly see accurate data until you're done entering the data. When these types of situations arise, changing the calculation options for Excel from Automatic to either Automatic Except Tables or Manual will save you a lot of time. Then, simply press the F9 key when you want to force Excel to perform an immediate and complete calculation.

With worksheets that rely on circular formula references or the Goal seek feature of Excel, multiple iterations are often required to refine the results of those calculations. When this is the case, calculation may take a long time to perform. You can save time by limiting the number of iterations Excel performs by selecting the Iteration check box and the two fields (Maximum Iterations and Maximum Change) that define how Excel knows when to stop iterating such formulas. Later, you can increase the limits using these iteration fields again when you want to achieve the greatest possible accuracy.

▶ **See** "Solving Problems with Goal Seek," **p. 506**

The Workbook options section of the Calculation tab contains some check boxes that let you further refine certain aspects of calculation:

- You can embed objects in Excel that link to other applications such as Microsoft Word or Microsoft Access. And, of course, you can also reference other Excel workbooks as external references. Recalculating such references can be time-consuming. When calculations are taking too long and you are working with a worksheet that includes remote references, you can save time by deselecting the Update Remote References check box until you want final calculations performed. You can also clear this check box to save time when you are certain that the remote references are unchanging and have already been calculated properly.
- It's rare, but sometimes a worksheet may take a long time to calculate because of the precision of the numbers that Excel is using. By default, Excel uses full precision during calculation, which runs to 15 digits long. Selecting the Precision As Displayed check box causes Excel to truncate any values in the worksheet to the precision that is displayed, which can speed calculation.

CAUTION

Be extremely careful when using the Precision As Displayed check box. Selecting it causes all values in the open workbooks to be truncated to their displayed precision. For instance, if a cell contains the value 123.456 but you are only displaying 123.5 (only displaying one decimal point and rounded up), and you choose the Precision As Displayed check box, the value permanently becomes 123.5. Any further precision detail that isn't displayed is lost forever.

- Excel stores date values as a serial number where the serial number 1 corresponds to January 1, 1900. Other programs, in particular Excel for the Macintosh, use the 1904 date system where serial number 1 corresponds to January 1, 1904. If you are using a worksheet developed with another spreadsheet application that uses the 1904 date system, you should select the 1904 Date System check box so that any serial number calculations performed in the worksheet operate as they were designed.
- Making sure the Save External Link Values check box is selected can save time in some cases. When you open a workbook that contains links to other workbooks, it can take a lot of time for Excel to open all of those linked workbooks and retrieve the values they are storing. Instead, with Save External Link Values checked, the values from those linked workbooks are stored along with the workbook you're working with. Excel doesn't have to update those external links every time you open the workbook in order to contain the data from those externally linked workbooks. However, keep in mind that the data in those linked workbooks may have changed, and so periodically, you should update the external link values. When you open a workbook, Excel asks if you want external linked values to be updated (if any exist).

TIP To manually update links in an active destination workbook, choose Edit, Links. In the Source File list box, select the source workbook, then click the Update Now button.

Editing Options

The Edit tab of the Options dialog box controls how Excel's editing functions operate (see Figure 8.3). You can customize these options so that editing cells works the way that you want. Table 8.3 details the options you find on the Edit tab.

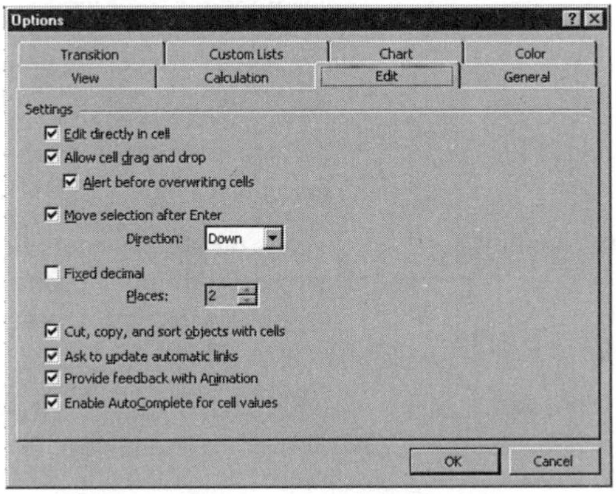

FIG. 8.3
Use the Edit tab to change how Excel's editing functions operate.

Table 8.3 Editing Settings in the Options Dialog Box

Option	Function
Edit Directly in Cell	Allows editing directly in cells. When deselected, data can only be edited in the formula bar.
Allow Cell Drag and Drop	Enables the fill handle to copy and fill data, as well as the ability to drag cell contents to other worksheet locations.
Alert Before Overwriting Cells	Only available when Allow Cell Drag and Drop is enabled; causes a warning message to appear if a cell drag-and-drop operation will overwrite existing data.
Move Selection After Enter	Enables you to press Enter after typing data into a cell to move the active cell in the direction indicated by the Direction setting. When this is disabled, the active cell remains the same when you press Enter.

continues

Table 8.3 Continued

Option	Function
Direction	Determines the direction the active cell moves after you enter data.
Fixed Decimal	Much like an adding machine that assumes a fixed decimal location, this setting performs the same function.
Places	Determines the number of decimal places assumed for the Fixed Decimal setting.
Cut, Copy, and Sort Objects with Cells	Embedded objects maintain their relationship to cells as the cells are cut, copied, or sorted.
Ask to Update Automatic Links	Causes a confirmation message to appear every time an automatic link is updated.
Provide Feedback with Animation	Turns on Excel's animation features, which can provide additional feedback to show what Excel is doing. This option is very useful for people new to Excel.
Enable AutoComplete for Cell Values	When this option is selected, Excel's AutoComplete feature is active.

Most of the options found on the Edit tab of the Options dialog box are self-explanatory, but there are a few that deserve some special attention.

When Allow Cell Drag and Drop is enabled, it is always a good idea to also enable Alert Before Overwriting Cells. It is easy to misdrag a cell from one location to another, and if Alert Before Overwriting Cells is not selected, you will have to rely on the Undo button to restore any overwritten data.

For many accountants who work with currency amounts, the Fixed Decimal option along with the Places option can make Excel emulate a 10-key adding machine's operation. With Fixed Decimal enabled and Places set to 2, entering the digits "12345" results in 123.45 being entered into the cell. You can override the default decimal place by typing it manually, just like an adding machine.

General Options

The General tab of the Options dialog box holds a plethora of different settings that don't fall into any single category, but are often changed by people. Figure 8.4 shows this tab, and Table 8.4 details the settings found within it.

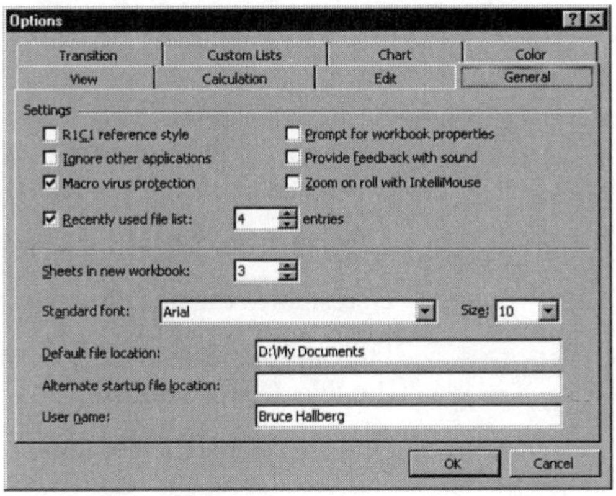

FIG. 8.4
Use the General tab to set a host of miscellaneous Excel options.

Table 8.4 General Settings in the Options Dialog Box

Option	Function
R1C1 Reference Style	Switches Excel into the old-style R1C1 reference style for referring to cells in formulas. See Chapter 3, "Entering and Editing Data," for more information on this option.
Ignore Other Applications	Causes Excel to ignore DDE/OLE requests from other running applications.
Macro Virus Protection	Enables Excel's macro virus protection that warns you when a workbook is opened that contains auto-start macros.
Recently Used File List	Controls the number of recently used files that appear at the bottom of Excel's File menu. The default is four files and the maximum is nine files.
Prompt for Workbook Properties	Automatically prompts for workbook property settings whenever a workbook is saved. You otherwise access these settings through the File, Properties command.
Provide Feedback with Sound	When a sound card is available and this option is selected, certain Excel actions provoke a suitable sound.
Zoom on Roll with Intellimouse	If an Intellimouse is installed (along with the appropriate Windows driver), this option causes the wheel to zoom in and out of a worksheet. When this is deselected, the wheel instead scrolls the worksheet up and down.

continues

Table 8.4 Continued

Option	Function
Sheets in New Workbook	Controls the default number of sheets created with new workbooks.
Standard Font	Allows you to choose Excel's default font.
Size	Determines the default size of the Standard Font.
Default File Location	Indicates the first folder you will see when you use the File, Open command.
Alternate Startup File Location	Sets an alternate folder for startup worksheets.
User Name	Displays the name used for any worksheet comments or revision marks made. This is an important setting to complete.

Most of the settings on the General tab, when changed, require that you exit Excel and restart it for them to take effect. Examples of this include Recently Used File List, Standard Font, and the file location settings.

You should avoid turning off the Macro Virus Protection option unless you frequently work with workbooks that have embedded macros that you are sure are safe. It is possible to transmit computer viruses using Visual Basic for Applications programs in Excel, and the Macro Virus Protection setting warns you when possibly suspicious workbooks are opened before they can cause problems for you.

CAUTION

Large companies external to your own that work with many Word and Excel documents are common sources for document-based macro viruses. Be particularly careful with documents coming from larger law firms and accounting firms, as document viruses propagate through such environments very quickly, and then often multiply when documents are sent to clients by diskette or e-mail. Making sure that a general-purpose virus scanner is always running on your workstation is very prudent protection from both document-based viruses and the more commonly seen program-based or boot sector-based viruses.

When indicating a folder for the Default File Location field, remember that you specify server-based folders using their Universal Naming Convention names. The syntax for UNC names is \\server_name\folder_name.

If you always open certain workbooks every time you start Excel (such as workbooks that contain VBA programs you always use), place those workbooks in their own folder and indicate that folder with the Alternate Startup File Location field. Any workbooks in the folder referenced by that setting are opened every time Excel starts.

CAUTION

Avoid placing any non-Excel files in the alternate startup folder, as Excel will try to open those files and this can cause Excel to behave erratically afterward.

You can help new Excel users get used to Excel by enabling the Provide Feedback with Sound option, provided their computer has a way of generating sounds.

Transition Options

The Transition tab in the Options dialog box contains settings designed for people migrating from another spreadsheet application, such as Lotus 1-2-3 or Quattro Pro. Figure 8.5 shows you this dialog box, and Table 8.5 details the options you find.

FIG. 8.5
The Transition tab contains options that help when you have been using another spreadsheet application.

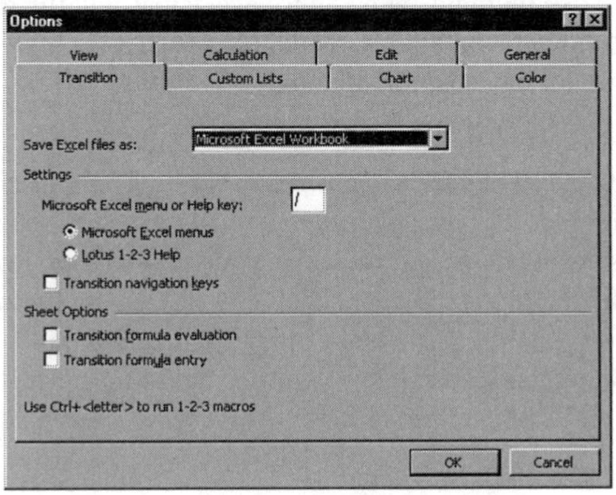

Table 8.5 Transition Settings in the Options Dialog Box

Option	Function
Save Excel Files As	Determines the standard file format into which Excel files are saved.
Settings Section	
Microsoft Excel Menu or Help Key	Determines the alternate key that activates either the Excel menus or Lotus 1-2-3 help.
Microsoft Excel Menus	Determines that Excel's menus are activated when the menu or Help key is selected.
Lotus 1-2-3 Help	Determines that Lotus 1-2-3 help in Excel is activated when the menu or Help key is selected.

continues

Table 8.5 Continued

Option	Function
Transition Navigation Keys	Forces Excel to use Lotus 1-2-3 navigation key commands.
Sheet Options Section	
Transition Formula Evaluation	Enables the Lotus 1-2-3 method of evaluating formulas.
Transition Formula Entry	Automatically converts formulas entered using the Lotus 1-2-3 method into normal Excel formulas.

Transitioning from one spreadsheet product to another is difficult. The people who use spreadsheets in their jobs often use them for many hours every day, and the habits formed are long-lasting. To make transitioning from other spreadsheets such as Lotus 1-2-3 to Excel easier, Microsoft provides a number of transition options.

Use the Save Excel Files As drop-down list to set a default file format to use when saving Excel workbooks. This option is very helpful when a group of people are gradually transitioning from one product to Excel. In cases like this, everyone should agree on a common file format (which is typically the previous application), and then everyone should save worksheets using that format so that people still using the old application can still access the work of others. You should be aware, however, that file formats for other applications will not support all of Excel's features, and saving worksheets into any format other than Microsoft Excel Workbook will cause some formatting and other information to be lost.

You use the options in the Settings section of the Transition tab to control how navigation keys work in Excel. Lotus 1-2-3 handles navigation keys differently than Excel. For instance, Lotus 1-2-3 moves your active cell to A1 when you press the Home key, while Excel moves to column A but leaves the active cell in the current row. Other keys also behave differently in the two programs. Use the Transition Navigation Keys option to cause Excel to emulate Lotus 1-2-3's navigation keys as closely as possible. You can also set a key that activates either Excel's menus or the Lotus 1-2-3 Help in Excel using the Microsoft Excel Menu or Help Key setting. The default, a forward slash, is the menu activation key in 1-2-3, and is a good choice to use to call up either Excel's menus or the 1-2-3 help.

Lotus 1-2-3 and Excel calculate formulas differently. Several differences are allowed for when the Transition Formula Evaluation check box is selected:

- *Some similarly named functions in Excel and 1-2-3 operate differently.* For example, VLOOKUP and HLOOKUP in Excel assume that the underlying data is sorted and simply look for the first match without considering the entire list. @VLOOKUP and @HLOOKUP in 1-2-3 instead examine all cells in a range.

- *Logical calculations in Excel and 1-2-3 return different results.* Excel returns TRUE or FALSE, while 1-2-3 returns 1 or 0. Turning on the Transition Formula Evaluation option causes Excel to use the numerical codes for TRUE and FALSE logical calculations.
- *Excel does not let you mix text and number entries inappropriately in formulas.* When you try, for instance, to SUM a range of values when one of the values is a text string, Excel returns a #VALUE error. 1-2-3, on the other hand, treats text entries referred to in this way as being equivalent to 0.
- *Database criteria operate differently.* Excel finds exact matches, whereas 1-2-3 assumes the equivalent of a wild card at the end of database criteria references.

It takes a long time to get used to function names in a spreadsheet application. Turning on the Transition Formula Entry check box lets you enter formulas using 1-2-3 methods. For example, you can use the @ character before Excel function names and the function name is automatically converted to a native Excel function name upon entry when Transition Formula Entry is selected. You can also use two periods when defining a range instead of the Excel-standard colon (for example, B1..B10 vs. B1:B10).

TIP Without any transition options selected, you can begin Excel formulas with the + sign (1-2-3 method) instead of the = sign (Excel method). You can also type the @ character before function names and Excel will simply ignore them.

Custom Lists

The Custom Lists tab of the Options dialog box lets you create lists that Excel uses when you copy a cell into adjacent cells using the AutoFill handle. For example, if you commonly create a long list of headings that names the different sales regions in your company, you can create a custom list to make this job easier. Define the custom list, and then in the future, you only have to type the first entry and then use the AutoFill handle to complete the remaining entries. The Custom Lists tab is shown in Figure 8.6.

NOTE There are a number of series that Excel automatically fills, such as times, dates, and numbers. These fills do not show on the Custom Lists tab; they are built into Excel.

There are several ways to use the Custom Lists tab:

- Create a new list by clicking NEW LIST in the Custom Lists window. Then click in the List Entries window and type each list member, pressing the Enter key after each entry. Click the Add button when you're done.
- Create a new list by selecting a range of cells in the Import List from Cells field. Once the range of cells that contains the list is entered, click the Import button to create that new list. Remember that you can direct-select the range in the Import List from Cells field by first clicking in the field, and then clicking the Collapse button at the end of the field, selecting the range, and clicking the Expand button to restore the dialog box.

FIG. 8.6
Use the Custom Lists tab to create your own AutoFill lists.

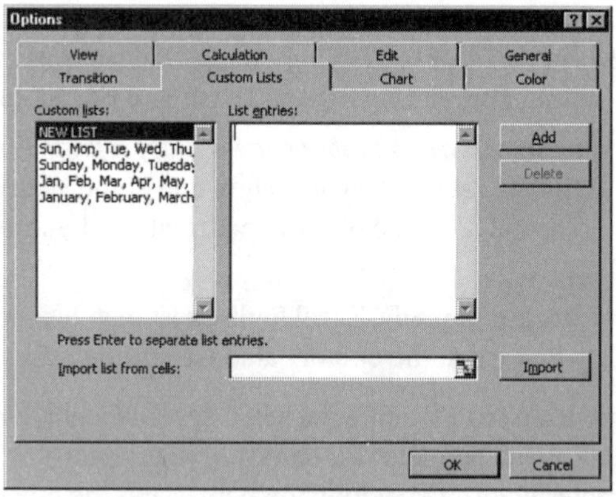

- Delete a list by selecting it in the Custom Lists window and clicking the Delete button. You can only delete custom lists that you create; you can't delete Excel's built-in lists.

Custom lists are used automatically when you use the AutoFill handle to copy a cell entry into adjacent cells, provided the cell entry matches either one of the predefined Excel AutoFill lists or an entry in the Custom Lists tab. You do not have to start with the first element of a Custom List before using AutoFill; any entry in the list will work.

Chart Options

97

The Options dialog box contains a tab that lets you set certain parameters for your charts. An improvement in Excel 97 now lets you define these options for each chart. Most of the settings on the Chart tab only apply to the active chart on your screen, whereas in previous versions of Excel you had to choose these options for all charts. Figure 8.7 shows the Chart tab.

FIG. 8.7
The Chart tab lets you control how charts are plotted.

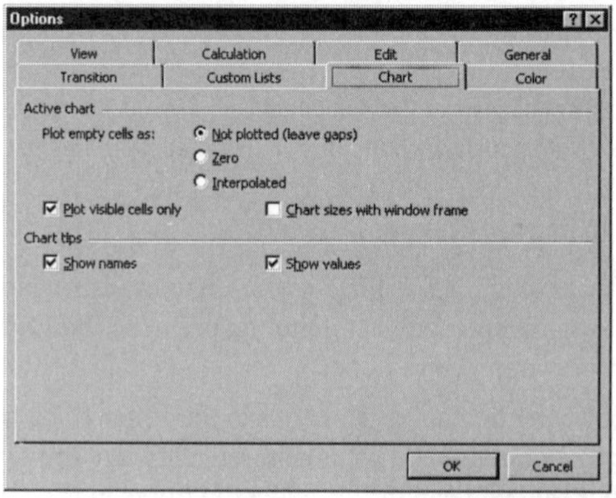

The settings in the Active Chart section of the Chart tab affect only the currently selected chart. The first setting lets you choose three different ways that missing data in a series will be plotted:

- Not Plotted (Leave Gaps) will skip any missing data in a series. This option generally makes the most sense for column or bar charts. On line charts, using this option leaves large gaps in the lines.
- Zero assumes that any missing values are zero and plots them accordingly. This option is rarely useful, as it is generally misleading to suggest that missing data is equal to zero.
- Interpolated causes any missing data to be skipped, but the line continues directly to the next valid point (in effect, interpolating the missing data). This option is only available if you are working with a line or scatter chart.

Selecting Plot Visible Cells Only is useful when you want to create a chart that dynamically shows only visible cells referenced by the chart. When you hide some of the chart's underlying cells in any way, those cells become skipped on the chart.

Choosing Chart Sizes with Window Frame causes any chart sheets being viewed to automatically scale to the size of the window in which they reside. This option is not available for embedded charts.

Finally, you can choose whether Excel's Chart Tips—on-screen pop-ups that work like ToolTips—show the names of series (Show Names) or the values of the data point (Show Values) when you rest your mouse pointer over a chart point or series.

Color Options

The Color tab of the Options dialog box lets you control what colors are available in Excel's color palette (see Figure 8.8). The colors you choose on the Color tab are then available in any of Excel's coloring options. Needing to change Excel's color palette is rare but can be useful when a particular color doesn't image well on your screen, or when you need to access a color that isn't in the default palette.

FIG. 8.8
Use the Color tab to change Excel's color palettes.

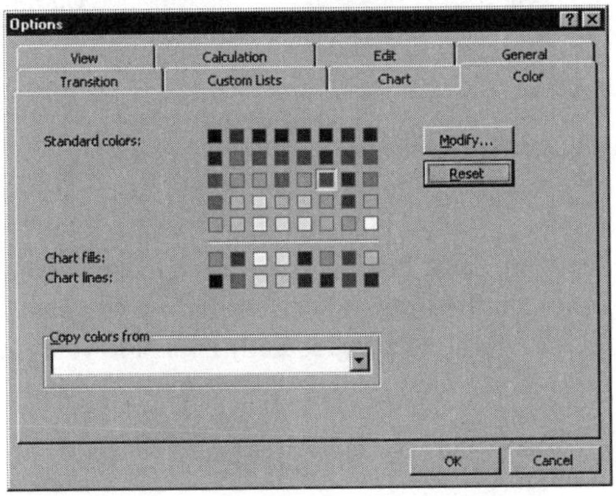

To change any of the colors in any of the three color palettes shown (Standard Colors, Chart Fills, and Chart Lines), click that color. Then click the Modify button, which reveals the Colors dialog box shown in Figure 8.9.

FIG. 8.9
The Standard tab of the Colors dialog box lets you choose from a number of typical colors.

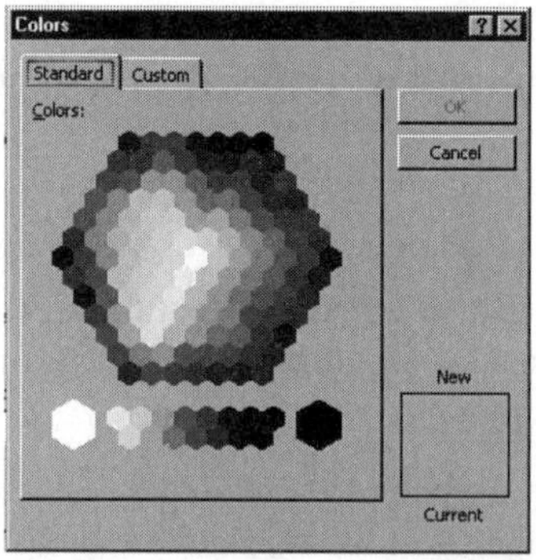
Colors
Standard
Custom
Colors:
OK
Cancel
New
Current

Choose from the colors shown on the Standard tab and click OK to choose that color for the previously selected color in one of Excel's palettes. If you don't find the color you want to use on the Standard tab, click the Custom tab in the Colors dialog box. The Custom tab of the Colors dialog box lets you choose exactly the color you want using any of several different methods (see Figure 8.10). Once you define the color you want, click OK to return to the Color tab of the Options dialog box.

FIG. 8.10
The Custom tab of the Colors dialog box lets you select a variety of colors.

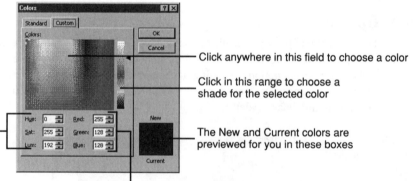

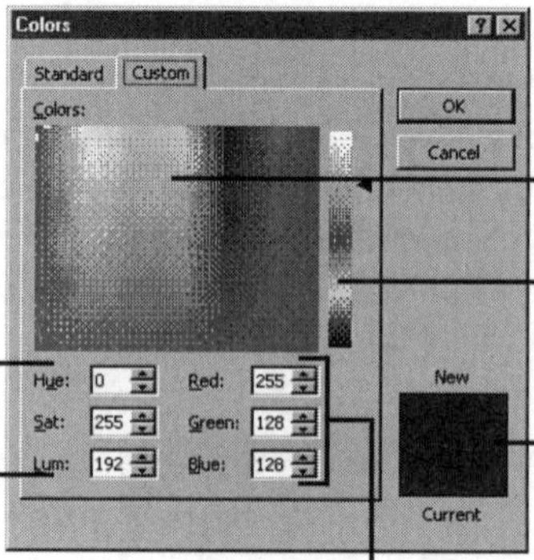
Colors
Standard
Custom
Colors:
OK
Cancel
Hue: 0
Sat: 255
Lum: 192
Red: 255
Green: 128
Blue: 128
New
Current
Click anywhere in this field to choose a color
Click in this range to choose a shade for the selected color
You can use the Hue, Sat (Saturation), and Lum (Luminescence) spin boxes to use that model of color definition
The New and Current colors are previewed for you in these boxes
You can use the Red, Green, and Blue spin boxes to use the RGB model of color definition

On the Color tab of the Options dialog box, you can also choose to copy a set of color palettes from another open workbook. In the Copy Colors From drop-down list, select one of the listed workbooks. The colors in that workbook are instantly copied to your current workbook.

Customizing Toolbars and Menus

Excel is extremely flexible in letting you control its built-in toolbars and menus, and in letting you build your own. You can change any aspect of the toolbars and menus in Excel. There are a number of reasons that you might want to do this:

- Building a new toolbar that contains functions that you commonly use lets you quickly access menu commands on a toolbar.
- You can change Excel's built-in toolbars to fit the way that you work or your personal tastes.
- You can access macros you've recorded or written from toolbars so that they're easy to run.
- Create new menus that contain VBA macros you use.
- Distribute custom menus and toolbars to others as part of a workbook. These custom menus and toolbars can be part of an Excel-based application you've developed.

All of the menu and toolbar customizations in Excel are handled with the Customize dialog box open. When you open this dialog box (by choosing Tools, Customize), Excel goes into "customization mode" in which its menus and toolbars can be edited. In this mode, clicking a toolbar button or menu command doesn't activate its normal function; rather it simply selects it for further editing.

Changes you make to Excel's menus and toolbars are stored in your system's \WINDOWS folder. The file name is *username*8.xlb, where *username* is the name under which you logged into the computer. If you are using a stand-alone system without a login prompt, the settings are stored in EXCEL8.XLB.

Understanding the Customize Dialog Box Tabs

The Customize dialog box is broken into three tabs. Figure 8.11 shows the first tab: Toolbars.

FIG. 8.11
The Toolbars tab of the Customize dialog box gives you broad control over toolbars.

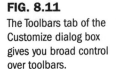

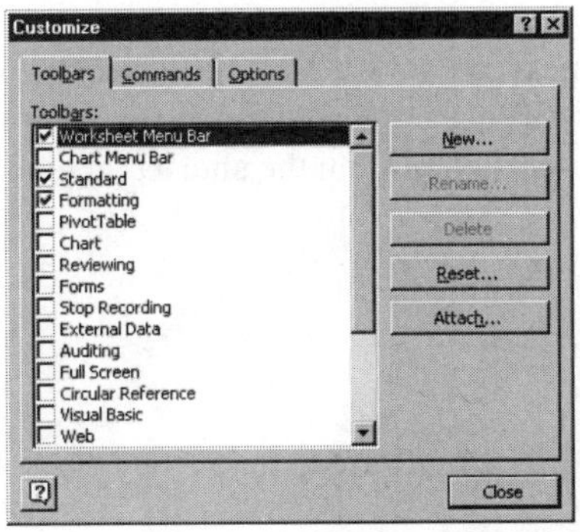

You can perform the following actions from the Toolbars tab:

- Activate toolbars by selecting the check boxes in the Toolbars window.
- Create a new, empty toolbar with the New button.
- Rename an existing custom toolbar with the Rename button. Built-in toolbars in Excel can't be renamed, only custom toolbars.
- Delete a custom toolbar with the Delete button.

- Reset a selected toolbar to its original configuration with the Reset button.
- Save a custom toolbar as part of a workbook by using the Attach button.

NOTE To edit the menu bar that appears when working with a chart, select the Chart Menu Bar in the Toolbars tab of the Customize dialog box. This causes the Chart menu bar to appear, after which you can edit it just like any other menu.

The second tab, the Commands tab, lets you choose command categories and then displays a list of commands in the selected category (see Figure 8.12). The listed commands in the Commands window can be directly dragged to toolbars or menus to add those functions. You can also select a command in the Commands window and click the Description button to see a brief description of the selected command.

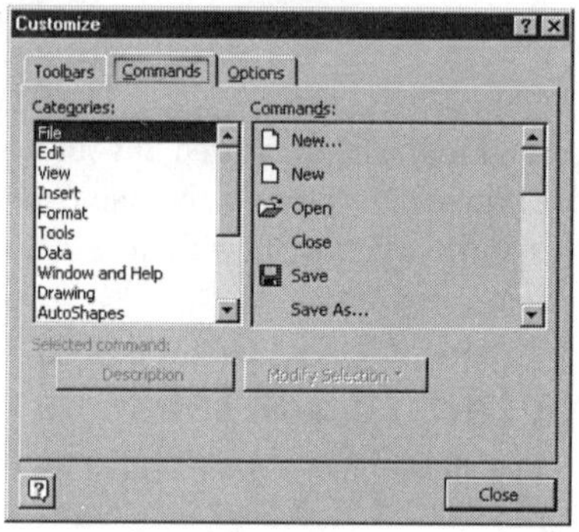

FIG. 8.12
The Commands tab lets you drag commands to toolbars.

The Modify Selection button activates a menu that lets you control many aspects of menu commands and toolbar buttons. You first select a menu command or toolbar button. Then click the Modify Selection button and choose an action from the shortcut menu shown in Figure 8.13.

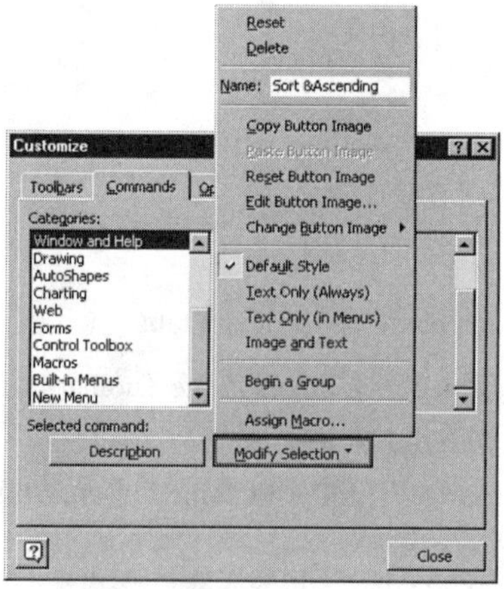

FIG. 8.13
Use Modify Selection to access all of the settings for a selected toolbar button.

The final tab of the Customize dialog box, Options, lets you control settings for Excel's toolbars and menus (see Figure 8.14). Click Large Icons to substitute larger icons for all toolbars (the change is immediate so you can preview the effect). Activate or deactivate the pop-up names of toolbar buttons with the Show ScreenTips on Toolbars check box. Finally, you can enable different animations for how Excel opens menus. Choose from (None), Random, Unfold, and Slide in the Menu Animations drop-down list.

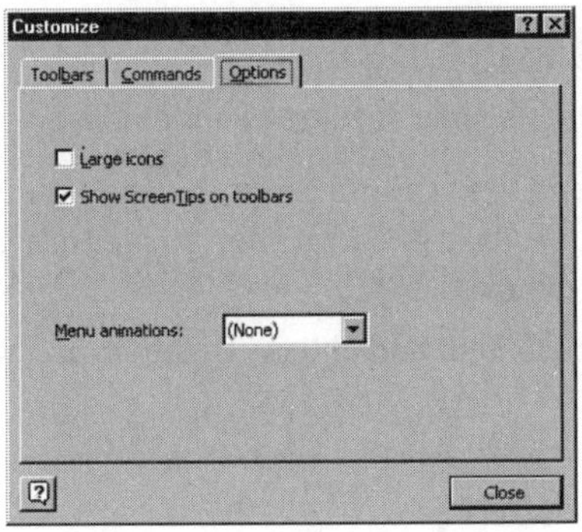

FIG. 8.14
The Options tab lets you choose system-wide settings for menus and toolbars.

Moving Menu and Toolbar Elements

While the Customize dialog box is displayed, you can easily move menu and toolbar elements by dragging them to new locations. When you do so, an insertion point shows you where the element will be dropped. Figure 8.15 shows a toolbar button being moved to a new location. The Align Right button is being dragged to a new location, and the insertion point appears between the Comma Style and Increase Decimal buttons.

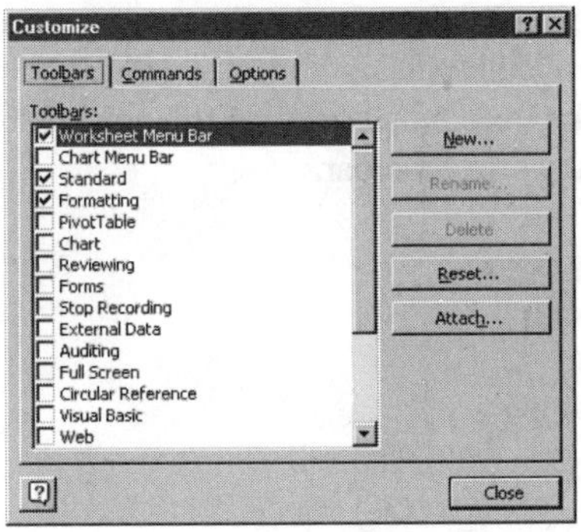

FIG. 8.15
To move a toolbar element, just drag it to a new location, paying attention to the insertion point that shows where it will appear.

Moving menu elements works the same way. Simply drag the menu element to its new location while the Customize dialog box is displayed. You can drag an individual menu item to another location on the same menu, to the menu bar, or to another menu (other menus open automatically as you drag the element to them).

Adding Commands to Menus and Toolbars

To add a new command to a menu or toolbar, make sure that the Commands tab in the Customize dialog box is selected. Then choose a command type in the Categories window, which lists the available commands from that category in the Commands window. You can then drag one of the listed commands to a toolbar or menu. The pointer changes to a plus sign to indicate that you will create the new button or menu entry with the dragged command.

Deleting Menu and Toolbar Elements

To delete a menu or toolbar element, use one of these two methods:

- Drag the element off of its container. Drag a menu element off of its menu, or a toolbar element off of its toolbar. As you drag, the icon your pointer drags includes an X to indicate that element will be removed.
- Right-click a menu or toolbar element and choose Delete from the shortcut menu that appears.

Creating New Menus and Toolbars

You can create new menus in three locations:

- On a toolbar, which creates a drop-down menu on the toolbar
- On the menu bar, which creates a new menu
- Inside an existing menu, which creates a submenu

To create one of these menus, display the Commands tab of the Customize dialog box, select New Menu in the Categories list, and then drag the New Menu entry in the Commands window to one of the three locations (a toolbar, the menu bar, or a menu).

To create a new toolbar, display the Toolbars tab of the Customize dialog box, and click the New button. This displays the New Toolbar dialog box, into which you type the name of your new toolbar (see Figure 8.16). Click OK to finish creating the new toolbar. You can then add commands to the toolbar just like any other toolbar.

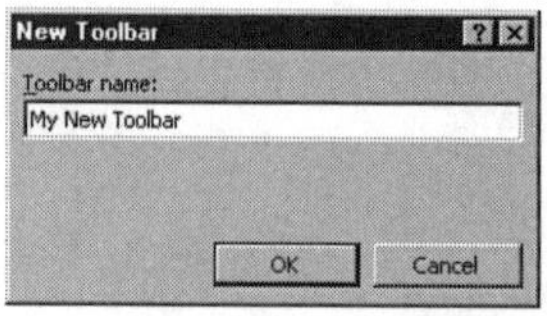

FIG. 8.16
After clicking the New button, you can assign a name for the new toolbar.

Changing Button and Menu Images

Most toolbar elements, and many menus, have icons associated with them. You can select different icons to associate with these elements, and you can even draw your own.

To choose a different icon for an element, right-click the menu command or toolbar button and use the Change Button Image submenu, which is shown in Figure 8.17. You can choose from any of the icons shown in the submenu.

FIG. 8.17
Select from 42 predefined icons to use for toolbar buttons or menu commands.

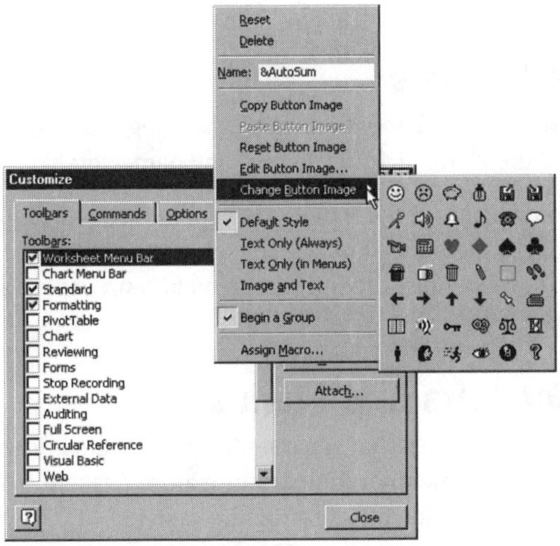

You can edit any element's image with the Edit Button Image command found on the element's shortcut menu. You then see the Button Editor shown in Figure 8.18. Select a color (or the Erase "color"), and then click individual squares to turn the color on and off. The Preview area shows you what the icon will look like at normal size as you draw. Click Clear to remove all drawing from the icon, and then you can draw an icon from scratch.

TIP If there is room to move an icon's image within the Picture box, you can click the arrows in the Move section of the Button Editor to reposition the image, one square at a time.

FIG. 8.18
The Button Editor lets you change existing icons or draw your own.

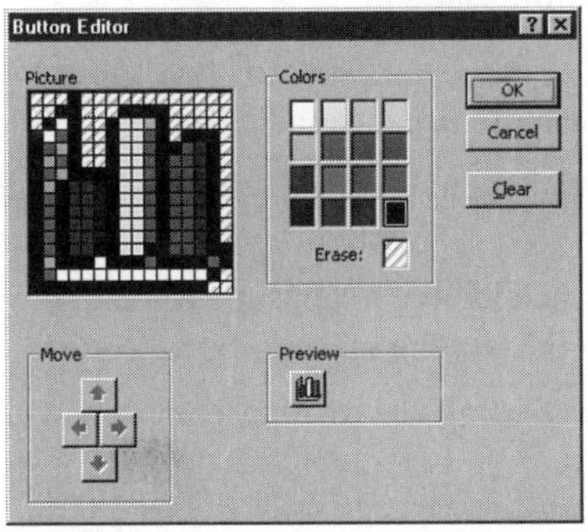

You can copy a button image from one toolbar element to another. Right-click the menu or toolbar element you want to copy and choose Copy Button Image. Then, right-click the menu or toolbar element that you want to receive the image, and choose Paste Button Image from the shortcut menu.

If you need to restore an image to its default, right-click the image and select Reset Button Image from the shortcut menu.

Changing an Element's Name

Right-clicking a menu or toolbar element and then choosing Name from the shortcut menu lets you change the name of the element. You can type any name you like, including spaces.

For menu elements, precede any of the letters of the name with an ampersand (&) to cause that letter to be used for the element's hot key (the character in the menu item that appears underlined on-screen). For example, the Format menu is represented as `F&ormat` in the Name field of its shortcut menu.

Creating Groups in Toolbars and Menus

Most toolbars and menus have lines that separate their elements into groups. These lines have no function except to make the menu or toolbar more attractive and to help visually separate the elements. You can create groups by following these steps:

1. Right-click the menu command over which you want the group line, or the toolbar button to the left of which you want the group line.
2. Choose Begin a Group.

To remove a group line, right-click the same element (the menu command under a group line, or the toolbar icon to the right of a group line), and choose the Begin a Group command from the shortcut menu. This action toggles the group line off.

Choosing an Element's Style

There are four styles you can choose for menu and toolbar elements. Each of these styles is selected from the shortcut menu for the element:

- Default Style causes menu commands to display as text along with any associated icons displayed to their left. Toolbar buttons appear as icons.
- Text Only (Always) causes an element to always appear as text, even when placed in a toolbar.
- Text Only (in Menus) causes an element to appear with text, only when placed in a menu. Toolbar elements with this setting still appear as icons.
- Image and Text causes the element to always display both text and an icon, even when used in a toolbar.

Assigning a Macro to an Element

You can assign any VBA macros to menu command or toolbar elements. Right-click the element and choose Assign Macro. From the resulting Assign Macro dialog box, select a macro and click OK. You can also type a new macro name in the Assign Macro dialog box and click the Record button to record a new macro that will be assigned to the element.

Displaying a Worksheet in Full-Screen View

In the normal worksheet view, screen elements such as the title bar, toolbars, the formula bar, and the status bar take up on-screen space. Excel enables you to switch the display to a full-screen view, in which only the worksheet is displayed along with the menu bar and sheet tabs. This enables you to see more data in the worksheet on-screen at one time. You can switch between these views at any time.

To display the current worksheet full screen, choose View, Full Screen. The worksheet display changes to full-screen view. To return to normal view, click the Close Full Screen button that appears in its own toolbar on-screen.

You can add one or more toolbars to the full-screen view by choosing View, Toolbars and selecting the toolbar you want to display.

Displaying Worksheets in Separate Windows

In the default workbook view, you only see one worksheet at a time in the workbook's window. When you click a sheet tab to display a different worksheet, that worksheet then displays using the entire workbook window. Excel enables you to display multiple worksheets in separate windows if you want to see them on-screen at one time.

To display worksheets in separate windows, follow these steps:

1. Open the workbook containing the worksheets you want to display in multiple windows. Close all other workbooks.
2. Choose Window, New Window once for each additional worksheet you want to see. This opens a new workbook window each time you choose the command.
3. Choose Window, Arrange, and select the option you want to use to arrange the windows on-screen: Tiled, Horizontal, Vertical, or Cascade.
4. Click OK. The workbooks now appear in separate windows on-screen. To see different worksheets in the additional workbooks you added, click the window to activate it, and then click the sheet tab for the worksheet you want to see.

Hiding Workbooks and Worksheets

Workbooks can become quite cluttered as you work with them. To simplify your workspace, you can hide an entire workbook window. If only one workbook is open in Excel, when you hide the window, the entire workbook is hidden. To hide a workbook, select a cell in the workbook you want to hide. Then, choose Window, Hide.

If you need to modify or view a hidden workbook, you will first need to restore the workbook. Choose Window, Unhide. In the Unhide dialog box, select the name of the workbook you want to display; then click OK.

CAUTION

If you hide a workbook and then quit Excel, the workbook will still be hidden the next time you use Excel. If you will not be using your workbook for some time, or if others need to access the same workbook, you should remember to unhide workbooks each time you exit Excel.

You may decide that you want to hide only selected worksheets in a workbook. Perhaps you have three worksheets and want to work with just two of them, or you may want to hide a worksheet in a shared workbook so that others will not see the worksheet. To hide a worksheet, click the sheet tab for the worksheet you want to hide. Then, choose Format, Sheet, Hide.

If you need to modify or view a hidden worksheet, you will first need to restore the worksheet. Choose Format, Sheet, Unhide. In the Unhide dialog box, select the name of the worksheet you want to display; then click OK.

TIP You can hide more than one worksheet in a workbook. Click the first sheet tab, then hold down Ctrl and click the other sheets you want to hide. Then follow the instructions above to hide the selected worksheets.

NOTE If your workbook includes just one worksheet, you cannot hide that worksheet.

Changing International Character Sets

In Windows, you can switch among different international character sets, time and date displays, and numeric formats. The international settings you choose show up in the formatting in your Excel worksheets as well as other Windows applications. When you choose Format, Cells in Excel, for example, the Number, Date, and Time categories on the Number tab display formats for the country or regions you have selected in the Windows Control Panel.

The Regional Settings Properties dialog box enables you to change the country, language, date, currency, and other formats. Changes to these settings aren't permanent—you can change them again at any time.

To change the international character set, follow these steps:

1. To choose the international settings you want to use, click the Start button on the Windows taskbar and then choose Settings, Control Panel. Double-click the Regional Settings icon.
2. To automatically change the settings for the Number, Currency, Time, and Date tabs to those used in a particular region, select the region you want from the drop-down list in the Regional Settings tab. Or, to change the number, currency, time or date formats individually, click the appropriate tab and select the formats you want to use.
3. Click OK when you have finished. The settings you chose take effect in all your Windows applications that use these settings.

Opening a Workbook from the Start Menu or the Desktop

In the section titled "General Options," previously in this chapter, you learned how to use the Alternate Startup File Location option to automatically open a specified workbook each time you start Excel. A similar method is to place a workbook you use frequently on the Windows 95 Start menu. Then, when you click the workbook icon on the Start menu, both Excel and the workbook open automatically.

To place an Excel workbook on the Start menu, follow these steps:

1. Open Windows Explorer, and find the workbook you want to open each time you start Excel.
2. Drag the icon to the Start Menu folder (normally located in the Windows folder).
3. Windows 95 places an icon for the workbook on the Start menu. Click the icon to start Excel with your workbook open.

Another variation on this method, which would probably work best if you use several Excel workbooks on a frequent basis, is to place an icon for each workbook on the Windows desktop. Double-clicking the desktop icon also opens both Excel and the workbook.

To create a desktop shortcut for an Excel workbook, follow these steps:

1. Open Windows Explorer, and find the workbook you want to place on the Windows desktop.
2. Right-click the workbook file name, then drag it to the desktop area and release the mouse button (make sure the Windows desktop is visible before you perform this step).
3. Select Create Shortcut(s) Here from the shortcut menu that appears.
4. Windows 95 places an icon for the workbook on the desktop. Double-click the icon to start Excel and open the workbook.

Setting Startup Switches for Excel

You can set a number of switches to control how Excel starts. For instance, you might not want to see the Excel startup screen and a new, blank workbook each time.

To set a startup switch for Excel, follow these steps:

1. In Windows Explorer, find the Microsoft Excel shortcut icon (open the Windows folder, then open the Start Menu folder and click the Programs folder.)
2. Right-click the Microsoft Excel icon, and then click Properties. Click the Shortcut tab.
3. In the Target text box, place the insertion point after the path to Microsoft Excel, type a space, and then type the switch you want to use. If you type `/e`, for example, the startup screen and blank workbook won't display. Click OK to close the Properties dialog box.

For information on other available startup switches in Excel, search on "switches" in the Excel on-line Help.

Common Problems and Solutions

You can run into a couple of different problems when modifying Excel's menus and toolbars. You can also use the Options dialog box in Excel to solve certain problems. In the following sections, some common problems encountered in this area are discussed, along with their solutions.

Displaying Formulas to Audit a Workbook

On the View tab of the Options dialog box is a setting named Formulas. Selecting this setting causes your worksheets to display their formulas, instead of the results of the formulas. Printing the workbook with this option selected also prints a version that shows all of the formulas in the cells. Figure 8.19 shows a worksheet displayed using this option.

You can use this feature in several important ways:

- To ensure a worksheet is accurate, display or print the worksheet with formulas displayed. You can then examine each formula closely.
- If you're explaining a worksheet you've created to someone else, it can often be useful to bring both the worksheet itself and a separate copy that shows the formulas you used. You can then refer to the formula printout to help explain your analysis or answer other questions about the worksheet you're presenting.

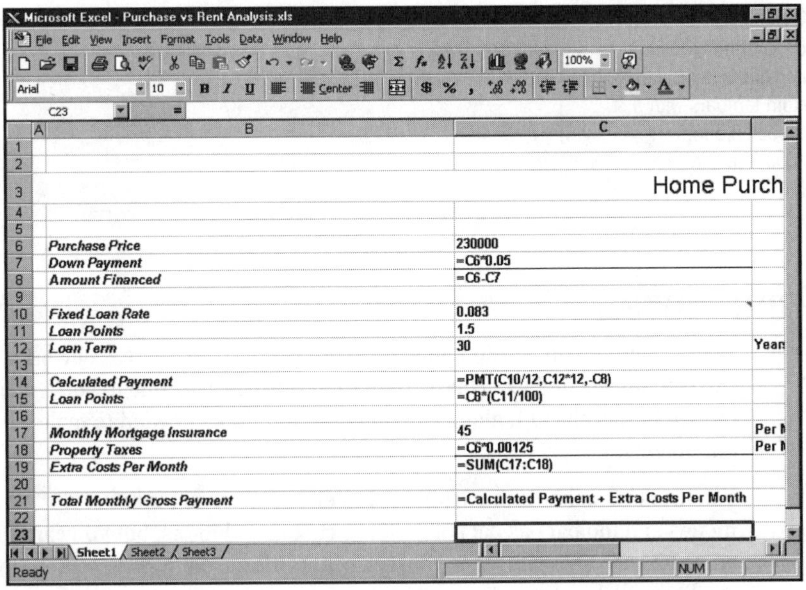

FIG. 8.19
You can cause Excel to display formulas instead of results in worksheets.

Restoring the Toolbar and Menu Customize Commands

If you've removed the menu commands that give you access to the Customize dialog box (the Tools menu, or the Customize command in the Tools menu), you can still follow these steps to access the Customize dialog box:

1. Right-click any of the displayed toolbars. (Add a toolbar to the display, if necessary.)
2. Choose Customize from the shortcut menu that appears.

After displaying the Customize dialog box, you can reset the appropriate menu to restore the Customize command or move the Customize command back to any menu or a toolbar.

A similar problem exists if you remove the Toolbars command from the View menu, or the entire View menu. Without the Toolbars command, you must choose which toolbars are visible by right-clicking an open toolbar and then selecting the appropriate toolbar from the shortcut menu that appears. Each toolbar listed on the shortcut menu can be displayed or hidden by clicking it.

Distributing Custom Toolbars

If you've created one or more custom toolbars that work with an Excel-based application you've developed, you need to distribute those toolbars along with the workbook. You do this with the Attach command on the Toolbars tab of the Customize dialog box.

After building the custom toolbars, click the Attach button to display the Attach Toolbars dialog box shown in Figure 8.20. You can then select from the listed Custom toolbars and click Copy to attach them to the open workbook.

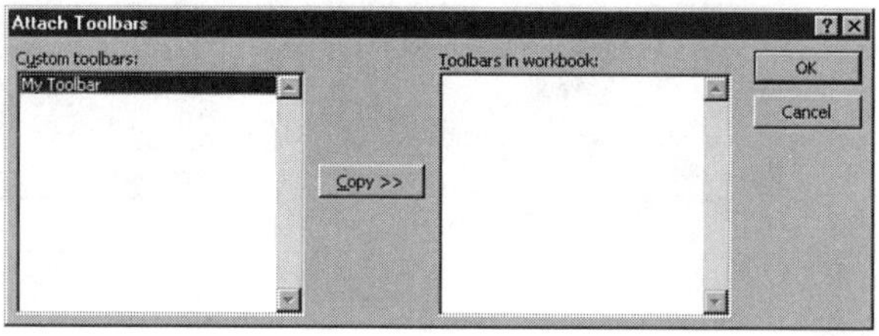

FIG. 8.20
Use the Attach Toolbars dialog box to associate custom toolbars with a workbook file for distribution.

From Here...

In this chapter you learned how to customize the way that Excel works, by making changes in the Options dialog box. There are myriad settings available to you, each of which was discussed in this chapter, along with any tips and tricks needed to make the best use of the different options.

You also learned how to customize Excel's menus and toolbars. Not only can you customize menus and toolbars as part of building custom solutions, but you can also make Excel more convenient to use, either for yourself or for others, by making frequently-used commands more readily available. From here, consider reading the following chapters:

- Chapter 9, "Excel Solution Templates," discusses all of the spreadsheet solutions that are included with Excel, which you can put to work immediately.
- Chapter 10, "Creating Charts," shows you how to start creating charts in Excel. The following chapters show you advanced charting techniques, explain all of the different chart types available to you, and describe how to annotate your charts and worksheets with graphic drawings.
- Chapter 14, "Building Excel Databases," teaches how to build simple yet flexible databases within Excel. You don't always need a full-fledged database program, because you can use Excel to meet many database needs.

CHAPTER 9

Excel Solution Templates

Microsoft Excel 97 comes with a variety of already-developed workbooks—called *templates*—that you can use to start solving problems immediately, without all the work of creating similar solutions by hand.

Four of these solutions are installed along with Excel when you choose a Complete installation, but there are another seven solutions available on the Office 97 CD-ROM, and there may be additional solutions available on Microsoft's Web site. Excel's Spreadsheet Solutions are extensive and include the following:

- Auto Lease Analysis
- Business Planner
- Change Request Tracker
- Expense Statement *
- Family Budgeter
- Invoicing *
- Loan Analyzer and Amortizer
- Purchase Order *
- Sales Quote
- Time Card
- Village Software Information Request Form

Installing Excel's Spreadsheet Solutions from the Office CD-ROM

Even when you perform a complete installation of Excel and all of its components as part of Office 97, all the available spreadsheet solutions aren't included. You can easily install them from the Office 97 CD-ROM, and you learn how in this section.

Downloading Spreadsheet Solutions from the Web

Microsoft occasionally makes additional Spreadsheet Solutions available for free download from their Web site. This section shows you how to locate, download, and install them.

Using Excel's Spreadsheet Solutions

The Spreadsheet Solutions included with Excel perform some useful tasks that save you from having to develop your own solutions. Learn how to use all the Spreadsheet Solutions in this section.

In this chapter, you learn about these various solutions, how to install them, what they provide you, and how to use them. ■

Installing Additional Solutions

Before exploring all of the Spreadsheet Solutions included with Excel, you first need to install the supplemental solutions. In the next two sections, you learn how to install the Spreadsheet Solutions that aren't automatically installed with Excel 97, and you learn how to check Microsoft's Web page for new Spreadsheet Solutions that are now available.

NOTE If you own Microsoft Excel 97 for Windows 95 and Windows NT, as opposed to the complete Microsoft Office suite, then the Spreadsheet Solutions will already have been installed along with Excel. ■

From the Office 97 CD-ROM

There are seven additional Spreadsheet Solutions found on the Office 97 CD-ROM that you can easily install. To do so, follow these steps:

1. Insert your Office 97 CD-ROM and open Windows Explorer using the Start menu's Programs group.
2. Expand the Office CD-ROM's folders to open the folder \VALUPACK\TEMPLATE\EXCEL.
3. Ctrl+click on each of the .XLT files displayed in the folder. Choose Edit, Copy to place the files on the Clipboard.
4. Using Windows Explorer, find the folder in which you installed Office 97. Typically, this is \Program Files\MSOffice (or \Program Files\Microsoft Office) on your C: drive, but you may have chosen a different folder during installation.
5. In the MSOffice folder, open the Templates\Spreadsheet Solutions folder by clicking on that folder. Choose Edit, Paste to paste the files in the Clipboard into the Spreadsheet Solutions folder.
6. Place the help file for the new Spreadsheet Solutions in the appropriate Office folder. First, return to the \VALUPACK\TEMPLATE\EXCEL folder using Windows Explorer; then, select the VSTMPLT.HLP file and choose Edit, Copy.
7. In Windows Explorer, navigate back to your home MSOffice folder. In the MSOffice folder, there will be a subfolder called Office. Select that folder, then choose Edit, Paste in Windows Explorer to copy the Solutions help file into the Office folder.

To test to see the new Spreadsheet Solutions in Excel, start Excel and choose File, New. In the New dialog box, choose the Spreadsheet Solutions tab (see Figure 9.1).

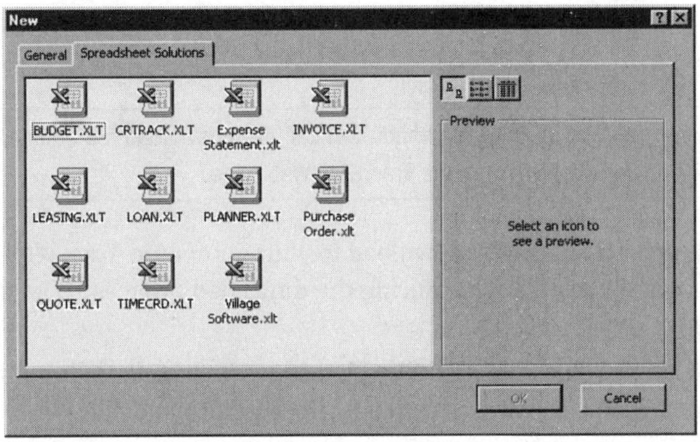

FIG. 9.1
After installing the additional Spreadsheet Solutions, you should find them in the New dialog box automatically.

From the Internet

Microsoft occasionally makes additional tools, such as Spreadsheet Solutions, available on their Web site. If you have Internet Web access on your computer, you can find additional Spreadsheet Solutions by following these steps:

1. Start Excel 97. Then choose Help, Microsoft on the Web, and then Free Stuff from Excel's menus. If you're not already connected to the Internet, your Web browser will start automatically and will attempt to connect to the Web.
2. Once connected you will automatically be taken to the Excel 97 Free Stuff page on **www.microsoft.com**, as shown in Figure 9.2.

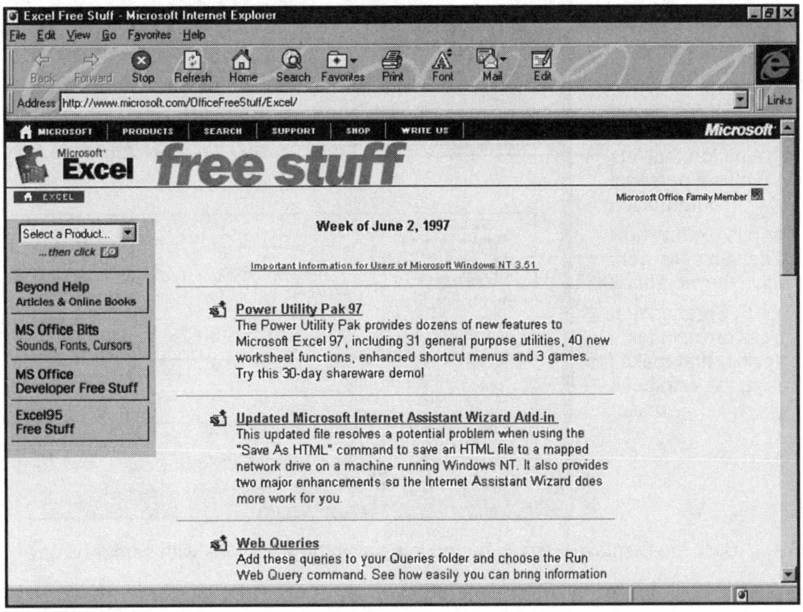

FIG. 9.2
The Microsoft Excel 97 Free Stuff page contains a variety of goodies for Excel that you can download.

3. Scroll through the list of Free Stuff items to locate the solution you want and click its link.

TIP If you don't have your Office 97 CD-ROM handy, you can even download the additional solutions found in the Value Pack on the CD-ROM from the Free Stuff Web page.

4. The file will automatically download to your computer. Your Web browser will prompt you to confirm the filename during the download process. (The default filename should be fine.)
5. Double-click the downloaded file. This starts its installation routine, which places the template files in the correct Office 97 folders automatically.

Each Spreadsheet Solutions will take about one to two minutes to download over a 28.8 Kbps modem connection.

Spreadsheet Solutions Overview

Although each spreadsheet solution provides fields and features to solve unique problems, there are several features common to all of the Spreadsheet Solutions that you should know about before learning about each solution. Figure 9.3 shows the Family Budgeter workbook open on the screen with some of these special features pointed out.

FIG. 9.3
The Family Budgeter workbook demonstrates the features common to all of the Spreadsheet Solutions.

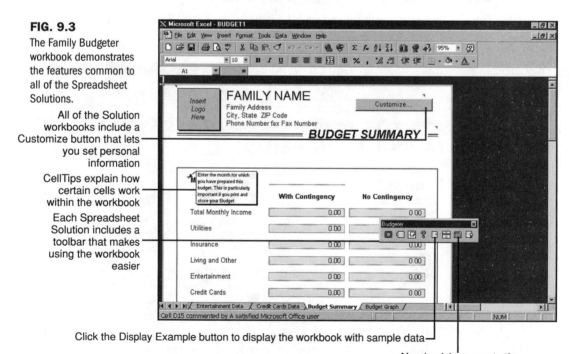

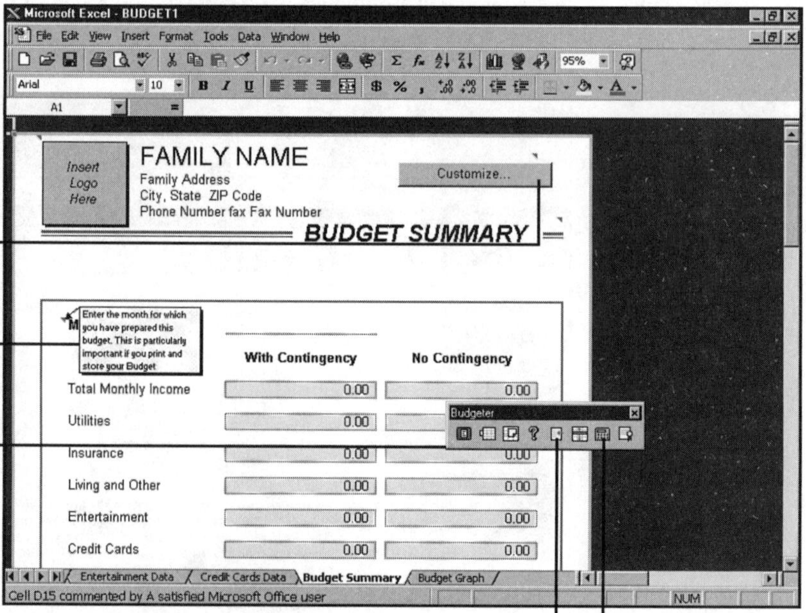

All of the Solution workbooks include a Customize button that lets you set personal information

CellTips explain how certain cells work within the workbook

Each Spreadsheet Solution includes a toolbar that makes using the workbook easier

Click the Display Example button to display the workbook with sample data

Need quick access to the Windows Calculator? Click here!

NOTE The Spreadsheet Solutions included with Excel 97 are from a company called Village Software. If you want additional Spreadsheet Solutions prepared with the same design standards as the ones you see here, you can use the Village Software template to request additional information on other templates they have available for sale.

CAUTION

The Spreadsheet Solutions included with Excel 97 are intended to be samples only. They may not comply with generally accepted accounting principles (GAAP). You should always seek advice from an attorney or Certified Public Accountant when making important financial decisions. Microsoft and Village Software have disclaimed any liability for the use of these samples.

You can use the various Spreadsheet Solutions included with Excel as solutions to problems you may encounter, or as learning tools that can guide you in developing your own worksheets along similar lines. In fact, developing your own solutions can be a good idea, because doing so lets you completely understand the dynamics of the worksheet required to solve the problem, and also lets you customize the worksheet to your specific needs without a lot of extraneous information that isn't relevant.

In the following sections, you learn about each of the Spreadsheet Solutions included with Excel and about any special features they include that you might be able to apply to building your own solutions.

About Macro Virus Protection

All of the Spreadsheet Solutions discussed here have macro programs included within the workbooks. Excel 97 warns you about opening such workbooks, because computer viruses can be transmitted within these sorts of macro programs. Figure 9.4 shows the warning you see when you open any of the Spreadsheet Solutions.

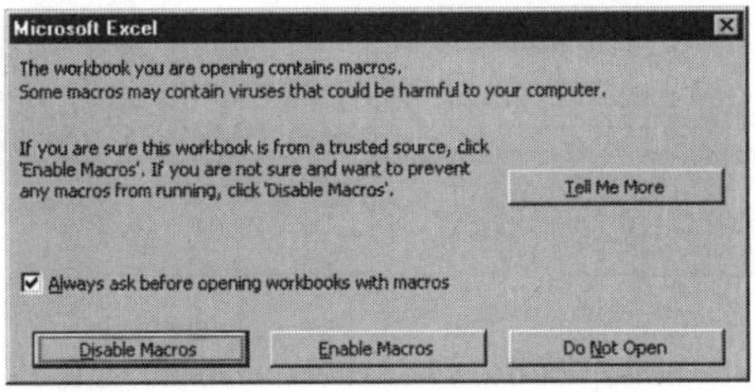

FIG. 9.4
Opening any workbook that includes macro programs elicits this warning from Excel 97.

For the Spreadsheet Solutions included with Excel 97, it's safe to click the Enable Macros button and open the workbook with the macros intact and running. (In fact, the Spreadsheet Solutions rely on these macros to function.)

CAUTION

If someone sends you an Excel workbook, be cautious when you see the Macro warning. Check with the person who sent you the workbook to find out if they included any macros deliberately. If not, choose Disable Macros when opening most workbooks to protect your computer from viruses.

There are many good anti-virus programs available that can watch for viruses, including Excel macro viruses. One good one is Symantec's Norton Anti-Virus. Find out more about it at: **http://www.symantec.com/avcenter/index.html**.

Family Budgeter

When you first open the Family Budgeter template (BUDGET.XLT), you see the Budget Summary sheet shown in Figure 9.5. Before this sheet will have any relevance, however, you first need to enter information into a number of other sheets within the Family Budgeter.

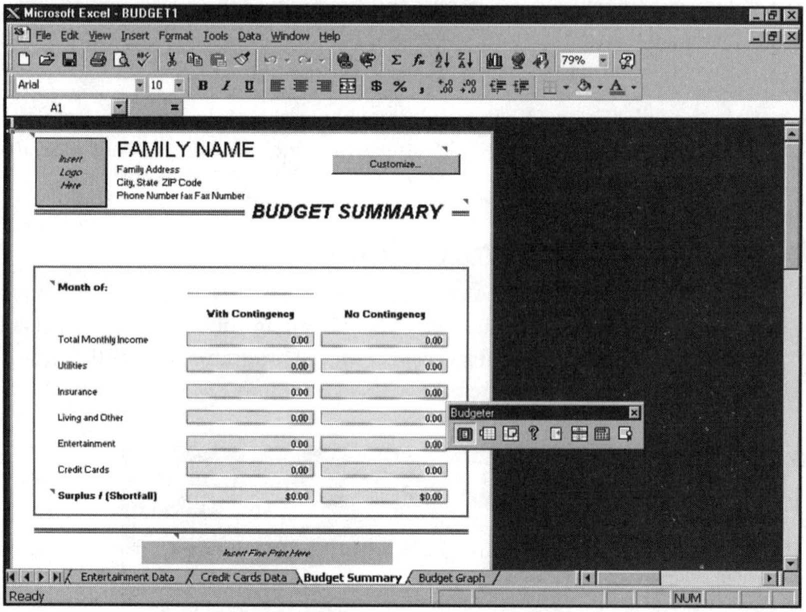

FIG. 9.5
Starting the Family Budgeter template displays the Budget Summary worksheet.

Click the Customize button at the top of the worksheet to move to the Customize Your Budgeter worksheet. In this worksheet, shown in Figure 9.6, you can enter key data about your family.

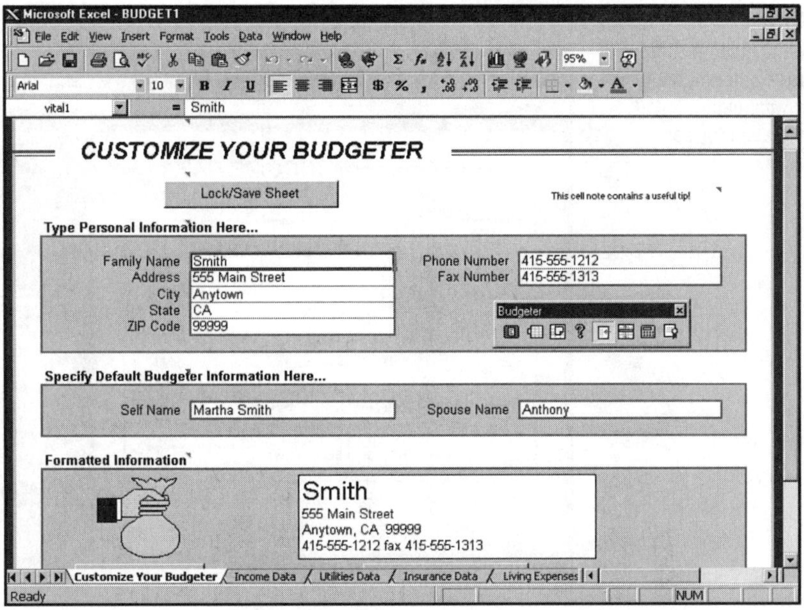

FIG. 9.6
Start the Family Budgeter by providing family information. You also can choose a logo that's displayed on all the pages.

CAUTION

As soon as you start entering information in the Family Budgeter, or any of the Spreadsheet Templates, make sure to save the template to a new filename, and then save it every time you enter any amount of information that you would hate to re-enter. Press Ctrl+S each time you want to quickly save your changes.

Entering Income Data Using the workbook tabs, move to the Income Data sheet, shown in Figure 9.7. Taking the information from your paycheck stubs, enter the monthly totals in the spaces provided.

TIP If you receive two paychecks a month, you can use Excel to enter the total monthly amount for you without using a calculator. In each of the cells below each spouse's name, enter the formula **=999.99+999.99** with the nines replaced with the actual numbers from each paycheck.

If you receive a check every two weeks, then use this formula to enter the information: **=(*check_amount**26)/12** to arrive at average monthly pay and withholding amounts. For weekly paychecks, use **=(*check_amount**52)/12** to arrive at a monthly figure. These formulas are more accurate than assuming that there are four weeks in every month.

Utilities Information Next, enter your utility expense information on the Utilities Data sheet, shown in Figure 9.8. For each utility class, enter in six months' worth of billings to get a reasonable average amount within the budget you're building.

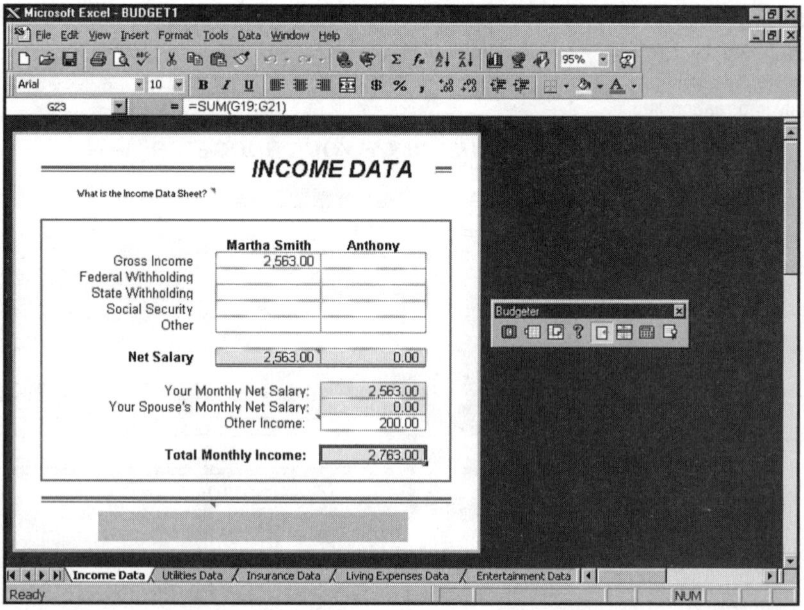

FIG. 9.7
Use the Income Data form to enter income and withholding information for each spouse.

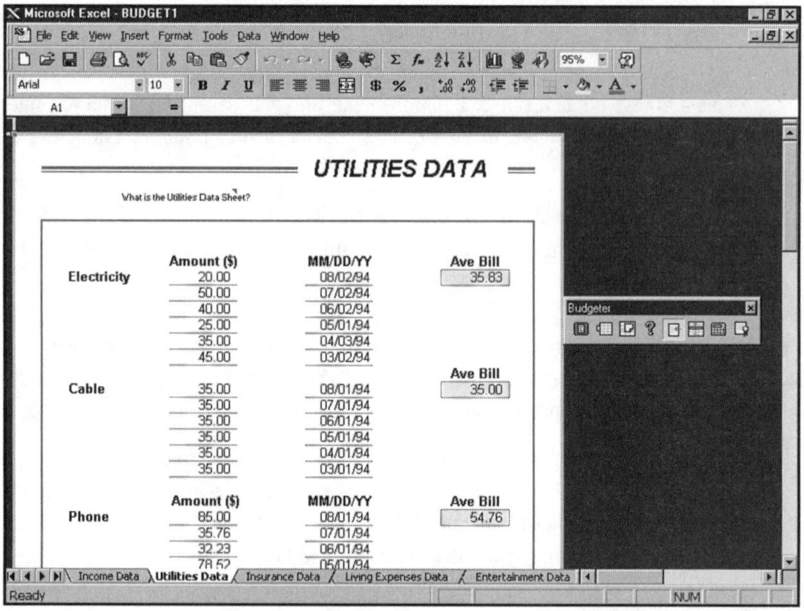

FIG. 9.8
Enter six months' worth of utility expenses into the Utilities Data worksheet.

TIP An important part of entering expense data in the Family Budgeter is to fill out the Contingency Percentage near the bottom of each expense form. As a rule, enter 15 percent for the contingency amount. This 15 percent is automatically added to your expenses in a separate column on the Budget

Summary worksheet. Optimally, your budget should be able to allow for at least a 10–15 percent contingency for any emergencies or higher priorities that come up.

Insurance Information Use the Insurance Data worksheet to record all of your insurance policies, their starting and ending dates, policies numbers, and, of course, their costs (see Figure 9.9). Like the other expense worksheets, make sure to choose a contingency percentage near the bottom of the worksheet that suits your needs.

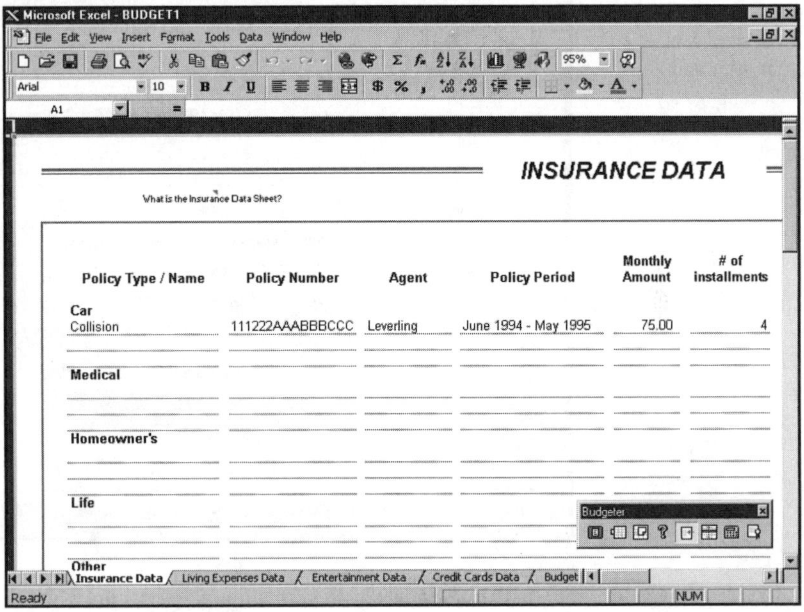

FIG. 9.9
Enter all of your insurance policy information and costs into the Insurance Data worksheet.

NOTE A nice feature of the Family Budgeter is that it not only helps you prepare a budget, but it also gives you places to record key personal information, such as insurance policy numbers, credit card accounts, and so on. After finishing the Family Budgeter, you can print out the workbook and keep a copy of this information in a readily accessible location.

Other Expense Worksheets Similar to the other worksheets you've already filled out, complete the remaining worksheets:

- *Living and Other Data* holds information about your rent or mortgage, auto loan or lease payments, commuting expenses, groceries, and any other miscellaneous loans you pay on. These figures are all entered using monthly totals.
- *Entertainment Data* lets you enter information for eating out, going to the movies, music, books, and a budget for vacations. Enter each amount as a monthly total.
- *Credit Cards Data* contains information about all of your credit cards, their interest rates, account numbers, and so on.

The Payoff After entering all of the data requested on the worksheets already discussed, you can move back to the Budget Summary worksheet shown in Figure 9.10. The example shown looks pretty good! It provides a good level of savings when there are no contingencies that arise, but even when the allowed-for contingency percentages arise, there's still some room in the budget.

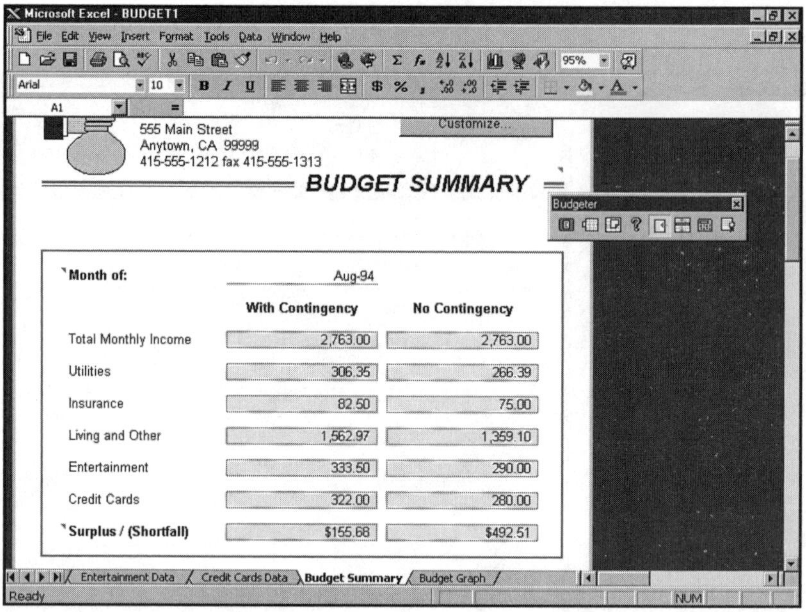

FIG. 9.10
A complete Family Budget Summary shows you your surplus or shortfall, with and without contingency amounts taken into account.

If you want to get a better feel for where your money goes, click the Budget Graph worksheet tab (see Figure 9.11) and take a look at a pie chart that shows how your expenses break down.

TIP You can choose to view the information shown on the Budget Graph page using different types of charts. Click the Change Graph button to select from any of Excel's built-in chart types.

Change Request Tracker

You can use the Change Request Tracker Spreadsheet Solution to document problems with a product or process. Change Requests can come from many different departments within a manufacturing organization, and are then responded to by either the Engineering, Assembly, or Final Fit functions (or perhaps a Quality function). Figure 9.12 shows an example Change Request form, ready to be printed and then distributed.

To make the best use of the Change Request Tracker, you should first fill out the Customize worksheet, and then save the template under a new name to the \MSOffice\Office\Templates\Spreadsheet Solutions folder. Now, when you open the customized template to create a new change request, you only need to complete the unique information. Save the file under a different filename to keep a copy of each change request.

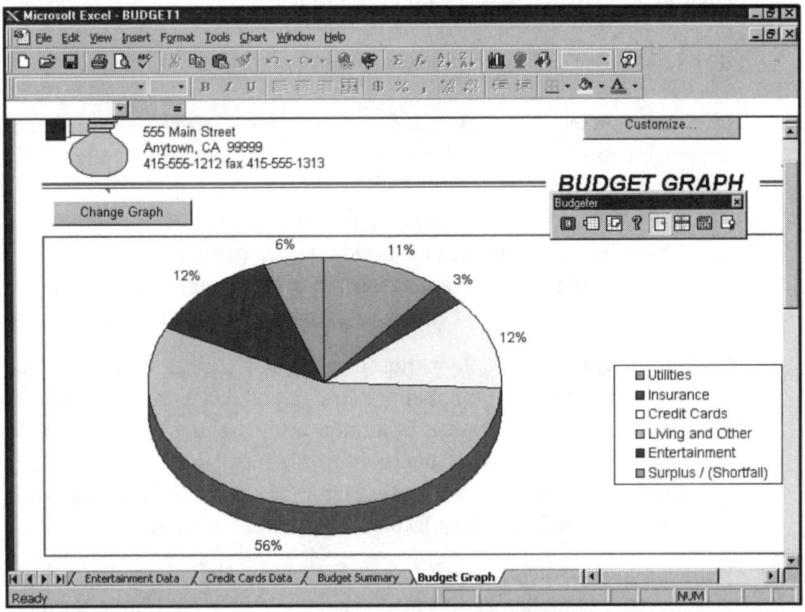

FIG. 9.11
Get a birds-eye view of how your spending breaks down with the Budget Graph.

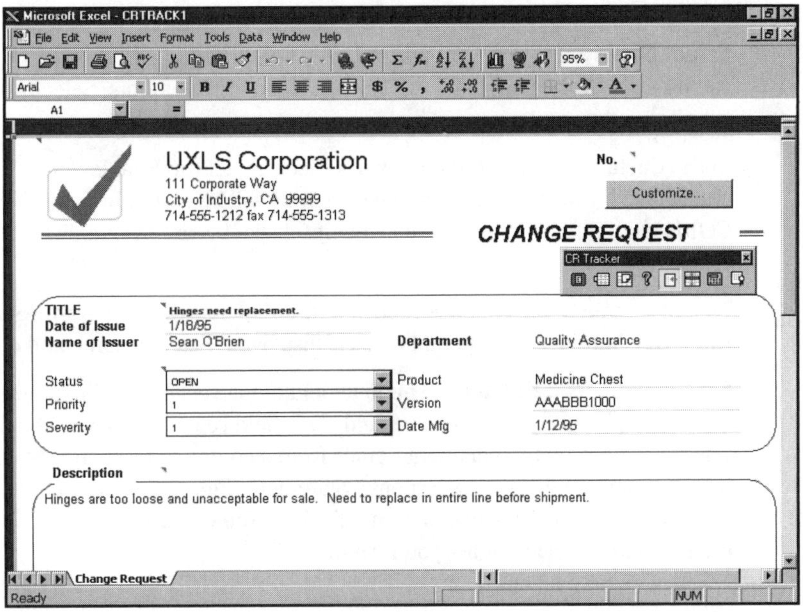

FIG. 9.12
The Change Request Tracker provides a form that documents product or process problems.

Expense Statement

The Expense Statement template lets you easily complete a standard expense report, and it illustrates some neat Excel features as well.

NOTE Before using the Expense Statement Spreadsheet Solution, you must have one of Excel's add-ins installed and selected. Using the Tools, Add-Ins command in Excel, ensure that the Template Wizard with Data Tracking Add-In is installed and selected. If it is not listed, you will need to first install it. See Chapter 7, "Using Excel Add-Ins," for information on doing so.

There are three interesting functions on the Expense Statement Customize Your Statement worksheet. You can establish a shared counter (which assigns a sequential number to each expense statement), create a database of employee information that is used when completing the expense statement, and create a database to track expense reports.

Shared Counter If people within the company use the Expense Statement worksheet to complete and turn in their expense reports, you can establish a shared counter so that each Expense Statement worksheet is automatically assigned a sequential, unique number. To do this on the Customize Your Statement worksheet, select the Share Expense Statement Numbers On Network check box. In the Counter Location field, fill in a directory on the network to which everyone filling out an Expense Statement will have access.

When employees fill out the Expense Statement, they then click the Assign a Number button on the Expense toolbar. This button examines the shared number file stored in the directory previously mentioned, and assigns an incremental number to the Expense Statement the employee is filling out.

Select Employees You can maintain a list of employees in a different Excel workbook that can be used by the people filling out the Expense Statements. Selecting a name from a database saves time and prevents errors.

In the Customize Your Statement worksheet, select the Enable Select Employee Function check box. By default, valid employee names will be stored in the \Office\Library folder's COMMON.XLS worksheet. You can edit this list by simply opening it in Excel and adding new employees.

To add a name to the expense report, in the Expense Statement worksheet, click the Select Employee button. A list of employees is displayed. Select a name and choose OK.

Expense Report Database The final field of interest on the Customize Your Statement screen is the Template Wizard Database field. This field references a workbook called EXPDB.XLS. In this worksheet, all the pertinent details from a completed Expense Statement are stored when the user saves and exits the Expense Statement. Figure 9.13 shows the EXPDB.XLS worksheet along with a single Expense Statement's data. You can use EXPDB.XLS to automatically keep track of expense statements you turn in.

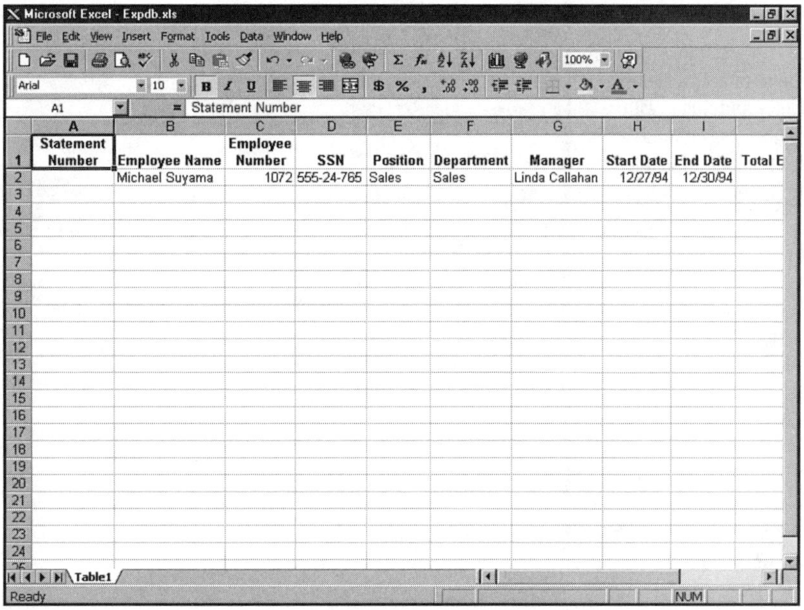

FIG. 9.13
The EXPDB.XLS workbook contains details about all of the Expense Statements completed and saved.

Invoicing

The Invoicing Spreadsheet Solution helps you create professional-looking invoices, easily and painlessly. The template for Invoicing shares a couple of the features discussed for the Expense Statement template, such as the use of a shared counter directory for sequential, unique numbering.

NOTE Before using the Invoicing Spreadsheet Solution, you must have one of Excel's add-ins installed and selected. Choose Tools, Add-Ins in Excel to ensure that the Template Wizard with Data Tracking Add-In is installed and selected. If it is not listed, you will need to first install it. See Chapter 7, "Using Excel Add-Ins," for information on doing so.

Using the Invoicing template, shown in Figure 9.14, is straighforward. Customize the company information as you've learned about in previous templates. You'll see that you can define special tax rates in the Customize Your Invoice worksheet, and can list the types of credit cards your company accepts.

Auto Lease Analysis

Just about every family would like to buy a new car. These days, people often wonder if all the hype about auto leasing makes sense for them. It's a difficult analysis, because there are many different leasing options, each one having a different overall effect on your bottom-line costs. The Auto Lease Analysis template included with Excel 97 can help you to better understand lease options, and can help you to compare leases offered from different sources.

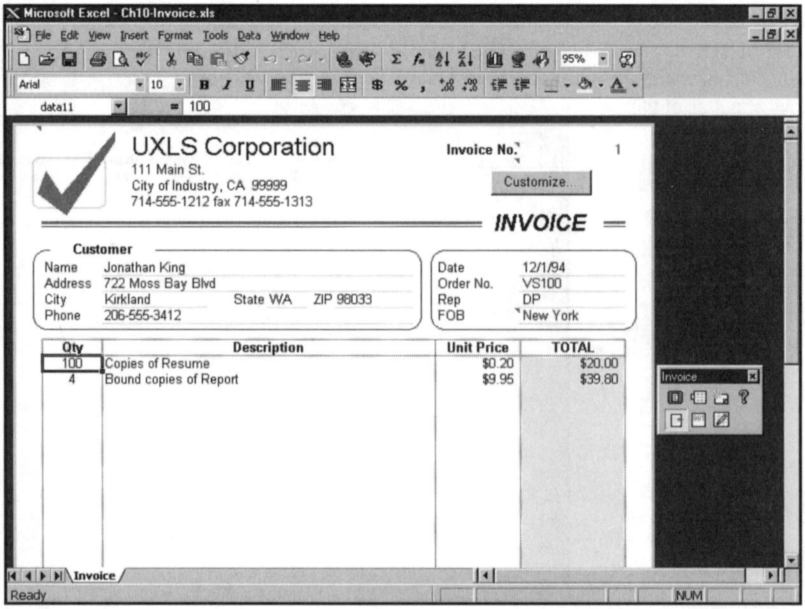

FIG. 9.14
You can produce professional invoices quickly and easily with the Invoicing Spreadsheet Solution included with Excel 97.

CAUTION

If you are seriously considering an auto lease, consult your accountant for advice. Not only will he be familiar with lease laws in your state, but he will be able to better relate how a lease may fit in your personal financial picture, as well as how it compares to a loan on the same automobile. You can use the Spreadsheet Solution included with Excel that analyzes auto leases to better understand the dynamics of auto leases, but you should rely on a professional who you know and trust when making these types of decisions, and not just an example spreadsheet analysis!

Using Auto Lease Analysis is very straightforward, but you'll need to gather a lot of information from the leasing company prior to completing the form (see Figure 9.15). In fact, one strategy may be to print several copies of the form and take them with you when shopping for an auto lease so you can gather all of the relevant information. Later, you can enter the information into the Auto Lease Analysis template for analysis.

The key to the Auto Lease Analysis lies with the Results Comparison worksheet, shown in Figure 9.16. Here, you can see the effects of various changes to a proposed lease. Fill in the different options on the Lease Options worksheet, and then examine the results on the Results Comparison worksheet.

Loan Analyzer and Amortizer

People often need to analyze or amortize a loan. Perhaps you're saving up for a home purchase and want to play around with the relationship between amount financed, percentage rate, and loan payment. Or perhaps you have an existing mortgage and want to prepare an amortization table so that your accountant can know how much to deduct for the interest portion of the payments. Whatever your loan analysis needs, the Loan Analyzer and Amortizer template can help you get the job done.

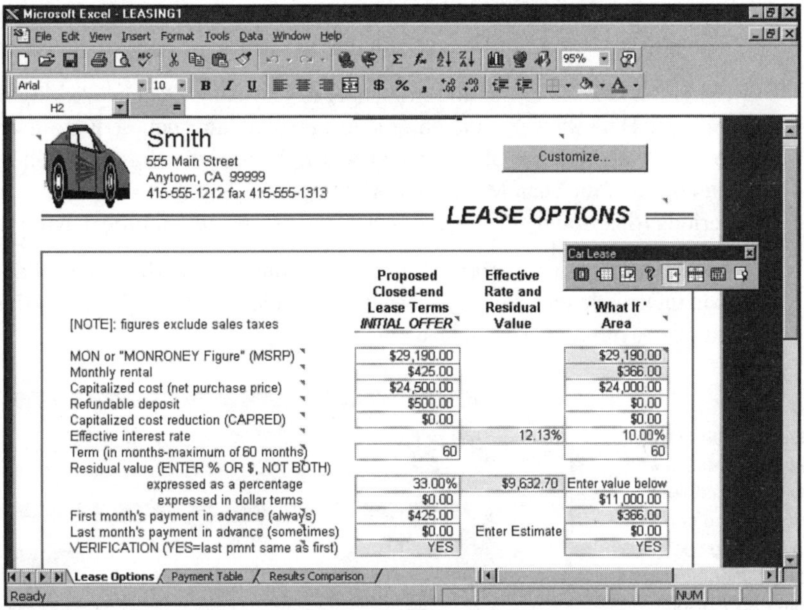

FIG. 9.15
The Auto Lease Analysis template lets you estimate costs and play with "what-if" scenarios.

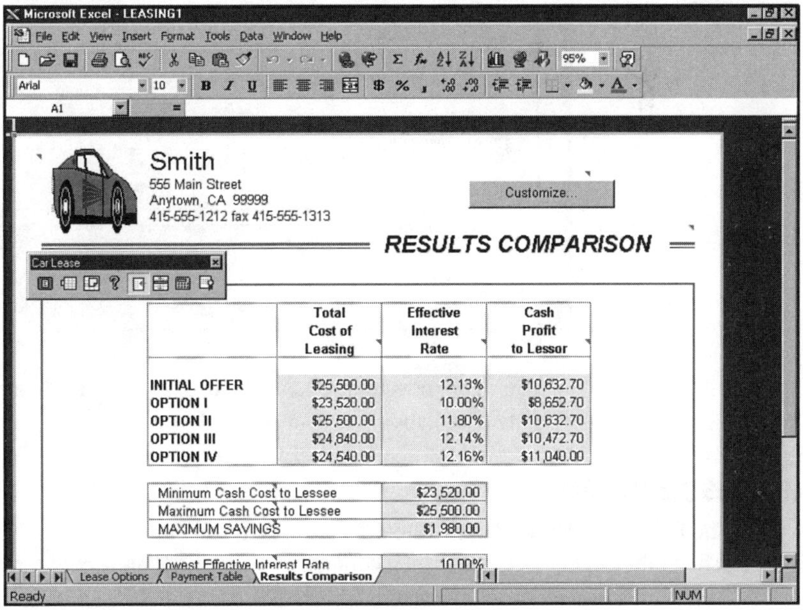

FIG. 9.16
The Results Comparison worksheet shows you the effects of different lease options that you may negotiate.

CAUTION

Always rely on your accounting professional for detailed loan analyses or amortization calculations. Although you can use this template to prepare information for your taxes, you should have the results double-checked by your accountant.

Using the Loan Analyzer and Amortizer is very easy. Start by clicking the Customize button on the Loan Data worksheet to enter your personal information. For amortizations, you also need to specify the number of periods for which the amortization table will be calculated on the Customize Your Loan Manager worksheet. The default is 48, but you can specify up to 720 periods (this would correspond to a 60-year loan with monthly payments).

After entering your customization information, move to the Loan Data worksheet and enter the loan information for which you want information. Figure 9.17 shows this worksheet with a sample 36-month personal loan entered.

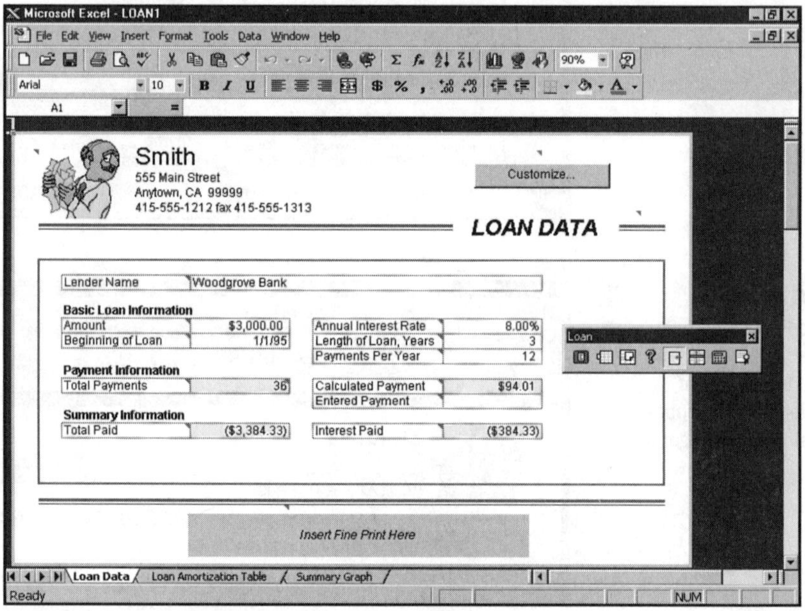

FIG. 9.17
Enter information about the loan into the Loan Data worksheet, and then use the other two worksheets to see detailed information about the loan you specified.

After entering the loan data, move to the Loan Amortization worksheet or the Summary Graph worksheet to see information about the loan you entered.

Business Planner

The Business Planner Spreadsheet Solution is for business owners or accountants who want to project the financial condition of a company. If you're not an accountant, most of it will probably be inexplicable to you. If you do have knowledge of accounting, you may find the Business Planner useful for your forecasting needs.

CAUTION

Before using the Business Planner, you should take into account this disclaimer made by Microsoft regarding its use:

"This product includes sample forms only. Using these forms may have significant legal implications; these vary from state to state and depend on the subject matter. Use of these forms may not necessarily comply with generally accepted accounting principles (GAAP) or other accounting principles or standards. Before using any of these forms for your business, you should consult with a lawyer, a financial advisor, and/or an accountant. Microsoft and its suppliers are not responsible for any action you take based on the use of this template."

Furthermore, you should not rely on the text or figures in this book for tax, legal, or financial decisions.

To use the Business Planner, first click the Customize button and complete the company information on that worksheet. On the Customize Your Planner worksheet, also select whether the business being planned for is a C-Corporation (leaving that check box blank assumes that it is an S-Corporation). If you select the check box indicating that the business is a C-Corporation, the Business Planner template will calculate estimated corporate taxes. Leaving the check box blank assumes that an S-Corporation is being planned for (S-Corporations pass along their tax liability to the individuals who own them).

After completing the customization worksheet, move to the Data Sheet worksheet, shown in Figure 9.18, to enter the key information about the business for which you are planning. You can enter statistics about how quickly Accounts Receivable are collected, how long finished goods stay in inventory, and other key statistics. You also enter key percentages from prior years that help estimate costs as a percentage of sales, and also company debt information. The shaded cells on the worksheet contain the calculated results based on the statistics you enter.

Next, move to the Balance Sheet worksheet and enter the closing balances from the prior year for the business's balance sheet accounts, such as cash on hand, accounts receivable, and so on (see Figure 9.19). Again, the shaded cells are calculated values driven by other data that you enter into the Business Planner.

Finally, move to the Income Statement worksheet shown in Figure 9.20. Here you enter your estimated sales volumes, expected amortizations, and other key income statement information that cannot be calculated.

When you're finished entering data, you can start examining the results. View the Data Chart, Asset Chart, Income Chart, and Cash Flow Sheet worksheets to see the results of all the information you entered.

Purchase Order

Another Spreadsheet Solutions included with Excel 97 is the Purchase Order template shown in Figure 9.21. You can use this template to generate purchase orders for your business. When using the Purchase Order template, you'll find that it functions almost identically to the Invoice template discussed in a previous section. Read the section on the Invoice template ("Invoicing") if you require more information on using the Purchase Order template.

FIG. 9.18
To start using the Business Planner, complete the Data Sheet worksheet.

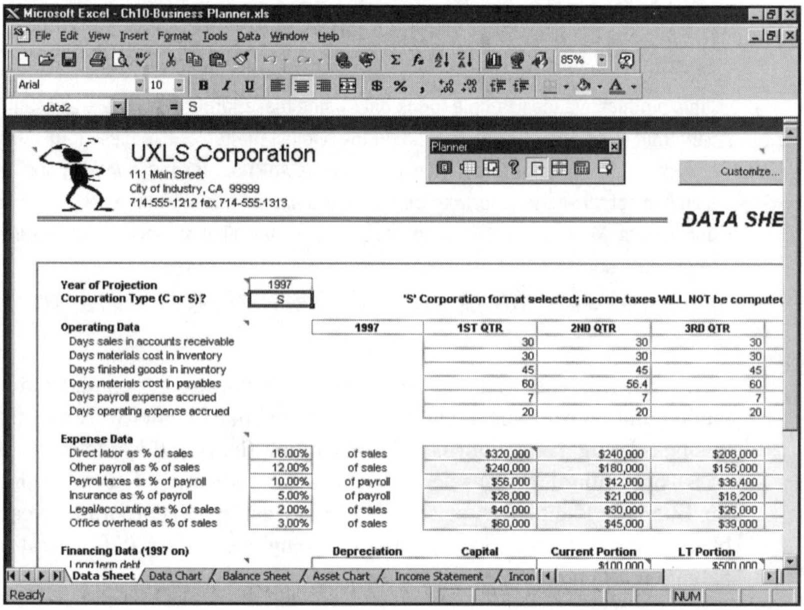

FIG. 9.19
Use the Balance Sheet worksheet to enter in the prior year's closing balances.

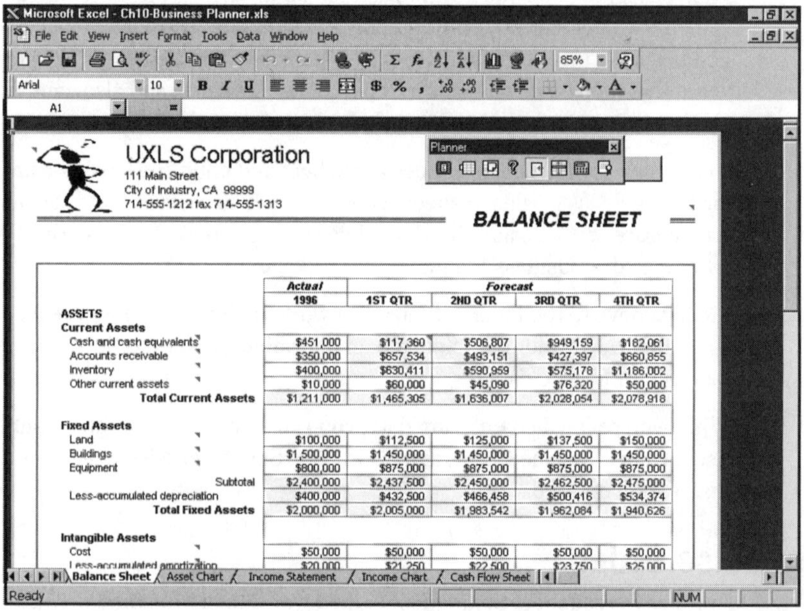

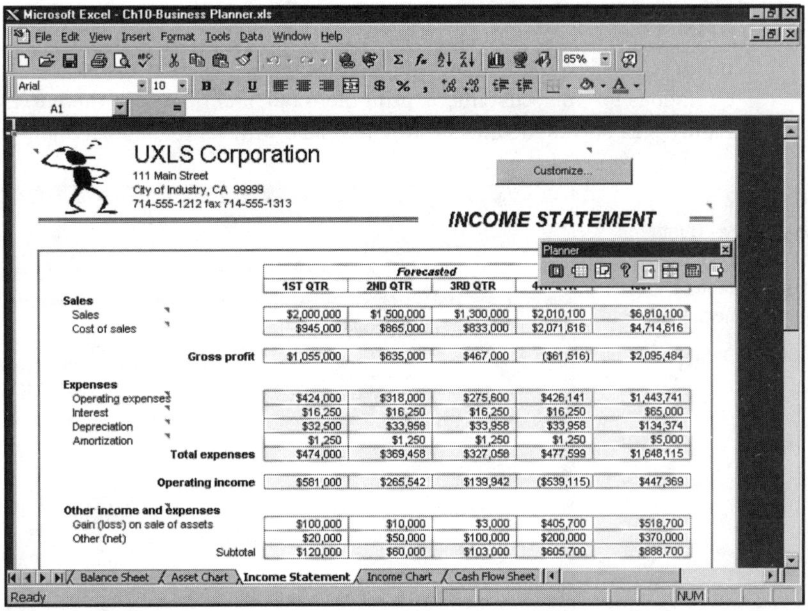

FIG. 9.20
Use the Income Statement worksheet to enter sales projections as well as other information that isn't calculated.

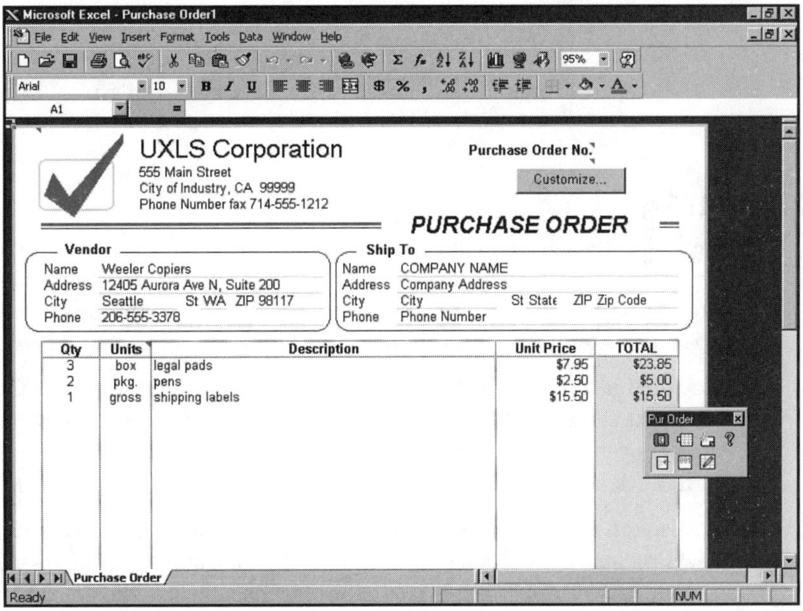

FIG. 9.21
You can generate quick and easy Purchase Orders with the Purchase Order template.

Sales Quote

If you're in sales, the Sales Quote template may be of interest to you. It lets you prepare sales quotations for your customers, print them out, and then save them to a file for future reference. Figure 9.22 shows the Sales Quote template with sample information.

FIG. 9.22
Use the Sales Quote template to prepare sales quotations for your customers.

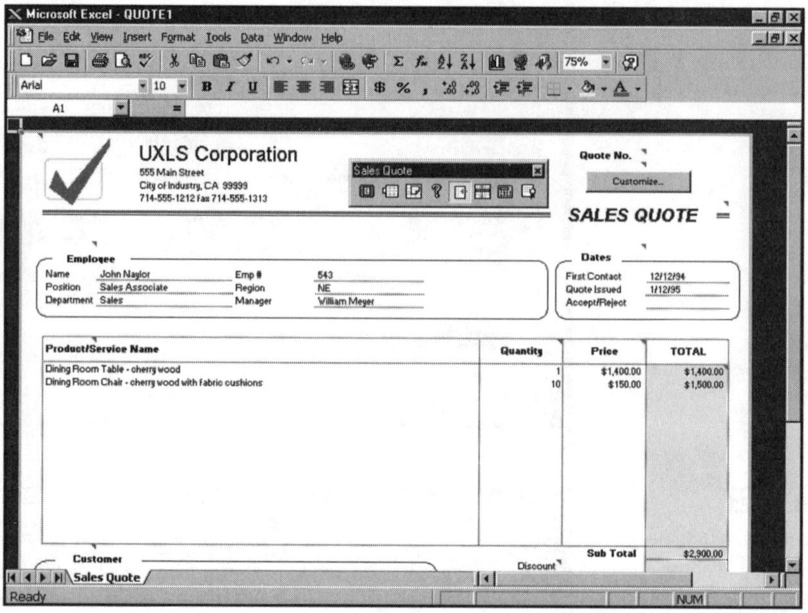

Time Card

The final Spreadsheet Solution included with Excel 97 is the Timecard template, shown in Figure 9.23. You or your employees can use this template to enter their time allocations. The information provided not only lets the payroll department properly charge their time to various departments or functions, but it also gives you a graphical view of how the time is spent.

Click the Customize button to enter specific company information in the fields provided. The Customize screen also lets you control the standard number of hours in a work week and whether overtime is approved or not. Then, the Timecard information is completed for the entire week, with the appropriate accounting codes assigned as shown in Figure 9.23.

You also can get an overview of how the time spent is being allocated by looking at the Personal Productivity worksheet. You can see the total number of hours allocated to each accounting code, as well as view a pie chart showing visually how the time allocations break down.

FIG. 9.23
The Timecard Spreadsheet Solution is terrific for tracking and accounting for how employees spend their time.

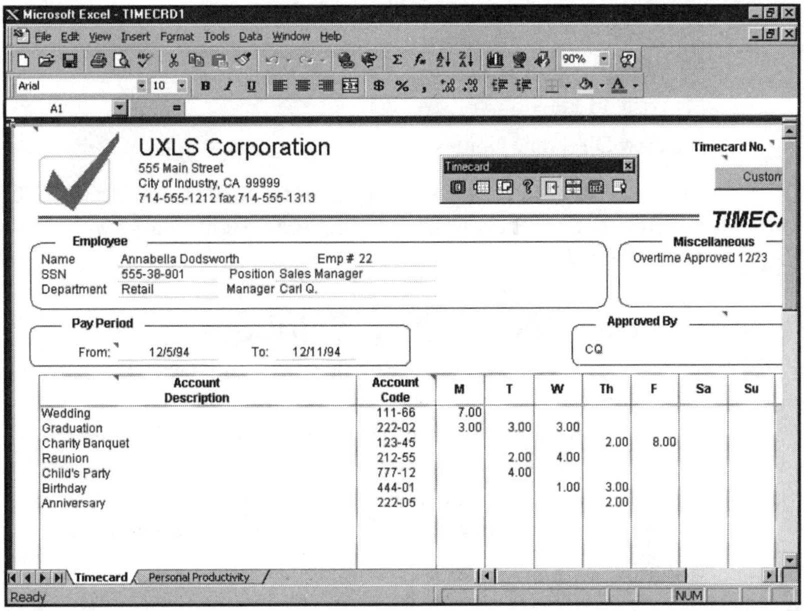

Common Problems and Solutions

The Spreadsheet Solutions included with Excel are complete and have been tested; however, there are a couple of problems you may want to watch out for. The following sections discuss some of the most common problems and their solutions.

No Logo Choices Available

When you use your first Spreadsheet Solution and click the Select Logo button on one of the template's Customize worksheets, the directory first shown doesn't contain any useful clip art that you might assign to the logo field. Of course, you can use your own company logo if you have a graphic image of the logo, but you can also spruce up the templates with the Office 97 clip art collection. In the dialog box that appears when you click the Select Logo button, navigate to the \MSOffice\Clipart folder and then look in the various subfolders there for suitable clip art for the logo art.

Shared Database Problems

Some of the Spreadsheet Solution templates let you establish shared databases for lookup information on the templates, for keeping track of a sequential set of numbers for each form used, or for collecting data about templates that have been completed and saved. To use these features, you need to establish a folder on a network server to which all of the users of the templates have permissions. It's best to work with your company's MIS department in establishing this shared folder.

To prevent possible problems, grant the following minimum access rights to the shared folder:

- Read from Files
- Write to Files
- View Directory Names

Consider removing any rights to create or delete files in that shared directory to prevent accidents. However, test how well restricting these rights works with the shared database files on your specific network.

Pre-Customized Spreadsheet Solutions

If you are using the Spreadsheet Solutions that come with Excel 97 in your company, you no doubt want to create versions that already have all of the company data filled in for the users, so that they only have to concentrate on the form itself. You can create a set of Solution templates for use in your company, including the ones discussed here as well as any others you develop. See Chapter 23, "Collaborating with Excel," for information on setting up shared template directories that everyone in your company can access automatically.

From Here...

In this chapter you learned about the Spreadsheet Solutions—custom workbook templates designed for different tasks—included with Excel. You learned how to install the Spreadsheet Solutions that don't get installed as part of the Office 97 installation, and how to locate additional Spreadsheet Solutions on the Web. From here, you may want to read the following chapters:

- Chapter 23, "Collaborating with Excel," offers more information on establishing shared templates within workgroups.
- Chapter 28, "Understanding VBA Macros," offers information on programming Excel, often a key component of developing your own Spreadsheet Solutions.
- Chapter 27, "Building Online Forms," includes information on developing Excel-based forms for use on the Internet.

PART III

Creating Charts and Graphics

CHAPTER 10

Creating Charts

by Bruce Hallberg

Charts are an exciting feature in Excel. Once you have all of your data entered and analyzed, you usually need to communicate it to others. And there's no better way to communicate data and results more concisely and powerfully than with attractive, well-designed charts. A good chart lets the reader instantly see the point that you want to make. Different charts draw readers to different conclusions, and cause them to ask different questions about what they're seeing. If you're selling something—an idea, result, plan, or opportunity—charts let you get across your thoughts with clarity and power. ■

Using the Chart Wizard

The Chart Wizard in Excel makes creating charts quick and easy. Extensively redesigned in Excel 97, the Chart Wizard is both more powerful and easier to use than in Excel 95.

Working with charts

You can use the Chart Wizard to quickly create powerful charts, but you often then want to further modify your charts to get just the right effect that you need. Work with Excel's detailed charting features to change different elements within the charts you create.

Formatting charts

Once you have all the data you need shown in your charts, and the data is arranged the way you want, you can then use Excel's chart formatting capabilities to create the most attractive charts possible.

Creating Charts with the Chart Wizard

To create a chart with the Chart Wizard, you first select the data you want charted (you don't have to do this, but it saves time to select the data before you begin the Wizard). When you select data to chart, you select both the data itself along with any labels that describe the data. Excel automatically recognizes the labels and uses them in the resulting chart. Figure 10.1 shows you a sample worksheet that is used for this example with the relevant portion (cells A5:E10) selected for the Chart Wizard.

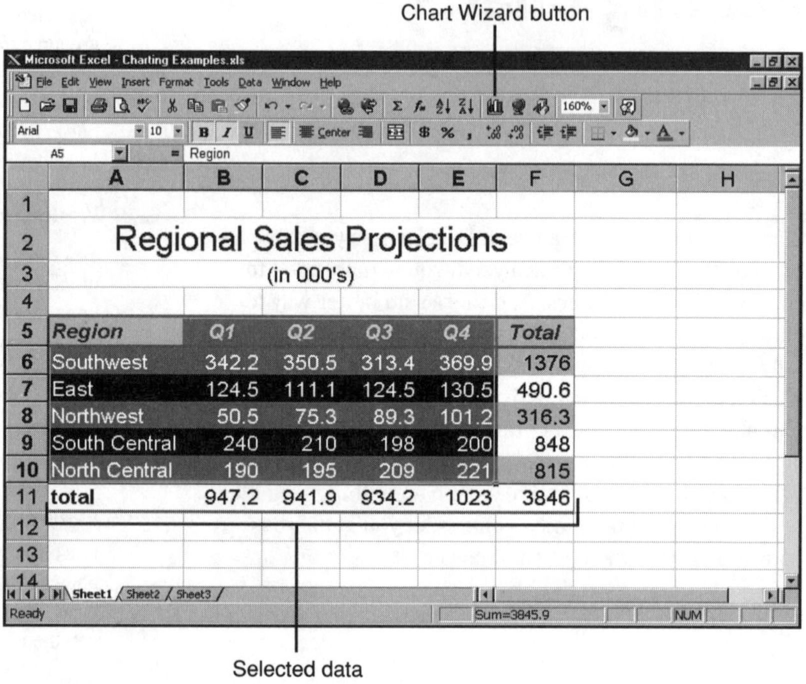

FIG. 10.1
Select your data and data labels before starting the Chart Wizard.

Step 1: Choosing the Chart Type and Sub-type

After selecting the data, click the Chart Wizard button. The Chart Wizard is divided up into four main steps, each of which defines a different aspect of the chart you create. Step 1 of the Chart Wizard is shown in Figure 10.2.

On the Standard Types tab you see the main types of Excel charts. Chapter 12, "A Field Guide to Excel Charts," discusses each one of these types in detail, and points out important distinctions between them. You can also choose from a variety of other chart types by clicking the Custom Types tab, shown in Figure 10.3. The Custom Types are charts that are created using all of Excel's capabilities to modify the standard chart types. You can also define your own custom chart types, which can also be selected on the Custom Types tab using the User-defined option button.

FIG. 10.2
Step 1 of the Chart Wizard lets you choose the type of chart you want to create.

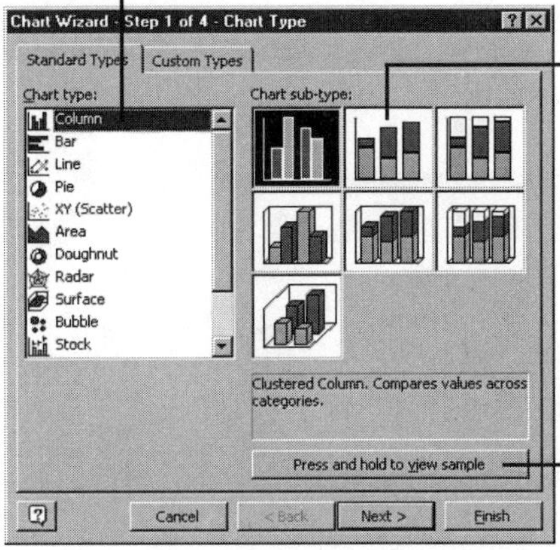

FIG. 10.3
The Custom Types tab lets you choose from a number of special chart types built into Excel.

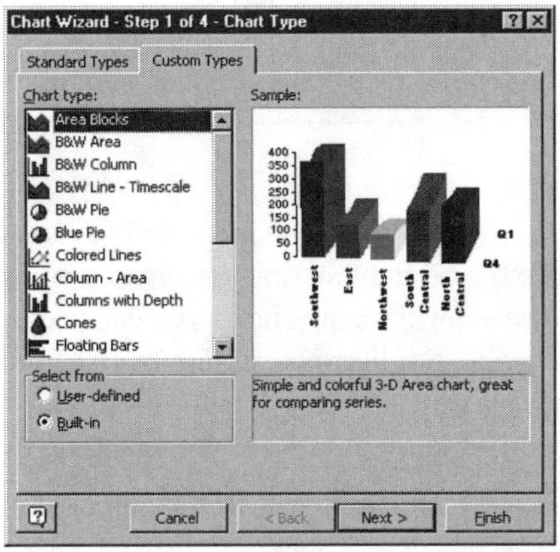

Part III
Ch 10

For this example, the Clustered Column chart is selected in the Standard Types tab. The Clustered Column is the upper-left sub-type within the Column chart type. After selecting it, click Next to continue.

Step 2: Select and Orient the Data Range and Series

In the second step of the Chart Wizard you see the dialog box shown in Figure 10.4. You can perform the following tasks on the Data Range tab:

- Select (or reselect) the range on which the chart is based using the Data Range field. If you didn't select the range of data to be charted before starting the Chart Wizard, you can select the data range at this time with this field. Use the Collapse/Expand button to move the dialog box out of your way when direct-selecting the range.

- Orient the range of data on the chart using the Rows and Columns option buttons. When you choose Rows, each row of data on the worksheet will be treated as a chart series. Choosing Columns causes each column of data to become a chart series. In Figure 10.4, the Rows option button is selected. Choosing either option button immediately previews the change in the window on the Data Range tab.

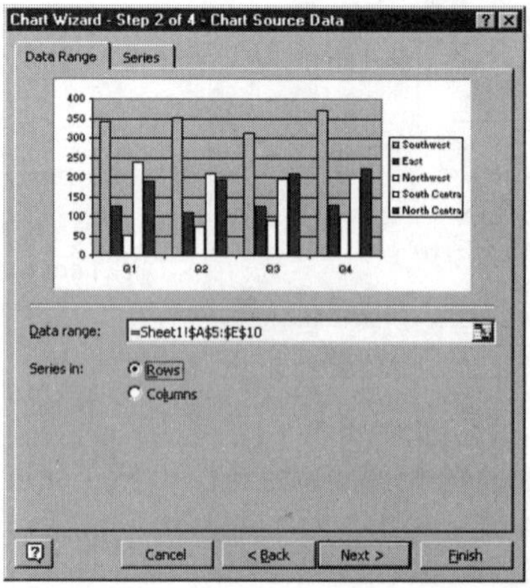

FIG. 10.4
Use the Data Range tab in Step 2 of the Chart Wizard to select and orient your data.

Why change the orientation of the chart series? The most obvious answer to this question is that Excel didn't correctly choose the orientation that you wanted and the default choice displays the data nonsensically. However, with many charts you can present your data differently depending on which choice you make. For instance, in Figure 10.4 you can see in the chart preview how selecting Rows shows a time-series of data for each region in the example data. This data would be examined in order to see how sales are changing over time for each region.

However, now consider the preview shown in Figure 10.5, in which the Columns option is chosen. This chart orientation does two things. First, it lets the reader see more easily how the sales are changing for each region across the four quarters, because the quarters for each region are right next to each other. More importantly, it does something that the example in Figure 10.4 doesn't do very well: It lets the reader easily see the gross differences between regions. It becomes painfully obvious, for example, that the Northwest region, while growing at a steady clip, is far behind the other regions. Switch back to the Rows option before proceeding.

The Series tab on the Chart Wizard's Step 2 dialog box lets you control each series of the chart. Figure 10.6 shows the Series tab. You can perform the following operations on the series shown:

- *Add or Remove a series.* When you click Add, a new series is instantly created, and you then use the other fields on the Series tab to fill in the details of that new series. To remove a series, select it in the Series list and then click Remove.

FIG. 10.5
Choosing an alternate orientation for the data suggests a different meaning.

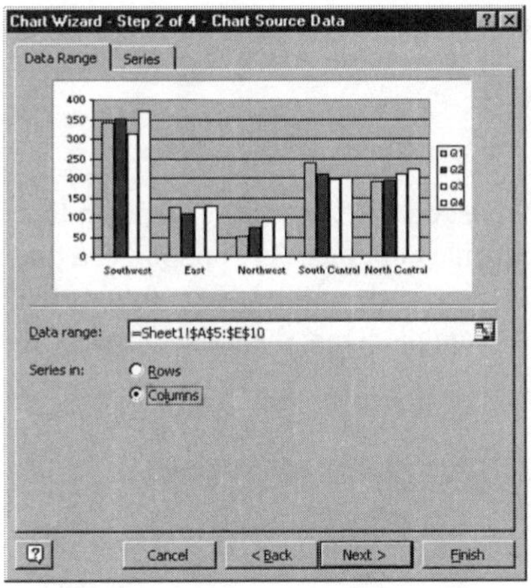

Part III Ch 10

- *Name a series.* Select a series in the Series list and then use the Name field to choose a different chart cell that contains the label for that series. You can also type any label that you want in the Name field.
- *Select (or reselect) the data on which a series is based.* Choose one of the series listed in the Series list and then use the Values field to choose a new range of data. You can also type the values you want to use by entering them directly with each value separated from the next with a comma.
- *Change the category labels.* Use the Category (X) Axis Labels field to change the names used to identify each chart category along the bottom axis of the chart. You can choose a new worksheet range in this field, or you can type each label, separating each from the next with a comma.

FIG. 10.6
The Series tab of Step 2 of the Chart Wizard lets you control each series on the chart.

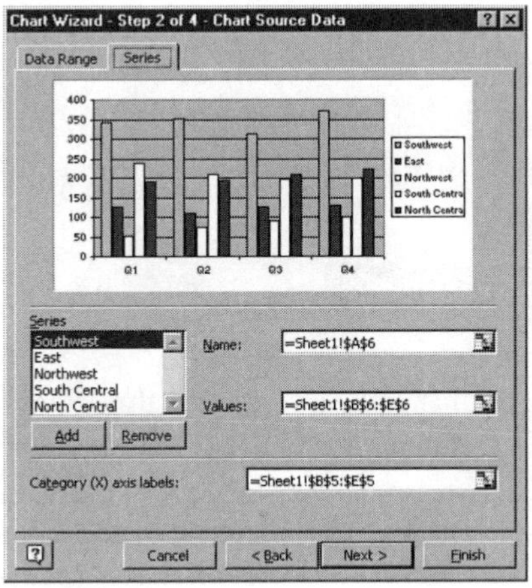

After checking and changing any necessary settings on the Data Range or Series tabs, click Next to continue.

Step 3: Set Chart Options

Step 3 of the Chart Wizard is the most complex of all the steps. In this dialog box you can choose from a plethora of different chart options. Any options you don't change use default values. Figure 10.7 shows the first tab, Titles, of the Chart Options dialog box. Several titles have already been typed in for the example. Only the fields for titles that are appropriate for a particular chart type are available.

FIG. 10.7
In the Titles tab of Step 3 you can enter different titles for your chart.

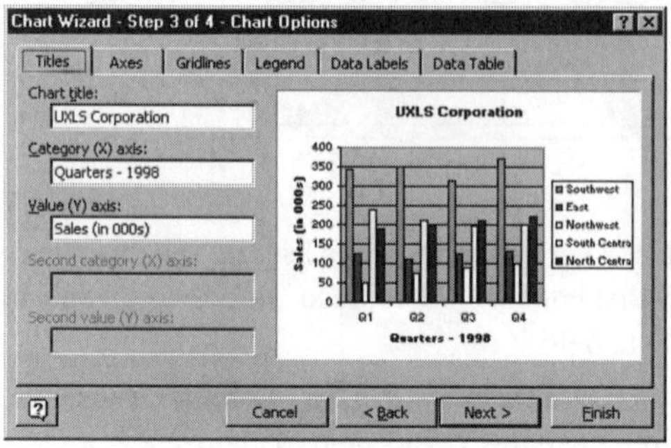

The Axes tab, shown in Figure 10.8, lets you control the category and value axes on the chart. You can toggle each axis on or off, and with the Category axis you can determine if the axis shows categories or a time-scale (or automatically determines the axis type).

FIG. 10.8
The Axes tab lets you control the category and value axes.

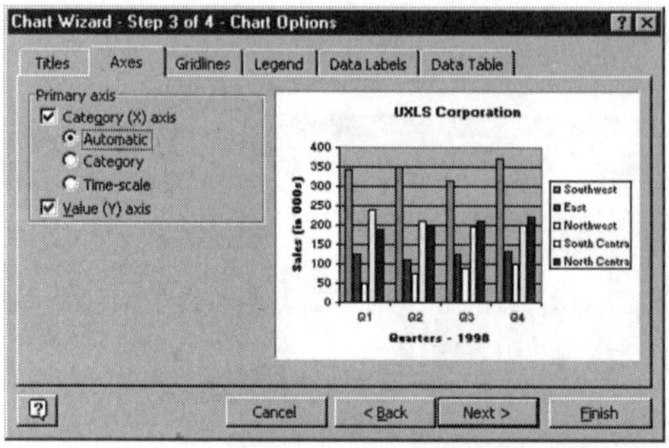

You can add gridlines to your charts that make interpreting the values on the chart easier. The Gridlines tab lets you select major and minor gridlines, as shown in Figure 10.9.

TIP Gridlines should be used only when necessary to help the reader align data points with the axis labels. Often gridlines are used in such a way that they clutter charts unnecessarily. Just as you wouldn't use unnecessary words when writing, you don't want to use chart elements that don't add anything.

FIG. 10.9
Select from four grid options for your chart with the Gridlines tab.

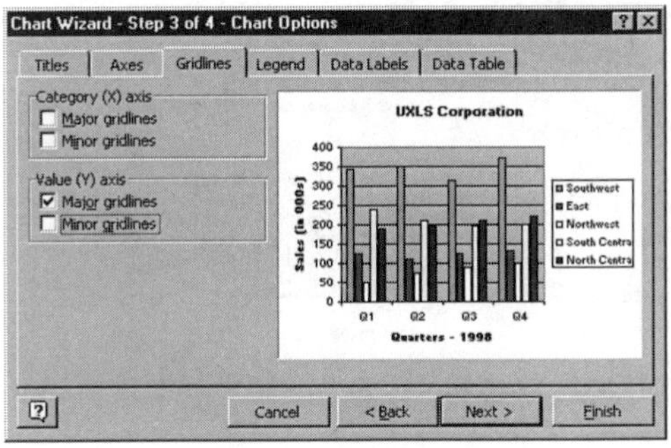

The Legend tab (see Figure 10.10) lets you determine whether or not a legend is shown for your chart, and if shown, lets you determine its position.

FIG. 10.10
Select whether you want a legend and the legend's position with the Legend tab.

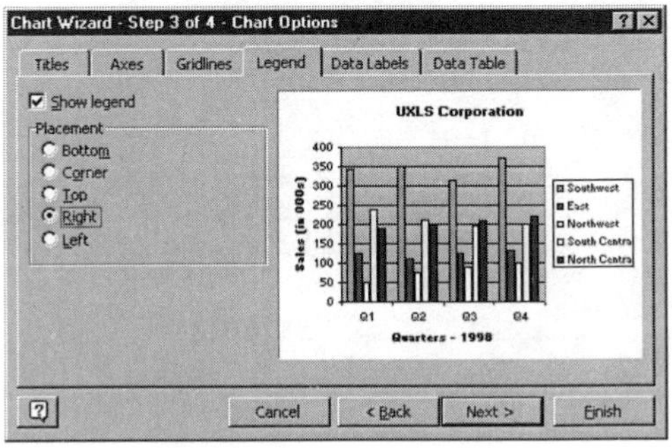

A data label is an on-chart label that shows the actual value or label of each data point. There are different data labels depending on the type of chart you're designing, and you control these data labels on the Data Labels tab (see Figure 10.11). Data labels appear in the chart immediately next to the data point they reference, although you can move them later when editing the chart.

TIP You should generally avoid data labels unless absolutely necessary. Data labels can clutter a chart, and they can also focus attention on the actual values being shown instead of emphasizing the "big picture" for the data.

One of the nicest new features in Excel 97's charting package is the addition of data tables in charts. A data table appears next to the chart and shows the actual data being charted. Because the numbers don't appear in the chart as with data labels, they tend not to clutter the appearance of the chart, and yet are readily visible should the reader need to reference the actual values being charted. Figure 10.12 shows the Data Table tab. Refer to the section titled "Data Tables," later in this chapter, to see how data tables look when used with charts.

FIG. 10.11
Data labels can help readers quickly see the actual values being charted.

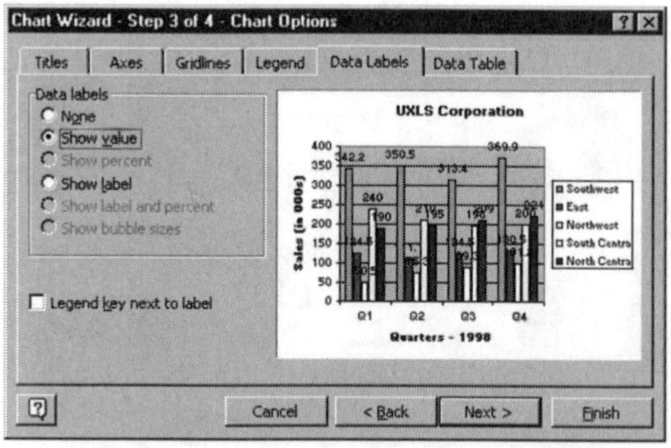

When you have finished making your selections from each tab, click Next to continue.

FIG. 10.12
Include quick and easy data listings in your charts with the Show Data Table check box.

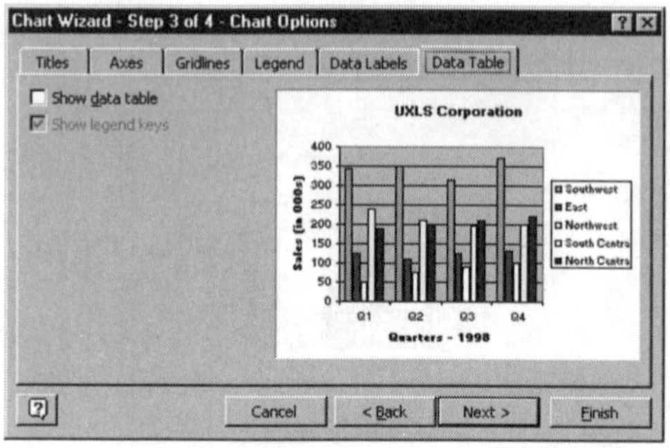

Step 4: Choose a Location for the Chart

In the final step of the Chart Wizard you determine the location for the chart you are creating. You can either embed the chart as an object in a worksheet, or you can create a separate *chart sheet* in the workbook that displays the chart. Figure 10.13 shows the Step 4 dialog box. Choose either As New Sheet or As Object In, and then make the appropriate changes to the associated fields. The As New Sheet field lets you name the resulting chart tab in the workbook, while the As Object In field lets you select from existing worksheets into which the resulting chart will be placed. Figures 10.14 and 10.15 show you the effect of both choices. After you've made your selection, click Finish to close the dialog box and view the chart in the worksheet.

FIG. 10.13
Use the final step of the Chart Wizard to determine where your new chart will appear.

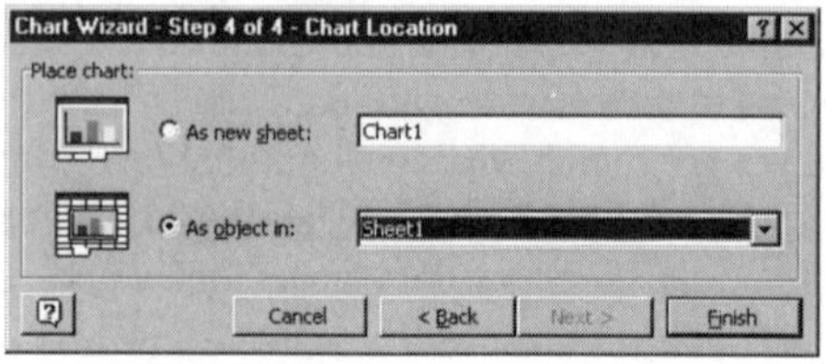

FIG. 10.14
The new chart created as a Chart sheet.

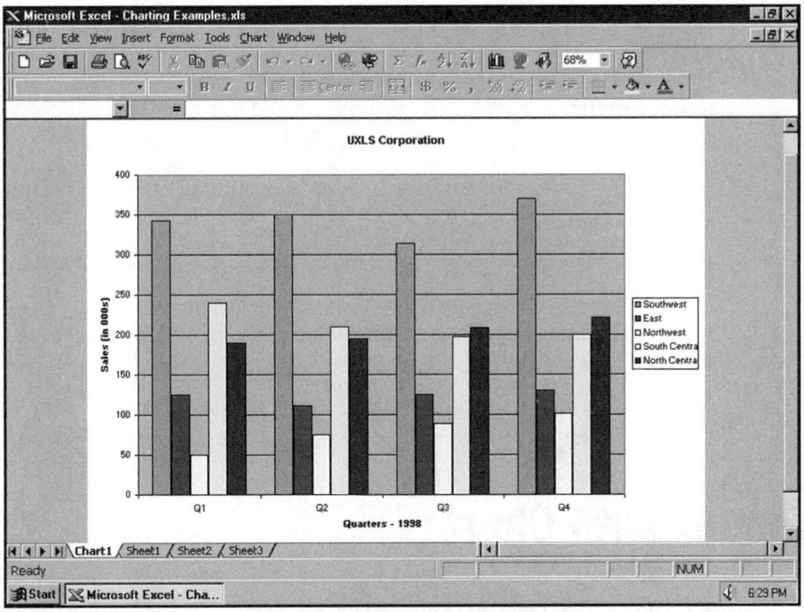

FIG. 10.15
The new chart embedded as an object in a worksheet.

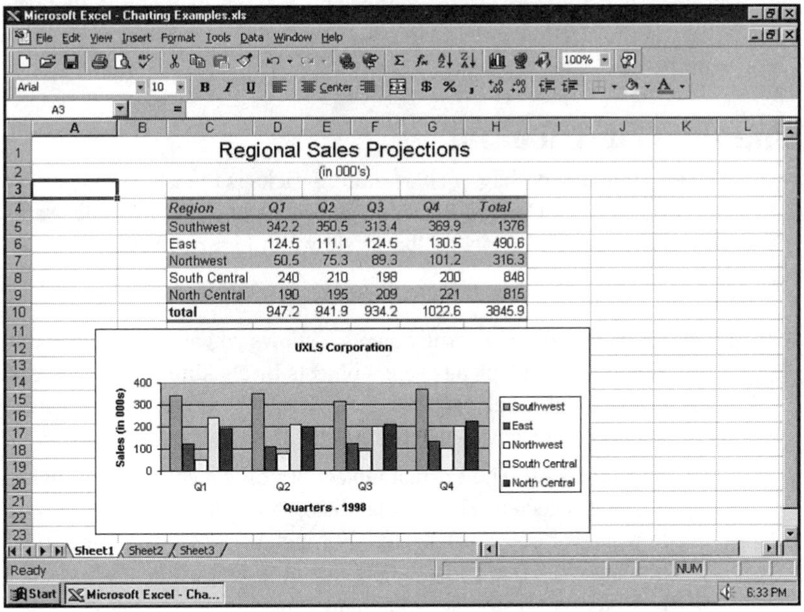

Modifying Charts with Wizard Dialog Boxes

The Chart Wizard isn't only for creating charts. You can also use it to modify existing charts. Each step of the Chart Wizard can be accessed individually through commands in the Chart menu (you must select the chart to see the Chart menu):

- Chart Type opens the Step 1 dialog box of the Chart Wizard in which you choose the type of chart.
- Source Data opens the Step 2 dialog box in which you can specify the data used in the chart.
- Chart Options opens the Step 3 dialog box, in which you can set a number of chart formatting and display options.
- Location opens the Step 4 dialog box in which you can relocate the chart between being embedded on a worksheet or included as a separate chart sheet in your workbook.

Working with Charts

The Chart Wizard is a useful tool for building and modifying charts. However, it falls short when you need to make certain specific changes to a chart. For example, the Chart Wizard's dialog boxes don't let you choose chart element colors, add floating text to the chart, or choose different data markers. To make these other types of changes, you have to edit the chart directly. In this section, you learn how to do that in order to create charts that are exactly as you want them.

Using the Chart Toolbar

The first tool in your bag of chart-editing tricks is the Chart toolbar, which displays by default when you select a chart. If it isn't displayed, right-click any toolbar and choose Chart from the shortcut menu. The Chart toolbar is shown in Figure 10.16.

The buttons on the Chart toolbar operate as follows:

- *Chart Objects.* This drop-down list shows you all of the selectable objects on the chart. While you can typically select objects by clicking them, sometimes with complex charts it is difficult to select the object you want. You can use the Chart Objects drop-down list to choose any of the chart's objects for further editing.
- *Format Object.* The Format Object button displays the Format dialog box for whatever object is selected. The Format dialog box contains different tabs which are appropriate to whatever object is selected. For instance, choose a line series, and the Format dialog box has a tab that lets you edit data markers. Choose a text label, and the Format dialog box has options that let you change how the text displays.
- *Chart Type.* This drop-down list lets you quickly choose different types of charts. You can use this to quickly try a number of different chart types until you find the one that works best for your data.

FIG. 10.16
Use the Chart Toolbar to edit parts of your chart.

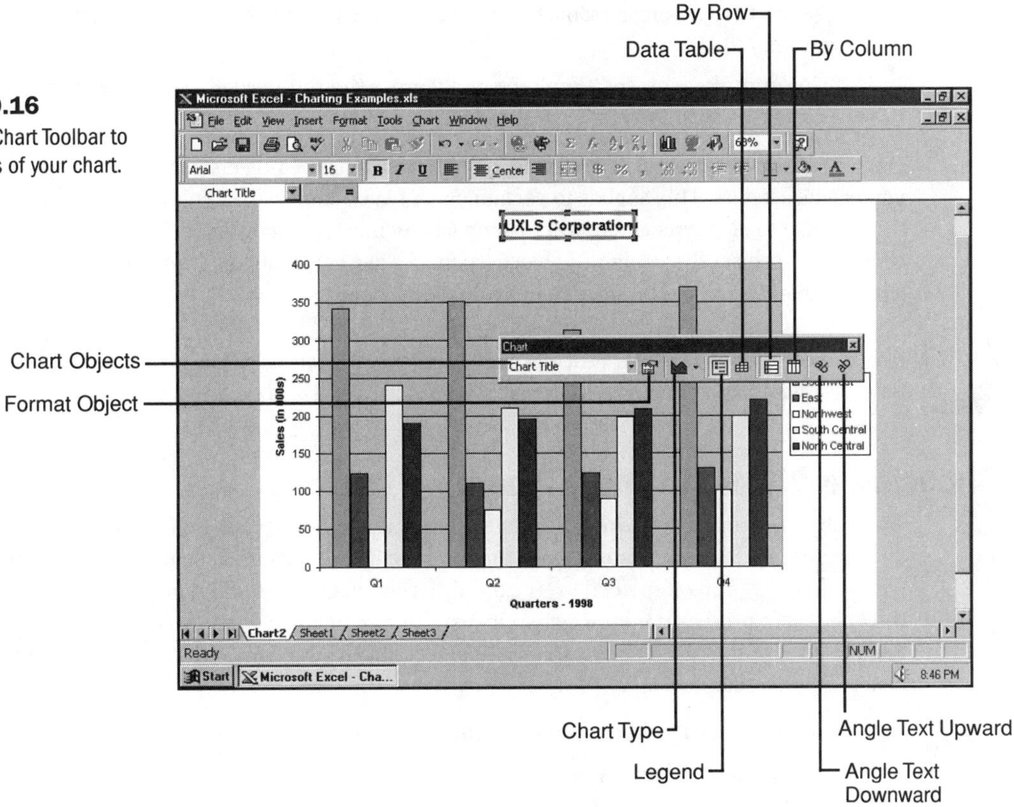

- *Legend.* The Legend button is an on/off toggle that lets you add or remove a legend in the chart.
- *Data Table.* Like the Legend button, the Data Table button is an on/off toggle that lets you add or remove a data table in the chart.
- *By Row and By Column.* The By Row and By Column buttons are mutually exclusive. They determine whether the data series being charted are arranged with the series being derived from rows in the worksheet's data, or from columns. You can toggle between these two options quickly and view the results instantly.
- *Angle Text Downward and Angle Text Upward.* A new feature in Excel 97, you can rotate text to any angle you want. These two buttons let you quickly choose 45-degree up or down angles for any selected text. To remove the rotation, click the selected angle button a second time to deselect it.

Selecting Chart Elements

You normally select elements in a chart by simply clicking them. Sometimes, though, a certain chart may not let you easily select one of its elements in this way. If this happens, there are two routes open to you:

- Use the Chart toolbar's Chart Objects drop-down list to choose the element with which you want to work.
- Select any element, and then repeatedly press the right or left arrow keys until the chart element you want to modify is selected.

One exception to the single-click selection rule is this: some objects contain sub-objects that you can also select. This applies to certain chart types, such as bar, column, line, and XY scatter, and also to elements and markers in chart legends. To choose sub-objects like these, first click once to select the container object (such as a series), wait a brief moment, and then click again to select a sub-object (like an individual data point).

TIP Excel 97 now supports ChartTips. Rest your mouse pointer over a data point on a chart, and a Chart Tip appears that displays the series name and shows you the actual data value being plotted.

Choosing a Different Chart Type

There are more than a hundred different chart types and sub-types from which you can choose. Mix in different custom types that you can develop yourself, and the assortment becomes dizzying. You often need to "try on" different chart types with your data in order to find the one that expresses the information in just the way that you want. Accordingly, you often need to change the type of chart that is being displayed. You can do this in two ways once the chart is generated:

- Use the Chart Type button on the Chart toolbar to select a different type.
- Choose Chart, Chart Type to select a different type.

The first method is faster, but yields fewer choices. The second method activates the same dialog box that you see in Step 1 of the Chart Wizard (refer to Figure 10.2), in which you can see and preview all of the chart types available in Excel. Refer to Chapter 12, "A Field Guide to Excel Chart Types," for more detailed information on specific chart types, and when you should choose a particular type.

TIP You can select an individual series and then use the Chart Type button on the Chart toolbar. Doing so causes that series to display using the selected chart type, while the remaining series remain in the default chart type. With this method you can superimpose line-based series in column or bar charts, for example.

Adding Elements to Charts

There are many elements that you can add to charts to increase their effectiveness. They range from simple text labels that may annotate a part of the chart, or might serve as a subtitle, to drawn annotations, added ranges, legends, and data tables. In the following sections you learn how to add these elements to your charts.

Legends Legends, such as the one shown in Figure 10.17, are often required to distinguish the different series on a chart. Excel automatically creates legends for you in one of two ways:

- Click the Legend button on the Chart toolbar.
- Choose Chart, Chart Options to open the Chart Options dialog box. Click the Legend tab and select the Show Legend check box. You can further select the location for the legend with the Bottom, Corner, Top, Right, and Left option buttons.

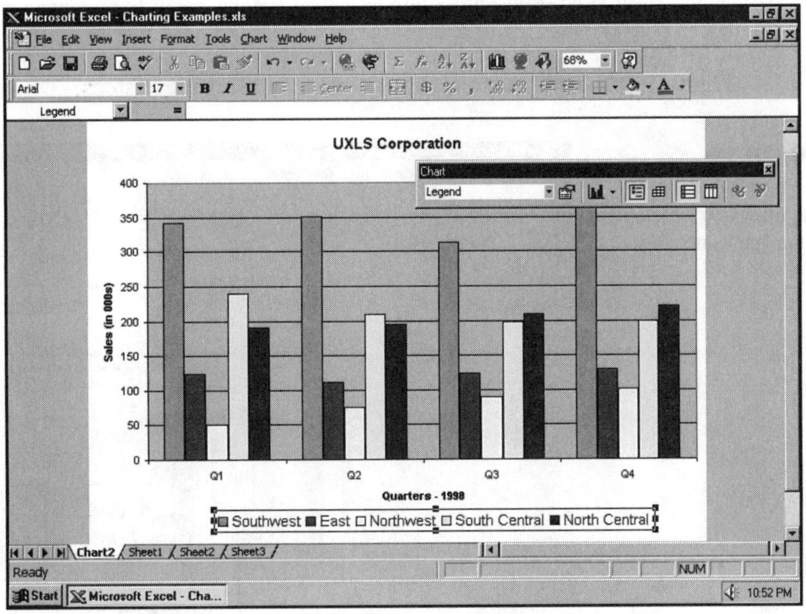

FIG. 10.17
Legends are often required to explain chart series.

Once a legend is created, you can reposition it by simply dragging it to its new location. If you want to change its orientation (for example, a bottom legend is shown in Figure 10.17, while a right legend is shown in Figure 10.14), you use the option buttons on the Chart Options dialog box to change the legend accordingly.

Labels There are a variety of different types of labels that you can use on charts. The main types are the chart title and the axis titles. You can also have free-floating text labels.

To create one of the main types of titles, choose Chart, Chart Options and click the Titles tab. You can then type the titles you want in the available fields.

To add a free-floating label, select the chart area by clicking the chart's background. Then, simply type whatever text you want. The text is created in a box that appears in the middle of the chart when you press Enter. You can then drag the text to any location that you want, and can right-click it to access its formatting properties on the shortcut menu.

Callouts Charts often beg for callouts. A *callout* is typically a line (with or without an arrow) pointing out a particular area of interest on a chart. You create callouts on Excel charts by first drawing the callout line, and then you add the text for the callout.

To draw a line for a callout, follow these steps:

1. Activate the Drawing toolbar.
2. Choose either the Line or Arrow line types on the Drawing toolbar.
3. Draw the line directly on the chart.
4. Add the text for the callout by selecting the chart background and typing the text you want. Press Enter when done.
5. Move the text (and the line or arrow, if necessary) to an appropriate location for the callout.

Figure 10.18 shows an example callout added using these steps.

FIG. 10.18
Add a callout to a chart with the Drawing toolbar and a free-floating text label.

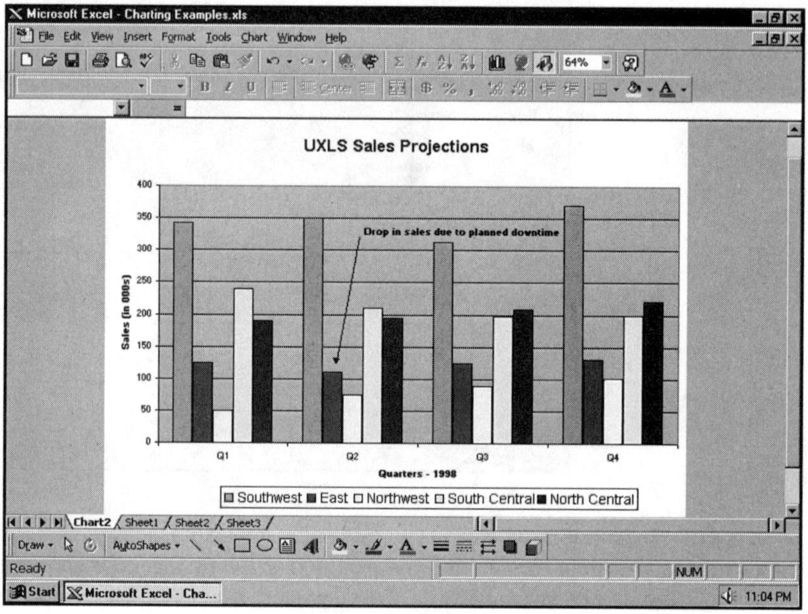

Data Tables Data tables can be extremely useful for some charts. They offer the reader the ability to see the actual numbers used for the data in the chart. In earlier versions of Excel, you had to insert data tables by embedding charts on worksheets, and then formatting a data table below the chart. With Excel 97, you can create data tables automatically, right in the chart.

To create a data table, use one of these methods:

- On the Chart toolbar, click the Data Table button.
- Choose Chart, Chart Options and click the Data Table tab on the Chart Options dialog box. Select the Show Data Table check box to activate the data table.

Figure 10.19 shows a chart with a data table included.

FIG. 10.19
Data tables can be extremely useful to show underlying data on which a chart is based.

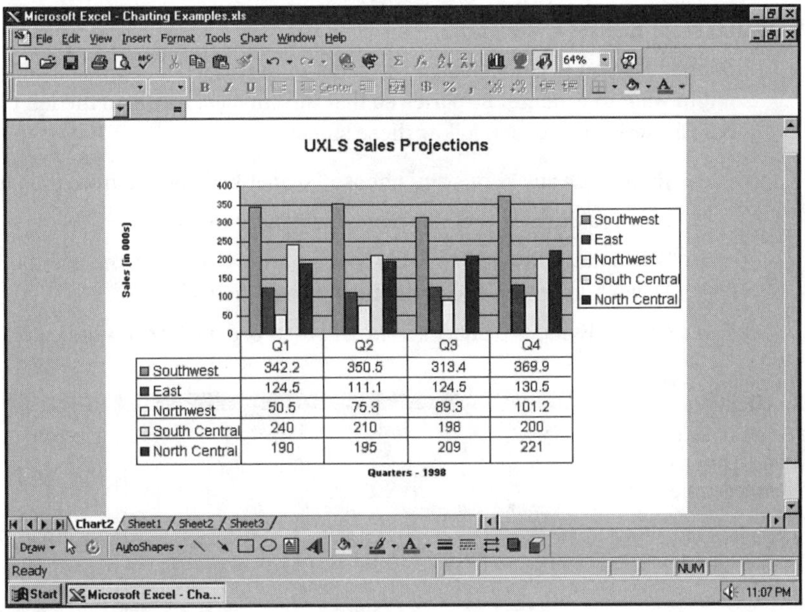

New Series Adding a new series of data to a chart is often required, particularly with charts that you update on a periodic basis. Instead of having to recreate the chart every time a new series of data is available, you can more easily add the new range as a new series.

To add a series to an existing chart, follow these steps:

1. With the chart selected, choose Chart, Source Data.
2. In the Source Data dialog box that appears, click the Series tab.
3. Click the Add button.
4. Complete the Name and Values fields as appropriate. You can type a name directly into the Name field or provide a cell reference from which the series name will come. You can type the values for the series in the Values field, separating each from the next by a comma, or you can supply a cell range reference that contains the data for the new series.
5. Click OK to close the dialog box.

TIP There is a quick shortcut to adding a series to an existing chart. Select the data (including the label) and copy the data onto the clipboard. Move to the chart, select the chart area, and then choose Paste from the Edit menu. The series is added automatically, and you then can "fine-tune" it if necessary using the Source Data dialog box.

Reordering Chart Series

Sometimes you need to change the order of the series that are charted. For example, you might want to arrange the series so that the smallest one is to the left of larger series. To reorder the series in a chart, follow these steps:

1. Right-click any series and choose Format Data Series from the shortcut menu.
2. Move to the Series Order tab, shown in Figure 10.20.
3. Select any of the series listed in the Series Order list and use the Move Up and Move Down buttons to reposition the series in the list.
4. Click OK and the chart series' will be reordered as you indicated.

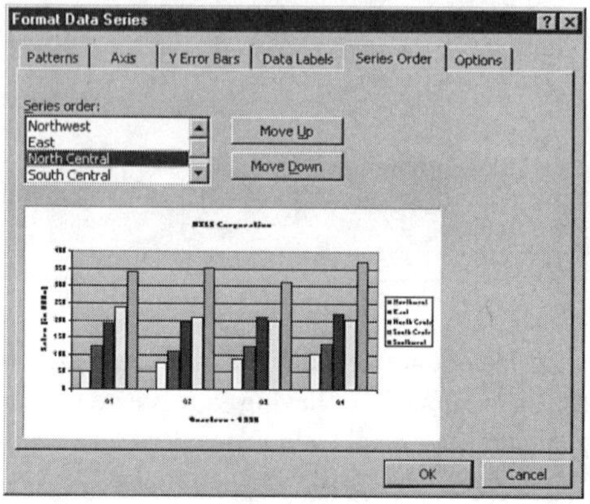

FIG. 10.20
The Series Order tab lets you choose how the different series are ordered.

Formatting Charts

Although the built-in formatting defaults for Excel charts are typically quite good, the most professional results occur when you spend extra time formatting different chart elements so that they are as attractive and communicative as possible. The general way in which this is done is by use of the Format Object command, which you can access in three ways (in all cases you must first select the object you want to format):

- Click the Format Object button on the Chart toolbar.
- Right-click an element and from the shortcut menu that appears, choose Format *object*, where *object* changes in the command name depending on what object you've selected.
- Choose Format, Selected *object*, where *object* changes in the command name depending on what object you've selected.

The Format dialog box differs depending on the type of element you're formatting. Only tabs that are appropriate to a given chart element appear in the dialog box. Each tab can also change depending on the object that you're formatting.

Changing Chart Colors, Line Styles, and Patterns

You can choose the colors, line styles, and drawing patterns that Excel uses for any aspect of its charts. You can change the colors for data series, individual data points, data markers, the chart background, and text on the chart. You can change the line style for any element that uses lines or borders. Finally, you can change the patterns of any filled object on the chart. To format the color, line style, or pattern of some element, follow these steps:

1. Right-click the element to be formatted.
2. Choose Format from the shortcut menu.
3. Click the Patterns tab, shown in Figure 10.21.

FIG. 10.21
Use the Patterns tab of the Format dialog box to select colors, line widths, and drawing patterns.

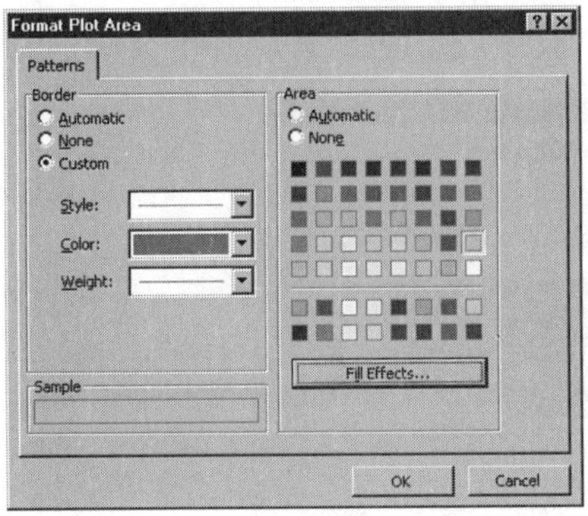

4. Use the Border and Area sections of the Patterns tab to make your choices.

97

Excel 97 adds some new pattern effects not available in previous versions of Excel. You access these additional effects with the Fill Effects button on the Patterns tab. You can perform the following color and pattern operations with the Fill Effects dialog box:

- Use a color gradient effect with the Gradient tab shown in Figure 10.22. You can choose the number and type of colors used in the Colors section of the tab, and the method of shading the gradient with the Shading Styles area. Once you've selected a shading style, choose from the Variants shown by clicking them.
- You can choose from a variety of predefined textures with the Texture tab shown in Figure 10.23. There are different wood grains, marble, weave textures, and others. You can also load a graphic image to use as a texture with the Other Texture button.
- You can choose from different predrawn patterns with the Pattern tab shown in Figure 10.24. The patterns are particularly useful when preparing black and white printouts where you can't really distinguish the colors that Excel otherwise uses on the hard copy printout.

FIG. 10.22
Gradients can make powerful effects on charts.

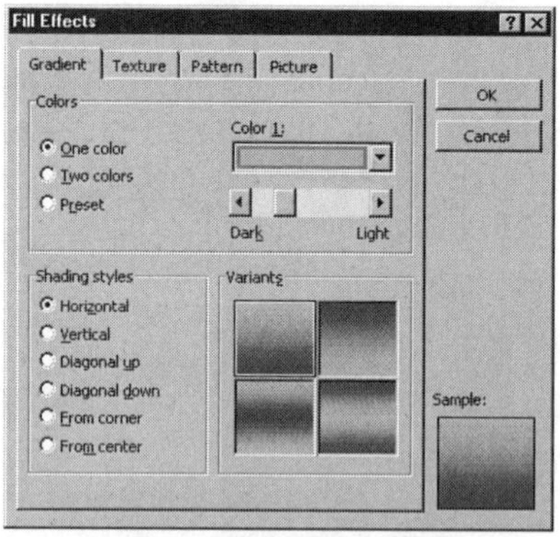

FIG. 10.23
Choose from different textures to use for a color fill with the Texture tab.

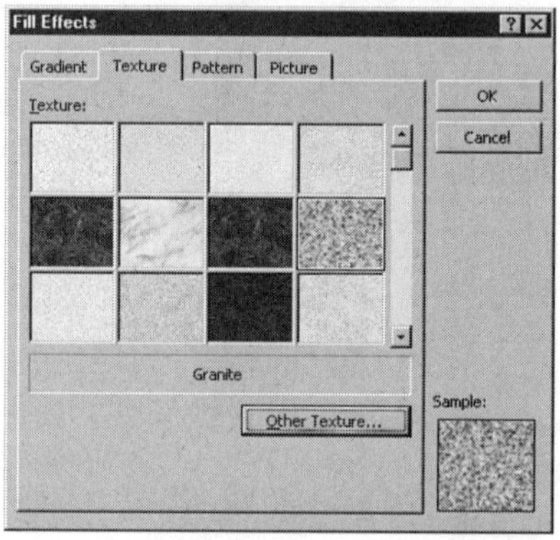

FIG. 10.24
Patterns can be helpful when designing charts to look good on black and white printouts.

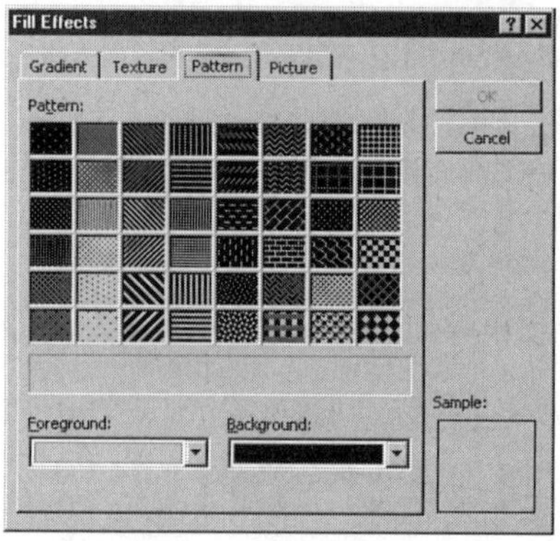

▶ **See** "Using Graphic Images as Data Markers," **p. 318**

Formatting Axes

There are a variety of formatting options for the axes on a chart. You can change the formatting of the text on the axis, the style of the axis, and the scale used for the axis.

To format an axis, right-click it and choose Format Axis from the shortcut menu. You see the dialog box shown in Figure 10.25.

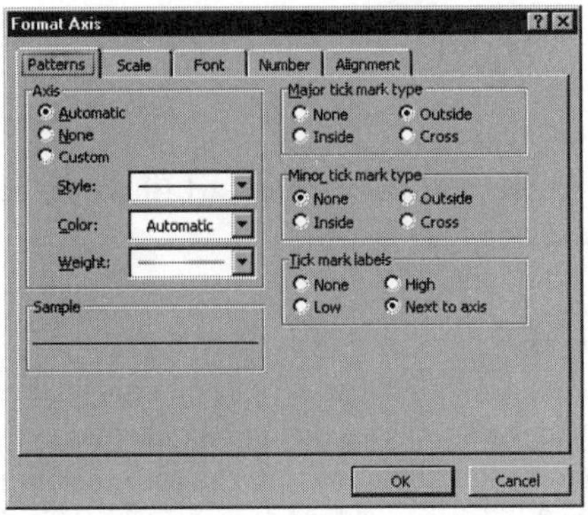

FIG. 10.25
The Format Axis dialog box lets you control how axes appear.

The following tabs are available in the Format Axis dialog box:

- *Patterns Tab.* The Patterns tab lets you select the line style for the axis, and also the style used for drawing the tick marks. You can also choose whether or not to include tick mark labels, which describe the value or category being shown.
- *Scale Tab.* The Scale tab of the Format Axis dialog box is critical to creating effective charts. With it, you control the range of values shown on the value category, or how the category axis displays. Figure 10.26 shows the Scale tab for the value axis.

If necessary, you also can use the options on the Font, Number, and Alignment tabs in the Format Axis dialog box to fine-tune the format and appearance of your axes.

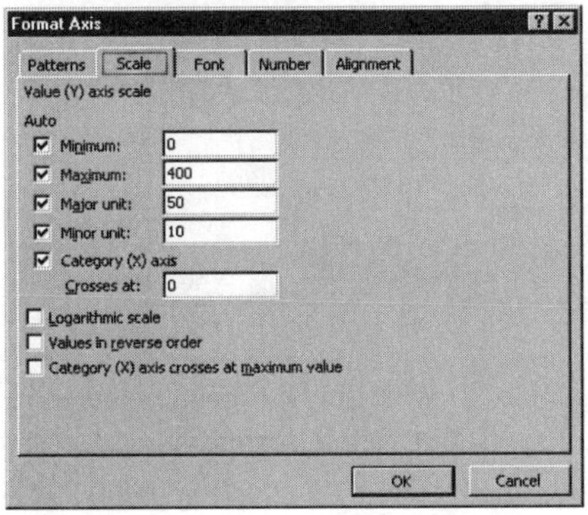

FIG. 10.26
Use the Scale tab to control how the axis plots its data.

You use the Scale tab with value axes to control how the axis divides up its data. You can control the major and minor units used for gridlines and tick marks. More importantly, you can control the top and bottom values for the axis. In a chart with tightly-clustered data, you can show much more detail by limiting the axis values to the range that encompasses only the values being plotted. For instance, if the minimum value plotted is 100, and the maximum is 101, your chart will be much more detailed if you set the axis Minimum and Maximum values to 100 and 101 respectively, rather than using 0 for the Minimum setting.

The Scale tab also lets you select a Logarithmic scale, which is discussed in more detail in Chapter 11, "Advanced Chart Topics."

The remaining options on the Scale tab let you reverse the order of the axis, and also let you move the axis to the maximum category value of the chart (this only has an effect when the category axis is displaying values or a time scale).

Changing Series Formatting

To format a data series on a chart, right-click the series and choose the Format option on the shortcut menu. You see the Format Data Series dialog box in which you can control how the series displays. The Patterns and Data Labels tabs are the same as earlier examples in this chapter. The Axis tab is discussed in Chapter 11, "Advanced Chart Topics," as is the Error Bars tab.

Use the Options tab to control how the series is arrayed on the screen. Different options will be operative for different chart types. Figure 10.27 shows the Options tab for a column series in which you can control the Overlap (the amount that each series overlaps the one next to it) and the Gap Width (the amount of space that divides the different categories).

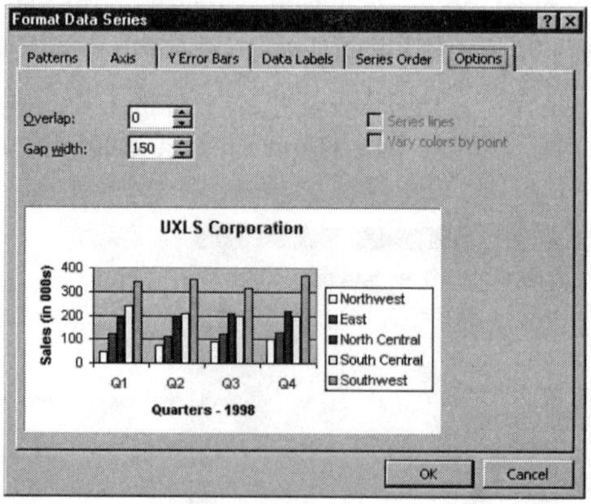

FIG. 10.27
The Options tab changes depending on the type of series you have selected. This is the Options tab for a column chart.

Contrast the Options tab in Figure 10.27 with the Options tab shown in Figure 10.28, which displays when a line series is selected. With a line series, you can create drop lines (lines from each marker to the minimum value), you can vary colors by each point, you can create high-low lines that show the spread between the high and low value (among lines), and you can choose up-down bars for stock (open-high-low-close) charts.

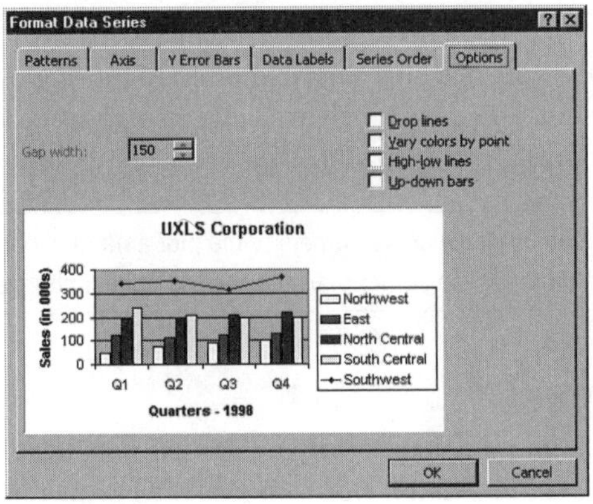

FIG. 10.28
The Options tab with the different options available for a line series.

Changing Chart 3-D View Angle

Excel lets you create attractive 3-D charts that are really eye-catching. With these charts, however, you often need to control the view angle from which the chart is displayed. Usually this is so that the viewer of the chart can see all of the data on the chart. You might, for instance, need to change the displayed 3-D view so that the 3-D chart is viewed from a higher position in order to see all of the information.

To change the perspective for a 3-D chart type, right-click the chart area and choose 3-D View from the shortcut menu. You see the 3-D View dialog box shown in Figure 10.29.

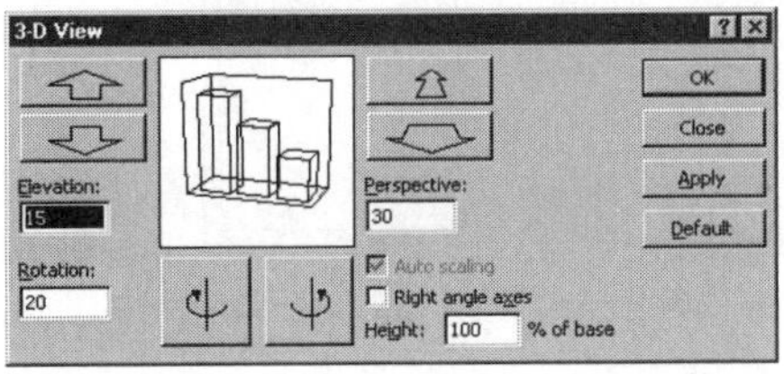

FIG. 10.29
The 3-D View dialog box lets you control 3-D perspective.

To use the 3-D View dialog box, click the different arrow buttons to rotate the wire-frame chart in the direction you want to move it. You can also specify the Perspective, Elevation, and Rotation fields directly (this is useful when you take pains to determine these numbers for a chart you frequently do and want to be able to reproduce the chart perfectly every time). Once the wire-frame preview displays as you want, click the Apply button to apply the 3-D view to the chart in the background for a more detailed preview. If the new view is acceptable, click OK or Close to exit the dialog box with your changes intact.

The Right Angle Axes check box in the 3-D View dialog box forces the chart axes to always remain at 90 degree angles with respect to each other, independent of the rotation or elevation you select. The Perspective option is preset when you choose Right Angle Axes and cannot be changed.

The Auto Scaling check box, which is only available when Right Angle Axes is selected, scales the chart automatically so that it uses as much available display space as possible. With Auto Scaling deselected, sometimes Excel draws 3-D charts smaller than their 2-D counterparts.

TIP When viewing a 3-D chart, you can drag any of the corners of the plot area to choose a new view angle with a wire-frame preview. Start dragging the corner marker when the pointer changes to a crosshair.

Choosing 3-D Bar Shapes

97

Excel 97 adds a number of different shapes that you can use with 3-D bar or column charts. Right-click a series in a 3-D bar or column chart, choose the Format option from the shortcut menu, and then click the Shape tab shown in Figure 10.30. You can choose from a bar, a cylinder, and two different types of pyramids and cones.

FIG. 10.30
Excel 97 adds new shapes to 3-D bar and column charts.

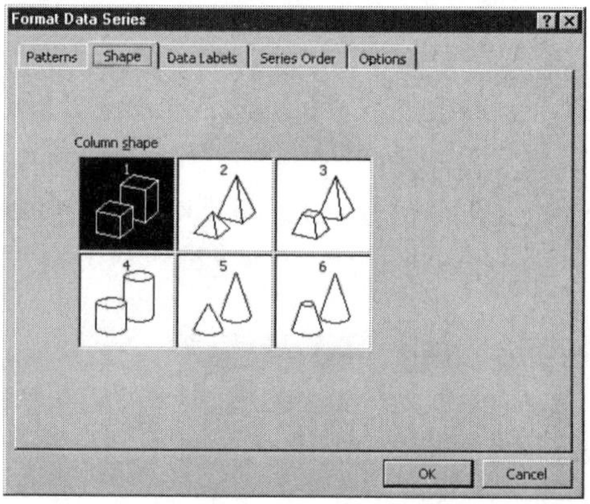

Using Rotated Text on Charts

Excel 97 lets you rotate the text objects on charts to any angle you want. Right-click the text object you want to rotate and choose the Format command from the shortcut menu; then click the Alignment tab (see Figure 10.31).

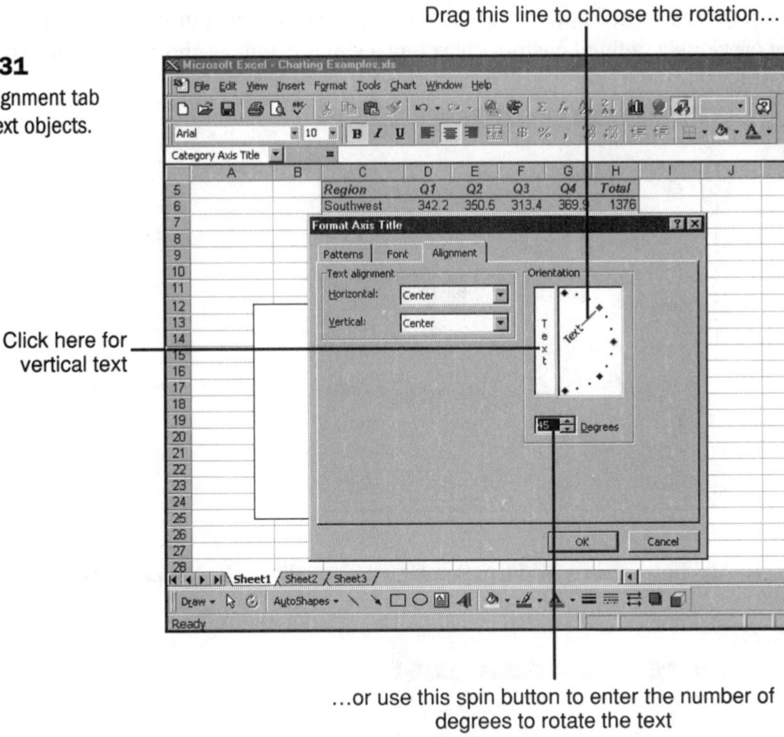
Drag this line to choose the rotation...
Click here for vertical text
...or use this spin button to enter the number of degrees to rotate the text
Format Axis Title
Patterns
Font
Alignment
Text alignment
Horizontal:
Center
Vertical:
Center
Orientation
Degrees
OK
Cancel

FIG. 10.31
Use the Alignment tab to rotate text objects.

Creating Custom Chart Types

Once you hit on a set of chart formatting settings that you like, it's a real pain to have to duplicate all of the settings each time you create another chart. Sometimes doing so can take five to ten minutes per chart created, and you run the risk of making mistakes and forgetting some crucial piece of formatting. If you're preparing a presentation with many charts, such mistakes can look unprofessional.

You solve this problem by creating a custom chart type once you've chosen all of the formatting options you want. Then, you can choose your custom chart type to instantly apply all of those settings to any new charts you create.

To create a custom chart type that you can reuse, follow these steps:

1. Format the chart the way that you want it. Spend as much time as it takes to make it perfect, because you'll apply the formatting choices you make to other charts and you want the formatting to be right.
2. Select the chart, and choose Chart, Chart Type.
3. Click the Custom Types tab.

4. Click the User-Defined option button. You see a preview of your current chart and a list of any previously defined custom chart types you created, as shown in Figure 10.32.

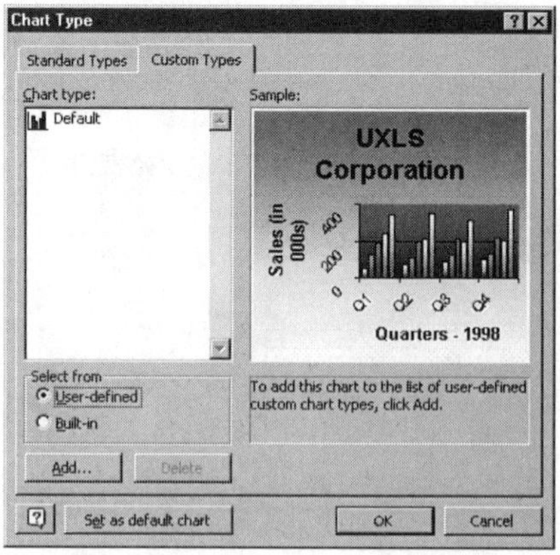

FIG. 10.32 The User-Defined option button lets you access and create your own custom chart types.

5. Click the Add button. The Add Custom Chart Type dialog box appears (see Figure 10.33).

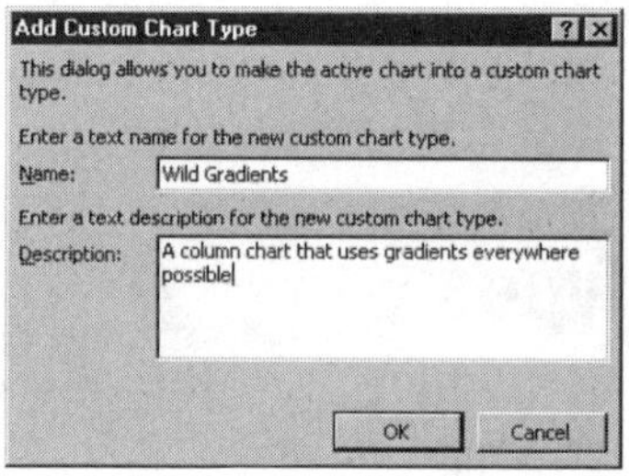

FIG. 10.33 The Add Custom Chart Type dialog box lets you enter a name for your new chart type and a description that you can refer to later.

6. Fill in the Name and Description fields on the Add Custom Chart Type dialog box and click OK.

Your custom chart type is added to the chart type list and can be chosen for new charts you create.

Common Problems and Solutions

Because creating and modifying charts in Excel is usually straightforward, you should run into few problems when working with charts. The following sections cover a few minor problems that you may encounter when printing to a laser printer or working with chart fonts.

Producing Attractive Black and White Charts

If you've been using Excel for very long, you've probably noticed how the colors that Excel chooses for data series often don't print attractively on laser printers. There is an easy fix for this:

1. Select the chart, and then choose File, Page Setup.
2. Click the Chart tab.
3. Select the Print in Black and White check box; then choose OK or Print.

When you choose this option Excel automatically adjusts the colors used in the chart when you print, so that your charts will look better when printed on black and white laser printers.

Keeping the Font Size Constant in Charts

When you resize a chart, you may notice that the font size used in the chart changes proportionally to the chart size. If you prefer that the font sizes used in a chart remain constant, follow these steps:

1. Right-click the chart area (outside of the plot area), then choose Format Chart Area from the shortcut menu.
2. In the Format Chart Area dialog box, click the Font tab.
3. Deselect the Auto Scale check box, then click OK.

From Here...

This chapter showed you how to use the Chart Wizard to create and modify charts. You also learned how to modify charts by using the Chart menu, as well as the shortcut menu that appears when you right-click a chart element. Refer to the following chapters for more information on working with charts in Excel:

- Chapter 11, "Advanced Chart Topics," takes the topic of charts one step further, and explains advanced chart features such as adding a second y-axis, inserting a trend line, and creating map charts.
- Chapter 12, "A Field Guide to Excel Chart Types," provides details on all the chart types available in Excel, and suggests when you should use particular chart types.

CHAPTER 11

Advanced Chart Topics

by Bruce Hallberg

This chapter builds on the previous chapter by providing instructions for using some of Excel's advanced charting features. After creating a standard chart with the Chart Wizard, you may find that you want to fine-tune your chart to include features such as trend lines, a second Y-axis, or data markers that use graphic images to represent data.

In this chapter, you'll also learn how to create map charts that enable you to plot data on a geographical map in Excel. For example, you can use the map feature to show how sales and commissions are distributed by region. This chapter also covers how to work with error bars and time-scale axes, in addition to several other advanced charting topics.

Editing chart series formulas

For advanced users, the ability to directly edit chart series formulas often comes in handy. Here, you learn how chart series formulas work and how to edit them.

Adding a second Y-axis

When plotting data that includes a series that uses a radically different set of values, a second Y (or value) axis often makes sense.

Using logarithmic scales

Excel lets you designate certain axes as using a logarithmic scale, which can often reveal detail that you otherwise can't see.

Creating trend lines

Trend lines typically represent linear regressions of the chart data, and often can be used to predict future trends.

Using graphic images as data markers

Excel lets you use graphic images for certain chart types, much like the graphs that you often see in newspapers where charts are created with stacked cars or dollar bills.

Creating map charts

Map charts let you easily create charts that incorporate maps of parts of the world.

Editing Chart Series Formulas

You've probably noticed, when selecting a series in a chart, that a SERIES formula appears in the formula bar for each series on your chart. The SERIES formula can be directly edited by you, which often comes in handy when you want to quickly change an aspect of a series being plotted; it's often faster to edit the SERIES formula than to use the dialog boxes. Figure 11.1 shows an example chart with one of its SERIES formulas shown in the formula bar.

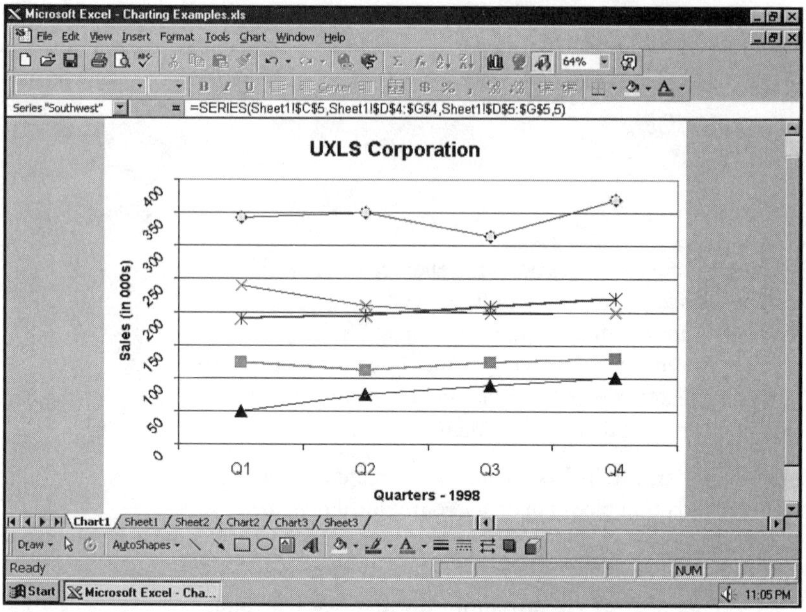

FIG. 11.1
The formula bar shows the SERIES formula for the selected series.

The SERIES formula is made up of 4 parts, ordered as follows:

- The first part describes the cell that contains the label for the series. This is the same label that appears when you activate the chart legend.
- The second part describes the category labels that align with each data point in the series. Typically, this part of the SERIES formula is shared by all of the series on the chart.
- The third part describes the actual data for each data point.
- The fourth part indicates the order of the series. Each series will have a different number in the final position of the SERIES formula.

Expressed as a psuedo-code formula, the SERIES formula looks like this:

```
=SERIES(series_label,series_category_labels,series_data,series_order_number)
```

There are some rules that you should observe when changing different aspects of the SERIES formula:

- While you can change the *series_order_number*, you cannot have two series with the same number. All of the remaining series are automatically renumbered when you change the *series_order_number.*
- You can change the *series_category_labels* in a SERIES formula, but Excel only creates the labels for the category axis on the chart from the first series (the series with the value 1 in the *series_order_number* position).
- Series formulas always refer to cells with absolute cell references (note the dollar signs in each cell reference in the SERIES formula in Figure 11.1). While you can remove the dollar signs, they are immediately added back into the series formula once you press Enter.
- To supply either the *series_category_labels* or *series_data* as absolute numbers that don't rely on cell references, use curly braces for the individual data, and then separate each data point from the rest with a comma within those curly braces. For instance, if you want to change the SERIES formula in Figure 11.1 to use the values 100, 150, 200, and 250 instead of using the data contained in cells $D$5:$G$5, you enter the series formula as follows:

  ```
  =SERIES(Sheet1!$C$5,Sheet1!$D$4:$G$4,{100,150,200,250},5)
  ```

  Similarly, you can supply the *series_category_labels* in the same way. For example, consider this SERIES formula with fixed category labels:

  ```
  =SERIES(Sheet1!$C$5,{"First Quarter","Second Quarter","Third
  Quarter","Fourth Quarter"},{100,150,200,250},5)
  ```

- The *series_order_number* controls where in a legend or data table the series appears in relation to the others.

Adding a Second Y-Axis

Some charts require that some data be plotted against a secondary Y-axis. This typically happens when one or more series use radically different values than the other series. Sometimes you still need to plot all of the series together in order to look for correlations between the two sets of numbers, and a secondary Y-axis helps you do this. For example, consider the chart in Figure 11.2.

In the example in Figure 11.2, you really can't see much of the data! Three of the series (Purple, Yellow, and Green) are completely hidden against the zero value. But are they truly zero entries, or are they clustered down there simply because the values of Blue and Red are so large? To find out, you can move the Blue and Red series to a secondary Y-axis that plots their values independently of the other series. To do this for each series you want to move to a secondary Y-axis, follow these steps:

1. Right-click the series. From the shortcut menu that appears, choose Format Data Series. (Or, choose the series from the Chart Objects drop-down list in the Chart toolbar, then click the Format Data Series button.)
2. Click the Axis tab.

FIG. 11.2
Can you see any correlation between the Blue and Red series and the rest?

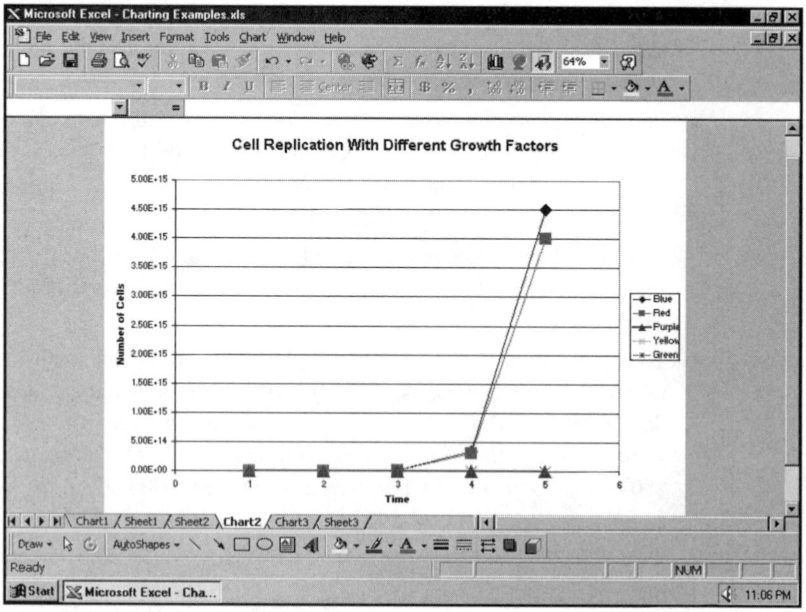

3. Select the Secondary Axis option button.

Figure 11.3 shows the result of this change. Notice how you can now see all of the series on the chart. In this example, both the Blue and Red series were moved to a secondary axis. Notice how you see the exponential numbers against the secondary Y-axis, while the primary Y-axis shows the much lower values required to chart the other series.

Using Logarithmic Scales

If you look again at the chart in Figure 11.3 (in the previous section of this chapter), notice how you can't see much detail in certain parts of the chart. For example, the first three time categories don't let you see much difference for most of the series being plotted; they're all right next to one another. Also notice how the later categories show very steep rises in the data. You see this pattern when you chart values that increase by orders of magnitude from one chart category to the next. You can address this problem by using a logarithmic scale for the value axes on the chart. For this example, a logarithmic scale will be chosen for both value axes. To do this for each axis, follow these steps:

1. Right-click the axis you want to change and choose Format Axis from the shortcut menu.
2. Click the Scale tab on the Format Axis dialog box.
3. Select the Logarithmic Scale check box and click OK to close the dialog box.

NOTE Charts that use a logarithmic scale on any axis cannot chart negative values for any data points.

FIG. 11.3
With the Blue and Red series charted against a secondary Y-axis, you can now see all of the series.

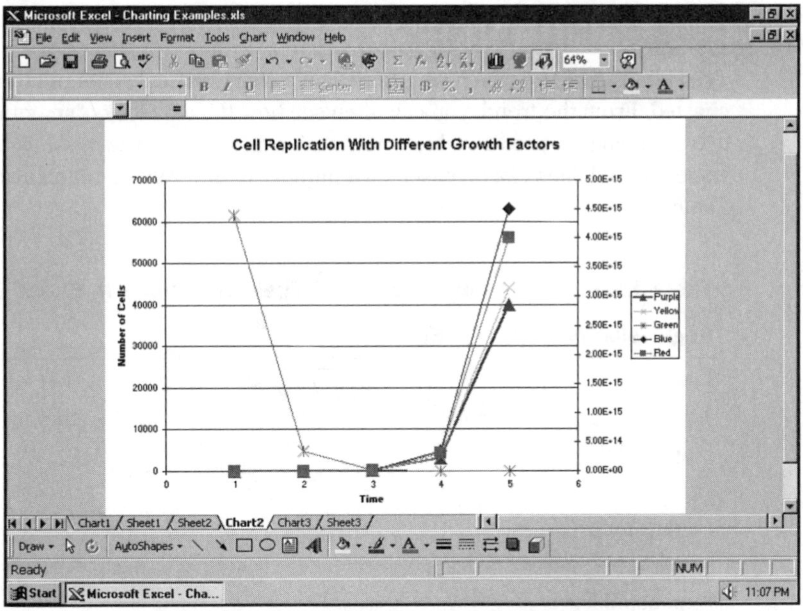

Figure 11.4 shows the result of changing both value axes to use logarithmic scales. While some of the series now coincide very closely with one another with a logarithmic scale, notice how you can now see the relationship between all of the series. For instance, all of the series except Green grow in similar ways, while the Green series shows an inverse-reversed relationship to the others.

FIG. 11.4
With logarithmic scales, you can see relationships between the series.

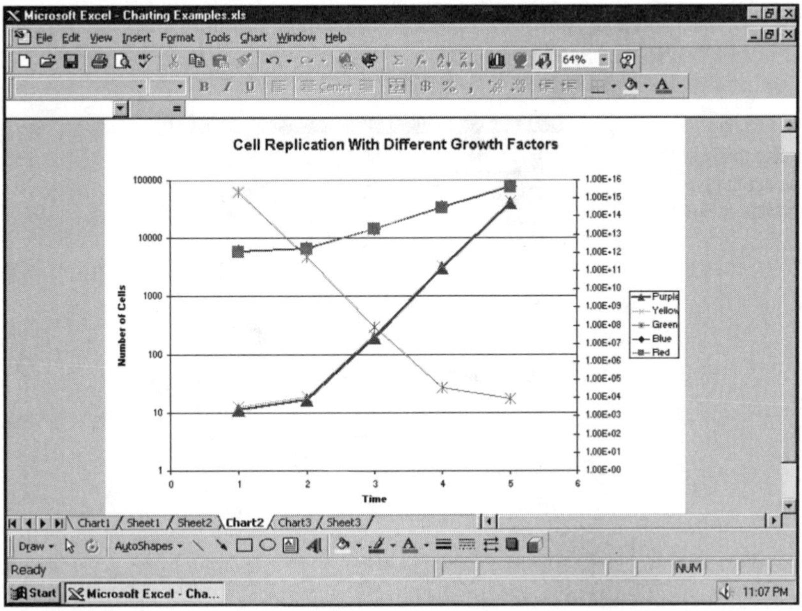

Creating Trend Lines

Trend lines take the data from a series on a chart, and calculate the trend of the data being charted. From the trend, you can often see how the data looks "smoothed," and you can also use trend lines to predict values that aren't available, such as missing data or forward-looking values. Trend lines can be based on a number of different mathematical models, as shown in Table 11.1.

Table 11.1 Trend Line Types and Their Equations in Excel 97

Regression Type	Equation
Linear	$y = mx + b$
Polynomial	$y=b+c_1x+c_2x^2+c_3x^3+\ldots+c_6x^6$
Logarithmic	$y = c \ln x + b$
Exponential	$y = ce^{bx}$
Power	$y = cx^b$

To insert a trend line in a chart, follow these steps:

1. Right-click one of the series on the chart.
2. Choose Add Trendline from the shortcut menu. You see the Add Trendline dialog box shown in Figure 11.5.

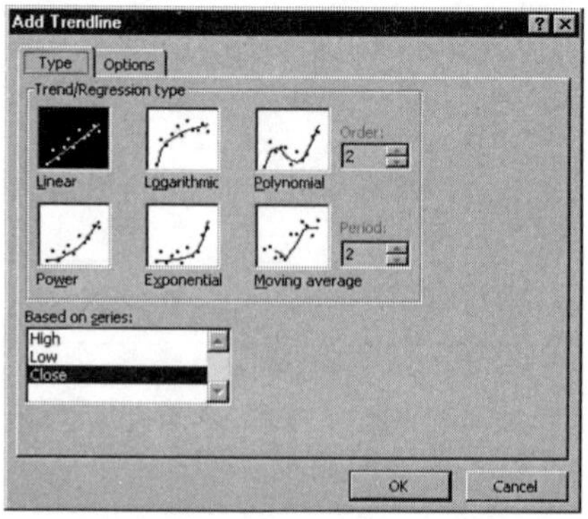

FIG. 11.5
You use the Type tab to select the type of trend line to create.

3. Choose a regression type by clicking it. If you choose Polynomial, set the Order in the spin box. If you choose a Moving Average (which is not a regression), set the Period in the spin box.

NOTE The Order spin box for the Polynomial regression sets the maximum order of magnitude that is used when calculating the regression. The Period spin box for the Moving Average trend line sets the number of periods used to calculate the moving average.

4. Check that the series for which you want a trend line is selected in the Based on Series list. If it is not, select the series that you want to use.
5. Click the Options tab, shown in Figure 11.6.

FIG. 11.6
You select other aspects of trend lines with the Options tab.

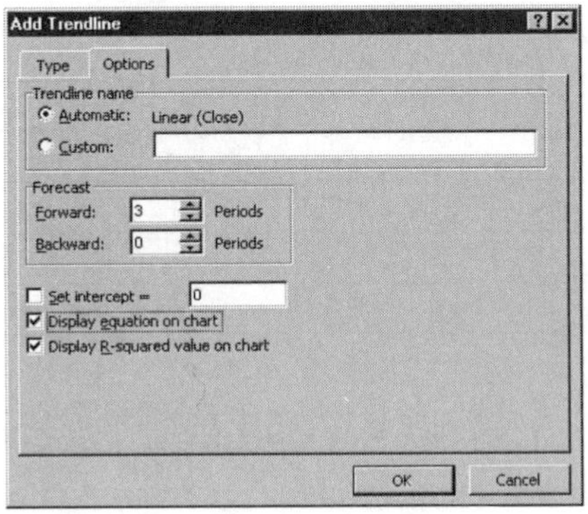

6. In the Trend Line Name section, select either Automatic or Custom, then type a name in the field provided. The name used for the trend line appears in the chart's legend.
7. If you are creating a trend line using any formula *except* a moving average, you can set the number of periods that you want the trend line to predict, either backwards or forwards, with the appropriate spin boxes.
8. Select the remaining options that you want (and that are available based on the trend line type you chose). You can choose to set the intercept, display the regression equation on the chart, and to display the regression's R^2 value.
9. Click OK to complete the trendline.

TIP When you create a custom user-defined chart type that includes a trend line, the trend line is automatically created as part of the chart type. The trend line will be created for the same series number as in the original chart.

Figure 11.7 shows a chart of stock prices with a linear regression trend line created for the stock's closing price each day. Above the trend line you can see the equation that results in the trend line, with the R^2 value.

TIP A trend line's R^2 value indicates how closely the trend line agrees with the data being forecasted. The closer an R^2 value is to 1, the closer the trend line agrees with the values being trended and forecast. Different trend line types will predict different data in different ways. In order to get the best prediction values based on the data, try the different trend line types until you find the one that yields the highest R^2 value.

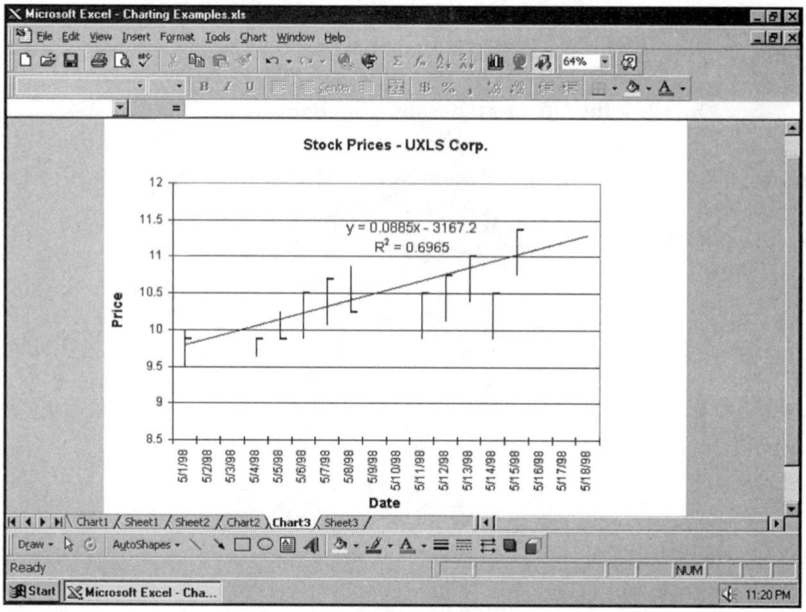

FIG. 11.7 A sample stock chart with a linear trend line added, along with the trend line's formula and R^2 value.

Using Graphic Images as Data Markers

You've probably seen those charts that often appear in newspapers and magazines, where the columns of the chart are made using some representative picture in place of normal bars or columns. For instance, if auto sales are being charted, the charts use stacked cars instead of simple column bars. Creating charts that use images like this can involve your audience more than charts that are more pedestrian, particularly when the data you're showing is fairly simple.

TIP You can format any column or bar chart to use a graphic image for its bars. Keep in mind, though, that image-based charts work best when they represent simple data. Otherwise, the charts tend to be too complex visually to capture the reader's interest.

To create a chart using a graphic image in place of the default Excel column or bar, follow these steps:

1. Create a column or bar chart with your data.
2. Right-click the series for which you want to substitute a graphic image and choose Format Data Series from the shortcut menu.
3. On the Patterns tab of the Format Data Series dialog box, click the Fill Effects button, which opens the Fill Effects dialog box.
4. Click the Picture tab of the Fill Effects dialog box.
5. Click the Select Picture button. This button allows you to choose a graphic image from a disk. Choose the image you want and click OK to return to the Picture tab of the Fill Effects dialog box (see Figure 11.8).
6. Choose the Format options for the picture you selected and click OK to display the graph using the picture.

FIG. 11.8
Use the Picture tab of the Fill Effects dialog box to select and format the picture you will use in your chart.

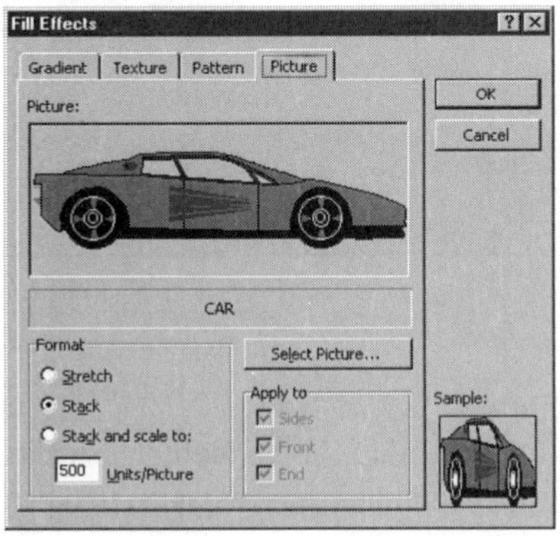

The Picture tab of the Fill Effects dialog box has a number of formatting options that let you control how the picture is used in the chart. You have three choices for how the picture is scaled to the chart. Choosing Stretch forces the picture to be stretched to the length of the bar. Select Stack to let Excel stack the image within the bar. Finally, you can choose Stack and Scale To if you want to determine how many copies of the image will be forced into each of the bars. As a rule of thumb, you will get the best images using the Stack option, because the picture won't be distorted within the bar, as happens with the other two choices.

For 3-D bars, you can further select options in the Apply To area of the Picture tab. There are three check boxes, Sides, Front, and End, that let you choose which sides of the bar will display the image you select.

Figure 11.9 shows an example sales chart using one of Office 97's clipart images in place of Excel's standard bars.

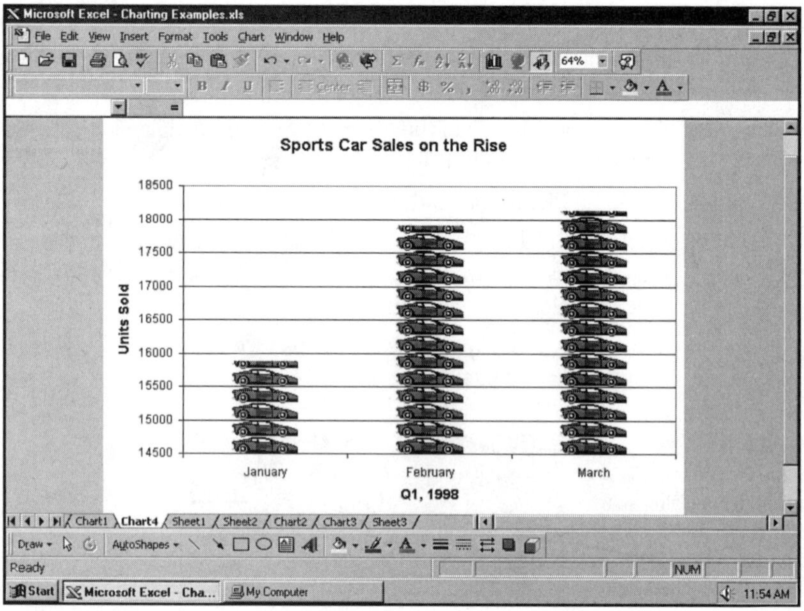

FIG. 11.9
You can spruce up certain charts by using graphic images in place of the normal chart elements.

Creating Map Charts

Included with Excel is a program that generates embedded maps called Microsoft Map. With it, you can chart data against geographical maps. For instance, you can chart sales against states, or countries, or population statistics, or just about any data that has a geographical component. Map-based charts can often help the reader to instantly comprehend geographically-based data.

When you create data to use with Microsoft Map, the first column of the data needs to contain the geographical data, which is a series of place names (cities, states, and countries). Figure 11.10 shows a sample worksheet from which an example map will be built.

TIP You can also create maps without using any data. Simply click the Map button without first selecting a range of cells on the worksheet. Such maps can then become the basis for a Pin Map or can be used to chart data you can query from Microsoft Access, within Microsoft Map.

TIP The data for this example is taken from a worksheet included with Microsoft Map called MAPSTATS.XLS. You can find it in the folder C:\Program Files\Common Files\Microsoft Shared\Datamap\Data\. This worksheet contains a variety of sample demographic data for a number of areas in the world.

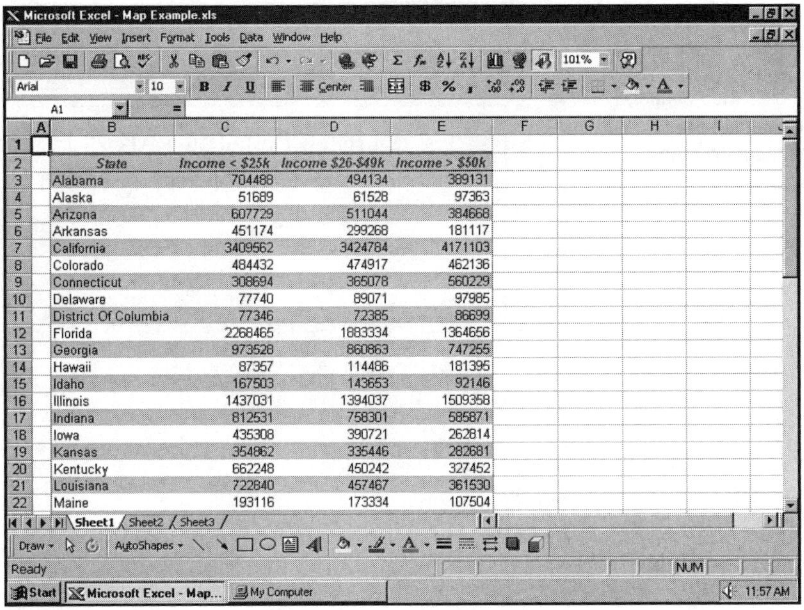

FIG. 11.10
Be careful to organize your data so that the geographical listing is in the first column.

To create a Microsoft Map image, follow these steps:

1. Select the data you want to chart.

2. Click the Map button on the Standard toolbar. Your cursor becomes a crosshair. Use the crosshair cursor to draw an area in the worksheet that will contain the map image.
3. Microsoft Map will try to determine which of its built-in maps should be used based on the data you provide. If it is unable to select the correct map, you will see either the Unable to Create Map dialog box (shown in Figure 11.11) or the Multiple Maps Available dialog box (not shown, but similar to the one shown in Figure 11.11). Use this dialog box to select a map that best fits the data you are charting, and click the OK button to continue.

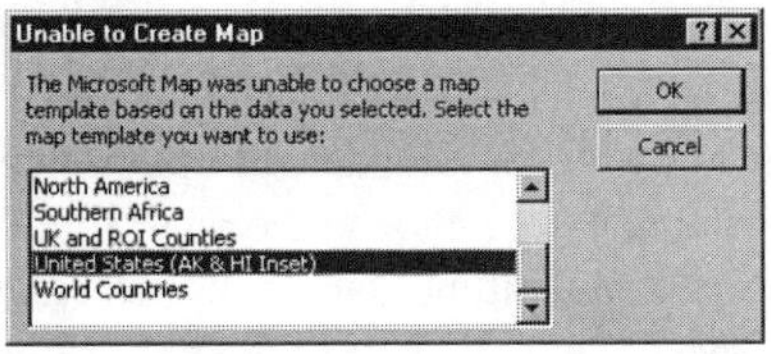

FIG. 11.11
If Microsoft Map can't determine which map to use, you see this dialog box in which you can select the appropriate map.

4. The map you selected appears in the worksheet, and includes the data from the first column of data values (the data from column C, in this example). You see this new map along with the Microsoft Map Control dialog box and the Microsoft Map toolbar (see Figure 11.12).

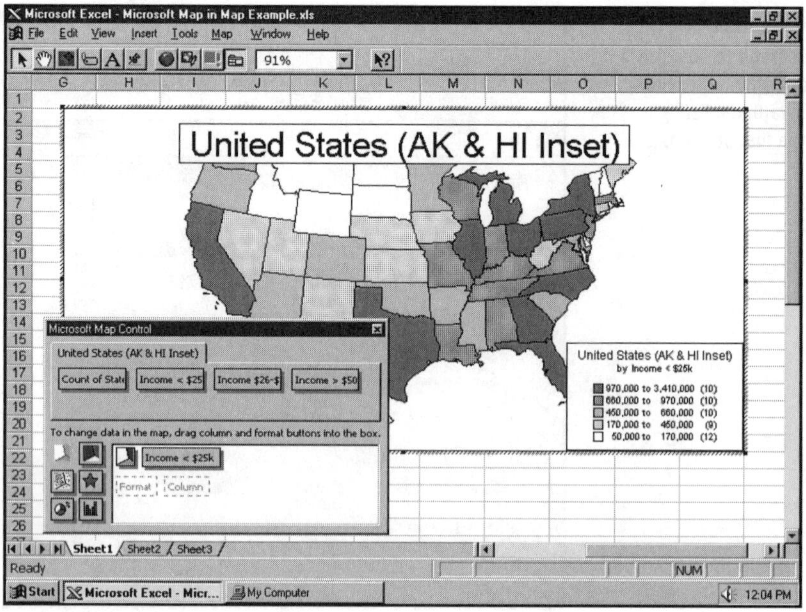

FIG. 11.12
A map is created for you automatically. Using Microsoft Map Control, you can then adjust what data the map charts.

TIP Microsoft Map is an Excel add-in written by MapInfo Corporation. Although the maps and data that come with Excel may suit your needs, you also can purchase add-in maps, data, and feature extensions directly from MapInfo. For more information on how to contact MapInfo and purchase these items, activate a map in Excel and choose Help, How to Get More Data.

Adding Map Features

There are a number of map features from which you can choose to further enhance your map's appearance. For the U.S. map, you can include cities, airports, and interstate highways. To select these features, right-click the map and choose Features from the shortcut menu. You see the dialog box shown in Figure 11.13.

You can choose from the features already attached to your selected map by simply clicking the Visible check box next to each feature. You can also add other features by clicking the Add button, which then lists all features available for all maps. For any selected feature, use the Fill Color section of the Map Features dialog box to choose the color that the feature is drawn with. The features are then added to the map, but without labels (see the following section on labeling map features). Figure 11.14 shows the example map with U.S. cities shown.

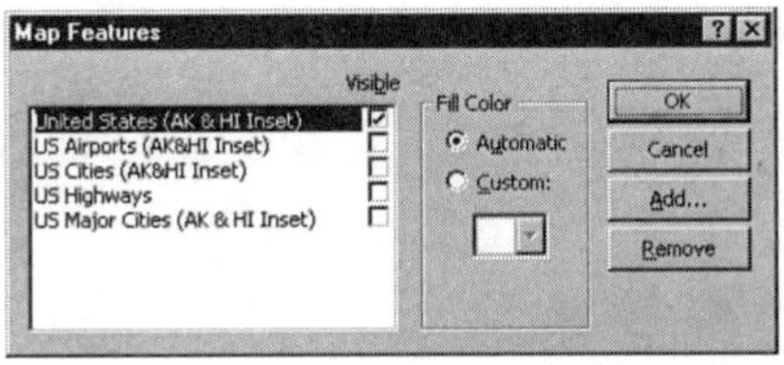

FIG. 11.13
Several additional map features can be added to embellish your maps.

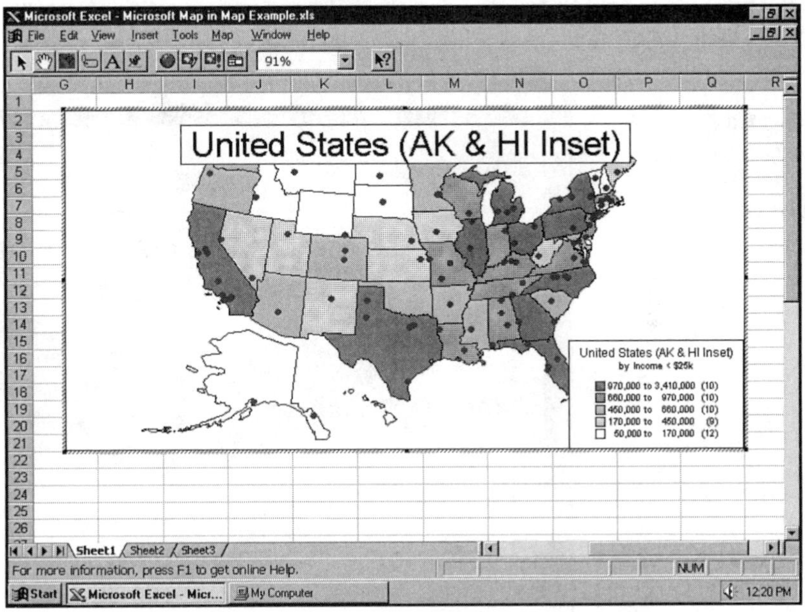

FIG. 11.14
The example map with U.S. Cities shown as an additional feature.

Labeling Maps

Microsoft Map includes a tool called the Labeler that lets you choose what labels are shown on your maps (you typically don't want to label everything on most maps, because they would become too busy). Access the Labeler by clicking the Map Labels button on the Microsoft Map toolbar, or choose Labeler from the Tools menu.

When you activate the Labeler you see the Map Labels dialog box that lets you choose which map feature you will label, as shown in Figure 11.15. Use the drop-down list box to choose which of the included features will be labeled.

After clicking OK in the Map Labels dialog box, your cursor changes to a crosshair. As you drag the crosshair over features of your map that have a name (and that correspond to the choice you made in the Map Labels dialog box), the name appears as a ToolTip. When a ToolTip appears over a feature, clicking the left mouse button causes that individual feature to be labeled. After the label is created, you can drag its border to reposition it on the map. Figure 11.16 shows the example map with several cities labeled in this fashion.

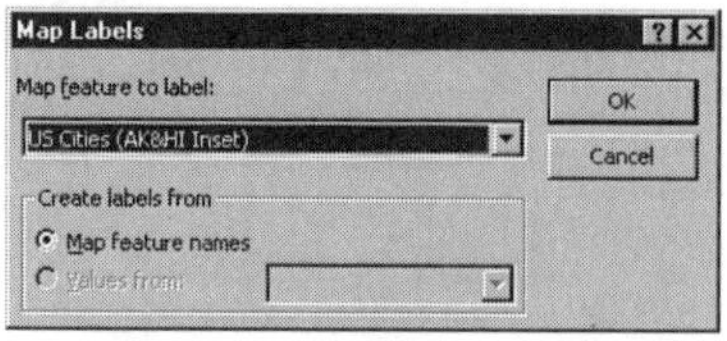

FIG. 11.15
The Map Labels dialog box lets you select which map feature will be labeled.

TIP You can also use the Add Text button on the Microsoft Map toolbar to add free-form text anywhere you want in the map.

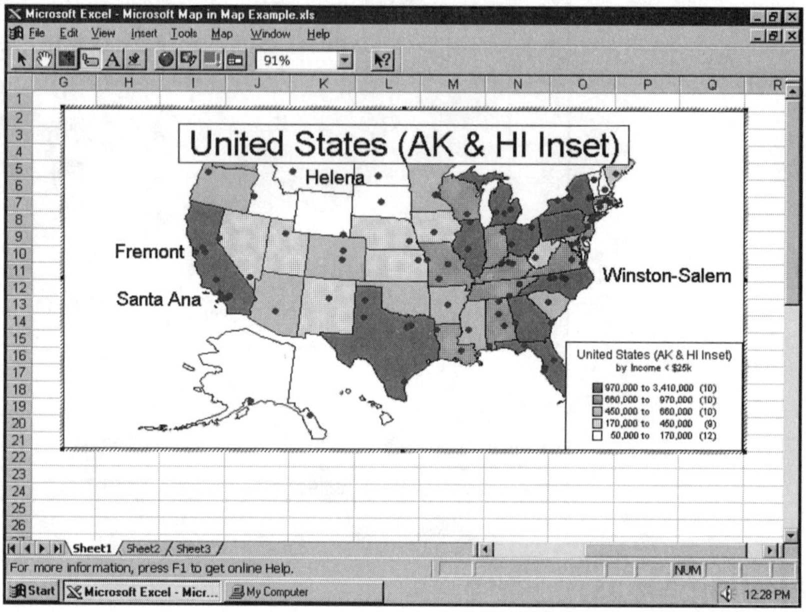

FIG. 11.16
Use the Labeler to add labels to features of your maps.

Repositioning and Zooming Maps

Maps are created inside of object frames on your Excel worksheets. You can, of course, resize the entire object frame using the handles on any of its sides. You can also, however, reposition the map within the frame. There are two ways to do this:

- The first, and most accurate method, is to click the Grabber button on the Microsoft Map toolbar, which lets you drag within the map to reposition the entire map within the frame. With this method, you can position the map exactly to your preferences.

- The second method uses a command that re-centers the map within the frame. Click the Center Map button on the Microsoft Map toolbar to automatically re-center the map.

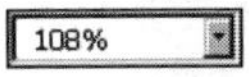

In combination with the above methods, you can also zoom in on your map using the Zoom Percentage of Map drop-down list in the Microsoft Map toolbar. Select a zoom level, and then use the Grabber to reposition the map within the frame.

Selecting Map Chart Data

There are a number of ways that data can be plotted against a map. These include:

- Shaded regions that correspond to data values
- Shaded regions that correspond to data categories
- Column charts superimposed on each map region
- Pie charts superimposed on each map region
- Dots placed in each region where the dot density corresponds to the data
- Symbols in each map region where the size of the symbol corresponds to the data

You create all of these map chart effects with the Microsoft Map Control dialog box. You can access this dialog box by clicking the Show/Hide Microsoft Map Control button on the Microsoft Map toolbar. Figure 11.17 shows the Map Control dialog box.

Part III Ch 11

FIG. 11.17
The Microsoft Map Control dialog box is the key to charting data used in a map.

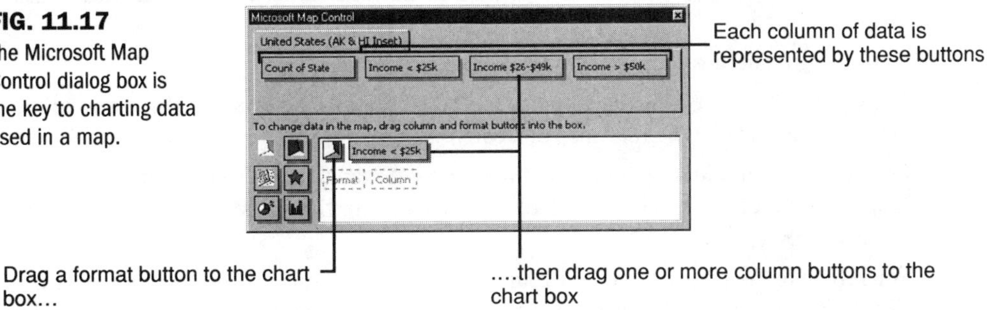

To use the Microsoft Map Control dialog box, you drag format and column buttons into the box. To remove a chart element, you drag its button from the box to some area outside of the box (a wastebasket appears to indicate that dropping the button there will remove it from the active chart). In Figure 11.18, you can see the example chart changed so that each region shows a column chart, where each column within the region indicates the number of households with the income levels shown by the legend.

Creating a Pin Map

Pin maps are useful for indicating events or locations. For instance, you might create a pin map to show all the locations in which your company has offices, or salespeople, or customers, or even places you have traveled. To create a pin map, follow these steps:

1. Start without selecting any data on a worksheet and click the Map button on the Standard toolbar.

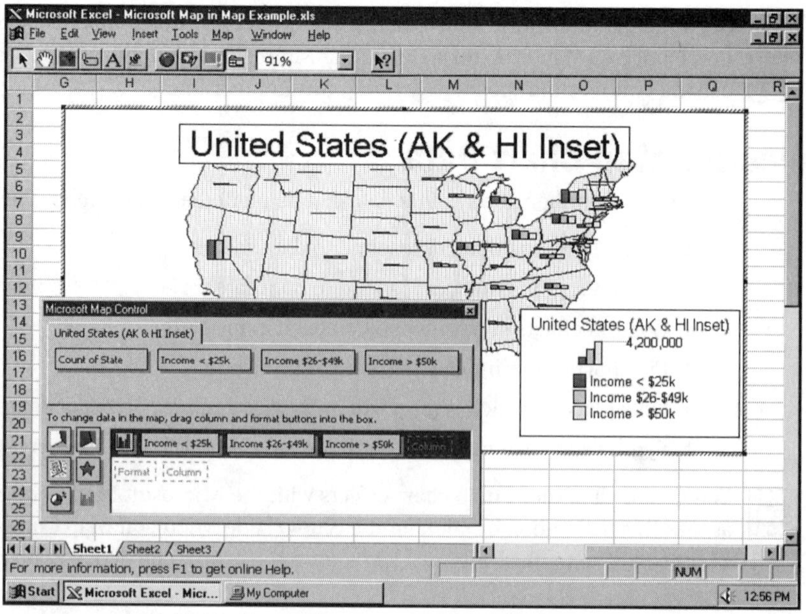

FIG. 11.18
You can flexibly choose what sort of information is shown on your map, as this map/column chart demonstrates.

2. Draw a region on the worksheet that will display the map.
3. The Unable to Create Map dialog box appears. Choose a map from the list shown in the dialog box and click OK. Your map is created without any data.

4. Click the Custom Pin Map button on the Microsoft Map toolbar. You see the Custom Pin Map dialog box shown in Figure 11.19. Type a name for the Pin Map in the field provided and click OK.
5. You return to the map display, and your cursor changes to an icon of a pushpin. Click each location in which you want a pin to appear. A small symbol appears in each location you click.

6. Exit the Pin cursor by clicking the Select Objects button on the Microsoft Map toolbar.

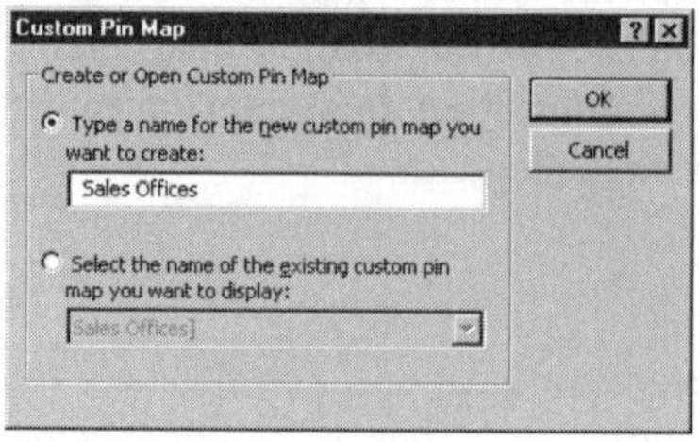

FIG. 11.19
Use the Custom Pin Map dialog box to name the Pin Map you'll create. You can have multiple pin map versions attached to a single map.

Working with Error Bars

Most technical charts often need to display error bars for the data they show. Error bars may show a variety of different types of error information about each data point, including standard deviation, fixed percentage of error, fixed value, standard error, and individual error values that you provide.

To add error bars to a time- or category-based series, follow these steps:

1. Right-click the series and choose Format Data Series from the shortcut menu.
2. Click the Y Error Bars tab, shown in Figure 11.20.
3. Choose whether you want both positive and negative error bars, either type, or no error bars by clicking the appropriate option.
4. Select the value for the error bar using one of the option buttons in the Error Amount section and click OK to add the error bars to the chart.

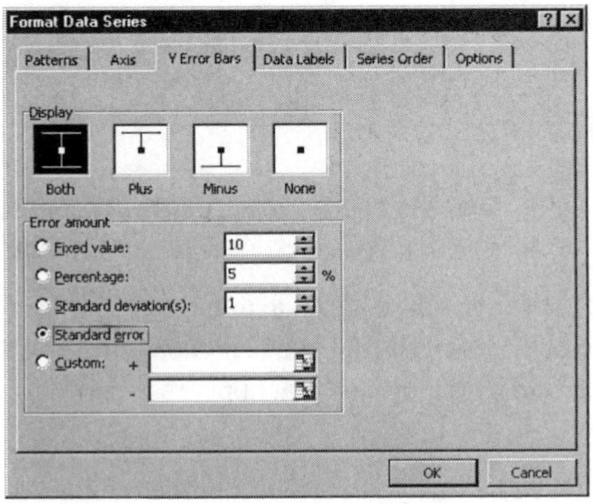

FIG. 11.20
Use the Y Error Bars tab to create error bars based on different error methods.

If you choose to provide your own error values with the Custom fields on the Y Error Bars tab, you can provide those values either by typing them into the fields, separating each error value from the next with a comma, or you can indicate a range of cells that contains the error information. Figure 11.21 shows a simple line chart with positive and negative error bars using the Standard Deviation method.

Changing Chart Data

Certain types of charts, most particularly the Bar, Column, Line, and XY Scatter charts, let you directly modify their data by selecting a data point and moving it manually. When you do this, the underlying data in the worksheet changes to reflect the new position of the data point. To change a data point in this fashion, follow these steps:

1. Click once to select a series.
2. Pause for a second, then click again on an individual data point to select it (you pause to avoid executing a double-click).

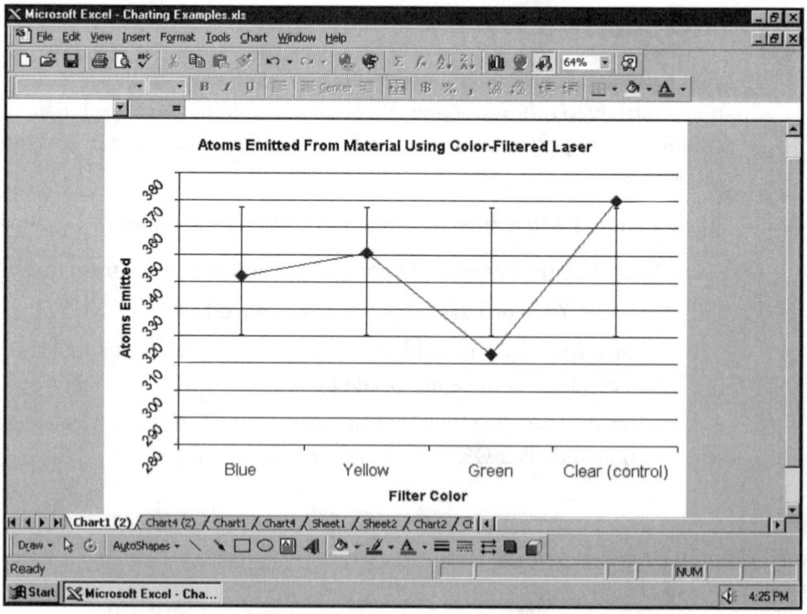

FIG. 11.21
An example of double-sided error bars showing Standard Deviation for the data.

3. Drag the data point up or down, as appropriate. A ToolTip appears that shows you the exact value that will be achieved when you "drop" the data point.

If you drag a data point that is the result of a calculation on your worksheet, Excel automatically invokes the Goal Seek dialog box so that you can determine how the new value will affect the precedent cells. The Goal Seek dialog box that appears is shown in Figure 11.22.

In the Goal Seek dialog box, the Set Cell field is set to the cell that you changed in the chart. The To Value field shows the value that you set by dragging the data point. All that is needed is to complete the By Changing Cell field to indicate which source cell should change so that the cell you affected maintains the correct formulaic relationship. With your cursor in the By Changing Cell field, click the cell that you want to change (or type and click the OK button). Goal Seek will then try to find a value, working backwards, and will show you its results. You can then either accept or reject its results by clicking either OK or Cancel.

Working with Time-Scale Axes

A new feature in Excel 97 gives you the ability to more easily work with data that uses time as its category axis. When you chart data that uses time or dates for the category axis, Excel automatically sorts the data using the time or dates so that they are in chronological order on the chart. You can also change other settings for time-based category axes. Access the Format Axis dialog box by double-clicking the time-based axis, and then clicking the Scale tab, shown in Figure 11.23.

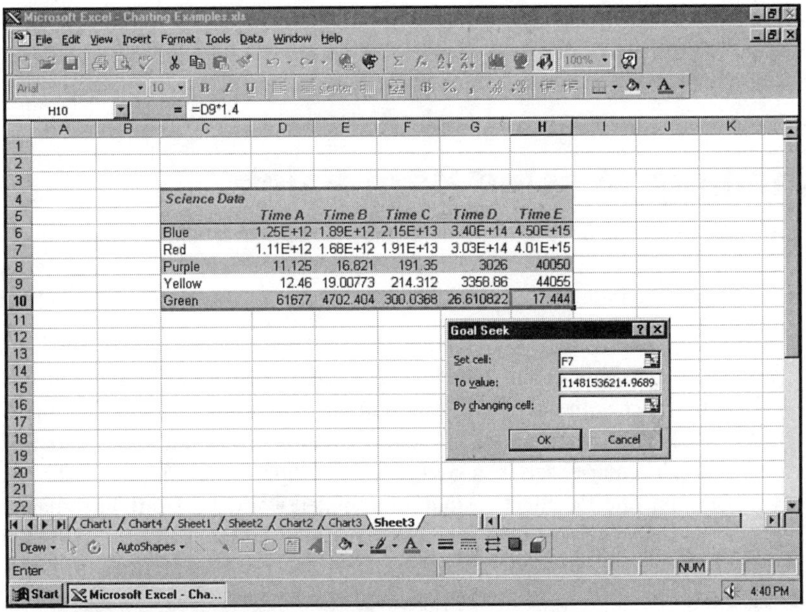

FIG. 11.22
When you change a data point that is based on a calculated value, the Goal seek dialog box appears to let you control how the source data is changed.

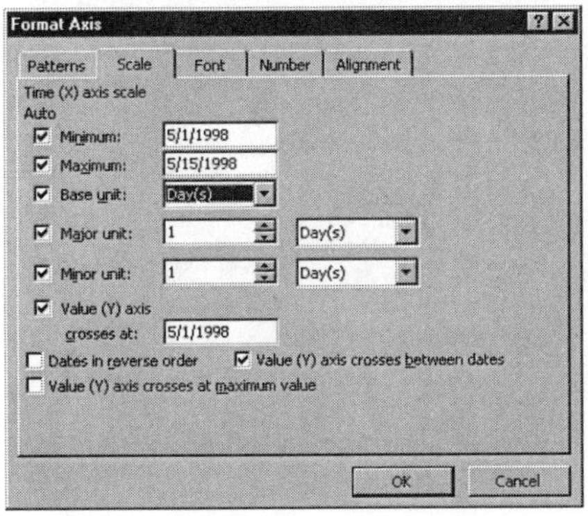

FIG. 11.23
New settings are available on the Scale tab for time-scale axes.

Of primary interest on the time-scale based Scale tab, the Base Unit drop-down list box lets you choose the increment of time shown on the chart. Using this setting, you can instantly rechart your data using different base units of time or days. The other settings on the Scale tab also reflect the time-scale nature of the axis, although they work the same as when you have a category-based or value-based X-axis.

NOTE Excel will insert dates when they are missing in your data if it identifies an axis as being time-based. For instance, when you chart stock data and have no entries for weekends, Excel will still create those missing dates in the chart. You can control this behavior by forcing the axis to be category-based instead of time-based. To do this, choose Chart, Chart Options, click the Axes tab, and choose the Category option button. This will also cause the dates to appear in the same order as they do in the worksheet, as opposed to being sorted by date as happens when a time-scale is used for the axis.

Handling Missing Data Points

Many charts have missing data, and you need to be able to chart them accordingly. In some cases, you simply want the missing data to be skipped, while in others you want the missing data to be interpolated. And in still other cases you might even want to show missing data as being equal to zero.

To change how a chart handles any missing data points, first create the chart with the missing data. Then, with the chart active, choose Tools, Options and click the Chart tab (see Figure 11.24). Then select which of the three options you want to use to handle missing data points on that particular chart. As a general rule of thumb, Not Plotted works best with XY Scatter, Bar, Column, and Pie charts, while Interpolated works best with line charts or XY Scatter charts that use lines to connect each scatter point. You also can choose the Zero option.

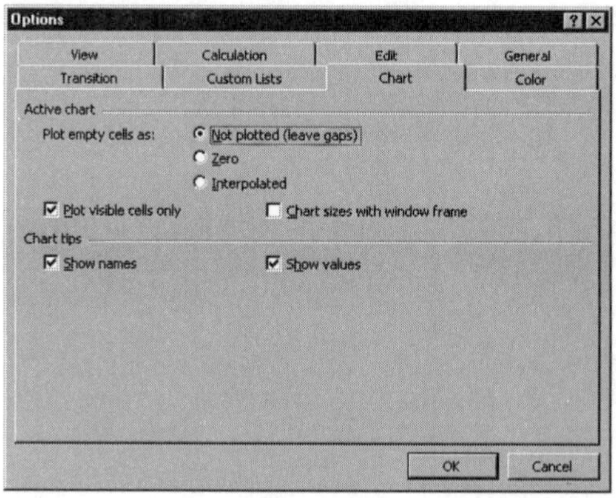

FIG. 11.24
You can choose how each chart in a workbook handles missing data.

TIP You can cause a chart series to automatically use the Interpolated option by marking any missing cells with the #N/A cell error. Just type **=NA()** into any cells with missing data, and when you plot a range that includes such cells, the chart series will interpolate across the missing data.

Plotting with a Recommended Range

A very common need in Excel charting is the capability to chart data against a recommended range. The reader of the chart can then instantly see when data falls outside of this range. For example, it is handy to plot medical lab data against the recommended ranges, or to plot machine tolerances against a recommended range.

You can easily create such charts. What you do is create two additional series of data, one of which describes the minimum recommended value, and one of which describes the maximum recommended value. Figure 11.25 shows some example data properly formatted for creating this chart. Notice that the high recommended value comes before (to the left of) the low recommended value.

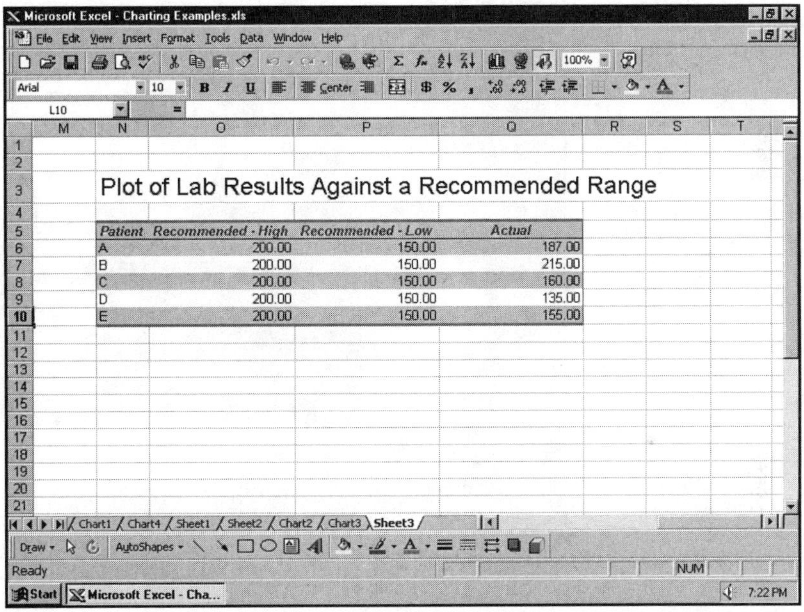

FIG. 11.25
Some example data showing how to set up the chart data when using a recommended range.

To create the chart, follow these steps:

1. Select the data and use the Chart Wizard to create an Area chart. Choose the Stacked Area sub-type (the middle one on the top row of Area sub-types). After selecting the sub-type, click Finish to create the chart (for this example, you can otherwise use the Chart Wizard to set other options you might be interested in, such as chart titles).
2. Activate the Chart toolbar (right-click the toolbar area and choose Chart if it's not visible).

3. Select the Actual data series, and then use the Chart Type button on the Chart toolbar to select the line chart type. Only the selected series changes to a line.

4. Right-click the Actual data series and choose Format Data Series from the shortcut menu. Click the Axis tab in the Format Data Series dialog box and choose the Secondary Axis option button. Click OK to close the dialog box.
5. Click either of the two recommended series, and then choose Chart, Chart Type. Choose the Area chart type, and the standard Area sub-type (upper-left corner in the sub-type display). Click OK to change the chart. The result up to this point is shown in Figure 11.26.
6. Select the bottom area series (which should be "Recommended - Low") and access its Format dialog box. Click the Patterns tab, and change the color of the series so that it matches the chart background. Click OK.

FIG. 11.26
Creation of a recommended range chart.

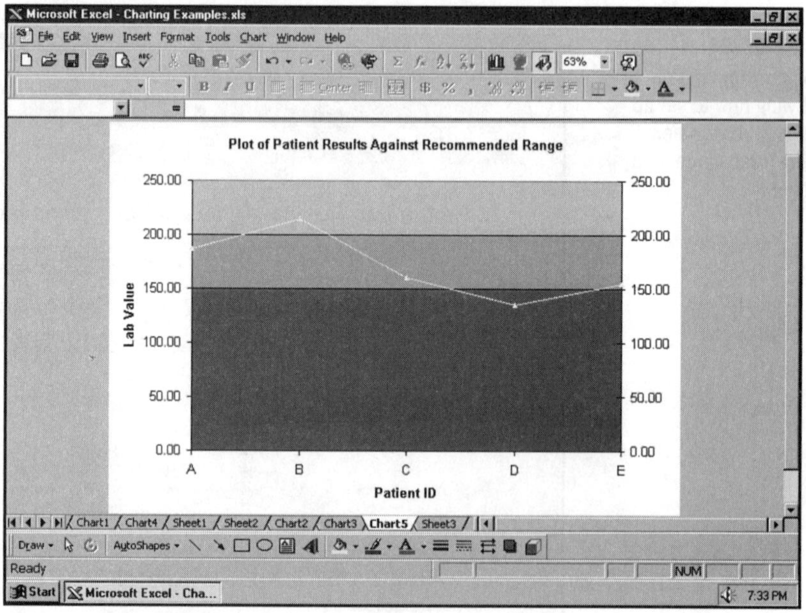

The final chart, shown in Figure 11.27, shows only the recommended range against which the actual values are plotted. (The line thickness and color of the Actual data range have been changed, to make this data range stand out.) Note that creating a legend for a chart like this will be a challenge, because the automatic legend will show the "invisible" Recommended Low series. Instead, arrange the chart so that a legend is not required.

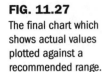

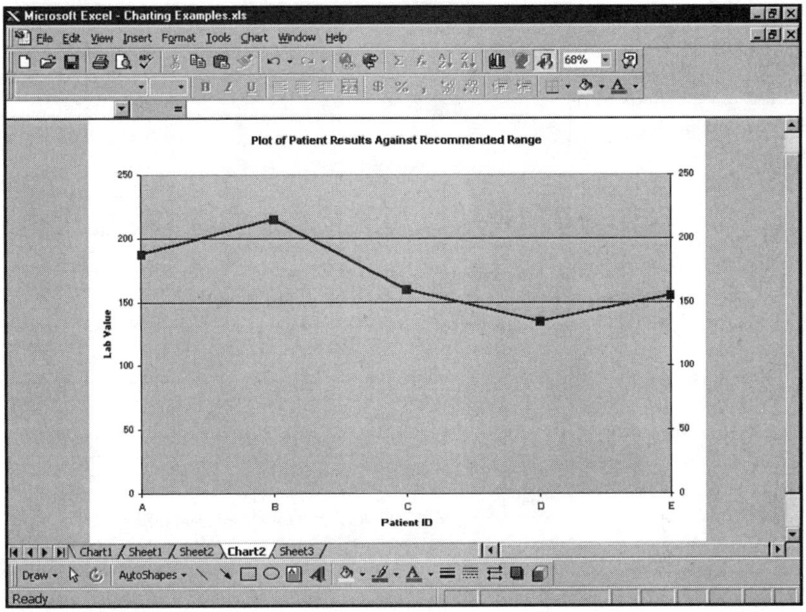

FIG. 11.27
The final chart which shows actual values plotted against a recommended range.

Common Problems and Solutions

Although creating a standard chart in Excel is simple, you may occasionally run into difficulties when using the advanced charting features. The following sections cover a few problems that you may run across when using these advanced features.

Using Logarithmic Scales with Line Charts

People often create line charts where the numbers are used for the category axis and they want to use a logarithmic scale on that axis. For instance, consider the chart shown in Figure 11.28.

The problem is this: When you go to change the X-axis to use a logarithmic scale, the choice doesn't exist! What's going on?

The problem is that line charts are designed to show changes across categories, or across time. Because of this, they can't treat the X-axis as numbers, and therefore don't let you choose a logarithmic scale for the X-axis, no matter what you use to label that axis. The solution is to use an XY Scatter chart, but use the sub-type that includes lines between each data point. If you change a line chart to an XY Scatter chart (using the "Scatter with data points connected by lines" sub-type) you can then use a logarithmic scale on the X-axis. More importantly, the X-axis is then proportional to the value being plotted.

Figure 11.29 shows the results of this change.

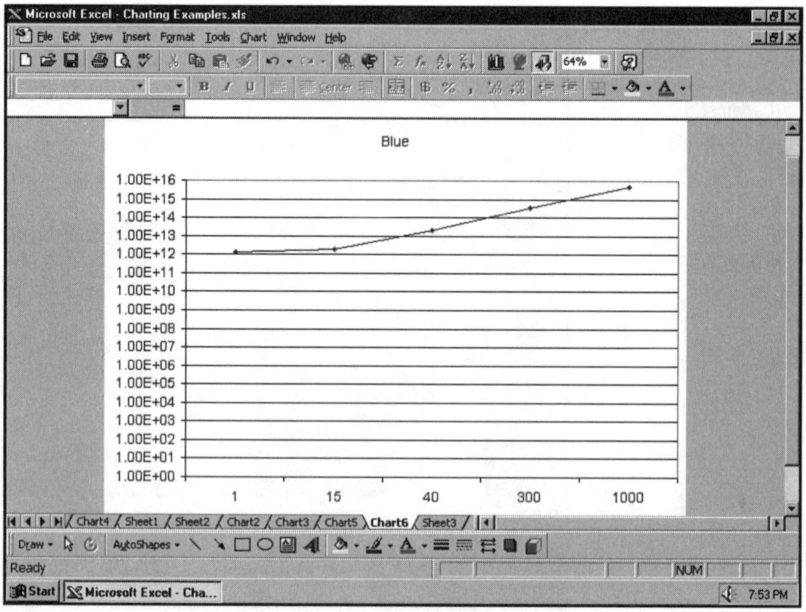

FIG. 11.28
A simple line chart where the numbers on the X-axis are the times that measurements were taken.

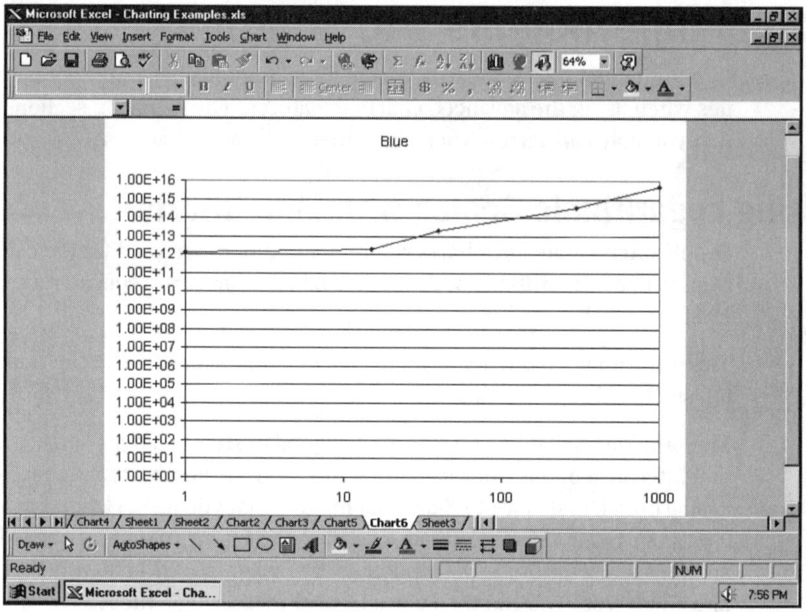

FIG. 11.29
Changing a line chart to an XY Scatter chart lets you use logarithmic axes.

Can't Rename an Embedded Chart

A handy improvement in Excel 97 is the capability to single-click select elements in embedded charts. Earlier versions of Excel forced you to double-click an embedded chart to edit it, and then click another time to select the element you wanted to work with. The new single-click method is far faster and easier.

However, you cannot click an embedded chart and use the Name box on the formula bar to change the chart's name. Instead, to select a chart so that you can change its name, first select a cell on the worksheet, and then select the chart with Ctrl+Click. You'll know you've selected the embedded object instead of the contents of the chart because the handles surrounding the chart are white instead of black. You can now use the Name box normally with the chart.

Save Charts as GIF Images

It's often very useful to convert charts to GIF images which can then be viewed by anybody who has a GIF file viewer (they're very common and easily downloaded from the Internet). However, there is no command that saves a chart into GIF format.

If you want to create a chart as a GIF image, choose File, Save as HTML. When you do this, all of the charts in the active workbook will be saved as GIF images.

TIP Once you save a chart into GIF format, you can use most graphics programs to convert that image to other formats you might want, such as JPG, TIF, PCX, or BMP.

From Here...

This chapter showed you how to use advanced charting features such as trend lines, logarithmic scales, and map charts. You also learned how to use graphic images as data markers, add a second Y-axis, work with error bars, and handle missing data points.

Refer to the following chapters for more information on Excel charts:

- Chapter 10, "Creating Charts," introduces the topic of charts. You learn how to use the Chart Wizard to create and modify charts, as well as additional ways to change the data in your charts.
- Chapter 12, "A Field Guide to Excel Chart Types," provides details on all the chart types available in Excel, and suggests when you should use particular chart types.

CHAPTER 12

A Field Guide to Excel Chart Types

by Bruce Hallberg

A picture can truly be worth a thousand words. A chart, on the other hand, can be worth a thousand numbers. Charts take advantage of how people best process and understand information. With a chart, you convey data metaphorically. Even if the underlying data is clear, it still might be difficult to understand. A chart tells a visual story about the data in a way that makes the information easy to understand. A good chart communicates its information clearly, quickly, concisely, and—most importantly—powerfully. ■

Communicating with charts

Charts of data can be powerful means of conveying ideas or helping others understand the points you're trying to make. In this section you learn how to use charts effectively.

Understanding and using different chart types

Excel contains many different types of charts, each of which is good in particular situations, with particular data, or for certain audiences. This section covers each of the chart types and shows example figures that illustrate how the charts work best.

Communicating with Charts

Choosing how to chart data is an art form. Different types of charts are designed to show data in different ways. Using the wrong type of chart to make a point usually confounds the audience. For example, while you can show a trend of sales figures using a 3-D surface chart, such a chart is less likely to strike a chord with the audience than a simpler (and expected) column or line chart might.

Consider the following when choosing what type of chart to use to convey your data:

- *Is the chart type designed to convey the information you're presenting?* For example, a column chart is perfect for comparing series and showing how the comparison changes over time. A pie chart, on the other hand, shows only parts of a whole. They're totally different types of charts designed for different purposes.
- *How does the audience expect to see the data?* When preparing charts to illustrate data, make sure you use chart types that your audience will understand and that correspond to how they expect to see the data. Experimenting with different types of charts in presentations is rarely a good idea!
- *Can the chart type you choose be formatted in such a way that it tells the story more powerfully?* For example, if you imagine a series of numbers that fall between 99.00 and 101.00, can you format the value axis so that it shows only that range, instead of showing the entire range from 0.00 to 101.00? If you can restrict a value axis to show only the top and bottom values of a needed scale, the differences between the values appear much larger and have more impact.
- *What questions does the chart suggest to the audience?* Different charts will suggest different questions to your audience. It's vital that you know what questions are being suggested and that you have answers to those questions. While every audience differs in what they notice about information and how they pursue a more complete understanding, you can often fine-tune your charts so that they lead the audience in the direction you want. For important presentations, it's a good idea to show your suggested charts (and alternatives) to people you trust to get their feedback and find out what questions they ask about the data. You can then be better prepared for a presentation.

Excel contains 14 basic chart types, 73 chart subtypes, and 20 built-in custom chart types. Each of these charts is different from the others. In some cases, a chart subtype is only slightly different from another subtype; however, in other cases, chart subtypes are like night and day in what they are designed to represent.

Column Charts

Column charts are designed for two primary purposes:

- They are excellent when you need to compare categories; in fact, this is what they are best at.
- They are good at showing changes over time, with time on the X-axis.

NOTE You can use error bars with column and bar charts. However, because of the way the chart bars appear, you are often limited to showing only positive errors. Negative error bars are harder to see against the column or bar itself, but you can change their color if necessary.

Table 12.1 describes the different column charts available.

Table 12.1 Column Charts in Excel 97

Subtype	Description
Clustered Column	Clustered Column (see Figure 12.1) compares categories. Within each category, you can further compare values. This subtype is also available with a 3-D effect.
Stacked Column	Use Stacked Column when you want to show how different values contribute to a total across different categories or time. There is also a variant available with a 3-D effect. You can see the Stacked Column in Figure 12.2.
100% Stacked Column	This type differs from the Stacked Column in that it shows the *percentage* contribution of each value across categories or time. You can choose from the normal version or one with a 3-D effect.
3-D Column	The 3-D Column chart adds a third dimension (a Z-axis) to the Clustered Column and often allows a clearer look at the changes in each series. An example of the 3-D column is shown in Figure 12.3.

FIG. 12.1
Use the standard Clustered Column chart to compare values across categories or time.

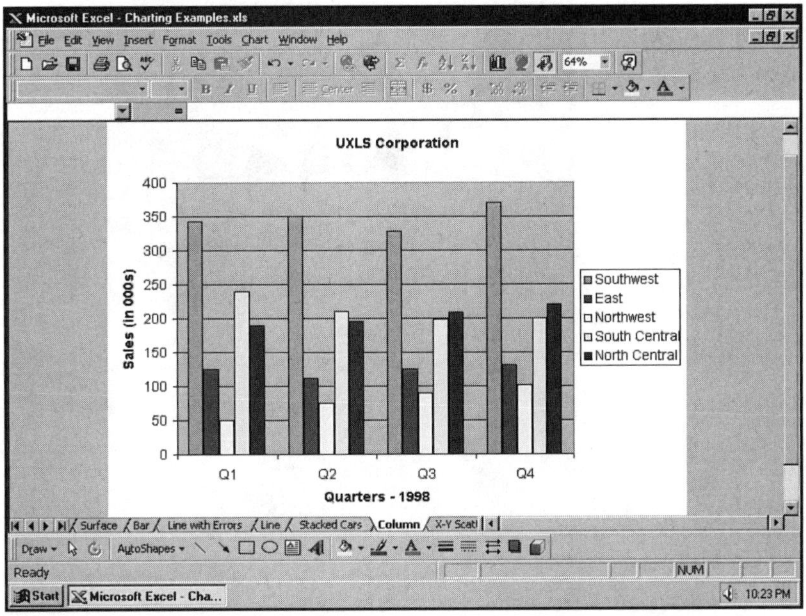

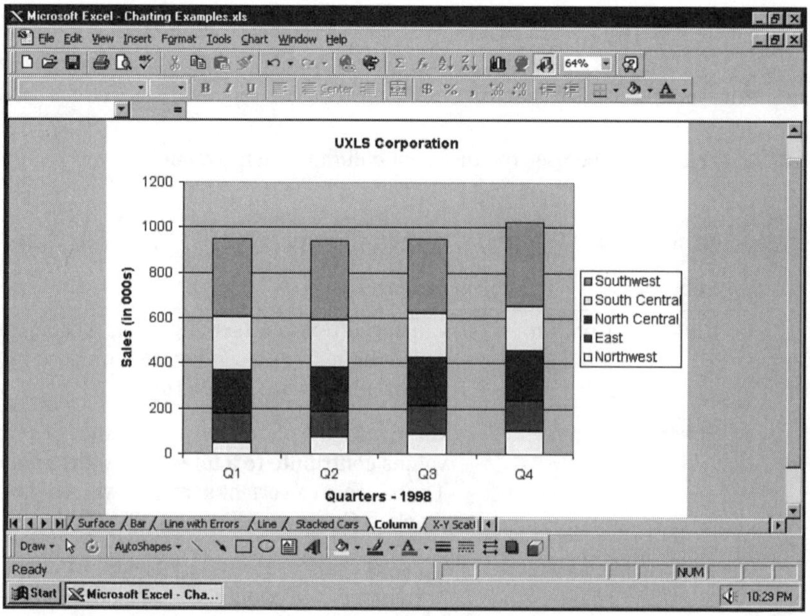

FIG. 12.2
The Stacked Column differs from the Clustered Column in that you can more easily see the total of all the series. However, it is harder to measure the actual values for each series.

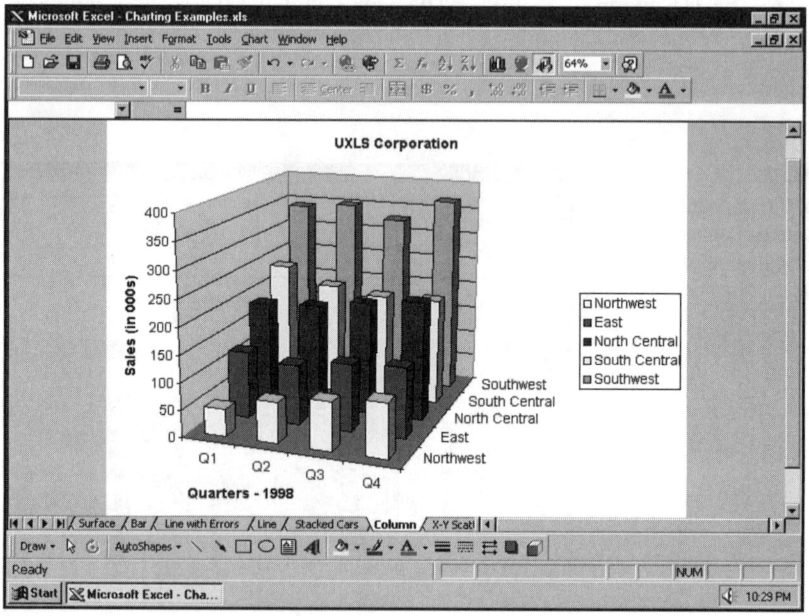

FIG. 12.3
The 3-D Column makes it easy to see how each series is changing across categories.

TIP When using the 3-D Column subtype, you may have to change the series order so that the tallest bars are to the rear of the chart and don't obscure series with lower values. The easiest way to reposition the series is to edit the series formula, changing the series order parameter at the end of the series formula for each series. Editing series formulas is covered in Chapter 11, "Advanced Chart Topics."

Bar Charts

Bar charts are similar to column charts except that the bars extend horizontally instead of vertically. Otherwise, they work the same way. However, this orientation change causes people to look at them differently. Although the difference is subtle, it can get you into trouble if you're not careful. Bar charts are not good for showing changes across time because most people spatially perceive time as moving from left to right. Because a bar chart orders the categories up and down, it typically causes the reader confusion when a time-based scale is used for categories. Many people in financial organizations, for example, are aware that using a time-based scale on the vertical category axis of a bar chart will reduce the credibility of the presentation.

The subtypes available for bar charts are the same as those for column charts, except that there is no equivalent to the 3-D Column chart. Bar charts are available in clustered, stacked, and 100% stacked formats, and each of those types are also available with a 3-D visual effect. Figure 12.4 shows an example Clustered Bar chart.

FIG. 12.4
Use the bar chart when you are comparing categories of information that are not time-based.

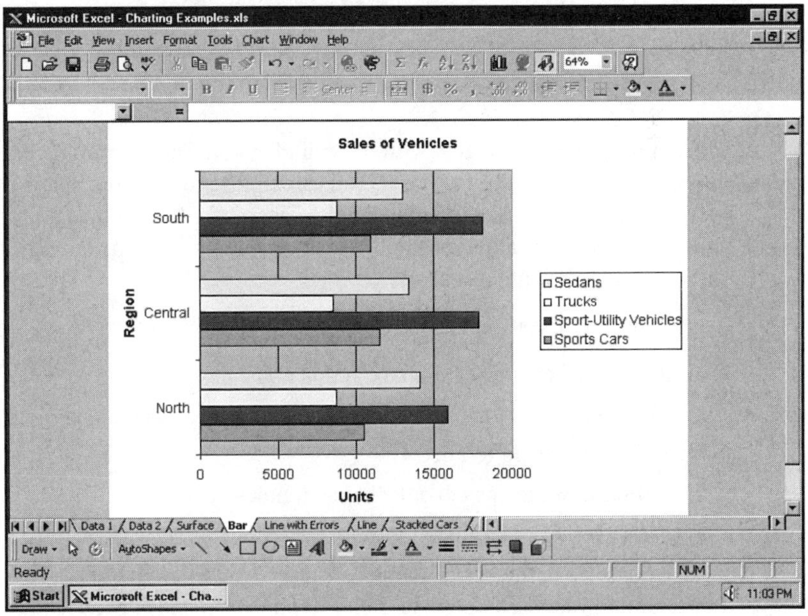

Cylinder, Cone, and Pyramid Charts

The column and bar charts you have already seen are also available with different formatting styles in which the bars or columns appears as cylinders, cones, or pyramids. All of the subtypes of the Column and Bar charts are available in these other shapes. Figure 12.5 shows an example 3-D Cone chart that corresponds to the 3-D Column chart.

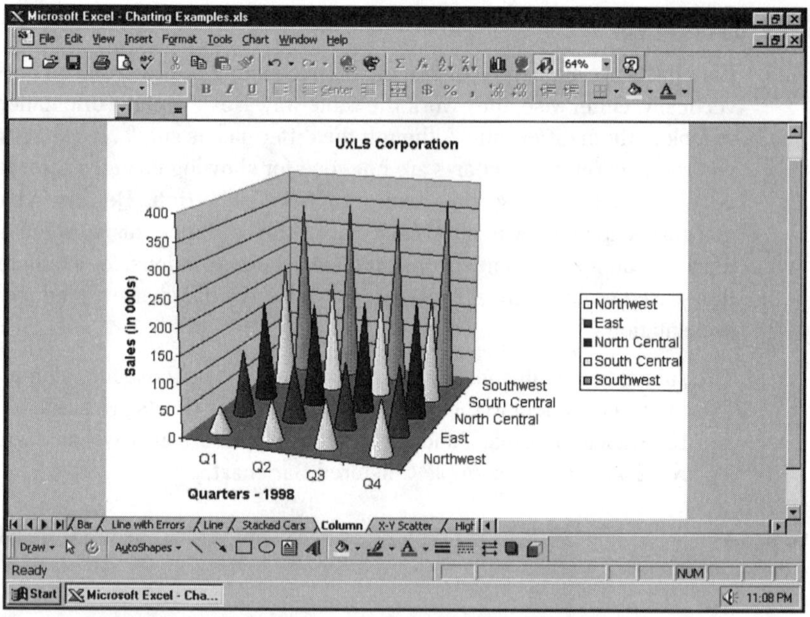

FIG. 12.5
Use a cylinder, cone, or pyramid type to spruce up a boring column chart.

There is one feature available with the cylinder, cone, and pyramid chart types that is not available with the bar or column charts. You can choose to have the shape of the bars correspond to the percentage of the maximum value they represent for each series. To access this feature, right-click any series and choose Format Data Series from the shortcut menu. Then move to the Shape tab, shown in Figure 12.6.

On the Shape tab, you can select:

- A standard column/bar shape (choice 1)
- Either of two forms of pyramid shapes (choices 2 and 3)
- A cylinder shape (choice 4)
- Either of two forms of cone shapes (choices 5 and 6)

For the pyramid and cone shapes, you can choose whether each shape is drawn the same way for all categories in the series (choices 2 and 5), or whether each shape is drawn according to the maximum value (choices 3 and 6). For choices 3 and 6, each shape is "chopped off" for the lower values on the chart. This effect often reinforces how the lower values compare to the maximum values. Figure 12.7 illustrates how this looks.

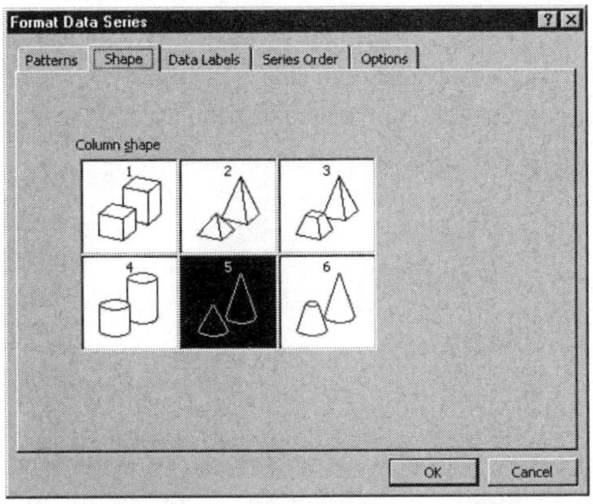

FIG. 12.6
Use the Shape tab with cylinder, cone, or pyramid charts to control how the shapes for a series are drawn.

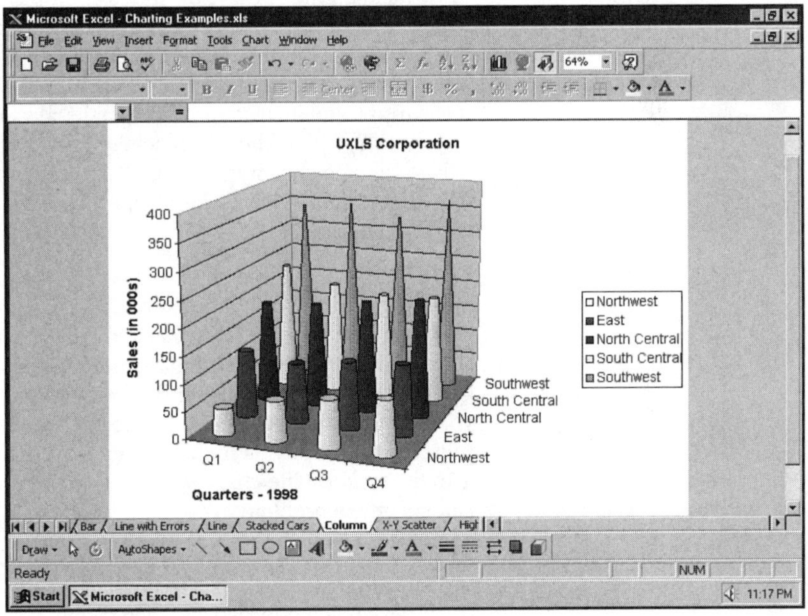

FIG. 12.7
With the pyramid and cone shapes, you can choose to draw them so that they more clearly indicate the relative proportions between the maximum value and lower values.

Line Charts

Line charts are similar to Column charts in that they best show changes in a series across categories or—even better—across time. Because the data points are interconnected, however, a line chart has somewhat different implications from a column chart.

The suggestion in a line chart is that the period between the points is continuous. In other words, the unmeasured data may be assumed to be continuing between the measurement points. A column chart, on the other hand, suggests discrete units across the categories. Table 12.2 outlines the types of line charts available.

NOTE Because line charts are designed to use time or categories along the X-axis, you cannot select a logarithmic scale for the X-axis of a line chart, even when your X-axis represents values. Instead, you must use the X-Y Scatter Chart and choose the chart subtype that connects the data points with lines when you need a logarithmic scale on the X-axis.

Table 12.2 Line Charts in Excel 97

Subtype	Description
Line	In a standard line chart, each series is represented by a simple line from one point to the next. The standard line chart does not use data markers for each data point; however, a variant is available that does. Figure 12.8 shows an example line chart.
Stacked Line	The Stacked Line shows how much each series contributes to the whole. You should be very careful with this chart subtype, as with the Stacked Column. It is easy to misunderstand the data being presented because it appears that each series is showing its measured value instead of its proportional value to the whole. In Figure 12.9, which shows a Stacked Line chart, compare the value axis to the one shown in Figure 12.8 to see why you must be careful with this chart subtype. The Stacked Line chart is also available with data markers.
100% Stacked Line	The 100% Stacked Line chart shows the percentage (of the maximum series) that each other series represents. The main thing to watch out for with the 100% Stacked Line is that the maximum series will coincide with the maximum gridline, so horizontal gridlines should typically not be used with this chart subtype. (If you simply must use a major gridline, be sure to use the variant of this chart subtype that includes data markers.) Figure 12.10 shows a 100% Stacked Line chart with the gridlines; you can see why this can become a problem.
3-D Line	This chart is a simple line chart drawn with a 3-D effect. Each series is distributed along a Z-axis to further differentiate one series from the others (each one also varies in color). Because of the Z-axis, a legend is not typically needed with a 3-D Line chart.

TIP Figures 12.8, 12.9, and 12.10 show the line chart with its default horizontal gridlines. Notice that the gridlines can make it hard to see the series lines in some cases.

When preparing line charts, make sure that your lines are distinct from the gridlines, either by eliminating or reformatting the gridlines or by reformatting the line styles. Also keep in mind that while the color series lines that you see on your screen make it clear which lines are the data and which are the gridlines, the colors will not be obvious on a laser printout.

FIG. 12.8
A standard Line chart is good for showing changes across time.

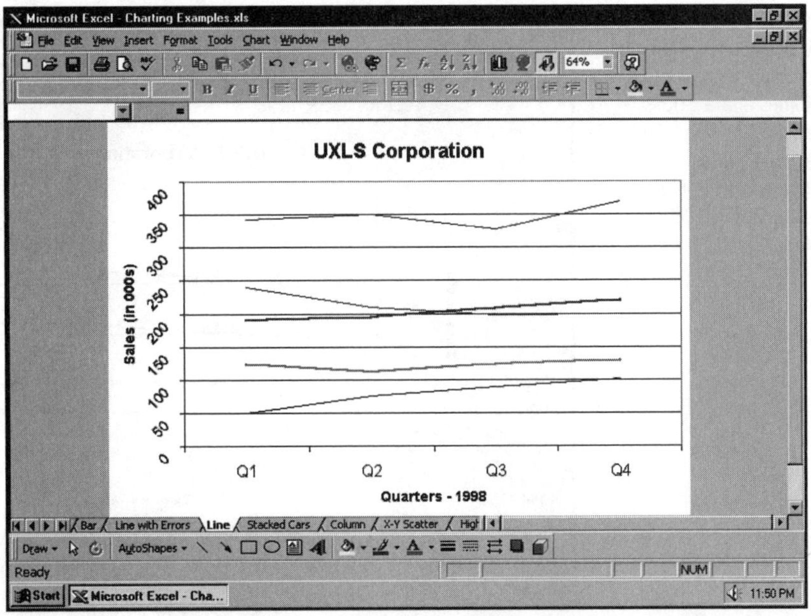

FIG. 12.9
With the Stacked Line chart, it is not immediately obvious that the values shown for each series represent their contributions to the whole.

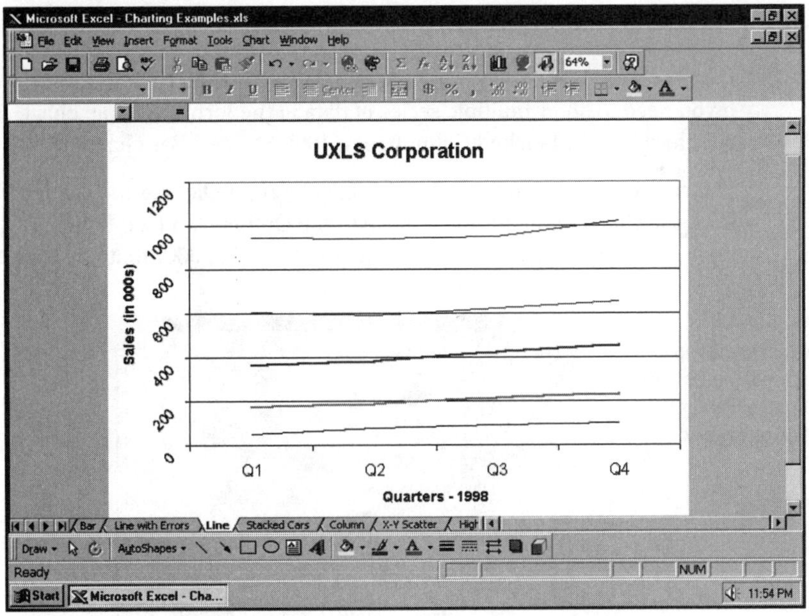

Part III

Ch 12

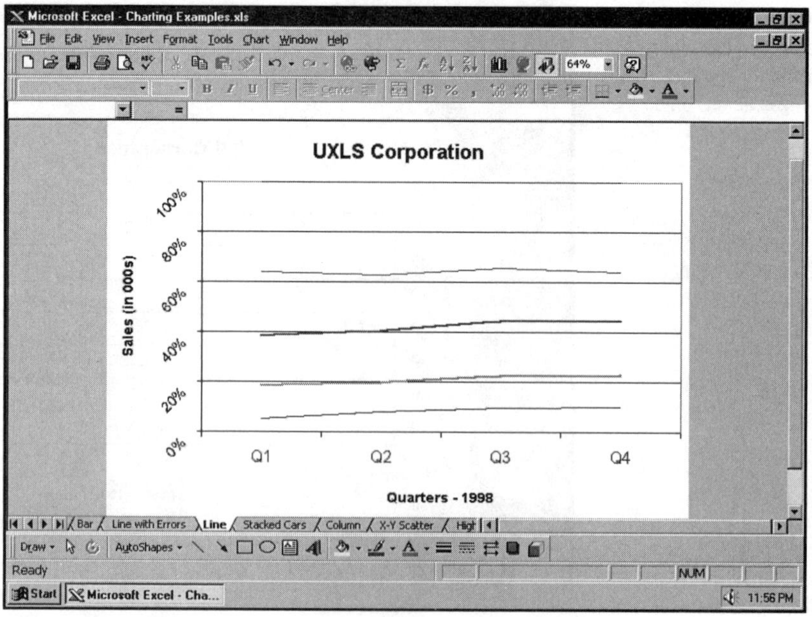

FIG. 12.10
You can see why there is a problem with using gridlines and a 100% Stacked Line chart. The maximum series is obscured by the major gridline at the 100% position

Pie Charts

Pie charts are best for showing percentages of a whole. They can show only one series of data. If you need to show multiple series of data in the format of a pie chart, consider using a Doughnut chart, a 100% Stacked Column, or a 100% Stacked Bar chart.

You can control the angle of the pie chart by right-clicking the pie and choosing Format Series from the shortcut menu. Then move to the Options tab (see Figure 12.11). With the Angle of first slice spinner button, select the angle (from 0 to 360) that you want the first slice drawn at.

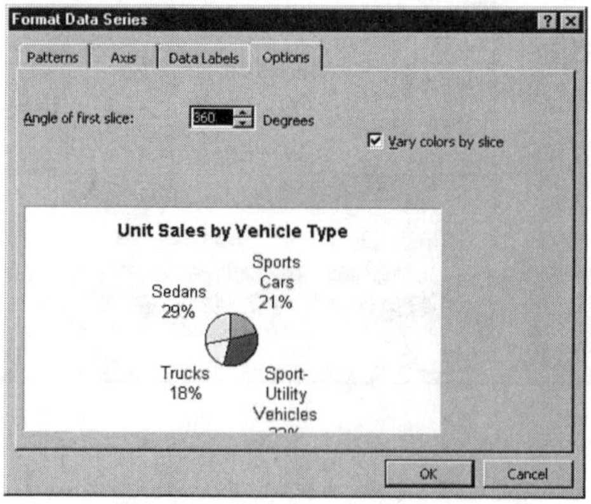

FIG. 12.11
You can rotate a pie chart with the Options tab of the Format Data Series dialog box.

There are two main variants of the standard pie chart: the Pie and the Exploded Pie (which sounds messy!). They are basically the same, but the Exploded Pie lets you "pull out" one or more slices to emphasize their values. Figure 12.12 shows an Exploded Pie chart. Both the Pie chart and the Exploded Pie chart are available in 2-D and 3-D formats.

FIG. 12.12
The Exploded Pie chart lets you emphasize one or more of the slices, as is demonstrated here with the Sport Cars slice.

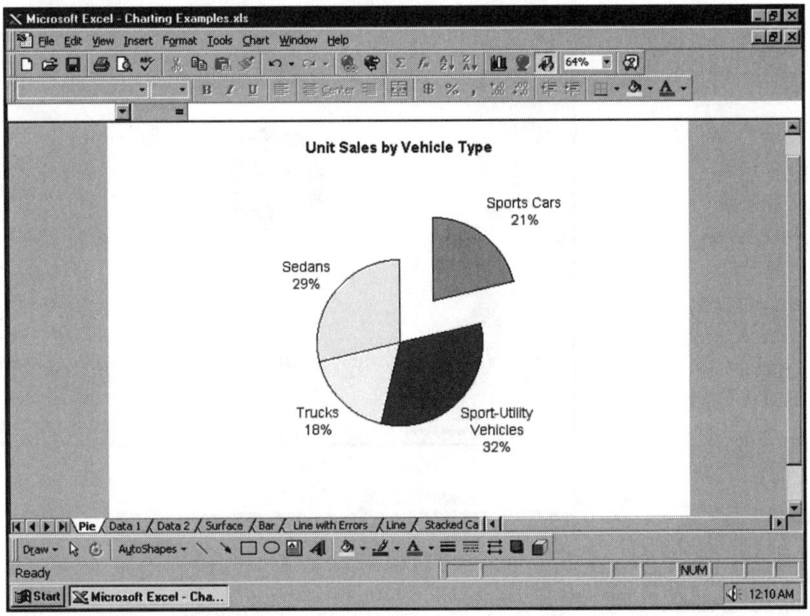

When working with the Exploded Pie chart, you control the amount of "explosion" by dragging any slice in or out. Doing so explodes all of the slices equally. To explode only one slice, click once on the slice to select the series, click once more to select just that slice, and then drag it outwards from the rest of the pie.

97

New in Excel 97, you can now have Bar of Pie and Pie of Pie charts, which show more detail for any of the slices in the main pie. Figure 12.13 shows a Pie of Pie chart with truck sales broken out from passenger car sales.

There are new options to control Pie of Pie and Bar of Pie charts and how they are displayed. To access these options, right-click any slice of a pie and choose Format Data Series from the shortcut menu. Then choose the Options tab (see Figure 12.14). Table 12.3 describes the options that are available.

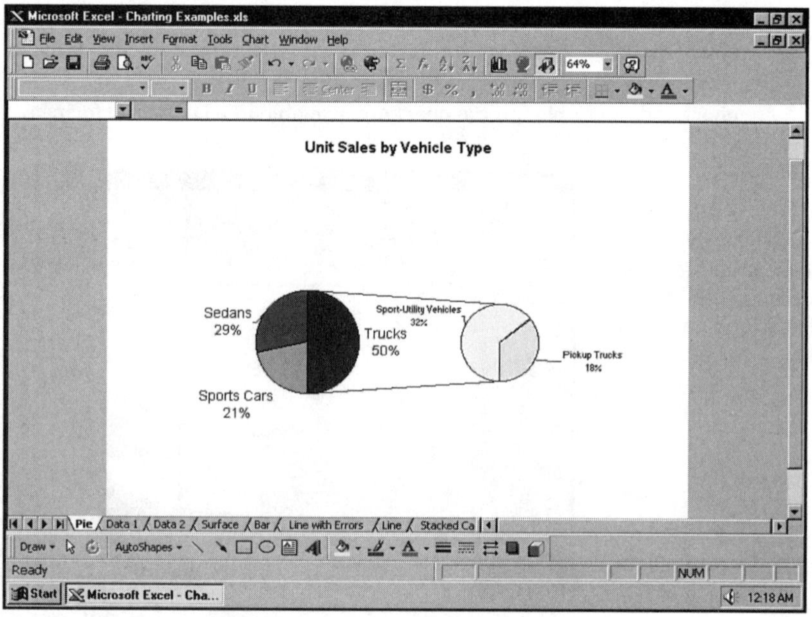

FIG. 12.13
The Pie of Pie and Bar of Pie charts let you break out some of the details from the main pie.

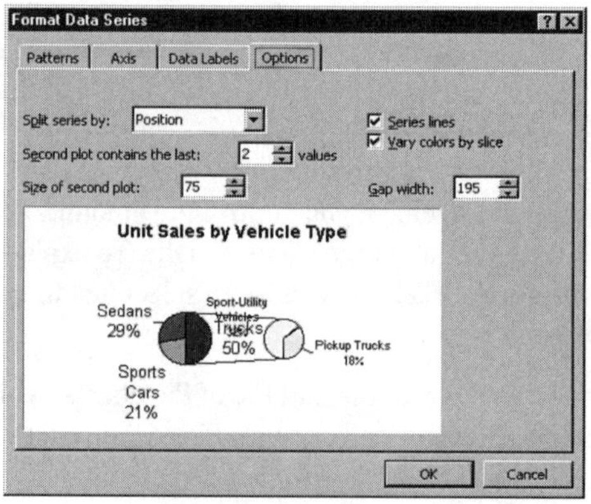

FIG. 12.14
Use the Options tab in the Format Data Series dialog box to control how Pie of Pie and Bar of Pie charts appear.

Table 12.3 Controls on the Options Tab for Pie of Pie and Bar of Pie Charts

Option	Description
Split Series by	There are four ways in which you can choose to break out detail from the main pie: by Position, Value, Percent Value, and Custom.
Second Plot Contains the Last	This is available only when Position is selected in the Split Series by drop-down list. You use this setting to control which data points are in the second plot, according to the order in which they are listed in the source worksheet range.

Option	Description
Second Plot Contains All ValuesLess Than	Available only when Value is selected in the Split Series by drop-down list, this setting specifies which values are included based on their value. You set the limit under which values are placed on the sub-pie or sub-bar. When you choose Percent Value in the Split Series by drop-down list, this same setting lets you choose the percentage limit under which values will be shown on the second plot.
Size of Second Plot	Use this setting to determine the percentage at which the second plot is displayed relative to the main pie. You can choose values from 5% to 200%.
Series Lines	Series lines are lines that link a pie slice data label to the slice itself.
Vary Colors by Slice	This setting lets you choose to use automatically varying colors for each slice of the pie.
Gap Width	The Gap Width setting controls the amount of space between the main pie and the sub-pie or sub-bar.

Scatter (XY) Charts

Scatter charts are used to show correlations between two sets of values, one on the Y-axis and one on the X-axis. While you can represent time on the X-axis, the line chart is somewhat better designed for that purpose in most cases. (The exception is when you need to show time as a value—in numbers of seconds or minutes, for example—and you may want to use a logarithmic scale.) Scatter charts come in five subtypes, as outlined in Table 12.4.

Table 12.4 Scatter Charts in Excel 97

Subtype	Description
Scatter	The standard Scatter chart uses data markers only to show where data values intersect between the X- and Y-axes. Figure 12.15 shows a standard Scatter chart.
Scatter with Data Points Connected by Smooth Lines	This subtype connects the data points for each series with smoothed lines between data markers. You can also choose this variant without data markers, where only lines are shown.
Scatter with Data Points Connected by Lines	Use this subtype as an alternative to the line chart when you need to chart values along the X-axis. An example of this variant is shown in Figure 12.16.

FIG. 12.15
The standard Scatter chart shows intersections between two value axes.

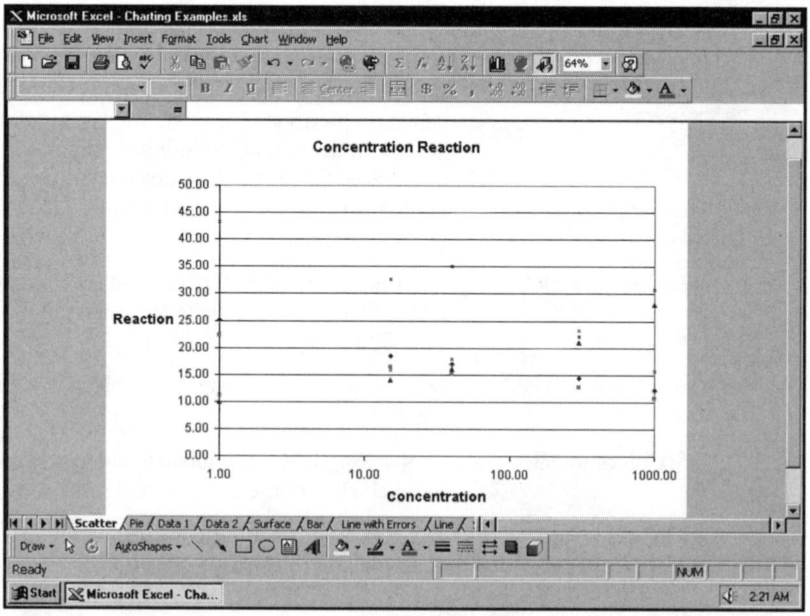

FIG. 12.16
Use the Scatter with Data Points Connected by Lines subtype when you want to show suggested trends in the data more clearly.

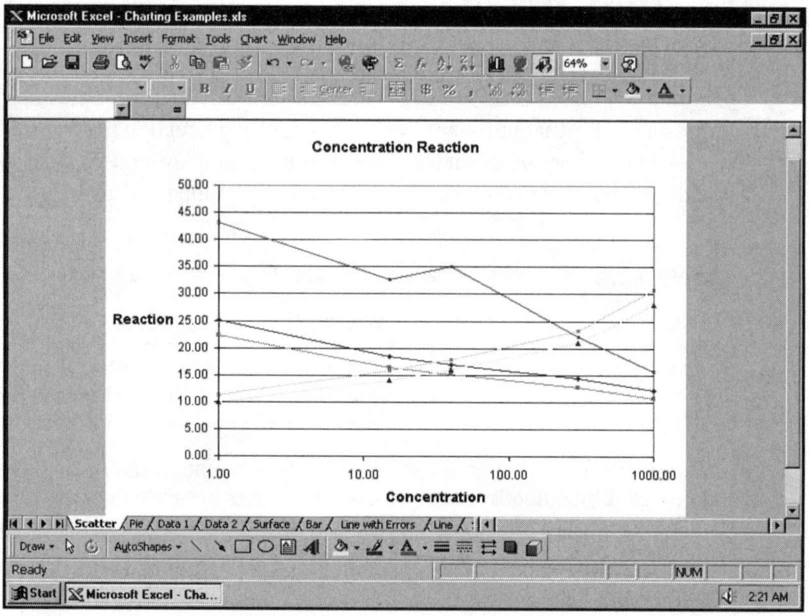

NOTE Because scatter charts use two value axes, they also support error bars in both directions. In the Format Data Series dialog box, you can choose both X and Y Error Bars.

Area Charts

Area charts combine aspects of line, pie, and stacked column charts for when you want to show changes over time but also put an emphasis on the total of all series combined. For instance, Figure 12.17, shows sales figures for four quarters displayed with an area chart. Notice how easy it is to see how the contribution of each series contributes to the whole at each measurement point, how trends in that contribution are made clear, and how easy it is to see the total for all series combined. Table 12.5 lists the area chart subtypes available.

FIG. 12.17
A Stacked Area chart is a good choice for when you want to show contributions of each series to a total, as well as trends across the categories or over time.

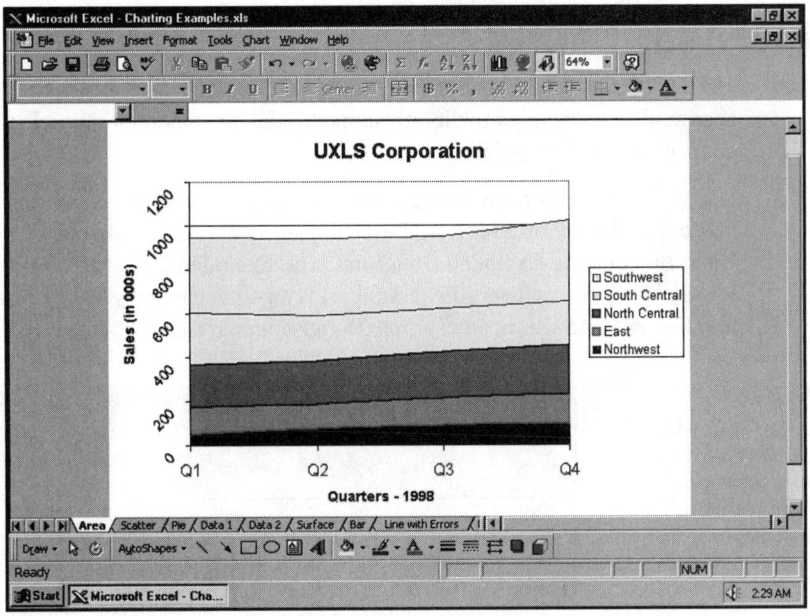

Table 12.5 Area Charts in Excel 97

Subtype	Description
Area	This subtype plots each series "on top" of one another. Because of this, the standard area chart can often obscure important data. This subtype is best when all values for each series allow each series to be visible (you may have to change the series order number in order to achieve the ordering you need). The area type also offers a 3-D effect that arrays the series along a Z-axis (which can help solve the problem of obscured data that's common in the 2-D Area type).
Stacked Area	Possibly the most useful variant of the Area chart, the Stacked Area shows trends and contributions to the total of all series combined. This subtype is also available with a 3-D effect.

continues

Table 12.5 Continued

Subtype	Description
100% Stacked Area	The 100% Stacked Area shows the percentage contribution of each series to the total of all series combined. This subtype is closest to showing what a pie chart shows (contribution to total), but it also shows trends across categories, which a pie chart can't do.

Doughnut Charts

The Doughnut chart is not often seen in business (at least in the United States), and that's a shame. When you need to directly compare the equivalent of multiple pie charts, the Doughnut chart is perfect for the job.

Doughnut charts show multiple series, in which each series shows how various values contribute to the whole for that series. Two subtypes of Doughnut charts are available: the normal Doughnut and the Exploded Doughnut. The Exploded Doughnut works just like the Exploded Pie chart in that it allows you to emphasize any one category by "pulling it out" from the others. Figure 12.18 shows an example Doughnut chart.

FIG. 12.18
Use the Doughnut chart when you want to see how each value in different series contributes to each whole.

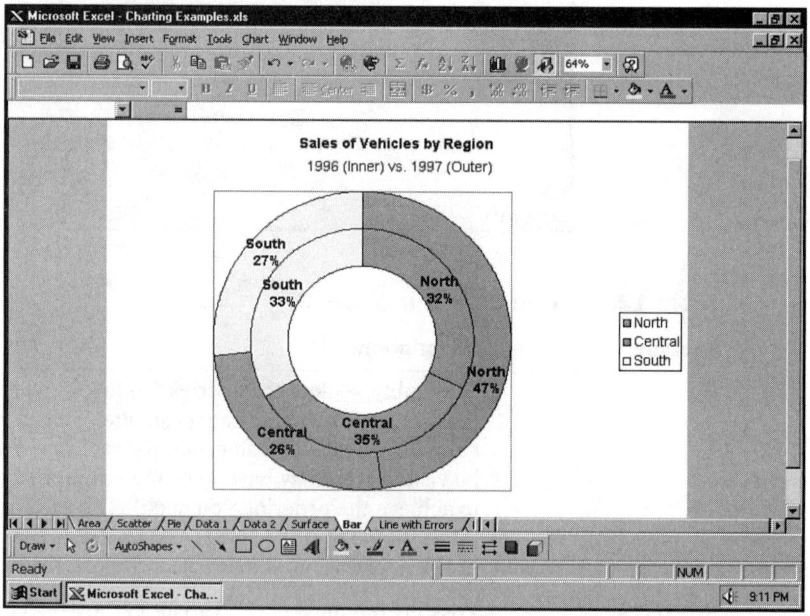

Radar Charts

Radar charts are not commonly seen in the United States; they are used more often in Europe and Asian countries. A radar chart uses a separate axis (although representing the same values) for each category radiating out from the center. It's almost like a line chart that has each line end folded back so it connects to its beginning.

There are three versions of the radar chart: one that uses data markers for the intersections, one that uses simple lines, and a third that uses filled areas within each series. All types let you use a logarithmic scale for the value axis. Figure 12.19 shows an example radar chart.

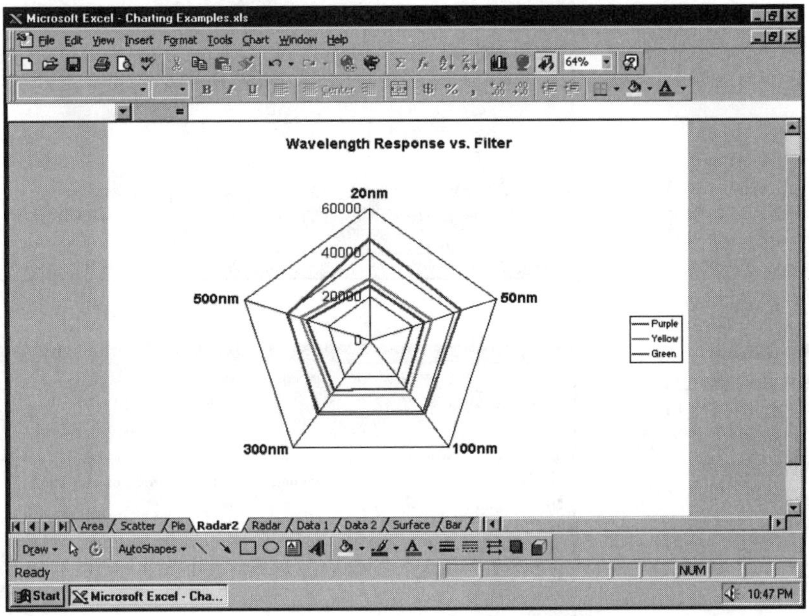

FIG. 12.19
The radar chart is similar to the line chart, but it gives an impression of the overall area (value) covered by each series.

Surface Charts

A surface chart uses three axes (X, Y, and Z) to show how three independent sets of data interact. Each range of values along the X-axis is drawn in a different color to help you see similar values. Surface charts often give a good overall "feel" for 3-D data, and they may help viewers see overall patterns that are not very apparent with other chart types. Figure 12.20 shows a surface chart.

Bubble Charts

97

Bubble charts are new to Excel 97. They are very similar to X-Y Scatter charts, except that the size of each data point indicates a third dimension of the data. Bubble charts use three columns of data. The first column indicates the X-axis on the chart, the second indicates the Y-axis, and the third controls the size of each bubble. Figure 12.21 shows an example of a bubble chart.

FIG. 12.20
The Surface chart gives shape to 3-dimensional data in ways that other charts don't.

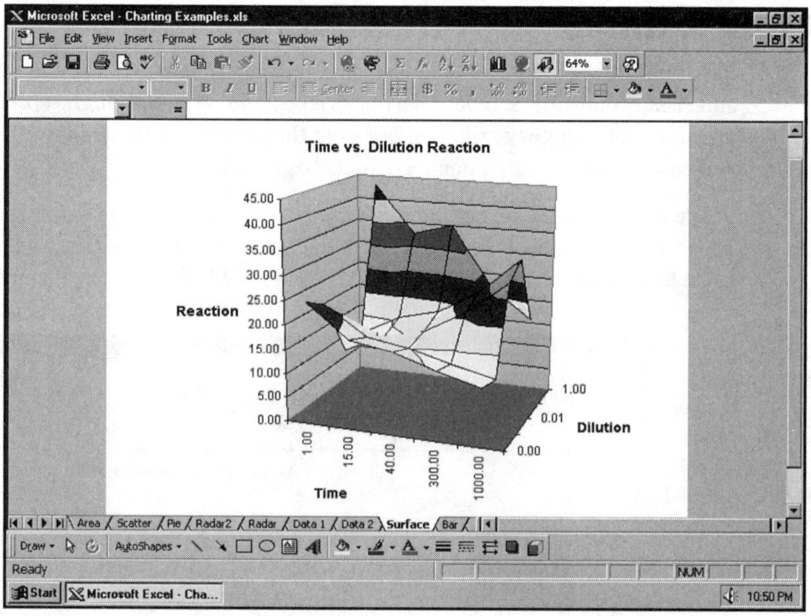

FIG. 12.21
The bubble chart is a great addition to Excel 97's charting package, almost like a supercharged XY Scatter chart.

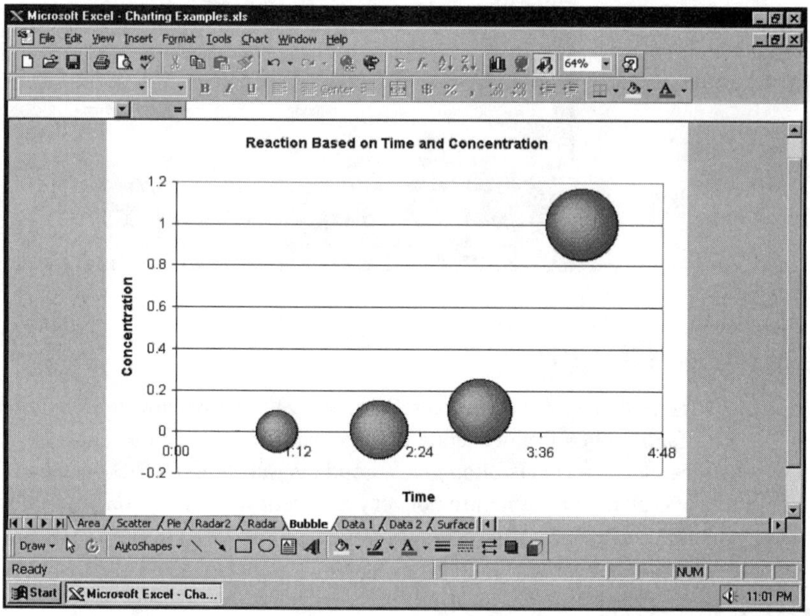

The Format Data Series dialog box's Options tab contains some settings specific to Bubble charts (Figure 12.22). You can use the Size Represents options to control whether the bubble's area or its width should represent the value being displayed. You can also choose how large the bubbles are with the Scale Bubble Size To spinner box. If Show Negative Bubbles is selected, negative bubbles are drawn in a different color from the positive bubbles. Finally, you can vary the bubble color from value to value with the Vary Colors by Point check box.

FIG. 12.22
You can control bubble chart-specific options with the Format Data Series dialog box's Options tab.

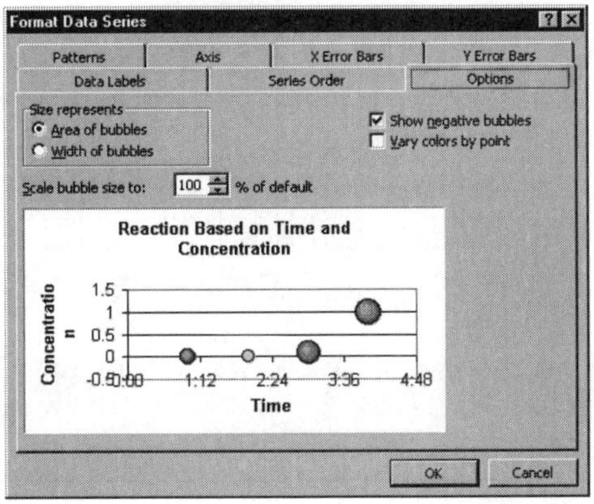

Stock Charts

Excel includes several built-in chart types specifically designed for charting stock activity. The name of each subtype corresponds to the data that the chart shows about a stock being charted:

- High-Low-Close
- Open-High-Low-Close
- Volume-High-Low-Close
- Volume-Open-High-Low-Close

For all four types, your data must be arranged in the order the subtype name suggests. In other words, in order to create a High-Low-Close chart, you must have four columns of data: the date, the high price for each date, the low price for each date, and the closing price for each date. Figure 12.23 shows an example Volume-High-Low-Close chart. The columns represent the volume of shares traded, the drop-lines show the range of prices (high and low), and the tick mark on each drop-line indicates the closing price for that day's trading.

Custom Chart Types

Excel 97 includes a host of custom chart types that incorporate features from many of the main chart types. When you want some pizzazz in your charts, examine the various custom types available for a special look. Figures 12.24, 12.25, and 12.26 show some of the more notable custom chart types available.

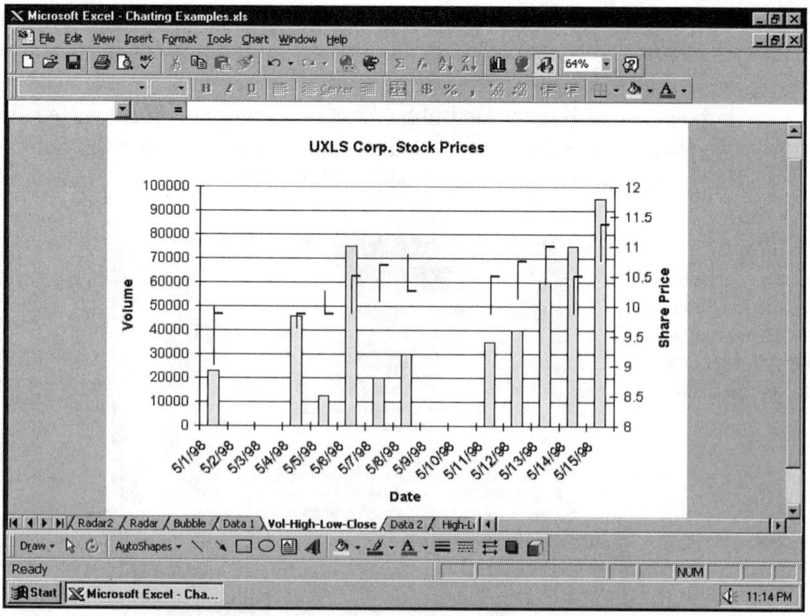

FIG. 12.23
Of the four stock charts in Excel 97, the Volume-High-Low-Close is one of the more popular.

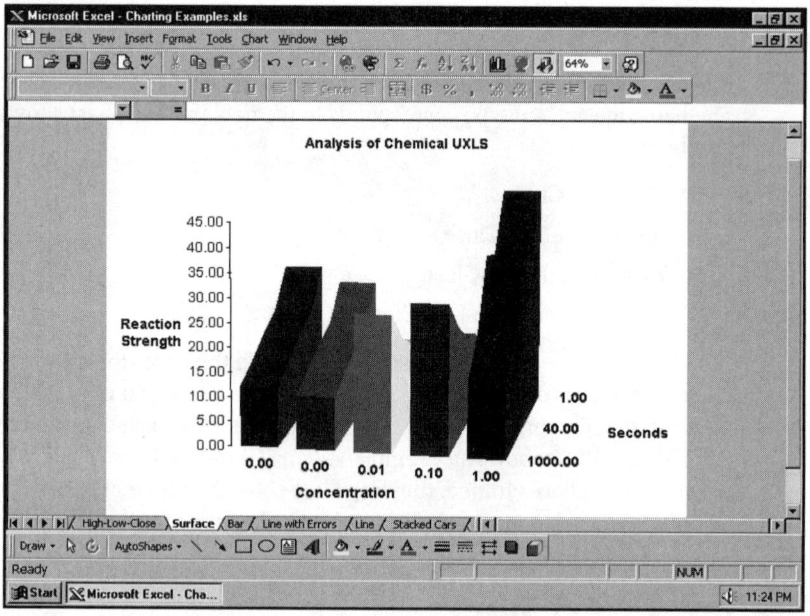

FIG. 12.24
The Area Blocks chart offers an attractive way to plot series of data.

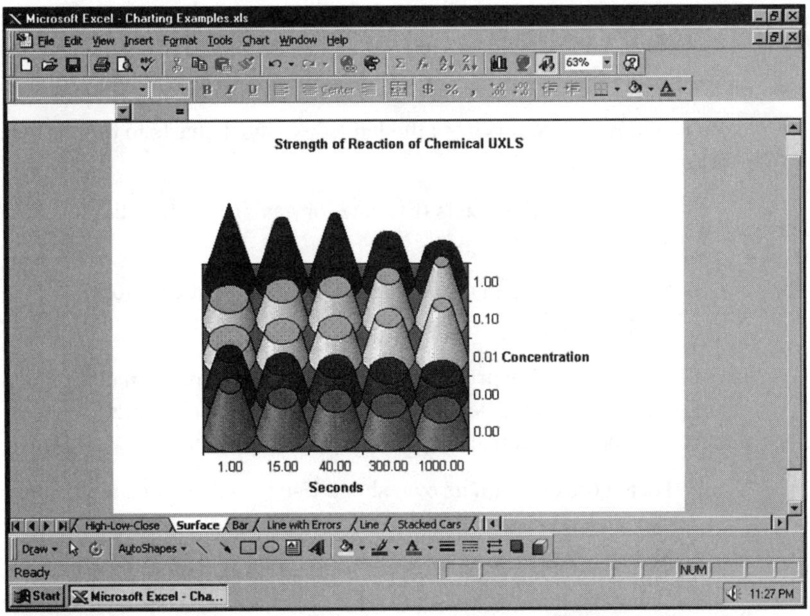

FIG. 12.25
The Cones Custom chart really drives home values that indicate strength.

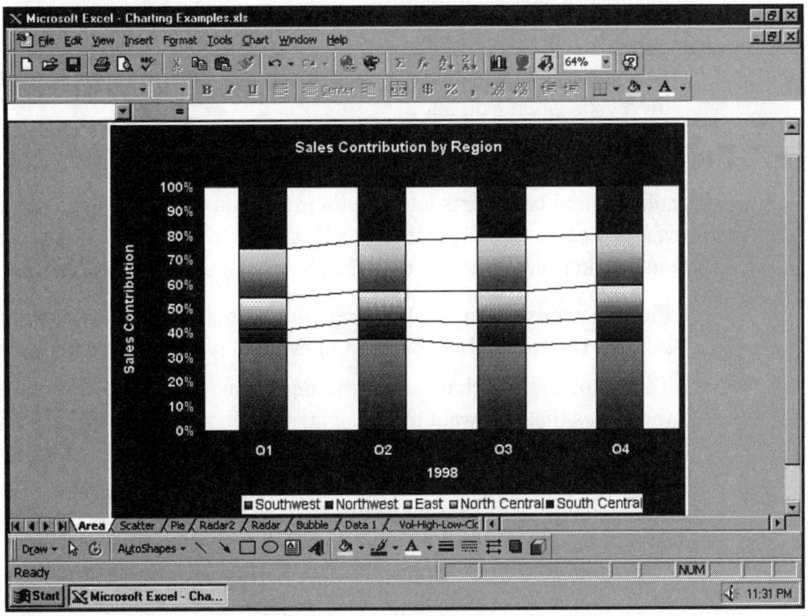

FIG. 12.26
The Stack of Colors chart is a very nice variation of the Stacked Column chart.

Common Problems and Solutions

Can I move the Y-axis from left side of chart to the right side?

You can move the Y-axis from the left side of most charts to the right side by following these steps:

1. Double-click the X-axis (the category axis) to access the Format Axis dialog box.
2. Move to the Scale tab.
3. Select the Value (Y) Axis Crosses at Maximum Category.
4. Click OK to close the dialog box.

While you can use this procedure for line, area, and column charts, you cannot perform the same feat for the 3-D variants of those charts. If you absolutely must do this with one of the 3-D chart subtypes, you can attempt a difficult workaround:

1. Locate the chart on its own sheet. Use the Chart, Location command to relocate the chart from being embedded on a worksheet to its own chart sheet.
2. Activate the Drawing toolbar.
3. Using the Rectangle tool, draw a box over the Y-axis labels on the left side.
4. Format the rectangle so that it uses no lines and contains a color that exactly matches the chart's background.
5. Using the Text Box tool, manually create the Y-axis labels on the right side of the chart. Your job will be easier if the chart has horizontal gridlines against which you can align the Y-axis labels you add.

Can I use a secondary axis in my 3-D charts?

Line, column, and bar charts let you plot individual data series against a secondary Y-axis. However, you cannot do this with the 3-D variants of the line, column, and bar charts. There is a difficult workaround, but it is only feasible for relatively simple charts.

1. Plot the series of data that will remain against the left-hand (primary) Y-axis normally. Do not plot the series that you want to eventually show against a secondary Y-axis.
2. Take a look at the chart and try to determine what measurements will make sense for the series that you want to plot against a secondary Y-axis, making sure that they fit within the primary Y-axis. For example, all of the primary Y-axis series might fit on a Y-axis that runs from 0 to 100 with axis labels every 10 units. The series that you want to plot against a secondary axis will fit if the secondary axis runs from 0 to 1000 with axis labels every 100 units.
3. Transform the data for the secondary axis so that it complies with the primary axis. In the example given in step 2, you could divide the secondary axis numbers by 10 so that they fit in the 0–100 scale of the primary axis but are still proportionately correct.
4. Add the transformed secondary axis series data to the chart.

5. Manually add the secondary axis labels using the Text Box tool on the Drawing toolbar.
6. Manually add an axis title to the secondary axis side of the chart.

From Here...

This chapter explained all of the Excel chart types, what each one is good (and bad) for, and any special features or properties of the various chart types and subtypes. This chapter, along with the previous two chapters, gives you a solid grounding in creating Excel charts and in using them to present data effectively. From here, consider the following topics:

- Chapter 13, "Drawing with Excel," explains how to use all of Excel's drawing tools. The built-in drawing tools in Excel are powerful and can meet many needs. Of particular interest are the creative ways they can be used to annotate your charts.
- Learn all about Excel databases in Part IV, "Creating and Using Excel Databases." Excel databases often provide data that needs to be charted.
- Part V, "Analyzing Your Data," shows you tools and features that make it easier to analyze your worksheet data.

CHAPTER 13

Drawing with Excel

by Bruce Hallberg with Joyce Nielsen

Excel 97 contains a surprisingly complete set of drawing tools. You can use these tools to create drawings ranging from simple worksheet or chart annotations to more complex drawings, such as diagrams, artistic drawings, simple maps, and so forth. With the addition in Excel 97 of AutoShapes—predefined shapes that you can easily incorporate in your drawings—sophisticated drawing effects are now a snap. And with 3-D and lighting effects now available, you can really produce impressive results! ■

Drawing in Excel 97

Excel contains a powerful suite of drawing tools with which you can draw just about anything, from diagrams to renderings.

Editing drawn objects

After drawing objects, you can use a host of available formatting settings to make your objects appear just the way you want. You can also add a variety of special effects to your drawn objects.

Advanced drawing

After you've mastered the basics of drawing in Excel, use this section to learn about more advanced topics, such as 3-D perspective, simulated light sources, connector lines, and embedding WordArt in Excel.

Drawing in Excel 97

To start drawing with Excel, first move to the worksheet or chart that you want to contain your drawing, and activate the Drawing toolbar (right-click in the toolbar area and select Drawing from the shortcut menu). Figure 13.1 shows the Drawing toolbar, and Table 13.1 details the tools available within it.

FIG. 13.1
Use the Drawing toolbar in Excel for easy access to the drawing tools.

Table 13.1 Drawing Toolbar Icons

Icon	Name	Description
	Draw	Activates a menu containing drawing control commands
	Select Objects	Chooses the pointer tool, with which you select drawn objects to manipulate
	Free Rotate	Places a selected drawn object into Free Rotate mode, with which you can quickly rotate the object to different angles
	AutoShapes	Lets you choose from a variety of predrawn shapes that you can incorporate into your drawings
	Line	Draws a straight line
	Arrow	Draws a line with an arrow at either end
	Rectangle	Draws a rectangle or square
	Oval	Draws an oval or circle
	Text Box	Draws a box into which you can type text
	WordArt	Inserts a WordArt drawing
	Fill Color	Chooses the fill color for a selected object, or new objects
	Line Color	Chooses the line color for a selected object, or new objects

Icon	Name	Description
	Font Color	Chooses the font color for a selected object, or new objects that contain text
	Line Style	Chooses the line drawing weight (thickness) for a selected object, or new lined objects
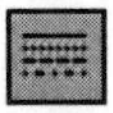	Dash Style	Chooses the line drawing style for a selected object, or new lined objects
	Arrow Style	Chooses the style of arrows to use with an arrow object or line object
	Shadow	Chooses a shadow effect for a selected object, or new objects
	3-D	Chooses a 3-D effect for a selected object, or new objects

Drawing Objects

There are really only three fundamental shapes you draw using Excel's drawing tools: lines, rectangles, and ovals. While there are a variety of predefined complex shapes also available, these three are the fundamental tools (see the section "Drawing Complex AutoShapes," later in this chapter, for information on the more complex shapes). By using a combination of these fundamental tools and the various effects you can apply to shapes, you can draw just about anything.

NOTE When you use Excel's drawing features, every single drawing—a line, rectangle, or oval, plus AutoShapes—is an *object*. Each individual object can be formatted, moved, rotated, and colored individually. ■

To draw an object using one of the fundamental shapes, click once on the appropriate Drawing toolbar button to select the drawing tool. Your pointer changes to a crosshair that makes it easier to see where each point of your drawing will be placed. Then, drag in the document to draw the shape. Release the mouse button, and the object is created.

Constrained Drawing While you are dragging in the document to draw an object, you can hold down the Shift key to *constrain* the object.

- When drawing a line, holding down the Shift key forces the line to be drawn only in 15-degree increments.
- When drawing a rectangle, the Shift key causes a perfect square to be drawn.
- When drawing an oval, the Shift key forces a perfect circle to be drawn.
- When you draw a complex AutoShape, such as a happy face or large arrow, the Shift key forces the object to maintain a predefined height:width ratio.

TIP To draw a quick circle or square, click the Oval or Rectangle tool, and then click once in the drawing area. A standard circle or square is instantly drawn. You can then drag it to a new position or use its handles to resize it. The position at which you click your mouse button defines the upper-left corner of the circle or square.

You can also use this trick with the more complex AutoShapes discussed in the section "Drawing Complex AutoShapes," later in this chapter.

Alternative Drawing Method Normally, when you draw an object, you drag from the object's upper-left corner to its lower-right corner, or vice-versa. In the case of a line, dragging draws from its starting point to its ending point.

As you draw an object, you can hold down the Ctrl key to draw the object using an alternate method, where the drag action draws the object from its *center* to one if its sides. For instance, if you hold down Ctrl and draw an oval, dragging defines the radius of the oval, rather than its approximate diameter. Holding down Ctrl and drawing a line defines the line from its center to one end.

TIP Use the Ctrl key drawing method when you know exactly where you want an object centered. The point at which you begin dragging will define that center.

Repeatedly Using a Drawing Tool When you choose any of the drawing tools and then draw an object, the tool is deselected after the object is drawn. To draw another object of the same type, you have to select the tool again. Most of the time, this is the easier way to work with drawn objects, because you typically want to modify them in some way once drawn, before drawing the next object.

When you are drawing many objects of the same type in succession, you can save time by double-clicking the drawing tool, which causes it to stay selected. You can then draw as many of a particular type of object as you want. To deselect the tool when you're done, click the tool once more.

Drawing Complex AutoShapes

You can quickly draw a number of predefined objects by using the AutoShapes tool on the Drawing toolbar. Clicking the AutoShapes tool opens a menu, from which you can choose a type of AutoShape. For each type of AutoShape, you can then choose a particular shape from a submenu that appears. Figure 13.2 shows the AutoShapes menu open, and the Stars and Banners submenu open.

Once you choose an AutoShape from the appropriate sub-menu, you then draw the object the same as any other object: drag in the drawing area to create the object. You can hold down the Shift key to constrain the AutoShape to the same proportions for which it was designed, and you can hold down the Ctrl key to draw the AutoShape's radius.

FIG. 13.2
Excel's wide variety of AutoShapes make drawing common objects quick and easy.

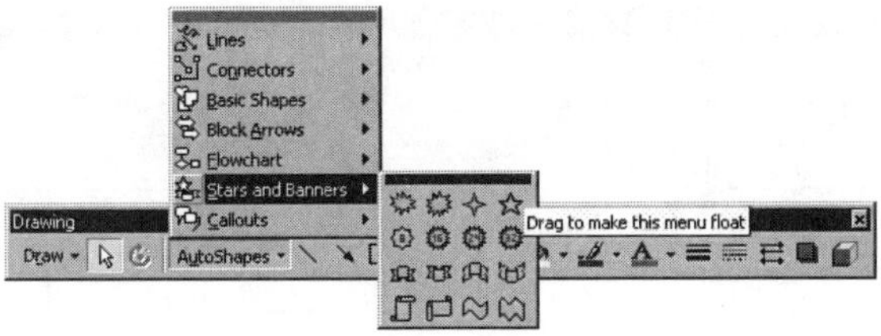

Drawing Text Boxes

Use the Text Box tool on the Drawing toolbar to draw a box designed to contain text. You can use text boxes to create labels and titles on your drawings. Text boxes can have a lined border (the default), or no border at all.

When you draw a text box, a cursor appears within the box. You can start typing the text immediately. Within the text box, you can use Excel's text formatting commands to format selected parts of the text.

TIP You can add text to any closed AutoShape, not just to rectangles. (A *closed* AutoShape is any shape besides a line.) For any drawn object that doesn't normally contain text, right-click the object and choose Add Text from the shortcut menu. A cursor then appears within the shape, and you can begin typing.

Editing Drawing Objects

Drawing most objects is only half the battle. You almost always have to perform some sort of formatting on each object so that it appears exactly as you want. Aside from such basic formatting as choosing a fill color or line style, you typically need to edit drawn objects to access some of the exciting new drawing effects available in Excel 97, such as 3-D perspectives, textures, and simulated light sources. In this section, you learn all about editing the objects you draw and accessing the more advanced effects.

Selecting Drawn Objects

Most editing functions are used after you select a particular object. There are several ways to select objects, and each method is appropriate in different circumstances.

The easiest way to select an object is to simply click it. As you move your pointer over a drawn object, the pointer changes to a pointer with a four-sided arrow. Click once to select the object for editing. Figure 13.3 shows a selected object.

You can select more than one object at a time. Two methods accomplish this. By clicking the Select Objects button on the Drawing toolbar and dragging the selection pointer around a set of objects, you can select all of the objects within a marquee when you release the mouse button. You can also Shift+Click each object you want selected.

FIG. 13.3
Once you select an object, you can reshape it in various ways.

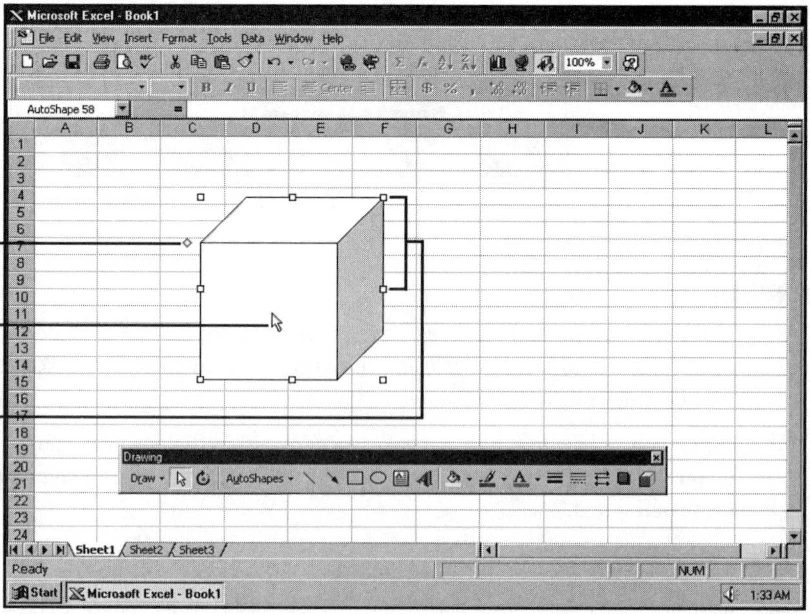

For 3-D objects, you see a perspective handle

This pointer selects an object

Handles on the sides of an object allow you to reshape it

Copying and Moving Drawn Objects

You can easily create exact duplicates of objects you've already drawn. In addition, you can move objects to a different position in the worksheet.

To copy a drawn object, press and hold down the Ctrl key. Then select the object you want to copy and drag the object. As you drag, a copy of the object moves with the pointer. Release the mouse button when the copied object is in the desired position.

To move a drawn object, select the object and then drag it to the position you want.

Using Formatting Toolbar Buttons

There are eight quick formatting buttons on the Drawing toolbar. After selecting an object, you can perform most formatting jobs using these buttons. The formatting buttons on the Drawing toolbar are:

- Fill Color
- Line Color
- Font Color
- Line Style
- Dash Style
- Arrow Style
- Shadow
- 3-D

All of these buttons open icon-based menus when you click them. From the menu that appears, you can choose the exact formatting option you want for the selected drawing objects. Figure 13.4 shows the Fill Color menu open.

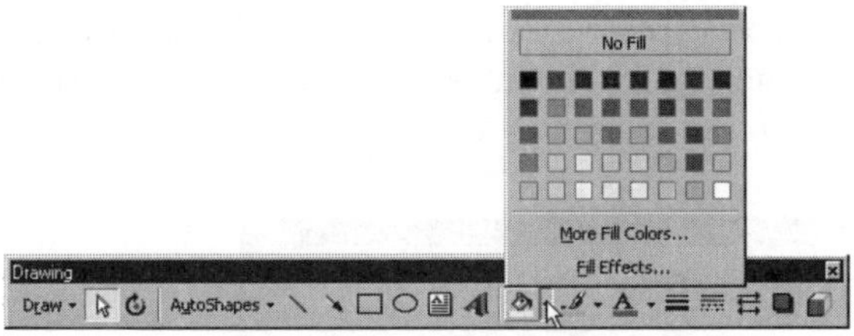

FIG. 13.4
Use the various formatting buttons, such as Fill Color, to quickly choose the formatting you need.

TIP Three of the formatting buttons—Fill Color, Line Color, and Font Color—can be "torn off" the toolbar and left floating on your screen. Drag the bar at the top of their menus to move them away from the toolbar. They'll stay open and can be quickly accessed.

Accessing an Object's Formatting Properties

You can double-click any drawn object to access its properties dialog box. You can also right-click an object and choose Format AutoShape from the shortcut menu. When you do either action, the Format AutoShape dialog box appears, as shown in Figure 13.5.

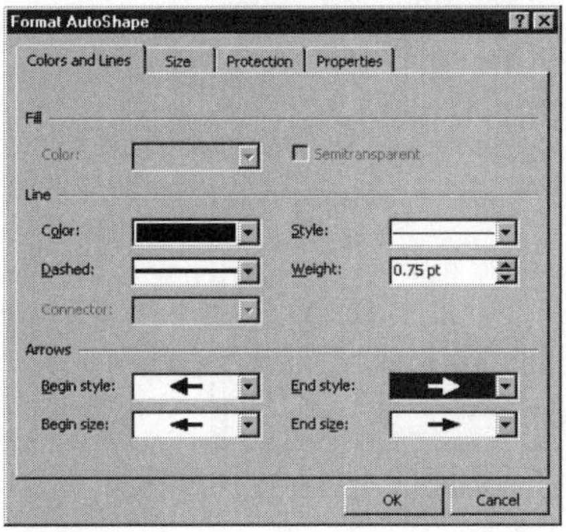

FIG. 13.5
The Format AutoShape dialog box lets you make more precise formatting adjustments than the Drawing toolbar's formatting buttons.

These four tabs appear in the Format AutoShape dialog box:

- *Colors and Lines* lets you choose a fill color (for closed objects), line characteristics, and arrow styles (for lines).
- *Size* lets you enter exact numbers for an object's height, width, and rotation angle. You can also choose to scale objects to different proportions. Figure 13.6 shows the Size tab.

- *Protection* lets you choose whether an object is locked or not. A locked drawing object, once the worksheet or workbook is protected, cannot be edited until the worksheet or workbook is unprotected.
- *Properties* lets you choose how a drawn object moves if the underlying cells in a worksheet are moved, resized, or insertions or deletions occur. You can also choose whether or not the object will print when the worksheet on which it rests is printed. Figure 13.7 shows the Properties tab.

FIG. 13.6
The Size tab of the Format AutoShapes dialog box lets you control an object's size and scaling.

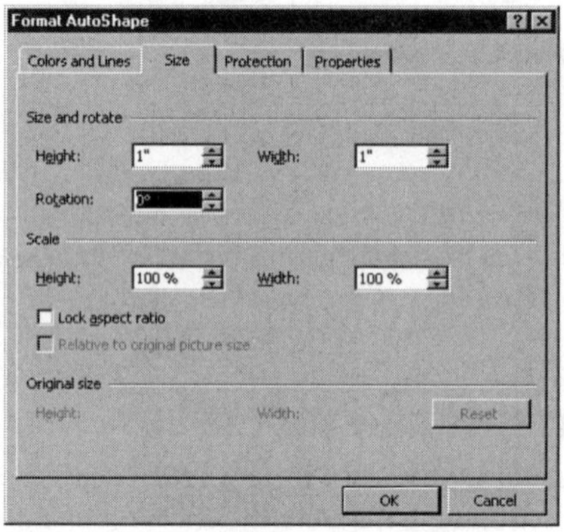

FIG. 13.7
The Properties tab of the Format AutoShapes dialog box lets you choose how an object is moved when the underlying worksheet cells are moved.

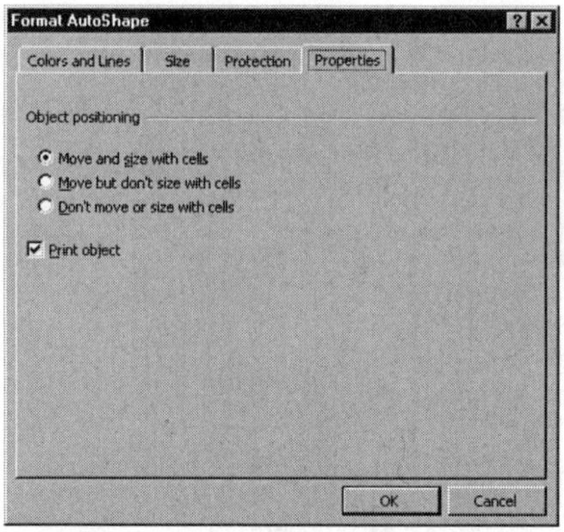

Using the Draw Menu on the Drawing Toolbar

The Draw menu on the Drawing toolbar contains a host of commands you can't find in Excel's normal menus. Most of the commands on the Draw menu concern object formatting and placement. Figure 13.8 shows the Draw menu; Table 13.2 details the commands you find on the Draw menu.

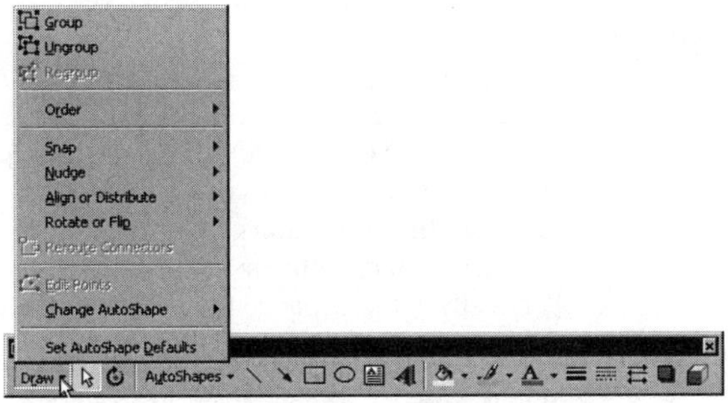

FIG. 13.8
Use the Draw menu for various formatting and placement commands.

Table 13.2 Draw Menu Commands

Command	Effect
Group	When multiple objects are selected, this command groups them so that they behave as a single object.
Ungroup	After grouping objects, you may need to ungroup them with this command in order to work with the individual objects within the group.
Regroup	This command is just like an "Undo Ungroup." After ungrouping a set of objects, instead of selecting them individually again and using the Group command, it's faster to use the Regroup command which restores the previous grouping.
Order	Use the submenu that appears when you access this command to choose in what order objects are displayed. You do this to control which opaque objects are "on top of" another. For a selected object, you can choose Bring to Front, Send to Back, Bring Forward, and Send Backward. Bring Forward and Send Backward move the object one layer up or down.
Snap	When drawing, it can often be helpful to have your drawn objects "snap" to locations on the screen. There are two options you can choose within the Snap command: To Grid and To Shape. Choosing To Grid causes any drawn objects to align with the underlying cells in a worksheet, while choosing To Shape causes any drawn objects to align with previously drawn objects.
Nudge	Use the four commands found in the Nudge submenu—Up, Down, Left, and Right—to move the selected object slightly in the direction you choose. You also can use the Ctrl key with an arrow key to achieve the same result.
Align or Distribute	There are eight commands found within the Align or Distribute submenu. These commands are only available when you have selected more than one object (using Shift+Click). With these eight commands, you can automatically align or distribute

continues

Table 13.2 Continued

Command	Effect
	objects relative to one another. For example, you can vertically align the middles of two or more objects, without moving any of them in other directions. When you have more than two objects selected, you can choose Distribute Horizontally or Distribute Vertically, which spaces the objects evenly from one another.
Rotate or Flip	Use the five commands in this menu to rotate or flip a selected object. You can choose from Free Rotate, Rotate Left, Rotate Right (both rotate 90 degrees), Flip Horizontal, and Flip Vertical.
Reroute Connectors	When you select a connector AutoShape (a line that connects other AutoShapes and is anchored to a place on each AutoShape), you can use the Reroute Connectors command to force all the connectors to be routed so that they connect in the same place on each object.
Edit Points	Use this command on a selected line object to edit the line's points. You can then right-click the line to add new points and segments to the line.
Change AutoShape	When you use an AutoShape and later decide that a different AutoShape would have been better, you don't have to delete and redraw the AutoShape. Instead, select it and then use this command to choose a different AutoShape.
Set AutoShape Defaults	After you format an AutoShape, choose this command to cause all of your formatting choices to be applied to other AutoShapes you draw. You can also select any AutoShape before choosing this command to use that shape's formatting as the new default.

Grouping and Ungrouping Drawn Objects When drawing objects, you may find that you want to format or edit many objects at once. Instead of having to select each object and format it individually, you can group the objects so they all act as if they are part of the same object. When you group objects, their individual handles disappear, and the entire group becomes surrounded by sizing handles.

To group drawn objects, follow these steps:

1. Select the first object you want to group.
2. Hold down the Shift key and select all other objects you want in the group. All the objects should remain selected.
3. Choose Draw, Group from the Drawing toolbar.
4. Move or format the objects as a group.

To ungroup a set of grouped objects, select the group. Then choose Draw, Ungroup from the Drawing toolbar. If you ungroup objects and later want to regroup the objects you previously had grouped, choose Draw, Regroup from the Drawing toolbar.

Rotating and Flipping Drawn Objects You can adjust the placement and position of a drawn object by using the Rotate or Flip command. You can rotate the object left or right 90 degrees at a time. You also can flip the object horizontally or vertically to reverse the position of the object. This feature is useful when you want a mirror image of an object.

To rotate or flip a drawn object, follow these steps:

1. Select the object you want to rotate or flip.
2. Choose Draw, Rotate or Flip from the Drawing toolbar.
3. Choose the desired option from the Rotate or Flip submenu: Rotate Left, Rotate Right, Flip Horizontal, or Flip Vertical.

TIP

If you need more flexibility when rotating or flipping objects, use the Free Rotate button on the Drawing toolbar. Then drag one of the rotation handles surrounding the object to the position you want. Click the Free Rotate button again to disable the feature.

Creating 3-D Objects

To take a 2-D AutoShape and convert it to a 3-D AutoShape, first draw the AutoShape. Then, with the AutoShape selected, open the 3-D menu on the Drawing toolbar (see Figure 13.9). Choose a 3-D perspective from the illustrations shown on the menu, and your shape is modified accordingly.

FIG. 13.9
Use the 3-D menu to choose from a wide variety of 3-D perspective effects.

Part III

Ch 13

After creating a 3-D object, you can use the 3-D Settings toolbar to make even more 3-D effect choices. Open the 3-D Settings toolbar by choosing 3-D, 3-D Settings from the Drawing toolbar. Figure 13.10 shows the 3-D Settings toolbar; Table 13.3 details the buttons on the 3-D Settings toolbar.

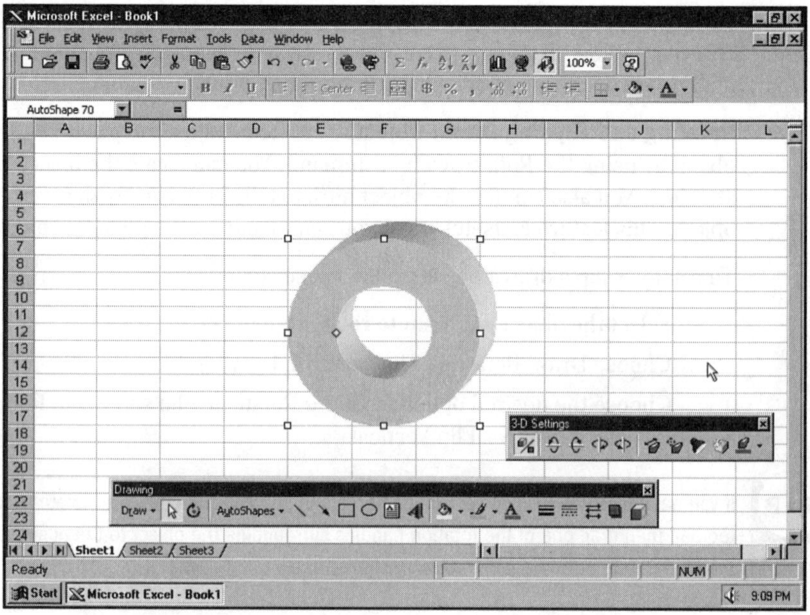

FIG. 13.10
The 3-D Settings toolbar contains a host of commands for formatting 3-D objects.

Table 13.3 3-D Settings Toolbar Buttons

Button	Name	Description
	3-D On/Off	Toggles the 3-D effect of the object.
	Tilt Down	Tilts the perspective of a 3-D object down slightly.
	Tilt Up	Tilts the perspective of a 3-D object up slightly.
	Tilt Left	Tilts the perspective of a 3-D object left slightly.
	Tilt Right	Tilts the perspective of a 3-D object right slightly.
	Depth	Opens a submenu from which you can choose the number of points (1/72 of an inch is a *point*) for the object's depth.
	Direction	Opens a submenu from which you can choose the direction (in 45 degree increments) from which the 3-D perspective is shown.

Button	Name	Description
	Lighting	Opens a submenu from which you can choose the direction from which simulated light is shined on the object. This affects the shading of the object's surfaces accordingly. You can also choose the brightness of the simulated light.
	Surface	Opens a submenu from which you can choose the surface texture of an object. Choose from Wire Frame, Matte, Plastic, and Metal.
	3-D Color	Chooses the color for the 3-D effect portion of the object.

Figure 13.11 shows three examples of 3-D objects created using the tools discussed in this section.

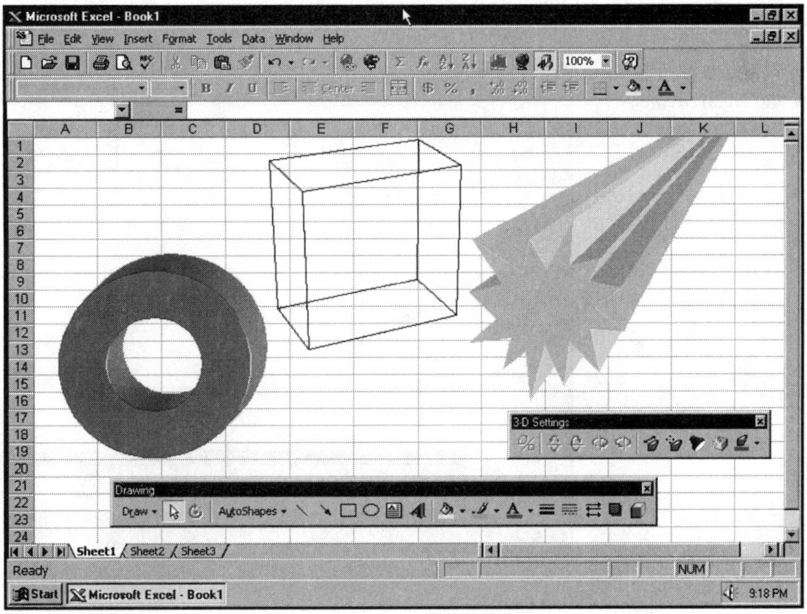

FIG. 13.11
You can create spiffy 3-D objects with Excel's 3-D drawing tools.

Creating Organization and Flow Charts

While there are many good dedicated programs designed to create organization and flow charts, you can easily create your own in Excel using various AutoShapes. Begin by drawing the boxes, circles, or other shapes that you need. (There are a variety of Flowchart shapes in the AutoShapes menu on the Drawing toolbar). Then use the AutoShapes menu to choose from a variety of Connectors, and use the connectors to connect the shapes.

TIP You can also generate organization charts in Excel using Microsoft Organization Chart, an OLE server application that comes with Office 97. Open the Insert menu, choose Picture, and then Organization Chart to access this program.

Connectors are drawn unlike other lines. When you choose a connector line, you first move your pointer over an existing shape. The existing shape displays a number of blue handles automatically when you move your pointer over the shape. Click the blue handle on the first shape, then click a blue handle on the second shape to anchor the connector to that place on the shape. Thereafter, moving either of the shapes causes the connector to be redrawn so that it always connects those two shapes in the two locations you chose.

Using a combination of AutoShapes and connectors, you can easily draw charts, such as the organization chart shown in Figure 13.12.

FIG. 13.12
Use Block AutoShapes and Connector AutoShapes to create flow and organization charts like this one.

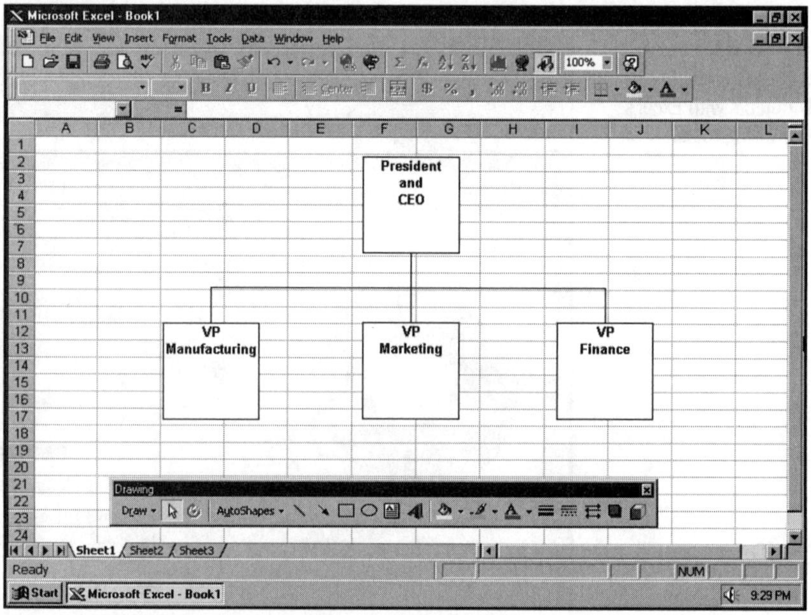

Using Clip Art in Excel

Clip art is a collection of graphics and pictures that is available for use in programs such as Excel. Clip art enables you to illustrate ideas with pictures. You can use clip art in place of columns or bars in a chart to add interest to a presentation, for example. You also can use clip art to create a company logo for a company invoice or expense statement. Many of Excel's built-in templates include a placeholder for you to insert a clip art logo. Be careful not to overdo your use of clip art; generally one effective use of clip art in a worksheet is sufficient.

Many clip art collections are sold in categories like business graphics, medical graphics, entertainment graphics, and so on. To locate clip art, look for ads in the back of computer magazines, particularly desktop publishing magazines. You also may find clip art packages available for purchase at your local software store.

Some programs, such as Excel, include free clip art collections. You use the Microsoft Clip Gallery in Excel to easily access these clip art images. You also can find collections of clip art on the Internet and online services such as CompuServe, America Online, and Prodigy.

To insert a clip art image, follow these steps:

1. In your worksheet, select the cell where you want the upper-left corner of the clip art to appear.
2. Choose Insert, Picture, Clip Art. Select the Clip Art tab in the Microsoft Clip Gallery dialog box.
3. Select a category from the list box on the left side of the dialog box. Then click the clip art symbol you want to use and select Insert.

NOTE If you cannot access the Microsoft Clip Gallery, you probably did not install this feature with Excel. For more information on how to install the Clip Gallery, search for "clip art" in Excel's Help system.

To insert a clip art image from a source other than the Microsoft Clip Gallery, choose Insert, Picture, From File. Then navigate to the drive and folder where the image is stored, select the file name, and choose Insert. You can use the Import Clips button in the Microsoft Clip Gallery dialog box if you want to add clip art images from other sources to the Clip Gallery.

Using WordArt in Excel

WordArt is a program that can generate text with a variety of different effects. Originally intended to be used with Word, since WordArt is an OLE server, its objects can be embedded in most OLE-aware applications.

To create WordArt in Excel, follow these steps:

1. Click the WordArt button on the Drawing toolbar. You see the WordArt Gallery shown in Figure 13.13. The gallery shows a number of different WordArt styles from which you can choose.
2. Select one of the displayed WordArt styles and click the OK button. You then see the Edit WordArt Text dialog box shown in Figure 13.14.
3. Type the text you want for your WordArt in the Text field, making sure that you choose the font, size, and attributes you want for the font. Click OK when you are done.
4. Your selected WordArt is generated and embedded onto the worksheet, and the WordArt toolbar is opened for you to use to further edit the WordArt, as shown in Figure 13.15.

FIG. 13.13
Use the WordArt Gallery to choose the basic style of WordArt you want...

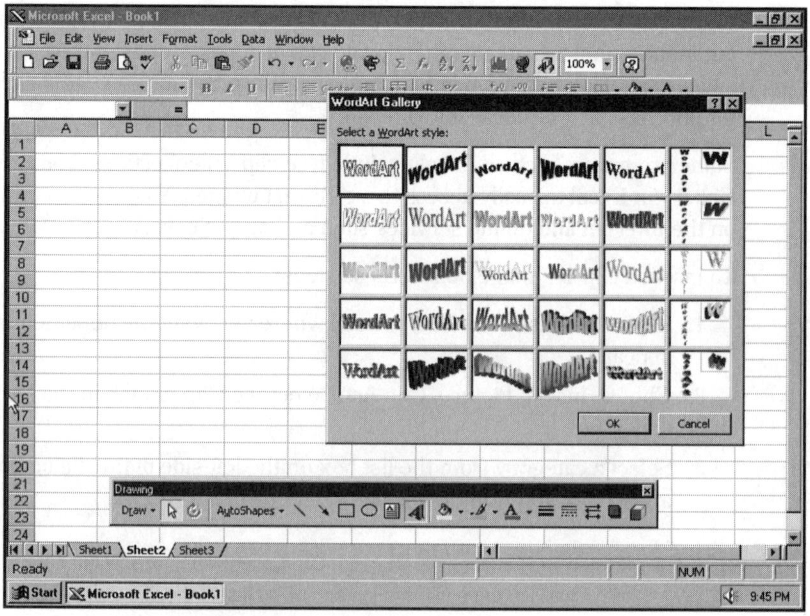

FIG. 13.14
...then enter the text for the WordArt with the Edit WordArt Text dialog box, and choose a font and font style...

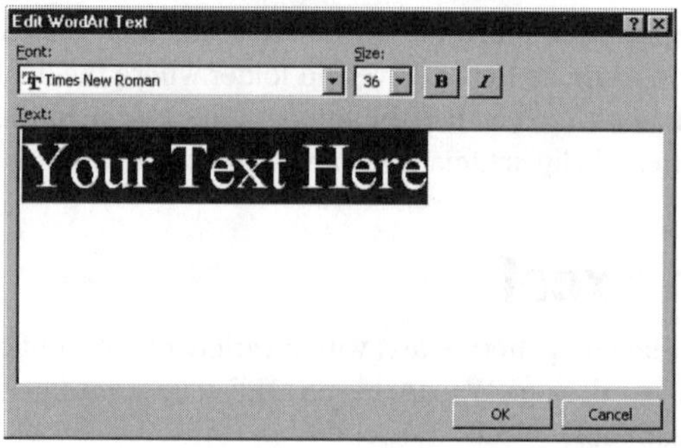

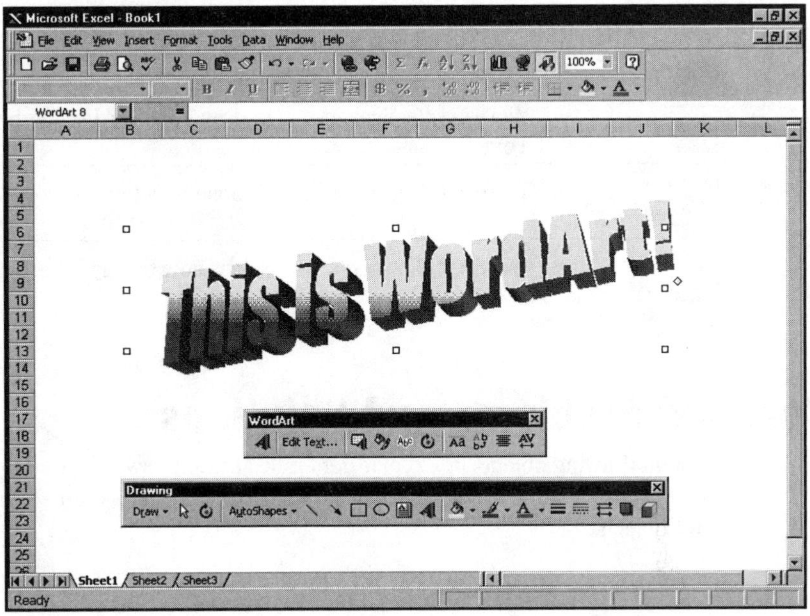

FIG. 13.15
...and your WordArt is created!

The WordArt toolbar is used to edit WordArt you create. Table 13.4 details the WordArt toolbar's buttons.

Table 13.4 WordArt Toolbar Buttons

Button	Name	Description
	Insert WordArt	Add WordArt (same as WordArt button on Drawing toolbar)
Edit Text...	Edit Text	Recall the Edit WordArt Text dialog box to change WordArt text
	WordArt Gallery	Choose a different WordArt gallery effect
	Format WordArt	Access the WordArt object's formatting dialog box
	WordArt Shape	Choose from additional shapes to which your WordArt is drawn
	Free Rotate	Rotate selected WordArt object
	WordArt Same Letter Heights	Cause all letters in selected WordArt to be drawn to the same height

continues

Table 13.4 Continued

Button	Name	Description
	WordArt Vertical Text	Redraw the WordArt with vertical text
	WordArt Alignment	Choose how text in WordArt is justified
	WordArt Character Spacing	Select how tightly letters within the WordArt are spaced

Common Problems and Solutions

Although drawing objects in Excel is generally straightforward, you may occasionally need some help to fine-tune your drawings. The following sections offer several tips for working with drawn objects.

Difficult to Align Objects

Sometimes when using the alignment commands to align a number of objects in certain ways, you cannot use the alignment commands to get the objects aligned the way you want. For example, examine Figure 13.16.

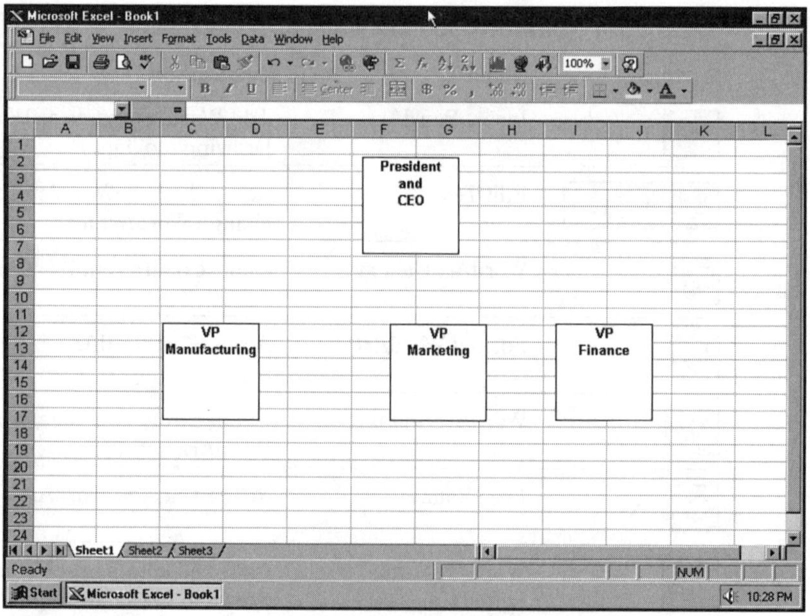

FIG. 13.16 Sometimes it's difficult to align objects exactly as you want.

If you're having trouble aligning a number of objects, consider these tips:

- If the alignment commands aren't working the way you want, consider drawing a line and then using that line as a guide to position the objects. Once the objects are arranged the way you want, delete the line.
- Consider using the Group command before using alignment commands. For instance, to evenly distribute the three VP boxes and then align the VP Marketing box with the President and CEO box, you could follow these steps:
  1. Select the three VP boxes and use the Align Middle command so that they're aligned top to bottom.
  2. With the three VP boxes still selected, use the Distribute Horizontally command so that they're evenly spaced.
  3. Group the three VP boxes together into one object.
  4. Select the grouped boxes and the President and CEO box, and then use the Align Center command so that all four boxes are arranged properly.
- It can be easier to align objects when you set one of the two Snap drawing options in the Draw menu of the Drawing toolbar. Try choosing To Grid, and then moving each object so that they align to the worksheet cell grid.
- If you use an alignment command and your objects get moved to a position you don't like, remember that you can activate the Undo command to reverse the alignment.

Trouble Getting Attractive Results

Until you gain experience with Excel's drawing tools, some things you might try could result in poor results. When drawing in Excel, keep these tips in mind:

- When drawing fine details, set the Zoom in Excel to 200%.
- When drawing curves, don't use the Scribble AutoShape. Instead, use the Curve AutoShape.
- Even if a curve or angled line looks jagged on the screen, it might print smoothly (particularly with a circle or the curved line AutoShapes). Don't waste a lot of time worrying about "jaggies" until you see how the drawing prints.
- If your mouse is too jumpy to draw with precisely, change its properties so that it tracks more slowly in the Control Panel.
- To see colors and gradients as clearly as possible, make sure your monitor and video board are using at least 256 colors.
- If you're trying to get good-looking results on a black and white laser printer, use shades of gray for your color selections, and test how they print on your printer. Try creating a "proof sheet" that contains objects that use different shades of gray, and then print it and keep it near your computer as a guide to what different shades look like on the printer. Every printer prints grays differently, and what looks great on your screen may look terrible when printed (and vice-versa).

- Using all of the special-effects features in Excel's drawing tools, such as light sources, 3-D effects, and shadows, should be done with care. Elegant, simple drawings often look more professional than busy, cluttered drawings with lots of whiz-bang effects.
- A drawing that looks great on a black and white laser printer may look lousy when you transfer it to an overhead transparency and use it with a projector. If you're generating transparencies, make sure to test your drawing the way you'll use it to see how it looks.
- If you're drawing lines to connect existing shapes, use the line connector AutoShapes instead of the line tool. When you move the connected shapes later, you won't have to worry so much about positioning the lines.

From Here...

In this chapter, you learned how to use Excel's drawing tools to draw objects in the worksheet. You then discovered how to edit drawn objects by formatting the objects, copying and moving objects, rotating and flipping objects, and so on. In addition, you learned how to create 3-D objects and organization charts, and how to use clip art and WordArt in Excel. Refer to the following chapters for related topics:

- Chapter 10, "Creating Charts," provides step-by-step information on using the Chart Wizard to create and modify charts.
- Chapter 11, "Advanced Chart Topics," explains how to fine-tune your charts by creating trend lines, adding data markers, and so on.
- Chapter 12, "A Field Guide to Excel Chart Types," covers each of Excel's chart types in depth and explains which chart type best fits the data you want to represent in the chart.

PART IV

Creating and Using Excel Databases

CHAPTER 14

Building Excel Databases

by Gail A. Perry

In its simplest form, a database is an organized list. The more complex your database, the more information your list will contain. The row and column structure of the spreadsheet program lends itself well to creating lists of information. It presents you with the opportunity for organizing your data in meaningful and easily retrievable order.

In this chapter, you will learn about the advantages and disadvantages of using Excel instead of a program designed specifically to manipulate data. You also will learn how to create your own database in Excel, how to add data to a database, and how to search for data meeting particular criteria. ■

Understand the concept of the database

A database can be a sophisticated tool for managing information. This chapter explains the basic theory behind the use of the database.

Prepare to create your own database

Learn how to plan a database and about what to consider before you start entering data.

Set up your database

Create the structure of your database on your Excel spreadsheet.

Enter your data

Learn efficient ways to get the data into your database.

Find specific data

How to retrieve information after you've entered the data you need to know.

Sort your data

Rearrange the information in your database in ways that make the information work for you.

Understanding Basic Database Concepts

Your database will contain pieces of information that are related to one another. For example, a database containing the names and addresses of your employees will include first names that go with last names, addresses that go with employee names, cities than go with addresses, states that go with cities, and so on.

To have a sensible way of grouping this information, place related information in a single row, with a separate column for each individual item. To continue the example of the employee list, one employee's information would occupy a single row in a database, with a separate column for each item, such as first name, last name, address, city, and state. In this way, you can build the database by presenting a separate row for individual members of the group but using the same columns for like pieces of information. Each employee's first name will appear in one column, each employee's last name will appear in another column, and so on.

In a database, individual items are referred to as *records*. Pieces of information within each record are referred to as *fields*. Continuing the above example, each person for whom you enter information in the employee list database would represent one record. Each piece of information about the person, such as the first name, last name, or job description, represents a field. Each person, or record, in the database can have information in every field.

Generally speaking, a row in a database is synonymous with the concept of a record, and a column in a database represents a field.

The format of the database remains constant: rows for individual members of the group, columns for pieces of information that repeat throughout the group. The beauty of the database is in the planning and design. The better designed your database or list, the more effortless the retrieval of your data will be.

A *flat database* is a two-dimensional database: rows and columns on a single screen. This is the type of database you create when you use Excel or any spreadsheet program. The employee list previously discussed is an example of a flat database. Figure 14.1 shows a flat database.

A *relational database* adds a third dimension to your data. Data is stored in many different tables or files that are linked to one another by a pre-determined relationship (thus the name, relational).

NOTE You can create a flat database in a spreadsheet program (such as Excel), a word-processing program (such as Word), or a database program (such as Access). To create a relational database, you must use a database program such as Access, Paradox, or dBase.

Think of a computerized library catalog in which a particular book is a member of a larger listing of all the books at the library. In addition, the book is linked to a listing of the branches of the library where copies of that book can be found. The book also is linked to the library card number of the customer who has checked out that book. The customer number is linked to a database of the library customers, a database that includes the address and telephone number of each customer. Each database—the book titles, the library branches, the customer names—is separate, yet they're associated with one another by a common link (book call number, customer library card number, library branch name) so that information can be gathered from all databases simultaneously. Thus with one request to this relational database, you can determine the name of a book, the name and location of the library branch that houses the book, and the name and telephone number of the customer who currently possesses the book.

FIG. 14.1
An example of a flat two-dimensional Excel database.

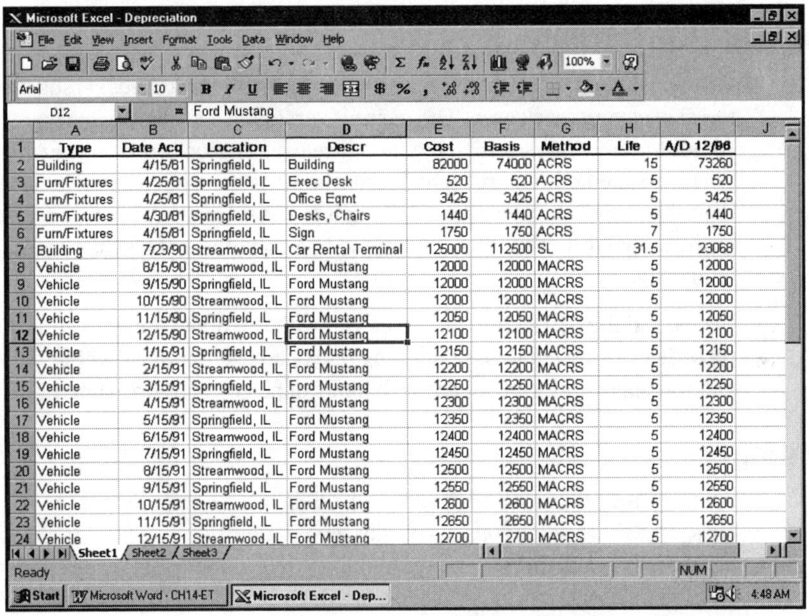

	A	B	C	D	E	F	G	H	I
1	Type	Date Acq	Location	Descr	Cost	Basis	Method	Life	A/D 12/96
2	Building	4/15/81	Springfield, IL	Building	82000	74000	ACRS	15	73260
3	Furn/Fixtures	4/25/81	Springfield, IL	Exec Desk	520	520	ACRS	5	520
4	Furn/Fixtures	4/25/81	Springfield, IL	Office Eqmt	3425	3425	ACRS	5	3425
5	Furn/Fixtures	4/30/81	Springfield, IL	Desks, Chairs	1440	1440	ACRS	5	1440
6	Furn/Fixtures	4/15/81	Springfield, IL	Sign	1750	1750	ACRS	7	1750
7	Building	7/23/90	Streamwood, IL	Car Rental Terminal	125000	112500	SL	31.5	23068
8	Vehicle	8/15/90	Streamwood, IL	Ford Mustang	12000	12000	MACRS	5	12000
9	Vehicle	9/15/90	Springfield, IL	Ford Mustang	12000	12000	MACRS	5	12000
10	Vehicle	10/15/90	Streamwood, IL	Ford Mustang	12000	12000	MACRS	5	12000
11	Vehicle	11/15/90	Springfield, IL	Ford Mustang	12050	12050	MACRS	5	12050
12	Vehicle	12/15/90	Streamwood, IL	Ford Mustang	12100	12100	MACRS	5	12100
13	Vehicle	1/15/91	Springfield, IL	Ford Mustang	12150	12150	MACRS	5	12150
14	Vehicle	2/15/91	Streamwood, IL	Ford Mustang	12200	12200	MACRS	5	12200
15	Vehicle	3/15/91	Springfield, IL	Ford Mustang	12250	12250	MACRS	5	12250
16	Vehicle	4/15/91	Streamwood, IL	Ford Mustang	12300	12300	MACRS	5	12300
17	Vehicle	5/15/91	Springfield, IL	Ford Mustang	12350	12350	MACRS	5	12350
18	Vehicle	6/15/91	Streamwood, IL	Ford Mustang	12400	12400	MACRS	5	12400
19	Vehicle	7/15/91	Springfield, IL	Ford Mustang	12450	12450	MACRS	5	12450
20	Vehicle	8/15/91	Streamwood, IL	Ford Mustang	12500	12500	MACRS	5	12500
21	Vehicle	9/15/91	Springfield, IL	Ford Mustang	12550	12550	MACRS	5	12550
22	Vehicle	10/15/91	Streamwood, IL	Ford Mustang	12600	12600	MACRS	5	12600
23	Vehicle	11/15/91	Springfield, IL	Ford Mustang	12650	12650	MACRS	5	12650
24	Vehicle	12/15/91	Streamwood, IL	Ford Mustang	12700	12700	MACRS	5	12700

Excel or Access: Which Program Should You Choose?

There are some basic considerations to contemplate when deciding which program to use for your data—some of these considerations have little to do with the results you expect to achieve from your database:

- If you only have Excel on your computer, that's probably the program you want to use.
- If Excel is the only program you know how to use, you might not want to or be able to take the time to learn how to use a dedicated database program, such as Access.
- If others are going to use your database, you will want to consider their skills as well. Which program is available to the other people who will use this database? With what program are they more comfortable? What is their preference?

The decision to use one program over another also depends on many factors, including the size of the database, the limitations of your computer, the type of information you want to analyze, and the use you want to make of the information once it is collected.

NOTE If you need to learn to use Access because your database requires a relational database rather than a flat database, you will be pleased to know that many of the commands and techniques you have learned in Excel carry over to other Microsoft programs, including Access. Also, you might be interested in purchasing the book, *Special Edition Using Access 97*, to help you learn the intricacies of using Access.

Size of the Database

Perhaps the most obvious difference between the worksheet versus the database program is the size of your work area. The current version of Excel provides you with 65,536 rows (2^{16}). Although this represents a hefty increase over earlier versions of Excel, which featured 16,384 (2^{14}) rows, and other spreadsheet programs that provide only 8,192 (2^{13}) rows, this can severely limit the size of your database. Taking into consideration the need to include headings above each row, your database will be limited to a maximum of 65,535 records or individual pieces of information.

Access, on the other hand, provides you with the opportunity to enter more than two billion records in a single database. Linking one database to others within the Access program gives you the opportunity to categorize billions of pieces of information.

Memory

Spreadsheet programs, such as Excel, utilize your computer's RAM (random access memory) for spreadsheet operations. Typically, a computer has 8–32M of RAM with which to work. This necessarily limits the size of your database because the database cannot exceed your RAM. Such database programs as Access, on the other hand, utilize hard drive space for database operations. Therefore, the size of your database is limited only by the size of your hard drive, which can range anywhere from several hundred megabytes to several gigabytes.

Is a Single Set of Records Enough?

As mentioned before, the flat database model in Excel lets you enter information on a single sheet. You can enter a list of your inventory items in a flat database, and a list of your vendors with addresses, phone numbers, and names of sales personnel, in a different flat database, but you need a relational database if you want to simultaneously retrieve information from both flat databases, such as the name of an inventory item, and the name of the salesperson with whom you deal when you order the item from a particular vendor.

Number Crunching

Excel is a number program. If you plan to perform complicated calculations on the results derived from information extracted from your database, you can't do better than to perform your work in Excel. You can perform mathematical operations in a database program, of course, but the more math you plan to do, the more your spreadsheet shines.

Planning an Excel Database

Ask yourself the following questions:

- Why do you want your information listed in an Excel database?
- What types of reports do you want to generate?
- Who else will need to use your data and for what purpose?
- What is the computer/Excel skill level of others who will use your database?
- What information do you have, and what information do you need to generate?
- For the information you have, in what order of entry can it be most efficiently accessed?
- What methods (formulas and so on) will you use to generate the information you require?

Consider the case of a company that wants to catalog its fixed assets so it can produce various asset reports and depreciation reports. The following list examines the previous questions in more detail:

- *Why do you want your information listed in an Excel database?* You want your asset information cataloged in one place where it is easy to access and study. You need to generate financial and tax reports using some or all of the assets in your possession. You and your coworkers are familiar with Excel and are comfortable using the program. Your data lends itself to a flat database because you don't need to enter such information as vendor data, you don't need to access information about the employees who use the assets, and you don't need a history of the use of the assets (if any of these items are a requirement, you should consider using a relational database program).
- *What types of reports do you want to generate?* All potential reports you will need to compile from this data should be considered at this early stage; otherwise, important information might be left out of your database or might not be placed conveniently, which would make it difficult to generate reports. In this example, you will need to produce the following:

  A list showing the cost and accumulated depreciation of assets owned for financial statements

  A cost list of assets owned, arranged by location for property tax reports

  A report of calculated depreciation expense for income tax purposes

- *Who else will use your data and for what purpose?* Your property acquisitions manager will use the data to produce a report of assets owned at each location and their condition. Your data entry person will enter information into the database.
- *What is the computer/Excel skill level of others who will use your database?* Your skill level is high (of course it is—you're reading this book!). Your property acquisitions manager has limited Excel skill. Your data entry person is comfortable with entering information into a spreadsheet as long as your directions are clear.

- *What information do you have versus what information do you need to generate?* The cost, depreciation methods used, locations of the assets, and dates acquired of your assets are written in a paper journal. You must generate depreciation expense information for the assets.
- *For the information you have, in what order of entry can it be most efficiently accessed?* Your written records contain the following information for fixed assets that will be useful in this database:

  Date acquired
  Description of item
  Type of asset
  Asset number
  Vendor from whom asset was purchased
  Location of item
  Cost
  Depreciable basis
  Method of depreciation
  Depreciable life of asset
  Accumulated depreciation through the most recent year-end, such as 12/31/96

  You organize your assets by type for your financial report. You organize your assets by date acquired and then by type for the tax depreciation report. You organize your assets by location and then by type for your property tax report. Because each of these reports relies in part on an organization by type, and because you produce financial reports monthly, tax depreciation reports quarterly, and property tax reports annually, the asset type seems to be the most important organizing field for your assets. Therefore, you should use asset type as the first field in your database. Date acquired seems to be of secondary importance, based on the reports you want to produce from this database, so that should be your second field.
- *What methods (formulas and so on) will you use to generate the information you require?* Your depreciation report will require the use of mathematical formulas for calculating depreciation. Check your tax guides or ask your accountant to get the proper depreciation formulas.

This is the type of thought process you want to put yourself through as you plan the organization of your database. Plan your entire database structure by organizing pieces of data in order of importance and by excluding any data you don't need, such as the vendor, in the previous example.

Setting Up the Structure

After you've planned the information you need for the entire body of information available to you, you are ready to determine the structure of your database:

- The first row of your database will contain column headings. Provide a unique name for each column of your database. This is the *field name.*
- Determine which column of your spreadsheet you want to use for the first column of your data. The first column of your database doesn't necessarily have to begin in column A.
- Set up columns so they are adjacent to one another.
- Use a separate column for each *field,* or piece of information relating to individual records (or assets, to continue the previous example).

TIP Field names should be short and succinct, yet descriptive enough so that anyone using your database will know immediately what information goes in that particular field.

Following the fixed asset and depreciation example, the spreadsheet looks like the one shown in Figure 14.2.

FIG. 14.2
Enter a brief heading in each column of your database. The heading corresponds to the type of data that will appear in the column.

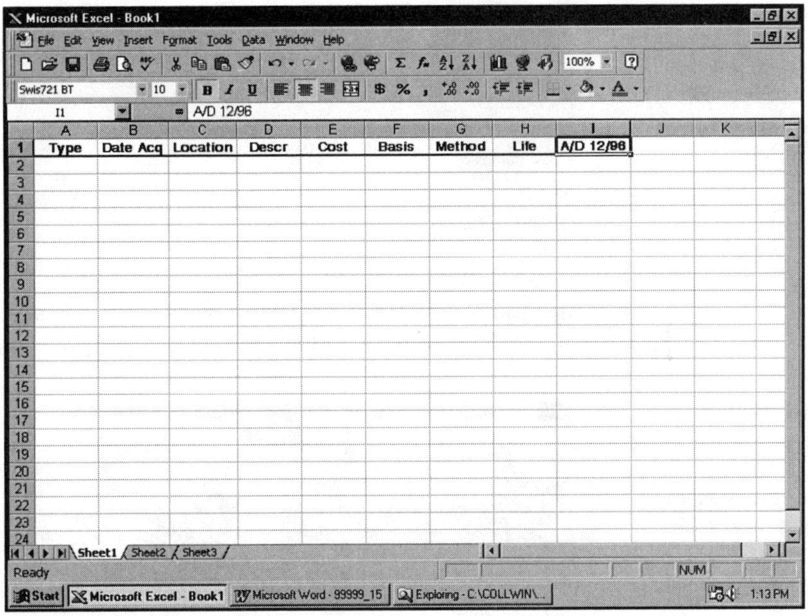

TIP When entering column headings, you only need to enter a heading for each piece of information your database requires. Remember, your records can contain data that doesn't need to be entered in the database.

After you've entered all your headings, you might want to adjust column widths, typeface, alignment, or other formatting styles. Changing the formatting of your headings makes them stand out from the rest of the data in your database.

▶ **See** "Formatting Your Worksheets," **p. 129**

Using the Database Form to Enter Data

Although you can directly enter your data into the spreadsheet, it will be easier for you and those who will use the database if you create a database form:

- The data entry person will be less likely to enter information into the wrong fields because the fields in the form are easy to distinguish.
- The data entry person doesn't have to posses any particular Excel skills enter data.
- Using the database form for data entry ensures that all data gets associated with the database.

Follow these steps to create a database form for entering data:

1. Select any cell in the row beneath your column headings (in the example, it's row 2). This is the first record that will receive data. Choose Data, Form (see Figure 14.3).

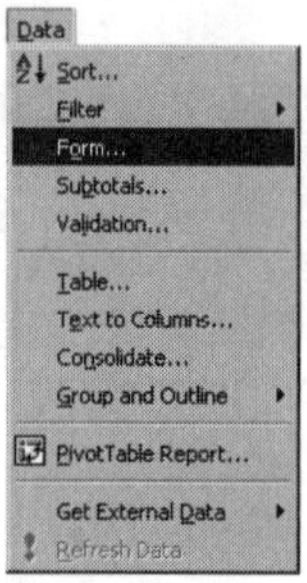

FIG. 14.3
Place the cursor in the row beneath the column headings, and then choose Data, Form to begin entering data.

2. The first time you choose Data, Form in a new database, you see an alert box (see Figure 14.4). Click OK in the alert box, and you are ready to begin entering data.

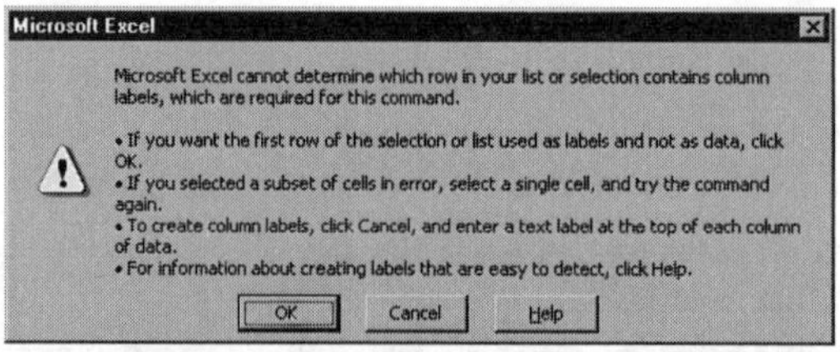

FIG. 14.4
The alert box appears if you choose Data, Form when the database is empty. Clicking OK allows you to proceed to the next step of data entry.

3. The data entry dialog box appears (see Figure 14.5). You will see an input text box corresponding to each data field (column heading) in your database.
4. Fill in the blanks in the data entry dialog box, as demonstrated in Figure 14.6. You can press Tab to get from one box to the next (press Shift+Tab to move backwards one box at a time), or you can click each box to progress. Press Enter or choose New to continue to the next record.

FIG. 14.5
This data entry dialog box has been customized for your database. Notice there is a text box for each of your column headings.

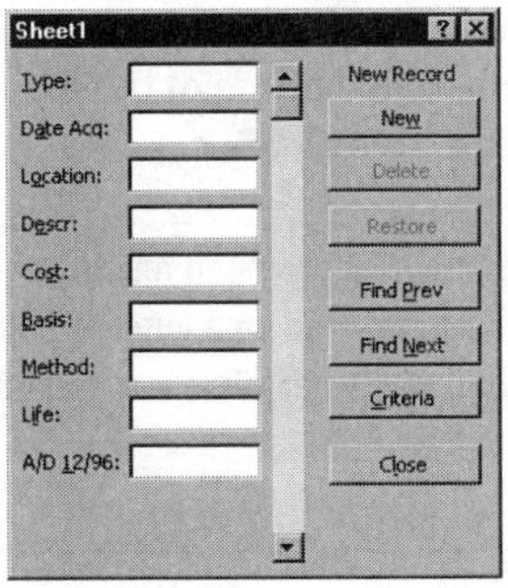

FIG. 14.6
Choose the Data, Form command to display this data entry and edit form, on which you can enter or change data for your database.

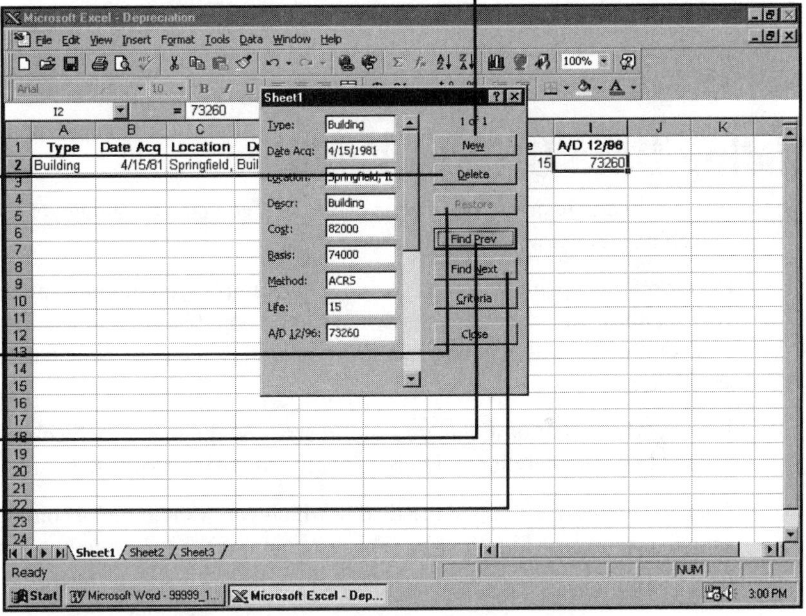
Click here to create a new record
Click here to permanently remove the current record
Click here to undo changes made in the current record
Click here to see the previous record
Click here to see the next record

As you enter data, you will see it displayed on the spreadsheet screen behind your data entry box. You don't have to enter all your data at once. If you are finished entering data for now, choose the Close button. The data entry box will close, and your database will appear onscreen.

TIP When entering figures in your database, enter the raw numbers with no commas or dollar signs. Instead, change the number format of the columns in the database to incorporate the style you wish to see. It will be easy to change the style at a later time.

▶ **See** "Mastering Number Formats," **p. 148**

At any time, you can add additional data by clicking anywhere in the database and choosing Data, Form. New data is automatically entered at the bottom of the list. You will learn about sorting data in the "Sorting Data" section later in this chapter.

TIP When you view your database, you might notice that some columns need resizing so you can view all the data within it. Simply double-click the bar to the right of the column letter to adjust a column width to the Best Fit. A nice side effect to resizing columns is that the next time you open the data entry dialog box, the input text boxes will be larger as well.

TIP You don't have to use the data entry dialog box to enter data into your database. This database is, after all, a spreadsheet. The form should be used as a timesaver, but if you find it quicker to enter information directly into the spreadsheet (for example, if you have several records with repeating data that can be copied from one cell to another), by all means do so.

▶ **See** "Entering Text and Values," **p. 86**

Finding Data Using AutoFilter

It's easy to find information in your database if you take advantage of the tools available for searching and extracting data.

First, determine what you want to find. For example, you might want to find all the records in your database that share one particular field. To find items with a common field (such as all the assets located in one city, or all the assets purchased on the same date), choose Data, Filter, AutoFilter.

When you choose AutoFilter, you see an arrow at the top of each column in your database (see Figure 14.7). You might need to scroll to the top of your spreadsheet to see these arrows.

Click the arrow at the top of the field in which you want to find a common feature. A drop-down list will appear (see Figure 14.8). This list contains the following options:

- *(All...)* Redisplays the entire list of unfiltered records.
- *(Top 10...)* Displays the 10 most repeated objects in this field (other options as well as this feature are covered in Chapter 15).
- *(Custom...)* Lets you customize the filter (see Chapter 15).
- *Exact values* A complete list of all the unique items that appear in that particular field. Choose one item and the resulting database will include only records containing that item.
- *(Blanks...)* Displays all records containing a blank in this field.
- *(NonBlanks...)* Displays all records that contain data of any kind (non-blanks) in this field.

Choosing one of the unique items in the AutoFilter drop-down list results in a database display of only the items that match the item you chose. Other items in your database will be hidden from sight.

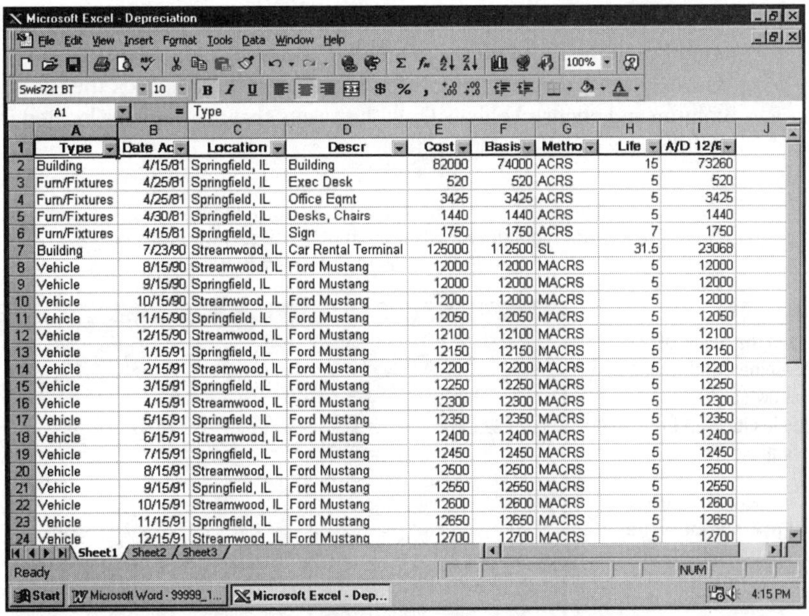

FIG. 14.7
AutoFilter places an arrow at the top of each column; you can use the arrow to view a list of all the unique records in that particular field.

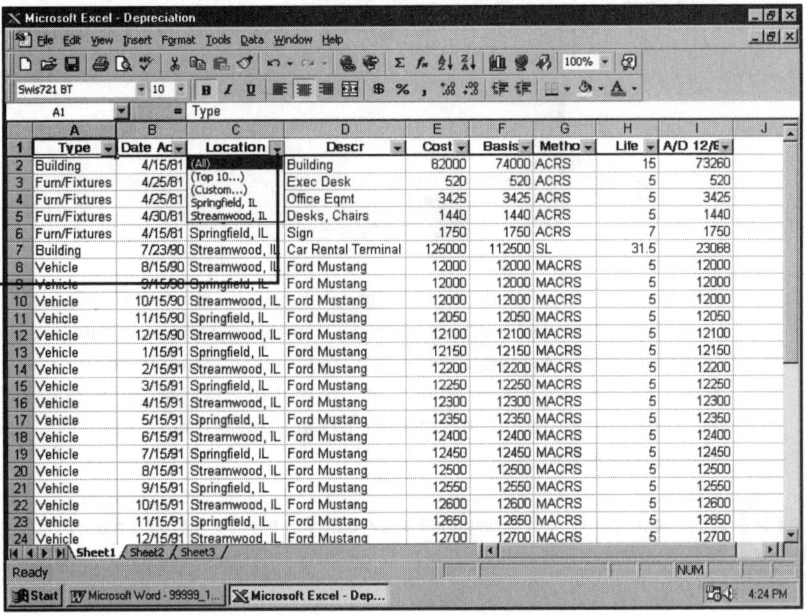

FIG. 14.8
Click the arrow at the top of any column, and then click any option in the drop-down list to display records meeting the selected criteria.

Click here to open a drop-down list of choices

To further isolate specific items in your database, click the AutoFilter arrow at the top of another column and choose an item from that list.

In the fixed asset example in this chapter, to find vehicles from the Springfield, IL, location, you would click the AutoFilter arrow in the Location column and choose Springfield, IL. A list of the assets located in Springfield, IL, will appear on-screen. Click the AutoFilter arrow in the Type column and choose Vehicle. Only the assets that are vehicles located in Springfield, IL, will be visible on-screen (see Figure 14.9).

FIG. 14.9
This is the result of searching the database to show only the vehicles located in Springfield, IL.

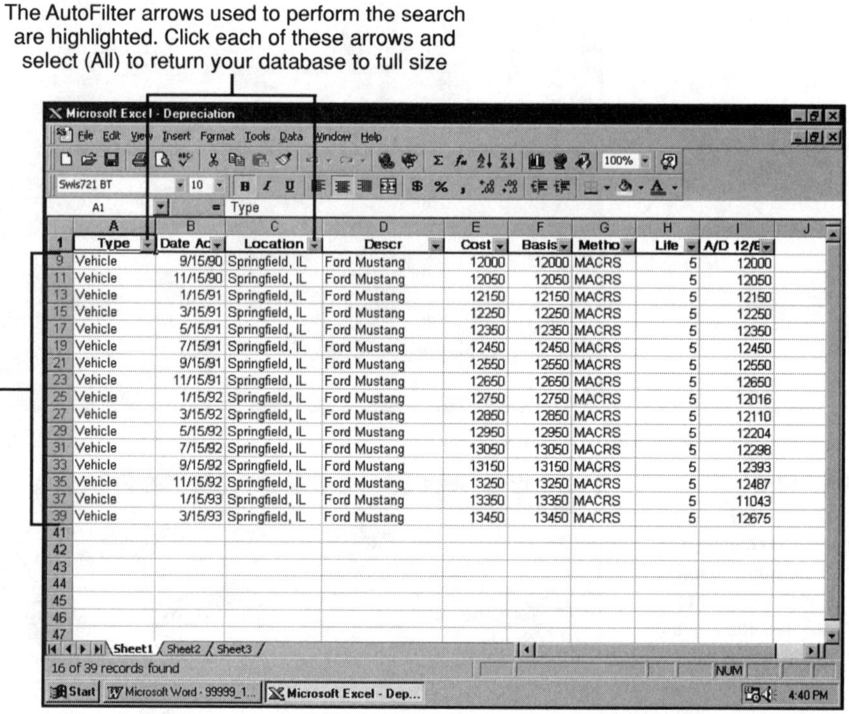

When you perform a search of your database, the arrows are highlighted at the top of the AutoFilter columns that have been used in the search. This way you quickly know which columns were used to isolate records from your database. In addition, notice that the row numbers appear in a different color than the rest of your spreadsheet and there are gaps between the numbers of rows. The missing rows are those that contain records that didn't meet your search requirements.

TIP While your filtered data is displayed on-screen, you might want to print a report. You can also copy the filtered data to a new worksheet and save it there to preserve the filtered list.

Viewing Your Entire Database After a Search

When you use the AutoFilter, the resulting on-screen database contains only the records that met your filtering requirements. The rest of the database is still there, it is just blocked from view. To quickly return your entire database to screen, choose Data, Filter, Show All. The entire database reappears and the filter arrows remain at the top of each column so you can perform other searches.

Alternatively, you can choose Data, Filter, AutoFilter. This turns off the AutoFilter feature (the arrows disappear from the tops of the columns) and at the same time returns the entire database to the screen.

What if your search resulted in isolating information from two columns (both the Location column and the Type column in the previous example) and you want to return all the items to the Type column but retain the search of the Location column. You can click the AutoFilter arrow at the top of any filtered column and select (All...). This has the effect of returning all items that had been filtered from the selected column, but leaving other searches in place. In the previous example, a search was performed to list only the records of assets located in Springfield, IL; then a further search resulted in only the vehicles among the Springfield, IL, assets. Clicking the arrow at the top of the Type column and selecting (All...) would return all of the assets from the Springfield, IL, location to the screen. The search for the Springfield, IL, location is still intact.

Saving Your Database

You can save your database at any time, whether or not the entire database is showing onscreen. You don't have to restore all of your database to the screen to save the entire database. Even if you have searched the database and only one or two records are showing of a total of thousands of records, saving your database file will save the entire file, including assets not currently showing.

Sorting Data

Sort your database quickly by the items in any single field. Click any cell (even the header row) in the field by which you want to sort, then click the A-Z sort button to sort alphabetically or chronologically from A to Z or lowest to highest number. Click the Z-A sort button to sort in reverse. Excel knows the boundaries of your database and knows that the first row contains headers; it sorts the entire database by the field you have chosen.

CAUTION

Sorting your database using the sort buttons on the Excel toolbar results in a sort of the *visible* database. If part of your database was hidden by the AutoFilter feature, the sort will apply only to the records you see onscreen. When you return the entire database to the screen, resort the database if you want to enforce a particular sort for the entire database.

TIP When you sort a database, the original order of items is lost. You can recover the original order of items in the database if you have a saved version of the database in which records are ordered in the

continues

continued

original order. However, if you save a sorted database, replacing the original file, the original order may be lost forever. If you think you might need to display or print the database in its original order sometime in the future, include a number field as one of the columns in the database and number the items chronologically as you enter them. In the future, you can perform a sort of the database using the number field as your main sorting field, thus restoring the original order of the records.

You can perform a more sophisticated sort, sorting up to three fields at a time:

1. Choose Data, Sort.
2. The Sort dialog box appears (see Figure 14.10). Select the first (primary) field on which you want to sort in the first text box.

FIG. 14.10
The Sort dialog box gives you the opportunity to sort your data by up to three levels, and you can choose ascending or descending order for each level.

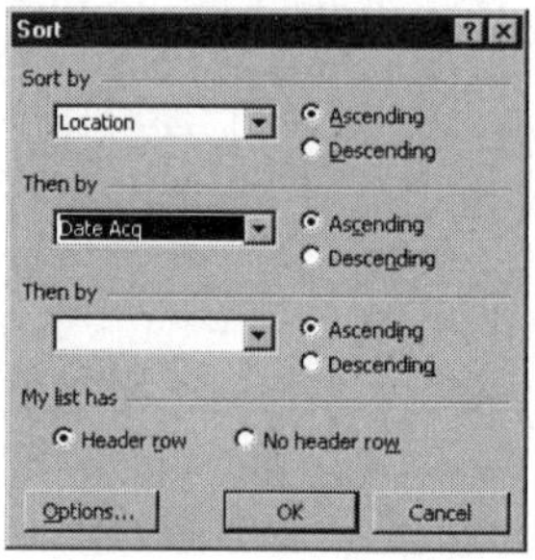

3. Select the second and third fields (if required) on which you want to perform your sort.
4. Indicate whether your sort should be in ascending (A-Z) or descending (Z-A) order. Make sure the My List Has a Header Row check box is selected.
5. Choose OK. The entire visible portion of the database will be sorted in the order you selected.

Common Problems and Solutions

The following is a list of common problems encountered when designing a database in Excel.

The initial design of the database is formed from knowledge of the data at hand rather than the output requirements of the database.

Take the time up front to determine exactly what you want this database to accomplish. This point can't be emphasized enough.

Repeating data is entered into the spreadsheet using the data form.

If you have data that repeats in several cells of the database (such as the same state for a list of employee names and addresses), use the copying skills you learned previously in this book to copy the information to the cells of your spreadsheet, rather than entering the state name again and again on each screen of the data form.

Searching is performed by scrolling through the database, looking at one item at a time.

Old habits can be hard to break, but this is one habit worth breaking. If you are looking for a particular item or group of items in your database, use the AutoFilter feature to search quickly for field information.

From Here...

In this chapter, you learned the basic operations for working with a database in Excel. By now you should be ready to experiment with the advanced techniques for filtering and working with your data, which are covered in Chapter 15. In addition, you may find the following sections of this book of related interest.

- Chapter 5, "Printing Worksheets," discusses creative ways in which you can print selected areas of your worksheet and repeat titles on each page.
- Chapter 10, "Creating Charts," shows you how you can chart the numerical data you extract from your database.
- The section "Partnering Access with Excel," in Chapter 24, "Integrating Excel with Other Office Applications," provides a discussion of ways in which you can combine the best of both programs to achieve control over your database.

CHAPTER 15

Using Advanced Excel Database Techniques

by Gail A. Perry

You created a database and you have a lengthy list of important items. Now take a look at some of the many ways to get at those items, use them in mathematical functions, and extract the data you need.

You can apply the features you learn about in this chapter to your entire database, or you can filter a portion of the data and use only that portion with the techniques you will learn. ■

Use mathematical totals with your data

Learn to perform totaling and subtotaling functions on your data.

Filter your data using advanced techniques

View and print only the data that meets the criteria you select.

Create custom lists

Learn to use sophisticated filtering techniques to customize your data further.

Use functions to find the data you need

Twelve functions designed just for databases will make your work easier.

Subtotaling Data

You don't have to dust off your math skills to generate totals and subtotals from the numbers in your database. Excel will subtotal your data for you.

Excel provides several subtotal functions that can give you interesting insights into your data:

- *Sum*. Returns the sum of numbers in a group.
- *Count*. Returns the quantity of items in a group.
- *Average*. Returns the average value of numbers in a group.
- *Max*. Returns the highest value of a group of numbers.
- *Min*. Returns the smallest value of a group of numbers.
- *Product*. Returns the product of all the numbers in a group multiplied together.
- *Count Nums*. Returns the quantity of all items in a group that have numeric value.
- *StdDev*. Returns an estimated measure of how widely numbers in a group vary from the average of the group.
- *StdDevp*. Returns a true measure of how widely numbers in a group vary from the average of the entire population.
- *Var*. Returns an estimated measure of the variance of numbers in a group.
- *Varp*. Returns a true measure of the variance of the numbers compared to the entire population.

To create subtotals in your database, follow these steps:

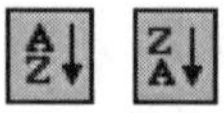

1. Click the column (field) for which you want to create subtotals, and then use the sort buttons to sort the database. In the fixed asset database (refer to Chapter 14), you might sort the list first by asset type so you can subtotal to find out the total cost of each type of asset, as shown in Figure 15.1.

CAUTION

It is imperative that you sort your database before creating subtotals. Otherwise, you will be subtotaling every change in a field from one record to the next.

2. Choose Data, Subtotals. The Subtotal dialog box appears (see Figure 15.2).
3. Make the following selections in the Subtotal dialog box:
   - In the At Each Change In drop-down list, select the field by which you want to subtotal. You can select only one field. In this example, select the Type field.
   - In the Use Function drop-down list, click the type of function you want to execute. For this example, choose Sum.
   - In the Add Subtotal To drop-down list, choose the fields you want to subtotal. You can choose as many fields as you want. However, when using the Sum function, only the fields containing numbers will produce results.

FIG. 15.1
This database has been sorted by the Type field; you can now apply subtotals by type.

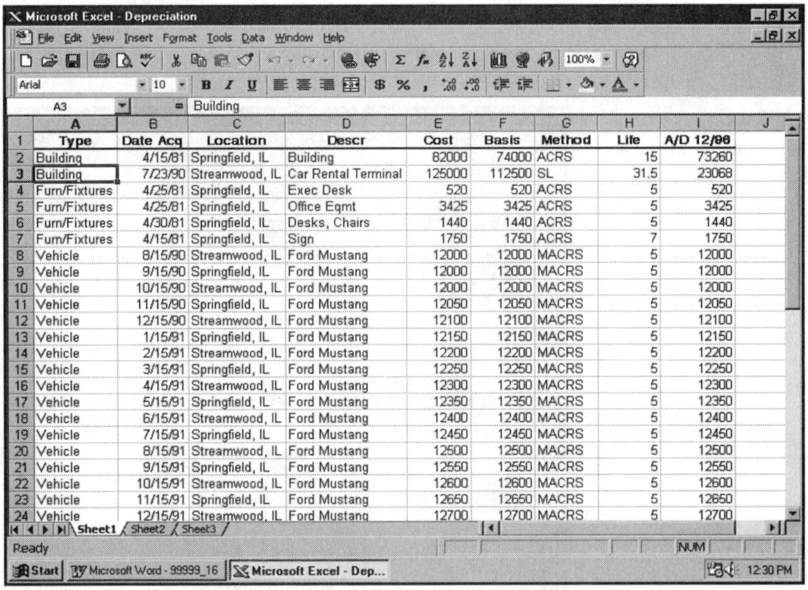
Microsoft Excel - Depreciation
A3 = Building

	A	B	C	D	E	F	G	H	I
1	Type	Date Acq	Location	Descr	Cost	Basis	Method	Life	A/D 12/96
2	Building	4/15/81	Springfield, IL	Building	82000	74000	ACRS	15	73260
3	Building	7/23/90	Streamwood, IL	Car Rental Terminal	125000	112500	SL	31.5	23068
4	Furn/Fixtures	4/25/81	Springfield, IL	Exec Desk	520	520	ACRS	5	520
5	Furn/Fixtures	4/25/81	Springfield, IL	Office Eqmt	3425	3425	ACRS	5	3425
6	Furn/Fixtures	4/30/81	Springfield, IL	Desks, Chairs	1440	1440	ACRS	5	1440
7	Furn/Fixtures	4/15/81	Springfield, IL	Sign	1750	1750	ACRS	7	1750
8	Vehicle	8/15/90	Streamwood, IL	Ford Mustang	12000	12000	MACRS	5	12000
9	Vehicle	9/15/90	Springfield, IL	Ford Mustang	12000	12000	MACRS	5	12000
10	Vehicle	10/15/90	Streamwood, IL	Ford Mustang	12000	12000	MACRS	5	12000
11	Vehicle	11/15/90	Springfield, IL	Ford Mustang	12050	12050	MACRS	5	12050
12	Vehicle	12/15/90	Streamwood, IL	Ford Mustang	12100	12100	MACRS	5	12100
13	Vehicle	1/15/91	Springfield, IL	Ford Mustang	12150	12150	MACRS	5	12150
14	Vehicle	2/15/91	Streamwood, IL	Ford Mustang	12200	12200	MACRS	5	12200
15	Vehicle	3/15/91	Springfield, IL	Ford Mustang	12250	12250	MACRS	5	12250
16	Vehicle	4/15/91	Streamwood, IL	Ford Mustang	12300	12300	MACRS	5	12300
17	Vehicle	5/15/91	Springfield, IL	Ford Mustang	12350	12350	MACRS	5	12350
18	Vehicle	6/15/91	Streamwood, IL	Ford Mustang	12400	12400	MACRS	5	12400
19	Vehicle	7/15/91	Springfield, IL	Ford Mustang	12450	12450	MACRS	5	12450
20	Vehicle	8/15/91	Streamwood, IL	Ford Mustang	12500	12500	MACRS	5	12500
21	Vehicle	9/15/91	Springfield, IL	Ford Mustang	12550	12550	MACRS	5	12550
22	Vehicle	10/15/91	Streamwood, IL	Ford Mustang	12600	12600	MACRS	5	12600
23	Vehicle	11/15/91	Springfield, IL	Ford Mustang	12650	12650	MACRS	5	12650
24	Vehicle	12/15/91	Streamwood, IL	Ford Mustang	12700	12700	MACRS	5	12700

FIG. 15.2
Enter your subtotaling requirements in the Subtotal dialog box.

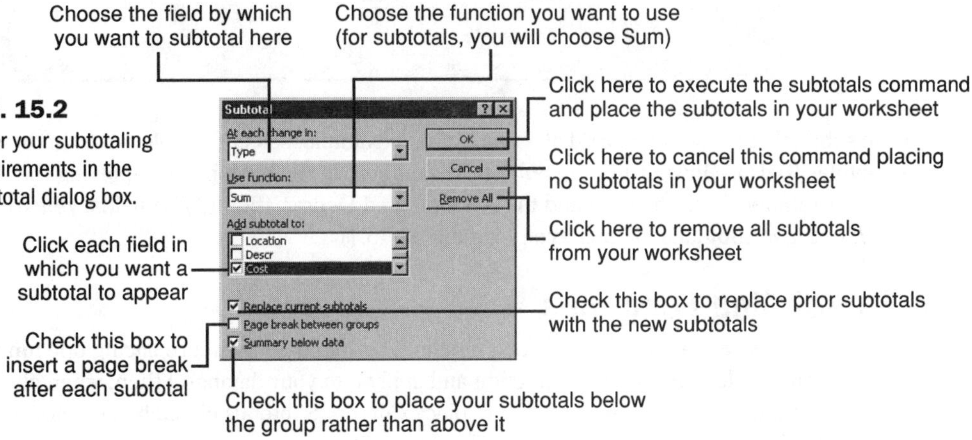
Choose the field by which you want to subtotal here
Choose the function you want to use (for subtotals, you will choose Sum)
Subtotal
At each change in:
Type
Use function:
Sum
Add subtotal to:
Location
Descr
Cost
Replace current subtotals
Page break between groups
Summary below data
OK
Cancel
Remove All
Click here to execute the subtotals command and place the subtotals in your worksheet
Click here to cancel this command placing no subtotals in your worksheet
Click here to remove all subtotals from your worksheet
Check this box to replace prior subtotals with the new subtotals
Click each field in which you want a subtotal to appear
Check this box to insert a page break after each subtotal
Check this box to place your subtotals below the group rather than above it

- Select the Replace Current Subtotals check box if a prior calculation of subtotals exists on your worksheet and you want to remove them while inserting your new subtotals. If this is the first time you are placing subtotals in your worksheet, do not select this check box.
- Select the Page Break Between Groups check box if you want each subtotaled group to appear on a separate page.
- Select the Summary Below Data check box if you want your subtotal to appear beneath your group; Otherwise, the subtotal will appear at the top of each group.

4. Choose OK, and the subtotal operation will be performed. In Figure 15.3, the cost of each type of asset has been subtotaled.

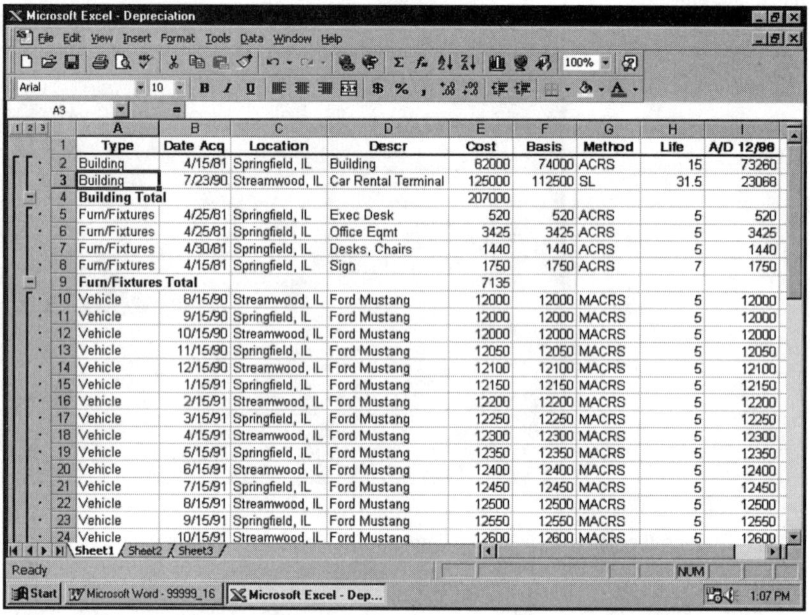

	A	B	C	D	E	F	G	H	I
1	Type	Date Acq	Location	Descr	Cost	Basis	Method	Life	A/D 12/96
2	Building	4/15/81	Springfield, IL	Building	62000	74000	ACRS	15	73260
3	Building	7/23/90	Streamwood, IL	Car Rental Terminal	125000	112500	SL	31.5	23068
4	Building Total				207000				
5	Furn/Fixtures	4/25/81	Springfield, IL	Exec Desk	520	520	ACRS	5	520
6	Furn/Fixtures	4/25/81	Springfield, IL	Office Eqmt	3425	3425	ACRS	5	3425
7	Furn/Fixtures	4/30/81	Springfield, IL	Desks, Chairs	1440	1440	ACRS	5	1440
8	Furn/Fixtures	4/15/81	Springfield, IL	Sign	1750	1750	ACRS	7	1750
9	Furn/Fixtures Total				7135				
10	Vehicle	8/15/90	Streamwood, IL	Ford Mustang	12000	12000	MACRS	5	12000
11	Vehicle	9/15/90	Springfield, IL	Ford Mustang	12000	12000	MACRS	5	12000
12	Vehicle	10/15/90	Streamwood, IL	Ford Mustang	12000	12000	MACRS	5	12000
13	Vehicle	11/15/90	Springfield, IL	Ford Mustang	12050	12050	MACRS	5	12050
14	Vehicle	12/15/90	Streamwood, IL	Ford Mustang	12100	12100	MACRS	5	12100
15	Vehicle	1/15/91	Springfield, IL	Ford Mustang	12150	12150	MACRS	5	12150
16	Vehicle	2/15/91	Streamwood, IL	Ford Mustang	12200	12200	MACRS	5	12200
17	Vehicle	3/15/91	Springfield, IL	Ford Mustang	12250	12250	MACRS	5	12250
18	Vehicle	4/15/91	Streamwood, IL	Ford Mustang	12300	12300	MACRS	5	12300
19	Vehicle	5/15/91	Springfield, IL	Ford Mustang	12350	12350	MACRS	5	12350
20	Vehicle	6/15/91	Streamwood, IL	Ford Mustang	12400	12400	MACRS	5	12400
21	Vehicle	7/15/91	Springfield, IL	Ford Mustang	12450	12450	MACRS	5	12450
22	Vehicle	8/15/91	Streamwood, IL	Ford Mustang	12500	12500	MACRS	5	12500
23	Vehicle	9/15/91	Springfield, IL	Ford Mustang	12550	12550	MACRS	5	12550
24	Vehicle	10/15/91	Streamwood, IL	Ford Mustang	12600	12600	MACRS	5	12600

FIG. 15.3
The subtotal of the cost each asset type appears under each group.

You can subtotal more than one field at a time. In this example, select multiple boxes in the Add Subtotal To drop-down list in the Subtotal dialog box. In the example, by applying the subtotal operation to both the Cost and the Accumulated Depreciation (A/D) fields, you are provided with two subtotals for each type (see Figure 15.4).

Types of Subtotaling Functions

You can present more than one function at a time in your database by not replacing one function with another. Select one subtotal function and apply it to your database; then, when choosing a second subtotal function, deselect the Replace Current Subtotals check box to show the results of both functions simultaneously (see Figure 15.5).

Collapsing a Subtotaled Database

Notice, when you present subtotals in your database, vertical lines appear at the left side of the database, with minus signs in little boxes (refer to Figure 15.5). Click the minus signs to collapse the database, showing only the subtotals. Click the resulting plus signs in a collapsed database to redisplay the entire detail (see Figure 15.6).

FIG. 15.4
Selecting more than one field for your subtotals provides you with additional information in one step.

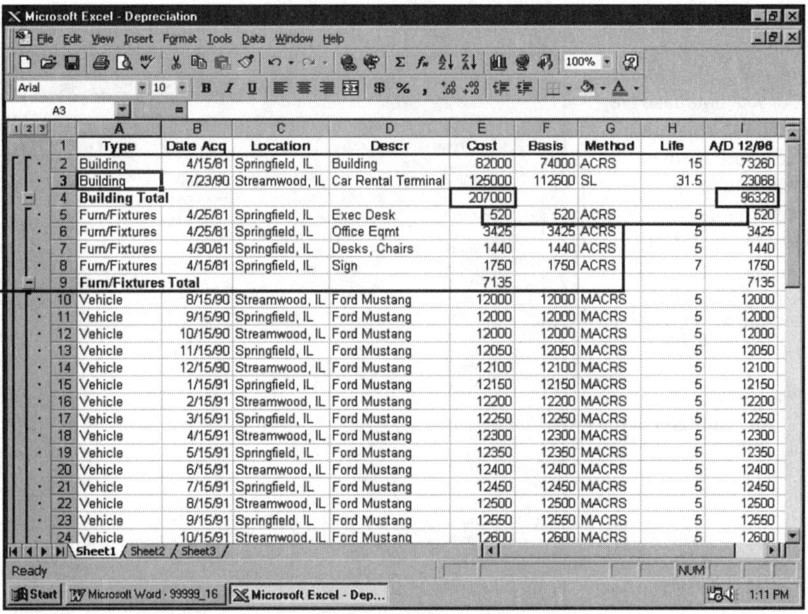

FIG. 15.5
Show more than one subtotal at one time by not replacing prior subtotals when requesting new ones.

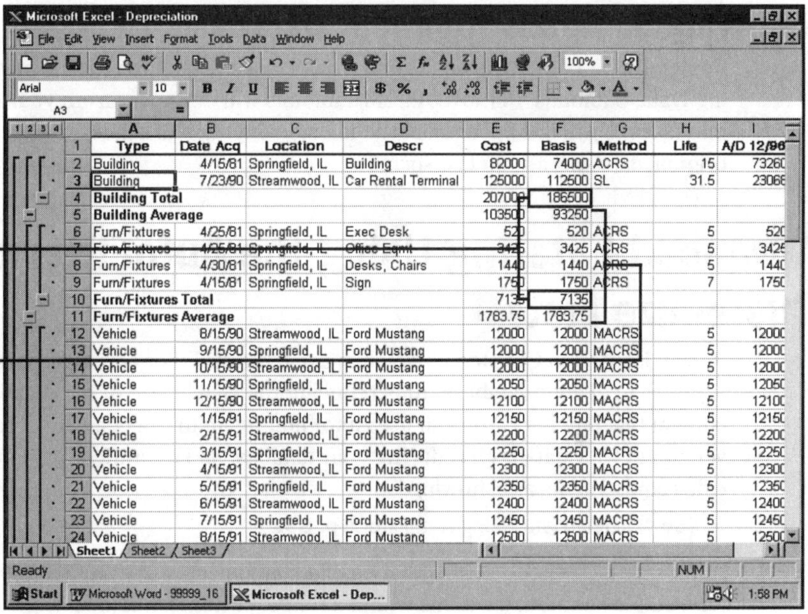

FIG. 15.6
The plus and minus signs that appear to the left of your database are expand and collapse buttons; use them to switch between a detailed view and a view of just the subtotals.

Click here to redisplay the details that make up the Building type

Click here to show just the Subtotal of the Furn/Fixtures type

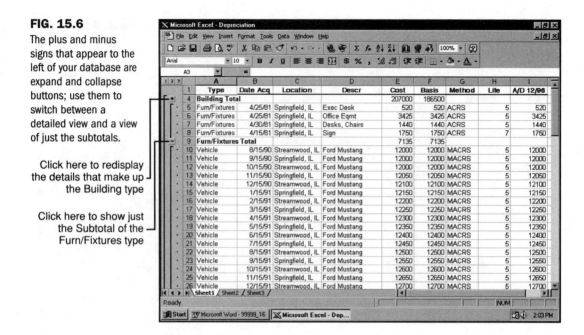

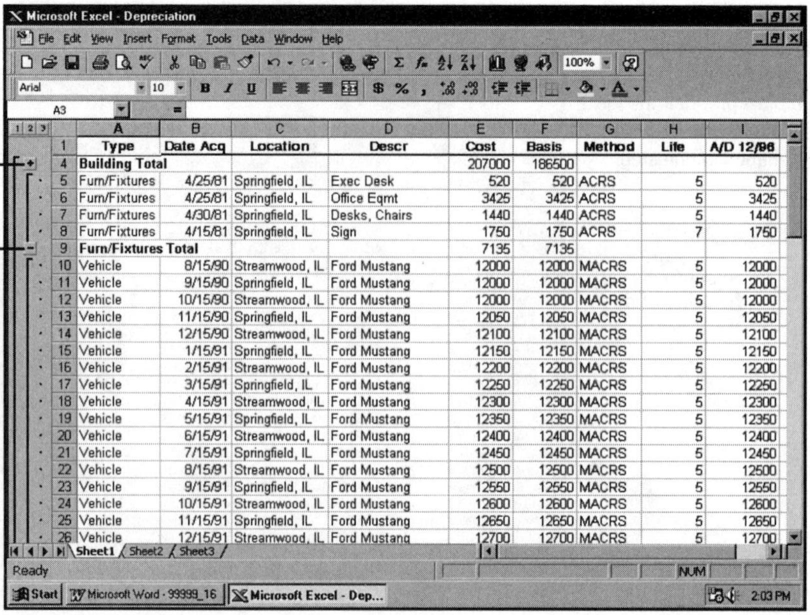

	A	B	C	D	E	F	G	H	I
1	Type	Date Acq	Location	Descr	Cost	Basis	Method	Life	A/D 12/96
4	Building Total				207000	186500			
5	Furn/Fixtures	4/25/81	Springfield, IL	Exec Desk	520	520	ACRS	5	520
6	Furn/Fixtures	4/25/81	Springfield, IL	Office Eqmt	3425	3425	ACRS	5	3425
7	Furn/Fixtures	4/30/81	Springfield, IL	Desks, Chairs	1440	1440	ACRS	5	1440
8	Furn/Fixtures	4/15/81	Springfield, IL	Sign	1750	1750	ACRS	7	1750
9	Furn/Fixtures Total				7135	7135			
10	Vehicle	8/15/90	Streamwood, IL	Ford Mustang	12000	12000	MACRS	5	12000
11	Vehicle	9/15/90	Springfield, IL	Ford Mustang	12000	12000	MACRS	5	12000
12	Vehicle	10/15/90	Streamwood, IL	Ford Mustang	12000	12000	MACRS	5	12000
13	Vehicle	11/15/90	Springfield, IL	Ford Mustang	12050	12050	MACRS	5	12050
14	Vehicle	12/15/90	Streamwood, IL	Ford Mustang	12100	12100	MACRS	5	12100
15	Vehicle	1/15/91	Springfield, IL	Ford Mustang	12150	12150	MACRS	5	12150
16	Vehicle	2/15/91	Streamwood, IL	Ford Mustang	12200	12200	MACRS	5	12200
17	Vehicle	3/15/91	Springfield, IL	Ford Mustang	12250	12250	MACRS	5	12250
18	Vehicle	4/15/91	Streamwood, IL	Ford Mustang	12300	12300	MACRS	5	12300
19	Vehicle	5/15/91	Springfield, IL	Ford Mustang	12350	12350	MACRS	5	12350
20	Vehicle	6/15/91	Streamwood, IL	Ford Mustang	12400	12400	MACRS	5	12400
21	Vehicle	7/15/91	Springfield, IL	Ford Mustang	12450	12450	MACRS	5	12450
22	Vehicle	8/15/91	Streamwood, IL	Ford Mustang	12500	12500	MACRS	5	12500
23	Vehicle	9/15/91	Springfield, IL	Ford Mustang	12550	12550	MACRS	5	12550
24	Vehicle	10/15/91	Streamwood, IL	Ford Mustang	12600	12600	MACRS	5	12600
25	Vehicle	11/15/91	Springfield, IL	Ford Mustang	12650	12650	MACRS	5	12650
26	Vehicle	12/15/91	Streamwood, IL	Ford Mustang	12700	12700	MACRS	5	12700

Removing Subtotals from Your Database

Remove subtotals entirely and return to a display of just the details of your database by choosing Data, Subtotals, Remove All. All subtotals will disappear from your database, all plus and minus signs will disappear from the left side of your worksheet, and you'll be left with your original database as you last sorted it.

Advanced Filtering Using the AutoFilter to Customize Lists

As you learned in Chapter 14, you can use the AutoFilter command to select one item from a single field of your database, thus reducing the visible size of the database to records that contain that one item. You can use AutoFilter again to select a single item from that smaller version of your database, reducing your database in size until only the records that meet specific requirements are showing.

▶ **See** "Finding Data Using AutoFilter," **p. 392**

AutoFilter has other qualities that enable you to perform searches on your database, not just for a single item, but for items within a range, or items that meet a set of specific requirements.

To find items in your database that fall within a specific range, follow these steps:

1. With your database displayed on-screen, choose Data, Filter, AutoFilter to turn on the AutoFilter feature.

2. Click the AutoFilter arrow at the top of the field you want to search. A drop-down list will appear.
3. Click (Custom...). The Custom AutoFilter dialog box appears.
4. Choose from the following options to specify ways to include or exclude items from the designated field.

Feature	
equals	begins with
does not equal	does not begin with
is greater than	ends with
is greater than or equal to	does not end with
is less than	contains
is less than or equal to	does not contain

5. Identify what you want to apply the above option to (for example, all items whose cost is greater than **20,000**, or all items whose location contains the state abbreviation, **IL**).
6. Choose OK to apply the AutoFilter feature to your database.

TIP After using the AutoFilter feature, you can always redisplay the entire database by choosing Data, Filter, AutoFilter, Show All.

To search for items that meet specific requirements, follow these steps:

1. Open your database so it's displayed on-screen. Then follow steps 1–5 of the previous procedure.
2. Choose a second option to limit the selection further using the "and" feature (for example, all items whose cost is greater than 20,000 but less than 40,000, all items whose location contains the state abbreviation, IL, and does not contain the city, Springfield), or using the "or" feature (for example, all items whose cost is greater than 20,000 or less than 10,000, or all items whose location contains the state abbreviation, IL or IN).
3. Choose OK to apply the AutoFilter features to your database.

Advanced Filtering Using a Criteria Range

You can get about as precise as you want when filtering information out of your database when you use a criteria range and indicate the exact criteria for which you are searching. This technique takes a small amount of set up before you can begin to use it.

1. Display your database on-screen and turn off the AutoFilter feature if it is turned on.
2. Insert at least four blank rows at the top of your database. This area is your criteria range.

TIP You can quickly insert blank rows by selecting the rows you want to be blank and then pressing Ctrl++ (plus sign).

NOTE The most convenient place for a criteria range is often the first few rows of your spreadsheet. The criteria range must be on the same sheet as your database, but can actually appear anywhere on the sheet. It is not recommended that you place your criteria range beneath your data because there is no room for the database to grow if the criteria range blocks such growth.

3. Copy the header row of your database to the first blank row (see Figure 15.7).

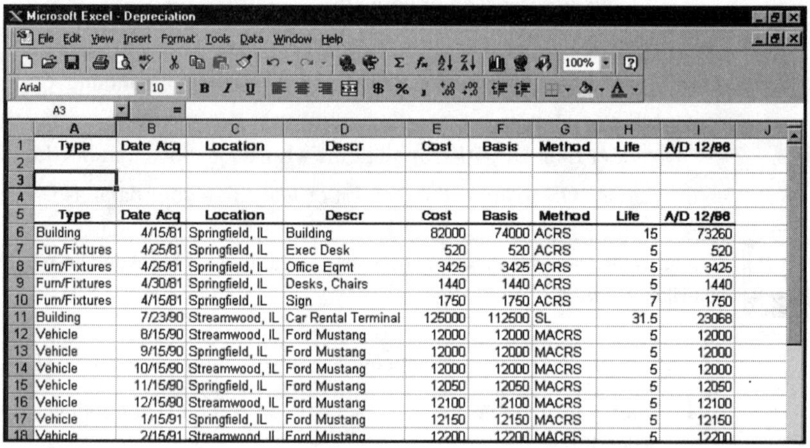

FIG. 15.7
The top row of your criteria range will contain the same headers as your database.

TIP Use the Copy and Paste features to copy your header row to the first row of your criteria range, rather than retyping the headers. This way there is no chance of making a typographical error. The header row of the criteria range must exactly match the header row of your database

4. In the first blank row of the criteria range (row 2 on your worksheet), enter criteria you want to match in your database search. For example, if you search for items from a particular location, enter the name of the location in the first blank row of the location field (see Figure 15.8).
5. (Optional) If you want to search for matches in other fields at the same time, enter that information in the first criteria row as well. By entering all search criteria in one row, you are requesting that the search results meet all of the criteria. You can use greater than (>) and less than (<) operatives in your search to indicate that you will accept any records that include data greater than or less than the specified amount (see Figure 15.9).

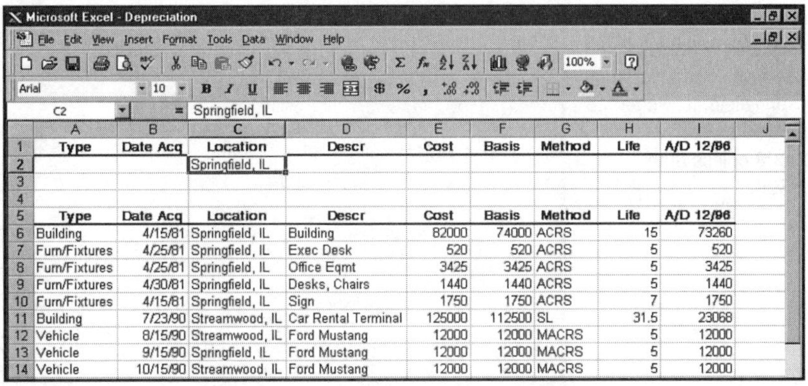

FIG. 15.8
Use the first blank row of the criteria range to display an example of the information you want to match in your database.

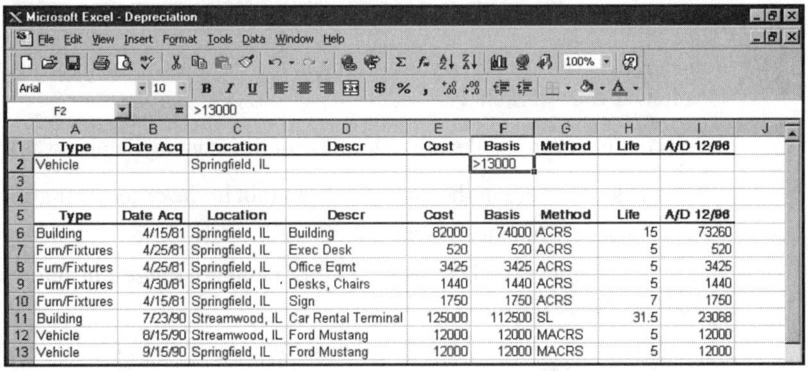

FIG. 15.9
Using the fields in the criteria range, enter any additional information for which you want to find records that match.

6. (Optional) To establish an either/or criteria search, enter one set of criteria in the first row of the criteria range, and enter a second set of criteria in the second row (see Figure 15.10). Results of the search will display records that meet all of the criteria in the first row *or* all of the criteria in the second row. You can enter as many rows of criteria as you like as long as no blank rows separate the criteria. Each row of criteria presents an "or" situation for your search.

NOTE There must be at least one blank row separating your criteria range from your actual database.

CAUTION

If you use the criteria range to filter data and the resulting data includes all the items in your database, your criteria range probably contains a blank row. The blank row has the effect of not filtering out any data, thus returning all records in the database. When selecting your criteria range, be sure to only select the rows that contain filtering information!

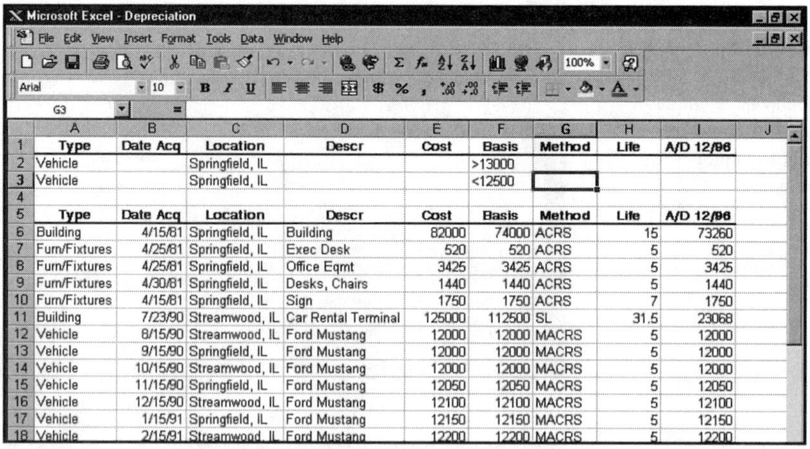

FIG. 15.10
This search will result in a list of vehicles located in Springfield, IL, with a cost greater than 13,000 or less than 12,500.

You can place the results of your search in the location of the existing database, or in a new location on your worksheet.

To place the search results in the location of the existing database, follow these steps:

1. Click anywhere in the main database (not in the criteria range).
2. Choose Data, Filter, Advanced Filter. The Advanced Filter dialog box appears.
3. Choose Filter the List, In-Place. Your database range will automatically be entered in the List Range box.
4. Click the Collapse Dialog button at the right of the Criteria Range box to move the Advanced Filter box out of the way (see Figure 15.11).

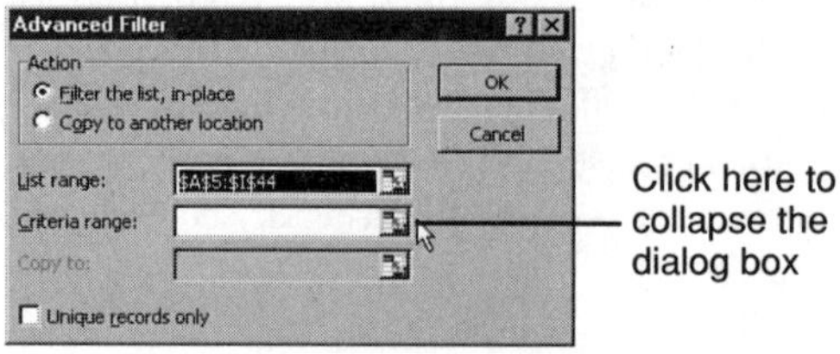

FIG. 15.11
The Collapse Dialog button returns you to your spreadsheet so you can select cells.

5. Drag over the entire criteria range (including the header row) while the Advanced Filter dialog box is collapsed (see Figure 15.12).
6. Click the Collapse Dialog button again to restore the Advanced Filter dialog box.

TIP After collapsing your dialog box, you can press Enter to quickly return to the dialog box.

7. Choose OK to perform the search. The results of your search will appear in place of your original database (see Figure 15.13).

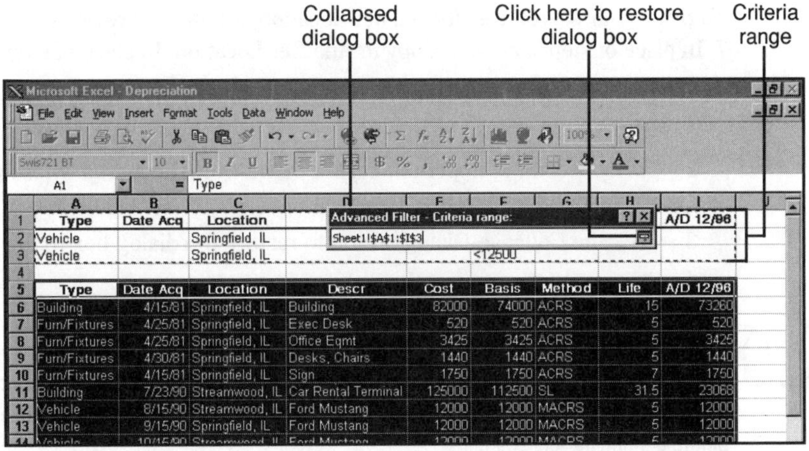

FIG. 15.12
Drag over your entire criteria range to select it.

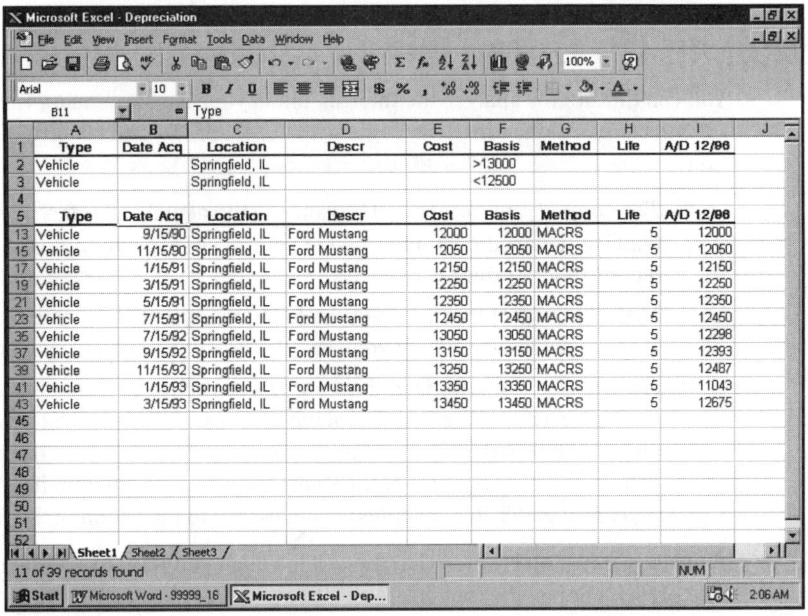

FIG. 15.13
The results of the Advanced Filter search appear in place of the original database.

To keep the appearance of your original database intact, you can place your search results in a new location on the current sheet of your worksheet.

NOTE You cannot place filtered data on a different sheet than that which contains the original data. If you want your filtered data to appear on a different sheet, perform the filter on the current sheet and use the Clipboard to move or copy the filtered data to a different sheet later.

To place your search results in a new location, follow the previous steps except step 3 and step 7. In place of step 3, choose Copy to Another Location. In place of step 7, perform these steps:

1. Click the Collapse Dialog button to the right of the Copy To box. The dialog box will collapse.
2. Click once in the upper-left corner of the worksheet area where you want to see the results of your search.
3. Click the Collapse Dialog button to restore the dialog box to the screen.
4. Choose OK to perform the filter.

TIP Each time you perform an Advanced Filter search on your database, there is a chance the ranges you indicated in the Advanced Filter dialog box may change, depending on where the pointer is located in the spreadsheet. It's always a good idea to double-check the ranges in the Advanced Filter dialog box before performing your search.

Looking Up Data Using Functions

You can thoroughly analyze the information in your database using Excel's database functions, or *Dfunctions*. All the functions begin with the letter "D" and require three pieces of information:

- *The range of your database.* The range is the actual cell references of your database, from (and including) the left-most cell of your header row to the right-most cell of the last record (bottom row) of data.
- *The field.* To perform the database functions, you will indicate a particular field (column) of your database on which you want the function to be performed.
- *The criteria.* The criteria in this case is a reference to the cell locations that contain criteria specific to the function being performed. This is synonymous with the criteria range established earlier in this chapter, although you don't have to use the entire criteria range if only part of the range (one or more column headings with criteria appearing under the headings) is necessary to the action of the function.

A database function is entered in the cell in which you want to see the results of the function. The presentation of the function is as follows:

```
FUNCTIONNAME(DataRange,"FieldName",CriteriaRange)
```

So, for example, the DCOUNT function, which counts the number of items in the database that meet particular requirements as set out in the criteria range, might appear as follows:

```
=DCOUNT(A5:I44,"Cost",A1:E2)
```

In this example, the function name is DCOUNT; the database range is from A5 to I44, which may be your entire database or just a selected portion of your database; the field you want to analyze is the "Cost" field, and the criteria controlling your analysis is located in the area from A1 to E2. The cell containing the DCOUNT function will return a result of the number of items in the specified database that meet the criteria set out in the criteria range (see Figure 15.14).

TIP When entering functions, you can either type the function or use the Paste Function feature.

NOTE Remember: all functions must begin with the "=" sign! This is automatic if you use the Paste Function feature.

FIG. 15.14
Cell J4 contains the count of the number of items in the database meeting the criteria set out in the criteria range.

The DCOUNT function

The results of the search

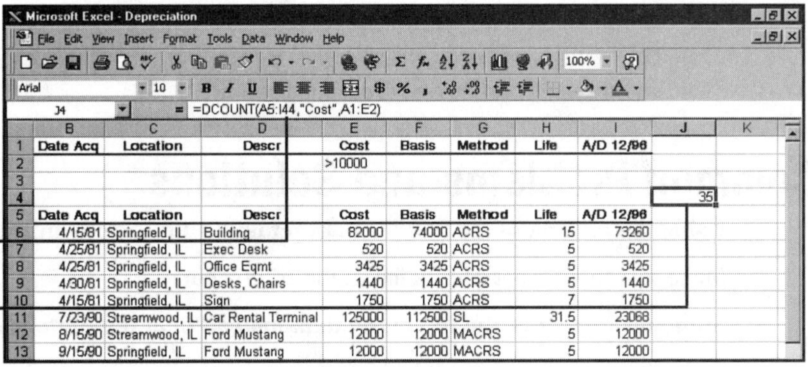

TIP When using database functions you will find it is often easier to refer to your database and criteria ranges by name rather than by cell reference. It's hard to remember the cell references, but easy to remember a name. Try naming the ranges before performing database actions.

▶ **See** "Naming Ranges," **p. 92**

The database functions available to you are similar to the subtotaling options you encountered earlier in this chapter:

- *DCOUNT.* Returns a count of the number of items in the database that meet the designated criteria. Only records containing numbers in the designated field are counted.
- *DCOUNTA.* Returns a count of the number of items in the designated field of the database that are not blank.
- *DMAX.* Returns the maximum value of the items in the particular field that meet the criteria.
- *DMIN.* Returns the minimum value of the items in the particular field that meet the criteria.
- *DSUM.* Returns the sum of all items in the particular field that meet the criteria. Text fields are ignored in this formula.

- *DPRODUCT.* Returns the product of all items in the particular field that meet the criteria. Text fields are ignored in this formula.
- *DAVERAGE.* Returns the average of all items in the particular field that meet the criteria. Text fields are ignored in this formula.
- *DSTDEV.* Returns the estimated standard deviation in the field for items meeting the criteria, if the data is a sample of the total database.
- *DSTDEVP.* Returns the true standard deviation in the field for items meeting the criteria, if the data is the entire database.
- *DVAR.* Returns the estimated variance in the field for items meeting the criteria, where the data in the field is a sample of the total database.
- *DVARP.* Returns the true variance in the field for items meeting the criteria, where the data in the field is the entire database.
- *DGET.* Returns the single item that meets the criteria. If more than one item meets the criteria an error message is encountered.

Common Problems and Solutions

Using the criteria range to filter data returns all the items in the database.

Make sure there is not a blank line in the criteria range.

Subtotals appear at the top of my data instead of at the bottom of the list.

In the Subtotals dialog box (which you access by choosing Data, Subtotals), check the Summary Below Data box to place subtotals at the bottom of each data range.

Original subtotals still appear after new subtotals are requested.

When selecting a subtotal, check the Replace Current Subtotals check box to replace old subtotals with new ones.

When I enter a function, the function name appears in the cell, not the results of the function.

Make sure you've started the function with an equals sign (=). If you don't use that sign, Excel reads the function as text.

From Here...

In this chapter, you learned some advanced filtering techniques, and you learned about using many functions for analyzing your data. So what else is there to learn about databases? In Chapter 16, you'll learn efficiency—easier ways to retrieve data using the Query Wizard. You'll also learn how to save your queries so you don't have to create a query every time you want to extract data from your database.

This chapter also covered advanced techniques for analyzing and presenting your data in Excel. Chapters 16 and 17 present you with tools for working with larger databases that you import from outside sources. In addition to those chapters, you may find the following related chapters of this book of interest.

- Chapter 6, "Using Excel Functions," introduces you to the Paste Function feature and shows you how to create functions easily.
- Chapter 10, "Creating Charts," and Chapter 11, "Advanced Chart Topics," will show you how you can chart the numerical data you extract from your database.
- Chapter 20, "Analyzing Data: PivotTables!," teaches you additional techniques for working with your data.

CHAPTER 16

Retrieving Data with the Query Wizard

Setting up Microsoft Query

Quickly install Microsoft Query and you can use the Query Wizard to choose the data you want to extract from your external database.

Choosing data to query

Choose the database that contains information you want to use in your worksheet.

Working with your data

Choose the items you want to use in your query. Then you can filter your data so that you use only the data you need. And you can save your queries so you can use them over again.

If you use a dedicated database program such as Access, Paradox, or dBase, you may find yourself faced with a desire to pull information from your database right into an Excel spreadsheet where you can manipulate numbers more easily. Microsoft Query is a program that enables you to do just that.

Use the Query Wizard in Excel to make simple queries and import straightforward data into your spreadsheet. For more complex queries and more detailed selection of data, bypass the Query Wizard and use the Microsoft Query program (see Chapter 17, "Advanced Queries Using Microsoft Query").

Remember that you have the option of importing the entire database into Excel if the quantity of data you want to use is not so large that it exceeds the bounds of the Excel worksheet. If, however, you want to examine or manipulate only a portion of the data in a database, the Query Wizard gives you the power to pinpoint data that meets specific criteria, thus enabling you to import only the portion of the database that you need.

Using the Query Wizard, you can view the fields in your database and request information for import into your Excel program. When you query, you select only the data that fits particular requirements, much like filtering.

Using the Query Wizard

Before you can use the Query Wizard, you may have to install Microsoft Query on your computer. First, check to see if the program is there. In Excel, choose Data, Get External Data, Create New Query. If Microsoft Query has not been installed, you will see a message like the one in Figure 16.1.

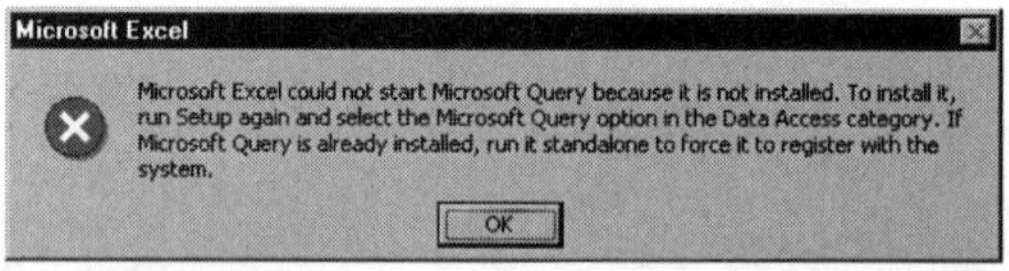

FIG. 16.1
Microsoft Query has not been installed.

Installing Microsoft Query

Install the Query program by following these steps:

1. Close all programs that are currently running on your computer.
2. Using the CD-ROM or disks that you used to install Excel (this would be the Microsoft Office 97 CD-ROM if you installed the entire Office package), run the Setup program.
3. In the Options list, make sure Data Access is checked. Do not uncheck any items. Click Data Access, then click the Change Option button.
4. Click Database Drivers, then click the Change Option button.
5. Indicate the drivers you want to install. Your choice will correspond with the database programs you will be using. See Table 16.1 for a list of compatible database programs and formats.
6. Click Continue. The setup program will install Microsoft Query to your hard drive.

CAUTION

When installing Microsoft Query, do *not* uncheck any items in the Options list of your setup screen. This will uninstall those items, which you don't want to do!

Table 16.1 Choosing a Database Driver

Driver Choices	What the Driver Does
Microsoft Access	Reads files with .mdb extension
dBase	Reads files with .dbf extension
Microsoft FoxPro	Reads files with .dbf extension
Microsoft SQL Server	The driver used to query data
Text and HTML	Reads files with extensions such as .txt, .csv, .asc, and .tab

Preparing to Query a Database

A small amount of advance preparation will save you time when you get ready to import information from an external database. Take a few minutes to perform these tasks before you use Microsoft Query:

- Know the file name and location of the file containing your database.
- Determine the exact elements that should be contained in the data you extract.

Selecting a Data Source

Before launching the Query Wizard you must identify the source of the data you want to extract. In other words, you tell Excel where to find the database from which the data will be chosen and what kind of driver will be needed in order to read information in that database. To identify a data source in Excel, follow these steps:

1. Choose Data, Get External Data, Create New Query. The Choose Data Source dialog box appears (see Figure 16.2).

   If you have used this feature previously, there may be some data selections from which you may choose listed in the box, or you can choose to create a new data source. Click your choice, make sure the Use Query Wizard box is checked, and then click OK.

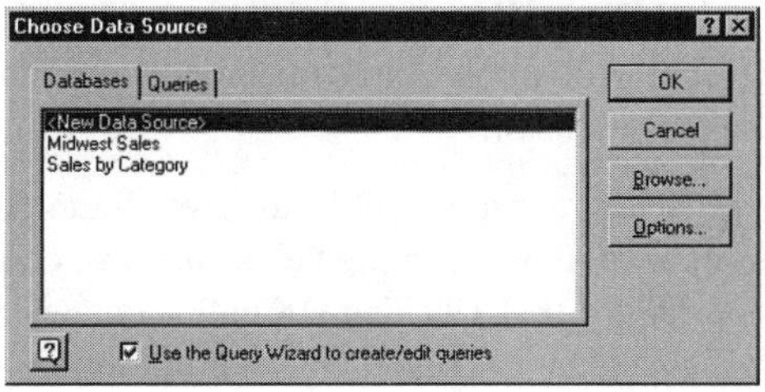

FIG. 16.2
Opening this window enables you to indicate the location of your data.

2. In the Create New Data Source window that appears, you are asked for four pieces of information:
   - *What name do you want to give your data source?* The name you choose for your data source will help you identify this source if you want to use it in the future.
   - *Select a driver for the type of database you want to access.* From the drop-down list provided, choose the driver that fits your type of database.
   - *Provide information appropriate to the database you have chosen.* Then click the Connect button and answer the on-screen questions.
   - *Select a default table for your data source.* The drop-down list gives you a choice of the tables associated with your data source. The table you choose will be the first one presented to you when you are ready to begin choosing fields for your query. This step is optional. Choosing a default table does not limit the fields available to you when creating your query.

3. When you finish entering the information requested in the Create New Data Source dialog box, click OK. The Choose Data Source dialog box reappears.
4. With your new data source selected, click OK. Excel starts the Query Wizard.

Choosing Tables and Fields

On the left side of the Query Wizard window is a list of the tables in your database. If you chose a default table with your data source, that table will appear first. Tables are marked with a plus sign on the left indicating multiple fields within the table. Clicking the plus sign expands the list to display the fields beneath the table name. Clicking the resulting minus sign compresses the list of fields.

You can choose fields for your database using any of the following techniques:

- Click a field name on the left side of the Query Wizard box and click the Add Field button (the first arrow button between the two lists) to add the specific field to your list of fields to query.
- Click a table name and click the Add Field button to add all the fields from the selected table to your list of fields to query.
- If you place a field in your query list and you decide later that you don't want to use it, click the field name in the query list, and then click the Remove Field button (the second arrow button between the two lists) to send the field back to the list on the left.
- To remove all fields from the query list, click the Remove All Fields button (the third arrow button between the two lists).

When you finish selecting fields for your query, click the Next button to begin filtering your data. If there is no obvious connection between the fields you have chosen to query, you will see a message like the one in Figure 16.3. Clicking OK in this box will take you completely out of the Query Wizard and will cause the Microsoft Query program to open. (Defining the connection between fields using Microsoft Query is covered in Chapter 17.) Clicking Cancel returns you to the Query Wizard, where you can alter your field selection.

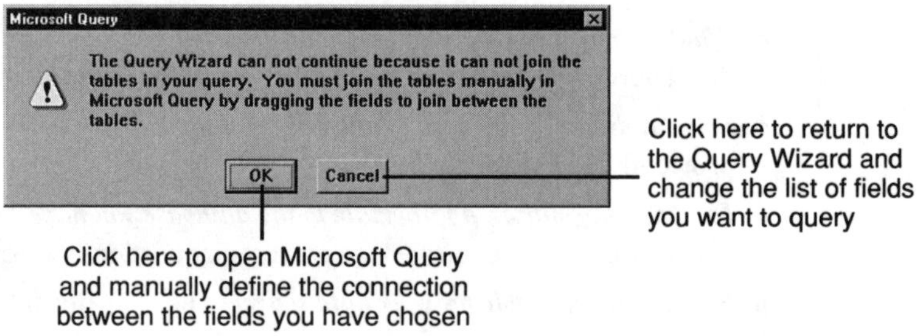
Microsoft Query
The Query Wizard can not continue because it can not join the tables in your query. You must join the tables manually in Microsoft Query by dragging the fields to join between the tables.
OK
Cancel
Click here to return to the Query Wizard and change the list of fields you want to query
Click here to open Microsoft Query and manually define the connection between the fields you have chosen

FIG 16.3
This message appears when the Query Wizard is unable to find a connection between the fields you have chosen to query.

Filtering Data

When selecting data with the Query Wizard, you can specify restrictions on the data that appears. If you don't specify any restrictions, the Query Wizard returns all of the records in the fields you have chosen. By setting restrictions or filtering your data, you request the Query Wizard to return only the data that you want to use for your analysis.

The Query Wizard gives you the opportunity to filter your data by letting you first select a field, and then indicate the limits you want to place on information coming from that field (see Figure 16.4). You can limit items in any field by choosing from the following options:

- equals
- does not equal
- is greater than
- is greater than or equal to
- is less than
- is less than or equal to
- begins with
- does not begin with
- ends with
- does not end with
- contains
- does not contain
- like
- not like
- is Null
- is Not null

NOTE You can specify up to 45 separate criteria for each field of your data.

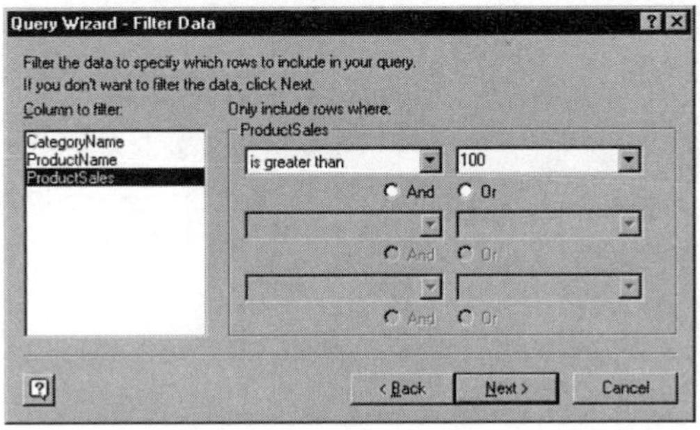

FIG. 16.4
Specify the criteria for selecting records from your chosen fields. If no criteria are specified, the Query Wizard will display all records from your fields.

When specifying criteria, follow these steps:

1. Select the first field for which you want to specify criteria.
2. Indicate your criteria choices.
3. Select additional fields if you want to limit your data selection further.
4. When you finish entering filtering criteria, click Next.

For example, suppose you are drawing data from a list of customers and their purchases and you want to limit the data to include only customers who made purchases in 1996 of $50,000 or more and who are located in a five-state region. The fields with which you are working are CustomerName, 1996Purchases, and State. You would first filter your data to exclude customers with sales less than $50,000 by selecting the 1996Purchases field, choosing Is Greater Than or Equal To, and entering **50000**. Next you would choose the State field, choose Equals, and enter the first of the five states. Choose the Or button, and in the second line of filtering (still within the State field), choose Equals and enter the second state. Continue this process until you have entered all five states with the or option separating them.

After specifying the filtering criteria, you will have the option of pre-sorting your data before it is displayed in your Excel worksheet.

Sorting Data

In the next screen of the Query Wizard (after you finish filtering), you have the opportunity to request that your data be sorted before it is presented to you on your worksheet. This can save you the steps of sorting later; however, you can always change the sort once you see the data displayed.

To sort your data, follow these steps:

1. Click the Sort By drop-down arrow and select the first field by which you want to sort your data (see Figure 16.5).
2. Choose ascending order (A-Z or lowest to highest) or descending order (Z-A or highest to lowest) for your sort.

FIG. 16.5
Sort your data while you're still in the Query Wizard.

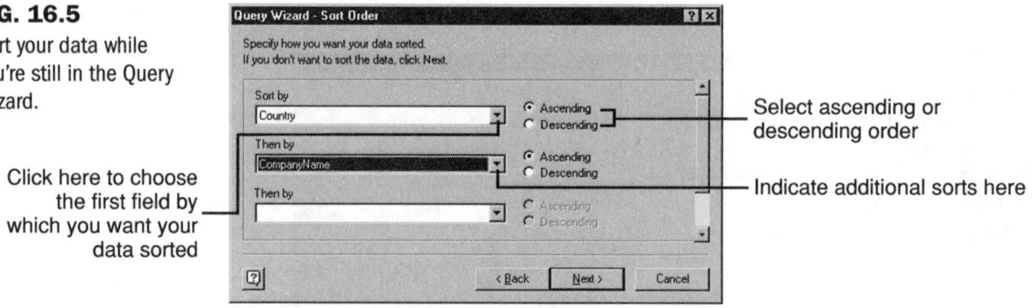

3. (Optional) If you want your data sorted further (for example, you might want the entire list of customers sorted by state and then want the list for each state alphabetized by customer name), add additional sort fields after the first.
4. When you finish indicating your sort request(s), click Next.
5. You will be asked if you want to view your (filtered and sorted) data in Excel, or if you would like to use Microsoft Query to further filter your data (see Figure 16.6). Choose Return Data to Microsoft Excel and click the Finish button.

FIG. 16.6
Click Finish to tell the Query Wizard where to send your data.

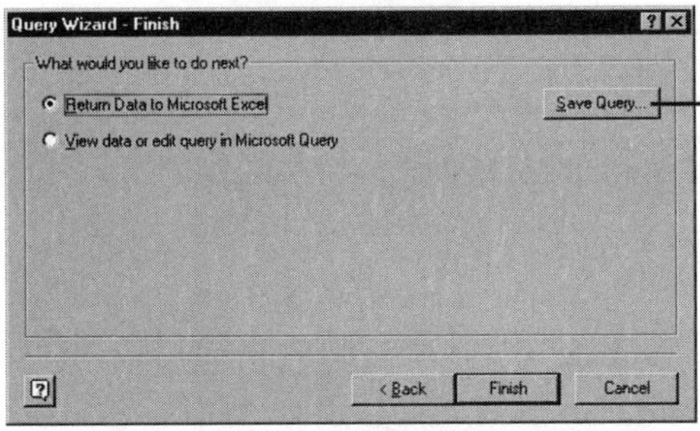

Click here to save your query for future use

NOTE Before you click the Finish button (in step 5), you have the opportunity to save your query. To do so, click the Save Query button. The Save As dialog box appears. For details on how to save your query, see the section "Saving and Reusing Queries," later this chapter.

6. You'll see a final screen (shown in Figure 16.7), which gives you three choices for displaying your data:
   - *Existing Worksheet.* Accept the default of cell A1 as the starting cell for your data, or click the Collapse Dialog button to move the dialog box out of the way and click the worksheet cell at the upper-left corner of the worksheet where you want the data to be displayed.
   - *New Worksheet.* Place your data in a worksheet other than the one currently displayed.
   - *PivotTable Report.* Place your data in a PivotTable.

FIG. 16.7
Choose one of three options for displaying the results of your query.

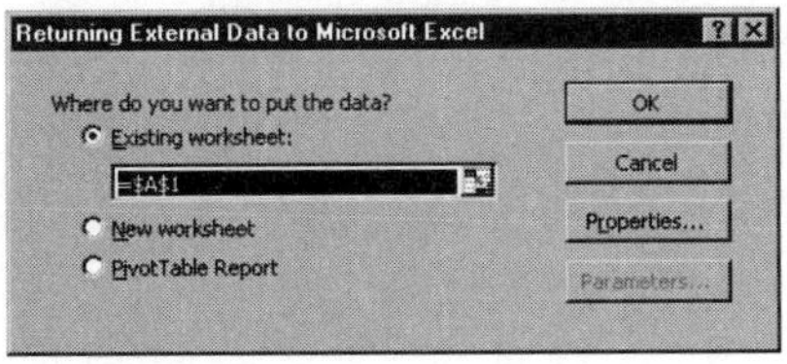

7. Click OK, and the results of your query are displayed based on the option you chose.

▶ **See** "Analyzing Data: PivotTables!," **p. 473**

Saving and Reusing Queries

After you've gone to all the work of creating your query in the Query Wizard, it seems a shame to have to start all over again the next time you want to use the same data. Save your query and you won't have to recreate it.

Click the Save Query button in the Query Wizard (refer to Figure 16.6). The Save As dialog box appears, and you are asked to give your query a name (see Figure 16.8).

After you name your query and click the Save button, you will be returned to the final Query Wizard window. Click the Finish button, and the results of your query are transferred to your Excel worksheet.

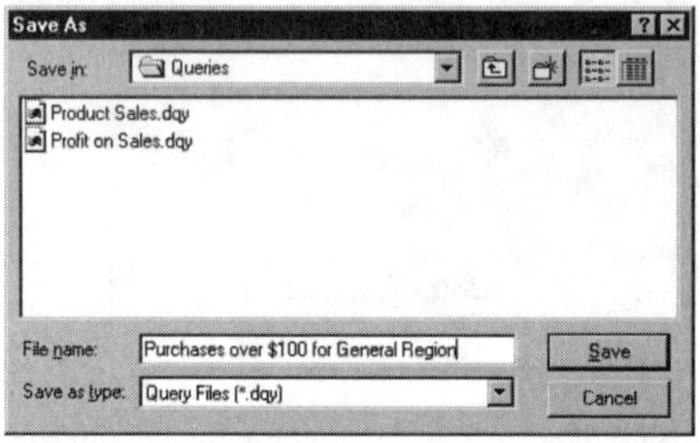

FIG. 16.8
Give your query a name so you can use it again.

To use your query again in the future, choose Data, Get External Data, Run Database Query. The Run Query window appears. Select the query you want to run from the list that is displayed (see Figure 16.9). Then click the Get Data button to run the query.

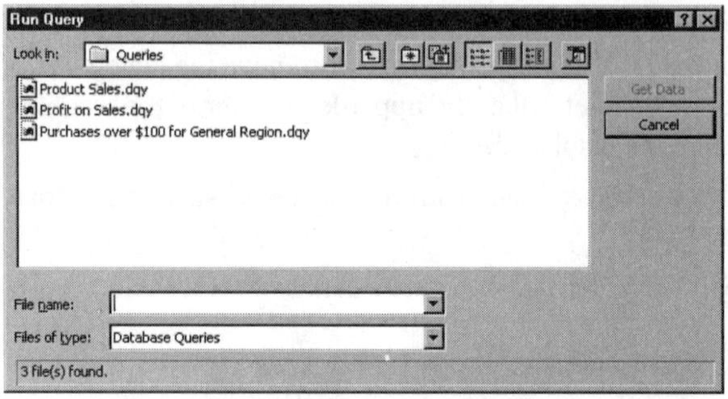

FIG. 16.9
Select your query and click Get Data to run it.

Common Problems and Solutions

Microsoft Query isn't installed on my computer.

Run the Office 97 Setup program, make sure Data Access is selected, and choose appropriate drivers.

I saved a query, and now I want to run it again. What do I do?

Choose Data, Get External Data, Run Database Query. Then select the query you want to run and click the Get Data button.

The Query Wizard can't find a common link among my fields.

When this happens, you are given the opportunity to leave the Query Wizard and open the Microsoft Query program, in which you can define the connection between fields.

From Here...

The Query Wizard is great for simple, straightforward queries of your data. For more complex queries you need the full power of Microsoft Query.

- Once you've got the data you need to work with, Chapter 6, "Using Excel Functions," can give you insight into applying mathematical and other functions to your data.
- Chapter 10, "Creating Charts," and Chapter 11, "Advanced Chart Topics," can spruce up your data with graphical elements.
- Chapter 17, "Advanced Queries Using Microsoft Query," gives you an in-depth description of the Microsoft Query program, which is part of the Microsoft Office package.

CHAPTER 17

Advanced Queries Using Microsoft Query

by Gail A. Perry

The Query Wizard, described in Chapter 16, provides you with the groundwork for extracting data from your database and into your Excel worksheet. Microsoft Query goes further. Using Microsoft Query, you can extract data from databases that would be too large to save in Excel, work with data in formats unreadable in Excel, and extract data from databases that include multiple tables.

In this chapter, you will learn how to use the Microsoft Query program to extract data from your database by building complex queries. You'll learn how to save your queries for future use, how to control the sort of the data, how to query more than one database, and how to make sense of SQL code. ■

Get to know Microsoft Query

Learn your way around the toolbar options associated with this program.

Build advanced queries

Go beyond the limitations of the Query Wizard and build queries that link fields from several different tables and that ask sophisticated questions of your database.

Accessing Microsoft Query

If you plan to use Microsoft Query to query your database, begin your data request in the same manner as you would if you were using the Query Wizard. First, make a note of the file name and location of your data. Next, take a few minutes to think about what you want from your data. Determine the exact elements that describe the information you wish to cull from your database. Then follow these steps:

NOTE If you find that Microsoft Query is not installed on your computer, you can install the software by following the instructions set out in the section "Installing Microsoft Query," at the beginning of Chapter 16.

1. Choose Data, Get External Data, Run New Query from the Excel menu.
2. In the Choose Data Source dialog box, deselect the Use Query Wizard check box.
3. Choose to use an existing data source by selecting one of the data sources listed (if any appear), or choose Create New Data Source. Use an existing data source if the data source you need is listed. If you are selecting data from a new source, you will choose Create New Data Source.
4. Click OK. If you chose to create a new data source, the Create New Data Source dialog box appears. Make your data source selections (as described in the section "Selecting a Data Source" in Chapter 16). When you finish, the Microsoft Query window opens, along with the Add Tables window (see Figure 17.1). If you chose an existing data source, the Microsoft Query window opens immediately (see Figure 17.2).

NOTE You also can access Microsoft Query from the Query Wizard. After making your query selections in the Query Wizard, instead of choosing to display your data in your Excel worksheet, you are presented with an option to view your data in Microsoft Query.

In the Microsoft Query window, you will identify the fields and tables you want to use in your query. This process is described in the next section.

Understanding the Microsoft Query Toolbar

When the Microsoft Query window opens, it displays its own toolbar. Figure 17.2 describes the toolbar buttons available to help you set up your query.

The top third of the Microsoft Query dialog box (under the toolbar) is called the Table pane. In the Table pane, your tables and their fields are shown. Lines connecting the fields show how fields are linked from one table to the next.

The middle section of the Microsoft Query dialog box is the Criteria pane. This section describes the query you've created. Field titles appear across the top row, and acceptable values appear in the next rows.

The bottom section of the dialog box, the Data pane, shows the results of your query.

FIG. 17.1
In the Add Tables window, you should indicate which tables from your database you want to use in your query.

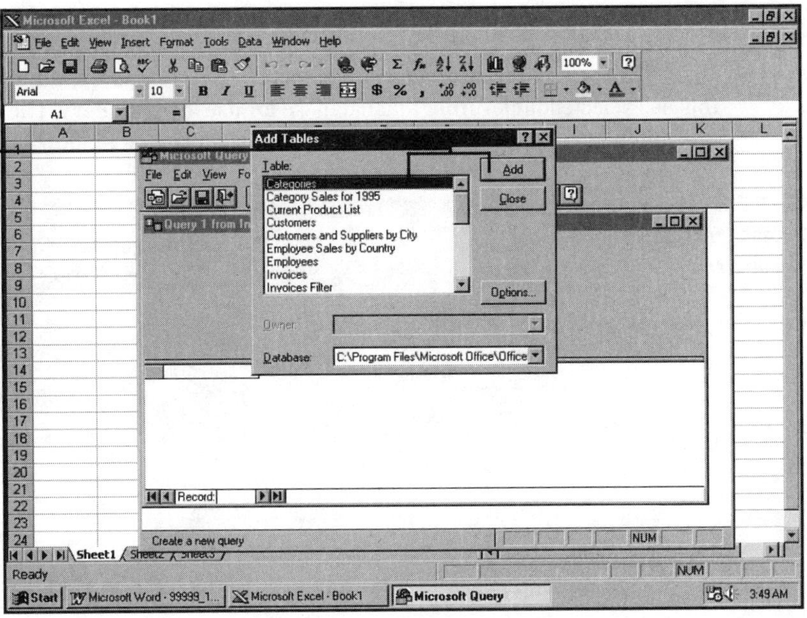

Click a table name and choose OK to make the fields in the table available for your query

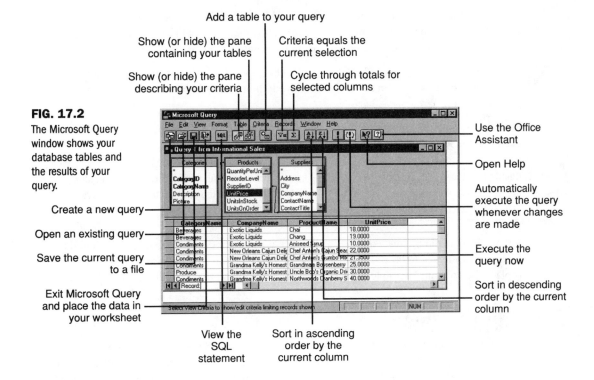

FIG. 17.2
The Microsoft Query window shows your database tables and the results of your query.

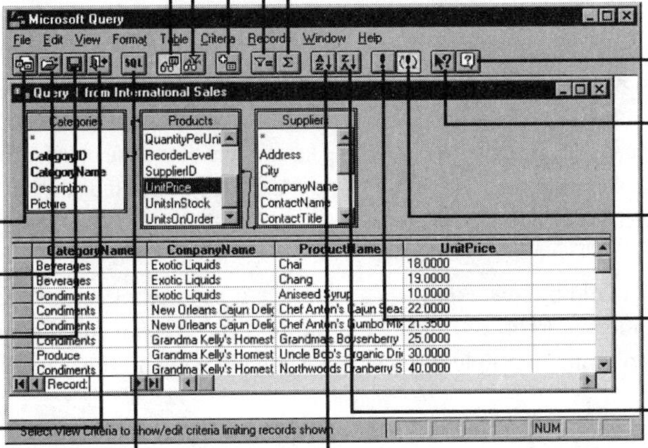

Selecting Fields

When you opened Microsoft Query, you chose the data source with which you wanted to work. You also selected tables from that database for use in your query. The tables you chose appear in the upper pane (the Table pane) of the Microsoft Query window (see Figure 17.3).

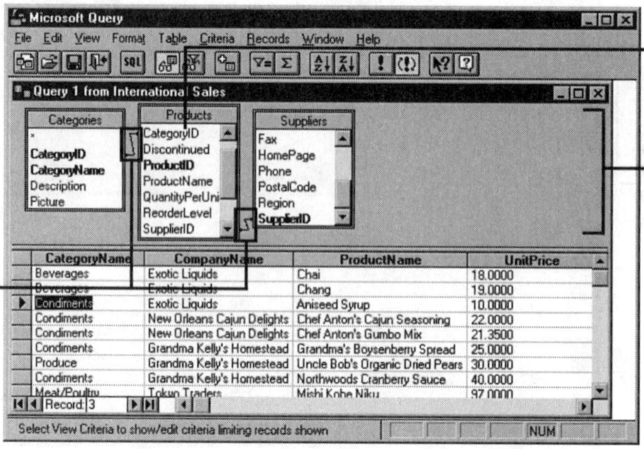

FIG. 17.3
Microsoft Query displays the tables you have chosen to use in your query.

Microsoft Query places a line between linked tables, indicating the fields on which the tables are linked. There must be a commonality among the tables—a field that is duplicated in multiple tables—in order to create a query using information from all the tables.

If you determine that you need to add a table, click the Add Table button on the Microsoft Query toolbar. Choose from the tables displayed; then click Add to add that table to your group.

Double-click any field in any of the tables to use that field in your query. The field will be displayed in the lower portion (the Data pane) of the Microsoft Query window.

TIP Double-click the bar (or drag the bar) separating fields in the data pane of the Microsoft Query window to expand the column if data is being cut from view. Likewise, you can drag the bar to reduce the size of a column to see more columns.

If you added a field by mistake, you can remove it by clicking anywhere in the unwanted column, then choosing Records, Remove Column. Change your mind again? Choose Edit, Undo to replace the column, or simply double-click the field again in the Table pane.

Building Queries

A query is a request for specific information from your data. So far, you've chosen a data source, selected tables from that data source, and the chosen fields you want to display. Creating a query will limit the selected information so that only records that meet specific requirements will be included in your final data output.

You will design your query by indicating *criteria*, or requirements to be met from the entire body of data. When you run your query, only data that meets the requirements you set out will be displayed.

Selecting Criteria from the Data Pane

If you want to limit your data to include only one type of item from a field (for example, if you only want to see addresses that include a particular zip code, or if you are only looking for a particular inventory part), select the item you want to focus on in the Data pane of the Microsoft Query window. Click the Criteria Equals button. Only data containing the selected item will remain in your data pane.

TIP Remember, as you're working with criteria selection, you can always turn to Edit, Undo if you change your mind about a selection.

Adding Criteria in the Criteria Pane

Click the Show Criteria Pane button to display the Criteria pane on your Microsoft Query screen. The Criteria pane includes columns that begin with a Criteria Field row. The name of the field you want to use for filtering your data is entered in this row. Click the first row, and then click the down arrow to display the field names (see Figure 17.4). Choose a field you want to use for limiting the data selection.

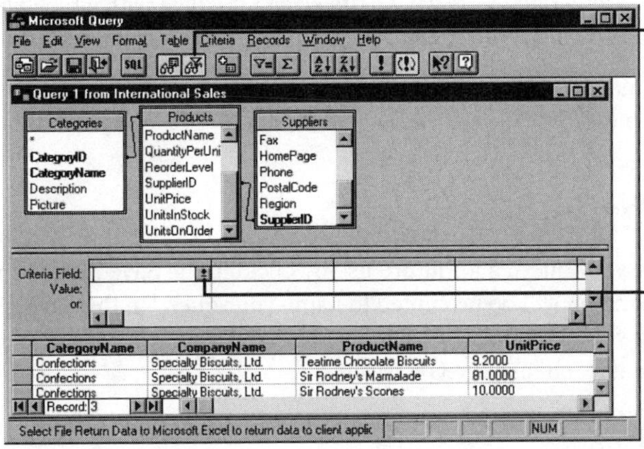
Click here to display the Criteria pane
Click in a cell of the Criteria field row, and then click the down arrow to display field choices

FIG. 17.4 Enter criteria options in the Criteria pane.

Choose as many fields as you need for your criteria. The fields you choose do not have to be the same fields displayed in the data area of the Microsoft Query screen. You may use criteria from one field to limit the presentation of the data without actually showing the field used for filtering. For example, in an employee database, you might want to display employees whose salaries exceed a particular amount, without displaying the actual salary figure. Your Criteria pane would include a field for salary in which you will set a limitation. Your Data pane might only include employee names and job descriptions.

Choose Criteria, Add Criteria to add items to the Criteria pane. Criteria items entered on the same row are "AND" items, meaning that each of the criteria need to be met for a data item to be included in the resulting group. Criteria items on separate rows in the Criteria pane are "OR" items, meaning that any of the criteria can be met for a record to be included in the resulting group (see Figure 17.5).

FIG. 17.5
The results of this query provide a list of all items whose reorder level is less than 25 AND whose units in stock is less than 25, as well as all items whose units in stock is less than 10, no matter the reorder level.

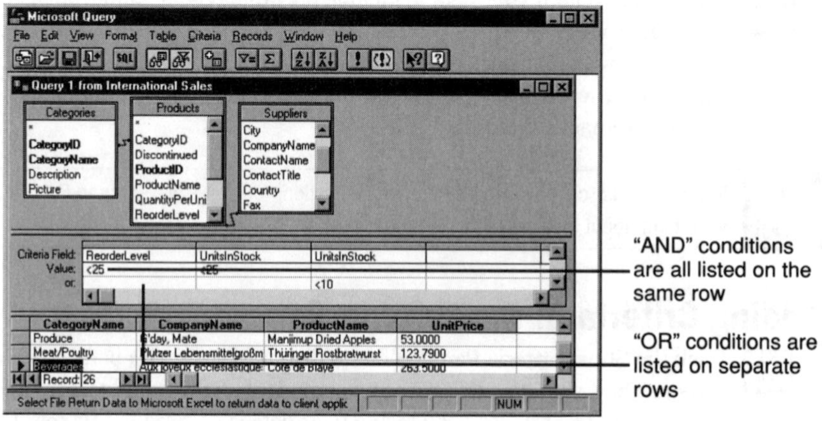

As long as the Auto Query button is depressed (which it is by default), whenever you change or add criteria in the Criteria pane, your data is automatically updated. If this is distracting, or if it is taking too long due to the very large size of the data with which you are dealing, you can turn off the Auto query feature by clicking the Auto Query button.

When the Auto Query feature is not in use, you can execute a query at any time by clicking the Query Now button.

Storing Queries

You can save your queries for future use by clicking the Save File button on the Microsoft Query toolbar. You will be prompted to name your query in the Save As dialog box. Use a name that will help you distinguish it from other queries you have saved. When you have entered your query name, choose the OK button.

You can modify an existing query, then save it with a different name. To save a query with a new name, follow these steps:

1. Choose File, Save As. The Save As dialog box appears.
2. Enter the name for your query.
3. Click Save. Your query will be saved with its new name. The original query is still intact with its original name.

Once you have saved your query, you can use it again by choosing Data, Get External Data, Run Database Query.

Query Expressions

As when you learned to filter your database (in Chapter 15), there are options for filtering your queries so that no unwanted data appears in your results. Table 17.1 lists expressions to use when creating your query.

Table 17.1 Query Expressions

Expression	The Way You Type It	How It Works
Equals	=	The field must equal the indicated value
Does not equal	<>	The field does not equal the indicated value
Is greater than	>	The field is greater than the indicated value
Is greater than or equal to	>=	The field is greater than or equal to the indicated value
Is less than	<	The field is less than the indicated value
Is less than or equal to	<=	The field is less than or equal to the indicated value
Is one of	In (*x*,*y*,*z*)	The field is one of a list of items shown in parentheses, separated by commas
Is not one of	Not in (*x*,*y*,*z*)	The field is not one of a list of items shown in parentheses, separated by commas
Is between	Between *x* and *y*	The field is between two values, separated by commas
Is not between	Not between *x* and *y*	The field is not between two values, separated by commas
Begins with	Like '*x*%'	The field begins with the value (shown as *x*)
Does not begin with	Not like '*x*%'	The field does not begin with the value (shown as *x*)
Ends with	Like '%*x*'	The field ends with the value (shown as *x*)
Does not end with	Not like '%*x*'	The field does not end with the value (shown as *x*)
Contains	Like '%*x*%'	The field contains the value (shown as *x*)

continues

Table 17.1 Continued

Expression	The Way You Type It	How It Works
Does not contain	Not like '%*x*%'	The field does not contain the value (shown as *x*)
Like	Like '*x*'	The field is like the value (shown as *x*), using wildcard characters * and ?
Not like	Not like '*x*'	The field is not like the value (shown as *x*), using wildcard characters * and ?
Is Null	Is Null	The field is empty
Is not Null	Is not Null	The field is not empty

Use these expressions when entering query information. Choose Criteria, Add Criteria from the menu in the Microsoft Query dialog box, and the Add Criteria dialog box appears (see Figure 17.6). You can enter as many criteria items as you like while this box is open, by entering an item, then clicking Add. When you have entered all your criteria in this box, click Close to close the box and return to your Microsoft Query screen.

FIG. 17.6
You can enter all of your criteria in the Add Criteria box.

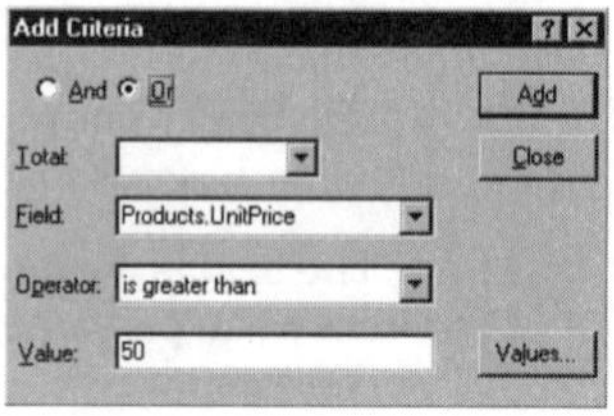

Controlling Sort Order

Before transferring your data over to your Excel worksheet, you can arrange it in the order in which you want it to appear. Sort your data right in Microsoft Query using the tools provided.

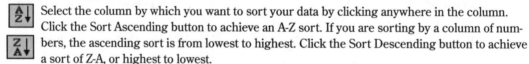

Select the column by which you want to sort your data by clicking anywhere in the column. Click the Sort Ascending button to achieve an A-Z sort. If you are sorting by a column of numbers, the ascending sort is from lowest to highest. Click the Sort Descending button to achieve a sort of Z-A, or highest to lowest.

Continue sorting by additional columns, retaining the first sort, by holding down the Ctrl key, clicking in the next column by which you want to sort, then choosing an ascending or descending sort.

You also can sort by several columns at once. First, move the columns into the order in which you want to have them sorted.

TIP Move columns in Microsoft Query by clicking at the top of the column to select the entire column, then clicking again so that your mouse pointer looks like an arrow with a box attached. Drag the column to its new location.

When the columns are arranged in the order by which you want them sorted, select all of the columns on which you want to sort; then click the Sort Ascending or Sort Descending button. The columns will be sorted in the chosen order, starting with the left-most column. When you sort, the entire database is sorted simultaneously, so entire records are kept together. You don't have to worry about one person's name becoming associated with another person's address.

You also can sort using the Sort dialog box by following these steps.

1. In the Microsoft Query dialog box, choose Records, Sort. The Sort dialog box appears.
2. Choose the column on which you want to base your sort in the Column drop-down list. If you have already sorted by a column, that column will not be in the list.
3. Choose Ascending or Descending for your sort type.
4. Choose Add. Your data will be sorted by the choices you made. The dialog box stays open for you to add additional sorts.
5. You can remove a sort by clicking the sort at the bottom of the box and choosing Remove.
6. Choose Close when you have finished making your sort selections.

Running the Query

When you are satisfied with your query results and the sorted order of your data, and you have saved your query, send the data to Excel by clicking the Exit button. Microsoft Query will close, and the Returning External Data to Microsoft Excel dialog box will appear (see Figure 17.7).

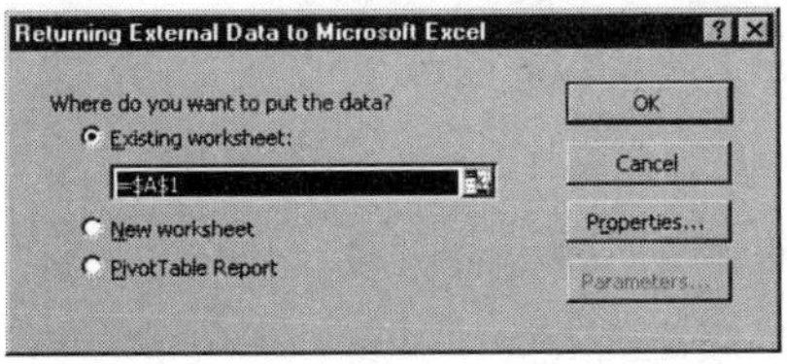

FIG. 17.7
Click the OK button to return your data to your Excel worksheet.

In the Returning External Data to Microsoft Excel dialog box, indicate where in your worksheet you want the data to appear (by default, it will begin at cell A1). Alternatively, you can choose New worksheet and your data will appear in a new Excel worksheet. Incoming data will overwrite any existing information in your current Excel worksheet. You also have an option for sending your information to a PivotTable. See Chapter 20, "Analyzing Data: PivoTables!" for a discussion of this feature. Click OK to display the query results in the chosen location.

Viewing and Editing SQL Code

Each time you create a query, Microsoft Query creates a little program written in SQL (Structured Query Language). If you are comfortable using SQL code, you can edit your queries directly in this format.

While creating a query, click the SQL button on the Microsoft Query toolbar. The SQL dialog box appears, displaying the SQL-coded version of your query (see Figure 17.8).

SQL language is based on an ANSI standard specification and appears in many database programs. You may want to obtain a SQL manual for your particular database if you plan to edit SQL code.

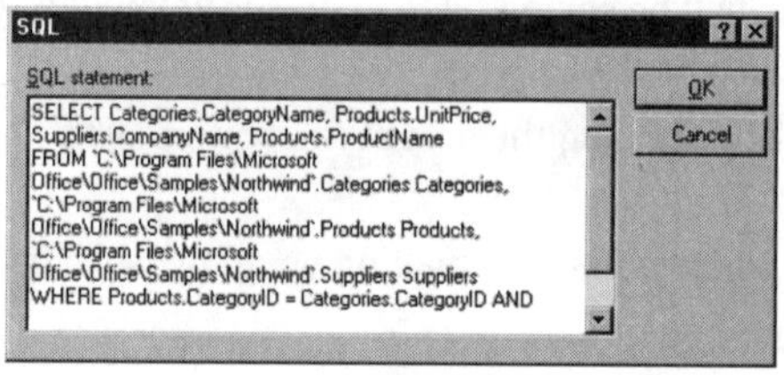

FIG. 17.8
Clicking the SQL button displays the SQL code, which you can edit.

Make any changes you need to in the SQL code, and then click the OK button to execute your changes.

Common Problems and Solutions

I forgot to include a table that I need for data.

Click the Add Table button on the Microsoft Query toolbar.

I can't read everything in the data columns of Query.

Double-click (or drag) the bar separating fields in the Data pane of the Microsoft Query window.

Oops! I added a field by mistake!

Click anywhere in the unwanted column and choose Records, Remove Column.

I entered a criteria choice, but it's not the one I wanted.

Don't forget your old buddy, Edit, Undo, when you change your mind.

From Here...

In the next part, you will learn about analyzing data:

- In Chapter 18, "Building Scenarios and Outlines with Excel," you will encounter techniques for creating scenarios and outlines in Excel.
- In Chapter 19, "Auditing and Validating Worksheets," you'll learn how to create an audit trail on your workbook, and you'll work with ranges.
- In Chapter 20, "Analyzing Data: PivotTables!," you'll learn about the magic of PivotTables.

PART V

Analyzing Your Data

CHAPTER 18

Building Scenarios and Outlines with Excel

by Bruce Hallberg with Joyce Nielsen

When working with business budgets or projections, you typically need to consider a variety of different scenarios in order to understand the dynamics arising from different decisions. You may have heard this referred to as *what-if analysis*, especially when using spreadsheet programs to analyze the data. While examining the data, you need to take into account the best- and worst-case assumptions for factors outside your direct control, so that you can exercise control over the final results by affecting controllable factors. Each set of variables that you examine is a *scenario*.

Outlining enables you to expand or contract worksheets or reports so that you see more or less detail. In a sales report, for example, you might need to display various levels of detail depending on who will read the report. With the outline feature, you can hide or display up to eight levels of detail in rows or columns. ■

Working with scenarios

Many business people need to create and manage different scenarios of data, particularly those that need to perform complex budgeting, business analysis, and other such tasks. Excel's Scenario Manager makes analyzing different cases easy.

Summarizing and printing scenarios

Excel provides a command that enables you to summarize all your scenarios in one worksheet. You can then print the worksheet to make simple comparisons between the different case scenarios.

Outlining worksheets

Many worksheets are very large, and contain both detailed data and different levels of summarization data. You can make working with such worksheets easier by using Excel's outlining feature.

Moving and copying outlines

You can use the Cut and Copy commands to move or copy an entire outline to another location. If you have collapsed an outline, you also can choose to move or copy only the visible cells.

How Scenario Manager Works

Understanding how Scenario Manager works can illuminate for you how to best utilize it. For each defined scenario, Scenario Manager stores the scenario name, a comment, whether the scenario is protected or hidden, and the changing cell information. The changing cell information consists of a list of the changing cells, and the values that those cells should contain for that scenario. When you choose to activate a scenario, the Scenario Manager inputs those changing cell values into the specified changing cells, almost as if you had typed those values yourself.

Because Scenario Manager works by typing values into the changing cells, any formulas in those cells will be overwritten with the values Scenario Manager stores. Moreover, any formulas in your base worksheet model will be overwritten as you use Scenario Manager with the values you substitute in those cells. (For this reason, it's critical that you save a copy of your base worksheet model to a different file name before you begin using Scenario Manager.)

If you want to use a combination of values and formulas as part of scenario planning, make the formulas dependent on cells that contain simple values. Then change those value cells with Scenario Manager, which will automatically affect their dependent formulas. For example, in the UXLS Proforma Income Statement used in this chapter, if you want to build projections based on percentages of growth, you would add cells that contain those growth percentages, and then use formulas within the income statement to build results based on those growth percentages. In Scenario Manager, you would only define the growth percentage cells to be changed, thereby maintaining the formulas in the income statement.

Working with Scenarios

You could develop different scenarios by using different worksheets in a workbook, with each sheet containing the different assumptions. However, this approach can waste a lot of time. For example, imagine that you have 10 different scenarios, each one in a different sheet, and you need to change your model by adding a new condition to each scenario. You would then have to make the identical change to each of the 10 worksheets. Aside from the waste of time involved in approaching the problem this way, you also improve the chance of making a mistake.

Instead, it is far easier to use Excel 97's built-in Scenario Manager to track, display, and manage your different scenarios. In the following sections you learn how to take advantage of this important planning tool.

Creating Scenarios

Consider the worksheet shown in Figure 18.1. In it, you see a five-year proforma (projected) income statement for UXLS Corporation. The income statement is divided into three main categories: revenues; cost of goods sold; and selling, general, and administrative costs. For the projected five years, many things can change in the business, different goals may be realized, and different directions pursued. In order to analyze the impact from all of these possibilities, you use the Scenario Manager to examine the different cases.

FIG. 18.1
A proforma income statement is where different scenarios will be explored.

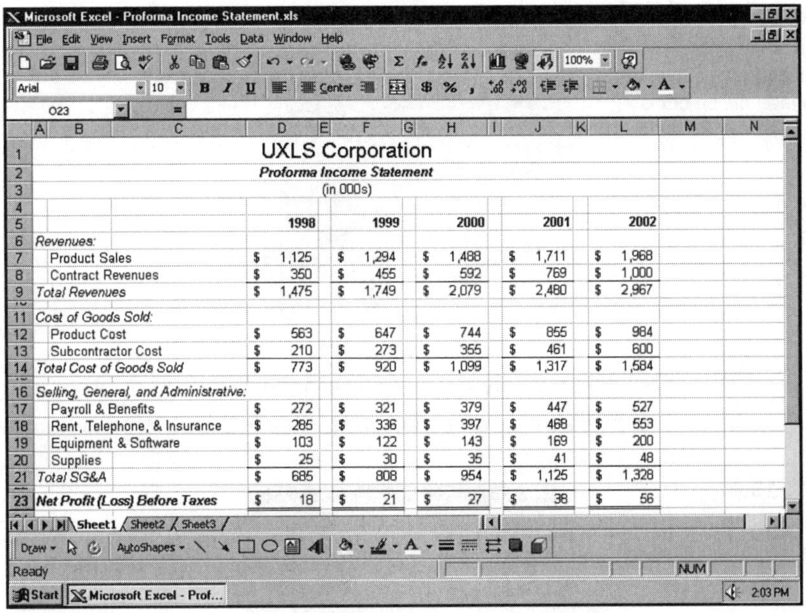

UXLS Corporation
Proforma Income Statement
(in 000s)

	1998	1999	2000	2001	2002
Revenues:					
Product Sales	$ 1,125	$ 1,294	$ 1,488	$ 1,711	$ 1,968
Contract Revenues	$ 350	$ 455	$ 592	$ 769	$ 1,000
Total Revenues	$ 1,475	$ 1,749	$ 2,079	$ 2,480	$ 2,967
Cost of Goods Sold:					
Product Cost	$ 563	$ 647	$ 744	$ 855	$ 984
Subcontractor Cost	$ 210	$ 273	$ 355	$ 461	$ 600
Total Cost of Goods Sold	$ 773	$ 920	$ 1,099	$ 1,317	$ 1,584
Selling, General, and Administrative:					
Payroll & Benefits	$ 272	$ 321	$ 379	$ 447	$ 527
Rent, Telephone, & Insurance	$ 285	$ 336	$ 397	$ 468	$ 553
Equipment & Software	$ 103	$ 122	$ 143	$ 169	$ 200
Supplies	$ 25	$ 30	$ 35	$ 41	$ 48
Total SG&A	$ 685	$ 808	$ 954	$ 1,125	$ 1,328
Net Profit (Loss) Before Taxes	$ 18	$ 21	$ 27	$ 38	$ 56

Before creating different scenarios, it's wise to establish your starting scenario (often called the *base case*) as a defined scenario in Scenario Manager. That way, you can return to the base case and view it again at any time. Otherwise, you run the risk of losing the base case because it is not automatically stored for you once you start using Scenario Manager. You define the starting base case scenario in the same way that you add other scenarios. After you do that, you can then start adding and evaluating different scenarios.

TIP Before using Scenario Manager with a workbook model, it's a good idea to save the completed model to a different file name so that, if something goes wrong, you can return to the base case. Then, create and analyze scenarios using a copy of the workbook with a different file name.

For each scenario you create, you name the scenario, and then designate the changing cells for the scenario. The *changing cells* are those cells that will be different in that scenario. You can have up to 30 changing cells per scenario.

You should consider designing the workbook model so that the changing cells are either adjacent to one another or in close proximity. This will make your workbook more efficient, and it enables others to more easily view the inputs you are using as changing cells. Excel doesn't require that you use a particular layout when creating scenarios, however.

To add a scenario to Scenario Manager, follow these steps:

1. First, completely develop your worksheet model.
2. Choose Tools, Scenarios. You initially see the Scenario Manager dialog box shown in Figure 18.2.

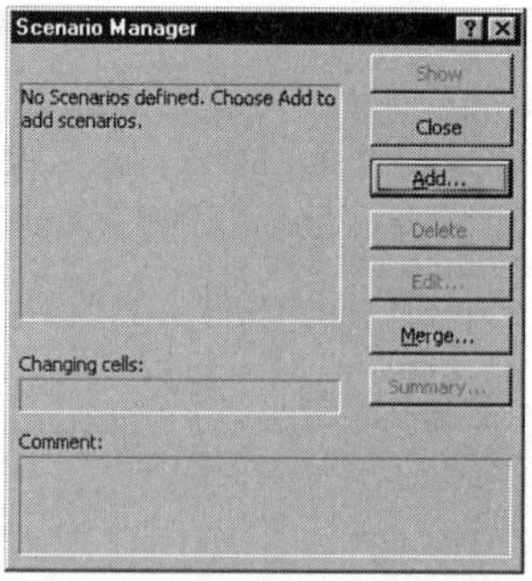

FIG. 18.2
Before you add scenarios, the Scenario Manager dialog box is empty.

3. Click the Add button. The Add Scenario dialog box displays.
4. For the base case scenario, type the name in the Scenario Name field (see Figure 18.3).

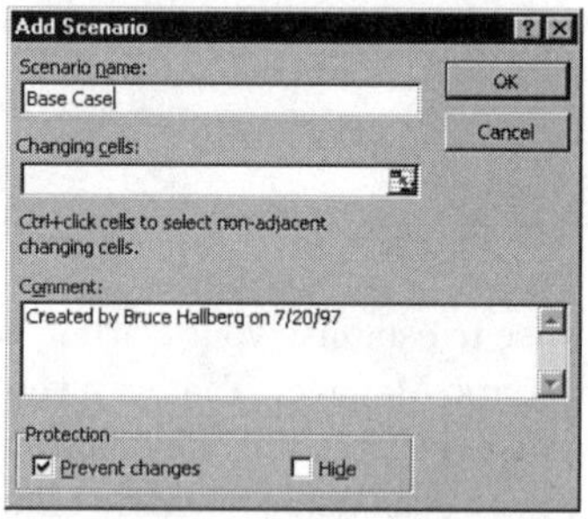

FIG. 18.3
The Add Scenario dialog box lets you define the name for new scenarios.

5. Using the Changing Cells field, select each of the cells that will be different for the scenario you're defining. For the first base case scenario you define, select one of the cells that doesn't contain a formula. To select the cells, click the Collapse button to the right of the Changing Cells field, and then either click and drag to select a contiguous range or use Ctrl+Click to select nonadjacent cells. Then click the Expand button to return to the dialog box.
6. Click OK to continue creating the scenario. If you selected any changing cells that contain formulas, you see the warning dialog box shown in Figure 18.4. This warning lets you know that one or more of the changing cells you selected contains a formula and that formulas will be changed to constant values when you view the scenario. You don't need to fix anything, but you might want to make a note of this so that you can restore formulas later. Click OK to continue.
7. You now see the Scenario Values dialog box shown in Figure 18.5. Each of the changing cells you selected is shown in the dialog box, along with its pre-scenario value. For each of the changing cells, enter a new value to reflect in the scenario.
8. Click OK to save the scenario and return to the Scenario Manager dialog box, or click the Add button to save the scenario and immediately create another scenario (you are taken to the Add Scenario dialog box instead).

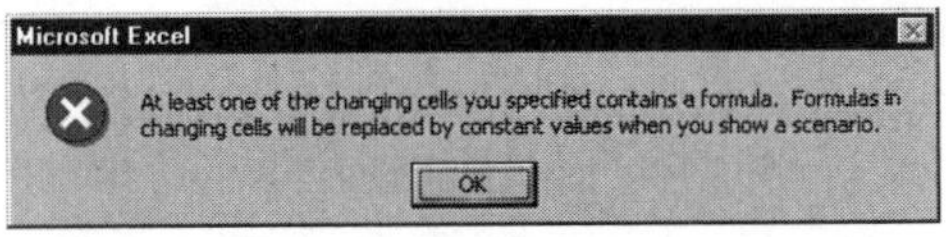

FIG. 18.4
Changing cells in scenarios are converted from formulas to values for each scenario.

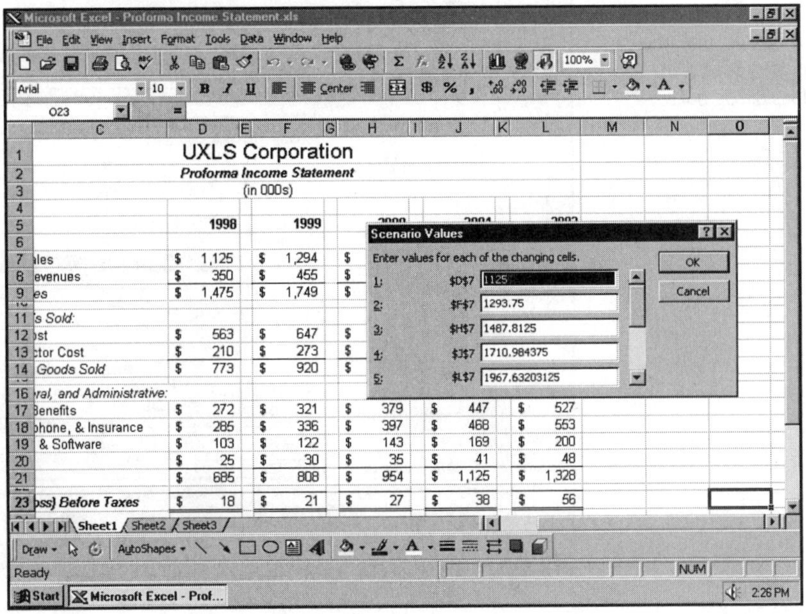

FIG. 18.5
Use the Scenario Values dialog box to control the values in each of the changing cells.

After you have defined additional scenarios, you can quickly switch between them. Choose Tools, Scenarios to display the Scenario Manager dialog box, select a scenario in the Scenarios list, and then click the Show button. The selected scenario is instantly activated. You can close the Scenario Manager dialog box to view it in more detail.

Tips for Creating Scenarios

As you are viewing different scenarios, it can become difficult to determine which scenario case you are viewing. You can easily rectify this problem. When you build your base worksheet model, include a cell that will contain the name of the scenario. Then, select that cell as one of the changing cells, and type in the name of the scenario in the Scenario Values dialog box for that cell. When you select scenarios to show, you can then see on the worksheet which scenario you are working with.

Sometimes you want to use formulas when deciding what values to enter into the Scenario Values dialog box. While Scenario Manager won't store formulas for you, you can enter them into the Scenario Values dialog box. For example, suppose you want to enter the value for cell H7 as being 12 percent higher than the value in cell F7. You can enter the formula **=F7*1.12** into the changing cell information for cell H7, as shown in Figure 18.6. When you click OK to store the changing cell values, the results of any formulas you entered are calculated and stored along with the scenario. Using this trick can save time when entering values for different scenarios.

FIG. 18.6
You can perform one-time calculations when using the Scenario Values dialog box.

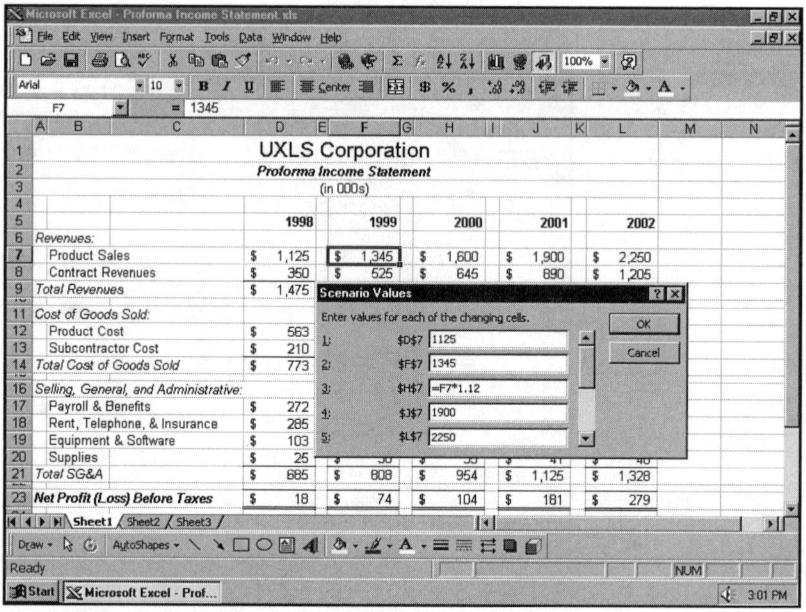

Naming worksheet cells, particularly those you use as changing cells, makes it less likely that you will enter incorrect information for scenarios. The quickest way to name cells is to select the cell or range you want to name, click in the Name Box (to the left of the formula bar), type the name, and press Enter. The Scenario Values dialog box automatically displays any assigned cell names in place of the cell references (see Figure 18.7).

▶ **See** "Naming Ranges," **p. 92**

Merging Scenarios

More than one person on a team may develop different scenarios. For example, it may be one person's job to research and develop a scenario that projects cost savings based on what is likely and possible. Another person may research the most likely possibilities for increasing sales. Yet another may be able to use his knowledge of manufacturing to develop scenarios for reducing the cost of goods sold.

After these scenarios are developed by these different people, each using their own copy of the base scenario model, you typically need to consolidate their scenarios into one "master scenario" where you can examine all possibilities.

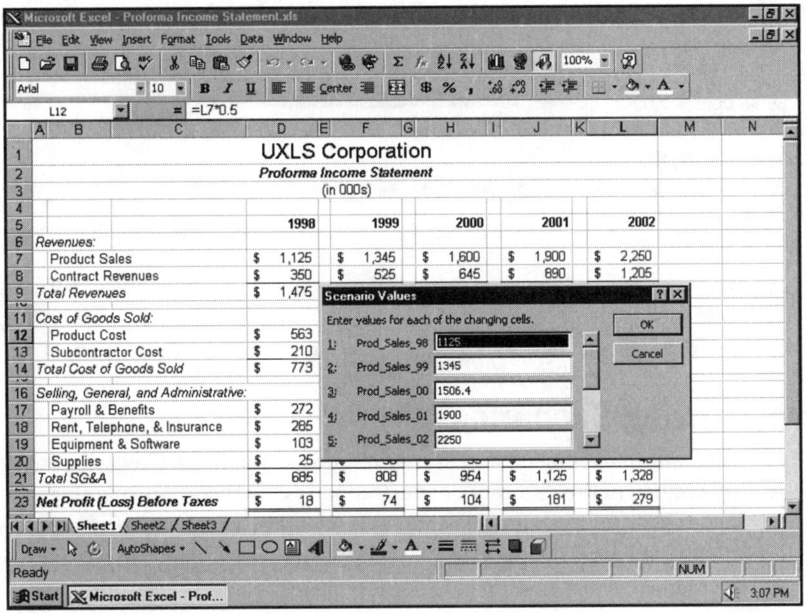

FIG. 18.7
There are many benefits for naming cells in Excel, one of which is the Scenario Values dialog box, which displays any cell names automatically instead of cryptic cell references.

In order to consolidate scenarios, each of the subsidiary scenario workbooks *must be* built in the same way, with each cell in the workbook indicating the same information (except for the changing cells, of course). To merge scenarios from multiple sources, follow these steps:

1. Open all of the scenario workbooks. Then display the workbook in which you plan to consolidate the information from the subsidiary scenario workbooks.
2. Choose Tools, Scenarios to access the Scenario Manager dialog box.
3. Click the Merge button.
4. Use the Merge Scenarios dialog box to choose the open workbook and sheet that contain the scenarios of interest (see Figure 18.8).
5. Click OK to merge the scenarios from the selected workbook to the active workbook. You return to the Scenario Manager dialog box with the new scenarios added to the list.

Protecting and Hiding Scenarios

When you define a scenario, there are two check boxes on the Add Scenario dialog box that let you protect or hide the scenarios (refer to Figure 18.3). These two options become active when you protect the worksheet and are otherwise not available.

- *Prevent Changes.* This option inhibits the ability to change a scenario in any fashion once the worksheet in which the scenarios exist is protected. A user of the workbook can still view the different scenarios when they're protected, but he cannot change them.
- *Hide.* This option causes a protected scenario to be invisible to anyone who cannot unprotect the worksheet (assuming you protect it with a password). With the Hide option selected and activated, others cannot view the hidden scenario's values.

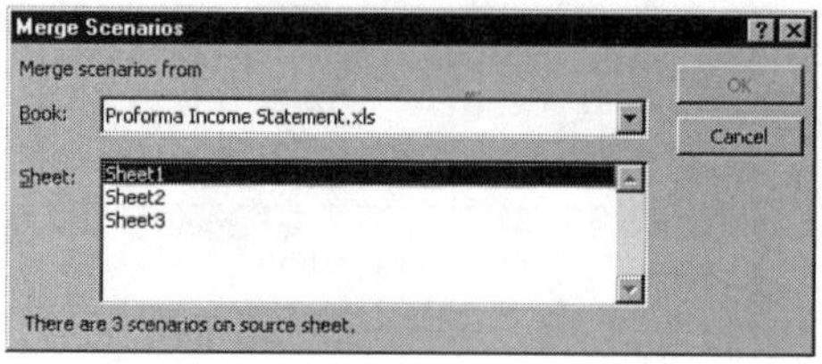

FIG. 18.8
Use the Merge Scenarios dialog box to choose an open worksheet that contains scenarios that you want to merge to your active worksheet.

In both cases, when you protect the worksheet, you must make sure that the Scenarios check box is selected in the Protect Sheet dialog box in order for these settings to operate. You choose Tools, Protection, Protect Sheet to display the Protect Sheet dialog box.

Summarizing Scenarios

As a way to document your scenarios and assumptions, Scenario Manager can prepare a summarization of the different defined scenarios. This scenario summary report lists all the inputs and results for all defined scenarios in a workbook. The following procedure summarizes three defined scenarios: Base Case, Best Case, and Worst Case. In addition, the current values of the changing cells are included in the report.

To prepare a summary report, follow these steps:

1. Make the scenario worksheet active.
2. Choose Tools, Scenarios to display the Scenario Manager dialog box.
3. Click the Summary button. You see the Scenario Summary dialog box shown in Figure 18.9.
4. Choose Scenario Summary as the Report Type, and choose the result cells in the field provided. To select the cells, click the Collapse button to the right of the Result Cells field, and then either click and drag to select a contiguous range or use Ctrl+Click to select nonadjacent cells. Then click the Expand button to return to the dialog box.

NOTE *Result cells* are the cells you want to recalculate when you view a new scenario, such as the cells containing net profit and loss calculations. The result cells must include formulas that are related to the changing cells. ■

5. Click OK to create the scenario summary.

A new worksheet is created in your current workbook called Scenario Summary. In it, you see the changing cells for each scenario in the workbook, and the results for each scenario. Figure 18.10 shows you a sample scenario summary report.

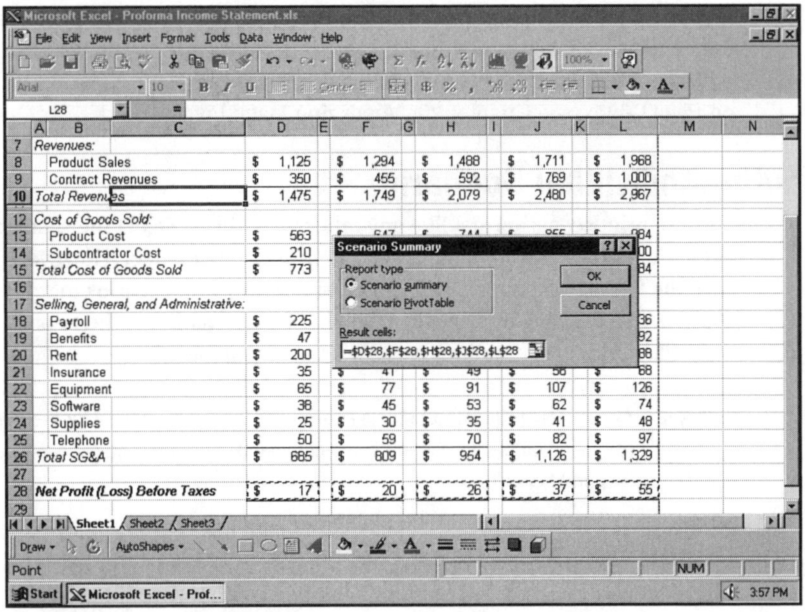

FIG. 18.9
The Scenario Summary dialog box lets you choose how the summary is created.

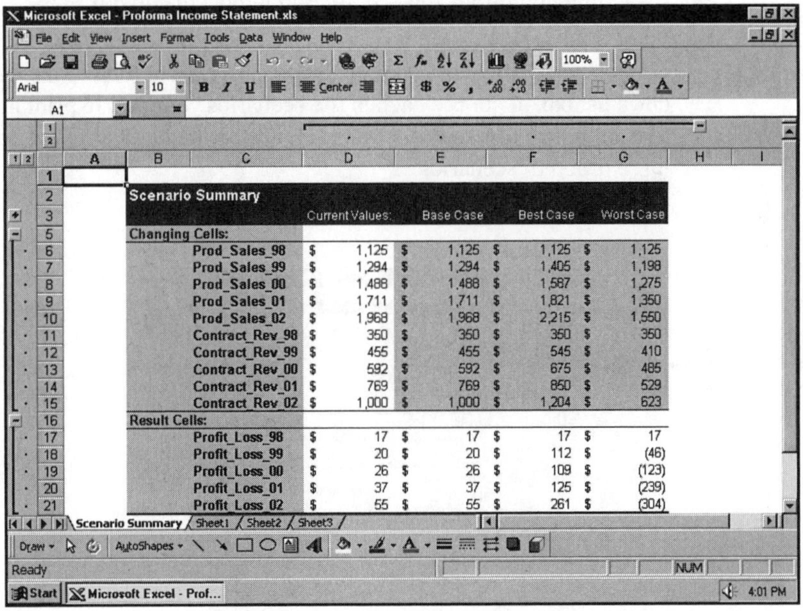

FIG. 18.10
The Scenario Summary report helps you summarize the results of your scenarios and to document your changing assumptions.

If your model contains multiple sets of changing cells provided by multiple users, you can create a PivotTable for the scenarios in step 4 of the preceding set of steps. The PivotTable provides a different way to analyze the results of complex scenario sets. For more information on PivotTables, see Chapter 20, "Analyzing Data: PivotTables!"

Printing Individual Scenarios

You can print scenarios just like any other worksheet. Select the scenario to show, close the Scenario Manager dialog box, and then print the worksheet. However, there is a way to combine the Report Manager (an Excel add-in) with your scenarios to print more than one scenario at a time. You do this by choosing the different scenarios in the Report Manager. Once they're defined, you can print multiple scenarios simultaneously.

NOTE You can tell if the Report Manager add-in is loaded by looking for the Report Manager command on the View menu. If the command is not present, choose Tools, Add-Ins to activate the Report Manager.

To print one or more scenarios, follow these steps:

1. Access the Report Manager dialog box by choosing View, Report Manager. You see the Report Manager dialog box.
2. Click the Add button. You see the Add Report dialog box.
3. In the Add Report dialog box, type a name for the report, and then use the Section to Add portion of the dialog box to define each part of the report. Use the Scenario drop-down list box to choose each of the scenarios you want to print in the report. Click Add after defining each report section. Figure 18.11 shows a report defined that will print three different scenarios.
4. Click OK to close the Report Manager dialog box.

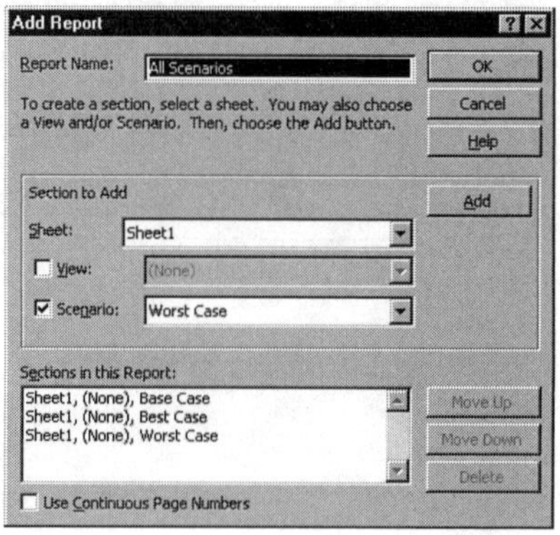

FIG. 18.11
The Add Report dialog box lets you choose scenarios for each section of a report.

Finally, to print a Report Manager report, access the Report Manager dialog box, select the report you want, and click the Print button. You must indicate how many copies you want to print in the subsequent Print dialog box. Click OK to print.

▶ **See** "Report Manager," **p. 228**

Outlining Worksheets

Large worksheets often make it difficult to look at the big picture represented by the data. Sometimes you want to hide some of the detail and only look at totals, for example. Or, perhaps you want to hide the monthly or quarterly detail and look at annual totals. There are several ways to do this sort of thing in Excel, but the easiest way to handle it is to use Excel's outlining feature.

A worksheet outline lets you select ranges of data that you can easily hide or reveal. You can create multiple levels of outline levels so that if your data is organized with multiple levels (with subtotals and grand totals, for example), you can select just the level you want at any time. Both rows and columns can be outlined.

NOTE With the outline feature in Excel 97, you can hide or display up to eight levels of detail in rows and columns.

Creating and Removing Outline Levels Manually

Consider the example worksheet shown in Figure 18.12. In it, sales are shown of different products, with a subtotal for each category of product. Because this worksheet continues for 86 rows, it's hard to see just the sales by each product category. This is a perfect application for outlines.

When you select rows or columns to outline, you choose just the rows or columns that will be hidden when the outline is collapsed. For example, to create an outline level that will hide the detail of the Beverage sales in the example, you would select row 2 through row 13. If you wanted to hide the quarterly sales detail, you would choose column C through column F prior to creating the outline.

Outlined areas cannot be immediately adjacent to other outline areas you want to create. For example, you cannot create an outline for row 2 through row 10, and then another outline for row 11 to row 18. If you try to do this, the result is row 2 through row 19 being outlined together. Instead, you have to insert a row or column between two areas that you want to outline at the same outline level. In our example, this is a subtotal line for each product.

To create an outline level, follow these steps:

1. Select the rows or columns to be outlined.
2. Choose Data, Group and Outline, Group. The outline is instantly created.

In Figure 18.13, you can see that rows 2 through 13 have been outlined.

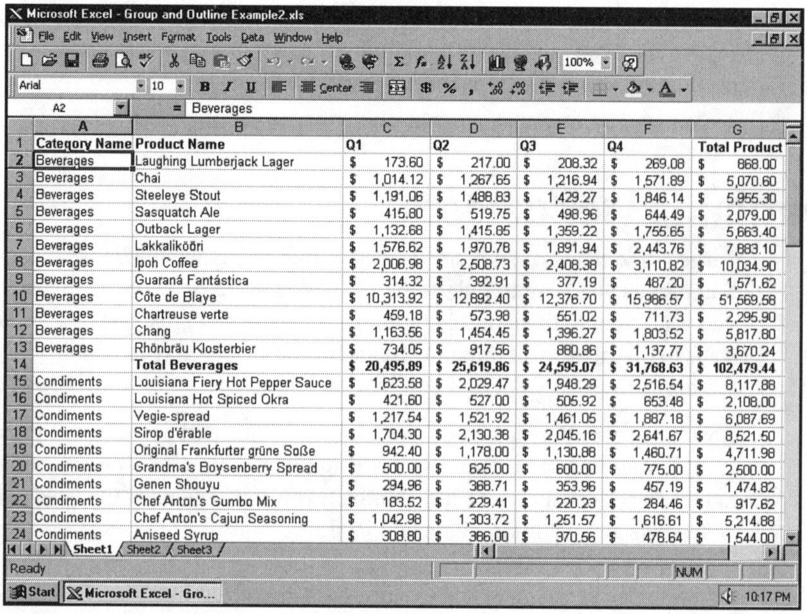

FIG. 18.12
Lists of data are one good place to use outlines.

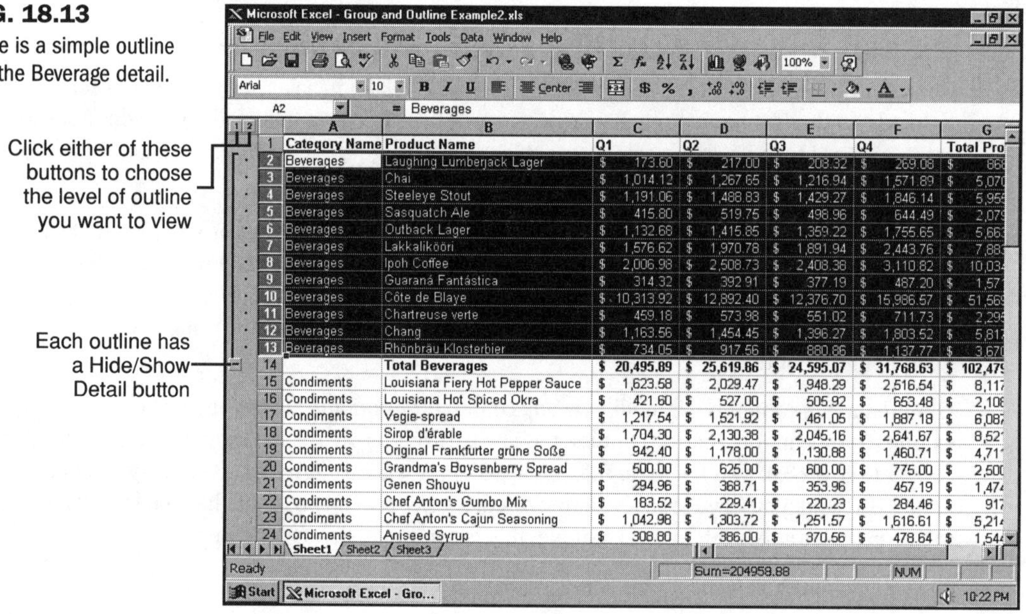

FIG. 18.13
Here is a simple outline for the Beverage detail.

TIP Instead of using the Group command, you can select the rows or columns and press Alt+Shift+right arrow.

After creating an outline, click the Show/Hide Detail buttons (the plus and minus buttons) to selectively display or hide the contents of the outlined region.

NOTE You can find the toolbar buttons for the Group, Ungroup, Hide Detail, and Show Detail commands on the PivotTable toolbar.

Removing outlines is just as easy as creating them. To remove an outline, follow these steps:

1. Select the rows or columns that make up the outline you want to remove.

   or

   To clear the entire outline, select a single cell in the worksheet.
2. Choose Data, Group and Outline, Ungroup. The outline is instantly removed.

TIP Instead of using the Ungroup command, you can select the rows or columns and press Alt+Shift+left arrow.

When you ungroup an outline level with hidden data (because its outline is closed), the data remains hidden. To reveal the data, select the rows or columns that surround the hidden rows or columns, and then use the Unhide command from the shortcut menu for the selected range.

Creating Outline Levels Automatically

In a large, complex worksheet, creating outline levels can be a real bore. It's not uncommon to have worksheets with thousands of rows, and a hundred or so places to create outline levels. It can take a lot of time to create outlines in such a worksheet. Fortunately, Excel can automatically create outlines for you.

Excel can examine worksheet data and determine where outlines should be placed. It does this by examining where the summarization functions, such as SUM or AVERAGE, are located in the data. Based on that information, it creates all the possible outlines given the layout of the data. To automatically outline a worksheet, follow these steps:

1. Select any cell in the worksheet you want to outline.

   or

   Select all the cells in which you want the outlines automatically created.
2. Choose Data, Group and Outline, Auto Outline. The outline areas that Excel can determine are instantly outlined.

When you create automatic outlines, Excel uses special automatic outline settings that you can control. To access these settings, choose Data, Group and Outline, Settings. You see the Settings dialog box shown in Figure 18.14.

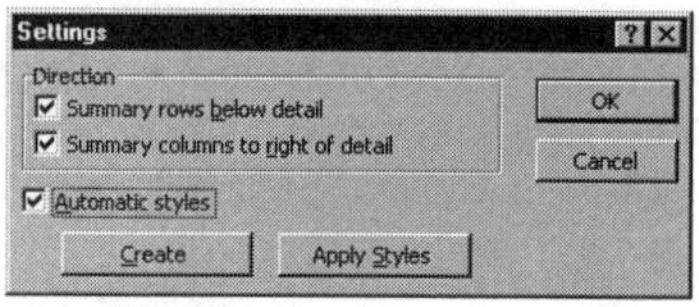

FIG. 18.14
The Settings dialog box in the Data, Group and Outline submenu lets you control how automatic outlines are created.

In the Settings dialog box, you indicate whether the summary rows are below the data they summarize (select Summary Rows Below Detail), and whether the summary columns are to the right of the data they summarize (select Summary Columns to Right of Detail). Unchecking either option means that the summary rows and columns are above or to the left of the data they summarize, respectively. You can click the Create button in the Settings dialog box to create (or recreate) the outlines based on your choices. (Clicking Create is the same as choosing Auto Outline from the Group and Outline submenu).

TIP You can clear all outlines in a worksheet with a single command. First, select the entire range of cells that is outlined (or select any single cell in the worksheet). Then choose Data, Group and Outline, Clear Outline.

Using Styles with Outline Levels

Excel can automatically apply style codes to different outline levels. These style codes enable you to format different outline levels as a group. To do this, follow these steps:

1. Choose Data, Group and Outline, Settings to open the Settings dialog box. Make sure that Automatic Styles is selected.
2. Click the Create button to create an automatic outline, or click Apply Styles to simply apply style codes to an existing outline.

CAUTION

Choosing the Create button will overwrite any previous outline levels, including any you may have added manually. Instead, set up the outlines as you want, and then use the Apply Style button to maintain existing outline levels.

Excel assigns style codes ColLevel_1 through ColLevel_7 and RowLevel_1 through RowLevel_7 to the outline levels in your worksheet. You can then format each level by opening the Style dialog box (choose Format, Style), choosing the style whose format you want to modify in the Style Name dialog box, and then using the other formatting options in the Style dialog box to make whatever formatting changes you want.

Moving and Copying Outlined Data

You can move and copy outlined data just the same way as you do other ranges in your workbooks. Whether the outlines are collapsed or opened, all of the underlying data is included when you use the Cut and Copy commands. However, what if you have collapsed several levels of outlines, and only want to copy the visible data to another worksheet?

You can copy only visible cells in an outline by using these steps:

1. Select the range of visible cells that you want to copy.
2. Choose Edit, Go To to open the Go To dialog box.
3. In the Go To dialog box, click the Special button to open the Go To Special dialog box.
4. Click the Visible Cells Only option button.
5. Click OK.

The result of these steps is that only the visible cells within the range you first specified are selected. You can then use the Copy command normally to place those cells on the Clipboard and paste them elsewhere.

TIP When you print outlined worksheets, visible cells are all that are printed. Therefore, make sure that the outline detail you want to print is revealed before printing.

Common Problems and Solutions

The scenarios and outlining features in Excel may pose concepts that are difficult to grasp initially, but with practice, you will learn to create scenarios and outlines with ease. The following sections discuss problems you may encounter while learning to use these features.

Do I really need more than 30 variables in a scenario?

It's true that you can only have 30 changing cells in a single scenario. However, many real-life scenarios have far more changing cells than this. How can you deal with this problem?

When you come across situations like this, break up your scenarios into multiple parts. Each part of the scenario controls a different set of changing cells. Then, to completely display a given scenario, use the Show button in the Scenario Manager dialog box for each part.

Recall that Scenario Manager works by inputting cell values into the changing cells. Because of this, there's no problem with using a collection of scenarios where each scenario inputs values into different collections of changing cells.

The danger with this approach is that you have to remember to show each of the component scenarios in order to display the complete scenario. You can make this a bit easier to remember by preceding each scenario name with a number. For example, to completely define a best case scenario, you might create scenarios with these names: 1-Best Case, 2-Best Case, and 3-Best Case. This gives you a reminder as you change complete scenarios that you need to use the Show button with each defined scenario.

Data is not grouped correctly in outlines.

When you're creating outlines, it's important to keep some points in mind so that they are created correctly.

If you are creating automatic outlines, make sure that the options in the Settings dialog box are set correctly for your worksheet's data. For example, if your summaries are below the detail they summarize, make sure that the appropriate option for the direction of the data is selected.

If you have parts of a list that summarize at the bottom of detail and parts that summarize at the top of detail, and you want to create an automatic outline, you have to break the process into steps. First, select all of the rows or columns where the summarization is in one direction, and then use the Auto Outline command. Then, select the other region where the summarization is in the other direction, and use the Auto Outline command again.

When you select rows or columns prior to using the Auto Outline command, make sure that you include all of the detail *and* the summarization rows or columns, because those rows and columns are used to determine where the automatic outlines are placed.

Conversely, when creating outlines manually, make sure that you do not select the summarization rows or columns before issuing the Group command. Otherwise, closing that outline will also close the summarization row or column.

Don't forget, as you create and remove outlines, that the Undo command reverses successive Group commands. If you make a mistake when creating an outline, simply click Undo and select the right set of rows or columns.

From Here...

In this chapter, you learned how to use Excel's scenario and outlining features to view the data you are analyzing in many different ways. Excel provides many additional features for analyzing your data. Refer to the following chapters for more information:

- Chapter 19, "Auditing and Validating Worksheets," explains how to trace errors in your workbooks, validate user input, and use names instead of cell references to help reduce the chance of errors in formulas.
- Chapter 20, "Analyzing Data: PivotTables!," shows you how to build PivotTables, which enable you to quickly analyze and manipulate complex data.
- Chapter 21, "Mastering Excel's Solver and Goal Seek," covers how to use the Solver add-in to find an optimal solution to a problem with multiple variables and the Goal Seek feature to find a specific solution to a problem involving one variable.
- Chapter 22, "Mastering the Analysis ToolPak," explains how to use Excel's analysis tools for business, engineering, and statistical applications.

CHAPTER 19

Auditing and Validating Worksheets

by Bruce Hallberg with Joyce Nielsen

Excel enables you to set up relationships among the various cells in the worksheet. However, if you run into an error in the worksheet, you may need to trace those various relationships to find the error. You can use the Auditing toolbar when you need to trace an error.

If you are setting up worksheets that others will use to enter data, you need to make sure that the data entered is valid. Many data fields can use simple rules that let you know that a typographical error was made. For example, if a user is entering dates, it may be that only dates within a certain range are valid. You can use Excel to determine whether data entered by others is or isn't acceptable.

This chapter also explains how using named ranges can significantly help reduce the amount of errors in your worksheets. You also can use cell comments to explain the data in your worksheets, especially if the worksheets will be used by others besides you. ■

Using Excel's auditing tools

Excel provides tools for error-checking worksheets on the Auditing toolbar. These tools enable you to trace formula precedents and dependents, find cells that contribute to error results, and display the formulas in a worksheet.

Validating user input

You have to allow for mistakes in workbooks you create. Excel's data validation features make checking for errors during data entry quick and easy.

Using names in Excel to improve worksheet accuracy

Cell or range names that you define are generally easier for you to remember and type in formulas than obscure cell references. Therefore, using names whenever possible can help reduce the number of errors in your worksheets.

Working with cell comments

Wouldn't it be nice if you could attach yellow sticky notes to your worksheets? With Excel's cell comments, you can do just that. Use cell comments to document individual cells in ways that make your worksheets more understandable.

Auditing Workbooks

Excel workbooks can often grow large and complex. The more complex a workbook is, the harder it is to ensure that it's doing its job correctly. With cell values and formulas used throughout the worksheet, finding the source of errors can be a real chore—unless you use Excel's built-in auditing features.

With Excel, you can display *tracer lines* to find *precedents* (cells that are referred to by a formula), *dependents* (cells that contain formulas that refer to other cells), and errors in any cell. Most of the time when you use the auditing feature, you probably want to trace the precedents to a formula to find out what other cells contribute to the formula in that cell. Once you find the source of your error, you can remove all tracer lines from the display with the click of a button.

In this section, you learn how to use Excel's auditing features to easily test the accuracy of your workbooks (or other people's workbooks).

Activating the Auditing Toolbar

The auditing tools in Excel are accessed on the Auditing toolbar. You cannot access this toolbar by using the View, Toolbars command. Instead, you must use the Tools, Auditing, Show Auditing Toolbar command. You also can right-click in the toolbar area, choose Customize, and select the Auditing option in the Customize dialog box. The Auditing toolbar is shown in Figure 19.1, and its buttons are described in Table 19.1.

FIG. 19.1
Use the Auditing toolbar to access Excel's auditing features.

Table 19.1 Auditing Toolbar Buttons

Button	Name	Description
	Trace Precedents	Graphically shows the source of a cell's result
	Remove Precedent Arrows	Removes the arrows generated with the Trace Precedents button
	Trace Dependents	Graphically shows what cells rely on a cell's contents or results
	Remove Dependent Arrows	Removes the arrows generated with the Trace Dependents button
	Remove All Arrows	Removes all precedent and dependent arrows on a worksheet

Button	Name	Description
	Trace Error	Locates cells that contribute to an error result in a cell
	New Comment	Inserts a comment into a cell
	Circle Invalid Data	Draws circles around data outside the valid range defined with the Validation feature (see "Validating User Input" later in this chapter)
	Clear Validation Circles	Removes circles drawn using the Circle Invalid Data button

Tracing Dependents and Precedents

Cells that refer to other cells, either directly or indirectly, can be thought of as having a precedent-dependent relationship. A ***precedent cell*** is one that contributes to a cell's result. A ***dependent cell*** is one that relies on the selected cell's contents or result. Excel 97 lets you graphically see these precedent-dependent cell relationships.

To trace the precedents or dependents of a cell, follow these steps:

1. If the Auditing toolbar isn't displayed, choose Tools, Auditing, Show Auditing Toolbar.
2. Select the cell for which you want to examine its precedents.
3. Click either the Trace Precedents or Trace Dependents button.

After clicking one of the Trace buttons, an arrow (or set of arrows) appears showing cells that directly relate to the selected cell's result. For example, in Figure 19.2 the precedents of cell B23 are displayed. The arrows show that cells B22 and B16 are being used by cell B23. And, if you examine the formula bar in Figure 19.2 you'll see that this is indeed the case.

You can use the Trace commands as many times as you want for a cell. Each time you issue the command, additional arrows are drawn showing even deeper precedent relationships. For example, Figure 19.3 shows the same worksheet with the Trace Precedents button used one additional time. You can now see that cell B22 relies on cells B19:B21, and that cell B16 relies on cells B14:B15.

After you're finished viewing the arrows created with the Trace Precedents or Trace Dependents commands, you can use the Remove Precedent Arrows and Remove Dependent Arrows commands to remove the arrows, one level at a time. You can also click the Remove All Arrows button to remove every arrow in a worksheet with one click.

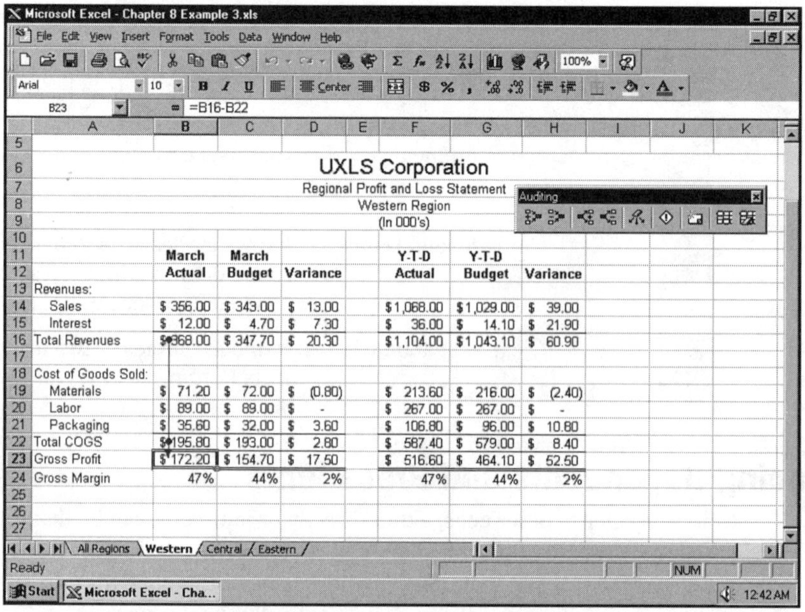

FIG. 19.2
Tracing precedents lets you quickly see what cells are being used to achieve a selected cell's result.

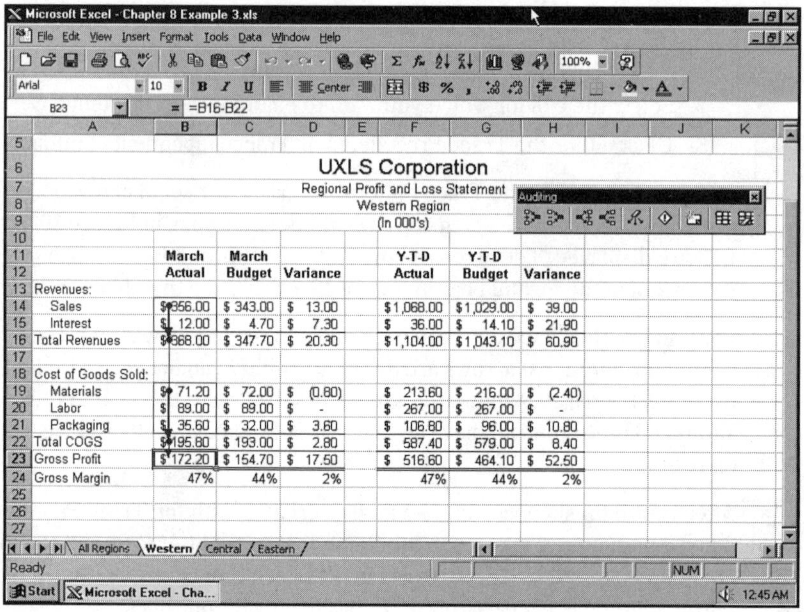

FIG. 19.3
Keep clicking the Trace Precedents button to see deeper relationships.

Jumping Through Trace Arrows

Large worksheets may have precedent and dependent arrows that extend across many pages of information. Having to scroll through a large worksheet to find the source or destination of an arrow can take a long time. To speed the process of tracking down arrow sources and destinations, you can double-click the arrow line. If the other end of the arrow indicates a cell on the current worksheet, you will be taken instantly to that cell. Double-click the arrow again to move back to the source.

Sometimes precedent or dependent arrows indicate a cell on another worksheet. For example, Figure 19.4 shows that cell B23 relates to another worksheet by the black dependent line and the worksheet icon. Double-clicking a worksheet arrow activates the Go To dialog box, which prompts you for the worksheet and cell reference to which you want to jump.

FIG. 19.4
Double-clicking a worksheet trace arrow takes you to the traced data in the referenced worksheet.

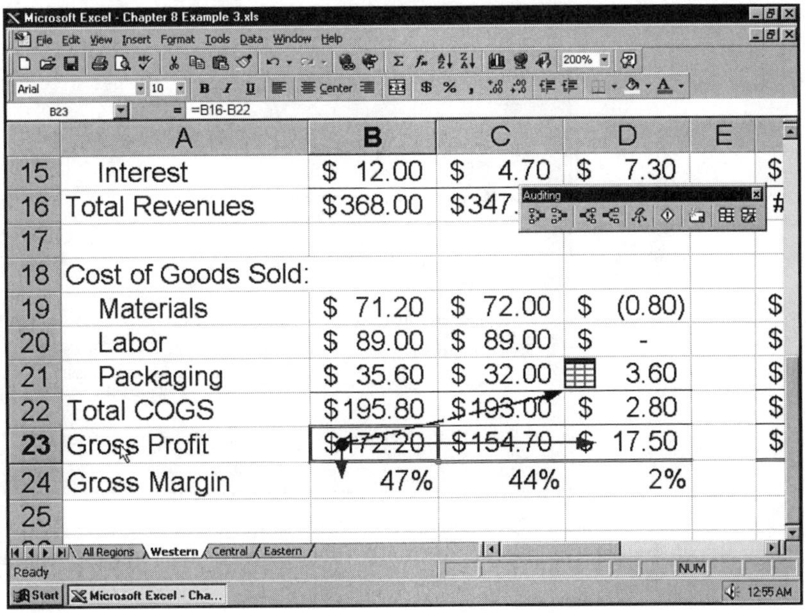

Tracing Errors

When cells return an error result, such as #VALUE!, select the cell with that result and click the Trace Error button. The normal trace arrows are drawn and let you track down the source of the error message.

Displaying Formulas Instead of Results

The tracing arrows are useful when auditing a worksheet because they show you graphically how different cells relate to one another. Reviewing a worksheet using precedent and dependent arrows is a lot faster than examining all of the formulas and checking them by hand.

Just the same, sometimes you have to check all of your formulas by hand to be completely sure that they're all referencing the cells you want in the way that you want. One quick way to do this is to set the worksheet to display its formulas, rather than the results of those formulas. Use the Tools, Options command to activate the Options dialog box, click the View tab, and choose the Formulas check box. Your worksheet then displays its formulas instead of their result. Figure 19.5 shows you how this looks.

TIP You can document a worksheet by displaying its formulas and then printing it.

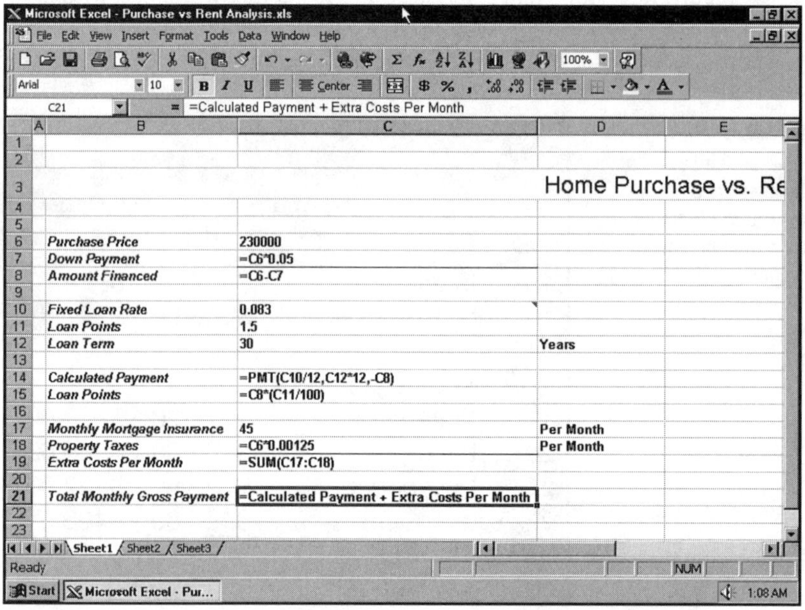

FIG. 19.5
View the formulas for a worksheet to perform a complete audit of the formula references.

To return the worksheet to normal, re-access the Options dialog box and deselect the Formulas check box.

Validating User Input

97

You can help ensure that the worksheets you create contain valid data entered by others (or even by yourself) through the use of Excel's Data Validation feature. New to Excel 97, Data Validation lets you define rules for cells on worksheets in a flexible way, including automatic pop-up reminders and messages if invalid data is entered. Through the use of the Data Validation feature, you can reduce the need to audit information in worksheets.

Set Validation Rules and Responses

Consider the worksheet shown in Figure 19.6. You see a worksheet designed to collect information on General Ledger journal entries. People in accounting use this worksheet to enter data about needed entries to the General Ledger, after which the General Ledger clerk enters the actual journal entries into the accounting system. There have been a number of problems with people entering invalid account and cost center numbers, dates, and descriptions that are too lengthy to fit into the accounting system. Each time an error occurs, a lot of employee time is wasted trying to sort out the problem. By setting up data validation rules in the worksheet, you can reduce the amount of confusion and the potential for these time-consuming problems.

FIG. 19.6
An example Journal Entry worksheet. How do you ensure that correct information is entered?

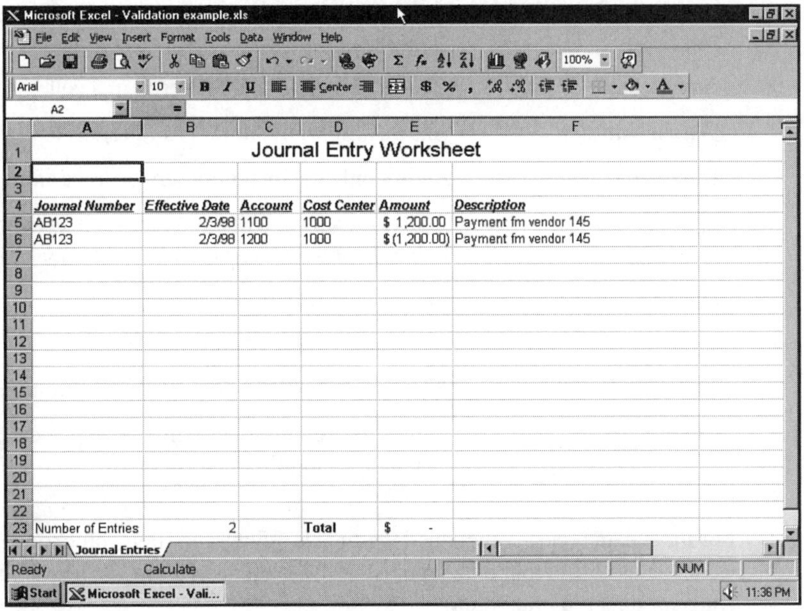

To access the Data Validation dialog box, first select the range of cells to which you want to apply a data validation rule. In this example, cells B5:B22 will be set so that only dates in the current year can be entered. After selecting the cells, choose Data, Validation. You see the Data Validation dialog box shown in Figure 19.7.

FIG. 19.7
Use the Data Validation dialog box to create validation rules and messages.

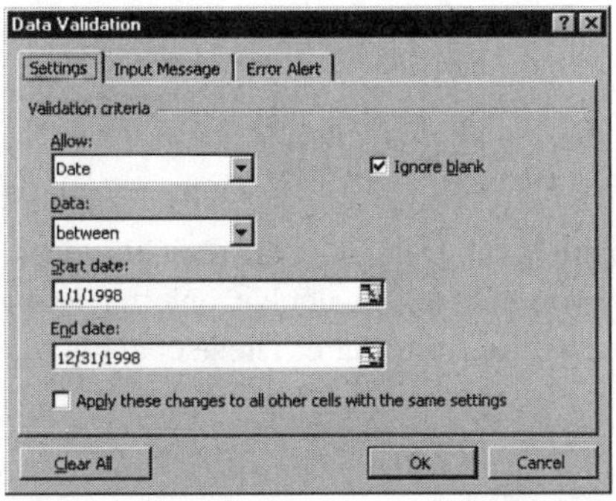

The Data Validation dialog box has three tabs. In the first, Settings, you set the actual rule for the selected cells. You first choose a type of data that can be entered in the Allow text box, and you then complete the remaining fields on the Settings tab to set the rules for that data type.

Part V
Ch 19

The remaining fields change based on the data type you choose in the Allow text box. Table 19.2 details the different data types available.

Table 19.2 Data Types for Data Validation

Data Type	Description
Any Value	Allows any value to be entered in a cell
Whole Number	Allows only whole numbers (integers)
Decimal	Allows only decimal numbers or fractions
List	Allows data from a defined list, such as a range of entries, a defined name, or typed entries separated by commas
Date	Allows only values entered as dates
Time	Allows only values entered as times
Text length	Allows only text of a defined length (number of characters)
Custom	Allows data entered as formulas, expressions, or references to calculations in other cells

For most data types, you choose the type in Allow, and then you choose how you will define valid values within that data type using the Data drop-down list box. You can use the following rules for data type validation:

- Between
- Not between
- Equal to
- Not equal to
- Greater than
- Less than
- Greater than or equal to
- Less than or equal to

Depending on the choice you make in the Data field, other fields appear on the dialog box. For example, if you choose Between, you then see two fields, one that lets you define a minimum value and one that lets you define a maximum value. These changing fields let you set the ***value limits***.

For most value limits, you can enter a value in the fields that appear, or you can choose a worksheet cell to use for the comparison. Using a cell reference lets you create flexible data validation rules that change based on a worksheet cell. For example, if a worksheet cell calculates and displays the current date, you could reference that cell for fields that the user will enter that should be the same as the current date. Formulas are also allowed in the value limit fields.

Setting Input Messages The second tab of the Data Validation dialog box lets you create input messages that remind the people using the worksheet of what data is required. The Input Message tab is shown in Figure 19.8.

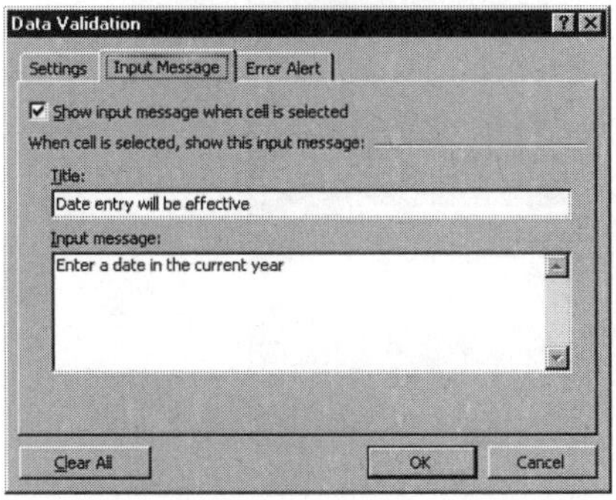

FIG. 19.8
Create input messages to remind people what data is required.

When a cell is selected that has an input message defined, a comment appears with the information you type in the dialog box. For example, Figure 19.9 shows the effective date field's input message.

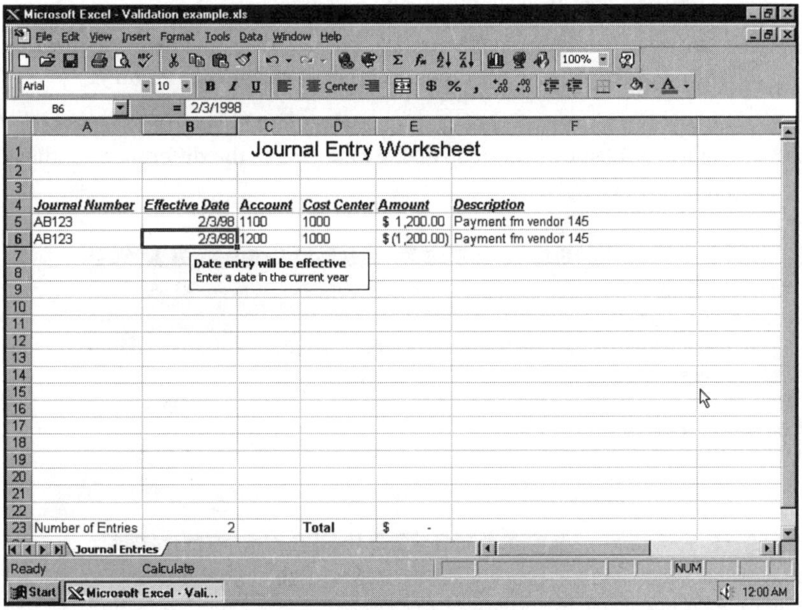

FIG. 19.9
Input messages unobtrusively tell people what information is required quickly, without disrupting their data entry.

Setting Error Alerts Even after defining entry rules and input messages, people will still try to enter incorrect data. Usually this is due to mistyped information, but sometimes it's also because they don't understand what data is required. You can define error alerts that appear when invalid data is entered. Not only do error alerts require attention by the user of the worksheet, but they can also contain helpful information. Figure 19.10 shows the Error Alert tab in the Data Validation dialog box.

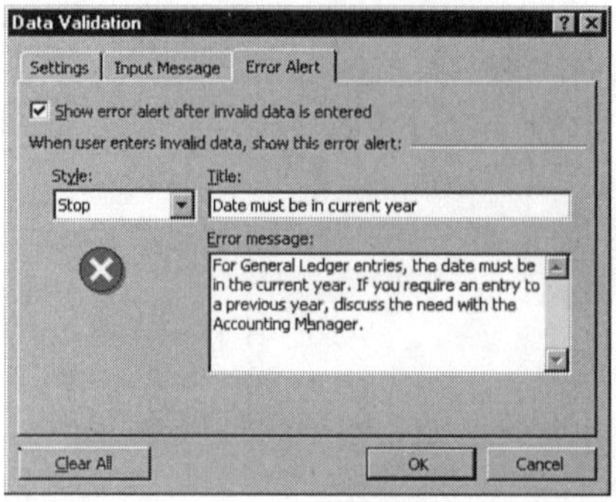

FIG. 19.10 Create an error message that appears when incorrect information is entered into a cell.

There are three types of error alerts you can define:

- *Information.* An Information message displays a dialog box, which the user can simply acknowledge and continue, leaving the invalid data intact.
- *Warning.* A Warning displays a dialog box in which the user must acknowledge that they want to leave the invalid data intact.
- *Stop.* A Stop displays a dialog box that doesn't allow the user to continue with invalid data in the cell; they must correct or reverse their entry.

Figure 19.11 shows an Information dialog box, Figure 19.12 shows the Warning dialog box, and Figure 19.13 shows the Stop dialog box. Notice the differences in the acknowledgment buttons for each one.

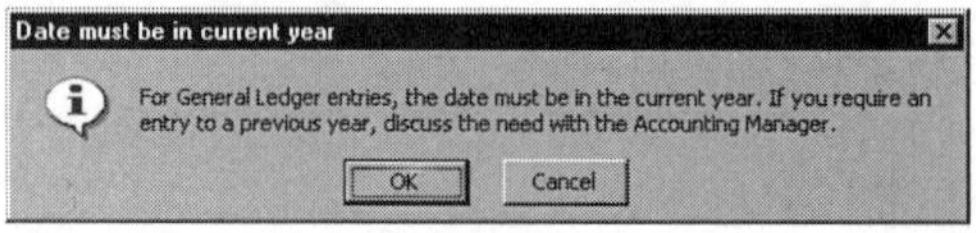

FIG. 19.11 An Information error alert simply displays a dialog box that the user can acknowledge and continue. Invalid data can be entered into the cell.

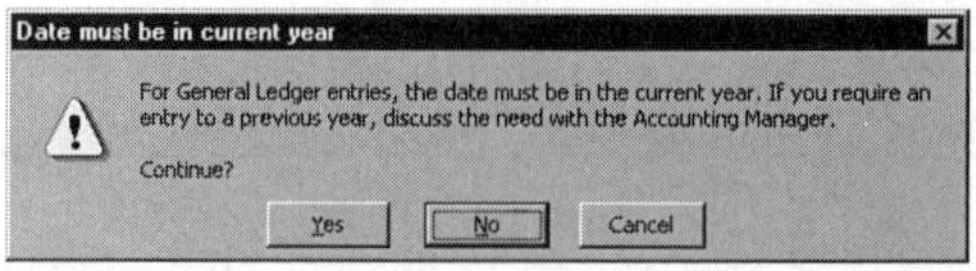

FIG. 19.12 A Warning error alert displays a dialog box in which the default action (No) lets the user re-enter the data. They must click Yes to leave the invalid data in the cell.

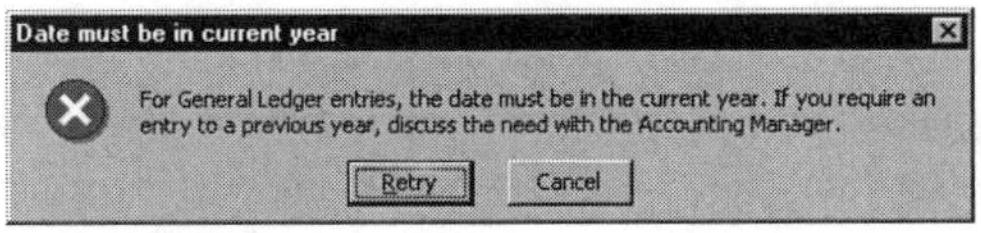

FIG. 19.13
The Stop error alert does not allow the user to leave a cell with invalid data entered; they must reverse or correct their entry.

Circle Invalid Data

Excel's Auditing toolbar contains a command that automatically circles data that doesn't meet the data validation criteria you've created. This can occur when you use Information or Warning messages and the user has continued past the error alert and left the invalid data intact. To circle invalid data, follow these steps:

1. Access the Auditing toolbar (choose Tools, Auditing, Show Auditing Toolbar).

2. Click the Circle Invalid Data button. Information on the worksheet that doesn't fit the data validation rules is circled, as shown in Figure 19.14.

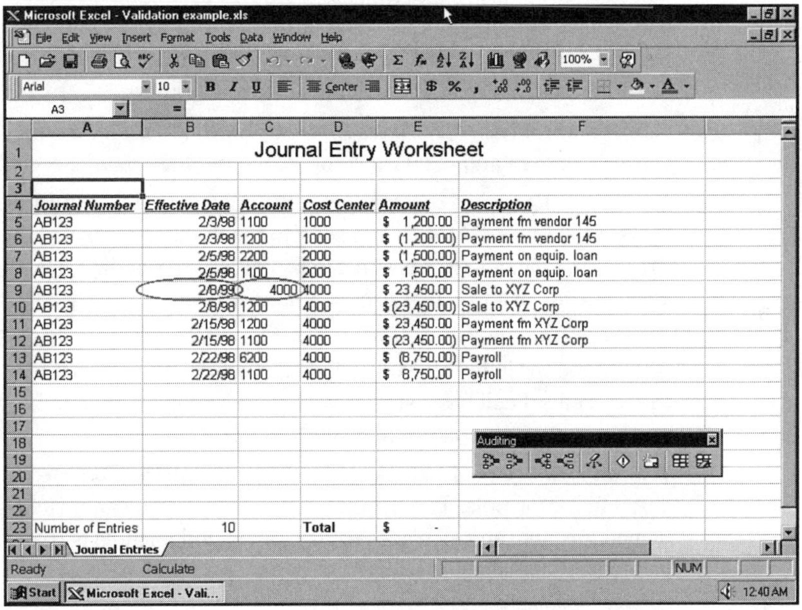

FIG. 19.14
Use the Circle Invalid Data command to quickly review the validity of worksheet data.

For each of the circled cells, you can examine the cell contents and correct them if appropriate. To remove the circles, click the Clear Validation Circles button on the Auditing toolbar. The circles also automatically disappear when you correct the cell contents to comply with the validation rules.

TIP The data validation settings along with the Circle Invalid Data command can be used not only for entering and checking data, but also for existing data. For example, if you have a large worksheet that you need to review, you can enter data validation rules after the worksheet is complete. Existing data is not affected by applying validation rules, and no errors occur when you apply the rules (unless you try to edit any of the validated cells afterwards). After applying the validation rules, use the Circle Invalid Data command to quickly see if any of the data appears incorrect.

Using Names in Excel to Improve Worksheet Accuracy

Excel lets you name cell ranges, constant values, and formulas. These names can then be used in formulas instead of cell references. Using names makes it much easier not only to enter formulas, but also to instantly see if a formula is entered correctly. Names help reduce the chance of errors in your formulas because in most cases, you are more likely to type a name correctly than a cell or range address. There are many advantages to using names in Excel:

- *You can use named ranges with Excel's Go To command.* For example, you can press Ctrl+G (Go To) and then type **Sales**, one of your named ranges. You are instantly transported to the named range of cells. You can also use the Name drop-down list box to choose one of the defined names to which to jump.
- *Names make it easier for others to quickly understand your worksheet models.* It's much easier to understand =Square_Footage*Lease_Rate than to see what =A5*D15 refers to.
- *You can create named constants.* For example, you can create a constant named **Days_in_Current_Month** and set it to the number of days in the current month. When the month changes to one with a different number of days, just change the constant value and all formulas that use that name will automatically adjust.
- *Names are inherently less prone to error than cell references.* If a cell reference you type is one number or letter off, you can get an incorrect result that may appear correct because the referenced cell has a similar value to the cell you intended. Typing a name with even one letter wrong displays the `#NAME?` error.
- *You can create named formulas.* These names can then be used in cells instead of typing a traditional formula. The advantage here is that you can make a single change to the named formula, and all places where the named formula is referenced will receive the change automatically.

▶ **See** "Naming Ranges," **p. 92**

Using Named Constants

You can use the Define Name dialog box, discussed in Chapter 3, "Entering and Editing Data," to create named constants. A *named constant* is a fixed value that you can refer to in your formulas. For example, you might define a named constant for the prime lending rate.

The prime lending rate changes infrequently, and you may not want to devote a cell to storing its current value. Instead, use a named constant and refer to that name when appropriate. Should you need to change the constant value, you can do so and all formulas will use the new value.

To create a named constant, type the constant name in the Names in Workbook field, and then type the constant value in the Refers To field. You enter the constant value in the form ***=value*** where value is a number or text. Surround text values with quotation marks.

TIP In order to distinguish constants from other types of names, use some common rule in creating their names. For example, you might begin all constant names with the letter C followed by a period (for example, **C.Prime_Rate**). When you examine formulas that use constants, you can then easily tell which names are named cells or ranges, and which are named constants.

Using Named Formulas

Excel lets you create named formulas. You use named formulas when you want to use a formula in your worksheet that may change at some time. You can then change the formula defined for the name, and the change is carried out everywhere the name is referenced.

You define a named formula using the Define Name dialog box. Type a name in the Names in Workbook field, and then enter the formula in the Refers To field using the form ***=formula***. For example, **=C.Prime_Rate/365** would yield the prime rate for use in calculations that perform daily compounding of that interest rate.

Removing Names

You can quickly remove names from your workbooks. Access the Define Name dialog box, click a name in the list, and then click the Delete button.

CAUTION

If you remove a name from a workbook that is being used in formulas, all such formulas will return the #NAME? error. Those formulas will need to be edited to correct the problem, or you can redefine the name.

Applying Range Names

Imagine that you're updating a workbook to use names when possible instead of cell references. You use the Insert, Name, Create command to automatically assign names to the cells. Now, instead of changing any formulas in the workbook to make use of the names you created, you can use the Apply Names command to automatically adjust all of the formulas so that they use the available names.

To automatically adjust formulas to use names, follow these steps:

1. Select the range of cells in which you want to adjust the formulas.
2. Choose Insert, Name, Apply to access the Apply Names dialog box, shown in Figure 19.15.

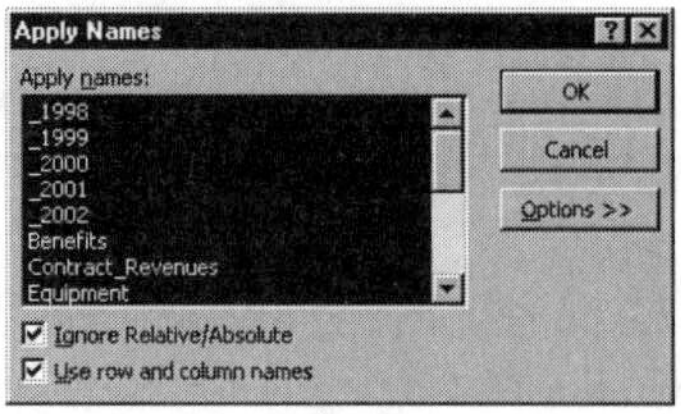

FIG. 19.15
The Apply Names dialog box lets you quickly substitute cell references in formulas with existing names.

3. In the Apply Names list, select all of the names that you want to have substituted in any formulas.
4. Check the Ignore Relative/Absolute check box if you want to replace all references with names, whether or not the reference type is relative or absolute. Deselecting this check box only replaces relative references in formulas with relative names, and absolute references with absolute names.
5. Check the Use Row and Column Names check box if you want Excel to use range names if specific cell names can't be found.
6. Click OK to apply the names.

You can use the Options button in the Apply Names dialog box to control how the Use Row and Column Names check box works.

Pasting Names

Sometimes worksheets will contain names that are long and difficult to type without error. You can use the Paste Name dialog box to type any defined names for you, eliminating the chance for error.

At any time that you are entering or editing a formula, access the Paste Names dialog box by choosing Insert, Name, Paste. The Paste Name dialog box is shown in Figure 19.16. Choose one of the names from the Paste Name list and click OK to have the name typed for you.

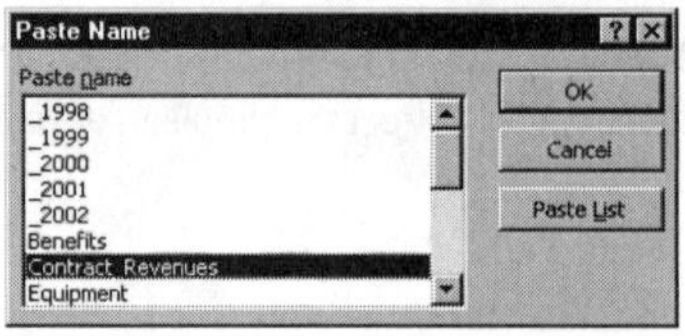

FIG. 19.16
Use the Paste Name dialog box when you aren't sure how a name is spelled or you don't want to type the entire name.

TIP You can use the Paste Names dialog box to quickly create a list of all of the names in your workbook. Select a two column area of a worksheet, access the Paste Names dialog box, and click the Paste List button. You can use this as a way to document the names in your workbook.

Defining Label Ranges

In some worksheets it may not be possible for Excel to correctly determine which cells contain labels for the data, and which cells contain the data itself. Trying to use labels in formulas when this is the case is tricky at best. What you can do, however, is tell Excel which cells contain the labels. You can then create natural language formulas that will be correctly interpreted by Excel.

To define a range of labels, follow these steps:

1. Use the Insert, Name, Label command to display the Label Ranges dialog box shown in Figure 19.17.
2. Click the Add Label Range field, and then select the range on the worksheet that contains the labels to which you want to refer.
3. Click either the Row Labels or Column Labels option button, as appropriate for the range you selected.
4. Click the Add button.

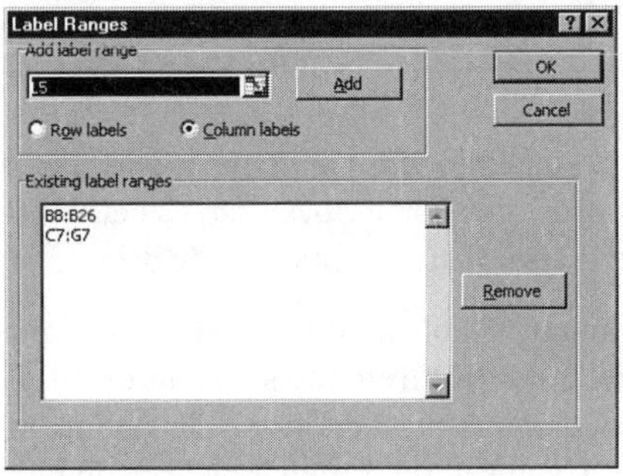

FIG. 19.17 You can define which cells contain labels for use in formulas with the Label Ranges dialog box.

Working with Cell Comments

It's often useful to include comments on specific cells in a worksheet. Comments can serve to document why you set up a cell in a particular way, why a particular result was achieved, or even to ask a question of someone else reviewing a worksheet for you.

To insert a cell comment use these steps:

1. Right-click the cell to which you want to add a comment.
2. Choose Insert Comment from the shortcut menu.
3. A box appears with your name at the top and an arrow to the cell that will contain the comment (see Figure 19.18). Type whatever comment you want in the space provided. Use the white handles around the comment to resize it, or drag one of its borders to move it to another place on the worksheet (it still indicates the same cell; you move it to create space to see underlying detail).
4. Click another cell to close the comment.

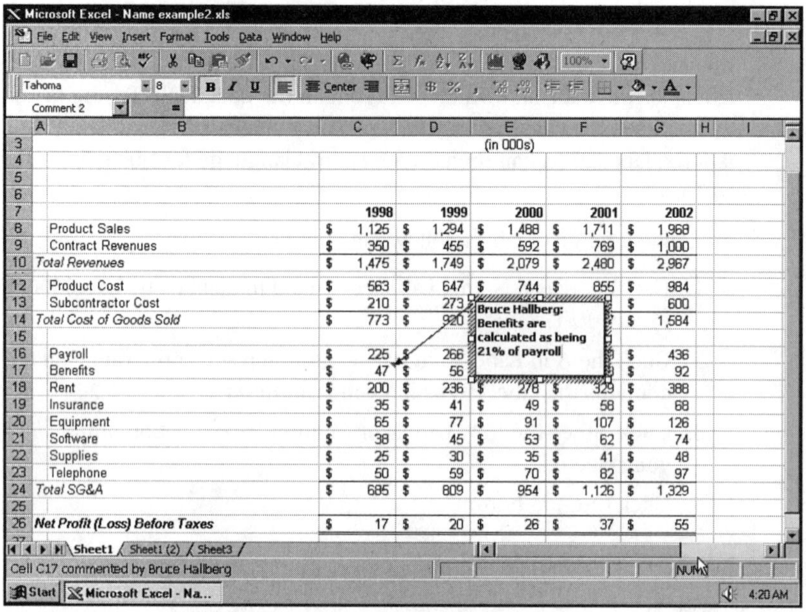

FIG. 19.18
Excel's cell comments simulate yellow sticky notes on your worksheets.

Cell comments are indicated by a small red triangle in the upper-right corner of each cell that contains a comment. Pausing your mouse pointer over such a cell causes the comment to appear in a comment box. You can review comments quickly using this technique.

You can make comments permanently visible in the worksheet by right-clicking the cell with the comment and choosing Show Comment from the shortcut menu. To hide the comment again, right-click the cell with the comment and choose Hide Comment from the shortcut menu. While a comment is shown, you can reposition it by dragging its border. You can also edit it by clicking in the comment window.

To edit an existing comment, right-click the cell containing the comment and choose Edit Comment from the shortcut menu. To remove a comment, choose Delete Comment from the shortcut menu.

Common Problems and Solutions

You should run into few problems when auditing your worksheets or validating user input. The following sections discuss a few minor difficulties that you may experience while validating data in your worksheets or trying to reference names in other worksheets.

The `Recalculate` message keeps appearing during data validation. How can I get rid of the message?

If you set up data validation rules that involve calculations, and your worksheet is set to manual recalculation, you may see a message prompting you to recalculate the worksheet when you find incorrect entries. To avoid seeing this message each time Excel discovers invalid data, choose Tools, Options, and then click the Calculation tab. In the Calculation section, click Automatic to switch to automatic calculation; then click OK.

How do I reference named cells in other worksheets?

If you want to refer to other cells or ranges from other sheets in a workbook, you must include a sheet reference as well as a cell reference or name in a formula. Use an exclamation mark (!) to separate the sheet reference from the cell reference or name.

If the cell you want to reference on Sheet2 is named Q1Sales, you would use `Sheet2!Q1Sales` as the reference. If you have named the sheet, simply use the sheet name and then the cell name, such as `Details!Q1Sales`. If the sheet name includes spaces, you must surround the sheet reference with single quotation marks, such as `'Sales Details'!Q1Sales`.

From Here...

This chapter showed you how to trace errors, validate user input, and use names and comments to help reduce the chance of errors in workbooks.

Excel provides many other features for analyzing your data. Refer to the following chapters for more information:

- Chapter 18, "Building Scenarios and Outlines with Excel," shows you how to use Excel's scenario and outlining features to view the data you are analyzing in many different ways.
- Chapter 20, "Analyzing Data: PivotTables!," shows you how to build pivot tables, which enable you to quickly analyze and manipulate complex data.
- Chapter 21, "Mastering Excel's Solver and Goal Seek," covers how to use the Solver add-in to find an optimal solution to a problem with multiple variables, and the Goal Seek feature to find a specific solution to a problem involving one variable.
- Chapter 22, "Mastering the Analysis ToolPak," explains how to use Excel's analysis tools for business, engineering, and statistical applications.

CHAPTER 20

Analyzing Data: PivotTables!

by Bruce Hallberg with Joyce Nielsen

Excel's PivotTable feature enables you to summarize, analyze, and manipulate data in lists and tables. When you use the PivotTable Wizard to create a PivotTable, you tell Excel which fields in the list you want to arrange in rows and columns. You also can specify a page field that appears to arrange the data in a stack of pages. PivotTables are called such because you can quickly rearrange the position of PivotTable fields to give you a different view of the table.

You can create a PivotTable from several sources. The default (and most common) choice is to create a PivotTable from an Excel list or database. In addition, you can create the PivotTable from data in an external data source, multiple consolidation ranges, or another PivotTable. ■

What are PivotTables?

PivotTables, introduced in Excel for Windows 95 and significantly enhanced in Excel 97, are an incredibly powerful tool for quickly analyzing complex data.

Building PivotTables

PivotTables are easy to build with the PivotTable Wizard, a four-step tool that guides you through the process of creating PivotTables.

Manipulating and analyzing PivotTables

Once the PivotTable is built, the work isn't yet done. There are numerous options that let you control just how PivotTables appear and work. You learn how to manipulate PivotTables to achieve the results you need and how to analyze PivotTable data.

The Magic of PivotTables

You've learned in other chapters how to analyze data using outlines, subtotals, filters, and other techniques. For relatively simple analysis of data, these tools work fine. However, they fall short when you need to analyze larger, more complex data, or when you need more flexible analysis tools.

PivotTables, introduced in Excel 95, are a powerful weapon in your analysis arsenal. In this chapter, you learn how to create and use PivotTables to explore relationships in your data that aren't available using other tools. As you will see, PivotTables are a major analysis feature of Excel and learning to make the most of them will greatly benefit you.

What Are PivotTables Good For?

Consider the worksheet shown in Figure 20.1. You see an Excel list that contains a number of fields describing detailed sales order records. There are 2,155 rows of data, and the following fields for each record:

Field	Description
OrderID	Order number
OrderDate	Date of order
ProductID	Product ID ordered
ProductName	Name of product ordered
Quantity	Quantity ordered
UnitPrice	Price for each unit of the product
Amount	Extended dollar amount ordered
CustomerID	Customer number
CompanyName	Name of ordering customer
EmployeeID	ID number of salesperson
LastName	Last name of salesperson

Now consider that you want to ask certain questions of the data, such as:

- What are sales for each product?
- What are sales for each salesperson?
- What is the product mix sold for each salesperson?
- Who is the best customer?
- Which salespeople sell the most to the top 10 customers?
- Are there seasonal (monthly) variations to product sales?

A PivotTable is a tabular representation of a set of data. Different fields in your source data are summarized in different dimensions. For example, Figure 20.2 shows a very simple PivotTable that summarizes amounts by customer names.

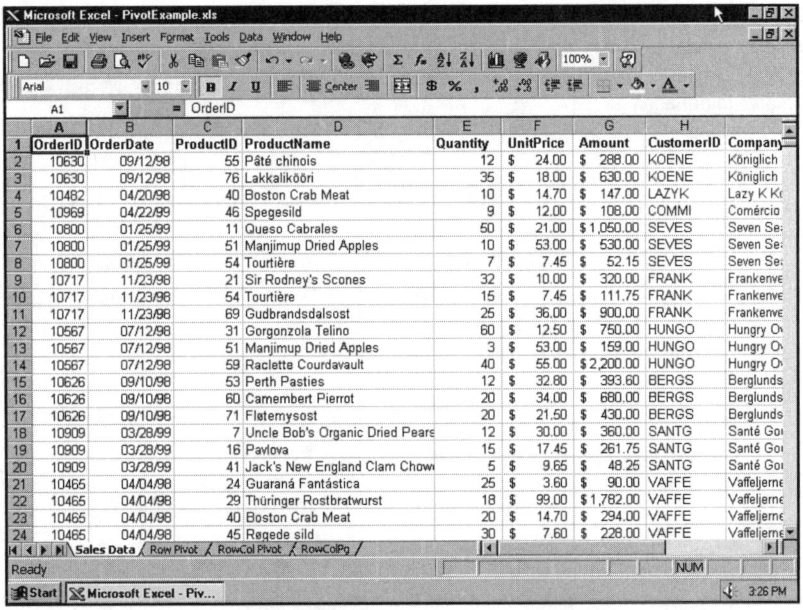

FIG. 20.1
An Excel worksheet can contain so much data that it becomes difficult to find out what you want to know.

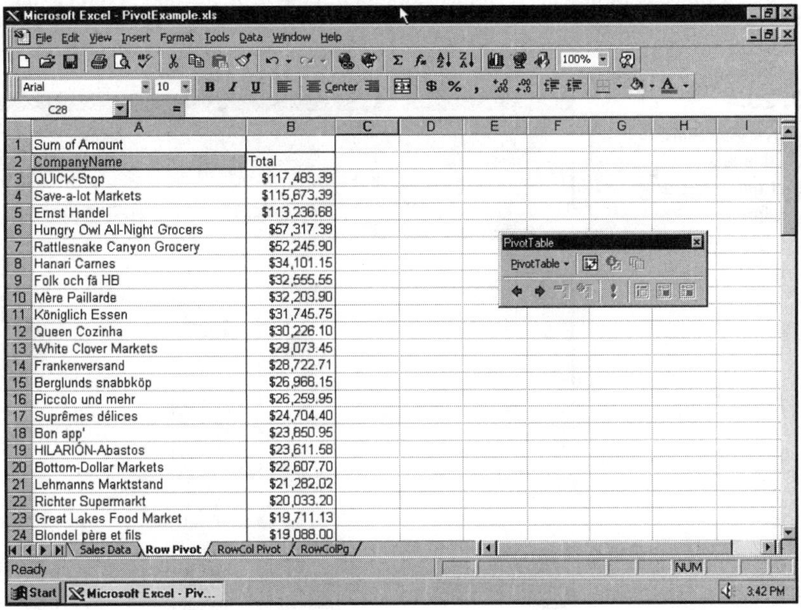

FIG. 20.2
The simplest form of PivotTables summarizes two fields in your data.

A more complex PivotTable may use two dimensions to summarize the data. For example, Figure 20.3 shows a PivotTable that summarizes salespeople by the name of the ordering customer, where salespeople are summarized in the rows and customer names are summarized in the columns.

FIG. 20.3
A two-dimensional PivotTable lets you summarize information in two directions.

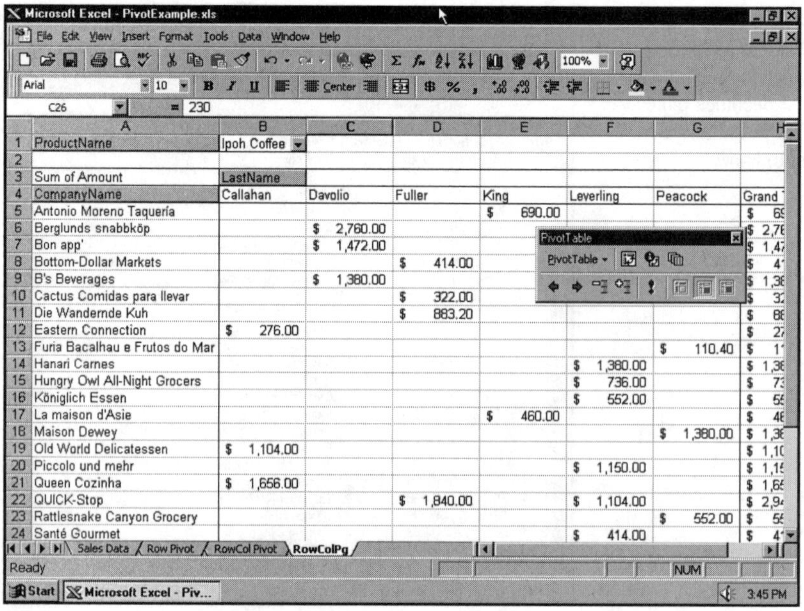

A more complex PivotTable is shown in Figure 20.4. Here, a field called a *page field* summarizes one field, limiting the data summarized by the row and column of the PivotTable.

FIG. 20.4
Adding a page field to a PivotTable lets you restrict the data being summarized.

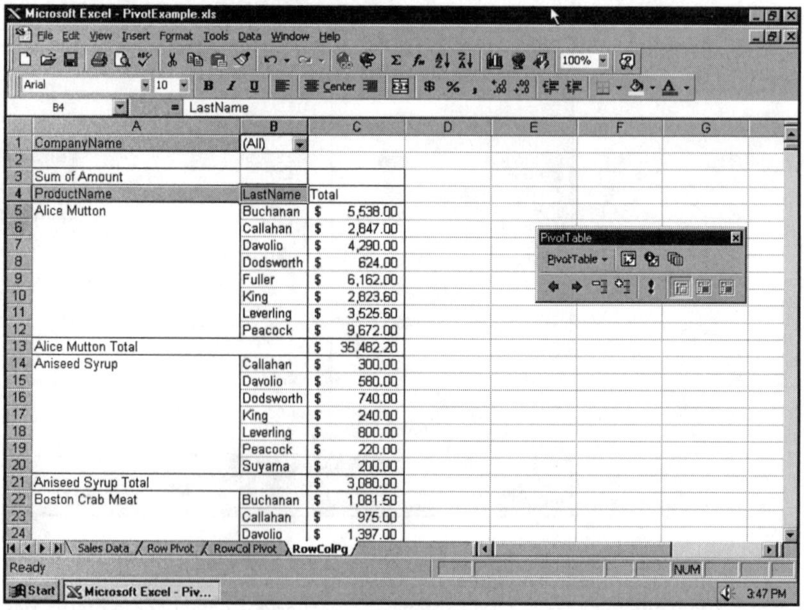

The real beauty of PivotTables comes when you drag one of the fields to another position in the PivotTable. When you do this, you pivot the data so that you can instantly explore a different arrangement of data. For example, Figure 20.5 shows the same data that is displayed in Figure 20.4, but the fields have been dragged to different positions in the PivotTable to show the data differently.

FIG. 20.5
Drag and drop PivotTable fields to different positions to instantly explore different data arrangements.

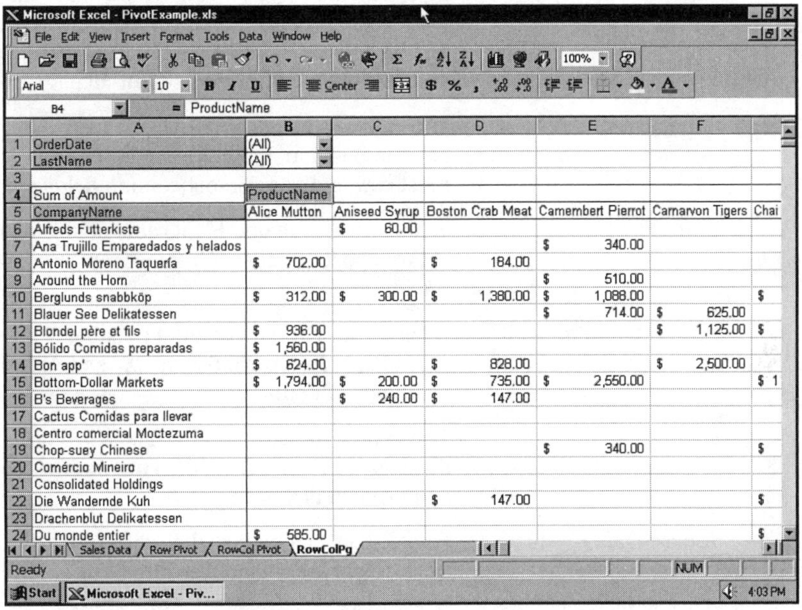

There are a number of additional features of PivotTables that make them even more powerful. For example, you can create calculated fields within the PivotTable, set up complex summarization rules, and restrict the data shown in the PivotTable in interesting ways to look at different views of the data. PivotTables make analyzing complex data easy.

Learning PivotTable Vocabulary

In order to get the most from this chapter, you should spend a moment reviewing the names of the different parts of PivotTables. Table 20.1 describes the key terms used when working with PivotTables. See Figure 20.6 as described in the table to see how specific terms appear in a PivotTable.

Table 20.1 PivotTable Terms

Name	Description
Column Field	A PivotTable field that summarizes across columns. In Figure 20.6, ProductName is the only column field.

continues

Table 20.1 Continued

Name	Description
Row Field	A PivotTable field that summarizes information across rows. In Figure 20.6, CompanyName is the row field.
Page Field	A page field lets you select which data is included in the PivotTable. In Figure 20.6, there are two page fields: OrderDate and LastName. If you set a criteria for the page fields, only data that meets the conditions set for all page fields is shown.
Outer Field	When more than one PivotTable field is displayed in the row or column position, they have an inner-outer relationship. The left-most row and upper-most column fields are the outer fields.
Inner Field	When more than one PivotTable field is displayed in the row or column position, the right-most row and lower-most column are the inner fields.
PivotTable Item	A particular row and column heading represents an item. For example, in Figure 20.6 Bon app' and Aniseed Syrup are both examples of items.
Data Area	The central area of the PivotTable is where the actual data displays. In Figure 20.6, the sum of the amount for each company and product is shown.
Source Data	PivotTables can be based on different types of source data such as an Excel list, a database query, or another PivotTable's data.
Refresh Data	If the underlying data for a PivotTable changes, you have to refresh the PivotTable to reflect the new data.

Building PivotTables

You build PivotTables with the PivotTable Wizard, a four-step tool that walks you through the process of creating PivotTables. To start the PivotTable Wizard, open the Data menu and choose PivotTable Report. You see the PivotTable Wizard - Step 1 of 4 dialog box shown in Figure 20.7.

In the PivotTable Wizard - Step 1 of 4 dialog box you choose the source of the data you want to analyze with a PivotTable. You have the following choices:

- *Microsoft Excel List or Database*. Choose this option when your source data already resides in a worksheet.
- *External Data Source*. This option invokes Microsoft Query in order to extract data in an external database.

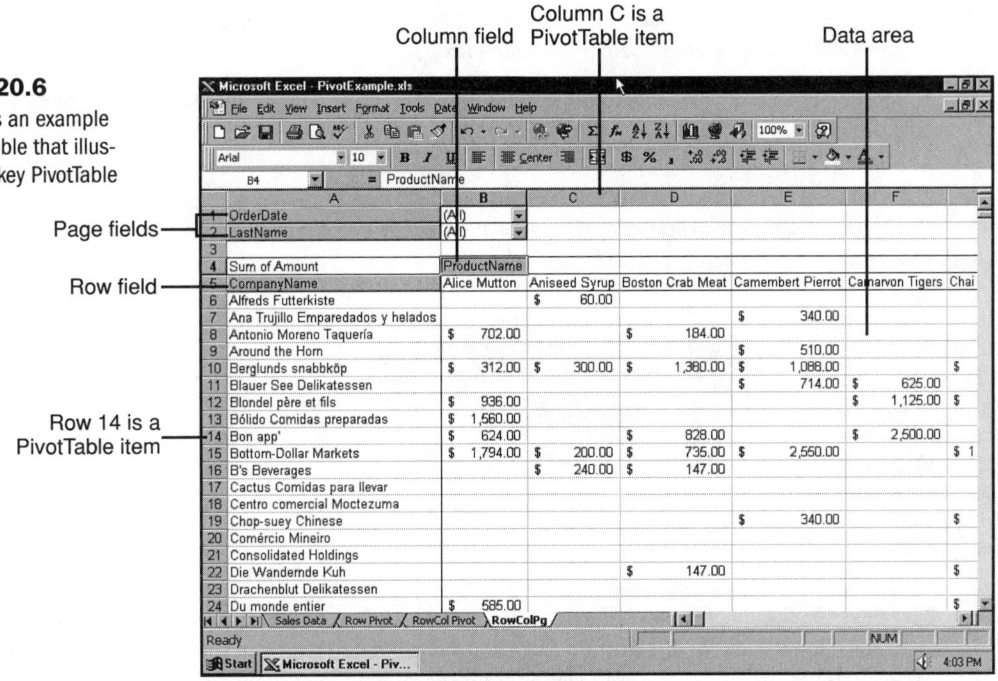

FIG. 20.6
Here is an example PivotTable that illustrates key PivotTable terms.

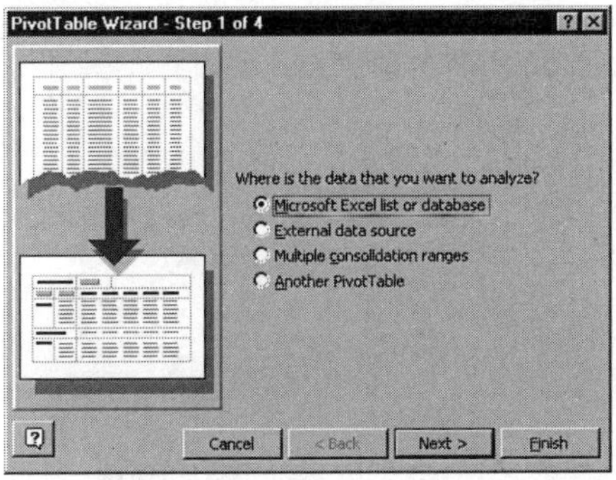

FIG. 20.7
Use the PivotTable Wizard - Step 1 of 4 dialog box to choose the source of the PivotTable data.

- *Multiple Consolidation Ranges.* If you have a series of worksheet lists, all arranged in the same way and with the same field headings, you can choose Multiple Consolidation Ranges to consolidate and analyze the data with PivotTables.
- *Another PivotTable.* PivotTables store a copy of the data they are analyzing for performance and memory utilization reasons. If you want to create multiple PivotTables from a single set of data, use this option to avoid having duplicate copies of the data consuming system resources.

Make your selection and click the Next button to continue. For this example, Microsoft Excel List or Database is selected before clicking Next.

In the PivotTable Wizard - Step 2 of 4 dialog box (see Figure 20.8) you define the range of cells that defines the worksheet list you want to use. Select the range and click the Next button to continue.

TIP If your active cell is within a list before starting the PivotTable Wizard, the range will be automatically entered for you in the Step 2 of 4 dialog box.

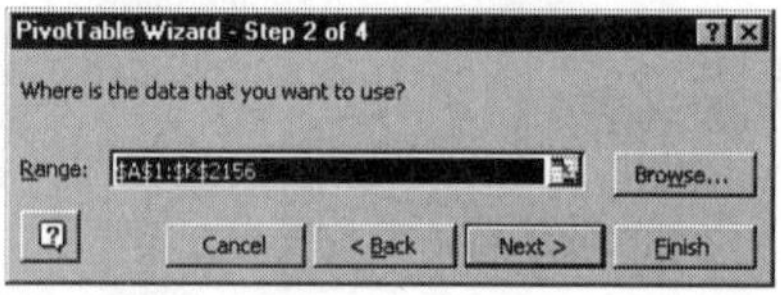

FIG. 20.8 In the PivotTable Wizard - Step 2 of 4 dialog box, you choose the range of cells on which to base the PivotTable when you are summarizing an Excel list.

You next see the PivotTable Wizard - Step 3 of 4 dialog box in which you make your initial decisions about how the fields of the data source will be arranged in the PivotTable. As Figure 20.9 illustrates, you drag the field names from the right side of the dialog box into the different PivotTable areas. After doing so, click Next to continue.

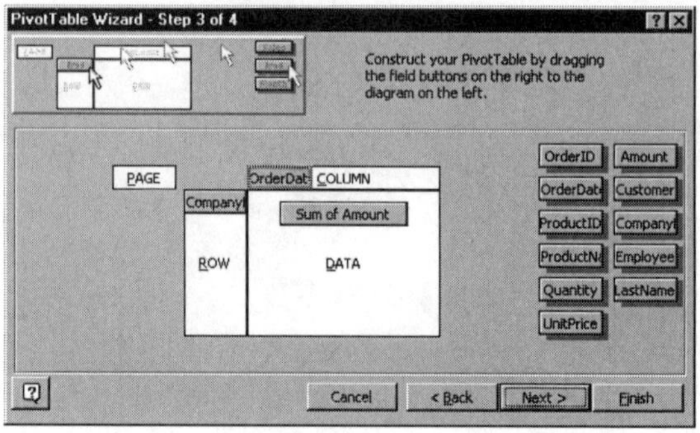

FIG. 20.9 Use the PivotTable Wizard - Step 3 of 4 dialog box to drag field names from the right side of the dialog box into the PivotTable areas.

In the final step of the PivotTable Wizard, you determine where the new PivotTable will be created. Choose the destination of the PivotTable using one of the choices shown in Figure 20.10 and click Finish to create the PivotTable. In this example, the New Worksheet option was selected. Figure 20.11 shows the completed PivotTable. (The Order Date field has been reformatted to show quarters before the figure was created.)

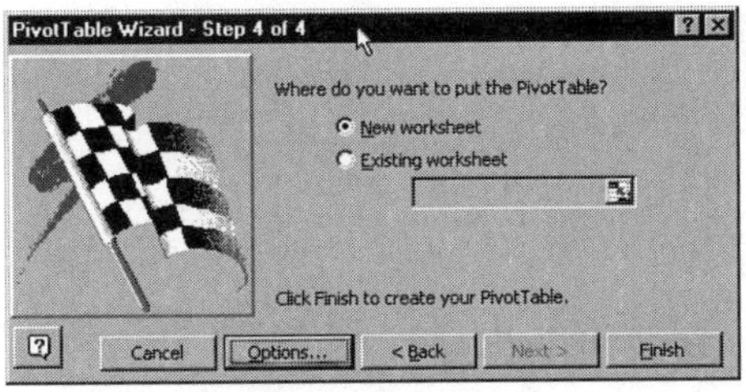

FIG. 20.10
In the PivotTable Wizard - Step 4 of 4 dialog box, you determine where you want the PivotTable to be created.

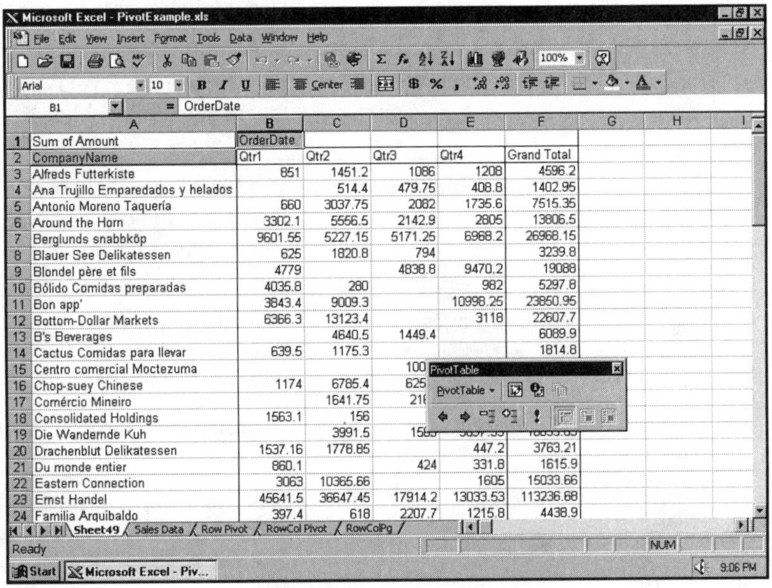

FIG. 20.11
Here is a completed PivotTable built with the PivotTable Wizard.

Manipulating and Analyzing PivotTables

Half the fun of working with PivotTables lies in the way you can quickly manipulate them to show different data. You can not only rearrange data, but you can create new fields, change how fields are grouped, and so on. By creating new fields and rearranging data, you gain a larger understanding of the data and can make better strategic decisions based on what you learn from the different views of the data. In the following sections you learn several methods for changing your PivotTables.

Using the PivotTable Toolbar

To control PivotTables easily, use the PivotTable toolbar shown in Figure 20.12. After you build a PivotTable, the PivotTable toolbar should automatically be visible. If it doesn't appear on-screen, right-click inside the toolbar area and select PivotTable. Table 20.2 shows you what each PivotTable toolbar button does.

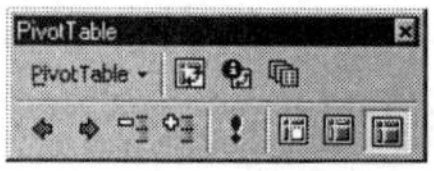

FIG. 20.12
Use the PivotTable toolbar to quickly and easily control PivotTables.

Table 20.2 PivotTable Toolbar Buttons

Button	Name	Description
PivotTable ▾	PivotTable	Use the PivotTable button to access a menu of PivotTable commands.
	PivotTable Wizard	You can use the PivotTable Wizard not only to create new PivotTables, but also to edit existing PivotTables.
	PivotTable Field	The PivotTable Field button activates the PivotTable Field dialog box, in which you can control how a particular PivotTable field displays and summarizes associated data.
	Show Pages	Click the Show Pages button to create another PivotTable on a new worksheet, one of which is created for every possible page field setting.
	Ungroup	Ungroups summarized PivotTable fields.
	Group	Lets you group a particular PivotTable field in different ways. For example, select a date field to group it by days, months, quarters, years, and so on.
	Hide Detail	Hides a selected PivotTable field's data.
	Show Detail	Reveals hidden PivotTable data.
	Refresh Data	Refreshes the PivotTable with any changed data in the data source.
	Select Label	Lets you select a PivotTable field's label so that you can change it.
	Select Data	Lets you select a PivotTable field's data for formatting.
	Select Label and Data	Lets you select a PivotTable field's label and data for formatting.

Dragging and Dropping Headings

The most rudimentary way to change PivotTables is to simply drag and drop field headings into new areas on the PivotTable. There are three places to which you can drag the field headings: row, column, and page fields. You can have multiple headings in each field.

Figure 20.13 shows a PivotTable prior to being changed. The PivotTable presently shows the sales of each product summarized by each salesperson.

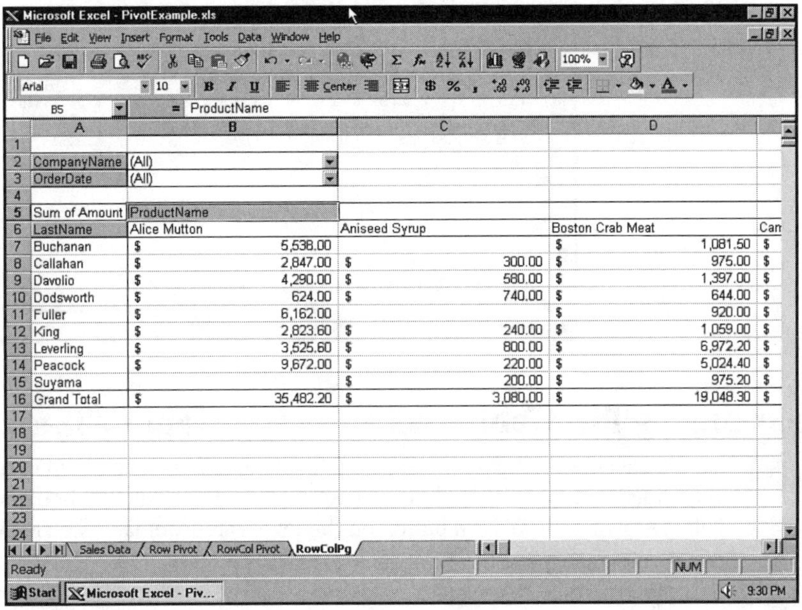

FIG. 20.13
You've finished examining product sales by salesperson. Now you want to see how well each salesperson did each quarter.

To change the PivotTable so that you can see the salespeople's sales for each quarter, you would perform the following steps:

1. Drag the ProductName field to the Page field area.
2. Drag the OrderDate field to the Column field area.

TIP Instead of deleting PivotTable fields that you don't want to use, drag them to the Page field area and set them so that they display all records. That way they don't affect the PivotTable results, but are still handy if you want to drag them back into the PivotTable.

As you can see in Figure 20.14, you now have a radically different PivotTable that shows different information. The PivotTable now shows you how much each salesperson sold during each quarter.

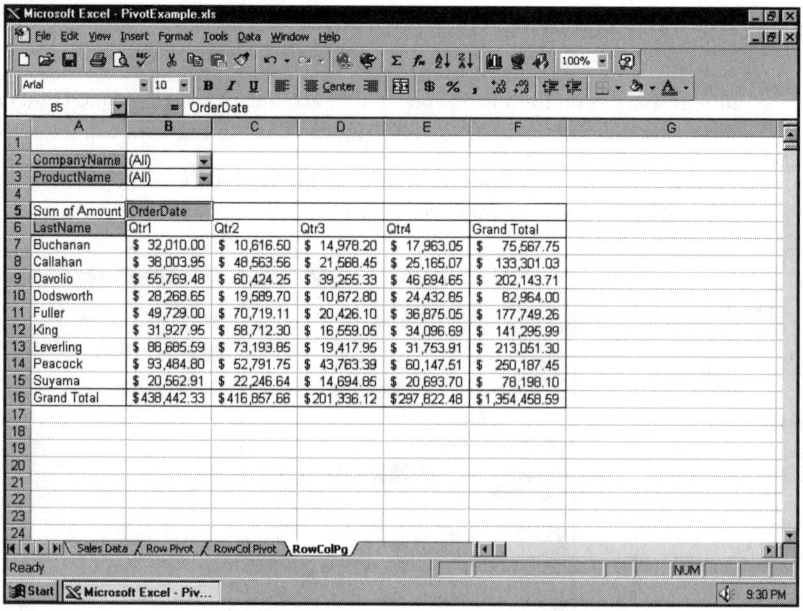

FIG. 20.14
With two quick drags, the PivotTable now shows very different information.

Rearranging PivotTables with the PivotTable Wizard

You can also use the PivotTable Wizard to change the arrangement of the PivotTable fields. To access the PivotTable Wizard for this purpose, first click one of the PivotTable fields, and then click the PivotTable Wizard button on the PivotTable toolbar. (Alternatively, you can open the Data menu and choose the PivotTable Report command.) Step 3 of 4 of the PivotTable Wizard, shown in Figure 20.15, instantly appears.

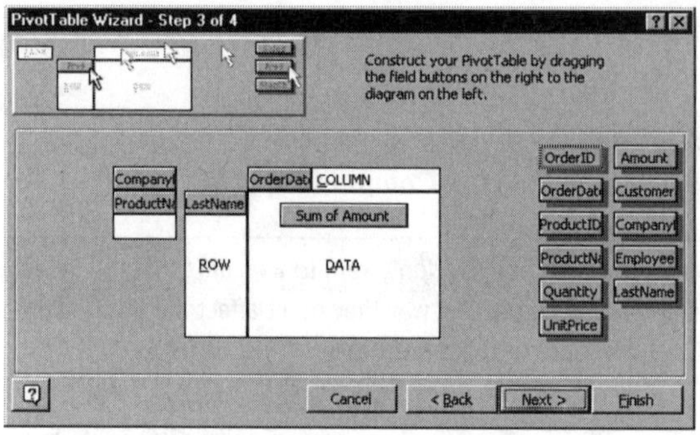

FIG. 20.15
You can reaccess the PivotTable Wizard to rearrange PivotTable fields.

After the PivotTable Wizard is open, you can remove fields, drag new fields from the right side of the dialog box into PivotTable fields, and so on. Click Finish to save your changes and redisplay the PivotTable.

Use the PivotTable Wizard to add fields to your PivotTable that exist within your data source. Access the wizard and drag the appropriate fields into the PivotTable area in the dialog box.

To remove PivotTable fields, drag any fields you don't want into a blank area of the PivotTable Wizard dialog box and drop them there to remove them from the PivotTable area.

TIP A quick way to remove PivotTable fields is to right-click the field heading in the PivotTable and choose Delete from the shortcut menu.

Adding Calculated Fields

You can create new PivotTable fields from calculations and include them in your PivotTables. The calculated fields are based on existing fields and a formula that you specify. To do this, follow these steps:

1. Right-click within the PivotTable. Choose Formulas, Calculated Field from the shortcut menu. You see the Insert Calculated Field dialog box shown in Figure 20.16.
2. Assign a name for the new field in the Name field.
3. Use the Formula field to create the formula that will calculate your new field. You can use any of Excel's functions in the field. To insert a field name from the PivotTable in the formula, select the field in the list and click the Insert Field button.
4. Click Add to create the new field.

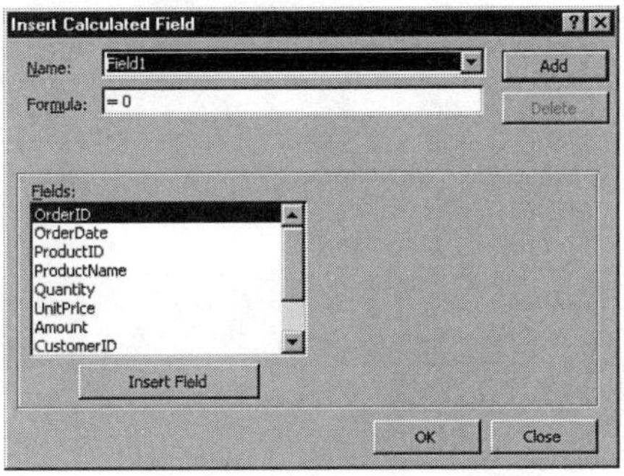

FIG. 20.16 Use the Insert Calculated Field dialog box to create new fields based on existing fields.

For example, you could create a new calculated field with the formula =AVERAGE(Quantity) to calculate the average quantity sold for each order, and then use the new field within your PivotTables.

Hiding and Revealing Data

You can hide detail within PivotTables. You can hide entire PivotTable fields, as well as detailed items within the PivotTable. However, you cannot hide subtotals or totals shown in rows or columns.

To hide detail within a PivotTable, select the data you want to hide, right-click it, and choose Group and Outline, Hide Detail from the shortcut menu.

To reveal hidden data, right-click the field that contains the hidden detail and choose Group and Outline, Show Detail from the shortcut menu.

Grouping Items

Your data isn't always grouped into nice, neat packages that are the way that you want to view them in your PivotTable. For example, Figure 20.17 shows a PivotTable that is virtually unusable because its data spans so many columns. In cases like this, you can group the data in different ways, depending on the type of data contained in the field.

FIG. 20.17
This PivotTable would be much more usable if the order dates were grouped in some meaningful way.

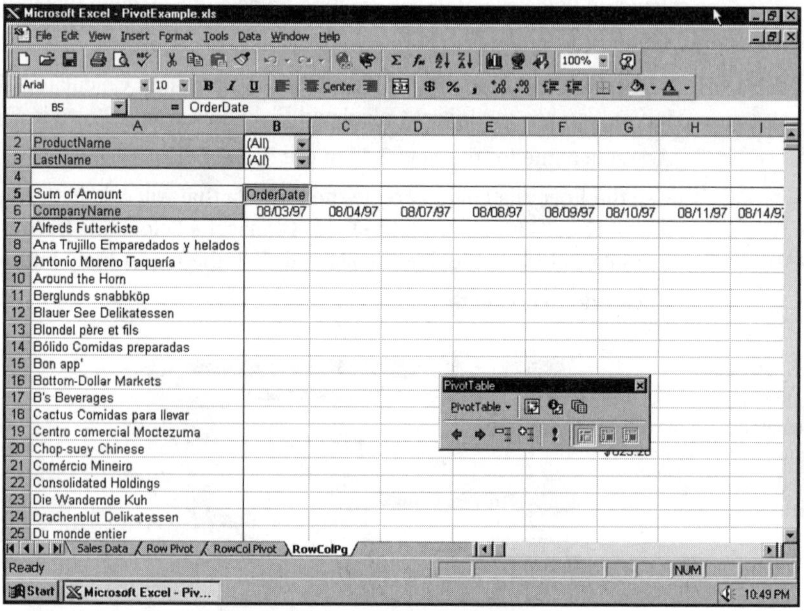

To group data, follow these steps:

1. Click the Group button on the PivotTable toolbar, or right-click the field you want to group and choose Group and Outline, Group. You see the Grouping dialog box shown in Figure 20.18.
2. Select a range of data to display. By default, all data is selected in the range fields (Starting At and Ending At).
3. If there are other types of groupings available, such as the ones shown in the By list in Figure 20.18, select them. Notice that you can select multiple groupings if you want.
4. Click OK to create the new grouping.

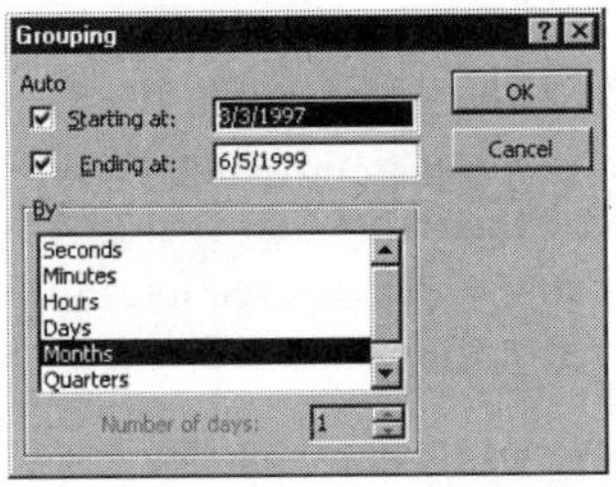

FIG. 20.18
Use the Grouping dialog box (which changes based on the data type being grouped) to restrict and group the data.

Figure 20.19 shows the effect of grouping the OrderDate field into quarters, which makes the PivotTable much easier to understand in this example.

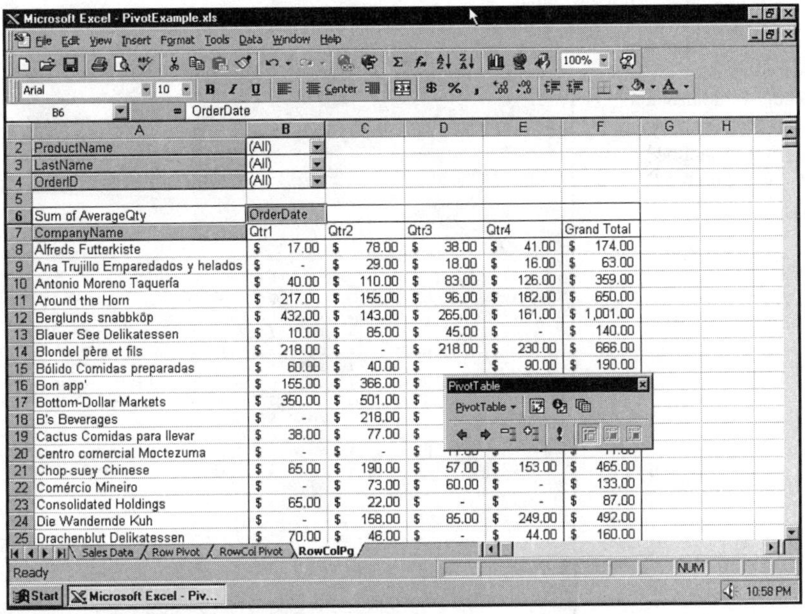

FIG. 20.19
After grouping OrderDate into quarters, you see a more usable PivotTable.

Fields that display numerical data show a different Grouping dialog box. Figure 20.20 shows the Grouping dialog box for the OrderID field, which contains numerical data. In this Grouping dialog box, you can still set a range for the grouped data, but you can also set an increment. For each increment that you select, all the records that fit within that increment will be combined.

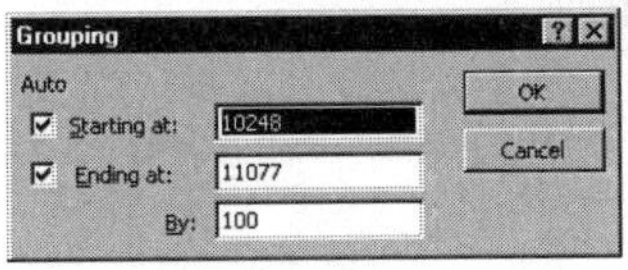

FIG. 20.20
When grouping numerical data, you see this Grouping dialog box.

There's still another way to group detail in a PivotTable: arbitrary groupings. You can group selected detail records together to make a single record within the PivotTable. For example, you could choose several salespeople in a PivotTable and group them together arbitrarily. You might do this when there's a way of grouping them together that isn't apparent in the data, but is known to you. For example, you might know which salespeople cover which regions, and using arbitrary groupings, you can reflect the regions in the PivotTable.

After you've created an arbitrary group, you can select the group labels (which are assigned names like Group1, Group2, and so on) and type new names. Figure 20.21 shows quarterly sales by salesperson, but with the salespeople grouped into their regions.

NOTE Arbitrary groupings become new PivotTable fields that you can move to other dimensions in the PivotTable.

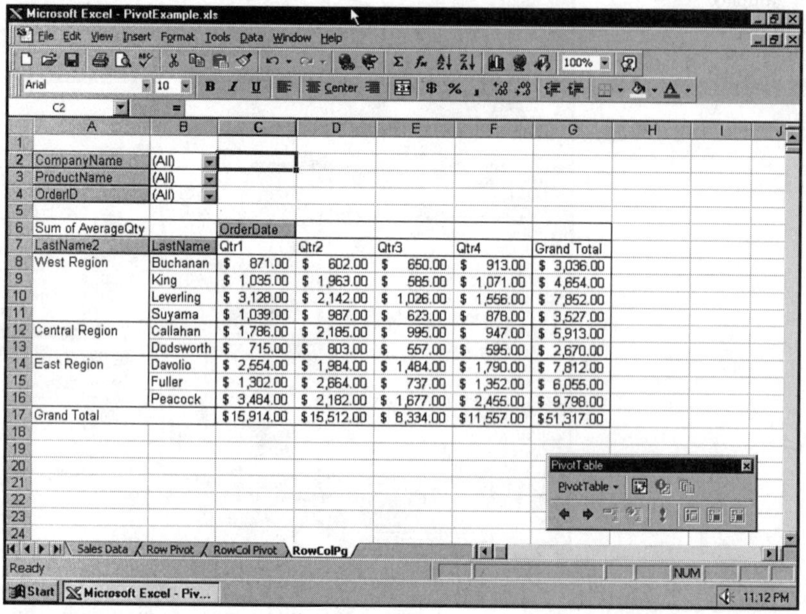

FIG. 20.21
Arbitrary groupings can let you group data in ways that cannot be done based on the data.

To reverse the effect of a grouping and restore all of the detail, right-click the grouped field heading and choose Group and Outline, Ungroup from the shortcut menu.

TIP You can also right-click the grouped field heading and then click the Ungroup button on the PivotTable toolbar to quickly remove groupings.

Editing PivotTable Fields

You can edit various properties for each PivotTable field. To do this, double-click the field heading, which displays the PivotTable Field dialog box shown in Figure 20.22.

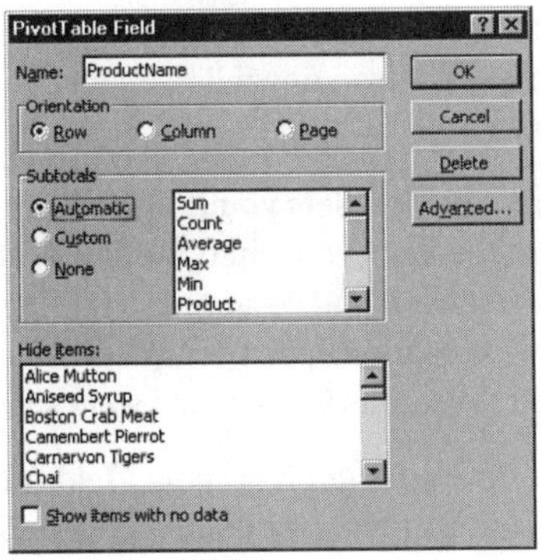

FIG. 20.22
The PivotTable Field dialog box lets you edit PivotTable field properties.

In the PivotTable Field dialog box, you can:

- Change the name of the PivotTable field.
- Delete the PivotTable field with the Delete button.
- Select where the PivotTable field is located (choose Row, Column, or Page).
- Select subtotals (including different types of subtotals) for an inner PivotTable field's data using the Subtotals area of the dialog box.
- Selectively hide items using the Hide Items list.
- Choose to Show Items With No Data, which displays all detailed records whether or not they contain any data.

You can also access AutoSort and AutoShow features using the Advanced button. These features are discussed in the following two sections.

AutoSort and AutoShow Fields

AutoSort is a feature that keeps a PivotTable field's data in sorted order, even when it is moved to another PivotTable dimension. You access the AutoSort feature by clicking the Advanced button in the PivotTable Field dialog box, which displays the PivotTable Field Advanced Options dialog box shown in Figure 20.23.

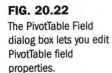

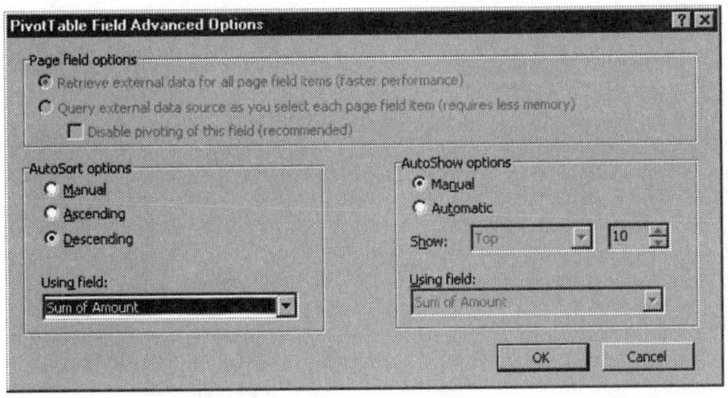

FIG. 20.23
The PivotTable Field Advanced Options dialog box lets you apply AutoSort rules to a particular field.

In the AutoSort options area of the dialog box, choose the type of sort you want. If you choose Ascending or Descending, in the Using Field drop-down list, choose the field by which the records will be sorted in the PivotTable.

The Manual AutoSort option (the default choice) lets you drag and drop PivotTable records. The records will maintain their place in the list, even when the PivotTable field is moved to other dimensions, or when the field is removed and re-added to the PivotTable. To move a PivotTable field, select the record (row or column) and then drag its border to position it elsewhere in the table, just as you drag and drop cells in standard worksheets.

AutoShow is another feature accessed through the PivotTable Field Advanced Options dialog box. AutoShow lets you choose the top or bottom records in a PivotTable field. For example, if you want to see the top 10 customers, you first arrange your PivotTable so that it displays all customers. Then use the AutoShow feature to display only the top 10 customers. Figure 20.24 shows this example set.

FIG. 20.24
AutoShow lets you show only the top- or bottom-most records in a PivotTable field.

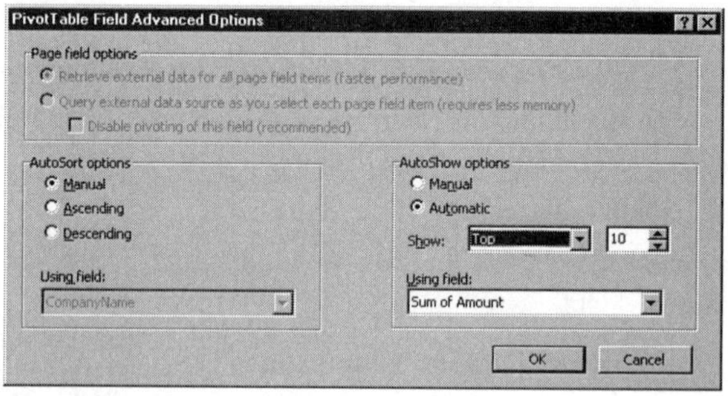

Setting PivotTable Options

Each PivotTable has a set of options that you can set that control how the PivotTable works. Access a PivotTable's options by right-clicking in the PivotTable and choosing Options from the shortcut menu. Figure 20.25 shows the PivotTable Options dialog box, while Table 20.3 details the options found in the dialog box.

FIG. 20.25
The PivotTable Options dialog box lets you control how PivotTables work.

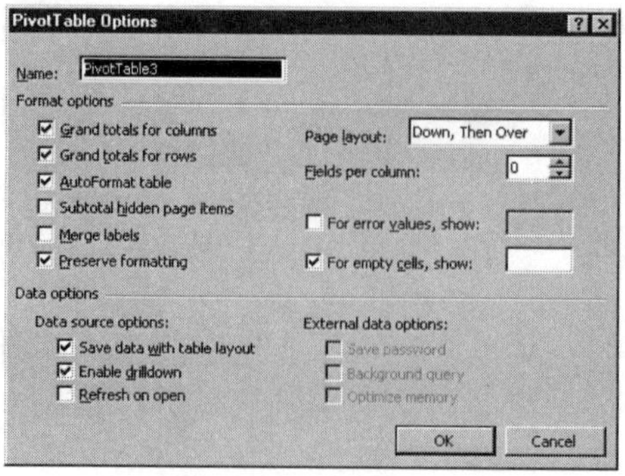

Table 20.3 PivotTable Options Dialog Box Settings

Setting	Description
Name	Lets you set the name for the PivotTable.
Grand Totals for Columns	Includes grand totals at the bottom of each column.
Grand Totals for Rows	Includes grand totals to the right of each row.
AutoFormat Table	Maintains the PivotTable's formatting using the default AutoFormat.
Subtotal Hidden Page Items	Causes any hidden page field records to be reflected within PivotTable subtotals.
Merge Labels	Merges outer row and column fields in the PivotTable. This option can make a PivotTable more attractive, but has no functional purpose.
Preserve Formatting	Lets you format a PivotTable, and maintains any formatting settings you make even after you change the PivotTable.
Page Layout	Controls how page fields in the PivotTable appear. You can choose Down, then Over; or Over, then Down. All of the figures in this chapter show pages arranged vertically, which occurs when Down, then Over is selected.
Fields Per Column	Selects the number of page fields that are displayed before the next column or row is used to display additional page fields.
For Error Values, Show	Lets you supply a value that is displayed in place of any error messages in cells.
For Empty Cells, Show	Lets you supply a value that is displayed for empty cells.
Save Data With Table Layout	Saves a copy of the data on which the PivotTable is based along with the PivotTable. Keeping this option selected makes PivotTables consume less memory and operate more quickly, at the expense of you needing to manually refresh the source data if it changes.
Enable Drilldown	When selected, you can double-click a cell in the data area of the PivotTable to jump to the source data.
Refresh on Open	Automatically refreshes the PivotTable data when the workbook is opened.
Save Password	Stores the password used for an external data query.

continues

Table 20.3 Continued

Setting	Description
Background Query	For external data source queries, this setting allows the query to run in the background. Background queries take longer, but let you continue to work with the workbook while the query is carried out.
Optimize Memory	If you are running out of memory resources while using PivotTables that use external data sources, you can select this check box to conserve memory at the price of decreased performance.

Formatting PivotTables

97

New to Excel 97, PivotTables now support ***persistent formatting***. This feature lets you format a PivotTable, and your formatting is maintained even after you change the PivotTable. Previously, you had to manually reformat the PivotTable every time you changed it.

In order for persistent formatting to work, the Preserve Formatting option must be selected in the PivotTable Options dialog box (refer to Figure 20.25 and Table 20.3).

You can format portions of your PivotTables using all of Excel's normal cell-formatting tools. Select a range of cells in the PivotTable, or an entire field, and then choose Format Cells from the shortcut menu for the selection.

You can achieve very attractive results with PivotTable formatting by using the AutoFormat command in Excel's Format menu. Choose from all of the list formatting options available in the AutoFormat dialog box.

Common Problems and Solutions

Although Excel 97 makes PivotTables easier to use than they were in previous versions, you still may encounter a few problems when using this feature. Here are a few possibilities:

I can't select just a row or column label.

PivotTables support something called ***structured selection***. This means that when you click a row or column label, you select the entire row or column in the PivotTable. When you click a row or column heading field, you select all the data for that field. Generally, structured selection makes selecting areas that you want to work with in PivotTables faster and easier.

Sometimes, though, you want to select just a label so that you can change it by typing a new label. To do this, first click the label, which selects the entire row or column. Then click the Select Label button on the PivotTable toolbar. The label alone is then selected, and you can type a new label.

TIP To toggle structured selection on and off, right-click anywhere in the PivotTable and choose Select from the shortcut menu, then choose Enable Selection from the submenu.

I need to summarize calculated fields.

In PivotTables that have many calculated fields, you may need to summarize them as part of documenting the PivotTable. Right-click in the PivotTable, choose Formulas from the shortcut menu, and then choose List Formulas from the submenu. A new tab is inserted in the worksheet that summarizes all of the calculated fields in the PivotTable.

From Here...

This chapter showed you how to build PivotTables, which enable you to quickly manipulate and analyze complex data using many different views. Excel provides other features for analyzing your data. Refer to the following chapters for more information:

- Chapter 18, "Building Scenarios and Outlines with Excel," shows you how to use Excel's scenario and outlining features to view the data you are analyzing in many different ways.
- Chapter 19, "Auditing and Validating Worksheets," explains how to trace errors in your workbooks, validate user input, and use names instead of cell references to help reduce the chance of errors in formulas.
- Chapter 21, "Mastering Excel's Solver and Goal Seek," covers how to use the Solver add-in to find an optimal solution to a problem with multiple variables and the Goal Seek feature to find a specific solution to a problem involving one variable.
- Chapter 22, "Mastering the Analysis ToolPak," explains how to use Excel's analysis tools for business, engineering, and statistical applications.

CHAPTER 21

Mastering Excel's Solver and Goal Seek

by Bruce Hallberg with Joyce Nielsen

Not many people take the time to understand and use Solver, which is a shame. Solver is an incredibly valuable part of Excel, and it can solve problems that you cannot otherwise easily solve. It's a good idea to spend some time understanding the capabilities of this powerful tool so that you can apply it to problems of your own that may crop up from time to time.

Solver is an Excel Add-in that can solve problems that have multiple variables that are interdependent—that is, the variables operate on one another through various formulas. Solver is designed to find the optimal solutions to such problems. Using a combination of linear algebra and iterative techniques to "try" different possible solutions, Solver quickly calculates the answers to such problems.

In this chapter, you'll also learn how to use Excel's Goal Seek feature to solve simpler problems that have only one changing variable (as opposed to the multiple changing variables that require the use of Solver).

Learning Solver through included examples

Included with Excel is a sample workbook that contains different examples of Solver problems. Use these examples to understand how Solver works.

Optimizing credit card payments with Solver

A sample Solver model that you can build is demonstrated. Use this example to see how to build your own Solver problems from scratch.

Solving problems with Goal Seek

Learn how to use Goal Seek to achieve a specific result in problems with only one changing variable.

Learning Solver Through Included Examples

One of the best ways to learn how Solver works is to try it with different problems. Included with Excel is a workbook with a number of problems suited for use with Solver. You can find this set of Solver examples in the file \Microsoft Office 97\Office\Examples\Solver\solvsamp.xls. Opening this workbook shows the first Solver example, as shown in Figure 21.1. Each worksheet contains an explanation of the example and description of the key worksheet cells that make up the problem.

FIG. 21.1
Use the SOLVSAMP.XLS workbook to see Solver in action.

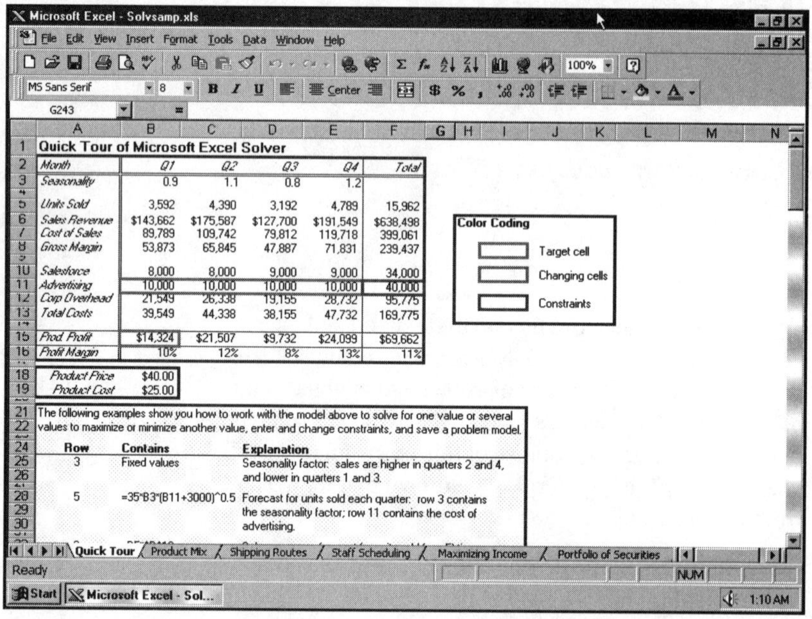

Included in the SOLVSAMP.XLS workbook are the following Solver examples:

- *Quick Tour.* This is the first worksheet in SOLVSAMP.XLS. In it, you find the problem of optimizing profitability for a company through selecting the best amount of money to spend on advertising.
- *Product Mix.* This example shows you the problem of optimizing product mix based on known costs and impacts from increasing production for different products.
- *Shipping Routes.* This demonstrates the problem of juggling multiple manufacturing plants' capacities against the needs of different distribution warehouses, as well as optimizing costs while ensuring that all warehouses get the amount of product that they need.
- *Staff Scheduling.* This demonstrates a common problem in most businesses: scheduling employees so that changing labor needs are met, balanced against the requirement to meet those needs at the lowest possible cost.

- *Maximizing Income.* This optimizes the interest earned on different investment vehicles (one-, three-, and six-month CDs are used in this example), while also meeting the company's need to use parts of the income at various times.
- *Portfolio of Securities.* This determines the best mix of stocks to hold in order to maximize the return while minimizing risk.
- *Engineering Design.* This shows a problem in designing a circuit that meets certain design criteria.

For most of the sample problem worksheets, Solver will start with the appropriate settings for solving the problem. For example, use these steps to start Solver for the Staff Scheduling problem:

1. Move to the Staff Scheduling worksheet.
2. Choose Tools, Solver. Excel displays the Solver dialog box shown in Figure 21.2.

TIP If you cannot find the Solver command in Excel's Tools menu, you need to load the Solver add-in. Access the Tools, Add-Ins command to activate the Solver add-in. If the Solver add-in isn't shown in the Add-Ins dialog box, you will need to use the Add/Remove Programs icon in the Windows Control Panel to access the Excel (or Office) installation program in which you can install the Solver add-in.

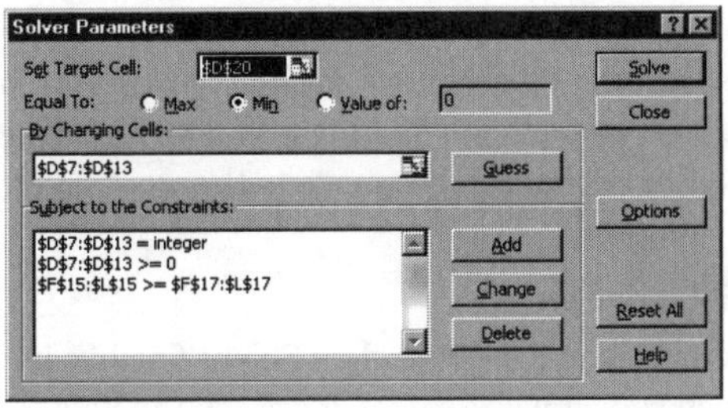

FIG. 21.2
This is the main Solver dialog box in which you set Solver parameters.

You will set three main parameters in the Solver Parameters dialog box:

- Set Target Cell field
- By Changing Cells field
- Subject to the Constraints list

The first is the Set Target Cell field. Every Solver problem optimizes the result of one cell in your worksheet. The target cell is related to other cells on the worksheet through formulas. Solver uses the formulas that result in the target cell's answer in order to know how to try different possible solutions. For the target cell, you use the Equal To settings to tell Solver how you want to optimize the result in the target cell. You can choose to find the maximum or minimum values for the target cell, or a set value.

The second main Solver parameter is the By Changing Cells field. The *changing cells* are those cells that Solver will modify in order to optimize the solution in the target cell. You can have up to 200 changing cells in a Solver problem. The changing cells have two main requirements:

They must not contain formulas, and changing their values must result in a change in the target cell. In other words, the target cell is dependent on the changing cells.

Finally, the third main parameter you set for Solver is the Subject to Constraints list. The *constraints* are rules that Solver must observe in order to find a correct answer. Without properly chosen constraints, Solver may try to provide solutions that are nonsensical such as scheduling people for negative time, or suggesting that a plant build quantities of product that are impossible (or even negative).

Starting Solver in the Staff Scheduling worksheet automatically places all of the correct settings into the Solver Parameters dialog box. You can simply click the Solve button to have Solver search for a solution. When Solver finds a solution, you see the Solver Results dialog box shown in Figure 21.3.

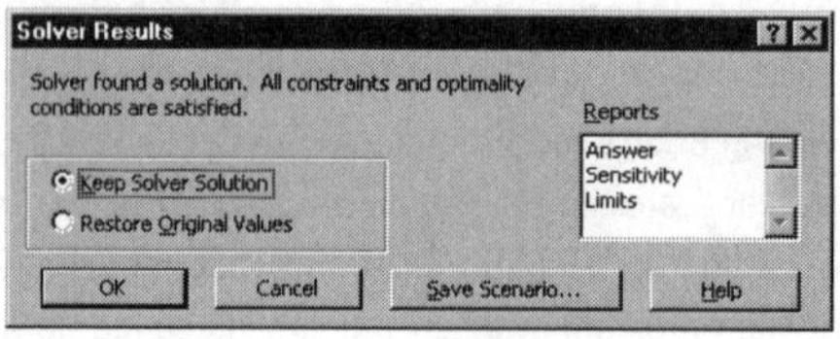

FIG. 21.3
Use the Solver Results dialog box to accept or reject Solver's proposed solution. You can also request reports that show how Solver found its solution.

Before accepting Solver's solution, you can move the Solver Results dialog box out of the way and examine the result that Solver suggests. If it makes sense and appears acceptable to you, you can accept the results and the changes are made to the worksheet.

Viewing Solver Result Reports

There are three possible reports you can view when Solver finishes its work: Answer, Sensitivity, and Limits. You click each report name that you want in the Solver Results dialog box before clicking the OK button. Each report is created in a new worksheet in the workbook.

The Answer report, shown in Figure 21.4, documents the results that Solver attained. Included in the report are the original and final value for the target cell, all changing cells revisions, and the effect of the constraints that were set for the problem.

The Sensitivity report, shown in Figure 21.5, shows you some of the underlying details about the sensitivities Solver observed in finding a solution.

The Limits report, which you can see in Figure 21.6, details the changing cell limits that Solver had to observe.

FIG. 21.4
The Answer report shows you how Solver arrived at its answer.

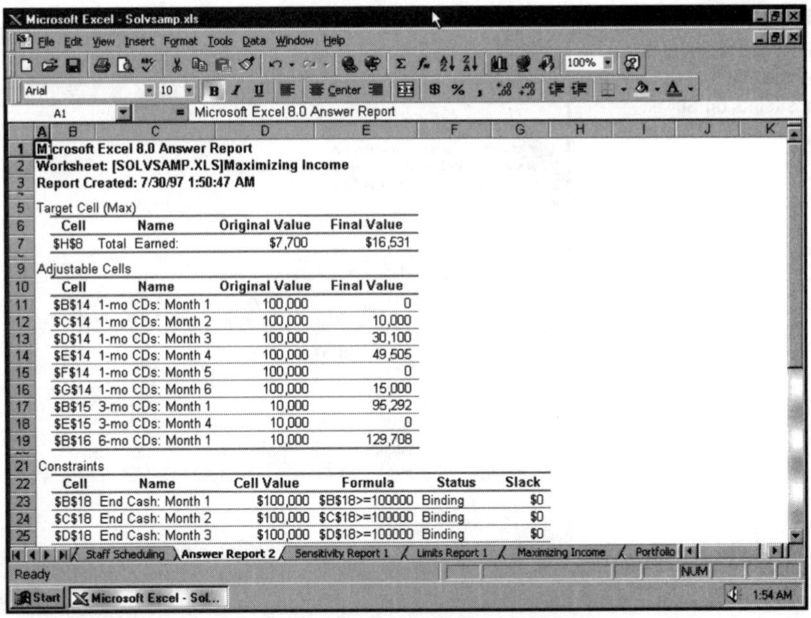

FIG. 21.5
The Sensitivity report reveals how Solver calculated the relative sensitivity of each changing cell in impacting the target cell.

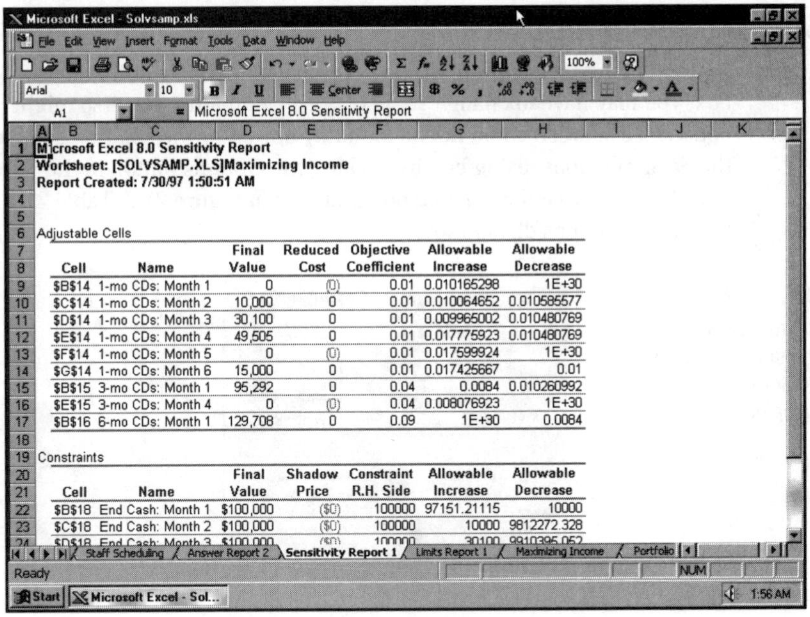

FIG. 21.6
The Limits report shows you the effect of the constraints on Solver.

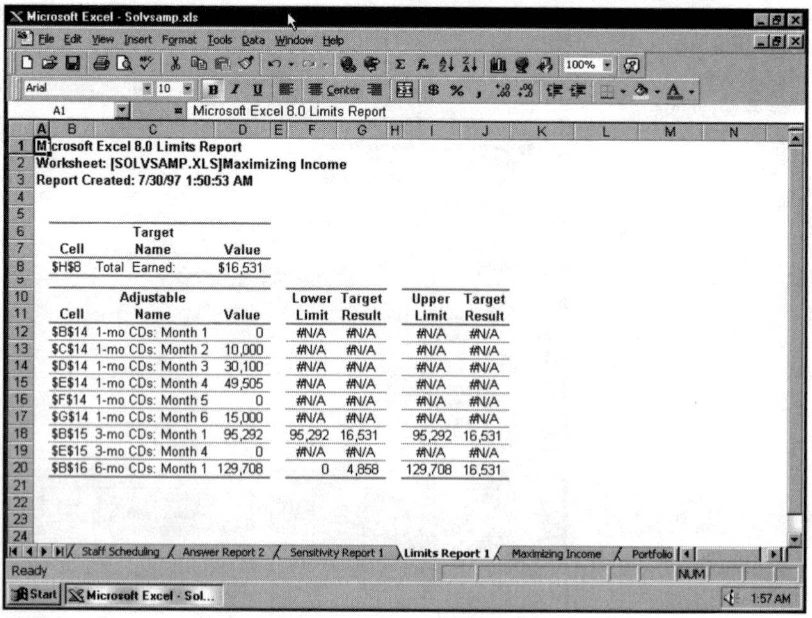

Setting Solver Options

Before finding the solution to a problem using the Solve button in the Solver Parameters dialog box, you may have to change some of Solver's options. You also might have to change Solver's options if a solution could not be found by Solver, or the solution appears inaccurate. Access the Solver Options dialog box by clicking the Options button in the Solver Parameters dialog box. The Solver Options dialog box is shown in Figure 21.7. Table 21.1 details the settings in the Solver Options dialog box.

FIG. 21.7
Control how Solver works by changing settings in the Solver Options dialog box.

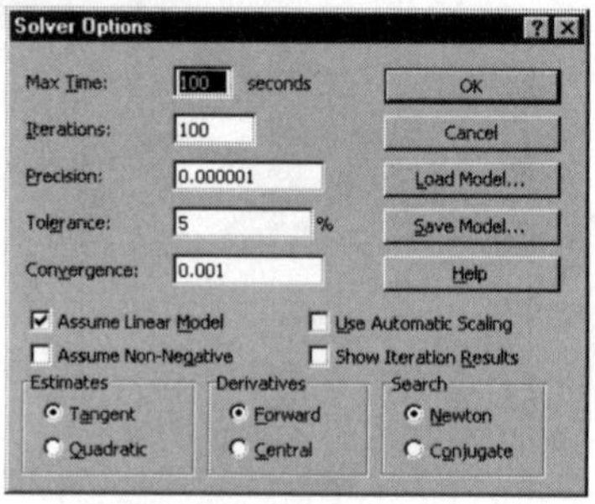

Table 21.1 Solver Options Settings

Setting	Description
Max Time	Controls the maximum amount of time that Solver will work toward finding a solution. You can enter up to 32,767 seconds (a bit more than nine hours) in this field.
Iterations	Controls the number of possible solutions that Solver will try before giving up, or offering you the best answer it could find within that number of iterations. You can enter up to 32,767 iterations.
Precision	This setting controls how accurately Solver attempts different possible solutions to a problem. Numbers with a higher precision (such as the default .000001) yield more accurate solutions than numbers with a lower precision (such as .01), but they cause Solver to take more time to solve the problem.
Tolerance	Problems that contain integer constraints are more difficult for Solver to solve. You can set higher tolerances for problems with integer constraints to allow Solver to work more quickly at the expense of some accuracy.
Convergence	For nonlinear problems, the convergence setting indicates the minimum amount of change that Solver should see for each iteration. If the change in the target cell falls below the convergence setting for five iterations, Solver stops and offers the best solution. Smaller convergences result in Solver taking longer to find solutions.
Assume Linear Model	If you know that a problem is linear in nature, select this check box to shorten the amount of time that Solver needs to find a solution.
Assume Non-Negative	When selected, Solver cannot attempt any negative values in any of the changing cells. You can also control this through the use of explicit constraints for those cells (in other words, set constraints that all changing cells must be greater than or equal to 0).
Use Automatic Scaling	When the changing cells and the target cell differ by orders of magnitude (powers of 10), select this option to ensure accuracy in Solver's results.
Show Iteration Results	When selected, Solver pauses after each iteration it attempts. Doing so can help you debug Solver problems.
Load Model	Loads a model—a set of Solver parameters—from a stored set of parameters on the worksheet.

continues

Table 21.1 Continued

Setting	Description
Save Model	Saves a Solver model to a cell or set of cells in the worksheet so that it can be recalled. Use the Load Model and Save Model settings to store the model in between sessions, or to work with multiple models for the same problem.
Estimates	
Tangent	Select this option when your problem is linear in nature.
Quadratic	Select this option when your problem is nonlinear in nature.
Derivatives	
Derivatives Forward	This default setting is correct for most problems; use it when the cells controlled by constraints change slowly as each iteration is attempted.
Central	When the constraint cells change rapidly and by large amounts, selecting this option can improve Solver's accuracy.
Search	
Newton	One of two methods that Solver uses to search for a solution, the Newton method uses more memory but results in fewer iterations.
Conjugate	The conjugate method of searching for a solution consumes less memory but requires more iterations. Select this option when working on very large problems, or when the computer's memory is exhausted while Solver is running (exhausted memory is usually indicated by excessive disk swapping).

Optimizing Credit Card Payments with Solver

In order to learn how to build Solver problems from scratch, you'll explore a simple Solver problem and walk through its creation and solution.

Consider this situation: you have a number of credit cards, each of which you make monthly payments against. Each credit card has different interest rates and default payment terms. Some cards require very small payments but take forever to pay off, while others require larger payments and are designed to be paid off in a relatively short period of time.

CAUTION

In the following example, fictitious credit cards, balances, and monthly payments are used to illustrate how a Solver problem works. You should not draw any conclusions about the relative cost of different credit card types from the examples given, and you should also not assume that real credit cards will fit the model used in this example.

The goal in this example is to minimize your monthly payments while paying off your credit cards in the most financially efficient and expeditious way. Because each card has different payment terms (basically, the ratio of the payment to the balance), you have to choose which cards to pay down wisely in order to get the best possible result.

Figure 21.8 shows the example worksheet that contains all of the credit card data and formulas needed for Solver to work on this problem.

FIG. 21.8
This is the example Credit Card Optimizer worksheet.

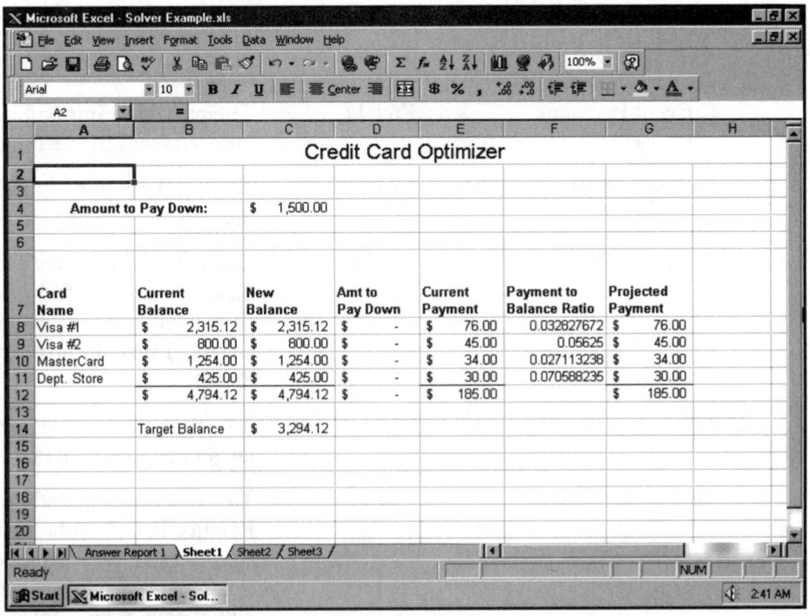

Table 21.2 shows all of the data and formulas included in the Credit Card Optimizer worksheet. You can use this data along with Figure 21.8 to build this model yourself.

Table 21.2 Credit Card Optimizer Worksheet Cells

Name	Cell(s)	Description
Amount to Pay Down	C4	The amount of money available to pay down credit cards.
Card Name	A8:A11	A list of credit card names.

continues

Table 21.2 Continued

Name	Cell(s)	Description
Current Balance	B8:B11	The current credit card balances typed into the worksheet.
New Balance	C8:C11	The new balances after Solver suggests how to pay down the credit cards. These cells will be the *changing cells* for Solver.
Amt to Pay Down	D8:D11	A calculated value (column B minus column C). These cells show how much to pay down on each card. Because Solver will suggest the new balances in C8:C11, these cells will show the difference between the starting balances and the Solver-suggested balances.
Current Payment	E8:E11	The current minimum payment for each card entered from the last monthly statement.
Payment to Balance Ratio	F8:F11	The amounts in column E (current payment) divided by the balance.
Projected Payment	G8:G11	The new payment for each card based on the balances suggested by Solver. This column is calculated by multiplying column C (New Balance) by column F (Payment to Balance Ratio).
Total Projected Payment	G12	A sum of cells G8:G11, this cell will be the target cell; the goal is to minimize this amount.
Target Balance	C14	This cell is calculated by taking the Current Balance in cell B12 and subtracting the Amount to Pay Down in cell C4. Solver will use this balance in order to know how much it can adjust each card's balance.

Setting Solver Parameters

After creating the worksheet, you start Solver and use the following steps to set all the parameters:

1. Select cell G12 for Set Target Cell. This cell is what you're aiming to minimize.
2. Choose the Min setting because you want Solver to find the minimum possible value for the target cell.
3. Select cells C8:C11 for the By Changing Cells field. These cells will be the credit card balances after carrying out the pay-downs.

4. Add three constraints:

   - The first constraint tells Solver to find a solution in which the total new balance is equal to the target balance. The constraint is $C$12 = $C$14.
   - The second constraint makes sure that Solver doesn't suggest transferring credit card balances from an expensive card to a less-expensive card. (While you can certainly do this in real life, for this example you decide that you don't want to.) Set the constraint $C$8:$C$11 <= $B$8:$B$11.
   - The third constraint ensures that Solver doesn't suggest paying off a credit card to a negative balance. Because Solver is only solving the mathematical problem presented, an optimal solution might include a negative balance on a credit card, where you'll receive income from that credit card instead of a payment. Because the real world doesn't work this way, you add this third constraint so that Solver doesn't suggest such nonsensical solutions. The constraint to add is $C$8:$C$11 >= 0.

After following the preceding steps, the Solver Parameters dialog box should look like the one shown in Figure 21.9.

FIG. 21.9
Here is the finished Solver Parameters dialog box.

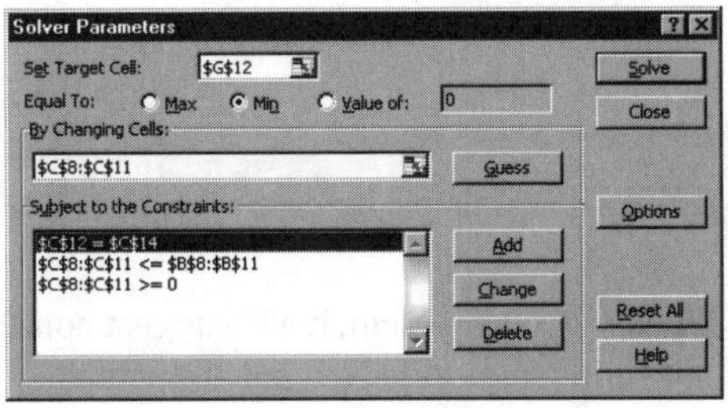

You can now click the Solve button to let Solver work on finding a solution. For this problem, you will see a solution in just a few seconds. In the Solver Results dialog box, choose to Keep Solver Solution and click the OK button. The result calculated by Solver is shown in Figure 21.10.

In the solution, you can see that Solver suggests completely paying off the Dept. Store credit card and the Visa #2 credit card. Because this doesn't use up all of the $1,500 you have budgeted to pay down credit cards, the remainder ($275) should be applied to the third most expensive card, which is Visa #1. Based on Solver's calculations, the monthly minimum payments will drop from $185 to a little over $100 after carrying out the pay-down.

Checking Solver's Solution

It's always a good idea to apply some common sense to solutions suggested by Solver. In the example presented in the preceding section, you can see that Solver has suggested the correct answer. Examine the Payment to Balance Ratio calculated in column F. The higher the ratio, the higher the monthly payment is in relationship to the balance on each credit card. Using the Payment to Balance Ratio, you can see that the most expensive card (in terms of monthly payment) is the Dept. Store card, followed by Visa #2, followed by Visa #1, followed by Master

Card. Using the ratios, you can see that Solver suggests paying down the cards that have the highest payment ratio to their balances. Looked at in another way, changing the balances for the cards with the highest ratios results in the largest decrease in monthly payment.

FIG. 21.10
This is the calculated solution to the Credit Card Optimizer.

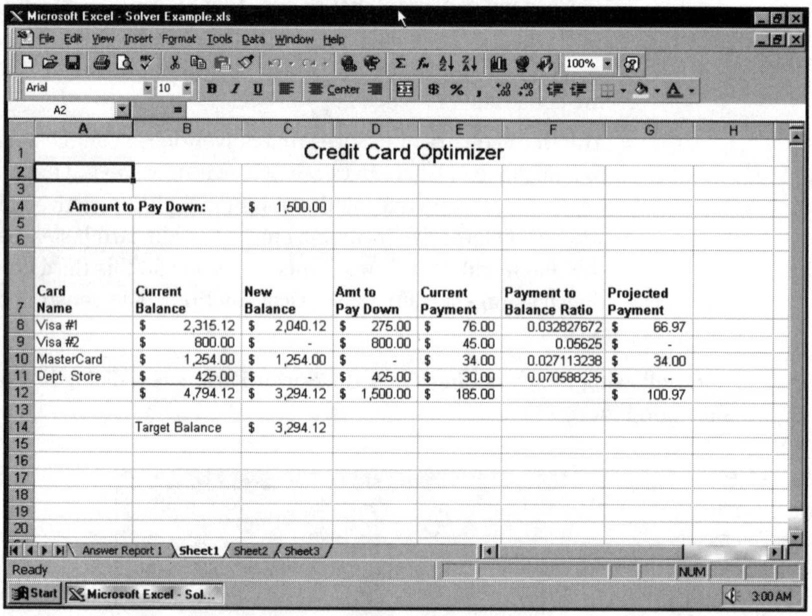

Amount to Pay Down:		$ 1,500.00				
Card Name	**Current Balance**	**New Balance**	**Amt to Pay Down**	**Current Payment**	**Payment to Balance Ratio**	**Projected Payment**
Visa #1	$ 2,315.12	$ 2,040.12	$ 275.00	$ 76.00	0.032827672	$ 66.97
Visa #2	$ 800.00	$ -	$ 800.00	$ 45.00	0.05625	$ -
MasterCard	$ 1,254.00	$ 1,254.00	$ -	$ 34.00	0.027113238	$ 34.00
Dept. Store	$ 425.00	$ -	$ 425.00	$ 30.00	0.070588235	$ -
	$ 4,794.12	$ 3,294.12	$ 1,500.00	$ 185.00		$ 100.97
	Target Balance	$ 3,294.12				

Often when you start using Solver with a problem, it will suggest nonsensical answers. Usually, the poor answers are not due to limitations in Solver, but are limitations in the real world that aren't yet reflected in the mathematical model that you ask Solver to solve. You typically have to run Solver several times, and add constraints to the problem each time to keep Solver from suggesting results that don't make sense.

Sometimes a problem is simply too complex or too large to check manually to see if the solution makes sense. In cases like this, consider setting up a smaller model with a subset of the data you're working with, and testing that model carefully. After you develop confidence that the model works correctly, you can add in the rest of the data and be reasonably sure that you're getting good results from Solver.

Solving Problems with Goal Seek

Although Excel's Goal Seek feature is similar to Solver, it is generally faster and easier to use because it doesn't provide as many options as Solver does. Use Goal Seek if you want to produce a specific value in a formula cell by adjusting only one input cell that influences a value; otherwise, if you have one or more input cells and have constraints on the solution, or if you want to maximize or minimize a formula cell, you must use Solver.

To find out how much you can afford to borrow in order to purchase a car, for example, the formula cell would contain the PMT function, which you decide should return an amount of $400 (representing your budgeted auto loan payment of $400 per month). Figure 21.11 shows a sample worksheet for this auto loan example. The formula bar shows the PMT function entered in cell C6, which calculates the monthly loan payment based on a $20,000 loan, a 48-month term, and an interest rate of 10 percent. You decide that you can't afford a payment of $507.25 per month for a $20,000 car, so you want to find out exactly how much car you can afford for $400 per month.

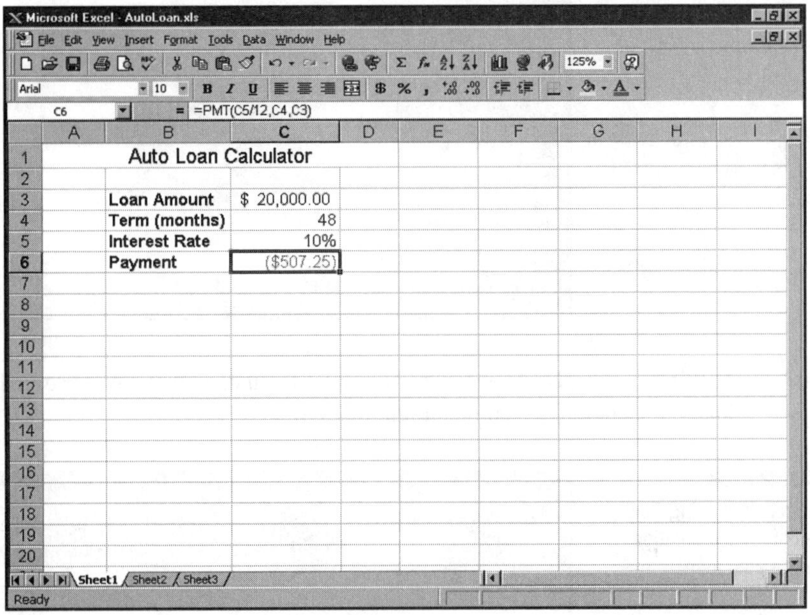

FIG. 21.11
This example auto loan worksheet shows you how Goal Seek works.

Follow these steps to use Goal Seek:

1. Select Tools, Goal Seek to display the Goal Seek dialog box.
2. In the Set Cell text box, reference the cell containing the formula you want to force to produce a specific value. In the auto loan example, select cell C6, which is the cell containing the PMT function.
3. In the To Value text box, type the target value you want the formula cell to reach. In this example, type **400** because you want the monthly payment amount to be $400.
4. In the By Changing Cell text box, type the cell reference of the input cell (the cell you want to change). Because you want to change the loan amount to achieve a monthly payment of $400, select cell C3. After these steps, the Goal Seek dialog box should look like Figure 21.12.
5. Click OK to start the Goal Seek process. The Goal Seek Status dialog box appears, stating whether or not Goal Seek found a solution.

FIG. 21.12
This is the completed Goal Seek dialog box.

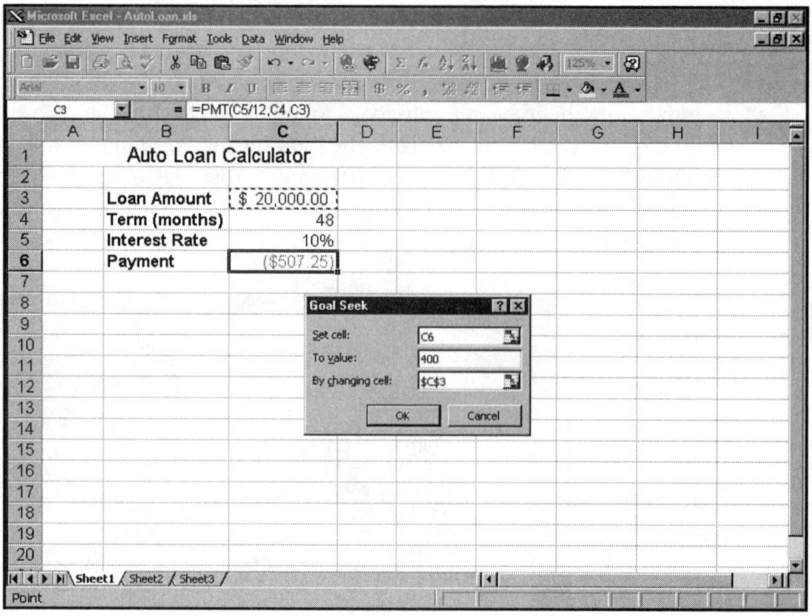

In this example, Goal Seek determines that you can afford to borrow $15,771.26 for a monthly loan payment of $400.00 (see Figure 21.13).

FIG. 21.13
The result of using Goal Seek to find a solution for the auto loan worksheet.

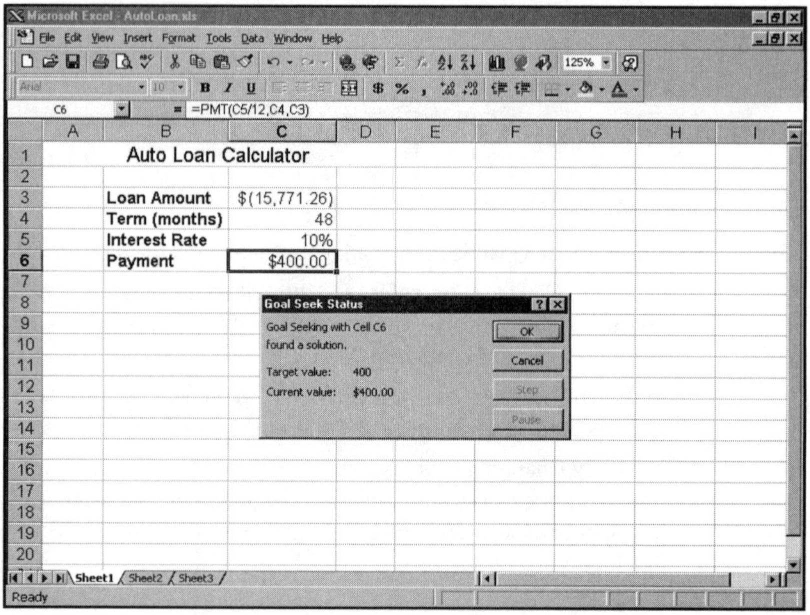

Common Problems and Solutions

The Solver add-in can be a challenge to understand and use correctly until you become more familiar with exactly how the feature works. This section provides tips to help you resolve problems you may encounter while using Solver.

Solver didn't find a solution.

Solver doesn't always find solutions to problems. When Solver finishes, it shows you a message in the Solver Results dialog box. The message tells you what Solver was able to accomplish, and it usually gives you a clue about what you need to fix if Solver wasn't able to come to a solution.

There are two normal result messages that indicate that Solver found a solution. The first one, `Solver found a solution. All constraints and optimality conditions are satisfied,` tells you that Solver found a solution. The second normal result message is `Solver has converged to the current solution. All constraints are satisfied.` If you see this second message, you may be able to improve on Solver's answer by decreasing the value in the Convergence field in the Solver Options dialog box. You also may have to increase the number of iterations or maximum time so that Solver can work on the problem for a longer period of time.

There are also a number of messages that indicate that better results may be achieved by taking some action:

> `Solver cannot improve the current solution. All constraints are satisfied.` If you see this message, Solver is indicating that it might be able to find a better solution if you increase the Precision setting in the Solver Options dialog box.
>
> `Solver could not find a feasible solution. No solution appears possible to Solver that meets all constraints.` Consider revising the constraints, and also increasing the precision in the Solver Options dialog box.
>
> `Solver encountered an error value in a target or constraint cell.` The most recent iteration Solver attempted resulted in an error in one of the cells. Check the formulas in the target and constraint cells, and also double-check the constraints to see that they're properly created.
>
> `Stop chosen when the maximum iteration was reached.` Try increasing the Iterations parameter in the Solver Options dialog box.
>
> `Stop chosen when the maximum time limit was reached.` Try increasing the Max Time parameter in the Solver Options dialog box.
>
> `The conditions for Assume Linear Model are not satisfied. The problem does not fit the linear model within Solver.` The problem may be nonlinear. Try clearing the Assume Linear Model setting in the Solver Options dialog box.

`The Set Target Cell values do not converge.` The target cell value is changing radically for each iteration, and Solver is not able to correlate the changing target cell value with the changing cells or the constraints. You should look for any missing constraints to the problem, such as minimum or maximum constraints for the changing cells.

`There is not enough memory available to solve the problem.` Try to free up available memory on the computer (close other running programs). If that doesn't work, try selecting the Conjugate setting in the Solver Options dialog box to conserve memory.

From Here...

This chapter showed you how to use the Solver add-in to find an optimal solution to a problem. You learned how to use the sample Solver worksheets provided with Excel, as well as how to build your own Solver problem from scratch. In addition, you learned how to use the Goal Seek feature to find a specific solution to a problem involving only one adjustable cell.

Excel provides many other features for analyzing your data. Refer to the following chapters for more information:

- Chapter 18, "Building Scenarios and Outlines with Excel," shows you how to use Excel's scenario and outlining features to view the data you are analyzing in many different ways.
- Chapter 19, "Auditing and Validating Worksheets," explains how to trace errors in your workbooks, validate user input, and use names instead of cell references to help reduce the chance of errors in formulas.
- Chapter 20, "Analyzing Data: PivotTables!," shows you how to build pivot tables, which enable you to quickly analyze and manipulate complex data.
- Chapter 22, "Mastering the Analysis ToolPak," explains how to use Excel's analysis tools for business, engineering, and statistical applications.

CHAPTER 22

Mastering the Analysis ToolPak

by Forrest Houlette

Install the Analysis ToolPak

The Analysis ToolPak is an add-in that gives you advanced statistical functions. It enables you to conduct more robust analyses than you can perform with run-of-the-mill Excel functions.

Use the business analysis tools

The business analysis tools allow you to examine business problems and predict trends.

Use the engineering analysis tools

The engineering analysis tools are perfect for analyzing complex data.

Use the statistical analysis tools

The statistical analysis tools allow you to analyze both experimental and nonexperimental problems.

Excel 97 provides some exceptionally useful business analysis tools. Imagine wanting to know whether the decline in sales for this quarter represents a dangerous trend that needs attention or a seasonal aberration. If the decline represents a trend, you would obviously want to examine the reasons behind it. You would start by surveying clients to find out what their attitudes toward your goods and services happen to be. You would then focus on sales force training, improving the product, developing new clients, improving management philosophy, or whatever else the surveys suggest. Your goal would be to boost sales in order to protect revenue.

An example is United Airlines' recent United Rising advertising campaign. United surveyed its customers and did not like the analysis of the numbers that came back. The analysis did not support United's opinion of its services and its vision of itself as a company—they thought they were better than their customers did. As a result, United is inculcating a corporate philosophy they hope will lead to vastly improved service.

A seasonal aberration requires a different strategy. You would want to attract customers who are typically loyal to purchase at a time when they focus their attention elsewhere. You might try a special product promotion, a sale, some seasonal version of the product or service, or a similar sales effort designed to boost the volume of sales in the slump period.

Examples are McDonalds' summer sandwich promotions (for a limited time only at participating restaurants). Disney promotes home video sales by releasing the videos like they do a film, for a defined period of time. Toward the end of the release, when sales tend to drop, Disney drives sales by reminding you that it's the last time to get that classic film this century. The consumer market responds by providing a rise in sales up to the ending date of the release. Excel can help you to plan these strategies using the tools in the Analysis ToolPak.

NOTE This chapter focuses on providing the context for making plans once you have the evidence you want to analyze. As a result, we will suggest some strategies as examples of decisions you might make. Each decision you make, however, must be based on the data you have at hand. Each data set will suggest different strategies.

Installing the Analysis ToolPak

Even though Excel can help you to define such strategies, it cannot help you in its default installed condition. You need to know where to look to find the tools. Even if you have chosen to have them installed on your disk, they do not appear on your menu until you install them as an add-in to Excel. To undertake this installation, follow these steps:

1. Open the Tools menu.
2. Select the Add-Ins option.
3. In the Add-Ins dialog box shown in Figure 22.1, check Analysis ToolPak (and Analysis ToolPak—VBA if you want to use the tools from within Visual Basic forms and macros).
4. Click the OK button.

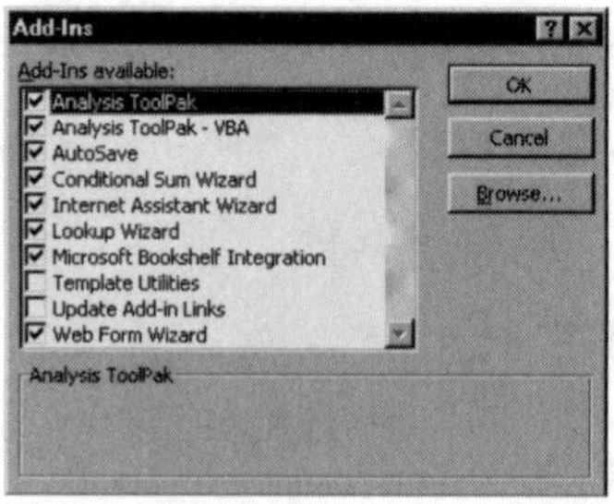

FIG. 22.1
Check the check boxes to activate the Analysis ToolPak in the Add-Ins dialog box.

After undertaking this simple installation, you will see a new item on the Tools menu. At the bottom, you see Data Analysis (see Figure 22.2). This menu option gives you access to the business analysis tools that Excel provides.

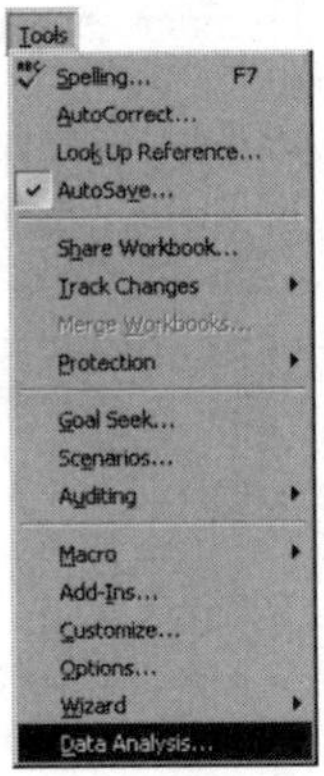

FIG. 22.2
The Data Analysis menu item gives you access to the Analysis ToolPak.

Using Business Analysis Tools

Using the business analysis tools is straightforward. You need to understand, however, that you have two ways of running the analysis. The first is to conduct the analysis interactively while running a spreadsheet. The second is to run the analysis from a macro using a line of Visual Basic code to script which form of the analysis to run. To run an analysis interactively, follow these steps:

1. Open the Tools menu.
2. Select the Data Analysis option.
3. In the Data Analysis dialog box, select the type of analysis you want to undertake (see Figure 22.3). (You'll learn more about the analysis tools later in the chapter.)

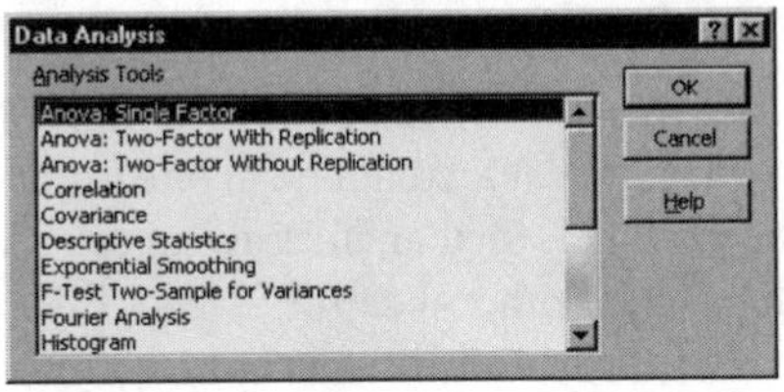

FIG. 22.3
The Data Analysis dialog box allows you to choose the method of analysis.

4. Click the OK button.

After you click the OK button, you see a dialog box that guides you through the selection of the data for analysis and the options for the analysis. You fill in the data range, choose your options, and then generate the output by clicking an OK button.(The exact steps for performing such a procedure will be covered later in the chapter.)

Running an analysis from Visual Basic requires you to use a line of VBA code that has the following form:

```
Application.Run "ATPVBAEN.XLA!Macroname", argument1, argument2, argument, ...
```

When you run the macro, the analysis tool specified by the macro name, which is stored in the workbook ATPVBAEN.XLA, runs to carry out the analysis. The exact form of the analysis depends on the arguments you specify. One of these is, of course, the data range to operate on. The others represent the settings of various controls in the dialog box that sets up the analysis when you run it from the Data Analysis dialog box. For example, the following line runs the Descriptive Statistics option using the range $A$1 through $A$10 and invoking the summary statistics option but none of the others:

```
Application.Run "ATPVBAEN.XLA!Descr", ActiveSheet.Range("$A$1:$A$10"), "" , "C",
➥False, True
```

TIP To find the Visual Basic for Applications syntax for any of the analysis tools, turn on the macro recorder and invoke the tool using dummy data and examine the macro you recorded. Try typing the command from left to right on a separate line, and VBA opens a tool tip with the correct syntax. Try this technique to explore the various arguments to the descriptive statistics code preceding this tip.

The next few sections discuss how to use the various business analysis tools found in the Data Analysis dialog box (refer to Figure 22.3). They show you the basics of choosing each statistical method you could apply, and work you through a problem that demonstrates using the method.

Correlation

The correlation tool calculates the Pearson product-moment correlation value that describes the two sets of data. Translating that statement, the correlation tool calculates a value named r, the coefficient of correlation, that describes the relationship of two sets of data. It also attempts to create a line that describes the relationship between the two data sets. The fit of this line to describe the trend in the data is done according to a method called the product moment or least squares method.

What Does Correlation Mean? r may take any value ranging from –1 to +1. If r=0, the two sets of data have no relationship whatsoever. Fluctuations in one set of data are not paired in any way with fluctuations in the other. If r=1, then an increase in the values in one data set is paired with an increase in the values in the other data set. If r=–1, then the reverse is true; an increase in the values in one data set is paired with a decrease in the values of the other data set. Values in between these extremes indicate the relative strength of the relationship.

Consider this practical example. Suppose you have picked one great stock: Its value has done nothing but increase steadily over the time you have owned it. But your other picks haven't been so great. You wonder whether you might be able to capitalize on one great choice by using it to predict whether other choices might be good.

You can acquire the daily price information for any set of stocks. Your excellent choice is one data series. The stock you are speculating on is another data series. Say you have entered the daily price figures for the last three months into two columns in an Excel spreadsheet and run the correlation tool on them. The value of r returned by the analysis is .76. That looks like a good strong value, but what does it really tell you?

First, this value tells you that the two stocks are positively correlated. When one increases in value, the other increases in value. This relationship is much better than if the value of r was –.76. In this case, when the index stock went up, the stock of interest went down. You wouldn't want to buy under those circumstances.

Is .76 a good enough relationship to indicate that the stock you are speculating on will do well? Here is where a judgment call is required. The total percentage of the relationship that the numbers you have analyzed can explain is calculated by squaring the value of r. In this case r^2 is .5776, or 57.76 percent. This figure means that almost 43 percent of the relationship you see between the data sets is caused by unexplained or unknown factors. At this point, your investment advisor would have a discussion with you about your risk tolerance. The odds are 43 in 100 that the relationship you see is incorrect. (That is, if you repeated the analysis on 100 independent data sets, you would make a mistake in accepting the relationship in 43 of these analyses.)

TIP It's wise to remember that correlation does not mean causation. Just because shoe size can correlate with ability to spell long words does not mean that the shoes you wear will make you a good speller.

How Do You Conduct a Correlation Analysis? We will now conduct a sample correlation analysis, using data stored in an Excel workbook named UESample.xls. This sample workbook contains data relating to a startup company over its first six quarters. The spreadsheet contains columns labeled Quarter, Items Sold, Gross Sales, and Net Sales (see Figure 22.4). If you examine this data, you notice that Net Sales fluctuates rather widely. A good question is whether these figures represent any sort of trend over time. Correlation analysis allows us to characterize the nature of this relationship.

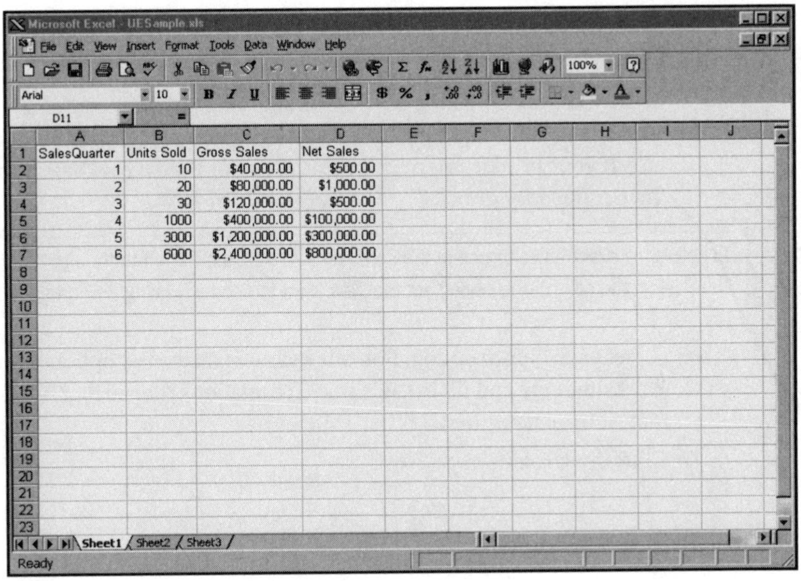

FIG. 22.4
The UESample.xls spreadsheet provides sample sales figures.

To conduct a correlation analysis, follow these steps:

1. Because the input range for the correlation analysis must be a contiguous set of cells, select the cells that represent the quarters and copy them into a new range of cells.
2. Copy the Net Sales cells to a new range contiguous with the quarter cells. Your spreadsheet should now look like the one shown in Figure 22.5.

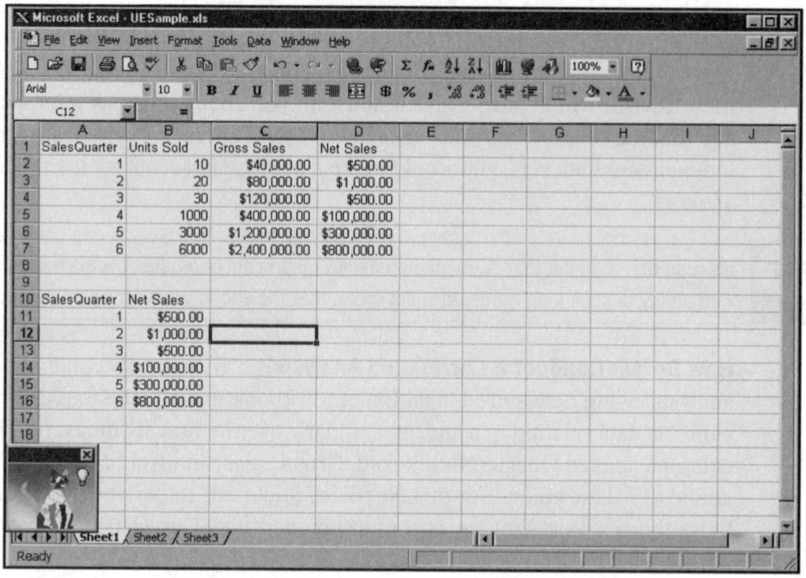

FIG. 22.5
The result of copying to two columns to be used as input to the correlation problem.

3. Open the Tools menu and select the Data Analysis option.
4. In the Data Analysis dialog box, select Correlation and click the OK button.
5. In the Correlation dialog box, the Input Range text box automatically shows the selected range. If you have also copied the column headers, check the Labels in First Row check box. If your headers were in a column rather than a row, select the Rows option button in the Grouped By group.

TIP To select the exact range to use in the spreadsheet, click the button to the right of the range text box. Then select the cells in the worksheet that you want to use by clicking and dragging.

6. Select your output option. For this example, leave the option button set on New Worksheet Ply and fill in the name Correlation. Your dialog box should now have the look shown in Figure 22.6.
7. Click the OK button.

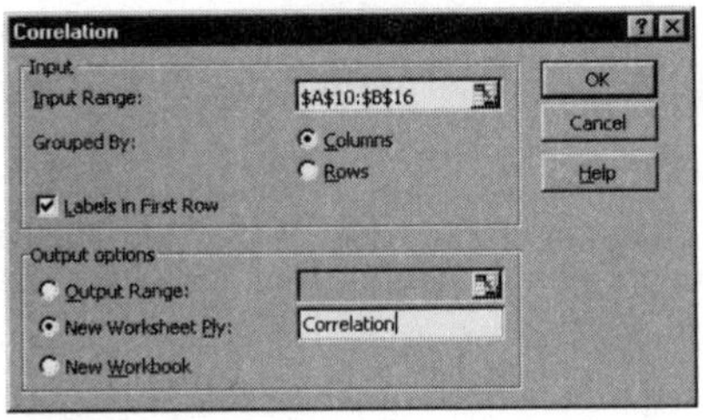

FIG. 22.6
The Correlation dialog box is ready to conduct the sample analysis.

Excel creates a new worksheet named Correlation that presents the solution of the correlation analysis (see Figure 22.7). The result, r=0.8448154487994184, indicates that you probably can assume that the variations in the linear trend evident in the data are flukes. In general, you have a strong positive relationship between time and the net sales in the company. With r^2= 0.7137132087545, you can be confident that the data you see accounts for 71.37 percent of the relationship. Chance factors are affecting sales, but the trend you see is likely to continue. You need not rush to have a drastic sale yet.

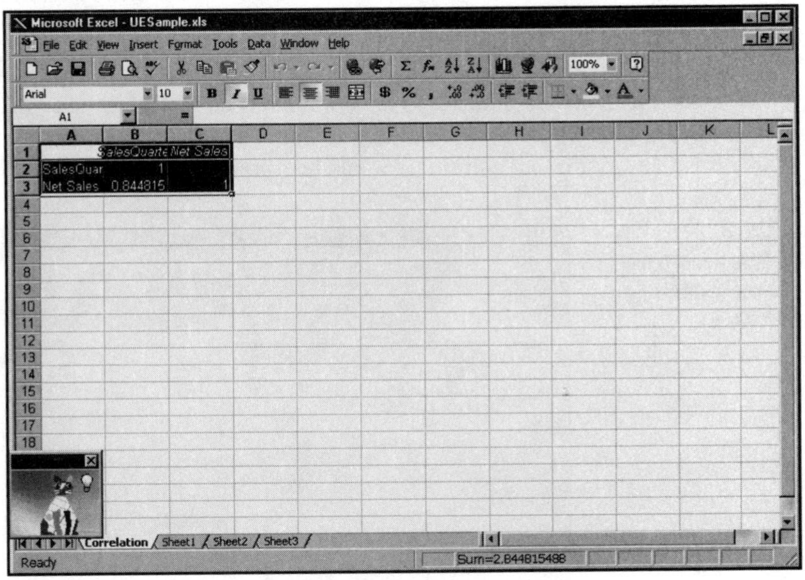

FIG. 22.7
The outcome of correlation analysis is presented in a 2 × 2 table.

Covariance

Like correlation, covariance measures the strength of a relationship between two data sets. Instead of using the product moment or least squares method, covariance measures the average deviation from the mean. Translated, this difference in method means that you are not trying to find a linear relationship between the two data sets. You are asking whether large values in one data set are associated with large values in another data set, in which case you get a positive covariance. If large values in one set are associated with small values in the other set, you get a negative covariance. If you get a covariance of zero, you cannot assume that the data sets have a relationship.

What Does Covariance Mean? Let's turn to a slightly different forecasting analysis. Assume that you are in the software business, head of your own custom programming shop. To fill in the slack times, you also do corporate training as a contractor. You notice that when you get offered lots of training courses, you also get calls requesting your services as a contractor. You know that this trend is cyclical, because over three years you have noticed three peaks of business about two or three months apart. You know that the training company is aware of its enrollments several months in advance. Could you use your enrollments to project upswings in your software contracts?

You would want some stronger sense of the relationship before banking on it. You could run an analysis of covariance to evaluate whether the large values in one data set were associated with large values in the other data set. You would set up enrollments for the training company in one range on the spreadsheet and number of contracts for software in another column. You could track over whatever time period you wanted. You would then run an analysis of covariance.

Figure 22.8 shows the outcome for a simple run of such an analysis. To accept that you could use the trend in training enrollment to predict growth in your software business, you would be looking for a positive number in the lower-left cell of the covariance matrix. A value near zero would indicate that you could not trust your observation. A negative value would indicate that growth in your training business would be paired with a downturn in your software business.

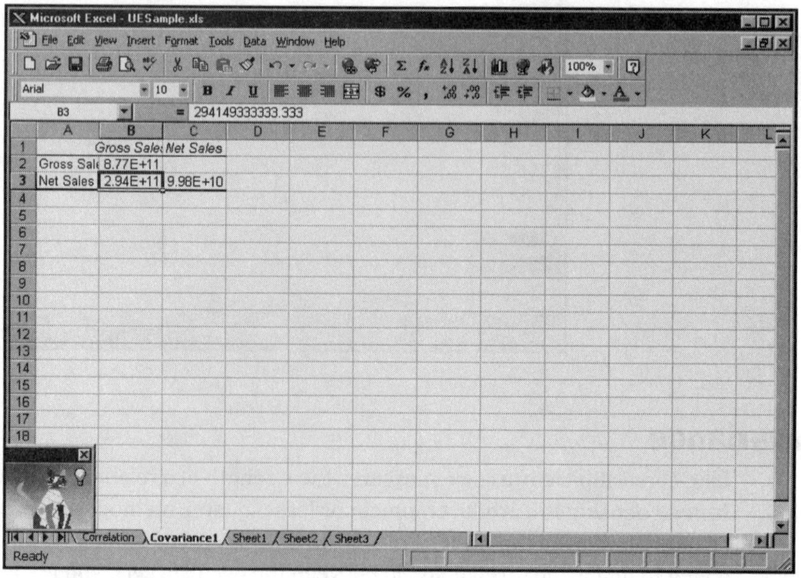

FIG. 22.8
The critical value in the covariance matrix is the lower-left cell.

How Do You Conduct an Analysis of Covariance? To conduct an analysis of covariance, follow these steps:

1. Select the cells that represent the two sets of data to be compared. Your spreadsheet should now look like the one shown in Figure 22.9.

TIP You may have to copy the two ranges of cells so that they are contiguous to one another.

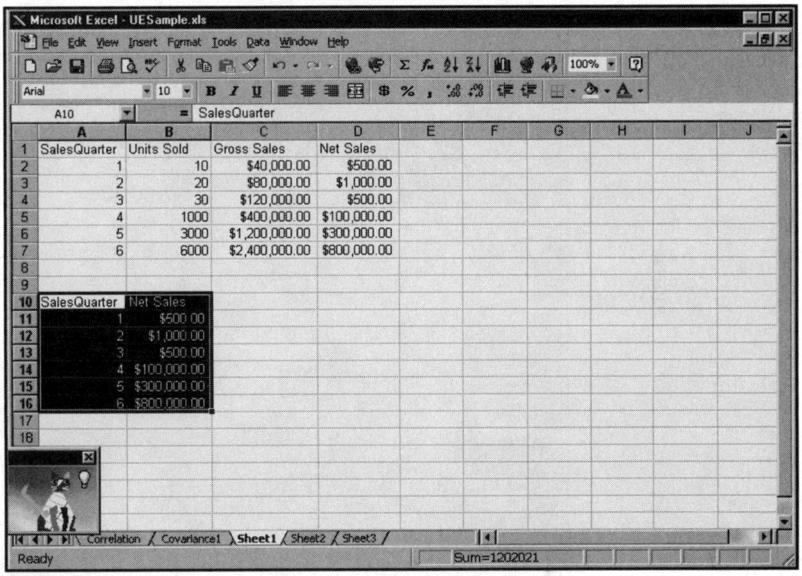

FIG. 22.9
The covariance tool operates on contiguous ranges of data.

2. Open the Tools menu and select the Data Analysis option.
3. In the Data Analysis dialog box, select Covariance and click the OK button. The Covariance dialog box appears.
4. In the Covariance dialog box, the Input Range text box automatically shows the selected range. If you have also copied the column headers, check the Labels in First Row check box. If your headers were in a column rather than a row, select the Rows option button in the Grouped By group.
5. Select your output option. For this example, leave the option button set on New Worksheet Ply and fill in the name **Covariance** (see Figure 22.10).
6. Click the OK button.

Excel creates a new worksheet named "Correlation" that presents the solution of the covariance analysis (see Figure 22.11). The result shows a positive number in the lower-left cell, indicating that the large values in one data set are associated with large values in the other data set. You can trust the trend you see.

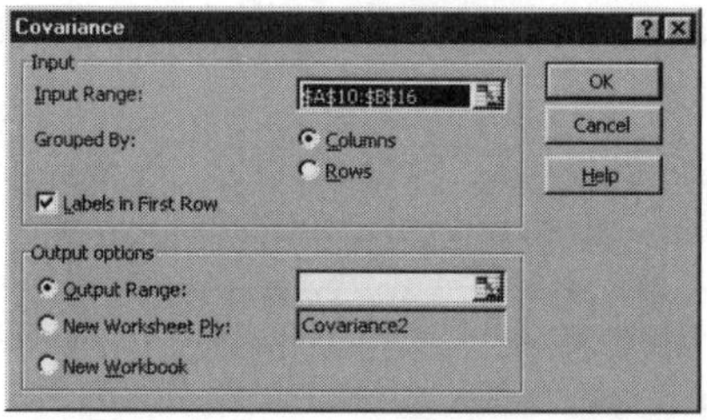

FIG. 22.10
The Covariance dialog box is ready to conduct the sample analysis.

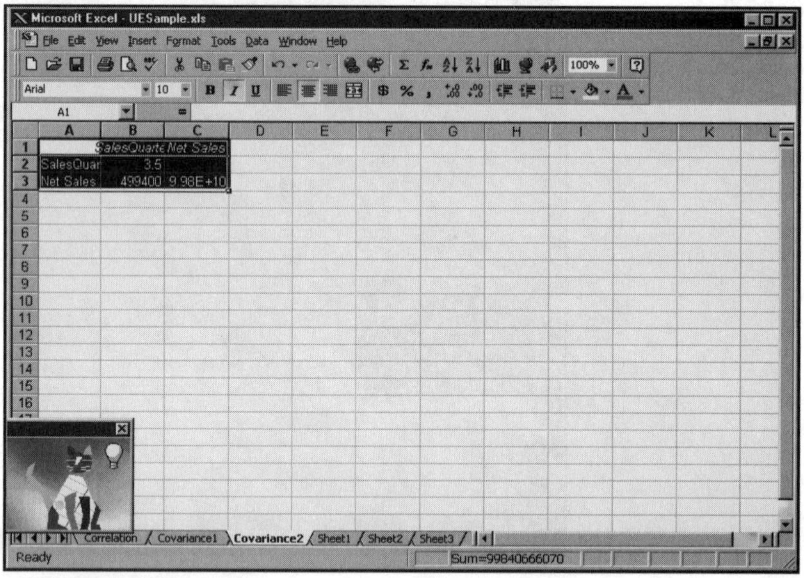

FIG. 22.11
The output of the covariance tool is presented in a 2 × 2 cell.

Exponential Smoothing

So you have done a correlation analysis between quarters and net sales, and you have charted the data points you analyzed. You have a strong value of r and you have placed a trend line on your chart, which shows graphically the linear relationship the correlation analysis tool calculated. You can now make a prediction about what sales ought to be for the next four quarters.

Excel allows you to make such predictions by examining the line on the chart visually, or you could use the TREND function to make the prediction. Whichever method you use, you will get four numbers. You could use these numbers to predict the next four quarters as well, but the nature of correlation and trend lines guarantees that the prediction is less accurate the farther in the future you go. The error values increase as the line is extrapolated farther into the future.

Exponential smoothing is a technique for adjusting such error in forecasts. This technique introduces a correction factor to reduce the error that creeps into the calculation, usually by about 20 to 30 percent. Your prediction of future values is less astounding because the correction typically lowers the value of the forecast; however, because the prediction is more conservative, it is more realistic.

What Is Exponential Smoothing? Exponential smoothing means that you, as the data analyst, will engage in adjusting the numbers on which you are basing your forecast. How much you adjust them depends on experience in the particular problem domain. Sometimes statisticians working in a particular field have shown that 20 percent is an appropriate adjustment. Other fields may have demonstrated that 30 percent is better. The demonstrations are based on trial-and-error forecasts. You try an adjustment and see if it works out. Based on this experience, you choose your adjustment. Your adjustment is known as the ***damping factor*** in the analysis.

If you have no clue about what adjustment is appropriate, be conservative. It is better to be surprised by achieving more than your forecast or having a little extra inventory on hand. The other surprise, being caught short on supplies or revenue, can lead you quickly to readjust your smoothing factor.

How Do You Conduct an Analysis Using Exponential Smoothing? To conduct an analysis using exponential smoothing, follow these steps:

1. Select the cells that represent the set of data on which to base the forecast. Your spreadsheet should now look like the one shown in Figure 22.12.

TIP You need to have at least four cells in the range that you input into the exponential smoothing tool; five, when standard errors are checked.

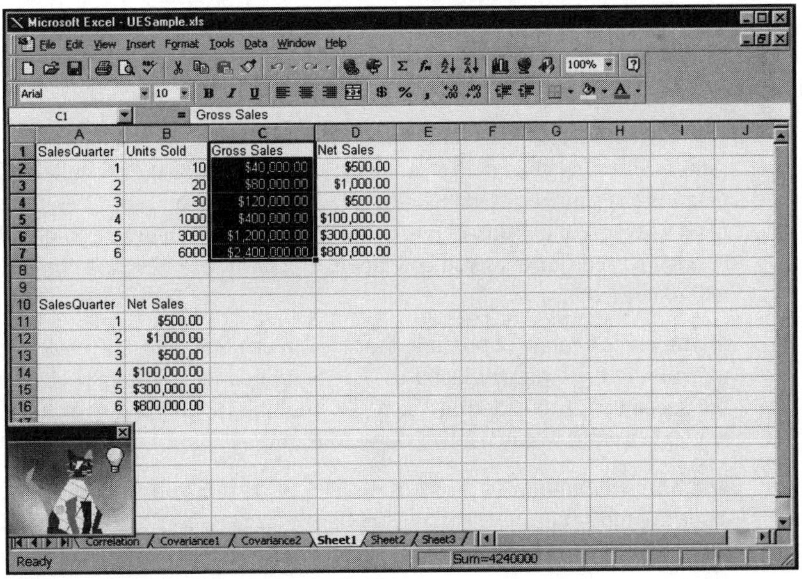

FIG. 22.12
The exponential tool operates on a single range of data.

2. Open the Tools menu and select the Data Analysis option.
3. In the Data Analysis dialog box, select Exponential Smoothing and click the OK button.

   In the Exponential Smoothing dialog box that appears, the Input Range text box automatically shows the selected range. (If not, click the button to the right of the box and select the appropriate range.
4. Click the button to its right again (after selecting the range) to return to the main dialog box. Enter your chosen Damping Factor as a decimal fraction, such as .2. The default factor is .3.
5. Select your output option. You can specify an output range, but you can also choose to chart the trend and to look at standard errors. Your dialog box should now have the look shown in Figure 22.13.

FIG. 22.13
The Exponential Smoothing dialog box is ready to conduct the sample analysis.

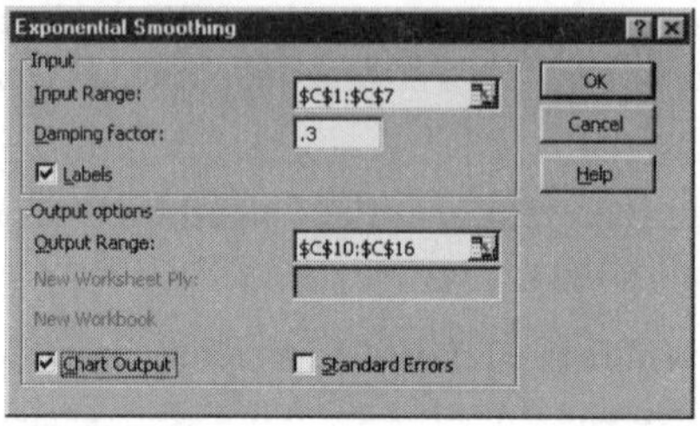

6. Click the OK button.

Excel reports the extrapolated forecast into a range of cells (see Figure 22.14). If you selected the appropriate options, a chart of the trend appears, as does standard error information. You can then evaluate the new forecast to see what course of action it suggests for you.

Histograms

The Histograms analysis tool takes you in a different direction. This tool does not describe relationships between data sets. Instead, it determines the cumulative frequencies in a set of data. As a result, you could use this tool to describe the score frequencies on an in-house certification exam for a group of twenty examinees. You can get a count of the number of students receiving each score, or you could define a set of data bins and obtain the number of scores falling in each bin.

A *data bin* is a range of possible scores. You can find out how many fall into the various quartiles of the scale, for instance. The first bin on a 100 point scale would be defined as 0–25, the second as 26–50, the third as 51–75, and the last as 76–100. You can then find how many students scored within each of these four ranges.

What Are Histograms? *Histograms* are charts that you interpret by visual inspection. They are tools that allow you to summarize large collections of data in interpretable ways. They show how many employees achieved a particular score on a screening test, for example. They can add percentages to summarize the frequency in a particular category as a portion of the whole. In general, they are your first step in dealing with a collection of data that makes no sense when you eyeball its listing in raw form. When you build histograms, you make pictures of the general trends in the data set.

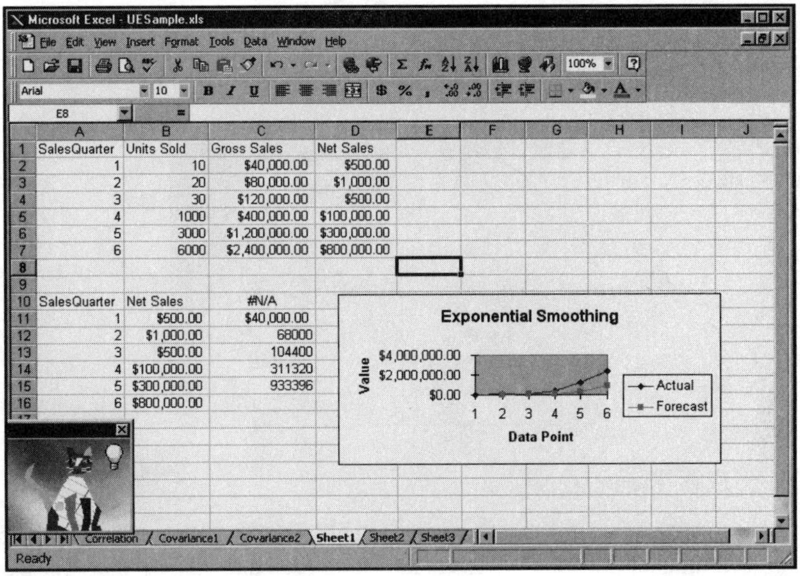

FIG. 22.14
The output of the exponential smoothing tool is presented in the cell range and (optionally) in a chart.

How Do You Conduct an Analysis Using Histograms? To conduct an analysis using histograms, follow these steps:

1. Select the cells that represent the set of data on which to base the analysis. Your spreadsheet should now look like the one shown in Figure 22.15.

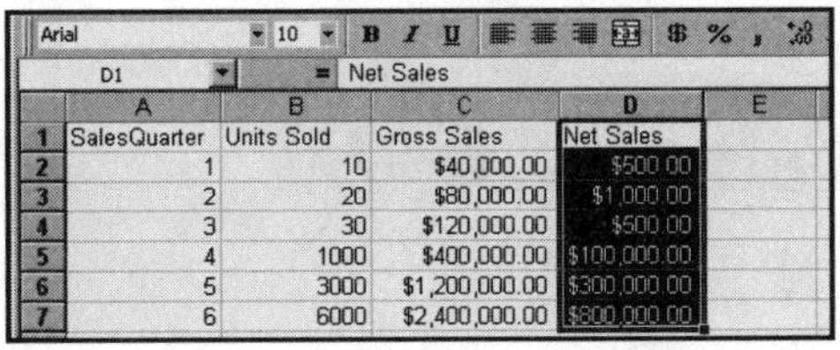

FIG. 22.15
The exponential tool operates on a single range of data.

2. Open the Tools menu and select the Data Analysis option.
3. In the Data Analysis dialog box, select Histograms and click the OK button.
4. In the Histograms dialog box, the Input Range text box automatically shows the selected range. (If not, click the button to the right of the box and select the appropriate range using the mouse cursor. After the range is selected, click the button to its right again to return to the main dialog box.) The Bin Range text box can contain an optional set of

cells that define the boundary values for dividing the data into bins. (Excel will choose an even division of the scale into bins.) Check the Labels check box if the input range contains labels.

5. Select your output option. You can specify an output range, a new ply, or a new workbook. You can also choose to chart the data in a Pareto chart or an Excel chart. You may choose to show cumulative percentages on the output. Your dialog box should now look like Figure 22.16.

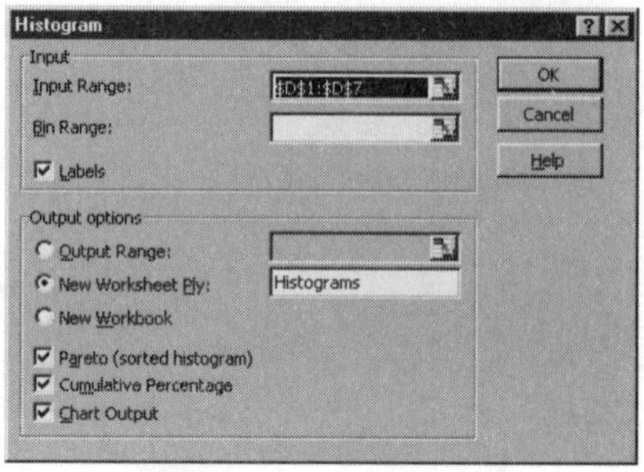

FIG. 22.16 The Histogram dialog box.

6. Click the OK button.

Excel creates the histograms (see Figure 22.17). It divides the scale into bins and reports the frequency of the data items that fell into each bin. You can scan this information to begin your interpretation of what the data might tell you. Perhaps you would see that an unacceptable number of employees scored in the lower ranges of the screening test, and you might introduce training to remedy the problem.

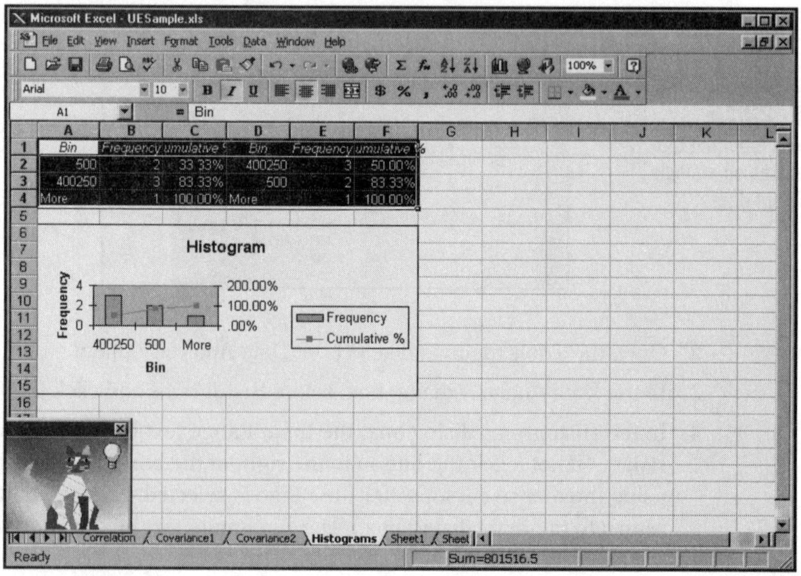

FIG. 22.17 The output of the histograms tool is presented two types of histograms.

Moving Average

Averages have curious properties. The picture of the data they present is center-weighted. That is, a mean tends to find the center of the data and then claim that the center between the two extremes is an accurate estimate of the ordinary state of affairs. If you are estimating average household income, however, an average is a very poor estimate of what a typical family faces financially each month. A few individuals like William H. Gates III included in any sample of households skew the average impossibly high, making it seem like you and I are making lots more than we really do.

For many business factors—sales, inventory, and expenses, for example—averages are good enough, but an average over a long period of time masks some of the realities that affect forecasting. The average cost of inventory over the last year might be $100,000 per month; but during the spring, that cost might be significantly more, on average, than in the fall. The technique of moving averages adjusts for the hidden factors that a single average over a long period of time might mask. The technique breaks the entire historical period into subperiods and bases the forecast on the averages of the subperiods.

What Is a Moving Average? A *moving average*, like exponential smoothing, means that you are adjusting your data to overcome error factors. This method is especially valid for inventory counts and similar variables. You decide that there are enough outlying data points to justify applying this technique, because you suspect that means are either too high or too low to give valid forecasts. How do you know to apply this technique? You can inspect a plot of your data. If you see several values that are significantly higher or lower than the rest, make the adjustment.

How Do You Conduct an Analysis Using Moving Average? To conduct an analysis using moving average, follow these steps:

1. Select the cells that represent the set of data on which to base the forecast. Your spreadsheet should now look like the one shown in Figure 22.18.

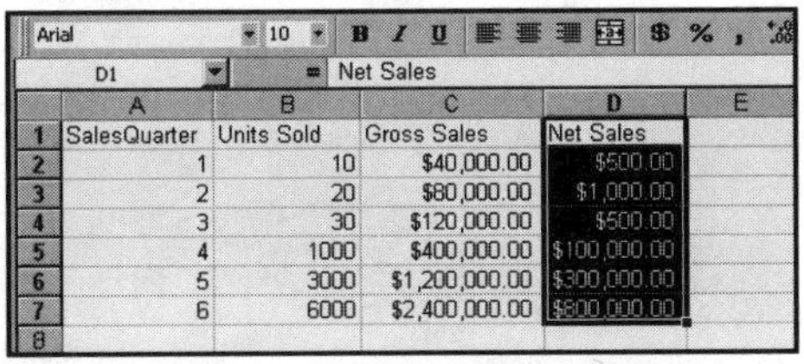

FIG. 22.18
The moving average tool operates on a single range of data.

TIP Moving averages work with a single column of data, and you must have at least four cells in the range.

2. Open the Tools menu and select the Data Analysis option.
3. In the Data Analysis dialog box, select Moving Average and click the OK button.

   In the Moving Average dialog box, the Input Range text box automatically shows the selected range. (If not, click the button to the right of the box and select the appropriate range using the mouse cursor.)

4. Click the button to its right again (after selecting the range) to return to the main dialog box. Check the Labels check box if the input range contains labels. Check the Chart Output and Standard Errors check boxes if you want to chart the forecast and view standard error information.
5. The Output Range text box must contain a set of cells where the output table will be placed. Your dialog box should now have the look shown in Figure 22.19. Click the OK button.

FIG. 22.19
The Moving Average dialog box is ready to conduct the sample analysis.

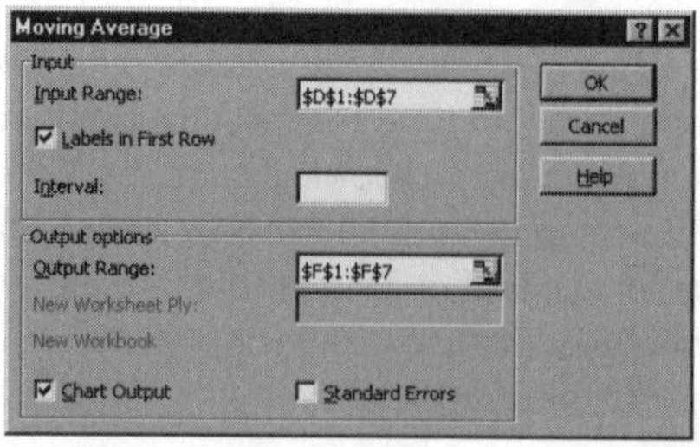

Excel creates the forecast (see Figure 22.20). You see your projected values adjusted according to the moving averages formula, which gives you a more conservative and accurate estimate of the future values.

FIG. 22.20
The output of the moving average tool is presented as a range of cells.

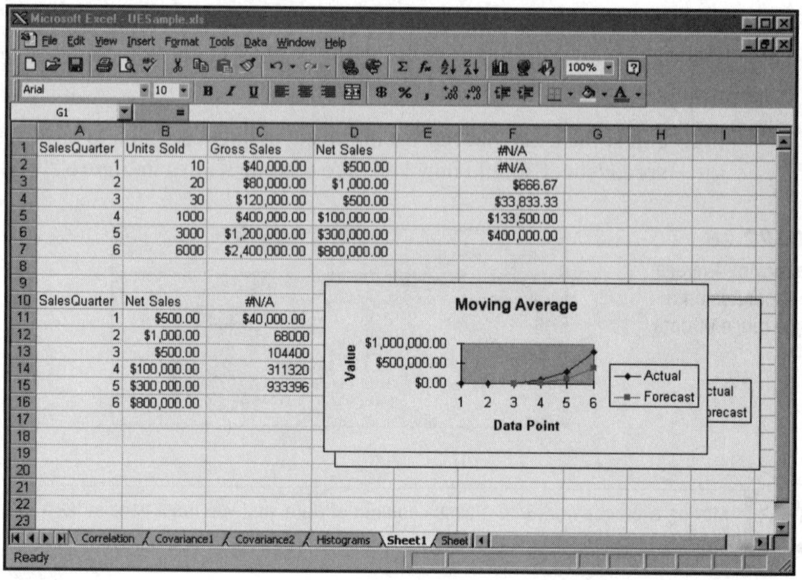

Random Number

Often in conducting an analysis, you must generate random numbers. You may need such a table to help you select a random sample. Or such a table may simulate a set of events, like the frequency of successful outcomes in a promotional game. The Analysis ToolPak provides a random number generator over which you have a great deal of control. You can specify the distribution to use for simulations, and you can specify the seed to use in creating the random numbers. Once you know the seed, you can recreate the same table of random numbers by supplying the seed number to the analysis tool.

To generate random numbers, follow these steps:

1. Open the Tools menu and select the Data Analysis option.
2. In the Data Analysis dialog box, select Random Number Generation and click the OK button.
3. Enter the number of columns of random numbers to create in the Number of Variables box. Enter the number of random numbers to create per column in the Number of Random Numbers box. Select the distribution you want to use using the Distribution drop-down list box. If you want to use a seed number, enter it in the Random seed box. (Note that Excel defaults to completely filling the output range you define with random numbers drawn from the distribution you choose.)
4. Select your output option. You can specify an output range, a new ply, or a new workbook. Your dialog box should now have the look shown in Figure 22.21.
5. Click the OK button.

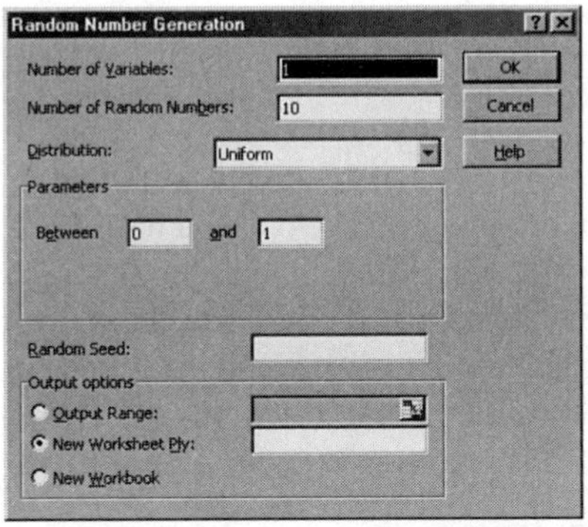

FIG. 22.21
The Random Number Generation smoothing dialog box is ready to generate the table of numbers.

Excel creates the table of random numbers (see Figure 22.22). You could then use these numbers to create random samples or to create sample data sets to test experimental designs you plan to undertake. For example, if you were designing a promotional game, you would want to simulate player choices to make sure that the odds of awarding prizes worked in your favor. You would greatly prefer not to be awarding more prizes than you had planned to award.

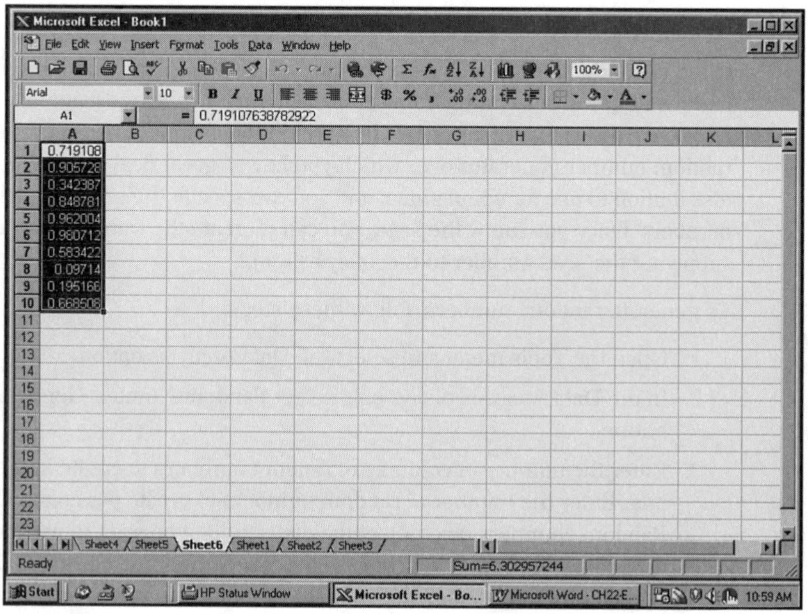

FIG. 22.22
The output of the random number generation tool is presented in the table format you specified.

Rank and Percentile

Often you will have a data set and you just want to know what the percentile rankings are. Such data sets could be scores on certification or entrance exams. They could be sales figures for your entire sales force. You would be using the rankings to evaluate the relative success of the employees involved, for example. The Rank and Percentile tool accepts a range of data and partitions it into such rankings.

What Are Ranks and Percentiles? Ranks and percentiles are ways of quickly evaluating who is better than whom, or what is better than what else. If you have a sales staff of fifty and you want to know who is doing the best, you can rank their monthly numbers and you have a quick answer. You know who is in fiftieth place and who is in first place. If you have 100 test scores and you want to know who scored better than 89 percent of the rest of the pool, get percentiles. The chart will tell you quickly who falls into this category.

How Do You Conduct an Analysis Using Ranks and Percentiles? To conduct an analysis using ranks and percentiles, follow these steps:

1. Select the cells that represent the set of data on which to base the analysis. Your spreadsheet should now look like the one shown in Figure 22.23.
2. Open the Tools menu and select the Data Analysis option.
3. In the Data Analysis dialog box, select Ranks and Percentile and click the OK button.
4. In the Ranks and Percentile dialog box, the Input Range text box automatically shows the selected range. (If not, click the button to the right of the box and select the appropriate range using the mouse cursor.)

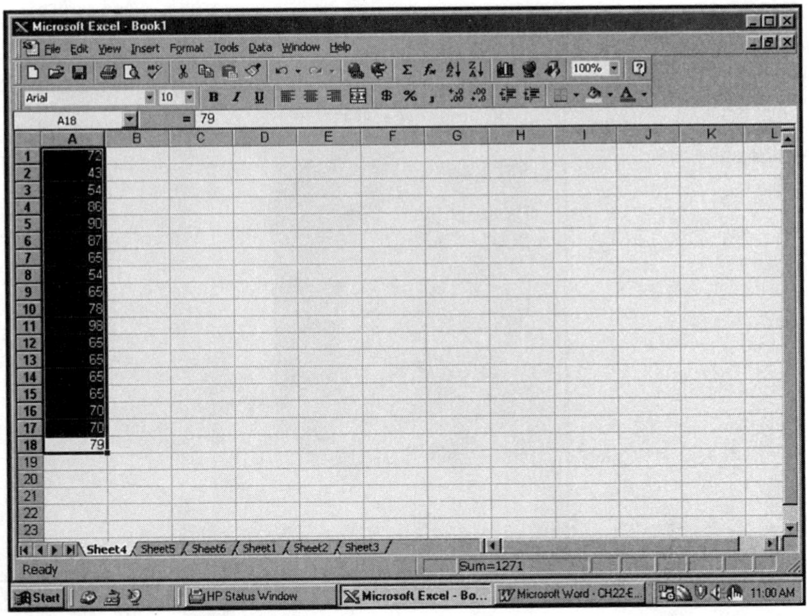

FIG. 22.23
The ranks and percentile tool operates on a single range or multiple ranges of data.

5. Click the button to its right again (after selecting the range) to return to the main dialog box. If you have also copied the column headers, check the Labels in First Row check box. If your headers were in a column rather than a row, select the Rows option button in the Grouped By group. Check the Labels check box if the input range contains labels.
6. Select your output option. You can specify an output range, a new ply, or a new workbook. Your dialog box should now look like Figure 22.24.
7. Click the OK button.

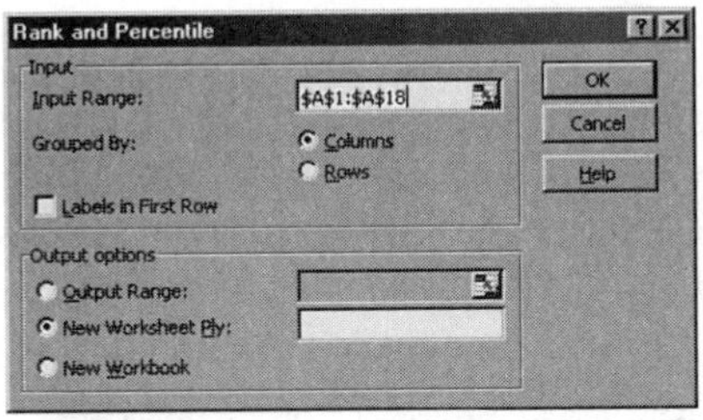

FIG. 22.24
The Ranks and Percentile dialog box is ready to conduct the sample analysis.

Excel creates a rank and percentile table (see Figure 22.25). In the first column, you see an ordinal number representing the original ordinal position of the data point in the range that Ranks and Percentiles operated on. The next column provides the actual value of the data point. The third column provides the rank of the data point. The last column provides percentile rank of the data point. For a set of test scores, for instance, you would find out where the person with the score ranks, in order, in relation to the rest of the test takers, and what percentage of the total pool they outscored.

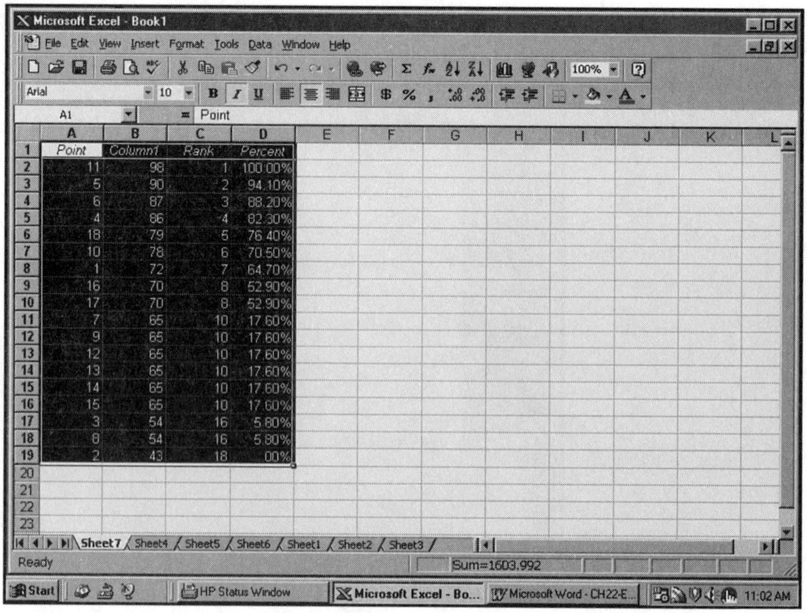

FIG. 22.25
The output of the ranks and percentile tool is presented as a table indicating rankings and percentiles.

Using Engineering Analysis Tools

Excel's Analysis ToolPak also provides some tools that are primarily of use to engineers. Anyone working with signal processing or time domain data can use the Fourier analysis tool to describe the types of frequencies common in the data. In addition, the sampling engine simplifies the process of sampling data for later analysis, as when you want to apply quality control procedures and extrapolate to determine whether a lot of manufactured goods is acceptable. The next two sections describe how to use these tools in more detail.

Fourier Analysis

Classically, Fourier analysis is used in signal processing to decompose a complex sine wave into its formants. For example, an equation can describe the oscilloscope output that represents a human speech stream. *Fourier analysis* can decompose the wave presented into separate waves, each one representing the band of frequencies that represent particular resonators in the human vocal tract.

What Is Fourier Analysis? Fourier analysis can also be applied to any set of time domain data (or time dependent data) to decompose the data set into complex constants that represent the frequencies of component data. Human speech, therefore, can be broken out into constants that represent the vibration of the vocal chords, the resonation of the mouth cavity, the resonation of the nasal cavity, and so forth. In typical wave forms, Fourier analysis can be used to break out harmonics.

How Do You Conduct a Fourier Analysis? To conduct an analysis using histograms, follow these steps:

1. Select the cells that represent the set of data on which to base the analysis. Your spreadsheet should now look like the one shown in Figure 22.26.

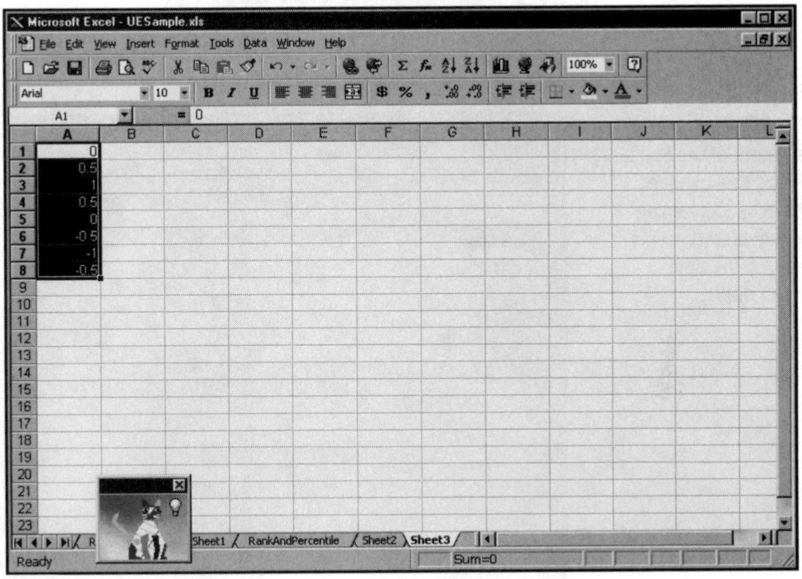

FIG. 22.26
The Fourier analysis tool operates on a single range of data with a number of cells that is a power of 2.

2. Open the Tools menu and select the Data Analysis option.
3. In the Data Analysis dialog box, select Fourier Analysis and click the OK button.

   In the Fourier Analysis dialog box, the Input Range text box automatically shows the selected range. (If not, click the button to the right of the box and select the appropriate range using the mouse cursor.)
4. Click the button to its right again (after selecting the range) to return to the main dialog box. Check the Labels check box if the input range contains labels.
5. Select your output option. You can specify an output range, a new ply, or a new workbook. You can choose to perform the inverse Fourier transform if you want. Your dialog box should look like Figure 22.27.
6. Click the OK button.

Excel creates a table that represents the frequencies associated with this time domain data (see Figure 22.28). In this case, you see the harmonics of the sine wave form defined by the data in the input range.

FIG. 22.27
The Fourier Analysis dialog box is ready to conduct the sample analysis.

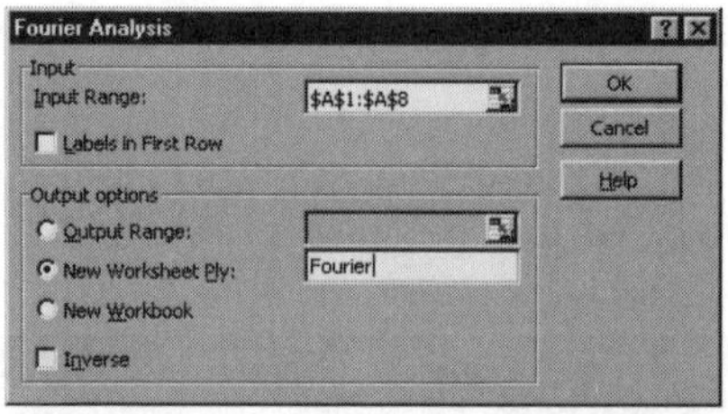

FIG. 22.28
The output of the Fourier analysis tool provides a data range containing the frequencies associated with the time domain data.

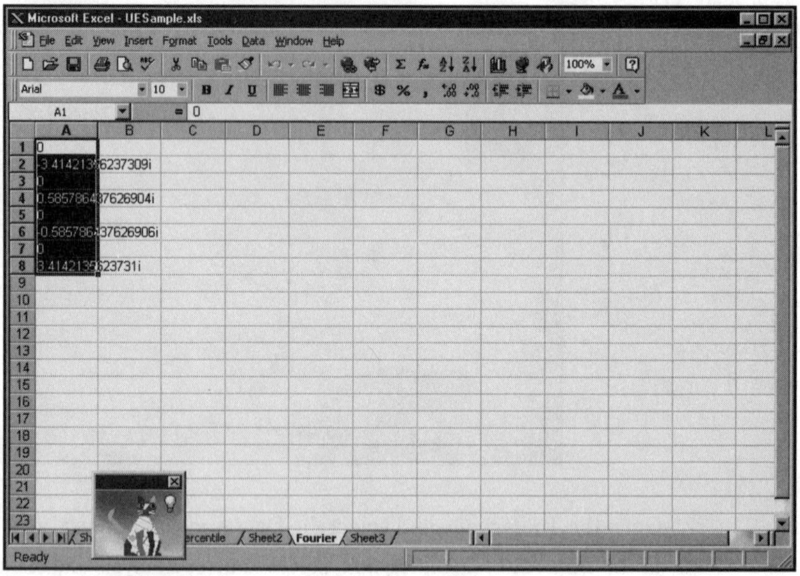

Sampling

The Analysis ToolPak's Sampling method allows you to sample data that you might have stored in an Excel spreadsheet. Often you might have more data points than you wish to analyze in summary statistics. For instance, if you have 30,000 client transactions stored in a spreadsheet, you may not want to invest the time in calculating a summary of all of them. You can, however, sample the data and use statistical inference procedures to make inferences about the entire population that are good enough for most work.

You can have quarterly summaries prepared by analyzing a sample of the transactions each quarter. These calculations will be faster and just as accurate as calculating the same summaries based on all transactions. If you must pull your data from a server-based database, and if you are looking at the hundreds of thousands (or more) of transactions to include, samples might make a great deal of sense.

Using the Analysis ToolPak, you can create either random samples or periodic samples. A random sample uses a table of random numbers to draw a subset of the data, such that each data point has an equal chance of inclusion in the sample. A periodic sample selects every k[th] data point, where k is a number representing a fixed interval, like every 5th transaction.

What Are Samples? You take samples when working with the entire population is either inconvenient or too costly. For example, if, like Radio Shack, you track each customer with each purchase, you can acquire information about the buying habits of your customers. However, you may have thousands of records representing customers. If you attempt to work with all these records, you could waste valuable time and effort generating information about your customers. Using statistical inference procedures is just as accurate and cheaper. To accurately estimate opinions among registered voters within five percentage points, for example, you need only take a sample of around 1200 voters. You can work with such a sample much more efficiently than trying to obtain an opinion from every voter.

How Do You Conduct a Sampling? To conduct an analysis using the sampling tool, follow these steps:

1. Select the cells that represent the set of data on which to base the sample. Your spreadsheet should now look like the one shown in Figure 22.29.

FIG. 22.29
The sampling tool selects a sample from a range of data.

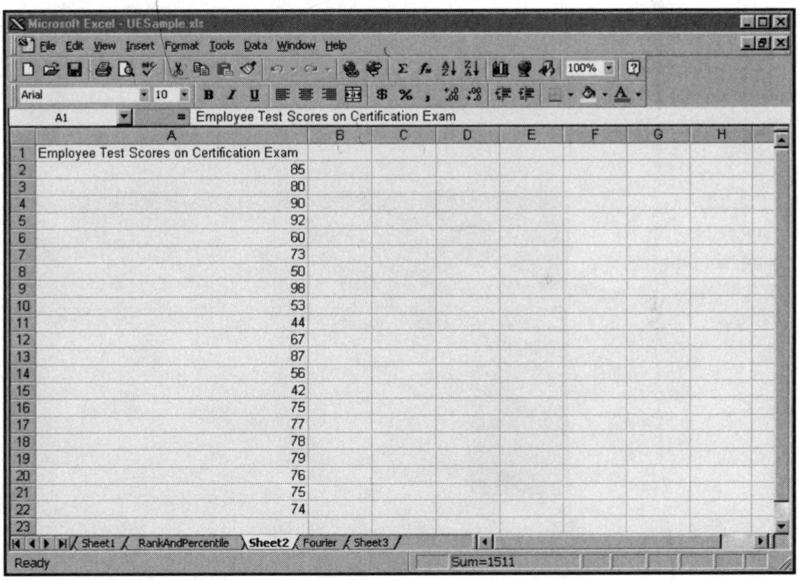

2. Open the Tools menu and select the Data Analysis option.
3. In the Data Analysis dialog box, select Sampling and click the OK button.

   In the Sampling dialog box, the Input Range text box automatically shows the selected range. (If not, click the button to the right of the box and select the appropriate range using the mouse cursor.)

4. Click the button to its right again (after selecting the range) to return to the main dialog box. Select the type of sample you would like to generate and enter either the period (every kth item) or the number of samples (the sample size) you want. Check the Labels check box if the input range contains labels.
5. Select your output option. You can specify an output range, a new ply, or a new workbook. Your dialog box should now look like Figure 22.30.

FIG. 22.30
The Sampling dialog box is ready to conduct a random sample of size 30.

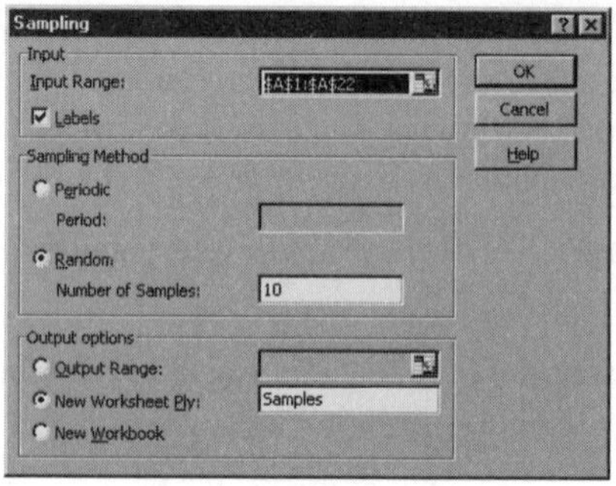

6. Click the OK button.

Excel creates the sample and displays it in a range of cells (see Figure 22.31). You can then use this range of cells as input to another statistical procedure that requires a sample.

FIG. 22.31
The output of the sampling tool presents the sample you requested.

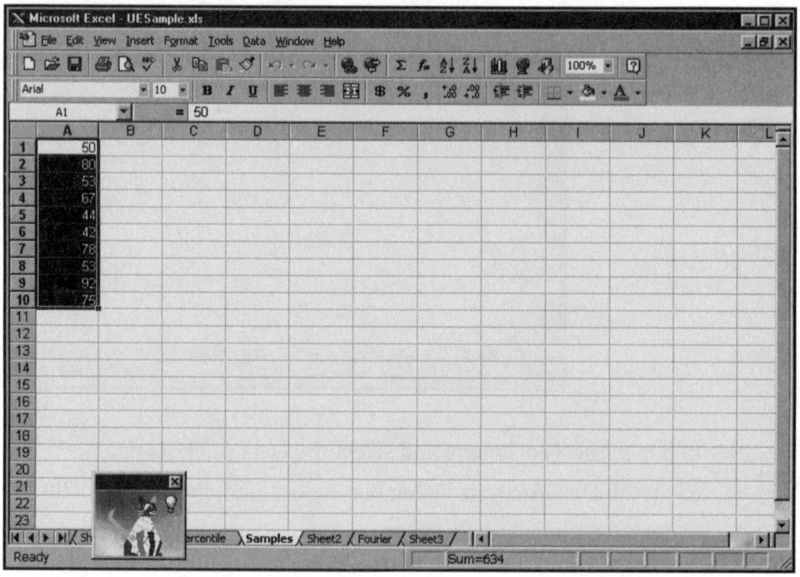

Using Statistical Analysis Tools

The remaining tools in the Analysis ToolPak are more focused on straight statistical analysis of data. The descriptive statistics package calculates the basic summary statistics associated with any data set. The *Z, T, and F tests* allow you to conduct a variety of tests on the means and variances of both small and large samples. The Anova package allows you to conduct three types of analyses of variance, allowing you to work with three experimental designs. The regression analysis tool helps you to describe complex linear trends in data.

Descriptive Statistics

In dealing with any data, you often need to have some sense of its central tendency and some sense of its variability. You can look at a range of cells all day long, even if you sort them by value, and not be able to say whether the data are closely packed about some center or widely spread out. The descriptive statistics package calculates for you several measures of central tendency and several measures of dispersion for a single set of measurements, or a variable. Because these descriptive statistics apply to a single measure or variable, they are often called ***univariate measures.***

What Are Descriptive Statistics? You can measure the center of a data set in various ways. You can look at the arithmetic average, or ***mean***. You can look at the most frequent score, or the mode. You can look for the score that divides the data set in half, or the ***median***. You can measure dispersion in various ways, as well. You can take the mean average deviation from the mean. (In doing so, you square the deviations to get rid of negative signs, otherwise the deviation may sum to be equal to zero.) You can look at the variance, which has special properties associated with the inflection points on the normal curve. Or, you can look at the standard deviation (the square root of the variance), which also has special properties associated with the inflection points of the normal curve.

Each of these measures gives you a sense of what the typical data point represents and what the range of the data is. Each method can be used for different purposes. Usually, a descriptive statistics package calculates a grab bag of these numbers and lets you choose which one suits your purposes.

How Do You Conduct an Analysis Using Descriptive Statistics? To conduct an analysis using descriptive statistics, follow these steps:

1. Select the cells that represent the set of data on which to base the analysis. Your spreadsheet should now look like the one shown in Figure 22.32.
2. Open the Tools menu and select the Data Analysis option.
3. In the Data Analysis dialog box, select Descriptive Statistics and click the OK button.

   In the Descriptive Statistics dialog box, the Input Range text box automatically shows the selected range. (If not, click the button to the right of the box and select the appropriate range using the mouse cursor.)
4. Click the button to its right again (after selecting the range) to return to the main dialog box. You need to indicate whether the data are grouped by columns or rows. Check the Labels check box if the input range contains labels.

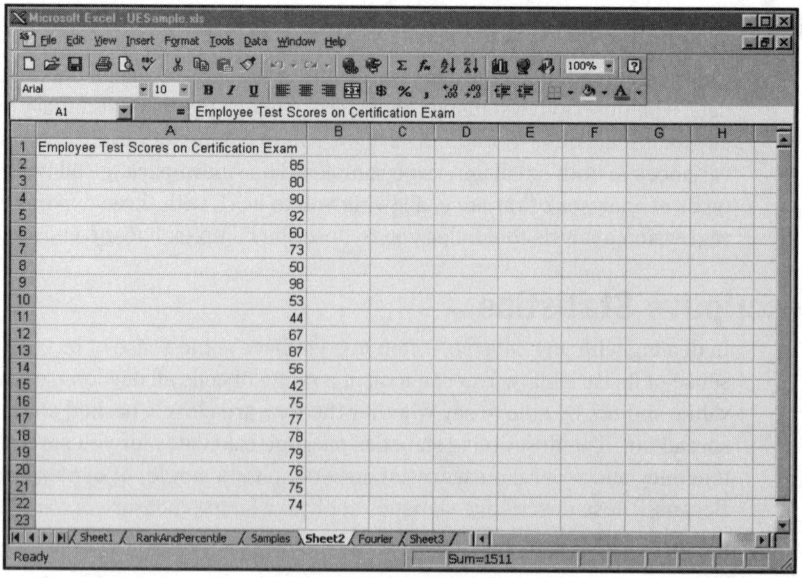

FIG. 22.32 The descriptive statistics tool operates on a range of data.

5. Select your output option. You can specify an output range, a new ply, or a new workbook. You can also choose to include summary statistics, a confidence level for the mean, and the kth largest and smallest values. You need to enter the percentage value for the confidence interval, and the value of k. Your dialog box should now look like Figure 22.33, if you have chosen all options.

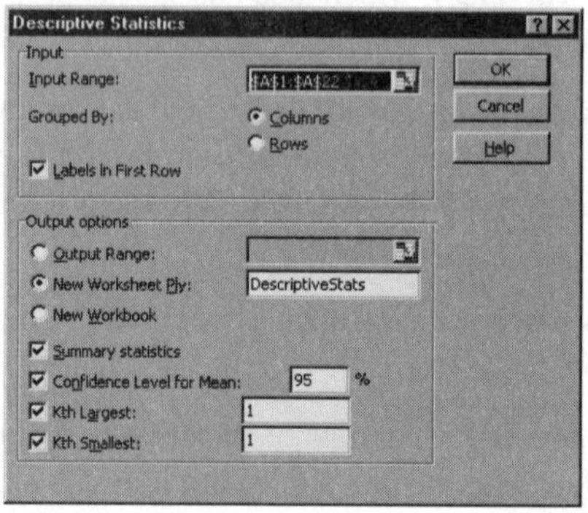

FIG. 22.33 The Descriptive Statistics dialog box is ready to deliver the statistics requested.

6. Click the OK button.

Excel creates a table containing the statistics you requested (see Figure 22.34). It divides the scale into bins and reports the frequency of the data items that fell into each bin. You can scan this information to begin your interpretation of what the data might tell you. Perhaps you would see that an unacceptable number of employees scored in the lower ranges of the screening test, and you might introduce training to remedy the problem.

FIG. 22.34
Descriptive statistics presents a table of summary statistics.

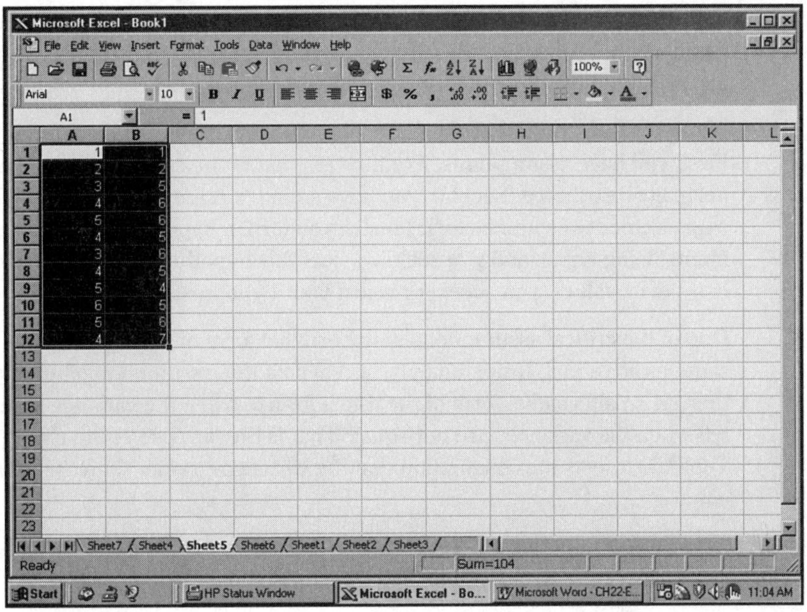

Z, T, and F Tests

This alphabet soup of tests determines whether means are equal or different and whether variances are equal or different. The *Z-test* is a test to see whether two samples have means that should be considered equal or different. It works well on large samples, and you must assume that the samples both came from populations in which the variable of interest was normally distributed. The *T-test* is similar to the Z-test, but it works better on small samples (less than 30 data points) than the Z-test does. Like the Z-test, you assume that the variable of interest is normally distributed in the population.

To understand what these tests do, take a brief look at Student, the creator of the T-test, and the problem he faced. *Student* was a pseudonym for a statistician who was solving the problem of how to determine when a vat of beer had finished fermenting. Student had to use a pseudonym because his employer would not allow him to publish his results under his own name. As beer ferments, the concentration of alcohol varies depending on where you pull the sample for analysis from the vat. To determine whether the beer has finished fermentation, you evaluate the alcohol content.

However, if you pull ten samples from the vat and they each show a slightly different concentration of alcohol, you must have a means of analysis that will estimate whether the mean of the ten samples is the same as, or different from, the mean alcohol concentration you need to achieve. Student created the T-test to compare his sample mean and the desired mean to test the hypothesis of whether the two means are equal. The test is based on analyzing the squared deviation from the mean in each sample. You sample a vat of finished beer and keep this data on record. Then you sample the vat in question. If you cannot reject the hypothesis that the two mean alcohol concentrations are equal, then the vat in question is ready to be bottled. If you can reject the hypothesis, you continue fermenting the beer.

What Are Z, T, and F Tests? This story illustrates some critical features of statistical tests. First, you have assumptions, like the variation in the concentration of alcohol in the vat being normally distributed. Second, you have an index criterion to examine (in these cases, the mean measurement of some factor). Finally, you form a hypothesis that is based on two measurements being equal, and you seek to reject this hypothesis. You compute a statistic, and on the basis of its values, you accept or reject your hypothesis.

One of the critical assumptions in the original form of the T-test is that the variances of the two samples are equal. Unfortunately, in real data this assumption often does not hold. As a result, there is an alternative form of the T-test for use when the variances are not equal. How do you tell when the variances are not equal? That is the purpose of the *F-test* provided in the Analysis ToolPak. It tests the assumption that the variances, rather than the means, of two samples are equal.

How Do You Conduct a Z-Style Test? To conduct an analysis using a Z-style text, follow these steps. The T-test for Paired Sample Means is shown as an example:

1. Open the Tools menu and select the Data Analysis option.
2. In the Data Analysis dialog box, select t_Test: Paired Two Sample for Means and click the OK button.
3. Enter the ranges for the two data sets to be compared (Variable 1 and Variable 2) in the select t_Test: Paired Two Sample for Means dialog box. Click the button to the right of each text box and select the appropriate range using the mouse cursor. After the range is selected, click the button to its right again to return to the main dialog box. Enter a value of 0 for the hypothesized means difference, which indicates that your hypothesis is that the means are equal. Select a value of alpha, the probability of making the least favorable type of error. Check the Labels check box if the input range contains labels.

NOTE The value for the hypothesized means difference can be `0` or a positive number. Excel does not document what the positive numbers mean, but they have unusual effects on the calculation of the t statistic. The value of alpha, the probability of the least favorable type of error, must be between `0` and `1`. Usually `.05` is accepted for most business analysis, but `.01` is considered by many to be the safer bet.

4. Select your output option. You can specify an output range, a new ply, or a new workbook. Your dialog box should now look like Figure 22.35.
5. Click the OK button.

Excel creates the output table (see Figure 22.36). The critical values on this table are all labeled `P(T<=t)`. These are the values that must be lower than your critical alpha in order for you to reject your hypothesis. You use the two-tailed value to test for the hypothesis that the means are not equal. You use the one-tailed value to test for the hypothesis that one mean is greater than, or lesser than, the other.

FIG. 22.35
The t-Test dialog box is ready to conduct the sample analysis.

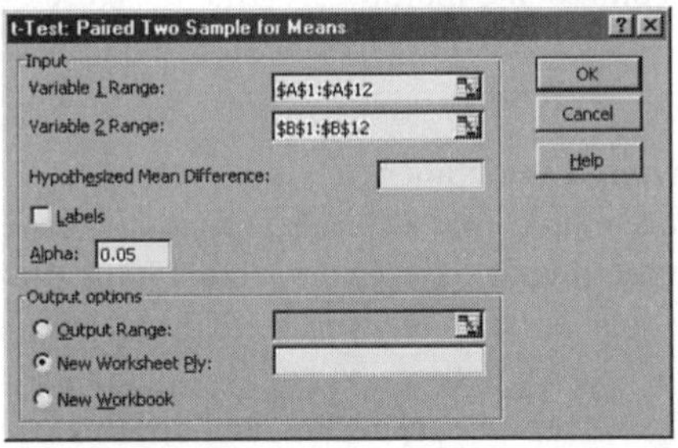

FIG. 22.36
The output of the t-test tool is presented in a table.

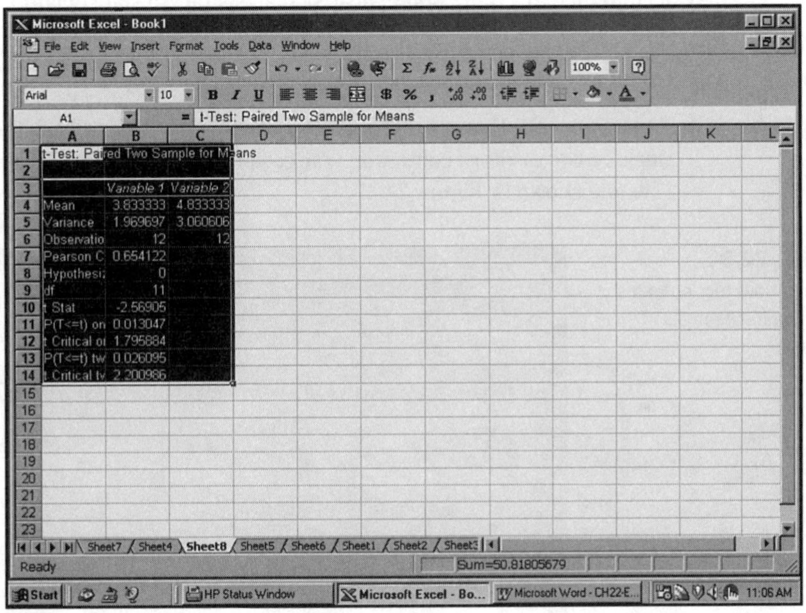

Anova (Analysis of Variance)

Analysis of variance, popularly abbreviated Anova, is a method for determining whether two means are equal. In some respects, it is an extension of Student's T-test. What it does is best understood in light of Student's T-test.

The T-test is a good enough test, but it works on two samples. What if you have a plot of four fields and you give each field a different pesticide treatment. If the pesticide has no effect, the mean crop yields from each field should be equal. If they are not equal, you can assume that your treatment had some effect. Analysis of variance was designed to deal with this more complex problem of evaluating whether means are equal. In this example, you must test whether four means are equal to one another. You sample each of the four fields and then examine how each of the sample data points vary from their mean, hence the name analysis of variance.

Anova has the flexibility to accommodate multiple treatments, paired trials, and multiple factors. Excel can do analysis of variance that incorporates one or two factors (or ways) and repeated trials.

What Is an Anova? Anova typically examines the means of multiple sample sets and tests the hypothesis that these means are equal. You, as the experimenter, are hoping that they are not equal, because you have structured your experiment so that if the means are equal, nothing has happened. So, if you have sampled data on average daily sales from four regions over the last four years, and you want to know whether one region is significantly higher than the others, you hypothesize that all the means are equal, and you hope to reject that hypothesis. However, once you achieve this rejection, Anova will not tell you which mean is actually higher. You may need to turn to a more sophisticated analysis (and a statistician) to confirm such facts.

How Do You Conduct an Anova? To conduct an analysis using Anova, follow these steps. We will present a single factor analysis of variance as an example:

1. Select the cells that represent the set of data on which to base the analysis. You must include two or more contiguous ranges of cells. Your spreadsheet should now look like the one shown in Figure 22.37.

FIG. 22.37
The Anova tool operates on multiple ranges of data.

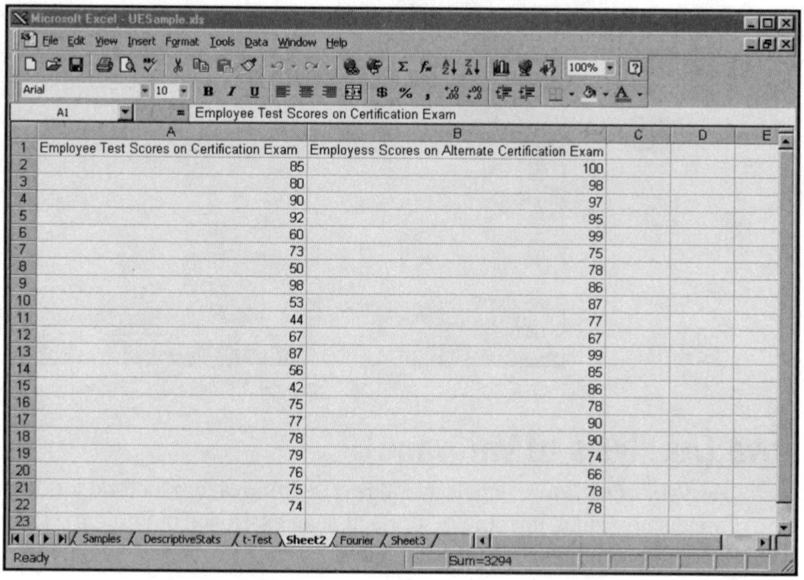

2. Open the Tools menu and select the Data Analysis option.

3. In the Data Analysis dialog box, select Anova: Single Factor and click the OK button. In the Anova: Single Factor dialog box, the Input Range text box automatically shows the selected range. (If not, click the button to the right of the box and select the appropriate range using the mouse cursor.)
4. Click the button to its right again (after selecting the range) to return to the main dialog box. Enter a value of alpha to use for the analysis, and indicate whether ranges are grouped by rows or columns. Check the Labels check box if the input range contains labels.
5. Select your output option. You can specify an output range, a new ply, or a new workbook. Your dialog box should now have the look shown in Figure 22.38.

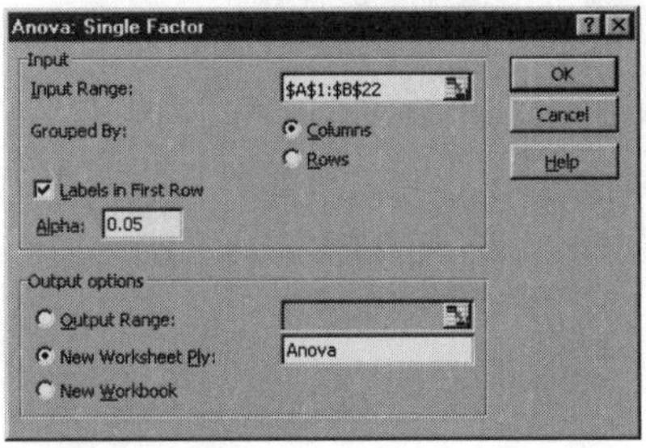

FIG. 22.38
The Anova: Single Factor dialog box is ready to conduct the sample analysis.

6. Click the OK button.

Excel creates the output table for the analysis (see Figure 22.39). The critical value on the table is labeled `P-value`. If this value is lower than your selected value of alpha, you can reject the hypothesis that the means are equal and accept that the differences among the ranges included in the test are real.

Regression Analysis

Regression analysis is like the correlation analysis that we examined earlier in this chapter, but it can include multiple factors. You assume that some measurement (the dependent variable) is dependent on some other set of measurements (the independent variables). Regression analysis examines the strength of this dependency, and yields a statistic R that gives a sense of the strength of this relationship. If R=0, there is no relationship. If R=1, then a perfect relationship exists, and the independent variables in the equation perfectly explain the value of the dependent variable.

What Does Regression Mean? Normally the value of R falls somewhere in between 0 and 1, so you must perform some secondary analysis to determine the exact nature of the relationship. A typical method is to square R to determine what percentage of the perceived relationship is explainable by the independent variables. Another is to look at the values of the constants associated with each of the independent variables, the so-called beta weights. If the beta number is negative, you have the same relationship between that independent variable and the dependent variable as a negative correlation coefficient implies. If the beta is positive, you have the same relationship as a positive correlation coefficient describes. Other methods include examining residuals and hypothesis testing, some of which is performed by the Regression Analysis tool. Interpretation of these results, however, is a bit beyond the scope of this book.

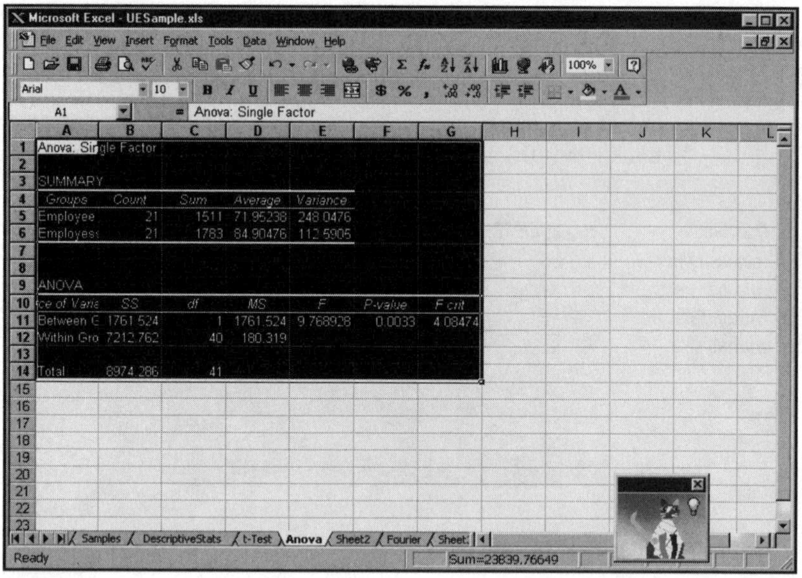

FIG. 22.39
The output of the Anova tool is presented as a table.

How Do You Conduct an Analysis Using Regression? To conduct an analysis using histograms, follow these steps:

1. Open the Tools menu and select the Data Analysis option.
2. In the Data Analysis dialog box, select Regression and click the OK button.
3. In the Regression dialog box, select the single range of cells that represents the dependent variable using the Input Y Range text box. Select the range or ranges that represent the independent variables using the Input X Range text box. Click the button to the right of the box and select the appropriate range using the mouse cursor. After the range is selected, click the button to its right again to return to the main dialog box. Check the Labels check box if the input range contains labels. Check the Constant is Zero check box to force the regression line to go through the origin of the Cartesian grid. Check the Confidence Level check box to select a confidence level other than 95 percent to be applied within the regression calculation.
4. Select your output option. You can specify an output range, a new ply, or a new workbook. You can also choose to plot residuals or normal probabilities, activities that can help you detect whether you should apply a curvilinear model to your data rather than a linear model. (If you need a curvilinear model, you should consult a statistician for assistance. Interpretation of residual plots is covered in most statistics manuals.) Your dialog box should now look like Figure 22.40.

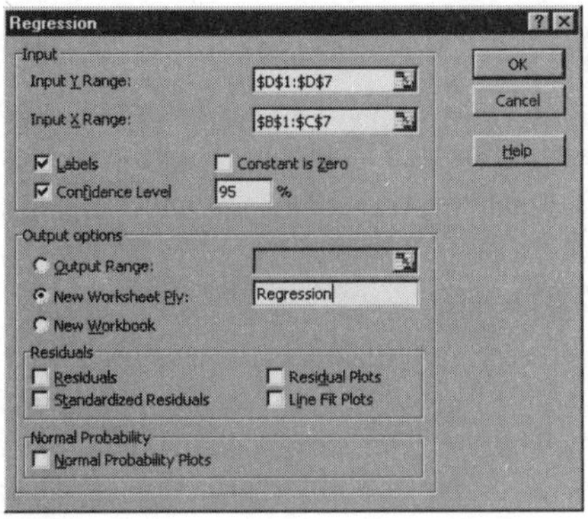

FIG. 22.40
The Regression dialog box is ready to conduct the sample analysis.

5. Click the OK button.

Excel creates several tables to summarize the regression output (see Figure 22.41). Interpretation of all these values goes well beyond the scope of this book. The critical values are R, which, like a correlation coefficient, gives you the strength of the relationship; R^2 which gives you the percentage of the relationship explainable by variables in the model; and Significance of F, which tests the hypothesis that R=0. As long as Significance of F is lower than your chosen alpha, which you entered as the Confidence Level (which is equal to 1 minus alpha) in the Regression dialog box.

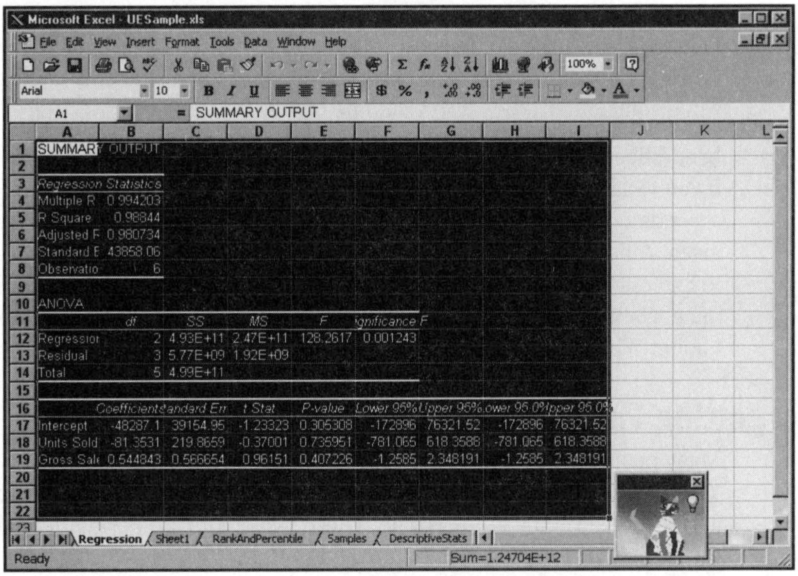

FIG. 22.41
The output of the Regression tool is presented as a series of tables and charts.

Common Problems and Solutions

When you work with analytical procedures, you can easily make mistakes. If you make mistakes in procedure, the course of action you chart based on the results may be completely mistaken. As a result, you want to avoid some very common errors.

Making the Wrong Assumptions

Many statistical procedures require you to make certain assumptions about your data. One of the most common is that the sample was generated from a population in which the measurement in question is normally distributed. The normal distribution has a venerable status in the life of any student who was graded on the curve. It fits the types of measurements that we often make. Perhaps one of the great mysteries of life is why such measurements typically have the frequencies described by this curve in the general population.

The types of measurements that behave according to the normal distribution have particular characteristics. They can be represented by scalar numbers, that is, numbers that can be arranged along a scale, like the scale on a thermometer. Typically, such numbers can represent fractions or fractional parts, like tenths of a degree, although often we do not express our scales in such terms. The scale of scores on a test, for example, typically has whole number values, not tenths of points. One thing that these values may not represent is categories, like male or female.

Other types of distributions represent other types of events. Flipping a coin is best described by the binomial distribution. Populations of animals in a given area are better described by the Poisson distribution. When one of these other distributions apply, different statistical procedures apply. You need to make sure that you are not mistakenly using analysis of variance when some other procedure would be better.

In addition, other assumptions may apply. One form of the T-test assumes equality of variances. If you violate this assumption, you increase the probability that you have made a mistake in accepting or rejecting your hypothesis. You never want to violate the assumptions behind a given statistical procedure. If you are not certain that the assumptions hold, you can apply tests to find out. The F-test we described tests for equality of variances. There are also tests to determine whether the data came from a normal distribution or is better described by another distribution. When in doubt, test to find out.

Forgetting That Error Is Always with You

Many people forget that statistical procedures are a compromise between two types of errors. You can mistakenly accept a hypothesis when it is really not true, or you can mistakenly reject a hypothesis when it really is true. These two errors are best understood in life and death cases.

Assume that you are testing a new life saving drug. You have reached the stage of human trials. Half your sample has a horrible disease that will kill them, and they have taken the new drug therapy. The other half have the same disease, but they have taken placebo treatments. We test the mean cure rate for both groups and compare them using a statistical test. We have formulated our hypothesis to say the two means are equal, and we want to reject that hypothesis. If the two means really are equal, the drug has no effect. If they are different, then the drug has an effect. (Of course, if the cure rate for the group that took the drug is lower than for the group that took the placebo, the drug had a very unfortunate effect.)

Consider the first type of error. If we accept the hypothesis that the two means are equal, when in fact they really are different, what cost have we incurred? We stay with the standard treatment for the disease, and we incur no liability as a drug company. We continue the search for new treatments.

Consider the second type of error. If we reject the hypothesis that the two means are equal when it really is true, what costs have we incurred? We rush to market with a new drug and we claim that it cures the disease. When in fact it fails to do so, angry relatives sue us, and we have incurred great liability for our mistake. This type of error is far more serious than the other type, and all statistical procedures are usually designed to minimize this type of error. The alpha statistic often quoted in relationship to statistical procedures is, in fact, the probability that this type of error will occur.

You never want to forget that you are making errors when you make decisions based on statistics. By minimizing the probability of one type of error, we increase the likelihood of the other. In addition, if we handle our sampling or statistical procedures inappropriately, we inflate the value of alpha artificially. Once such inflation occurs, your chance of being in error when you choose your course of action is very high. When dealing with very important matters, therefore, have a statistician verify your procedures.

From Here...

This chapter focused on using Excel 97 as a business analysis tool. You've seen how to conduct trend analyses, engineering analyses, and statistical analyses. These tools help to examine common business problems so that you can make informed decisions about how to proceed from a particular problem or question to a solution or answer. You will find that Excel has other facilities that can assist with such analyses. For further information, turn to these chapters:

- For more information on functions that can perform statistical analyses, see Chapter 6, "Using Excel Functions," and Appendix B, "Excel Function Reference."
- For more information about add-ins, see Chapter 7, "Using Excel Add-Ins."

PART VI

Networking and Integration with Excel

CHAPTER 23

Collaborating with Excel

by Diane Koers

Networks are more and more common today than even a few years ago. Even the smallest offices frequently have more than one computer. Connecting computers gives people access to common files so everyone in the office can strive for greater accuracy and productivity.

When a group of people work on the same document, it is important to know how Microsoft Excel will react. Although Excel was designed to be used over a network, certain restrictions will apply when two or more users are accessing the data at the same time. This is done to protect the integrity of the data.

This chapter shows you how to work with an Excel worksheet within your workgroup and communicate any changes via your network. You will also learn how to protect the privacy of your data.

Set up a shared template

You will learn how to share templates, set up a standard spreadsheet where each user can input his or her information, and explore one of Excel's Spreadsheet Solutions templates.

Use shared workbooks

You will learn what features will and will not be available when a workbook is shared.

How Excel handles conflicts

Discover what course Excel will take when two or more users enter conflicting information.

Track changes to workbooks

You can have Excel identify what changes have been made to a workbook, when the changes occurred, and who made the changes.

Set workbook properties

Learn how to define and locate criteria specific to a workbook such as who the author is, the subject of the workbook, or specific contents in the workbook.

Secure the privacy of workbooks

Learn how to add passwords, lock cells and sheets, and safeguard your workbooks from accidental changes.

Working with Shared Templates

A great timesaving feature of Excel is the ability to use shared *templates*. A template is a spreadsheet with formatting, styles, and frequently used text already applied. Each new worksheet you create is based on a template. Because styles and text are already built-in, you aren't "reinventing the wheel."

The settings saved in a template determine the characteristics of any new workbook based on the template.

The following settings are stored in a template:

- The number and type of sheets in a workbook
- Cell and sheet formats and styles
- Page formatting and print settings for each sheet
- Text such as row and column headings, as well as data, formulas, graphics, and other information you want each new workbook to have
- Custom toolbars, macros, and hyperlinks
- Protected or hidden areas of the workbook
- Calculation and display options

Creating a Customized Template

A template is really a workbook that has been saved in a template format. You can create your own customized templates by entering information in a workbook that would be standard for a particular project. It could consist of a report, a list, a chart, or anything that you do in Excel.

An example of this might be a monthly profit and loss statement. You would create a standard profit and loss worksheet including all data but the actual monthly figures, then save the worksheet as a template.

Each month, a new profit and loss statement would be created from the template, and all you have to do is fill in the blanks. It's very quick and very easy! Another advantage is that you are able to maintain consistency in the appearance of each profit and loss statement.

To create a new template, use the following steps:

1. Set up a blank workbook with any boilerplate text and any formatting you want. See Figure 23.1 for an example of a simple profit and loss statement workbook.
2. Choose File, Save As. The Save As dialog box will appear.
3. Click the Save as Type drop-down list and select Template (*.xlt).

Notice in Figure 23.2 that Excel automatically jumps to the Templates folder. You should save custom templates in the Templates subfolder in which you installed Excel. Template (.xlt) files you save in the Templates folder are displayed on the General tab when you choose File, New. To group your custom templates on a separate tab, save the templates in a subfolder in the Templates folder.

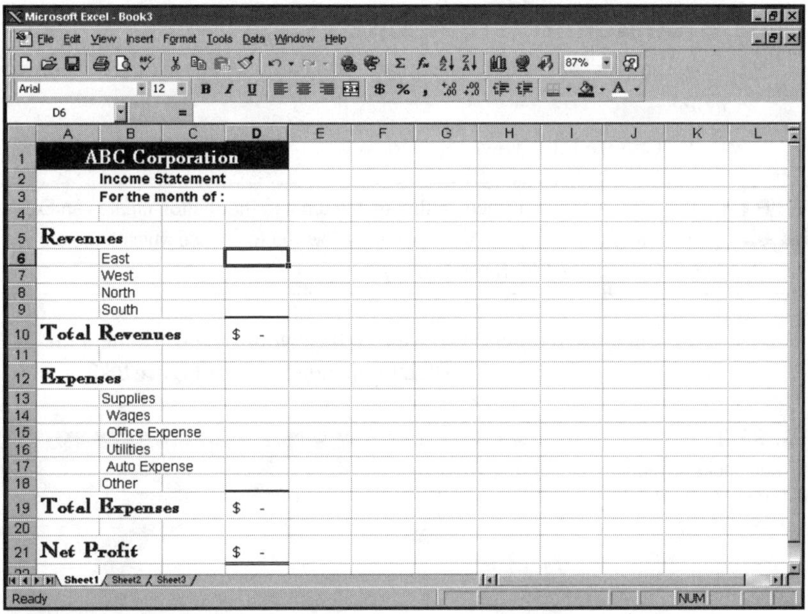

FIG. 23.1
This profit and loss statement has formulas and formatting already entered.

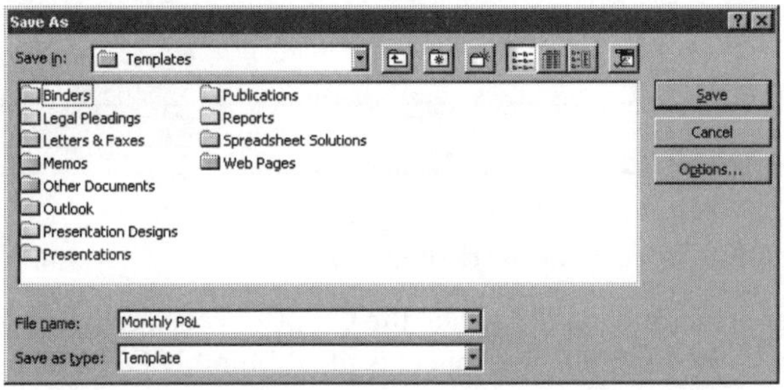

FIG. 23.2
You can create a new subfolder to store your personal templates.

TIP You can make a custom template available to others by storing the template on a network location. Place the template in a folder in a network location that is accessible by all users in your group. Then create a shortcut to the folder or template, and have users place the shortcut in their Templates folder.

4. Give the template a name in the File Name text box. Excel will add a .xlt extension to the file name. For the sake of this example, we'll call it Monthly P&L.
5. Choose Save to accept the choices and save the template. The Save As dialog box will close.

The template has been saved and is now ready for you to use. Close the template file so you can create a new workbook based on it.

Using a Customized Template

Now that you've created a template, you can use it to create a blank workbook. Follow these steps:

1. Choose File, New.

TIP Do not use the New Worksheet button on the toolbar. That button creates an Excel worksheet based on the normal generic template and does not allow you to choose which template you want to use. The same is true for the Ctrl+N shortcut key.

2. Click the template you want to base your new worksheet on. In this example, we'll choose the Monthly P&L template shown in Figure 23.3.

FIG. 23.3
Any workbooks saved in the Templates folder will be displayed here.

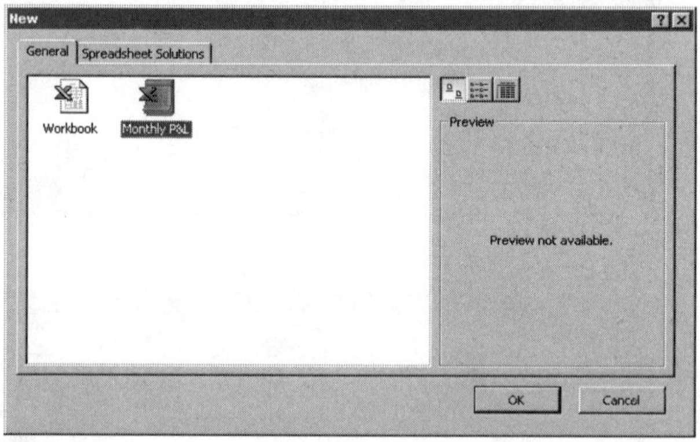

3. Choose OK to open a new worksheet.

The worksheet opens and looks just like the template you created earlier. What's the difference? Look at the title bar. The worksheet is titled Monthly P&L1 instead of Book1, which you would normally see when you open a new workbook.

When you go to save the file after you fill in the information necessary for this month's statement, you will be prompted to assign it a new name such as July 1997 P&L. You are not going to overwrite the existing template file, so you can use it again and again.

When the time rolls around next month to do the profit and loss statement, you will repeat this procedure and then name that file differently, for example, August 1997 P&L.

Using the Spreadsheet Solutions Templates

Excel includes three predefined templates for invoices, expense sheets, and purchase orders. These templates automate the tasks of filling in these forms. They also have built-in macros to assist the user in filling out the forms.

▶ **See** "Excel Solution Templates," **p. 261**

TIP Additional templates, for example, for planning personal finances, are available at Microsoft's Web Site **http://www.microsoft.com**. Choose Free Stuff. (A quick easy way to access this site is to click Help, Microsoft of the Web, Free Stuff.)

For this example, you will use the Invoice template to customize and create an invoice to send to our customers. If this is the first time you have used this template, one of the first things you will want to do is customize it with your company information.

To customize a Spreadsheet Solutions template, follow these steps:

1. Choose File, New.
2. From the New dialog box, click the Spreadsheet Solutions tab. From here you see the templates such as Invoice, Purchase Order, or Expense Statement provided by Excel.
3. Double-click Invoice to open it. A virus warning dialog box may appear.

   Because these templates are automated, they contain macros. Macros can contain viruses, so Excel is warning you of the potential.
4. Choose Enable Macros to proceed.

   ▶ **See** "Managing Workbooks, Windows, and Sheets," **p. 61**
5. Click the Customize button (shown in Figure 23.4). The Customize Your Invoice worksheet appears on top.

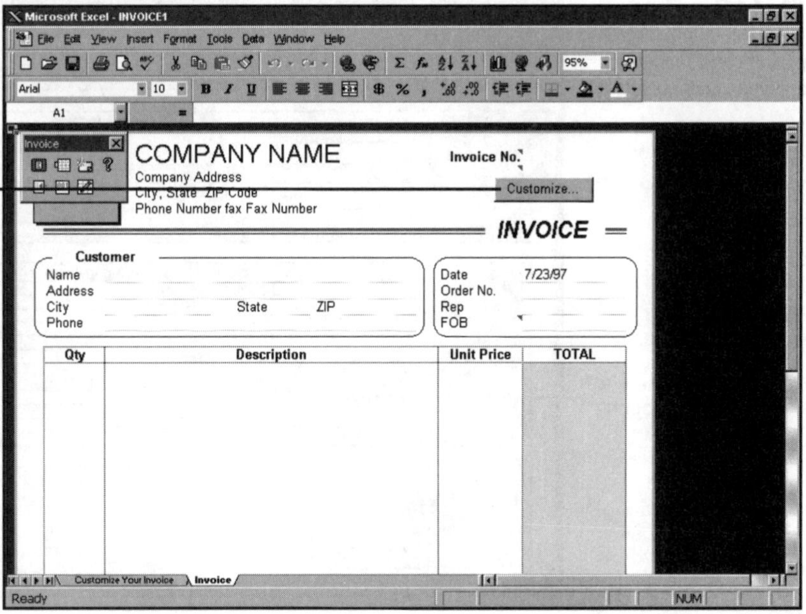

Click here to customize the template

FIG. 23.4
Preserving a customized template saves you time.

6. In the fields provided, type your company name, address, city, state, ZIP code, phone, and fax. Be sure you are entering them in the white fields, not the gray shaded ones.

TIP If any cell has a small red triangle in it, you can position your mouse pointer on top of that cell for further information about what is required in any cell.

7. In the bottom half of the customize screen, you will need to fill in other default information such as your state and its sales tax rate, any standard shipping charges, and which (if any) credit cards your company accepts. All of this information will be carried over to the actual invoice.
8. Choose the Select Logo button. (It's located at the bottom of the customize invoice screen.) The Insert Picture dialog box will open.
9. Select the graphic that is your company logo, changing the Look In folder if necessary.
10. Click Insert. The logo will appear in the logo box and will be resized and formatted to fit in the box.
11. (Optional) If you would like to generate sequential invoices from more than one computer on a network, check the Share Invoice Numbers on a Network check box and specify a server location in the Counter Location text box (see Figure 23.5). Excel creates a counter file called Invoice in the location you specify. It will track and increment invoice numbers for you.

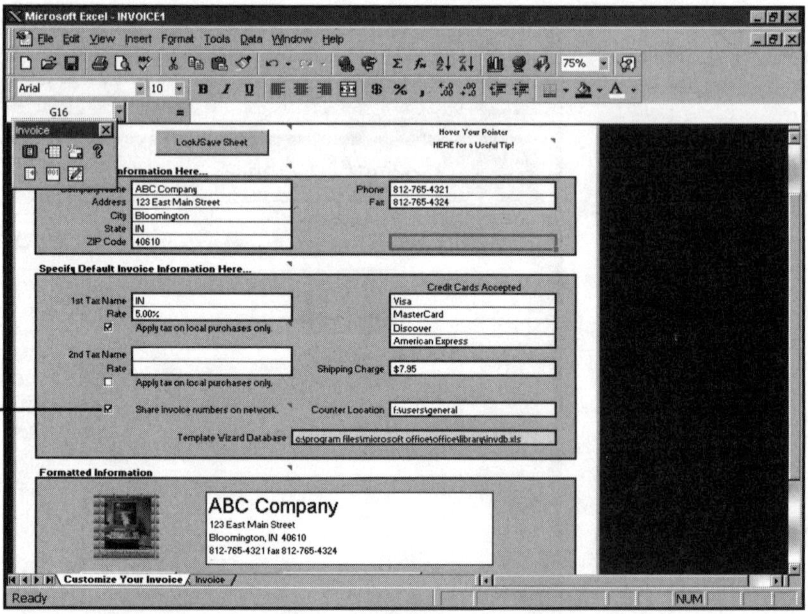

Click here to share numbering

FIG. 23.5
Sequential numbering by Excel can eliminate duplicate numbering.

> **TIP** For more information on locking and unlocking a worksheet, see the section "Hiding and Protecting Worksheets from Changes," later in this chapter.

12. Click the Lock/Save Sheet button. A Lock/Save Sheet dialog box will appear. Click OK to lock and save the customized template. The Save Template dialog box appears, prompting you for a template file name.
13. Enter a name for the template in the File Name box. In this example, call it ABC Invoice. Click Save to save the template.
14. Click OK to acknowledge the message box and close the template file.

You are now ready to use the customized template.

Follow these steps to use the customized Spreadsheet Solutions template:

1. Choose File, New.
2. Double-click ABC Invoice to open it.
3. Click Enable Macros to proceed with the invoice.

The invoice is now displayed with your company name, address, logo, and other information.

You can now fill out the rest of the invoice with your customer's name and address as well as the quantity, description, and unit price of their purchases. Excel calculates the total invoice for you.

You probably noticed a new toolbar appear when you created the new invoice. This toolbar was specifically designed to be used with the invoice. It has choices available to change the view of your invoice as well as to add a sequential invoice number to it.

To add a sequential invoice number use the following steps:

1. Click the Assign a Number button on the Invoice toolbar.
2. Click OK to proceed with the numbering. The next sequential number is assigned to your invoice (see Figure 23.6).

The invoice is now ready to be printed and mailed to your customer. You can also save the invoice for your permanent record.

To save the invoice, follow these steps:

1. Click File, Save or press Ctrl+S.
2. If you have a database designed to track the records, choose Create a New Record. If you do not have a database designed to track the invoices, choose Continue Without Updating.
3. Click OK to continue. The Save As dialog box will appear.
4. In the File Name text box, enter a name for the invoice and choose OK to save the file.

FIG. 23.6
This is the completed invoice with sequential numbering.

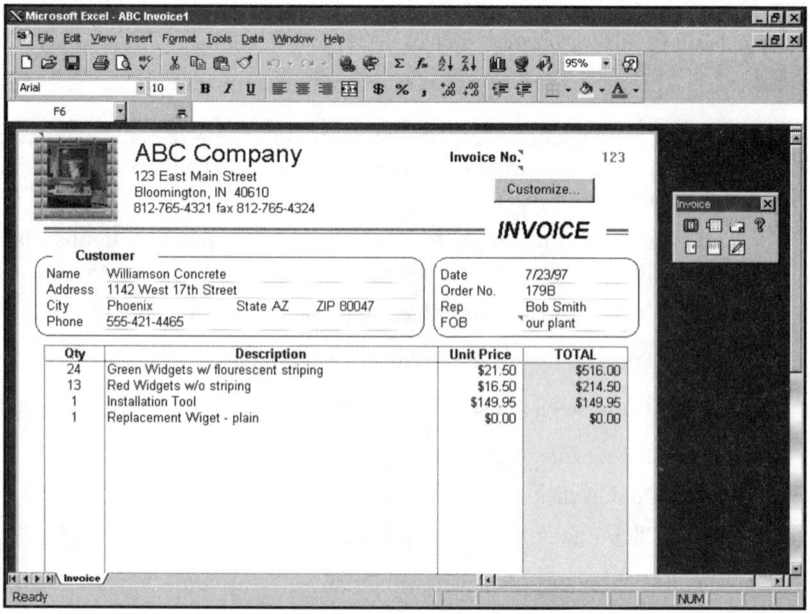

How Do Different Excel Versions Interoperate?

Many features are new to Excel 97. By default, Excel workbooks are saved in Excel 97 format. If someone you work with is using an earlier version of Microsoft Excel and he opens a workbook saved in Excel 97 format, a message will be displayed recommending that he open the file as read-only. If he ignores the recommendation and saves the workbook in an earlier version of Excel, features and formatting available only in Excel 97 are lost.

You can prevent this feature and formatting loss if other users on your network are still working in Excel 95 or Excel 5.0. You can save your Excel 97 workbook in a special dual file format that can be read by all three products: Excel 97, Excel 95, and Excel 5.0. Excel 95 and Excel 5.0 have the same file format. Users of Microsoft Excel 97 can then continue to work in a workbook saved in the dual format without losing any features or formatting unique to this version.

To save a file in the dual format, use these steps:

1. Choose File, Save As.

TIP If this is the first time the file has been saved, you can click the Save button on the toolbar instead.

2. Type a name for the file in the File Name text box.
3. Click the arrow on the Save as Type drop-down list. A list of file choices will appear as seen in Figure 23.7.

FIG. 23.7
Saving a workbook in a dual file format will allow users of earlier versions of Excel to work on an Excel 97 workbook.

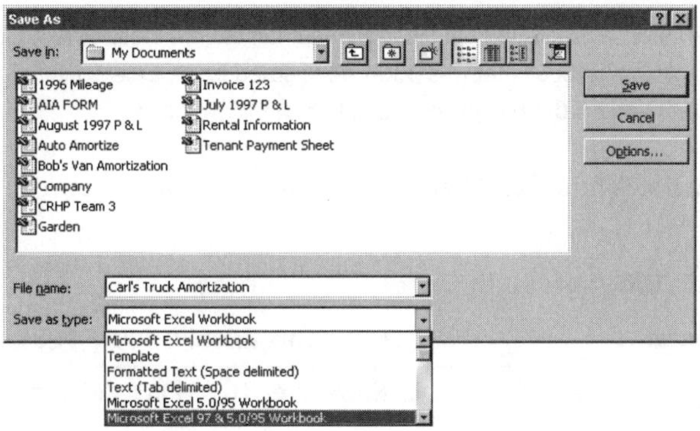

4. Choose Microsoft Excel 97 & 5.0/95 Workbook.
5. Choose Save to close the Save As dialog box and save the file in the dual format.
6. If you are prompted to replace an existing file, choose Yes.

If Excel 95 or Excel 5.0 is still widely used in your company, you should consider changing the default Excel 97 file format to the dual file format. All workbooks will be saved in the new default dual format unless you specify a different one by using the Save As feature.

To change the default file format, use these steps:

1. Choose Tools, Options.
2. Click the Transition tab to bring it to the top of the stack.
3. Click the down arrow in the Save Excel Files As list box and select Microsoft Excel 97 & 5.0/95 Workbook (see Figure 23.8).

FIG. 23.8
There are many customization options available in the Options dialog box.

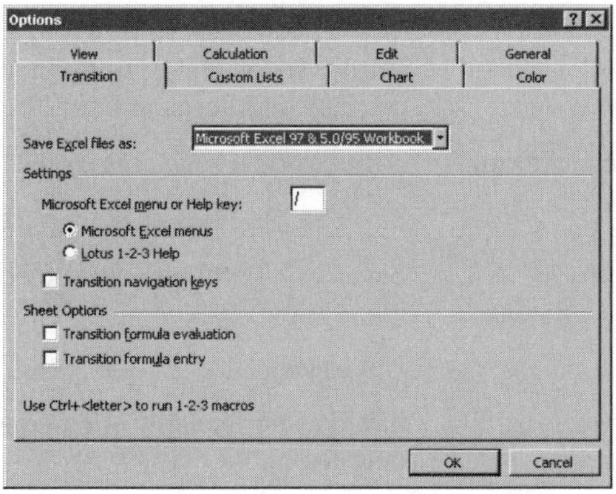

4. Choose OK to close the dialog box.

Now by default, all workbooks will be saved in the dual file format.

NOTE Workbooks saved in the dual file format are larger than those saved in a single format. For example, a workbook that was 330K when saved in the Excel 97 format is 665K when saved in the Excel 97 and 5.0/96 workbook dual format.

Table 23.1 illustrates how Excel handles a few of the changes between the two file formats.

Table 23.1 Differences in Excel File Formats

Excel 97 Feature	Microsoft Excel 5.0/95 Feature
65,536 rows per worksheet	Rows after 16,384 are deleted.
32,000 characters per cell	Characters after 255 are deleted.
Text formatted with Shrink to Fit option on the Alignment tab of the Cells dialog box (Format menu)	Text is the original point size (before the Shrink to Fit option was applied).
Rotated text	Text rotated at angles other than 90 degrees, -90 degrees, or 0 (zero) is changed to horizontal orientation.
Indentations within cells	Indentation is removed, and the contents of cells are left-aligned.
Merged cells	Merged cells are split into their original configuration. Data is placed in the top-left cell.
Conditional formatting	Conditional formatting is lost, and cells are reformatted with the Normal style.
Sheet backgrounds	Not saved.
New border styles	Border styles are converted to the closest border style available in Microsoft Excel 95 or 5.0.
Pie of pie/Bar of pie chart format	Saved as type 1 pie chart.
Bubble chart	Saved as type 1 xy scatter chart.
3-D marker shape (cylinder, pyramid, and cone)	Saved as 3-D column chart (rectangular shape).
Data tables in charts	Not saved.
Rotated text on axis and data labels	Saved as horizontally oriented text (0 [zero] degrees).
Gradient fills and patterns on chart items	Saved as the closest available solid color and pattern.
Shading in surface charts	Shading is not saved.

Excel 97 Feature	Microsoft Excel 5.0/95 Feature
Time-scale axis (x-axis categories with date format)	Special scaling information is lost, and the axis is converted to a normal category axis.
Shadows on series and points	Not saved.
Sizable line and xy scatter data markers	Not saved.
Special placement of data labels	Saved in the default location for chart items.
New worksheet functions: AVERAGEA; MAXA; MINA; STDEVA; STDEVPA; VARA; VARPA; HYPERLINK; GETPIVOTDATA	Not supported. However, Microsoft Excel calculates the function before saving the file and replaces the formula with the resulting value. The HYPERLINK function is resolved to the value =#N/A.

Benefits and Constraints of Sharing Workbooks

Suppose, for example, you are managing a project that is requiring information from several other team members. Rather than each person handing you a sheet of paper with his or her data and you having to key all of it in, you can create a shared workbook and allow each team member to work on his or her section.

A shared workbook is one that has been designed to allow other users on a network to view or make changes at the same time. Each time a shared workbook is saved the changes are tracked, and each user will see any changes made by other users.

Sharing a workbook has several benefits including saving time and improved accuracy.

Some features of Microsoft Excel are not available when you use a shared workbook. If you need to use these features, you should do so before you share the workbook, or remove the workbook from shared use.

In a shared workbook, you cannot do the following:

- Delete worksheets.
- Merge cells.
- Insert or delete blocks of cells. (You can insert or delete entire rows and columns.)
- Insert or change charts, pictures, objects, or hyperlinks.
- Use the drawing tools.
- Assign a password to protect individual worksheets or the entire workbook. Protection that you applied before sharing the workbook will remain in effect after you share the workbook.
- Change or remove passwords. Passwords that you assigned before sharing the workbook will remain in effect after you share the workbook.

- Save, view, or make changes to scenarios or data tables.
- Group or outline data.
- Define or apply conditional formats.
- Set up or change data validation restrictions and messages.
- Insert automatic subtotals.
- Create or modify PivotTables.
- Create or modify macros. You can run macros that were created before you shared the workbook; however, if you run a macro that includes an unavailable operation, the macro will stop running when it reaches the unavailable operation.

Setting Up a Shared Workbook

When a shared workbook is opened the word `[shared]` will be displayed at the top of the window next to the workbook name. If `[shared]` is not displayed, the workbook is not shareable and multiple users cannot work on it simultaneously.

NOTE To make changes to a shared workbook created in Excel 97, you must use Excel 97. You cannot use earlier versions of Microsoft Excel.

Set Shared Workbook Options

There are several options available when you decide to share a workbook. You will need to tell Excel to allow multiple users at the same time, how to save the shared workbook, and when to save the shared workbook.

To share a workbook, use these steps:

1. Choose Tools, Share Workbook. The Share Workbook dialog box seen in Figure 23.9 is displayed.

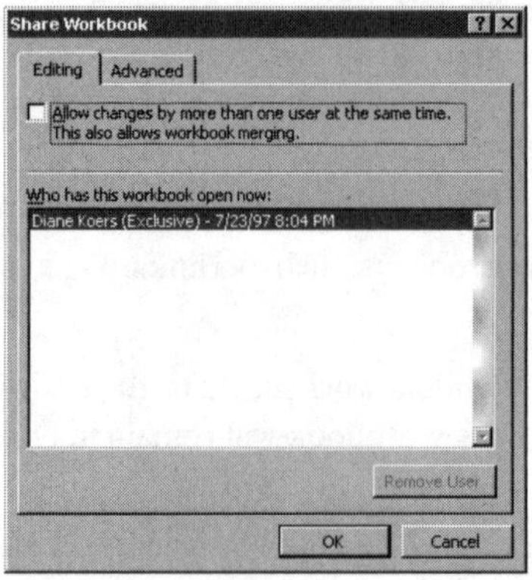

FIG. 23.9
The Share Workbook dialog box also displays other users of the workbook.

2. From the Editing tab, click Allow Changes by More Than One User at the Same Time.
3. Click the Advanced tab of this dialog box (shown in Figure 23.10) and choose from the other shared options in the following list.
   - The Track Changes section sets how many days Excel should keep track of the changes made to this workbook. The change history includes information about how users resolved conflicting changes to the workbook, including the data from changes that was discarded. Each time you close the workbook, Excel erases any part of the stored change history that is older than the number of days you specified. The actual changes are retained.
   - The Update Changes section allows you to choose when everyone's changes will be updated: either upon saving the workbook, or automatically every xx number of minutes.
   - If you choose to save at xx number of minutes you also have two more choices. The Save My Changes and See Others' Changes option will save any changes you make as well as update the worksheet with other current users' changes. The Just See Others' Changes Option will not save your changes, just update the workbook with other current users' changes.
   - In the Conflicting Changes Between Users area, you can tell Excel to automatically accept your changes over the other users, or to ask you which change it should save.

Part VI
Ch 23

FIG. 23.10
Setting options here determines how some conflicts will be resolved.

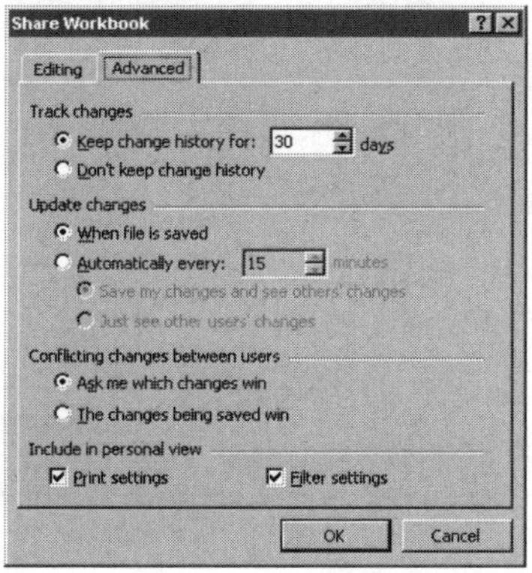

4. Make the desired selections from the Advanced tab.
5. Choose OK to close the dialog box.
6. When prompted, choose Save to save the workbook. The Excel file must be saved to activate the sharing feature.

TIP Save the shared workbook to a shared folder accessible to the other users on the network.

If you copy the shared workbook to a network location, make sure any links to other workbooks or documents are intact. If necessary, use the Edit, Links command to make corrections to the link definitions.

▶ **See** "Managing Objects and Links," **p. 588**

To unshare a workbook, use these steps:

1. Choose Tools, Share Workbook.
2. Click Allow Changes by More Than One User at the Same Time to remove the check mark and turn this feature off.
3. Choose OK to close the dialog box.
4. Excel will warn you that you are removing the workbook from shared use (see Figure 23.11). Choose Yes to continue.

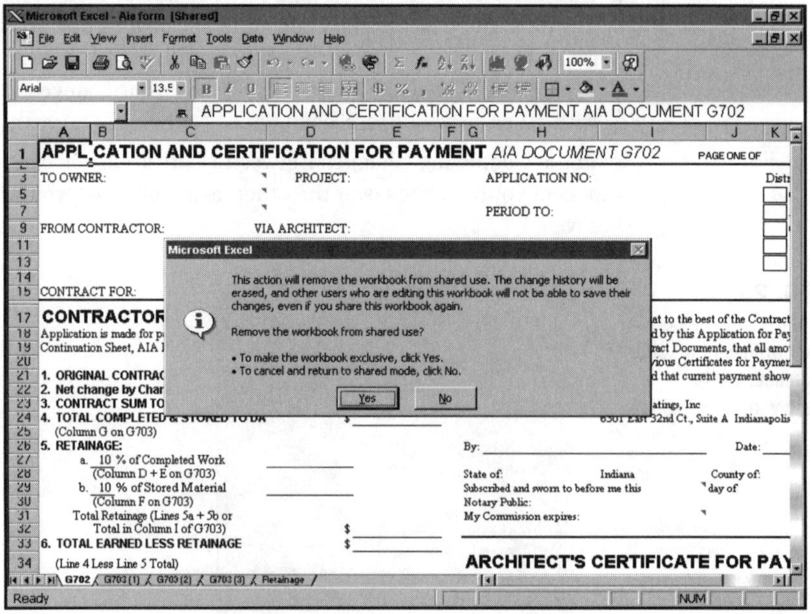

FIG. 23.11
A warning here can protect your data if someone else is currently editing the workbook.

The word `[Shared]` no longer appears in the title bar. Any history of the changes to this workbook are lost.

Open a Shared Workbook

Opening a shared workbook is just like opening any other Excel workbook. Editing the shared workbook is also done the same way, with the exception of the unavailable features listed in the previous section "Benefits and Constraints of Sharing Workbooks."

Follow these steps to open a shared workbook:

1. Click the Open button on the Standard toolbar or press Ctrl+O.
2. Click the file name to be opened and choose Open. The file opens, and the word `[shared]` appears in the title bar next to the file name.

If the workbook is not shared and a second user tries to open it while one user already has it open, the second user will get the message as seen in Figure 23.12.

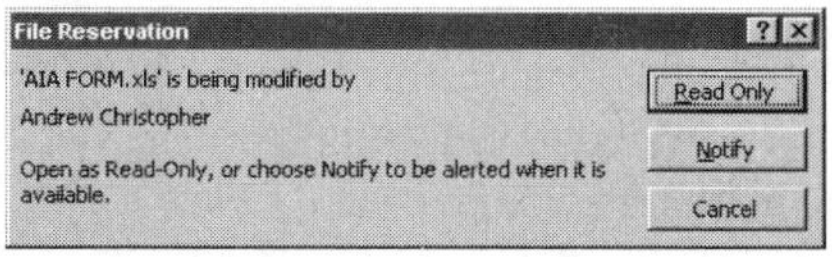

FIG. 23.12 Someone else is currently using this workbook.

When you get the above message, you have two options:

- Open it as Read-only which means you will not be able to save any changes unless you save the file under a different file name.
- Choose Notify to be notified when the file becomes available.

If you choose the Notify option, the file will open as read-only, but when the other user is finished Excel's file reservation system will send you a message like the one you see in Figure 23.13. A dialog box will advise you that the *filename*.xls file is now available for editing.

At this point, you can click Read-Write to open the file.

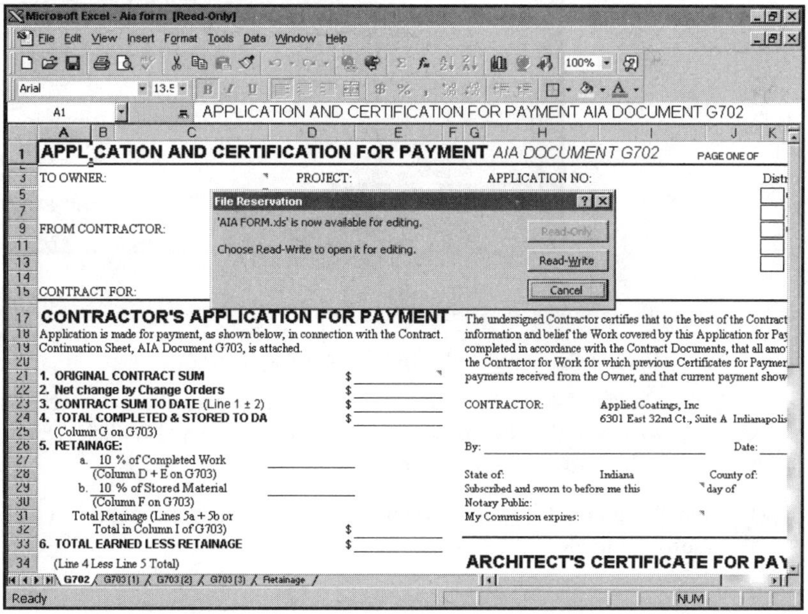

FIG. 23.13 You are now eligible to save your changes to this workbook.

If you have Excel minimized when the file becomes available, the Excel button on the Windows task bar will begin to flash. Upon restoring the Excel program, you will see the notification dialog box.

Handling Conflicts

When two or more users of a shared workbook make changes that conflict with each other, such as typing different values in the same cell, Excel has several options available to help manage the conflicting changes.

Each time the workbook is saved, all the changes made to the workbook are updated. When you try to save the workbook and a conflict is detected, the Resolve Conflicts dialog box (see Figure 23.14) appears, notifying you of the conflict.

FIG. 23.14
A dotted line surrounds the cell in question.

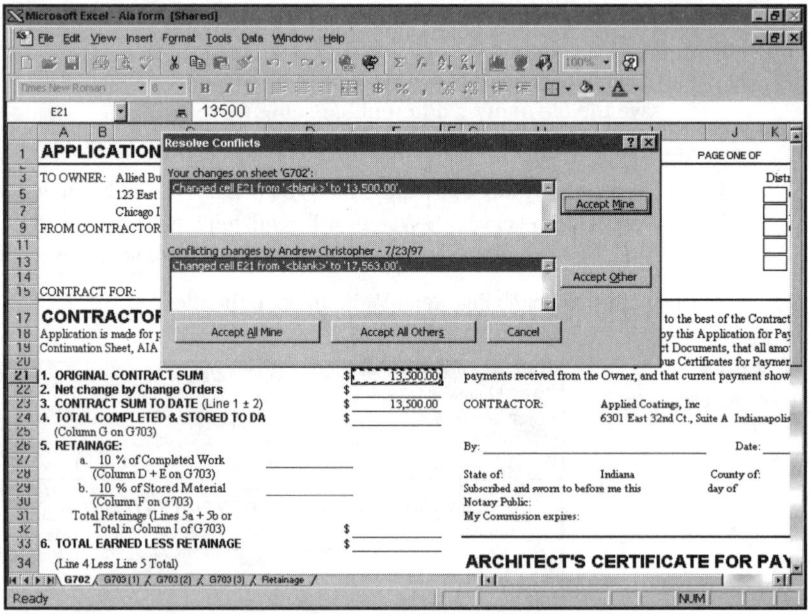

To handle conflicts, use these steps:

1. Review the conflict shown in the dialog box.
2. Choose Accept Mine to have your change placed in the workbook, or click Accept Other to accept the change of the other user. You can also click Accept All Mine or Accept All Others to accelerate the conflict review.

This dialog box will appear for each conflict in the workbook. When all conflicts have been resolved, the file will be saved.

CAUTION

Use caution when reviewing changes. There is no Undo feature available after you have accepted a change.

Tracking and Merging Changes to Workbooks

You worked like crazy on your spreadsheet yesterday, but today you cannot remember where you left off. (The older you get the more frequently this happens!) Excel can help you with this problem using its tracking feature.

Excel also has the ability to merge different copies of a workbook together to see the changes made by different users.

Tracking Changes

The tracking feature can keep you up-to-date about any changes made to a spreadsheet whether they were made by you or someone else.

The tracking feature tracks only changes made to the contents of cells. It does not track formatting changes such as boldface, fonts, or column width.

NOTE A workbook does not have to be shared prior to turning on tracking, but Excel will make it shareable when the tracking feature is invoked.

To turn on the tracking feature, use these steps:

1. Choose Tools, Track Changes.
2. Choose Highlight Changes. The Highlight Changes dialog box appears as seen in Figure 23.15.
3. Click the Track Changes While Editing check box.
4. In the Highlight Which Changes area, there are three ways you can filter the tracking information:
   - *When*. You can decide to only track the changes that have been made since you last saved your file.
   - *Who*. You can track only the changes made by a particular user.
   - *Where*. You can even track only the changes made to a particular range of cells.

   If none of these three boxes are selected, Excel will track all changes made by any user at any time. For now, deselect the check box labeled When.
5. Next you must decide where to track the changes:
   - If you choose Highlight the Changes on the Screen, Excel displays a small colored triangle in the upper-left corner of the modified cell. The modified cell will also have a colored border around it.

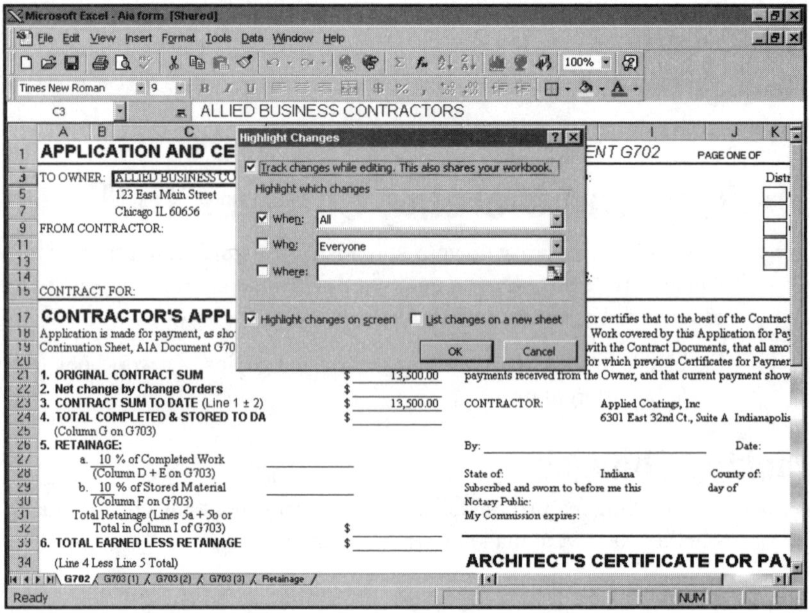

FIG. 23.15
The choice to list the changes on a new sheet will only be available if the workbook has been saved as a shared workbook.

- If you choose to List the Changes on a New Sheet, a new worksheet will be added titled History, like the one shown in Figure 23.16. This sheet will display each change in a row/column format showing who made the change, when the change was made, the type of change, where the change was made, and what the value was before and after the change. It will also display any conflicts and how they were resolved as well. When you save the workbook, Excel removes the History worksheet. To view the History worksheet after you have saved the workbook, you must repeat this procedure to display it again.

6. Click Highlight the Changes on the Screen to activate that feature.
7. Choose OK to close the dialog box.

Now any cells that have content changes will be displayed on your screen. As you move the mouse pointer on top of a revision triangle, a box will appear telling you who made the change, when the change was made, and what the change was. See Figure 23.17 for an example.

If the option to maintain change history was set when the workbook was shared, you can view information from past editing sessions as well, including which changes were kept, replaced, or discarded, as well as the author and data that was entered and later replaced.

The revision triangles will not print on the worksheet, but the borders will print. If you do not want them to print, you must turn this feature off. Your changes can still be tracked, but the changes will not be displayed on-screen and the revision borders will not print.

To turn off revision marks, use these steps:

1. Choose Tools, Track Changes.

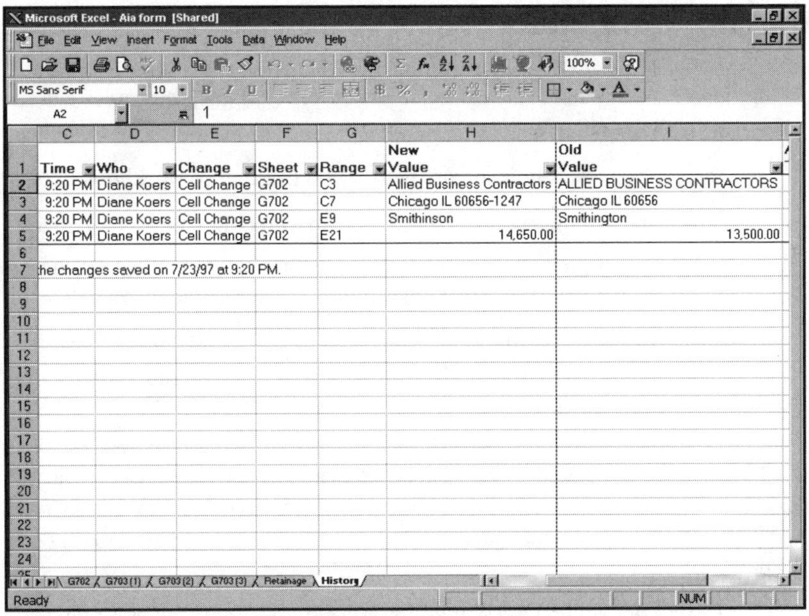

FIG. 23.16
The history sheet displays the types of changes that have been made since the worksheet was last saved.

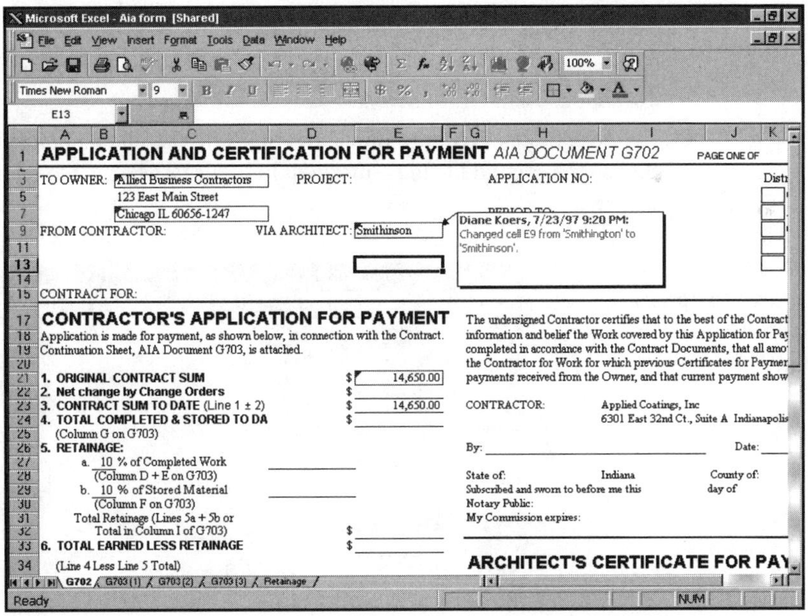

FIG. 23.17
The comment box displays information about the changed cell.

2. Choose Highlight Changes.
3. Click Highlight Changes On Screen to deactivate this feature.
4. Choose OK to close the dialog box.

Merging Workbooks

Another method of maintaining shared workbooks is to send a copy of the workbook to other users. After each user has made his or her changes, the copies can then be united into one file with all the changes.

Excel has a few requirements before you can merge workbook copies:

- The original workbook must be shared before copies are made.
- The original workbook must have the change history setting enabled, and the merging must occur prior to the expiration of the change history date.
- Each copy of the workbook must have come from the original.
- Each copy of the workbook must have a different file name and contain no passwords to open the file.

TIP To make sure other users don't turn off the change history, choose Tools, Protection, and select Protect Shared Workbook. From the dialog box, turn on Protect Workbook for Sharing with Tracking Changes and optionally add a password. The workbook cannot be shared when you assign the password.

To merge the changes of multiple workbooks, follow these steps:

1. Open the shared workbook that will be the main copy for all changes to be merged into.
2. Choose Tools, Merge Workbooks.
3. If the workbook has any unsaved changes in it, you will be prompted to save the workbook. Click OK to save it.
4. The Select Files to Merge Into Current Workbook dialog box will appear. From here, choose the second file to be merged. In Figure 23.18 the file named Drew's AIA form is selected.

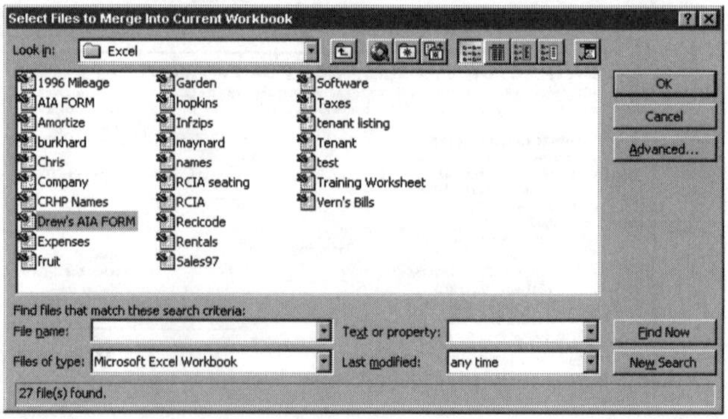

FIG. 23.18 You can merge several copies of a workbook into one master copy.

5. Click OK.
6. Repeat steps 2 through 5 for each copy of the workbook to be merged.

As the copies are merged together, revision marks are made to each cell that has been modified. Figure 23.19 illustrates how Excel will show any modified cells with a small colored triangle in the upper-left corner of the modified cell, as well as a border around each cell. Each user's change will be designated with a different color.

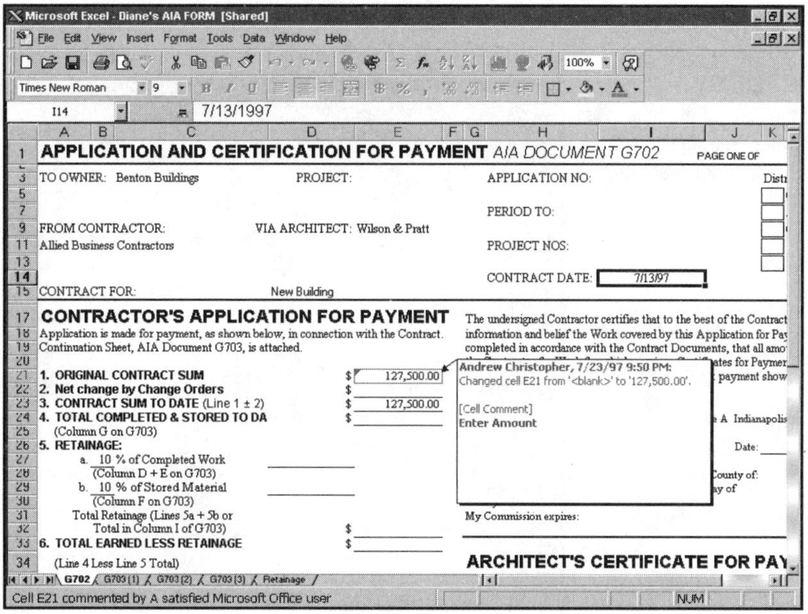

FIG. 23.19
The comment will display the other users' changes.

Accepting or Rejecting Tracked Changes

After any changes have been made, you can now decide to accept or reject them. You will have the opportunity to accept or reject all the changes at once, or you can review each change individually.

To turn on the tracking feature, use these steps:

1. Choose Tools, Track Changes. Then choose Accept or Reject Changes. The Select Changes to Accept or Reject dialog box will appear.
2. You can now filter which changes you want to review:
   - In the When area you can specify only the changes made on the worksheet during a time interval you designate.
   - In the Who area you can examine the edits made by specific users of the shared workbook. All users who have accessed and changed the workbook are displayed.
   - In the Where area you can specify the changes made to a particular range of the worksheet.

In this example, I want to review the changes made by anyone other than myself. From the Who drop-down list box, choose Everyone But Me. The Who selection becomes checked.

3. Choose OK to begin the review session. The first cell Excel finds that has been modified by someone else is selected, and a history of all changes to that cell is displayed in the Accept or Reject Changes dialog box like the one shown in Figure 23.20.

FIG. 23.20
In the case of multiple changes, you must click the change you want to accept.

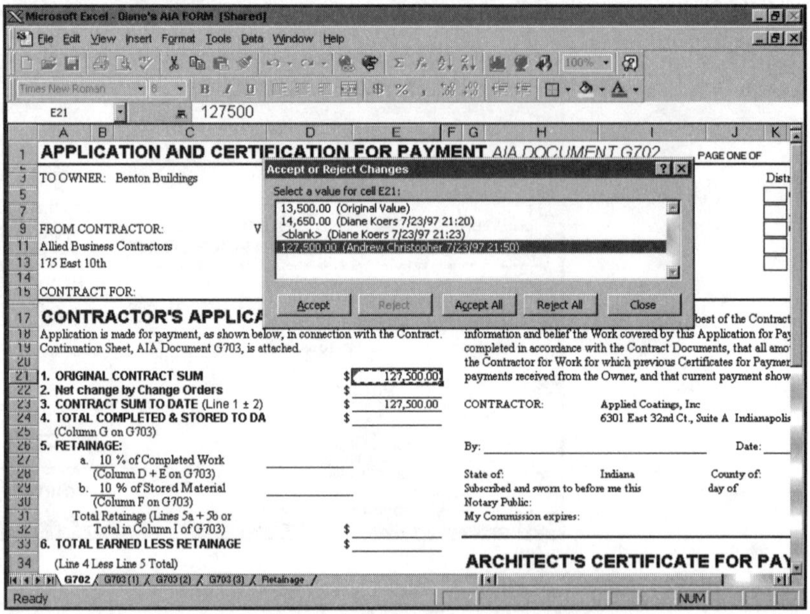

4. Depending on how many changes were made to this cell, you can accept the current change or pick one of the prior changes. Click Accept to keep the changes or click Reject to revert to the prior setting. Excel then moves to the next modified cell.

5. You can continue to review each change independently, or you can click the Accept All or Reject All buttons to review them all at one time. The modified cells no longer display the revision triangles and borders around the cell.

NOTE When you reopen a worksheet, you need to turn on the tracking feature again to make the revisions visible.

Setting Workbook Properties

Each workbook has a set of properties that tracks statistics about the workbook and will allow you to create summary information such as the author, subject, keywords or comments, and revision information. This information can be very helpful if you are trying to locate a spreadsheet and you don't know the exact name of the file.

Set Properties

Workbook properties can be viewed by anyone with access to a shared workbook, but they cannot be modified. Therefore, the property information should be set prior to allowing sharing.

The file properties are not actually associated with the file until you save the file.

TIP You can choose to automatically display the Properties dialog box when saving workbooks the first time by choosing Tools, Options. From the General tab, select Prompt for Workbook Properties.

When you assign properties to a workbook you'll have several areas of information to work with:

- The General tab displays the type, location, and size of the file as well as the creation date and the last modification date. You can also see the MS-DOS file name that Windows 95 has assigned to this file. Excel completes the information on this tab for you.
- The Summary tab allows you to fill in specific information such as the subject and author of the workbook. You can also categorize the workbook and list comments about it.
- The Statistics tab shows who last modified the workbook and the total amount of time spent on editing it. This information is useful for someone who bills for a project by the amount of time it was worked on. Excel completes the information on this tab for you as well.
- The Contents tab displays the names of all worksheets in a workbook. This includes any worksheets that are hidden. Again, Excel completes the information on this tab for you.
- The Custom tab allows you to define specific fields in which to store information.

To assign properties to a worksheet, use these steps:

1. Click File, Properties. The Properties dialog box like the one seen in Figure 23.21 appears.
2. Click the Summary tab. Several blank fields are available for you to enter information.
3. Enter any desired information in the Title, Subject, Category, Keywords, or Comments text boxes (see Figure 23.22).

NOTE Excel has picked up the Author name from the User Name area on the Options dialog box. It picked up the Company name from information that was entered when Excel was installed.

4. Choose OK to accept the information for the Properties dialog box.

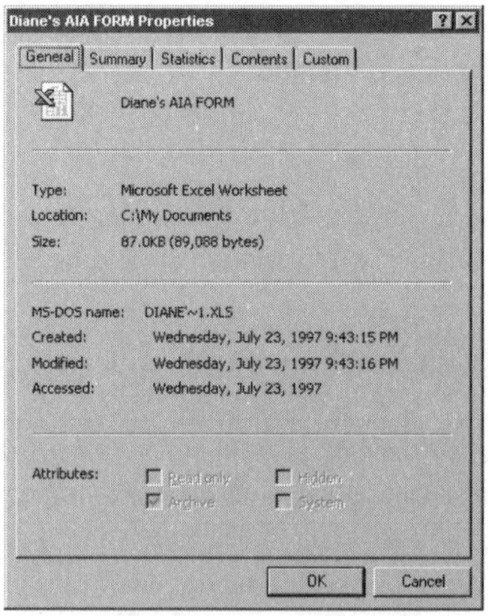

FIG. 23.21
The Properties dialog box displays file statistics.

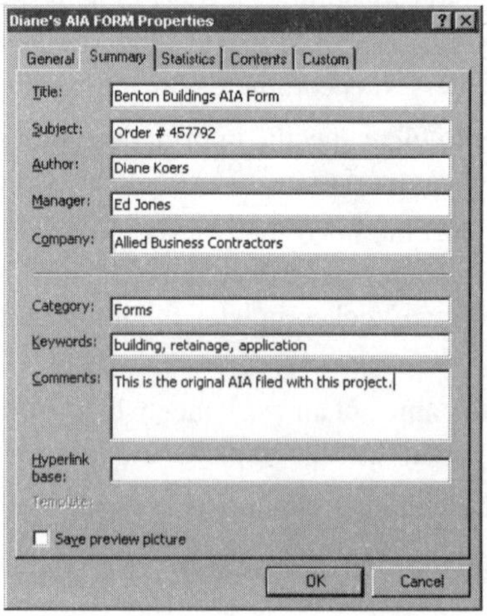

FIG. 23.22
Enter any information you want to store about the workbook.

Searching for Properties

Now that you have assigned properties to the workbook, you can use the search feature of Excel to locate it. This is really handy when you've forgotten the name of the workbook.

To search for a workbook by properties, follow these steps:

1. Choose File, Open.
2. Click the Advanced button in the Open dialog box. The Advanced Find dialog box appears with many options for you to select from.
3. Click the Property drop-down list box. A list of choices appears. Many of these choices were fields displayed in the File, Properties dialog box shown earlier.

4. Choose the field Text or Property.
5. From the Condition drop-down list box, select the condition you want to match. The condition choices are explained here:
   - *Includes words*. Your search will include the words you specify in the Value text box, but not in any particular order, nor do the words need to be together.
   - *Includes phrase*. Your search will include the phrase you specify in the Value text box, and the words must be in that exact order.
   - *Begins with phrase*. Your search will specify that a field must begin with the phrase you enter in the Value text box, and the words must be in that exact order.
   - *Ends with phrase*. Your search will specify that a field must end with the phrase you enter in the Value text box, and the words must be in that exact order.
   - *Includes near each other*. A field must include each of the words you specify in the Value text box, but not in any particular order.
   - *Is (exactly)*. A field in the search must be exactly the words you specify in the Value text box. No extra words are allowed.
   - *Is not*. Your search will specifically exclude the word(s) you specify in the Value text box.
6. In the Value text box, enter the words or phrase you want to search.
7. Click the Add to List button. The search criteria are added to the Find Files That Match These Criteria list box. Your dialog box should resemble the one shown in Figure 23.23.

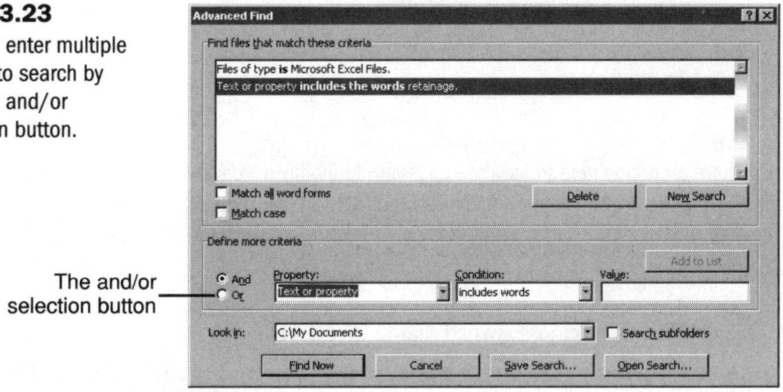

FIG. 23.23
You can enter multiple criteria to search by with the and/or selection button.

8. Click the Look In drop-down list box to specify a folder to begin the search in. Optionally, click the Search Subfolders check box to include subfolders.
9. Choose Find Now to begin the search. Excel will search the folders you specified and display any Excel workbook that matches the criteria.
10. Double-click the desired file to open it.

Securing Workbooks

All users who have access to the network location where a shared workbook is stored have the same access to the shared workbook. If you want to prevent certain types of access to a shared workbook, you can protect the shared workbook and the change history. You'll find there are several levels of protection you can place on a worksheet.

Setting a Password to Open a File

One method of protection you can assign is password protection for the entire workbook. If you assign a password to a workbook, anyone who tries to open the file must know the password to gain access. A workbook cannot be shared when you assign a password to it.

Follow these steps to assign a password to a workbook:

1. Choose File, Save As.
2. Click the Options button. The Save Options dialog box appears.
3. In the Password to Open text box, type a password. The password you are typing will not display; only a series of asterisks can be seen like the ones in Figure 23.24.

   The password can be up to 15 characters long and can include spaces. Also, passwords are case-sensitive. That means you need to type the password exactly as you want users to enter it, taking upper- and lowercase letters into account.

FIG. 23.24
Passwords are hidden from prying eyes.

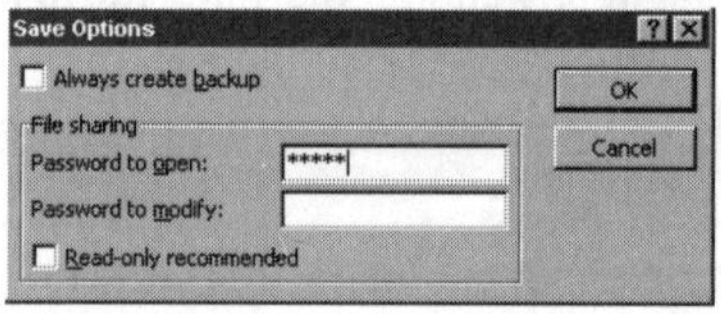

NOTE You also have an option here to assign a password to modify a workbook. If you assign a password here, the user must know this password to make any changes to a workbook. The user will have the option to open it and view it, but cannot save any changes to the file unless he gives the file a different name.

4. Choose OK, and the Confirm Password dialog box appears.
5. In the Reenter Password to Open text box, type the password again, and then click OK. The reason you are reentering the password is to verify your typing.
6. Click Save.
7. If prompted, click Yes to replace the existing workbook with the open workbook.

When you create a password, write it down and keep it in a secure place. If you lose the password, you cannot open or gain access to the data in a password-protected workbook.

The password is now required to open the workbook.

To open a password-protected workbook, use these steps:

1. Choose File, Open.
2. Double-click the file name to be opened.
3. Enter the password in the Password dialog box (see Figure 23.25).

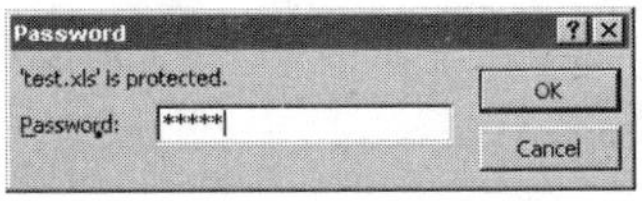

FIG. 23.25
Remember the password is case-sensitive.

4. Choose OK to open the file. The workbook is now ready for you to begin editing.

If you type the password incorrectly, Excel will notify you with the message box shown in Figure 23.26. Click OK.

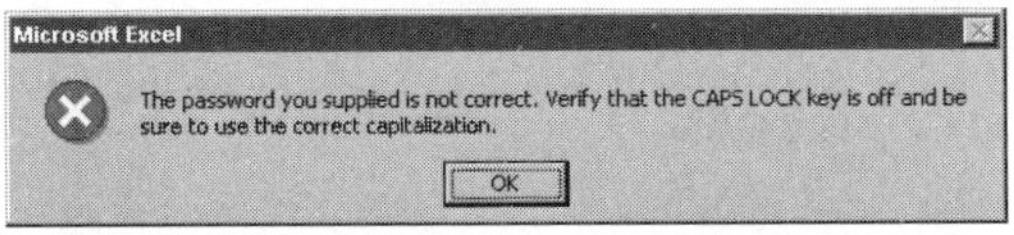

FIG. 23.26
If you type an incorrect password you will have to open the workbook and try again.

To remove a password from a workbook, use the following steps:

1. Choose File, Save As.
2. Click the Options button and delete any of the asterisks in the password box.
3. Choose OK, and then click Save.
4. Choose Yes to replace the existing workbook with the open workbook if prompted to overwrite the existing file.

Protecting Shared Change History

Earlier in this chapter you learned how to share a workbook and how to keep track of changes that have been made. Excel also has a method to protect sharing for a workbook and to prevent users from removing the workbook from shared use or turning off the change history.

In a workbook that is already shared, you can turn on protection for sharing and the change history, but you cannot assign a password for this protection. To assign a password, you must first remove the workbook from shared use.

To protect shared change history, use these steps:

1. Choose Tools, Share Workbook.

2. Temporarily turn off the sharing feature by removing the check mark from the Allow Changes From More Than One User at a Time option.
3. Click OK to close the dialog box.
4. Choose Tools, Protection, Protect and Share Workbook.
5. Click Sharing with Track Changes to activate this feature.
6. As you can see in Figure 23.27, the Optional Password area becomes available. Enter a password for this feature, then choose OK.

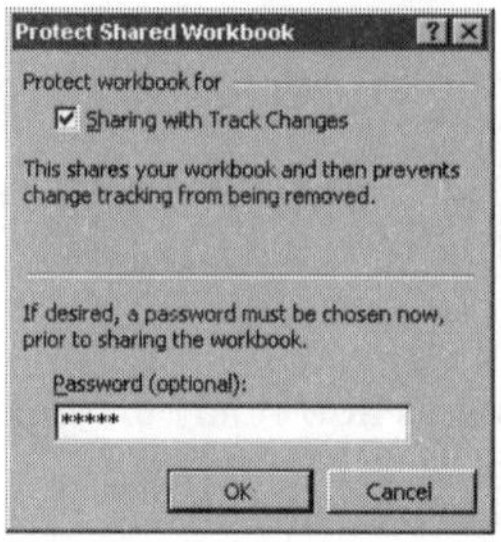

FIG. 23.27
The password can be up to 15 characters in length and is case-sensitive.

7. In the Reenter Password to Open text box, type the password again, and then click OK. You're reentering the password to verify your typing.
8. Click OK to accept the selection.
9. Click OK to save the workbook.

As shown in Figure 23.28, the title bar indicates that the workbook is now shared. If a user chooses Tools, Share Workbook, the features for turning off sharing and tracking changes are unavailable.

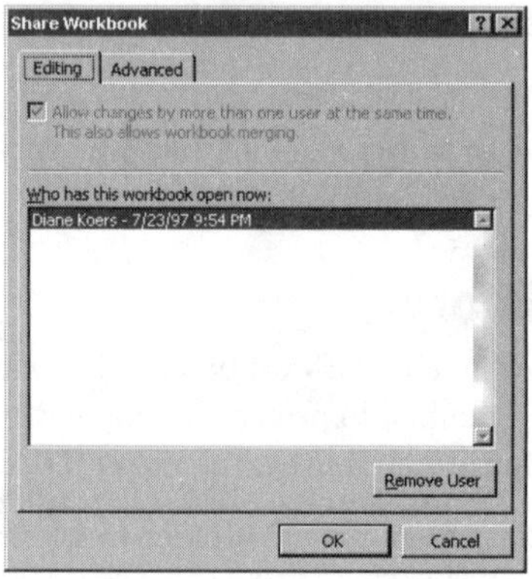

FIG. 23.28
Sharing changes is not allowed in a protected workbook.

To remove shared change history protection, follow these steps:

1. Choose Tools, Protection, Unprotect Shared Workbook.

2. Enter the Password to unprotect sharing and click OK. Remember that passwords are case-sensitive.
3. A dialog box appears advising you that the workbook will no longer be shared and the change history will be erased. Click Yes to remove the workbook from shared use.

CAUTION

If other users are currently editing the shared workbook and you turn off the shared change history protection, the other users will not be able to save their current changes even if you share the workbook again.

Hiding and Protecting Worksheets from Changes

If you don't want others to see specific worksheets in the shared workbook, you can hide them and then protect them from being redisplayed without a password.

To hide and protect worksheets, use these steps:

1. Click the worksheet to be hidden from view.
2. Choose Format, Sheet, Hide. The current worksheet is no longer in view. Repeat these steps for each worksheet to be hidden.

After you hide the worksheets, you must protect the workbook to keep other users from redisplaying the hidden worksheets. They will also not be able to insert, delete, hide, move, or rename the worksheets without supplying the password.

1. Choose Tools, Protection, Protect Workbook.
2. Click the Structure check box to activate protection for the underlying structure of the workbook (see Figure 23.29).

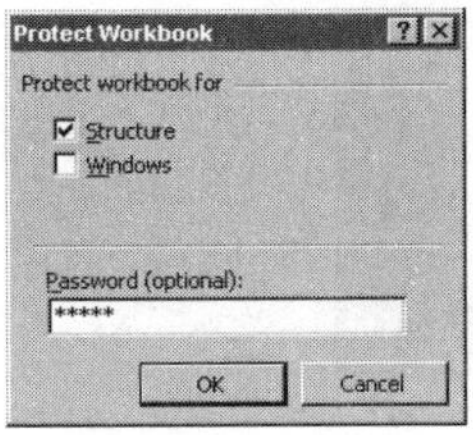

FIG. 23.29
Protecting the structure of a workbook includes inserting other worksheets.

3. In the Password text box, type a password then choose OK to accept the changes. The password can be up to 15 characters in length and is case-sensitive.
4. In the Reenter Password to Open text box, type the password again, then click OK.

To remove worksheet protection, use these steps:

1. Choose Tools, Protection, Unprotect Workbook.

2. Enter the appropriate password in the Password text box. Remember that passwords are case-sensitive.

The protection is removed and any user can now hide, unhide, insert, delete, move, or rename the worksheets.

Protecting Cells from Changes

Excel has a feature that will allow you to protect specific areas of a worksheet. A great reason to use this feature is to protect your worksheet formulas. It's very easy to accidentally type something in a cell that already had a formula in it. The formula gets overwritten by the new entry, and that certainly could be disastrous to your entire workbook. This type of protection is done on a worksheet-by-worksheet basis.

When you apply this type of protection, Excel assumes every cell in the current worksheet is to be protected from changes. You must then tell Excel which cells are permitted to be modified.

To protect cells from changes, follow these steps:

1. Select any cells that you want to allow to be modified.
2. Choose Format, Cells.
3. The Format Cells dialog box appears. Click the Protection tab.
4. Click the Locked check box to remove the check from it and unlock the selected cells. Then choose OK to close the dialog box (see Figure 23.30) .

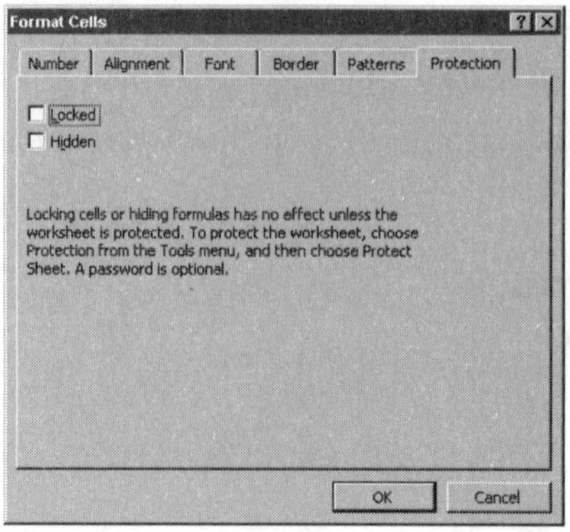

FIG. 23.30
Excel assumes cells are to be locked unless you turn the locked cell check box off.

5. Choose Tools, Protection, Protect Sheet. The Protect Sheet dialog box appears prompting you for the type of protection you are looking for. By default, Excel will protect everything on the current worksheet except for the cells you excluded in step 4.
6. In the Password text box, type a password and then click OK. The password can be up to 15 characters in length and is case-sensitive. (A password is optional here. Not putting a password in is mainly used to protect yourself from accidental changes.)
7. In the Reenter Password to Open text box, type the password again, then click OK.

If you try to enter data into a protected cell, Excel will advise you that the cell is protected and it is not changeable (see the error message in Figure 23.31). Instructions for removing cell protection are also provided in this information box. Click OK to acknowledge the message box.

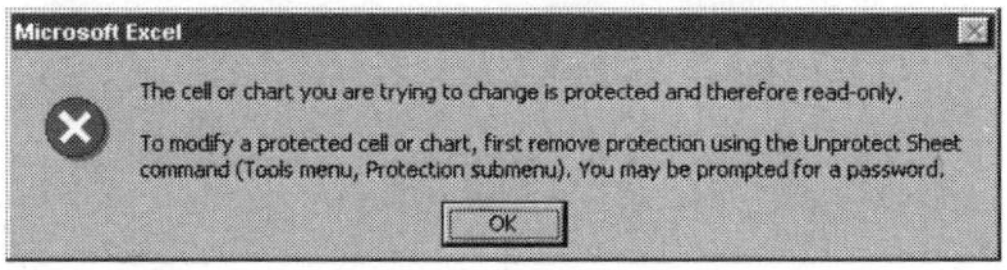

FIG. 23.31
No formatting or content change can be done on a locked cell.

To remove protection from specific cells, follow these steps:

1. Choose Tools, Protection, Unprotect Sheet.
2. Enter the password in the Password text box, then click OK. Remember that passwords are case-sensitive.

You can now make any desired editing changes to all cells in that sheet of the workbook.

Common Problems and Solutions

I created a worksheet at home that included some cells with the text rotated to a 45° angle. When I brought the worksheet into the office to print it, the rotated text was no longer rotated.

Check the version of Excel in the office. Versions earlier than Excel 97 could only rotate text to 90 degrees or –90 degrees. Any rotations other than those were changed to horizontal orientation.

I'm trying to delete a worksheet from my Excel workbook, but the Delete option is unavailable.

Excel will not let you delete worksheets if a workbook is shared. You must first unshare the workbook by selecting Tools, Share Workbook and deselecting Allow Changes by More Than One User at the Same Time.

I need to open a workbook that has a password assigned to it, but it won't accept my password.

Passwords are case-sensitive. Check to see if your Caps Lock key is turned on by mistake.

From Here...

In this chapter, you learned how you and others can share an Excel workbook across a network. In earlier chapters, you learned how Excel could be used as a database. A common Excel database can also be integrated with other applications—whether or not they are Microsoft Office applications. For more information see these other chapters:

- Chapter 24, “Integrating Excel with Other Office Applications,” examines how Excel interacts with Word, PowerPoint, and Access.
- Chapter 25, “Integrating Excel with Any Other Applications,” discusses importing and exporting data to or from Excel using other software (such as accounting software).

CHAPTER 24

Integrating Excel with Other Office Applications

by Bill Ray

- **Using objects in Excel**
  You'll learn how Excel enables you to embed and link objects from other Office applications.
- **Managing object links**
  Find out how Excel keeps linked data up to date.
- **Creating hyperlinks to Office documents**
  Create a web-like collection of information out of regular Office documents.
- **Using the Windows Clipboard**
  You'll see how Excel uses the Clipboard for importing and exporting data dynamically.
- **Working with Access databases**
  Use Excel and MS Query to use Access databases directly.
- **Using Microsoft Office Binder**
  Use Office Binder to assemble documents from multiple applications.

Microsoft Excel is just one application included with Microsoft Office 97. The Standard Edition of Office also includes Microsoft Word 97 for word processing, Microsoft PowerPoint 97 for creating graphical presentations, and Microsoft Outlook 97 for managing personal information, such as electronic mail, names and addresses, and your calendar of meetings and appointments. The Professional Edition of Office 97 also includes the Microsoft Access 97 relational database management system.

Each of these applications uses its own format for organizing and storing information. Fortunately, Excel and the other Office applications offer several different methods for you to exchange and share data among them. This chapter will show you how to use information from other Office applications in your Excel workbooks and to use Excel's data in other Office applications. ■

Using Objects in Excel

Many applications that you create in Excel may benefit from the features of other Office applications. You may want to include text passages that you format by using Word's word processing power. You may want to include presentation graphics from PowerPoint or event audio and video clips.

The most common method for sharing data among Windows applications is Object Linking and Embedding (OLE). As its name implies, OLE provides two methods for communication between applications.

- *Object Linking* enables you to place a reference in one application, known as the client, to data that is stored in a file created by another application, known as the server. Any changes to the linked file will be updated automatically in the client application's document.
- *Object Embedding* enables you to store the data from the server application directly in the client document. There is no link to the server document and, in fact, you may never even create and save the file in the server application.

There is more to OLE than simply storing data. The linked or embedded application automatically remembers the application in which it was created. If you want to update the data in the object, you can activate the object, and the server application is activated automatically. By updating the data in the object, you can edit the application by using all the features and commands of that server application.

Not all applications fully support OLE linking and embedding. Some applications can create OLE objects, acting as an OLE server, but can't be an OLE client, receiving OLE objects. Two examples of such applications are the Microsoft Paint and WordArt accessories that come with Windows. Other applications can be clients but not servers. An example of such an application is the WordPad accessory.

The Office 97 applications have good support for OLE and generally can serve as both OLE clients and servers. In this chapter, you'll learn how each of the major Office applications can work with Excel using OLE and other techniques. Excel, in particular, can serve as both an OLE client and an OLE server. In other words, you not only can place objects from other applications in an Excel workbook, but you can place objects created in Excel, such as worksheets and charts, into other applications.

In Chapter 25, "Integrating Excel with Any Other Applications," you'll learn to use Excel to work with non-Office applications, including some that don't support OLE.

Comparing Embedding and Linking

How do you know whether you should use embedding or linking when you need to create an OLE object? To help you make the decision in your own case, consider the differences between linking and embedding, as listed in response to the following questions.

Where are the data for the object stored?

- Data for embedded objects are stored in the client document. You do not need to save a server document separately unless you need it for other purposes.
- Data for linked objects are stored in the server application's document in a separate file, which is especially useful if you need to share the source document with other users on a network or if you want to reuse the same source document for several applications. If you delete the server file, you will not be able to update the object.

What is the impact of embedding or linking objects on file size?

- Embedded objects may dramatically increase the size of the client document because all the data for the object must be stored in that document.
- Linked objects have a minimal impact on the size of the client document. The value of this advantage is multiplied if you create several client applications that link to the same server document. You also may edit the linked document independently of the client document, thereby using less memory.

What if I need to send the client document via e-mail or disk?

- If you use embedded objects, you do not need to send any additional files. Because the client document contains the data for the object, you only have to send one file.
- If you use linked objects, you'll have to send the server document as well as the client document. Because the linked file might be stored in a different location on the recipient's computer, the recipient also might need to edit the link so that he or she can see the changes in the linked document.

Inserting Objects into Workbooks

You can use several methods to place an OLE object in an Excel workbook. You can select the method you want to use based on convenience as well as the degree of control you want over the process of creating and manipulating the objects.

Using the Insert Object Command

The most formal method for creating OLE objects is to use the Insert Object command. This command gives you the most control over the process of creating objects and enables you to choose whether to create linked or embedded objects.

Creating a New Embedded Object With the Insert Object command, you can create a new object by using another application without first saving that object with the other program.

1. In Excel, position the cell pointer where you want to place the new object.
2. Choose Insert, Object. The Object dialog box appears, as shown in Figure 24.1.
3. Click the Create New tab on the dialog box if it is not already selected.
4. Select the object type you want to create.

FIG. 24.1
The Object dialog box enables you select the type of object you want to embed in your workbook.

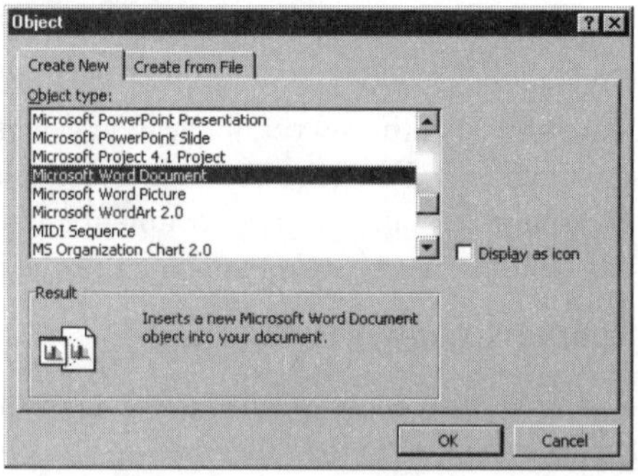

CAUTION

The Object Type list reflects the applications that have been installed on your computer, according to the information that is stored in the Windows Registry. If you decide to remove an application from your computer, it is important that you run the uninstall routine for that program so that its registry information is also removed.

5. Check the Display as Icon check box if you want to see only an icon representing the object in your workbook instead of the normal appearance of the object.
6. Click OK to complete the command. The object is embedded in the Excel workbook, and the server application is activated.
7. Edit the object using the server application's commands and features.
8. Click outside the boundaries of the embedded object to exit the server application and store the embedded object in the Excel worksheet.

The embedded object you have created is not saved in a separate file but, rather, is part of the Excel workbook you have open. When you save your Excel workbook, the object is saved with the workbook. If you copy the workbook to a disk or send the workbook as an e-mail attachment, you need to include only one file—the Excel workbook. Of course, the Excel file will be larger than normal because it contains all the data of the embedded object.

As you select the object, notice the contents of the Excel formula bar. . The formula bar will contain a formula, such as `=EMBED("Word.Document.8","")`, which indicates that this is an embedded object created by the application Word, version 8.

NOTE When you edit an object created in another Office 97 application, Excel's menus are modified to contain the functionality of the server application. This feature is known as *menu merging*. Many non-Office applications may not use the menu merging feature and may open the object in a separate application window for the server application.

NOTE The server application determines the appearance of the embedded object. Some server applications, such as Word or PowerPoint, create an object that looks just like a document in the original application. Other servers, such as audio programs, may not have a useful graphical presentation for the object and may be limited to displaying an icon to represent the object. ■

Creating an Object from an Existing File Another feature of the Insert Object command is the capability to create an object based on an existing file that was created in another application.

1. In Excel, position the cell pointer where you want to place the new object.
2. Choose Insert, Object. The Object dialog box appears.
3. Click the Create from File tab on the dialog box if it is not already selected. The Object dialog box should now look like Figure 24.2.

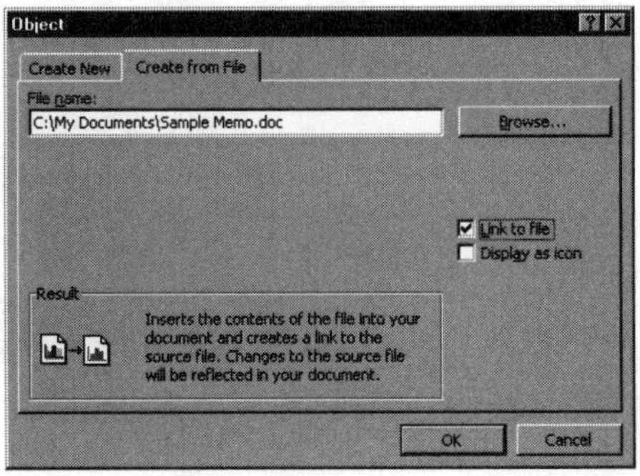

FIG. 24.2
Also use the Object box for inserting objects from an existing file.

4. Type the file name in the File Name box, or click the Browse... button to search for the file you want to use.
5. Check the Display as Icon check box if you want to see only an icon representing the object in your workbook instead of the normal appearance of the object.
6. Check the Link to File check box if you want the object to be linked to the original file. Leave the check box unchecked if you want to embed a copy of the file.
7. Click OK to complete the command. The linked or embedded object is placed in the Excel workbook.

If you chose to create a linked document, the formula bar may contain a formula such as `=Word.Document.8¦'C:\My Documents\Memo.doc'!''''`. This formula indicates that the object is an external reference to a Word document and shows the path and file name of the document.

Using the Drag-and-Drop Technique to Create Objects

Another way to place an object from one application into another is by using the drag-and-drop technique. Just as you can move or copy ranges within Excel by dragging them with the mouse or move text passages in Word by dragging them, you can use the same technique to copy and move data between two applications, creating an OLE object in the destination document.

1. Arrange the windows of the source and destination applications on the screen so that you can see the locations from and to which you want to copy the data.
2. Select the data that you want to copy or move in the source application. Figure 24.3 shows the Word and Excel application windows with some text selected in Word in preparation for copying.

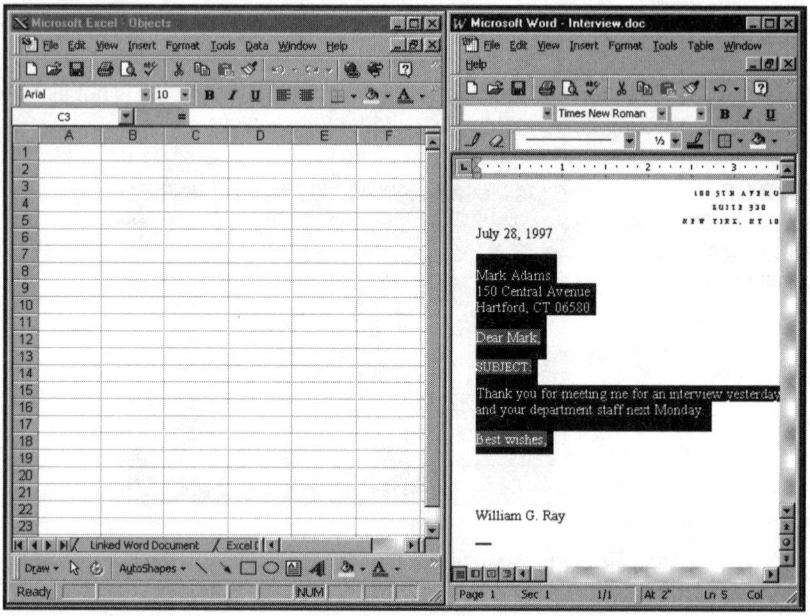

FIG. 24.3
Word and Excel are arranged on the screen so that you can copy information from one window to another.

3 Using the right mouse button, drag the selected data to the destination window. Do not release the mouse button.

4. Position the mouse cursor over the location in the destination window where you want to place the object.
5. Release the mouse button when you have positioned the mouse where you want to place the object. A shortcut menu appears, as shown in Figure 24.4.
6. Select the command that indicates the operation you want to complete.

TIP Sometimes when you try to drag data from one application to another, one of the application windows may begin to scroll, making it difficult for you to position the data.

To prevent this scrolling, hold the Alt key while you drag data from one window to another.

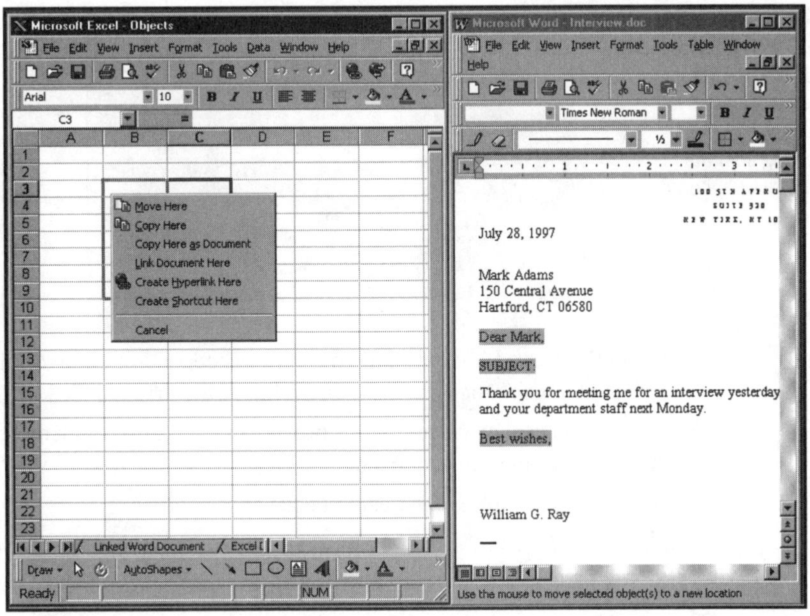

FIG. 24.4
The shortcut menu enables you to select how you want to place an object.

Using the Windows Clipboard for OLE

Another method for copying and moving data between programs is to copy and paste data using the Windows Clipboard. The Clipboard has more flexibility than many people think. When you copy data from an application to the Clipboard, the application may place several different forms of data on the Clipboard. The number of formats copied to the Clipboard varies by the program from which you are copying.

When you paste data from the Clipboard into another program using the Edit, Paste command or one of the common Paste shortcuts, the receiving program selects the most appropriate data format from the Clipboard based on the rules defined by the receiving program. Fortunately, most programs also contain a Paste Special command, which enables you to override the normal selection process and to select the format you want to use in the destination program.

To use the Clipboard for creating objects in a destination program, follow these steps.

1. Select the data that you want to copy in the source application.
2. Copy the data to the Clipboard by pressing Ctrl+C.
3. Activate the destination document and select the location where you want to place the data.
4. Choose Edit, Paste Special. The Paste Special dialog box appears (see Figure 24.5).
5. Select the result format you want to paste from the Clipboard by making a selection from the As list.

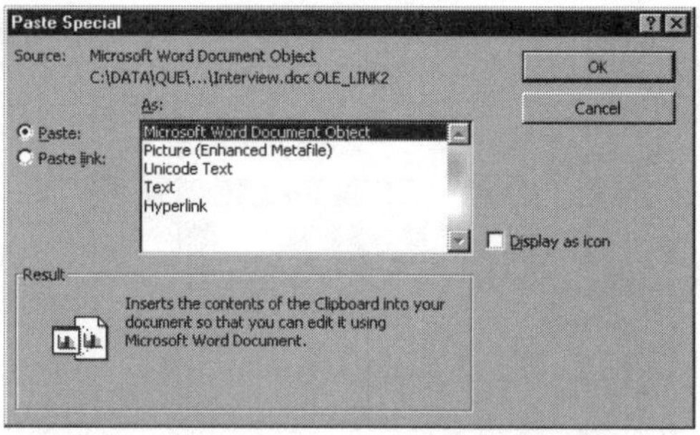

FIG. 24.5
The Paste Special dialog box enables you select the data format you want to use when pasting from the Windows Clipboard.

6. Select the Paste Link button if you want to keep a link to the original file. Select Paste if you want to copy the data without linking to the original file.
7. Check the Display as Icon check box if you want to see an icon representing the object instead of seeing the actual data.
8. Click OK to complete the Paste Special command.

Managing Objects and Links

Once you have embedded an object in a workbook, you may need to make changes to the object. You can change the position and appearance of the object in the Excel workbook or work with the data from the server application

Formatting and Positioning Objects

If you have placed an object in Excel, you have several options for changing the appearance, location, and size of the object. It is important to understand, however, that Excel does not have complete control over the appearance of the object. When you place an object, the server application is responsible for defining the general appearance of the object. For example, a Word object looks like a Word document and a PowerPoint object looks like a PowerPoint slide. If you want to change the appearance of some internal aspect of the object, such as its font, color, or the actual contents of the object, you must first activate the server application. You'll learn to activate an object in the section, "Activating an Embedded Object."

You can change some aspects of the object's appearance by using Excel, however.

Changing the Size and Position of an Object with the Mouse You can easily change the size and position of an object by using the mouse.

1. Click the object to select it. Figure 24.6 shows an object in an Excel workbook that has been selected.
2. To move the object, click the object and drag it to a new position.
3. To resize the object, click one of the sizing handles on the selected object and drag the handle to a new position.

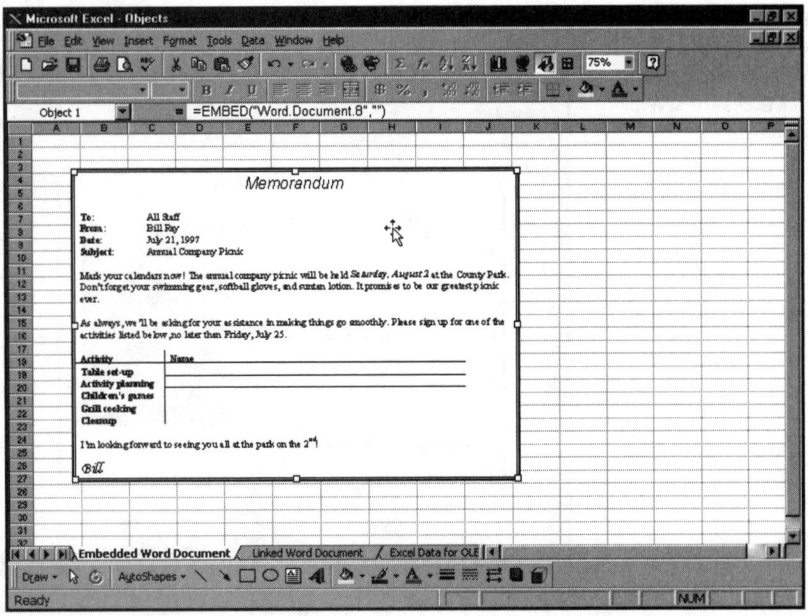

FIG. 24.6
You can easily identify a selected object by the selection handles along its borders.

CAUTION

Resizing an object may give you unexpected results. Depending on the server application's method of displaying the object, the appearance of the object may be stretched, compressed, or distorted after you resize it. In this case, you can use the Undo command to restore the object to its original size.

Using the Shortcut Menu to Change the Appearance of an Object You can modify several aspects of an object by using the shortcut menu that is available for editing objects. You can use this menu to change the style and color of the border lines of an object, to set precisely the size of the object, to crop the object, and to set the protection and positioning properties of the object.

To display the shortcut menu shown in Figure 24.7, right-click the object.

To modify the appearance of the object, select Format Object. The Format Object dialog box has five tabs. Figure 24.8 shows the Colors and Lines tab.

- Use the Color control in the Fill section to change the background color of the object. You can also use this control to set a background pattern or other special effect.
- Use the Color control of the Lines group to change the color of the border lines around the object. You can choose None with this control to remove the border lines if you don't want them.
- Use the Dashed, Style, and Weight controls to further modify the appearance of the border lines around the object.

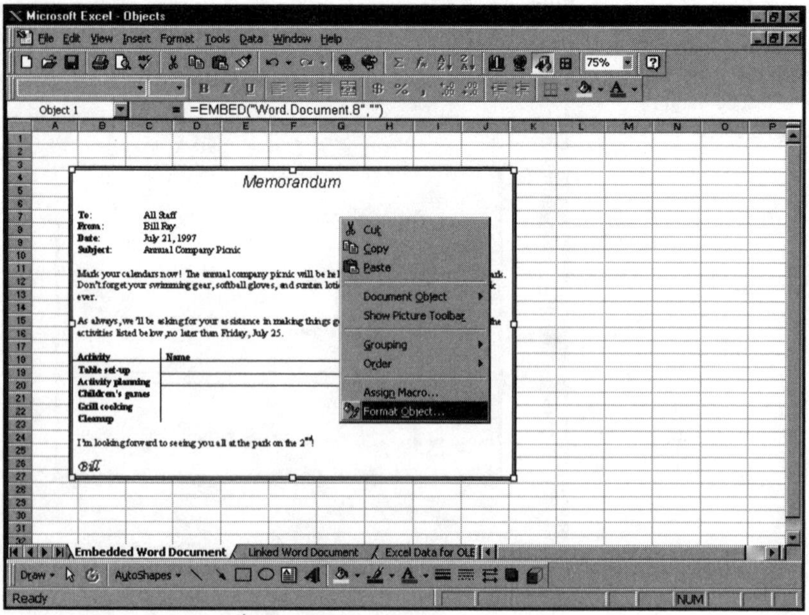

FIG. 24.7
The shortcut menu for an object gives you quick access to several commands.

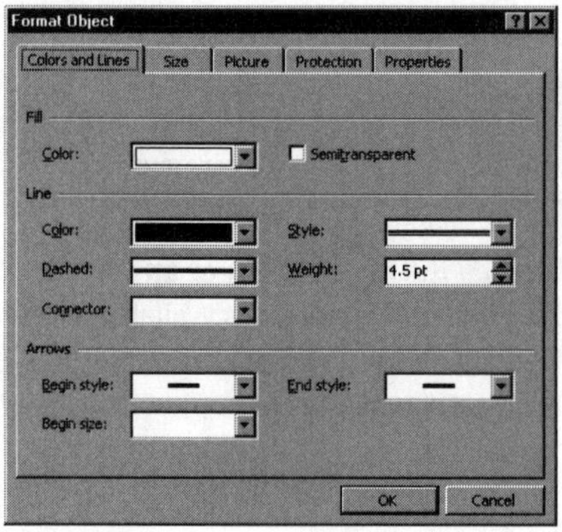

FIG. 24.8
With the Colors and Lines tab of the Format Object dialog box, you can change the appearance of the object's borders.

Figure 24.9 shows the Size tab of the Format Object dialog box.

- Use the Height and Width settings in the Size and Rotate group to control precisely the size of the object.
- Use the Height and Width settings in the Scale group to adjust the size of the object by a percentage of the object's original size.
- Click the Reset button to restore the object to its original size.

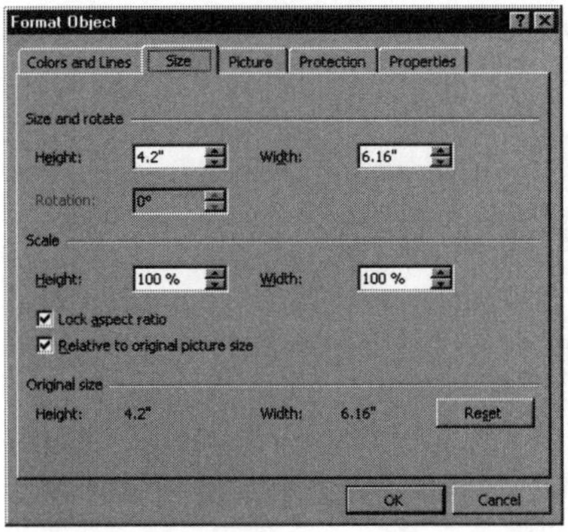

FIG. 24.9
The Size tab gives you precise control over the size of an object.

Figure 24.10 shows the Picture tab of the Format Object dialog box.

- Use the Crop From settings to hide a portion of the object by moving the appropriate border over the object's content.
- Use the image control settings to change the brightness, contrast, and color palette of the object.

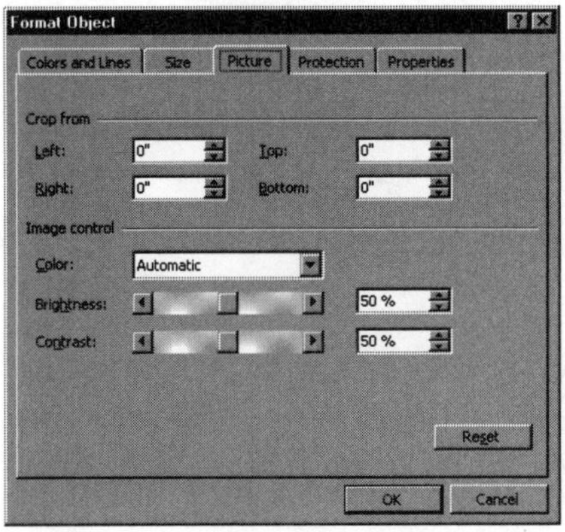

FIG. 24.10
The Picture tab enables you to crop the display of an object.

Figure 24.11 shows the Protection tab of the Format Object dialog box. Checking this box has no effect unless the sheet containing the object is protected. If the object is locked and the sheet is protected, you cannot activate the object.

▶ **See** "Securing Workbooks," **p. 574**

Figure 24.12 shows the Properties tab of the Format Object dialog box.

- Use the Object Positioning options to determine how the object moves and is resized if the cells containing the object are moved or resized.
- Uncheck the Print object check box if you don't want the object to be printed when you print the worksheet.

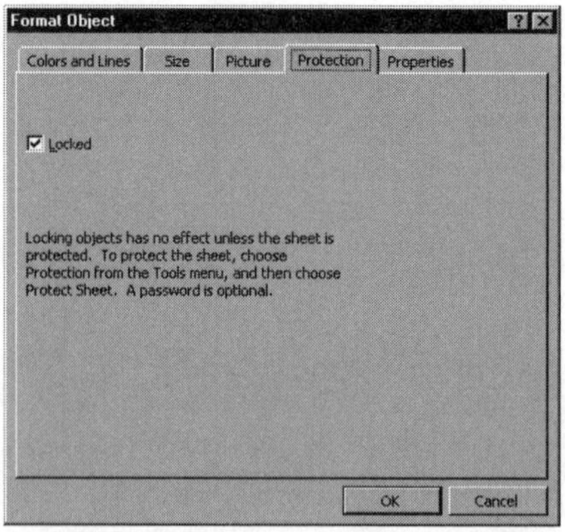

FIG. 24.11
The Protection tab enables you to lock an object against changes if the worksheet is protected.

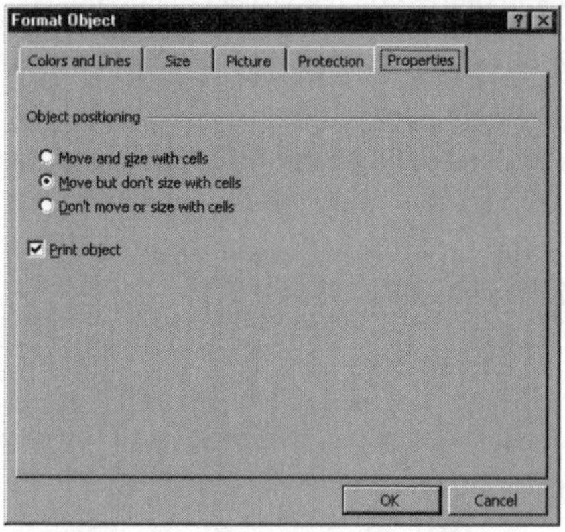

FIG. 24.12
With the Properties tab, you can control the positioning and printing options for an object.

Activating an Embedded Object

If you want to make changes to an embedded or linked object, you must activate the server application that created the object. In most cases, you can activate an object by simply double-clicking the object.

Different types of objects have different behaviors that are executed when you double-click the object. Though many objects open for editing, some object types, such as media objects, play when you double-click them.

To gain more control over the activation process, you can use the shortcut menu for the object. To display the shortcut menu, right-click the object. The shortcut menu is shown in Figure 24.13 with the Object submenu selected.

In this example, using a PowerPoint object, the submenu shows the *verbs*, or activities, for the object. Each selection has a different result, as described here.

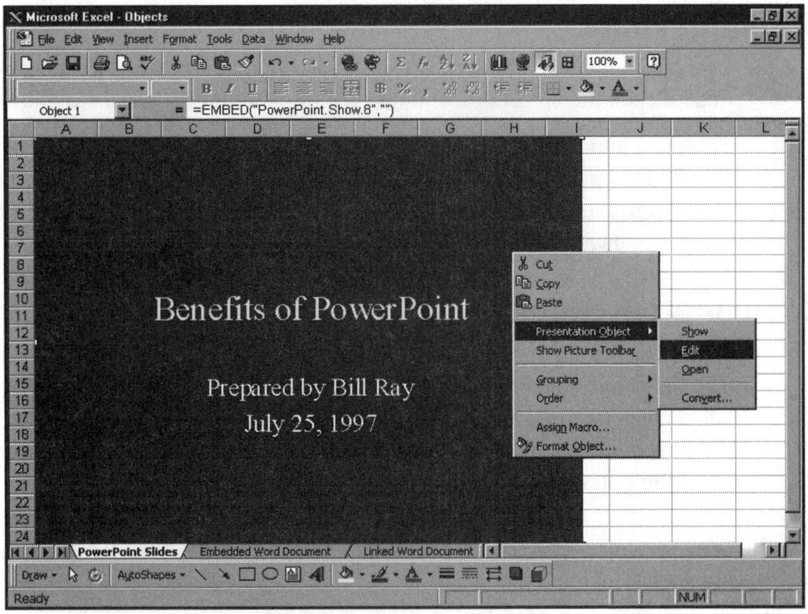

FIG. 24.13
You can use the shortcut menu to activate an object for editing or some other action.

- Show presents the PowerPoint presentation on your screen, just as the slide show operation in PowerPoint would.
- Edit activates PowerPoint's functionality inside the Excel application window. PowerPoint's menus and toolbars merge with Excel's, giving you direct access to PowerPoint's functionality. This process is known as *in-place editing*.
- Open activates PowerPoint in a separate application window. With this selection, you can maximize the PowerPoint window and work as you normally would in PowerPoint.

The list of verbs, or commands, on the Object shortcut menu will vary from one application to another. Some applications have several verbs and others have only one or two. Ideally, the meaning of the verbs for any application are self-evident. If you don't find them to be obvious, check the Help file for the server application.

Updating the Object After Editing If you have activated and edited an embedded object, the changes will be saved when you save the containing object. If you are editing an object *in-place*, as described in the previous section, "Activating an Embedded Object," the object is automatically updated as soon as you click outside it to deactivate it.

If you have opened the object in a separate application window, you must tell the server application that you want to update the object in the client document. Most applications have a command on the File menu when you are editing an object, with a name such as Close and Return to *Document*, where *document* is the name of the client document. Select this command to return to the client application with the changes to the object updated.

Updating Links

Updating a linked document is very similar to updating an embedded document. You can either double-click the object or use the shortcut menu for the object to edit the linked document.

The most important thing to remember about linked documents is that when you activate the server document, you are now editing the separately saved document. Remember to save the changes to the server document so the data will be up to date the next time you open either the client or server document.

Changing the Source of a Link

When you open a document that contains links to one or more other files, Excel displays a message box, shown in Figure 24.14, asking whether you want to update the data with the latest changes to the linked document. If you answer Yes, Excel reads the current data from the linked document. If you answer No, Excel displays the data that was inserted in the document the last time it was updated.

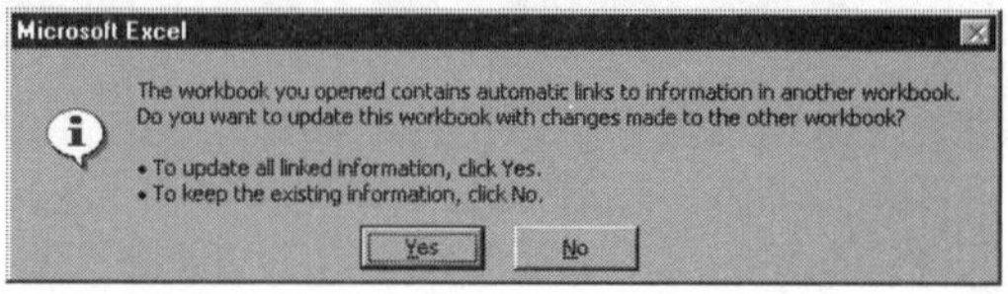

FIG. 24.14 Excel asks how you want to treat linked objects when you open a workbook.

When updating data from a linked document, Excel uses the same path and file name that was last used to update the workbook. Sometimes you may want to change the source document for the link. You may have moved the files to a different computer or network with a different file and directory structure. You may have developed a new document with alternate data that you want to substitute for the previously linked data.

You can change the source of a linked document by using the Edit, Links command.

1. Open the document that contains linked references to other documents.
2. Choose Edit, Links. The Links dialog box appears, as shown in Figure 24.15.

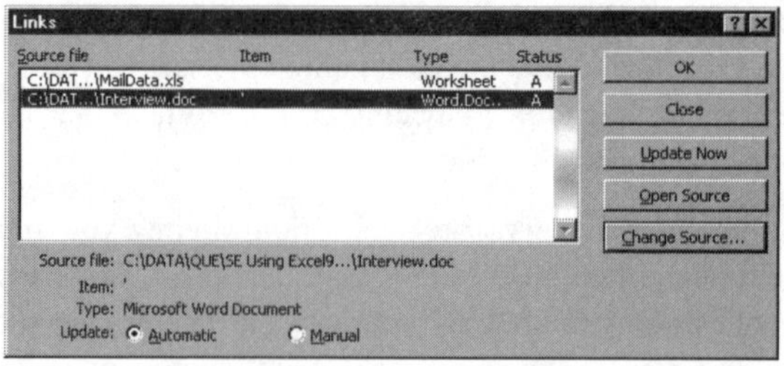

FIG. 24.15 Use the Links dialog box for updating and modifying link information.

3. Select the link you want to modify, then click the Change Source button. The Change Links dialog box appears, as shown in Figure 24.16.

FIG. 24.16
In the Change Links dialog box, you can replace a link with a different file name.

4. Enter a new link reference, then click OK.

You can also use the Links dialog box to update a link at any time by clicking the Update Now button. This process is useful if you have set a link as a Manual link instead of as Automatic and you now want to update the link with the latest data.

The Open Source button enables you to open the linked document in the application window of the server application.

Using Hyperlinks with Office 97 Applications

If you have used an Internet browser, such as Microsoft Internet Explorer, you are probably familiar with the concept of ***hyperlinks***. A hyperlink is text, a graphic, or another object on a Web page that is highlighted in some way, inviting you to click it. When you click the hyperlink, you automatically jump to another location. That other location may be a different spot on the same page, a different page on the same Web site, or an entirely different Web site anywhere on the Internet.

To learn more about creating hyperlinks to Web pages and about converting Word documents into Web pages, see Chapter 26, "Working with Web Pages."

97

Office 97 extends your ability to create an Internet-style system of documents to include hyperlinks to other Office documents as well as to standard Web pages. Once you have created and followed a hyperlink, all Office 97 applications, including Excel, have full Internet-style browsing features provided by the Web toolbar.

NOTE A hyperlink is a navigation tool with which you can easily jump from one location to another, even if that other location is in a document created in another application. A hyperlink does not imply any link to the data or content of the document at the destination of the link. ■

Creating a Hyperlink in Excel 97

Any Excel 97 workbook can contain a hyperlink. Before you create the hyperlink, make sure that the document to which you want to link exists and that its location is reliable. The document might be located on your local hard drive or in a directory on your network. If the document's location changes later, the hyperlink will not be updated automatically, and the link will fail.

Figure 24.17 shows an Excel spreadsheet that will contain some hyperlinks. A user has activated the Web toolbar by clicking the Web Toolbar button on the Standard toolbar.

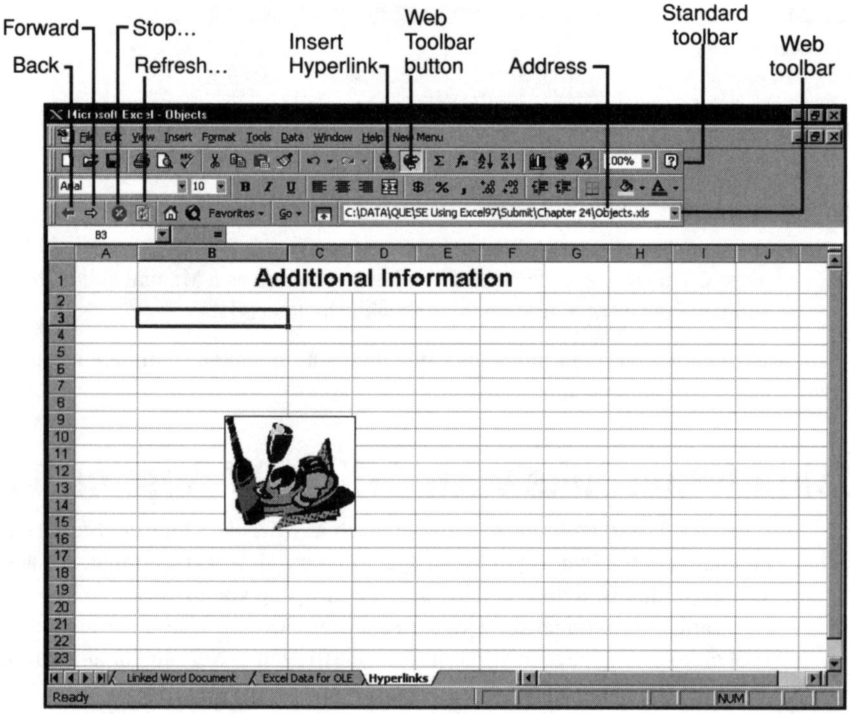

FIG. 24.17 The Standard and Web toolbars work together when you create and work with hyperlinks.

You can simply create a hyperlink in an empty cell in the worksheet.

1. Select the cell in which you want the hyperlink to appear.

2. Choose the Insert Hyperlink button on the Standard toolbar. The Insert Hyperlink dialog box appears, as shown in Figure 24.18.

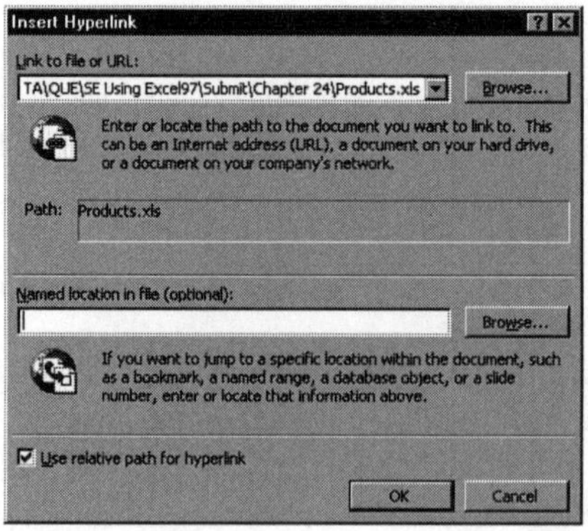

FIG. 24.18 The Insert Hyperlink dialog box enables you to choose the destination of the link.

3. Type the path and file name of the file to which you want to create the hyperlink in the Link to File or URL text box. If you don't want to type the name, click the Browse button to use a standard file selection dialog box to locate the file.

NOTE An URL is a Uniform Resource Locator, the type of address that is used to locate Web pages and other resources on the Internet. For more information on URLs and locating information on the Internet, see Chapter 26, "Working with Web Pages." ■

4. If you want to link to a specific location in the destination document, type the name of the location in the Named Location text box. To see a list of the available locations in the destination document, click the Browse button next to the text box.

NOTE The kind of locations available in other documents vary by the type of document. If the destination document is a Word document, for example, you can specify a bookmark name that has previously been defined in the document. If the destination document is a PowerPoint presentation, you can type the name of a slide as it is contained in the title area of the slide. If the destination file is an Excel workbook, you can select a range name or other named location in the workbook. ■

5. Select OK to complete the command. The hyperlink is placed in your worksheet at the location you selected.

Figure 24.19 shows the result of creating a hyperlink using this process. Notice that the mouse pointer has changed its shape to the familiar pointing hand shape that a Web browser uses. Excel also displays a ToolTip next to the mouse pointer, showing the details of the hyperlink.

FIG. 24.19
When you point to a hyperlink, the mouse pointer changes, and a ToolTip appears.

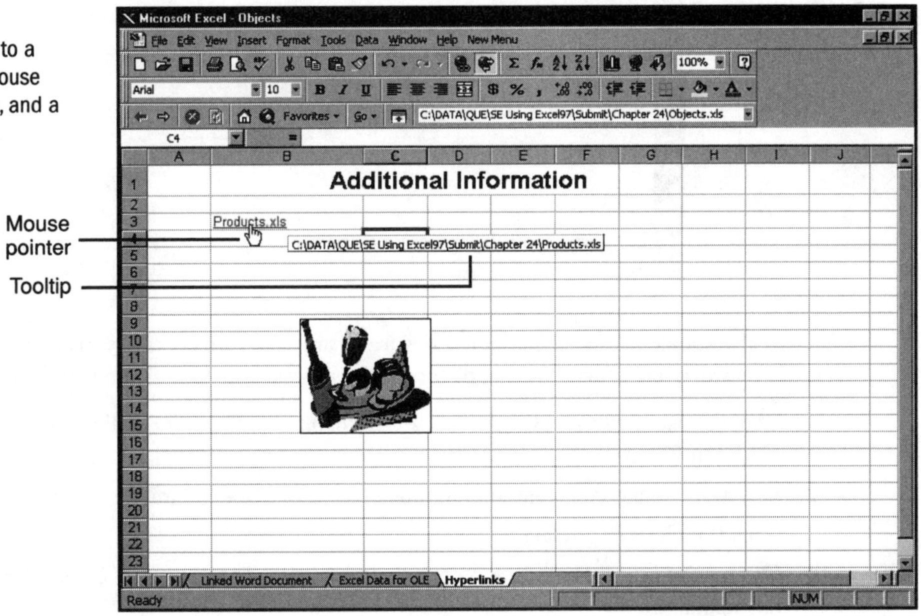

The text that appears as the hyperlink is provided automatically by Excel when you create a link in a blank cell. You can control the text that appears as the hyperlink by typing it first, then creating the link.

1. Type the text in a cell in your worksheet as you want it to appear in the link.
2. Choose the Insert Hyperlink button on the Standard toolbar. The Insert Hyperlink dialog box appears.
3. Complete the Insert Hyperlink dialog box, indicating the file and the named location for the link.
4. Select OK to complete the command. The hyperlink is placed in your worksheet at the location you selected with the text you typed as the hyperlink text.

Figure 24.20 shows a hyperlink that was created by typing the text for the link in a cell before creating the link.

FIG. 24.20
This hyperlink was created with text that was previously typed in the cell.

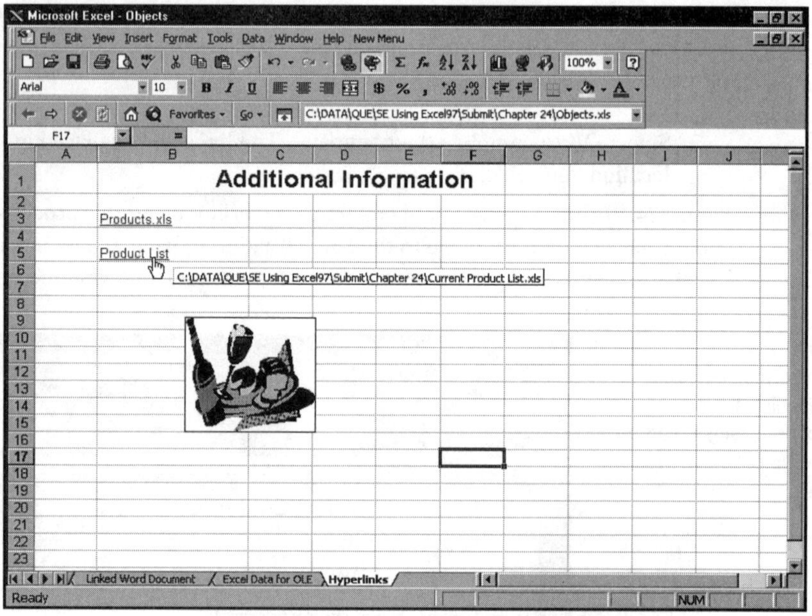

You can also create a hyperlink using a picture or any other object that you've embedded in your Excel workbook. Sometimes a picture is the easiest way to indicate what you're linking to.

1. Choose Insert, Picture, Clip Art. The Microsoft Clip Gallery 3.0 dialog box appears, as shown in Figure 24.21.
2. Select the image you want, then choose Insert to place the image in your worksheet.
3. Click the picture to select it.
4. Choose the Insert Hyperlink button on the Standard toolbar. The Insert Hyperlink dialog box appears.
5. Complete the Insert Hyperlink dialog box, indicating the file and the named location for the link.
6. Select OK to complete the command. The hyperlink is defined for the picture.

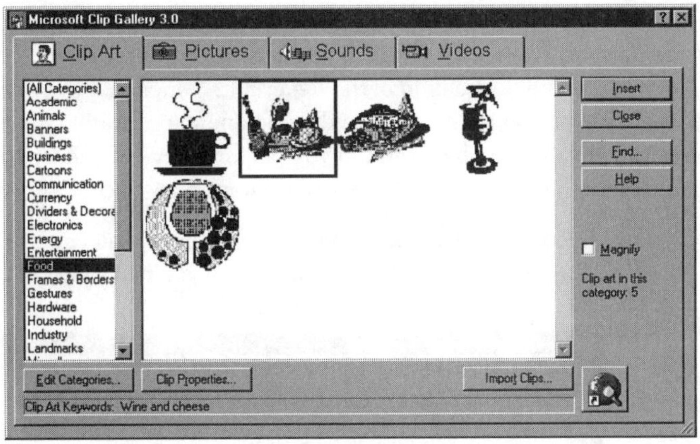

FIG. 24.21
Use the Microsoft Clip Gallery to select an image to place in your worksheet.

Figure 24.22 shows the appearance of a hyperlink that is created for a picture on a worksheet.

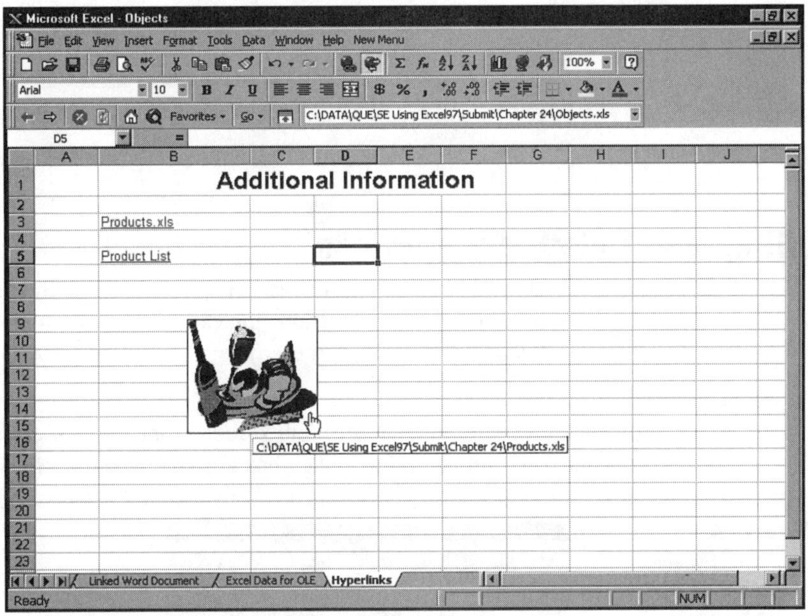

FIG. 24.22
A picture can serve as a hyperlink to another Office document.

Following the Link: Browsing in Office 97

Once you've created a hyperlink, you can use that link at any time to jump to the destination of the link. To follow the link, simply point to the hyperlink and click it.

The document at the destination of the hyperlink opens and displays. If the document belongs to another application, that application opens as well. The destination document might also contain hyperlinks, which you can follow by clicking them. In this manner, you can get to a lot of different information by following a few well-organized links.

When you follow a hyperlink, the Web toolbar appears if it wasn't already displayed. The Web toolbar has buttons with which you can easily navigate among documents. Figure 24.23 shows the Products table, the destination of the hyperlink. Notice that the Back button is now active. Clicking the Back button returns you to the document, or location, that you were viewing before you performed the last hyperlink. If you perform several consecutive hyperlinks, you can use the Back button repeatedly to retrace your steps back to the original location.

After you have clicked the Back button one or more times, you can use the Forward button to move "ahead" to the destination location from which you just returned.

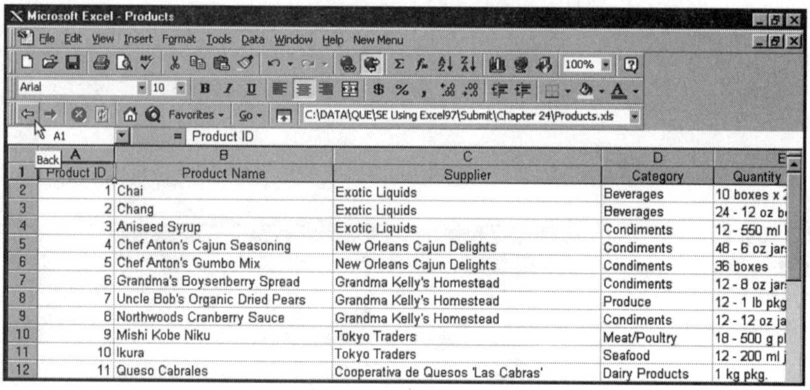

FIG. 24.23
Use the Back button to return to the document you were viewing before you activated a hyperlink.

Editing and Deleting Hyperlinks

After you have created a link, you might need to change or delete the link. If the destination document has been moved to a new location, you can edit the link to point to a new location. If you delete the destination document, you can delete the link to prevent an error from occurring when you try to link to the file.

1. Right-click the hyperlink. On the context menu that appears, choose Hyperlink, Edit Hyperlink. The Edit Hyperlink dialog box appears, as shown in Figure 24.24.

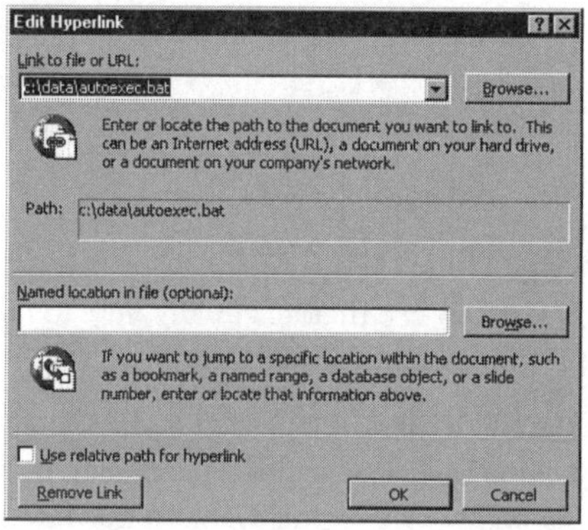

FIG. 24.24
Use the Edit Hyperlink dialog box to change or delete a hyperlink.

2. To change the destination for a hyperlink, type a new destination in the Link to File or URL text box, then choose OK.
3. To delete the hyperlink, choose Remove Link.

NOTE To edit or delete a hyperlink from an embedded object, such as a picture, you must first select the object by right-clicking it. The context menu for objects does not have a Hyperlink command. Instead, choose Insert, Hyperlink from the main menu of Excel to display the Edit Hyperlink dialog box. ■

When you remove a hyperlink, the text or object that contained the link remains in the worksheet. You can choose to leave the text or object there or to delete it.

Sharing Data Between Excel and Word

Word and Excel are probably the two most commonly used applications in Office 97 and are common candidates for sharing data using OLE. Because you can use both applications as both servers and clients, you can embed and link objects from either application into the other.

Using Word Objects in an Excel Workbook

Word provides two object types that you can embed in Excel or any other OLE-aware application. The most commonly used object is a Word document. As you might expect, a Word Document object contains all the normal word processing features of Microsoft Word. You will find that using the Word Document object in your Excel workbooks is especially useful when you need large passages of formatted text because the object enables you to use Word's advanced formatting features.

NOTE For simple, formatted text passages in an Excel workbook, you can place a Textbox object by using the Drawing toolbar. Use Word when you need more elaborate formatting or when you are using formatted text that is already created in Word.

For more information on the Drawing toolbar, see Chapter 13, "Drawing with Excel." ■

The second object type that Word can provide is a Word Picture object, which you can create by using Word's Drawing tools. Because the same tools are available in Excel, it is not very likely that you'll need to use OLE to embed a Word Picture object.

Using Excel Ranges in a Word Document

It is a common requirement to use financial or other numeric data in many types of reports you may develop in Word. If you have created the data in Excel, you can use an embedd linked Excel object in a Word document. Use any of the techniques described earlie chapter to place an Excel spreadsheet range, or an Excel chart, in any Word docu

Working with PowerPoint

PowerPoint presentations may benefit from supporting numeric data and charts that you develop in Excel. You can create Excel objects in a PowerPoint presentation either by copying the Excel data into a PowerPoint slide or by using the Insert, Object command from PowerPoint.

One thing to keep in mind when embedding Excel ranges in PowerPoint is that a PowerPoint slide has a fairly limited size. It is usually a good idea to use a limited amount of data on a PowerPoint slide so the slide doesn't become too hard to read.

You can also place PowerPoint presentations in an Excel workbook, which enables you to use Excel as a launcher for your PowerPoint presentations. The embedded presentation displays only the initial slide of the presentation when it is embedded in an Excel workbook.

Partnering Access and Excel

Excel has some built-in database capabilities, so you might wonder why you would have to bother using Access with Excel. Access has many advanced features for managing databases that go beyond the limited database features of Excel. Some of Access's major advanced features include the following.

- Access tables and attached tables can hold much larger amounts of data than an Excel worksheet, and Access is optimized to perform more efficiently than Excel when handling large amounts of data.
- Access has a system of indexes and keys that provide very rapid access to data for both look-up and sorting purposes. This system makes Access much more flexible than Excel for managing large, complex sets of data.
- Access is a *relational database management system*, which makes it very adept at managing complex relationships between multiple tables of data. Excel's database features are mainly used for working with a single database table at a time.
- Access has a very powerful *querying* capability built in. Querying allows you to ask complex analytical questions regarding the data in one or more tables. You can save and

e. While some of this capability is available to Excel
they are not as closely integrated as the querying tools in

d reporting tools that work closely with the tables and
se tools are optimized with many features designed for
as well as for performing common database operations,
ization.

ing multiuser applications, providing locking features that
m editing the same data simultaneously.

organizations store large amounts of strategic data in Ac-
manages very large sets of data as its primary function,

especially those involving multiple tables of related data, may be more appropriately designed as an Access application than as an Excel application.

When to Use Access and Excel

Consider usingAccess as your primary development tool when your application requirements include any of the following items:

- Large sets of data, organized into multiple tables
- Many reports that have to be generated from the same data
- Multiple users simultaneously performing data entry, querying, and reporting
- Access to remote data sources, such as SQL Server or mainframe data

Even if you have decided to use Access as a primary application development tool, you can still use Excel for certain operations. Excel is especially adept at some tasks with which Access may not be as familiar:

- Flexible calculations and what-if scenarios
- Ad hoc calculations and reporting with Excel Pivot Tables
- Charting using Excel's extensive graphing facilities

Unfortunately, you can't simply insert an Access object in your Excel workbook. The primary way to get data from Excel is by using the MS Query tools that you access by using the Data, Get External Data command. For more information on using this command, see the next section "Using MS Query with Access Data".

Another way to get data from Access to Excel is by exporting a table or query. Access can convert a table or query directly to an Excel file.

1. In Access, select the table or query that you want to export.
2. Chose File, Save As/Export. The Save As dialog box appears.
3. Select To an External File or Database, and click OK. The Save In dialog box appears.
4. Type a file name for the Excel file, and select Microsoft Excel 97 in the Save as type list. Click OK to save the table or query as an Excel file.

The new Excel file contains the field names in the first row and data records in the rows immediately below the first row of the sheet.

To use as a shortcut, you can select a table or query in Access and select the Analyze It with MS Excel tool on the Access toolbar. The current table or query opens in Excel.

Using MS Query with Access Data

Another way to use Access data in Excel is to use the querying tools that come with Office 97. A *query* is a request for data from a database. Excel 97 uses the Microsoft Query Wizard, which is included with Office 97, to create and execute queries against data stored in an Access database, which might be stored on your hard drive or on your company's network.

You can store the queries you create with Microsoft Query for later use. Each time you use a query to get external data, Microsoft Query retrieves the latest data from the Access database. The query you create can contain logic that determines which records are selected and which fields are to be included in the result.

NOTE Microsoft Access data is stored in tables. A table is a collection of related information, and a single Access database can contain many tables. For example, in the Northwind sample database that comes with Access, there are separate tables for employees, customers, products, and orders, as well as several others.

Each table is organized in rows and columns. Each row in a table is called a record. A record contains all the information about one item in the table. In the Employees table, for example, there is one record for each employee. The columns of the table are called fields. There is a field for each type of information that is stored. In the Employees table, there are fields for each employee's first name, last name, employee ID, phone extension, and several other items. ■

CAUTION

The amount of data that you return from an Access database can be very large. You should always save your Excel workbook before creating a query in case the operation can't be completed.

It is also a good idea to set aside a large area, preferably on its own sheet, for the data returned by a query so you don't accidentally overwrite any other data in your workbook.

Creating a Query with the Query Wizard

To use Access data in an Excel workbook, you can create a query using the Microsoft Query Wizard.

1. Select the location in the workbook where you want the results to appear. Because the results that are returned might be a large amount of data, it is a good idea to dedicate a sheet to the query.
2. Choose Data, Get External Data, Create New Query. The Choose Data Source dialog box appears, as shown in Figure 24.25.

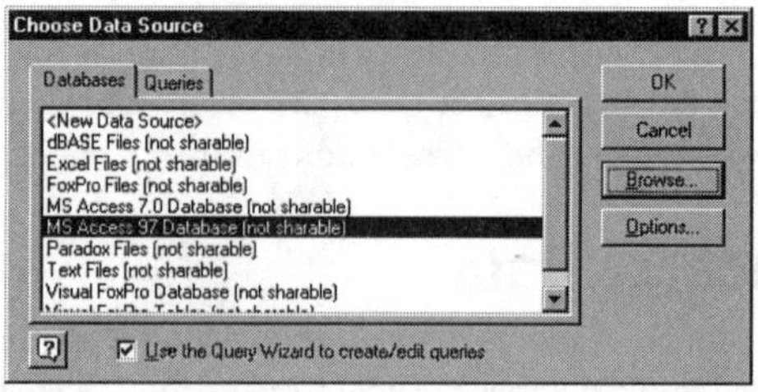

FIG. 24.25
You can get external data from any data sources that are installed on your computer.

3. Select the data source that contains the data you want to query, then choose OK. The Select Database dialog box appears, as shown in Figure 24.26.

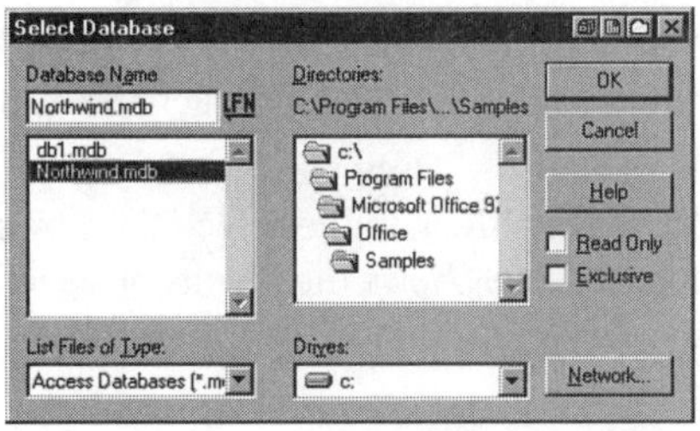

FIG. 24.26
You can select the database from your hard drive or your network.

4. Select the database, then choose OK. The Query Wizard dialog box appears, as shown in Figure 24.27. The names that appear in the Available tables and columns list include the tables and queries that are stored in the Access database you selected.

NOTE If you have enabled security features on the Access database, you are required to enter the password to give you permission to open the database. This is true for Access databases as well as for data from other sources, such as Microsoft SQL Server.

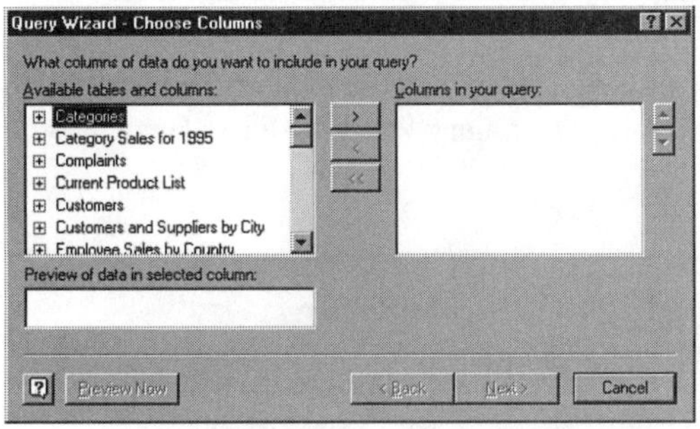

FIG. 24.27
Use the Query Wizard to select the columns in the query result.

5. Select the columns of data that you want to appear in the result set. To select an entire table or query, select the table name in the Available Tables and Columns list, then click the > button to move the fields from the table to the Columns in Your Query list. Figure 24.28 shows the result of selecting the Customers table.

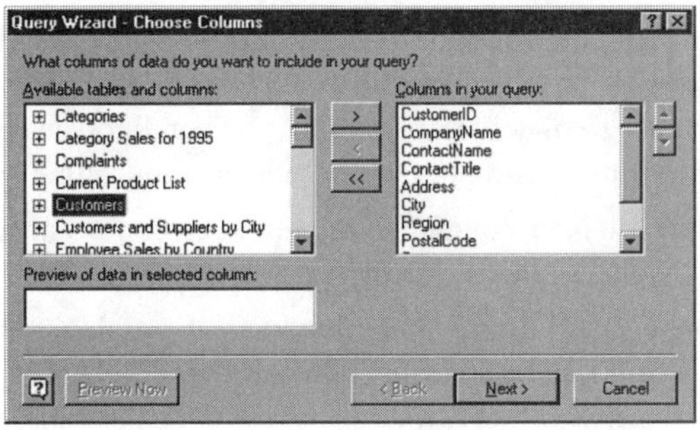

FIG. 24.28
The fields from the Customers table have been selected for the result set.

Part VI
Ch 24

To remove a field from the selected columns, select the field, then click the < button.

To remove all the fields from the selected columns, click the << button.

To select fields individually, click the + symbol next to the table or query name. Then select the fields individually, moving them to the selected list by clicking the > button or by double-clicking them. Figure 24.29 shows the results of selecting just a few fields from the Customers table.

FIG. 24.29
Only a few fields from the Customer table have been selected for the query results.

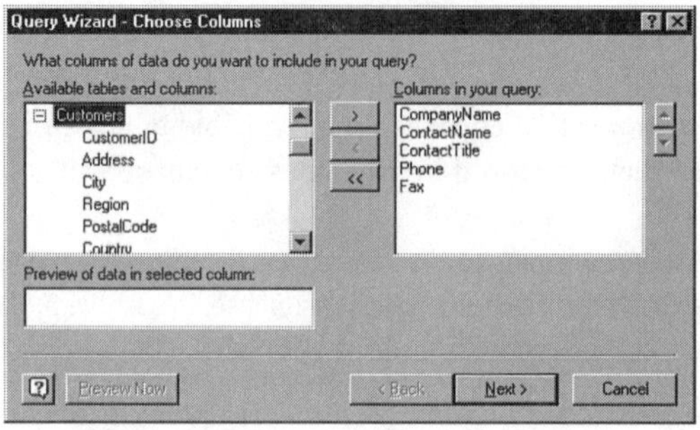

6. When you have completed selecting columns for the result, choose Next to continue with the Query Wizard. The Query Wizard—Filter Data dialog box appears, as shown in Figure 24.30.

FIG. 24.30
Use the Filter Data dialog box to determine which rows the Query Wizard should return.

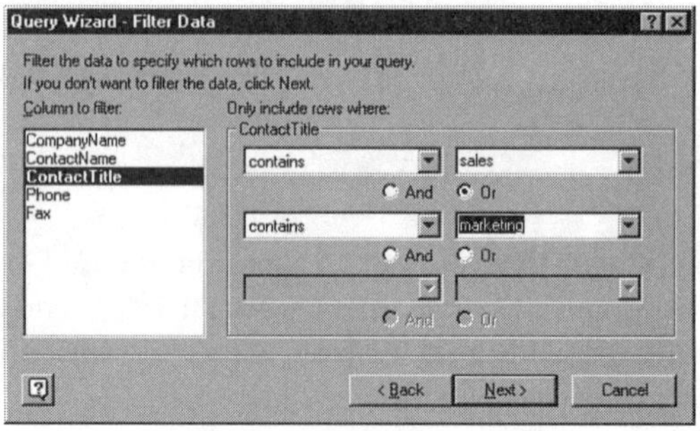

7. If you want to return all the rows in the table or query, you don't have to make any selections in this dialog box. To limit the results, select a condition, known as a filter, to limit the rows that are returned. For example, the condition selected in Figure 24.30 limits the results to those customers whose title contains either "sales" or "marketing."
8. Choose Next when you have completed the filter selection. The Query Wizard—Sort Order dialog box is displayed, as shown in Figure 24.31.
9. Select one or more records to use as sorting keys. If you don't make any selection in this dialog box, the records will be returned in whatever order Access uses to store them. The example in Figure 24.31 sorts the results by company name then by the name of the contact.

FIG. 24.31
Using the Sort Order dialog box, you determine the order of the rows that the Query Wizard returns.

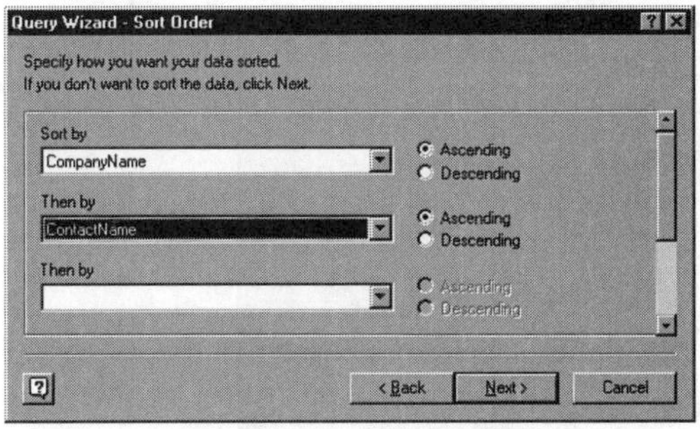

10. Choose Next when you have completed your Sort Order selection. The Query Wizard—Finish dialog box is displayed, as shown in Figure 24.32.

FIG. 24.32
Use the Finish dialog box to select whether you want to perform further customization with the Query Wizard or to return the results immediately to Excel.

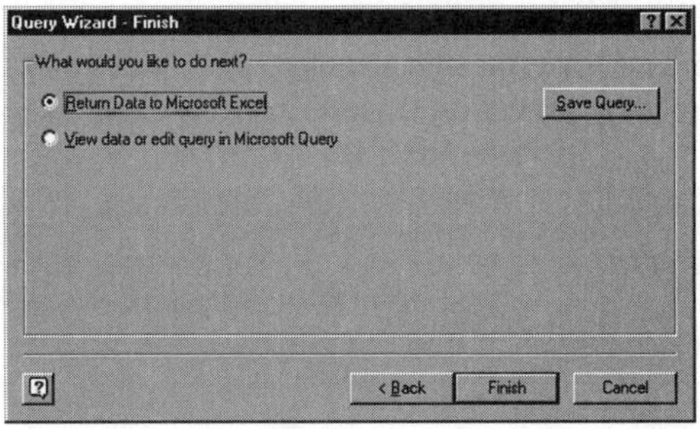

11. Choose whether you want to return the results immediately to Excel or to edit the query further in Microsoft Query. If you want to save the query for later use, Choose Save Query.
12. Choose Finish when you have completed your selection.
13. If you chose to return the data to Microsoft Excel, the Returning External Data to Microsoft Excel dialog box appears, as shown in Figure 24.33.

FIG. 24.33
When you return the data to Excel, you have the choice of where you want to place the results.

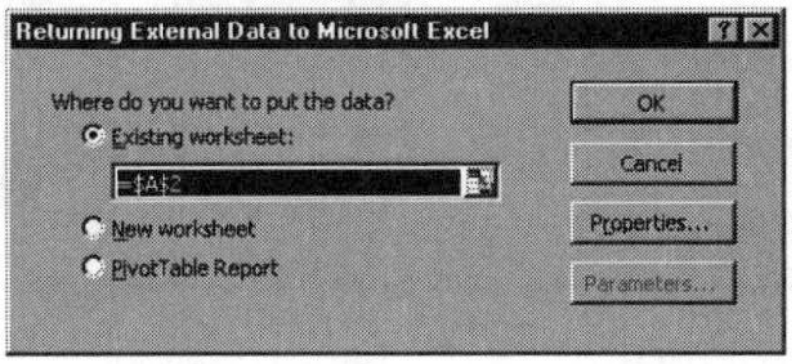

14. Select the destination for the results of the query. You can place the results in the current worksheet, a new worksheet, or in a pivot table.
15. If you want to view or change any of the properties of the query, choose Properties before completing this dialog box. The External Data Range Properties dialog box is shown in Figure 24.34. Choose OK to complete this dialog box.

FIG. 24.34
Using the External Data Range Properties, you determine the behavior of the data after you place it in your workbook.

16. Select OK to complete the command and place the results in the workbook. Figure 24.35 shows the data from the Access database as it appears in the Excel workbook.

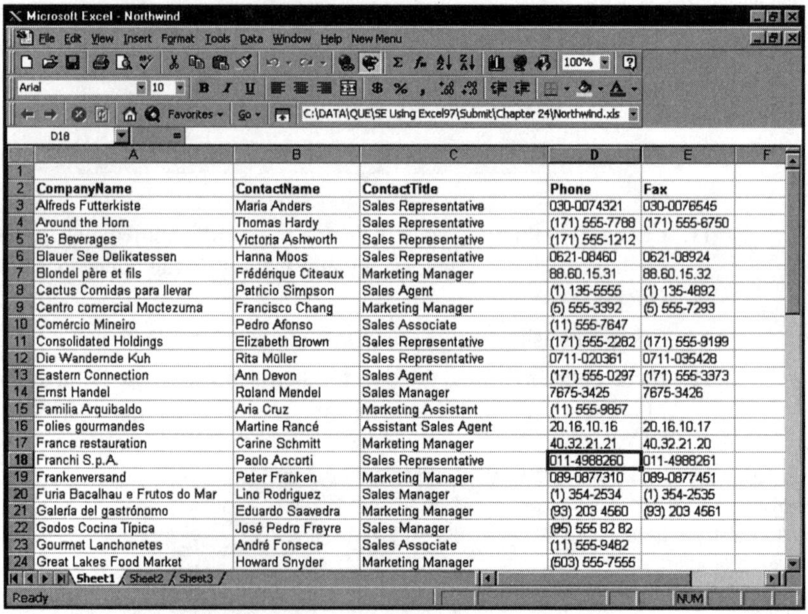

FIG. 24.35
The result of a database query displays the data from the Access table.

Understanding the Query's Properties

During the process of creating a query for external data using the Query Wizard, you had the option of modifying several properties of the query. You can display the External Data Range Properties dialog box at any time after you have completed the query by choosing Data, Get

External Data, Data Range Properties. It is important that you understand the purpose of these properties before making any changes to them.

- The Name property declares a range name that is used for the entire table.
- If you uncheck Save Query Definition, Excel does not maintain a link to the Access database, and the data can't be updated automatically.
- If you uncheck Save Password, you will be required to enter the password for the Access database each time Excel and Microsoft Query attempt to update the data. If you leave the box checked, Excel stores the password and enters it for you automatically.
- If you check Enable Background Refresh, the query runs in the background allowing you to do other work while the query is performed. This process is useful because some queries can take a long time to execute.
- If you check Refresh Data on File Open, Excel will update the external data automatically each time you open the workbook. Otherwise, the data will be updated only when you request an update.

  Checking this property also activates the next check box, Remove External Data from Worksheet Before Saving. Turning this feature on reduces the size of your saved workbook.
- The Include Field Names property determines whether the field names are copied from the Access database. You might want to disable this feature if you are providing more descriptive field names than those in the original database.
- If you check Include Row Numbers, Excel adds a column of numbers indicating the sequence of the records that are returned.
- If you check Autoformat Data, automatic table formatting is applied each time the data is refreshed. If you uncheck this property, automatic formatting is not applied, preserving any local formatting you have applied.
- The Import HTML Table(s) Only property is only available if your external data is from an HTML source. Enabling this property excludes all nontable data from the external source. Disabling this property allows all text from the HTML source to be returned, with each paragraph of text returned to a separate cell.

NOTE HyperText Markup Language (HTML) is the most common form of data storage in an Internet page. For more information on working with Internet data, see Chapter 26, "Working with Web Pages."

The next property describes how Excel should modify the data range if the number of data rows changes when the data is refreshed. Records may have been added to or deleted from the Access database, resulting in a data range of a different size. The options follow:

- *Insert Cells for New Data, Delete Unused Cells.* This option has the advantage of leaving cells to the right or left of the external data range undisturbed.

- *Insert Entire Rows for New Data, Clear Unused Cells.* Because entire rows are inserted into the worksheet, data outside the external data range will be moved down if additional rows are returned.
- *Overwrite Existing Cells with New Data, Clear Unused Cells.* In this case, no new cells or rows are added, leaving existing data intact unless the additional data that is returned overwrites it.

TIP It is generally a good idea to use a separate sheet for returning external data because the amount of data that is returned can vary widely. Excel's capacity of more than 65,000 rows might seem like a lot of data storage, but an Access table can contain more than 2 billion records.

The last property, *Fill Down Formulas in Columns Adjacent to Data,* is useful when you have created formulas next to the external data range. If you check this property, additional copies of the formulas are automatically created if the query returns additional rows, and extra copies of the formulas are deleted if the query returns fewer rows.

Getting Updated Data from Access

Once you have created a link to an external data source, such as Microsoft Access, you can get an updated copy of the data as frequently as you wish. As you learned in the previous section, one method of updating the data is to set the property that automatically refreshes the data each time your workbook is opened. You might not select this property, though, for a couple of reasons. First, the update might take a long time, and if you want to work in another area of the workbook, you really don't need to wait for the external data to be refreshed. Second, you might not even be interested in the updated data. Suppose you are working on a monthly report. If you last refreshed the data at the end of the previous month, you probably don't want to include data that may be new or changed since the beginning of the new month.

In this case you can manually refresh the data as often as you like. Here's how:

1. Select all or part of the external data range.
2. Choose Data, Refresh Data. Microsoft Query opens the external data source, returning a fresh copy of the data to the external data range.

Using Microsoft Office Binder

Microsoft Office Binder is tool for assembling a collection of Microsoft Office documents for editing and printing. Suppose you are preparing a report that contains data from a variety of sources, such as Word documents, Excel workbooks, and PowerPoint presentations. Office Binder enables you to print the entire report in one operation with a consistent header and footer and with consecutive page numbering.

You can assemble a binder file from existing documents, or you can create new documents within the Binder. Once you save a binder file, you have easy access to the group of files in the binder through a single location.

Creating a Binder File

You can create a new Binder file in two easy ways. The first method uses the Office 97 shortcut bar.

- Click the New Office Document button on the Office shortcut bar. The New Office Document dialog box appears, as shown in Figure 24.36.

FIG. 24.36
Use the New dialog box to create a new binder file.

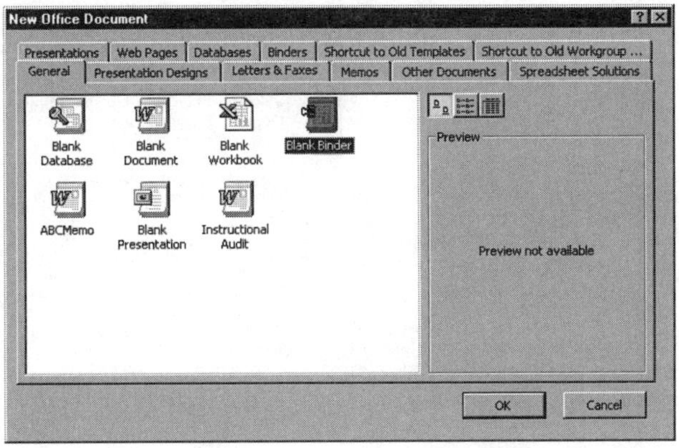

- Select Blank Binder and choose OK to create the binder file. The Microsoft Office Binder application window opens with a new binder file.

If you don't use the Office shortcut bar, you can start the Office Binder program from the Windows 95 Start menu.

- Choose Start, Programs, Microsoft Binder. The Microsoft Office Binder application window opens with a new binder file.

Adding an Existing File to the Binder

Each document in a binder file is stored in a separate section of the binder. To add documents to a binder, you add sections containing existing documents or newly created documents. If you have already created and saved the documents for your binder file, you can create sections for them in the binder file.

1. Choose Section, Add from File. A file section dialog box appears.
2. Select the file you want to add to the binder, then choose Add. The file is added to the binder. Figure 24.37 shows a new binder file with three existing Excel spreadsheets inserted.

TIP You can drag files from the Windows Explorer or from the desktop into the left pane of the Office Binder window.

The left pane of the Office Binder window displays icons representing the documents in the binder file. You can change the order of the documents in the binder file by dragging the icons up or down. The right pane of the Office Binder window displays the selected document. The menus in the right pane are a combination of the Office Binder menus and the menus of the applications that was used to create the the document.

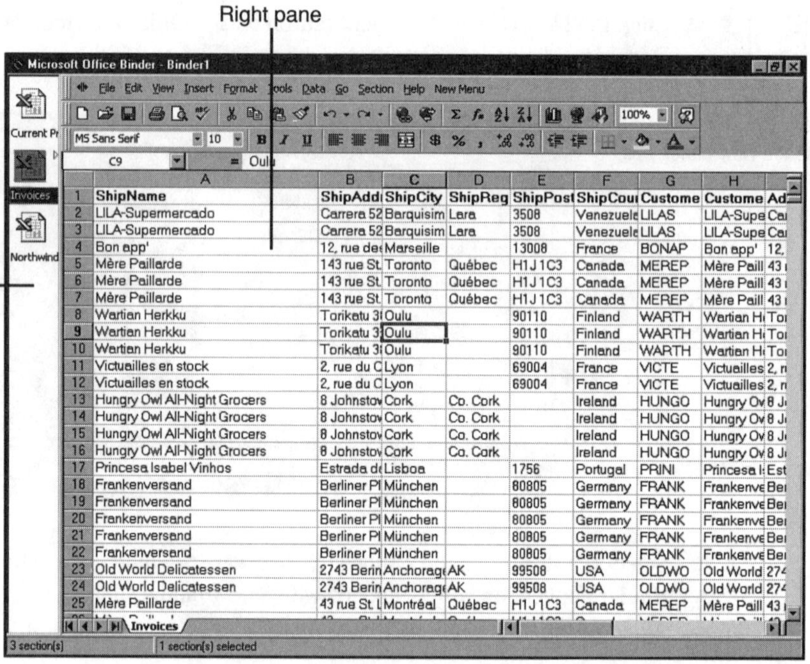

FIG. 24.37
The Office Binder displays the contents of Office documents in its application window.

Creating a New Document with the Binder

If you want to add a new document to the binder, you can create the document from within the Office Binder.

1. Click in the left pane of the binder window to select the location for inserting a new section. The new section will be inserted after the section you select.
2. Choose Section, Add. The Add Section dialog box is displayed, as shown in Figure 24.38. The icons that appear in the dialog box will vary depending on what applications are installed on your computer.
3. Select the icon for the document you want to create, then choose OK. The new blank document is added to the binder.

Printing with Office Binder

The Office Binder enables you to provide a consistent header or footer for a binder file and to control page numbering in the sections of the binder.

1. Select File, Binder Page Setup. The Binder Page Setup dialog box appears, as shown in Figure 24.39.

FIG. 24.38
The Add Section dialog box enables you to create a new document within a binder file.

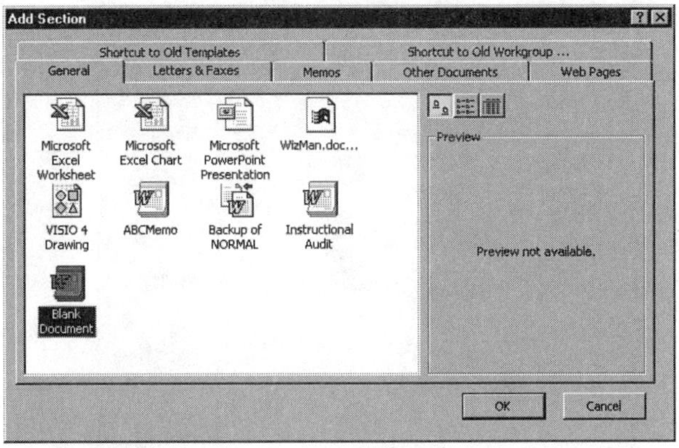

FIG. 24.39
Use the Binder Page Setup dialog box used to create headers and footers for an Office Binder file.

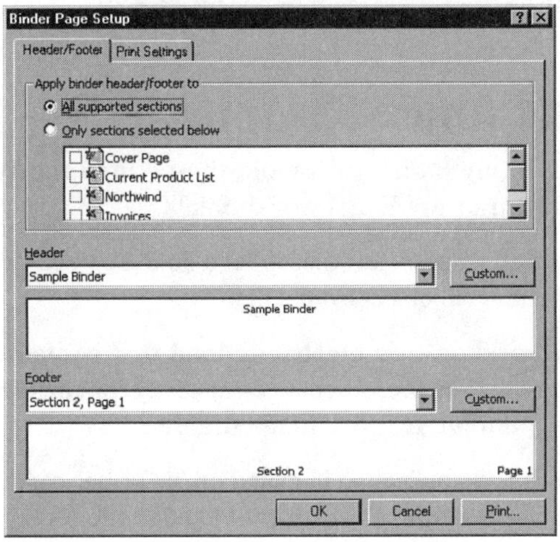

2. Select whether you want to set the header and footer for all supported sections of the binder or only selected sections.
3. Select a header and footer from the available lists or select the Custom buttons to create a customized header or footer.
4. To choose print settings for the binder file, select the Print Settings tab. The Print Settings page appears, as shown in Figure 24.40.
5. Choose the Print What option to indicate whether you want to print all visible sections of the binder or only those sections selected in the binder's left pane.
6. Choose the Page Numbering option to select whether you want consecutive numbering throughout the binder or you want to restart numbering for each section.
7. Then, to print, choose the Print button. To print later, choose OK.

You can print the contents of the binder at any time by choosing File, Print Binder.

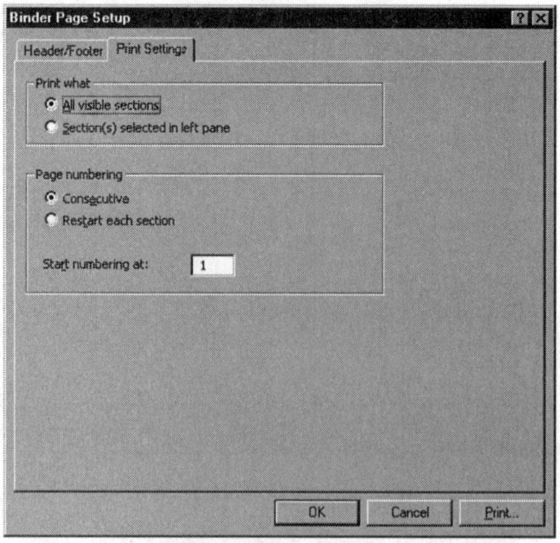

FIG. 24.40
The Print Settings page is used to print selected sections and to control page numbering.

Common Problems and Solutions

I placed a Word object in my Excel workbook, then edited the Word document. Why don't the changes show up in my Excel workbook?

You probably created an embedded object instead of a linked object. Create the object again, following the steps for creating an object from a file.

A coworker sent me a workbook via electronic mail that contained some embedded objects. When I double-clicked the objects, I got an error message and couldn't open the objects. What's happening? Did I damage the file?

Your coworker probably has an application installed on his or her computer that you don't have. When Excel tried to activate the object, it couldn't find the server application on your system. You didn't do any damage. Although you can't edit or activate the objects, they are still embedded in the workbook. You can edit the rest of the workbook and e-mail it back to him or her. The objects will still function on his or her system.

From Here...

In this chapter, you learned how Office 97 uses Object Linking and Embedding to share data among its applications. You can use data from other Office applications in your Excel workbooks, and you can use Excel data in your other Office applications.

- Chapter 25, "Integrating Excel with Any Other Applications," shows you how to use OLE with other non-Office applications and how to import and export data from Excel.
- Chapter 26, "Working with Web Pages," shows you how to use Excel to connect to the Internet and how to make your Excel workbooks available for use on the Internet.

CHAPTER 25

Integrating Excel with Any Other Applications

by Bill Ray

Microsoft Excel workbooks can work with the data from many other applications. In Chapter 24, "Integrating Excel with Other Office Applications," you learned how Excel can share data with other Office applications using Object Linking and Embedding (OLE). In this chapter, you'll learn to embed the objects from other programs in your Excel workbooks, and to import data from programs that can't create OLE objects.

You also may need to use the data in your Excel workbooks in other programs. This chapter will show you how you can export Excel data so that it can be used in other programs. ■

Linking to other applications

You'll learn how to identify the linking capabilities of other applications, and how to build, use, and update the links.

Using Object Linking and Embedding

You'll learn to use OLE with many different applications

Importing and exporting data

Use Excel's ability to import and export a variety of data formats, and use the File Conversion Wizard to convert several files at a time.

Object examples

You'll see several examples of using objects from other applications in your Excel workbooks.

Using Data from Other Applications

There are many reasons that you may need to share or exchange data with other applications. You may want to add features to your Excel workbooks, such as multimedia, or advanced drawing, that are not built-in features of Excel. You might need to include data that another user has entered into another application, or that has been downloaded from a mainframe computer. You also may need to make the data in your workbooks available to other users who don't use Excel.

Excel provides a variety of methods for meeting these requirements. You can select the method for sharing data with other programs based upon your needs and the ability of the other program to support these other features.

Working with OLE Objects

Many applications support the Object Linking and Embedding (OLE) technologies that are used by Excel and the rest of Microsoft Office. If a program uses OLE, you can use the same techniques that you learned about in Chapter 24 for working with these applications:

- Use the Insert, Object command to place an embedded or linked object created by the other program in your Excel workbook.
- Copy data from the other program to the Windows Clipboard, and use the Edit Paste Special command in Excel to select the appropriate data format for pasting into the workbook.
- Use Drag and Drop to place an object from another program into your Excel workbook.

Once you have placed an OLE object in your workbook, you can use the same techniques to work with the object that you can with an Office object:

- Click and drag the object to adjust its size and position.
- Right-click the object to use its shortcut menu for formatting, editing, and activation of the object.
- Double-click the object to activate the object. Depending upon the nature of the other application, activation may allow you to edit the object, play it, or perform some other activity that is relevant to that server application.

The applications that provide OLE features, such as linking and embedding, range from relatively simple applications such as media players and picture displays, to full-featured applications, such as graphics programs, word processors, and many other specialized applications.

Some OLE server applications are designed specifically for placing objects in an OLE client, and do not have the ability to save files on their own. An example is the Microsoft Equation Editor. You can't run the Equation Editor directly from the Windows Start menu. The only way to create an equation with the Equation Editor is to use an OLE client application such as Excel, and to use the Insert, Object command to create an embedded object. In this case, because you can't save the equation as a separate file, you can only create embedded equation objects, not linked objects.

In the section “Some Object Examples,” later in this chapter, you will see several examples of applications that can create OLE objects for use in your Excel workbooks. Some of these applications are accessories that come with Windows 95 or with Office 97. Others are independent applications that you may purchase separately.

Copying Excel Data to the Windows Clipboard

When you need to transfer data from Excel to another program, you might elect to transfer the data by copying with the Windows Clipboard, then pasting the data into the other application. This is one of the simplest and most direct ways to exchange data between two programs.

How the data will be received in the other program depends upon the ability of the other program to recognize the Excel data. Some other programs may let you paste an embedded or linked object, so that you can later activate the object and edit it with Excel. Other applications might not recognize the data as an Excel Worksheet object, but may be able to accept it in another format, such as text or as a bitmap.

When you copy data from Excel to the Windows Clipboard, Excel actually places several forms of the data in the Clipboard’s memory. You can examine the Clipboard contents by using the Clipboard Viewer accessory application that is included with Windows. Figure 25.1 shows the Clipboard viewer displaying some data that has been copied from an Excel workbook.

You can use the Display menu in the Clipboard Viewer to see a list of other data types that are stored on the Clipboard. Figure 25.2 shows the Clipboard Viewer with the Display menu open. As you can see from this figure, Excel copies an extremely large number of data types when it copies data to the Clipboard. This increases the likelihood that almost any other program will find some kind of data that it recognizes and can paste into its window or document.

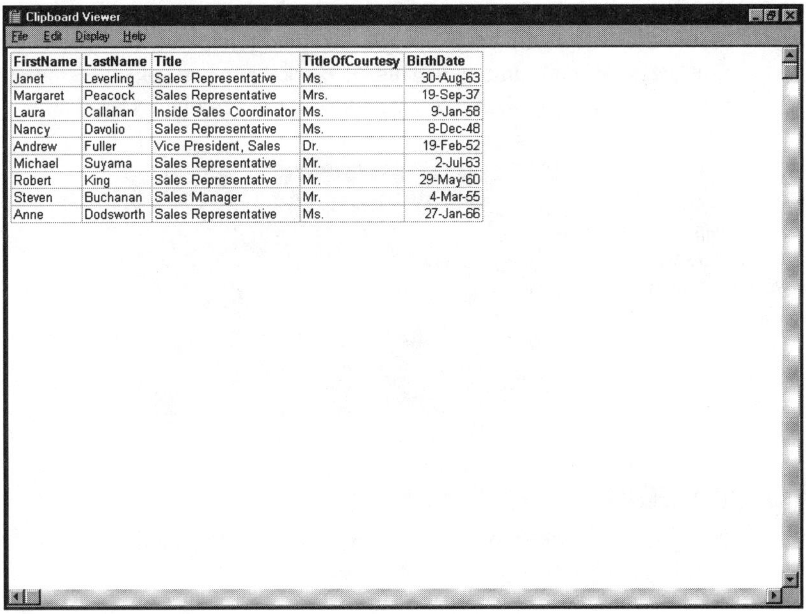

FirstName	LastName	Title	TitleOfCourtesy	BirthDate
Janet	Leverling	Sales Representative	Ms.	30-Aug-63
Margaret	Peacock	Sales Representative	Mrs.	19-Sep-37
Laura	Callahan	Inside Sales Coordinator	Ms.	9-Jan-58
Nancy	Davolio	Sales Representative	Ms.	8-Dec-48
Andrew	Fuller	Vice President, Sales	Dr.	19-Feb-52
Michael	Suyama	Sales Representative	Mr.	2-Jul-63
Robert	King	Sales Representative	Mr.	29-May-60
Steven	Buchanan	Sales Manager	Mr.	4-Mar-55
Anne	Dodsworth	Sales Representative	Ms.	27-Jan-66

FIG. 25.1
The Clipboard Viewer shows you the data that has been copied from any program to the Windows Clipboard.

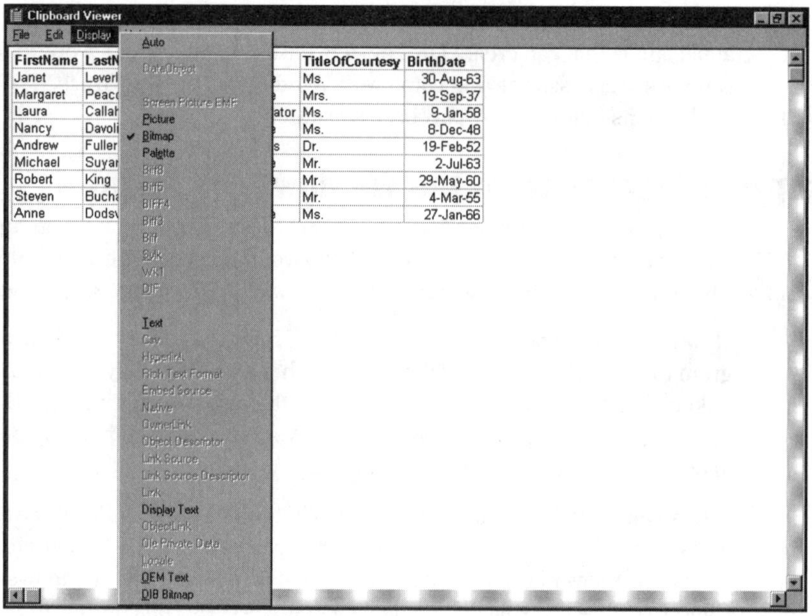

FIG. 25.2
The Display menu shows you what data formats are currently stored on the Clipboard.

When you use the Edit, Paste command that is available in just about any Windows program, that program looks through the list of data types that are available on the Clipboard, and selects the type that is most appropriate. For example, if you paste the Excel range into the Windows Paint program, the bitmap format is selected. If you paste the range into the Windows NotePad text editor, the text format of the data is selected.

Some programs have additional features to let you select the type of data that will be pasted. Figure 25.3 shows the Paste Special dialog box that WordPad displays when you select the Edit, Paste Special command. This dialog box lets you select the data type you want to paste, as well as whether you want to create a link to the original Excel file.

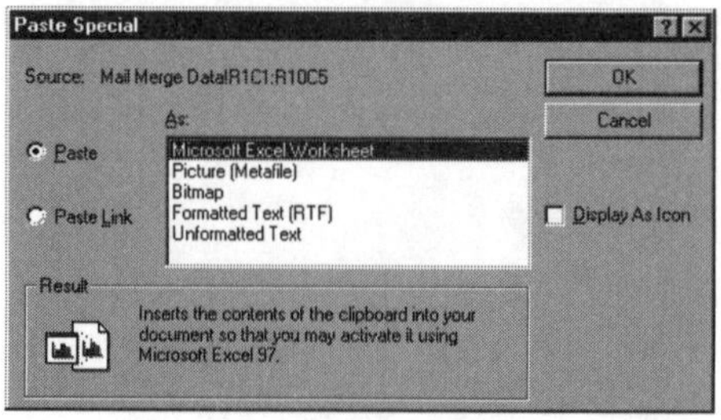

FIG. 25.3
The Paste Special dialog box in WordPad lets you choose the data type you want to paste from the Clipboard.

Importing Data from Text Files

It is not uncommon to receive text files that contain data that you need to use in Excel. These text files may come from a variety of sources:

- Mainframe computer reports are often captured and saved as text files, so you can use them on your personal computer.
- Many older programs, including word processors, databases, spreadsheets, and accounting packages may be able to export data to a text file format. In some cases, these files are created by allowing the other program to print its output to a file.
- Data contained in electronic mail messages or other files that have been transmitted to your computer may be in text file formats.
- Many text files are available for downloading or capture over the Internet.

Once you have identified that you have a text file to open, Excel automatically provides assistance in converting the file to an Excel spreadsheet. The challenge is to define how the data will be organized into rows and columns.

Many text files that contain rows and columns of data come in one of two common formats:

- *Delimited* text files contain some special character that defines the boundary between the columns of data. The two most common delimiting characters are commas and tab characters. Some programs that create delimited text files allow the user to specify the delimiting character, so almost any character can potentially be the delimiter. The following is an example of a comma-delimited text file.

```
,CompanyName,ContactName,ContactTitle,Phone,Fax
0,Alfreds Futterkiste,Maria Anders,Sales Representative,030-0074321,030-
0076545
1,Around the Horn,Thomas Hardy,Sales Representative,(171) 555-7788,(171)
555-6750
2,B's Beverages,Victoria Ashworth,Sales Representative,(171) 555-1212,
```

- *Fixed-width* text files are arranged so that each column lines up automatically. Instead of using a delimiting character to mark the column boundaries, each column has a designated width (often made up of spaces) as required by the data in that column. The following is an example of a fixed-width text file.

```
CompanyName           ContactName         ContactTitle          Phone
Alfreds Futterkiste   Maria Anders        Sales Representative  030-0074321
Around the Horn       Thomas Hardy        Sales Representative  (171) 555-77
B's Beverages         Victoria Ashworth   Sales Representative  (171) 555-1212
```

The process of importing a text file is like opening any other file.

1. Choose File, Open. The Open dialog box appears. In the Files of type list, select Text Files, so that you can see the text file instead of Excel files.

NOTE When you select Text File in the Files of Type list, Excel searches for files with a ".txt" extension. If the text file you want to import has a different extension, select All Files in the Files of Type list, and Excel displays all files no matter what their extensions.

2. Select the file you want to open and click OK. Excel automatically recognizes that the file you are opening is a text file, rather than an Excel workbook file. The Text Import Wizard dialog box appears, as shown in Figure 25.4.

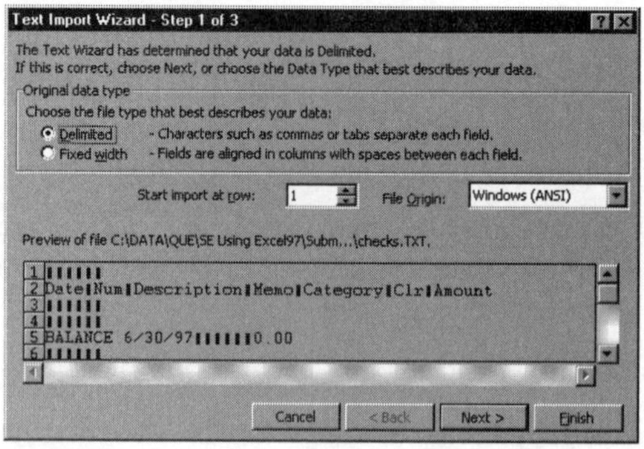

FIG. 25.4
The Text Import Wizard lets you select the type of text file you are opening.

3. Select either Delimited or Fixed width to indicate the type of file you are opening and click OK. If you are unsure which to choose, look at the Preview box to see which choice looks best. The next screen in the dialog box lets you preview the layout of the data in the imported text file.
4. Select the column delimiters for a delimited file as shown in Figure 25.5.
5. Select a text qualifier in this screen. The most common qualifier is the quotation mark ("). The qualifier is used to indicate the contents of a column. For example, a person's name that is entered in a column might be indicated as "John Smith" if the quotation mark is used as the qualifier. Click OK when you have made your selections.

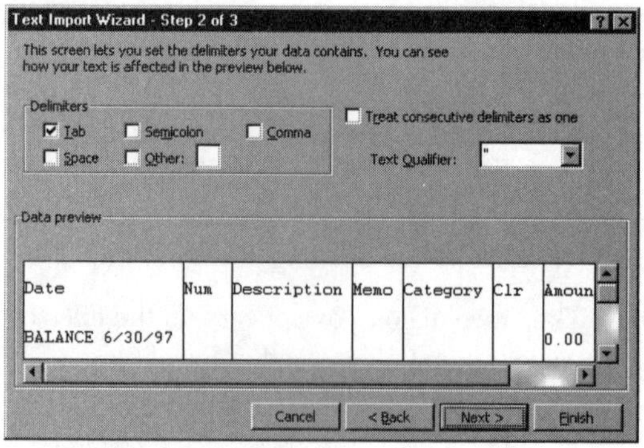

FIG. 25.5
The second step of importing a delimited text file is to select the delimiter character and a text qualifier.

6. Review the columns individually, confirming the data type of each column, or even choosing to skip over a column you don't want to import (see Figure 25.6). Click each column that is displayed in the dialog box and select the data type for the column by clicking the appropriate option button in the Column data format group.

NOTE The Text Import Wizard attempts to detect many of the attributes of the text file you are importing, such as the text qualifier and the data type of each column. However, it's a good idea to confirm the wizard's selections in case there are inconsistencies in the text file.

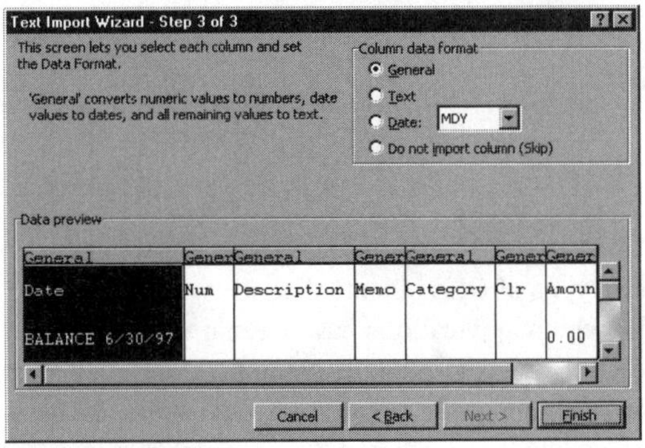

FIG. 25.6
The third step in importing text files is to confirm the data types of the individual columns.

7. Click OK when you have completed reviewing the columns, to proceed with the importing of the text file.

Once you have completed the importing process, you can save the workbook normally as an Excel workbook.

Exporting Data to Text Files

Just as you can use the Import Wizard to get text data into Excel, you can export your Excel data to a text file so that users who don't have Excel can use the data. Make sure that you know which type of text file is required by the user or program that will be receiving the file. This information can usually be found in the other application's documentation or Help files, or you might find it by experimenting with the application's importing options.

The method for importing text files into other applications varies with each application. Because the other application can even be a non-Windows program or a program that runs on a different type of computer, refer to the documentation of the other program for the text importing feature of the application. These steps indicate the basic procedure:

1. Activate the worksheet that you want to export to a text file. You can only export one sheet at a time.
2. Choose File, Save As. The Save As dialog box appears.
3. Type a name for the file and select the location where you want to save the file.
4. Use the Save as Type list to select the file format you want to create. The text formats are listed in Table 25.1.
5. Click OK to save the file in the selected format.

Table 25.1 Text File Formats You Can Select with the Save As Command

File Type	Description
Formatted Text (space delimited)	Creates a fixed-width text file
Text (Tab delimited)	Columns delimited by tabs
CSV (comma delimited)	Columns delimited by commas

Some Object Examples

The number of different types of OLE objects that are available to be inserted in your workbooks is limited only by which applications have been installed on your system. Each time you install a new application on your computer, its setup program may add one or more references in the Windows Registry, which lets Excel and other programs know what objects are available on the computer. This also lets Windows find the program that is needed when you want to activate the program.

The next few sections show some examples of objects that you might want to use in your workbooks.

Using Images in Excel

There are many sources of images that you can use in your applications. These images also come in many different file formats. There are many differences in the number of colors that an image format can display, as well as the quality of images that can be shown.

- Windows 95 and Office 97 both come with collections of clip art and other images that you can use in your document.
- Many other applications that you purchase and install on your computer come with libraries of artwork, clip art, and photographs.
- There are extensive libraries of images available for purchase on Compact Disk or other media.
- Many images are available for download from the Internet.
- Anything that you can display on your screen can be captured with screen capture software.
- You can use a scanner to convert your own photos, drawings, and other images into image files.
- Many commercial services will perform scanning and conversion of images to computer file formats.
- You can purchase hardware and software that lets you capture images from television, VCRs, and video cameras.

- Digital cameras are now available that let you take pictures without film, storing the images in memory that is in the camera. The images can then be transferred via cable to your computer.

No matter what the source of an image, it is easy to insert an image into your workbook.

1. Choose Insert, Picture, From File, as shown in Figure 25.7.

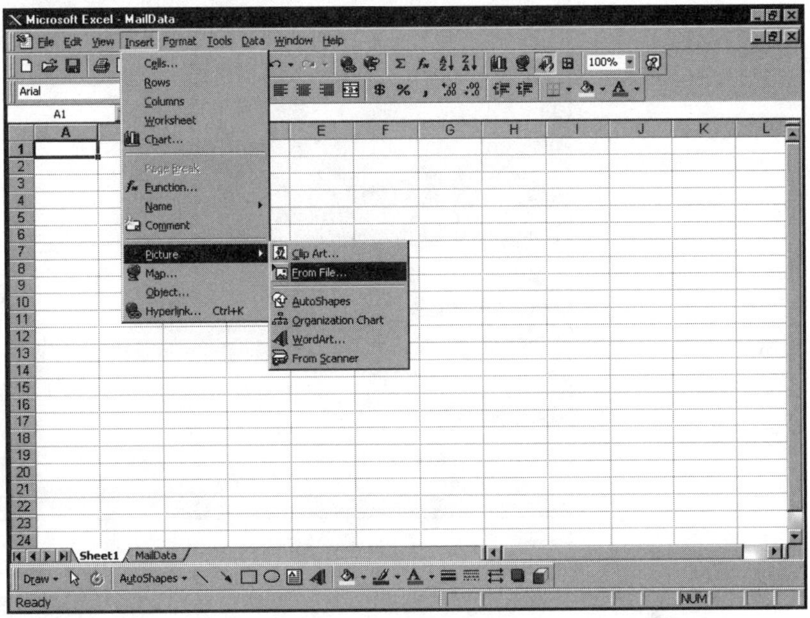

FIG. 25.7
The Insert Picture command lets you choose which type of picture you want to include in your workbook.

2. In the Insert Picture dialog box (see Figure 25.8), select the picture file you want to insert and click Insert.

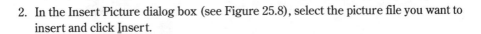

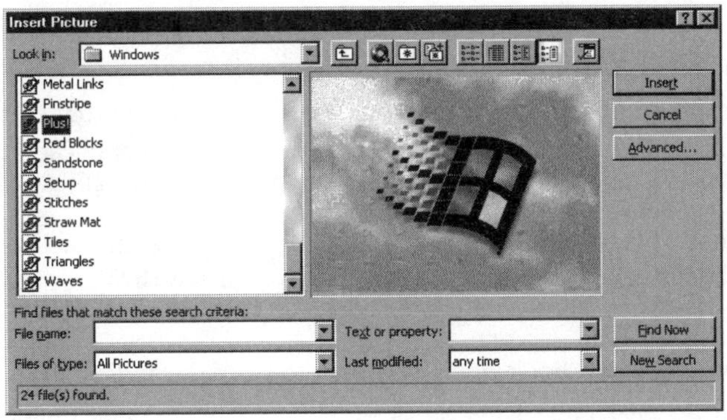

FIG. 25.8
The Insert Picture dialog box lets you preview your images before inserting them in a workbook.

3. The image is inserted into your workbook. Figure 25.9 shows a picture that has been inserted in a workbook.

▶ **See** "Managing Objects and Links," **p. 588**

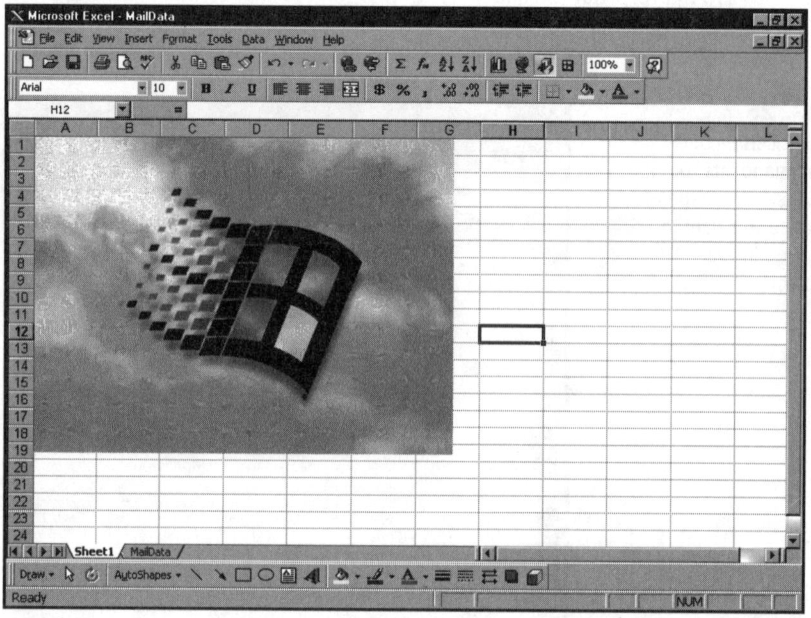

FIG. 25.9
An image in a workbook can be positioned wherever you want it.

> **CAUTION**
>
> Depending upon the source and type of the image files you use, they can be very large. If you add many large images to a workbook, the added memory and resource requirements may affect the performance of the workbook.

Using Sound and Video

Sound and Video clips can add even more interest to your workbooks. Sample audio and video files are included with Windows, as well as with many other applications. Many programs now include videos as part of the tutorials and help files that come with an application.

If your computer is equipped with a microphone, you can easily record an audio message in your workbooks, using the Sound Recorder that comes with Windows. To do so, follow these steps:

1. Activate the workbook where you want to place the audio object.
2. Choose Insert, Object and select Wave Sound as the Object type. Click OK to start the Sound Recorder. Figure 25.10 shows the Sound Recorder's window.

FIG. 25.10
The Sound Recorder can be used to create audio annotations in a workbook.

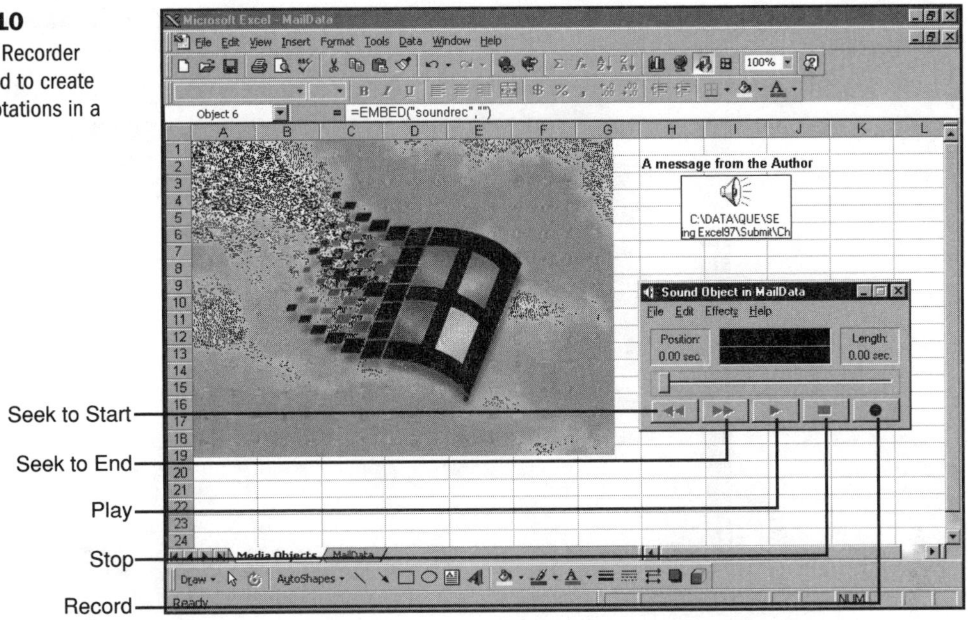

3. Use the recorder-style buttons to record and play back the audio object.
4. Choose File, Exit & Return to embed the audio object in your workbook.
5. An icon is placed in the workbook. To play back the audio object, double-click the icon.

Video files may be found on many CDs and are included with many programs. Creating your own videos requires additional hardware for converting the signal from your television, VCR, or video camera to a video file format. Once you have identified a video file, you can use the Insert Object to create either a linked or embedded object in your workbook. Figure 25.11 shows a video object that is embedded in a workbook. This is one of the instructional videos that comes with Windows. You can double-click the video object to play the video.

Creating Equations

The Microsoft Equation Editor, which is included with Microsoft Office, lets you create mathematical and scientific equations, chemical formulas, and other objects that would be difficult, if not impossible, to create directly in Excel.

The Equation Editor is activated with the Insert, Object command. Figure 25.12 shows the Equation Editor during the editing process. Clicking the buttons on the Equation Editor window gives you access to a variety of special symbols and frames for arranging the elements of an equation. The equation is edited directly in the Excel workbook, without opening a separate application window.

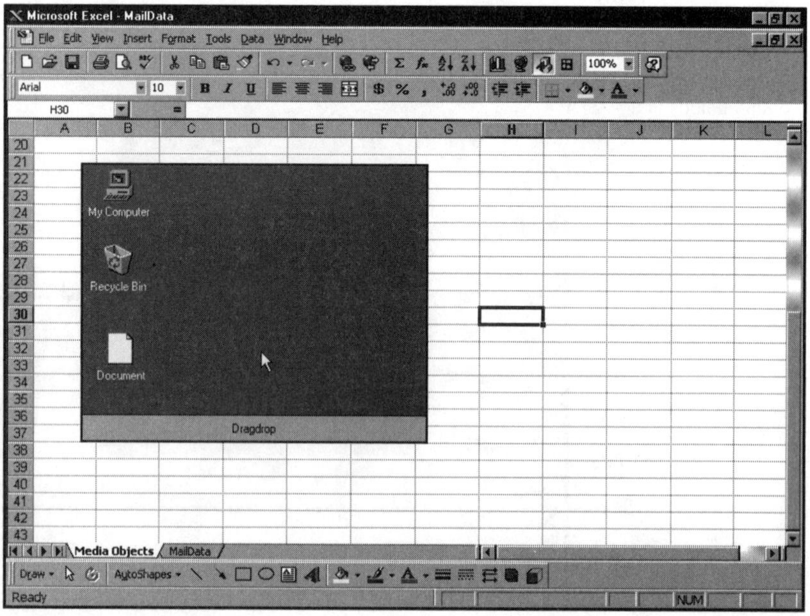

FIG. 25.11
A video object comes to life when you double-click it.

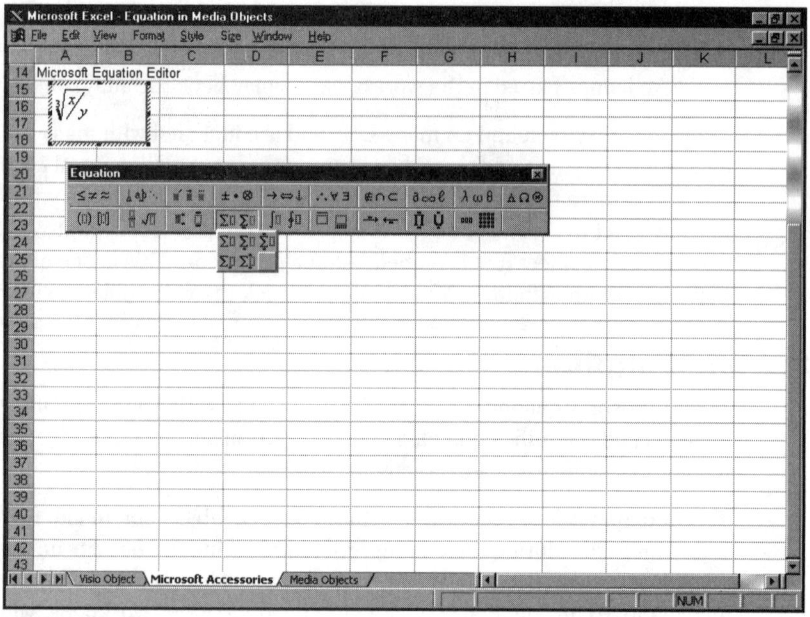

FIG. 25.12
The Equation Editor is used to create and modify equations.

The Equation Editor is used only to insert a new embedded object in a workbook—not to load the object from a file.

NOTE Some of the shared Windows applications, such as the Microsoft Equation Editor, are supplied by partners of Microsoft. These software companies often have more powerful versions of their applications available for separate purchase or upgrade. Information about these additional products is available from Microsoft in the online Help for the application and in the documentation. ■

Creating Organization Charts

The MS Organization Chart application lets you create a company organization chart, which can be embedded in the active workbook.

You can add boxes representing employees, draw lines to represent reporting responsibilities, and organize employees into groups. Figure 25.13 shows the Organization Chart window during the editing process. The chart is edited in its own application window.

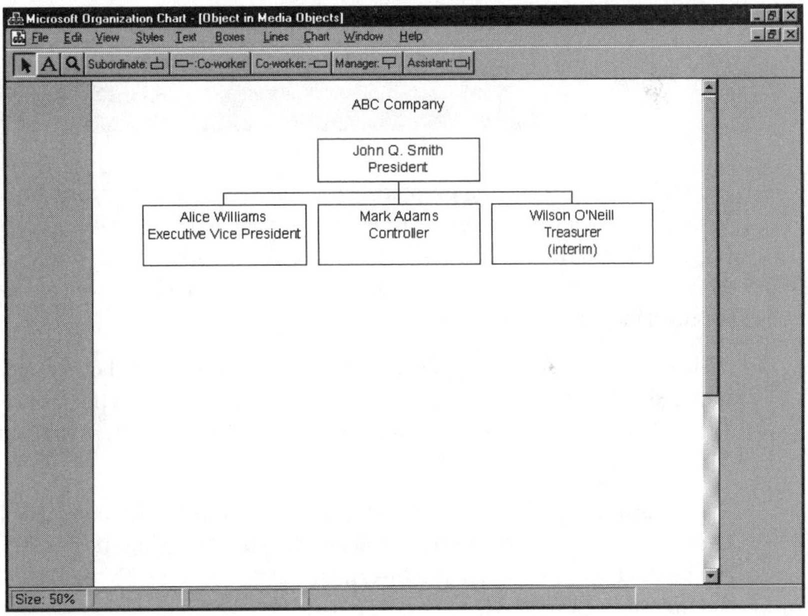

FIG. 25.13 The MS Organization Chart window is used to create and edit organization charts.

The Organization chart and equation objects display (see Figure 25.14) and print very naturally in the workbook.

▶ **See** "Creating Organization and Flow Charts," **p. 373**

Using Visio for Flow Charts and Diagrams

Whereas the accessory applications that come with Window and Office 97 are very convenient, you may want to use a more sophisticated tool for creating objects, such as charts, drawings, and multimedia. There are many commercially available applications that can create OLE objects which can be linked or embedded in your Excel workbooks.

FIG. 25.14
The finished organization chart and equation have been embedded in the workbook.

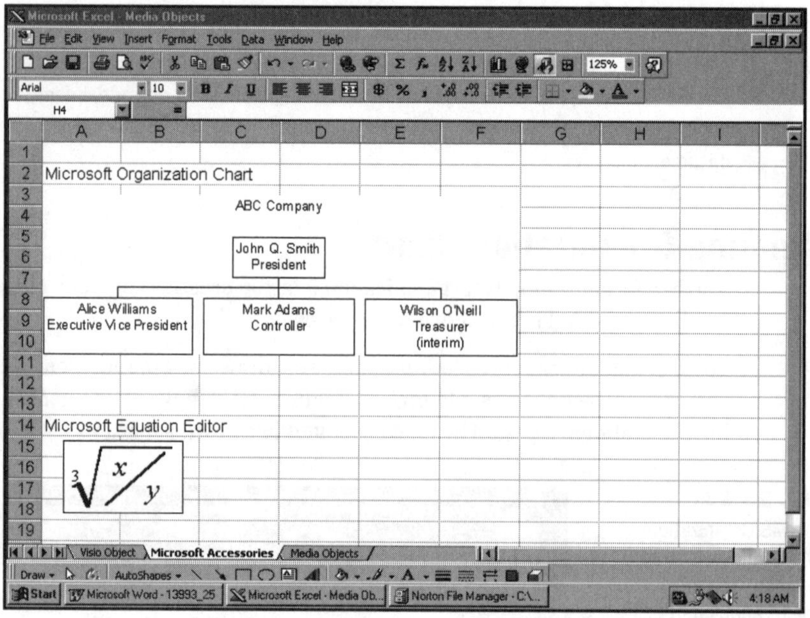

A popular tool for creating graphical OLE objects is Visio Corporation's Visio for Windows. Visio provides a wide variety of drawing templates and stencils for creating specialized drawings, such as flow charts, organization charts, blueprints, floor plans, maps, and many others. Additional templates and stencils are available from Visio, as well as some which are available for download from the Internet.

Visio drawings can store application data such as pricing and other application-specific information in the drawing. The latest version of Visio even includes the Visual Basic for Applications (VBA) programming language, so you can write VBA programs that automatically generate Visio drawings.

Visio drawings can be created directly in Excel by using the Insert, Object command with the Create New tab, or you can run Visio independently, saving the file in Visio's own file format. In the latter case, you can use the Insert, Object command with the Create form File tab to embed the object.

Figure 25.15 shows a Visio version of an organization chart that is embedded in a workbook.

Pasting Report Data from Quicken for Windows

Many valuable programs contain data that you might like to use in Excel, but do not support OLE embedding and linking. With programs such as these, you'll have to resort to techniques such as importing and exporting data, and copying data through the Windows Clipboard.

Intuit's Quicken for Windows is one of the most popular personal finance programs available. Using a checkbook-style window, you can enter all your financial transactions, including checks, withdrawals, deposits, interest, and investment accounts. You can categorize the data by budget accounts, and even export the data to tax preparation software for preparation of your annual tax return.

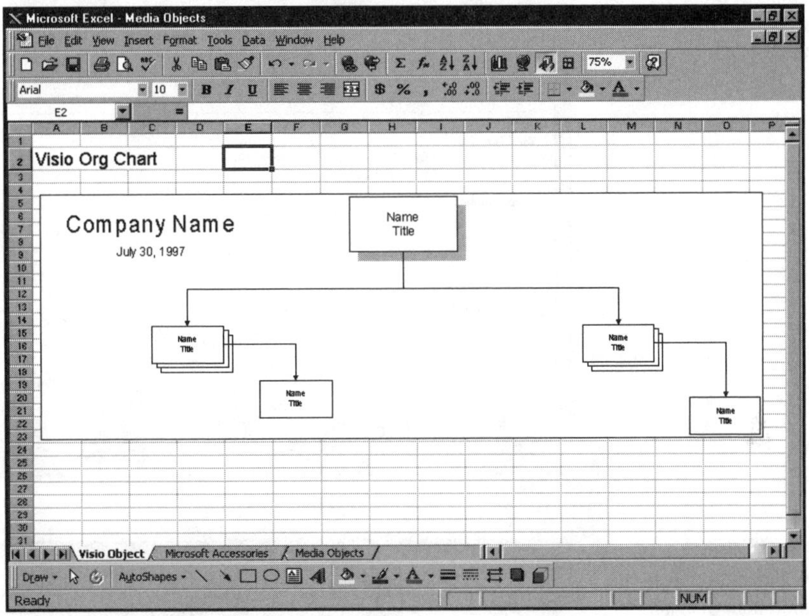

FIG. 25.15
A Visio drawing has many custom shapes and connectors for creating highly structured drawings.

Although Quicken has a lot of analytical power built-in, you may want to transfer some of the data to Excel for further analysis. Unfortunately, Quicken doesn't support OLE linking and embedding, and you can't manually copy and paste any significant amount of data directly from the Quicken check register.

There are two ways to get Quicken data into Excel:

- You can generate a Quicken report to the screen. Quicken then provides a Copy button that lets you copy the report output to the Windows Clipboard. Once you have the data in the Clipboard, you can paste it into Excel.
- Quicken also lets you print directly to a text file. You can select a delimited file format, which can be directly imported into Excel.

Figure 25.16 shows the Quicken report window, with an Itemized Categories Report displayed. The Copy button can be used to copy the report to the Windows Clipboard, so it can be pasted into Excel.

Figure 25.17 shows the same report after it has been pasted into Excel. As you can see from this figure, the report is not automatically formatted, but you can perform your own formatting on the Excel worksheet to improve the appearance.

FIG. 25.16
Quicken can generate a wide variety of automatic and memorized reports, based upon your financial data.

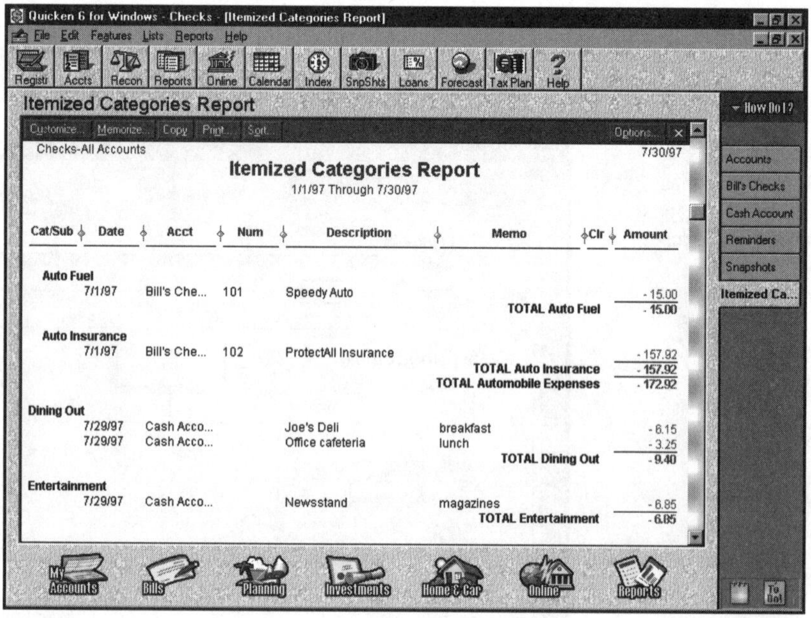

FIG. 25.17
The Itemized Category Report from Quicken has been pasted into Excel.

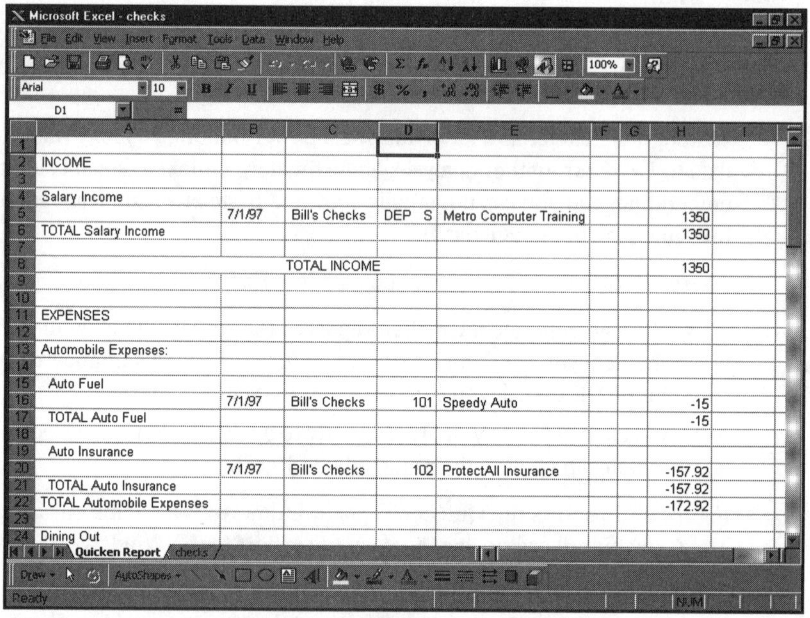

To export Quicken data to a delimited text file, you can choose Quicken's File, Print Register command, then click the Print button. The Print dialog box, shown in Figure 25.18, lets you select the destination for the printout. Select ASCII Disk File, or Tab-delimited Disk File to create the text file format you want to use and click OK to create the text file.

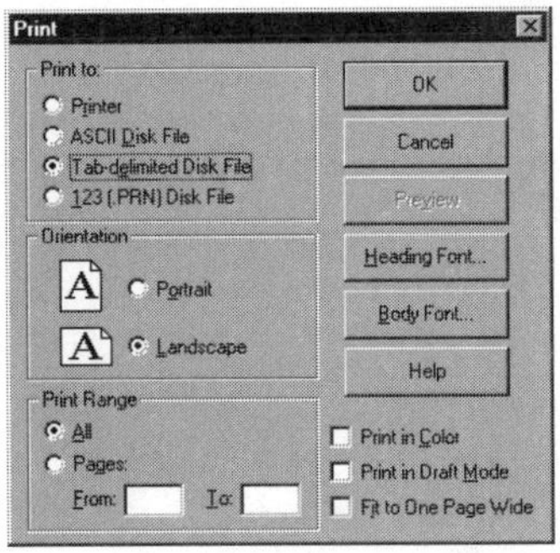

FIG. 25.18
The Print dialog box lets you choose a file as the destination of the Quicken printout.

Common Problems and Solutions

I used the Insert, Object command to create a new object with an application that is listed in the dialog box, but Excel can't seem to find the application. What's wrong?

You might have deleted the directory that contains the application without actually uninstalling the program. Because the information about the program is still in the Windows Registry, the program name appears when you choose Insert, Object. When you want to remove a program, make sure you use the Add/Remove Hardware icon in the Windows Control Panel. In order to use the object that isn't working, you'll probably have to reinstall the application.

How can I copy a multiple selection to the Clipboard?

You can't. There are several commands that Excel won't perform on a multiple selection, and copying is one of them.

I received a file with a .txt extension, but I can't import it using the Text Import Wizard. What's wrong?

It's possible that the file isn't a text file. Whoever created it may have mistakenly given the file a .txt extension even though it's not a text file. Check with whoever sent you the file to see what program it was created in and what file format was selected.

From Here...

This chapter showed you that Excel can share data with many different programs by embedding the OLE object created by those programs or by linking to the data files. You can share data with programs that don't support OLE by importing and exporting data in a text format or by using the Windows Clipboard.

- Chapter 26, "Working with Web Pages," shows you how to use Excel to connect to the Internet and how to make your Excel workbooks available for use on the Internet.

- Chapter 27, "Building Online Forms," shows you how to create interactive Web pages with Excel by using the Web Form Wizard to gather input from the persons who visit your Web site.

CHAPTER 26

Working with Web Pages

by Bill Ray

Until the late 1980s, the World Wide Web didn't exist. Today, the Web has become an integral part of our lives. Moreover, the technologies that it has spawned have been adapted to meet other computing needs. Organizations large and small have added intranets to their internal networks, making it easy for users to share information regardless of the type of computer that they are using.

Microsoft Excel 97, along with the other components of the Office 97 suite, incorporates many of these new technologies. This chapter and the next one will show you how to take full advantage of the Web-oriented features built into the program. ■

The concept and importance of intranets

The technologies spawned by the World Wide Web have been adapted to local and wide area networks, where they have been used to build intranets.

How Web technology has been integrated into Excel 97

Excel 97 is tightly integrated with Microsoft Internet Explorer and includes several features previously found only in Web browsers.

How to access and import information from a Web site

Excel's powerful new Web Query feature enables you to collect information from a Web site and import it directly into your workbook.

How to upload and download workbooks

Excel's Web capabilities make it easy to upload and download workbooks by using the FTP file transfer protocol or posting them to a Web page.

How to create hyperlinks to other documents

The hyperlink feature built into Excel 97 and other components of the Office 97 suite makes it easy to integrate your workbook with other documents.

Understanding Intranets

The purpose of a network, whether a Local Area Network (LAN) in a single facility or a Wide Area Network (WAN) linking several facilities, is to enable the people who use it to share information and resources. Most of us who have worked in an office environment are familiar with the benefits, as well as the limitations, of these types of networks.

Networking technology has made it possible to share files and resources, including software, more easily. Dedicated file servers have become an extension of your own system, providing disk storage space where you can upload and download files that you need to share with others. In some cases, where keeping information up-to-date is critical, you may work directly with files on the server. You can even run software directly from the network server, so that, in some cases, users can legitimately share licensed copies of software that they do not need to use all the time.

There are limitations to this scenario, however:

- Network drives are no easier to navigate than the drives on your own local system. You still have to know exactly what folder on what drive has the file that you need.
- Before you can do anything with the file, you need to have a copy of the software used to create it—or at least the ability to import it into the software that you do have.
- When files are copied to and from local and network drives frequently, it is all too easy to open an outdated version of a file, make changes to it, and then copy it over what had been the up-to-date version.
- Sharing files and resources across computing platforms is less than foolproof, if only because of the differences in file-naming conventions between PC and Macintosh systems, for example.

To understand why intranets have become so popular, all that we need to do is look at the reasons for the popularity of the World Wide Web itself:

- The Web uses a graphical interface. The fact that it might be slower than the command-line interface favored by some hard-core PC veterans is beside the point. The average user finds it easy to work with. Even relative novices have little trouble browsing the Web.
- While the visual appeal of many Web sites draws people to them, the feature that brings them back is the ease with which people can access and exchange information.
- The HTML markup language used to create Web pages was designed to be compatible with virtually every desktop-based computing platform. Versions of the most popular Web browsers, Netscape Navigator and Microsoft Internet Explorer, have been developed for many of these platforms. It doesn't matter whether you are using a PC, a Macintosh, or a UNIX workstation. As long as you have a Web browser and a connection to the Internet, you can access the information on the Web.

All of these advantages apply to corporate intranets as well. Through an internal Web site, organizations can disseminate up-to-date information quickly and easily. Departments and individuals can be given pages on the site for their own needs.

In creating an intranet, Information Technology professionals usually build upon an already-existing network structure, enhancing it by adding hardware and software originally designed for the World Wide Web. Users can access an intranet with the same Web browser that they use to surf the World Wide Web.

If you work for a medium- or large-sized organization, and you don't yet have an intranet, chances are very good that you will in the near future. This chapter and the next one will help you to take advantage of powerful new features in Excel that will help you to use it effectively in such an environment.

Opening Web Pages

97

If you have a Web browser on your system and a connection to the Internet, the Web browsing capabilities built into Excel 97 make it very easy for you to access the Web or your company intranet from within the program. The tool that makes this possible is the Web toolbar, found in each of the major Office 97 applications.

The Web toolbar includes many of the features common to Web browsers today (see Figure 26.1). Its icons are similar to those in Microsoft Internet Explorer, and if you are already familiar with that browser, you will have no problem using the toolbar.

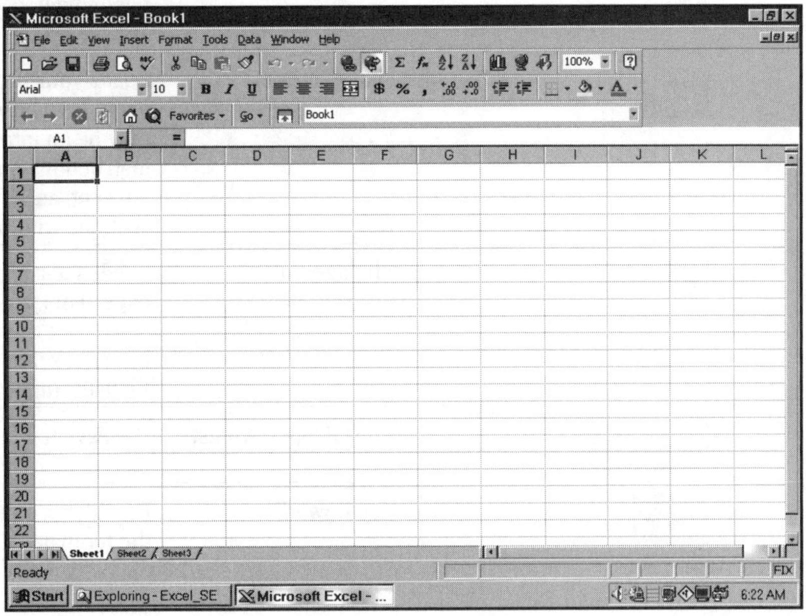

FIG. 26.1
The Web toolbar contains many of the icons and features familiar to users of Internet Explorer and other Web browsers.

The Web toolbar is not visible by default. The easiest way to display it on your toolbar set is to click the Web toolbar icon on the standard toolbar. If you want to add it permanently to your Excel setup, click Tools, Customize, Toolbars, and check the Web box near the bottom of the list.

Table 26.1 lists the icons on the toolbar and what they do. Icons are listed left to right as they appear on the toolbar.

Table 26.1 Icons on the Web Toolbar and What They Do

Icon	Icon Name	Action
	Left arrow	Returns you to the previous page in your browsing cycle. Applies to the current session only. Will be grayed out if there are no pages in the cycle.
	Right arrow	Returns you to the next page in your browsing cycle.
	Stop button	Aborts the loading of the page that you are attempting to jump to. Use this when the page is taking too long to download.
	Refresh button	Refreshes the current page. Use this when the content of the page has been updated, to make sure that you are seeing the latest version.
	Start page button	Loads your browser's default start page. If you are on an intranet, this may be an internal home page with instructions on how to use the intranet, as well as links to other sections within the intranet.
	Search page button	Loads your browser's default search page. This page may use the capabilities of one or more of the major Internet search engines, such as Alta Vista or Yahoo!.
	Favorites drop-down list	Displays the favorites list, or bookmarks, in your Web browser.
	Go drop-down list	Provides a menu of the commands on the toolbar.

Icon	Icon Name	Action
	Up arrow	Hides all toolbars except the Web toolbar, enabling you to see more of your page. This arrow is a toggle. Click it to hide the toolbars. Click it again to redisplay them.
	URL edit box and drop-down list	Shows the current document in the edit box. The drop-down list includes pages or documents that you have visited recently. To revisit one of these pages, click the drop-down list, and then select the item that you want to revisit. To browse to a new entry, type its URL address in the edit box; then press Enter.

TIP If your start or search page is a Microsoft Office document rather than one written in the HTML markup language, you will need a copy of the software used to create it. For example, if the document has been written in Word or PowerPoint, you will need that program to open the page.

If all that you need to do is view or print the file, however, you can install the Word or PowerPoint viewer that's included with the CD-ROM version of Excel. Microsoft provides these viewers at no charge, and you can distribute them to others who may need them to view your files.

I highly recommend that you install the Word and PowerPoint viewers in any case, if you don't have the full programs, because they act as extensions to your Web browser, enabling you to view files on the World Wide Web created with these industry-standard programs.

How Excel Integrates with a Web Browser

The distinction between Web browsers and traditional means of opening files on your network, or even your own computer, is becoming blurred. Internet Explorer 4.0 can be configured to replace the Windows Explorer or whatever means you have been using to run programs and open files in Windows 95.

This trend began with Internet Explorer 3.0, which can open Office 97 files directly. Netscape Communicator 4.01 has a similar capability. For example, if you were to open an Excel 97 workbook in Internet Explorer 3.0, your screen would look very much as it does in Excel itself (see Figure 26.2). All of the standard menus would be there. The only major difference is that Explorer substitutes its toolbar for the ones that you normally use in Excel. Netscape Communicator 4.01 works in much the same way.

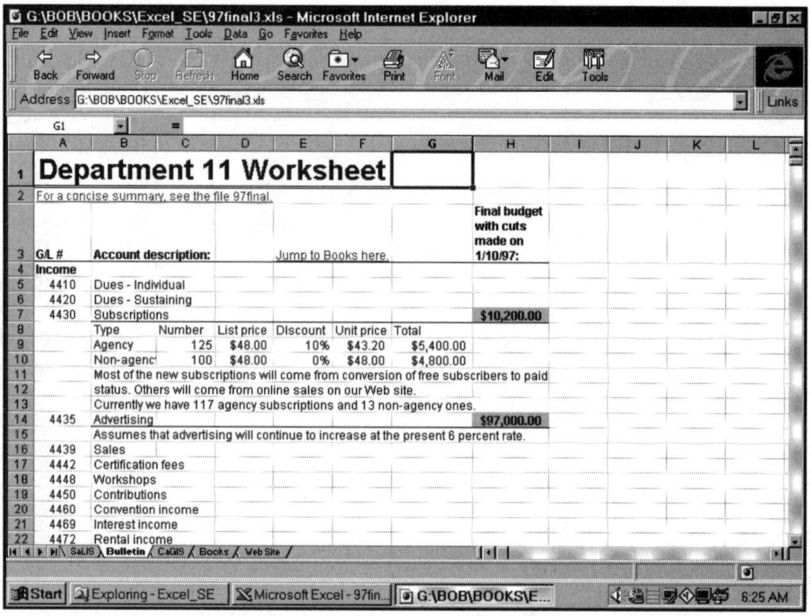

FIG. 26.2
If they have the necessary Office 97 applications on their systems, users can open, edit, and save Excel files in Internet Explorer.

NOTE When you attempt to open an Excel file in a Netscape Communicator 4.01 window, you may receive an error message saying that the "other program" is busy and you should activate it by clicking its icon on the taskbar. Presumably the "other program" is Excel. I have received this message even when Excel was not open.

If you receive this message, click the Retry button, and Netscape Communicator will eventually display an image of your file. To open the file in Excel from within Communicator, double-click the image. This opens the file in Excel. You might get the error message described above again. If so, click Retry and wait for Excel to open in the Communicator window.

This integration is possible because of ActiveX document technology. This technology enables Web browsers and other container applications to open Office 97 files in place. What this means to you and me is that we can open our working files, and navigate among them, by using the convenient navigation features of our Web browser.

Try it out. If you have Internet Explorer 3.0, start the browser; then click File, Open. In the Open dialog box, type the full pathname of an Excel file in the text box, or select the Browse button to navigate to the file (see Figure 26.3). Press Enter. The file will open within Internet Explorer, and you can edit it just as if you had opened it in Excel directly.

If you have Netscape Communicator 4.01, click File, Open Page. In the Open Page dialog box, select Choose File to open the Look In dialog box. Set Files of Type to All Files, and then navigate to the Excel file you want to open. Select the file, and Excel returns you to the Open Page dialog box. In the Open Location or File In section, make sure that the Navigator option button is selected, and then click Open to load the file in a Navigator window. (Netscape Communicator is a suite of Web tools; Navigator is the Web browser component of the suite.)

FIG. 26.3
To open an Office 97 file in Internet Explorer, be sure to set files of Type to All Files in the Browse/Open dialog box.

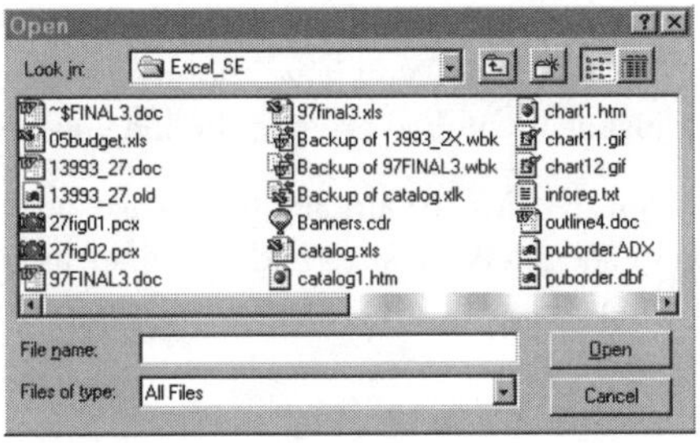

Navigator loads an image of your Excel file—but not Excel itself—in the Navigator window. To open the file in Excel from within the Navigator window, double-click the image. Excel opens, with your current toolbar and menu configuration. However, some of the menu options, such as the ability to add or remove toolbars, will be grayed out. (Between your Excel toolbars and the Navigator toolbars, the screen will be a bit crowded.)

TIP If you select Browse to access the File Open dialog box, the Files of Type option will default to "HTML Files," and you won't see your Excel files in the list. In the Files of Type list, select All Files.

If your document includes hypertext links to other Office 97 files, you can open these files from within Internet Explorer as well. For example, you might create your budget in Excel but explain it in a Microsoft Word file. You can add links in your Excel file to the relevant portions of your Word document. Click a link, and the Word document will open just as the Excel workbook did, with the standard Word menu bar.

If you're making extensive changes to a file located on your system or on an easily accessible network drive, then this feature may be of limited value to you. I certainly wouldn't want to be without my customized menus and toolbars in this situation. There are other situations, however, where you may need to access a file in a remote location and you might not even know the full pathname to the file. In such cases, being able to access the file easily with your Web browser can make your life much easier.

NOTE There are subtle differences between the Excel menus as they would normally appear and the Excel menus as they appear within the browser. For example, if you open an Excel file in Internet Explorer 3.0, the Save as HTML option on the File menu will not be available, nor will any additions or customizations that you have made to your Excel menus.

Running Web Queries

97

The HTML markup language and the World Wide Web have made it easy for us to receive and read up-to-date information in our browsers. Excel's Web Query feature goes beyond this, however, by enabling us to create queries for specific sites, download information directly into an Excel workbook, and update it as often as necessary. This is particularly useful for items such as stock quotes, sales and inventory tracking, and company financial information.

By using Web queries, you can import tabular information from sites on the World Wide Web, as well as from your own local intranet. Once you have captured the data, you can use Excel's powerful features to analyze it just as if you had created the file yourself.

Excel comes with several Web queries. More sample queries are available on Microsoft's Web site. These queries are geared to specific Web sites and new ones are added regularly. Check out Microsoft's Excel 97 Web Query page at **http://www.microsoft.com/excel/webquery/samples.htm**.

CAUTION

The sites accessed in the queries are not under Microsoft's control. Therefore, while the queries worked at the time they were posted, Microsoft does not guarantee that they will continue to do so. Nevertheless, they are worth downloading if only for the examples that they offer.

There are two types of queries that you can run with Excel: static and dynamic. A static query retrieves the same data each time, while a dynamic query asks you to specify the data to be retrieved.

Running a Static Query

Let's begin by using one of the static queries that ship with Excel. You'll need to have access to the Internet, so make sure that you are connected to the Internet before you start Excel. Open a new, blank workbook. By default, Excel creates three worksheets when you open a new workbook:

1. Place your cursor in the first cell of the first worksheet (or wherever you want the first cell of the imported data to appear) and click Data, Get External Data, Run Web Query. (If you don't see these options, the Web Query feature was not installed with Excel, and you need to install it from the installation CD-ROM.)

   This leads you to the Run Query dialog box with the names of all of the queries available to you (see Figure 26.4). Select the Dow Jones Stocks by PC Quote, Inc. query. You see the Returning External Data to Microsoft Excel dialog box, asking you where you want to put the data. Select the existing worksheet option.

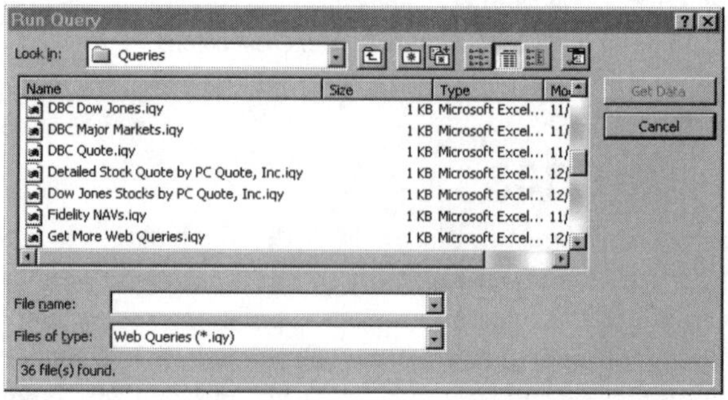

FIG. 26.4
The Run Query dialog box shows all of the queries installed on your system.

2. In the Returning External Data to Microsoft Excel dialog box, select the Properties button. This opens the External Data Range Properties dialog box (see Figure 26.5). Here are some of the choices that you might want to make:
   - In the Query Definition section, make sure that the Save Query Definition box is checked. This will embed the query in the workbook, enabling you to update the data later.
   - Under Refresh Control, select Enable Background Refresh if you have a fast computer with adequate random-access memory (RAM). This enables you to continue to work in Excel while the data is being downloaded to your system. If you have an older system or a limited amount of RAM, however, your system might run sluggishly with this option selected. In that case, deselect the box, and go get a cup of coffee while your data downloads.
   - Also under Refresh Control, select Refresh Data on File Open if you want Excel to update the data whenever you open the file. For the purposes of this practice query, leave the box deselected.
   - Under Data Layout, make sure that the AutoFit Column Width and Import HTML Table(s) Only boxes are checked. The first enables Excel to adjust the width of the columns to the data imported into them. The second limits the import to tabular data only; otherwise you may get the entire Web page.
   - Leave the remaining options at their default settings.
3. Click OK to return to the previous dialog box; then click OK again. Excel begins to retrieve the data. Watch the status bar at the bottom left of your Excel window. In about a minute, your worksheet should fill with the data.

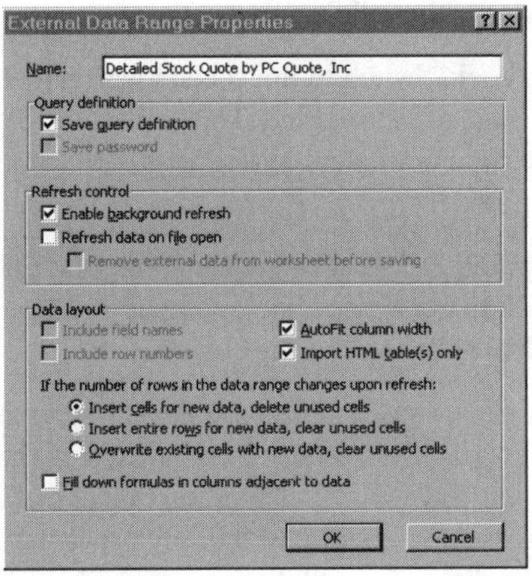

FIG. 26.5
The External Data Range Properties dialog box enables you to control how the information will be downloaded and how it will appear in your worksheet.

When the data has downloaded, you will also see the External Data toolbar (see Figure 26.6). This same toolbar is used for other types of queries covered elsewhere in this book. Some of its features do not apply to Web queries. Table 26.2 shows the buttons on the External Data toolbar.

Table 26.2 Icons on the External Data Toolbar and What They Do

Icon	Description
Edit Query	Opens the Query editor (grayed out for Web queries)
Data Range Properties	Opens the External Data Range Properties dialog box described above
Query Parameters	Allows you to enter parameters for dynamic queries
Refresh Data	Updates the data in the current external data range
Cancel Refresh	Aborts the update process
Refresh All	Updates the data in all external data ranges in the worksheet
Refresh Status	Reports the status of any refresh currently in progress

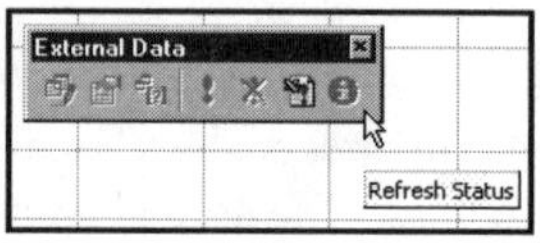

FIG. 26.6
The External Data toolbar appears on-screen when you are in a worksheet with the results of a query.

Running a Dynamic Query

The process for running a dynamic query is similar, except that you get to choose the data that will be retrieved. This is useful if, for example, you are interested in stock quotes for only a handful of companies rather than for the full Dow Jones list.

Let's return to our queries workbook. Switch to the second worksheet, place your cursor in the first cell, and repeat the previous steps 1 through 3. This time, select the Detailed Stock Quote by PC Quote, Inc. query. Ignore the Parameters button in the Returning External Data to Microsoft Excel dialog box for now.

When you click OK in the Returning External Data dialog box, the Enter Parameter Value dialog box opens. Enter the stock ticker symbol for a company on the New York Stock Exchange. For example, enter **MSFT** for Microsoft Corporation.

What if you need to "freeze" the data, as you might at the end of a fiscal quarter? Click the Data Range Properties icon on the External Data toolbar. This brings up the External Data Range Properties dialog box. Deselect the Save Query Definition box and click OK at the warning dialog box. This removes the embedded query and thereby prevents further refreshes. When you do this, related options in the dialog box will become grayed out.

Creating Your Own Web Queries

If you work for a large organization that maintains a Web site and has branch or regional offices, you may want to be able to download data from the Web site directly into an Excel worksheet. To do this, you may need to create your own Web query, particularly if the page that contains the data you need is a dynamic, interactive one.

A web query is nothing more than a small text file named with a file extension of .IGY. There are either three or four elements to the file, depending on circumstances. Each occupies a single line, which ends in a carriage return.

You can create a Web query file in Notepad or any other text editor. Each element must be on one continuous line. Some of the lines can get quite long, so be sure to turn off the editor's word wrap feature before you begin to create the query. (I recommend that you do not use a word processor, such as Microsoft Word, to create the query unless you know how to save its files in plain ASCII text format. Word processors embed non-text characters in their files and, therefore, should not be used for this purpose. Text editors such as Notepad do not embed such characters.)

Save the file to your \Program Files\Microsoft Office\Queries folder, so that it will show up in the list of queries installed on your system when you use the Web Query feature. After you run the query and save your worksheet, you will no longer need the query file. The query will be embedded in the worksheet itself, where you can run it again at any time. Nevertheless, you may want to keep the file to use as a sample or template for other such files.

The elements of a Web query include:

- Type of Query
- Version of Query
- URL
- POST parameters

The first two elements are optional in a Web query. If you omit them, Excel will apply default settings. I don't recommend leaving them out, however. If you should need to troubleshoot a query, it's always best if all of the elements are present.

The last element is required only when your query needs to refer to POST forms and data. POST is one of two methods used to transmit data from a Web server to the server's intermediary gateway software.

In this case, the data is your query. The gateway processes your query and returns the information that you have requested to the server. The server, in turn, passes it back to your Web browser or your Web-enabled software, including Microsoft Excel 97.

The second method is called GET. While somewhat simpler than POST, it is also more limited. The type of method you will use depends on the requirements of the Web server you are accessing and the amount of data you need to pass to that server at one time.

The Microsoft Excel Web Connectivity Kit, available from the Excel section of Microsoft's Web site (http://www.microsoft.com/excel/), contains examples of both types of methods. S.QUOTE.IQY is a three-line query that uses the GET method, while M_QUOTES.IQY is a four-line query that uses the POST method. If you have installed the connectivity kit, the files will be in your \Program Files\Microsoft Office\Webcnkit folder.

First, look at S_QUOTE.IGY. You'll recognize this from the Dow Jones Stocks by PC Quote query covered earlier in this chapter.

```
WEB
1
http://webservices.pcquote.com/cgi-bin/excelget.exe?TICKER=["TICKER","Enter your
➥stock symbol for a detailed quote."]
```

The first line defines the type of query being generated. For a Web query, there is only one valid type, called "WEB." Technically, the line is optional, and if you were to omit it, Excel would assume that you meant "WEB" in any case.

The second line includes the version of the query. Here, too, there is only one valid entry: the number "1." This element is paired with the first one, Type of Query. If you specify the type of query in line 1, you must also specify the version in line 2. If, however, you omit the first element, you must omit this one as well.

The third line contains the Uniform Resource Locator (URL) address of the file to which the query will be sent. The URL address format is used to access files on the Internet. In this case the file, EXCELGET.EXE, is located in a folder that contains executable files used by the PCQuote Web server's Common Gateway Interface software.

This line is an example of using the GET method to retrieve data. Although the line must be continuous, its elements can be divided into two distinct sections. The first section—everything *before* the question mark—is the URL of the executable file, EXCELGET.EXE, that will be used to process your request. Everything *after* the question mark is a parameter being passed to the executable file.

The operative parameter here is TICKER. The braced instructions following the equals sign tell Excel's Web Query feature to generate a dialog box in which you can enter the stock symbol for the quote you want. Whatever you enter will be passed to the parameter TICKER. For example, if you were to ask for a quote for MSFT (Microsoft Corporation), the parameter would become TICKER=MSFT.

If you wanted to retrieve data for the same company each time you ran the query, you could eliminate the dialog box. To do this, delete everything after the equals sign and replace it with the stock symbol. If you were retrieving Microsoft stock quotes, for example, the third line would read as follows:

http://webservices.pcquote.com/cgi-bin/excelget.exe?TICKER=MSFT

One limitation of the GET method is that you can run into problems if the line containing the URL and the parameters is more than 200 characters long. Therefore, it is best used for short, simple queries.

TIP It's very important that you enter the URL correctly. If you don't, your query will not work. One way to ensure that your URL is correct is to use your Web browser to access the Web page that contains the data you want. Then copy and paste the URL into the browser's address field to your query.

Open your query file in Notepad or any other Windows text editor that supports copying and pasting from the Windows Clipboard, and then open your browser and navigate to the page. If you are using Internet Explorer, place your cursor at the end of the URL that appears in the Address window below the toolbar. The URL should become highlighted when you do. If not, place your cursor at the end of the line and press Shift+Home to highlight it.

Next, press Ctrl+C to copy the line to the Clipboard. Return to your text editor, place your cursor where you want the URL to appear, and press Ctrl+V to paste it.

In Netscape Communicator 4.01, the URL appears in the Location window in the middle of the toolbar area. As you would in Internet Explorer, place your cursor in the window, copy the highlighted URL to the Clipboard, and paste it into your text editor.

If the page contains a table with data, that may be all you will need to do. When you access the page with a Web Query instead of browsing the HTML file, Excel retrieves only the data in the table and not the entire page.

If the site you are accessing uses the GET method of transmitting queries and you intend to use parameters, you can go a step further. Fill out the online HTML form that accesses the data you need. When your browser has retrieved and displayed the data, look at the URL in the Address window. You will see a line that includes both the URL and the parameters that have been passed to the CGI program. Copy and paste the URL into your query file and edit the parameters as needed.

If you do not see a string of parameters following the file name, it means the site's server uses the POST method.

Now let's take a look at M_QUOTES.IGY, which uses the POST method:

```
WEB
1
http://webservices.pcquote.com/cgi-bin/excel.exe
QUOTE0=["QUOTE0","Enter up to 20 symbols separated by spaces."]
```

As you can see, there are no parameters following the file name EXCEL.EXE on the third line. Instead, the parameters are on a separate line below. This enables you to construct longer, more complex queries than with the GET method. In the sample above, you could pass as many as 20 stock symbols to the QUOTED parameter.

Static and Dynamic Parameters

As we have seen, Web queries can be either static or dynamic. Static queries include all of the necessary information to be passed to the Web server, while dynamic queries prompt you for input. Thus, there are two types of parameters that you can include in your query file, static and dynamic.

Each parameter has both a name and a value. In the example TICKER=MSFT, TICKER is the parameter name and MSFT is the parameter value.

In a static query, the value is hard-coded into the query itself; in a dynamic query, the user supplies the value, which is then passed to the parameter. Those of you who have written DOS batch files will recognize the latter as *replaceable* parameters.

You can have more than one parameter in a query, separated by an ampersand (&). If you wanted to create a static query to retrieve stock quotes for both Microsoft and Intel, your parameters would look like this:

TICKER=MSFT&TICKER=INTL

Some Web servers also allow you to include more than one value for a single parameter, in addition to allowing multiple parameters. It would look something like this:

TICKER1=MSFT+INTL&TICKER2=ABCD+EFGH

To create a dynamic parameter in place of static values, use a pair of arguments. Each argument is contained in quotation marks, and the pair is enclosed within braces. For example:

QUOTE0=["QUOTE0","Enter up to 20 symbols separated by spaces."]

The braces signal Excel to generate a dialog box where you can enter a dynamic value. The first argument is the name of the value. The second is the message to be displayed in the dialog box. The value that you enter in the dialog box will take the place of the arguments when the query is sent to the Web server.

Determining Whether the Server Uses GET or POST

Before you can make a final decision whether to use the POST or GET methods of passing your query to the Web site's server, you need to be sure that the server supports the method you want to use. One way is to fill out a form online and observe the URL in your browser's Address window when the information you've requested has been downloaded to your browser. If the URL contains a question mark followed by parameters, the GET method has been used; if not, the server has used the POST method.

The best way to be certain, however, is to view the underlying HTML source file. In Internet Explorer, click View, Source. In Netscape Communicator, click View, Page Source.

Look for an HTML tag beginning with the word "FORM." The line would look something like this:

<FORM method="GET" action="/cgi-bin/excelget.exe">

or like this:

<FORM method="POST" action="/cgi-bin/excel.exe">

The value of the parameter "method" tells you what method to use in your query. The value of the parameter "action" tells you the file to be accessed.

URL Encoding

In order to send your query to a Web server, it must contain only characters acceptable in an URL address. Keep these points in mind:

- Upper- and lowercase letters from A to Z, numbers from 0 to 9, dashes (-), periods (.), and underscores (_) are all acceptable.
- Spaces are not allowed. Use the plus (+) sign instead.
- If you want to use any other characters, such as quotation marks, you must use the hexadecimal code for the character instead, preceded by the percentage sign (%).

For example, the hexadecimal code for a double quotation mark is 22. Thus, this line

value number “text”

would become:

value+number+%22text%22.

Using Excel's FTP Capabilities

97

Excel's Internet capabilities extend beyond the World Wide Web. The program also supports FTP. FTP, which actually stands for File Transfer Protocol, was the most common way of uploading and downloading data to and from remote servers on the Internet until the World Wide Web took off a few years ago. In many cases, FTP is still the method of choice for experienced, knowledgeable computer users.

FTP, which is a character-based protocol, is not as easy to use or intuitive as navigating a Web site with a graphical browser. It is not unlike navigating your own system with Windows Explorer or the Windows 3.1 File Manager. However, it is often faster and simpler than using a browser, particularly when you know where the file that you need to download is located or where the file that you are about to upload should be posted.

Many Web servers that host World Wide Web sites also support the FTP protocol. Web site developers frequently use this protocol to upload their Web pages. When you download a file from a World Wide Web page, you will often find that the hypertext link used to start the download is to a file on an FTP site.

The FTP names of many sites are similar to their World Wide Web names. For example, the URL address of the home page of Microsoft's World Wide Web site is **http://www.microsoft.com** while its FTP equivalent is ftp://ftp.microsoft.com. The term **ftp** is used in this context both to identify the protocol used to transfer data over the Internet (before the double slash) and to describe the type of site.

The user-friendly URLs to which we have become accustomed are aliases for a series of numbers that constitute the actual address of the site, whether World Wide Web or FTP. Not all FTP sites have an alias, however. Their URL may look something like 206.216.206.3. If you intend to upload or download files regularly from an FTP site, it's a good idea to find out its numerical address. You won't go wrong using it.

Access to an FTP site is controlled by password. Folders on the site that are open to the public usually require the password **Anonymous**. Your Web supplies this password transparently when you click a hypertext link to a file on an FTP site from a Web page.

To be allowed to upload a file to an FTP site, you will almost certainly need to have a password, which will be assigned by the site's administrator. This may give you access to folders on the site that are not available to anonymous users.

In Excel, the FTP feature is built into the File Open and File Save As dialog boxes. To use it, you must have access to the Internet. Before you can access an FTP site in Excel, you must add it to the list of sites recognized by Excel.

To add an FTP site to the Excel list, follow these steps:

1. Click File, Open, and then click the down arrow in the Look in drop-down box. At the bottom, you'll see Add/Modify FTP Locations. Select this to open the Add/Modify FTP Locations dialog box (see Figure 26.7).

FIG. 26.7
You can add FTP sites to your File/Open and File/Save As dialog boxes through the Add/Modify FTP Locations dialog box.

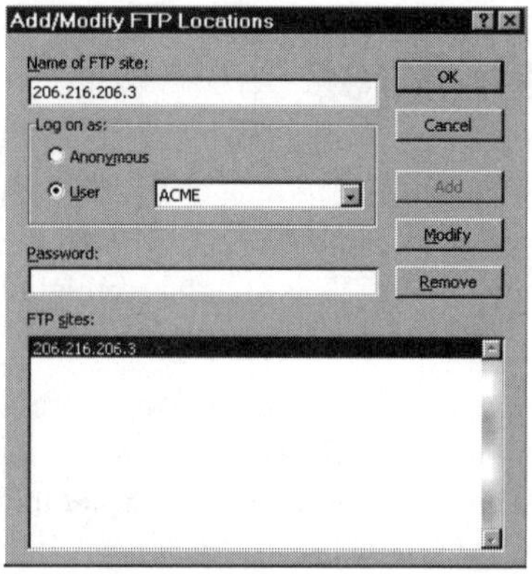

2. Under Name of FTP Site, type the URL address of the site. Enter the numerical address if you know it. If not, enter the user-friendly alias.
3. Under Log On As, the Anonymous option button will be selected by default. If you have been assigned a user ID and password, select the User button and enter your ID in the edit box next to the button.
4. Enter your password in the Password window. If you are logging on as Anonymous, enter your e-mail address here.
5. Click OK. The name of the site that you have just entered will now appear at the bottom of your Look In list.

NOTE FTP support is built into other Office 97 applications as well. When you add an FTP site to your list, it becomes available to all of them.

In the Office 97 environment, saving and opening workbooks on an FTP site can be done through the standard Open and File Save As dialog boxes. The folders to which you have access on an FTP site become an extension of your own system.

Here are the steps to follow in opening a file on an FTP site:

1. If necessary, establish a connection to the Internet.
2. Click File, Open, and then click the down arrow in the Look In drop-down box.
3. Scroll down to the Internet Locations (FTP) section at the bottom of the list, and select the site that you want to visit.
4. You may see a dialog box prompting you for your logon ID and password. Type the information as needed; then click OK.
5. The root folder of the ones available or assigned to you on the site will open in the file selection window. Double-click the folders as needed to navigate to the one with the file that you want to open.
6. When you have located the file, double-click it to open it in Excel.

To post an Excel file to an FTP server, open the file; then click File, Save As. Navigate to the proper folder on the FTP site as described in previous steps 1 through 4, and then click OK to save the file.

While it may be possible to work on an Excel file directly on the FTP server, you may find that response is very sluggish, particularly if you are connected to the Internet through a dial-up connection. If you are making extensive changes to the file, you will save time in the long run by copying the file to your own system. Click File, Save As to copy the file to your local drive and work on the copy.

When you finish, copy the modified file back to the server using the File, Save As method. Just reverse the process that you used to open the file:

1. Make sure you have an active connection to the Internet, and then click File, Save As.
2. In the Save As dialog box (shown in Figure 26.8), click the drop-down arrow next to the Save In window. Excel displays a list of all the elements in your my Computer setup.

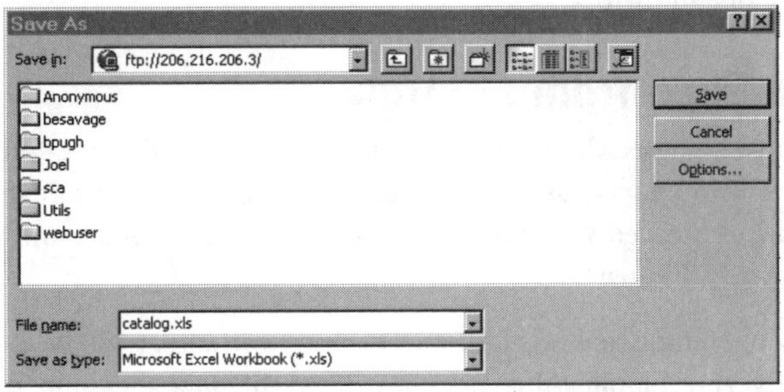

FIG. 26.8
When you open or save files to an FTP site, navigating the folders available to you is much like using Windows Explorer or My Computer.

3. Scroll down to the bottom of the list and select the FTP site to which you want to copy the file.

4. In the FTP Log On dialog box, make sure your user name and password are entered correctly, and then click OK.
5. Once a connection to the FTP site has been established, you will see a directory tree with the folders available to you. Open the folder in which you want to save the file and click Save.

TIP The FTP features in Excel 97 are adequate for opening and saving individual workbooks. If you need to use FTP to copy large numbers of files frequently, however, I would recommend that you obtain an FTP utility, such as WS_FTP32, which has many of the features of a good file manager. The shareware version is readily available. Also, Internet service providers often include an FTP utility in the software that they send you when you sign up.

Posting Workbook Content on the Web

97

Through the Web features in Excel 97, we can take just about anything that we can include in a workbook and create a Web page built around it without having to learn the HTML markup language used in developing Web pages. If we already have existing pages, we can export our data into them directly. If our site has been created with Microsoft FrontPage 97, a first cousin to the Office 97 siblings, we have even more options.

To use these features, you will need to have the Internet Assistant for Excel 97. If your File menu does not list a Save as HTML option, you will need to install the Assistant from the installation CD-ROM.

Excel 97 offers two basic options for posting content from your workbooks to a Web page:

- You can have Excel create a complete Web page for you with the appropriate header information required by HTML.
- You can export content to an existing page.

The latter requires a minor modification to the existing page that tells the Internet Assistant where to insert your data.

Let's take each one in turn.

Creating a Web Page from Scratch

By now, if you've followed the suggestions in this book, you've created a number of workbooks, including some with charts. Use these to practice the procedures described here. For illustration purposes, I've created workbooks for the usual, ever-popular, and fictitious ACME Widgets Company, shown in Figure 26.9.

Let's begin by opening a new workbook. The first worksheet will be a straightforward monthly sales report covering January through May. Type the data shown in Table 26.3.

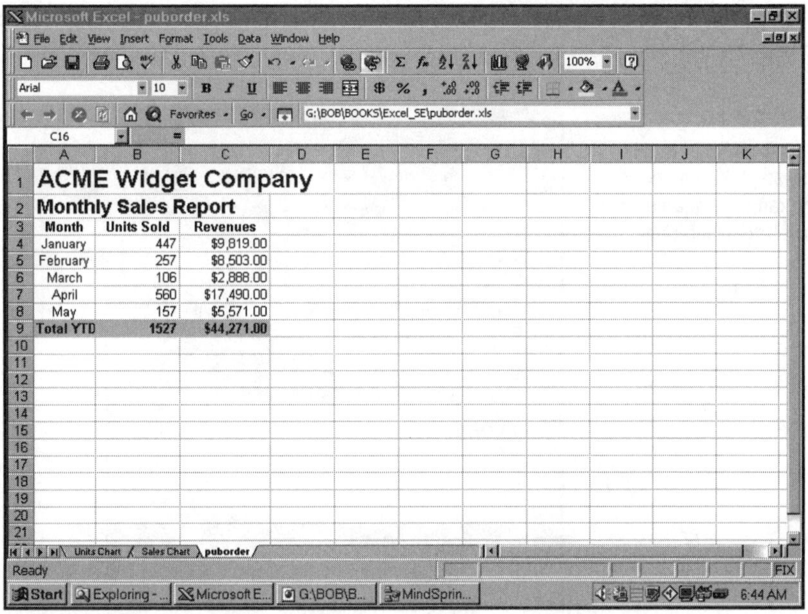

FIG. 26.9
The worksheet for the Monthly Sales Report is condensed and concise, ideal for posting on a Web page.

Table 26.3 ACME Widgets Monthly Sales Report

Month	Units Sold	Revenues
January	447	$9,819.00
February	257	$8,503.00
March	106	$2,888.00
April	560	$17,490.00
May	157	$5,571.00
Total YTD	1527	$44,271.00

You don't need to export the header row with the company name and the title of the report, because the Internet Assistant will allow you to enter this information in the main heading of the Web page itself. So just work with cells A3 through C9. Here are the steps to follow to export this data to an HTML page:

1. Highlight cells A3 through C9.
2. Select File, Save As HTML. This will bring up the Internet Assistant Wizard, which will walk you though a series of four steps. Click the Next button to move from step to step.
3. The wizard will list the ranges and worksheets in the workbook that can be exported (see Figure 26.10). Because this is a new worksheet, there should only be one range shown—the one that you've just highlighted. Later, as we add charts to this worksheet,

they will be listed as well. (You can add, remove, or change the order of the ranges; be sure to remove any that you don't want to export). Click Next.

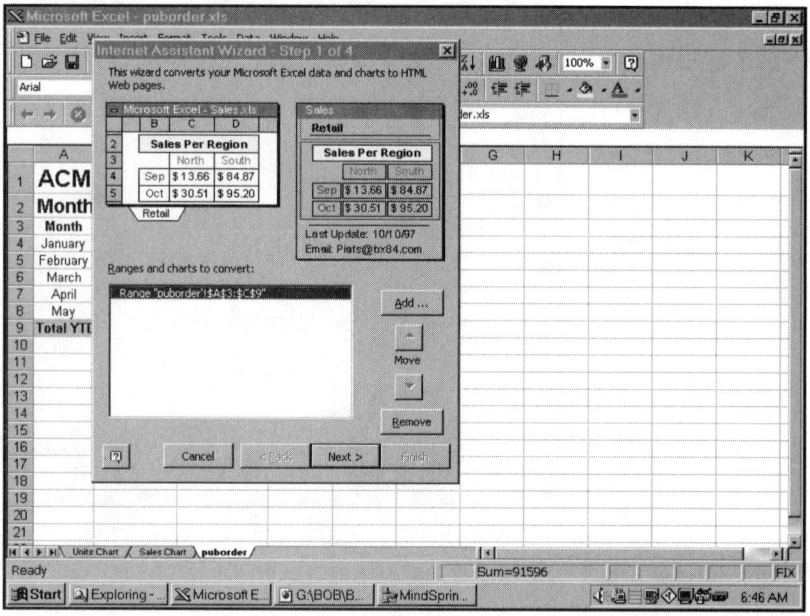

FIG. 26.10
Step 1 of the Internet Assistant Wizard shows the ranges available for export to a Web page.

4. Step 2 of the wizard asks you to choose whether to export the data to a separate file or copy it to an existing one (see Figure 26.11). Select the separate file option and click Next.

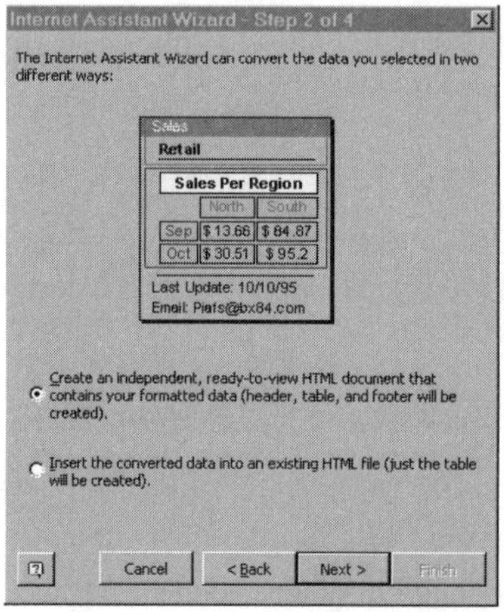

FIG. 26.11
Choose between creating an entire Web page or inserting your table into an existing page.

5. Next you'll be asked to type a title and header for your page (see Figure 26.12). The title will appear in the title bar of Web browsers and will be the first element picked up by Internet search engines. If you post the page to a site on the World Wide Web, make sure that the title accurately describes the page (it's best to limit your title to about 40 characters). The header will be the first thing that the user sees—a headline for the page. You don't have room for a very long header in a typical browser window, so keep it to five or six words. The dialog box also provides room for a descriptive paragraph and offers options to add horizontal rules above and below your table. The rules help set it off from the rest of the page. Finally, the wizard enters your name and today's date at the bottom of the page and provides a place for you to enter your e-mail address. (It's considered good form for authors of Web pages to identify themselves and provide a means for people browsing their page to contact them.) Click Next.

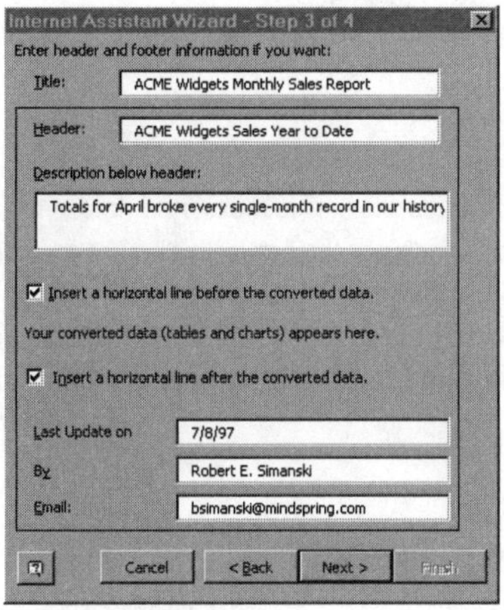

FIG. 26.12
In step 3 of the wizard, you enter information that will appear at the top and bottom of the new page.

6. The wizard asks you what code page to use (leave the default setting alone) and whether you want to create a separate HTML file or add the result to your FrontPage Web, assuming that you have FrontPage installed (see Figure 26.13). Select the separate file option. Excel suggests a name and location for the file. The default folder will be the one containing the Excel file itself. The location is fine but let's change the suggested file name to **sales1.htm**. Click Finish to create the file.

Now start your browser and open the file that you have just created. If you are using Internet Explorer, click File, Open, and then enter the full pathname to the file in the edit box. Or click the Browse button to navigate to the file. Once you select the file, you return to the Open/Browse dialog box with the full pathname of the file in the edit box. Click OK to load the file into the browser.

What you are likely to see is—to put it charitably—a deadly dull Web page. You'll probably want to create your Web pages in Microsoft Word 97, which has a better Internet Assistant Wizard, or in Microsoft FrontPage, and use the second means of exporting your content to HTML, which I will describe next.

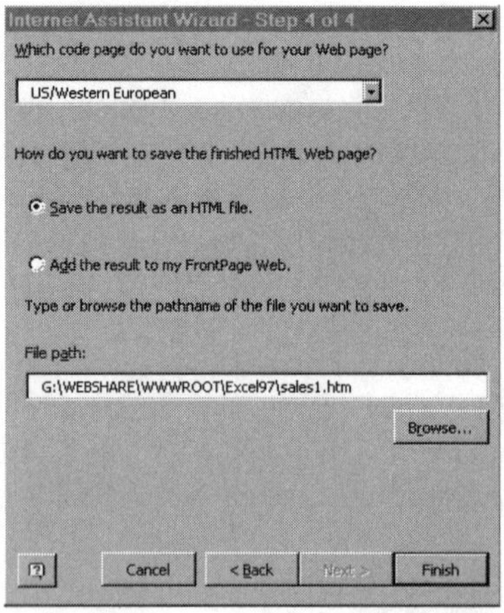

FIG. 26.13
In step 4 of the wizard, you determine how the results of the export will be saved.

CAUTION

Keep the tables that you export as small as possible. If your exported data is more than five or six columns wide, it either won't fit within the browser window or the browser will make the columns so narrow that each cell will be elongated and hard to read. Similarly, don't export more than a dozen rows or so if you can help it. Tables can take a longer time to download than straight text, and the users may have to scroll the page endlessly to get to the information that they need. Instead, break up the data into several smaller and more manageable pages.

Adding Content to an Existing Page

Now let's export the same sales report to an existing Web page. The process is about the same, with one major exception: The Internet Assistant Wizard has to know where in the page to insert your content. To do this, you have to add one line to the underlying HTML code.

To add the line, all you need is a simple text editor such as Notepad, because HTML files are in plain ASCII text format. This is one of the reasons they can be read by any browser on virtually any desktop-computing platform.

Here are two safe ways to enter the line of code. The first assumes that you have FrontPage 97 and that the page to which you want to add the code is already part of your FrontPage Web:

1. Open the file in FrontPage Editor. Add text, if necessary, to introduce your new content.
2. Click View, HTML. This opens a window where you can edit the HTML code directly. Look for the text that you have just entered; it should end with a trailing </p>.
3. Insert a carriage return at the end of the paragraph, and then type the table indicator line exactly this way:

```
<!--##Table##-->
```

The exclamation point at the beginning of the tag indicates that what is between the brackets is a comment or special code. This tells Web browsers to ignore it if they don't understand it.

4. Click OK to close the source code editor and return to the main FrontPage Editor window. The editor displays a small graphic where you have inserted the comment. Double-click the graphic, and FrontPage displays the comment itself. This graphic will not appear in your browser.
5. Save the file and exit FrontPage Editor.

The process is essentially the same if you have Internet Explorer:

1. Open the page in Internet Explorer as previously described.
2. Click View, Source. This opens the HTML file in Notepad.
3. Notepad doesn't display the HTML code as nicely as the source code editor in FrontPage, but the principle is the same. Look for a break between paragraphs to insert your code. Don't worry about line breaks or the extra spaces that Notepad inserts everywhere. Web browsers ignore them.
4. As described previously, insert a carriage return at the end of the paragraph, and then type the table indicator line exactly this way:

```
<!--##Table##-->
```

5. Click File, Save to exit Notepad. Click View, Refresh to force Internet Explorer to reload the saved file. You should not see any difference in the browser.

Now it's time to bring your content into the page you have modified. Refer to the procedure described under "Creating a Web Page from Scratch."

1. Highlight cells A3 through C9. Then click File, Save As HTML to open the Internet Assistant Wizard.
2. In step 1 of the wizard, make sure the correct range is selected and remove any unneeded ranges (refer to Figure 26.10). Click Next.
3. In step 2 of the wizard, select the second option to insert the data into an existing HTML file (refer to Figure 26.11). Click Next.
4. Step 3 of the wizard now takes on a different look (see Figure 26.14). You have the choice of opening the file directly or opening it from your FrontPage Web. Select the first option. Then click the Browse button to navigate to the file you modified to accept your table. Click Next.
5. In step 4 of the wizard, you can either save the result as a new HTML file or add it to your Web (refer to Figure 26.13). For the second option to work, however, you need to have the FrontPage Explorer open and your Web loaded in it, so go with the first option.

   You can also select the final output file. If you're feeling brave, make it the file that you designated in step 3 of the wizard. To be safe, save it to a new name in the same folder as the first file. If the results are satisfactory, you can always rename the files.
6. When everything is ready, click Finish.

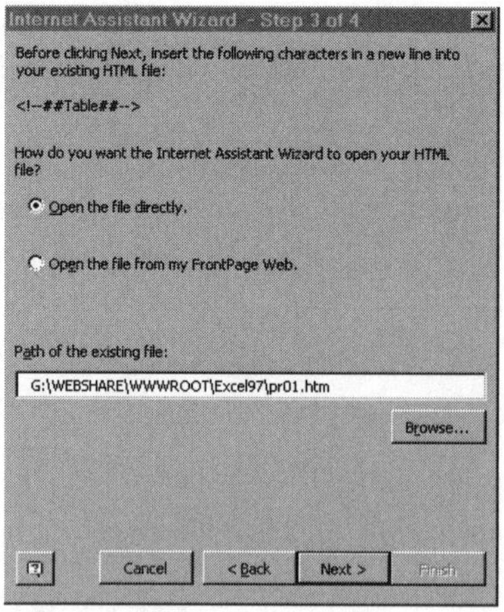

FIG. 26.14
Step 3 of the Internet Assistant Wizard when you are inserting a table into an existing page.

Now view the page in your Web browser. You should notice a big improvement, as you can see in Figure 26.15.

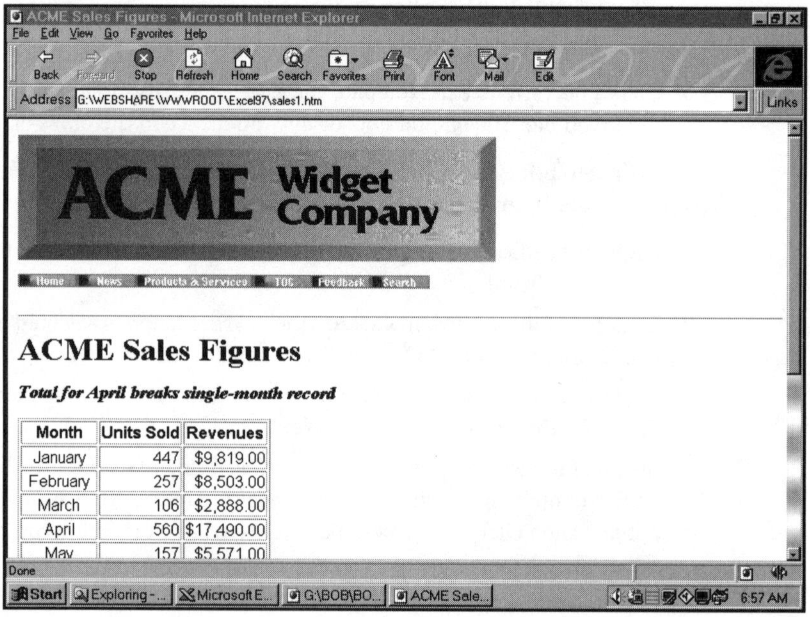

FIG. 26.15
The ACME Sales Figures worksheet after being imported into an existing FrontPage 97 Web page.

Basic Structure of an HTML File

I'm not going to attempt to teach you the ins and outs of HTML coding here. I couldn't do it justice in the space allowed. If you're interested, there are many excellent books on the subject. However, there are a few HTML rules that you need to be aware of to make sure that you put the line of code discussed above in the right place:

- There are two main sections to an HTML file: head and body. The head contains information about the file that your browser needs but that you don't see, so be sure that your content goes in the body section.
- All HTML codes are enclosed within less-than (<) and greater-than (>) brackets (see Figure 26.16). Many have both a beginning and an ending code, with the backward slash (/) the first character in the ending code. For example, the head section begins with <head> and ends with </head>. The body section, which follows the head immediately, is indicated with <body> and </body>.
- The best place to insert your content is between two normal paragraphs. Paragraphs begin with the <p> code and sometimes end with a </p>, although not all Web authoring tools add the ending code, which is not required by most browsers (see Figure 26.16).
- Be careful not to insert the line within a paragraph, particularly a heading paragraph, denoted by the letter h plus a number, as in <h2> (see Figure 26.16). Your content will take on the characteristics of the paragraph. If it's within a heading, your table will be very large.

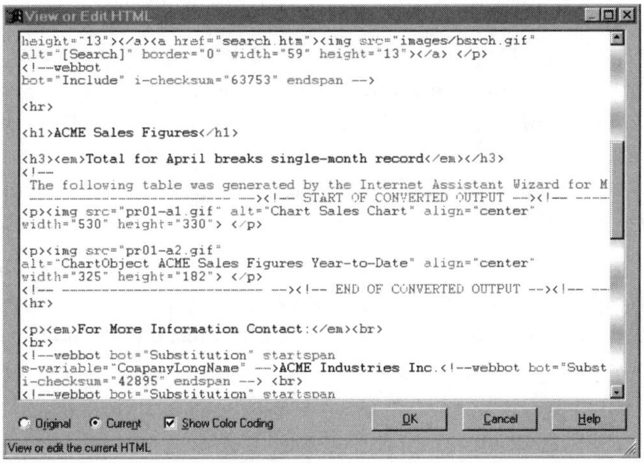

FIG. 26.16
HTML code as displayed in the FrontPage source code editor. You can edit this code to insert a pointer to the location of your table.

CAUTION

Don't use your word processor to edit an HTML file. If you forget to save the file in ASCII format, your word processor will add its own codes, which will destroy the page and make your Webmaster very angry.

Exporting Charts and Graphs to Web Pages

Eventually, you'll want to export charts and graphs to your Web pages. Unlike raw tabular data, they can add considerable visual appeal to your pages. When you do, there are some important considerations to keep in mind.

When you export a chart to HTML using Excel's Internet Assistant Wizard, the wizard converts the chart to one of two graphics formats commonly used on the World Wide Web: JPEG or GIF. However, it doesn't always optimize the graphics for the Web. Therefore, the size of the file may be larger than necessary. This makes some graphics slow to download and display on the other person's screen.

To improve performance, edit the graphic in an image editor such as Microsoft Photo Editor, which comes with Microsoft Word 97, to reduce the size and resolution of the file. Photo Editor is included on the Word 97 installation CD-ROM but may not have been installed on your system. You may need to rerun the Setup program to install it. However, almost any recent-vintage image editing program will have what you need to modify and prepare graphics for use on a Web site.

Here are some suggestions for optimal graphic size and resolution:

- Graphics created for use on the Web should be no larger than 500 by 350 pixels, the width of the default Netscape Navigator window at standard VGA resolution.
- The resolution (as opposed to the size) of the graphic should be no more than 120 dots per inch, the resolution of a display set for 1,024 by 768 pixels. In fact, a resolution of 96 dots per inch, matching that of an 800 by 600 screen, is adequate for most graphics.
- If the file is in JPEG format (the file name will have a JPG extension), your image editor may offer you several compression options. Select a middle-ground option, test the image in your browser, and experiment until you find the compression level that offers the best compromise between file size and image quality. Use that compression level on all of your JPEG files.

There is something else that you need to be aware of when creating charts that will be exported to your Web site. The Internet Assistant Wizard will export the charts in the size that they would appear on a printed page. If your chart fills the width of an 8.5×11 page, it will be much too large for the browser screen.

In a drawing or image editing program, the best way to control this would be to create a page size that's the same as the desired size of the final image—in this case, about 500 pixels wide by 350 pixels deep. Unfortunately, Excel doesn't allow you to create a custom page size. However, you can specify very wide margins.

The goal is to size your chart so that it is no more than about four inches wide by three inches deep. It's best to create a page of this size on a blank worksheet before you create your chart because Excel will size the chart to fit the page. However, you can also modify existing charts and worksheets to accomplish this goal.

To optimize the size of an existing chart for use on a Web page:

1. With the worksheet containing the Excel chart displayed, click File, Page Setup. In the Page Setup dialog box, set the page size to 8.5×11, and set the page orientation to landscape.
2. Next, click the Margins tab and set all of the margins to 3 inches (see Figure 26.17). This gives you a small, workable area of the right proportion. You may have to scale the chart to fit the page.
3. Click OK to close the Page Setup dialog box and return to the worksheet.
4. Select the chart. Then click and drag on one of the corner sizing handles and resize the chart to fit within the new dimensions of the page.

To set up a blank worksheet for a chart, follow steps 1 through 3 above, and then create your chart.

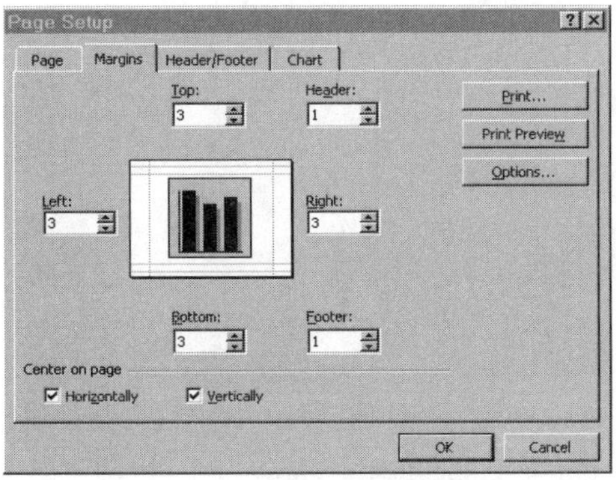

FIG. 26.17
Modify the margins in the Page Setup dialog box to reduce the size of your chart for use on a Web page.

Creating a Hyperlink from the Insert Menu

97

To set up links to locations in your own files, first create a foundation for the links by creating bookmarks in your Microsoft Word files or named ranges in your Excel files. To create a bookmark in a Word document, place your cursor where you want the bookmark to be, and then click Insert, Bookmark. In the resulting dialog box, enter a name for the bookmark; then click OK.

To create a named range in Excel, follow these steps:

1. Place your cursor in the cell where you want to locate the name, or highlight a group of cells to name a range. Click Insert, Name, Define.
2. In the Define Name dialog box, type a concise name with no spaces in it. (Use the underscore character in place of a space.) A window in the middle of the dialog box shows existing named cells and ranges. Click Add to create the name.
3. Highlight the name after it is added to the list. Make sure that the range of cells that is shown in the bottom window is correct; then click OK.

After you create a number of bookmarks or named ranges, you'll find it easier to generate hypertext links to them. In Excel, place your cursor in an empty cell where you want your link, and then follow these steps:

1. Click Insert, Hyperlink.
2. In the Insert Hyperlink dialog box (see Figure 26.18), under Link to File or URL, enter the full pathname of the file to which you are linking, if it is on your computer or your Local Area Network. If it is on a remote Web site, enter the Internet URL address for the file (which can be a Web page). If you have visited the file or page recently, click the down arrow to view a recent history list. If the file is on the list, select it and the proper path or URL will be entered for you. Most likely you will want to click Browse to locate the file.

FIG. 26.18
In the Insert Hyperlink dialog box, enter the name of the file to which you are linking and, optionally, the name of a bookmark or named range in the file.

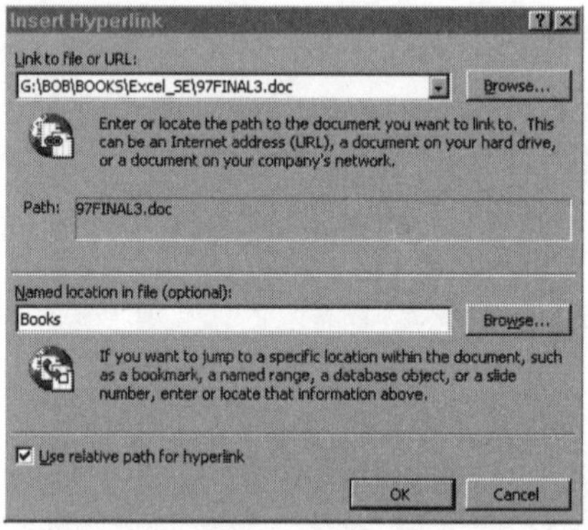

3. Under Named Location in File, type the name of the bookmark or named range that you want to link to. This is optional. If you don't fill this in, the link will go to the beginning of the file. Click OK to create the link.
4. Excel creates a link in the selected cell using the file pathname or URL. You can change this to something more useful by editing the text in the cell. Changing the text will not remove the link.
5. To edit or remove a link, highlight the link and click Insert, Hyperlink. You will see the same dialog box used to create the link originally, except now it contains a Remove Link button. (This button does not appear until after a link has been created.) Make the necessary change or check the Remove Link box at the bottom of the dialog box.

NOTE When you remove a link, the text that was entered for it remains.

You can use this same method to enter a link to a page on a remote Web site, or even a mailto e-mail link.

Using the HYPERLINK() Function

There is a second method of adding hypertext links to your Excel files. You do this with the HYPERLINK() function. The syntax is:

=HYPERLINK(*location,description*)

The end result is much the same as using the first method of creating a hyperlink, but if you already know the location of the linked file, this second method can be easier and faster. Begin by placing your cursor in a blank cell where you would like to locate the hyperlink. Then follow these steps:

1. Click the equals sign to the left of the cell text edit window just below your toolbars. The drop-down Function menu should appear at the left of your screen.
2. Select the HYPERLINK option from the Function menu. This will open a dialog box with two edit boxes (see Figure 26.19).
3. In the first edit box, enter the full pathname, UNC (local network) address, or URL address of the file. Be sure to place quotation marks around the pathname, particularly if it contains blank spaces.
4. In the second edit box, enter the text that will overlay the link.
5. Click OK. Excel creates the link in the cell that you select.

For more information about this function, see Appendix B, "Excel Function Reference."

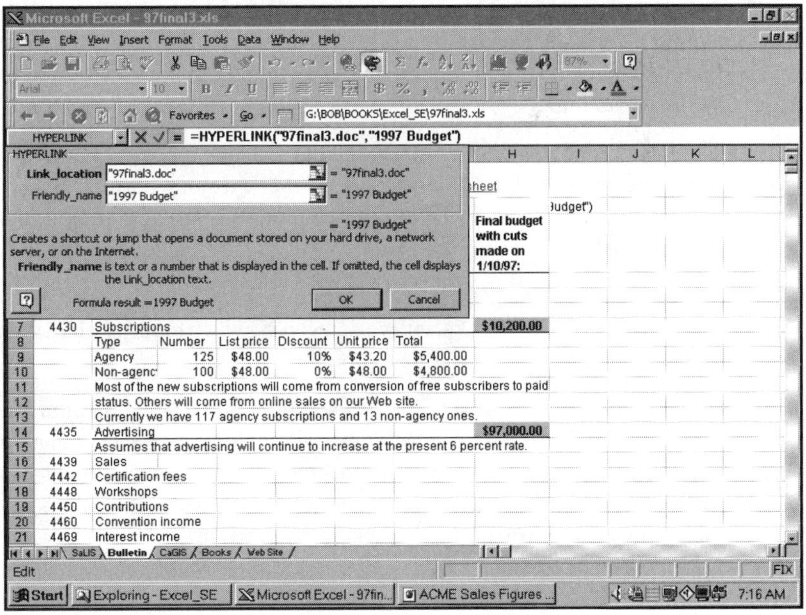

FIG. 26.19
If you know the location of the linked file, it's often easier and faster to create a link with the HYPERLINK() function.

Relative versus Absolute Hyperlinks

In working with Web-oriented technology, it's important to understand the difference between relative and absolute hyperlinks. Keep in mind that it is the relative relationship between files, in terms of their physical location, that makes a Web work properly. As long as the relative relationship remains intact, the link will work properly, even if the files are moved to an entirely different system.

An absolute link defines the actual physical location of a file. For example, the word processing file for this chapter is in the folder **g:\bob\books\excel_se** on my computer system. Other Excel and Word files used to create the examples for this book are also in that directory.

Some of these files contain hypertext links to each other. If I were to use absolute links to these files and then decide to move the files to another drive, the links would no longer work, even if the files were in the same folder. The links from my Excel file to my Word document would look for the document in the old directory on drive G and nowhere else.

A relative link, on the other hand, looks for a relative location, not an absolute one. For example, if I create relative links between my Word and Excel files, when I selected a link to a Word document, Excel would expect the document to be in the same folder as the Excel file. If I were to move the files to another drive, the links would still work as long as they were in the same folder. The only thing that would appear in the link would be the name of the file itself. The pathname, showing its place in the directory structure of my drive, would be unnecessary.

While the files need not be in the same folder for relative links to work, they must, however, be on the same drive. Thus, if I were to create a folder for images one level below the one containing my text files (often referred to as a child folder) and place some linked images there, there would be no problem. The link to divider.gif in the \images folder would be simply images\divider.gif.

The folder need not even be below the current one. I could just as easily create an \images folder below the \bob folder (where it would be a sibling, rather than a child of the folder with my text files). The relative link to the graphics file would then be ..\images\gif. The two dots and the slash mean go up one level (to \bob) and then down to the \images folder.

As long as I preserve the directory structure from \bob on down, and keep the files in their respective folders, the links will work, even if I were to move all of them to a different computer.

Relative links are essential to the development and management of Web sites and should be used instead of absolute links whenever possible. Relative links enable developers to create sites on one system and copy them to another without losing their sanity. As we begin to use the Web-oriented features of Excel and other Office 97 applications, they will become increasingly important to you and me as well.

Here is how to create a relative link in Excel:

1. Whenever you have an Excel file to which you plan to add hypertext links, begin by clicking File, Properties. In the edit window at the bottom of the dialog box, enter the full path to the current file. This will become the base address for the hypertext links that you will create from within that file. In other words, the folder containing the Excel file will become the root folder for your hypertext links.
2. Whenever you use Insert Hyperlink to create a link, make sure that the Use Relative Path for Hyperlink box is checked. The link will become relative to the base address for the file on which you are working.

As useful as relative links are, however, they only work with files on the same drive. When you create a link to a file on another drive or to a remote Web site, you have no choice but to use absolute links.

Common Problems and Solutions

Excel 97 is a powerful, feature-rich applications program. In this chapter, you have learned how Excel can interact with other programs and even work from within those programs. Anytime two programs interact with each other, however, things can go wrong—and occasionally they do.

These are some of the problems you may encounter. Fortunately, most of them are merely annoyances.

Disappearing Excel Files

Sometimes when you use the hyperlink features in Excel and Word to toggle between files and are also running Internet Explorer, when you return to your Excel window, the file on which you were working has disappeared. Don't panic, it has just been closed. Click File and the file will be at the top of your recently used list. Select the file to reopen it.

HTML Files Are Not Quite There

If you are using Microsoft FrontPage 97 to manage your Web site and you create an HTML file with Excel's Internet Assistant, one option is to save the file to your FrontPage web. A quick check with Windows Explorer shows that the file has been saved to the folder for your Web's home page. When you open the Web in FrontPage, however, the file does not show up in FrontPage Explorer. To add the file to your Web, so that you can open it in FrontPage Editor, open FrontPage Explorer, click File, Import and select the file. To properly integrate the file into your site, you'll need to add the necessary hypertext links to and from other pages.

Missing Links

If you've modified pages in your existing Web and saved the modified pages to a different folder than the original page, chances are very good that the existing hypertext links on the new page will be broken. Graphics simply won't appear and text links won't work. The reason is that the relationship between the location of your target files and the links to them on your page is critical. Let's say you're editing a page and you create a hypertext link to a file or graphic in the same folder as the page that you're editing. Your Web server or authoring tool is expecting to find the linked files in the same folder as the page with the links, ***no matter where that page may be.*** That information will be hard-coded into the HTML markup. If you copy or move the page to another folder and don't take the linked files with it, the links will be broken. The solution, however, is simple: When you are using the Internet Assistant Wizard to modify an existing page and you save the modified file under a new name, be sure to save it in the same folder as the original file.

From Here...

In Chapter 27, "Building Online Forms," you'll learn how to create online forms using Excel's form design tools. Specifically, you'll learn about these things:

- Modifying the sample forms that come with Excel.
- Creating a form from scratch for use on your Local Area Network or intranet.
- Creating a form for use on a Web site.

Subsequent chapters will cover related topics such as programming in Visual Basic for Applications. This information will help you to enrich and enhance what you create in the next chapter.

CHAPTER 27

Building Online Forms

by Robert Simanski

Until recently, the process you used to collect data from other persons was very inefficient. You would either have the person fill out a paper form, or you would ask them questions and fill out the form yourself. Either way, the data then had to be entered into a computer database, by yourself or by a data entry worker. The process was inefficient, time consuming, and prone to error.

Microsoft Excel 97, with its versatile form design and automation features, can help us to eliminate much of this work. You can create online forms for use on your Local Area Network, corporate intranet, or Web site. Users can access the forms whenever they need to and fill them out online. When they do, the information that they enter can be captured automatically to an Excel worksheet set up as a database. No matter how often you update or modify these forms, your users will always be working with the latest version. ■

Design principles

In this section, you learn basic principles of effective form design and about factors you should consider before beginning to work on your form.

Modifying a sample form

Look at the sample forms that come with Excel and learn how to customize them to meet your needs.

Creating a form from scratch

In this section, which constitutes the bulk of the chapter, you build an online Purchase Order form from the ground up, applying the principles of design discussed earlier.

Using the Template Wizard

Here you apply the Template Wizard to your Purchase Order form to create an Excel database for use on a Local Area Network. This database will capture information that users enter into the form.

Using the Web Form Wizard

Here you will learn how to use the Web Form Wizard to enable users to fill out the form from a Web page, using their browser, and capture the information to a database.

Online Forms in Excel 97

In Microsoft Excel 97, you can develop two basic types of online forms—one for use on your own local system and another for use on a corporate intranet or World Wide Web site. In fact, you can use the same basic form for both purposes, and both types are covered in this chapter.

In either case, Excel creates a new template, based on your form, for users to fill out online, and a separate workbook for use as a database. This database is an ordinary Excel file, with each column in the first worksheet serving as a field and with one record per row. By inserting additional worksheets, you can analyze and manipulate the data that has been collected when people enter data using the form.

In the case of a form intended for use on a Web site, Excel also generates the intermediate files necessary to transmit the information collected to either Microsoft's Internet Information Server or the Common Gateway Interface used on other Web servers.

As you learned in the last chapter, recent versions of the two most popular Web browsers, Microsoft Internet Explorer and Netscape Navigator, are able to load Excel 97 directly into the browser window, along with its standard menu and toolbar. You can add a hyperlink to a Web page to access the new form, and users can edit it directly from within their browser. Because of this, you need not be concerned with the limitations of the user's Web browser, as you would be when designing a worksheet that is to be converted to an HTML page.

Principles of Good Form Design

Whether you are designing a form for printed output or online use, there are several basic principles of good design that will help you to get effective results with your form. Keep them in mind whenever you begin to work on a new form.

Planning the Form

Good form design requires thoughtful planning. Ask yourself these questions before you crank up Excel:

- What is the purpose of the form? What should be the most important information or section on the form?
- How will the form be used? If it is for another department, such as Finance, does it have all of the information that the staff will need, and is it in a format that they will be able to use easily? If it is a purchase order, does it provide the vendor with all of the information that they will need to fill your order accurately and quickly?
- What information should be on the form? Start by creating a checklist of the information that you will need, then review it with others who will use the form. Taking the time to do this up front will save you from having to make major revisions later on. No doubt, you'll want to make refinements after you've laid out the form, but if you've done your homework, they should be relatively minor ones.

- Who will be filling out the form? Will it be used to collect demographic or mailing list information from people outside of your organization? If so, you will want to take extra care to ensure that your questions and instructions are clear, unambiguous, and easily understood by people from a wide variety of backgrounds. (You should do this in any case, of course, but it becomes even more important when you don't know who will be using the form.) Will it be used to expedite an internal process or provide for financial accountability, as would be the case with a purchase order or expense report? You will then want to take extra steps to make sure that the information is entered accurately and completely.
- How should the information be organized? Chances are that the data will fall into several clearly distinct categories. A purchase order, for example, would have information about the vendor, data needed for financial accounting, and a place for approvals and signatures, as well as a table for entering the order itself. Organizing this material into logical sections that flow naturally from one to the other will help users to fill out the form correctly and completely.

Designing with the User in Mind

When designing a form, you must never lose sight of the fact that you are usually designing it for someone else to use, perhaps someone you have never met. Thus, the design of your forms should be attractive, understandable, and logical. It should lead the user through the process from beginning to end. Excel makes it easy to do this through its extensive support of graphics and its invaluable Comments feature.

Here are some points to keep in mind as you design forms that others will use:

- Use colors, borders, and AutoShapes or other graphics to organize and distinguish the different sections of your form, and use them consistently. For example, use one color as a background for your heading area at the top of the form and another as a background in the main data area, separated by a border at the bottom of the last row in the heading. Use rounded rectangles or similar devices to group small sections.
- Use colors judiciously. Keep in mind that there are many people with varying degrees of color blindness or similar visual problems. In areas where you have a large amount of text, stay with light pastel backgrounds. Avoid whole-sheet background images; even the most subtle of them tend to get in the way.
- Clearly distinguish the cells used for data entry. If you are using a background color in an area with data entry cells, change the color of these cells to white and add a border around each cell, or at least at the bottom, to help set them off even more.
- Use comments and text blocks liberally to explain the fields on your form. Comments have several advantages over text blocks, because they can be embedded in a cell with other content and pop up only when you move your cursor into the cell so they don't take up any space on your form.
- Design the form to be as compact as possible. Keep in mind that many users, particularly those with older monitors, are still using standard 640×480 VGA resolution. Wherever possible, design each section of your form so that it fits within the standard VGA screen.

If you can't do this, it's better to make the form a little too long rather than a little too wide, for the simple reason that it's easier to move up and down within a form than side to side.

- Users may also need to print paper copies of the form; therefore, it should be designed for the standard portrait paper sheet as well as for the screen. This means that you should avoid color on top of color, which translates into shades of gray in most black-and-white laser printers. If you have text on top of a dark color background, make the color of the text white or at least light yellow. Also, a form that completely fills a standard paper sheet will be two or three screens deep, which is about as deep as you want to go for an online form. If your form is more than one printed page long, you may want to redesign it. Keep in mind also that people don't like to fill out lengthy forms.
- Use fonts that everyone who uses the form is likely to have on their system. The fonts that come with Windows 95 itself include Arial, Courier, Times New Roman, Symbol, and Wingdings, so you can safely use them. I recommend that you use Arial for forms because it reproduces well, even in smaller sizes. If you find this selection too limiting, use one of the fonts that come with Excel or Microsoft Office. Be aware, however, that many software installation programs, including those from Microsoft, install fonts in your Windows setup without informing you. If you don't know the source of the font, you can't assume that another person will have the same fonts that you have. If you use a font that they don't have, their software will substitute another font and the results may not be satisfactory.

In the sections that follow, you'll learn how to implement these guidelines, particularly when you build a form from scratch. You'll see how to use each of the features just described.

Creating Forms for a Local Area Network

In this section, you'll develop two forms for use on a Local Area Network. For the first one, you'll modify one of the sample templates that come with Excel 97. For the second, you'll build a form from the ground up.

Modifying a Sample Template

To modify one of the sample form templates that should already be on your system. Click File, New and select the Spreadsheet Solutions tab, and then open the Purchase ORDER.XLT template. The subject of customizing templates is covered in detail in Chapter 9, "Excel Solution Templates," and Chapter 24, "Integrating Excel with Other Office Applications," so I won't duplicate the information here.

Now customize the template according to what you learned in those chapters. Remember to save your file often.

TIP If you don't find the Purchase Order template, it might not have been installed on your system. In that case, you'll need to run Setup from the Excel installation CD-ROM and select the option to add or remove individual components.

A Note from the Author

The Spreadsheet Solutions folder contains sample templates, including several that were created by Village Software of Boston, Massachusetts. Essentially, they are samples of products available from this developer. (One of the templates is actually an order form for their products.) You may find them useful "as is." Each one can be customized to a certain extent, using features built into the templates. For example, you can substitute your family or company name and address and even your company logo.

However, I recommend that you do not attempt to modify or change these templates in any major way. The reason is that they use a large number of macros that depend on certain data being in specific cells. Some of these forms–specifically the Purchase Order, Expense Statement, and Invoice templates–export the information that you enter to an associated Excel worksheet database. If you make major changes to these forms, you'll get an error message every time you save them.

To play it safe, be sure to save them under another name before you make any changes to them, even if you only use the customization options built into them.

To test the template, fill out the purchase order and click the Capture Data in a Database button on the floating custom toolbar. (It's the last button on the toolbar.) You'll see a Create and Interact with Database dialog box. Select the Update Existing Database option.

Next you'll see the Template File – Save to Database dialog box again. This time, select the Create a New Record option, and Excel saves the information you have entered into the form in the associated database worksheet.

To view the database, open the worksheet PODB.XLS. If the default folder names were used when Excel was installed, it will be in the \Program Files\Microsoft Office\Office\Library folder.

Finally, return to the "Customize Your Purchase Order" worksheet in the Purchase Order workbook and click the Lock/Save Sheet button at the top of the form. This prevents users from inadvertently changing the information in the customization sheet. You will see two options, "Lock but Don't Save" and "Lock and Save Template." If you are finished with your customization, select the lock and save option, which opens the Save Template dialog box. Save your template under an appropriate name. I suggest that you save it in the Spreadsheet Solutions folder. If you are not ready to save the template, select the lock but don't save option and continue working.

You'll notice that the Lock/Save Sheet button is a toggle. When the worksheet is locked, the button reads Unlock This Sheet. You can click the button to see a brief explanation of locking and unlocking. Press OK.

When you have finished customizing the form, make it available to others by providing them with the network address for the template.

Creating a Form from Scratch

As useful as the sample Purchase Order template may be, you've probably found that it doesn't meet all of your requirements for a company purchase order. For example, you may need a place to enter accounting codes or department names. You may also want a form that's easier to navigate, in which the data entry fields are better defined. To meet these needs, you'll want to build a form from scratch. Although the example form you create here is for a Purchase Order (see Figure 27.1), the techniques can be applied to any form you may want to create. The following sections take you through the process step by step.

FIG. 27.1
This is what the completed form will look like.

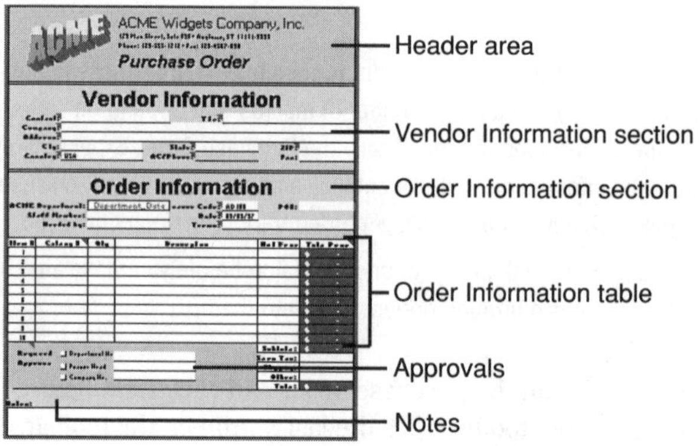

Preparing the Worksheet Before you begin to build your form, you need to prepare the worksheet and customize the formatting toolbar:

1. Click File, New to open a new blank workbook. Save the file to your working folder. It's always a good idea to name and save a new file right away so that Excel's AutoSave feature will work properly. (It will not work unless you have already named the file.)
2. Click Tools, Options and select the View tab (see Figure 27.2). Under Window Options, make sure that all of the boxes are checked except for Formulas. This will display the row and column headers, gridlines, and page breaks. In the Excel help file, Microsoft recommends that you turn off those features when creating forms. You will turn them off eventually, but you most definitely want them on while you are building the form.
3. In the General tab, set the standard font to Arial 10-pt. Then click OK to return to the worksheet.
4. Click File, Page Setup and make sure that letter-sized paper and portrait orientation are selected.
5. Click Format, Column, Standard Width and set the width to 6 (see Figure 27.3). This should give you rows A through M within the margins of your page. The sheet should also be about 50 rows deep. Look for the dotted lines that indicate the edges of your printed page. In designing the form, you'll leave Row 1 and Column A blank, so you can use them as borders later on.

TIP One of the secrets to using tables and worksheets for creating forms is to have a large number of narrow columns—at least 12—and then to merge cells as needed. This gives you good control over the placement of elements in your form and is far better than having to resize columns frequently.

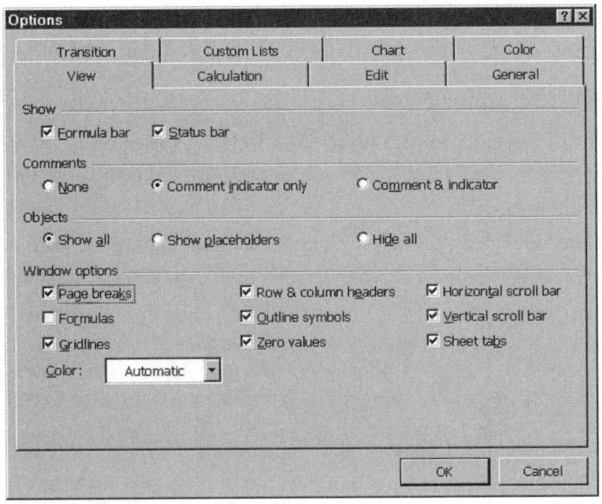

FIG. 27.2
When you create your own template, make sure that all of the boxes in the Window Options section of the Options, View tab are checked, except for formula display.

FIG. 27.3
Set the default column width to a smaller-than-normal number, such as 6, when creating a new form.

6. You'll be doing quite a bit of cell formatting, so add some icons that you'll need frequently to the Formatting toolbar. Click Tools, Customize, select the Commands tab, and click the Format category (see Figure 27.4). Drag and drop the following icons from the List of Commands to the formatting toolbar (the one with the typeface name and size) at the top of your screen: Merge Cells, Unmerge Cells, and Lock Cell. Also make sure that the Border and Fill Color icons (part of the default toolbar) are showing.

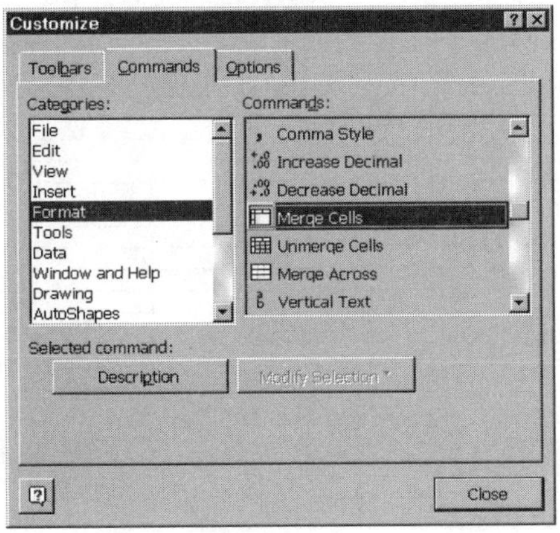

FIG. 27.4
Add new icons to your existing toolbars by dragging and dropping them from the Tools, Customize, Commands tab.

Setting Up the Header You'll use cells B2 through M9 for the header area, where you'll place the company name, address, and logo. Now you'll create the header:

1. Select cells B2 through M9 and click the Merge Cells icon.
2. Import your company logo, or use WordArt to create one, and place it at the top-left of the header area. Size it so that it doesn't take up more than a third of the area.

NOTE If you need to create your own logo, do it in a drawing program, such as Corel Draw, Adobe Illustrator, or Macromedia Freehand, rather than in a paint or image editing program such as Adobe PhotoShop or Corel PhotoPaint. Drawing programs create vector graphics, which are essentially mathematical formulas. These graphics can easily be scaled to whatever sizes you need, and will always print or display at the resolution of the output device. Unless the drawing is very complex, file sizes tend to be small and manageable.

Paint programs, on the other hand, generate bitmapped images made up of pixels, or dots, that are turned on or off. Bitmapped graphics are best created at the size at which they will be used, do not scale easily, and will print or display at the resolution inherent in the image, not that of the output device. The higher the resolution of the image, the more pixels in it–and the larger the file size.

Even if you intend to use your logo on a Web page, which requires a bitmapped image, use a drawing program to create it. Most good drawing programs today are able to export high quality bitmapped versions of the files that you create in them.

3. Click the Drawing icon in the standard toolbar. The Drawing toolbar will appear at the bottom of your screen, above the status bar (see Figure 27.5).

FIG. 27.5
The Drawing toolbar appears at the bottom of your screen.

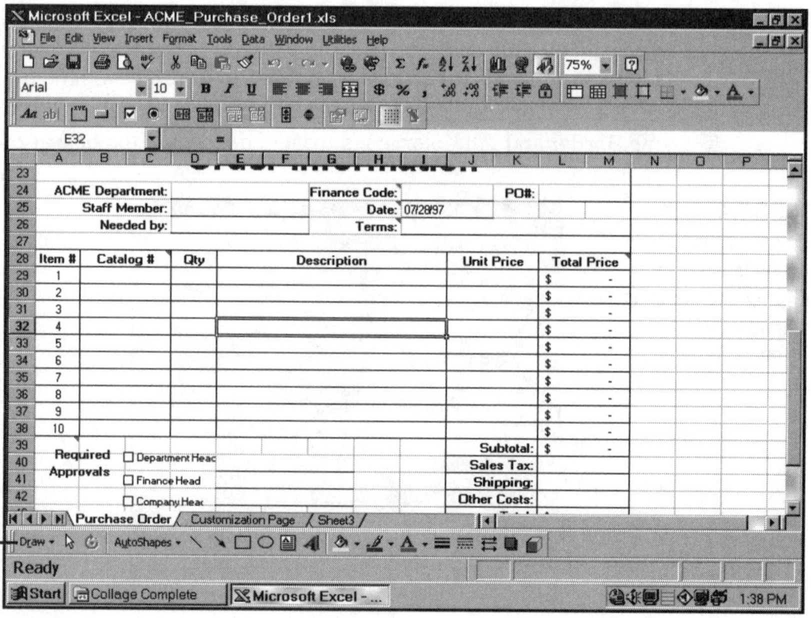

The Drawing toolbar

4. Select the Text Box icon on the Drawing toolbar. Your cursor will become a crosshair. Draw the Text Box in the remaining free area of the header.
5. With the Text Box selected, type your company name and address information. Press Shift+Insert to create a line break. On the last line, type **Purchase Order**.
6. Use the options on the formatting toolbar to change the typeface, size, or style (see Figure 27.6) of your Company name and the Form title. In the example, the company name is 18-pt. Bold. The words Purchase Order are set to 24-pt. Bold.

FIG. 27.6
A text box created with one of the drawing tools.

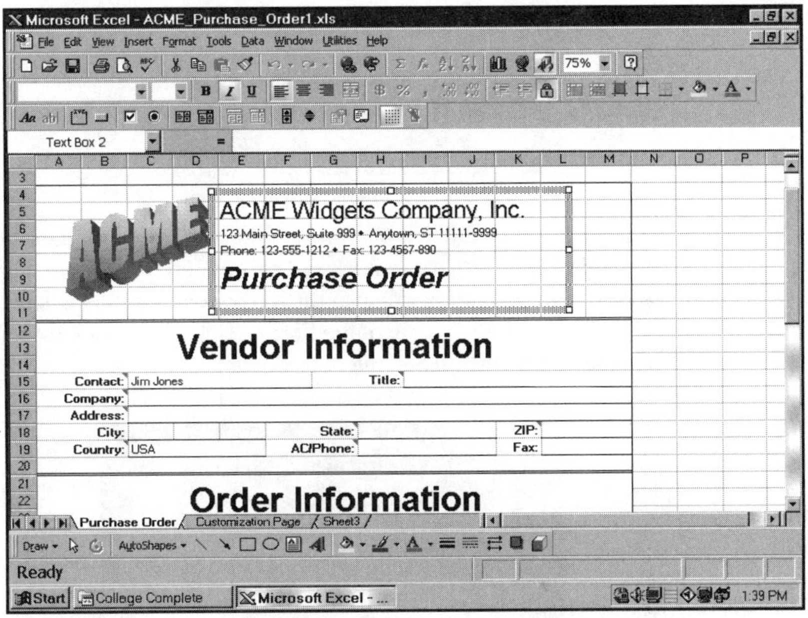

7. Right-click the cell containing the header and select Format Cells from the context-sensitive menu. In the Border tab, select the double rule for the bottom of the cell (see Figure 27.7).

TIP When should you use a Text Box, as in the example, rather than simply merging cells and formatting the text within them to create a large heading, as is done later? If you have only one line of text, all of which will be the same size and font, place it in a group of merged cells. If you have several lines of text, and you want to use more than one font or type size, create a Text Box. You'll find it much easier to format the text, and you can easily move or resize the box as needed.

Setting Up the Vendor Information Section In this section, you add the data entry fields for vendor information. Follow these steps:

1. Select and merge cells B10 through M12.

FIG. 27.7
The Border tab in the Format Cells dialog box allows you to place rules, or borders, on any side of the selected cell. You can use more than one type of rule in the same cell.

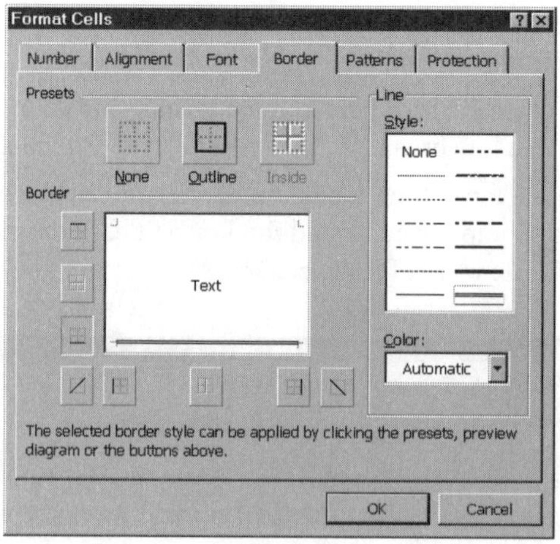

2. Type the line **Vendor Information** in the merged cell and use the options on the formatting toolbar to make it 28-pt. Arial, centered, and bold. If the line of text is at the bottom of the cell, rather than at the top or center, right-click the cell and select Format Cells. In the Alignment tab of the Format Cells dialog box (see Figure 27.8), set both horizontal and vertical alignment to Center.

FIG. 27.8
Adjust the alignment of text within a cell in the Alignment tab of the Format Cells dialog box.

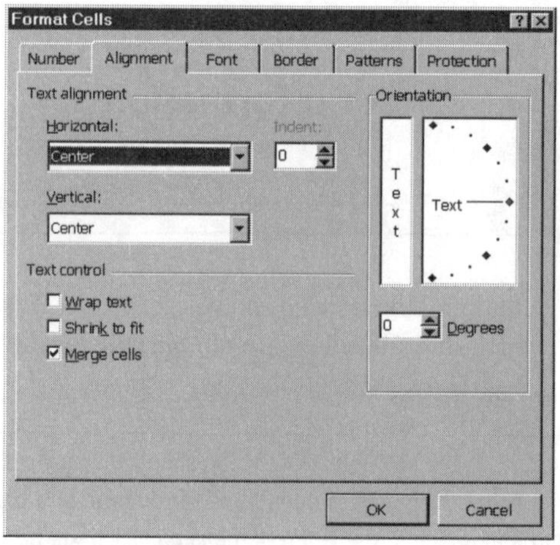

TIP If you find yourself changing Excel's default settings often, consider creating a blank template that has the settings the way you want them. Place the template in your Spreadsheet Solutions folder and use it whenever you need to create a new workbook. Be aware, however, that some settings in the Tools, Options dialog box, such as visible page breaks, don't "stick" from session to session.

3. Merge cells B13 and C13. Type **Contact** and make it bold, aligned right.

4. Similarly, merge B14-C14, B15-C15, B16-C16, and B17-C17, respectively. Type the following in the merged cells: **Company**, **Address**, **City**, and **Country**, respectively. Use the Format Painter on the standard toolbar to copy the formatting from B13 to each of these cells (see Figure 27.9).
5. Merge cells H13 and I13 and type **Title**. Format as in step 4. Do the same with G16-H16 (**State**) and G17-H17 (**AC/Phone**). Type **ZIP** in K16 and **Fax** in K17.
6. Merge cells D13 through G13. Click the arrow on the Border icon that you've added to the formatting toolbar and select the Bottom Border. Place a bottom border in the merged cell. This becomes the data entry field for the Contact name.
7. Do the same for cells J13-M13, D14-M14, D15-M15, D16-F16, D17-F17, I16-J16, I17-J17, L16-M16, and L17-M17, respectively.
8. Select and merge B18-M18 and place a double rule at the bottom (see Figure 27.9).

TIP The labels that you create at this stage will become column headings in an Excel database worksheet that you will generate and may eventually wind up as field names in a full-fledged database such as Microsoft Access or Lotus Approach. If this is likely, you'll make life easier for yourself by creating labels that conform to the dbase field name standard; that is, no more than 10 characters, and no spaces. (Use an underscore in place of a space.)

This may seem limiting, but if you ever have to import the data from a worksheet to an industry-standard database, you'll be glad you've done this. In fact, if your company uses databases at all, it is recommended that you standardize on commonly used field names, such as those for name and address information. This will make it much easier to import data from a variety of company sources.

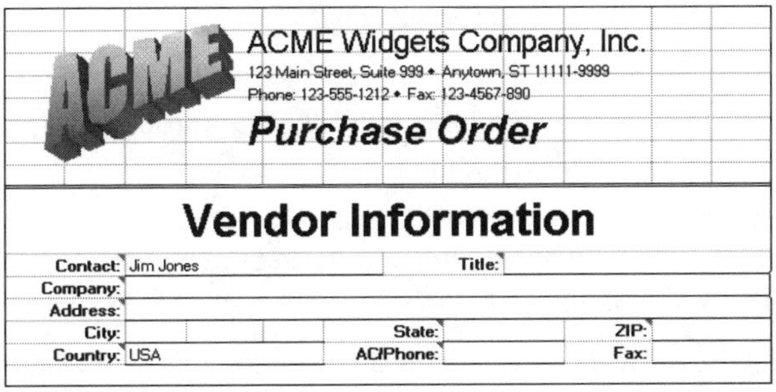

FIG. 27.9 The header and Vendor Information sections of the custom Purchase Order form.

Setting Up the Order Information Section Next you'll set up the Order Information area (see Figure 27.10), the largest section on the form. This portion of the form has two areas. The second area, where the actual order information is entered, looks and functions just like a spreadsheet.

To create the first area, follow these steps:

1. Merge cells B19 through M21. Type **Order Information** and use the Format Painter to copy the formatting from cell B10.

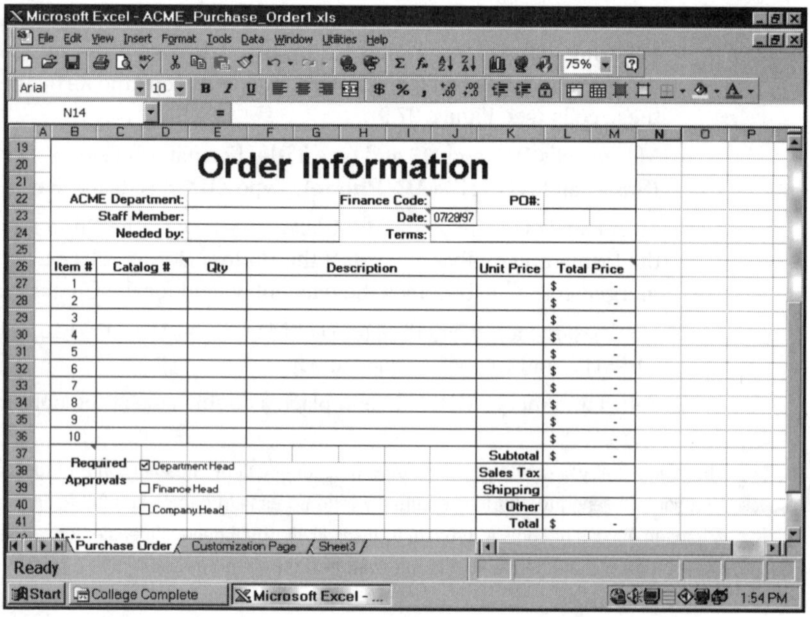

FIG. 27.10
The Order Information table portion of the custom Purchase Order form.

2. Merge B22 through D22, B23 through D23, and B24 through D24, respectively. Type **Department**, **Staff Member**, and **Needed by**, respectively, in the merged cells, and make the text bold and aligned right.
3. Merge H22-I22, H23-I23, and H24-I24, respectively. Type **Finance Code**, **Date**, and **Terms**, respectively, in the merged cells.
4. In K22, type **PO#**.
5. Merge E22 through G22, E23 through G23, E24 through G24, L22-M22, and J24 through M24, respectively. Apply a bottom border to each.
6. In J23, type the formula **=TODAY()**. Right-click the cell and select Format Cells. In the Number tab, select the Date category and set the type to 03/04/97 or any other short format that will fit in the cell.

In the second area, rows 26 through 41 will become a table for the actual order information. Follow these steps to create the second area:

1. Highlight cells B27 through M41. Right-click the highlighted area and select Format Cells. In the Border tab, apply a single line border to both inside and outside.
2. In row 26, merge cells C and D, F through J, and L and M. Then merge the same cells in each of the rows 27 through 36.
3. In row 26, type the following table headings: **Item#**, **Catalog#**, **Qty**, **Description**, **Unit Price**, and **Total Price**.
4. In column B, rows 27 through 36, type the numbers **1** through **10** respectively.

5. In cells K37 through K41 (respectively), type the following: **Subtotal**, **Sales Tax**, **Shipping**, **Other**, and **Total**. Make the text bold and aligned right.
6. In cell L27, type the formula **E27*K27**. This multiplies the quantity by the unit price. Copy and paste this formula into cells L28 through L36, respectively.
7. In cell L37, type the formula **SUM(L27:L36)**. This adds the total prices of items 1 through 10.
8. In cell L41, type the formula **SUM(L37:L40)**. This adds shipping charges, sales tax, and other charges to the subtotal in cell L37.
9. Highlight the cells in the Item#, Catalog#, and Description columns. Right-click and select Format Cells. In the Number tab, select the Text category.
10. Similarly, apply the Number category to the cells in the Qty column. Apply the Currency category to the cells in the Unit Price and Total Price columns.

NOTE The Order Information table allows for 10 items. If you don't need that many, leave out some rows. On the other hand, if you need more, go ahead and add them now. Whatever you do, however, be sure to adjust the SUM formulas in column L accordingly.

Adding Space for Approvals and Notes At this point the form is nearly complete. However, you still need to provide space for approvals, and it's always good to have a place to write notes or add information that doesn't fit anywhere else. Cells B37 through J41, at the bottom left of the Order Information table, are not being used, so you'll provide for approvals there. Follow these steps:

1. Highlight cells B37 through J41. Right-click and select Format Cells. In the Border tab, clear all borders.
2. Create a Text Box with the words **Required Approvals** and place it over cells B37 through C40. Make the text bold and right aligned.
3. Click View, Toolbars, Forms to add the forms toolbar to your toolbar area.
4. Click the Checkbox icon on the forms toolbar. Your cursor will become a crosshair.
5. Click the cursor next to the Text Box that you have just created. A check box object appears, already selected, with placeholder text. Move your cursor over the check box so that it becomes a text cursor, and then change the text to something appropriate for your organization, such as **Department Head**.

NOTE Normally you would attach a macro to a check box. The macro would most likely place the checked or unchecked value returned by the check box in a designated cell elsewhere in the worksheet. Other macros or formulas would use that value, in turn. For example, in the checked state that value might be Y, while in the unchecked state it might be N. However, in this case, the purpose of the check box is simply for the user to indicate what approvals are required, so you don't need a macro.

6. Create a check box for each level of approval required by your organization. There's room for up to four within the Order Information table. If you need more than that,

consider placing them below the table. Note that you cannot modify the font, type size, or style of the Checkbox label.

7. Align each check box with the top-left corner of a convenient cell. Each check box should occupy the space of only two cells. Stack them in the area D37 to E41 (see Figure 27.11).
8. Merge three or four cells to the right of each check box and apply a bottom border to each. This is for signatures on paper copies of the Purchase Order.

If you have included space for 10 items in the Order Information table, you should now have eight or nine rows left above the page break indicator. You'll use some of this space for the user to add notes.

1. In cell B43, type **Notes** and make it bold.
2. Merge cells B44 through M46. This will leave a cushion of about three rows at the bottom of the form, giving you room to add items as needed.

The basic form is now complete. This is a good time to save the file, print out a copy for proofreading, and check it over to make sure that you've covered all the bases.

Adding Comments and Color and Validating Data With the basics in good shape, you can now add some of the finishing touches that will make the form attractive and easy to use. You will add embedded messages to explain the purpose of an item or give the user instructions. You will take steps to ensure that the form is protected from user error and that the user enters the data correctly. Finally, you will add color to make it attractive and easier to use.

There are two ways to enter embedded comments or instructions. One is to select the Comment option on the Insert menu (or Insert Comment from the context-sensitive, right-click menu). Another is to include a message as part of Excel's validation feature (available from the Data menu). In either case, the end result is about the same.

When you add a comment to a cell, Excel places a red marker at the top-right corner. The comment pops up whenever you place your cursor over the marker for a second or two. It disappears as soon as you move your cursor. Validation messages, on the other hand, pop up automatically whenever you place your cursor in the cell itself. The message stays on the screen, just below the cell, as long as your cursor is in it.

TIP The comment feature is more flexible. You can format the type or resize the window, which you can't do with a validation message, and the message can be fairly long. Validation messages are limited in length and can become annoying because you can't avoid them. Comments are more accessible when you need to edit or delete them.

Use comments for general information or lengthy instructions and reserving validation messages for short, specific instructions to help the user enter data in a cell properly. There may be situations where you would want to use both features together. For this reason, adding comments to the text cell that contains the label for the data entry cell is suggested, rather than to the data cell itself.

Follow these steps to add a comment:

1. Right-click the cell to which you want to add a comment and select Insert Comment. This opens a box in which you enter and edit text in the usual way. By default, it will already have your name, in bold, followed by a colon. You may want to replace your name with the name of the field being explained.
2. Move your cursor to the right of the colon, which will take you out of the boldface area to the next line, and type your text. When you are finished, click outside of the text box. It disappears, but you see a red comment marker in the upper-right corner of the cell.
3. Move your cursor over the marker to check a comment and it pops up (see Figure 27.11).
4. To edit or delete a comment, right-click the cell containing it and select Edit Comment or Delete Comment, respectively, from the context-sensitive menu.

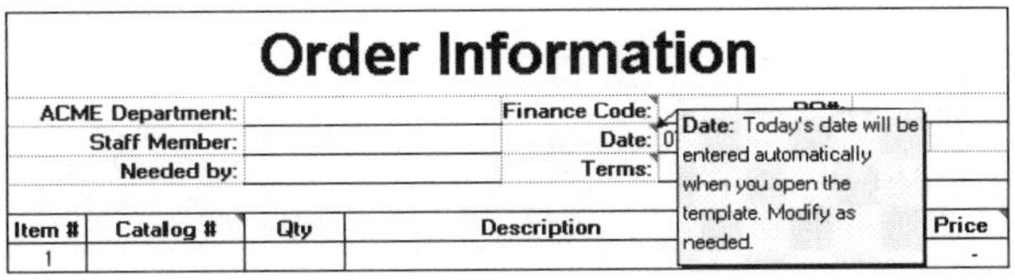

FIG. 27.11 Embedded comments can be used to provide information or instructions.

TIP Excel's default setting for Comment text is 10-pt., which is very easy to read at 1024×768 resolution but perhaps a bit large at lower settings, such as 800×600 (Super VGA) or 640×480 (standard VGA). You might want to make your comment text 9-pt. instead, which is a good compromise and is still readable at 1024×768 on a decent monitor, or even 8-pt. if most of your users have relatively low resolution settings. Avoid using text smaller than 8-pt.

In addition to providing the user with helpful comments and instruction, you also want to take steps to make sure that they enter the data correctly. For example, you could add a drop-down list of acceptable codes to the `Finance Code` data cell, prevent a user from ordering any item over a certain price, or remind the user to follow date format in the `Needed by` cell. You begin first with the drop-down list, as outlined here:

1. To create the items for the list, move your cursor to an off-screen column, such as Q. Create a list of the codes that you will need in a single vertical column, as shown in Figure 27.12, then save your file.
2. Select cell J22 and click Data, Validation.
3. In the Settings tab of the Data Validation dialog box (see Figure 27.13), under Validation Criteria, select the List criteria from the Allow drop-down box. Make sure that both the Ignore Blank check box and the In-Cell Dropdown check box are checked.
4. Click the button at the bottom of the Source window under the list of criteria. Figure 27.14 shows a minimized Data Validation dialog box and the order form worksheet.

FIG. 27.12

A column of data to be included in a validation list.

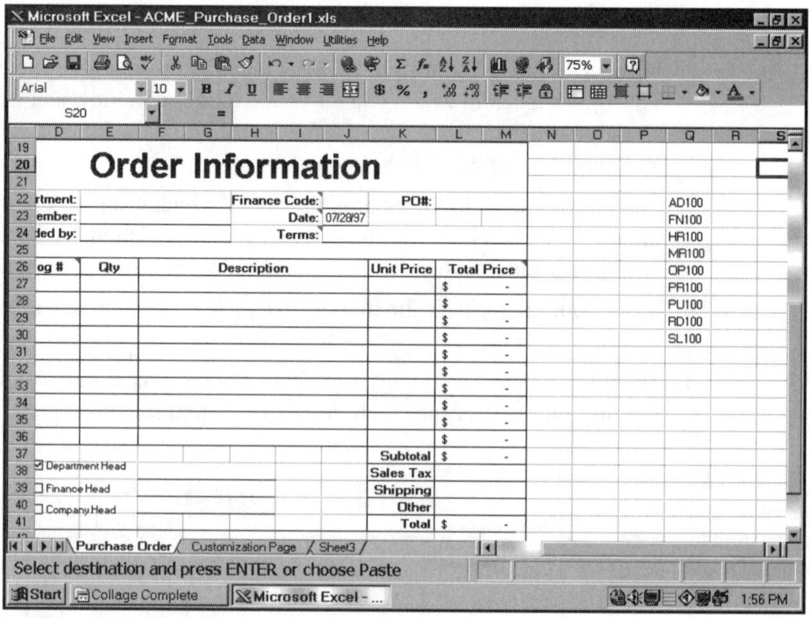

FIG. 27.13

The Settings tab of the Data Validation dialog box, with List selected as the criteria.

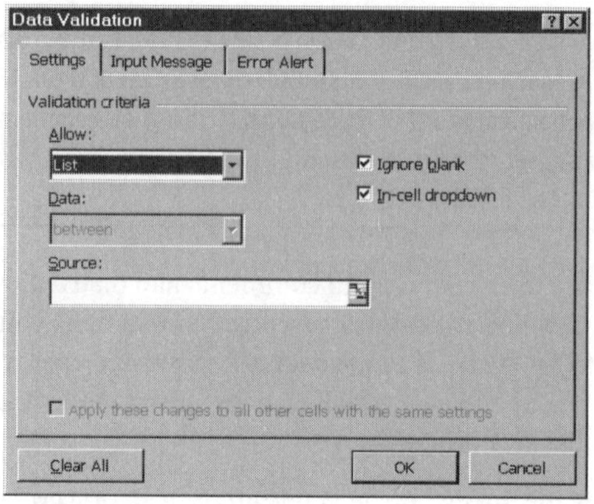

5. Highlight the cells with the finance codes that you have just entered in step 1. The range will appear in the Data Validation window.
6. Click the button at the bottom-right of the window to return to the Validation dialog box and click OK. You should now see a drop-down box in the `Finance Code` data cell, with a list of the codes that you have defined (see Figure 27.15).

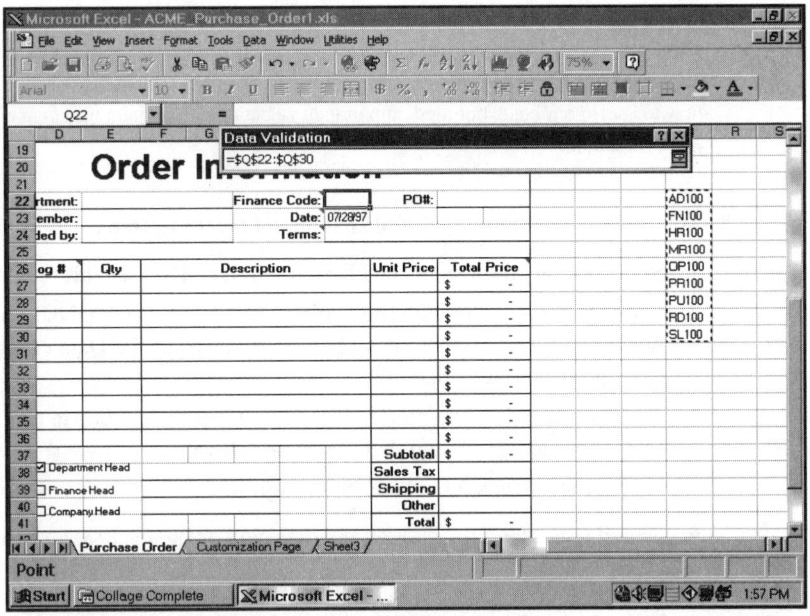

FIG. 27.14
The Data Validation Source window opens to allow you to select the data to be included in the list.

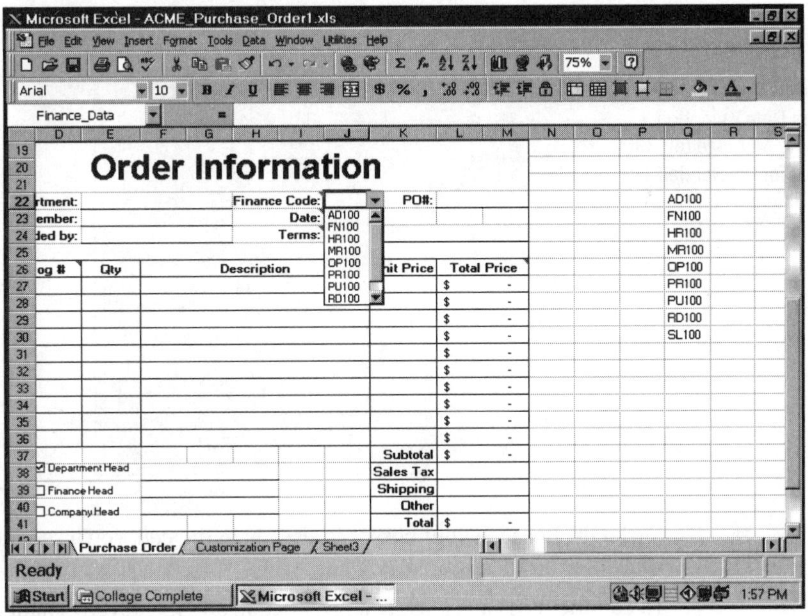

FIG. 27.15
The drop-down list box created by list validation.

CAUTION

When creating a validation list, do not select any of the other tabs in the Validation dialog box. They don't apply to lists in any case, but more importantly, selecting one of them may cause Excel to crash. It did on my system, repeatedly.

To set a ceiling on the unit price of an item, follow these steps:

1. Save your file, then select cell K27, the first cell in the Unit Price column.
2. Click Data, Validation. On the Settings tab, select Decimal or Whole Number as the Allow criteria and select Less Than or Equal To as the Data criteria. Type **1000** in the Maximum window. Click OK.
3. Test the validation by entering a number larger than 1000 in cell K27. You should see an error message indicating that the value is invalid.
4. Repeat these steps for cells K28 through K36.

Now you add a message to cell E24, the data cell for the `Needed by` field. Here's how:

1. Select cell #24 and click Data, Validation.
2. In the Input Message tab (see Figure 27.16), check the box at the top of the dialog box. Then type a title for your message in the Title window, and type the message itself in the Input message window.

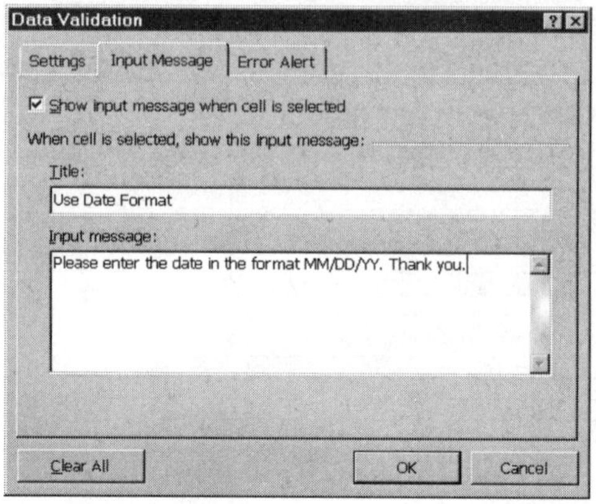

FIG. 27.16
The Data Validation Input Message tab, with text for the Needed by data entry cell.

3. Click OK. Because your cursor is already in the cell, you'll see the message as soon as you close the Validation dialog box.
4. To edit the message, click Data, Validation and make your changes.

To remove a validation, click Data, Validation and click the Clear All button.

Judicious use of colors can help to make the form more pleasing to the eye, as well as easier to use. Colors can also help to delineate the various sections within the form. Follow these steps to add some color to the header at the top:

1. Select cell B2 and click the Fill Color button on the formatting toolbar. Select a color that complements your logo.
2. Highlight the Vendor Information area and click the drop-down arrow on the Fill Color icon to select a new color—perhaps a light blue. Do the same for the top part of the Order Information section, above the table, as well as the rows between the table and the Notes window.
3. Highlight the Required Approvals portion of the table and select a suitable light color.
4. At this point the Order Information table and the Notes window should still be white. If not, select them and change them to white.
5. Highlight the cells L27 through L37 as well as L41. Right-click and select Format Cells. In the Patterns tab, set the fill color to red. On the Fonts tab, change the text color from automatic to white and the style from normal to bold. (If the red and white combination doesn't work for you, make the background color yellow and set the text color to black instead.) The logic here is to indicate that these cells contain formulas and that the user cannot enter data in them.
6. Highlight the rows and columns around the form and select a dark color for them.
7. Click Tools, Options. In the View tab of the Options dialog box, uncheck the Page Breaks, Gridlines, and Row & Column Header boxes.
8. Print out a proof of the page.

The last thing you need to do is protect all but the data entry cells, so that they cannot be inadvertently changed. Follow these steps:

1. Highlight the entire form, right-click, and select Format Cells
2. On the Protection tab of the Format Cells dialog box (see Figure 27.17), click several times on the Locked check box until the check mark appears against a white background. This means that all of the cells have been locked.

NOTE Locking a cell has no effect until you protect the entire worksheet.

3. Select the cells in which the user can enter data, all of which should be white by now. (Select multiple cells with Control+Click.)
4. Right-click and select Format Cells. In the Protection tab, clear the Lock check box.
5. Click Tools, Protection, Protect Sheet (see Figure 27.18). In the Protect Sheet dialog box, make sure that all of the check boxes are checked. Think twice about entering a password, because if you forget it, you won't be able to modify the worksheet. If you do use one, be sure to write it down someplace.

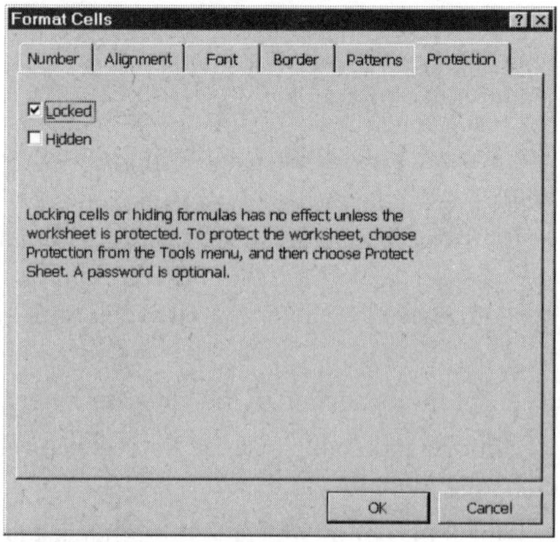

FIG. 27.17
Highlight the entire form and click the Locked check box in the Protection tab of the Format Cells dialog box to lock all of the cells. Later, unlock only those cells used for data entry.

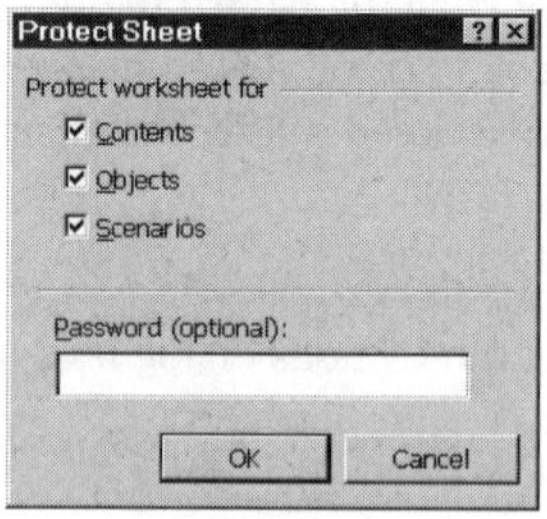

FIG. 27.18
Use the Protect Sheet dialog box to prevent others from inadvertently modifying your form.

6. Test the protection by placing your cursor in the first available cell and tabbing through the form. You should move smoothly from left to right, from one data cell to another. If your cursor winds up in a non-data cell, click the Lock icon that you've added to the formatting toolbar to protect it.
7. To unprotect a sheet, click Tools, Protection, Unprotect Sheet. Figure 27.19 shows the completed form.

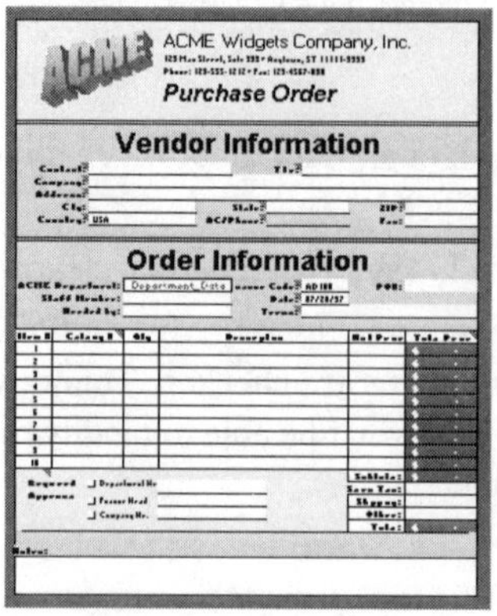

FIG. 27.19
The finished custom Purchase Order form.

Adding Form Controls

The purchase order worksheet, as it now stands, is quite attractive and functional. However, it does not make extensive use of interactive devices such as option buttons and command buttons—nor does it require them. As you develop more complex forms, however, you will want to use some of those available devices.

Excel 97 provides two means of adding these elements: the Forms toolbar and the Control Toolbox. To display these tools, click View, Toolbars, Forms and View, Toolbars, and Control Toolbox.

At first glance, these groups of tools appear to be very similar. Each contains the same basic elements, such as option buttons, check boxes, and list boxes. The difference is in the means in which they are implemented.

The Forms toolbar controls are designed to work solely within Excel. Many of them require the use of existing Excel macros. You use these controls to run macros that you have created within Excel.

The Control Toolbox contains ActiveX controls, including custom controls that may have been installed on your system by other applications. They use macros that have been written specifically for the controls, rather than for Excel worksheets. Use them to manage specific events that are triggered when the control itself is used.

ActiveX controls cannot be used on a form designed for use on a Web site. For that type of form, you must use the controls on the Forms toolbar.

The Forms Toolbar In this section, you learn about the controls available on the Forms Toolbar and how to set the properties for these controls. Table 27.1 lists the toolbar buttons and their descriptions.

Table 27.1 Contents of the Forms Toolbar

Button	Control	Description
	Label	Use this control to add a brief amount of text to your form (for example, to provide information about another control or to highlight something else on the form). The label is independent of any cell; however, you cannot change the typeface or size of the text.
	Edit Box	This is a data entry box for text, numbers, dates, or cell references. It's used in Visual Basic dialog box controls; it is often grayed out when you are in a worksheet.
	Group Box	This is a rectangle with a label and a border. Use this to group related controls, such as option buttons or check boxes.

continues

Table 27.1 Continued

Button	Control	Description
	Command Button	Use this to create a button you can click to run a macro. Define the macro before creating the button.
	Check Box	This box is used to select or deselect an option. Even when enclosed within a group box, check boxes are independent of each other; that is, more than one box can be checked. The control returns True when checked and False when unchecked.
	Option Button	Option buttons are grouped; only one button within the group can be selected at any time. Each button has an assigned number. The number of the selected button is returned.
	List Box	This box contains a list of items related to the content of a group of cells elsewhere in the worksheet. Selecting an item from the list returns the position of the selected item within the list.
	Combo Box	A list box with a text box and a drop-down arrow. The selected item is shown in the text box.
	Combination List/Edit Box	A text list with an edit box. Used in dialog box controls, it's often grayed out in worksheets.
	Combination Drop-Down Edit Box	A drop-down list with an edit box. Used in dialog box controls, it's often grayed out in worksheets.
	Scroll Bar	Use this when you have a long list of values. Users can click the scroll arrows to move in small increments or use the scroll box to move more quickly through the list.
	Spin Button	This button has up and down arrows and can be attached to a cell. Use it to increase or decrease values in controlled increments.
	Control Properties	Opens the Properties dialog box for the selected control.
	Edit Code	Select this to edit the code assigned to the selected control.
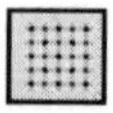	Toggle Grid	This button turns worksheet gridlines on or off.
	Run Dialog	This is used to test dialog boxes you have added to a dialog sheet. It's often grayed out in worksheets.

To add a Forms toolbar control to your worksheet, follow these steps:

1. Click the control on the toolbar and move your cursor to your worksheet. The cursor turns into a small crosshair.
2. Click and drag to draw the dimensions of the control.
3. With the control still selected, right-click and select Format Control from the shortcut menu. The Format Control dialog box opens.

The Format Control options will differ depending on the control you selected. For example, the label control has only three tab sheets (Size, Protection, and Properties) while the List Box and Combo Box controls add a fourth (called Control). Check Boxes and Option Buttons add a fifth tab (Colors and Lines).

The following list outlines the Format Control options:

Colors and Lines. Here you can select the control's fill color, line color, style and weight, and in some cases, arrow styles.

Size. In this dialog box, you can change the height and width of the control and, in some cases, its rotation. If you prefer to work with percentages, you can scale the height and width. By default, the current size of the control is shown, and scaling is set at 100 percent.

Protection. Here you can lock the control itself to prevent it from being resized, moved, or deleted, and you can lock the text within the control to prevent it from being changed.

Properties. Here you can determine whether the control can be moved or resized as the cells over which it has been placed are moved or resized, as well as whether the control appears when you print your worksheet.

Control. In this last tab, you can change the default value of the check box and select the cell to which the control will be linked. The value options are Checked, Unchecked, and Mixed. Checked returns True, Unchecked returns False to the linked cell, and Mixed (where the check box itself is grayed out) returns N/A. The data returned by the control can be used in a macro or formula.

To use a list or combo box, you will need to go through several additional steps:

1. Create the items to be included in the list by entering them in a single column in a blank area of your worksheet. See the section "Validating Data," earlier in this chapter for further information.
2. Draw the control.
3. Right-click and select Format Control. Then click the Control tab.
4. Define the input range. You can enter the cell coordinates of your list manually; however, you might find it easier to click the icon at the right of the input range edit window, highlight the cells with the list you've just created, and then click the icon again to define your selection and return to the Control tab. The proper cell coordinates should appear in the input range window.

5. Using the method described in step 4, define the cell to which the results of the control will be linked.
6. Set Selection Type to Single.
7. Click OK to exit the Format Control dialog box.
8. To test your control, click outside of the control to deselect it, and then use the control to select an item. The position of the selected item in your list should appear in the linked cell.
9. To move a control, select it and drag it to the new location.
10. To resize a control, select it, and then click and drag a sizing handle.

The Control Toolbox The ActiveX controls available in the Control Toolbox are similar in function to those on the Forms Toolbar. However, the way that you use them is very different. When you right-click a Control Toolbox control and select Format Control, you see only three tabs in the dialog box: Size, Protection, and Properties.

Noticeably absent, even from the Check Box and List Box controls, are the Colors and Lines tab and the Control tab. To control the appearance and behavior of a Control Toolbox control, you need to be familiar with Visual Basic.

To edit the properties, right-click the control and select Properties. This displays a list of the properties associated with that control, expressed in Visual Basic terminology. Double-clicking a control opens the underlying code in the Visual Basic editor, where you can edit the code.

To edit only the text in a text box, check box, or option button, right-click the control. The name of the control appears in the middle of the context-sensitive shortcut menu. Select the name, and then select Edit. A text cursor appears inside the control. Edit the text, and then click outside of the control to deselect it. Be aware that while you can edit the text itself in this mode, you cannot change its properties.

Table 27.2 shows each of the available controls and provides a description of it.

Table 27.2 Contents of the Control Toolbox

Button	Control	Description
	Design Mode	Activate this to enable yourself to edit and manipulate the controls.
	Properties	Click this to open the Properties list for the selected control.
	View Code	Click this to open the underlying code for the selected control in the Visual Basic editor.
	Check Box	This box is used to select or deselect an option. Even when enclosed within a group box, check boxes are independent of each other; that is, more than one box can be checked.

Button	Control	Description
	Text Box	This is similar to the Label control, but more suitable for longer amounts of text.
	Command Button	Use this to create a button that initiates an action when pressed.
	Option Button	Options buttons are used to select one item among a group.
	List Box	This type of box contains a list of items.
	Combo Box	A list box with a text box and a drop-down arrow. The item selected is shown in the text box. You can also enter data manually in the text box portion.
	Toggle Button	This button remains pressed when it's clicked, and it is not released until it is clicked again.
	Spin Button	This button has up and down arrows and can be attached to a cell. Use it to increase or decrease values in controlled increments.
	Scroll Bar	Use this when you have a long list of values. Users can click the scroll arrows to move in small increments or use the scroll box to move more quickly through the list.
	Label	Use this to add small amounts of text to the worksheet.
	Image	This control enables you to embed an image in a form.
	More Controls	Select this to see a list of additional ActiveX controls installed on your system.

Using the Template Wizard to Create a Database

When you are satisfied with the final worksheet (refer to Figure 27.19), you can proceed to creating the database that will enable you to capture the data. This is the easy part because Excel does most of the work for you. But before you plunge ahead, think about what data you want to export to the database worksheet that will be generated.

To begin with, you probably don't need all of the vendor information, just the name. Chances are you already have a vendor database, or at least a good Rolodex file. In any case, if the vendor is used frequently, much of the data will be redundant.

On the other hand, you probably do need all of the information at the top of the Order Information section, above the table, and you may want to include the Notes data as well. You will certainly want to include the totals and other costs in cells L37 through L41, particularly if you are using the data to manage a budget.

What about the individual items on the order? That information would probably be useful as well, but you'll skip it this time around.

With this in mind, invoke the Template Wizard by selecting Data, Template Wizard. (If that option does not appear, the wizard was not installed and you'll need to rerun the Excel setup program from the installation CD-ROM to add it.) The Template Wizard has five steps:

1. Step 1 has two edit boxes, one for the name of the source worksheet or template and another for the name of the template to be generated from it. The new Purchase Order template is identical in appearance to the workbook that you have just created. Check to make sure that the default information is correct and click Next.
2. In step 2, decide what type of database you want to create and what folder will contain it. You can choose between Microsoft Excel Workbook and several industry-standard database formats. Accept the default settings for now and click Next.
3. Decide on the cells that you want to export and the names to give the fields in step 3 (see Figure 27.20). Use the default setting for the name of the worksheet to which the data will be exported.
4. Under the Sheet title are two columns, Cell and Field Name. Place your cursor in the first Cell field and click once in the `Company` data cell to place a reference to that cell in the Template Wizard. Click in the next Cell field and the label from the cell to the left of the data cell automatically is added to the Field Name list.
5. Repeat the process for the remaining fields (see Figure 27.20). Keep in mind that they will be exported in the order you place them in the Template Wizard. Make sure that the field names conform to the standards required by your full-fledged database program, if you have one. When everything is ready, click Next.

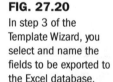

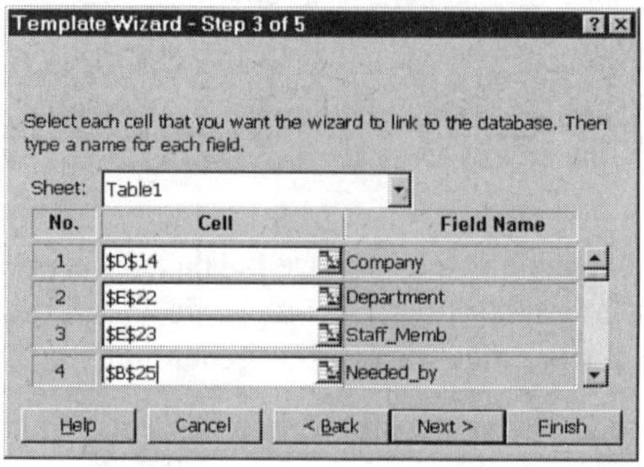

FIG. 27.20 In step 3 of the Template Wizard, you select and name the fields to be exported to the Excel database.

6. In step 4, the wizard asks you if you want to add information from an existing workbook to the new one. Select the No, Skip It option button and click Next.

7. In step 5, the wizard tells you where the new template and database will be placed and offers instructions for making the template available to others. The wizard seems to have a problem with pathnames that have a space in them (as in "\Program Files\ Microsoft Office", which it truncates to "\Program Files\Microsoft") but it does save the file in the expected location. Click Finish.
8. Open the new template and test it by entering some data, and click File, Save. When you do, you'll get a message asking you if you want to create a new record in the attached database or continue without creating one. Select the option to create a new record and close the template without saving it.
9. Open the new database to make sure that your data was exported correctly (see Figure 27.21). Adjust the width of the columns to accommodate your field names and format each column as needed.

FIG. 27.21
The new database generated by the Template Wizard. Adjust the widths of the columns as needed.

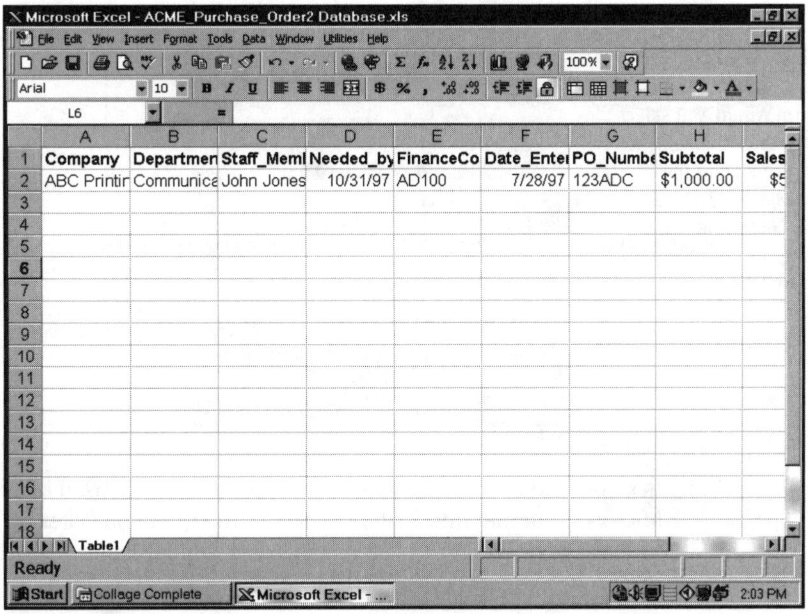

CAUTION

Do not add anything to the worksheet containing your data! If you do, it may not function properly as a database. Instead, add worksheets as needed and either copy the data to another worksheet or create references to the cells in the first one.

When you check out the new template, you'll probably find a few mistakes. You can modify the template as long as you don't alter the location of the cells containing data to be exported. Unprotect the sheet and make your changes or corrections.

Using the Web Form Wizard

You'll use the same Purchase Order worksheet to create a template that can be posted on a Web site. You'll first need to unprotect the sheet, then click Tools, Wizard, Web Form. This wizard involves six steps:

1. Step 1 tells you what the wizard does. Click Next.
2. In step 2 (see Figure 27.22), you'll see a list of controls and cell references. Begin by deleting obvious ones that you don't need, such as the references to the check boxes.
3. By default, the field name will be the same as the cell reference. Select a reference, and the wizard will highlight the cell. If you don't need it in the database, delete the reference. If you do, type a meaningful field name in the edit box below the list of references, then click the Change Name button. The field name next to the cell reference will now reflect your change. When everything is ready, click Next.

FIG. 27.22
In step 2 of the Web Form Wizard, you select and name the fields to be exported to the database. By default, the field name is the same as the cell reference.

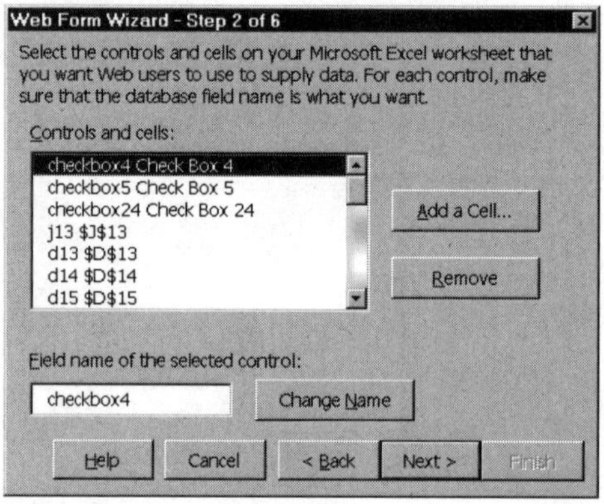

4. In step 3, the wizard asks you for the type of interface used by your Web server, either Microsoft Internet Information Server or the Common Gateway Interface. If you are not sure, ask your Webmaster or your network administrator.
5. In step 4, you must choose between saving the result as an Excel file or adding it to your FrontPage Web. To add it to your Web, FrontPage Explorer must be running and your Web site must be open in it. For now, select the option to save the results as an Excel file. (Whatever your choice, the wizard generates the same basic files.) The default file name is MYFORM, which you will probably want to change to something such as MYPURCHASEORDER. Click Next when ready.
6. In step 5 (see Figure 27.23), you're asked to provide the information that will appear on the confirmation page sent to the user's browser after they have submitted the form. Use the default options, which can easily be changed later on, and click Next.

FIG. 27.23
In step 5 of the Web Form Wizard, you provide the information that will appear on the confirmation page seen by the user after they submit the form to your Web site.

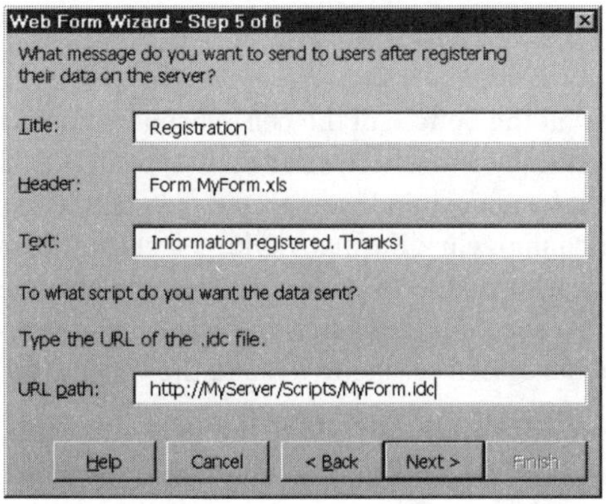

7. In step 6, the wizard tells you what you must now do with the files it has created for data collection. These files will have the extensions XLS, IDC, HTX, and MBD. They must be moved to the appropriate directory on your Web server for them to work properly. That location will differ from one server to another. You will also need to configure the ODBC data source, and you might need to create a new one. Finally, you must edit the IDC file to reflect the proper name for your data source.

One final comment: The Web Form Wizard generates the intermediary files required by the Web server interface. For example, it creates the HTX, IDC, and MDB files required by Microsoft Internet Information Server. In spite of Excel 97's excellent Web connectivity features, one file that the Web Form Wizard does *not* generate is an HTML page with the form in it. All that you or your Webmaster can do is create a hypertext link to the file from a Web page. Users browsing your site must still have Excel 97 to be able to use the form. This may work well in a corporate intranet environment where many people have the necessary software, but not on a World Wide Web site. If you are designing forms for the World Wide Web, and you have FrontPage 97, you may be better off using its excellent HTML forms feature to create forms for Web pages.

Common Problems and Solutions

The bottom of a comment is truncated.

Right-click the cell containing the comment and select Edit Comment. Drag one of the handles on the border surrounding the box to enlarge it.

The Web Form Wizard keeps changing my field names.

The wizard will not allow you to include anything other than letters and numbers in the field name, nor will it allow you to begin a name with a number. It will change the name automatically if you attempt to create one that it can't handle.

Excel aligns text at the bottom of the cell, making it difficult to enter text in large merged cells.

By default, Excel aligns text at the bottom of the cell. Normally this is not a problem. However, if you have merged cells vertically and you then begin to type in the merged cell, your text will start at the bottom. This can be annoying. If you prefer your text to align differently, such as top (vertical) and left (horizontal), click Format, Style, select the Normal style, and click Modify. You'll get the familiar Format Cells dialog box, but the changes that you make will affect the entire worksheet (except for items that you have already modified on-the-fly). In the Alignment tab, change the horizontal setting to left and the vertical setting to top.

When I look at a form on my computer, all of the text and data fit inside the cells with room to spare. However, when I look at the same form on my assistant's system, sometimes the text or data is truncated. This is true even though we are both using the same fonts and the same screen resolution.

The quality of your video system, which includes your monitor, video card, and video driver, can be a major factor in how text is displayed on your screen. Chances are that you have a good-quality system, while your assistant may have a lesser-quality system. These systems tend to "fatten" the text because the pixels, or dots, on the screen are not as fine as they ought to be. The best way to avoid the problem is to leave as much of a safety margin as possible around the text in each cell. If possible, try to avoid resorting to a smaller font size, which can be hard to read on a poor-quality video system.

When the Validation List Source window is open, you can't select data from another worksheet.

Creating a validation list by highlighting data to be included in the list works only within the same worksheet. The Source validation window will allow you to move within the active worksheet but not to switch worksheets. Place the data on the same worksheet as the form, in an off-screen column where it will be out of sight.

From Here...

In developing effective forms for online use, many factors come into play, including graphic design, database connectivity, and even programming (if you want to use advanced features such as ActiveX controls). The following chapters will provide more information on related topics:

- See Chapter 14, "Building Excel Databases," for a better understanding of Excel databases.
- See Chapter 19, "Auditing and Validating Worksheets," for more information about validating user input.
- See Chapter 29, "Introducing VBA Programming," as well as Chapters 30 through 32 to learn about programming in Visual Basic for Applications.

PART VII

Programming Excel

CHAPTER 28

Understanding VBA Macros

by Bill Ray

Microsoft Excel 97 contains a powerful macro language called Visual Basic for Applications, which is commonly known as VBA. Macros allow you to automate your work in Excel by turning a whole series of actions into a single command. An Excel macro can be as simple as a series of recorded steps, or as complex as a custom application. ■

What is a macro?

Excel 97 contains the powerful VBA programming language, which is used to create and run macros. Macros provide timesaving shortcuts for many everyday activities.

Record and play back macros

By recording macros, you can take advantage of the automation of VBA without learning to program. Later, you can edit your recorded macros to add features and improve performance.

Assign shortcut keys and toolbar buttons

By defining shortcut keys and customizing your toolbars, you will be able to run you macros quickly, at any time.

How macros are stored

Because macros are stored in your workbooks, you can easily distribute your macros with any spreadsheet application.

What Is a VBA Macro?

Throughout the history of personal computing, many application programs have had macro programming facilities available. Generally, these macro languages have allowed a user of the program to record a series of actions, and play them back at a later time. In some programs, the macros are simply a sequence of keystrokes, such as those you would use to operate the menu commands of the program. In other programs, the macro language is more of a complete programming language, allowing the experienced user to use complex programming logic to create fully functional applications.

Microsoft Excel 97, as well as the other major applications in Microsoft Office 97, contains a powerful macro programming facility that combines the best of both worlds. You can easily record and play back macros, assigning the macro to be run when you press a convenient key combination, or when you click on a customized toolbar or menu command. The macros that you record are created automatically in the Visual Basic for Applications programming language, also known as VBA. You are not required to do any programming to work with recorded macros.

As you learn more about working with macros, you can add programming features to your recorded macros, or even create entirely new macros by typing in all the VBA code yourself. You'll learn more about advanced programming in VBA in Chapters 29 through 32. This chapter will show you how to create and work with recorded macros, which are the foundation of working with VBA in Excel.

When Do You Need a Macro?

One of the first signs that you may need a macro is when you find yourself performing the same series of actions over and over again. By recording these actions as a macro, you can speed up your work and make it more reliable. But first, you should check to see whether Excel has built-in features you can use instead of creating a macro.

There are many time-saving features built into Excel 97. Here are just a few examples of the kinds of features you should consider before creating a macro:

- Find and Replace. See "Find and Replace Strategies" in Chapter 3, "Entering and Editing Data."
- PivotTables and other Data Management commands. See Chapter 20, "Analyzing Data: PivotTables!"
- AutoFormat, Conditional Formatting, and Styles. See Chapter 4, "Formatting Your Worksheets."
- Views, Scenarios, and the Report Manager. See "Report Manager" in Chapter 7, "Using Excel Add-Ins," and "Working with Scenarios," in Chapter 18, "Building Scenarios and Outlines with Excel."

If none of these will do the job, or if you need to use several features and actions in a sequence, then you will probably benefit from creating a macro.

The number of uses for macros is limited only by your imagination and the requirements that you are faced with. Nonetheless, there are certain operations that are very common candidates for macros. A few of the most popular uses for macros are:

- *Printing macros*. These may automate the selection of various print ranges, page layout settings, headers and footers, and other printing layout features.
- *Data entry macros.* A macro can enter text, numbers, and formulas directly into cells throughout your worksheet.
- *Formatting macros*. Macros might systematically apply formatting throughout a workbook, combining different formats such as fonts, colors, shading, numeric formats and borders.
- *Charting macros.* A macro may automate the process of creating charts, or applying formatting or labeling to a chart.
- *Any or all of the above!* The real power of macros begins when you combine many features together in a sequence, saving you time and effort, and repeating your actions reliably.

Creating a Macro

There are two ways to create a macro:

- Use the built-in macro recorder
- Type the VBA code of the macro directly into the Visual Basic Editor

Recording a macro creates VBA code, just as though you had typed the code in yourself, starting from a blank editing window. When you record your first macro, you may be surprised at the large amount of VBA code that Excel generates to perform even the simplest of actions.

Recording a macro is certainly easier and quicker than typing code. You can just turn on the recorder, perform the actions you want in the macro, and Excel creates the code, with no need for any programming on your part. Even as you learn the VBA language, you probably will find that there are so many details involved in the VBA language, that it is convenient to create a "first draft" of a VBA macro by recording it. You can always go back into the Visual Basic Editor to revise and add advanced features to your recorded macros.

However, there are some disadvantages to recording macros. The macro recorder is very literal, and it pays attention to every action you perform while recording. You may notice that when you record a series of actions into a macro, Excel has recorded a lot more that you intended! As you become more familiar with the VBA language, you will probably find that it is often simpler, and more accurate, to type the VBA code yourself, rather than relying on the macro recorder.

Many advanced capabilities of VBA, such as custom forms and dialog boxes, using variables, and other advanced programming logic, can only be entered into your VBA macros by typing the code yourself. The macro recorder has no way of capturing this code. You can learn more about using the programming and editing features of VBA in Chapters 29 through 32. For the rest of this chapter, you'll get acquainted with Excel macros by using the recorder.

Planning a Macro

One of the most important steps in creating a macro is to plan what the macro needs to do. After you turn on the macro recorder, every action you perform is recorded. If you have not planned your activities carefully, your macro may contain many unnecessary actions. These extra actions will often slow down your macro, or may even have unexpected side effects, resulting in incorrect results.

The simplest way to plan your macro before recording it, is to perform all the actions that the macro needs to carry out, one step at a time. Write down all the steps you take on a piece of paper. Be very careful, and don't leave anything out. Take note of every time you type something into a cell, click a toolbar button, or select a command from the menus. Remember, everything you do once the recorder is on will be recorded exactly, so you want to be careful to perform only those actions that you want recorded.

Try out the macro recorder with a very simple example. Suppose you need to enter some formatted text into a workbook. Figure 28.1 shows an example of a cell that contains an approval statement which is formatted with a distinct font, and border formatting. Instead of typing this information in, and applying the formatting, you can record a macro that will insert the approval statement anywhere you need it in the workbook.

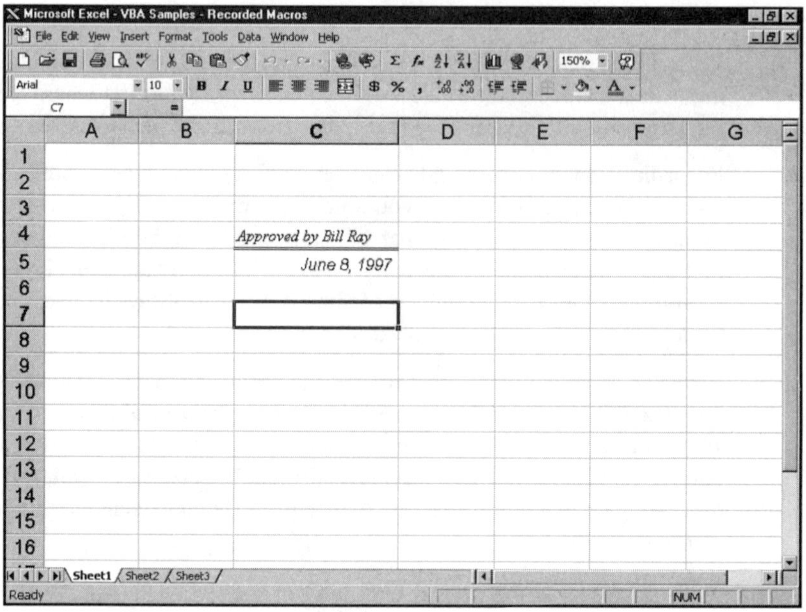

FIG. 28.1 Entering this approval notice throughout a workbook will be easy work for an Excel macro.

Here are the steps necessary to perform these actions in Excel 97:

1. Type the text **Approved by Bill Ray** into the active cell, and press Enter.
2. Because pressing Enter usually moves to the cell below, press the up arrow key, or click with the mouse, to return to the original cell for formatting.
3. To apply the Font formatting to this cell, choose the Format, Cells command, and select the Font tab in the dialog box. Use Times New Roman, 8 point, Italic. Leave the dialog box open.
4. Select the Border tab in the Font dialog box to apply a double-line border along the bottom of the cell. Choose OK to finish the formatting.
5. Move down one cell by pressing the down arrow key or by clicking into the new cell with the mouse.
6. Enter the formula "=TODAY()" in this cell.
7. Choose the Format, Cells command to apply 8 point italic formatting. This time don't switch to Times New Roman. Leave the dialog box open.
8. Select the Number tab in the Font dialog box, to apply the appropriate date format for this cell. Select the format "March 4, 1997."
9. Select both cells in which you've entered information. This will allow you to adjust the column width to fit the selection.
10. Select the Format, Column command, and select Autofit Selection from the submenu. The width of the column is automatically adjusted to match your entries.

As you can see, what looks like a very simple entry often involves a lot of specific steps. If you have to repeat this process many times throughout a workbook, the process may become both time-consuming and cumbersome.

CAUTION

When you plan your macro, take special care to consider where the Excel selection and active cell will be at the beginning of the macro, and where you want to leave the selection when the macro is finished. Many macros begin by positioning the active cell in a specific location. Because the sample macro doesn't begin by positioning the active cell, it carries out its actions wherever the user positions the active cell before running the macro. In this case, because the macro begins by typing text into a cell, any previous cell contents will be overwritten.

Naming Your Macros

An important part of the planning stage of a macro is to define a name for the macro. If you don't enter your own name for the macro that you record, Excel assigns a default name, such as Macro1, Macro2, and so on. The default names are not descriptive, and don't tell you much about the meaning or purpose of the macro.

Excel lets you use long, descriptive names, subject to the following rules:

- Macro names must begin with a letter.
- Names can contain letters, numbers, and the underscore (_)character.
- Spaces are not allowed in macro names, but you can use an underscore instead of a space to separate words.
- Macro names can be up to 255 characters in length.

Based upon these naming rules, the following names are legal for Excel VBA macros:

PrintOne

Print1 -
rint_One

These names would not be legal for Excel VBA macros:

1Print

Print One

Print/One

At the same time that you name your macro, you will have an opportunity to enter a description of the macro. Excel automatically fills in your name and the date that you created the macro. You may want to add more text to the description, to describe the purpose of the macro in greater detail. Figure 28.2 shows the Record Macro dialog box, which appears just before you begin recording a macro. The sample macro used for this chapter could be named *ApprovalDate.*

FIG. 28.2
The Record Macro dialog box allows you to enter the name of the macro, a shortcut key, the storage location, and a description for the macro.

Recording Your Macro

When you're confident that you know the exact steps your macro needs to perform, you're ready to turn on the macro recorder and create your macro. Follow these steps to record a macro:

1. Open the workbook and activate the worksheet where you want the macro to be recorded, and position the active cell where the macro should begin. I started out in cell C5 when I recorded my macro.
2. Choose Tools, Macro, Record New Macro. The Record Macro dialog box appears.

3. Type the name you want to use for your macro. Use the name *ApprovalDate* for the sample macro. You can enter a shortcut key for your macro at this time, or you can assign a shortcut key later.
4. Select a storage location for the macro. For now, select This Workbook in the Store Macro In list box.
5. Choose OK to begin recording. The dialog box closes, and the Stop Recording toolbar appears.
6. Perform the actions you have planned for your macro.
7. To turn off the recorder, click the Stop Recorder button on the Stop Recording toolbar, or choose Tools, Macro, Stop Recorder.

NOTE The macro recorder records only the actions that you complete. For example, if you begin typing into a cell, but press Cancel before completing the entry, none of your typing is recorded. If you begin typing, press Backspace a couple of times, finish your typing, and then press Enter, Excel records the result of your typing as though you had typed it flawlessly the first time, without the typing and retyping. If you open a dialog box, and make some selections, but cancel the dialog box, none of that action is recorded.

Also, the act of selecting the Stop Recorder button is not recorded.

Running Your Macro

After you have recorded your macro, you probably will want to test it, to see how it works. The simplest way to test your macro is to run it using the menu command.

1. Choose Tools, Macro (or press Alt+F8) to open the Macro dialog box, as shown in Figure 28.3.
2. Click the name of the macro you want to run and choose the Run button to execute your macro.

FIG. 28.3
The Macro dialog box lets you select a macro to run, edit, or delete.

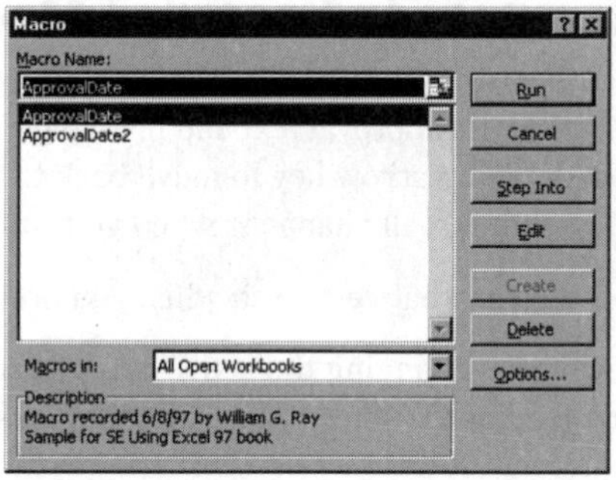

If you have been following along carefully, and have tested the macro that you recorded in this chapter, you may discover a problem with the ApprovalDate macro. Try running the macro several times, but click into a different starting cell each time you are about to run the macro. You should get a result that looks something like Figure 28.4.

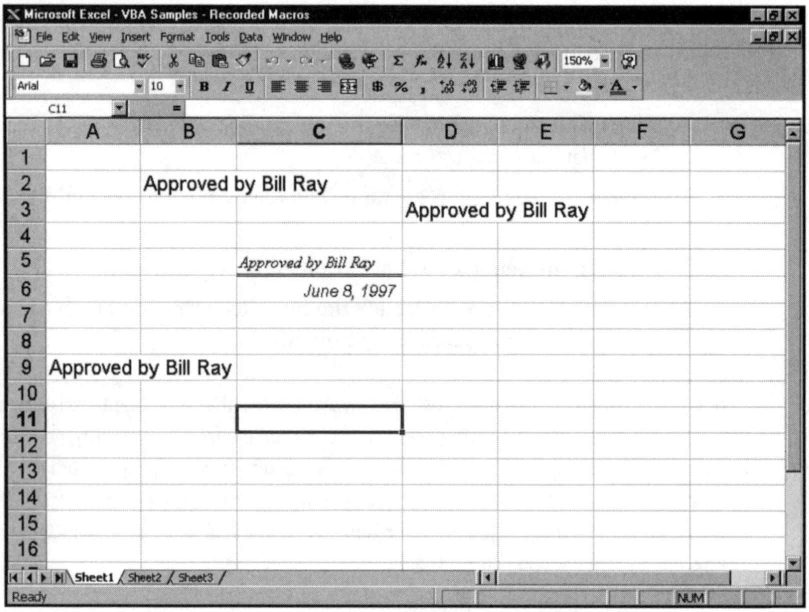

FIG. 28.4
The results of running the ApprovalDate macro are not what we expected.

The problem with the macro is that every time it runs, Excel types the first line of text into the active cell, but then goes back to the original cells where you recorded the macro and performs the rest of the steps of the macro. However, the macro should enter the name and date, and do all the formatting that you recorded, wherever you place the active cell when you run the macro each time.

To understand exactly what is causing this problem, and, more importantly, how to solve the problem, you need to understand a little about relative and absolute references in recorded macros.

Relative and Absolute References in Recorded Macros

Think about the second step you recorded when you created the macro using the recorder, earlier in this chapter. Because typing the approval text and pressing Enter moved the active cell down one cell, you had to press the up arrow key to move back to the original cell so you could apply the font formatting. But what really happens when you "press the up arrow key?"

Excel has two possible ways to interpret what you mean when you press the up arrow key:

- Pressing the up arrow key means changing the active cell so it refers to the cell one row up, in the same column, depending on where you are in the worksheet when you get to this point in the macro.
- Because the cell you just moved to is cell C5, every time you come to this point in the macro, you'll move to C5, no matter where you are in the worksheet.

In the sample macro, the intention of pressing the up arrow key is like the first of these two statements. You're asking Excel to move up one cell, relative to the cell that is active at the time.

Unfortunately, Excel's normal assumption is in line with the second statement. Because you moved to cell C5 when you recorded the macro, Excel will absolutely always move to cell C5, when it runs the macro.

The reason for this behavior is that Excel uses *absolute references* when recording macros unless you tell Excel to use the alternative method, known as *relative references*. Fortunately, it's easy to switch back and forth between absolute and relative references while recording a macro.

▶ **See** "Relative and Absolute References in Recorded Macros," **p. 704**

Figure 28.5 shows the Stop Recording toolbar, as it appears while recording a macro. Notice that the ToolTip for the Relative Reference button is being displayed, because the mouse pointer is over the Relative Reference button. Clicking this button toggles between relative and absolute references while recording your macro:

- When the Relative Reference button is depressed, the relative method is used for cell addresses in the recorded macro.
- When the Relative Reference button is not depressed, the absolute method is used for cell addresses in the recorded macro.

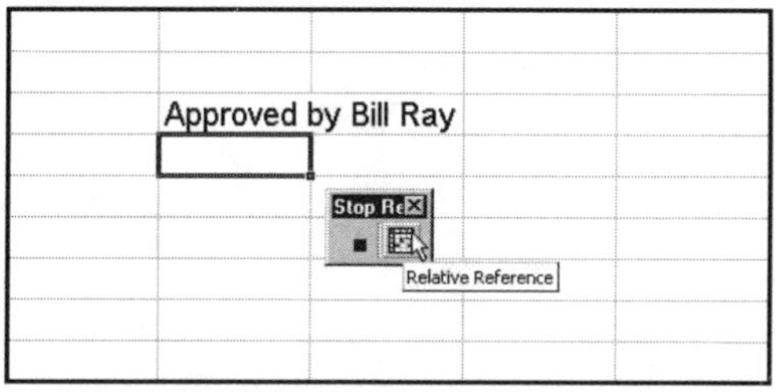

FIG. 28.5
The Relative Reference button lets you switch between relative and absolute references while recording macros.

You can switch back and forth between relative and absolute addresses as often as you like while recording a macro. You might decide to begin with absolute references, switch to relative addresses after a while, then switch back to absolute references for the rest of the macro.

Recreating Your Macro with Relative Addresses

Now that you know you need relative addresses in the macro, you can correct the ApprovalDate macro in one of two ways. One method would be to edit the macro using the Visual Basic Editor. Because you haven't really looked at any code yet, try the easier method: recording the macro over again with relative addresses.

1. Open the workbook and activate the worksheet where you want the macro to be recorded, and position the active cell where the macro should begin. Select cell C5 again for this macro.

2. Choose Tools, Macro, Record New Macro. The Record Macro dialog box appears.
3. Type the name you want to use for your macro. This time you can call the macro ApprovalDate2.
4. Select a storage location for the macro. Again, select This Workbook in the Store Macro In list box.
5. Choose OK to begin recording. The dialog box closes and the Stop Recording toolbar appears.
6. Click the Relative Reference button on the Stop Recording toolbar to switch to the relative method for cell references.
7. Perform the actions you have planned for your macro.
8. To turn off the recorder, click the Stop Recorder button on the Stop Recording toolbar, or choose Tools, Macros, Stop Recorder.

As always, once you have finished recording you can begin testing the macro by running it several times. This time the macro should produce the desired result, as displayed in Figure 28.6.

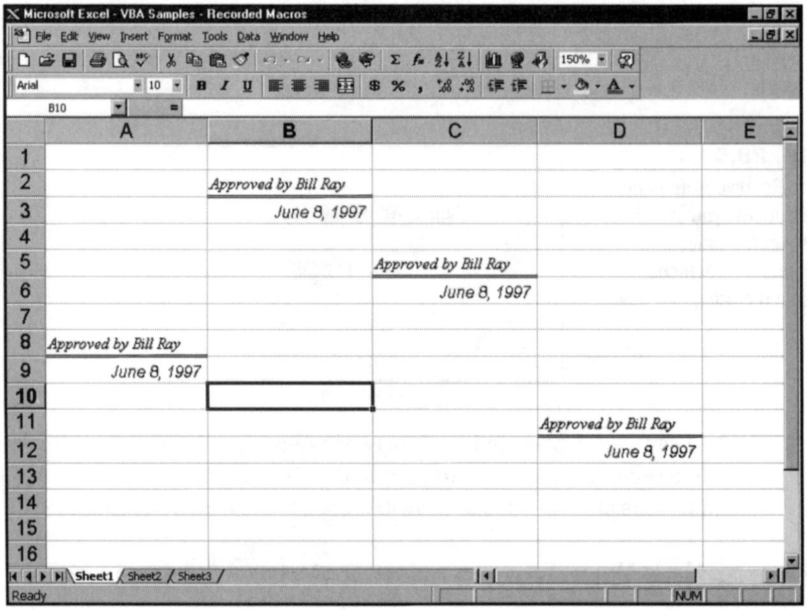

FIG. 28.6
The results of running the second version of the ApprovalDate macro match the original design goals of the macro.

Later in this chapter, you'll take a look at the VBA code that was produced by the two versions of the sample macro, so you can see both the relative and absolute references in the macros.

Deleting a Macro

If you decide that you don't need a macro any longer, you can delete it. Follow these steps:

1. Choose Tools, Macro, Macros. The Macro dialog box appears.
2. Select the name of the macro you want to delete.
3. Choose the Delete button. A message appears, asking if you want to delete the macro.
4. Choose Yes to delete the macro. Choose No if you don't want to delete the macro.

Once you delete the macro, you won't be able to get it back without recording it again or typing it in the Visual Basic Editor.

Assigning a Shortcut Key

Earlier in this chapter, you learned to run a macro using the Tools, Macro command (or by pressing Alt+F8), then selecting the macro from the list of available macros. However, for a macro to be a really great shortcut, you need an even quicker way to run your macros. If you prefer using the keyboard rather than reaching for the mouse, the quickest way to run a macro is by pressing a shortcut key that you assign to run the macro.

To set or change a shortcut key:

1. Press Alt+F8 to open the Macro dialog box.
2. Click the name of the macro whose shortcut key you want to change, then choose the Options button. The Macro Options dialog box appears, as shown in Figure 28.7.
3. Type a letter in the Shortcut Key text box. Choose OK to complete the command.

If you type an uppercase letter in the Shortcut Key text box, you will need to press the Shift key when you want to run the macro. For example, if you type a capital A, as in Figure 28.7, you can run your macro by pressing Ctrl+Shift+A. If you type a lowercase a, you will run your macro by pressing Ctrl+A.

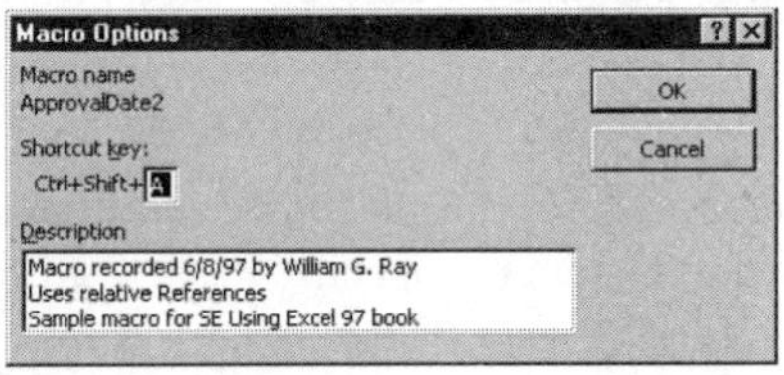

FIG. 28.7
The Macro Options dialog box lets you set a shortcut key or edit the description of a macro.

Adding a Macro to a Toolbar

If you think about the way you execute built-in commands in Excel, you often have a choice between several methods. These usually involve a choice between shortcut keys, buttons on a toolbar, or commands on a menu. Shortcut keys are great for commands that you use every day, because you'll be more likely to remember the shortcut key than you will for a less frequently used command. For those occasionally used macros, it's easier to find them on a toolbar or menu, where there is no need to memorize the shortcut key.

In all the Office 97 applications, you can easily modify toolbars and menus. Toolbars and menus are really special features within the *command bar* environment. Creating and organizing menus and toolbars is covered in detail in Chapter 8, "Customizing Excel." In that chapter, you learned how to add buttons to toolbars and menus to execute built-in commands. You can just as easily add buttons to toolbars and menus to run your macros. You can even add menu items, or entirely new menus, to a command bar. In fact, you might decide to mix built-in commands with your custom macros on a custom toolbar or menu, selecting those commands that are most likely to be grouped together in a particular spreadsheet application.

In the following section, you learn how to create a new toolbar, just for your custom macros, and place buttons or custom menu items on the toolbar for the two versions of the ApprovalDate macro you recorded in this chapter.

Creating a New Toolbar You can add new buttons to an existing toolbar, or create a new toolbar just for your application. Follow these steps to create a new toolbar, and name it "Using Excel 97 Macros":

1. Activate the workbook that contains the macros you have recorded.
2. Choose Tools, Customize, and click the Toolbars tab.
3. Choose the New button to create a new toolbar.
4. Type the name for the new toolbar, *Using Excel 97 Macros*, and choose the OK button.

The new toolbar is created, and appears next to the Customize dialog box.

Adding Buttons to a Toolbar Now that you have a new toolbar, you can add buttons or text to the toolbar to run your macros easily, whenever you need them.

1. If the Customize dialog box is not already open, choose Tools, Customize.
2. Click the Commands tab to display the list of Excel's built-in commands that can be added to the toolbar.
3. In the Categories list box, select Macros. The Commands list is updated to allow for adding a custom menu item or a command button to the toolbar.
4. To add a custom button, drag the button image from the Custom Button list item to the position on the toolbar where you want to place the button.
5. To add a custom menu item, drag from the Custom Menu Item list to the position on the toolbar where you want the menu item to appear.

After you've placed the command buttons and custom menu items on your toolbar, there are several ways to customize their appearance. Here are a few of the most useful changes you might want to make, all of which can be made only while the Customize dialog box remains open:

- To change the image on a command button, right-click the button and select the Change Button Image command. You can select from any of the 42 predesigned images that are included with Excel.

- To draw your own button image, right-click the button and select the Edit Button Image command. The Button Editor window opens, allowing you to create new button images or to modify existing images.
- To change the text of a custom menu item, right-click the menu item and edit the text in the Name item on the shortcut menu.

Assigning a Macro to a Toolbar Button After you've added a command button or custom menu item to a menu, you can assign the macro that you want to run when the user clicks the button:

1. If the Customize dialog box is not already open, choose Tools, Customize.
2. Right-click the button or custom menu item that you want to assign a macro to. A shortcut menu appears.
3. Choose the Assign Macro command. The Assign Macro dialog box appears.
4. Select the macro you want to assign, and choose OK.

Editing the Text of a Toolbar Button or Menu Item You can customize the text of a custom menu item or of a toolbar button, so that it is easier for the user to understand. Here's how:

1. If the Customize dialog box is not already open, choose Tools, Customize.
2. Right-click the button or custom menu item whose text you want to edit. A shortcut menu appears.
3. Select the text to the right of the Name command, and then edit it by typing or using the Backspace and delete keys.
4. Press Enter to complete the change.

TIP When editing the text for a custom menu item, you can easily provide the same kind of underlined shortcut key that you find in built-in menu items. When typing the text for the custom menu item, simply place an ampersand (&) immediately before the letter you want to be underlined. For example, if you type **&Approval Date**, the resulting text on the custom menu item will be displayed as Approval Date.

Where Your Macros Are Stored

In Excel 97, macros are not stored in a separate "macro file," but instead are part of the workbook you were in when you created the macro.

NOTE In previous versions of Excel, macros were stored in a visible sheet in the workbook, called a *module sheet*. You could click the sheet tab for a module sheet, just like any other sheet, to view and edit the code in your macros.

Excel 97 stores the macros and other VBA code invisibly in *projects* within the workbook. The only way to see your code is by using the Visual Basic Editor. When you convert an Excel, version 5, or Excel 95 workbook to Excel 97, the module sheets are removed, and the code is moved to VBA projects automatically.

When you first recorded a macro, The Record Macro dialog box displayed a combo box labeled Store Macro In. There are three options you can select in this list:

- *This Workbook.* This is the usual selection. The macro you are about to create will be stored in, and saved with, the workbook you are currently using. The macro will be available any time you open this workbook, but will not be available when this workbook is not open. If the macro that you are creating is specifically designed to help you with the work of this workbook, this is the natural selection.
- *New Workbook.* Selecting this option creates a new workbook, and stores the macro with the new workbook. This selection is useful when you are just starting out on a new spreadsheet application, or when you want to create a general-purpose macro, that is not specific to this workbook. In that case, you will have to remember to open the workbook that contains the macro before you will be able to run it.
- *Personal Macro Workbook.* When you select this option, Excel creates the macro in a hidden workbook that is automatically opened behind the scenes, every time you start Excel. If the personal workbook doesn't already exist, Excel creates it at the time you record this macro. You'll learn more about this option in "Using the Personal Macro Workbook," later in this chapter.

A Word About Macro Viruses

When you open a workbook that contains macros, Excel may display a dialog box warning you about the possibility of viruses (see Figure 28.8).

A macro virus is simply a macro that is designed to spread itself from workbook to workbook. Some macro viruses do damage to files, by deleting contents, overwriting contents, or other harmful actions. Other macro viruses may not do any damage, but waste your time with unwanted messages or other activities. Macro viruses are an unfortunate side effect of such a powerful programming language as VBA. In recent years, the number of macro viruses known to exist has multiplied dramatically, making it very difficult to be familiar with all the existing viruses.

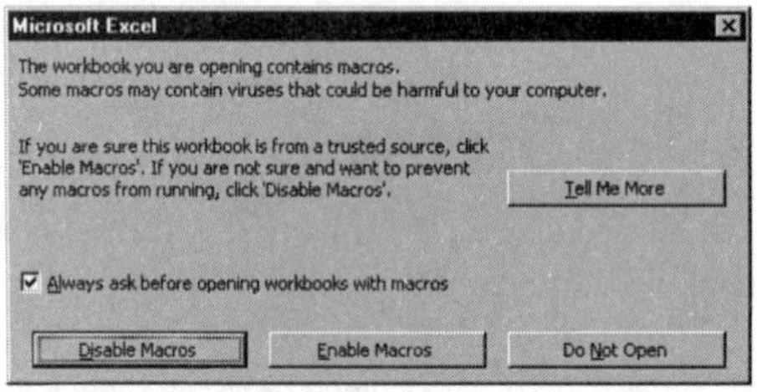

FIG. 28.8
This warning dialog appears anytime you open a workbook containing macros, unless you have disabled virus protection.

You have three choices of action when the virus warning dialog box appears:

- *Disable Macros.* The workbook is opened, but the macros in the workbook will not run. This protects you from any macro viruses that may be in the workbook, but at the cost of disabling all the macro functionality as well.

- *Enable Macros.* The workbook is opened, and the macros work normally. This allows you to use your macros, but at the risk of damage by a virus.
- *Do Not Open.* The workbook is not opened at all. This is a good choice if you are opening a workbook that should not contain any macros, or a workbook from an unknown source. The presence of unexpected macros is a strong indication of macro viruses.

Deselecting the Always Ask Before Opening Workbooks with Macros check box turns off macro virus protection when you open workbooks in the future. If you are likely to use workbooks created by others, no matter what the source of these files, it is highly recommended that you do not turn off virus protection.

If you have turned off macro virus protection, you can easily turn it back on.

1. Choose Tools, Options and click the General tab.
2. Select the Macro Virus Protection check box, and choose OK.

TIP Excel's built-in virus protection warns you about the possibility of viruses, but does not reliably identify viruses, or take any action to repair them. It is highly recommended that anyone who shares files of any type with others, using a network, disks, e-mail, or the Internet, should invest in one of the widely available commercial or shareware anti-virus applications.

Most of these programs provide frequent updates, distributed via the Internet, or by disk subscription. These updates allow the program to identify the latest viruses, and in many cases will disable or remove the viruses entirely.

Using the Personal Macro Workbook

If you selected Personal Macro Workbook when you recorded your macro, it was saved in the hidden workbook that Excel opens every time you start Excel. This workbook is named Personal.XLS, and is stored in your startup directory. The startup directory is normally a subdirectory named XLStart, which is a subdirectory of your Excel program directory.

Any files that you put in your startup directory are loaded automatically, each time you start Excel. Because this file will contain any general-purpose macros that you have created, those macros will always be available to run, no matter what workbook is active.

If you are working on a network with a shared installation of Excel, the XLStart directory may be a shared, read-only directory, so you won't be able to save your changes there. Fortunately, Excel lets you specify an alternate startup directory, which you would probably create either on your local hard disk, or in your private area on a network. To specify an alternate startup directory for Excel:

1. Make sure the directory you want to specify already exists. If necessary, use the Windows Explorer to create the new directory.
2. Choose Tools, Options, and click the General tab.
3. In the Alternate Startup File Location text box, type the complete path to the directory where you want to store your personal macro workbook, and choose OK.

The alternate startup file location will not be activated until the next time you start Excel.

Viewing Your Recorded Macros

Beginning in Chapter 29, "Introducing VBA Programming," you'll learn how to edit your recorded macros and to create new macros by typing the code directly into the Visual Basic Editor. Even if you never intend to edit your code, you may want to know how to view the code that you've recorded. In the following sections, you learn how to use the Visual Basic Editor to view your code.

Understanding Modules and Projects

Before you open the Visual Basic Editor to look at your recorded macros, it is important to understand how Excel organizes VBA code.

VBA code is stored in modules, which in turn are stored in projects. What exactly are modules and projects?

- A *module* is simply a collection of VBA code, such as procedures, declarations, and statements. These elements are defined in detail in Chapter 29, "Introducing VBA Programming." For now all you need to know is that recorded macros are actually VBA procedures. A module can contain any number of procedures.
- A *project* is a collection of modules. There may be any number of modules in a project.

Each Excel 97 workbook contains a single project. When you record a macro, Excel creates a module in the project for that workbook, and puts the VBA code for the recorded macro into that module. If you record additional macros in the same Excel working session, those new macros will be stored in the same module. If you record additional macros the next time you run Excel, those macros will be recorded in a new module.

Modules are simply a way of organizing macros, and for now, it doesn't matter too much how many modules are in a given workbook's project, or how many macros are in any module. As you get more experience in working with the Visual Basic Editor, and with managing many macros, you'll find that it's easy to copy or move entire modules from one project to another.

Meeting the Visual Basic Editor

To view, edit, or type VBA code, you need to use the Visual Basic Editor, also known as the VBE. The VBE is a separate program from Excel, and is shared by all the Office 97 applications. In Chapter 29, "Introducing VBA Programming," you'll learn to go directly to the VBE to begin editing or entering code, but for now, there's a quick way to view any macro you've recorded.

1. Make sure the workbook that contains your macro is open.
2. Choose Tools, Macro, Macros. The Macro dialog box appears.
3. Click the name of the macro you want to view and choose the Edit button. The VBE opens, with your macro displayed in a code window, as shown in Figure 28.9.

FIG 28.9
The ApprovalDate macro is displayed in a code window of the VBE.

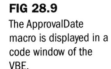

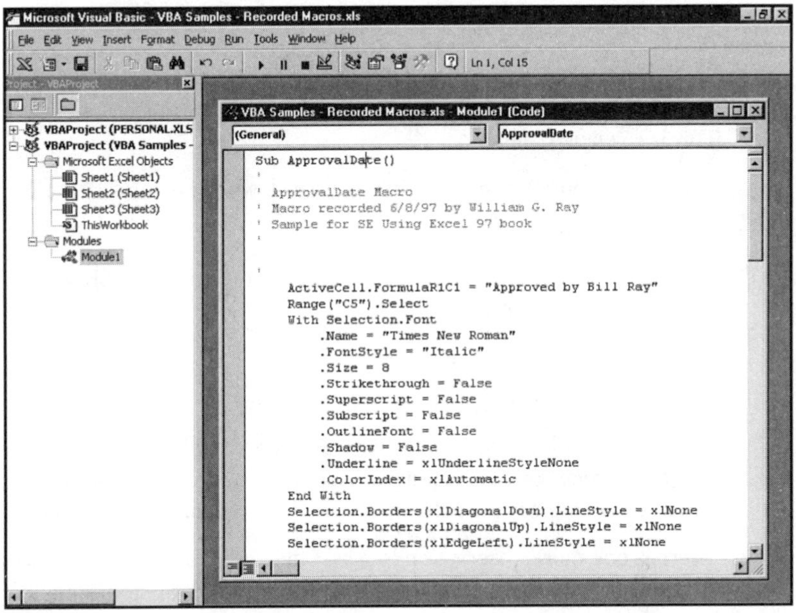

The first thing you might notice is that the ApprovalDate macro is long enough that it can't be entirely displayed on-screen at one time. Of course, you can use the scroll bars of the code window to move through the code as you read it. For now, don't make any editing changes to the macro.

There are a couple of other commands you may want to know about at this time.

- The Tools, Macros command lets you select another macro in this project for editing or viewing.
- The File, Print command lets you print the code for a module or an entire project.
- The File, Close and Return to Microsoft Excel command closes the VBE, and returns to the active workbook in Excel. The shortcut key for this command is Alt+Q.

In case you're curious about the VBA code produced by recording the two sample macros, they are printed in Listing 28.1, which is the ApprovalDate macro, and Listing 28.2, which is the ApprovalDate2 macro.

These two listings have a lot in common, with the only differences being the use of absolute references in ApprovalDate, and relative references in ApprovalDate2. Take a look at a couple of specific differences.

Near the beginning of Listing 28.1, you'll find the following statement:

```
Range("C5").Select
```

Loosely translated, this statement says, "Select the range (or cell) identified as 'C5'." That's how VBA represents the absolute reference.

Now look at the same line in Listing 28.2:

```
ActiveCell.Select
```

This statement simply says, "Select the active cell." It doesn't specify an identifier for the cell. This is a relative reference.

Look at one more example. A little further down in Listing 28.1, you'll find the following line:

```
Range("C6").Select
```

That doesn't come as too much of a surprise. You can probably guess that it means, "Select the range (or cell) identified as 'C6'."

In Listing 28.2, the same line looks like this:

```
ActiveCell.Offset(1,0).Range("A1").Select
```

Now that really looks different! The translation of this statement is not as obvious, but it roughly means, "Select the range (or cell) whose reference is different from the active cell by one row, but in the same column." Wow! All that from just pressing the down arrow key!

There is one more observation to make about the code in the sample macros. One of the reasons the listings are so long is that Excel recorded a lot of information that you probably didn't intend to include. Look at this example from Listing 28.1:

```
With Selection.Font
     .Name = "Times New Roman"
     .FontStyle = "Italic"
     .Size = 8
     .Strikethrough = False
     .Superscript = False
     .Subscript = False
     .OutlineFont = False
     .Shadow = False
     .Underline = xlUnderlineStyleNone
     .ColorIndex = xlAutomatic
End With
```

This code corresponds to the use of the Format, Cells command to apply font formatting to the selection. Although Excel accurately captured your choices for the font name, style, and size, it also recorded the current state of the strikethrough, superscript, subscript, outline font, shadow, underline, and color attributes of the selection. Because you didn't really intend to record this information, it is unnecessary, and will slow down the execution of the macro. Worse, it may have a side effect in some situations, applying those recorded attributes to cells where you don't want them to be applied.

The solution is simple. You can use the VBE to delete the unnecessary lines of code, as well as to make other changes to the sample macros.

If this new language seems a little difficult and unusual just now, don't worry. In the next few chapters, you'll learn how to read and write VBA code. For now, you can just be glad that the macro recorder can do all that work for us.

Listing 28.1 VBA SAMPLES - RECORDED MACROS (The first version of the ApprovalDate macro contains absolute references.)

```
Sub ApprovalDate()
'
' ApprovalDate Macro
' Macro recorded 6/8/97 by William G. Ray
'   Sample for SE Using Excel 97 book
'
'
    ActiveCell.FormulaR1C1 = "Approved by Bill Ray"
    Range("C5").Select
    With Selection.Font
        .Name = "Times New Roman"
        .FontStyle = "Italic"
        .Size = 8
        .Strikethrough = False
        .Superscript = False
        .Subscript = False
        .OutlineFont = False
        .Shadow = False
        .Underline = xlUnderlineStyleNone
        .ColorIndex = xlAutomatic
    End With
    Selection.Borders(xlDiagonalDown).LineStyle = xlNone
    Selection.Borders(xlDiagonalUp).LineStyle = xlNone
    Selection.Borders(xlEdgeLeft).LineStyle = xlNone
    Selection.Borders(xlEdgeTop).LineStyle = xlNone
    With Selection.Borders(xlEdgeBottom)
        .LineStyle = xlDouble
        .Weight = xlThick
        .ColorIndex = xlAutomatic
    End With
    Selection.Borders(xlEdgeRight).LineStyle = xlNone
    Range("C6").Select
    ActiveCell.FormulaR1C1 = "=TODAY()"
    Range("C6").Select
    Selection.NumberFormat = "mmmm d, yyyy"
    With Selection.Font
        .Name = "Arial"
        .FontStyle = "Italic"
        .Size = 8
        .Strikethrough = False
        .Superscript = False
        .Subscript = False
        .OutlineFont = False
        .Shadow = False
        .Underline = xlUnderlineStyleNone
        .ColorIndex = xlAutomatic
    End With
    Range("C5:C6").Select
    Selection.Columns.AutoFit
End Sub
```

Listing 28.2 VBA SAMPLES - RECORDED MACROS (The ApprovalDate2 macro uses relative references when moving from cell to cell.)

```
Sub ApprovalDate2()
'
' ApprovalDate2 Macro
' Macro recorded 6/8/97 by William G. Ray
'   Uses relative References
'   Sample macro for SE Using Excel 97 book
'


'
    ActiveCell.FormulaR1C1 = "Approved by Bill Ray"
    ActiveCell.Select
    With Selection.Font
        .Name = "Times New Roman"
        .FontStyle = "Italic"
        .Size = 8
        .Strikethrough = False
        .Superscript = False
        .Subscript = False
        .OutlineFont = False
        .Shadow = False
        .Underline = xlUnderlineStyleNone
        .ColorIndex = xlAutomatic
    End With
    Selection.Borders(xlDiagonalDown).LineStyle = xlNone
    Selection.Borders(xlDiagonalUp).LineStyle = xlNone
    Selection.Borders(xlEdgeLeft).LineStyle = xlNone
    Selection.Borders(xlEdgeTop).LineStyle = xlNone
    With Selection.Borders(xlEdgeBottom)
        .LineStyle = xlDouble
        .Weight = xlThick
        .ColorIndex = xlAutomatic
    End With
    Selection.Borders(xlEdgeRight).LineStyle = xlNone
    ActiveCell.Offset(1, 0).Range("A1").Select
    ActiveCell.FormulaR1C1 = "=TODAY()"
    ActiveCell.Select
    Selection.NumberFormat = "mmmm d, yyyy"
    With Selection.Font
        .Name = "Arial"
        .FontStyle = "Italic"
        .Size = 8
        .Strikethrough = False
        .Superscript = False
        .Subscript = False
        .OutlineFont = False
        .Shadow = False
        .Underline = xlUnderlineStyleNone
        .ColorIndex = xlAutomatic
    End With
    ActiveCell.Offset(-1, 0).Range("A1:A2").Select
    Selection.Columns.AutoFit
End Sub
```

From Here...

This chapter introduced you to creating VBA macros for Excel 97 by using the macro recorder. The next few chapters will show you how to expand your skills in working with macros by editing your recorded macros and creating your own macros from scratch in the VBE.

- Chapter 29, "Introducing VBA Programming," shows you how to use the powerful VBE to create and modify macros, and gives you an introduction to the elements of the VBA programming language.
- Chapter 30, "Taking Control of Excel with VBA," describes the object model used by VBA for controlling the features of Excel, and shows you how to let your macros interact with the user.
- Chapter 31, "Advanced VBA Programming," shows you how to create custom forms for your VBA applications, and how to extend the reach of VBA through the Windows Application Programming Interface.
- Chapter 32, "Building Solutions with VBA," demonstrates the process of creating complete Excel 97 applications, incorporating spreadsheet design together with advanced VBA coding techniques.

CHAPTER 29

Introducing VBA Programming

by Bill Ray

To go beyond recording and playing back macros, you have to learn to create and edit macros using the Visual Basic Editor. This chapter introduces the many powerful features of the editing environment in Excel, and the Visual Basic language that Excel uses for VBA macros.

The power of VBA

VBA is a powerful programming language. You learn how it enables you to develop powerful applications for Excel and the rest of Office 97.

Modifying recorded macros

You learn how to make changes to the macros you have recorded. You use the Visual Basic Editor to make macros more efficient, as well as to make sure they do what you want them to.

Creating macros in the Visual Basic Editor

You can create your VBA macros directly in the Editor, typing the code instead of recording it. Entering your own code can result in simpler, faster, and more accurate macros than using the recorder.

Using the Visual Basic Editor

You learn how to use the powerful editing and debugging tools of the Visual Basic Editor to enter and test your code.

The elements of VBA

You learn how your code is organized, and about many of the language components you can use in any VBA program.

VBA—What It Can Do for You

VBA is the macro programming language for Excel 97, as well as for Word 97, PowerPoint 97, and Access 97. Earlier versions of each of these products used different macro languages, such as WordBasic, AccessBasic, and in the case of PowerPoint, there was no macro language at all until PowerPoint 97. Even Excel used a different macro language prior to the addition of VBA in Excel, version 5.0. This macro language has become known as the Excel 4.0 macro language, because it was the last version of Excel that used this earlier macro language exclusively.

NOTE Outlook 97 uses a scaled-down version of VBA, called Visual Basic Scripting Edition, more commonly known as VBScript. To learn how to develop custom solutions in Outlook 97, see Chapters 27–29 (written by Helen Feddema) of *Special Edition Using Microsoft Outlook 97* (also published by Que).

VBA has several advantages over these early macro languages and has much to offer if you take the time to learn it.

- *Logical control.* Macros can behave differently depending upon conditions at run time, such as the value of data in a cell, the result of a calculation, or the preferences of the user.
- *Repetitive execution.* Besides performing a sequence of recorded actions very quickly, a VBA macro can repeat its actions many times at a very high speed, either for a set number of repetitions or until some special event occurs. This type of action is commonly known to programmers as *looping*.
- *Interaction with the user.* VBA provides functions for presenting messages, asking questions, and allowing input of information. The built-in form design tools let you create custom dialog boxes with list selection, check boxes, push buttons, grids, and a virtually limitless collection of ActiveX controls which extend the interactive power of VBA.
- *Database connectivity.* VBA's built-in support for Open Database Connectivity (ODBC) lets you interact with many different types of data sources, including Microsoft Access, Microsoft FoxPro, and Microsoft SQL Server, as well as non-Microsoft products such as dBase, Paradox, and countless others. Your VBA programs can read data from these data sources, as well as updating the data in their data tables.
- *Control of Excel.* Through the powerful object model that allows access to virtually all the features of Excel, you can write code that performs just about anything that Excel can do. You can also write code that checks the value of various settings, such as whether a workbook is protected, or whether calculation is set to automatic or manual.
- *Control of other programs.* The same system of controlling object models that is built into Excel extends to the other Excel applications, as well as many other Windows applications. You can write an Excel VBA macro that types text into a Microsoft Word document, or that counts the number of slides in a PowerPoint presentation.

- *Direct use of Windows functions.* By using the Windows Application Programming Interface (API), you can use many of the functions of Windows itself directly in your VBA programs. This allows you to extend the language even beyond the reach of VBA.
- *Automation.* By using Automation, formerly called OLE Automation, you can write macros that communicate with a different Office application. For example, you can write Excel macros to retrieve data from Access, perform calculations in Excel, and generate output in the form of PowerPoint presentations and Word documents.
- *Editing Tools.* In addition to the programming language, all the Office 97 programs use the same editing environment, the Visual Basic Editor. Not only do you get the consistency of using the same editor for all your programming, but you also get a powerful set of tools for developing and debugging your programs, and managing your programming projects.

NOTE It is worth noting that VBA can be used only within a program that supports it. In other words, you can't write an Excel 97 VBA macro and run that macro on a computer that doesn't have Excel 97 installed. This is one of the major differences between VBA and VB. You can create a program with Visual Basic for Windows, and run that compiled program on another machine that doesn't have VB installed.

In addition to using VBA in Microsoft Office and other Microsoft applications (such as Microsoft Project) Microsoft has licensed VBA for use by the producers of other software applications. One of the first programs to have VBA built in was Visio, the powerful drawing package developed by Visio Corporation. The inclusion of VBA in Visio lets programmers create automated applications for producing data-driven drawings, as well as communication with Office 97 data files and applications.

A Little Bit of BASIC History

VBA is a descendant of the BASIC programming language. First developed at MIT in the 1960's, BASIC (short for Beginner's All-purpose Symbolic Instruction Code) became known to many early personal computer users. Versions of BASIC were included with just about every brand of early computer, including those from Commodore, Apple, Atari, and the IBM PC. Those early versions of BASIC were not very elegant programming languages. The programs used line numbers before every line of code, there were very limited data types, and the programming language didn't have many of the "structured programming" features of other languages that existed. However, the fact that BASIC was included with just about every computer sold contributed to its becoming one of the most widely known programming languages.

Microsoft has long been involved in the development of the BASIC language. In addition to the inclusion of Microsoft Basic on early computers, there were several separate versions of BASIC produced by Microsoft. Microsoft QuickBasic was an inexpensive compiler for MS-DOS development, placing the capability to create standalone programs within the reach of many programmers. For the professional, the Microsoft Basic Professional Development System provided a high-power optimizing compiler, moving BASIC into the same class as Pascal, Fortran, Cobol, and other professional development platforms. QBasic is a version of BASIC included with recent versions of DOS and Windows, that brings a more modern, structured approach to every day programming of text-mode programs.

The most revolutionary product in the BASIC line, however, had to be Microsoft Visual Basic for Windows. Creating stand-alone Windows applications had previously been a complex, expensive, and time-consuming chore, requiring the use of the C programming language, or its successor, C++. Visual Basic lets programmers design a program graphically, by placing controls (such as text boxes, list boxes, and push buttons) on a form, then writing relatively simple code to bring the form alive. VB was also the first experience for many programmers in the world of *event-driven* programming, in which the execution of the code in the program was controlled by events that occurred at run-time. The click of a mouse button, opening or closing a form, or pressing a shortcut key, would send a message to VB to run a previously written procedure, placing control in the user's hands.

The tremendous popularity of Visual Basic led to the development of hundreds of add-on components, mostly in the form of custom controls, which were then known as VBXes. You could buy VBXes from many utility vendors, to provide your VB programs with all kinds of visual controls, such as grids, editors, gauges, graphical tools, and endless others. Unfortunately, these VBXes could not be used, with a few rare exceptions, in any of the Microsoft Office applications. Microsoft Office applications used different programming languages, and an inconsistent environment for creating dialog boxes and menus.

The incorporation of VBA throughout Office 97 brings the programming power of Visual Basic to the macro programmer. The Visual Basic Editor, with its integrated debugging and project management tools, dramatically improves the programmer's productivity. The form design capabilities bring not only a consistent set of tools for creating dialog boxes, but a full event programming model, and support for ActiveX controls, which have succeeded VBXes and OCXes as the tools for extending the power of the Visual Basic programming environment.

VBA ensures that Office 97 is not only a great application suite, but also a great development platform. From simple macros to complex applications, Office 97 and VBA work together as a great team.

Using the Visual Basic Editor

The Visual Basic Editor (VBE) is the home for all editing operations with VBA in Office 97. The VBE is new to Office 97, replacing the various code editing features of the applications in previous versions of Office. The VBE puts a consistent and powerful editing and debugging platform in the hands of the Office developer. As a matter of fact, the VBE is virtually identical to the Visual Studio 97 editing environment that is used to create programs using Microsoft Visual Basic 5.0, as well as Visual C++ and Visual J++.

Starting the VBE

The VBE is easy to start from Excel. To start the VBE directly, choose Tools, Macro, Visual Basic Editor. The VBE opens in a separate program window. Figure 29.1 shows the VBE display.

FIG. 29.1
The VBE has a variety of tools and windows to help you edit VBA code.

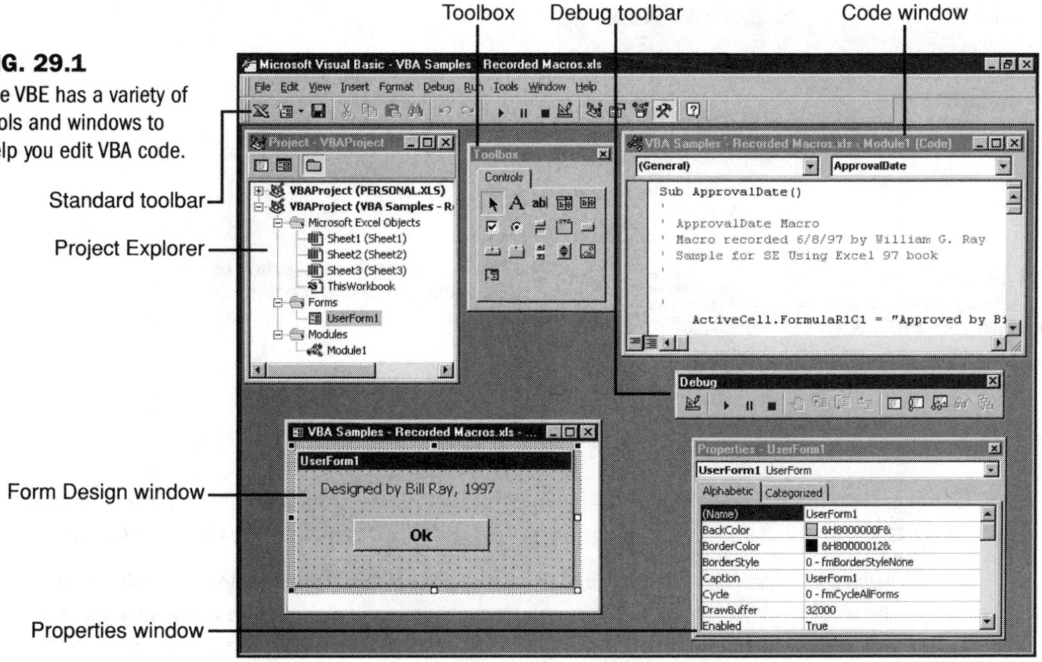

To edit a macro that already exists, you can have the VBE display that macro's code when you open the VBE window:

1. Choose Tools, Macro, Macros. The Macro dialog box appears.
2. Select the name of the macro you want to edit, and then choose the Edit button.

TIP If you like shortcut keys, there are two combinations that will get you into the VBE even quicker than the menus. Alt+F11 immediately opens the VBE, while Alt+F8 opens the Macro dialog box, so you can select a specific macro to edit.

Using the Project Explorer

The VBE Project Explorer works like a table of contents for any VBA projects you have open. You can use it to quickly gain access to the modules and procedures you need to view and edit. You also can use the Project Explorer to copy and move modules among projects, or to delete modules from projects. As its name implies, the Project Explorer looks and works much like the Windows Explorer.

The Project Explorer lets you work with any projects that are currently open. Because each workbook in Excel contains a project, the Explorer shows a project for each open workbook. This includes any hidden workbooks, such as the Personal.xls workbook that you can create when you record a macro with the macro recorder. Figure 29.2 shows the Project Explorer as it might appear with two open workbooks, along with the Personal.xls hidden workbook.

FIG. 29.2
The Project Explorer displays the projects for all open workbooks.

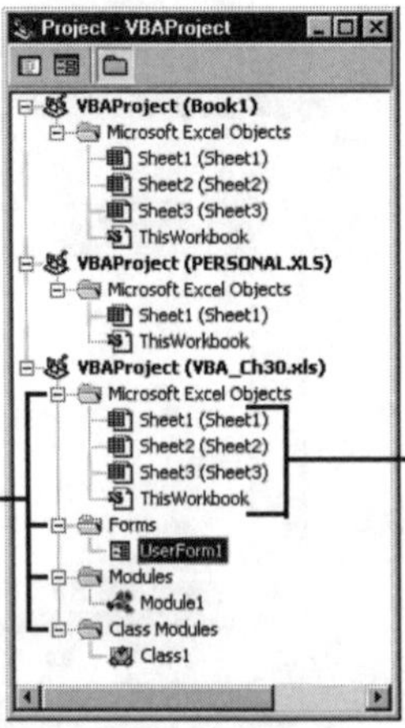

A VBA project is organized into modules, which contain your VBA code

A module is simply a collection of VBA declarations and procedures

Each project in the Project Explorer is organized into folders that contain different kinds of objects. Figure 29.2 shows that the project VBA_Ch30.xls contains four different folders.

- *Microsoft Excel Objects*. The objects are the sheets that make up a workbook, as well as the workbook itself. VBA automatically creates a module for each of these objects. You will mainly use these modules for entering *event-driven* code for each sheet or workbook. To learn about event-driven programming, see the section "Programming with Events" in Chapter 30.
- *Forms.* Using the built-in form design tools of VBA, you can create custom dialog boxes, also known as forms, for presenting data to the user, and for getting input from the user. Each form also contains a VBA module, which holds the event-driven code for working with that form. To learn how to create your own custom forms, see the section "Creating Custom Forms in the VB Editor," in Chapter 31.
- *Modules.* VBA creates a module the first time you record a macro in a workbook. You also can add as many modules as you wish to any workbook. These modules are the containers for most of the sub-procedures and functions that make up your VBA applications. You'll work with these modules throughout the next two chapters.
- *Class Modules.* In addition to the many built-in objects available to your VBA macros, you can create your own objects, complete methods and properties. This practice makes your code easier to reuse, and easier to call from other procedures when you need to use it. To learn more about using class modules, see the section "Creating Objects with Class Modules," in Chapter 31.

Expanding and Collapsing Folders

Because you will often spend most of your time working with the normal modules in a workbook, you might choose to collapse away the details of the other folders in the Project Explorer. Figure 29.3 shows the effect of collapsing the folders that you're not working on for the time being.

You can expand or collapse a branch of the Project Explorer window by clicking the plus or minus sign to the left of any branch.

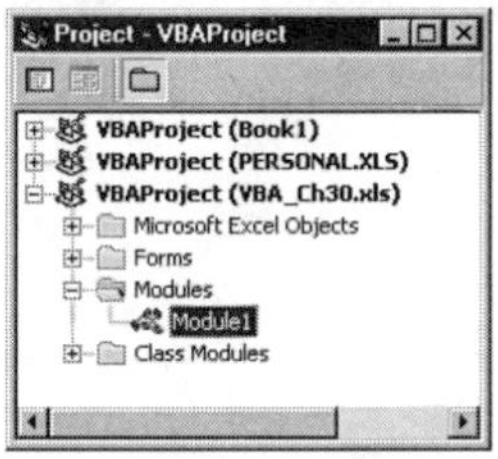

FIG. 29.3
All the folders except for the Modules folder have been collapsed to simplify the display of the Project Explorer.

Toggling the Display of the Folders

If you don't care to see the folders in the project folder, you can hide their display, as shown in Figure 29.4. You can toggle the display of the folders by clicking the Toggle Folders button in the Project Explorer's toolbar.

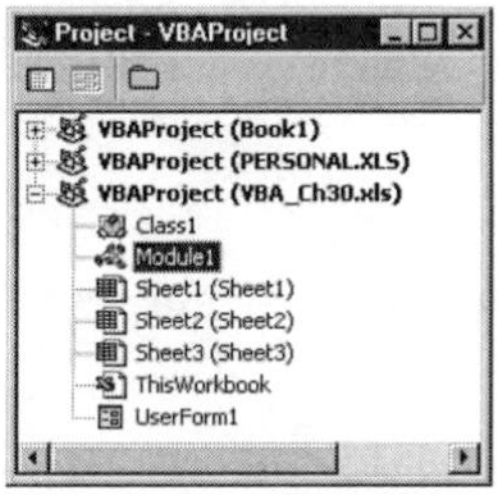

FIG. 29.4
Click the Toggle Folders button to remove the folders from the display in the Project Explorer.

Opening a Module in the Project Explorer

After you locate the module that you want to work with, you can open the code window for that module, allowing you to view and edit the code in that module. After selecting the module, you can open its code window in any of the following ways:

- Choose View, Code.
- Press F7.
- Double-click the module name in the Project Explorer window.

Figure 29.5 shows the result of double-clicking the Module1 entry in the Project Explorer.

Moving and Copying Modules

Because more than one project can be open at a time in the Visual Basic Editor, you can use the Project Explorer as an easy way to copy a module from one project to another, or to move code between modules.

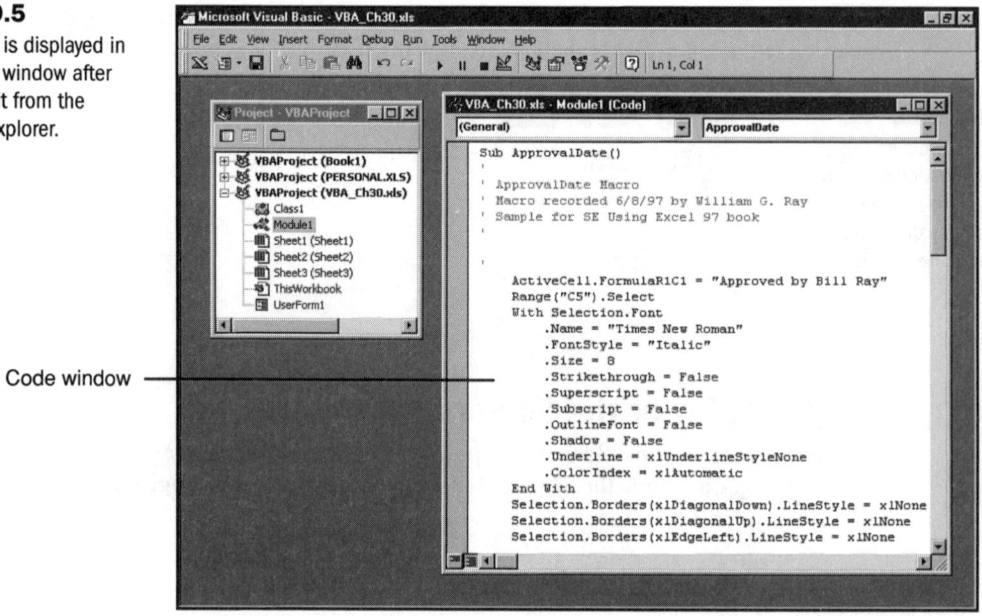

FIG. 29.5 Module1 is displayed in the code window after opening it from the Project Explorer.

To copy a module between two projects:

1. Use Excel to open the workbooks containing the two projects you want to work with.
2. Press Alt+F11 to activate the VBE.
3. Select the module you want to copy in the source project.
4. Hold the Ctrl key and drag the module to the destination project. An identical module is created in the destination project.

To move a module from one project to another:

1. Use Excel to open the workbooks containing the two projects you want to work with.
2. Press Alt+F11 to activate the VBE.
3. Select the module you want to copy in the source project.
4. Drag the module to the destination project. The module is removed from the source project, and added to the destination project.

TIP It's up to you how to organize your code in modules. Suppose you have a project that contains six macros. You might choose to have one module that contains all six macros, six modules each containing one macro, or any combination in between.

The main purpose of combining or separating code in modules is for your own organization. VBA allows you to copy and move entire modules in one operation, so you may want to combine any group of related macros or other procedures in a single module, so you can easily copy them to new projects as needed.

Deleting a Module from a Project

Sometimes you might find that you no longer need a module that has been added to a project. Maybe you created a module for testing purposes, and no longer need your test macros. Maybe you reorganized your modules by moving procedures into other modules. In any case, you can delete an unneeded module from a project, simplifying the project and reducing the size of the project in memory.

To delete a module from a project:

1. In the Project Explorer, select the module you want to delete from the project.
2. Choose File, Remove *modulename* (where *modulename* is the name of the module you want to delete).
3. The Microsoft Visual Basic dialog box appears, shown in Figure 29.6, asking whether you want to export the code before deleting the module. Choose Yes to copy the code from this module to a text file with a .bas extension (for Basic Code). Choose No to continue the deletion of the module without copying the code. Choose Cancel if you changed your mind, and you don't want to delete the module after all.

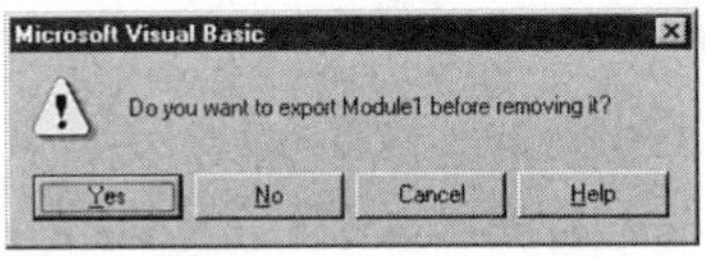

FIG. 29.6
VBA asks for confirmation before allowing you to delete a module from a project.

Renaming a Project

In the examples you've seen so far, the projects have been automatically named VBAProject by Excel VBA. You can give a project a more descriptive name, if you like.

1. In the Project Explorer, select the project you want to rename.
2. Choose Tools, *projectname* Properties (where *projectname* is the current name of the project).
3. The VBAProject - Project Properties dialog box appears (see Figure 29.7). Type a new name for the project in the Project Name text box. You might also want to type a description in the Project Description text box. Choose OK to complete the command.

NOTE Because a project is also a type of object, the names of projects must follow the naming rules of other objects, such as macros. The object name must start with a letter, can contain letters, numbers, and underscores (_) and cannot contain spaces.

Saving Your Work from the VB Editor

As with any computer work, it is important that you save your work often. This is especially true when you are programming, because it's easy to make mistakes when you're learning a new language.

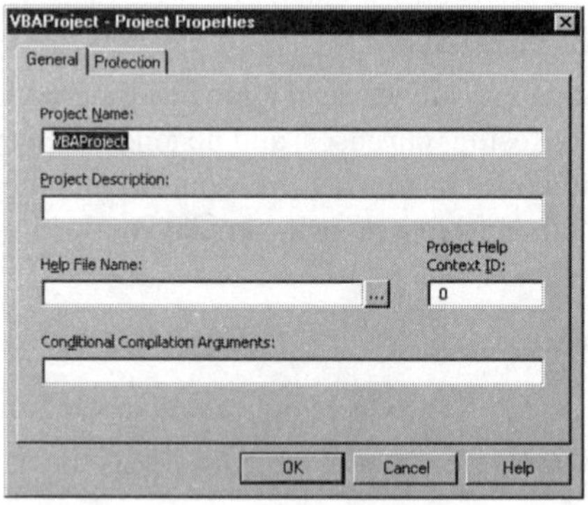

FIG. 29.7
The VBAProject - Project Properties dialog box can be used to change the name and description of a project.

Because the VBA code for a project is actually a part of a workbook, simply saving the workbook also saves all the modules and forms associated with that workbook. If you're in the VBE, you may want a quicker way to save your work, without switching back to Excel in order to save the workbook.

1. Select the project you want to save in the Project Explorer.
2. Choose File, Save, or press Ctrl+S. The workbook containing the project is saved.

CAUTION

Any time you modify your VBA code, it is tempting to immediately test the code by running the macros. Get in the habit of saving your work before giving the macro a test run. It is possible to create VBA code that will result in an endless loop, or even to cause Excel to stop running (especially if you are doing advanced Windows API programming). Once such a crash occurs, you will have no opportunity to go back and save your work.

Using the Properties Window

When you work with objects using VBA, one of the most common elements you must manage is the properties of those objects. Later, you will learn how to manage properties using VBA code. Often, though, it is useful to view and change properties using the Properties window in the VBE. This process is known as making *design-time* changes to properties.

A property is an attribute, or characteristic, of an object. You'll see many examples of objects and their properties as we continue to use VBA code. Here are a few examples of properties that are available in the VBE environment.

- Each project has a Name property. The initial value for this property is VBAProject. You can change this value to a more descriptive name.
- Each Workbook has a PrecisionAsDisplayed property, which corresponds to the corresponding setting in the Tools, Options command. This property is initially set to False. Changing it to True is the same as selecting the check box in the Options dialog box.

- Each sheet in a workbook also has a Name property. This is the same as the name that appears on the sheet tab when you have a workbook open in Excel. Changing the value of the Name property for a sheet in the VBE property window actually changes the name on the sheet tab in Excel.

These are just a few of the many properties available at design time. Even more properties will become available as you add procedures and forms to your projects. For now, see how you can use the Properties window to view and modify properties.

The Properties window is one of several windows in the VBE that you can leave open all the time, or open and close as you want. If you leave this window open all the time, it takes up room on the screen, and might obscure other windows.

Use any of the following methods to open the Properties window:

- Choose View, Properties Window.
- Press F4.
- Click the Properties Window button on the Standard toolbar.

Understanding the Properties Window

The Properties window, shown in Figure 29.8, is used to view and modify properties at design-time. The main part of the display lists the names of the available properties in the first column. The second column displays the current value for each property.

FIG. 29.8
The properties of the active workbook are displayed in the Properties window.

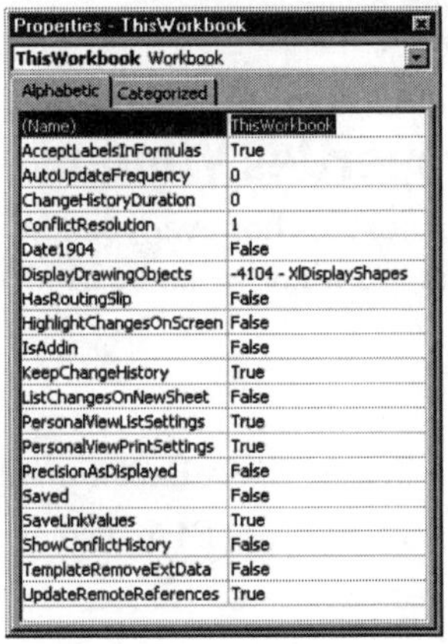

Each property may be of a particular type. For example, in Figure 29.8, the (Name) property is a text value, the AcceptLabelsInFormulas property is a logical value, and the UpdateFrequency property is a numeric value.

If you choose to leave the Properties window open while you work, it will automatically keep itself updated with the available properties of each object that you select in another window, such as the Project Explorer or a form editing window. Different types of objects have different properties, so the list of available properties will grow and shrink as you go about your work.

You can modify a property's value by clicking into the second column of the Properties window, and typing a new value. In some cases, a drop-down list will appear to display the available choices. In other cases, you might be able to enter just about any value that you want to. For details on the appropriate values for any particular property, check the online help for that property.

NOTE Not all properties are available at design-time. Some are only available while your macros are running. These are known as *run-time* properties. For example, the ActiveSheet property of a workbook object tells you which sheet is currently active for editing or viewing at any time during the execution of your macro. The ActiveSheet property is a read-only property, so your VBA macro can read its value, but can't modify it.

CAUTION

Before you modify a property, make sure you understand the purpose of the property, and what its legal values are. Many properties have important effects on the way Excel works, and changing a property may affect these behaviors.

If you aren't sure of the meaning or the available values for a property, click the property in the Properties window, and press F1 to see the help screen for that property.

Renaming a Module Using the Properties Window

Because you can organize your macros into modules however you like, you may want to give your modules descriptive names. The Properties window can be used to modify the Name property of a given module.

To change the name of a module:

1. Select the module you want to rename in the Project Explorer window.
2. If the Properties window is not already open, press F4 to display it.
3. Click the Name property of the module.
4. Edit the name or type a new name, and press Enter to complete the change.

Using the Code Window

The Code window is where you'll do most of the hard work of VBA programming. This is where your code is displayed for viewing, editing, and printing. Because advanced programming in VBA requires you to type and edit much of your VBA code, you'll spend a pretty fair amount of time with the Code window open. Figure 29.9 shows the Code window displaying a recorded macro.

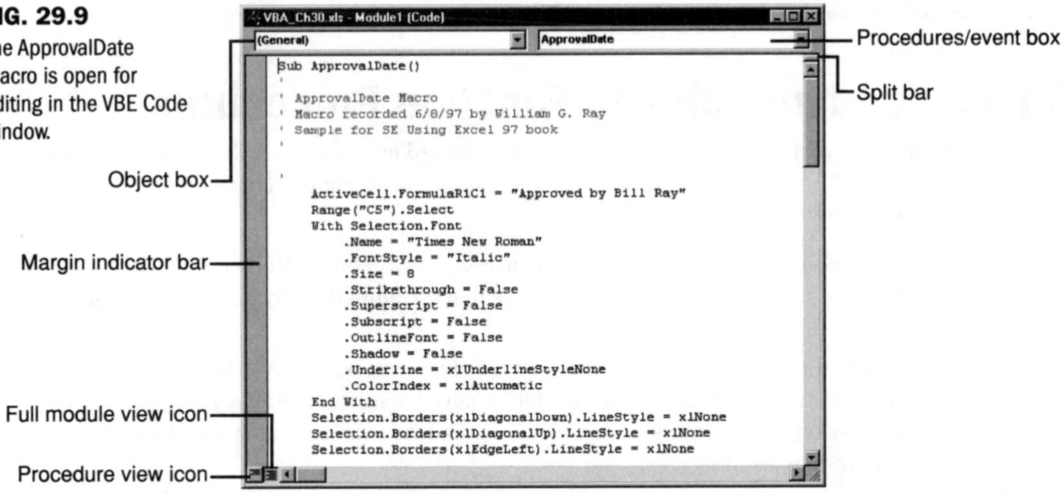

FIG. 29.9
The ApprovalDate macro is open for editing in the VBE Code window.

These are the key elements of the Code window:

- The *object box* displays the selected object that contains the VBA code. In a standard module, the object will always be (General). When you use a form module to create event-driven VBA code for forms, all the controls and parts of the form will be listed in this box as well.
- The *procedures/events box* lists the available procedures for editing, including the automatically generated event procedures in a form module. Clicking this list lets you select the procedure you want to edit. If your selection in the object box is (General), the procedures/events box will also contain an item called (Declarations), which selects the area of the module where you would type declarations of module-level variables, constants, and user-defined types.
- The *split bar* allows you to divide the Code window into two panes by dragging it vertically to a position in the Code window. This is useful for view two sections of a long procedure, or a different procedure in each pane, for comparison as well as for copying and pasting code.
- The *margin indicator bar* can contain various visual indicators of the status of your code during editing and debugging.
- The *procedure view icon* selects the view that displays only one procedure at a time in the code window, even if there is room to display more than one procedure. You can select another procedure for editing by using the procedures/events box.
- The *full module view icon* selects the view that displays all the procedures in the module as though they were a continuous document. You can scroll through the code using the scroll bar.

At first glance, the Code window looks and works like most text editing windows. But after typing just a few lines of code, you'll almost surely find that it is paying a lot of attention to what you type! The VBE detects many errors in your code and then makes suggestions for how to complete a line of code.

Understanding Sub and Function Procedures

The majority of the VBA code you create will be stored in procedures. A procedure is simply a series of VBA statements that is collected together for execution. There are two types of procedures in VBA:

- *Sub procedures* are designed to perform a series of actions. All recorded macros are sub procedures, as are the event procedures that are automatically created for working with custom forms.
- *Function procedures* may perform a series of actions, but can also return a resulting value. Function procedures are useful for performing calculations, manipulating text expressions, or for verifying the success or failure of an operation by setting an appropriate result.

Because recorded macros are stored in sub procedures, they'll probably be the most common type of procedures you use. To learn how to create and use function procedures, see the section "Creating User-Defined Functions," in Chapter 30, "Taking Control of Excel with VBA."

The macro in Listing 29.1 was recorded by selecting the Format, Cells command and making only two selections in the Font tab:

- The Size was changed to 24 points.
- The Font Style was changed to Bold.

The VBA macro recorder picked up a lot of other details while it was recording. You'll learn how to improve this macro as you continue with this chapter. First, though, let's make sure you understand the parts of the procedure.

Listing 29.1 VBA_CH29.XLS—The LargeFont macro was recorded using the Format, Cells command.

```
Sub LargeFont()
'
' LargeFont Macro
' Macro recorded 6/23/97 by William G. Ray
'

'
    With Selection.Font
        .Name = "Arial"
        .FontStyle = "Bold"
        .Size = 24
        .Strikethrough = False
```

```
        .Superscript = False
        .Subscript = False
        .OutlineFont = False
        .Shadow = False
        .Underline = xlUnderlineStyleNone
        .ColorIndex = xlAutomatic
    End With
End Sub
```

- The statement Sub LargeFont() declares the beginning of a Sub procedure and indicates the name of the procedure.
- Lines beginning with an apostrophe (') are *comments*. These lines do not perform any action, but they are useful for documenting the purpose of the macro, as well as any other important information.
- The statement End Sub marks the end of the Sub procedure.
- Everything else between the Sub and End Sub statements is the executable code of the macro.

This macro uses the With...End With block statement to work with the Font object of the current selection. The lines within the block represent the different Font options in the Format Cells dialog box.

One of the common problems with recorded macros is that you end up recording more than you want to. In this case, you intended to record only the Size and FontStyle properties of the Font object. However, VBA recorded the Font Name, Strikethrough, and the rest of the properties because they were displayed in the dialog box when the recorder was on.

Why is this a problem? Suppose you decide later to run the LargeFont macro in another area of your worksheet to make a selection 24-point bold. Suppose, too, that the font in that area is Times New Roman instead of Arial. When you run the macro, it will not only make the selection 24-point bold, it will also change the font to Arial. The macro would do more than you intended. To correct it, you would have to edit the macro.

NOTE VBA macros perform most of their work by using *objects*, *methods*, and *properties*. To learn more about the object-based system of programming in VBA, see Chapter 30, "Taking Control of Excel with VBA."

Modifying Recorded Macros

To edit a recorded macro, you must first display that macro in the code window. If the VBE is not already running, you can open the code window for the desired macro in this way:

1. Choose Tools, Macro, and then select the Macros command from the submenu. The Macro dialog box is displayed.
2. Select the name of the macro you want to edit, and then click the Edit button.

If you are already in the VBE, you can get directly to a desired macro by following the same steps using the Tools menu in the VBE.

When the code window is open, you can use either the mouse or the keyboard to scroll through the code in the macro and to select, or highlight text. While you have text highlighted, if you begin typing, your new text will replace your highlighted text. If you press the Delete key, your highlighted text will be deleted.

One of the first things you may notice is that the VBE checks your code syntax one line at a time as you type. As soon as you move the cursor off the line of code you are editing or you press Enter to move to the next line, the VBE checks to see whether the statement you just edited is constructed according to VBA's coding rules. Figure 29.10 shows the kind of response you might get if you make a mistake while editing your code.

FIG. 29.10
Pressing Enter in the middle of a line of code resulted in an error that was caught by the VBE syntax checker.

In this example, the line of code that previously read:

```
.FontStyle = "Bold"
```

now has been split into two lines:

```
.FontStyle =
"Bold"
```

Because VBA can't interpret the incomplete expression .FontStyle =, an error message occurs.

One of the best ways to get started editing recorded macros is to remove unnecessary lines of code that the recorder picked up. You can select an entire line of code to be deleted by clicking to the left of the line you want to remove. Figure 29.11 shows the result of clicking to the left of a line of code to select it. Notice that the mouse pointer has changed to a reverse arrow (pointing right), which indicates that it is positioned in the area where a click selects the line. Pressing the Delete key now will delete the line of code.

FIG. 29.11
The highlighted line of code is ready for deletion.

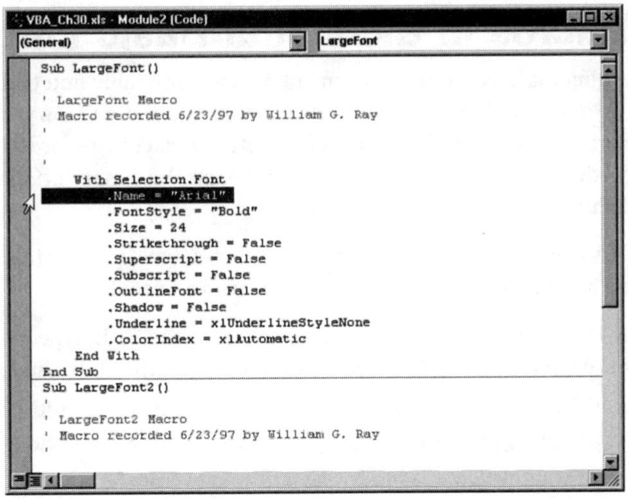

To meet your original objectives for recording the LargeFont macro, you should edit it so that it reads as shown in Listing 29.2.

Listing 29.2 VBA_CH29.XLS—The simplified LargeFont macro will do just what you want...and no more.

```
Sub LargeFont()
'
' LargeFont Macro
' Macro recorded 6/23/97 by William G. Ray
'

'
    With Selection.Font
        .FontStyle = "Bold"
        .Size = 24
    End With
End Sub
```

This modified macro has two advantages over the original recorded macro:

- Without the extra lines, the macro may run faster (although the difference won't be noticeable in a macro as small as this one).
- The edited macro performs more accurately the actions you intended, without the side effects of the recorded macro.

This example is not intended to suggest that you shouldn't use the macro recorder, but rather that you should inspect the results of your recorded macros carefully to see whether they do exactly what you had in mind. Recording and editing macros is one of the easiest ways to learn the VBA language and will remain a timesaver, even for experienced programmers.

Creating Macros in the Visual Basic Editor

While recording macros is often convenient, you will probably find that sometimes it's just simpler to go ahead and type the code for a new macro yourself. As you learn more about the VBA language, you will find that many VBA methods can't be recorded at all. In other cases, while a recorded sequence works properly, there may be a more efficient or more flexible way to accomplish your goals by typing your own code.

Because VBA macros are created as Sub procedures, typing a new macro means you'll have to create a new Sub procedure. There are a few ways you can do this:

- Using the Macros dialog box in either Excel or the VBE, type a name for your macro and click the Create button. Your new macro opens in the code window.
- In the VBE, choose the Insert, Procedure command. The Add Procedure dialog box appears (see Figure 29.12). Type a name and click OK to create the procedure.
- In a code window, go to a blank line between two procedures, or select the (Declarations) section using the Procedure list box. On the blank line, type Sub *ProcName*, where *ProcName* is the name for your new procedure. The new procedure will be created in the code window.

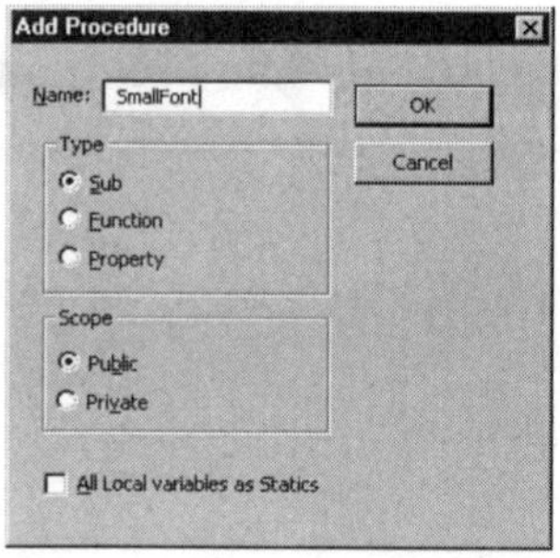

FIG. 29.12
The Add Procedure dialog box automatically creates a new procedure in the VBE.

In any case, you will end up with an empty procedure that looks something like this:

```
Sub SmallFont()

End Sub
```

The first statement declares the name of the procedure you are creating and marks the beginning of the code for that procedure. The empty parentheses indicate that this procedure does not have any ***arguments***, which are additional data items that can be passed to a Sub procedure. Simple macros will not take any arguments. They are only used in procedures that are called by another macro or procedure.

Every Sub procedure must end with the End Sub statement. There must be one, and only one, such statement in every Sub procedure.

At this point, you have a new macro with a name, but it doesn't do anything. Now comes the hard part. It's time to start typing your own code.

How the VBE Helps You Write VBA Code

The Visual Basic Editor is a great tool for entering code. It is more than just a simple text editor. It has been designed to understand the rules of the VBA language and to assist you in several ways as you type your code.

- *Automatic Syntax Checking*. Each time you complete a line of code, the VBE checks to see whether you have made an obvious mistake, such as misspelling a statement name or leaving out some required punctuation. This won't catch every possible error, but it certainly picks up a lot of typos.
- *Require Variable Declaration*. This optional rule requires you to declare variables before using them. The main benefit is that it catches misspelled variable names, which might otherwise lead to logical errors that are hard to identify.
- *Auto List Members*. Many statements, methods, and functions have lists of items you can choose from when entering code. Instead of having to remember (or look up) the list items, you can select from a list that is automatically displayed by the VBE.
- *Auto Quick Info*. This feature displays the ***parameters*** of statements, methods, and functions as you type them in so you don't have to remember them.
- *Auto Data Tips*. When your macro is in break mode, this displays the value contained in a variable. This is used during the debugging process.
- *Auto Indent*. Automatically aligns each new line of code with the previously entered line. This makes it easy to create neatly formatted code, which is easier to read and to debug.
- *Color-Coded Editing*. The VBE automatically applies different colors to different types of text, such as language keywords, comments, and normal text. This not only makes your code easier to understand, it also helps you catch spelling errors that might result in logical errors.
- *Tool Tips*. This automatically displays additional information about the toolbar buttons that are available in the VBE.
- *Edit, Complete Word Command*. Completes the word you are typing, so you don't have to key in the full name. This not only saves time, it also reduces the number of errors.

Setting Options for the VBE

The VBE offers a variety of options for editing your VBA code. The Tools, Options command provides a multipage dialog box with four groups of settings you can customize or turn off or on.

Figure 29.13 shows the Editor tab, which contains two groups of settings. The Code Settings control whether the VBE provides the automatic features to help you edit your code. You turn each feature on or off by clicking its corresponding check box. The Window Settings controls the appearance of the code editing window.

Figure 29.14 shows the Editor Format tab, which allows you to set the font appearance of text in the code editing window. This makes it easy to distinguish different types of text, such as VBA language keywords, or comments.

FIG. 29.13
The Editor tab of the Options dialog box controls the code editing window.

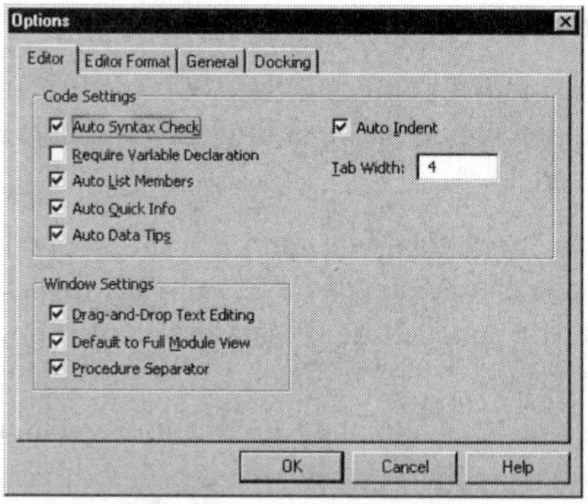

FIG. 29.14
The Editor Format tab of the Options dialog box controls the appearance of text in the code editing windows of the VBE.

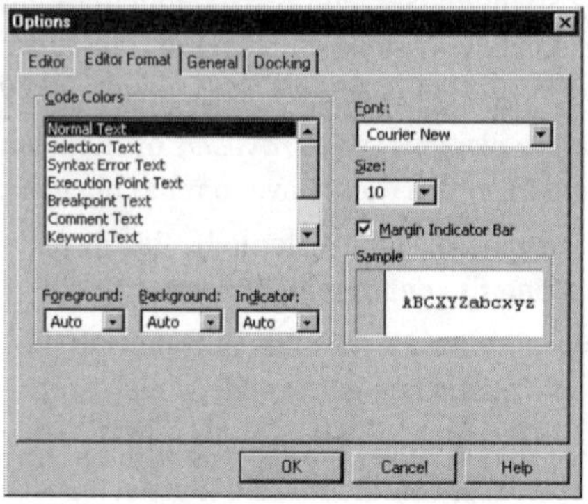

Figure 29.15 shows the General tab, which has settings for controlling form design, error trapping, and compiling. A simple but useful option in this pane is the Show ToolTips option, which helps you identify different parts of the VBE window and toolbars.

FIG. 29.15
The General tab of the Options dialog controls a variety of appearance and performance attributes of the VBE.

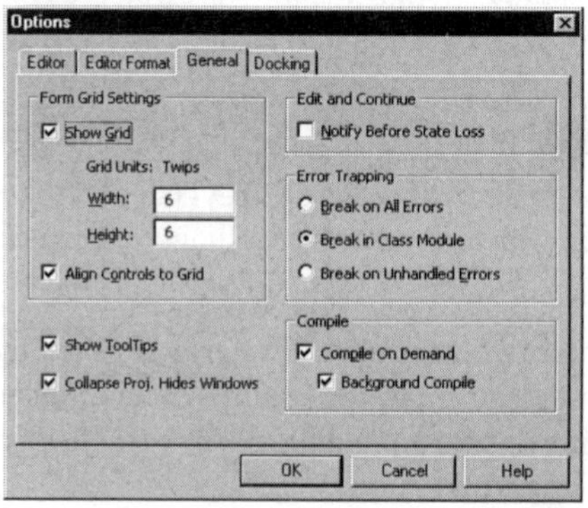

Figure 29.16 shows the Docking tab. By declaring a window as dockable, you are allowing it to attach itself to the edge of the VBE window, instead of floating freely on the screen. You can make any combination of selections here to suit your preferences.

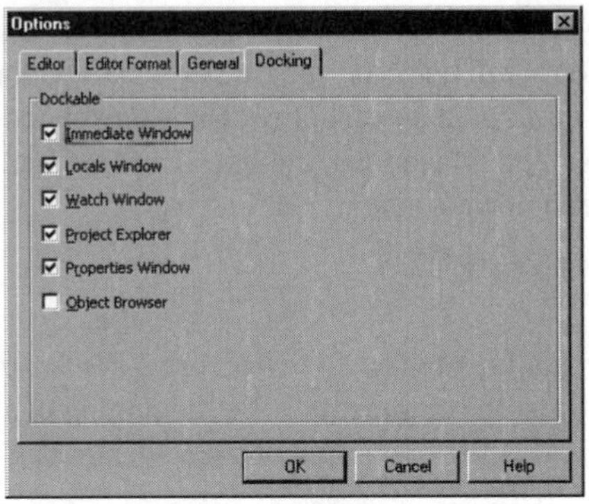

FIG. 29.16
The Docking tab of the Options dialog lets you select the Dockable property of the VBE's different windows.

An Introduction to the VBA Language

Once you have declared a Sub procedure, you can begin entering the code that tells VBA what you want your macro to do. The code that you enter must follow the rules of the VBA language. These rules are known as the *syntax* of the language. The syntax defines how you can combine the different elements of the language into expressions and statements that VBA can execute.

How to Enter VBA Code

VBA is pretty flexible in allowing you to enter code in a variety of layouts. In some cases, VBA will even correct your code to make it follow its syntax rules. Here are a few things to keep in mind:

- Enter one VBA statement on a line, and then press Enter to move to a new line. Although you can put multiple statements on a line and separate them with colons (:),that makes your code harder to read.
- If the line of code is very long due to functions and methods that have many arguments, you can continue a statement on the next line by typing an underscore (_) at the end of a line and continuing the statement on the next line. For example, take a look at this single line of code:

  ```
  Selection.MoveDown Unit:=wdLine, Count:=2, Extend:=wdExtend
  ```

  The following is the same line of code split across three lines using the line continuation character:

  ```
  Selection.MoveDown Unit:=wdLine,
  Count:=2,
  Extend:=wdExtend
  ```

- Between statements, you can leave blank lines to make your code easier to read. This helps divide longer macros into sections of related statements.

- You can indent a line by pressing Tab at the beginning of the line as many times as necessary. The VBE will automatically indent the following line by the same amount. This is another way of setting off a group of related statements, such as those statements inside a loop. To reduce the indention (also called *outdenting*), press Shift+Tab.
- Use comments freely to explain your code. If you or someone else has to edit the code months later, the comments will help you remember what you had in mind when you were creating the code. Putting an apostrophe (') in a line of code makes the rest of that line a comment. In this sample, the entire first line is a comment, and the second line contains a comment after a normal statement.

```
'The next line sets the font size
Selection.Font.Size=24       'Very large font
```

It is generally not necessary to comment every line because VBA is a pretty expressive language. However, it's a good idea to use comments at the beginning of a procedure to describe the purpose of the procedure, and at the beginning of each section of a long procedure.

Building Statements in VBA

Each line of code that will execute in your VBA procedures is known as a *statement*. Several elements can be combined to create statements in VBA:

- *Keywords* are elements of the VBA language that have predetermined purposes. Sub and End Sub are examples of VBA keywords that you have already seen.
- *Expressions* combinations of variables, constants, operators, and keywords that produce a value of some type. Expressions can be simple or very complex. Here are some examples of simple expressions:

```
"Microsoft Excel 97"
4.5 * Width
Age >= 65
City & ", " & State
```

- *Variables* let you use a name to represent and store a value for later use. To learn about variables, see "Declaring and Using Variables," later in this chapter.
- *Constants* are also names that refer to values, but the value of a constant cannot be changed during the execution of a procedure.
- *Literals* are simple expressions of particular values in any data type. The following examples are numeric, string, and data literals:

```
1600
"Los Angeles"
#12/31/99#
```

- *Operators* are used to combine simple expressions into more complex expressions, resulting in a value of a particular data type. There are several different types of operators in VBA, which perform arithmetic, comparisons, logical evaluation, and string manipulation.

Here are some simple examples of the use and result of operators in expressions:

Expression	Result
15.8-12.2	3.6
75=(25*3)	True
"John" & " Doe"	"John Doe"

- *Methods* and *properties* are elements of the objects used by your program. Excel provides a very large collection of objects, methods, and properties. Excel uses these methods and properties to do most of its work in a macro. Objects are covered in greater detail in Chapter 30, "Taking Control of Excel with VBA."

Declaring and Using Variables

A variable is a named location for storing data during the execution of a VBA procedure. The value of a variable may be modified during the execution of the procedure by assigning a new value to the variable.

In VBA, you can introduce a new variable at any time by using it in your procedure. Consider the simple VBA macro shown in Listing 29.3.

Listing 29.3 VBA_CH29.XLS—The ChangeFontSizes macro uses the NewSize variable without declaring it first.

```
Sub ChangeFontSizes()
'
' ChangeFontSizes Macro
' Macro recorded 6/26/97 by William G. Ray
'

    NewSize = 12        'Assign a value to a variable
    Selection.Font.Size = NewSize     'Use variable to update a property
    ActiveCell.Offset(1, 0).Range("A1").Select
    NewSize = 11        'Assign a new value to the variable
    Selection.Font.Size = NewSize     'Use variable to update a property
End Sub
```

This macro sets the font size of the current selection to 12 points and then moves down one cell and sets the font size of the cell below to 11 points. In this macro, NewSize is a variable that contains the numeric value of the font size to be assigned. The variable does not exist until the first time it is used. This is known as ***implicitly*** declaring the variable. In other words, you are declaring the variable simply by using it.

Now look at a slightly modified version of that macro in Listing 29.4.

Listing 29.4 VBA_CH29.XLS—This version of the ChangFontSizes macro uses the Dim statement to declare the variable NewSize.

```
Sub ChangeFontSizes()
'
' ChangeFontSizes Macro
' Macro recorded 6/26/97 by William G. Ray
'
    Dim NewSize As Integer

    NewSize = 12        'Assign a value to a variable
    Selection.Font.Size = NewSize     'Use variable to update a property
    ActiveCell.Offset(1, 0).Range("A1").Select
    NewSize = 11        'Assign a new value to the variable
    Selection.Font.Size = NewSize     'Use variable to update a property
End Sub
```

The only difference in the two listings is the line Dim NewSize As Integer. The Dim keyword declares a variable and allows you to specify a data type for the variable. Following the keyword As, you can use any of the data types that are defined in this chapter.

So why would you bother with this extra step? Declaring the exact data type of a variable can improve performance and memory usage of your macros. If you don't tell VBA what the data type for a variable is, it uses the data type known as *variant*. The variant data type allows for the use of just about any kind of data, but also requires more storage space and is usually slower than other data types. This may not make much difference in very small macros, but will be increasingly important as your macros get larger and more complex.

Also, if you declare a specific data type, VBA can enforce the rules of that data type on the macro, often preventing errors. Suppose you entered the following line of code into either of the two versions of the ChangeFontSizes macro:

```
NewSize = "Large"
```

This statement attempts to assign a text value to the variable. In the first version of the macro, this statement would be allowed to execute because variant variables can contain text values. This may be dangerous, however, because using the text value later in the same macro may produce incorrect results.

On the other hand, if you try to run this statement in the second version of the macro, you'll get an error with the message "Type mismatch." Because you have declared that the variable can contain only Integer values, any attempt to assign a different data type results in an error. This prevents you from making such a mistake, which might result in logical errors in your macros.

Requiring Variable Declaration

Because declaring variables before they are used is such a good idea, VBA allows you to change the rules so that you are required to declare all variable before they are used.

In order to require the declaration of variables, type the following statement in the Declarations section of a module:

```
Option Explicit
```

If the Option Explicit statement is present in a module, VBA will allow the use of variables only after they are declared. The rule applies to that module only, however, so you should get in the habit of entering the Option Explicit statement into every module.

You can have the VBE put the Option Explicit statement into new modules for you automatically. Follow these steps:

1. In the VBE, choose Tools, Options, and select the Editor tab.
2. Check the Require Variable Declaration box, and then click OK to complete the command.

After you activate this option, the Option Explicit statement is added to each new module you create. It will not affect any existing modules, so you'll have to add the statement to existing modules yourself if you want to enforce the variable declaration requirement.

Using Option Explicit has an additional benefit, which is illustrated by the version of the ChangeFontSizes macro found in Listing 29.5.

Listing 29.5 VBA_CH29.XLS—This version of ChangeFontSizes has a spelling error. With Option Explicit enabled, the VBA compiler will catch this error.

```
Sub ChangeFontSizes()
'
' ChangeFontSizes Macro
' Macro recorded 6/26/97 by William G. Ray
'
    Dim NewSize As Integer

    NewSize = 12        'Assign a value to a variable
    Selection.Font.Size = NewSize      'Use variable to update a property
    ActiveCell.Offset(1, 0).Range("A1").Select
    NewsSize = 11        'Ooops! I spelled it wrong!
    Selection.Font.Size = NewSize      'Use variable to update a property
End Sub
```

Notice that there is a spelling error near the end of the macro. NewSize was typed as NewsSize. If Option Explicit is not present in this module, a subtle error creeps in. VBA would have to assume that NewsSize is simply a new variable and would allow the assignment of the value 11 to the new variable. The previously assigned variable NewSize would still contain the value 12. Because the next line in the macro uses the correct spelling, the second cell would get the font size of 12, and no error message would be generated. Therefore, you might not notice the error until much later—if at all.

However, if you have Option Explicit in effect in this module, the attempt to assign a value to an undeclared variable results in the error message "Compile error: Variable not defined." This catches the error before it allows your code to execute with incorrect results.

Now that you know how to declare a variable, you need to know what the different data types of variables in VBA are.

Understanding Data Types

VBA allows for several different data types. When you declare a variable, it's a good idea to declare the most appropriate data type for the job, so that VBA will store the data most efficiently and give you the best performance. Sometimes the data type is determined by how you are going to use the variable. The example of the NewSize variable in the previous section was used to set the Size property of the Font object. The Size property is numeric, so it was appropriate for you to select a numeric data type. Selecting another data type might have resulted in an error in your macro or in unexpected results.

Numeric Data Types There are several different numeric data types, as listed in Table 29.1. The *storage* for each data type indicates how much space is required by VBA to hold the variable in memory. The range of the data type tells how large and small the values can be that are stored in variables of that data type.

Table 29.1 VBA Numeric Data Types

Data Type	Storage	Range
Byte	1 byte	0 to 255
Integer	2 bytes	-32,768 to 32,767
Long	4 bytes	-2,147,483,648 to 2,147,483,647
Single	4 bytes	approx. -3.403E38 to -1.401E-45 for negative numbers approx. 1.401E-45 to 3.403E39 for positive numbers
Double	8 bytes	approx -1.798E308 to -4.941E-324 for negative numbers approx. 4.901E-324 to 1.798E308 for positive numbers
Currency	8 bytes	-922,337,203,685,477.5808 to 922,377,203,685,477.5807
Decimal	14 bytes	+/- 79,228,162,514,264,337,593,543,950,335 with no decimal point +/-7.9228162514264337593543950335 with 28 places to the right of the decimal point

The main thing to notice is that for greater numeric range and greater accuracy, you will require more storage. You should also notice that the Byte, Integer, and Long types do not support fractional values of any type. However, these types are usually much faster than Single, Double, or Decimal types if you are doing a lot of calculation and you don't need to store decimal values.

String Data Types String data types are used for storing text information. There are two types of string variables:

- *Variable-length* strings are most commonly used and allow you to store text of up to about 2 billion characters in length. Each string variable of this type uses 10 bytes of storage in addition to the actual string value that is stored.
- *Fixed-length* strings can hold no more than about 65,400 characters. Fixed-length strings usually have the advantage of being faster than variable-length strings. They also let you limit the length of the strings you allow to be stored in order to eliminate data you don't want to allow in your application.

You can declare a variable-length string when you don't want to place a specific limit on the length of the value that can be contained in the variable.

```
Dim Remarks As String
```

You should use a fixed length string if you want to limit the length of the text value that can be stored in the variable. The following declaration allows no more than three characters to be stored in the new variable.

```
Dim Initials As String * 3
```

Other Data Types There are three other simple data types in VBA:

- *Boolean* variables are for storing logical values. The only two values you can store in a Boolean variable are True and False.
- *Date* variables are double-precision numeric values used for storing dates and times. VBA can store dates from January 1, 100 to December 31, 9999.
- *Object* variables are used for storing references to objects within an application. These objects may be part of Excel, other Office 97 applications, or many other Windows applications that support Automation with objects.

To assign a value to a Boolean variable, use the keywords True and False as shown here.

```
Dim ExamPassed As Boolean
ExamPassed = False
```

To assign a literal value to a date variable, you must enclose the data between two number signs (#) like this:

```
Dim StartDate As Date
StartDate = #15 Jun 97#
```

Using object variables is covered in greater detail in Chapter 30, "Taking Control of Excel with VBA."

The Variant Data Type VBA includes a data type not found in most programming languages: the *variant* data type. You can declare a variable to be of the Variant data type in three ways:

- Use an explicit declaration: Dim MyVariable As Variant.
- Leave out the As keyword: Dim MyVariable.
- If you aren't using Option Explicit, simply use a new variable without declaring it first.

Variants can hold data of any of the simple data types previously defined in this chapter, except for fixed-length strings. Variants give you the flexibility of being able to change the data type of a variable during the execution of a procedure and to combine different data types without producing run-time errors. Consider the example in Listing 29.6.

Listing 29.6 VBA_CH29.XLS—The Variant variables in this message can be combined to perform arithmetic or to create a longer message.

```
Dim Sales As Variant
Dim Message as Variant
Dim Target As Variant
Sales = 125000
Message = "The current sales level is " & Sales & "."
Target = Sales * 1.1
```

In this example, the Sales variable contains numeric data, but it can be combined with a text expression to produce a message. The same variable can also be used in the numeric calculation of a target value for the new year's sales.

Variant variables can contain three special values:

- *Empty.* This value indicates that a variant variable has been declared but has not yet been assigned a value. You can't assign the Empty value to a variable. It simply results from the variant not having been assigned a value.
- *Null.* This is a value you can assign to a variant to indicate that the variable does not contain any data. You assign the Null value in your code like this:

  ```
  Sales = Null
  ```
- *Error.* The Error value indicates that an error has occurred. You can use the CVErr function to convert numbers to error values.

The variant data type is the most flexible data type, but you should use it only when you need this flexibility. Selecting one of the other simple data types will usually use less memory, result in faster performance, and ensure the accuracy of your use of data types.

Using Program Control Statements

Any recorded VBA macro will execute ***sequentially***. The code begins executing at the Sub statement and executes one line at a time until it reaches the End Sub statement. Then the macro is finished.

This sequential execution is good enough for simple macros, but as you try to do more complex activities with your macros, you may want your code to be more flexible.

VBA, like just about any programming language, has a variety of program control statements that let you code make logical decisions about which statements will execute, perhaps depending upon the value of data in a spreadsheet cell. These statements sometimes let you skip from one part of the macro to another or to repeat statements in the macro.

Making Decisions with If...Then...End If

Perhaps the most common control structure is the If...Then...End If statement. This statement lets VBA conditionally execute some of your code, depending on a logical condition.

The simplest way to use this statement is as a one-liner. The syntax for the simple If statement is as follows:

```
If condition Then [statements] [Else elsestatements]
```

NOTE In the syntax examples for VBA, any expression enclosed in brackets is optional. The programmer has the choice of including or omitting these portions of the syntax.

In this structure, the *condition* is a logical expression that can be either True or False. If the expression is True, VBA executes the statements. If the expression is False, it skips over the statements. If there is an Else portion in the statement, it is executed when the logical expression is False. Consider the example in Listing 29.7.

Listing 29.7 VBA_CH29.XLS—The IfTest macro displays a rating message that depends on the value of the active cell.

```
Sub IfTest()
Dim ThisCell, Rating

Rating = "Average"
ThisCell = ActiveCell.Value
If ThisCell >= 10 Then Rating = "Excellent"
If ThisCell <= 5 Then Rating = "Poor"
MsgBox Rating
End Sub
```

Depending on the value in the active cell of the spreadsheet when this macro is run, a message will be presented. The variable Rating is initially assigned the value "Average." If the value of the current cell is 10 or more, the Rating is changed to "Excellent." If the value is 5 or less, the Rating is changed to "Poor." If neither condition is true (i.e, the value is between 5 and 10), the Rating will not have changed and will still be "Average."

The more complete version of the If statement is the block structure of the If...Then...End If statement. The complete syntax of this statement follows:

```
If condition Then
  [statements]
[ElseIf condition-n Then
  [elseifstatements]...
[Else
  [elsestatements]]
End If
```

The block structure gives you more flexibility in handling conditions and lets you execute many statements depending upon the logical condition. This is demonstrated by the SetCommission macro shown in Listing 29.8. Note that this macro refers to the sheet named "Sales Data." If the sheet does not exist, an error will occur.

Listing 29.8 VBA_CH29.XLS—This macro calculates a sales commission and generates a rating depending on the sales level.

```
Sub SetCommission()
Dim Sales As Long, Commission As Single, Rating As String

Sheets("Sales Data").Activate
Sales = Cells(2, 1).Value
If Sales > 150000 Then
    Commission = Sales * 0.012
    Rating = "Superior"
ElseIf Sales > 100000 Then
    Commission = Sales * 0.08
    Rating = "Satisfactory"
Else
    Commission = Sales * 0.04
    Rating = "Unsatisfactory"
End If
Cells(2, 2).Formula = Commission
Cells(2, 3).Formula = Rating
End Sub
```

This macro first checks to see whether the sales level (stored in cell A2) is over the "superior" level of $150,000. If so, it calculates the commission and sets the rating text. If the sales level is not over $150,000, the macro checks for the "satisfactory" level of $100,000. It sets the "unsatisfactory" level if neither of the two conditions is met. Finally, the macro updates cells B2 and C2 with the Commission and Rating values.

Notice that the block structure allows for the execution of as many statements as you want within each portion of the block structure. This offers a lot of flexibility.

Choosing with the Select Case Statement

The Select Case statement is easier to use than the If statement when you need to choose among several values for a single expression and you need to perform a different action for each value. The syntax of the Select Case statement follows:

```
Select Case expression
Case value1
   [statements]
[Case valuex
   [statements]]
[Case Else
   [statements]]
End Select
```

Each Case *value* is compared to the Case *expression*. Only the statements following the matching value are executed. You can list as many different cases as you need for your testing. If there are no matching values, the statements following the Case Else statement are executed.

The SetTaxes macro, shown in Listing 29.9, uses the Select Case statement to calculate the tax rate on commission in several states, each of which uses a different method for calculating its taxes.

Listing 29.9 VBA_CH29.XLS—The SetTaxes macro uses the Select Case statement to calculate taxes using different methods for each state.

```
Sub SetTaxes()
Dim Commission As Single, State As String, Taxes As Single

Sheets("Sales Data").Activate
Commission = Cells(2, 2).Value
State = Cells(5, 1).Value
Select Case State
Case "NY"
    Taxes = Commission * 0.08
Case "FL"
    If Commission > 2000 Then
        Taxes = Commission * 0.05
    Else
        Taxes = Commission * 0.03
    End If
Case "CA"
    Taxes = (Commission - 1000) * 0.1
Case Else
    Taxes = 0
End Select
Cells(5, 2).Formula = Taxes

End Sub
```

Repeating with the Do...Loop Statement

One of the most common requirements of any programmer is to repeat one or more statements some number of times. This process is known as *looping*, and VBA provides a block structure for looping called the Do...Loop structure.

The Do...Loop statement is simple yet very flexible. There are four different ways to use the Do...Loop structure:

- **Syntax 1:** Do While...Loop

```
Do While condition
  [statements]
Loop
```

- **Syntax 2:** Do Until…Loop

```
Do
  [statements]
Loop Until condition
```

- **Syntax 3:** Do…Loop While…

```
Do
  [statements]
Loop While condition
```

- **Syntax 4:** Do…Loop Until…

```
Do While condition
  [statements]
Loop Until condition
```

The Statements inside the loop are repeated as many times as is allowed by the evaluation of the logical condition. In the first two variations, the logical condition is tested before the loop has executed, so it's possible that the statements will not be executed at all. In the last two variations, the logical test is applied after the loop statements have executed, which ensures that the execution of at least one statement will occur.

The other difference is the use of either a While test or an Until test. With the While test, the loop continues as long as the condition is True. Using the Until test, the loop is repeated as long as the condition remains False. Generally, it's up to you to select which is the easier logical choice. You may find it easier to express the testing condition as either True or False in any particular situation.

Using the For...Next Statement

The For…Next block statement is another looping statement that makes it easy to repeat a set of VBA statements a given number of times. This statement will be familiar to programmers of many other languages.

```
For counter = start To end [Step stepvalue]
  [statements]
Next [counter]
```

In this structure, ***counter*** must be a numeric variable that is automatically increased each time through the loop. The first time the loop is executed, ***counter*** is set to the value of start, and the loop repeats until the last time through the loop, when ***counter*** is equal to end.

If you omit the optional Step portion, the variable is incremented by 1 each time through the loop. You can have the loop variable incremented by a different value by using the Step keyword and supplying a numeric value for stepvalue, which can be either positive or negative.

The ElectionYears macro, shown in Listing 29.10, uses a For Next loop to count from 2000 back to 1792, listing every fourth year. The Step -4 phrase allows the loop to count backward four years at a time.

Listing 29.10 VBA_CH29.XLS—This macro uses a For...Next loop to find all the election years from 2000 back to 1792.

```
Sub ElectionYears()
Dim Year
Worksheets.Add.Move after:=Worksheets(Worksheets.Count)
For Year = 2000 To 1792 Step -4
    ActiveCell.Formula = Year
    ActiveCell.Offset(1, 0).Select
Next Year
End Sub
```

NOTE VBA also supports the use of the GoTo statement to jump directly to another location in a procedure. Use of the GoTo statement is generally discouraged, but you should typically be able to accomplish its functionality using the structured control statements explained in this chapter. For more information on the GoTo statement, check the online help for VBA.

Looping Through Collections with the For Each...Next Statement

VBA has some control statements designed especially for working with objects. You will learn more about the objects that are built into Excel in Chapter 30, "Taking Control of Excel with VBA." However, you'll learn about the control statements in this chapter because they work much like the other looping structures.

Many objects in Excel come as *collections* of objects. Collections occur when groups of similar objects are organized together. Probably the easiest way to understand the nature of a collection is to consider a few examples.

- The Application object contains a collection of Workbooks.
- Each Workbook object contains a collection of Worksheets.
- Each Workbook contains many collections, such as the collections of rows, columns, and cells.

One characteristic of collections is that there may be almost any number of items in a collection, including zero. For example, a workbook might have any number of worksheets.

When you need to perform some action on every item in a collection, the For Each...Next loop comes in handy. This loop executes a block of statements once for each member of a collection. This is especially convenient if you don't know how many items are in a collection.

```
For Each element In collection
  [statements]
Next [element]
```

Suppose you wanted to make a list of all the sheets in the active workbook. The macro in Listing 29.11 creates such a list, beginning at the active cell, by navigating through the collection of sheets. Notice that nothing in the macro indicates how many sheets are in the workbook.

Listing 29.11 VBA_CH29.XLS—The SheetLister macro uses a For Each...Next loop to find the name of each sheet in the current workbook.

```
Sub SheetLister()
Dim Sheet As Object
For Each Sheet In ActiveWorkbook.Sheets
    ActiveCell.Formula = Sheet.Name
    ActiveCell.Offset(1, 0).Select
Next Sheet
End Sub
```

While it is often possible to use other methods to accomplish the same effect, the For Each…Next structure is usually a good choice. It makes your code easy to read and understand, and it often executes faster that other looping methods with built-in collections of objects.

Using With...End With to Control Objects

Another characteristic of objects in Excel, is that a given object may have many methods and properties. You can discover the methods and properties of an object by using the Object Browser, as described in Chapter 30, "Taking Control of Excel with VBA." VBA code that refers to objects can be very repetitive. Consider the macro in Listing 29.12, which clears a cell, applies several formatting properties, and initializes the contents of the cell.

Listing 29.12 VBA_CH29.XLS—The InitializeCell macro clears any old contents from a cell and initializes it to a consistent value and appearance.

```
Sub InitializeCell()
    ActiveCell.ClearContents
    ActiveCell.Font.Name = "TimesNewRoman"
    ActiveCell.Font.Size = 14
    ActiveCell.Font.Bold = True
    ActiveCell.BorderAround LineStyle:=xlDouble
    ActiveCell.Formula = "***"
    ActiveCell.HorizontalAlignment = xlHAlignCenter
End Sub
```

This macro references the ActiveCell object in every line and the Font object in three lines. While there is nothing terribly wrong with this, VBA must reference the objects for each statement, which will take longer as your macro becomes more complex. The macro in Listing 29.13 uses the With…End With structure twice. The main loop captures the properties and methods of the ActiveCell object, while the inner loop refers to the Font object of the ActiveCell. This code only has to refer to the ActiveCell and Font objects once and will perform faster than the original version.

Listing 29.13 VBA_CH29.XLS—The improved version of InitializeCells runs faster because it makes fewer object references.

```
Sub InitializeCell()
    With ActiveCell
        .ClearContents
        With .Font
            .Name = "TimesNewRoman"
            .Size = 14
            .Bold = True
        End With
        .BorderAround LineStyle:=xlDouble
        .Formula = "***"
        .HorizontalAlignment = xlHAlignCenter
    End With
End Sub
```

VBA usually is able to apply the With structure to a group of similar properties when you record a macro, but you may be able to improve upon the recorded macro, especially if you didn't perform all the activities of the macro in the most efficient order.

From Here...

This chapter has taught you how to go beyond recorded macros in Excel 97 by editing and creating your own code in the Visual Basic Editor. The next three chapters expand upon these new skills to show you how to take advantage of the power of VBA.

- Chapter 30, "Taking Control of Excel with VBA," describes the object model used by VBA. You'll use the VBE to create macros that use the Excel object model to control your spreadsheet application.
- Chapter 31, "Advanced VBA Programming," shows you how the custom form design features of VBA let you create interactive Windows applications. You'll also learn how use the Windows Application Programming Interface to add even more features to VBA.
- Chapter 32, "Building Solutions with VBA," builds upon your VBA skills to let you create a complete application, combining the power of VBA with the rich features of Excel.

From Here...

CHAPTER 30

Taking Control of Excel with VBA

by Bill Ray

The real power of working with VBA comes from its ability to directly control Excel and the rest of the Microsoft Office 97 suite of applications. The key to using this power is to understand the object models that are built into each Office 97 program. This chapter introduces you to the Excel 97 object model, and shows you how to use the object model to control and to get information from Excel. ■

Understanding object models

You'll learn how the object model gives VBA access to the full power and functionality of Excel 97.

Key objects for Excel VBA

You'll get a detailed look at some of the most important objects in Excel, which let you control workbooks, worksheets, and ranges.

Interacting with the user

You'll learn how to use VBA's functions for gathering data from your users and presenting messages to them.

Creating user-defined functions

You'll use VBA to create your own functions, which can be used just like Excel's built-in worksheet functions.

Programming with events

You'll run your own macros when certain events occur in Excel, such as opening a workbook or activating a specific sheet.

Object Models and VBA

Most of the real work that an Excel macro performs involves the use of the Excel 97 object model. The actions in a recorded macro are mostly the result of executing the methods and modifying the properties of the built-in objects. When you write your own VBA code, you need a thorough understanding of the object model of Excel to select the best course of action for your code.

By incorporating the use of object models into the VBA development environment, VBA is able to use a relatively simple, consistent language that can work with any application. (The core elements of VBA were presented in Chapter 29, "Introducing VBA Programming.") Of course, the recorded macros and other examples in that chapter made use of the Excel object model, but the detailed description of objects was saved for this chapter.

The object model for an application describes the structure and functionality of the program. In Excel, for example, there are predefined objects that represent the application itself, workbooks, individual sheets, cells, and ranges, as well as many other objects. In Word, the object model contains references to the application, documents, sections, paragraphs, and so on. Each application's object model must define those elements that make that program unique, while providing a consistent way for the programmer to interact with the program.

Each application in Office 97 has its own object model, which is automatically installed when you install Office 97. The object models give VBA programmers a consistent programming interface for controlling Excel, Word, PowerPoint, Access, and Outlook. Many other Windows programs have object models, too. In Chapter 32, "Building Solutions with VBA," you'll learn how to create an Excel 97 macro that controls the object model of another Office 97 program. For the rest of this chapter, you'll concentrate on the extensive object model of Excel 97.

What Is an Object?

The object model of Excel 97 describes the content and functionality of Excel. The content of Excel includes the application, workbooks, sheets, cells, and other items that together make up the material of Excel, along with the characteristics of those object, including colors, sizes, and other attributes. The functionality of Excel includes all the operations you can perform with Excel, including entering data into cells, opening and closing files, printing, and many other commands and actions of Excel.

All these items in Excel are represented by objects. An object is simply a way of thinking about is single item or group of related functionality in the application. For example, there is a Workbook object, representing the workbook and all its behaviors and characteristics. Some of the things you can do with the Workbook object are:

- Find out the name of the workbook.
- Count how many sheets are in the workbook.
- Open, close, save, or print the workbook.

This is all possible because of the built-in functionality of the object model. In this chapter, you will learn about some of the major object of the Excel object model, and how to tap into the functionality of the objects. This functionality is realized by using the properties and methods of the objects.

Methods and Properties of Objects

Although an object represents an item in Excel, to really make use of the object, you must work with the methods and properties of the object.

A *property* describes some information about the content or some other attribute of an object. For example, many objects have a Name property, which contains the text of the name of that object. The following statement shows how to display the name of the active sheet in a message box, by reading the Name property of the sheet.

```
MsgBox ActiveSheet.Name
```

You also can use properties to change the attributes of an object. The next statement shows how to change the name of a sheet by assigning a new value to the Name property of the sheet object.

```
ActiveSheet.Name = "Sales Report"
```

Different types of objects have their own set of properties. You can use the online help or the built-in Object Browser to find the available properties for an object. The Object Browser is described later in this chapter, in the section "Using the Object Browser."

A *method* is like a predefined procedure that performs some action with an object. For example, the Close method of a Workbook object, does just what it sounds like; it closes the workbook.

```
ActiveWorkbook.Close
```

Many methods have one or more ***arguments***. An argument is some type of information that tells the method exactly how you want it to work. For example, the SaveAs method of a workbook object can be used to save the workbook with a new name. For the method to work, you have to supply the name for the new file by providing the FileName argument.

```
ActiveWorkbook.SaveAs FileName:="MySheet"
```

Some arguments are optional. The SaveAs method for workbook objects has several optional arguments. One of these allows you to provide a password when you save the file.

```
ActiveWorkbook.SaveAs FileName:="MySheet", Password:="OpenSesame"
```

As with properties, you can learn about the methods of an object by using the online help or the Object Browser.

NOTE The methods and properties of an object are accessed using *dot notation*. In its simple form this is represented as Object.Property or Object.Method. For example, in the expression ActiveWorkBook.Close, ActiveWorkBook is an object reference, and Close is a method.

continues

continued

Often, one object will contain properties that refer to other objects, so you may get a string of several dots in a single expression. For example, the expression ActiveCell.Font.Name refers a Cell object that has a Font property. The Font property refers to a Font object, which has a Name property.

The dot notation gives you a concise method for precisely referring to objects, methods, and properties in the extensive Excel 97 object model.

Using Collections of Objects

Many objects are commonly found in *collections*. A collection is a set of items as they are defined in Excel, with a specific order. There are many common examples of collections you can access in Excel with VBA:

- The Application object contains a collection named Workbooks, which contains all the currently open workbooks.
- A Workbook object contains a collection named Sheets, representing all the sheets in the workbook.
- A Sheet object contains a collections named Cells, which corresponds to the cells in the sheet.

To work with a specific item in a collection, you can use the index of the item. For example, to find the name of the first sheet in a workbook, you could use the following statement:

```
MsgBox ActiveWorkbook.Sheets(1).Name
```

In addition to using a numeric index, you can use the name of the item in a collection as the index. To close a specific workbook, you can use this statement.

```
Application.Workbooks("Expenses").Close
```

This technique is especially useful, because many collections change dynamically, and the number of the index for an item may change. In the case of the Workbooks collection, the exact index number of any workbook will change as workbooks are opened and closed.

Understanding Excel's Object Model

Of all the Office applications, Excel was the first to support VBA and object models. This concept was introduced to Excel programmers in Excel 5, and has been further developed in Excel for Windows 95 (version 7), and now has been updated for Excel 97 (version 8). Excel's object model is very extensive, and might even seem a little overwhelming at first. Remember, the object model contains references to all the features of Excel, and Excel 97 is certainly a feature-rich program. Additionally, as you will see in this chapter, there are objects designed specifically for VBA programmers, such as the Range object. There is no way to take advantage of this object without programming, and, as you will see, it gives you lots of added power in your VBA applications.

No macro developer should expect to memorize the entire Excel 97 object model. You will get to know those objects that you use frequently very well, but you'll need help with others. Even frequently used objects will have many features that you use only occasionally, so you'll need help with them, too. There are a few things to remember in beginning to learn the Excel object model, to keep you from losing your way in this rich and extensive model:

- *Use the macro recorder.* When you record a macro, the result contains lots of objects, methods and properties. Interpreting and modifying this recorded code is a great way to get to know the Excel object model.
- *Use the Object Browser.* This powerful tool, which is accessed through the VBE, lets you search through the object hierarchy of Excel, as well as of other applications that you may need to control in your VBA macros.
- *Use the VBE's built-in tools.* The VBE has many tools that are designed to help you enter your code in the code window.
- *Use the online Help system.* The objects, collections, methods, and properties of the Excel object model, as well as the statements and functions that make up VBA, are documented in the online help. In most cases, there are useful code examples of the language elements in action. You can print out the help pages and code examples, or even copy and paste them into your application.

Figure 30.1 shows the help screen for the Microsoft Excel object model. Clicking the bar representing one of the objects displays detailed help for that object, and may lead to many additional help screens about that object's methods, properties, and other related objects. Figure 30.2 shows the detailed help for the Application object, the first object you need to understand in working with the Excel object model.

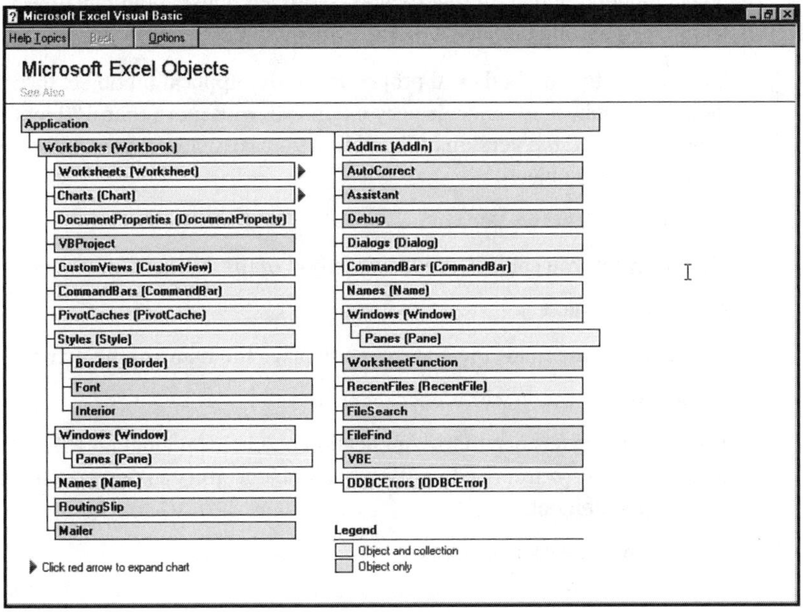

FIG. 30.1
The Microsoft Excel 97 object model is documented in the online help. Clicking an object displays detailed information about the object.

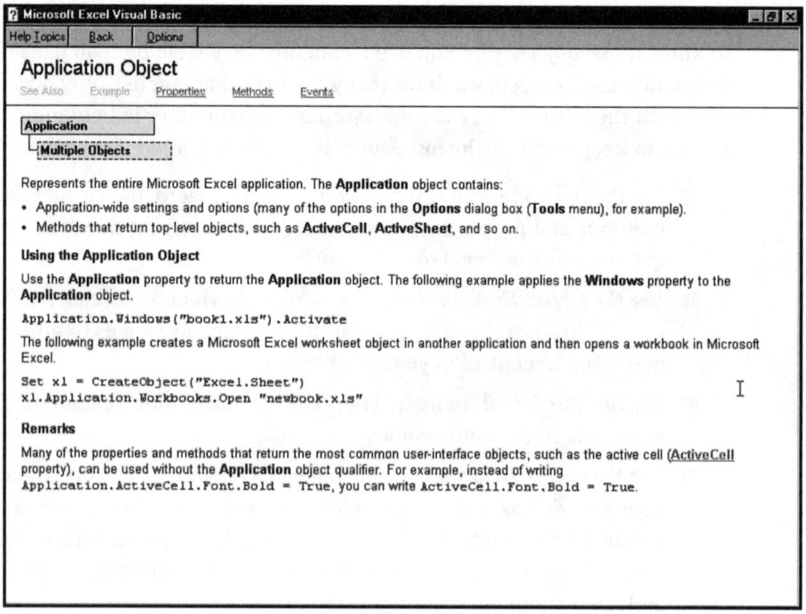

FIG. 30.2
The Application object is the first object to understand in any object model, because it contains methods and properties that lead to the rest of the object model.

The Application Object

Most applications that provide object models have an Application object that is the first place to look for information about the program. Excel 97 uses the Application object to provide properties and methods that refer to Excel 97 as a whole, as well as providing access to the rest of the object model of Excel. In theory, you could begin just about any object reference in Excel VBA with the Application object, although it is often not necessary.

You can use the methods and properties of the Application object directly, using the dot notation. The Application object is very extensive, with more than 180 methods and properties. For example, to find the version of Excel that you are using, you can use the Version property of the Application object.

```
MsgBox Application.Version
```

To exit Excel, you can use the Quit method of the Application object.

```
Application.Quit
```

For example, the following statement displays the name of the active workbook:

```
MsgBox Application.ActiveWorkbook.Name
```

However, the reference to the Application object is optional for the ActiveWorkbook property, which returns a reference to a Workbook object. You can perform the same action with the following statement:

```
MsgBox ActiveWorkbook.Name
```

As with any object, the key to using the Application object is to become familiar with its properties and methods.

Properties of the Application Object The Application object has too many properties to list and describe them all in this chapter. Instead, let's get a flavor for the Application object, by looking at some of its most useful properties. Table 30.1 shows some of these properties, along with descriptions of each.

Table 30.1 Some Useful Properties of the Application Object

Property	Description
ActiveCell	Returns a range object referring to the active cell
ActivePrinter	Returns or sets the active printer
ActiveSheet	Returns a sheet object referring to the active sheet
ActiveWindow	Returns a window object referring to the active window
ActiveWorkbook	Returns a workbook object referring to the active workbook
Calculation	Returns or sets the calculation mode
Caption	Returns or sets the text of the Excel title bar
CommandBars	Returns an object representing Excel's command bars
DefaultFilePath	Returns or sets the location Excel uses for saving new workbooks
DisplayFormulaBar	Shows or sets whether the Excel formula bar is displayed
MailSystem	Returns a number indicating which mail system, if any, is installed
MemoryFree	Returns the number of bytes of free memory
Name	Returns the name of the application
OperatingSystem	Returns the name and version number of the operating system
PreviousSelections	Returns an array of the last four ranges or names selected
RecordRelative	Tells whether macro are recorded with relative references
ScreenUpdating	Tells whether Excel's display is updated during macro execution
StatusBar	Returns or sets the text in the status bar
UserName	Returns the name of the current user
VBE	Returns a reference to the VBE
Workbooks	Returns a collection of all the open workbooks

The macro in Listing 30.1 shows how to display the values of a variety of Application object properties by entering them into a worksheet.

Listing 30.1 VBA_CH30.XLS—The ApplicationProperties macro displays Excel's properties by updating a spreadsheet.

```
Sub ApplicationProperties()
Sheets(1).Select
Cells(2, 2).Formula = Application.ActivePrinter
Cells(3, 2).Formula = Application.ActiveWorkbook.Name
Cells(4, 2).Formula = Application.AltStartupPath
Cells(5, 2).Formula = Application.Build
Cells(6, 2).Formula = Application.Caption
Cells(7, 2).Formula = Application.DefaultFilePath
Cells(8, 2).Formula = Application.DefaultSaveFormat
Cells(9, 2).Formula = Application.MemoryFree
Cells(10, 2).Formula = Application.MemoryTotal
Cells(11, 2).Formula = Application.MemoryUsed
Cells(12, 2).Formula = Application.OperatingSystem
Cells(13, 2).Formula = Application.StandardFont
Cells(14, 2).Formula = Application.UserName
Cells(15, 2).Formula = Application.Version
End Sub
```

Methods of the Application Object The methods of the Application object define actions that you can take at the application level. Table 30.2 lists some of the methods of the Application object that you may find useful.

Table 30.2 Some Methods of the Application Object

Method	Description
ActivateMicrosoftApp	Runs a Microsoft program, such as Word or Access
Calculate	Calculates all open workbooks
FindFile	Displays the Open dialog box, and opens the selected file
GetOpenFileName	Displays the Open dialog box, but doesn't open any files
GetSaveAsFileName	Displays the SaveAs dialog box, without saving any files
Help	Displays a help topic
MailLogon	Logs onto a MAPI Mail or Exchange session
Quit	Exits Microsoft Excel
Run	Executes a VBA or Excel 4.0 macro
SaveWorkspace	Saves the current workspace
Undo	Undoes the last user action
Wait	Pauses your Excel macro until a specified time

Using Workbook Objects

The Application object contains a collection called Workbooks, which refers to all the open workbooks. Here are a few useful operations with the Workbooks collections.

To create a new workbook, you just add a new item to the Workbooks collection:

```
Workbooks.Add
```

To close a workbook, you need to refer to the specific workbook in the Workbooks collection:

```
Workbooks("Sales Report").Close
```

You will probably be more interested in the workbook you are currently working with than the entire Workbooks collection, most of the time. You can use the ActiveWorkbook property, to refer to the object representing the current workbook.

```
ActiveWorkbook.Save
```

There are many useful properties of a Workbook object. Table 30.3 lists some of them.

Table 30.3 Some Properties of the Workbook Object

Property	Description
ActiveSheet	Returns a sheet object referring to the active sheet in the workbook
BuiltinDocumentProperties	Returns a collection of the document properties of a workbook, such as the Title, Author, and Keywords
CustomDocumentProperties	Returns a collection of the custom properties that have been defined for a workbook
FileFormat	Returns a value representing one of the file formats available for a workbook object
FullName	Returns the file name of the workbook (including the path)
Name	Returns the name of the workbook
Names	Returns a collection of the names defined within the workbook
Path	Returns the complete path of the workbook, without the file name
Saved	Tells whether any changes have been made since the workbook was last saved
Sheets	Returns a collection of the sheets in the workbook
Styles	Returns a collection of the styles in the workbook
VBProject	Returns a reference to the Visual Basic project for the workbook

continues

Table 30.3 Continued

Property	Description
Windows	Returns a collection of the currently open windows in the workbook
Worksheets	Returns a collection of the worksheets in the workbook

Working with Worksheet Objects

Because each workbook in Excel may contain many worksheets, you can use the Worksheets collection to refer to all the worksheets in a workbook. Each individual worksheet is represented by a Worksheet object.

NOTE In addition to the Worksheets collection, a workbook contains a Sheets collection. The Sheets collection contains both the Worksheets and Charts collections. Likewise, a Sheet object may refer to either a Worksheet object or a Chart object.

To add a new worksheet to a workbook, use the Add method.

```
ActiveWorkbook.Worksheets.Add
```

To remove a worksheet form a workbook, use the Delete method.

```
ActiveWorkbook.Worksheets("Old Data").Delete
```

You can easily print a worksheet.

```
ActiveSheet.Printout
```

Or you can display the Print Preview window for a worksheet.

```
ActiveSheet.PrintPreview
```

To make a particular sheet the active sheet, use the Activate method.

```
Worksheets("Sheet1").Activate
```

Table 30.4 lists some of the most useful properties of the Worksheet object.

Table 30.4 Some Properties of the Worksheet Object

Property	Description
Cells	Returns a Range object containing all the cells on the worksheet
Columns	Returns a collection of the columns in the worksheet
DisplayPageBreaks	Tells whether page breaks are displayed
Name	Returns or set the name of the worksheet
Names	Returns a collection of the worksheet-specific names on the sheet

Property	Description
PageSetup	Returns a PageSetup object, containing the page setting for the workbook
ProtectionMode	Tells whether the worksheet has protection enabled
Range	Returns a Range object on the worksheet
Rows	Returns a collection of the rows in the worksheet
UsedRange	Returns a Range object that refers to the used area on the worksheet
Visible	Returns or sets the visibility of the worksheet

TIP The Visible property of a worksheet has a special value, available only to VBA macros. If you set the Visible property of a worksheet to `xlVeryHidden`, the only way to make the sheet visible is to execute VBA code that sets the Visible property to `True`. The user will not be able to unhide the worksheet using the menus.

Working with the Selection and Range Objects

The Range object is one of the most commonly used objects in Excel VBA. Range objects are used any time you want to get information about the cells in your worksheets, or to put information into or change the properties of the cells of the worksheet. Range objects may refer to anything from a single cell to any number of cells, including 3-D range of cells.

There are several ways to generate a reference to a Range object. The important thing to remember is that each of these methods returns a reference to a Range object, with all the methods and properties of a Range object.

- Use the `Selection` property of the Application or of a window. As long as the current selection is one or more cells, this will return a Range object. If another object, such as a chart, or drawing object, is selected, a Range object will not be returned.
- Use the ActiveCell property of the Application or of a window. This property will always return a single cell, unless the active windows is not a worksheet.
- Use the Range property of the Application or of a window, or even of another range. The Range property can refer to a named range, or to a collection of cells, referenced by rows and column.
- Use one of the other methods or properties that returns a Range object. There are many of these objects and methods in Excel's object model. The following list shows the objects and methods that return Range objects. You can learn more about each of these methods and properties in the online Help.

ActiveCell	Offset
BottomRightCell	PageRange
Cells	Precedents
ChangingCells	Range
CircularReference	RowFields
Columns	RowRange
CurrentArray	Rows
CurrentRegion	Selection
Dependents	TableRange1
DirectDependents	TableRange2
EntireColumn	TopLeftCell
EntireRow	UsedRange
Next	VisibleRange

Because there are so many uses for working with ranges in Excel VBA, it is worth taking a look at some examples of some methods of working with ranges.

Using a Range Name You can use the Range property together with a previously defined name to refer to a cell. The following example selects the range named "InputArea" in the active workbook.

```
Range("InputArea").Select
```

Working with A1-Style References You can use the familiar A1-style references of Excel together with the Range property to refer to one or more cells. The following example enters a formula into cell B10 on the active sheet.

```
Range("B10").Formula  = "=SUM(B2:B9)"
```

NOTE Cell references in Excel VBA come in two forms. The most familiar form for most people is the A1-style reference. In this reference style, a letter represents the column of the referenced cell, and a number represents the row of the referenced cell.

The R1C1 style reference uses numbers for both the row and the column. Notice that in this reference style, the row comes before the column, while in the A1-reference style, the column comes first.

As an example, the cell that is referred to as B10 in the A1-style reference is known as R10C2 in R1C1 reference style.

You also can use A1-style references to refer to more than a single cell using the Range property. By supplying both the beginning cell and the ending cell, the following statement selects an entire rectangular range.

```
Range("B5","G10").Select
```

You also can use a more complete reference to the Worksheets collection, together with the Range property, to refer to a range on another worksheet.

```
Worksheets("User Information").Range("UserName") = Application.UserName
```

TIP It is usually not necessary to select cells in your VBA macros. A recorded macro usually reflects the fact that you have selected a cell or range before performing an action, such as formatting or editing. In the code that you write, however, you can simply refer to a cell without selecting it, and inspect or set a property of the cell or range. For example, it is easy to understand the following code:

```
Range("B10").Select
ActiveCell.Formula = 0
Range("B11").Select
ActiveCell.ClearContents
```

However, this code is simpler and executes much faster:

```
Range("B10").Formula = 0
Range("B11").ClearContents
```


Using the Cells Property to Work with Ranges The Cells property provides an easy way to return a reference to one or more cells in a range. This property may be applied to the Application object, to a worksheet, or to a range. The Cells property usually takes two arguments: a row number and a column number. Omitting the arguments refers to all the cells in the selected object.

The following example fills the cells of the current selection with the value 0.

```
Selection.Cells.Value = 0
```

By supplying the row and column indices for the Cell property, you can refer to an individual cell. The following statement assigns the value in cell B10 to a variable.

```
Sales = Cells(10,2)
```

TIP When referring to rows and columns with the Cells property, remember that you indicate the row first and then the column. This is the opposite of the A1-style reference, in which the column reference comes first.

If you apply the Cells property to a Range object, it returns a Range object referring to only the cells in the range. The following statement deletes the contents of the second row, third column within the range named Sales.

```
Range("Sales").Cells(2,3).ClearContents
```

Using the Offset Property The Offset property is a convenient way to get a reference to a range that is located a certain number of rows and columns away from another range. Offset takes two arguments, representing the number of rows and columns to adjust the cell reference.

This statement selects the cell below the active cell, offset from the active cell by one row, and zero columns.

```
ActiveCell.Offset(1,0).Select
```

The row and column arguments to the Offset property also can be negative, returning references above or to the left of the original range. The following statement adjusts the current selection, moving it up two rows and to the left one column.

```
Selection.Offset(-2,-1).Select
```

If the Offset method attempts to refer to an address beyond the edge of the sheet, an error is generated.

Some Properties That Return Useful Ranges Several properties are included in Excel VBA to return ranges that are especially useful:

- CurrentRegion returns the current region, which is the area surrounded by empty rows or the edge of the worksheet. This is often a useful range to select for formatting, printing, copying, and many other actions.
- UsedRange returns the range containing all the used cells in a worksheet.
- TopLeftCell returns the cell at the upper-left corner of the object to which it is applied.
- BottomRightCell returns the cell at the bottom-right corner of the object to which it is applied.

Looping Through a Range It is often useful to perform a series of actions on every cell in a range. This requires a way to visit or reference each cell in a range. Usually, the best way to do this is with the `For Each...Next` block statement. This statement treats the cells in a range like items in a collection.

The code in Listing 30.2 checks each cell in a named range and applies formatting based upon the value in the cell.

Listing 30.2 VBA_CH30.XLS—The ColorFormat macro formats each cell differently, depending on its value.

```
Sub ColorFormat()

Dim R As Object
For Each R In Range("InputData")
    If R.Value > 800 Then
        R.Font.Color = RGB(0, 0, 255)
        R.Font.Bold = False
        R.Font.Italic = False
    ElseIf R.Value < 500 Then
        R.Font.Color = RGB(255, 0, 0)
        R.Font.Bold = False
        R.Font.Italic = True
    Else
        R.Font.Color = RGB(0, 128, 0)
        R.Font.Bold = True
```

```
        R.Font.Italic = True
    End If
Next R
End Sub
```

If your code modifies the range, for example by inserting and deleting rows or columns, the `For Each...Next` loop might not work right, because the collection is established at the beginning of the loop. You may move past the original range, or not get to every cell in the range. In this case, you can use another method for looping through a range, the Do...Loop structure. The advantage of the `Do...Loop` approach is that you can apply a logical test each time through the loop, to make sure that the end of the range has been reached properly.

The DeleteDiscontinued macro in Listing 30.3 loops through a products table. In each row, the macro looks in column G, which contains a 1 if the product is discontinued, and 0 if it is not discontinued. By checking the value of this cell, the macro decides whether to delete the row containing the product from the worksheet. This process continues until an empty cell is found, indicating that the end of the table has been reached.

Listing 30.3 VBA_CH30.XLS—The DeleteDiscontinued macro loops through the products table, deleting the discontinued items.

```
Sub DeleteDiscontinued()
Dim CurrentCell As Object, NextCell As Object
ActiveWorkbook.Sheets("Products").Select
Set CurrentCell = ActiveSheet.Range("G2")
Do While Not IsEmpty(CurrentCell)
    Set NextCell = CurrentCell.Offset(1, 0)
    If CurrentCell.Value = 1 Then
        CurrentCell.EntireRow.Delete
    End If
    Set CurrentCell = NextCell
Loop
End Sub
```

Using Object Variables

In many cases, you can use the built-in objects of Excel without declaring variables to represent them. Sometimes, however, you may find it useful to declare a variable to refer to an object. Declaring object variables may improve the performance of your macros as they become more complex, especially if your macro must reference an object many times. Object variables also can make your code easier to understand, by using a descriptive name rather than the built-in name for an object. In Chapter 31, "Advanced VBA Programming," you will learn how to create your own objects, which will also require the use of object variables.

Object variables are declared using the Dim statement, just as you declare other objects.

```
Dim AW As Object
```

If you use the keyword Object when you declare an object variable, you can later create an instance of the object by using the Set keyword.

```
Set AW = Application.ActiveWorkbook
```

TIP Assigning an object to an object variable always requires the use of the Set keyword. A common mistake in using object variables is to omit this keyword and to attempt a simple assignment.

```
Dim MyVar as Object
MyVar = ActiveWorkbook
```

TIP This produces the error message, "Object variable or With block variable not set," when you try to run your code. Remember to use the Set keyword with object variables, as in:

```
Dim MyVar as Object
Set MyVar = ActiveWorkbook
```

Now you can use your newly assigned object variable in the same manner as you would use the object reference itself. For example, you can use the methods and properties of the object.

```
MsgBox AW.Name
AW.Close
```

When you declare an object variable, it is a good idea to be more specific about the object type than using the general type `Object`. Declaring a variable with a specific object type improves performance and enforces more accurate error checking.

```
Dim objWS As Worksheet
Dim strSheetname as String

Set objWS = ActiveWorkbook.Sheets(1)
Sheetname = objWS.Name
```

When you no longer need a reference to an object in your code, you should destroy the object reference by setting the object variable with the keyword `Nothing`. This removes the object reference, freeing the memory and system resources used by that object.

Using the Object Browser

As you can tell by looking at the macros that we've been creating, most of the functionality of an Excel VBA macro comes from the Excel 97 object model. The same is true of macros using other Office 97 applications, as well as many other Windows programs. Therefore, one of the key skills in VBA programming is understanding the object models of Excel and other applications. Of all the Office 97 applications Excel probably has the most extensive and powerful object model.

The VBE provides the Object Browser as a tool for exploring the object models of Excel and other Windows applications. From within the VBE you can display the Object Browser window by choosing View, Object Browser, or pressing F2. Figure 30.3 shows the Object Browser window.

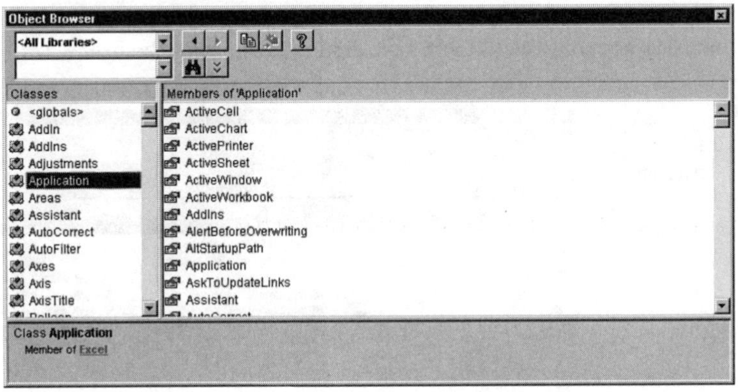

FIG. 30.3
The Object Browser shows the object, methods, and properties available to the current project.

When the Object Browser is displayed, you can use the many different parts of the window to navigate the available object models. The Object Browser shows the classes, properties, methods, events, and constants that are available to your project.

- Use the Project/Libraries Box to select the object library you want to work with. All open libraries that are available to the current VBA project are available.
- Use the Classes list to select the object you want to inspect. A class is simply the formal definition of an object.
- The Members list shows the members of the selected class. The members of a class may include properties, methods, and constants.
- The Details pane shows detailed information about the selected class or member, including the type of the object, and where it is defined.
- The Go Back and Go Forward buttons let you move to previously viewed object displays, and then to return to where you started.
- The Search button lets you search through the libraries for the name of an object or other item that you want to find. Type the text you are looking for in the Search Text box. The Search Text box keeps a list of the last four items you searched for.

When you perform a search, the Search Results pane appears, as shown in Figure 30.4.

Interacting with the User

It is often necessary to have your macros communicate with the user while the macro is running. You may want to display some information or a message to the user, or you may want to ask the user to make a selection or to answer a question. VBA has two simple methods of interacting with the user. The MsgBox function displays messages and receives simple responses from the user. The InputBox function allows you to ask the user a question and provides a text box for the user to enter his or her response.

For applications that require lots of user interaction, you will probably want to develop custom forms using the form design tools provided by the VBE. These tools are discussed in detail in

Chapter 31, "Advanced VBA Programming." For simple messages and questions, MsgBox and InputBox are convenient tools for communicating with the user.

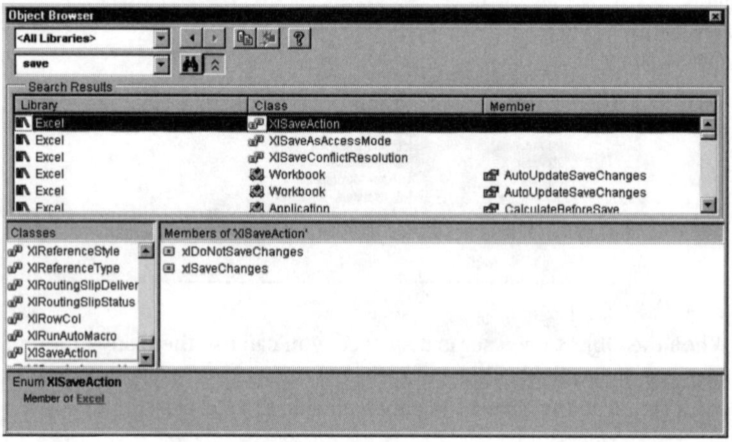

FIG. 30.4
The Search Results pane shows the results of searching for all items containing "save."

Displaying Messages with Message Boxes

A message box displays information in a simple dialog box, as shown in Figure 30.5. One or more buttons are available to the user, to close the message box and respond to the message, which might be in the form of a question.

FIG. 30.5
The message box is a simple tool for presenting messages to the user.

Message boxes are created in VBA by using the MsgBox function. The syntax of the MsgBox function is as follows:

```
Result = MsgBox(messagetext [, buttonoptions] [, titletext] [, helpfile,
➥context])
```

Here are the components of the MsgBox function:

- *Messagetext* is the text you want to appear in the message. This may be a literal string, or a string variable.
- *Buttonoptions* is a numeric value representing which buttons you want to appear in your message box, as well as some other option for the display and behavior of the message.
- *Titletext* is an optional argument to supply the caption at the top of the message box. This may be a literal or variable string expression.

- *Helpfile* and *context* let you specify the name of a Windows help file the user can access for more information. Context is a numeric expression for a specific location within the help file.
- *Result* is the numeric value returned by the function when the message box is dismissed. This value lets you know which button was pressed to dismiss the message.

Using the Button Options for a Message Box The Buttonoptions argument for a message box lets you indicate several details about the appearance and behavior of the message box. To make these options available, several constants are predefined in VBA. These constants are listed in Table 30.5.

To use the MsgBox constants, you can simple add together the constants you want to use. For example, suppose you want to present the message, "Have a Nice Day!" You only need one button, the OK button. The message is not critical, so you may want to display the Information Message icon. Since there is only one button, you don't need to worry about the default button. The following code presents the message box shown in Figure 30.5.

```
MsgBox "Have a Nice Day!", vbOkOnly + VbInformation
```

Because there is only one button, there is no need to return the value of the MsgBox function, and it is used like a simple statement.

Table 30.5 Button Option Constants for the MsgBox Function in VBA

Name	Value	Description
vbOKOnly	0	Display OK button only.
VbOKCancel	1	Display OK and Cancel buttons.
VbAbortRetryIgnore	2	Display Abort, Retry, and Ignore buttons.
VbYesNoCancel	3	Display Yes, No, and Cancel buttons.
VbYesNo	4	Display Yes and No buttons.
VbRetryCancel	5	Display Retry and Cancel buttons.
VbCritical	16	Display Critical Message icon.
VbQuestion	32	Display Warning Query icon.
VbExclamation	48	Display Warning Message icon.
VbInformation	64	Display Information Message icon.
VbDefaultButton1	0	First button is default.
VbDefaultButton2	256	Second button is default.
VbDefaultButton3	512	Third button is default.
VbDefaultButton4	768	Fourth button is default.

continues

Table 30.5 Continued

Name	Value	Description
VbApplicationModal	0	Application modal; the user must respond to the message box before continuing work in the current application.
VbSystemModal	4096	System modal; all applications are suspended until the user responds to the message box.

You also can use the MsgBox function to as a simple question, and find out what the user's response is. The result returned by the MsgBox function tells which button was pressed to dismiss the dialog. The values that can be returned by the function are listed in Table 30.6.

Table 30.6 Return Values of the MsgBox Function

Constant	Value	Description
vbOK	1	OK
vbCancel	2	Cancel
vbAbort	3	Abort
vbRetry	4	Retry
vbIgnore	5	Ignore
vbYes	6	Yes
vbNo	7	No

Suppose the user runs a macro that can exit Excel. You may want to ask the user whether she really wants to do this. Based upon her response, you can either exit Excel, or end the macro and stay in Excel. The macro in Listing 30.4 displays the dialog box shown in Figure 30.6 and responds to the user's selection.

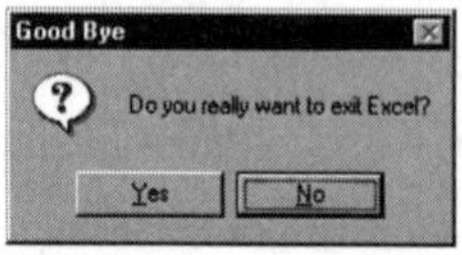

FIG. 30.6
The Good Bye message box not only asks a question, but receives the user's answer.

Listing 30.4 VBA_CH30.XLS—The TryToExit macro will exit excel unless the user clicks the no button.

```
Sub TryToExit()
Dim txtMsg As String, txtTitle As String
Dim Buttons As Integer, Result As Integer
```

```
txtMsg = "Do you really want to exit Excel?"
txtTitle = "Good Bye"
Buttons = vbYesNo + vbQuestion + vbDefaultButton2
Result = MsgBox(txtMsg, Buttons, txtTitle)
If Result = vbYes Then
    Application.Quit
Else
    MsgBox "Exit cancelled.", vbOKOnly, "Hello, again"
End If
End Sub
```


While VBA's custom form design tools let you create complex interactive forms relatively, the one-line simplicity of the MsgBox function is still a useful tool.

Getting Input with Input Boxes

The only problem with the MsgBox function is that the user's response is limited to the choice of buttons that can be displayed. What if you want to ask the user's name, or for some other information. The InputBox function provides an easy way to ask such a question and get an answer. Here is the syntax for the InputBox function:

```
ResultText = InputBox(prompt[, title] [, default] [, xpos] [, ypos] [, helpfile,
context])
```

- *Prompt* is the question or message you are presenting to the user.
- *Title* supplies the caption for the input box.
- *Default* lets you supply an answer, so the user doesn't have to type it. This is useful when a question usually has a consistent answer. The user can still edit or replace this value while the input box is open.
- *Xpos* and *ypos* allow you to position the input box on the screen. By omitting these arguments, the input box is automatically centered on the screen.
- *Helpfile* and *context* allow you to specify a Windows help file and a particular topic within that help file. The user can display the help topic by pressing F1.
- *ResultText* is the text that the user typed in response to the input box.

The macro in Listing 30.5 shows how to use the results of the InputBox function in a worksheet.

Listing 30.5 VBA_CH30.XLS—The GetCompanyName macro asks for the user's name and then updates the sample input sheet.

```
Sub GetCompanyName()
Dim txtMsg As String, txtTitle As String
Dim txtResult As String, txtDefault As String

txtMsg = "What is your name?"
txtTitle = "InputBox Example"
txtDefault = "Unknown User"
```

continues

Listing 30.5 Continued

```
txtResult = InputBox(txtMsg, txtTitle, txtDefault)
Worksheets("Sample Input").Select
ActiveSheet.Range("A1").Formula = "This worksheet was prepared by: " & txtResult
End Sub
```

Creating Subroutines and Functions

As your macros grow in number, length and complexity you will probably find that you create the same code over and over again. If you do, you are ready to create a subroutine. Of course, every macro you have created is already a subroutine, but you've probably just run each macro, or sub procedure, on its own. In this section, you'll see how to create and call sub procedures from your macros. You'll also learn how to create your own functions, to perform calculations in your macros, as well as in an Excel 97 workbook.

Reusing Code with Subroutines

A subroutine is nothing more than a VBA sub procedure that you call from another procedure or macro. To be a little more formal about it, a sub procedure is a named collection of VBA statements, which can be executed as a unit. The formal syntax for a sub procedure is as follows:

```
Sub ProcName([argumentlist])
[statements]
End Sub
```

As with a simple VBA macro, the *ProcName* is any valid name. *Argumentlist* is a comma-separated list of values that can be passed when calling the subroutine. You'll look at one example without any arguments, and another with arguments.

Listing 30.6 contains the code for the HighlightRow subroutine, which applies formatting to the entire row containing the active cell. The HighlightProducts macro moves through the Products table, selecting those rows that have a value of 0 in column 6, which contains the number of units in stock. If the value is 0, HighlightProducts calls HighlightRow to do the formatting.

Listing 30.6 VBA_CH30.XLS—The HighlightRows macro calls the HighlightRow subroutine to add formatting to products that need to be reordered.

```
Sub HighlightRow()
Dim CurrentRow As Range
Set CurrentRow = ActiveCell.EntireRow

With CurrentRow.Font
     .Bold = True
     .Italic = True
     .Color = RGB(255, 0, 0)
```

```
End With
End Sub

Sub HighlightProducts()
Dim R As Range
Worksheets("Products").Select
For Each R In ActiveSheet.UsedRange.Rows
    If IsNumeric(R.Cells(1, 6)) Then
        If R.Cells(1, 6).Value = 0 Then
            Cells(R.Row, 1).Select
            HighlightRow
        End If
    End If
Next
ActiveSheet.Cells(1, 1).Select
End Sub
```


Listing 30.7 contains the EnterYears subroutine, and the macro Next10Years, which calls EnterYears. EnterYears is designed to type a consecutive list of years, given a starting year and the number of years to enter. The arguments StartingYear and HowMany provide the direction necessary for it to do its work.

The Next10Year macro selects a sheet and starting cell, then calls EnterYears, passing 1997 as the StartingYear argument, and 10 as the HowMany argument. EnterYears types the values 1997 through 2006 into the Sample Input sheet beginning at cell C1.

Listing 30.7 VBA_CH30.XLS—The Next10Years macro calls the EnterYears subroutine, passing the starting year and the number of years to enter.

```
Sub EnterYears(StartingYear As Integer, HowMany As Integer)
Dim YearCount As Integer
Dim CurrentCell As Range

For YearCount = 1 To HowMany
    Set CurrentCell = ActiveCell.Offset(YearCount - 1, 0)
    CurrentCell.Formula = StartingYear + YearCount - 1
Next YearCount
End Sub

Sub Next10Years()
Worksheets("Sample Input").Select
Range("C1").Select
Call EnterYears(1997, 10)
End Sub
```

Creating User-Defined Functions

A function is a special type of VBA procedure, which returns a result. You can create custom functions to perform calculations in your macros, and to use directly in your workbooks, just like the built-in functions that come with Excel. Custom functions are defined in VBA as function procedures. The syntax for a function procedure is similar to the syntax for a sub procedure.

```
Function FuncName ([argumentlist]) [As Type]
    [statements]
    FuncName = expression
End Function
```

FuncName is the name of the function you are declaring. *Argumentlist* is a comma-separated list of data arguments that are passed to the function. The *As Type* phrase declares the data type of the value returned by the function. If you omit this phrase, the implied return type is the variant type.

Notice the final statement before the End Function statement. The function name is used as though it were a variable, and a value is assigning to the name. This value must be of the data type that you declared for the value to be returned by the function.

The function in Listing 30.8 accepts two arguments, representing a person's first and last names. The result of calling the function is a string, arranged as last name, followed by a comma and space, then the first name.

Listing 30.8 VBA_CH30.XLS—The CommaName function accepts FirstName and LastName string arguments and returns the last name first, with a comma inserted before the first name.

```
Function CommaName(FirstName As String, LastName As String) As String
Dim CName As String
CName = LastName & ", " & FirstName
CommaName = CName
End Functioncx
```

After you have declared a function such as CommaName, you can use the function in your workbook, just as if it were a built-in function. Figure 30.7 shows the results of entering the CommaName function into an Employees sheet, using the cell references to the names in columns A and B of the sheet to provide the input arguments. The result of the functions is displayed in column E.

Programming with Events

There are several ways to tell Excel that you want to run a macro. Most of these were discussed in Chapter 29, "Understanding VBA Programming." You can run a macro by choosing the Tools, Macros command, or by pressing a shortcut key you have assigned to the macro. You also can assign a macro to a custom toolbar or menu.

Another way to run a macro is to allow Excel to run it automatically, when some predetermined event occurs. This technique is known as *event programming*. This system relies upon the built-in events that are recognized by Excel and its object model. You may want to run a macro automatically every time a user opens a workbook, enters a value into a cell, or prints a worksheet. These are examples of the kinds of events your code can respond to.

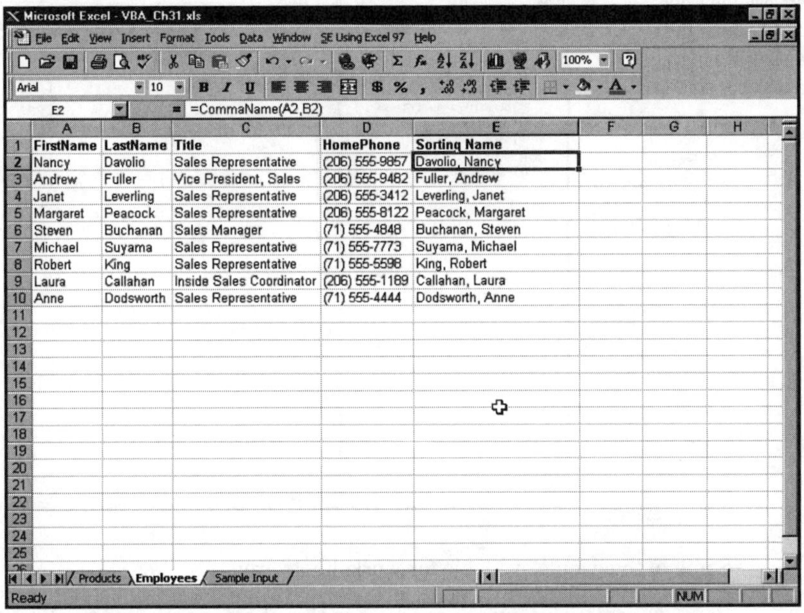

FIG. 30.7
The CommaName function has been entered into column E of the Employees table.

Excel VBA has already defined the procedures that you can use for event programming. The procedures initially contain no statements, but are there for you to use for your own purposes. You can find these procedures by using the Project Explorer. Figure 30.8 shows the VBE with the Project Explorer docked at the left side of the window. In addition to the module you have been using for your VBA macros, VBA automatically creates a module for each workbook and each worksheet. These modules contain the event procedures for each object. In Figure 30.8, the code window for the ThisWorkbook module has been opened by double-clicking its name in the Project Explorer. The procedure list shows the events that are available for this module.

The name of the event procedure indicates the nature of the event that causes the procedure to run. A few examples of useful events for a workbook module are:

- *Open.* This even occurs immediately after opening the workbook.
- *Activate.* The workbook becomes active, either by opening it, or switching from another open workbook.
- *Deactivate.* The workbook is about to be deactivated, either by closing it or switching to another workbook.
- *BeforePrint.* This event occurs just before printing is executed.
- *BeforeClose.* This event occurs just before the workbook is closed.
- *BeforeSave.* This event occurs just before the workbook is saved.

FIG. 30.8
The Project Explorer displays the modules in a project. The Code window makes the event procedures available for editing.

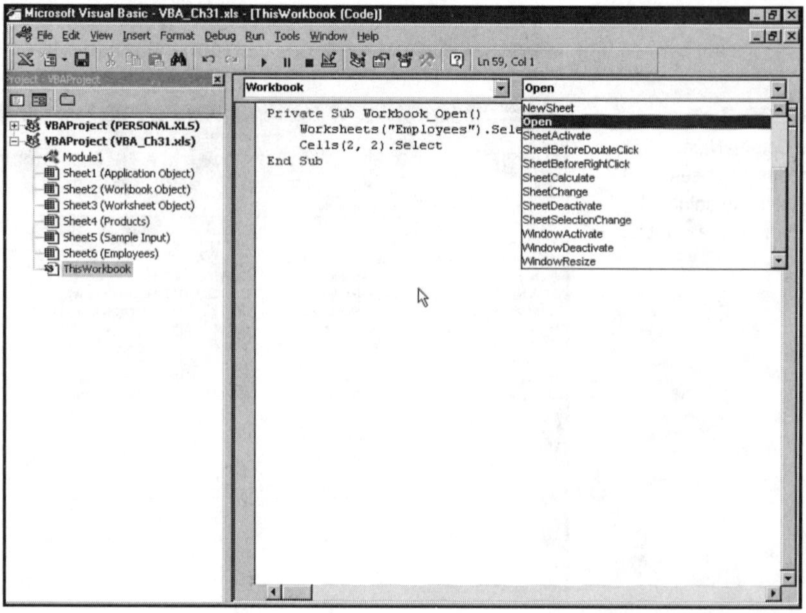

Some of the events available for worksheets are:

- *Activate.* This event occurs when this sheet is activated, such as when the workbook is opened, or when you switch to this sheet from another sheet in the same book.
- *Deactivate.* This event occurs when the sheet is deactivated, by moving out of this sheet.
- *Change.* This event occurs when the value in a cell changes.
- *Calculate.* This event occurs after a worksheet has recalculated.
- *BeforeDoubleClick.* This event occurs when the user has double-clicked an object, but before the normal double-click behavior is performed.
- *BeforeRightClick.* This event occurs when the user has right-clicked an object, but before the normal right-click behavior is performed.
- *SelectionChange.* This event occurs when the selection changes on the worksheet.

Additional events are provided for forms and the controls placed on the forms you create. These events will be covered in detail in Chapter 31, "Advanced VBA Programming."

There are many examples of how event programming can make your applications easier to use. For example, you may want to activate a particular sheet in a workbook, and even select a range, when you open the workbook. To do this you would write event code in the Workbook_Open event procedure.

```
Private Sub Workbook_Open()
    Worksheets("Employees").Select
    Cells(2, 2).Select
End Sub
```

This procedure causes Excel to select the Employees sheet and select cell B2 when the workbook is opened.

One of the things you can do with an event procedure is to cancel the event that is scheduled to occur, preventing the event from proceeding. The procedure shown in Listing 30.9 prevents the Employees sheet from being printed. If the user attempts to print this sheet, a message box is displayed and the Print event is canceled. Any other sheet in the workbook can be printed as usual.

Listing 30.9 VBA_CH30.XLS—The Workbook_BeforePrint event procedure lets you capture, and even cancel, the printing of a sheet.

```
Private Sub Workbook_BeforePrint(Cancel As Boolean)
If ActiveSheet.Name = "Employees" Then
    MsgBox "The employee list is confidential, and should not be printed.", _
        vbOKOnly + vbExclamation, _
        "Employee Confidentiality Policy"
    Cancel = True
End If
End Sub
```

Enabling and Disabling Events

What if you have written an event procedure that modifies an event, but now you want the event to occur normally, without running your event code? VBA provides the EnableEvents property of the Application object to take care of this situation. The following code shows how you could turn off event processing so that a macro can print the Employees table, then turn event processing back on so the user can't print the sheet individually.

```
Application.EnableEvents = False
Worksheets("Employees").Printout
Application.EnableEvents = True
```

From Here...

In this chapter, you learned how the Excel 97 object model provides the functionality of Excel for your VBA macros. The next two chapters address more advanced topics in VBA programming.

- Chapter 31, "Advanced VBA Programming," shows you how advanced forms can go far beyond the simple message box and input box, to provide a completely interactive programming environment. You'll also see how to extend the power of VBA through the Windows Application Programming Interface.
- Chapter 32, "Building Solutions with VBA," takes all your VBA skill, together with Excel workbook design, to build a complete Excel 97 solution. You'll also learn to use VBA to control other Office 97 applications and to work with even more of Excel's rich object model.

CHAPTER 31

Advanced VBA Programming

by Bill Ray

After you've mastered the basic functionality of Excel VBA macros, you can use the advanced features of VBA to add features beyond what's built into Excel. Using Excel's custom form design tools, you can create dialog boxes that make data entry easier, faster, and more reliable for your users. You can design your own objects, complete with methods and properties, to making features beyond what's built into Excel. Using Excel's custom form design tools, you can create dialog boxes that make data entry easier, faster, and more reliable for your users. You can design your own objects, complete with methods and properties, which your macros run faster and use less memory.

The features you learn about in this chapter will enable you to create macros that don't just provide the minimal functionality, but that are easy and interesting to use, and that add value beyond the basic recorded macro. ■

Creating custom forms

You learn to use VBA's integrated forms editor to create custom dialog boxes for interacting with the user.

Using ActiveX controls

You add ActiveX controls to your forms to create dynamic, interactive applications, controlled by VBA.

Creating your own objects

This advanced feature of VBA lets you define your own data objects, and reuse their code in many applications.

Introduction to API programming

Using the programming libraries that are built into Windows, you can add even more functionality to your programs than is provided by VBA.

Creating PivotTables with VBA

Use VBA to automate the creation of Excel PivotTables so you and your users can easily analyze data.

Creating toolbars with VBA

Provide custom toolbars under VBA control, giving your users an easy and intuitive method for running your macros.

Creating Custom Forms in the VB Editor

One of the most visible characteristics of the Windows family of operating systems is the dialog box. Every user quickly learns to use dialog boxes to perform everyday operations, such as opening and saving files, applying formatting, and selecting from the options of any program. Users like working with dialog boxes, because they're easy to use and pleasant in appearance. Applications that don't use dialog boxes often require users to answer a series of questions, one at a time, in a designated order. It might be difficult, or impossible, to go back and change an answer in a system designed in this fashion. Another scenario, which some spreadsheet designers might use, is to require users to make entries in cells scattered throughout one or more worksheets in a workbook. This process might be error prone, relying on the user to put data in the right place, and to know what the valid data values are.

Dialog boxes can relieve these problems in many applications. By gathering required data entries into a dialog box, you can make sure the user doesn't forget any entries, and that all data is entered in the correct location. You can make it easier for the users to select the right values by providing list boxes, check boxes, option buttons, and other controls that are easy and quick to use. The VBA code that goes with the dialog box can check to see if the entered data is valid, and then can update the spreadsheet with all the correct values. Dialog boxes can also allow the users to move about the dialog in any order, filling out the values as they like.

97

Office 97 introduces a new form design system that can be used in all the Office applications to create custom dialog boxes. This facility is built into the VB Editor, and provides a powerful and consistent set of tools for designing, editing, and coding your custom forms. This system replaces the custom form or dialog design tools in previous versions of Excel and the other Office applications.

In VBA terminology, dialog boxes are created as *forms*. As with any other Excel functionality, Excel VBA provides a complete object model for working with the form object and its methods and properties. The process of working with Excel forms will be familiar to those who have experience working with forms in Microsoft Access or Microsoft Visual Basic for Windows.

97

NOTE Excel 5.0 and Excel 95 dialog boxes were designed on dialog sheets that were visible in the workbook. When you convert a workbook from one of these versions to Excel 97, the dialog sheets are converted to Excel 97 forms automatically.

Adding a Form and Working with Form Properties

Forms are created in the VB Editor.

1. In the VBE Project Explorer, select the project to which you want to add a form.
2. Choose Insert, UserForm. A new form is added to the project and opened for editing. The control toolbox is also opened. Figure 31.1 shows the VBE immediately after adding the first form to a new project.

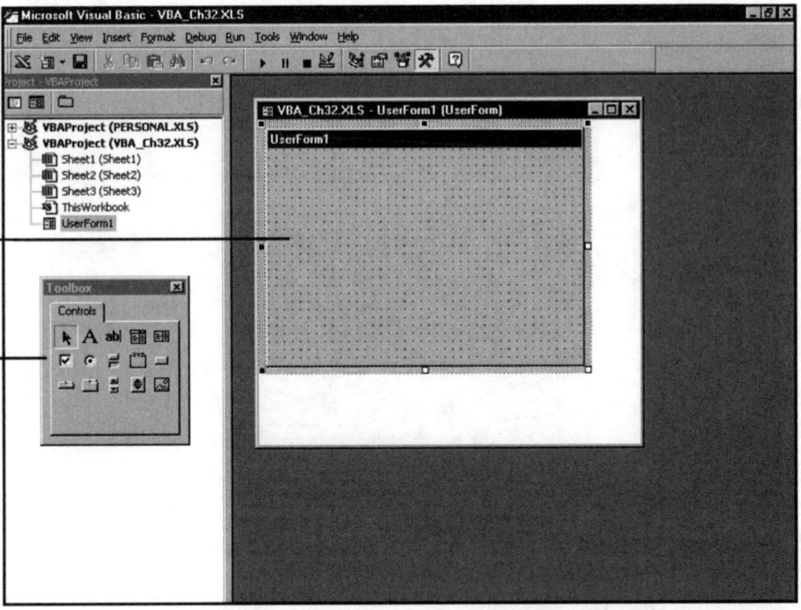

FIG. 31.1
A new form has been added to the current project, and the toolbox window is displayed.

A form isn't very interesting, or useful, until you add some controls to it. Before you do so, however, you might want to set some of the properties of the form. VBA forms and controls have a very large number of properties available for your design and customization.

To open the Properties window, choose View, Properties Window, or press F4. There are a few properties that you may want to set at the time you design your form.

- The *Name* property provides the name you will use in your VBA code to refer to this form. It's a good idea to supply a descriptive name for the form, to make your code easier to understand.
- The *Caption* property contains the text that appears in the title bar of the form.
- *BackColor* enables you to change the color of the background of the form, using either a Windows system color or a color you select from a palette of additional colors. If you select a system color, the form display the system color selected on the user's machine at the time the form is used.

Figure 31.2 shows the Properties window for a new form whose Name and Caption properties have been modified. The Properties window appears, using the Categorized tab, which groups the properties by functional category instead of alphabetically. Notice that the name of the form appears in the Form window and in the Properties window.

Using TextBoxes, Labels, and CommandButtons

The toolbox is used to add different controls, such as command buttons, text boxes, and labels, to your forms. The toolbox is shown in Figure 31.3. You can display the toolbox by choosing View, Toolbox.

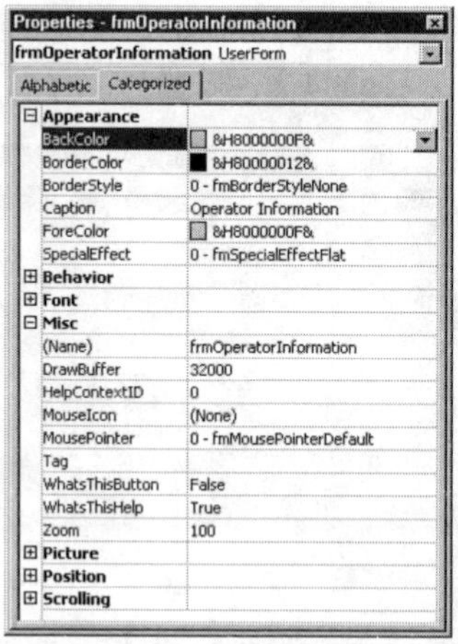

FIG. 31.2
The Properties window is used to change the appearance and behavior of a form.

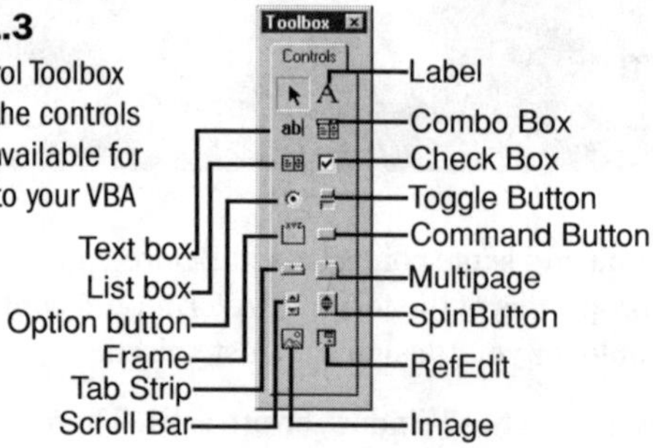

FIG. 31.3
The Control Toolbox displays the controls that are available for addition to your VBA forms.

Controls are the objects on a form that are used to display information and to allow the user to enter information or to cause events to occur. Several standard controls are often used in VBA forms. Let's start with three of the most commonly used controls.

- *Textbox* controls allow the user to enter and edit text. You might also use a Textbox control to display the result of a calculation, or some other result.
- *Label* controls are used to display text. The user can't edit the contents of a label, or even select the text in a label.
- *CommandButton* controls are buttons that the user can click with the mouse or operate with the keyboard. CommandButtons are used to by the operator to signal some event, such as the completion of the dialog, or that he wants to cancel a command.

You can add a control to the form in the VBE with the following steps:

1. Click the Toolbox on the control you want to add to your form.
2. Click the form in the location where you want the control to appear.
3. Drag the control to position and size it as you like.

Figure 31.4 shows the results of placing a Label, TextBox, and CommandButton on the Operator Information form. Now you need to change the appearance of the controls.

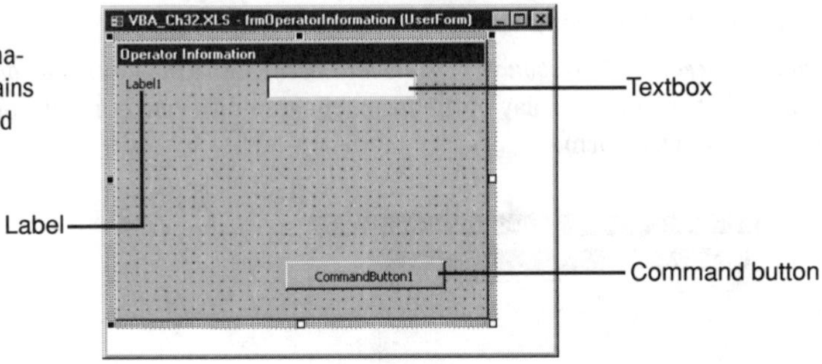

FIG. 31.4
The Operator Information form now contains a label, text box, and command button.

Each of the controls you place on a form is an object, just as the form itself is an object. Therefore, the controls have properties and methods. The properties of a control define many attributes of the control, such as the color, size, and position of the control. Each type of control has different properties, so it's worth getting to know the commonly used properties of a control.

- The *Caption* property of a Label control contains the text that appears on the label. For this example, change the Caption property to `Name:`, because the label will appear next to the text box where the operator will enter his or her name.
- The *Name* property of any control, allows you to refer to the control by name in your VBA code. Change the TextBox control's Name property to `OperatorName`.
- The *Caption* property of a CommandButton contains the text that appears on the button. Set the Caption of the CommandButton to `Ok`.
- Setting the *Default* property of a CommandButton to True makes it the default button of the form. This means that if the user presses Enter while the form is displayed, that button will be clicked automatically. Only one button per form can have the Default property set to True. Set the Default property of our CommandButton to True.
- Setting the Cancel property of a CommandButton to True makes it the cancel button of the form. This means that if the user presses Esc while the form is displayed, that button will be clicked automatically. Only one button per form can have the Cancel property set to True. For now, you don't have a Cancel button.

Figure 31.5 shows the results of making these property changes.

Programming the Form and Its Controls

While the form that you've created so far looks attractive, it still doesn't do anything useful. You'll have to write some VBA code to accomplish that. Creating a useful form usually requires the creation of two or more procedures:

- *A macro to display the dialog box.* This macro might simply be a macro in the workbook project, or it might be an event procedure of some other object in the workbook.
- *A procedure to dismiss the dialog box, which makes it disappear.* This is usually an event procedure of one of the command buttons on the form.
- *Additional procedures to respond to events that occur while the form is displayed.* These might include the initial display of the form, clicking different controls, or entering data in the controls of the form.

FIG. 31.5
After you modify the properties of the controls, the purpose of this form is clear: The operator will enter his or her name and click OK.

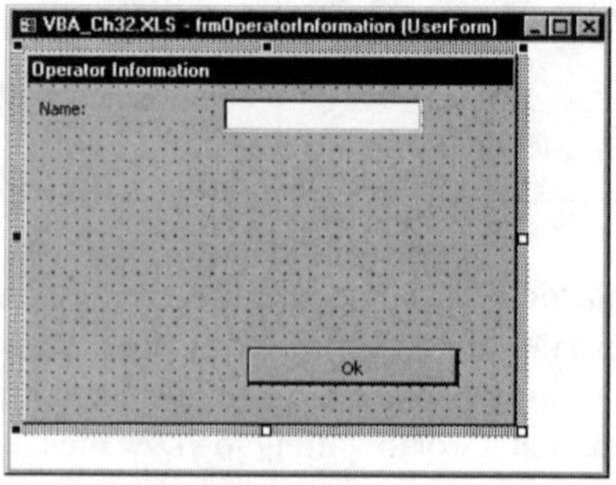

To display the form, you can create a macro as simple as the GetOperatorInformation macro shown in Listing 31.1. This macro calls the `Show` method of the form, which displays the form.

Listing 31.1 VBA_CH31.XLS—The GetOperatorInformation macro displays your custom form.

```
Sub GetOperatorInformation()
    frmOperatorInformation.Show
End Sub
```

Each form you create in Excel automatically contains a module for storing VBA code. A form module contains a general section, as well as many predefined procedures for responding to the events that occur while a form is open. One of the first event procedures to think about is one to respond to the user clicking the OK CommandButton.

You can easily find the events procedures for a control by double-clicking the control, which opens the code window for the form. Another method is to right-click the control, and choose View Code from the shortcut menu that appears. Figure 31.6 shows the code window open with the Click event for CommandButton1 ready for editing.

Notice that the keyword Private has been added before the customary Sub keyword in the procedure definition. This declares the procedure as private to the current module (in this case the form module). Private procedures are available to be called only from within the same module. In other words, a procedure in another module of the current project, such as the workbook module, will not be able to call this procedure.

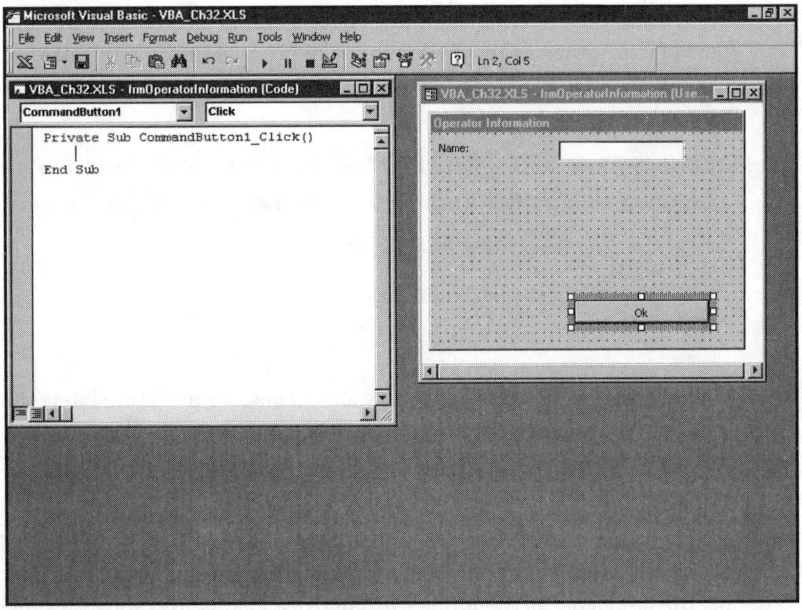

FIG. 31.6
The Sub procedure CommandButton1-Click will run whenever the user clicks the button.

What should a Click event procedure do? One thing it might do is to make the form disappear. A simple way to do this is to call the `Hide` method of the form. As you might guess, Hide is the opposite of Show, and makes the form invisible. Therefore, you could use the following line of VBA code:

```
frmOperatorInformation.Hide
```

A simpler way to write the code is to replace the name of the form with the keyword `Me`.

```
Me.Hide
```

The Me keyword refers to the current object class, which in this case is the form named frmOperatorInformation. You couldn't use Me when you showed the form, because the GetOperatorInformation macro is stored in the workbook module, not the form module for this form.

NOTE An alternative to the Hide method is the Unload statement. The Hide method makes the form invisible, but doesn't remove it from memory, so your VBA code can still use the properties of the form and its controls after it is hidden. The Unload statement completely removes the form from memory, making the form and its controls unavailable to your VBA code, and freeing up the memory and resources associated with the form.

Another thing you probably want this form to do is to take the information entered by the user and enter it into the workbook. You can set the Formula property of a cell in the workbook using the Text property of the OperatorName text box. Listing 31.2 shows the code necessary to hide the form and update the cell named Operator with the name entered into the text box.

Notice that the Me keyword is used once again to indicate that the OperatorName control is a part of the current form. While the use of Me is optional in this case, it makes the code easier to understand than if it were omitted.

Listing 31.2 VBA_CH31.XLS—The Click event for a CommandButton may be used to hide the form and use the data in the controls of the form.

```
Private Sub CommandButton1_Click()
    Me.Hide
    Range("Operator").Formula = Me.OperatorName.Text
End Sub
```

Before adding more controls to this form, consider one more interesting event. Sometimes you may want to set the value of a control at the time the form first appears. In this form, for example, if the operator name has already been entered into the Operator range on the worksheet, it would be nice for that name to appear in the text box when the form is shown.

The form itself has many event procedures, and one of these is for the Initialize event. This event occurs when the form is loaded, but before it is displayed. This is a convenient time to set the properties of the form or its controls. Listing 31.3 shows a simple procedure for placing the current value of the Operator range into the text box during the form's initialization. The Initialize procedure for a form is one of the predesigned event procedures of the form.

To edit the *UserForm_Initialize* procedure, follow these steps:

1. In the Project Explorer, double-click the form to open the form design window.
2. Double-click the background of the form to open the code window for the form.
3. From the Procedure list, select Initialize to display the UserForm_Initialize procedure.

Listing 31.3 VBA_CH31.XLS—The Initialize Procedure can be used to set the values of a form's controls.

```
Private Sub UserForm_Initialize()
    Me.OperatorName.Text = Range("Operator").Text
End Sub
```

Using ListBoxes and ComboBoxes

If the only type of control you could place in a form was a text box, forms would be only a small improvement—if any—over entering text into the workbook directly. Other controls make using the forms easier because they do not require the user to type complete entries into the form. One of the more common controls is a list the user can select items from. Figure 31.7 shows an updated version of our operator information form, which now provides two lists for selecting the operator's department and title.

FIG. 31.7
The Operator Information dialog box now allows the user to select a department and a title.

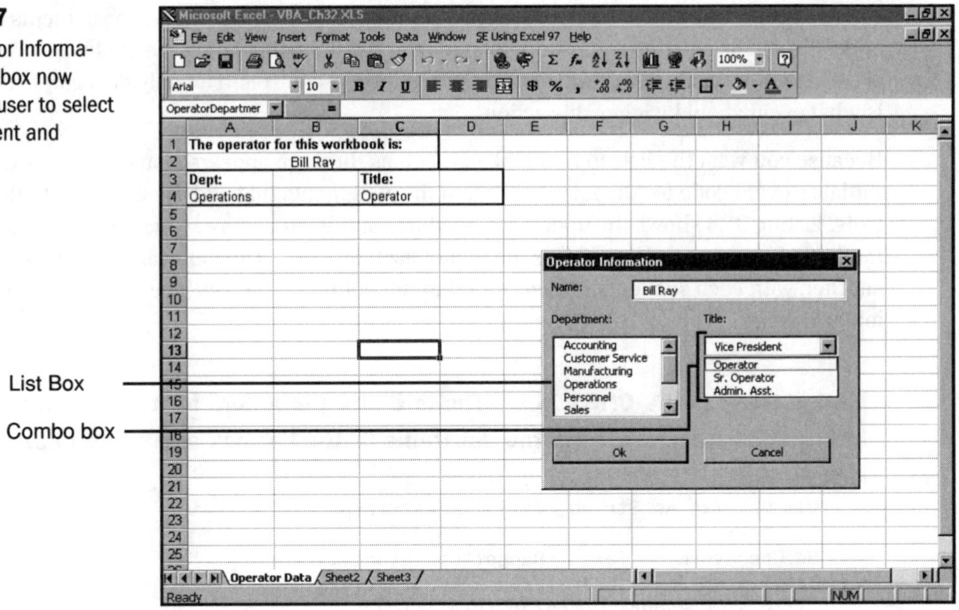

The department is selected using a ListBox control. List boxes are good for selecting from a fixed list, when only those entries on the list are valid choices. The Name property of this list box has been set to *DeptList*.

The title is entered using a ComboBox control. The Name property of this controls has been set to *TitleList*. In Figure 31.7, the drop-down arrow for the list has been clicked, showing the items on the list.

One difference between a combo box and a list box is that a combo box contains a built-in text editing box so the user can type an entry instead of selecting from the list. Using the text editing capability of a ComboBox property relies upon the Style property.

The *Style* property of a ComboBox control offers two options:

- Choose `fmStyleDropDownCombo` to allow the user to type the entry or select from the list.
- Choose `fmStyleDropDownList` to restrict the user to only selecting from the drop-down list.

There is one other difference to consider between the ListBox and ComboBox controls. A ListBox control takes up the amount of space in the form that you allow for it, even when the user is working in another area of the form. A ComboBox control only takes up the space occupied by the text editing portion of the control, until the user clicks the list arrow to expand the list. ComboBoxes are an effective way to use space and simplify the visual effect of a complex form.

There's a very important detail missing so far. How do the names of the departments and titles appear in the lists? These items are not added at the time you define the controls, but rather are supplied by calling the AddItem method of the list controls. The only decision left to make is what event should trigger this action.

Because you want the lists to be visible as soon as the form appears, you can enhance the Initialize event code for the form to contain the statements that add the list items to the controls. Listing 31.4 shows the updated procedure. In this procedure, you simply call the AddItem method of each control, supplying the text of each list item. The items are added one after another, with each subsequent item added to the bottom of the list. The code in this listing also initializes the Text property of the lists.

Listing 31.4 VBA_CH31.XLS—The Initialize procedure for the Operator Information form now adds the list items to the list box and combo box.

```
Private Sub UserForm_Initialize()
    Dim DeptTxt As String, TitleTxt As String

    Me.OperatorName.Text = Range("Operator").Text
    DeptTxt = Range("OperatorDepartment").Text
    TitleTxt = Range("OperatorTitle").Text

    With Me.DeptList
        .AddItem "Accounting"
        .AddItem "Customer Service"
        .AddItem "Manufacturing"
        .AddItem "Operations"
        .AddItem "Personnel"
        .AddItem "Sales"
        .AddItem "Shipping"
        .AddItem "Telemarketing"
        .AddItem "Vendor Relations"
        .Text = DeptTxt
    End With

    With Me.TitleList
        .AddItem "Operator"
        .AddItem "Sr. Operator"
        .AddItem "Admin. Asst."
        .Text = TitleTxt
    End With
End Sub
```

Now that the lists have been filled, the only remaining issue to address is how to transfer the user's selection to the worksheet. This turns out to be as simple as reading the Text property of the controls, just as you did with the text box. You can update the OK command button with the code as shown in Listing 31.5.

Listing 31.5 VBA_CH31.XLS—The Click event of the OK button now updates the worksheet with the values from the list boxes.

```
Private Sub CommandButton1_Click()
    Me.Hide
    Range("Operator").Formula = Me.OperatorName.Text
    Range("OperatorDepartment").Formula = Me.DeptList.Text
    Range("OperatorTitle").Formula = Me.TitleList.Text
End Sub
```

Another feature that you should add to most dialog boxes is a Cancel button. All you need to do in most cases is to add a command button with the Cancel property set to True, and the following line of code in the Click event, to hide the form:

```
Me.Hide
```


Using CheckBoxes, OptionButtons, and Frames

The CheckBox and OptionButton controls are familiar to any user of Excel or any other Windows application. Frames are used to group controls in a form, and are especially useful in working with forms, as you will see in this section.

OptionButton controls are used to select one item from a group of two or more items. Although an option button group can contain any number of items, it is most common to use option buttons for relatively short lists, of no more than about six items. Option button groups take a lot of space on the form, and a long option button group is harder to use than a list box or combo box.

A *Frame* control is used to contain a group of option buttons. If you have only one group of option buttons on a form, you don't have to enclose them in a frame. However, if you have more than one group of option buttons in a form, you must enclose each group in a frame because only one button in a group may be selected at a time. If you're going to use frames, it's easiest to place the frame first, and then place the option buttons inside the frame.

CheckBox controls are used for asking simple True/False or Yes/No questions. Check boxes act independently of one another, unlike option buttons, so you can check or uncheck any or all the check boxes on a form.

Figure 31.8 shows a form that can be used to get input regarding an employee's office information and benefits eligibility. There are two groups of option buttons: one for selecting an employee's home office and another for selecting the employee's employment status. A frame encloses each group. Checkboxes are used to indicate the eligibility of an employee for the health plan and the 401K plan.

This form has the same requirements as the Operator Information form. You must have some initialization code to update the form with any information that is already in the worksheet, and there must be a response to the Click event of the Ok Button. The procedures that respond to these two events are shown in Listing 31.6. Notice that the initialization code for the option buttons only has to set the True value for the appropriate button. The other buttons in the group are set to False automatically, because only one button in a group can be True at a time.

FIG. 31.8
The Office Information dialog box uses option buttons and check boxes to gather information from the user.

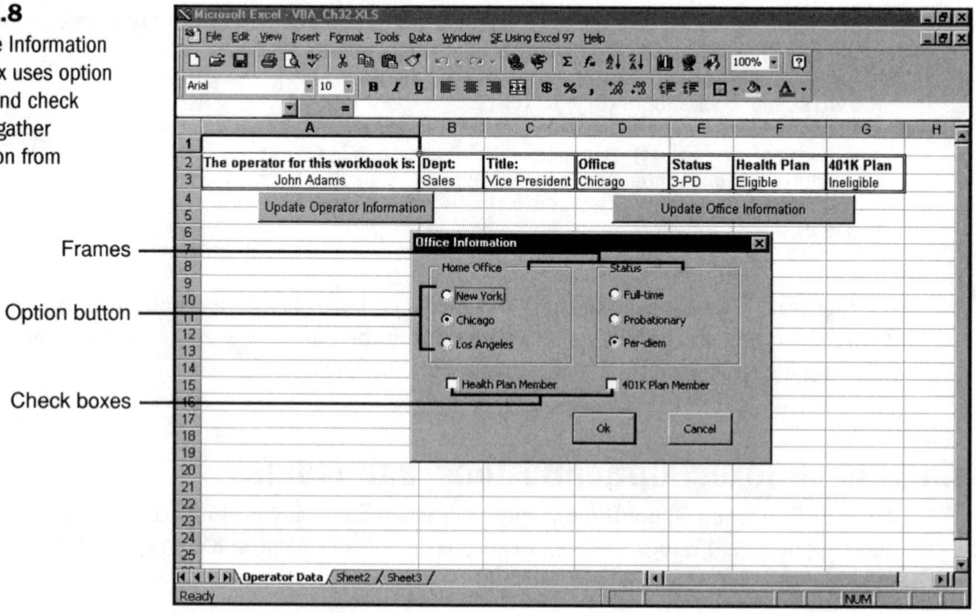

Listing 31.6 VBA_CH31.XLS—The Initialize and Click procedures transfer data between the worksheet and the OfficeInformation form.

```
Private Sub UserForm_Initialize()

  Select Case Range("Office").Text
  Case "New York"
    btnNewYork.Value = True
  Case "Chicago"
    btnChicago.Value = True
  Case "Los Angeles"
    btnLosAngeles.Value = True
  Case Else
    btnNewYork.Value = True
  End Select

  Select Case Range("Status").Text
  Case "1-FT"
    btnFullTime.Value = True
  Case "2-PR"
    btnProbationary.Value = True
  Case "3-PD"
    btnPerDiem.Value = True
  Case Else
    btnFullTime.Value = True
  End Select
End Sub

Private Sub OkButton_Click()
  Me.Hide
```

```
    If btnNewYork.Value = True Then
      Range("Office").Formula = "New York"
    ElseIf btnChicago.Value = True Then
      Range("Office").Formula = "Chicago"
    Else
      Range("Office").Formula = "Los Angeles"
    End If

    If btnFullTime.Value = True Then
      Range("Status").Formula = "1-FT"
    ElseIf btnProbationary.Value = True Then
      Range("Status").Formula = "2-PR"
    Else
      Range("Status").Formula = "3-PD"
    End If

    If chkHealthPlan.Value = True Then
      Range("HealthPlan").Formula = "Eligible"
    Else
      Range("HealthPlan").Formula = "Ineligible"
    End If

    If Chk401KPlan.Value = True Then
      Range("Plan401K").Formula = "Eligible"
    Else
      Range("Plan401K").Formula = "Ineligible"
    End If
  End Sub
```


Using ToggleButtons and SpinButtons

Another pair of useful controls for your VBA forms are ToggleButton and SpinButton controls. These are examples of controls that work much like other controls, but can add variety and ease of use to your forms.

A *ToggleButton* control works much like a CheckBox control, and has essentially the same function. The difference is primarily in how it is displayed. The ToggleButton has the appearance of a CommandButton, but its *state* corresponds to the value associated with the control. When the button appears to be depressed, its state represents the True value, and when the button appears to be raised, the state represents the False value.

Toggle buttons provide one stylistic advantage over check boxes. You can modify the Picture property of a toggle button so that an image—not text—appears on the button, which makes for an interesting display. Figure 31.9 shows a form that contains two ToggleButton controls, one with a text caption and one with a picture of a car.

A *SpinButton* control appears as a pair of arrows, representing two directions, such as Up and Down or Right and Left. There is no data associated with a spin button, but clicking either of the arrows triggers an event—either the SpinUp or SpinDown event, depending on which arrow is clicked. It is up to you to determine what should happen when one of these events occurs.

A common use of spin buttons is to change the numeric value of a text box by some convenient value. The Commuting Information form, shown in Figure 31.9, has a spin button control that can be used to modify the value of the number of miles in the text box, increasing or decreasing it by 10 miles. In Listing 31.7, the SpinUp and SpinDown procedures perform the calculations. Of particular interest is the SpinDown procedure, which must make sure not to reduce the average daily mileage below zero.

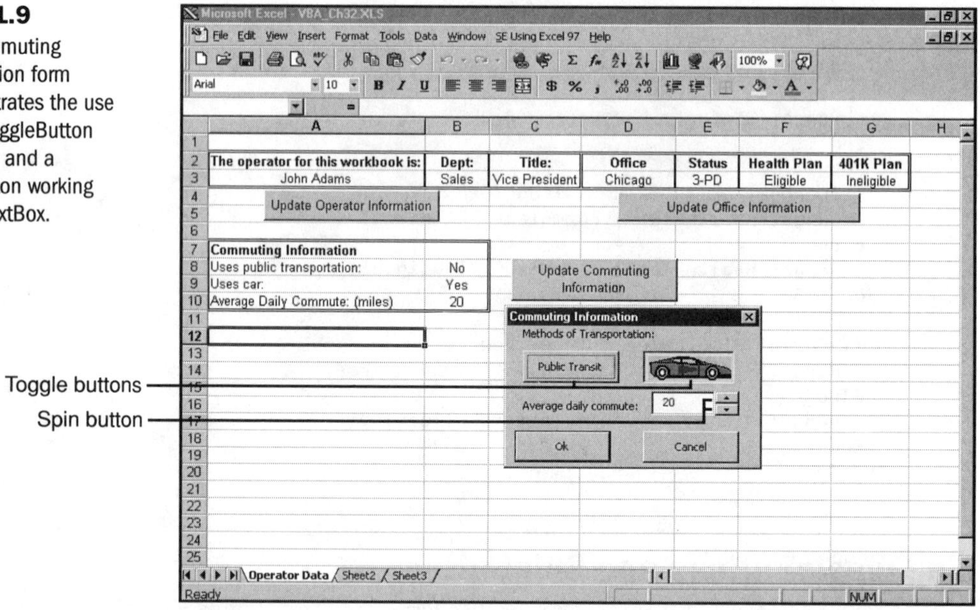

FIG. 31.9 The Commuting Information form demonstrates the use of two ToggleButton controls, and a SpinButton working with a TextBox.

The rest of the code in Listing 31.7 should appear familiar. The values are taken from the cells on the worksheet, and are transferred to the controls upon initialization of the form. Clicking the OK button causes the values in the form to be transferred to the worksheet.

Listing 31.7 VBA_CH31.XLS—The event code for the Commuting Information form takes care of initialization of the controls, handling the SpinButton events and updating the worksheet when the OK button is clicked.

```
Private Sub UserForm_Initialize()
    If Range("Public").Text = "Yes" Then
        Me.TogglePublic.Value = True
    Else
        Me.TogglePublic.Value = False
    End If
    If Range("Auto").Text = "Yes" Then
        Me.ToggleCar.Value = True
    Else
```

```
        Me.ToggleCar.Value = False
    End If
    Me.txtCommuteMiles.Text = Range("CommuteMiles").Text
End Sub

Private Sub SpinCommute_SpinUp()
Dim Miles As Variant
Miles = Me.txtCommuteMiles.Text
If Miles = "" Then
    Miles = 10
Else
    Miles = Miles + 10
End If
Me.txtCommuteMiles.Text = Miles
End Sub

Private Sub SpinCommute_SpinDown()
Dim Miles As Variant
Miles = Me.txtCommuteMiles.Text
If Miles = "" Then
    Miles = 10
Else
    Miles = Miles - 10
    If Miles < 0 Then Miles = 0
End If
Me.txtCommuteMiles.Text = Miles
End Sub

Private Sub OkButton_Click()
    Me.Hide
    If Me.TogglePublic.Value = True Then
        Range("Public").Formula = "Yes"
    Else
        Range("Public").Formula = "No"
    End If
    If Me.ToggleCar.Value = True Then
        Range("Auto").Formula = "Yes"
    Else
        Range("Auto").Formula = "No"
    End If
    Range("CommuteMiles").Formula = Me.txtCommuteMiles.Text
End Sub

Private Sub CancelButton_Click()
    Me.Hide
End Sub
```

Using TabStrip and MultiPage Controls

Recent Windows applications have made extensive use of tabbed controls in commonly used dialog boxes. The Options dialog box of Excel 97 is a good example. The use of categorized tabs lets you put many controls into a single dialog box.

VBA provides two tabbed controls, each of which serves a different purpose.

- The *MultiPage* control lets you define two or more pages in a form. Each page contains its own collection of controls, which act independently of one another. This lets you divide a complex form into sections, simplifying the visual effect on the user.
- The *TabStrip* control lets you use a single set of controls for multiple sets of data. This is useful when you have a collection of data in a form that uses a similar set of related controls.

Figures 31.10 and 31.11 show the two pages of a form that contains a MultiPage control. The first page contains some text boxes to gather name and address information for the worksheet. The second page contains a different set of controls to gather information about the operator's phone numbers for home, work, car phone, and fax.

FIG. 31.10
The first page of this multipage form is used to gather address information.

MultiPage control

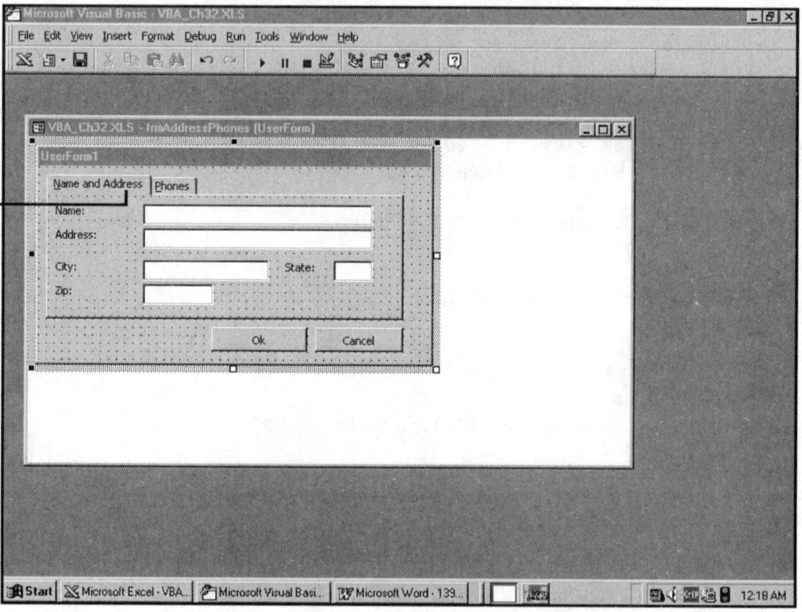

To set up a MultiPage control, add it to the form and then place the controls on the form. You can add pages to the MultiPage control and rename the tabs on the pages. While the form is running, the Value property of the MultiPage control tells you which page is currently displayed. The Value of the control is 0 when the first page is displayed, 1 when the second page is displayed, and so on.

In Figure 31.11, the second page of the form contains a TabStrip control. In this case, because you want to allow for gathering four different phone numbers, there are four tabs on the tab strip. However, with a tab strip, there is only one set of controls. Each type of phone number requires an area code and a number, so the same pair of text boxes will work for all four numbers.

FIG. 31.11
The second page of the form is used to gather four different phone numbers.

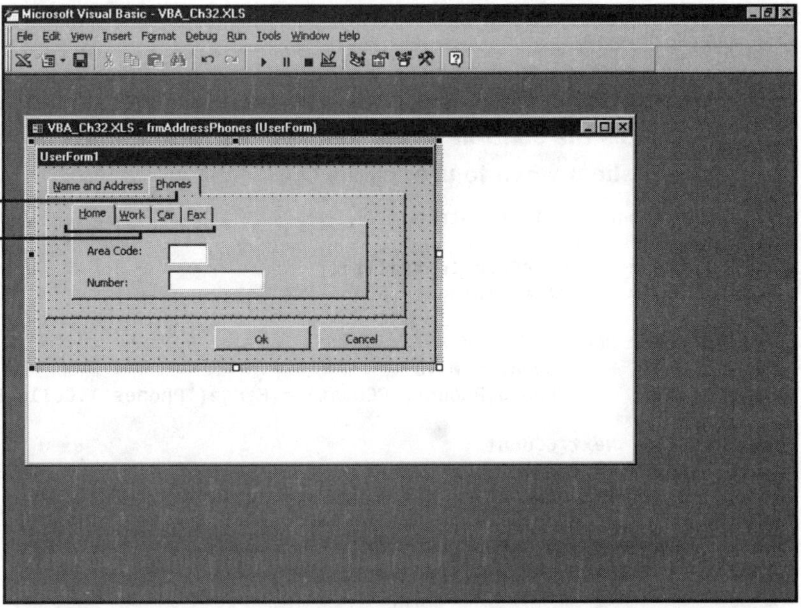

The use of the tab strip requires us to find a different way to keep track of the data for the form, because there is not a separate control for each data item. For this purpose, you can use a form-level variable. In this case, an array variable named Phones will hold the data. This variable is defined as a 4-row by 2-column array to hold the required data. The following declaration appears in the General section of the form module.

```
Dim Phones(3, 1) As String
```

Declaring the array variable in this location makes it a form-level variable. This means that the array is only available to the procedures of this form module. The array is initialized in the form's Initialize event procedure. Each of the cells in the Phones range is used to update one element of the Phones( ) array.

The TabStrip control is used to provide an event procedure that is coded to update the text boxes that are on the tab strip, each time the user selects a different tab button. The Change event procedure contains the code, which copies values from the Phones() array into the text boxes, depending upon which tab on the tab strip is selected. The TabStrip control also has a Value property, and just like the MultiPage control, the Value is 0 if the first tab is selected, 1 if the second tab is selected, and so on.

Another detail to take care of is the updating of the Phones() array anytime the user edits a phone number or area code. This is easy to do with the Change event for each of the text boxes, which is called every time the user changes the value of the text boxes.

Finally, the Click event of the OK button updates the spreadsheet with the results of the editing session using the form. The data for the Phones range is copied item-by-item from the Phones() array.

The complete VBA code for the form *frmAddressPhones* is shown in Listing 31.8.

Listing 31.8 VBA_CH31.XLS—The code for the frmAddressPhones form initializes the controls of the form, responds to events, and updates the spreadsheet when to user clicks OK.

```
Dim Phones(3, 1) As String

Private Sub UserForm_Initialize()
    Dim RCount As Integer, CCount As Integer

    For RCount = 0 To 3
        For CCount = 0 To 1
            Phones(RCount, CCount) = Range("Phones").Cells(RCount + 1, CCount +
➥1).Text
        Next CCount
    Next RCount
    Me.txtName.Text = Range("Operator").Text
    Me.txtAddress.Text = Range("Address").Text
    Me.txtCity.Text = Range("City").Text
    Me.txtState.Text = Range("State").Text
    Me.txtZip.Text = Range("Zip").Text
    Me.MultiPage1.Value = 0
End Sub

Private Sub MultiPage1_Change()
' This makes sure the TabStrip is updated when we change to
' the second page.

Call TabStrip1_Change
End Sub

Private Sub TabStrip1_Change()
'Update the Text boxes from the Phones array

    txtAreaCode.Text = Phones(TabStrip1.Value, 0)
    txtPhone.Text = Phones(TabStrip1.Value, 1)
End Sub

Private Sub txtAreaCode_Change()
'Update the Phones array if the Area Code changes
    Phones(TabStrip1.Value, 0) = txtAreaCode.Text
End Sub

Private Sub txtPhone_Change()
'Update the Phones array if the Phone number changes
    Phones(TabStrip1.Value, 1) = txtPhone.Text
End Sub

Private Sub OkButton_Click()
    Dim RCount As Integer, CCount As Integer

    Me.Hide
    'Upadte the Phones range from the Phones array
```

```
    For RCount = 0 To 3
        For CCount = 0 To 1
            Range("Phones").Cells(RCount + 1, CCount + 1).Formula =
Phones(RCount, CCount)
        Next CCount
    Next RCount

    'Update the remaining worksheet cells
    Range("Operator").Formula = Me.txtName.Text
    Range("Address").Formula = Me.txtAddress.Text
    Range("City").Formula = Me.txtCity.Text
    Range("State").Formula = Me.txtState.Text
    Range("Zip").Formula = Me.txtZip.Text

End Sub

Private Sub CancelButton_Click()
    Me.Hide
End Sub
```


Using ActiveX Controls on Worksheets and Forms

Excel 97 comes with a variety of controls for use on your forms and on your worksheet. The controls you've seen so far in the chapter are the built-in controls of VBA. Office 97 and VBA also allow you to add a virtually limitless collection of additional controls through the use of ActiveX technology.

ActiveX is an open programming standard, developed by Microsoft, that allows developers to create additional controls that can be used in Office 97 applications. These controls also can be used in Visual Basic for Windows applications, Internet Explorer, and any other application that supports ActiveX. You can develop your own ActiveX controls using Visual Basic for Windows, Control Creation Edition.

You can add the ActiveX controls to your forms just as you have added the built-in controls, or you can add them directly to your worksheets. Using controls directly on a worksheet makes them immediately accessible to the user, without the user having to run a macro to get to the control.

A control that's often added to a workbook is the CommandButton control. This is most commonly used as a shortcut for running a macro. Adding a CommandButton to a worksheet is simple; follow these steps:

1. If the Forms toolbar is not visible, choose View, Toolbars, Forms.
2. Click the CommandButton control on the Forms toolbar, and click the location where you want to place the button. The Assign Macro dialog box appears.
3. Select the macro you want to assign to the button and choose OK.

Now that the macro has been assigned, you can click the button to run the macro. To modify the button or its properties, right-click the button.

In your custom forms, you can add even more controls in the form of ActiveX controls that are installed on your system. Some sample ActiveX controls are installed with Office 97, and hundreds more are available from tool vendors. Figure 31.12 shows the use of a Calendar control that comes with Office 97. Before you can create a form like this, you have to add the control to your toolbox if it is not already there.

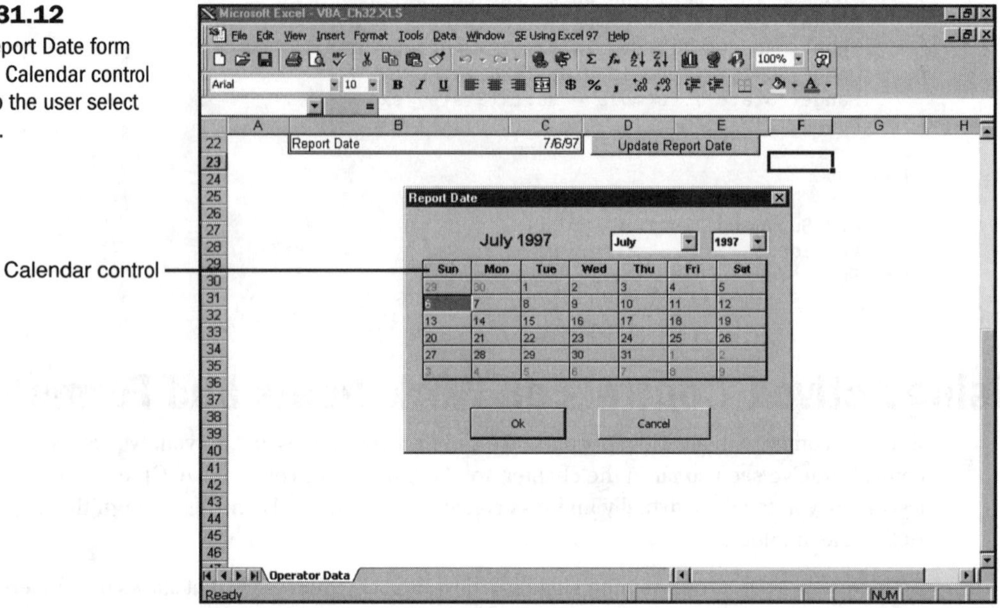

FIG. 31.12
The Report Date form uses a Calendar control to help the user select a date.

Follow these steps to add a control to your toolbox:

1. In the VBE, display the Control Toolbox.
2. Right-click the toolbox and choose Additional Controls from the shortcut menu that appears. The Additional Controls dialog box appears.
3. Select the check box next to any control you want to add to your toolbox; then choose the OK button.

After you have added a control to the toolbox, you can add the control to your forms, just like a built-in control. You also can modify the properties of the control, and write VBA code to respond to the events supported by the control. Of course, the specific properties, methods, and events supported by each control will vary, and should be documented in the manual or online help that comes with the control.

The Report Date form is a relatively simple form, with code to initialize the form using the current entry in the ReportDate range, and event code to process the OK button updating the spreadsheet from the Calendar control. The code for the form is shown in Listing 31.9.

Listing 31.9 VBA_CH31.XLS—The Report Date form uses only three procedures to initialize the form and respond to the form's events.

```
Private Sub UserForm_Initialize()
    Dim ReportDate As Variant
    ReportDate = Range("ReportDate").Text
    If IsDate(ReportDate) Then
        Me.Calendar1.Value = ReportDate
    Else
        Me.Calendar1.Value = Date
    End If
End Sub

Private Sub OkButton_Click()
    Me.Hide
    Range("reportDate").Formula = Me.Calendar1.Value
End Sub

Private Sub CancelButton_Click()
    Me.Hide
End Sub
```


The *RefEdit* control is a special toolbox control for use in Excel 97 that allows you to work with ranges on a worksheet. The RefEdit control is very unusual in a couple of ways:

- While you are using the RefEdit control, you can click into the worksheet in the background, using the mouse to select a range whose reference will be displayed in the control's text area.
- While you are selecting a range with the RefEdit control, the rest of the form collapses away, so you have more room on your screen to see and select the range in the background.

The result of selecting a range with the RefEdit control is the address of the selected range. You can use this address to perform any action with ranges that you would with any other range object.

Figure 31.13 shows a custom form that has a RefEdit control, along with a label to be used for displaying information about a selected cell reference. A command button is used to update the label with information about the reference.

The code in Listing 31.10 shows how to use the information returned by the RefEdit control. First, the control is initialized using the Address property of the selection at the time the form is displayed. When the command button is clicked, the UserSelection variable is assigned as the range of the reference returned by the control. Then it's a simple matter to assemble a message concerning several statistics about this range.

Listing 31.10 VBA_CH31.XLS—The code for the RefEdit Sample form initializes the control, updates the output label, and closes the form.

```
Private Sub UserForm_Initialize()
    Me.RefEdit1.Value = Selection.Address
    Call CommandButton1_Click
End Sub

Private Sub CommandButton1_Click()
    Dim UserSelection As Range
    Dim AreaCount As Integer
    Dim FirstCell As String, RangeInfo As String

    Set UserSelection = Range(Me.RefEdit1.Value)
    RangeInfo = "Number of Cells: " & UserSelection.Cells.Count
    RangeInfo = RangeInfo & Chr$(10) & "Number of Areas: " &
Selection.Areas.Count
    FirstCell = UserSelection.Cells(1, 1).Text
    RangeInfo = RangeInfo & Chr$(10) & "Contents of first cell: " & FirstCell
    Me.OutputLabel.Caption = RangeInfo
    UserSelection.Select
End Sub

Private Sub CancelButton_Click()
    Me.Hide
End Sub
```

FIG. 31.13
A RefEdit control lets the user select a range while a form is displayed.

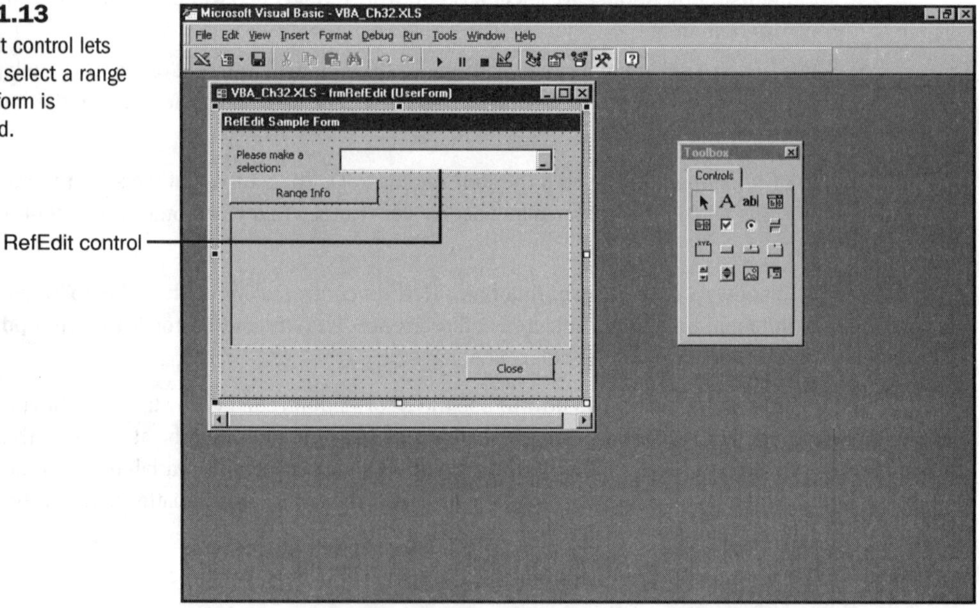

Creating Objects with Class Modules

Throughout your work with VBA, you've seen that Excel 97 macro programming consists largely of working with the Excel object model. The objects, methods, and properties in the object model give you a consistent way to relate to the application in your VBA code.

VBA allows you to create your own objects, complete with their own methods and properties. To create your own objects, you must insert a *class module* into your workbook project.

For the example in this section, you'll create an `Operator` object. This object will represent the person operating the workbook. The Operator object will have properties such as *Name, Title, Office, Department, Rating* and *DateHired*. The object also will have some calculated properties, such as *Seniority* and *EmpClass*, which will represent an employment class that is based on the operator's Seniority and Rating. These calculated properties can't be set directly, but can only be read by your VBA code.

Creating a New Class Module

In the VBE, with the Project Explorer open, choose Insert, Class Module. A new class module is assigned to the project.

The first thing you'll usually do with a new class module is give it a meaningful name. With the Project Explorer open and the new class module selected, open the Properties window. The class module has only one property, the Name property. Type a new name for the class you are creating. In the sample object, set the name to `Operator`.

Defining Properties and Methods

Now that you have a new class module, you can open the code window for that object, to define the properties and methods of the object.

Properties can be defined by declaring Public variables in the Declarations section of the class module. These properties can later be set by your VBA code, and read just like any other property.

```
Public Name As String
Public Title As String
Public Department As String
```

Calculated properties, which will be read-only to your VBA code, are defined by creating a Property Get procedure.

```
Property Get Seniority()
    Seniority = Year(Date) - Year(DateHired)
End Property
```

This procedure defines a new property, *Seniority*, and calculates its value by subtracting the year in which the operator was hired from the current year. Listing 31.11 includes the complete definition of the Operator class, including a more complex property, EmpClass, which calculates the property based upon the values of the Rating and Seniority properties.

Methods can be defined by declaring a public Sub procedure inside the class module. Listing 31.11 includes a *ShowInfo* method, which uses a message box to display information about the operator object.

Listing 31.11 VBA_CH31.XLS—The class module code for the Operator class defines the properties and methods of the Operator object.

```
'Properties of the Operator object class
Public Name As String
Public Title As String
Public Department As String
Public Office As String
Public DateHired As Date
Public Salary As Double
Public Rating As Integer

Property Get Seniority()
'Calculates Seniority for Operator Class
    Seniority = Year(Date) - Year(DateHired)
End Property

Property Get EmpClass()
'Calculates Employee class of operator
' based upon Rating and Seniority

    Select Case Rating
    Case 1
        If Seniority > 10 Then
            EmpClass = "Master Operator"
        Else
            EmpClass = "Senior Operator"
        End If
    Case 2
        If Seniority > 8 Then
            EmpClass = "Senior Operator"
        Else
            EmpClass = "Junior Operator"
        End If
    Case 3
        If Seniority > 6 Then
            EmpClass = "Junior Operator"
        Else
            EmpClass = "Apprentice Operator"
        End If
    Case 4
        If Seniority > 4 Then
            EmpClass = "Apprentice Operator"
        Else
            EmpClass = "Probationary Operator"
        End If
    Case Else
        EmpClass = "Probationary Operator"
    End Select
```

```
End Property

Public Sub ShowInfo()
'Defines the ShowInfo method of the Operator class

    Dim OpStatus As String

    OpStatus = Name & " was hired on " & DateHired
    OpStatus = OpStatus & " and has acheived the grade of " & EmpClass
    MsgBox OpStatus
End Sub
```

Using Your Custom Object

After you've defined a new object class, you can use the class in your VBA applications. First, you must declare an object variable, creating an instance of the object by using the New keyword.

```
Dim Op As New Operator
```

This statement creates a copy of the Operator class, so you can work with the methods and properties of the object.

Now you can assign values directly to the public properties of the object.

```
Op.Name = "Michael Wilson"
```

You also can call the methods of the object.

```
Op.ShowInfo
```

Listing 31.12 contains two macros that use worksheet values that work with the Operator class. The OperatorMessage macro gathers data for the operator properties from the worksheet; then it calls the ShowInfo method to display its message box. The message box is shown in Figure 31.14.

The YearsAndGrade macro uses the data on the spreadsheet to supply the necessary information for the calculated properties of the Operator object, and updates the worksheet with the results. Figure 31.15 shows the results of running this macro.

Listing 31.12 VBA_CH31.XLS—These macros from the workbook module show how to use the Operator object.

```
Sub OperatorMessage()
    Dim Op As New Operator
    Dim WS As Worksheet

    Set WS = Worksheets("Operator Object")
    With WS
        Op.Name = .Cells(1, 2).Text
        Op.DateHired = .Cells(5, 2).Text
        Op.Rating = .Cells(8, 2).Text
```

continues

Listing 31.12 Continued

```
    End With
    Op.ShowInfo

End Sub

Sub YearsAndGrade()
    Dim Op As New Operator
    Dim WS As Worksheet

    Set WS = Worksheets("Operator Object")
    With WS
        Op.Name = .Cells(1, 2).Text
        Op.DateHired = .Cells(5, 2).Text
        Op.Rating = .Cells(8, 2).Text
        .Cells(7, 2) = Op.Seniority
        .Cells(9, 2) = Op.EmpClass
    End With
End Sub
```

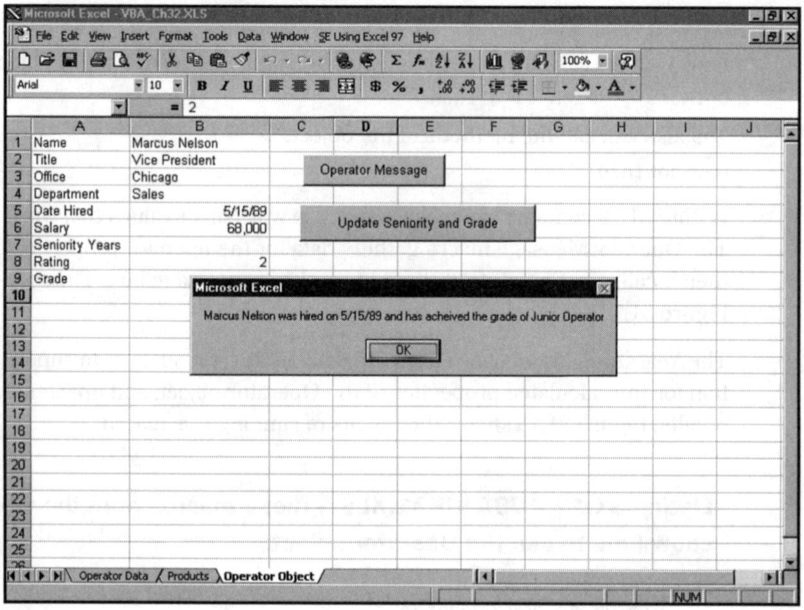

FIG. 31.14 The ShowInfo method of the Operator object class displays information about the operator. Here it is called by the OperatorMessage macro.

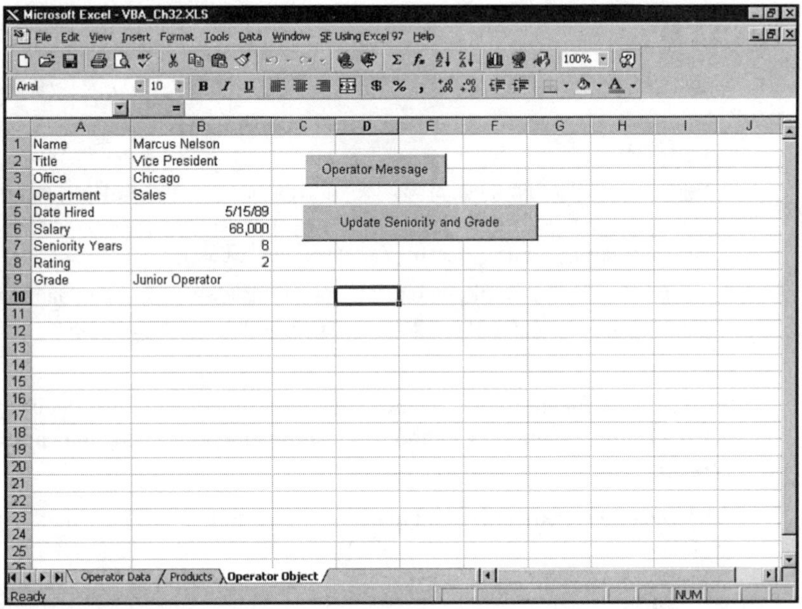

FIG. 31.15
The YearsAndGrade macro has been used to update this spreadsheet using the methods of the Operator class.

Extending VBA with the Windows API

Windows 95 and Windows NT contain an extensive set of code libraries that can be used directly in your VBA macros. These libraries, and the methods for using them in your macros, are know as the Windows Application Programming Interface, or the Windows API.

Windows is constructed of a special kind of code library, known as a Dynamic Link Library, or DLL. Each DLL file may contain many functions, usually written using the C++ programming language, that perform a variety of purposes in the operation of Windows and the applications that work in Windows. Many of these functions are low-level functions that would be of little use to your VBA programs. Others provide functions that are already present in VBA, such as Input boxes and message boxes. Some, however, provide functionality that is missing or incomplete in VBA.

In addition to the API functions that come with Windows, you can acquire additional DLL files from other sources.

- Many commercial programs and utilities come with a collection of DLLs.
- Many vendors sell DLLs for the developer market.
- You or someone in your organization can create DLLs using C++ or another programming language.

NOTE VBA cannot be used to create DLLs. Visual Basic for Windows, beginning with version 5.0, can be used to create DLLs.

CAUTION

Using DLL functions in your applications gives VBA access to the low-level functionality of Windows and other code libraries. If misused, functions called from DLLs can cause program errors which may stop not only your macros, but also Excel or other Office applications.

Before using any DLL function in your VBA macros, make sure you understand completely what the effects of the function are, and that you have complete documentation on the syntax and results of the function.

Using a DLL function requires two main steps. First, you must declare the function, so that VBA will understand how to find and call the function. Then, you can call the function in your VBA macros.

The Declare statement is used to define a DLL function. The syntax of the Declare statement is as follows:

```
Declare Function functionname Lib "libname" [Alias "aliasname"] [([arglist])]
[As type]
```

FunctionName is the name you will call your function when you call it in VBA. *Libname* is the name of the DLL file that contains the function you are declaring. The optional *aliasname* is the name of the function as it is defined inside the DLL. You only need to use an alias if you decide to use a different name for the function in your VBA macro than the original name of the function. *Arglist* is the list of arguments that can be passed to the function, as defined in the documentation of the DLL function. Finally, the optional *As Type* argument declares the return type of the function.

An example of a function defined in the Windows API is `GetTickCount`. This function, defined in the Windows DLL named `kernel32`, returns the number of milliseconds that have elapsed since Windows started running. This function can be called when you want to perform precise timing of the duration of events.

Listing 31.13 shows the declaration of the GetTickCount function and an example of how it can be used. The APITimerDemo macro uses two methods to update a worksheet and uses GetTickCount to determine which is the faster method. The first time through the loop, the macro selects each of the first 1,000 cells in the first column of a worksheet, typing a number into each cell. The second time through the loop, the first 100 cells in column 2 are updated directly, without selecting the cells.

GetTickCount is called four times, one before and once after each of the loops. For each loop, the starting tick count is subtracted from the finishing tick count to determine the duration of the loop.

The results are displayed in a message box, as shown in Figure 31.16.

FIG. 31.16
The GetTickCount function is used to show that it's faster to update a range directly than to select each cell.

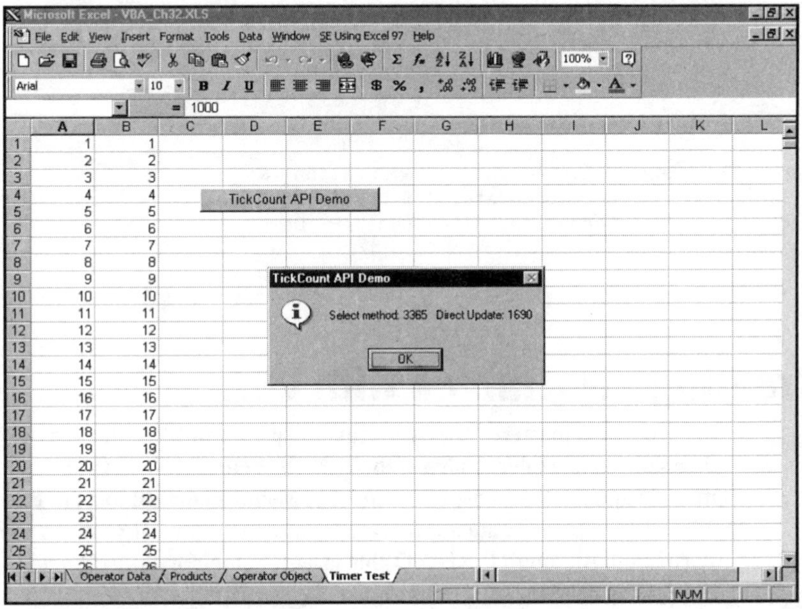

Listing 31.13 VBA_CH31.XLS—The GetTickCount API function can be used for very precise timing of events in Windows applications.

```
Declare Function GetTickCount Lib "kernel32" () As Long

Sub APITimerDemo()
Dim StartCount As Long, EndCount As Long
Dim i As Long, Total As Long
Dim Duration1 As Long, Duration2 As Long

Worksheets("Timer Test").Select
Application.ScreenUpdating = False

StartCount = GetTickCount()
For i = 1 To 1000
    Cells(i, 1).Select
    ActiveCell.Formula = i
Next i
EndCount = GetTickCount()
Duration1 = EndCount - StartCount
Application.ScreenUpdating = True
Application.ScreenUpdating = False

StartCount = GetTickCount()
For i = 1 To 1000
    Cells(i, 2).Formula = i
Next i
EndCount = GetTickCount()
```

continues

Listing 31.13 Continued

```
Duration2 = EndCount - StartCount

Application.ScreenUpdating = True

MsgBox "Select method: " & Duration1 & _
    "   Direct Update: " & Duration2, vbOKOnly + _
    vbInformation, "TickCount API Demo"

End Sub
```

Creating PivotTables with VBA

Once you have mastered the syntax and structure of VBA, the best way to build your programming skills is to explore more of the rich object model that is built into Excel and the other Office 97 applications. One of the most powerful analytical tools in Excel is the *PivotTable*, which is used to generate a wide variety of reports and calculations with Excel database information. Although the PivotTable is a great tool for skilled Excel users to manipulate interactively, it is also available for automated control under VBA. As with any application feature, the key to controlling PivotTables with VBA is understanding the PivotTable object model.

Figure 31.17 shows the data that is used to create the PivotTables in this chapter. This data represents product orders that have been placed for a variety of products that were purchased by many customers and several different salespersons.

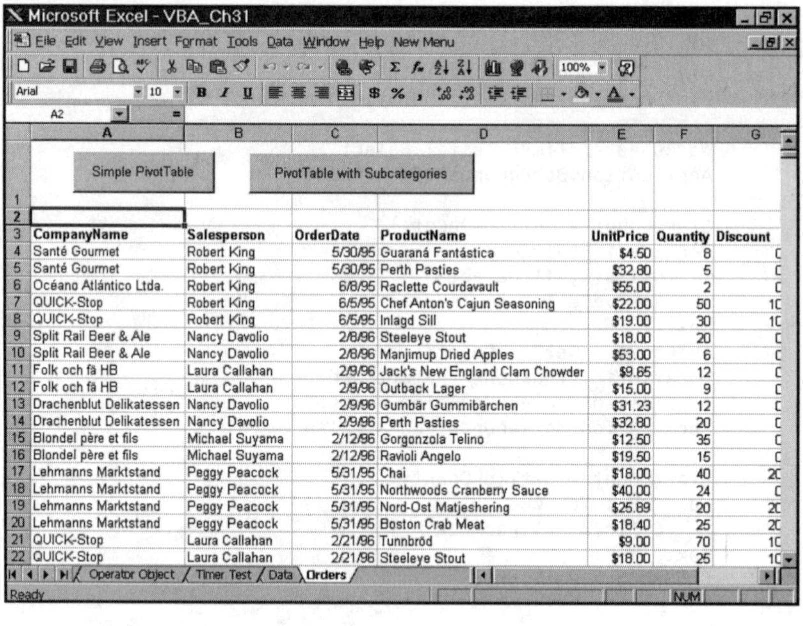

FIG. 31.17
The Orders sheet contains more than 2,000 records that can be analyzed in a PivotTable.

The easiest way to create a PivotTable object is by calling the *PivotTableWizard* method. The following code fragment creates a PivotTable on a new sheet in the current workbook, and initializes an object variable that is declared to be of the type *PivotTable.*

```
Dim objPivot As PivotTable
'...
' Make sure you select the database range before calling PivotTableWizard
'...
    Set objPivot = ActiveSheet.PivotTableWizard
```

After you create the PivotTable, you can designate the fields from your database that will be used for the row, column, and page headings of the PivotTable by calling the AddFields method of your PivotTable object.

```
    objPivot.AddFields RowFields:="ProductName", _
        ColumnFields:="Salesperson", PageFields:="OrderDate"
```


A PivotTable object contains a PivotFields collection that represents all the data fields available to the PivotTable. You can use the name of a field to assign a value to an object variable of the PivotFields type. Then you can set the properties of the PivotField variable. The following code uses a PivotField variable to make Extend Price the data field of the new PivotTable and sets the numeric formatting for the field.

```
Dim ptField As PivotField
'...
    Set ptField = objPivot.PivotFields("ExtendedPrice")
    ptField.Orientation = xlDataField
    ptField.NumberFormat = "$#,##0.00"
```

Finally, you can select the part of the PivotTable you want to display. The following statement places the selection on the Order Date field, which was designated earlier as the page field for the PivotTable.

```
    objPivot.PivotSelect "OrderDate[All]", xlLabelOnly
```

Listing 31.14 shows the complete process for selecting the data used to create a new PivotTable and then creating that table on a new sheet in the current workbook. The results of running the macro are shown in Figure 31.18.

Listing 31.14 VBA_CH31.XLS—The PivotTable object is used to create and manipulate PivotTable under VBA control.

```
Sub MakePivotTable()
'
' MakePivotTable Macro
'
Dim PTRange As Range
Dim objPivot As PivotTable
Dim ptField As PivotField
Dim ptItem As PivotItem
```

continues

Listing 31.14 Continued

```
    Cells(3, 1).Select
    Selection.CurrentRegion.Select
    Set objPivot = ActiveSheet.PivotTableWizard
    objPivot.AddFields RowFields:="ProductName", _
        ColumnFields:="Salesperson", PageFields:="OrderDate"
    Set ptField = objPivot.PivotFields("ExtendedPrice")
    ptField.Orientation = xlDataField
    ptField.NumberFormat = "$#,##0.00"

    objPivot.PivotSelect "OrderDate[All]", xlLabelOnly
End Sub
```

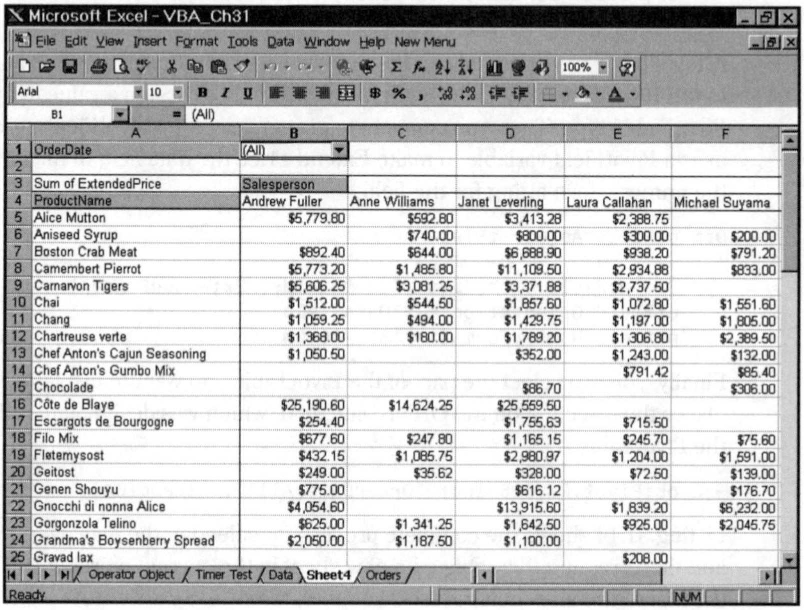

	A	B	C	D	E	F
1	OrderDate	(All)				
2						
3	Sum of ExtendedPrice	Salesperson				
4	ProductName	Andrew Fuller	Anne Williams	Janet Leverling	Laura Callahan	Michael Suyama
5	Alice Mutton	$5,779.80	$592.80	$3,413.28	$2,388.75	
6	Aniseed Syrup		$740.00	$800.00	$300.00	$200.00
7	Boston Crab Meat	$892.40	$644.00	$6,688.90	$938.20	$791.20
8	Camembert Pierrot	$5,773.20	$1,485.80	$11,109.50	$2,934.88	$833.00
9	Carnarvon Tigers	$5,606.25	$3,081.25	$3,371.88	$2,737.50	
10	Chai	$1,512.00	$544.50	$1,857.60	$1,072.80	$1,551.60
11	Chang	$1,059.25	$494.00	$1,429.75	$1,197.00	$1,805.00
12	Chartreuse verte	$1,368.00	$180.00	$1,789.20	$1,306.80	$2,389.50
13	Chef Anton's Cajun Seasoning	$1,050.50		$352.00	$1,243.00	$132.00
14	Chef Anton's Gumbo Mix				$791.42	$85.40
15	Chocolade			$86.70		$306.00
16	Côte de Blaye	$25,190.60	$14,624.25	$25,559.50		
17	Escargots de Bourgogne	$254.40		$1,755.63	$715.50	
18	Filo Mix	$677.60	$247.80	$1,165.15	$245.70	$75.60
19	Fløtemysost	$432.15	$1,085.75	$2,980.97	$1,204.00	$1,591.00
20	Geitost	$249.00	$35.62	$328.00	$72.50	$139.00
21	Genen Shouyu	$775.00		$616.12		$176.70
22	Gnocchi di nonna Alice	$4,054.60		$13,915.60	$1,839.20	$6,232.00
23	Gorgonzola Telino	$625.00	$1,341.25	$1,642.50	$925.00	$2,045.75
24	Grandma's Boysenberry Spread	$2,050.00	$1,187.50	$1,100.00		
25	Gravad lax				$208.00	

FIG. 31.18
The MakePivotTable macro creates a table showing the sales of each product by each salesperson.

At the time you create a PivotTable, you can include subcategories in your PivotTable. When you call the AddFields method, you can use the Array function to pass more than one field as one of the arguments. The following statement uses the Array function to make both Discount and Product Name row fields.

```
objPivot.AddFields RowFields:=Array("Discount", "ProductName"), _
    ColumnFields:="Salesperson", PageFields:="OrderDate"
```

Another option you can choose is to specify a page to be displayed. The following code sets the initial display of the PivotTable to show only those orders placed on January 5, 1995.

```
Set ptField = objPivot.PivotFields("OrderDate")
ptField.CurrentPage = "1/5/95"
```

Listing 31.15 shows how to create a PivotTable with subcategories in the row headings. Figure 31.19 shows the results of running this macro.

Listing 31.15 VBA_CH31.XLS—The MakePivotTable2 creates subcategories and shows only the orders for a single date.

```
Sub MakePivotTable2()
'
' MakePivotTable Macro
'
Dim PTRange As Range
Dim objPivot As PivotTable
Dim ptField As PivotField
Dim ptItem As PivotItem


    Cells(3, 1).Select
    Selection.CurrentRegion.Select
    Set objPivot = ActiveSheet.PivotTableWizard
    objPivot.AddFields RowFields:=Array("Discount", "ProductName"), _
        ColumnFields:="Salesperson", PageFields:="OrderDate"
    Set ptField = objPivot.PivotFields("ExtendedPrice")
    ptField.Orientation = xlDataField
    ptField.NumberFormat = "$#,##0.00"
    Set ptField = objPivot.PivotFields("OrderDate")
    ptField.CurrentPage = "1/5/95"

    objPivot.PivotSelect "OrderDate", xlLabelOnly
End Sub
```


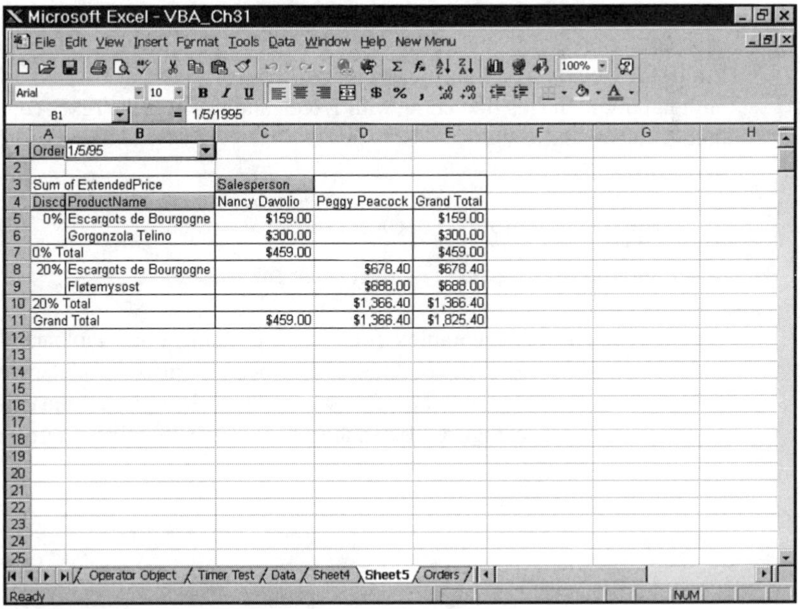

FIG. 31.19 The MakePivotTable2 macro creates a table with subcategories by Discount and Product Name.

Controlling Toolbars with VBA

Toolbars provide any easy way to select commands and options in any Windows application. Excel includes many built-in toolbars and lets you create your own custom toolbars. It is possible to customize the toolbars in Excel without any programming by using the customization tools in Excel.

▶ **See** "Customizing Excel," **p. 233**

Creating a toolbar under VBA ensures that you have complete control of the process and enables you to delete the toolbar when your workbook is closed. You can also customize the appearance of the buttons on your toolbar, assign a macro to a button, and customize the ToolTip text that appears when you position the mouse pointer over the toolbar. It is not possible to customize your ToolTips without using VBA.

As you might expect, the key to working with toolbars is working with an object model. Toolbars are actually one of two items you can create using the CommandBar object. (The other type of CommandBar object is a menu.) To create a new toolbar, you have to declare a CommandBar object variable to create a new toolbar.

The following code declares an object variable, cbToolbar, to represent the toolbar and then sets its value by adding a toolbar named Checkbook Tools to the collection of command bars. Notice that the Add method lets you specify the name of the toolbar, its position in the application window, whether it is a menu, and whether you are using it only temporarily.

```
Dim cbToolbar As CommandBar

Set cbToolbar = CommandBars.Add(Name:="Checkbook Tools", _
    Position:=msoBarFloating, MenuBar:=False, temporary:=True)
cbToolbar.Visible = True
```

After you create the toolbar, you can add buttons to it by calling the Add method of the Controls collection that is part of the toolbar object. The following code adds a button to the toolbar to run the GetOperatorInformation macro. The button's FaceId property is set with one of the built-in button images that come with Excel, and the ToolTipText property is set with a value that is helpful to the user.

```
With cbToolbar
    Set tbButton = .Controls.Add(Type:=msoControlButton)
    tbButton.OnAction = "GetOperatorInformation"
    tbButton.FaceId = 69
    tbButton.TooltipText = "Operator Information"
End With
```

Listing 31.16 shows the complete process for creating a new toolbar, adding several buttons, and assigning macros to the buttons. This procedure also includes error checking code to see if the toolbar already exists. If it does exist, you can just display the existing toolbar instead of creating another one. Figure 31.20 shows the toolbar that this macro creates.

Listing 31.16 VBA_CH31.XLS—The CreateToolbar adds a new toolbar to Excel and customizes the buttons on the toolbar.

```
Sub CreateToolbar()
Dim cbToolbar As CommandBar
Dim tbButton As CommandBarButton

On Error GoTo CreateError
Set cbToolbar = CommandBars.Add(Name:="Checkbook Tools", _
    Position:=msoBarFloating, MenuBar:=False, temporary:=True)
cbToolbar.Visible = True
With cbToolbar
    Set tbButton = .Controls.Add(Type:=msoControlButton)
    tbButton.OnAction = "GetOperatorInformation"
    tbButton.FaceId = 69
    tbButton.TooltipText = "Operator Information"

    Set tbButton = .Controls.Add(Type:=msoControlButton)
    tbButton.OnAction = "GetOfficeInformation"
    tbButton.FaceId = 591
    tbButton.TooltipText = "Office Information"

    Set tbButton = .Controls.Add(Type:=msoControlButton)
    tbButton.OnAction = "GetCommutingInformation"
    tbButton.FaceId = 29
    tbButton.TooltipText = "Commuting Information"

    Set tbButton = .Controls.Add(Type:=msoControlButton)
    tbButton.OnAction = "GetReportDate"
    tbButton.FaceId = 461
    tbButton.TooltipText = "Report Date"

    Set tbButton = .Controls.Add(Type:=msoControlButton)
    tbButton.OnAction = "OperatorMessage"
    tbButton.FaceId = 325
    tbButton.TooltipText = "Operator Message"

    Set tbButton = .Controls.Add(Type:=msoControlButton)
    tbButton.OnAction = "RefEditDemo"
    tbButton.FaceId = 485
    tbButton.TooltipText = "RefEdit Control Demo"

    Set tbButton = .Controls.Add(Type:=msoControlButton)
    tbButton.OnAction = "YearsAndGrade"
    tbButton.FaceId = 304
    tbButton.TooltipText = "Years and Grade"
End With
AlreadyExists:
Toolbars("CheckBook Tools").Visible = True
Exit Sub

CreateError:
Resume AlreadyExists
End Sub
```

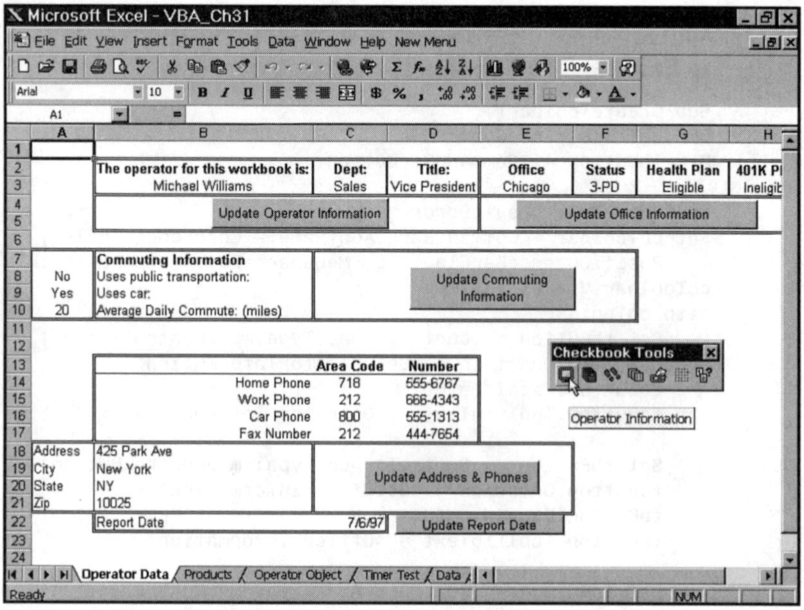

FIG. 31.20
The Checkbook Tools macro gives you an easy way to run your VBA macros.

If you know you don't need a toolbar anymore, you can delete it. As you can see in Listing 31.17, all you have to do is call the Delete method of the CommandBars object and pass the name of the toolbar you want to delete. The On Error statement ensures that you won't see an error message if you run this macro when the Checkbook Tools toolbar doesn't exist.

Listing 31.17 VBA_CH31.XLS—The ClearToolbars macro removes a toolbar from Excel.

```
Sub ClearToolbars()
    On Error Resume Next
    CommandBars("Checkbook Tools").Delete
End Sub
```

Once you have a macro that creates a toolbar and one that deletes a toolbar, how can you run these macros automatically? For example, you might want the CreateToolbar macro to run automatically each time you open the workbook in which it is defined, and you might want to run the ClearToolbars macro when you close the workbook. All you have to do is open the ThisWorkbook module of the workbook and enter the two procedures in Listing 31.18.

Listing 31.18 VBA_CH31.XLS—The Open and BeforeClose event procedures create and delete the toolbar automatically.

```
Private Sub Workbook_BeforeClose(Cancel As Boolean)
    ClearToolbars
```

```
End Sub

Private Sub Workbook_Open()
    CreateToolbar
End Sub
```

Common Problems and Solutions

I'm working on a custom form in the VBE, and there's not enough room to display the whole form.

The VBE has a very busy screen, especially if you have all the optional windows open. Try closing some of the windows, such as the Project Explorer, the Immediate window, and the Properties window. You can open them again when you need them.

I wrote some great code for one of my workbooks. How can I use it in another workbook?

Open both workbooks in Excel and open the VBE. The Project Explorer shows all the modules in all open workbooks. You can drag modules from one workbook to another to duplicate the code.

I had written some event code for a control in a form, but then I deleted the control from the form. Did I lose my work?

No. Look in the General section of the form's code module. The procedures for deleted controls are stored there.

I wrote some VBA macros for Excel 5.0 that used Windows API calls. Now they don't seem to work. What went wrong?

Excel 5.0 was designed to run in the 16-bit versions of Windows. Excel 7.0 and Excel 97 (8.0) are designed to work with Windows 95 and Windows NT, both of which are 32-bit operating systems. Almost every Windows API function was redefined for 32-bit Windows, and the code has to be rewritten. At a minimum, you'll have to correct the declarations of the functions. You might also have to change the data types of any variables or other data that you pass as arguments to the functions.

From Here...

In this chapter, you learned how to create and program custom forms in VBA. You also learned how to create your own object and extend the reach of VBA by using the Windows API.

Chapter 32, "Building Solutions with VBA," shows you how to put all your VBA knowledge together, incorporating the design of your workbook with your VBA applications. You'll also learn how to control other Office 97 applications with VBA, and you'll explore additional features of the Excel object model.

CHAPTER 32

Building Solutions with VBA

by Bill Ray

When you go beyond simple recorded macros, to creating a complete, automated application in Excel, you can use VBA as a tool to work closely with the features of Excel, enhancing your ability to control the Excel application environment. It is often necessary to create Excel applications that are easy to use, secure, and reliable, and which assist the user in such processes as data entry, reporting, and charting. ■

Designing an integrated solution

You'll learn to create an effective Excel application by taking advantage of VBA power, combined with effective workbook design.

Working with other Office 97 applications

You'll see how the concept of the object model can be extended beyond just working with Excel, to using the other Office 97 applications under VBA control.

Designing a Complete Excel Solution

It is a mistake to think that writing extensive VBA code will be the only solution to creating a complete Excel solution. In fact, you should give a lot of thought to the design of your Excel workbook and the data, formulas, and other objects that make up the application, before you write the first line of VBA code.

While creating complete applications using Excel and VBA has the potential to involve a lot of complexity, both in workbook design and in VBA coding, a relatively simple example can be used to show the principles of automated application design in Excel. The application developed throughout this chapter is a rather common one, modeled after a simple checkbook register. The workbook allows the user to enter transactions in a check register and to generate reports based upon the contents of the register.

An application such as this one can certainly be developed without any macro programming at all. There are several advantages to automating even a simple application such as this checkbook register:

- *Reliable data entry.* Instead of depending upon the user to enter the correct data in the correct location in a workbook, a form-driven application lets you validate the data entry, and to make sure the data gets to the right locations.
- *Saving time for the user.* By automating the data entry and reporting processes, you can eliminate many of the time consuming (and error prone) tasks, such as scrolling through large worksheets and selecting ranges. Your macro can automatically retrieve and update data in remote areas of the application.
- *Consistent results.* Even a well-designed spreadsheet may be used incorrectly by an end user. If you multiply this by the variety of results you may get when you distribute an application to many users, you may find it very useful to get more consistent results from an automated application.

Developing an automated solution in Excel requires you to balance your Excel workbook design skills with a developmental strategy. The first place to take action is in the design of the workbook.

The Workbook

In any Excel application, the workbook contains several elements that make up the functionality that the application must provide.

- *Data storage.* Whether the data is entered manually or imported from another application, it must be stored in some fashion. Of course, the data in an Excel workbook is stored in the cells of the workbook. This data consists mostly of text and numbers, as well as other types of data such as embedded objects. It is important to consider how the data should be organized, and how it can be found, reliably and efficiently.

- *Data entry.* Many Excel applications require data to be entered and edited directly in the workbook. Depending upon the volume of editing required, and the requirement for accuracy, you may decide to provide an automated facility for data entry, usually using custom forms.
- *Calculations and data manipulation.* Consider the calculations that must be performed upon the data when you determine how to organize it in the workbook. Whether you need to perform arithmetic calculations, lookups, sorting or filtering will help you determine whether to take a free-form or more structured approach to storing the data.
- *Output requirements.* Each application has its own set of requirements for displaying or printing results. Some applications have relatively simple requirements, allowing you to directly print an area of the worksheet where the data and formulas are stored. Other applications have more flexible requirements, which may result in a need to extract data to other parts of the workbook, or to use other applications for reporting purposes.

Consider a checkbook application. If you think about the kinds of information you typically store in a checkbook, it is easy to set up a data layout. Table 32.1 describes the data that might be required for this application.

Table 32.1 Information Typically Stored and Calculated in a Checkbook Register

Data Item	Source of Data	Notes
Date	User entry	Date of a check or deposit
Number	User entry	Check number or other transaction number
Type	User entry	Type of entry (check, deposit, ATM, and so on)
Description	User entry	Name of Payee or other descriptive text
Memo	User entry	Additional descriptive text
Payment	User entry	Amount of check or withdrawal
Deposit	User entry	Amount of deposited funds
Balance	Calculation	Current checkbook balance after the transaction
Cleared	User entry	Indicates the transaction has cleared the bank
Reconciled	User entry	Indicates reconciling with bank statement
Category	User entry	Used to indicate budget category

Most of the entries in Table 32.1 are self-explanatory. A few are worth explaining a little further. The *Type* and *Category* fields may be designed as selections from lookup lists. The category list, especially, will be most useful if the user can customize the categories to his own preference. Selecting the category from the list will make the register easy to use and less error prone.

Figure 32.1 shows the layout of the check register, with a few items entered. This table is stored on a sheet named Register, and no other data or workbook functionality is stored in this sheet. By creating separate sheets for each functional component of your workbook, the application is easier to maintain, and your VBA macros will have fewer complications in finding the correct data.

An important part of the design of this sheet is the definition of a range name called *RegisterList*. This range name will be used by the macros to place new data in the proper location at the bottom of the register. The macro will also update the range name when new rows are added to the register.

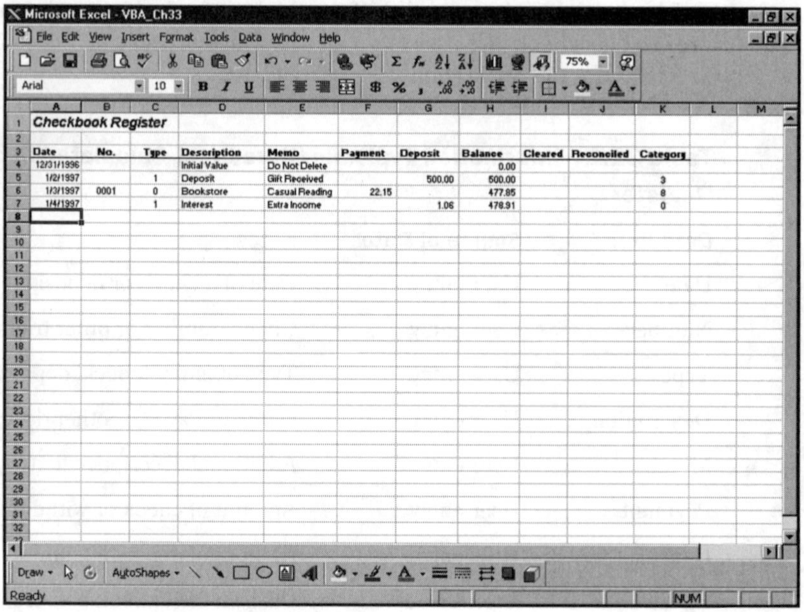

FIG. 32.1
The Register sheet is the main data storage and calculation area for the Checkbook application.

Figure 32.2 shows the lookup lists for the Category and Type lists. These are stored in a separate sheet named Lists. If you later need to add any additional lookup lists for your application, you can add them to this sheet, or store them in their own sheets.

As was the case on the Register sheet, the Lists sheet uses range names to identify the lists. In this instance, the names *TypeList* and *CategoryList* have been defined to correspond to the list contents.

FIG. 32.2
The Lists sheet contains the lookup lists for the Category and Type of each checkbook transaction.

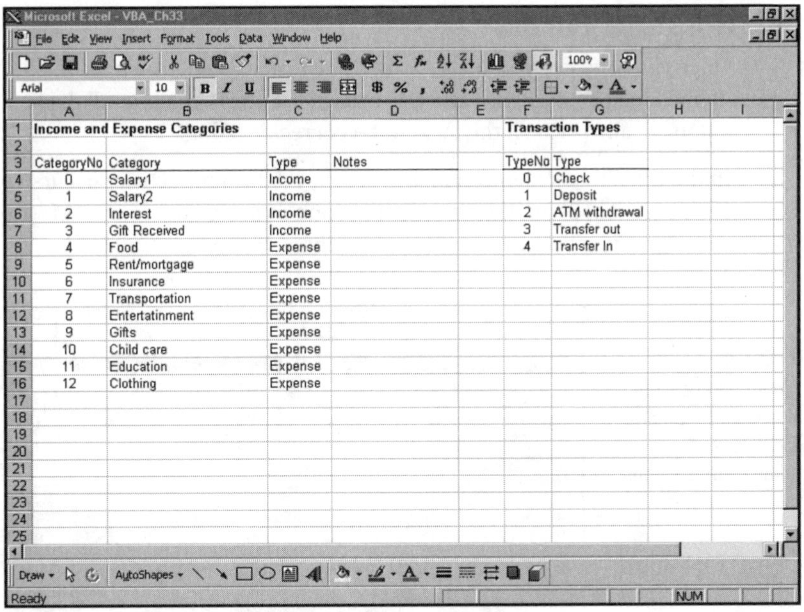

Figure 32.3 shows the Menu sheet, which appears when the workbook is opened. The buttons that appear on the Menu sheet are used to execute macros to carry out the automated functions of the application, such as data entry and report generation.

FIG. 32.3
The Menu page appears when the Checkbook application is opened, and has buttons for carrying out the automated operations.

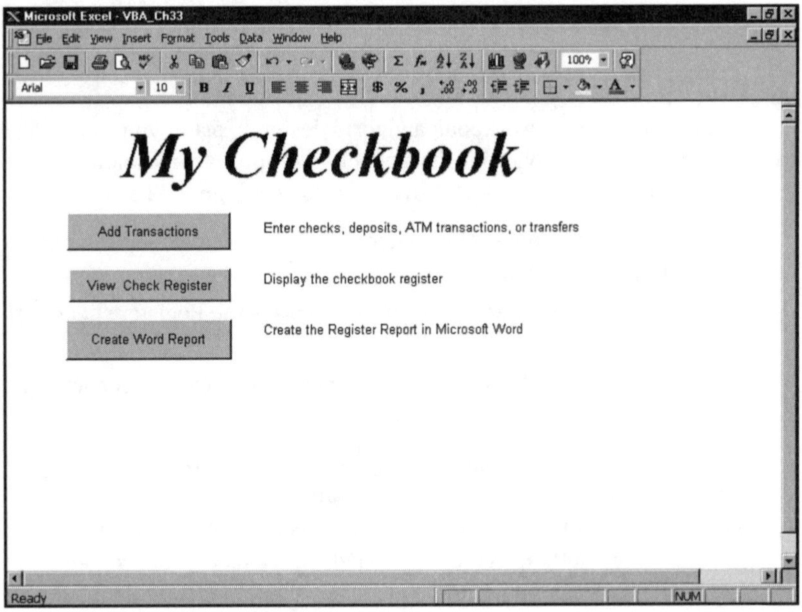

Designing the Forms

Once you organize your data, you can begin designing the look and feel of the application, as defined by form design. Custom forms allow you to monitor all data entry activities and to automatically place all the data in the correct location.

In the Checkbook application, the primary data entry activity occurs when the user writes a check or records another transaction such as a deposit or an ATM withdrawal. The form shown in Figure 32.4 is used to collect the data for any transaction.

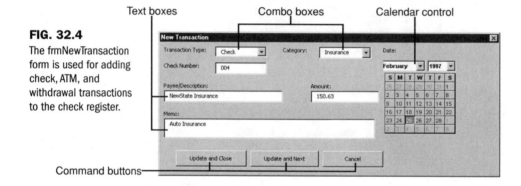

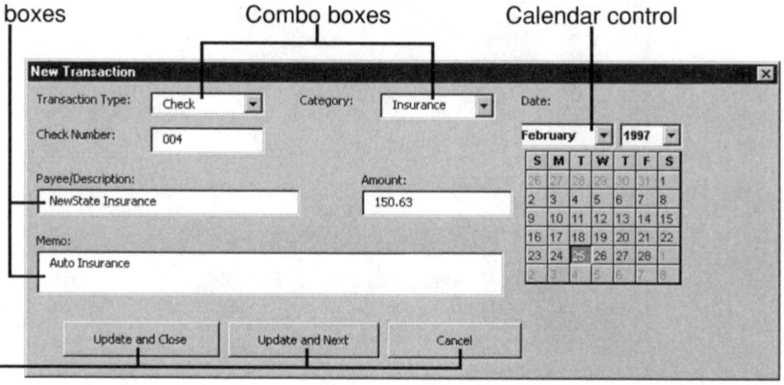

FIG. 32.4
The frmNewTransaction form is used for adding check, ATM, and withdrawal transactions to the check register.

In this form, text boxes are used for most of the data entry. The Transaction Type and Category are selected from combo box lists. The Date is selected using the calendar control that comes with Office 97. This control is much more reliable than depending upon a user to type a properly formatted date.

Organizing the VBA Code

Once you have the workbook and form design in place, you can begin creating the VBA code to automate the application. The checkbook application designed so far has three major automated functions, represented by the buttons in Figure 32.3.

- *Add Transactions.* This macro displays the frmNewTransaction form, which adds entries to the check register.
- *View Check Register.* This macro displays the Register sheet so the user may edit it directly.
- *Create Word Report.* This macro generates a custom report, using Word 97 to display the report results.

The code behind these buttons may be very simple or more complex. It is not unusual for a button such as the Add Transactions button to simply display a form. The form may contain much more VBA code to respond to the events that occur while the form displays. The Create Word Report button, on the other hand, calls a macro that contains all the functionality needed to create the final report. The code for this button is described later in this chapter, in the section "Automating Other Office 97 Applications."

The simplest macro on the Menu sheet is attached to the View Check Register button. This macro, shown in Listing 32.1, switches to the Register sheet and moves to the bottom of the table.

Listing 32.1 VBA_CH32.XLS—The ShowRegister macro selects the register form and moves the selection past the end of the table.

```
Sub ShowRegister()
    Application.ScreenUpdating = False
    Sheets("Register").Select
    Range("RegisterStart").Select
    Selection.End(xlDown).Select
    ActiveCell.Offset(1, 0).Range("A1").Select
End Sub
```

The Add Transactions button calls the Record Transactions macro, which does nothing more than display the frmNewTransaction form. This simple macro is shown in Listing 32.2.

Listing 32.2 VBA_CH32.XLS—The RecordTransaction macro displays the form that is used for entering transactions into the register.

```
Sub RecordTransactions()
    frmNewTransaction.Show
End Sub
```


The real functionality for entering transactions is stored in the form. First, the form is initialized by the UserForm_Initialize procedure, which is shown in Listing 32.3. This event procedure executes automatically each time the form appears. The VBA code in this procedure uses the two lists in the Lists sheets to provide the items for the combo box lists in the form. For example, to update the TransactionType list, you first need to know how many items are in the list. VBA can use the Count property of the Rows collection corresponding to the named range TypeList.

```
Dim CatRowCount As Integer, TypeRowCount As Integer
Dim I As Integer

TypeRowCount = Range("TypeList").Rows.Count
```

Now you can loop through the second column of the TypeList range, using the text in these cells to add items to the list.

```
For I = 1 To TypeRowCount
    Me.TransactionType.AddItem Range("TypeList").Cells(I, 2).Text
Next I
```

Finally, you can set an initial value for the list. Each item on the list has a corresponding ListIndex value. Setting the ListIndex property of the list to 0 selects the first item on the list, since the index values start counting from 0.

```
Me.TransactionType.ListIndex = 0
```

After a similar procedure is used to initialize the Category list, some of the other controls in the form are set to initial values.

```
Me.Amount = ""
Me.Description = ""
Me.Memo = ""
Me.TransactionDate = Date
```

Initializing the controls on the form results in a consistent and reliable behavior, each time the form appears.

Listing 32.3 VBA_CH32.XLS—The UserForm_Initialize procedure runs automatically whenever the form appears.

```
Private Sub UserForm_Initialize()
' Update category and transaction type lists
    Dim CatRowCount As Integer, TypeRowCount As Integer
    Dim I As Integer

    TypeRowCount = Range("TypeList").Rows.Count
    For I = 1 To TypeRowCount
        Me.TransactionType.AddItem Range("TypeList").Cells(I, 2).Text
    Next I
    Me.TransactionType.ListIndex = 0

    CatRowCount = Range("CategoryList").Rows.Count
    For I = 1 To CatRowCount
        Me.Category.AddItem Range("CategoryList").Cells(I, 2).Text
    Next I
    Me.Category.ListIndex = 0
    Me.Amount = ""
    Me.Description = ""
    Me.Memo = ""
    Me.TransactionDate = Date
End Sub
```

The two buttons that do most of the work on this form are *UpdateCloseBtn* and *UpdateNextBtn*. UpdateCloseBtn adds the contents of the form to the register and then hides the form, returning to the Menu sheet. UpdateNextBtn also adds the contents of the form to the register, but instead of hiding the form, it simply reinitializes the form so another entry can be made. The code for these two procedures is shown in Listing 32.4.

Listing 32.4 VBA_CH32.XLS—The procedures for the two buttons on the form are very similar, and both call the UpdateRegister procedure.

```
Private Sub UpdateCloseBtn_Click()

    Me.Hide
    Application.ScreenUpdating = False
    Call UpdateRegister
```

```
    Worksheets("Menu").Select
End Sub

Private Sub UpdateNextBtn_Click()
    Application.ScreenUpdating = False
    Call UpdateRegister
    Call UserForm_Initialize
End Sub
```

Because these two event procedures must update the register, it's a good idea to create a separate procedure that contains the code for this common activity. This procedure, shown in Listing 32.5, performs several important activities.

First, an object variable is declared and initialized to refer to the RegisterList range, and the number of rows and columns in the range is recorded.

```
Dim RegRange As Range, RegRowCount As Integer, RegColCount As Integer

Set RegRange = Range("RegisterList")
RegRowCount = RegRange.Rows.Count
RegColCount = RegRange.Columns.Count
```

The *Offset* property of this range object is used to refer to the first empty row below the range. Offset returns a reference that is different from the original range by the number of rows and columns indicated. Because you have already detected how many rows are in the range, you can use Offset to simply go down that number of rows from the beginning of the range, which results in the first empty row. This is where the values from the form are entered.


```
Worksheets("Register").Select
RegRange.Offset(RegRowCount, 0).Cells(1, 1).Formula = Me.TransactionDate
RegRange.Offset(RegRowCount, 0).Cells(1, 2).Formula = Me.CheckNumber
RegRange.Offset(RegRowCount, 0).Cells(1, 3).Formula =
➥Me.TransactionType.ListIndex
RegRange.Offset(RegRowCount, 0).Cells(1, 4).Formula = Me.Description
RegRange.Offset(RegRowCount, 0).Cells(1, 5).Formula = Me.Memo

RegRange.Offset(RegRowCount, 0).Cells(1, 9).ClearContents
RegRange.Offset(RegRowCount, 0).Cells(1, 10).ClearContents
RegRange.Offset(RegRowCount, 0).Cells(1, 11).Formula = Me.Category.ListIndex
```

The value of the Amount control must be entered in either column 6, if the transaction is a check or other withdrawal, or in column 7, if it is a deposit. The *ListIndex* property of the TransactionType combo box lets us know what type of transaction has been entered.

```
Select Case Me.TransactionType.ListIndex
Case 0, 2, 3    'Check, ATM Withdrawl, or Transfer Out
    RegRange.Offset(RegRowCount, 0).Cells(1, 6).Formula = Format(Me.Amount,
    ➥"#,##0.00")
Case 1, 4    'Deposit or Transfer In
    RegRange.Offset(RegRowCount, 0).Cells(1, 7).Formula = Format(Me.Amount,
    ➥"#,##0.00")
End Select
```

Another special entry is the formula for the Balance in the new row. This is entered as a relative reference in the R1C1 style. The following statement will always have the same meaning, whenever a new row is added to the register. The formula refers to the cell above the current cell (R[-1]C), the cell two columns to the left (RC[-2]), and the cell one column to the left (RC[-1]).

```
RegRange.Offset(RegRowCount, 0).Cells(1, 8).Formula = "=R[-1]C-RC[-2]+RC[-1]"
```

Now that the new data has been entered, the *RegisterList* name must be updated to include the new row. The following code selects the range that is one row taller than the existing RegisterList range and then deletes the old name and replaces it with a new name based upon the current selection.

```
Range("RegisterList").Select
Selection.Resize(RegRowCount + 1, RegColCount).Select
ActiveWorkbook.Names("RegisterList").Delete
NewAddress = "=Register!" & Selection.AddressLocal
ActiveWorkbook.Names.Add Name:="RegisterList", _
    RefersToLocal:=NewAddress
```

Listing 32.5 VBA_CH32.XLS—The UpdateRegister procedure transfers the data from the form to the Register sheet and updates the RegisterList range name.

```
Private Sub UpdateRegister()
    Dim RegRange As Range, RegRowCount As Integer, RegColCount As Integer

    Set RegRange = Range("RegisterList")
    RegRowCount = RegRange.Rows.Count
    RegColCount = RegRange.Columns.Count

    Worksheets("Register").Select
    RegRange.Offset(RegRowCount, 0).Cells(1, 1).Formula = Me.TransactionDate
    RegRange.Offset(RegRowCount, 0).Cells(1, 2).Formula = Me.CheckNumber
    RegRange.Offset(RegRowCount, 0).Cells(1, 3).Formula =
    ➥Me.TransactionType.ListIndex
    RegRange.Offset(RegRowCount, 0).Cells(1, 4).Formula = Me.Description
    RegRange.Offset(RegRowCount, 0).Cells(1, 5).Formula = Me.Memo
    Select Case Me.TransactionType.ListIndex
    Case 0, 2, 3    'Check, ATM Withdrawl, or Transfer Out
        RegRange.Offset(RegRowCount, 0).Cells(1, 6).Formula = Format(Me.Amount,
        ➥"#,##0.00")
    Case 1, 4    'Deposit or Transfer In
        RegRange.Offset(RegRowCount, 0).Cells(1, 7).Formula = Format(Me.Amount,
        ➥"#,##0.00")
    End Select
    RegRange.Offset(RegRowCount, 0).Cells(1, 8).Formula = "=R[-1]C-RC[-2]+RC[-
    ➥1]"
    RegRange.Offset(RegRowCount, 0).Cells(1, 9).ClearContents
    RegRange.Offset(RegRowCount, 0).Cells(1, 10).ClearContents
    RegRange.Offset(RegRowCount, 0).Cells(1, 11).Formula = Me.Category.ListIndex
    Range("RegisterList").Select
    Selection.Resize(RegRowCount + 1, RegColCount).Select
```

```
    ActiveWorkbook.Names("RegisterList").Delete
    NewAddress = "=Register!" & Selection.AddressLocal
    ActiveWorkbook.Names.Add Name:="RegisterList", _
        RefersToLocal:=NewAddress
End Sub
```

Controlling the Workspace Environment

In an automated application, you may want to change the appearance of the Excel workspace. You may want to hide certain sheets or workbooks, remove the formula bar or scroll bars, or change other view settings.

The Open event for the workbook is a natural place to put code for making such environmental changes. The Close event may be used to reset the settings to the original values.

If you expect the user to be working on more than one workbook at a time, it's a good idea to use the WindowActivate and WindowDeactivate procedures of the workbook to allow these settings to be adjusted automatically when you switch between workbooks.

Listing 32.6 shows three procedures that make changes to the environment when workbook events occur.

The Workbook_Open procedure turns off the display of the formula bar, which is an application setting, and then turns off the display of cell gridlines, row and column headings, and worksheet tabs, which are all settings of the active window. Additionally, this procedure makes the Lists sheet invisible, and selects the Menu sheet.

The Workbook_WindowDeactivate procedure simply restores the display of the formula bar. Since this is an application setting, it would be bad manners to turn it off and then leave it off when you switched to another workbook. It is also worth noting that the WindowDeactivate event procedure will be executed when the workbook is closed, so it is not necessary to create a separate procedure for the Close event.

The Workbook_WindowActivate procedure sets the same display attributes as the Workbook_Open procedure, with the exception of not needing to hide the Lists sheet or activate the Menu sheet.

Listing 32.6 VBA_CH32.XLS—These three event procedures make changes to the Excel environment when the workbook is opened, activated, or deactivated.

```
Private Sub Workbook_Open()
    Application.DisplayFormulaBar = False
    With ActiveWindow
        .DisplayGridlines = False
        .DisplayHeadings = False
        .DisplayWorkbookTabs = False
    End With
```

continues

Listing 32.6 Continued

```
    Sheets("Lists").Visible = False
    Sheets("Menu").Select
End Sub

Private Sub Workbook_WindowActivate(ByVal Wn As Excel.Window)
    Application.DisplayFormulaBar = False
    With ActiveWindow
        .DisplayGridlines = False
        .DisplayHeadings = False
        .DisplayWorkbookTabs = False
    End With
End Sub

Private Sub Workbook_WindowDeactivate(ByVal Wn As Excel.Window)
    Application.DisplayFormulaBar = True
End Sub
```

Automating Other Office 97 Applications

Because Excel 97 is a member of the Office 97 suite, you can take advantage of the features of the other Office programs as you develop your Excel automated solutions. Here are some examples:

- Use Word 97 to generate letters, memos, multicolumn reports, and other text formatting that would be difficult or impossible to generate in Excel.
- Automatically generate PowerPoint 97 slide shows based upon the data in your Excel workbook.
- Use Access 97 as a permanent storage location for data that you've entered or compiled in Excel. Access provides advantages such as greater storage capacity, indexing for faster retrieval of data, and flexible querying and reporting facilities.
- Interact with Outlook 97 to automatically update your calendar, contact list, or e-mail Inbox.

VBA lets you control other programs using Automation, which was formerly referred to as OLE Automation. Automation allows your Excel VBA code to gain control of the object model of another application, just as any Excel VBA macro can work with the Excel object model.

As you might expect, this can also work in the opposite direction. You can use VBA from within Word, PowerPoint, and Access to control Excel using Automation. This means, of course, the VBA code you've written in the other application has access to the Excel object model.

The first step in using Automation in your VBA macros is to get a reference to the other application.

Declaring a Reference to Another Program

An Excel VBA macro doesn't automatically know anything about the object models of Word, PowerPoint, Access, or Outlook, let alone applications that are not part of the Office 97 suite. There are several steps necessary for an Excel macro to control another application's object model.

1. Using the VBE, choose Tools, References; then select the reference that you want to use in your application. Activate the check box for any references you want to use, and then click OK to complete the command. Figure 32.5 shows the References dialog box.

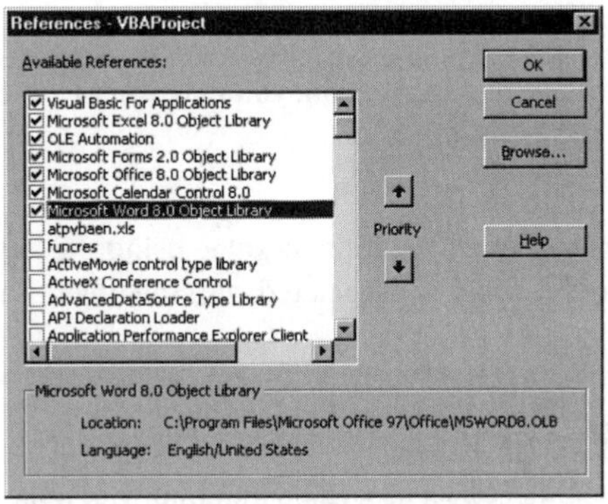

FIG. 32.5 The References dialog box establishes a link to the type library of another application.

NOTE When the other application you are controlling from your Excel macro is one of the Office 97 applications, you may not have to use the Tools, Reference command to set a reference to the application, since it may automatically be registered. If you need to set a reference to Word, for example, you would select Microsoft Word 8.0 Object Library in the dialog box.

2. Declare an object variable, using any of the objects in the application that you want to use.

```
Dim WordApp As Word.Application, WordDoc As Word.Document
```

3. Assign an object to the variable, using the Set statement, along with the CreateObject function.

```
Set WordApp = CreateObject("Word.Application")
```

NOTE The CreateObject function, as its name implies, creates a new object using the application to which you have previously established a reference. This is useful as long as you don't need to work with an existing document.

If you want to work with an existing document, use the GetObject function instead. This function lets you specify a file name, and then it automatically opens that file.

```
Dim WordDoc as Object
Set WordDoc = GetObject("C:\My Documents\JuneRpt.Doc")
```

4. Now you have access to the methods and properties of the other application. Refer to the Help file for that application to find out which methods and properties are available.

```
WordApp.Visible = True          'Make Word visible
WordApp.Selection.EndKey Unit:=wdStory     'Move to the end of the document
WordApp.Selection.TypeParagraph          'Insert a new paragarph
WordApp.TypeText "Current sales totals: "          'Type some text
```

TIP Just as you can learn about Excel's VBA methods and properties by recording macros, you can use the macro recorder with Word or PowerPoint to create VBA code that you can adapt for use in an Excel macro that must control these applications. Unfortunately, you can't record the VBA code you might need to control Access or Outlook.

5. When you finish using the other application, you may want to use the Quit method to close the program.

```
WordApp.Quit
```

6. You can clear the object variable by setting its value using the keyword Nothing. This releases the memory and resources associated with the object variable.

```
Set WordApp = Nothing
```

Controlling Word Using Excel VBA

The Checkbook application can use Word as a reporting tool. You may find that some users are more familiar with the formatting capabilities of Word and prefer to edit a report using Word. You may also want to use a particular formatting or layout feature that is available in Word but not in Excel.

An illustration of this technique is the WordReport macro, which is called when the Create Word Report button is clicked on the Menu sheet (in the earlier checkbook example). The code for this macro is shown in Listing 32.7.

First, the macro declares object variables for the Word objects you need to work with.

```
Dim WordApp As Word.Application
Dim WordDoc As Word.Document
Dim WordTable As Word.Table
Dim WordRange As Word.Range
Dim RegRange As Range
```

Next, the CreateObject function is called to start an instance of Word, and a new document is created by adding an item to the Documents collection in Word.

```
Set WordApp = CreateObject("Word.Application")
WordApp.Visible = True
Set WordDoc = WordApp.Documents.Add
```

Each Word document contains a collection of tables. When you want to add a table, you have to indicate the location of the table, in the form of a range. In this case, you simply add the new table at the range representing the current selection. The table will begin as one row by six columns, and you can add rows as required by the data that will come from Excel.

```
Set WordRange = WordApp.Selection.Range
Set WordTable = WordDoc.Tables.Add(WordRange, 1, 6)
```

To add the title row text, you can call the InsertAfter method for the Range of each cell in the table's first row.

```
With WordTable
    .Cell(1, 1).Range.InsertAfter "Date"
    .Cell(1, 2).Range.InsertAfter "Check #"
    .Cell(1, 3).Range.InsertAfter "Desc."
    .Cell(1, 4).Range.InsertAfter "Pmt."
    .Cell(1, 5).Range.InsertAfter "Dep."
    .Cell(1, 6).Range.InsertAfter "Balance"
End With
```

Using a range reference to the RegisterList range in the Excel workbook, you can work through the register row-by-row. Notice the use of the For Each...Next loop. Using this structure, you don't need to know how many rows are in the register. For each row, the macro simply adds a row to the Word table and then updates the values of the table cells with the data from the Excel RegisterList range.


```
Set RegRange = Names("RegisterList").RefersToRange
For Each R In RegRange.Rows
    WordTable.Rows.Add
    rowcount = WordTable.Rows.Count
    WordTable.Cell(rowcount, 1).Range.InsertAfter RegRange.Cells(rowcount -
    ➥1, 1).Text
    WordTable.Cell(rowcount, 2).Range.InsertAfter RegRange.Cells(rowcount -
    ➥1, 2).Text
    WordTable.Cell(rowcount, 3).Range.InsertAfter RegRange.Cells(rowcount -
    ➥1, 4).Text
    WordTable.Cell(rowcount, 4).Range.InsertAfter RegRange.Cells(rowcount -
    ➥1, 6).Text
    WordTable.Cell(rowcount, 5).Range.InsertAfter RegRange.Cells(rowcount -
    ➥1, 7).Text
    WordTable.Cell(rowcount, 6).Range.InsertAfter RegRange.Cells(rowcount -
    ➥1, 8).Text
Next R
```

Finally, you don't need the Word object variables anymore, so it's a good idea to free the variables by setting them to Nothing.

```
Set WordTable = Nothing
Set WordDoc = Nothing
Set WordApp = Nothing
```

Because this macro doesn't call the Quit method of Word, the Word application window is left open so the user can edit the document, print, or save it. Of course, you might choose to automatically perform any or all of these activities, by calling the appropriate methods of the Word object. Figure 32.6 shows the finished report as it appears in Word.

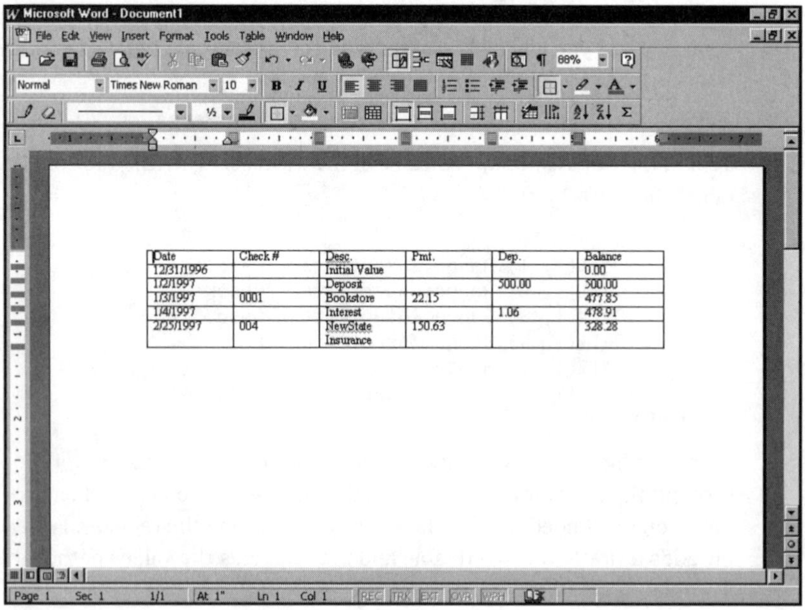

FIG. 32.6
The WordReport macro produces a new table in a Word document.

Listing 32.7 VBA_CH32.XLS—The WordReport macro uses the data in the Register sheet to create a new table in a Word 97 document.

```
Sub WordReport()
    Dim WordApp As Word.Application
    Dim WordDoc As Word.Document
    Dim WordTable As Word.Table
    Dim WordRange As Word.Range
    Dim RegRange As Range

    Set WordApp = CreateObject("Word.Application")
    WordApp.Visible = True
    Set WordDoc = WordApp.Documents.Add
    Set WordRange = WordApp.Selection.Range
    Set WordTable = WordDoc.Tables.Add(WordRange, 1, 6)
    With WordTable
        .Cell(1, 1).Range.InsertAfter "Date"
        .Cell(1, 2).Range.InsertAfter "Check #"
        .Cell(1, 3).Range.InsertAfter "Desc."
        .Cell(1, 4).Range.InsertAfter "Pmt."
        .Cell(1, 5).Range.InsertAfter "Dep."
        .Cell(1, 6).Range.InsertAfter "Balance"
    End With
    Set RegRange = Names("RegisterList").RefersToRange
    For Each R In RegRange.Rows
        WordTable.Rows.Add
        rowcount = WordTable.Rows.Count
```

```
        WordTable.Cell(rowcount, 1).Range.InsertAfter RegRange.Cells(rowcount -
        ➥1, 1).Text
        WordTable.Cell(rowcount, 2).Range.InsertAfter RegRange.Cells(rowcount -
        ➥1, 2).Text
        WordTable.Cell(rowcount, 3).Range.InsertAfter RegRange.Cells(rowcount -
        ➥1, 4).Text
        WordTable.Cell(rowcount, 4).Range.InsertAfter RegRange.Cells(rowcount -
        ➥1, 6).Text
        WordTable.Cell(rowcount, 5).Range.InsertAfter RegRange.Cells(rowcount -
        ➥1, 7).Text
        WordTable.Cell(rowcount, 6).Range.InsertAfter RegRange.Cells(rowcount -
        ➥1, 8).Text
    Next R
    Set WordTable = Nothing
    Set WordDoc = Nothing
    Set WordApp = Nothing
End Sub
```

Controlling Excel from Another Application

Just as you can use Excel to control Word or other applications using Automation, you can use Automation to control Excel. The steps are similar to the process that Excel used to control Word.

1. Using the VBE while creating a macro in the other application, choose Tools, References. Then select the reference you want to use in your application. This time you will select Microsoft Excel 8.0 Object Library.
2. Declare an object variable using any of the objects in Excel that you want to use.

   ```
   Dim XLApp As Excel.Application, XLSheet As Excel.Sheet
   ```

3. Assign an object to the variable using the Set statement, along with the CreateObject function.

   ```
   Set XLApp = CreateObject("Excel.Application")
   ```

   Now your macro in the other application has access to the methods and properties of Excel.

   ```
   XlApp.Visible = True            'Make Excel visible
   XlApp.Workbooks.Add             'Create a new workbook
   XLApp.ActiveWorkbook.Cells(1,1).Formula = 500      'Enter data into a cell
   ```

4. When you finish using Excel, you may want to use the Quit method to close the program.

   ```
   XlApp.Quit
   ```

5. You can clear the object variable by setting its value using the keyword Nothing. This releases the memory and resources associated with the object variable.

   ```
   Set XlApp = Nothing
   ```

Automating the Office Assistant

Your VBA code can control the appearance and behavior of the Office Assistant that comes with Office 97. The Assistant's message balloon functions much like a message box, presenting information and asking questions. You can also instruct the Assistant to perform one of its animations, which are predesigned by the creator of the Assistant.

The Assistant object in Excel gives you access to a set of properties and methods for working with the Assistant. It's a good idea to check the user's preferences for working with the Assistant before displaying the Assistant in your own code. The following code fragment checks the AssistWithAlerts property of the Assistant object to see whether the user wants to see the Assistant. If the property is set to True, the Assistant is displayed; if it's not, a more traditional message box is used.

```
If Assistant.AssistWithAlerts = True Then
    asstVis = Assistant.Visible
    Assistant.Visible = True
' ...Work with the assistant here
    Assistant.Visible = asstVis
Else
    MsgBox msgText, vbOKOnly, msgTitle
End If
```

To control the message displayed by the Assistant, you must work with a Balloon object. You can set the value of the object variable by calling the NewBalloon method of the Assistant object. Then you can use the properties and methods of the Balloon object.

```
Dim blln As Balloon
   Set blln = Assistant.NewBalloon
```

The Mode property determines how the user can interact with the workbook while the Assistant is displayed. The msoModeModal constant sets the performance as *modal*, meaning that the user can't work directly with the workbook while the balloon is displayed. Use msoModeModeless as the constant if you want to allow the user to continue working with the workbook while the balloon is displayed.

```
    blln.Mode = msoModeModal
```

Setting the Button property of the Balloon object controls which buttons appear in the balloon. The msoButtonSetOk constant is used to create an OK button without a Cancel button. For additional constants, see the online help for the Button property.

```
    blln.Button = msoButtonSetOK
```

The Heading and Text properties let you place any text you want in the title area and the main body of the balloon.

```
    blln.Heading = msgTitle
    blln.Text = msgText
```

Setting the Animation property causes one of the Assistant's animations to execute when the Assistant is displayed. You can include any of 34 standard animations when designing an Assistant. You can find the constant names for the animations in the online help for the Animation property. Some Assistants might not support all of these animations. On the other hand, some Assistants may provide more that one animation for one or more of the Animation constants. In those cases, you can't choose which of the multiple animations the Assistant will run.

The following statements set the Animation property and then display the Assistant:

```
blln.Animation = msoAnimationListensToComputer
ret = blln.Show
```

Listing 32.8 shows the entire process of displaying the Assistant with a custom message and animation. Figure 32.7 shows the results of running this macro.

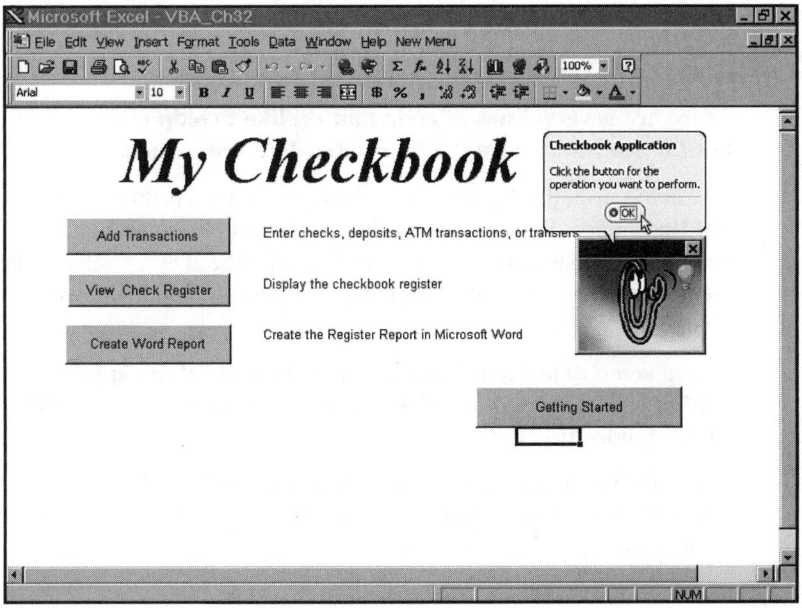

FIG. 32.7
The Office Assistant can display your own custom messages.

Listing 32.8 VBA_CH32.XLS—The AssistantDemo macro shows how to display and control the Office Assistant.

```
Sub AssistantDemo()
Dim blln As Balloon

msgTitle = "Checkbook Application"
msgText = "Click the button for the operation you want to perform."

If Assistant.AssistWithAlerts = True Then
    asstVis = Assistant.Visible
    Assistant.Visible = True
    Set blln = Assistant.NewBalloon
    blln.Mode = msoModeModal
    blln.Button = msoButtonSetOK
```

continues

Listing 32.8 Continued

```
        blln.Heading = msgTitle
        blln.Text = msgText
        blln.Animation = msoAnimationListensToComputer
        blln.Button = msoButtonSetOkCancel
        ret = blln.Show
        Assistant.Visible = asstVis
Else
        MsgBox msgText, vbOKOnly, msgTitle
End If
End Sub
```

Common Problems and Solutions

There are several lines of code that I'd like to skip over while I'm testing my code, but I'll need to restore the lines later. Is there a quick way to do this?

Yes. In the VBE, display the Edit toolbar, which has a pair of buttons named Comment Block and Uncomment Block. Select the lines you want to skip over and click the Comment Block button to put comment characters at the beginning of every selected line. To remove the comment characters, select the lines that you previously commented and click the Uncomment Block button.

I have some data I need to hide from the user of my application, but I like the ease of editing it on a worksheet. Can I prevent the users from unhiding the worksheets where I store this data?

Yes. In the Open procedure for the workbook, set the Visible property for the sheet to xlVeryHidden, as shown here. The user will not be able to unhide the worksheet using Excels commands.

```
Sheets("Lists").Visible = xlVeryHidden
```

You can write a separate macro that unhides the sheet by setting the Visible property of the sheet to True.

From Here...

This chapter covered designing an automated application in Excel and using VBA, custom forms, and automation. Using the techniques covered in the last five chapters, you can begin to design your own automated applications, taking advantage of Excel's built-in features and the power of VBA to control Excel.

The appendixes in Part VIII provide you with a lot of useful information. Be sure to use them for help with using the Financial Manager, functions, and Excel shortcuts; finding business sites on the World Wide Web; and taking advantage of the content on the CD included with this book.

PART VIII

Appendixes

APPENDIX A

Using Small Business Financial Manager

by Sherry Kinkoph

In addition to the great tools and templates found in Excel, Office 97 Small Business Edition also comes with the Small Business Financial Manager, a collection of useful worksheets and wizards designed specifically for the small business user. You can plug in data from other accounting packages and create professional reports and analyses using Excel 97. You can also speculate with what-if scenarios and forecast how changes in your finances affect your bottom line. This appendix will show you how to tap into Financial Manager and put more of Excel's features to work for you.

What is the Small Business Financial Manager?

Learn how to use the Small Business Financial Manager.

Working with the Import Wizard

Learn how to import data from other accounting packages to use with the Small Business Financial Manager.

Working with the Report Wizard

Find out how to create professional, accurate reports based on your accounting data, including balance and cash flow sheets.

Working with what-if scenarios

Speculate how changes you make to your financial data impact your overall financial status.

Analyzing lease options with the Lease Wizard

Take a look at the differences in your finances when you perform a what-if analysis examining buying versus leasing an asset.

Analyzing a new loan with the Add New Loan Wizard

Create a what-if scenario that examines the impact of adding another loan to your account.

Starting and Exiting Small Business Financial Manager

TIP If you've not yet installed the Small Business Financial Manager, stop and do so now.

The Microsoft Small Business Financial Manager works alongside Excel 97 to help you analyze, manipulate, and summarize your company's bookkeeping and financial records. The Small Business Financial Manager offers you several key tools to help you examine, manipulate, and analyze accounting data:

- **Import Wizard** If you use another accounting package, such as Peachtree or Quickbooks, you can import the data into Excel for analysis.
- **Report Wizard** Use the Report Wizard to create comprehensive, detailed reports for viewing your data more clearly.
- **What If Wizard** Use this feature to see how your decisions impact your data. Create and save scenarios that show you how a few important changes in your data can affect your bottom line.

Financial Manager is a great tool for helping you examine your business data and as a result, make better financial decisions. For example, use the Report Wizard to keep track of sales, inventory levels, and expenditures. You can view your entire company's financial data, or simply track an individual account. Then use the What If Wizard to create "what-if" analysis on the data, such as what happens when you increase product prices or increase service costs.

You can start the Small Business Financial Manager from the Excel window or from the Windows 95 desktop. When you install Financial Manager, the Accounting menu is added to Excel's menu bar. If you have the Excel program window opened, you can start any of the Small Business Financial Manager tools simply by opening the Accounting menu, as shown in Figure A.1, and selecting the appropriate Wizard you want to use.

After choosing a wizard from the Accounting menu, the Small Business Financial Manager startup screen appears briefly and the appropriate wizard dialog box appears.

You can also start the Small Business Financial Manager by double-clicking its shortcut icon on the Windows 95 desktop. (This shortcut icon, is automatically added when you install Financial Manager.) When you start the Small Business Financial Manager in this way, the startup screen shown in Figure A.2 appears. The startup screen displays the three Financial Manager Wizards as buttons—the same three wizards found on the Accounting menu in Excel (see Figure A.1). To start a particular wizard, move your mouse pointer over the area of the screen listing the wizard (the wizard names look like buttons), then click. This opens the appropriate wizard dialog box.

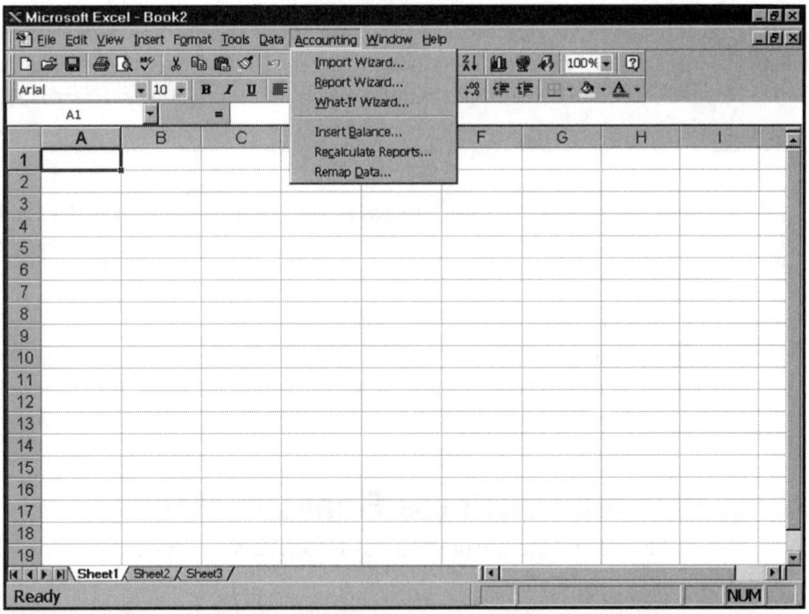

FIG. A.1
To start a Small Business Financial Manager tool from the Excel window, simply open the Accounting menu.

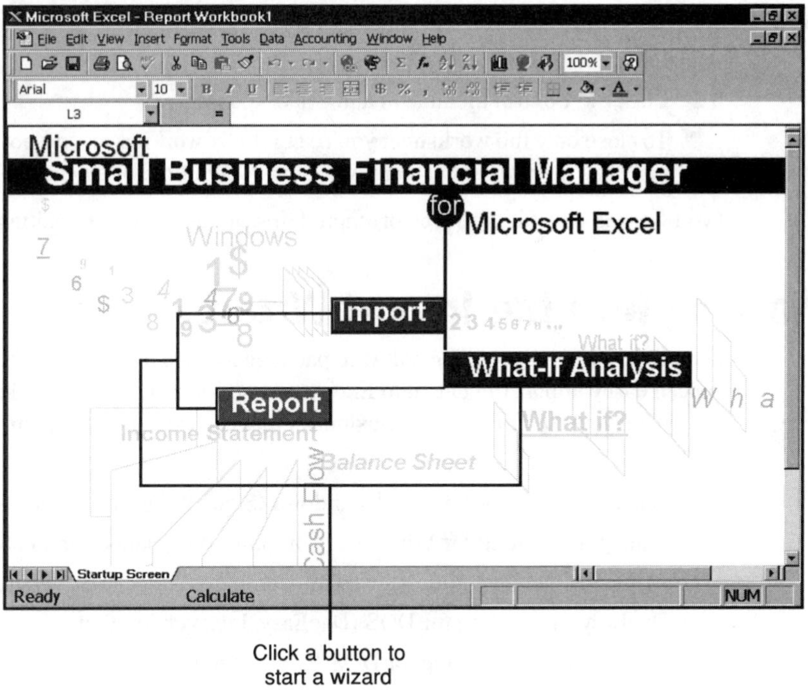

FIG. A.2
The Small Business Financial Manager startup screen.

TIP If you choose to start Financial Manager by using the shortcut icon, you may first encounter a warning box, that cautions you about using macros. Click the Tell Me More button to learn more about this topic. Or, click the Enable Macros button to display the Small Business Financial Manager startup screen.

NOTE Remember, the Small Business Financial Manager works alongside Excel, so when you double-click the Small Business Financial Manager shortcut icon, Excel opens onto your screen.

NOTE Unlike other Office 97 programs, you cannot start the Small Business Financial Manager from the Windows 95 taskbar. You can only launch the feature from the Excel program window or use the Small Business Financial Manager shortcut icon on the Windows 95 desktop.

Exiting the Small Business Financial Manager

To exit Excel and the Small Business Financial Manager, simply close the program using any of the following methods:

- Click the Close (X) button in the upper-right corner of the program window.
- Open the File menu and select Exit.
- Press Alt+F4 on the keyboard.
- Click the Control-menu icon and select Close.
- To close only the worksheet you're currently working on and not the entire program, just click the worksheet window's Close (X) button, or select File, Close.

If you worked on a file, you'll be prompted to save the file before exiting.

Working with the Import Wizard

If you use another accounting software package to keep track of your company's financial data, you can easily import the data into Excel and use Excel's features to view, summarize, and manipulate your data. The Small Business Financial Manager supports the following accounting packages:

- BusinessWorks for DOS and Windows (State of the Art, version 9.0)
- Simply Accounting for Windows (Computer Associates, version 3.0)
- ACCPAC Plus Accounting for DOS (Computer Associates, version 6.1)
- DacEasy Accounting for DOS (DacEasy, Inc., version 6.0)
- Great Plains Accounting for DOS (Great Plains Software, version 8.0, 8.1, 8.2)
- Quickbooks (Intuit, version 3.1, 4.0, Pro 4.0)

- M-A-S 90 Evolution/2 (State of the Art, version 1.51)
- One-Write Plus Accounting with Payroll for DOS (ADP Company, version 4.03)
- Peachtree for Windows (Peachtree Software, Inc., version 3.0, 3.5, 4.0)
- Peachtree Complete Accounting for DOS (Peachtree Software, Inc., version 8.0)
- Platinum Series for DOS and Windows (Platinum, version 4.1, 4.4)
- MV Server/MetaView (Timeline, Inc., version 2.3, 2.4, 2.5)

TIP If your accounting package isn't in the previous list, visit Microsoft's Web site (**http://www.microsoft.com/**) for new filters, or call the Microsoft Customer Support people at 1-800-426-9400 and ask about what's available for your software package.

When you import accounting data from another program into Excel, you don't necessarily have to have the accounting package installed on your computer, just the data files you use.

CAUTION

If you use Quickbooks, you must install the accounting program first in order to import data.

What Data Is Imported with the Import Wizard?

The more detailed your data from the accounting package you use to import from, the more detailed your analysis, reports, and scenarios can be with Small Business Financial Manager. Depending on your existing package, and the way it's set up, you may be limited in the kinds of analysis you can perform. For example, if you're keeping a general ledger on your accounting package and an accounts receivable subsystem, but don't update sales or invoicing data from the subsystem into the general ledger, then you won't be able to create an analysis on individual customers.

Table A.1 shows what kinds of data can be imported.

Table A.1 Types of Data to Import

Data Type	Imported Information
System information	Includes company name, fiscal year, and accounting periods.
Account information	Includes charts of accounts, posted transactions, product lists, sales force, services, customer/client information, and so on.

continues

Table A.1 Continued

Data Type	Imported Information
Balance sheet information	Beginning year balances for each account,including assets, liabilities, and equity.
General ledger information	Posted general ledger transactions.
Sales information	Includes sales invoice information, such as customers, services/products, quantities sold, and so on.
Product information	Includes inventory balances for stock items.

Budget information from your accounting package will not import into Small Business Financial Manager. Also keep in mind that you need to use a 12-period account in order to import into Financial Manager, plus the accounting system should be set up using accrual basis accounting not cash basis accounting.

CAUTION

Be sure to import your accounting data into Financial Manager before using your accounting software to close out fiscal periods. If you don't, Financial Manager won't be able to import all your transaction details. Some programs, like QuickBooks, don't have a year-end closing routine, so you won't need to worry.

In addition to data types, Small Business Financial Manager recognizes various account categories, listed in Table A.2.

Table A.2 Account Categories

Account Category	Credit or Debit	FSIC	Category Description
1110 Cash	D	CCE	Cash accounts and other assets that can be turned into cash
1111 Credit card receipts	D	CCE	Posted credit card receipts
1121 Accounts receivable	D	AR	Trade AR accounts
1122 Allowance debts	D	ABD	Noncollectible trade AR for bad accounts

Account Category	Credit or Debit	FSIC	Category Description
1130 Inventory	D	INV	Inventory accounts
1190 Other current assets	D	OCA	Current assets from other categories
1211 Property, plant, equipment	D	PPE	Cost of assets
1212 Accumulated depreciation	D	AD	Accumulated depreciation of property, plant, equipment
1290 Other noncurrent assets	D	ONCA	Other noncurrent assets aside from proper ty, plant, equipment
2110 Accounts payable	C	AP	Payable trade accounts
2120 Short-term debt	C	STD	Debts that are paid off within the current year
2130 Credit cards payable	C	OCL	Recorded credit card purchases
2190 Other current liabilities	C	OCL	Current liabilities (except accounts payable and short-term debt)
2210 Long-term debt	C	LTD	Debts recorded more than one year in duration
2240 Other	C	ONCL	All other noncurrent liabilities
3100 Equity	C	EQ	Accumulated dividends, capital stock, other pain-in capital
3200 Retained savings	C	RE	All prior retained earnings
3999 Revenue/ expense	C	RE	Year-end closing account for revenue and expenses clearing
4000 Net sales	C	NS	All sales accounts
5000 Cost of sales	D	COS	All direct costs of sales
6100 Amortization and depreciation	D	ADE	Depreciation and amortization costs
6200 Bad debt expense	D	BDE	All bad debt expense

continues

Table A.2 Continued

Account Category	Credit or Debit	FSIC	Category Description
6300 Officer compensation	D	OC	Expenses for compensation of company officers
6400 Interest expense	D	INT	Recorded interest expense
6500 Operating expense	D	OOE	All other expenses not recorded elsewhere
7100 Non-operating income	C	ONOI	All revenue not classified as net sales
7200 Non-operating expense	D	ONOE	Other non-operating expenses
8000 Income taxes	D	IT	State and federal taxes paid

CAUTION

Keep in mind that Financial Manager simply makes a copy of the data in your accounting software package. If you make changes to it in the accounting program, those changes will not be reflected in Financial Manager. You can easily update the information, select Accounting, Import Wizard from the Excel window and click the Update button.

Importing Data with the Import Wizard

Like other Office 97 Wizards, the Import Wizard walks you through the necessary steps to accomplish the task—in this case, importing accounting data or using an existing database. A series of four dialog boxes helps you with each step of the process. Simply enter the appropriate information and click Next to continue. To return to a previous step at any time, click the Back button. To exit the procedure without completing the import, click the Cancel button.

TIP If at any time during the import procedure you need some help, click the Help button in the wizard dialog box to open Financial Manager's Help system.

To import accounting data from another software package into Excel's Small Business Financial Manager, follow these steps:

1. From the Excel window, open the Accounting menu and select Import Wizard.

   Or, from the Financial Manager startup screen, click the Import button.

2. The Import Wizard dialog box appears, as shown in Figure A.3. Choose one of the following options:

   Select the Import option to import accounting data, then click Next to continue.

   If you're updating from an existing database, click the Update option, and then click Next.

FIG. A.3
The Import Wizard dialog box.

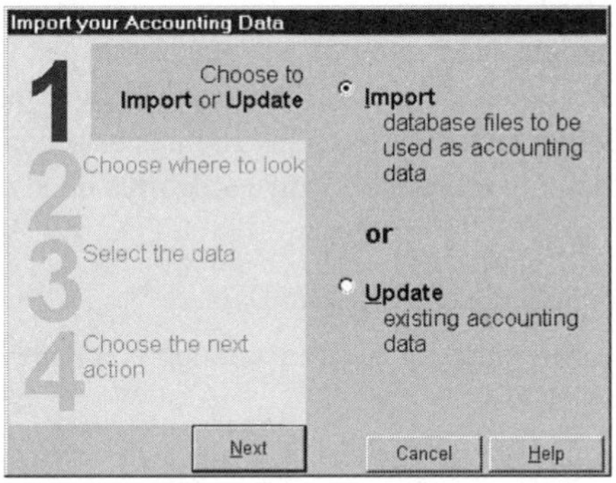

3. In the next Import Wizard screen (see Figure A.4), select the Look On option to search all of your drives for accounting data. To look only in specific folders, click the In Specific Folders option, and then select the folders you want to search. Click the folder from the list and click the Add Folder to List button. You can select several folders to search.

FIG. A.4
Specify where you want to look for accounting data on your system.

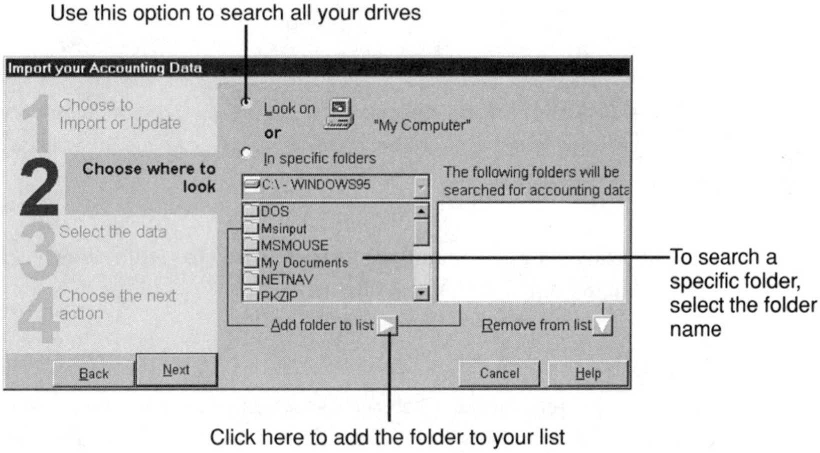

CAUTION

You won't see a list of files when you select a folder in step 3. You aren't looking for files, just indicating which folders to search. Instead of trying to remember where you've stored your accounting data, let Financial Manager find it for you; select the Look on My Computer option.

4. Click Next to continue.
5. The third box lets you select the accounting data for importing. Click the data you want and click the Next button to continue.
6. The next box prompts you about the amount of time the import will take; click Yes to continue.
7. When the import is complete, click Finish.

After importing the accounting data, it's a good idea to see how Small Business Financial Manager mapped the data into its account categories. Financial Manager may not be able to match the right account categories, which in turn affects any reports or scenarios you might generate. For that reason, take a moment and check. If any categories need correcting, you can do so now. Follow these steps:

1. Open the Accounting menu and select Remap Data.
2. The Select a Company for Remapping Accounts dialog box appears. Select the company you want to remap and click OK.
3. The Map Your Accounts dialog box appears. Use the + or – symbols in front of the account categories to expand or collapse the subcategories.
4. To move an account to another category, select the account and click Cut.
5. Locate the category where you want it moved and click Paste.
6. Continue following steps 3 through 5 to rearrange the categories as needed. Click OK when finished.

CAUTION

It's better to remap your data before creating reports or scenarios. If you don't, any reports and scenarios won't reflect the remapping changes you make using the preceding steps. This is especially true if you use an alphabetical chart of accounts. Financial Manager only uses numeric account numbers. Remapping will help you order the information.

After importing your accounting data, you're ready to create reports and what-if scenarios, as explained in the remainder of this chapter.

CAUTION

If Financial Manager can't find the accounting data you're trying to import or update, make sure the files are still available on your computer and have not been moved to a new location. In some instances, Financial Manager needs to locate not only the accounting data, but also the software used to create it. For example, Peachtree Complete Accounting for DOS stores proprietary files in a different location from the data files. If you import the data files, you'll leave out the necessary proprietary files. To fix this, place a copy of your accounting files with the accounting software folder and try again.

Working with the Report Wizard

You can create dozens of different reports with Small Business Financial Manager and your financial data. The Report Wizard can walk you through each step for generating a report. You can create seven basic financial reports plus many variations of each one. Here's a run-down of the basic reports you can create:

- **Balance Sheet** Use this type of report to reflect a snapshot of your company's financial status, such as assets, equity, and liabilities.
- **Trial Balance** Trace your account's audit trail of balance and net change for your company for a particular accounting period. The balance includes opening account balance, current period activity of debits and credits, and a closing balance.
- **Income Statement** Detail your company's performance over a specific amount of time, including profit or loss, with a report that summarizes revenues and expenses.
- **Cash Flow** Show your company's cash flow, in and out, and spot potential problems.
- **Changes in Stockholders Equity** Use this report to analyze how much stock ownership is controlled by you and your investors and your creditors.
- **Sales Analysis** Find out sales, expense, and gross profit using a PivotTable for each area of your business.
- **Ratios** Use this type of report to calculate ratios and quickly examine your company's financial status.

CAUTION

In order to generate reports, accounting information must be imported from an accounting package or created in Excel. Remember, a report is only as detailed as your accounting data.

For each of these report categories, you'll find specific types of reports you can use. For example, if you create a report based on your company's balance sheet, the Report Wizard lets you choose from a regular balance sheet (showing your company's financial condition at the end of a certain period of time), a balance sheet with scenarios (showing projected conditions based on what-if scenarios), or a balance sheet with prior year comparisons (showing your financial condition that includes a look at previous years' figures). The different types of reports you create allow you to look at different parts of your financial data.

TIP Small Business Financial Manager comes with several examples you can refer to based on a fictitious company called Volcano Coffee. Be sure to check them out.

Creating a Report with the Report Wizard

To build a report using Report Wizard, follow these steps:

1. From the Excel window, select Accounting, Report Wizard.

   Or, from the Small Business Financial Manager startup screen, click the Report button.

2. The Report Wizard dialog box appears on-screen, as shown in Figure A.5. From the Financial Reports list box, select the type of report you want to use.

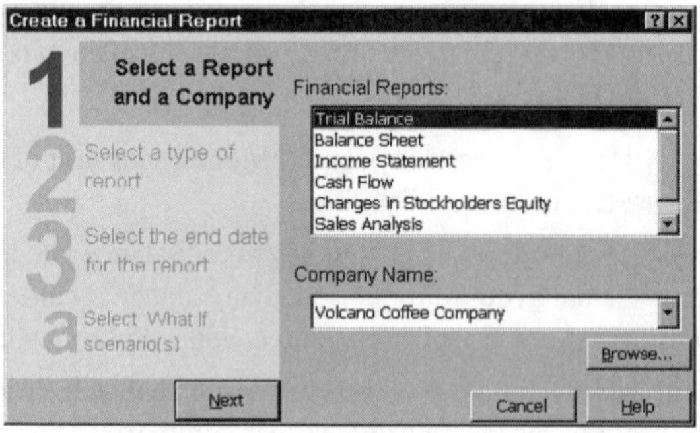

FIG. A.5
The Report Wizard helps you create a financial report.

3. From the Company Name drop-down list, select the financial database you want to use. If your company's database isn't listed, click the Browse button and locate the appropriate folder and file.

TIP You can use a database you just imported or use one from another folder or network server. Use the Browse button to help locate the database folder and file.

4. To continue, click the Next button.
5. The second step in the Report Wizard, shown in Figure A.6, lets you select a specific report type from the Report Types list box. Simply click the one you want to use. (Remember, the report types you see listed in this dialog box depend on the financial report style you selected in step 2.)

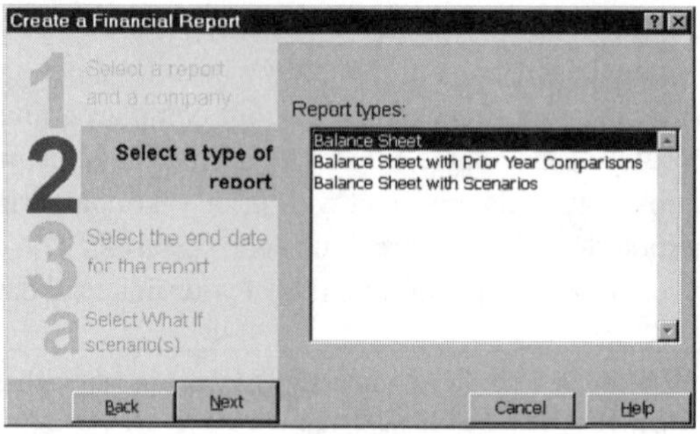

FIG. A.6
Select the type of report you want to use.

6. Click Next to continue.

7. The third step in the Report Wizard lets you choose the end date for your report (see Figure A.7). Click the end date you want to use. The Time Period area shows the start and end dates for the report.

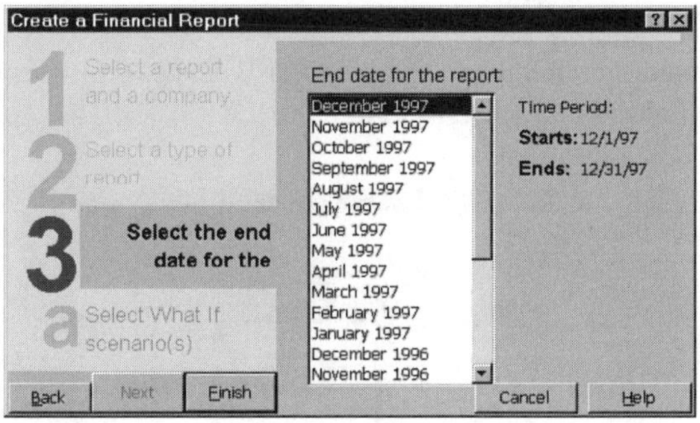

FIG. A.7 Select an end date for your report.

8. (Optional) If you selected Balance Sheet with Scenarios in step 6, click the Next button and select the scenario(s) you want to use.
9. After making selections for all three Report Wizard steps, click the Finish button. The report is displayed on your screen, as shown in Figure A.8.

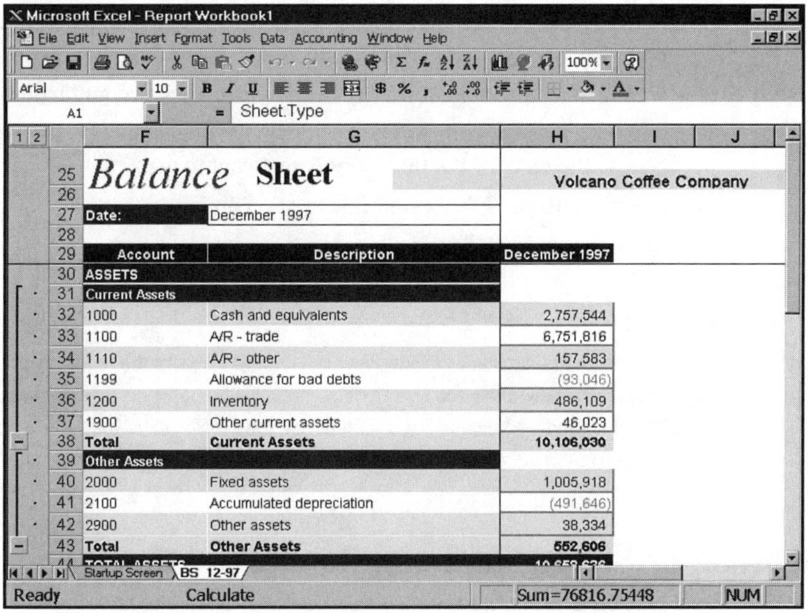

FIG. A.8 The new report appears in the Excel window.

You can now manipulate the data in your report, perform scenarios with the What-If Wizard, print your reports, and more, using Excel's spreadsheet tools.

Creating a Custom Report

If you prefer to create your own kind of accounting data report, you can easily do so from the Report Wizard dialog box. Follow these steps:

1. Open Excel's Insert menu and select Worksheet.
2. Open the Accounting menu and select Insert Balance. This opens the Insert Balance dialog box, similar to the one shown in Figure A.9.

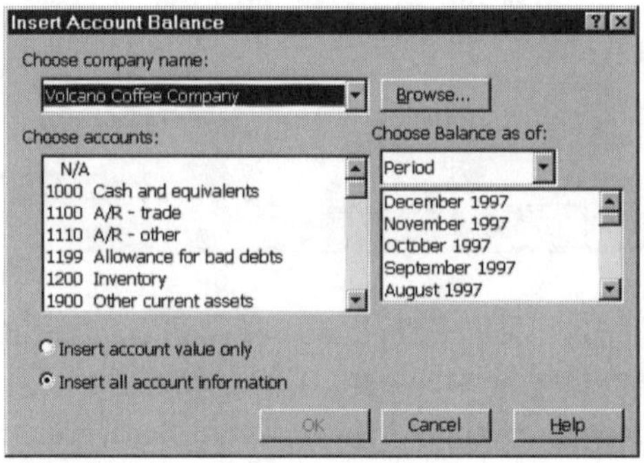

FIG. A.9
The Insert Balance dialog box.

3. In the Choose Company Name drop-down list box, select the database on which you want to base your report. (If your database isn't listed, locate it with the Browse button.)
4. In the Choose Accounts list box, click the accounts to be included. To select multiple accounts, simply hold down the Ctrl key and click account names.
5. In the Choose Balance As Of drop-down list box, select Period, Quarter, or Year; then choose the date for the time period you want to use.
6. Select the Insert All Account Information option.
7. Click OK, and you have a customized report.

CAUTION

When you open a report you've saved, Financial Manager checks the report against the accounting data. If you've made changes to the accounting data, Financial Manager displays a comment box asking you if you want to update and recalculate. If you update but don't recalculate, you'll see a comment in the report's Date box telling you the report is out of date. To update the report, choose Accounting, Recalculate Reports.

Showing or Hiding Financial Report Data

If you plan on sharing the report with others, you can choose to hide or show transaction details. The following methods can be used to show or hide details in your report:

- To show a detailed list of accounts for any account category, double-click the account category cell.

- To show details behind a particular calculated column, click the plus (+) button at the top of the column.
- To show a separate Drill Down report revealing transaction details for a particular value, double-click any cell bordered by a thick gray line on the bottom and right sides.
- To hide a detailed list for an account category, click the minus (–) button at the far left end of the row.
- To hide a column (collapse), click the minus (–) button at the top of the column.

Take a look at Figure A.10 to locate the hide/show controls.

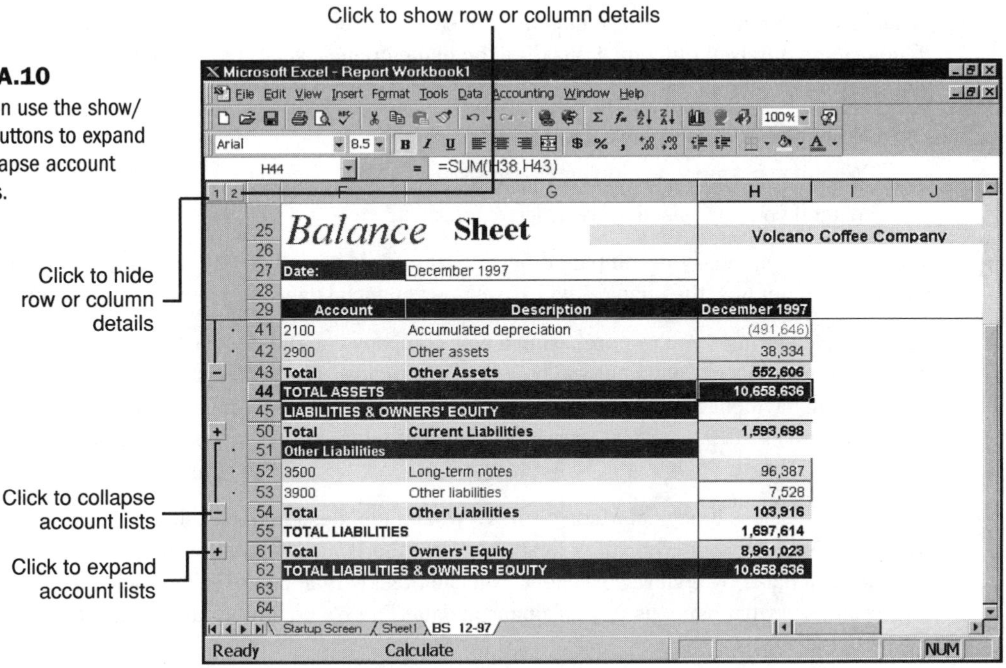

FIG. A.10
You can use the show/hide buttons to expand or collapse account details.

CAUTION

If you can't seem to display a Drill Down report, the accounting database may not include transaction details. Some software packages don't reflect new transactions until you post them. Financial Manager won't import nonposted transactions. Be sure to post necessary transactions in your accounting software, then update the Financial Manager report.

CAUTION

If you get a lot of error messages while using Financial Manager, you may need to turn off the Error Trapping option. From the Excel program window, choose Tools, Macro, Visual Basic Editor. From the Visual Basic window, choose Tools, Options and display the General tab. Deselect the Break on All Errors option under the Error Trapping area. Click OK and exit the Visual Basic window (click the window's Close button).

Working with What-If Scenarios

What-if scenarios are simply speculations you can make on your financial and accounting data to determine different outcomes. Just like the name implies, what-if scenarios involve playing with future projections, such as:

What if you increased product prices?

What if you dropped shipping charges?

What if you purchased more office equipment?

With what-if scenarios, you can plug different values into a copy of your existing spreadsheet data and find out how the changes will affect your financial data and your overall bottom line.

For example, perhaps you're purchasing a new company car and need a general idea of how much your monthly car payment will be. If you've already got a spreadsheet detailing your current loan payment for a $20,000 car at 3.9% interest, but want to find out what the payment might be for a $25,000 or $30,000 car using different interest rates, a what-if scenario can help you out.

The Small Business Financial Manager has a what-if tool designed specifically for creating what-if analyses on your company's financial data—the *What-If Wizard*. You can use the wizard to create a What-If Overview worksheet. You can quickly manipulate values, select analysis topics, and see what happens to your financial data. There's no limit to the scenarios you can create:

- Analyze your current pricing and see what would happen if you increased product prices.
- Analyze your sales revenue and see what happens if you increase your sales revenues by 10 percent.
- Find out the effects of changing your inventory stocking levels, or see a breakdown of products or services.
- Examine the effects of taking out another loan or paying off an existing one.
- What would happen to your numbers if you sold your property or used equipment?

These are just a few of the types of analyses you can perform using the What-If Wizard. You can designate the types of analyses you want to see and then let Financial Manager help you with the steps needed to perform them.

Using the What-If Wizard

To use the Small Business Financial Manager What-If Wizard, follow these steps:

1. From the Excel window, select Accounting, What-If Wizard.

   Or, from the Small Business Financial Manager startup screen, click the What-If Analysis button.

2. The What-If Wizard dialog box appears on-screen, as shown in Figure A.11. Choose a company financial database to use. If yours isn't listed, click the Browse button and locate the database.

FIG. A.11
The dialog boxes will walk you through the steps for building a what-if scenario.

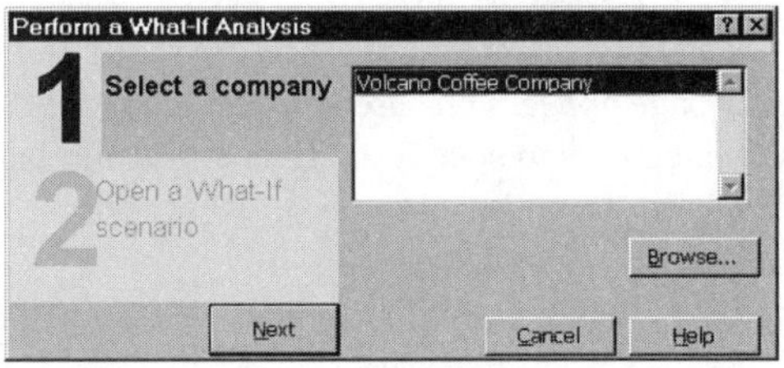

3. To continue, click the Next button, and the box displays options for opening a new or existing scenario (see Figure A.12).

FIG. A.12
In step 2 of the What-If Wizard, you can choose to open a new or existing scenario.

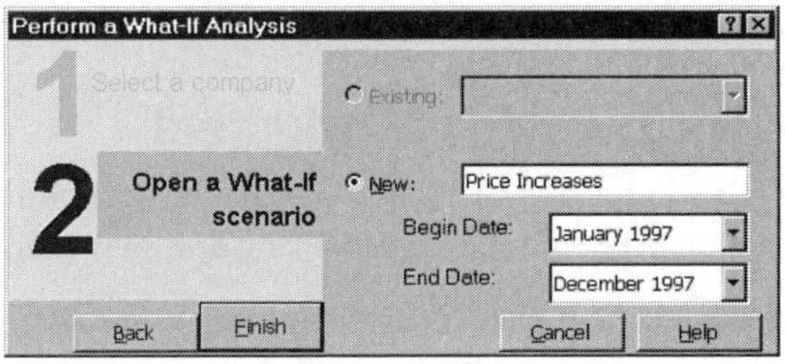

4. To create a new scenario, click the New option and type in a name for the scenario. To use an existing scenario, click the Existing option and select a previously saved scenario from the drop-down list.

TIP The scenario name you type in can be up to 50 characters long.

5. Next, select a starting date for the scenario in the Begin Date box and an ending date in the End Date box.
6. Click Finish to continue.
7. The Save Scenario Workbook As box appears, as shown in Figure A.13. Save your scenario by clicking the Save button.

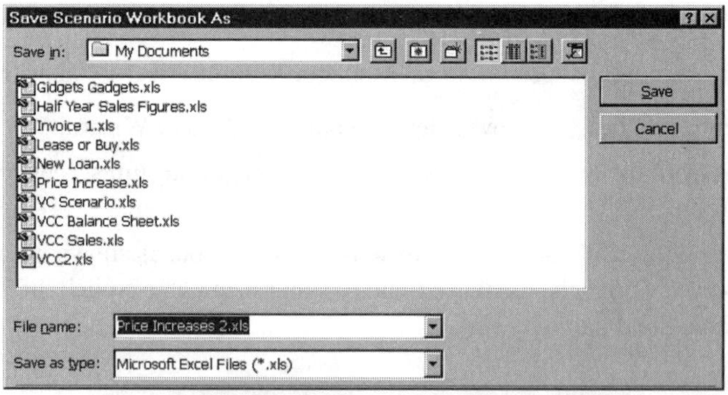

FIG. A.13
The Financial Manager prompts you to save your scenario.

8. The What-If Overview page appears on-screen (see Figure A.14). From here, you can use the various worksheet tools to specify analysis topics and build your what-if scenario.

CAUTION

If your what-if analysis looks odd or contains numbers you know aren't correct, it may be that Financial Manager is having some difficulty interpreting your accounting data. To verify information, choose the Accounting menu and select the Remap Data command. Check over the structure of your account charts and make remapping changes if necessary. You may also be able to use your accounting software to reorganize the data in a standard fashion.

Working with the What-If Overview Worksheet

Are you ready to perform a what-if analysis? The What-If Overview worksheet has three areas with which you need to familiarize yourself before trying a what-if analysis:

- The top rows of the worksheet have buttons for saving, opening, and deleting scenarios and a drop-down list for selecting other scenarios to view. Scroll to the right of the worksheet to see the New, Save, and Delete buttons.
- The middle area of the worksheet contains analysis categories: Profitability; AR (accounts receivable), AP (accounts payable), Inventory; Expenses & Taxes; Finance; Buy versus Lease. The topic buttons open other worksheets and wizards for changing what-if values.
- The bottom of the worksheet displays a miniature of your income statement and a graph that lets you see comparisons between the scenario you create and your actual data.

Figure A.14 points out each of these worksheet areas.

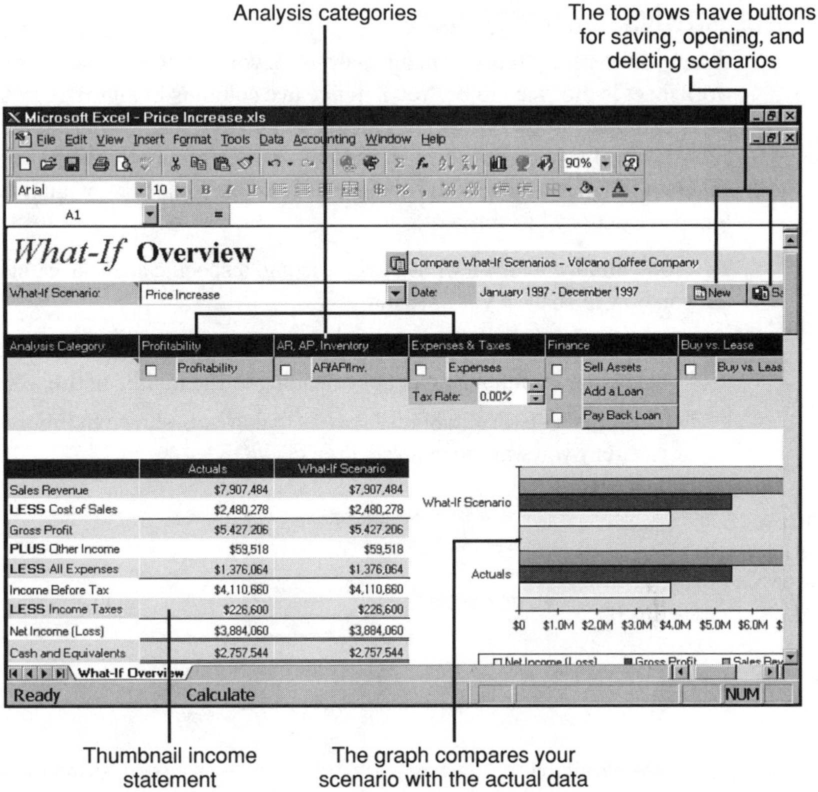

FIG. A.14
The What-If Overview has three areas in which to work.

As you can see from Figure A.14, the Overview sheet has buttons and drop-down lists you can use to help set up your scenarios. Table A.3 shows what the What-If Overview buttons do.

Table A.3 Overview Buttons

Button	Function
	Compares what-if scenarios on a Summary Page worksheet.
New	Starts a new scenario based on the values in the current scenario.
Save	Saves the current scenario.
Delete	Deletes the current what-if scenario.
?	Opens the Financial Manager Help window.

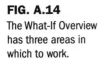

Using Analysis Categories

When you're ready to perform an analysis on your what-if scenario, the middle of the Overview worksheet is the place to be. You'll notice five columns in Figure A.14 that each represent a particular analysis category. The category buttons (located below the category headings for each column), when clicked, start wizards or open other worksheets pertaining to the selected category. Whereas most of the categories have only one type of analysis you can perform, the Finance category has three.

To show you how to use a what-if scenario and a specific analysis category, the following steps tell you how to analyze your pricing.

1. From the What-If Overview worksheet, click the Profitability button (located directly below the Profitability category heading in the middle of the worksheet).
2. This opens the Profitability Analysis dialog box, shown in Figure A.15. Select the type of category you want to analyze, then click OK.

FIG. A.15
The Profitability Analysis dialog box.

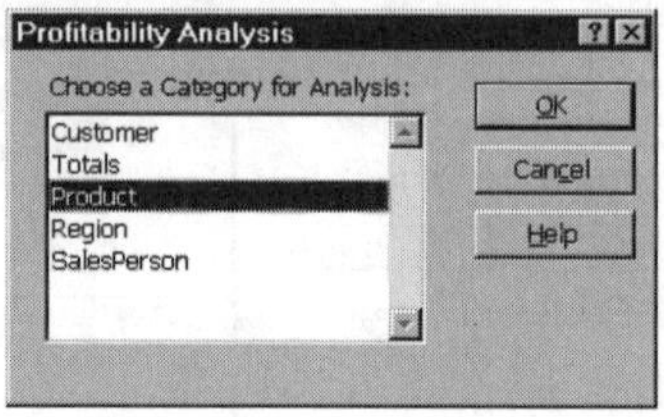

3. The Profitability Analysis worksheet opens on-screen, similar to the one shown in Figure A.16. From here, you can change values and view their effects on your data. For example, at the top of the worksheet, click the View drop-down list and select Price View.
4. The Unit Price column moves to the left of the worksheet, as shown in Figure A.17. In the Unit Price column, adjust the pricing for your products; type in new values for each item you want to change. In this particular scenario, you can find out what a difference pricing makes to your financial data.
5. To see a graph of your changes, scroll to the right of the worksheet to the Graphical View column, click the drop-down list and select Unit Price to reflect the price changes in the graph.

TIP To add a new item to your database, click the Add selection below the Items column heading and type in the appropriate information for the item as prompted. When you finish, the item is added to the worksheet.

After creating a what-if scenario, you can save it or print it out. It's a good idea to save the scenario under a unique name so you can easily find it and use it again. You can save a scenario just like you save a worksheet. Click the Save button and give it a name. Click the What-if Overview button to return to the What-If Overview sheet. You can then examine the graphs and compare the what-if scenario to your actual data.

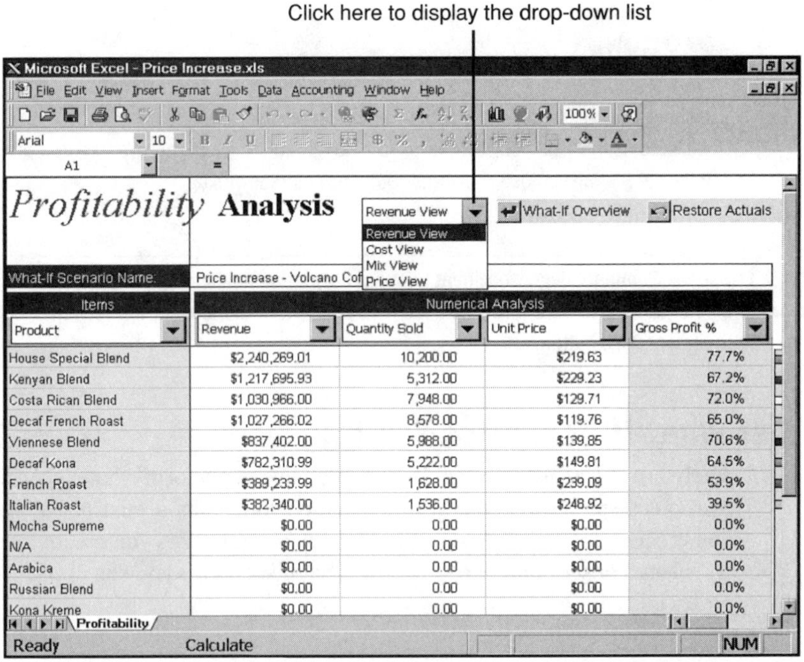

FIG. A.16
The Profitability Analysis worksheet.

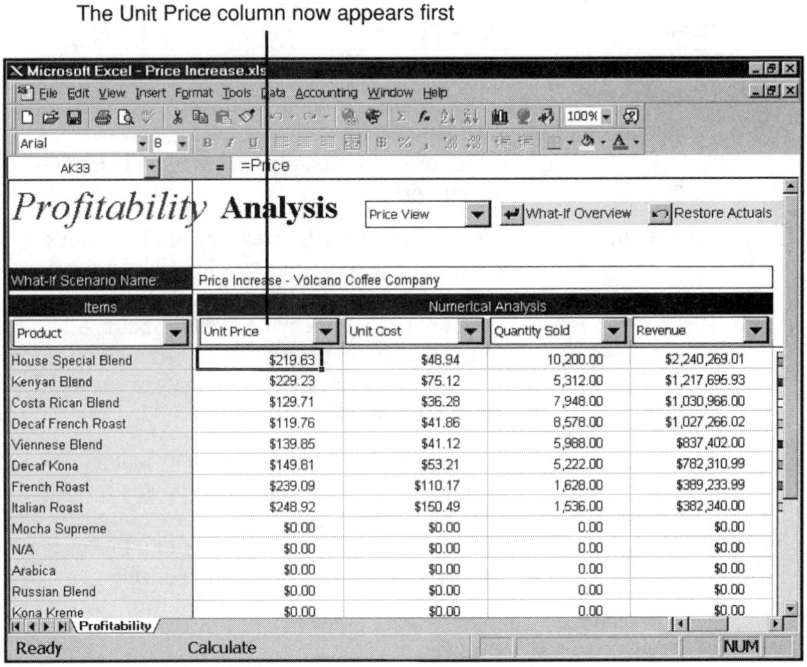

FIG. A.17
When you select Price View, the Unit Price moves to the left of the worksheet.

CAUTION

You may encounter long delays when Financial Manager saves a report or opens an existing report. This is because the calculations performed on the the accounting data take quite a bit of processing speed and available memory on your computer. To help speed things up, always free up system resources before using Financial Manager. Close programs you're not currently using.

TIP Use the Summary Page worksheet to compare your actual income statement to the scenarios you create. Be sure to save your scenarios first, then return to the What-If Overview sheet and select the Summary Page button.

Other What-If Scenarios You Can Use

There are five analysis categories you can use to perform what-if scenarios on your data. The previous steps showed you how to use the Profitability scenario. Each of the five categories lets you create a scenario whereas the Finance category lets you create three different ones. Table A.4 gives a description of each of the what-if scenarios you can create using the analysis category buttons.

Table A.4 What-If Scenarios

Scenario	Description
Profitability	Create a Profitability Analysis worksheet to view changes in your product mix pricing. You can choose to view revenue, total costs of sales or unit costs, product mix, and changes in unit prices.
AR/AP/Inv.	Opens the AR/AP/Inventory Analysis worksheet that you can use to adjust accounts receivable, accounts payable, and inventory dollar amounts or number of days. For example, find out what would happen if you reduced inventory to stock your product for 30 days of sales rather than 60.
Expenses	Creates an Expense Analysis worksheet that lets you adjust general expenses and see how the changes affect your profits. For example, what would happen if you gave your employees a raise or pared down your marketing costs?

Scenario	Description
Sell Assets	Opens the Sell Assests Wizard and creates a Finance Analysis worksheet that shows you a balance sheet summary of the effects of the sale of an asset, such as selling a computer or office copier machine.
Add a Loan	Opens the Add New Loan Wizard and creates a Finance Analysis worksheet that shows the effects of adding a new loan to your account. The worksheet details the effect on your company's cash position, and you can even view a payment schedule to see what the monthly payments would be like.
Pay Back Loan	Opens the Pay Back Loan Wizard and creates a Finance Analysis worksheet to show what a loan payoff will do to your finances.
Buy vs. Lease	Opens the Buy Versus Lease Wizard and creates a Lease Analysis worksheet you can use to compare costs of leasing, buying with a loan, or paying cash.

CAUTION

If your what-if analysis contains incorrect numbers, you may need to recheck your accounting data for partial detail transactions or errors. To update the information into Financial Manager, select Accounting, Import Wizard, and choose Update.

Analyzing Lease Options with the Lease Wizard

In the previous section, you learned how to use the What-If Wizard to speculate how changes you make to values in your accounting database will affect your financial bottom line. In this section, you continue building on those skills, by learning how to analyze a common decision among business owners—whether to lease or to buy.

The Small Business Financial Manager, in addition to all the other report and analysis tools, comes with the Analyze Buy Versus Lease Wizard. With this Wizard, you can carefully evaluate various financing options for accumulating assets of any kind. For example, if your company needs new office equipment or perhaps a new delivery truck. The Buy Versus Lease Wizard can help you determine which course to take, whether it's buy with a loan, lease, or pay cash (in full and up front).

Starting the Analyze Buy Versus Lease Wizard

The first step to using the Buy Versus Lease Wizard is to start a What-If Scenario or open an existing scenario. Next, you must start the Buy Versus Lease Wizard and enter the appropriate data. The last phase of the procedure will open the Lease Analysis worksheet where you can manipulate the data and see the results of making different decisions about buying and leasing.

The following steps walk you through the entire procedure:

1. From the Excel window, select Accounting, What-If Wizard.

   Or, from the Small Business Financial Manager startup screen, click the What-If Analysis button.
2. The What-If Wizard dialog box appears on-screen. Choose a company financial database to use. If yours isn't listed, click the Browse button and locate the database.
3. To continue, click the Next button, and the box displays options for opening a new or existing scenario.
4. To create a new scenario, click the New option and type in a name for the scenario. To use an existing scenario, click the Existing option and select a previously saved scenario from the drop-down list.
5. Next, select a starting date for accessing any particular portion of your financial data in the Begin Date box and an ending date in the End Date box.
6. Click Finish to continue.
7. The Save Scenario Workbook As box appears. Save your scenario by clicking the Save button.
8. The What-If Overview page appears on-screen, as shown in Figure A.18. Scroll to the right of the worksheet to locate the Buy vs. Lease category and click it.

TIP If you want to calculate tax benefits in your scenario, be sure to enter a tax rate in the Tax Rate cell before selecting the Buy vs. Lease button.

9. The Analyze Buy Versus Lease Wizard appears, as shown in Figure A.19. Fill out the fields for each of the options, as next described. You don't have to add dollar signs, percent signs, or commas to the entries. You must fill out all fields before continuing.
   - **Name of Asset** Type in a name of the asset, such as Car or Computer.
   - **Purchase Price** Enter the original price you expect to pay, including registration or license fees.
   - **Date of Purchase** Use the drop-down list to select a time period for the scenario.
   - **Sales Tax Rate** Enter sales tax that applies.
   - **Number of Months Asset Held** Type in how long you plan to hold the asset.
   - **Estimated Resale Value** Enter the amount you can get for selling the asset.

- **Opportunity Cost of Capital** Enter the opportunity cost of spending money for this asset—the money you'd lose by making this purchase instead of investing the money. (If necessary, use a Ratio report to help you with this number. Create a yearly rate Ratio report for a 12-month span of return on net worth ratios.)
- **Depreciation Life in Years** Estimate the depreciation life of the asset.

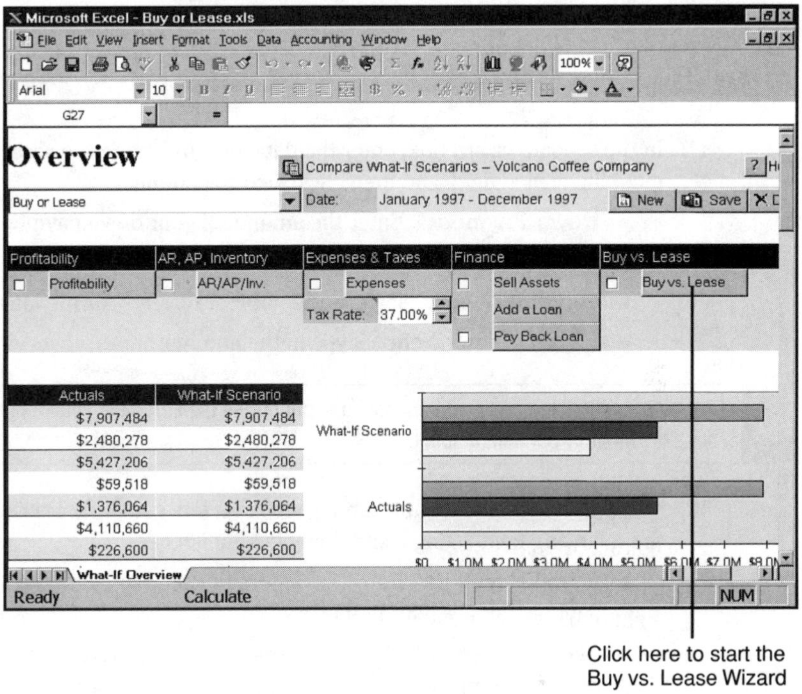

FIG. A.18 If necessary, scroll to the right of the What-If Overview worksheet to view the Buy vs. Lease category.

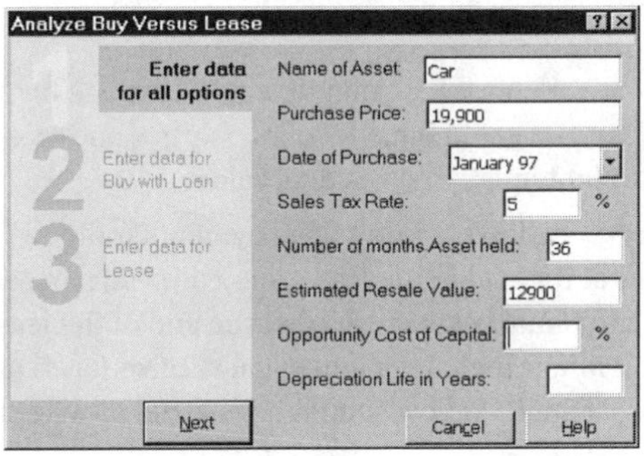

FIG. A.19 Use this wizard box to enter data for all options.

10. Click the Next button to continue, and the second wizard dialog box appears, as shown in Figure A.20.

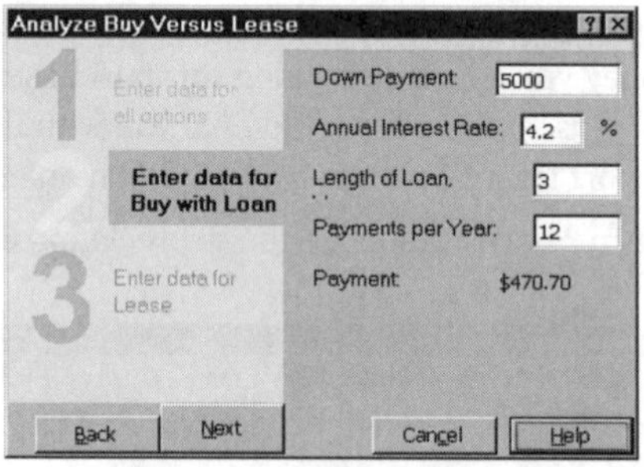

FIG. A.20
Use this wizard box to enter data pertaining to buying with a loan.

11. In the second wizard box, enter the data for purchasing the asset through a loan. You must fill in each field, and then click Next to continue.
    - **Down Payment** Enter the amount of your down payment if buying the asset.
    - **Annual Interest Rate** Enter an interest rate for the loan.
    - **Length of Loan** Type in the number of years for the loan.
    - **Payments per Year** Type in the number of payments you will make per year.

TIP After entering in all the pertinent information about buying the asset, the bottom of the dialog box shows the monthly payment amount.

12. The third wizard box, shown in Figure A.21, lets you enter leasing data. Fill out each of the following field listings, and then click Finish.
    - **Initial Payment** Enter the amount needed to begin the lease, including first payment and registration fees.
    - **Security Deposit** Enter the amount of a possible security deposit you may be required to make.
    - **Monthly Payment** Type in the amount you expect to pay each month, plus taxes.
    - **Residual Value** Enter the amount it would cost you to buy the asset at the end of the lease. Don't forget to include extra charges and fees (such as excess mileage) that might inflate the residual value.
    - **Other Outflows/Inflows** Enter any payments (outflow) or returns (inflow) you may encounter at the end of the lease, such as return of security deposit. Outflow includes any additional costs involved at the end of the lease or loan (such as appraisal fees); inflow includes money you receive (such as the resale amount if you sell the asset). (Net inflow should be entered as a negative number.)
13. The Lease Analysis worksheet now appears on-screen, as shown in Figure A.22. From here, you can experiment with different costs, interest rates, and other values to determine their affect on your finances.

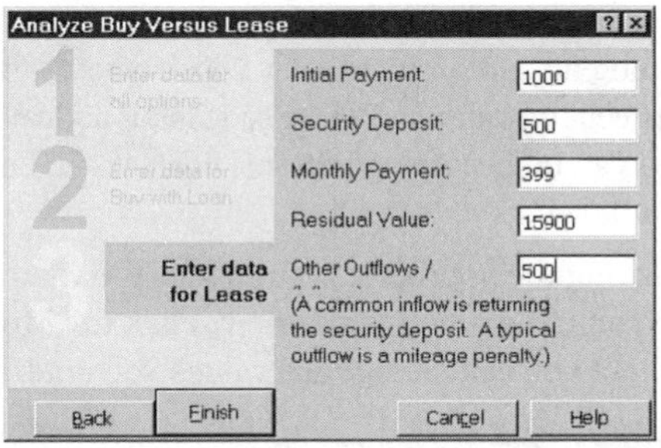

FIG. A.21
In the third Wizard box, enter data pertaining to the lease.

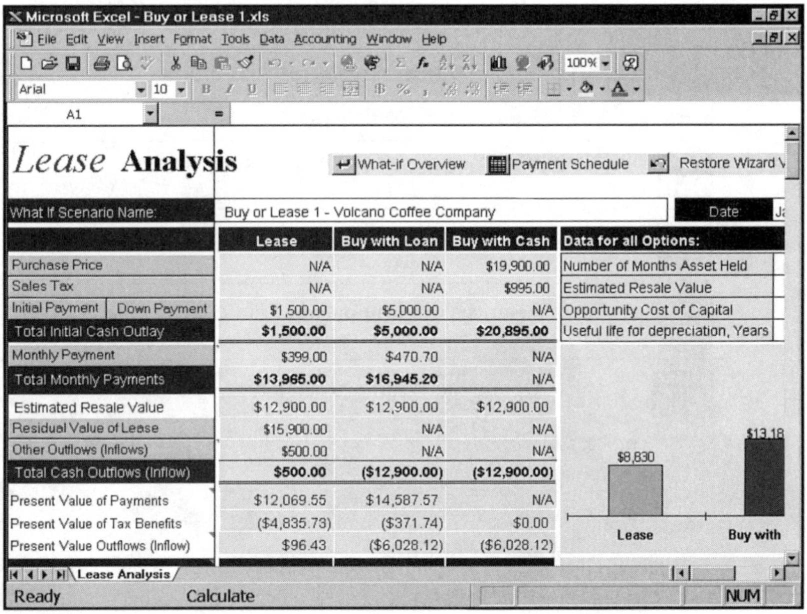

FIG. A.22
The Lease Analysis worksheet.

Working with the Lease Analysis Worksheet

The Lease Analysis worksheet (see Figure A.22) shows you cost comparisons of leasing, buying with a loan, or purchasing the asset with cash. You can change the values in this worksheet to see what different options may do to your costs. Notice the amounts are divided into three sections (rows) on the worksheet:

- **Total Initial Cash Outlay** This section summarizes upfront costs involved with starting the purchase or lease of the asset.
- **Total Monthly Payments** This section totals all the monthly payments involved for the loan or lease for the life of the loan or lease.

- **Total Cash Outflows (Inflow)** This row summarizes the costs involved at the end of the loan or lease, including any amount you may receive back. For example, if you sell the asset at its fully depreciated value, or if you're leasing and receive your security deposit back, the value is an inflow. Any additional costs tacked on at the end of your lease are considered outflows.

You can change a value by clicking the appropriate button for the value in the left column of the worksheet. For example, to change the monthly payment, click the Monthly Payment button. This opens the wizard box where you can change the values you entered.

The graph located at the far right of the worksheet shows comparisons of total costs for each option. Table A.5 explains how to use the buttons at the top of the worksheet.

Table A.5 Lease Analysis Worksheet Buttons

Button	Function
	Returns you to the Overview worksheet.
	Creates an amortization table of loan payments.
	Restores the original analysis values.
	Opens the Windows calculator.

CAUTION

If the calculations in the Lease Analysis worksheet use the wrong purchase option, you need to change the selection in the Choose One Option group at the bottom-right of the worksheet. Make sure you examine the different options and then select the most cost-effective one before returning to the What-If Overview worksheet.

TIP Click the Help button at the top-right side of the worksheet to access Financial Manager's Help window.

Analyzing a New Loan with the Add New Loan Wizard

You learned how to use the What-If Wizard to create different kinds of scenarios. Depending on the type of scenario you're creating, various wizards come into play. For example, you've already learned to use the Buy Versus Lease Wizard to make a Lease Analysis worksheet. In this section, you learn how to use the Add New Loan Wizard to create a Finance Analysis worksheet that you can use to see how a new loan will affect your company's finances.

Keep in mind that the Small Business Financial Manager has many wizards and worksheets you can use to help you clearly see the impact changes make on your financial data. Step-by-step, wizards help you pinpoint the data you want to examine—then it's up to you to manipulate the data and see what happens when you make changes.

Using the Add New Loan Wizard

The first step in using the Add New Loan Wizard is to start a What-If Scenario or open an existing scenario. Next, you must start the Add New Loan Wizard and enter the appropriate data. The last phase of the procedure will open the Finance Analysis worksheet, where you can manipulate the data and see the results of taking out a new loan.

Follow these steps to walk through the entire procedure:

1. From the Excel window, select Accounting, What-If Wizard.

   Or, from the Small Business Financial Manager startup screen, click the What-If Analysis button.
2. The What-If Wizard dialog box appears on-screen. Choose a company financial database to use. If yours isn't listed, click the Browse button and locate the database.
3. To continue, click the Next button, and the box displays options for opening a new or existing scenario.
4. To create a new scenario, click the New option and type in a name for the scenario. To use an existing scenario, click the Existing option and select a previously saved scenario from the drop-down list.
5. Next, select a starting date for accessing any particular portion of your financial data in the Begin Date box and an ending date in the End Date box.
6. Click Finish to continue.
7. The Save Scenario Workbook As box appears. Save your scenario by clicking the Save button.
8. The What-If Overview page appears on-screen, as shown in Figure A.23. Scroll to the right of the worksheet to locate the Finance category and click the Add a Loan button.
9. The Add New Loan Wizard appears, as shown in Figure A.24. Fill out the fields for each of the options, as next described. You don't have to add dollar signs, percent signs, or commas to the entries. You must fill out all fields before continuing.
   - **Loan or Lender Name** Enter the lender name or a name for the loan.
   - **Account Number** Select an account to place the loan in; use the drop-down arrow to display a list of your loan accounts.
   - **First Payment Date** Use the drop-down list to select a date for the first payment on this loan.
   - **Amount of Loan** Enter the total amount of the loan.
   - **Annual Interest Rate** Type in the interest rate you hope to use.

- **Length of Loan** Enter the number of years for the loan.
- **Payments per Year** Enter the number of payments you expect to make each year.

FIG. A.23
The What-If Overview worksheet.

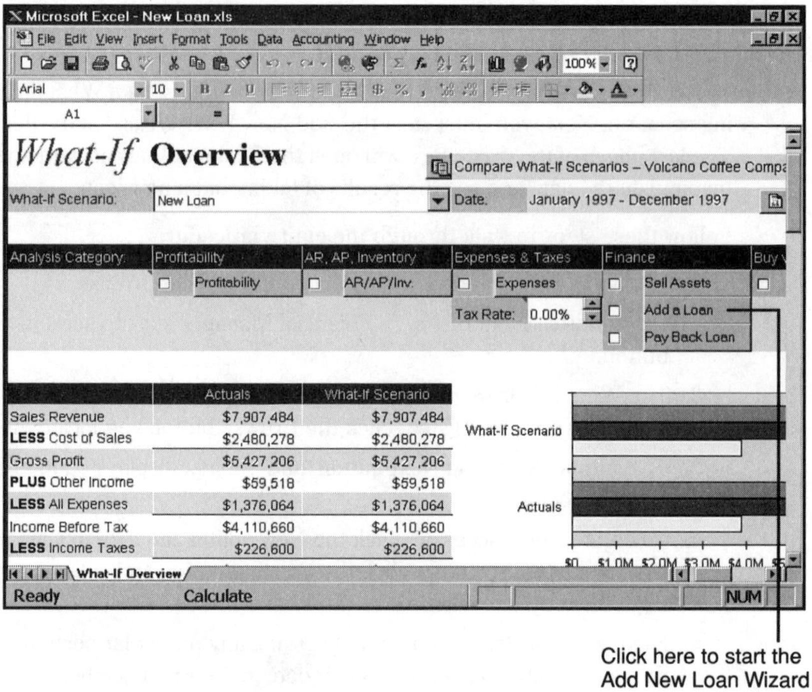

FIG. A.24
Fill out each field in the dialog box.

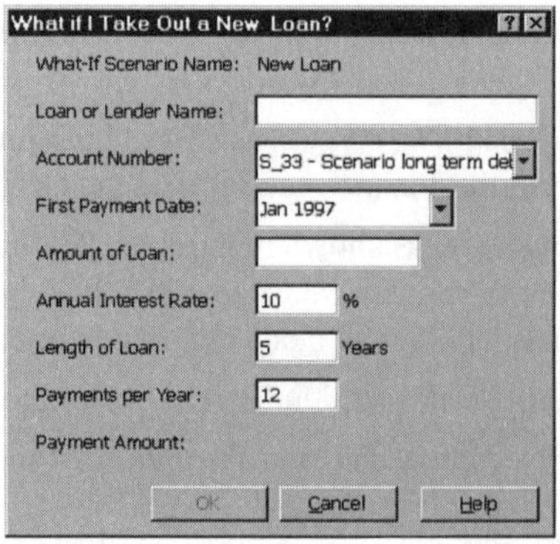

TIP After you enter all the pertinent information about the loan, the bottom of the dialog box shows the monthly payment amount.

10. Click the Finish button. The Finance Analysis worksheet now appears on-screen, as shown in Figure A.25. From here, you can experiment with different values involved with the loan and determine their effects on your finances.

FIG. A.25
The Finance Analysis worksheet.

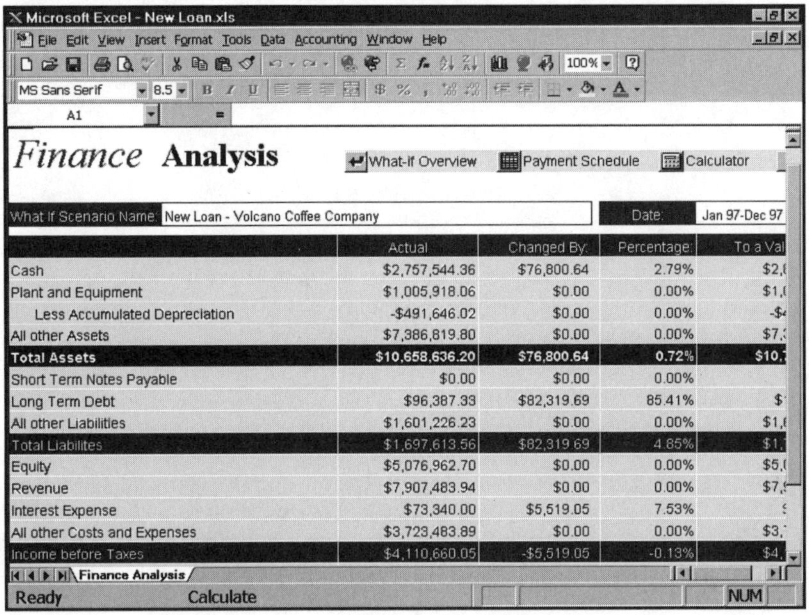

The Finance Analysis worksheet (refer to Figure A.25) shows you how your data changes when introducing a new loan. You can change the values in this worksheet to see what different options may do to your costs. Table A.6 explains how to use the buttons at the top of the worksheet.

Table A.6 Add New Loan Worksheet Buttons

Button	Function
	Returns you to the Overview worksheet.
	Creates an amortization table of loan payments.
	Opens the Windows calculator.
	Opens the Financial Manager Help window.

CAUTION

If you click the New button in the What-If Overview worksheet expecting to create a new what-if scenario, you won't be able to. Keep in mind that the New button copies the current scenario. You can then create a new scenario based on these values. If you want a completely new scenario, you'll need to use the What-If Wizard to build one.

APPENDIX B

Excel Function Reference

by Bruce Hallberg with Joyce Nielsen

- Database functions
- Date and time functions
- Financial functions
- Information functions
- Logical functions
- Lookup and reference functions
- Math and trig functions
- Statistical functions
- Text functions

Excel offers many functions to make your work easier. Although you certainly don't have to memorize all of the functions, having a sense of the functions and their uses will make your life easier when using Excel. Once you've located a function that you think will solve whatever problem you have, you can use a combination of the Paste Function dialog box, the Formula Palette, and the Office Assistant to guide you through using the function.

Spend some time browsing the following sections and tables so you have an idea of what is possible with the Excel functions. Then keep this information in the back of your mind as you use Excel in your day-to-day work.

If you need more detailed information on using and entering functions, refer to Chapter 6, "Using Excel Functions." You also can find extensive Help information in Excel for each of the individual functions, including examples of their use. To see Excel Help on a specific function, select the function category and function name for which you want help in the Paste Function dialog box, and then click the Office Assistant button in the lower-left corner of the dialog box. ■

NOTE In the syntax lines shown in the function tables of the following sections, all required arguments are indicated in ***bold italic***; optional arguments appear in *italic* only.

Database Functions

When you use Excel for data management, you often want to perform some of the simple mathematical operations on ranges of data, but only with a subset that matches some criteria. Using the database functions, you can do just that. Review Table B.1 to see what database functions are available for use in your data management projects.

Table B.1 Database Functions in Excel

Function Syntax	Returns
=DAVERAGE(***database,field,criteria***)	Average of cells within a database field that match the criteria
=DCOUNT(***database,*** *field*,***criteria***)	Count of cells within a database field that match the criteria
=DCOUNTA(***database,*** *field*,***criteria***)	Count of non-blank cells within a database field that match the criteria
=DGET(***database,field,criteria***)	Record from a database that matches the criteria
=DMAX(***database,field,criteria***)	Maximum value from a database field within records that match the criteria
=DMIN(***database,field,criteria***)	Minimum value from a database field within records that match the criteria
=DPRODUCT(***database,field,criteria***)	Product of cells within a field where the rows match the criteria
=DSTDEV(***database,field,criteria***)	Estimated standard deviation based on a sample of records that meet the criteria
=DSTDEVP(***database,field,criteria***)	Standard deviation based on an entire population of records that match the criteria
=DSUM(***database,field,criteria***)	Sum of a field within records that match the criteria
=DVAR(***database,field,criteria***)	Estimated variance of a field based on a sample of records that match the criteria
=DVARP(***database,field,criteria***)	Variance of a field (based on total population) within records that match the criteria
=GETPIVOTDATA(***pivot_table,name***)	Data stored within a PivotTable

Date and Time Functions

Date and time functions manipulate or calculate dates and times. These functions generally work using date *serial numbers*. A date serial number is a number that represents a date and time in our calendar, but that is easier to work with for calculations. Table B.2 details the date and time functions available in Excel.

Table B.2 Date and Time Functions in Excel

Function Syntax	Returns
=DATE(***year,month,day***)	Excel serial number of a specified date
=DATEVALUE(***date_text***)	Excel serial number for a text-based date entry
=DAY(***serial_number***)	Day of the month (1–31) for an Excel date serial number
=DAYS360(***start_date,end_date,****method*)	Number of days between two dates using a 360-day calendar
=HOUR(***serial_number***)	Hour (0–23) of an Excel serial number time value
=MINUTE(***serial_number***)	Minute (0–59) of an Excel serial number time value
=MONTH(***serial_number***)	Month (1–12) of an Excel serial number date value
=NOW( )	Current date and time
=SECOND(***serial_number***)	Second (0–59) of an Excel serial number time value
=TIME(***hour,minute,second***)	Excel serial number fraction (from 0 to 0.99999999) for specified time
=TIMEVALUE(***time_text***)	Excel serial number fraction for a text-based time entry
=TODAY( )	Serial number date for today's date, using the date set in the computer's clock/calendar
=WEEKDAY(***serial_number,****return_type*)	Day of the week (1–7) based on a date serial number
=YEAR(***serial_number***)	The year (from 1900 to 9999) an Excel date serial number represents

Financial Functions

Excel contains a number of financial functions that either directly or indirectly can solve just about any financial calculation you might require (see Table B.3). Common uses include calculating loan details, annuities, investment analyses, and so on. Broadly, these calculations are called *time value of money* calculations. The value of money changes with the passage of time because of interest that's charged (excepting any impact from inflation). Essentially, a dollar today is worth more than a dollar tomorrow because you can collect interest on that dollar over time. Similarly, a dollar borrowed today requires that you repay more than a dollar tomorrow because of the interest that you pay.

The financial functions accept some common arguments that you might not be familiar with if you don't have a business or financial background. These are the most common arguments found in the financial functions:

- *Present value.* The Present Value (PV) is what a stream of payments is worth at the beginning of the stream. It is directly affected by the interest rate used in the calculation. If no interest were charged whatsoever, the present value of a stream of payments would simply be the sum of all of the payments. Instead, almost all loans include interest (which may be good or bad depending on which side you're on). So the present value of the payments is less than the sum of the payments.
- *Number of periods.* The number of periods (Nper) corresponds to the *number of payments* made for an investment or loan. For example, a three-year loan with monthly payments would have 36 periods.
- *Payment.* Abbreviated by Excel as pmt, this is the amount either collected or paid for each period (keep in mind that not all transactions are monthly).
- *Future value.* The future value, or FV, of a loan or investment is its value at the end of all the periods. Examples of future values include loans with balloon payments and leases with purchase options. For example, consider a simple loan with no future value. Once the final payment is made, the amount originally borrowed, plus interest, is then repaid and no further monies are owed. The payments equal 100 percent of the amount borrowed. Some loans, however, defer some of the principle until the end of the term. In this case, the payments don't correspond to 100% of the principle, but rather to the difference between the present and future values. In such a loan, the payments are only for the *difference* between these two values.
- *Rate.* The rate is the interest rate being charged or paid. It is entered as a percentage *per period*. In other words, a loan with monthly payments that is quoted as having a 12 percent Annual Percentage Rate (APR) actually has an interest rate of *1 percent per period*, and it is the 1 percent that you would enter into the Excel function.
- *Type.* With a loan, you make payments at the end of each period, or *in arrears*. With a lease, you make rental payments at the beginning of each period, or *in advance*. Each method yields different values when calculating payments. Excel uses the Type argument to determine whether the calculation it will perform should be based on payments being made in advance or in arrears.

Table B.3 Financial Functions in Excel

Function Syntax	Returns
=DB(***cost,salvage,life,per***,*month*)	Depreciation of an asset using a fixed declining balance
=DDB(***cost,salvage,life,per***, *factor*)	Depreciation of an asset using the double-declining balance depreciation method or some other method that you specify
=FV(***rate,nper,pmt***,*pv,type*)	Future value of an investment using periodic payments and a fixed rate
=IPMT(***rate,per,nper,pv***,*fv,type*)	Interest payments required on an investment using a fixed rate
=IRR(***values***, *guess*)	Internal rate of return for a stream of cash flows
=MIRR(***values,finance_rate,reinvest_rate***)	Internal rate of return considering reinvestment of the stream of cash flows
=NPER(***rate,pmt,pv***, *fv,type*)	Number of periods required to achieve a target future value
=NPV(***rate,value1***,*value2,...*)	Net present value of an investment using a series of flexible payments
=PMT(***rate,nper,pv***,*fv,type*)	Payments on a fixed-rate loan
=PPMT(***rate,per,nper,pv***,*fv,type*)	Principle portion of payments on a fixed-rate loan
=PV(***rate,nper,pmt***,*fv,type*)	Present value of an investment
=RATE(***nper,pmt,pv***,*fv,type,guess*)	Interest rate returned or paid
=SLN(***cost,salvage,life***)	Straight-line depreciation on an asset for one period
=SYD(***cost,salvage,life,per***)	Sum of years' digits depreciation on an asset for a given period
=VDB(***cost,salvage,life,start_period, end_period***,*factor,no_switch*)	Depreciation amount for an asset for any period, using a variable-declining balance

Information Functions

Information functions typically answer questions about portions of your worksheet. For example, you can use an information function to find out if a specific cell is blank, what formatting is applied to it, its data type, or other types of information. Table B.4 covers the information functions in Excel.

Table B.4 Information Functions in Excel

Function Syntax	Returns
=CELL(***info_type,reference***)	Information on the formatting, location, or contents of a cell
=ERROR.TYPE(***error_val***)	Number that corresponds to an error value
=INFO(***type_text***)	Information about the current operating environment
=ISBLANK(***value***)	TRUE if value is a blank reference; otherwise, FALSE
=ISERR(***value***)	TRUE if value is any error (except #N/A); otherwise, FALSE
=ISERROR(***value***)	TRUE if value is any error value; otherwise, FALSE
=ISEVEN(***value***)	TRUE if value is even; otherwise FALSE
=ISLOGICAL(***value***)	TRUE if value is a logical value; otherwise, FALSE
=ISNA(***value***)	TRUE if value is the #N/A error value; otherwise, FALSE
=ISNONTEXT(***value***)	TRUE if value is not text; otherwise, FALSE
=ISNUMBER(***value***)	TRUE if value is a number; otherwise, FALSE
=ISODD(***value***)	TRUE if value is odd; otherwise FALSE
=ISREF(***value***)	TRUE if value is a reference; otherwise, FALSE
=ISTEXT(***value***)	TRUE if value is text; otherwise, FALSE
=N(***value***)	Number converted from a value using certain rules
=NA( )	Error value #N/A (value not available)
=TYPE(***value***)	Number indicating data type of a value

Logical Functions

Boolean algebra is based on a simple set of logical statements. For example, if value A is true and value B is true, the AND function will return true. You can use these types of logical functions to perform similar tests, and your functions can then provide some result based on whether a logical test is true or false. Table B.5 details the logical functions within Excel.

Table B.5 Logical Functions in Excel

Function Syntax	Returns
=AND(***logical1***,*logical2,...*)	TRUE if *all* arguments are true, or FALSE if any argument is false
=FALSE( )	The logical value FALSE

Function Syntax	Returns
=IF(***logical_test***,*value_if_true*, *value_if_false*)	Provides one of two results that you specify, based on whether the test evaluates to TRUE or FALSE
=NOT(***logical***)	Reverses a logical value; TRUE becomes FALSE and vice versa
=OR(***logical1***,*logical2*,...)	TRUE if any argument is true, or FALSE if *all* arguments are false
=TRUE( )	The logical value TRUE

Lookup and Reference Functions

When you work with lists of data in Excel, particularly large lists, you often need to find information within those lists as part of a worksheet function. The Lookup and Reference functions perform this job in a variety of ways to meet these needs. Some of these functions return cell references when the information is found, while others return the contents of the found cell (or nearby cells) using different data types. Table B.6 shows you the lookup and reference functions available in Excel 97.

Table B.6 Lookup and Reference Functions in Excel

Function Syntax	Returns
=ADDRESS(***row_num***,***column_num***, *abs_num*,*a1*,*sheet_text*)	Text for a given cell reference
=AREAS(***reference***)	Number of contiguous areas of data in a given cell range
=CHOOSE(***index_num***,***value1***,*value2*,...)	Value within a list based on an index
=COLUMN(*reference*)	Column number of a cell reference
=COLUMNS(***array***)	Number of columns in an array
=HLOOKUP(***lookup_value***,***table_array***, ***row_index_num***,*range_lookup*)	Value found in a cell using a horizontal (row-based) lookup in a table
=HYPERLINK(***link_location***,*friendly_name*)	Shortcut or jump to a document
=INDEX(***input***,*row_num*,*column_num*,*area_num*)	Value or cell reference from a table using an index value; use the *area_num* argument only in the cell reference form of this function
=INDIRECT(***ref_text***,*a1*)	Cell reference based on a text string
=LOOKUP(***lookup_value***,***array***)	Value from a single-dimension range (a one-row or one-column range)

continues

Table B.6 Continued

Function Syntax	Returns
=MATCH(***lookup_value,lookup_array,*** *match_type*)	Value indicating relative position of a matched item in an array
=OFFSET(***reference,rows,cols,****height,width*)	Cell reference that is indexed to a base position or range
=ROW(*reference*)	Row number of a cell reference
=ROWS(***array***)	Number of rows in an array
=TRANSPOSE(***array***)	Range of cells that is transposed from a base range (row becomes column or vice versa)
=VLOOKUP(***lookup_value,table_array, col_index_num,****range_lookup*)	Value found in a cell using a vertical (column-based) lookup in a table

Math and Trig Functions

Excel's math and trigonometric functions perform a wide variety of calculations. The functions can compute sines, cosines, factorials, exponents, logs, and other such functions. Table B.7 details these functions.

Table B.7 Math and Trig Functions in Excel

Function Syntax	Returns
=ABS(***number***)	Absolute (positive) value of a number, omitting any information to the right of the decimal place
=ACOS(***number***)	Arccosine of a number in radians
=ACOSH(***number***)	Inverse hyperbolic cosine of a number
=ASIN(***number***)	Arcsine of a number in radians
=ASINH(***number***)	Inverse hyperbolic sine of a number
=ATAN(***number***)	Arctangent of a number in radians
=ATAN2(***x_number,y_number***)	Arctangent of a coordinate in radians
=ATANH(***number***)	Inverse hyperbolic tangent of a number
=CEILING(***number,significance***)	Number rounded up to the nearest integer or multiple of specified significance
=COMBIN(***number,number_chosen***)	Number of combinations for a number of items
=COS(***number***)	Cosine of an angle

Function Syntax	Returns
=COSH(***number***)	Hyperbolic cosine of a number
=DEGREES(***angle***)	Number of degrees in the specified angle
=EVEN(***number***)	Number rounded up to the nearest even integer
=EXP(***number***)	Value of *e* raised to the power of the specified number
=FACT(***number***)	Factorial of a number
=FLOOR(***number,significance***)	Number rounded down to the nearest multiple of specified significance
=INT(***number***)	Number rounded down to the nearest integer
=LN(***number***)	Natural logarithm of a number
=LOG(***number,****base*)	Logarithm of a number using a base you specify
=LOG10(***number***)	Base-10 logarithm of a number
=MDETERM(***array***)	Matrix determinant of an array
=MINVERSE(***array***)	Inverse matrix for the matrix stored in a specified array
=MMULT(***array1,array2***)	Matrix product of two arrays
=MOD(***number,divisor***)	The remainder, after a number is divided by specified divisor
=ODD(***number***)	Number rounded up to the nearest odd integer
=PI( )	Value of π to 15 digits of accuracy
=POWER(***number,power***)	Number raised to the specified power.
=PRODUCT(***number1,****number2,...*)	Product of a series of numbers
=RADIANS(***angle***)	Radian of the specified angle
=RAND( )	Random number between 0 and 1 (result changes each time a worksheet is recalculated)
=ROMAN(***number,****form*)	Roman numeral representation of a number
=ROUND(***number,num_digits***)	Number rounded up to the specified number of digits
=ROUNDDOWN(***number,num_digits***)	Number rounded down (towards zero)
=ROUNDUP(***number,num_digits***)	Number rounded up (away from zero)

continues

Table B.7 Continued

Function Syntax	Returns
=SIGN(***number***)	Sign of a specified number (1=positive, 0=zero, -1=negative)
=SIN(***number***)	Sine of an angle
=SINH(***number***)	Hyperbolic sine of a number
=SQRT(***number***)	Square root of a number
=SUBTOTAL(***function_num,ref1,...***)	Subtotal in a series of numbers
=SUM(***number1***,*number2*,***...***)	Sum of an entire series of numbers
=SUMIF(***range,criteria***,*sum_range*)	Sum of a series of numbers that meet a certain criteria
=SUMPRODUCT(***array1***,*array2*,***...***)	Product of a series of arrays
=SUMSQ(***number1***,*number2*,***...***)	Sum of the squares of a list of numbers
=SUMX2MY2(***array_x,array_y***)	Sum of differences between two squares of corresponding numbers
=SUMX2PY2(***array_x,array_y***)	Sum of sums of squares of series of corresponding numbers
=SUMXMY2(***array_x,array_y***)	Sum of the squares of the differences of corresponding series of numbers
=TAN(***number***)	Tangent of an angle
=TANH(***number***)	Hyperbolic tangent of a number
=TRUNC(***number***,*num_digits*)	Number truncated to an integer with specified number of digits

Statistical Functions

Excel's statistical functions operate on lists of data. The simplest of these functions is AVERAGE, but this group of functions also can perform such jobs as calculating deviations, distributions, correlations, slopes, and even Poisson distributions. Table B.8 lists Excel's statistical functions.

Table B.8 Statistical Functions in Excel

Function Syntax	Returns
=AVEDEV(***number1***,*number2*,***...***)	Average of absolute deviations of data points from their mean

Function Syntax	Returns
=AVERAGE(***number1***,*number2*,...)	Arithmetic mean of a series of numbers
=AVERAGEA(***value1***,*value2*,...)	Arithmetic mean of a series of numbers or text entries (text and FALSE arguments evaluate to 0; TRUE arguments evaluate to 1)
=BETADIST(***x***,***alpha***,***beta***,*a*,*b*)	Cumulative beta probability density
=BETAINV(***probability***,***alpha***,***beta***,*a*,*b*)	Inverse of the BETADIST function
=BINOMDIST(***number_s***,***trials***, ***probability_s***,***cumulative***)	Individual term binomial distribution probability
=CHIDIST(***x***,***deg_freedom***)	One-tailed probability of a chi-squared distribution
=CHIINV(***probability***,***deg_freedom***)	Inverse of the CHIDIST function
=CHITEST(***actual_range***,***expected_range***)	Test for independence for a chi-squared distribution
=CONFIDENCE(***alpha***,***standard_dev***,***size***)	Confidence interval for population mean
=CORREL(***array1***,***array2***)	Correlation coefficient for two sets of data
=COUNT(***value1***,*value2*,...)	Number of entries in a series that contain number values
=COUNTA(***value1***,*value2*,...)	Number of non-empty cells within a series
=COUNTBLANK(***range***)	Number of empty cells in a specified range
=COUNTIF(***range***,***criteria***)	Number of cells that meet the specified criteria
=COVAR(***array1***,***array2***)	Covariance (average of the products of deviations) for two data sets
=CRITBINOM(***trials***,***probability_s***,***alpha***)	Smallest value for which the cumulative binomial distribution is greater than or equal to a set criteria

continues

Table B.8 Continued

Function Syntax	Returns
=DEVSQ(***number1***,*number2*)	Sum of squares of deviations of data points from their sample mean
=EXPONDIST(***x,lambda,cumulative***)	Exponential distribution
=FDIST(***x,deg_freedom1,deg_freedom2***)	F probability distribution (degree of diversity) for two data sets
=FINV(***probability,deg_freedom1,deg_freedom2***)	Inverse of the FDIST function
=FISHER(***x***)	Fisher transformation
=FISHERINV(***y***)	Inverse Fisher transformation
=FORECAST(***x,known_y's,known_x's***)	Predicted future value using a linear trend, based on existing values
=FREQUENCY(***data_array,bins_array***)	Array of value frequency within an array
=FTEST(***array1,array2***)	Result of an F-test (probability that the variances in the arrays aren't significantly different)
=GAMMADIST(***x,alpha,beta,cumulative***)	Gamma distribution
=GAMMAINV(***probability,alpha,beta***)	Inverse of GAMMADIST
=GAMMALN(***x***)	Natural logarithm of the gamma function
=GEOMEAN(***number1***,*number2,...*)	Geometric mean of an array or range of positive numbers
=GROWTH(***known_y's***,*known_x's,new_x's,const*)	Predicted exponential growth of a series, based on existing data
=HARMEAN(***number1***,*number2,...*)	Harmonic mean of a series of positive numbers
=HYPGEOMDIST(***sample_s,number_sample, population_s,number_population***)	Hypergeometric distribution
=INTERCEPT(***known_y's,known_x's***)	Point at which a line will intersect the y-axis, using given x- and y-values
=KURT(***number1***,*number2,...*)	Kurtosis of a series of numbers
=LARGE(***array,k***)	Kth largest value in an array

Function Syntax	Returns
=LINEST(***known_ y's***,*known_x's,const,stats*)	Least-squares linear estimate line
=LOGEST(***known_ y's***,*known_x's,const,stats*)	Array of values describing an exponential curve based on regression analysis
=LOGINV(***probability,mean,standard_dev***)	Inverse of the LOGNORMDIST function
=LOGNORMDIST(***x,mean,standard_dev***)	Cumulative lognormal distribution function of x
=MAX(***number1***,*number2,...*)	Largest value in a series
=MAXA(***value1***,*value2,...*)	Largest value in a series, including text and logical values
=MEDIAN(***number1***,*number2,...*)	Median (middle) value in a series
=MIN(***number1***,*number2,...*)	Smallest value in a series
=MINA(***value1***,*value2,...*)	Smallest value in a series, including text and logical values
=MODE(***number1***,*number2,...*)	Most frequently occurring value in a series
=NEGBINOMDIST(***number_f,number_s, probability_s***)	Negative binomial distribution
=NORMDIST(***x,mean,standard_dev,cumulative***)	Normal cumulative distribution
=NORMINV(***probability,mean,standard_dev***)	Inverse of the NORMDIST function
=NORMSDIST(***z***)	Standard normal cumulative distribution (uses a mean of zero, and a standard deviation of one)
=NORMSINV(***probability***)	Inverse of the NORMSDIST function
=PEARSON(***array1,array2***)	Pearson product moment correlation coefficient (*r*)
=PERCENTILE(***array,k***)	Kth percentile of values in an array
=PERCENTRANK(***array,x***,*significance*)	Rank of a value returned as a percentage of the set
=PERMUT(***number,number_chosen***)	Number of permutations
=POISSON(***x,mean,cumulative***)	Poisson distribution

continues

Table B.8 Continued

Function Syntax	Returns
=PROB(***x_range*,*prob_range*,*lower_limit***,*upper_limit*)	Probability that values are within upper- and lower-limit ranges
=QUARTILE(***array*,*quart***)	Quartile of a set of data
=RANK(***number*,*ref***,*order*)	Rank of a number in a list (relative size)
=RSQ(***known_y's*,*known_x's***)	Square of the Pearson product moment correlation coefficient
=SKEW(***number1***,*number2*,...)	Distribution skewness
=SLOPE(***known_y's*,*known_x's***)	Slope of a linear regression
=SMALL(***array*,*k***)	Kth smallest value in an array
=STANDARDIZE(***x*,*mean*,*standard_dev***)	Normalized value from a distribution
=STDEV(***number1***,*number2*,...)	Standard deviation based on a sample
=STDEVA(***value1***,*value2*,...)	Standard deviation based on a sample, including text and logical values
=STDEVP(***number1***,*number2*,...)	Standard deviation for entire population
=STDEVPA(***value1***,*value2*,...)	Standard deviation for entire population, including text and logical values
=STEYX(***known_y's*,*known_x's***)	Standard error for predicted y-value for each *x* in a regression
=TDIST(***x*,*degrees_freedom*,*tails***)	Student's t-distribution
=TINV(***probability*,*degrees_freedom***)	Inverse of the TDIST function
=TREND(***known_y's***,*known_x's*,*new_x's*,*const*)	Values from a linear trend, using the least squares method
=TRIMMEAN(***array*,*percent***)	Mean of interior portion of a set
=TTEST(***array1*,*array2*,*tails*,*type***)	Probability for Student's t-test
=VAR(***number1***,*number2*,...)	Variance of a sample
=VARA(***value1***,*value2*,...)	Variance of a sample, including text and logical values
=VARP(***number1***,*number2*,...)	Variance for an entire population

Function Syntax	Returns
=VARPA(***value1***,*value2,...*)	Variance for an entire population, including text and logical values
=WEIBULL(***x,alpha,beta,cumulative***)	Weibull distribution
=ZTEST(***array,x***,*sigma*)	Two-tailed P-value for a z-test

Text Functions

When working with text in worksheets, you often need to manipulate that text, or convert it to something else, or extract data from within the text strings. The text functions within Excel are like a Swiss Army Knife for manipulating text information. Table B.9 shows you these versatile functions.

Table B.9 Text Functions in Excel

Function Syntax	Returns
=CHAR(***number***)	Character based on a code number from within the selected character set
=CLEAN(***text***)	Text with all unprintable characters removed
=CODE(***text***)	Code number of the first character of a string
=CONCATENATE(***text1***,*text2,...*)	Joined text strings
=DOLLAR(***number***,*decimals*)	Text representation of a number using a currency format
=EXACT(***text1,text2***)	Logical TRUE or FALSE based on whether two pieces of text match (case-sensitive)
=FIND(***find_text,within_text***,*start_num*)	Index number locating a text string from within a larger string based on a criteria
=FIXED(***number***,*decimals,no_commas*)	Text form of a number, rounded
=LEFT(***text***,*num_chars*)	Left-most portion of a text string at a given length
=LEN(***text***)	Number of characters in a string
=LOWER(***text***)	Lowercase-only string based on another string
=MID(***text,start_num,num_chars***)	Middle of a text string based on a starting position and length that you specify

continues

Table B.9 Continued

Function Syntax	Returns
=PROPER(***text***)	Text string converted to title case (first letter of each word capitalized)
=REPLACE(***old_text,start_num, num_chars,new_text***)	Replaces part of a text string with another text string
=REPT(***text,number_times***)	Repeated set of text strings, a specified number of times
=RIGHT(***text***,*num_chars*)	Right-most portion of a text string at a given length
=SEARCH(***find_text,within_text,*** *start_num*)	Index number where search text is found within a text string
=SUBSTITUTE(***text,old_text, new_text***,*instance_num*)	Text with a portion of a text string replaced by another text string
=T(***value***)	Text of a specified value
=TEXT(***value,format_text***)	Text based on a value, in a given number format
=TRIM(***text***)	Text with extra spaces removed (except single spaces between words)
=UPPER(***text***)	Uppercase-only string based on another string
=VALUE(***text***)	Value of a numerical text string

APPENDIX C

Excel Shortcuts

If you prefer using the keyboard to navigate and select commands, Excel offers hundreds of key combinations you can use to build and work with Excel worksheets and tasks, as detailed in this appendix. If you're a mouse user, you too can benefit from learning to use shortcut keys. They can speed up data entry and worksheet navigation considerably, if you don't mind taking the time to memorize the key combinations.

Keyboard Shortcuts

For many users, the keyboard is a faster way to enter data than the mouse is. Instead of clicking your way around a worksheet and entering numbers and text, it's faster to type in the data and use the shortcut keys to navigate from cell to cell.

The keyboard also offers numerous shortcut keys to activate commonly used commands. Unfortunately, you must memorize keyboard shortcuts in order to use them to their best advantage. The Excel menus sometimes list keyboard shortcuts for some commands, but the best way to learn is through lots of Excel use.

The following tables list the various keyboard keys you can use, along with the menu commands they activate or a description of their functions.

Table C.1 Data Entry Shortcut Keys

Press	Result
Enter	Completes a cell entry and moves to next cell in the series
Tab	Completes a cell entry and moves to next adjacent cell to the right
Shift+Tab	Completes a cell entry and moves to next adjacent cell to the left
Shift+Enter	Completes a cell entry and moves up to next cell in the series
Alt+Enter	Starts a new line in the same cell
Esc	Cancels a cell entry
Delete	Deletes the character to the right of the insertion point
Backspace	Deletes the character to the left of the insertion point
Ctrl+Delete	Deletes text to the end of the current line
Home	Moves to the beginning of the line
End	Moves to the end of the current line
Arrow keys	Move up, down, left, or right by character
Ctrl+Y or F4	Repeats the last action
Shift+F2	Edits a cell comment note
Ctrl+D	Fills series down
Ctrl+R	Fills series right
Ctrl+Enter	Fills selected range with current entry
Ctrl+Shift+F3	Uses row and column labels to create names

Table C.2 Formula Bar Shortcut Keys

Press	Result
=	Starts a formula
Esc	Cancels entry
F2	Edits the selected cell
Enter	Completes a cell entry
Backspace	Clears the selected cell or deletes the preceding character
Ctrl+F3	Defines a name
F3	Pastes a name into the formula
Shift+F9	Calculates the current worksheet
F9	Calculates all open workbook sheets
Alt+=	Inserts the AutoSum formula
Ctrl+;	Enters the date
Ctrl+Shift+:	Enters the time
Ctrl+K	Inserts a hyperlink
Alt+Down Arrow	Displays the AutoComplete list
Ctrl+Shift+A	Inserts the argument names and parentheses for a function after you type a function name
Ctrl+A	Opens the Formula Palette
Ctrl+Shift+Enter	Enters a formula as an array
Ctrl+Shift+' or Ctrl+'	Copies the value from the cell above or the selected cell into the Formula bar
Ctrl+‘	Alternates between displaying values or formulas in a cell

Table C.3 Formatting Shortcut Keys

Press	Result
Alt+'	Displays the Style dialog box (Format, Style)
Ctrl+1	Displays the Format Cells dialog box (Format, Cells)
Ctrl+B	Applies bold formatting
Ctrl+I	Applies italics
Ctrl+U	Applies underline

continues

Table C.3 Continued

Press	Result
Ctrl+5	Applies strikethrough formatting
Ctrl+~	Applies General number format
Ctrl+Shift+$	Applies Currency number format
Ctrl+Shift+%	Applies Percentage number format
Ctrl+Shift+^	Applies Exponential number format with two decimal points
Ctrl+Shift+#	Applies the Date number format with day, month, and year
Ctrl+Shift+@	Applies the Time number format with hour, minute, and AM or PM
Ctrl+Shift+!	Applies the Number format with two decimal places
Ctrl+9	Hides rows
Ctrl+Shift+(	Unhides rows
Ctrl+0	Hides columns
Ctrl+Shift+)	Unhides columns
Ctrl+Shift+&	Adds outline border
Crtl+Shift+_(underscore)	Removes all borders
Ctrl+K	Inserts a hyperlink

Table C.4 Editing Shortcut Keys

Press	Result
Ctrl+C	Copies the selection
Ctrl+V	Pastes the selection
Ctrl+X	Cuts the selection
Delete	Clears selection or cell contents
Ctrl+-	Deletes selection
Ctrl+Z	Undoes the last action
Ctrl+Shift++	Inserts blank cells
F2	Edits current cell
Enter	Completes a cell entry
Esc	Cancels entry

Press	Result
Backspace	Deletes preceding character
F3	Pastes a name into the formula
Ctrl+P	Opens the Print dialog box
Ctrl+Y	Repeats your last action
Alt+Enter	Starts a new line in the same cell
Arrow keys	Move up, down, right, or left
Ctrl+Shift+*	Selects range adjacent to current cell
Shift+*arrow key*	Extends selection by one cell in specified direction
Ctrl+Shift+*arrow key*	Extends selection to last non-blank cell in specified direction
Shift+Home	Extends selection to beginning of row
Ctrl+Shift+Home	Extends selection to beginning of worksheet
Ctrl+Shift+End	Extends selection to last used cell in worksheet
Ctrl+Spacebar	Selects entire column
Shift+Spacebar	Selects entire row
Ctrl+A	Selects entire worksheet
Shift+Page Down	Extends selection down one screen
Shift+Page Up	Extends selection up one screen
Ctrl+Shift+Spacebar	Selects all objects on sheet
Ctrl+6	Hides or displays objects
Ctrl+P	Prints file
Ctrl+9	Hides rows
Ctrl+Shift+(	Unhides rows
Ctrl+0	Hides columns
Ctrl+Shift+)	Unhides columns
Ctrl+–	Deletes the selection
Crtl+Z	Undoes your last action
Ctrl+Delete	Deletes all the text to the end of the line
Ctrl+D	Fills down
Ctrl+R	Fills to right
Ctrl+Enter	Fills the selected range with the current data

Table C.5 Navigation Shortcut Keys

Press	Result
Tab	Moves from left to right
Shift+Tab	Moves from right to left
Shift+Enter	Moves from bottom to top within a selected range
Ctrl+.	Moves clockwise to the next corner within the selection
Ctrl+Alt+Right arrow	Moves to the right between nonadjacent selections
Ctrl+Alt+Left arrow	Moves to the left between nonadjacent selections
Home	Moves to the beginning of the row
Ctrl+Home	Moves to the beginning of the worksheet
Ctrl+End	Moves to the last cell of the worksheet
Page Down	Moves down one screen
Page Up	Moves up one screen
Alt+Page Down	Moves one screen left
Alt+Page Up	Moves one screen right
Ctrl+Page Down	Moves to the next worksheet in the workbook
Ctrl+Page Up	Moves to the previous worksheet in the workbook
Ctrl+F6 or Ctrl+Tab	Moves to the next workbook window
Ctrl+Shift+F6 or Ctrl+Shift+Tab	Moves to the previous workbook window
F6	Moves to the next pane
Shift+F6	Moves to the previous pane
Ctrl+Backspace	Scrolls to display the active cell
End	Turns End mode on or off
End+*arrow key*	Moves one data block in a row or column
End+Enter	Moves to last cell to the right that's not blank

Table C.6 Menu Shortcut Keys

Press	Result
Shift+F10	Displays the shortcut menu
F10 or Alt	Makes the menu bar active

Press	Result
Alt+Spacebar	Shows the program icon menu
Down arrow	Selects the next command on the menu or submenu
Up arrow	Selects the previous command on the menu or submenu
Home	Selects the first command on the menu or submenu
End	Selects the last command on the menu or submenu
Esc	Closes the active menu or submenu

Table C.7 Toolbar Shortcut Keys

Press	Result
Ctrl+Tab	Selects the next toolbar
Ctrl+Shift+Tab	Selects the previous toolbar
Arrow keys	Highlight an option from a drop-down list
Enter	Selects an option from a drop-down list
Tab	Selects the next toolbar button
Shift+Tab	Selects the previous toolbar button
Ctrl+7	Shows or hides Standard toolbar

Table C.8 Dialog Box Shortcut Keys

Press	Result
Ctrl+Tab or Ctrl+Page Down	Switches to next tab
Ctrl+Shift+Tab or Ctrl+Page Up	Switches to previous tab
Tab	Moves to next option
Shift+Tab	Moves to previous option
Arrow keys	Moves between options or list items
Spacebar	Performs action or clears the active check box
Alt+Down arrow	Opens drop-down list box
Esc	Closes drop-down list box or closes dialog box
Enter	Performs action, activates selection

Table C.9 Office Assistant Shortcut Keys

Press	Result
Alt+F6	Activates the Office Assistant message balloon
Alt+*topic number*	Chooses a help topic from the list
Alt+Down arrow	Displays more help topics
Alt+Up arrow	Displays previous help topics
Esc	Closes Office Assistant message or tips
F1	Opens Office Assistant
Alt+N	Displays next tip
Alt+B	Displays previous tip

Table C.10 Database and PivotTable Shortcut Keys

Press	Result
Alt+key	Selects a field or command button
Down arrow	Moves to same field in next record
Up arrow	Moves to same field in previous record
Tab	Moves to the next field to edit
Shift+Tab	Moves to previous field to edit
Enter	Moves to the first field in the next record
Shift+Enter	Moves to the first field in the previous record
Page Down	Moves to the same field 10 records forward
Page Up	Moves to the same field 10 records back
Ctrl+Page Down	Moves to the new record
Ctrl+Page Up	Moves to the first record
Home	Moves to the beginning of a field
End	Moves to the end of a field
Left arrow	Moves one character left
Right arrow	Moves one character right
Shift+Home	Extends a selection to the beginning of a field
Shift+End	Extends a selection to the end of a field
Shift+Left arrow	Selects the character to the left

Press	Result
Shift+Right arrow	Selects the character to the right
Alt+Down arrow	Displays the AutoFilter list for active column
Alt+Up arrow	Closes the AutoFilter list
Down arrow	Selects the next item in the AutoFilter list
Up arrow	Selects the previous item in the AutoFilter list

Table C.11 Function Keys

Press	Result
F1	Opens Excel's Help feature via the Office Assistant
Shift+F1	Activates the What's This? help command
F2	Activates the Formula bar
Shift+F2	Allows adding or Editing of comment notes
Ctrl+F2	Activates the Show Info option
F3	Activates the Paste Name command
Shift+F3	Activates the Paste Function command
Ctrl+F3	Activates the Define Names command
Ctrl+Shift+F3	Activates the Create Names command
F4	Repeats last action
Ctrl+F4	Closes the worksheet
Alt+F4	Closes Excel
F5	Opens the Go To command
Shift+F5	Activates the Find command
Ctrl+F5	Restores the window to original size
F6	Moves to next pane
Shift+F6	Moves to previous pane
Ctrl+F6	Opens the next workbook window
Ctrl+Shift+F6	Opens the previous workbook window
F7	Opens the Spell Check tool
Ctrl+F7	Moves the program window

continues

Table C.11 Continued

Press	Result
F8	Turns on Extend mode
Shift+F8	Turns on Add mode
F9	Activates the Calculate Now command
Shift+F9	Activates the Calculate Sheet command
Ctrl+F9	Minimizes the program window
F10	Activates the menu bar
Shift+F10	Displays the shortcut menu
Ctrl+F10	Maximizes the program window
F11	Activates the New Chart command
Shift+F11	Activates the New Worksheet command
Ctrl+F11	Activates the New Excel 4 Macro Sheet
F12	Opens the Save As dialog box
Shift+F12	Saves the file
Ctrl+F12	Opens the Open dialog box
Ctrl+Shift+F12	Prints the file

APPENDIX D

Business Sites on the Web

This appendix is a list of business resources you can find on the Internet. Whether you're just in the planning and startup phase of your business, you're involved in international trade, you need legal or accounting assistance, or you're interested in the latest trade shows and conferences, you'll find a Web site here that can help you find answers.

Business Startup and Planning

America's Brightest

http://www.americasbrightest.com/

This Santa Monica-based organization describes itself as the "one-stop shop" for small businesses and working professionals. A subscription-based service with a one-month free trial, America's Brightest offers giveaways and wide range of discussion groups.

Big Dreams

http://vanbc.wimsey.com/~duncans/

Big Dreams is an online newsletter dedicated to individuals starting their own businesses. Visit the site and play the Business Game to ask yourself key questions about your new business, or take a look through current and archived issues for topical articles.

BizTalk

http://www.biztalk.com/

BizTalk is an electronic magazine devoted to small business. Departments include news, finance, law, politics, technology, and more. *BizTalk* runs contests to provide seed money for start-ups.

Business Plan Resource File

http://www.aifr.com/startup.html

Sponsored by the American Institute for Financial Research, this site is designed to help emerging business with their first business plan. A full compendium of general advice is offered in addition to having information on interactive business plan software.

Business Research Lab

http://spider.netropolis.net/brl/brl1.htm

This site is dedicated to the development of market research, an essential element for start-ups. Filled with tips and articles on conducting surveys and focus groups, the site also has a large number of sample surveys on file.

BuyersZone

http://www.buyerszone.com/index.html

BuyersZone is an online buyer's guide for businesses. It includes articles on what to look for in everything from 401(k) plans to voice mail systems. Also featured is The Inside Scoop, which offers the latest tips and stories of "buying disasters."

CCH Business Owner's Toolkit

http://www.toolkit.cch.com/

CCH (Commerce Clearing House) features articles on Small Office, Home Office (SOHO) guides to everyday business, coupled with a comprehensive listing of business tools, including model business forms, financial templates, and check lists.

Education, Training, and Development Resource Center for Business and Industry

http://www.tasl.com/tasl/home.html

This page, sponsored by Training and Seminar Locators Inc., offers help in finding business education resources. It includes an index of qualified training providers and information about products and services.

Internal Revenue Service

http://www.irs.ustreas.gov/

An important step in planning your business is to establish your tax status and potential responsibilities. The new IRS site has a special "Tax Info for Business" section with many helpful tax guides, including the Tax Calendar to keep track of special deadlines, a Business Tax Kit (a downloadable package of forms and publications), and the interactive Tax Trails for Business.

LinkExchange

http://www.linkexchange.com/

LinkExchange is an online advertising network that claims more than 100,000 members. If you have a Web site to promote, you can join for free; you then display ads for other members, and they display ads for you. There are also low-cost paid services.

Marketing Resource Center

http://www.marketingsource.com/

A free service of Concept Marketing Group, Inc., the Marketing Resource Center has an extensive articles library on planning your business, marketing tools and contacts, a database of industry associations, and links to online business magazines.

Marketshares

http://www.marketshares.com/

Marketshares tracks the best commercial and corporate Web sites. You can use their built-in search engine or browse their categories including Arts & Entertainment, Business & Technology, Finance & Money, and Travel & Transportation. Most links include a paragraph describing the site.

PRONET

http://www.pronett.com/

PRONET is a Multilingual Interactive Business Centre: The corporate philosophy is to help small- to medium-sized businesses grow by helping them use the Internet as a natural extension of their communications and marketing programs.

Occupational Safety and Health Administration

http://www.osha.gov/

Aside from a wealth of information on health and safety regulations and statistics, the OSHA site features software advisors that you can download on confined space standards, and asbestos regulations to help you figure out your requirements.

Small Business Advisor

http://www.isquare.com/

A terrific collection of articles for the new businessperson forms the core of this site. Example titles include "Don't Make These Business Mistakes," "Getting Paid," and "Government Small Business Resources." You'll also find tax advice and a glossary of business terms.

Small Business Workshop

http://www.sb.gov.bc.ca:80/smallbus/workshop/workshop.html

Sponsored by the Canadian government, this site has a host of articles for any business around the world. Areas include Starting Your Business, Marketing Basics, Planning Fundamentals, Financing Your Business, and Basic Regulations.

Tax Planning

http://www.hooked.net/cpa/plan/index.html

"An ounce of prevention…" is certainly worth more than a pound when it comes to taxes. This site specializes in information on tax planning—for individuals, businesses, and even an IRS audit. Take the tax challenge to find out how much you don't know about taxes.

Tax Prophet

http://www.taxprophet.com/

Hosted by Robert Sommers, the tax columnist for the *San Francisco Examiner*, the Tax Prophet has a number of FAQ files on tax issues and tax information for foreigners living in the U.S. The Interactive Tax Applications is very informative; try the Independent Contractor versus Employee Flowchart to check your job status.

U.S. Small Business Administration

http://www.sbaonline.sba.gov/

SBA Online is your online resource to government assistance for the small businessman. The site is organized into special areas on Starting, Financing, and Expanding Your Business, as well as other information on SCORE, PRONET, and local SBA links.

Business Financing

Angel Capital Electronic Network

http://www.sbaonline.sba.gov/ADVO/acenet.html

Angel Capital Electronic Network, ACE-Net, the Internet-based network is sponsored by the SBA's Office of Advocacy. The site gives new options for small companies seeking investments in the range of $250,000 to $5 million.

America Business Funding Directory

http://www.businessfinance.com/

America Business Funding Directory is the first search engine dedicated to finding business capital. You can search categories ranging from venture capital to equipment lending to real estate, as well as a private capital network of accredited investors.

Bankruptcy FAQs

http://site206125.primehost.com/faqs.html

Sponsored by Gold & Stanley, P.C., commercial bankruptcy lawyers, this site answers many basic questions about the ins-and-outs of bankruptcy from all perspectives. Topics include "How to Recover Money" and "10 Things to Do when a Bankruptcy is Filed."

Closing Bell

http://www.merc.com/cb/cgi/cb_merc.cgi

Closing Bell provides a daily e-mail message containing closing prices and news for a personalized portfolio of market indices, mutual funds, and securities from the three major U.S. exchanges. Visitors can also sign up for news alerts during the day for followed companies.

Computer Loan Network

http://www.clnet.com/

Borrowers can use this Web site to add a loan Request for Proposal (RFP) directly to the CLN MortgageNet mortgage multiple listing service. Mortgage brokers, lenders, banks, and secondary marketers will search the system, locate your RFP, and then find ways to offer you a lower note rate than your currently quoted rate, if possible.

Currency Converter

http://www.oanda.com/cgi-bin/ncc

An interactive Web page designed to allow you to see current conversions for 164 currencies. Convert your U.S. dollars to everything to the Albanian lek ($1 = 155 leks) to the Zambian kwacha ($1 = 1,310 kwacha). You can also check the previous day's rates or download a customizable currency converter.

EDGAR Database

http://www.sec.gov/edgarhp.htm

EDGAR, the Electronic Data Gathering, Analysis, and Retrieval system, performs automated collection, validation, indexing, acceptance, and forwarding of submissions by companies and others who are required by law to file forms with the U.S. Securities and Exchange Commission (SEC). Its primary purpose is to increase the efficiency and fairness of the securities market for the benefit of investors, corporations, and the economy. EDGAR is also a great resource of filing examples.

Export-Import Bank of the U.S.

http://www.exim.gov/

The Export-Import Bank offers programs on loans and guarantees, working capital, and export credit insurance. All the necessary application forms can be found online here with additional literature on importing from and exporting to various countries around the world.

FinanceNet

http://www.financenet.gov/

FinanceNet was established by Vice President Al Gore's National Performance Review in Washington, D.C. in 1994 and is operated by the National Science Foundation. This site features a list of government asset sales including a subscription to daily sales.

Financial Women International

http://www.fwi.org/

Founded in 1921, Financial Women International serves women in the financial services industry who seek to expand their personal and professional capabilities through self-directed growth in a supportive environment. FWI's vision is to empower women in the financial services industry to attain their professional, economic, and personal goals, and to influence the future shape of the industry.

National Credit Counseling Service

http://www.nccs.org/

The National Credit Counseling Service's Web site features news about its Debt Management Program for businesses and individuals, as well a full range of information on credit, budgeting, and financial planning.

Prospect Street

http://www.prospectstreet.com/

Prospect Street is a venture capital firm specializing in resources for high-tech entrepreneurs: information technology, software, the Internet, and wireless communications. Its site has links to investment, stock, and technical research sources.

Securities and Exchange Commission

http://www.sec.gov/smbus1.htm

This page of the SEC site opens its small business area where you can find information on taking your small business public. In addition to a complete Q&A, you'll also find current and pending initiatives of interest.

U.S. Tax Code On-Line

http://www.fourmilab.ch/ustax/ustax.html

This Web page allows access to the complete text of the U.S. Internal Revenue Title 26 of the Code (26 U.S.C.). To make cross-referencing easy, hyperlinks are embedded throughout the text.

International Business and Trade

Asia-Pacific Economic Cooperation

http://www.apecsec.org.sg/

Based in Singapore, this organization's Web site carries information on the 18-member countries' economies, information on intellectual property rights overseas, and a financial procedures guidebook with government procurement outlines.

Bureau of Export Administration

http://www.bxa.doc.gov/

A key element of this site is the EAR Marketplace, a one-stop source for timely Export Administration Regulations data, including a current, searchable copy of the Export Administration Regulations online. You can also find current information on U.S. encryption policy here.

Central and Eastern Europe Business Information Center

http://www.itaiep.doc.gov/eebic/ceebic.html

CEEBIC is a primary information source for doing business in the emerging markets of central and eastern Europe. Each country has a full profile that includes market research and business and trade opportunities. A recently added page features tax and VAT rates for the area.

Contact! The Canadian Management Network

http://strategis.ic.gc.ca/sc_mangb/contact/engdoc/homepage.html

This bilingual (English and French) site features links to more than 1,500 Canadian small business support organizations. Here you'll also find a small business handbook on doing business in Canada and information on cross-cultural business strategies.

The Electronic Embassy

http://www.embassy.org/

The Electronic Embassy provides information on embassies for every country with special attention to those on the Internet. There is also an International Business Center that spotlights commercial and nonprofit organizations providing goods, services, or opportunities to international markets.

ExporTutor

http://web.miep.org/tutor/index.html

Is your business export ready? Follow this site's 10-Step Road Map to Success in Foreign Markets, developed by Michigan State University's International Business Center, to find out. There's also a Quick Consultant with valuable information on everything from Accounting to Value Chain Analysis.

India Market Place

http://www.indiaintl.com/

Here you'll find in-depth information on doing business in India, Indian business news updated every business day, extensive information about trade shows being held in India, and links to India-based business management resources, directories and databases, and associations.

TrADE-Net Italy

http://www.tradenet.it/

Italy is filled with small- to medium-sized companies known for their quality and desire to export. TrADE-Net Italy has a searchable industry directory organized by category—perfect for finding your company just the right import item.

Venture Web—Japan

http://www.venture-web.or.jp/

Searching for a Japanese connection? Whether you're looking for a partner in Japan or marketing your availability to the Japanese market, you can submit your request for posting on the site. Other areas of the site have information on export/import regulations and human resource links.

Web of Culture

http://www.worldculture.com/index.html

The Web of Culture is a wonderful site to visit before working with or going to a new country. The site includes information on business, religion, resources, and holidays. There's even a very visual page about gestures and their meanings in different countries.

Job Opportunities and Labor Resources

AFL-CIO

http://www.aflcio.org/

The AFL-CIO Web site focuses on information on unionization and other labor-related issues. New sections include an Executive Pay Watch, Ergonomics, Working Women, and Summer Jobs for Seniors.

America's Job Bank

http://www.ajb.dni.us/

A multi-state project of the public Employment Service, America's Job Bank is for both employers and employees. A section on Occupational Employment trends offers an interactive outlook handbook and answers to many surveys such as, "What's the fastest growing occupation?"

Computer Register

http://www.computerregister.com/

If you're in the market for computer consultants or related services, check out these extensive advertisements, including employment. Classifieds are provided for both job seekers and employers.

CareerPath.com

http://www.careerpath.com/

CareerPath.com posts more than 400,000 new jobs on the Internet every month, and is updated daily by newspapers across the U.S. You can search their help wanted database by category, newspaper, and keyword.

Department of Labor

http://www.dol.gov/

The government site has information on minimum wage regulations, labor protections and welfare reform, and small business retirement solutions. Visitors can access "America's Job Bank," as well as job banks for regulatory and statutory information.

Ernst & Young's Virtual HR Office

http://www.idirect.com/hroffice/

This site is a resource center for the human resource professional; it includes a chat room, bulletin board, newsletter, and links to other HR sites in both the U.S. and Canada.

E-Span

http://www.espan.com/

Connecting the right person with the right job is what E-Span is all about. Visitors can access a resume database, a reference and resource library, and information on career fairs.

JobWeb

http://www.jobweb.org/

Run by the National Associations of Colleges and Employers, JobWeb lists jobs, employer profiles, and career planning resources. One resource, the Catapult, offers a variety of career assessment tools.

National Center for Employee Ownership

http://www.nceo.org/

The National Center for Employee Ownership (NCEO) is a private nonprofit organization. The NCEO site is a leading source of information on employee stock ownership plans (ESOPs), stock options, and other forms of employee ownership.

Telecommuting, Teleworking, and Alternative Officing

http://www.gilgordon.com/

This site features telecommuting information from around the world—and from many different perspectives—on the subjects of telecommuting, teleworking, the virtual office, and related topics. Includes a FAQ section and a list of upcoming events.

Legal and Regulatory

American Law Source Online (ALSO)

http://www.lawsource.com/also/

This site is notable because it has links to all American online legal systems, including the Federal judiciary and all 50 states and territories. ALSO has equally far-reaching coverage of Canadian and Mexican law.

Business Law Site

http://members.aol.com/bmethven/index.html

Sponsored by Methven & Associates, the Business Law Site covers federal and state statutes, as well as legal research sites for both business and high-tech law. You can also find a full compendium of tax forms, information on international law, and a list of legal research sites.

Corporate Counselor

http://www.ljx.com/corpcounselor/index.html

The Corporate Counselor has resources including daily news columns and articles on employment law, securities, antitrust, and other business issues.

Department of Labor Poster Page

http://www.dol.gov/dol/osbp/public/sbrefa/poster.htm

A fixture in every American workplace finds its online equivalent: the Department of Labor mandatory notices. So far, you can download posters for the minimum wage requirements, OSHA, the Family Leave Act, and the Equal Opportunity Act. All posters are in PDF format; you'll need a PDF reader like Adobe Acrobat (**http://www.adobe.com**).

International Trade Law

http://itl.irv.uit.no/trade_law/

You can search this site (Sponsored by the Law Department at Norway's University of Tromsø) for virtually any subject related to international trade law. Typical topics include Dispute Resolution, Customs, Protection of Intellectual Property, GATT, and other free trade treaties.

The Legal Information Institute

http://www.law.cornell.edu/

Sponsored by Cornell University, the Legal Information Institute Web site houses its collection of recent and historic Supreme Court decisions, hypertext versions of the full U.S. Code, U.S. Constitution, Federal Rules of Evidence and Civil Procedure, and recent opinions of the New York Court of Appeals complete with commentary. It's fully indexed and searchable.

QuickForms Online

http://www.quickforms.com/

QuickForms is an easy-to-use interactive system that drafts sophisticated agreements automatically weighted in your favor. Answer a few questions online, and you have your draft agreement in 10 minutes. A wide range of contracts are available.

Magazines Online

Advertising Age

http://www.adage.com/

All the information you could ever need about the movers and shakers of advertising. The site features a section called NetMarketing that covers getting the most out of your Web site, and a section called DataPlace that features industry reports and statistics.

Barron's Online

http://www.barrons.com/

In addition to complete contents of their weekly publication, *Barron's Online* features the ability to examine most companies mentioned in their articles through the Barron Dossiers. *Barron's Online* requires a free registration.

BusinessWeek

http://www.businessweek.com/

BusinessWeek's online-only content includes Maven (the interactive computer shopper) and BW Plus (lists of the best business schools, business book reviews, and articles on the computer industry and the Information Age). You can also access BW Radio, hourly market reports in RealAudio format.

Disgruntled

http://www.disgruntled.com/

Describing itself as "The Business Magazine for People Who Work for a Living," *Disgruntled* provides an irreverent look at being employed. There's even a Boss Button on every page that you can hit when the boss is looking over your shoulder to jump to a proper-looking spreadsheet.

Entrepreneurial Edge Online

http://www.edgeonline.com/

Articles aimed at the innovative entrepreneur fill this site. You also find a Pointers from the Pros section, a SmallBizNet (with a full digital library), and the Interactive Toolbox (a series of self-calculating worksheets and benchmarking and assessment tools).

Fast Company

http://www.fastcompany.com/

A new edge business magazine with a host of "how-to" articles: how to make a group decision like a tribe, how to deal with the issues of dating and sexual harassment on the job, how to choose a career counselor, how to disagree (without being disagreeable), and more.

Financial Times

http://www.usa.ft.com/

The online edition of the *Financial Times* is divided into three sections: News & Comment, with "tastes" of articles from the newspaper, as well as stock market information updated every 30 minutes; Themes & Topics, for categorized articles; and Connect & Respond, where online visitors can find services such as recruitment advertising and a library of annual reports.

Forbes Digital Tool

http://www.forbes.com/

In addition to current and archived articles from Forbes, this Web site features the Toolbox, a collection of reports and indices; ASAP, Forbes' supplement on the Information Age; Angles, a section on media and politics; and access to a free Investment Monitor.

Fortune

http://www.pathfinder.com/fortune/

Can't wait to see if you made the 500 this year? Check out the digital version of the famous survey as well as online areas dedicated to the stock market, mobile computing, managing your money, and information technology. You'll also find a special Fortune Forum for exchanging views on investing and related matters.

Hispanic Business Magazine

http://www.hispanstar.com/

This site covers information for business owners and professionals with a Hispanic interest. There is also a national résumé referral service, a market research area focusing on the U.S. Hispanic economic market, and a special events department that provides a calendar of events.

Inc. Online

http://www.inc.com/

Self-described as the "Web site for Growing Companies," *Inc. Online* is actually several minisites, including Inc. itself, which offers articles and archives; Business & Technology, which contains statistics to benchmark your business; and Local Business News, where you can choose from more than 25 U.S. cities for local business news and resources.

MoneyWorld Online

http://www.money-world.net/

MoneyWorld Online features investing information and tips on the most promising investment opportunities. *MoneyWorld* offers "hot-pick" IPOs, a series of long and short picks and growth industry surveys.

Red Herring

http://www.herring.com/mag/home.html

Red Herring provides business information for the technology and entertainment industries with a special focus on emerging markets. Their online site features an Entrepreneurs Resource Center with workshops on the unique challenges facing business startups.

Success Magazine

http://www.SuccessMagazine.com/

The *Success* site includes a searchable archive of past articles, a survey of the best 100 franchises (with links), and the Source (a compendium of business-related links organized by subject).

The Wall Street Journal—Small Business Suite

http://update.wsj.com/public/current/summaries/small.htm

Although the interactive *Wall Street Journal* is a subscription service ($49 per year), this service is free. Articles of interest to small business are the primary feature here, along with a series of discussion groups, Web resources, and a business locator.

Marketing and Market Research

American Demographics/Marketing Tools

http://www.marketingtools.com/

At the American Demographics/Marketing Tools Web site, you can check out consumer trends, tactics and techniques for information marketers, or access *Forecast*, a newsletter of demographic trends and market forecasts.

American Marketing Association

http://www.ama.org/

AMA is a national organization of marketing professionals. Their Web site features a special section on Internet marketing ethics as well as a calendar of events, publications, and information on regional chapters.

Business Intelligence Center

http://future.sri.com/

What type of person is your customer? The Values and Lifestyles (VALS) program at SRI Consulting, hosts of this site, studies consumers by asking questions about their attitudes and values. You can answer an online questionnaire to determine your VALS type—and see how you fit with other consumers.

Business Wire

http://www.businesswire.com/

Business Wire is a leading source of news on major U.S. corporations, including Fortune 1000 and NASDAQ companies. You can look up a company, category, keyword, or region and find all the pertinent business news. You can sign up for their service online.

Commando Guide to Unconventional Marketing and Advertising Tactics

http://199.44.114.223/mktg/

This online reference covers such topics as how to market survey your competition, doing your own professional marketing and business plan, referral systems, barter exchanges, print advetorials, and telemarketing.

First Steps: Marketing and Design Daily

http://www.interbiznet.com/nomad.html

Developed by the Internet Business Network, First Steps contains a rich source of articles on market research and industry analysis regarding business-to-business transactions. Much of the marketing and design work is Internet-oriented.

International Public Relations

http://www.iprex.com/

IPREX specializes in international public relations. Its areas of expertise include business-to-business, crisis management, energy and environment, and technology. Its news section has valuable information on public relation trends.

Market Facts and Statistics

http://www.mightymall.com/sevenseas/facts.html

This 1996 survey covers the countries of the world's population, gross national product, and growth rate. Each country has a small paragraph on its economy and markets. The information is organized by major regions: Asia, Western Europe, Central Europe, Middle East, Atlantic, and West Indies.

Marketing Resource Center

http://www.marketingsource.com/

Sponsored by the Concept Marketing Group, the Marketing Resource Center maintains an articles archive with more than 250 business-related articles. Their Tools of the Trade section links to an association database and software for general business and project management.

Retail Futures

http://e1.com/RF/

Sponsored by the Institute for Retail and Merchandising Innovation, this site carries information on tracking customer preferences, category and brand management, regional marketing, and store and product design issues.

Sales Leads USA

http://www.abii.com/

This site is run by American Business Information, Inc., which specializes in generating company profiles. Free services include searching for businesses or people by name with American Directory Assistance or searching by type of business with American Yellow Pages.

Selling.com

http://www.selling.com/

This site is dedicated to salespeople and their needs. Here, you'll find a collection of selling concepts and exercises written by salespeople, for salespeople.

Sharrow Advertising & Marketing Resource Center

http://www.dnai.com/~sharrow/register.html

You have to register at first to visit this site, but it's well worth it; the Advertising Parody section is worth the time by itself. The BizInfo Resource Center has an overview of database marketing, a direct mail profit spreadsheet, and information on approaches to integrated marketing.

Top Marketing Tips, Tricks, and Techniques

http://www.disclosure.com/marketing/toptricks.html

What's the inside scoop? Check out this site, sponsored by Disclosure, Inc., for all the skinny on advertising, direct marketing, marketing law, marketing management, promotions, public relations, trade shows, and telemarketing.

U.S. Census Bureau

http://www.census.gov/

The Census Bureau is a great site to gather social, demographic, and economic information. The site has more than 1,000 Census Bureau publications featuring statistical information on such topics as the nation's population, housing, business and manufacturing activity, international trade, farming, and state and local governments.

World Business Solution

http://thesolution.com/

The World Business Solution is a free marketing manual available from TheSolution.com. There's also a section devoted to downloadable or lined handy forms and reference.

Nonprofit Information

Charity Village

http://www.charityvillage.com/cvhome.html

Hundreds of pages of news, jobs, resources, and links for the Canadian nonprofit community. Sponsored by Hilborn Interactive, Inc. this site is updated daily in both French ("Rue Principale") and English ("Main Street").

Council of Foundations

http://www.cof.org/index.html

The Council of Foundations is an association of foundations and corporations gathered to promote responsible and effective philanthropy. You'll find information on the various types of foundations as well as a Community Foundation Locator service.

The George Lucas Educational Foundation

http://glef.org/welcome.html

The George Lucas Educational Foundation, a tax-exempt, charitable organization based in Nicasio, California, was established to facilitate the innovative uses of multimedia technologies to enhance teaching and learning. The site has frequently updated information about innovative efforts to change education.

The Gen-X Group

http://www.globalserve.net/~genxgrp/

Gen. X Group is a not-for-profit Christian organization promoting charities and nonprofit organizations on the Internet. The site features a short course on how and why nonprofit organizations can get on the Web.

The Grantsmanship Center

http://www.tgci.com/

The Grantsmanship Center specializes in training for grant-writing and fundraising. Much of the site is designed to support their courses around the country. The site also contains a cross-referenced database of state and federal funding.

IdeaList

http://www.contact.org/

This site features a global directory of nonprofits with links to more than 10,000 sites in 110 countries. There is also an online library of tools for nonprofits, with information about fundraising and volunteering, accounting and management, legal issues, and nonprofit support organizations.

Nonprofit Resources Catalog

http://www.clark.net/pub/pwalker/

A personal project by the head of United Way Online, this site features meta-links (links to pages of links) dedicated to Interlink sites that benefit nonprofits. Categories include Fundraising and Giving, General Nonprofit Resources, and United Ways on the Internet.

Patents, Trademarks, and Copyrights

Basic Patent Information

http://www.fplc.edu/tfield/ipbasics.htm

Sponsored by the Franklin Law Center, this compendium of resources offers beginning information for artists, independent inventors, Internet authors and artists, programmers, and small business owners, including information on how to avoid being burned by fraudulent invention promotion schemes.

Copyright Clearance Center

http://www.copyright.com/

Copyright Clearance Center (CCC) is a not-for-profit organization created at the suggestion of Congress to help organizations comply with U.S. copyright law. CCC offers a number of catalogs that you can search to see if a work is registered.

Copyright Website

http://www.benedict.com/index.html

This lively site provides real-world, practical, and relevant copyright information including a look at famous copyright infringement cases, copyright fundamentals, and distribution of copyright information over the Web.

Intellectual Property Center

http://www.ipcenter.com/

News and information on intellectual property issues dominate this site. Government statutes and decisions are highlighted, along with memos from law firms on intellectual property issues.

Nerd World: Copyrights & Patents

http://www.nerdworld.com/users/dstein/nw427.html

This site provides a resource of links to many patent attorneys and intellectual property law firms from around the world. A recent survey showed many contacts in the U.S., Canada, and Japan.

Patent Application Drafting

http://w3.gwis.com/~sarbar/patapp01.htm

This Web site gives an overview of the steps necessary for writing a patent application, section by section. Aside from covering the statutory legal requirements, Intellectual Property Attorney R. Lawrence Sahr gives insightful comments on the target audience for your patent: the patent office itself.

Patent Pending Resource

http://silkpresence.com/patents/

Sponsored by the patent law firm of Ogram & Teplitz, this site covers new patents law, a FAQ on provisional patent application that allows the "Patent Pending" label to be used. There are also online forms that ask a patent attorney's questions before you schedule a visit.

U.S. Patent Office

http://www.uspto.gov/

The home page for the U.S. Patent Office gives you access to downloadable patent application forms and searchable databases. These include both the U.S. Patent Bibliographic Database (U.S. patents issued from January 1, 1976 to July 8, 1997), and the AIDS Patent Database (full text and images of AIDS-related patents issued by the U.S., Japanese, and European patent offices).

Procurement and Contracting

Acquisition Reform Network

http://www-far.npr.gov/

The Acquisition Reform Network (ARNet) provides services to members of the government acquisition community, both public and private sector. Its resource center, the Federal Acquisition Virtual Library, provides links to numerous other federal acquisition resources on the World Wide Web. Numerous opportunities are also listed.

BidCast

http://www.bidcast.com/

BidCast is a subscription service that allows you to browse and search thousands of U.S. federal government bids. You can sign up the e-mail service for personal notification. There is a free trial section that allows you to look at Commerce Business Daily listings.

Business Information and Development Services (BIDS)

http://www.bidservices.com/newindex.html

BIDS is an electronic publishing and consulting firm that informs small businesses about upcoming government contract opportunities and provides assistance in the procurement process. Their site offers information from both the Commerce Business Daily (U.S.) and Supply and Services Open Bidding Service (Canada).

Commerce Business Daily

http://www.govcon.com/public/CBD/

A sophisticated search engine for finding government procurement opportunities. You can search for a procurement or award under a specific category, by contract value or by a search phrase. You can even specify the level of "fuzzyness" the engine uses to find items bearing a close similarity to your search criteria.

Electronic Commerce Program Office (ECPO)

http://www.arnet.gov/ecapmo/

The Electronic Commerce Program Office (ECPO) is a multi-agency group assembled under the co-leadership of the General Services Administration and the Department of Defense to implement Electronic Commerce/Electronic Data Interchange (EC/EDI) for the federal acquisition programs. An online tutorial can help you get started.

Electronic Commerce Resource Center

http://www.ecrc.ctc.com/

The ECRC Program promotes awareness and implementation of Electronic Commerce and related technologies into the U.S.-integrated civil-military industrial base. Downloadable products can be found in the Electronic Commerce Testbed.

Environmental Protection Agency Procurement

http://www.epa.gov/epahome/Contracts.html

Visit this site for a full listing of business opportunities and EPA acquisition resources. In addition to covering policy and procedure, you can also find an acquisition forecast and a special section devoted to small business opportunities.

FAA Acquisition Center

http://www.faa.gov/asu/asu100/acq-reform/acq_home.htm

After you've checked out the FAQ page on supplying to the Federal Aviation Administration, visit FAST, the FAA Acquisition System Toolset. FAST is a interactive databank designed to guide users through the FAA's new Acquisition Management System (AMS); it contains examples, templates, instructions, tips, policy documents, and other automated tools.

Federal Acquisition Institute

http://www.gsa.gov/fai/

Trying to find your way through the maze of federal acquisition? Pay a visit to the Federal Acquisition Institute, a one-stop acquisition training shop. Here you can sign-up for the FAI Online University or download a Contract Pricing Reference Guide.

General Services Agency

http://www.gsa.gov/

The GSA's mission is to provide expertly managed space, supplies, services, and solutions at the best value to Federal employees. In addition to full information on buying practices, you can also visit its online shopping service, GAO Advantage.

Government Accounting Office

http://www.gao.gov/

The U.S. General Accounting Office (GAO) is a nonpartisan agency that conducts audits, surveys, investigations, and evaluations of federal programs. You can sign up for daily reports through the GAO Daybook service or visit the GAO FraudNET for allegations of fraud, waste, abuse, or mismanagement of federal funds.

Government Contractors Glossary

http://www.kcilink.com/govcon/contractor/gcterms.html

An excellent resource for finding your way through the verbiage of government contracts. A special Acronym Table appears at the end of this guide to enable you to identify the full meaning of the most common government acronyms.

National Technology Transfer Center

http://www.nttc.edu/

The National Technology Transfer Center's task is to take technologies off laboratory shelves and put them to work in U.S. businesses and industries where taxpayers get even more benefits from their investments. Full database services, a training center, and links to other business assistance sites are hallmarks of this Web site.

State and Local Procurement Jumpstation

http://www.fedmarket.com/statejump.html

This invaluable Web page gives you links to procurement sources for all 50 states, not to mention Washington, D.C. and Guam. Most states also have some local listings for specific cities as well as economic development links supplying market data.

U.S. Business Center

http://www.business.gov/

This one-stop shop is designed to streamline interactions between businesses and the government. Common questions and answers are organized by subject, and an expert tool area gives you forms and guidance in everything from Disaster Assistance to Finding a Zip Code.

U.S. Post Office

http://www.usps.gov/business/

The Post Office wants to give you the business! This Web site provides an overview of doing business with the USPS and even tells you how to submit an unsolicited bid. You can download the Procurement Manual, as well as check out business opportunities.

U.S. Veteran Affairs

http://www.va.gov/osdbu/

The online Department of Veteran Affairs site promotes increased use of small and disadvantaged businesses, including acquisition opportunities. A focus of this site is the VA's 1997 Forecast which supplies marketing information useful to the small business person in selling their goods and services, both to the VA and to the VA's large prime contractors.

Small Office/Home Office

America's Small Business Finance Center

http://www.netearnings.com/

Sponsored by Net Earnings, Inc., this one-stop shop offers business advice on insurance policies and prices, and on applying for loans and credit cards. You can also sign up for online payroll service here.

American Express Small Business Exchange

http://www.americanexpress.com/smallbusiness/

The American Express Small Business Exchange offers online classifieds (buying and selling); expert advice where you can ask a specific question, browse the categories, or check out the tip of the month; and business planning and resources with information on starting, managing, or expanding your business.

Bathrobe 'til 10

http://www.slip.net/~sfwave/

This guide for the home professional offers articles and information for the solo self-employed. Concerned about word use? Pay a visit to the Grammar Queen to clear up those business correspondence blues.

Biz$hop

http://www.bizshop.com/

Biz$hop is a virtual company specializing in helping entrepreneurs achieve success in their own businesses. Numerous reports and free business resources are available; be sure to download the free "First 25 Business Decisions" report.

BizResource.com

http://www.bizresource.com/

Dedicated to encouraging small businesses and entrepreneurs, BizResource offers an ongoing series of business tips (both via e-mail and archived online), a business chat area, and a series of audio, video, and computer resources.

Business@Home

http://www.gohome.com/

An electronic magazine dedicated to the working-from-home community, Business@Home includes articles on opportunity, marketing, and technology. Its Cool Tools department reviews recent hardware and software important to the general home office worker, while the Consultant's Corner focuses on the consultants work experience.

Business Resource Center

http://www.morebusiness.com/

This site hosts an excellent four-part primer with advice and activities to get you thinking about your business, its customers, development, and marketing. In addition, you can find templates and worksheets here for press releases and business plans.

Business Start Page

http://www.wp.com/fredfish/

Here's a great place to start your business day. This site offers a virtual desktop where you can find everything at your fingertips: Yellow, Blue, and International page telephone directories, links to shipping companies, a reference library, and a series of tips and tricks.

Center for Family Business

http://199.103.128.199/fambiznc/cntprovs/orgs/necfb/

Run by Northeastern University, this site features an on-going series of articles on running a family business (both home and office- or store-based). You'll find lots of information here on family business issues including generational change, sibling rivalries, and how to balance family and business priorities.

EGOPHER—The Entrepreneur Gopher

http://www.slu.edu/eweb/egopher.html

Sponsored by St. Louis University, EGOPHER is designed for people and organizations interested in new, small, or entrepreneurial businesses. A variety of Top 10 lists for entrepreneurs is available along with topical business resources and access to core research journal in entrepreneurship.

Electronic Money Tree

http://www.soos.com/$tree/

Aimed at the Internet savvy (or those who want to be) entrepreneurs, the Electronic Money Tree consists primarily of a digest of articles. Sample articles include "Can SOHO Really Compete?" "Biz Tips," "Better Press Releases," and "Time Management."

Entrepreneur's Bookstore

http://kwicsys.com/books/

There are more than 600 information reports offered at this site, most from $1 to $2 each. The reports are categorized. Sample topic areas include Mail Order, Multilevel Marketing, Legal, and Direct Response TV.

Entrepreneur Magazine's BizSquare

http://www.entrepreneurmag.com/

This site is chock-full of information for the SOHO businessperson. Visit the Resource Center to check out the online Franchise 500 and Business Opportunity 500 lists. Then go to the SOHO Mall for all your business-related software, books, magazines, and audio or videocassettes.

EntreWorld

http://www.entreworld.org/

The EntreWorld site is organized by business level. Visit the Starting Your Business area for information on business planning, finding the right people, or creating products that win loyalty. Running Your Business is devoted to later stage companies with information on expanding your customer base and exit strategies.

FranInfo

http://www.frannet.com/

Thinking about franchising? Visit FranInfo's site to find information on buying a franchise or franchising your own business. The site has several self-tests to determine if you're ready for franchising, as well as a listing of franchises for sale.

Guide to the Small Business Administration

http://www.geocities.com/WallStreet/2172/

Before you dive into the SBA bureaucracy, you might want to visit this site. It provides details about the various SBA programs available and information to help you find just the right one for your business.

Heath's Computer and Telecommunication Acronym Reference

http://www.sbri.com/acro2.htm

Visit this site before your next cocktail party where you want to impress others with statements like, "My GOSIP is about to go LUNI on Harv's LANE." Or maybe when you just want to find out what all those jargonese initials mean.

Home Office Association of America

http://www.hoaa.com/

There's power in numbers—even if you're working alone. The Home Office Association of America offers group health insurance, a long-distance calling plan, a debt collection service, home business and equipment insurance, and more. Be sure to visit their 50 Great Home Office Startup Ideas page.

Home Office Links

http://www.ro.com/small_business/homebased.html

Home Office Links is a full compendium of Web links for small and home-based offices including franchises, business opportunities, reference material, newsgroups, searching tools, and services for small business. It includes links to just about anything related to small- and home-based business.

Home Office Mall

http://www.the-office.com/

This is a centralized location for products and services catering to the home office professional. You'll find everything from computers for rent to computer furniture, to networks for female executives.

Home Realtors Information Network

http://www.realtors.com/

About the only thing all home business have in common is the home. This Web site, sponsored by the National Association of Realtors, has almost 900,000 listings of homes around the country—and, of course, a search engine to help you find your dream office.

NetMarquee Family Business NetCenter

http://nmq.com/

This site supplies news and information for owners and executives in family-owned businesses. There is a calendar of events, weekly articles, and a listserve for ongoing discussion related to family businesses.

Offshore Entrepreneur

http://www.au.com/offshore/

With the motto "Neither profit, nor opportunity, have any borders," the Offshore Entrepreneur takes you through the promise, pitfalls, and profit of basing your business in another country. The site offers abundant information on tax-planning and forming an off-shore corporation.

Opportunities for Women in Small Business

http://www.mindspring.com/~higley/project.htm

One path around the glass ceiling is to open your own business. This site is dedicated to helping women choose and run a business. It offers profiles of successful women, as well as financial and legal advice and tips on how to avoid failure.

Resource Center for Home-Based Businesses

http://www.masseypub.com/

Learn from someone who made the home-based business dream come true. Featuring information on self-published brochures, this site offers a FAQ section, details on seminars, and an area devoted to mail order scams.

Retail Business Resource Center

http://www.retailadvz.com/

Looking for a site where you can learn from the experts? The Retail Business Resource Center offers theme-oriented live business chats, live workshops, and even a business therapist offering real-world solutions to real-world problems.

Small Business Innovative Research

http://www.sbir.dsu.edu/

Small Business Innovative Research is a federally supported program aimed at funding small businesses with money from Federal agency and department's R&D divisions. This site assists small companies in applying for that funding by answering questions and providing online tests.

SOHO America

http://www.soho.org/

SOHO America is a small business benefits association. In addition to news of interest to the small office/home office market, this site offers a comprehensive list of health benefits, business tools, and personal discounts available to members.

Your Small Office

http://www.smalloffice.com/

This site is the online presence of *Small Office Computing* and *Home Office Computing* magazines and features articles from their magazines. The Web site visitor will find a great number of reviews of network, computer, and office equipment as well as a full "How To" department covering everything from Startup to Sales and Marketing.

U.S. Chamber of Commerce Small Business Institute

http://www.uschamber.org/programs/sbi/index.html

The U.S. Chamber of Commerce runs a Small Business Institute with a variety of resources both for free and for sale. There are self-study programs on Mastering Your Business on the Internet and the Small Business Institute Series, as well as information on the SOHO Conference.

Travel and Transportation

Airlines of the Web

http://w2.itn.net/airlines/

Where can you find a list of *all* the airlines, both passenger and cargo? At the Airlines of the Web site, of course. Passenger airlines are categorized by region, and you can also find airline-related information like 800 numbers and a link to a real-time reservation service.

American Airlines

http://www.americanair.com/aa_home.htm

The American Access Web site takes a full-service approach. Here, you can plan your travel, check out Advantage frequent flier miles, take advantage of the NetSaver fares, and download Personal Access, American's Windows-based software program that brings you dedicated AAdvantage information, travel planning, and up-to-the-minute information and specials.

American Movers Conference

http://www.amconf.org/

The American Movers Conference is an association of 3,000 professional moving companies in the U.S. Their site has information on how to prepare your move, how much a "self-haul" might cost, and lists of movers across the country.

Continental Airlines

http://www.flycontinental.com:80/index.html

Continental On-Line's main claim to fame is its C.O.O.L. Travel Assistant which can be used to schedule and book airline travel on Continental, Continental Express, and Continental Micronesia, as well as more than 40 rental car companies and 26,000 hotels around the world.

FedEX

http://www.fedex.com/

Not only can you now track your overnight package online, but you can also use their interactive rate finder, and even ship packages via the Internet to more than 160 countries from the U.S. and Canada. There's also a searchable database of drop-off locations and downloadable software for managing your shipping, including the airbill printing.

HomeBuyer's Fair

http://www.homefair.com/home/

While most of this site is dedicated to helping you buy or sell your home, the HomeBuyer's Fair has some amazing interactive tools in its Popular Exhibits area. There's a Salary Calculator for comparing the cost of living in hundreds of U.S. and international cities, a Moving Calculator for figuring the cost of a move, and a Relocation Crime Lab for comparing crime statistics.

InterKnowledge Travel Network

http://www.interknowledge.com/

When your business takes you to an exotic locale—meaning you've never been there before—stop by the InterKnowledge Travel Network site first. The site is characterized by beautiful images and full details on geography, culture, and climate.

Northwest Airlines

http://www.nwa.com/

This Northwest Airlines site has information on CyberSavers, their online low-cost tickets, as well as regular travel and frequent flier information. A full slate of vacation packages rounds out the site.

U.S. Air

http://www.usair.com/

Tune into the U.S. Air Web site to schedule and book a flight or check your frequent flyer miles. An extensive area of the site is devoted to its U.S. Airways Cargo service where you can use the software to track shipments with real-time information from airport drop-off to pickup.

United Parcel Service

http://www.ups.com/

Interactive functions featured at the UPS site include package tracking, cost-estimating, a drop-off locator, and pick-up scheduling. UPS also makes available free software for all of these functions as well as up-to-the-minute zone and rate charts.

Trade Shows and Conferences

EXPOguide

http://www.expoguide.com/

If you're thinking about selling your product through a trade show, stop by this site first. It has a full list of trade shows, conferences, and exhibitions as well as comprehensive coverage of show services and associations. Although primarily intended for trade show managers, it also offers plenty of information for exhibiting companies.

CD Information

http://www.cd-info.com/CDIC/Industry/TradeShows.html

Today, much of computing and information storage and retrieval revolves around the CD-ROM. This site is CD-centric and lists many upcoming exhibition, conferences, seminars, and workshops in a month-by-month format.

Guide to Unique Meeting Facilities

http://www.theguide.com/

A terrific resource for meeting planners, The Guide to Unique Meeting Facilities covers colleges and universities, retreat centers, camps and lodges, and cultural and historical venues, as well as traditional conference centers. There is also a Hot Date/Cool Rate area to highlight facilities with open, economical dates.

Major Trade Shows In Asia

http://www.tdb.gov.sg/trshow/tr_menu.html

You can start your search for Asian trade shows here, either by country, industry or by date. Fourteen countries, including Brunei, China, Japan, South Korea, and Vietnam, and more than 25 different industries are covered.

Trade Show Central

http://www.tscentral.com/

Sponsored by the International Association for Exhibition Management, Trade Show Central gives you easy access to information on more than 30,000 trade shows. Its searchable database links to an e-mail notification service where you can request more information. Its AudioNet connection broadcasts and archives keynote speeches from major events.

Wall Street Directory

http://www.wsdinc.com/index.html

Wall Street Directory offers a wide range of information for traders and investors. To see its up-to-the-minute conference information, select the Seminars-Shows-Conventions category and click the Search by Category button.

Small Business Administration Upcoming Events

http://www.sbaonline.sba.gov/gc/events.html

Organized on a monthly basis, the SBA keeps a listing of many business-related seminars and conferences. Although not hot-linked, all conferences have telephone contact information. Free seminars are prominently noted.

EventWeb

http://www.eventweb.com/

A free mailing list service for meeting, conference, and trade show promoters. Sample articles include "How to Exhibit at a Virtual Trade Show," "Expanding Educational Horizons in the Online World," and "Promote Your Speakers—Inexpensively!"

Tradeshow News Network

http://www.tsnn.com/

The Tradeshow News Network allows you to search for a trade show in the U.S. by location, date, or industry. Its Trade Show Education department offers tips on both exhibiting and attending, as well as an Ask the Expert section.

Virtual Online Trade Show

http://www.volts.com/

This site promotes the Virtual Trade Show concept, and is aimed at both exhibition managers and exhibitors. Exhibitors can see how they can save money, broaden their exposure, and communicate with their customers. ●

APPENDIX E

What's on the CD?

The contents of the CD-ROM are easily viewed and navigated through with any Web browser. If you do not have a browser, you can use Internet Explorer 3.02, which is provided. The contents of the CD are organized into the following categories: electronic books, software, business sites on the Web, and source code and samples from the book.

Detailed instructions on CD-ROM use and operation can be found in the README.DOC file on the CD-ROM. ■

Electronic Books

This CD-ROM is packed with several electronic (Web-based) versions of Que's leading titles. Some of these titles include:

Office 97 Quick References

- *Office 97*
- *Word 97*
- *Excel 97*
- *Access 97*

Operating Systems

- *Platinum Edition Windows 95*
- *Special Edition Using Windows NT Workstation 4.0*

Internet

- *Special Edition Using Internet Explorer 3.0*
- *Special Edition Using FrontPage 97*

Software

The CD-ROM includes many full, as well as trial-version, software products and utilities to make your Office 97 computing experience more productive and exciting. All of the software can be installed directly from the CD-ROM.

Office 97 Add-Ins and Tools

Village Software FastStart Sampler Excel Solutions The Village Software FastStart Sampler includes twelve ready-made Excel templates to provide spreadsheet solutions for common business and personal needs. These templates were hand-selected as a special sample package from Village Software's FastStarts product line.

ActiveOffice ActiveOffice, the "Essential Graphics Companion to Microsoft Office," instantly transforms text and numbers into compelling graphics that effectively communicate the key ideas, trends, and relationships in all of your documents, spreadsheets, and presentations.

ActivePresenter ActivePresenter gives you all of the tools you need to deliver high-impact, low-cost presentations on the Web. ActivePresenter—which features SPC's revolutionary Intelligent Formatting technology—includes everything you need to create, publish, and present in one powerful, simple-to-use solution.

Office Toys 97 Office Toys 97 is an add-in for Microsoft Word 97, which creates a toolbar filled with many great Word utilities. These utilities provide you with a quicker and smarter way to use Word 97 and the files you create. Some of the powerful utilities and functions include the following: Office Navigator, Project Manager, More Proofing Tools!, Formatting tools!, Auto-backup, Virus Alert!, Smart printing tools!, Style Management!, and much more.

Microsoft Office 97 Viewers Microsoft provides distributable viewers for three of their Office products. These viewers enable you to share Word, Excel, and PowerPoint documents with individuals who have not installed Microsoft Office applications on their computer systems.

Business and Professional

Pagis Pro97 Pagis Pro97 is a fully featured scanning application that allows you to scan documents (one or multiple pages) into your Windows 95/NT 4.0 desktop. With a color, grayscale or binary scanner, you can easily scan documents into your PC and then file, copy, print, send or use them with your favorite application by simply "dragging and dropping" them onto the application icon.

GoldMine GoldMine is the number one Workgroup Contact Manager. It is designed to automate business professionals—whether they work remotely in the field, alone on a desktop PC, or with others in networked offices. It combines contact management, day and time planning, sales automation, and mail list management with group calendaring, database design, data synchronization, and e-mail messaging.

WinFax Pro WinFax Pro gives you hassle-free faxing anywhere, anytime. Why waste time printing documents and feeding a fax machine? Fax right from your computer. WinFax PRO is easy to install and use—step-by-step wizards show you exactly what to do.

Paint Shop Pro Paint Shop Pro—a powerful and easy-to-use image viewing, editing, and conversion program—supports more than 30 image formats. With numerous drawing and painting tools, this might be the only graphics program you will ever need!

Internet

EarthLink Total Access Total Access offers a quick-start tool for connecting to the Internet. EarthLink Network specializes in providing inexpensive Internet access throughout the United States.

Microsoft Internet Explorer 3.02 Microsoft Internet Explorer is a must-have application for Web viewing. With the explosion of the Web, many companies, organizations, and individuals are generating Web-based documents. In order to view these documents, you need a Web Browser. Even if you already have Netscape installed on your computer, many sites optimize their Web pages for Internet Explorer. The version that is provided runs on both Windows 95 and NT.

Adobe Acrobat Reader with Search 3.01 The free Adobe Acrobat Reader enables you to view, navigate, and print PDF files across all major computing platforms. Adobe has created two flavors of Acrobat Reader 3.01, Acrobat Reader and Acrobat Reader with Search. Reader with Search includes additions that allow the user to search within a collection of PDF files on a hard disk, CD, or local-area network (for which an index file has been created with the Acrobat Catalog tool).

CuteFTP CuteFTP is a Windows-based Internet application that allows you to use the capabilities of FTP without having to know all the details about the protocol itself. It simplifies FTP by offering a user-friendly, graphical interface instead of a cumbersome command-line utility.

WinZip WinZip brings the convenience of Windows to the use of Zip files. It requires neither PKZIP nor PKUNZIP. The new WinZip Wizard makes unzipping easier than ever. WinZip features built-in support for popular Internet file formats, including TAR, gzip, UNIX compress, UUEncode, BinHex, and MIME. ARJ, LZH, and ARC files are supported via external programs. WinZip interfaces to most virus scanners.

WebPrinter 4-Pack WebPrinter instantly turns your valuable Internet, CD-ROM, and Windows data into attractive booklets with WebPrinter. With only two clicks, sports stats, custom travel itineraries, financial how-to guides, product literature, maps, and even photos are transformed into convenient, double-sided booklets.

PointCast Network Through personal news profiles, viewers are enabled to customize the information they receive. Viewers specify news topics of interest and the PointCast Network delivers current news to their desktops. They can modify personal news profiles at any time.

Business Sites on the Web

The CD includes a hyperlinked version of Appendix D, "Business Sites on the Web." To take advantage of Web publishing, click the hyperlink of any business site and go directly to its Web site. ●

Index

Symbols

A

B

C

E

G

I

M

N

O

P

Q

R

S

T

U

V

X

Y

Z

Complete and Return this Card
for a *FREE* Computer Book Catalog

Thank you for purchasing this book! You have purchased a superior computer book written expressly for your needs. To continue to provide the kind of up-to-date, pertinent coverage you've come to expect from us, we need to hear from you. Please take a minute to complete and return this self-addressed, postage-paid form. In return, we'll send you a free catalog of all our computer books on topics ranging from word processing to programming and the Internet.

] Mrs. ☐ Ms. ☐ Dr. ☐

(first) ☐☐☐☐☐☐☐☐☐☐☐☐ (M.I.) ☐ (last) ☐☐☐☐☐☐☐☐☐☐☐☐☐☐☐☐☐☐

ss ☐☐

☐☐

☐☐☐☐☐☐☐☐☐☐☐☐☐☐☐☐ State ☐☐ Zip ☐☐☐☐☐ ☐☐☐☐

☐☐☐ ☐☐☐☐☐☐☐☐☐ Fax ☐☐☐ ☐☐☐ ☐☐☐☐

any Name ☐☐☐☐☐☐☐☐☐☐☐☐☐☐☐☐☐☐☐☐☐☐☐☐☐☐☐☐☐☐☐☐☐☐☐☐

 address ☐☐☐☐☐☐☐☐☐☐☐☐☐☐☐☐☐☐☐☐☐☐☐☐☐☐☐☐☐☐☐☐☐☐☐☐

se check at least (3) influencing factors for chasing this book.

or back cover information on book ☐
ıl approach to the content ☐
leteness of content .. ☐
r's reputation ... ☐
her's reputation ... ☐
cover design or layout ☐
or table of contents of book ☐
of book .. ☐
ıl effects, graphics, illustrations ☐
(Please specify): _____ ☐

w did you first learn about this book?

ı Macmillan Computer Publishing catalog ☐
ımended by store personnel ☐
ıe book on bookshelf at store ☐
ımended by a friend ... ☐
ved advertisement in the mail ☐
ı advertisement in: _____ ☐
ıook review in: _____ ☐
(Please specify): _____ ☐

w many computer books have you chased in the last six months?

ıook only ☐ 3 to 5 books ☐
ks ☐ More than 5 ☐

4. Where did you purchase this book?

Bookstore ... ☐
Computer Store .. ☐
Consumer Electronics Store .. ☐
Department Store .. ☐
Office Club .. ☐
Warehouse Club ... ☐
Mail Order ... ☐
Direct from Publisher .. ☐
Internet site ... ☐
Other (Please specify): _____ ☐

5. How long have you been using a computer?

☐ Less than 6 months ☐ 6 months to a year
☐ 1 to 3 years ☐ More than 3 years

6. What is your level of experience with personal computers and with the subject of this book?

	With PCs	With subject of book
New	☐	☐
Casual	☐	☐
Accomplished	☐	☐
Expert	☐	☐

Source Code ISBN: 0-07897-1399-3

7. Which of the following best describes your job title?

Administrative Assistant ☐
Coordinator ☐
Manager/Supervisor ☐
Director ☐
Vice President ☐
President/CEO/COO ☐
Lawyer/Doctor/Medical Professional ☐
Teacher/Educator/Trainer ☐
Engineer/Technician ☐
Consultant ☐
Not employed/Student/Retired ☐
Other (Please specify): ____________ ☐

8. Which of the following best describes the area of the company your job title falls under?

Accounting ☐
Engineering ☐
Manufacturing ☐
Operations ☐
Marketing ☐
Sales ☐
Other (Please specify): ____________ ☐

9. What is your age?

Under 20
21-29
30-39
40-49
50-59
60-over

10. Are you:

Male
Female

11. Which computer publications do you read regularly? (Please list)

____

Comments: ____________

Fold here and tape

NO POSTAGE NECESSARY IF MAILED IN THE UNITED STATES

BUSINESS REPLY MAIL
FIRST-CLASS MAIL PERMIT NO. 9918 INDIANAPOLIS IN

POSTAGE WILL BE PAID BY THE ADDRESSEE

ATTN MARKETING
MACMILLAN COMPUTER PUBLISHING
MACMILLAN PUBLISHING USA
201 W 103RD ST
INDIANAPOLIS IN 46290-9042

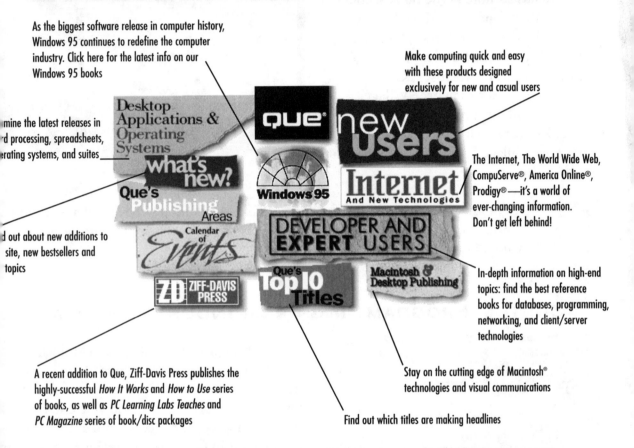

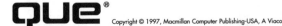

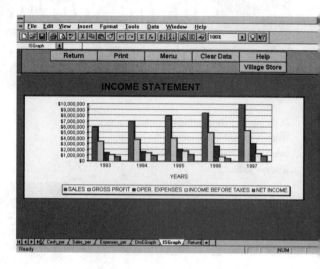

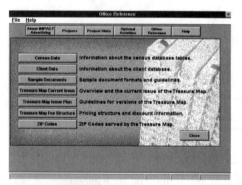

Licensing Agreement

By opening this package, you are agreeing to be bound by the following:

The software product contained on this CD is copyrighted and all rights are reserved by the publisher and author. You are licensed to use this software on a single computer. You may copy and/or modify the software as needed to facilitate your use of it on a single computer. Making copies of the software for any other purpose is a violation of the United States copyright laws. THIS SOFTWARE IS PROVIDED FREE OF CHARGE, *AS IS*, AND WITHOUT WARRANTY OF ANY KIND, EITHER EXPRESSED OR IMPLIED, INCLUDING BUT NOT LIMITED TO THE IMPLIED WARRANTIES OF MERCHANTIBILITY AND FITNESS FOR A PARTICULAR PURPOSE. Neither the publisher nor its dealers or distributors assumes any liability for any alleged or actual damages arising from the use of this program. (Some states do not allow for the exclusion of implied warranties, so the exclusion may not apply to you.)

Using Special Edition

Using MICROSOFT® Excel 97

Bestseller Edition

QUE®